Check out the animations, videos, and activities on your FREE CD-ROM

Chapter 1

- Offspring of Parents Homozygous and Heterozygous for Brown Eyes (animation)
- RNA, DNA, and Protein (animation)
- Selection and Random Drift (Try It Yourself)

Chapter 2

- The Parts of a Neuron (animation)
- Virtual Reality Neuron (virtual reality)
- Neuron Puzzle (drag & drop)
- Resting Potential (animation)
- Action Potential (AP) (animation)
- Action Potential: Na+ Ions (animation)

Chapter 3

- Postsynaptic Potentials (animation)
- Release of Neurotransmitter (animation)
- Cholinergic (animation)
- Release of ACh (animation)
- AChE Inactivates ACh (animation)
- AChE Inhibitors (animation)

Chapter 4

- Neuroimaging (video)
- Virtual Reality Head Planes (virtual reality)
- Planes Puzzle (drag & drop)
- 3D Virtual Brain (virtual reality)
- Left Hemisphere Function #1 (rollover with text pop-ups)
- Cortex Puzzle (drag & drop)
- Sagittal Section: Right Hemisphere #1 (rollover with text pop-ups)
- Sagittal Section: Right Hemisphere #2 (rollover with text pop-ups)
- Sagittal Section: Right Hemisphere #3 (rollover with text pop-ups)
- Brain Puzzle (drag & drop)
- The Motor Cortex (animation)
The Sensory Cortex (animation)
Illustration of Binding (Try It Yourself)

Chapter 5

- Sperry Experiment (animation)
- Brains on Ice (video)
- Phantom Limb (animation)

Chapter 6

- The Retina (animation)
- Virtual Reality Eye (virtual reality)
- Motion Aftereffect (Try It Yourself)
- Brightness Contrast (Try It Yourself)
- Blind Spot (Try It Yourself)
- Color Blindness in Visual Periphery (Try It Yourself)

Chapter 7

- Hearing Puzzle (puzzle)
- Hearing Loss (video)
- Somesthetic Experiment (drag & drop)
- Attention Deficit Disorder (video)

Chapter 8

- Major Motor Areas (animation)
- The Withdrawal Reflex (animation)
- The Crossed Extensor Reflex (animation)
- The Brain Pacemaker (video)

Chapter 9

- Sleep Cycle (video)
- Stages of Sleep on an EEG (static image)
- Awake (animation)
- Stage 1 (animation)
- Stage 2 (animation)
- Stage 3 (animation)
- Stage 4 (animation)
- REM (animation)

Chapter 10

- Pathways from the Lateral Hypothalamus (animation)
- Anorexia Patient: Susan (video)
- Stress & Fat (video)

Chapter 11

- Menstruation Cycle (animation)
- Erectile Dysfunction (video)
- Sex Dysfunction in Women (video)

Chapter 12

- Amygdala and Fear Conditioning (animation)
- Health and Stress (video)
- Stress and the Brain (video)
- CNS Depressants (animation)

Chapter 13

- Classical Conditioning (video)
- Amnestic Patient (video)
- Alzheimer's Patient (video)
- Implicit memories (Try It Yourself)
- Long Term Potentiation (Try It Yourself)
- Neural Networks and Memory (video)

Chapter 14

- Hemisphere Control (Try It Yourself)
- Lateralization and Language (animation)

Chapter 15

- Understanding Addiction (video)
- CNS Stimulants (animation)
- Opiate Narcotics (animation)
- Barbara 1 (video)
- Barbara 2 (video)
- Mary 1 (video)
- Mary 2 (video)
- Mary 3 (video)
- Frontal Neglect and the Wisconsin Card Sorting Task (video)
- Schizophrenia (video)
- Etta 1 (video)
- Etta 2 (video)

In addition to the above elements, you can review and test yourself using the chapter-specific Critical Thinking essay questions, the multiple-choice Chapter Quizzes, and the Interactive Biological Psychology Glossary.

Biological Psychology

Biological Psychology

8

James W. Kalat

North Carolina State University

THOMSON

WADSWORTH

Australia • Canada • Mexico • Singapore • Spain • United Kingdom • United States

THOMSON
~~~~~~~~~~~~~~~~
WADSWORTH

Psychology Editor: *Vicki Knight*
Development Editor: *Penelope Sky*
Assistant Editor: *Jennifer Wilkinson*
Editorial Assistant: *Monica Sarmiento*
Technology Project Manager: *Darin Derstine*
Marketing Manager: *Lori Grebe*
Marketing Assistant: *Laurel Anderson*
Advertising Project Manager: *Brian Chaffee*
Project Manager, Editorial Production: *Kirk Bomont*
Print/Media Buyer: *Kris Waller*
Permissions Editor: *Joohee Lee*

Production Service: *Nancy Shammas, New Leaf Publishing Services*
Art Editor: *Lisa Torri*
Photo Researcher: *Terri Wright*
Copy Editor: *Frank Hubert*
Illustrator: *Precision Graphics*
Text & Cover Designer: *Roy Neuhaus Design*
Cover Image: *Walter Hodges/Corbis; Yann Arthus-Bertrand/Corbis; Brand X Pictures; Photodisc/Getty Images; Rubberball; David Job/Getty Images*
Compositor: *Preface, Inc.*
Printer: *Transcontinental Printing/Interglobe*

For more information about our products, contact us at:
Thomson Learning Academic Resource Center
1-800-423-0563

For permission to use material from this text, contact us by:
Phone: 1-800-730-2214 **Fax:** 1-800-730-2215
Web: http://www.thomsonrights.com

Library of Congress Control Number: 2003106604

Student Edition: ISBN 0-534-58816-6

Instructor's Edition: ISBN 0-534-58859-X

International Student Edition: ISBN 0-534-58858-1

Wadsworth/Thomson Learning
10 Davis Drive
Belmont, CA 94002-3098
USA

Asia
Thomson Learning
5 Shenton Way #01-01
UIC Building
Singapore 068808

Australia
Nelson Thomson Learning
102 Dodds Street
South Melbourne, Victoria 3205
Australia

Canada
Nelson Thomson Learning
1120 Birchmount Road
Toronto, Ontario M1K 5G4
Canada

Europe/Middle East/Africa
Thomson Learning
HIgh Holborn House
50/51 Bedford Row
London WC1R 4LR
United Kingdom

Latin America
Thomson Learning
Seneca, 53
Colonia Polanco
11560 Mexico D.F.
Mexico

Spain
Paraninfo Thomson Learning
Calle/Magallanes, 25
28015 Madrid, Spain

About the Author

James W. Kalat (rhymes with ballot) is Professor of Psychology at North Carolina State University, where he teaches introduction to psychology and biological psychology. Born in 1946, he received an AB degree summa cum laude from Duke University and a PhD in psychology from the University of Pennsylvania, under the supervision of Paul Rozin. He is also the author of *Introduction to Psychology, Sixth Edition* (Belmont, CA: Wadsworth, 2002). In addition to textbooks, he has written journal articles on taste-aversion learning, the teaching of psychology, and other topics. A remarried widower, he has three children, two stepsons, and two grandchildren.

To My Family

Brief Contents

Contents

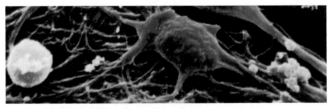

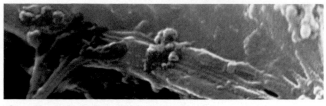

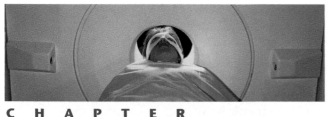

C H A P T E R

4 Anatomy of the Nervous System 73

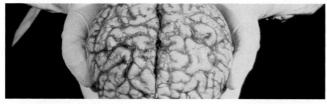

CHAPTER

5 Development and Plasticity of the Brain 107

CHAPTER

6 Vision 143

CHAPTER

7 The Other Sensory Systems and Attention 187

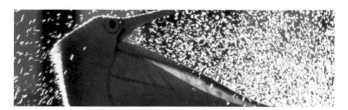

CHAPTER

10   Internal Regulation   293

C H A P T E R

11 Reproductive Behaviors 323

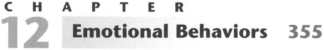

C H A P T E R
12 Emotional Behaviors 355

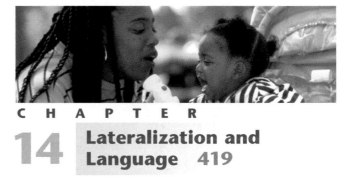

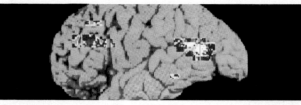

Preface

Much has changed since the first edition of this text was published in 1981. I wrote that book with pen on paper and then typed it with a manual typewriter. Compared to today's technology, that method seems as obsolete as churning your own butter. The first edition had only black-and-white illustrations and certainly no computerized test bank. CDs, email, and the Internet had not even been invented yet.

Biological psychology has changed almost as quickly as technology, and discussions of the topic become outdated almost as fast as computer technologies do. In the first edition, I remarked, "I almost wish I could get parts of this text . . . printed in disappearing ink, programmed to fade within ten years of publication, so that I will not be embarrassed by statements that will look primitive from some future perspective." An alternative to disappearing ink would be an expiration date, like those on milk cartons: "Best if used by this date . . . "

The most challenging aspect of writing a book is selecting what to include and what to omit. My primary goal has been to engage readers' interest. I have focused on the biological mechanisms relevant to key issues in psychology, such as language, learning and memory, sexual behavior, anxiety, aggression, abnormal behavior, and the mind-body problem. I hope that when they finish the book, readers will clearly see that the study of the brain has a great deal to do with "real psychology" and that they will want to learn more.

Each chapter consists of several modules, enabling instructors to assign part of a chapter per day instead of a whole chapter per week. This flexible format lets instructors assign modules in an order that suits their teaching styles. Indeed, of course, chapter order can be rearranged. I know one instructor who starts with Chapter 14.

I assume that the reader's background in psychology and biology is sufficient to understanding such basic terms as classical conditioning, reinforcement, vertebrate, mammal, gene, chromosome, and cell. Naturally, the stronger the background, the better. Although I assume a high-school chemistry course, Appendix A provides an adequate review.

CHANGES IN THIS EDITION

This edition has countless major and minor updates, well over 600 new references dated 2000 or later, new and improved illustrations, and fresh Try-It-Yourself exercises. The Instructor's Manual lists the changes in detail, but here are a few highlights:

- Recommended Web sites are cited within the text and listed again for quick reference at the end of the chapter.
- The seventh-edition Digressions have been taken out of boxes, renamed "Extensions and Applications," and moved into the text itself.
- The prospects and limitations of evolutionary psychology are discussed more fully in Chapters 1 and 11.
- The text has many new and updated sections on genetics, reflecting the enormous increase in research on this topic.
- Most of the material about drugs has been moved from Chapter 3 (synapses) to Chapter 15 (psychological disorders), and most of the material about hormones has been moved from Chapter 3 to Chapter 11 (reproductive behaviors). Consequently, Chapter 3 dropped from four modules to two.
- Chapter 4 has a new module that briefly surveys methods of research into the functions of the nervous system. When I first describe a study using a particular method, I then discuss that technique in more detail in a special Methods section.
- Chapter 7 (senses) includes a new module on attention, which gathers together material that was previously in other chapters.
- The first module of Chapter 15 (psychological disorders) has been broadened from alcohol abuse to drug use and addictions in general.

SUPPLEMENTS

Instructors who adopt the book may also obtain from the publisher a copy of the Instructor's Manual, written by Cynthia Crawford, California State University at San Bernardino. The manual contains chapter outlines, class demonstrations and projects, a list of video resources, additional Web sites, and the author's answers to the Thought Questions in the main text. The Exploring Biological Psychology CD-ROM that accompanies this book draws students into a multimedia world of animations, videos, quizzing, and interactive exercises. The Test Bank, by Jeffrey Stowell, Eastern Illinois University, offers multiple-choice test items and a few true-false and short-answer items. It also contains special files of questions for midterm and comprehensive final exams. The test items are available on ExamView, a cross-platform CD-ROM. The Study Guide, written by Elaine Hull of SUNY, Buffalo, may be purchased by students. Also available is the Multimedia Manager for Biological Psychology: A PowerPoint Link Tool, prepared by Duane Essex, Oxnard College.

I am grateful for the excellent work of Elaine Hull, Cynthia Crawford, Jeffrey Stowell, and Duane Essex.

ACKNOWLEDGMENTS

Let me tell you something about researchers in biological psychology: Nearly all are amazingly cooperative with textbook authors. A number of colleagues have sent me comments, ideas, and published materials; others supplied me with photos. I thank especially the following:

David Atkins, George Washington University

Stephen Black, Bishop's University

Anton Coenen, University Nijmegen, Netherlands

Juan Dominguez, University of Cincinnati College of Medicine

Martin Elton, University of Amsterdam

Edmund Gerstein, Leviathan Legacy, Inc.

Elaine Hull, State University of New York, Buffalo

Sam Kalat, North Carolina State University

William Moorcroft, Luther College

Edward Pollak, West Chester University

Dale Purves, Duke University Medical School

Aryeh Routtenberg, Northwestern University

Fred Toates, Open University, U. K.

I have received an enormous number of letters and email messages from students. Many included helpful suggestions; some managed to catch errors or inconsistencies that everyone else had overlooked. I thank especially the following:

E. Hayes Beckley, California State University, Chico

Eric DeWalt, West Chester University

Lynn Durel, University of Miami

Joel Fankhauser, Ouachita Baptist University

Michael Franklin, Tulane University

Garrett Hazelton, Matthew Keith, Joshua Ransom, and Tatyana Sivashinskaya, North Carolina State University

I appreciate the helpful comments provided by the following reviewers:

Tracie Blumentritthal, Texas A & M International University

Robin Bowers, College of Charleston

Richard Bruce, University of Alaska, Anchorage

Allen Butt, California State University, San Bernardino

Carl Cheney, Utah State University

Henry Gorman, Jr., Austin College

James Goss, University of Pittsburgh

Michael Havens, Montana State University—Billings

Susan Heidenreich, University of San Francisco

Elaine Hull, State University of New York, Buffalo

Gloria Lawrence, Wayne State College

Bill McClure, University of Southern California

Randy Nelson, Ohio State University

Robert Patterson, Washington State University

Heywood Petrie, University of Louisville

Michael Reich, University of Wisconsin—River Falls

Ronald Rogers, San Jose State University

William Schmidt, University of Buffalo

Barbara Shook, National University

Carlisle Skeen, University of Delaware

Jeffrey Stern, University of Michigan—Dearborn

Jeffrey Stowell, Eastern Illinois University

Scott Sugarman, City University of New York, College of Staten Island

Allen Szalda-Petree, University of Montana—Missoula

H. P. Zeigler, Hunter College

In preparing this text I have been most fortunate to work with Vicki Knight, a wise, patient, and very supportive acquisitions editor. She was especially helpful in setting priorities and planning the major thrust of this text. Penelope Sky, my developmental editor, has guided every step, from the review stage to the final draft. I have worked with her before, and each time I have greatly enjoyed and gained from the experience. Nancy Shammas supervised the production, a major task for a book like this one. As art editor, Lisa Torri's considerable artistic abilities helped to compensate for my complete lack. Jaime Olavarria made sure the figures were accurate. Terri Wright had charge of photos, another major task. I hope you enjoy the new illustrations in this text as much as I do. Many thanks to Kristina Seymour and team at Precision Graphics. Jennifer Wilkinson oversaw the development of supplements, such as the Instructor's Manual and Test Bank. Kirk Bomont guided the production of the text. I thank Roy Neuhaus for the text and cover design, Frank Hubert for the copyediting, and Do Mi Stauber for the indexes. All of these people have been splendid colleagues.

I also thank my wife, Jo Ellen, for keeping my spirits high, and my department head, David Martin, for his support and encouragement.

I welcome correspondence from both students and faculty. Please write to: James W. Kalat, Department of Psychology, Box 7801, North Carolina State University, Raleigh, NC 27695–7801, USA. Email: james_kalat@ncsu.edu

James W. Kalat

The Major Issues

Chapter Outline

Opposite:
A biological psychologist tries to explain any behavior, such as the behavior of this mother gorilla toward her baby, not in terms of subjective experiences such as "love," but in terms of its physiology, its development, its evolution, and its function. *Source: James Balog/Getty Images*

Main Ideas

1. Biological explanations of behavior fall into several categories, including physiology, development, evolution, and function.

2. Nearly all current philosophers and neuroscientists reject the idea that the mind exists independently of the physical brain. Still, the question remains as to how and why brain activity is connected to consciousness.

3. The expression of a given gene depends on the environment and on interactions with other genes.

4. Research with nonhuman animals can produce important information, but it sometimes inflicts distress or pain on the animals. Whether to proceed with a given experiment can be a difficult ethical issue.

It is often said that Man is unique among animals. It is worth looking at this term "unique" before we discuss our subject proper. The word may in this context have two slightly different meanings. It may mean: Man is strikingly different—he is not identical with any animal. This is of course true. It is true also of all other animals: Each species, even each individual is unique in this sense. But the term is also often used in a more absolute sense: Man is so different, so "essentially different" (whatever that means) that the gap between him and animals cannot possibly be bridged—he is something altogether new. Used in this absolute sense the term is scientifically meaningless. Its use also reveals and may reinforce conceit, and it leads to complacency and defeatism because it assumes that it will be futile even to search for animal roots. It is prejudging the issue.

Niko Tinbergen (1973, p. 161)

Biological psychologists study the "animal roots" of behavior, relating actions and experiences to genetics and physiology. In this chapter, we consider three major issues and themes: the relationship between mind and brain, the roles of nature and nurture, and the ethics of research. We also briefly consider prospects for further study.

MODULE 1.1

The Mind-Brain Relationship

Biological psychology is the study of the physiological, evolutionary, and developmental mechanisms of behavior and experience. Much of it is devoted to studying brain functioning. Figure 1.1 offers a view of the human brain from the top (what neuroscientists call a *dorsal view*) and from the bottom (a *ventral* view). The labels point to a few important areas which will become more familiar as you proceed through this text. An inspection of brain areas reveals distinct sub-areas and sub-subareas. At the microscopic level, we find two kinds of cells: the *neurons* (Figure 1.2) and the *glia*. Neurons, which convey messages to one another and to muscles and glands, vary enormously in size, shape, and functions. The glia, generally smaller than neurons, also vary and have functions that are less well understood. The activities of neurons and glia *somehow* produce an enormous wealth of behavior and experience. This book is about researchers' attempts to elaborate on that word "somehow."

Biological psychology is the most interesting topic in the world.

No doubt every professor and every textbook author feels that way about his or her field. But the others are wrong because biological psychology really *is* the most interesting topic. When I make this statement to a group of students, I always get a laugh. But when I say it to a group of biological psychologists or neuroscientists, they nod their heads in agreement, and I do in fact mean it seriously. I do *not* mean that memorizing the names and functions of brain parts and chemicals is unusually interesting. I mean that biological psychology addresses some theoretical issues that should be fascinating to anyone who thinks about them.

Actually, I shall back off a bit and say that biological psychology is about tied with cosmology as the most interesting topic. Cosmologists ask why the universe exists at all: Why is there *something* instead of *nothing*? And given that there is something, why this particular kind of something? Biological psychologists ask: Given the existence of this universe composed of matter and energy, why is there such a thing as consciousness? How does the physical brain give rise to vision, hunger, sexual desire, anger, fear, and other experiences? They also ask more specific questions such as: What genes, prenatal environment, or other factors predispose some people to psychological disorders? Is there any hope for recovery after brain damage? And what enables humans to learn language so easily?

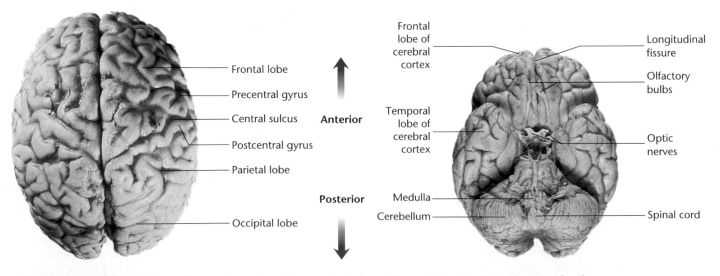

Figure 1.1   A dorsal view (from above) and a ventral view (from below) of the human brain
The brain has an enormous number of divisions and subareas; the labels point to a few of the main ones that are visible on the surface of the brain.

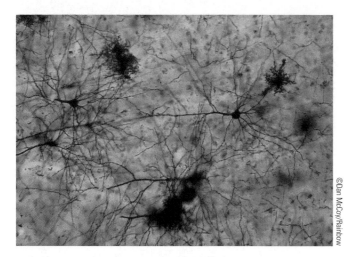

Figure 1.2 Neurons, magnified
The brain is composed of individual cells called neurons and glia.

Researchers continue to debate exactly what good yawning does. Yawning is a behavior that even people do without knowing its purpose.

BIOLOGICAL EXPLANATIONS OF BEHAVIOR

Commonsense explanations of behavior often refer to intentional goals such as, "He did this because he was trying to . . ." or "She did that because she wanted to . . ." But in many cases, we have no reason to assume any intentions. A 4-month-old bird migrating south for the first time presumably does not know why; the next spring, when she lays an egg, sits on it, and defends it from predators, again she probably doesn't know why. Even humans don't always know the reasons for their own behaviors. (Yawning and laughter are two examples. You do them, but can you explain what good they accomplish?)

In contrast to commonsense explanations, biological explanations of behavior fall into four categories: physiological, ontogenetic, evolutionary, and functional (Tinbergen, 1951). A **physiological explanation** relates a behavior to the activity of the brain and other organs. It deals with the machinery of the body—for example, the chemical reactions that enable hormones to influence brain activity and the routes by which brain activity ultimately controls the contractions of muscles.

The term *ontogenetic* comes from Greek roots meaning "to be" and "origin" (or genesis). Thus, an **ontogenetic explanation** describes the development of a structure or a behavior. It traces the influences of genes, nutrition, experiences, and the interactions among these influences in producing behavioral tendencies.

An **evolutionary explanation** examines a structure or a behavior in terms of evolutionary history. For example, when people become frightened, they

Unlike all other birds, doves and pigeons can drink with their heads down. (Others fill their mouths and then raise their heads.) A physiological explanation would describe these birds' unusual pattern of nerves and throat muscles. An evolutionary explanation states that all doves and pigeons share this behavioral capacity because they inherited their genes from a common ancestor.

sometimes get "goose bumps"—erections of the hairs, especially on the arms and shoulders. Goose bumps are useless in humans because our shoulder and arm hairs are so short. In hairier animals, however, hair erection makes a frightened animal look larger and more intimidating (Figure 1.3). Thus, an evolutionary explanation of human goose bumps is that the behavior evolved in our distant hairier ancestors and that we still have the mechanism for producing goose bumps.

A **functional explanation** describes *why* a structure or behavior evolved as it did. Within a small population, such as an isolated community, a gene can spread by accident through a process called *genetic drift.* (For example, sometimes one dominant male has an enormous number of offspring and thereby spreads all of his genes, including some that might be neutral or maladaptive.) However, the larger the population, the less powerful is genetic drift, and a gene that has become common in a large population presumably provides some advantage. A functional explanation identifies the advantage. For example, certain species have an appearance that matches their background (Figure 1.4). A functional explanation is that camouflaged appearance makes the animal inconspicuous to predators.

To contrast the four types of biological explanation, consider how they all apply to one example, birdsong (Catchpole & Slater, 1995):

Physiological explanation: A particular area of a songbird brain grows under the influence of

Figure 1.4   A seadragon, an Australian fish related to the seahorse, lives among kelp plants, looks like kelp, and usually drifts slowly and aimlessly, *acting like kelp.*
A functional explanation addresses why a structure or behavior has evolved and the purpose it serves. In this case, the purpose is that potential predators overlook a fish that resembles inedible plants.

testosterone; hence, it is larger in breeding males than in females or immature birds. That brain area enables a mature male to sing.

Ontogenetic explanation: In certain species, a young male bird learns its song by listening to adult males. Development of the song requires both the genes that prepare him to learn the song and the opportunity to hear the appropriate song during a sensitive period early in life.

Evolutionary explanation: In certain cases, one species' song closely resembles that of another species. For example, dunlins and Baird's sandpipers, two shorebird species, give their calls in distinct pulses, unlike other shorebirds. This similarity suggests that the two evolved from a single ancestor.

Functional explanation: In most bird species, only the male sings, and he sings only during the reproductive season and only in his territory. The functions of the song are to attract females and warn away other males. As a rule, a bird sings only loudly enough to be heard in the territory he can defend. In short, birds have evolved tendencies to sing in ways that improve their chances for mating.

We improve our understanding of behavior when we can combine as many of these approaches as possible. That is, ideally, we should understand the body mechanisms that produce the behavior, how it develops within the individual, how it evolved, and the function it serves.

Figure 1.3   A frightened cat with erect hairs
When a frightened mammal erects its hairs, it looks larger and more intimidating. (Consider, for example, the "Halloween cat.") Frightened humans sometimes also erect their body hairs, forming "goose bumps." An evolutionary explanation for goose bumps is that we inherited the tendency from ancestors who had long enough hair for the behavior to be useful.

1. What is the difference between an evolutionary explanation and a functional explanation?

Check your answer on page 8.

THE BRAIN AND CONSCIOUS EXPERIENCE

Biological psychology is an ambitious field. The explanations are still incomplete, littered with "maybe," "probably," and "this part to be filled in later." Nevertheless, researchers are optimistic about developing more thorough explanations.

Explaining birdsong in terms of hormones, brain activity, and evolutionary selection troubles few people. But how would you feel about a physical explanation of your own actions and experiences? Suppose you say, "I became frightened because I saw a man with a gun," and a neuroscientist says, "You became frightened because of increased electrochemical activity in the central amygdala of your brain." Is one explanation right and the other wrong? Or if both are right, what is the connection between them?

Biological explanations of behavior raise the **mind-body** or **mind-brain problem:** What is the relationship between the mind and the brain? The most widespread view among nonscientists is, no doubt, **dualism,** the belief that mind and body are different kinds of substance (thought substance and physical substance) that exist independently but somehow interact. The French philosopher René Descartes defended dualism but recognized the vexing issue of how an immaterial mind could influence a physical brain. He proposed that mind and brain interact at a single point in space, which he suggested was the pineal gland, the smallest unpaired structure he could find in the brain (Figure 1.5).

Although we credit Descartes with the first explicit defense of dualism, he hardly originated the idea. Nearly everyone starts as a dualist (except for the part about the pineal gland). We all grow up convinced that our thoughts control our actions, and when we are told that the brain controls behavior, we react, "Well, okay, then the brain communicates with the mind, and the mind controls the brain."

However, nearly all current philosophers and neuroscientists reject dualism. The decisive objection is that dualism conflicts with physicists' law of conservation of matter and energy: The only way to accelerate matter or transform energy, including the matter and energy in your body, is to act upon it with other matter or energy. If your mind is not composed of matter or energy, it cannot possibly influence anything in the entire physical universe, including your own body.

The alternative to dualism is **monism,** the belief that the universe consists of only one kind of existence. Various forms of monism are possible, grouped into the following categories:

- **materialism:** the view that everything that exists is material, or physical. According to one version of this view ("eliminative materialism"), mental events don't exist at all, and the common folk psychology based on beliefs and experiences is fundamentally mistaken. But most of us find it difficult to believe that our mind is a figment of our imagination. A less drastic version is that all psychological experiences can eventually be explained in purely physical terms.
- **mentalism:** the view that only the mind really exists and that the physical world exists only because we think about it, or perhaps only in the mind of God. This is not an easy position to disprove—go ahead and try!—but few philosophers or scientists take it seriously.
- **identity position:** the view that mental processes are the same thing as certain kinds of brain processes but described in different terms. In other words, the universe has only one kind of existence, but that existence is both material and mental. For example, one could describe the *Mona Lisa* as a beautiful painting by an extraordinarily skillful artist, or one could list the exact color and brightness of each point on the painting. Although the two descriptions appear very

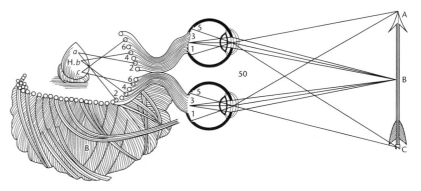

Figure 1.5 René Descartes's conception of brain and mind
Descartes understood that light from an object reached the retinas at the back of the eyes. From there, he assumed, the information was all channeled back to the pineal gland, a small unpaired organ in the brain.
Source: From Descartes' Treatise on Man.

different, they refer to the same object. According to the identity position, every experience *is* a brain activity, even though descriptions of our thoughts sound very different from descriptions of brain activities. For example, the fright you feel when you see a man with a gun *is the same thing* as a certain pattern of activity in your brain.

Has monism, or any version of it, been proved correct? No. In fact, most scientists avoid the word prove, except in mathematics. However, the arguments against dualism seem compelling, and the monist position leads to fruitful research. For example, as you will find throughout this text, stimulation of any brain area provokes changes in behavior and experience, and changes in experience evoke particular patterns of brain activity. Experiences and brain activities appear to be inseparable. We can still use the terms mind and mental activity if we make it clear that we regard these terms as another way of describing brain activity. However, if you lapse into using mind to mean a ghostlike something that is neither matter nor energy, don't underestimate the scientific and philosophical arguments that can be marshaled against you (Dennett, 1991).

(Does a belief in monism mean that we are lowering our evaluation of minds? Maybe not. Perhaps we are elevating our concept of the material world.)

If we accept some version of the monist position, such as the identity position, have we then solved the mind-brain problem? Hardly. Stating that mind and brain are the same thing does not solve the mystery; it merely restates it. The questions remain: *Why* is there any such thing as consciousness? *What kind* of physical structure is necessary to produce consciousness? And *how* does the physical structure produce consciousness?

The function (if any) of consciousness is far from obvious. People sometimes respond to signals that did not register consciously, and we perform skilled athletic acts *better* if we do them automatically instead of devoting conscious attention to them (Koch & Crick, 2001). Consciousness must perform a role in some tasks more than others and presumably depends on some brain areas more than others.

David Chalmers (1995) has proposed that in discussions of consciousness we distinguish between what he calls the easy problems and the hard problem. The **easy problems** pertain to many phenomena that we call *consciousness*, such as the difference between wakefulness and sleep and the mechanisms that enable us to focus our attention. These problems are in fact difficult scientifically, but they pose no philosophical problems.

On the other hand, the **hard problem** is the question of why and how any kind of brain activity is associated with consciousness. As Chalmers (1995) put it, "Why doesn't all this information-processing go on 'in the dark,' free of any inner feel?" (p. 203). Of all the research done on consciousness and its relationship to brain activity, little of it relates to the hard problem (Zeman, 2001). It is hard because we do not know how to do the research; we do not even have a clear hypothesis to test.

Chalmers's suggested answer is that consciousness is a fundamental property of matter—fundamental in the sense that it cannot be reduced to anything else. For example, mass and charge are fundamental properties; we cannot explain *why* matter has mass or charge; it just does. Perhaps in the same way, consciousness might be an unexplainable fundamental. If so, conscious experience may be a widespread phenomenon in the universe, found wherever matter and energy are arranged in information-rich ways.

And then again, maybe not. Noted philosopher Daniel Dennett (1991, 1996) argues that the hard problem really consists of an enormous number of easy problems. Once we fully answer all the easy problems, the hard problem will go away. By analogy, many people in the 1800s doubted that it was possible to explain life in physical terms. And then, step by step, biologists discovered the physical basis of metabolism, reproduction, embryological development, and other phenomena of life . . . except for consciousness, so far. Today, many researchers are trying to understand the physiology of consciousness, and perhaps they will succeed. Several other prominent philosophers and scientists also have stated their belief that consciousness can be explained in physical terms without any need for new assumptions (Churchland, 1996; Gell-Mann, 2001).

Do not expect an agreement on this issue soon. The problem is that consciousness is not observable. In contrast, mass and charge—properties that we agree are fundamental—cannot be explained, and they cannot even be observed directly, but at least they can be measured. Consciousness is different. Although I am directly aware of my own conscious mind, as you are of yours, we can only infer each other's. Indeed, how do you even know that other people are conscious? You don't, really. Maybe they are just very convincing robots.

Solipsism (SOL-ip-sizm, based on the Latin words *solus* and *ipse,* meaning "alone" and "self") is the philosophical position that I alone exist, or I alone am conscious. (There probably aren't many solipsists in the world, but there might be more than we know about. Solipsists don't have any reason to form an organization because each is convinced that all the other solipsists are wrong!) Although most people do not take solipsism seriously, it is hard to imagine evidence to refute it. The difficulty of knowing whether other people (or animals) have conscious experiences is known as the **problem of other minds.**

Nonsolipsists readily assume that other people are conscious, reasoning by analogy: "Other people look much like me and act much like me, so they probably have internal experiences much like mine." How about chimpanzees? Not everyone agrees, but I would say, "Sure. They look and act less like me, but close enough that I'll infer they have conscious experiences." How about dogs? Rats? Fish? Insects? Amoeba? Trees? Rocks? Most people hesitate at some point in this sequence, although different people hesitate at different points. At the extremes, some people believe that only humans are conscious, whereas others maintain that consciousness is a potential property of all matter. By that view, although a rock as a whole is not conscious, every atom within the rock or anything else has a primitive, "proto" consciousness (Hameroff, 2001). But most of us draw a hazy line somewhere separating animals we believe to be conscious from those we assume are not.

Or consider human development: If children are conscious and a just-fertilized egg is not (as I would assume), then at what point between egg and childhood does someone become conscious? And how could we possibly know?

Speculating on these issues leads most people to the conclusion that consciousness cannot be an all-or-nothing, yes-or-no question. We should draw no sharp dividing line between those having consciousness and those lacking it. Consciousness must have evolved gradually and no doubt develops gradually within an individual (Edelman, 2001).

What about computers and robots? Every year, they get more sophisticated and complicated. What if someone builds a robot that can walk, talk, carry on an intelligent conversation, laugh at jokes, and so forth? At what point, if any, would we decide that the robot is conscious?

Some people respond, "Never. A robot is just a machine, and it's programmed to do what it does." True, but the human brain is also a machine. (A machine is anything that converts one kind of energy into another.) And we, too, are programmed—by our genes and our past experiences. (We did not create ourselves.) Perhaps no robot of the kind we are building ever can be conscious, if consciousness is a property of carbon chemistry (Searle, 1992). But how would we know? Can you imagine any conceivable evidence that would persuade you that a robot is conscious? If you couldn't be persuaded by *any* evidence, then you're simply holding a prejudice. Try to think of evidence that could convince you of machine consciousness. If you are curious about the author's answer, check page 8. But think about your own answer first.

Many researchers originally became attracted to neuroscience because they were fascinated with the mind-brain problem and hoped to contribute at least slightly to its solution. As you will see throughout this text, losing various parts of the brain means losing parts of the mind, and stimulating certain brain activities can evoke experiences or behavioral tendencies. *Why* there is such a close relationship between brain and experience may still elude us, but at least we continue to explore and document the connection. If Dennett is right that answering the easy problems does answer the hard problem, then great. But if the hard problem really is unsolvable, the only way we will demonstrate its unsolvability is by vigorous attempts to solve it. In the process, we should at least provide guidance for our philosophical speculations.

If you would like to read more about these philosophical issues, go to the first Web site and then follow the links to *Journal of Consciousness Studies,* or visit the second link for the *Journal of Mind and Behavior.*
www.imprint.co.uk/
www.ume.maine.edu/~jmb/welcome.html

Stop & Check

2. What are the three major versions of monism?
3. What is meant by the "hard problem"?
Check your answers on page 8.

MODULE·1.1

In Closing: Your Brain and Your Experience

Biological psychologists are ambitious, hoping to explain as much as possible of psychology in terms of brain processes, genes, and the like. The guiding assumption is that the pattern of activity that occurs in your brain when you see a rabbit *is* your perception of a rabbit; the pattern that occurs when you feel fear *is* your fear. And so forth. This is not to say that "your brain physiology controls you" any more than one should say that "you control your brain." Rather, your brain *is* you! The rest of this book explores how far we can go with this guiding assumption.

SUMMARY

1. Biological psychologists try to answer four types of questions about any given behavior: How does it relate to the physiology of the brain and other organs? How does it develop within the individual? How did the capacity for the behavior evolve? And why did the capacity for this behavior evolve? (That is, what function does it serve?) (p. 3)

2. Biological explanations of behavior do not necessarily assume that the individual understands the purpose or function of the behavior. (p. 3)

3. Philosophers and scientists continue to address the mind-brain or mind-body relationship. Dualism, the popular view that the mind exists separately from the brain, is opposed by the principle that the matter and energy of the brain can be influenced only by other matter and energy. (p. 5)

4. Nearly all philosophers and scientists who have addressed the mind-brain problem favor some version of monism, the belief that the universe consists of only one kind of substance. That substance could be either material (materialism), mental (mentalism), or a combination of both (identity position). Still, the hard problem remains: Why is there such a thing as conscious experience at all and why does it emerge from certain kinds of brain activity? (p. 5)

ANSWERS TO *STOP AND CHECK* QUESTIONS

1. An evolutionary explanation states what evolved from what. For example, humans evolved from earlier primates and therefore have certain features that we inherited from those ancestors, even if the features are not useful to us today. A functional explanation states why something was advantageous and therefore evolutionarily selected. (p. 5)

2. The three major versions of monism are materialism (everything can be explained in physical terms), mentalism (only minds exist), and identity (the mind and the brain are the same thing). (p. 7)

3. The "hard problem" is why minds exist at all in a physical world, why there is such a thing as consciousness, and how it relates to brain activity. (p. 7)

THOUGHT QUESTIONS[1]

1. What would you say or do to try to convince a solipsist that you are conscious?

2. Now suppose a robot just said and did the same things you did in question 1. Will you be convinced that it is conscious?

AUTHOR'S ANSWER ABOUT MACHINE CONSCIOUSNESS (p. 7)

Here is a possibility similar to a proposal by J. R. Searle (1992): Suppose someone suffers damage to part of the visual cortex of the brain and becomes blind to part of the visual field. Now, engineers design artificial brain circuits to replace the damaged cells. Impulses from the eyes are routed to this device, which processes the information and sends electrical impulses to healthy portions of the brain that ordinarily get input from the damaged brain area. After this device is installed, the person sees the field that used to be blind, remarking, "Ah! Now I can see that area again! I see shapes, colors, movement—the whole thing, just as I used to!" Evidently, the machine has enabled conscious perception of vision. Then, the person suffers still more brain damage, and engineers replace the rest of the visual cortex with artificial circuits. Once again, the person assures us that everything looks the same as before. Next, damage occurs in the auditory cortex, someone replaces it with a machine, and the person reports normal hearing. One by one, additional brain areas are damaged and replaced by machines; in each case, the behavior returns to normal and the person reports having normal experiences, just as before the damage. Even brain areas storing memories are replaced. Eventually, the entire brain is replaced. At that point, I would say that the machine itself is conscious.

Note that all this discussion assumes that these artificial brain circuits and transplants are possible. I don't know whether they ever will be. My point is merely to show what kind of evidence might convince us of a conscious machine.

---

[1]Thought questions are intended to spark thought and discussion. The text does not directly answer any of them, although it may imply or suggest an answer in some cases. In other cases, there may be several possible answers.

MODULE 1.2

The Genetics of Behavior

Everything you are and everything you do depend on both your genes and your environment. Without your genes or without an adequate environment, you would not exist. So far, no problem. The controversies arise when we discuss why people differ from one another in their intelligence, weight gain, sexual orientation, mood, tendency toward alcoholism, and so forth. Do we differ mostly because of our genes or mostly because we grew up in different environments? This module certainly does not resolve the controversies, but it should help you understand them.

We begin with a review of elementary genetics. Readers already familiar with the concepts may skim quickly over the next few pages and start with the section on heritability.

MENDELIAN GENETICS

Prior to the work of Gregor Mendel, a late-19th-century monk, scientists thought that inheritance was a blending process in which the properties of the sperm and the egg simply mixed, much as one might mix red and yellow paint.

Mendel demonstrated that inheritance occurs through **genes,** units of heredity that maintain their structural identity from one generation to another. As a rule, genes come in pairs because they are aligned along **chromosomes** (strands of genes), which also come in pairs. (As an exception to this rule, a male's X and Y chromosomes are unpaired, having different genes.) A gene is a portion of a chromosome, which is composed of the double-strand chemical **deoxyribonucleic acid,** or **DNA.** A strand of DNA serves as a template (model) for the synthesis of **ribonucleic acid (RNA)** molecules. RNA is a single-strand chemical; one type of RNA molecules serves as a template for the synthesis of protein molecules. Figure 1.6 summarizes the main steps in translating information from DNA through RNA into proteins, which then determine the development and properties of the organism. Some proteins form part of the structure of the body; others serve as **enzymes,** biological catalysts that regulate chemical reactions in the body.

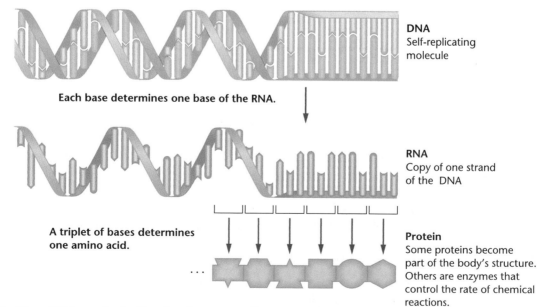

DNA
Self-replicating molecule

Each base determines one base of the RNA.

RNA
Copy of one strand of the DNA

A triplet of bases determines one amino acid.

Protein
Some proteins become part of the body's structure. Others are enzymes that control the rate of chemical reactions.

Figure 1.6   How DNA controls the development of an organism
The sequence of bases along a strand of DNA determines the order of bases along a strand of RNA; RNA in turn controls the sequence of amino acids in a protein molecule.

An individual who has an identical pair of genes on the two chromosomes is **homozygous** for that gene. An individual with an unmatched pair of genes is **heterozygous** for that gene. For example, a gene for blue eyes might be on one chromosome and a gene for brown eyes on the other.

Certain genes can be identified as dominant or recessive. A **dominant** gene shows a strong effect in either the homozygous or heterozygous condition; a **recessive** gene shows its effects only in the homozygous condition. For example, someone with a gene for brown eyes (dominant) and one for blue eyes (recessive) will have brown eyes, although he or she is a "carrier" for the blue-eye gene and can transmit it to a child. For a behavioral example, the gene for ability to taste moderate concentrations of phenylthiocarbamide (PTC) is dominant; the gene for low sensitivity is recessive. Only someone with two recessive genes has trouble tasting it. Figure 1.7 illustrates the possible results of a mating between people who are both heterozygous for the PTC-tasting gene. Because each of them has one high taste sensitivity (T)[2] gene, each can taste PTC. However, each parent transmits either a taster gene (T) or a nontaster gene (t) to a given child. Therefore, a child in this family has a 25% chance of being a homozygous (TT) taster, a

[2]Among geneticists, it is customary to use a capital letter to indicate the dominant gene and a lowercase letter to indicate the recessive gene.

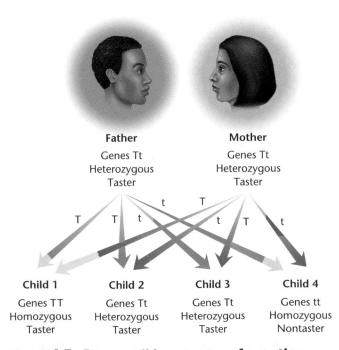

Father
Genes Tt
Heterozygous
Taster

Mother
Genes Tt
Heterozygous
Taster

Child 1
Genes TT
Homozygous
Taster

Child 2
Genes Tt
Heterozygous
Taster

Child 3
Genes Tt
Heterozygous
Taster

Child 4
Genes tt
Homozygous
Nontaster

Figure 1.7 Four possible outcomes of a mating between parents who are heterozygous for a given gene (Tt)
A child in this family has a 25% chance of being homozygous for the dominant gene (TT), a 25% chance of being homozygous for the recessive gene (tt), and a 50% chance of being heterozygous (Tt).

50% chance of being a heterozygous (Tt) taster, and a 25% chance of being a homozygous (tt) nontaster.

Chromosomes and Crossing Over

Each chromosome participates in reproduction independently of the others, and each species has a certain number of chromosomes—for example, 23 pairs in humans, 4 pairs in fruit flies. If you have a *BbCc* genotype, and the *B* and *C* genes are on different chromosomes, your contribution of a *B* or *b* gene is independent of whether you contribute *C* or *c*. But suppose *B* and *C* are on the same chromosome. If one chromosome has the *BC* combination and the other has *bc*, then if you contribute a *B*, you probably also contribute *C*.

The exception comes about as a result of **crossing over**: A pair of chromosomes may break apart during reproduction and reconnect such that part of one chromosome attaches to the other part of the second chromosome. If one chromosome has the *BC* combination and the other chromosome has the *bc* combination, crossing over between the *B* locus (location) and the *C* locus leaves new chromosomes with the combinations *Bc* and *bC*. The closer the *B* locus is to the *C* locus, the less often crossing over occurs between them.

Sex-Linked and Sex-Limited Genes

The genes located on the sex chromosomes are known as **sex-linked genes**. All other chromosomes are autosomal chromosomes, and their genes are **autosomal genes**.

In mammals, the two sex chromosomes are designated X and Y: A female mammal has two X chromosomes; a male has an X and a Y. (Unlike the arbitrary symbols *B* and *C* that I introduced to illustrate gene pairs, X and Y are standard symbols used by all geneticists.) During reproduction, the female necessarily contributes an X chromosome, and the male contributes either an X or a Y. If he contributes an X, the offspring is female; if he contributes a Y, the offspring is male.

The Y chromosome is small and carries few genes other than the gene that causes the individual to develop as a male. The X chromosome, however, carries many genes. Thus, when biologists speak of sex-linked genes, they usually mean X-linked genes.

An example of a human sex-linked gene is the recessive gene for red-green color vision deficiency. Any man with this gene on his X chromosome has red-green color deficiency because he has no other X chromosome. A woman, however, is color deficient only if she has that recessive gene on both of her X chromosomes. So, for example, if 8% of human X chromosomes contain the gene for color vision deficiency, then 8% of all men will be color deficient, but fewer than 1% of women will be (.08 × .08).

Distinct from sex-linked genes are the **sex-limited genes.** A sex-limited gene is present in both sexes but has an effect limited or almost limited to one sex. For instance, genes control the amount of chest hair in men, breast size in women, the amount of crowing in roosters, and the rate of egg production in hens. Both sexes have these genes, but the genes become active only under the influence of sex hormones.

1. Suppose you can taste PTC. If your mother can also taste it, what (if anything) can you predict about your father's ability to taste it? If your mother cannot taste it, what (if anything) can you predict about your father's ability to taste it?

2. How does a sex-linked gene differ from a sex-limited gene?

Check your answers on page 19.

Sources of Variation

If reproduction always produced offspring that were exact copies of the parents, evolution would not occur. One source of variation is **recombination,** a new combination of genes, some from one parent and some from the other, that yields characteristics not found in either parent. For example, a mother with curly blonde hair and a father with straight black hair could have a child with curly black hair or straight blonde hair.

A more powerful source of variation is a **mutation,** or change in a single gene. For instance, a gene for brown eyes might mutate into a gene for blue eyes. Mutation of a given gene is a rare, random event; that is, the needs of the organism do not guide it. A mutation is analogous to having an untrained person add, remove, or distort something on the blueprints for your new house. Random changes are only rarely helpful, but those rare events are critical for evolution.

Most mutations produce recessive genes. Thus, if you or one of your recent ancestors had a harmful mutation on one gene, your children will not show its effects unless your mate has the same harmful gene. For this reason, it is unwise to marry a close relative.

HERITABILITY

Unlike PTC sensitivity and color vision deficiency, most variations in behavior depend on the combined influence of many genes and environmental influences. You may occasionally hear someone ask about a behavior, "Which is more important, heredity or environment?" That question as stated is meaningless. No behavior can develop without both heredity and environment.

However, we can rephrase it meaningfully: Do the observed *differences* among individuals depend more on differences in heredity or on differences in environment? For example, if you sing better than I do, the reason could be that you have different genes, that you had better training, or of course, both.

In measuring the relative contribution of heredity, researchers use the concept of **heritability,** an estimate of how much of the variance in some characteristic within some population is due to differences in heredity. Heritability ranges from 0 to 1. A heritability of 0 means that genetic differences account for none of the observed variations in some characteristic within the tested population. A heritability of 1 indicates that genetic differences account for all of the observed differences. Naturally, a value such as .5 indicates an intermediate role.

Note that heritability is specific to the tested population; it could be high in one population and low in another. For example, in a community in which everyone is closely related, any variation in their behaviors would be largely due to differences in their environments, and therefore, heritability would be low. (Differences in heredity cannot account for much if everyone has the same genes!) Conversely, if all the people in some other community have nearly identical environments, the heritability of their behaviors will be high. (Environmental differences cannot account for much, so the remaining variability must be largely hereditary.)

Ways of Measuring Human Heritability

We omit the mathematics here and consider only the logic. First, researchers compare the resemblances between monozygotic (identical) twins and dizygotic (fraternal) twins. A stronger resemblance between monozygotic than dizygotic twins indicates high heritability; equal resemblance in both kinds of twins implies 0 heritability. Second, they examine adopted children. If adopted children resemble their biological parents and not their adoptive parents, we infer high heritability.

Based on these kinds of evidence, researchers have found fairly high heritability for details of brain anatomy (P. Thompson et al., 2001) and for an enormous range of behaviors, including loneliness (McGuire & Clifford, 2000), neuroticism (Lake, Eaves, Maes, Heath, & Martin, 2000), television watching (Plomin, Corley, DeFries, & Fulker, 1990), social attitudes (S. F. Posner, Baker, Heath, & Martin, 1996), and many others to be described in later chapters.

Overestimating Heritability

Humans are difficult research animals. Investigators cannot control people's mate choices and have only limited control over their environments. Some of the difficulties studying humans lead to overestimated heritabilities (Rutter, Pickles, Murray, & Eaves, 2001).

For example, the closer we come to providing everyone with the same environment, the higher the heritability becomes. (Tiny environmental differences will not produce much difference in outcome, so the remaining differences have to reflect heredity.) Such is the case for adopted children: Adoption agencies try to place them all in high-quality homes, and therefore, differences in their environments are generally small (Stoolmiller, 1999).

Furthermore, studies on humans seldom distinguish between genetics and prenatal influences. Most monozygotic (MZ) twins share a single chorion and therefore a single blood supply during prenatal life, whereas dizygotic (DZ) twins develop in separate chorions (Figure 1.8). Therefore, MZ twins resemble one another more closely in prenatal environment as well as heredity. In addition, consider the studies showing that biological children of low-

IQ, criminal, or mentally ill parents are likely to have similar problems themselves, even if adopted by excellent parents. The low-IQ, criminal, or mentally ill parents gave the children their genes, but they also gave them their prenatal environment. In many cases, those mothers had poor diets and poor medical care during pregnancy. Many smoked cigarettes, drank alcohol, and used other drugs that affect a fetus's brain development. Therefore, what looks like a genetic effect could be wholly or partly an effect of prenatal environment.

Still another problem is that your genes not only affect you but also influence how other people treat you (Kendler, 2001). For example, good-looking children get treated differently from less attractive children. If your genes cause you to be even-tempered, others react to you in a friendly way, thereby improving your already calm disposition. If your genes lead you to frequent temper tantrums, other people—including your parents—will react harshly, giving you still further reason to feel hostile. Dickens and Flynn (2001) call this tendency a **multiplier effect:** If genetic or prenatal influences produce even a small increase in some activity, the early tendency will change the environment in a way that magnifies that tendency.

Genes or prenatal influences ⟶ Increase of some tendency ⤸ Environment that facilitates ⤴

For a sports example, imagine a child born with genes promoting greater than average height, running speed, and coordination. Early in life, that child succeeds at basketball and thus is encouraged to play more. The increased practice fosters even greater skill and success and therefore still more encouragement. What was initially a small effect of genes or prenatal environment develops into a huge effect. It shows up in any research study as evidence for high heritability, despite the obvious importance of the environment. The research difficulty is that different genes predispose people to seek out different environments, which support the same behavioral tendencies as the genes themselves.

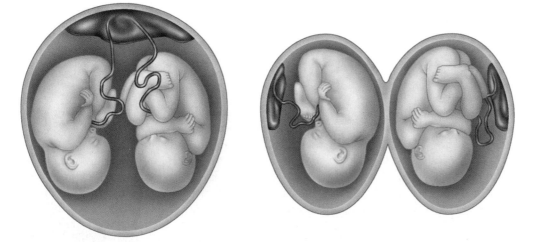

Figure 1.8 Prenatal development of monozygotic and dizygotic twins
In most cases, monozygotic (identical) twins develop in a single chorion and have the same blood supply. Dizygotic (fraternal) twins develop in separate chorions. Therefore, monozygotic twins have nearly the same prenatal environment as well as the same genetic inheritance, and dizygotic twins differ in both respects.

Environmental Modification of Heritable Behaviors

Even a trait with high heritability can be modified by environmental interventions. (A measure of heritability applies to a population in a specific environment; it cannot tell us about the effects of another environment.) For example, different genetic strains of mice behave differently in the *elevated plus maze* (Figure 1.9). Some stay almost entirely in the walled arms, like the mouse shown in the figure; others (more adventuresome? less nervous?) venture onto the open arms. But even when different laboratories use the same genetic strains and nearly the same procedures, strains that are adventuresome in one laboratory are less active in another (Crabbe, Wahlsten, & Dudek, 1999). Evidently, the effects of the genes depend on subtle differences in procedure, such as how the investigators handle the mice or maybe even the investigators' odors. (Most behaviors do not show this much variability; the elevated plus maze appears to be an extreme example.)

For a human example, **phenylketonuria** (FEE-nil-KEET-uhn-YOOR-ee-uh), or **PKU**, is a form of mental retardation caused by a genetic inability to metabolize the amino acid phenylalanine. Because of the PKU gene, phenylalanine accumulates to toxic levels, impairing brain development and leaving children mentally retarded, restless, and irritable. Approximately 1% of Europeans carry a recessive gene for PKU; fewer Asians and still fewer Africans have the gene (T. Wang et al., 1989).

Ordinarily, the heritability of PKU would be virtually 1. However, physicians in many countries routinely measure the level of phenylalanine or its metabolites in babies' blood or urine. If a baby has high levels, indicating PKU, physicians advise the parents to put the baby on a strict low-phenylalanine diet to minimize brain damage (Waisbren, Brown, de Sonneville, & Levy, 1994). Our ability to prevent PKU provides particularly strong evidence that *heritable* or *genetic* does not mean *unmodifiable*.

A couple of notes about PKU: The required diet is difficult. People have to avoid meats, eggs, dairy products, grains, and especially aspartame (NutraSweet), which is 50% phenylalanine. Instead, people with PKU must eat an expensive formula containing all the other amino acids. Physicians long believed that children with PKU could quit the diet after a few years. Later experience has shown that high phenylalanine levels damage teenage and adult brains, too, leading to mild mental retardation and increased risk of psychological disorders. A woman with PKU should be especially careful during pregnancy and nursing. Even a genetically normal baby cannot handle the enormous amounts of phenylalanine that an affected mother might pass through the placenta.

For more information about PKU, try the following:
web.ukonline.co.uk/nspku/

For more information about the distribution of the gene in various populations, see this Web site:
archive.uwcm.ac.uk/uwcm/mg/fidd/index.html

3. Suppose researchers measure the heritability of intelligence in two populations: one in which everyone shares a good, supportive environment and one in which certain individuals have a much better environment than others do. Which population will show the higher heritability? Why?

4. What example illustrates the point that even if some characteristic is highly heritable, a change in the environment may be able to change it?

Check your answers on page 19.

How Genes Affect Behavior

A biologist who speaks of a "gene for brown eyes" does not mean that the gene directly produces brown eyes. Rather, the gene produces a protein that alters body chemistry to make the eyes brown instead of another color. If we speak of a "gene for alcoholism," we should not imagine that the gene itself produces alcoholism. Rather, the gene produces a protein that under

Figure 1.9 An elevated plus maze
Different genetic strains of mice behave differently in this apparatus, presumably displaying different levels of anxiety. But the results vary from lab to lab because of minor, unintentional variations in procedure. In short, the effects of a gene can vary depending on the environment.

certain circumstances increases the probability of alcoholism. It is important to specify those circumstances as well as we can, of course.

Exactly how a gene increases the probability of a given behavior is a complex issue. In later chapters, we encounter a few examples of genes that control brain chemicals. However, genes also can affect behavior indirectly by changing other body characteristics. For example, a gene that increases a person's height increases the probability of playing basketball (if he or she lives where people play basketball). Because time spent on a basketball court is time not spent doing something else, the increased-height gene probably decreases the time that the person spends playing the violin, talking on the telephone, and so forth. Consequently, we should not be amazed by reports that almost every human behavior has some heritability. The point is that genes that affect the body in any way also affect behavior, and a gene that affects one behavior also influences other behaviors.

THE EVOLUTION OF BEHAVIOR

Every gene is subject to evolution by natural selection. **Evolution** is a change over generations in the frequencies of various genes in a population. Note that, by this definition, evolution includes *any* change in gene frequencies, regardless of whether it is helpful or harmful to the species in the long run. (Charles Darwin, in fact, did not like the term *evolution* because it implied progress. He preferred the term *descent with modification*.)

We must distinguish two questions about evolution: How *did* species evolve, and how *do* species evolve? To ask how species did evolve is to ask what evolved from what, basing our answers on inferences from fossils and comparisons of living species. For example, biologists find that humans are more similar to chimpanzees than to other species. These similarities point to the probability of a common ancestor from which both humans and chimpanzees inherited most of their genes. Similarly, humans and chimpanzees together have some striking resemblances to monkeys and presumably shared a common ancestor with monkeys in the remoter past. Using similar reasoning, evolutionary biologists have constructed an "evolutionary tree" that shows the relationships among various species (Figure 1.10). As new evidence becomes available, biologists occasionally change their opinions of what evolved from what; thus, any evolutionary tree is tentative.

Nevertheless, the question of how species *do* evolve is a question of how the process works, and that process is, in its basic outlines, a logical necessity. That is, any species that reproduces more or less the way we do *must* evolve. The reasoning goes as follows:

- Offspring generally resemble their parents for genetic reasons.
- Mutations and recombinations of genes occasionally introduce new heritable variations.
- Some individuals survive longer and reproduce more abundantly than others.
- The individuals who reproduce the most pass on the greatest number of genes to the next generation, which therefore resembles the individuals who reproduced most successfully. That is, any new gene or gene combination that is consistently associated with reproductive success will become more and more prevalent in later generations.

This principle has long been known by plant and animal breeders, who choose individuals with a desired trait and make them the parents of the next generation. This process is called **artificial selection,** and over many generations, it has produced exceptional race horses, hundreds of breeds of dogs, chickens that lay huge numbers of eggs, and so forth. Charles Darwin's (1859) insight was that nature also selects. If certain individuals are more successful than others in finding food, escaping enemies, attracting mates, or protecting their offspring, then their genes will become more prevalent in later generations.

Common Misunderstandings About Evolution

Let us clarify the principles of evolution by addressing a few misconceptions.

- *Does the use or disuse of some structure or behavior cause an evolutionary increase or decrease in that feature?* You have probably heard people say something like, "Because we hardly ever use our little toes, they will get smaller and smaller in each succeeding generation." That idea is a carryover of the biologist Jean Lamarck's theory of evolution through the inheritance of acquired characteristics, known as **Lamarckian evolution.** According to this idea, if giraffes stretch their necks as far out as possible, their offspring will be born with longer necks. Similarly, if you exercise your arm muscles, your children will be born with bigger arm muscles, and if you fail to use your little toes, your children's little toes will be smaller than yours. However, biologists have found no mechanism for Lamarckian evolution to occur and no evidence that it does. Using or failing to use some part of the body does not change the genes that one can transmit to the next generation.

(It is possible that people's little toes might shrink in future evolution if people with even smaller little toes have an advantage over other people. But we would have to wait for a mutation that decreases little

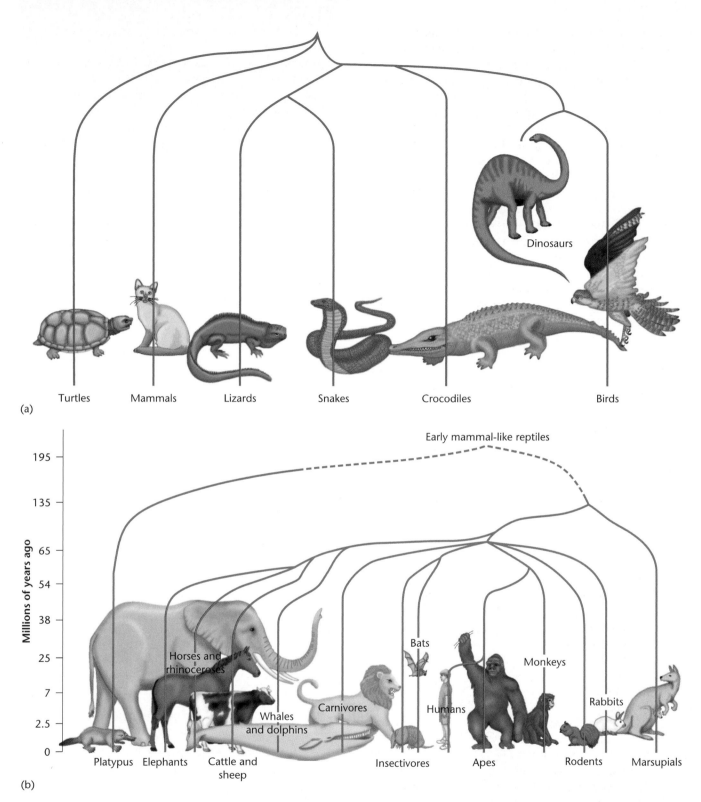

(a)

Turtles Mammals Lizards Snakes Crocodiles Birds

(b)

Early mammal-like reptiles

Millions of years ago

195

135

65

54

38

25

7

2.5

0

Platypus Elephants Cattle and sheep Whales and dolphins Carnivores Insectivores Apes Rodents Marsupials

Horses and rhinoceroses

Bats Monkeys Rabbits

Humans

Figure 1.10 Evolutionary trees
(a) Evolutionary relationships among mammals, birds, and several kinds of reptiles. **(b)** Evolutionary relationships among various species of mammals.

toe size—without causing some other problem—and then we would have to wait for people with this mutation to outreproduce people with other genes.)

• *Have humans stopped evolving?* Because modern medicine can keep almost anyone alive, and because welfare programs in prosperous countries provide the necessities of life for almost everyone, some people assert that humans are no longer subject to the principle of "survival of the fittest." Therefore, the argument goes, human evolution has stopped or at least slowed down a great deal.

The flaw in this argument is that the key to evolution is not survival, but reproduction. One must survive long enough to reproduce, but what counts in evolution is how many healthy children (and nieces and nephews etc.) one has. Thus, keeping everyone alive doesn't stop human evolution. If some people have more children than others do, their genes will spread in the population.

- *Does "evolution" mean "improvement"?* It depends on what you mean by "improvement." By definition, evolution improves the **fitness** of the population, which is operationally defined as *the number of copies of one's genes that endure in later generations.* However, genes that increase fitness at one time and place might be disadvantageous after a change in the environment. Consider, for example, the colorful tail feathers of the male peacock, which enable it to attract females. If the environment changes with the introduction of a new predator that responds to bright colors, the previously advantageous display becomes a handicap. In other words, the genes of the current generation evolved because they were adaptive for *previous* generations, and they may or may not be adaptive at present.
- *Does evolution act to benefit the individual or the species?* Neither: It acts to spread the genes! In a sense, you do not carry your genes around as a way of reproducing yourself; your genes carry *you* around as a way of reproducing *themselves* (Dawkins, 1989).

Sometimes a sexual display, such as the spread of a peacock's tail feathers, leads to great reproductive success and therefore to the spread of the associated genes. In a slightly changed environment, this gene could become maladaptive. For example, if an aggressive predator with good color vision enters the peacock's range, the bird's slow movement and colorful feathers could seal its doom.

A gene spreads through a population if—and only if—the individuals bearing that gene reproduce more than do the individuals with other genes. So, for example, imagine a gene that causes you to risk your own life to protect your children. That gene will spread through the population (if it really does benefit your children), even though it endangers you personally. A gene that caused you to attack other members of your species to benefit your children could also spread, even though it harmed the species in general—presuming, of course, that the behavior really did benefit your children and that others of your species did not attack you or your children in retaliation.

5. Many people believe the human appendix is useless. Should we therefore expect it to grow smaller from one generation to the next?

Check your answer on page 19.

Sociobiology

Sociobiology, or evolutionary psychology, deals with how social behaviors have evolved. The emphasis is on *functional* explanations, as defined earlier—how a behavior might be useful and why natural selection would favor it. The assumption is that any structure or behavior that is characteristic of a species must have

It is possible to slow the rate of evolution, but not just by keeping everyone alive. The Chinese government attempts to limit each family to one child. Successful enforcement of this policy would certainly limit the possibility of genetic changes between generations.

arisen through natural selection. For example, if nearly all healthy male peacocks have large, colorful tails, those tails must in some way help males spread their genes. The same goes for behavior.

Is that assumption valid? Often, it is at least an excellent guide to research. Consider a few examples:

- Some animal species have better color vision than others, and some have better peripheral vision. Presumably, these differences relate to something about different species' ways of life (see Chapter 7).
- We have brain mechanisms that cause us to sleep for a few hours each day and to cycle through several different stages of sleep. Presumably, we would not have such mechanisms unless sleep provided benefits, and we can do research to determine those benefits (see Chapter 9).
- Mammals and birds devote more energy to maintaining body temperature than to all other activities combined. We would not have evolved such an expensive mechanism unless it gave us major advantages (see Chapter 11).
- Bears eat all the food they can find; small birds eat only enough to satisfy their immediate needs. Humans generally take a middle path. The different eating habits presumably relate to different needs by different species (see Chapter 11).

On the other hand, some characteristics of a species have a more debatable relationship to natural selection. Consider two examples:

- People grow old and die, with an average survival time of about 70 or 80 years under favorable circumstances. Do we deteriorate because we have genes that cause us to die and get out of the way, so we don't compete against our own children and grandchildren? Or are aging and death inevitable? Different people do age at different rates, largely for genetic reasons (Puca et al., 2001), so it is not ridiculous to hypothesize that our tendency to age and die is controlled by selective pressures of evolution. But the conclusion is hardly obvious, either.
- More men than women enjoy the prospect of casual sex with multiple partners, and men and women tend to look for somewhat different qualities in a potential lifelong mate. Theorists have related these tendencies to different selective pressures on men and women: A man can have many children by impregnating many women, whereas a woman cannot multiply her children through sex with many men. Men can have children when they are old; women generally cannot. A woman can be sure any child she bears is her own; a man is less certain about which child is his own. And so forth (Buss, 1994). So, can we conclude that men and women are prewired to have different sexual behaviors? As we shall explore in Chapter 11, this question is a difficult one.

To further illustrate the sociobiological/evolutionary psychology approach, let's consider the theoretically interesting example of **altruistic behavior,** an action that benefits someone other than the actor. A gene spreads within the population if individuals with that gene reproduce more than those without it. A gene that encourages altruistic behavior would help other individuals, who might then spread their own genes. How could a gene for altruism spread, if at all?

We should begin with the question of how common altruism is. It certainly occurs in humans: We contribute to charities; we try to help people in distress; a student may explain something to a classmate who is competing for a good grade in a course. Among nonhumans, examples are abundant of parents devoting much effort and even risking their lives to protect their young, but altruism toward nonrelatives is rare. Even apparent altruism often has a selfish motive. For example, when a crow finds food on the ground, it caws loudly, attracting other crows that will share the food. Altruism? Not really. A bird on the ground is vulnerable to attack by cats and other enemies, and when it lowers its head to eat, it cannot see the dangers. Having other crows around means more eyes to watch for dangers.

Similarly, consider meerkats (an animal related to the mongoose). Periodically, one or another member of any meerkat colony stands and, if it sees danger, emits an alarm call that warns the others (Figure 1.11). Its alarm call helps the others (probably including its close relatives), but the one who sees the danger first and emits the alarm call is the one most likely to escape (Clutton-Brock et al., 1999).

In short, altruistic behavior is uncommon in nonhumans, and even in humans, we have no evidence that it is under genetic control. Still, for the sake of illustration, suppose some gene increases altruistic behavior. Is there any way it could spread within the population? One common reply is that most altruistic behaviors cost very little. True, but being almost harmless is not good enough; a gene spreads only if the individuals with it reproduce more than those without it. Another common reply is that the altruistic behavior benefits the species. True again, but the rebuttal is the same. A gene that benefits the species but fails to help the individual dies out with that individual.

A suggestion that sounds good at first is *group selection.* According to this idea, altruistic groups survive better than less cooperative ones (D. S. Wilson & Sober, 1994). However, what will happen when a mutation favoring uncooperative behavior occurs within a cooperative group? If the uncooperative individual has a reproductive advantage within the group, its genes will spread until the entire group is no longer cooperative. At best, group selection would produce an unstable outcome.

Figure 1.11 Sentinel behavior: altruistic or not? As in many other prey species, meerkats sometimes show sentinel behavior by watching for danger and warning the others. However, the meerkat who emits the alarm is the one most likely to escape the danger.

A better explanation is **reciprocal altruism,** the idea that animals help those who help them in return. Clearly, two individuals who cooperate with each other will prosper; however, reciprocal altruism requires that individuals recognize one another and learn to help only those who return the favors. Otherwise, it is easy for an uncooperative individual to accept favors, prosper greatly, and never repay the favors. In other words, reciprocal altruism requires good sensory organs and a well-developed brain. (Perhaps we now understand why altruism is more common in humans than in other species.)

Another explanation is **kin selection,** selection for a gene because it benefits the individual's relatives. For example, a gene could spread if it caused you to risk your life to protect your children, who share many of your genes, including perhaps the altruism genes. Natural selection can favor altruism toward less close relatives—such as cousins, nephews, or nieces—if the benefits to them outweigh the cost to you (Dawkins, 1989; Hamilton, 1964; Trivers, 1985). In addition, a mechanism that caused you to behave altruistically toward your children might accidentally trigger you to help nonrelatives who looked like them or acted childlike. The mechanism might also cause you to behave altruistically toward all who are emotionally close to you because many of them are genetically close as well (Korchmaros & Kenny, 2001).

At its best, sociobiology leads to research that helps us understand a behavior. For example, someone notices that males of one species help with infant care, but males of another species do not. The assumption that these behavior differences relate to evolutionary histories can direct researchers to explore species' different habitats and ways of life until we understand why they behave differently. However, sociobiology is criticized, often with justification, when its practitioners assume that every behavior must be adaptive and then propose an explanation without testing it.

6. What are two plausible ways for possible altruistic genes to spread in a population?

Check your answer on page 19.

MODULE 1.2

In Closing: Genes and Behavior

In the control of behavior, genes are neither all important nor irrelevant. Certain behaviors have a very high heritability, such as the ability to taste PTC. Many other behaviors are influenced by genes but also subject to strong influence by experience. Our genes and our evolution make it possible for us to be what we are today, but they also give us the flexibility to change our behavior as circumstances warrant.

Understanding the genetics of human behavior is particularly important but also particularly difficult. Separating the roles of heredity and environment is always difficult, but especially so with humans, because researchers have such limited control over environmental influences. Inferring human evolution is also difficult, partly because we do not know enough about the lives of our ancient "caveman" ancestors. Finally, we should remember that the way things *are* is not necessarily the same as the way they *should be*. For example, even if our genes predispose people to behave in one way or another, we still have great flexibility in acting on our predispositions.

SUMMARY

1. Genes are chemicals that maintain their integrity from one generation to the next and influence the development of the individual. A dominant gene affects development regardless of whether a person has pairs of that gene or only a single copy per cell. A recessive gene affects development only in the absence of the dominant gene. (p. 9)

2. Some behavioral differences demonstrate simple effects of dominant and recessive genes. More often, however, behavioral variations reflect the combined influences of many genes and many environmental factors. Heritability is an estimate of the amount of variation that is due to genetic variation as opposed to environmental variation. (p. 10)

3. Researchers estimate heritability of a human condition by comparing monozygotic and dizygotic twins and by comparing adopted children to their biological and adoptive parents. (p. 11)

4. The results often overestimate human heritability for several reasons. First, the environmental quality varies little for most adopted children. Second, most of our results do not distinguish between the effects of genes and those of prenatal environment. Third, after genes produce an early increase in some behavioral tendency, that behavior may lead to a change in the environment that magnifies the tendency, thus leading to what appears to be a huge effect of heredity. (p. 12)

5. The fact that some behavior shows high heritability for a given population does not necessarily indicate that it will show an equal heritability for a different population. It also does not deny the possibility that a change in the environment might significantly alter the behavioral outcome. (p. 13)

6. Genes influence behavior directly by altering chemicals in the brain and also indirectly by affecting virtually any aspect of the body. (p. 13)

7. The process of evolution through natural selection is a logical necessity because mutations sometimes occur in genes, and individuals with certain sets of genes reproduce more successfully than others do. (p. 14)

8. Evolution spreads the genes that are associated with the individuals who have reproduced the most. Therefore, if some characteristic is widespread within a population, it is reasonable to look for ways in which that characteristic is or has been adaptive. However, we cannot take it for granted that all common behaviors are adaptive; we need to do the research to test this hypothesis. (p. 16)

ANSWERS TO *STOP AND CHECK* QUESTIONS

1. If your mother can taste PTC, we can make no predictions about your father. You may have inherited a gene from your mother that enables you to taste PTC, and because the gene is dominant, you need only one copy of the gene to taste PTC. However, if your mother cannot taste PTC, you must have inherited your ability to taste it from your father, so he must be a taster. (p. 11)

2. A sex-linked gene is on a sex chromosome (almost always the X chromosome). A sex-limited gene is on one of the other chromosomes, but it is activated by sex hormones and therefore makes its effects evident only in one sex or the other. (p. 11)

3. Heritability will be higher in the population who all share a good, supportive environment. The less variation that occurs in quality of environment, the greater the ability of hereditary differences to account for any differences in performance. (p. 13)

4. Keeping a child with the PKU gene on a strict low-phenylalanine diet prevents the mental retardation that the gene ordinarily causes. The general point is that sometimes a highly heritable condition can be modified environmentally. (p. 13)

5. No. Failure to use or need a structure does not make it become smaller in the next generation. The appendix will shrink only if people with a gene for a smaller appendix reproduced more successfully than other people did. (p. 16)

6. Altruistic genes could spread because they facilitate care for one's kin or because they facilitate exchanges of favors with others (reciprocal altruism). (p. 18)

THOUGHT QUESTION

What human behaviors are you sure have a heritability of 0?

MODULE 1.3

The Use of Animals in Research

Certain ethical disputes seem likely to linger indefinitely, resistant to either agreement or compromise. One is abortion; another is the death penalty; still another is the use of animals for research. The animal research controversy is critical for biological psychology. As you will see throughout this book, most of what we know about the functioning of the nervous system stems from research done on nonhuman animals. That research ranges from mere observation of animals in nature through painless research on caged animals to other studies that inflict stress and pain. How shall we deal with the fact that on the one hand we want more knowledge and on the other hand we wish to minimize animal distress?

REASONS FOR ANIMAL RESEARCH

Given that most biological psychologists are primarily interested in the human brain and human behavior, why do they study nonhuman animals? Here are four reasons.

1. *The underlying mechanisms of behavior are similar across species and sometimes are easier to study in a nonhuman species.* If you wanted to understand how a complex machine works, you might begin by examining a smaller, simpler machine that operates on the same principle. We also learn about brain-behavior relationships by starting with simpler cases. The brains and behavior of nonhuman vertebrates resemble those of humans in many aspects of their chemistry and anatomy (Figure 1.12). Even invertebrate nerves follow the same basic principles as our own. Much research on nerve cells has been conducted on squid nerves, which are similar to human nerves but thicker and therefore easier to study.
2. *We are interested in animals for their own sake.* Humans are naturally curious. We want to understand why the Druids built Stonehenge, where the moon came from, how the rings of Saturn formed, and why certain animals do the strange things they do. Sometimes research done for theoretical

reasons produces results with surprising practical applications, but even if it doesn't, we would like to understand our universe just for the sake of understanding.
3. *What we learn about animals sheds light on human evolution.* What is our place in nature? How did we come to be the way we are? One approach to such questions is to examine other species. Humans did not evolve directly from chimpanzees, monkeys, or any other species currently alive, but we do share common ancestors with them, so studying them may provide important clues to our evolution.
4. *Certain experiments cannot use human subjects because of legal or ethical restrictions.* For example, investigators insert electrodes into the brain cells of rats and other animals to determine the relationship between brain activity and behavior. These experiments answer questions that investigators cannot address in any other way. They also raise an ethical issue: If it is unacceptable to do such research on humans, should we not also object to using nonhumans? (Remember from earlier in this chapter: The physical basis of conscious experience is unknown. Do rats have the same mental life as we do? None at all? Something in between? Clearly, we are making ethical decisions without full knowledge of what the animals experience.)

THE ETHICAL DEBATE

In some cases, researchers observe animals in nature as a function of different times of day, different seasons of the year, changes in diet, and so forth. These procedures do not even inconvenience the animals and raise no ethical problems (unless you want to worry about invasion of privacy). In other experiments, however, including many discussed in this book, animals have been subjected to brain damage, electrode implantation, injections of drugs or hormones, and so forth. Many people regard such experimentation as cruelty to animals and have reacted either with loud but peaceful demonstrations or with more extreme tactics, such as breaking into

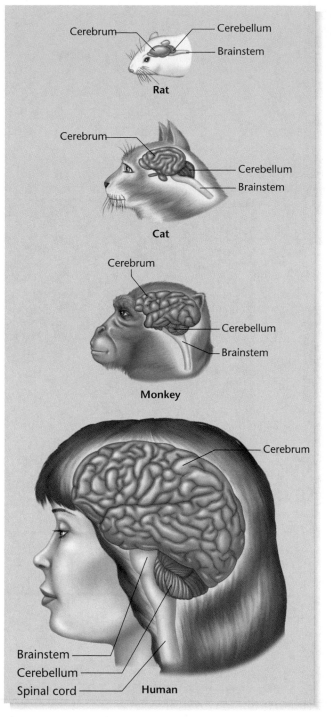

Figure 1.12 Brains of several species
The general plan and organization of the brain are similar for all mammals, even though brain size varies from species to species.

procedures that are admittedly not intended for their own benefit. Anyone with a conscience (including scientists) is bothered by this fact. On the other hand, experimentation with animals has been critical to the medical research that led to methods for the prevention or treatment of polio, diabetes, measles, smallpox, massive burns, heart disease, and other serious conditions. Most Nobel Prizes in physiology or medicine have been awarded for research conducted on nonhuman animals. The hope of finding methods to treat or prevent AIDS and various brain diseases (e.g., as Alzheimer's disease) depends largely on animal research. For many questions in biological psychology, our choice is to conduct research on animals or to make much slower progress and perhaps none at all (Figure 1.13).

Opposition to animal research ranges considerably in degree. At one end are the moderates, the "minimalists" who agree that some animal research is acceptable but wish it to be minimized and regulated. That is, they accept some kinds of research but wish to prohibit others, depending on the probable value of the research, the amount or type of distress to the animal, and perhaps the type of animal. (Most people have fewer qualms about hurting an insect, say, than about hurting a dolphin.)

At the other end are the "abolitionists," who see no room for compromise. Abolitionists maintain that all animals have the same rights as humans. They regard killing an animal as murder, regardless of whether the intention is to eat it, use its fur, or gain scientific knowledge. Keeping an animal (presumably even a pet) in a cage is, in their view, slavery. Because animals cannot give informed consent to an experiment, abolitionists insist it is wrong to use them in any research, regardless of the circumstances. According to one opponent of animal research, "We have no moral option but to bring this research to a halt. Completely. . . . We will not be satisfied until every cage is empty" (Regan, 1986, pp. 39–40). Advocates of this position sometimes claim that much animal research is extremely painful or that no animal research ever leads to important results. Note, however, that for a true abolitionist, none of those points really matter. Their moral imperative is that people have no right to use animals, regardless of how useful the research, regardless of how painless.

Some abolitionists have opposed environmental protection groups as well. For example, red foxes, which humans introduced into California, so effectively rob bird nests that they have severely endangered California's least terns and clapper rails. To protect the endangered birds, the U.S. Fish and Wildlife Service began trapping and killing red foxes in the areas where endangered birds breed. Their efforts were thwarted by a ballot initiative organized by animal

research labs, stealing lab animals, vandalizing lab property, and even threatening to kill researchers (Schiermeier, 1998).

The issues are difficult. On the one hand, many laboratory animals undergo painful or debilitating

A monkey learns to control an object on the screen for a sweet-liquid reward.

Many aquatic mammals can master surprisingly complex visual categorization tasks.

A young bird raised in captivity is imprinted on a model of its parent so it will respond socially to its own species.

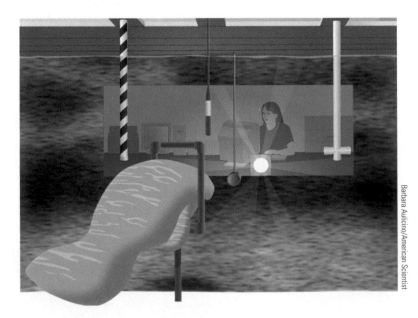

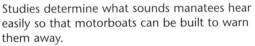

Studies determine what sounds manatees hear easily so that motorboats can be built to warn them away.

rights activists, who argued that killing any animal is immoral even when the motive is to protect another species from extinction (T. Williams, 1999). Similar objections were raised when conservationists proposed to kill the pigs (again a human-introduced species) that were destroying the habitat of native Hawaiian wildlife.

At times in the animal rights dispute, people on both sides have taken shrill "us versus them" positions. Some defenders of animal research have claimed that the research is almost always useful and seldom painful, and some opponents have argued that the research is usually painful and never useful. In fact, the truth is messier (D. Blum, 1994): Much research is both useful and painful. Those of us who value both knowledge and animal life look for compromises instead of either–or solutions.

Nearly all animal researchers sympathize with the desire to minimize painful research. That is, just about everyone draws a line somewhere and says, "I will not do this experiment. The knowledge I might gain is not worth that much distress to the animals." To be sure, different researchers draw that line at different places.

An organization of European researchers offered a series of proposals, which you can read at this Web site (see also van Zutphen, 2001):

www.esf.org/ftp/pdf/SciencePolicy/ ESPB9.pdf

Here are a few highlights:

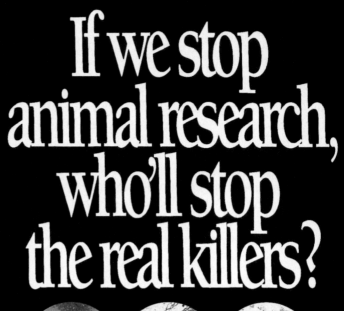

Figure 1.13 In defense of animal research
For many years, opponents of animal research have protested against experimentation with animals. This ad is a reply by supporters of such research. *Courtesy of the Foundation for Biomedical Research*

- Laboratory animals have both an instrumental value (as a means to an end) and an intrinsic value (for their own sake), which must be respected.
- While accepting the need for animal research, the European Science Foundation endorses the principles of reduction (using fewer animals), replacement (using other methods not requiring animals, when possible), and refinement (using less painful procedures).
- Research to improve animal welfare should be encouraged.
- Before any research starts, the research plan should be evaluated by someone other than the researchers themselves, to consider likely benefits and suffering.
- Investigators should assume that a procedure that is painful to humans is also painful to animals, unless they have evidence to the contrary.
- Investigators should be trained in animal care, including ethics and alternative research methods.
- Journals should include in their publication policy a statement about ethical use of animals.

Is this sort of compromise satisfactory? It can be to researchers and to minimalists, but true abolitionists have no interest in compromise. If you believe, as they do, that keeping any animal in any cage is the moral equivalent of slavery, you don't want to endorse doing it in moderation. The disagreement between animal researchers and abolitionists is a dispute between two ethical positions: "Never knowingly harm an innocent" and "Sometimes a little harm leads to a greater good." On the one hand, permitting research has the undeniable consequence of inflicting pain or distress. On the other hand, banning the use of animals for human purposes means a great setback in medical research as well as the end of animal-to-human transplants (e.g., using pig heart valves to help people with heart diseases). For this reason, many victims of serious diseases have organized to oppose animal rights groups (Feeney, 1987).

Although not everyone agrees to moderation and compromise, those principles are now the legal standard. In the United States, every college or other research institution that receives federal funds is required to have an Institutional Animal Care and Use Committee, composed of veterinarians, community representatives, and scientists, that evaluates proposed experiments, decides whether they are acceptable, and specifies procedures designed to minimize pain and discomfort. (Similar regulations and committees govern research on human subjects.) In addition, all research laboratories must abide by national laws requiring certain standards of cleanliness and animal care. Professional organizations such as the Society for Neuroscience publish guidelines for the use of animals in research (see Appendix B). The following Web site describes U.S. regulations and advice on animal care:

http://oacu.od.nih.gov/index.htm

1. Describe reasons biological psychologists conduct much of their research on nonhuman animals.

2. How does the "minimalist" position differ from the "abolitionist" position?

Check your answers on this page.

MODULE 1.3

In Closing: Humans and Other Animals

We began this chapter with a quote from the Nobel Prize-winning biologist, Niko Tinbergen. Tinbergen argued that no fundamental gulf separates humans from other animal species. Because we are similar in many ways to other species, we can learn much about ourselves from animal studies. Also because of that similarity, we identify with animals and we wish not to hurt them. Neuroscience researchers who decide to conduct animal research do not, as a rule, take this decision lightly. They want to minimize harm to animals, but they also want to increase knowledge. They believe it is better to inflict limited distress under controlled conditions than permit ignorance and disease to inflict much greater distress. In some cases, however, it is a difficult decision.

SUMMARY

1. Researchers study animals because the mechanisms are sometimes easier to study in nonhumans, because they are interested in animal behavior for its own sake, because they want to understand the evolution of behavior, and because certain kinds of experiments are difficult, illegal, or unethical with humans. (p. 20)

2. The ethics of using animals in research is controversial. Some research does inflict stress or pain on animals; however, many research questions can be investigated only through animal research. (p. 20)

3. Animal research today is conducted under legal and ethical controls that attempt to minimize animal distress. (p. 23)

ANSWERS TO *STOP AND CHECK* QUESTIONS

1. Sometimes the mechanisms of behavior are easier to study in a nonhuman species. We are curious about animals for their own sake. We study animals to understand human evolution. Certain procedures are illegal or unethical with humans. (p. 24)

2. A "minimalist" wishes to limit animal research to studies with little discomfort and much potential value. An "abolitionist" wishes to eliminate all animal research, regardless of how the animals are treated or how much value the research might produce. (p. 24)

Prospects for Further Study

This module, by far the shortest in the book, concerns careers related to biological psychology. The relevant careers fall into two categories: research and medicine. A research career ordinarily requires a PhD in psychology, biology, neuroscience, or other related field. Most people with a PhD in one of these fields hold college or university positions in which they teach and conduct research. Others have pure research positions in laboratories sponsored by the government, drug companies, or other industries. Depending on their specialized interests, researchers might identify themselves as one of the following:

- *Behavioral neuroscientist* (almost synonyms: psychobiologist, biopsychologist, or physiological psychologist). Investigates how functioning of the brain and other organs influences behavior.
- *Neuroscientist.* Studies the anatomy, biochemistry, and physiology of the nervous system.
- *Neuropsychologist.* Conducts behavioral tests to determine what various brain damaged people can and cannot do and how their condition changes over time. Most neuropsychologists work in hospitals and clinics and have a mixture of psychological and medical training.
- *Psychophysiologist.* Measures heart rate, breathing rate, brain waves, and other body processes that change as a function of people's activities and information processing.
- *Neurochemist.* Investigates chemical reactions in the brain and their consequences.
- *Comparative psychologist* (almost synonyms: ethologist, animal behaviorist). Compares the behaviors of different species and tries to relate them to evolutionary histories and ways of life.
- *Sociobiologist* (almost a synonym: evolutionary psychologist). Relates behaviors, especially social behaviors, including those of humans, to the functions they have served and therefore the presumed selective pressures that caused them to evolve.

The medical fields require a medical degree (MD) plus about 4 years of additional specialized study and practice. Most people with an MD work in hospitals and clinics; those who work in hospitals affiliated with a medical school also teach and conduct research. The related medical specialties are:

- *Neurologist.* Treats people with brain damage or diseases of the brain.
- *Neurosurgeon.* Performs brain surgery.
- *Psychiatrist.* Helps people with emotional distress or troublesome behaviors, sometimes using drugs or other medical procedures.

If you pursue a career in research or medicine, you need to stay up to date on new developments by attending conventions, consulting with colleagues, and reading the primary research journals, such as Journal of Neuroscience, Neurology, Behavioral Neuroscience, Brain Research, Nature Neuroscience, and Archives of General Psychiatry. However, what if you are entering a field on the outskirts of biological psychology or neuroscience, such as clinical psychology, school psychology, social work, or physical therapy? In that case, you probably don't want to wade through technical journal articles, but you do want to stay current on major developments in neuroscience, at least enough to converse intelligently with medical colleagues.

I used to have no good recommendations other than buying new editions of this textbook every time it is published (!) or reading *Scientific American* or *American Scientist*—excellent publications for the nonspecialist, including some articles on neuroscience and psychology. Beginning in 1999, there is now a comparable periodical devoted exclusively to neuroscience for the nonspecialist. The title is *Cerebrum*, published by the Dana Press, 745 Fifth Avenue, Suite 700, New York, NY 10151. Their Web site is www.dana.org and their email address is danainfo@dana.org. Their Web site is a good source of information about Alzheimer's disease, stroke, depression, schizophrenia, head injury, pain, addiction, and other psychological and neurological disorders.

Here are two other excellent Web sites for general reference. The first is an all-purpose source of information about the nervous system, its anatomy, and its disorders. The second offers biographies of the early pioneers in the study of the nervous system.

www.neuroguide.com
www.uic.edu/depts/mcne/founders

Key Terms and Activities

TERMS

altruistic behavior (p. 17)

artificial selection (p. 14)

autosomal gene (p. 10)

biological psychology (p. 2)

chromosome (p. 9)

crossing over (p. 10)

deoxyribonucleic acid (DNA) (p. 9)

dominant (p. 10)

dualism (p. 5)

easy problems (p. 6)

enzyme (p. 9)

evolution (p. 14)

evolutionary explanation (p. 3)

fitness (p. 16)

functional explanation (p. 4)

gene (p. 9)

hard problem (p. 6)

heritability (p. 11)

heterozygous (p. 10)

homozygous (p. 10)

identity position (p. 5)

kin selection (p. 18)

Lamarckian evolution (p. 14)

materialism (p. 5)

mentalism (p. 5)

mind-body or mind-brain problem (p. 5)

monism (p. 5)

multiplier effect (p. 12)

mutation (p. 11)

ontogenetic explanation (p. 3)

phenylketonuria (PKU) (p. 13)

physiological explanation (p. 3)

problem of other minds (p. 7)

recessive (p. 10)

reciprocal altruism (p. 18)

recombination (p. 11)

ribonucleic acid (RNA) (p. 9)

sex-limited gene (p. 11)

sex-linked gene (p. 10)

sociobiology (p. 16)

solipsism (p. 6)

X chromosome (p. 10)

Y chromosome (p. 10)

SUGGESTIONS FOR FURTHER READING

Blum, D. (1994). *The monkey wars.* New York: Oxford University Press. Informative and evenhanded account of the disputes between animal researchers and animal rights activists.

Dennett, D. C. (1991). *Consciousness explained.* Boston: Little, Brown. Regardless of whether Dennett has explained consciousness, he has dealt with the mind-brain issue in a deep and provocative manner.

Gazzaniga, M. S. (1998). *The mind's past.* Berkeley: University of California Press. A noted neuroscientist's attempt to explain the physical origins of consciousness. This book includes a number of fascinating examples.

Shear, J. (Ed.). (1997). *Explaining consciousness—The "hard problem."* Cambridge, MA: MIT Press. A collection of articles by philosophers, psychologists, biologists, and physicists attempting to understand the relationship between mind and brain.

WEB SITES TO EXPLORE[3]

You can go to the Biological Psychology Study Center at this address:

http://psychology.wadsworth.com/ kalatbiopsych8e

It would help to set a bookmark for this site because it will be useful for each chapter. In addition to sample quiz items and other information, it includes links to many other Web sites. One way to reach any of these

[3]Web sites arise and disappear without warning. The suggestions listed in this book were available at the time the book went to press; I cannot guarantee how long they will last.

sites is to go to the Biological Psychology Study Center, click the appropriate chapter, and then find the appropriate links to additional sites. The sites listed in this chapter are:

Imprint Academic (which includes the *Journal of Consciousness Studies*)
www.imprint.co.uk/

Journal of Mind and Behavior
www.ume.maine.edu/~jmb/welcome.html

National Society for Phenylketonuria Home Page
web.ukonline.co.uk/nspku/

National PKU News
http://www.pkunews.org/

Frequency of Inherited Disorders Data Base
archive.uwcm.ac.uk/uwcm/mg/fidd/index.html

Statement on Use of Animals in Research
www.esf.org/ftp/pdf/SciencePolicy/ESPB9.pdf

U.S. government statement on animal care and use
http://oacu.od.nih.gov/index.htm

Dana Foundation for brain information
www.dana.org

Neuroguide, a link to neuroscience sites on the Internet
www.neuroguide.com

Founders of Neurology (biographies of major researchers)
www.uic.edu/depts/mcne/founders

CD-ROM: EXPLORING BIOLOGICAL PSYCHOLOGY

Offspring of parents homozygous and heterozygous for brown eyes (animation)

RNA, DNA, and Protein (animation)

Selection and Random Drift (Try it Yourself)

Critical Thinking (essay questions)

Chapter Quiz (multiple choice questions)

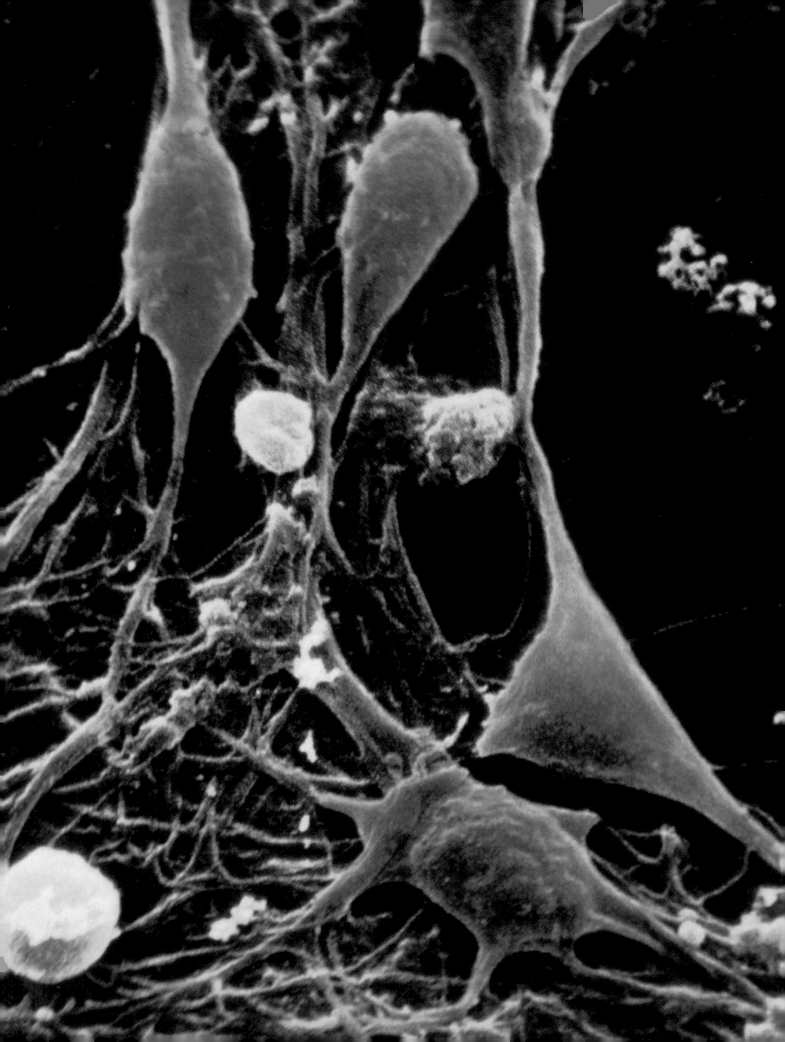

Nerve Cells and Nerve Impulses

2

Chapter Outline

Main Ideas

1. The nervous system is composed of two kinds of cells: neurons and glia. Only the neurons transmit impulses from one location to another.

2. The larger neurons have branches, known as axons and dendrites, which can change their branching pattern as a function of experience, age, and chemical influences.

3. Many molecules in the bloodstream that can enter other body organs cannot enter the brain.

4. The action potential, an all-or-none change in the electrical potential across the membrane of a neuron, is caused by the sudden flow of sodium ions into the neuron and is followed by a flow of potassium ions out of the neuron.

5. Local neurons are small and do not have axons or action potentials. Instead, they convey information to nearby neurons by graded potentials.

$\mathbf{A}$ nervous system, composed of many individual cells, is in some regards like a society of people who work together and communicate with one another or even like elements that form a chemical compound. In each case, the combination has properties and functions that are unlike those of its individual components. We begin our study of the nervous system by examining single cells; later, we examine the compounds of many cells acting together.

Advice: Parts of this chapter and the next require a knowledge of some basic chemical concepts such as *positively charged ions.* If you need to refresh your memory, read Appendix A.

Opposite:
An electron micrograph of neurons, magnified tens of thousands of times. The color is added artificially. For objects this small, it is impossible to focus light in order to obtain an image. It is possible to focus an electron beam, but electrons do not show color. *Source:* ©CNRI/Photo Researchers, Inc.

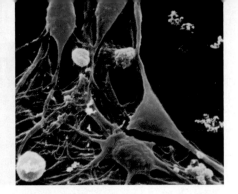

MODULE 2.1

The Cells of the Nervous System

Before you can build a house, you first assemble bricks or other construction materials. Similarly, before we can address the great philosophical questions such as the mind-brain relationship, or the great practical questions such as the causes of abnormal behavior, we have to examine our construction materials. We have to start with the building blocks of the nervous system—the cells, their components, and their interactions.

ANATOMY OF NEURONS AND GLIA

The nervous system consists of two kinds of cells: neurons and glia. **Neurons** are cells that receive information and transmit it to other cells; they are what people usually mean when they refer to "nerve cells." The adult human brain contains a great many neurons (Figure 2.1)—approximately 100 billion, according to one estimate (R. W. Williams & Herrup, 1988). (An accurate count would be more difficult than it is worth.) Glia perform a number of tasks other than conducting messages; their functions are difficult to summarize, and we shall defer that discussion until later in the chapter.

The idea that the brain is composed of individual cells is now so well established that we take it for granted. However, the idea was controversial and widely doubted as recently as the early 1900s. Until that time, the best microscopic views revealed little detail about the organization of the brain. Without special staining techniques, neurons are hard to distinguish from one another or from their backgrounds. Observers noted long, thin fibers between one neuron's cell body and another, but they could not see whether each fiber merged into the next cell or stopped before it (Albright, Jessell, Kandel, & Posner, 2001). Then, in the late 1800s, Santiago Ramón y Cajal demonstrated that a small gap separates the tips of one neuron's fibers from the surface of the next neuron. The brain, like the rest of the body, consists of individual cells.

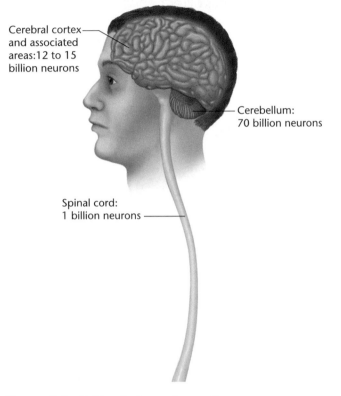

Figure 2.1 Estimated numbers of neurons in humans
Because of the small size of many neurons and the variation in cell density from one spot to another, obtaining an accurate count is difficult.

Labels in figure: Cerebral cortex and associated areas:12 to 15 billion neurons; Cerebellum: 70 billion neurons; Spinal cord: 1 billion neurons

EXTENSIONS AND APPLICATIONS

Santiago Ramón y Cajal: A Pioneer of Neuroscience

Generally, two scientists are recognized as the founders of neuroscience. One was Charles Sherrington, whom we shall discuss in Chapter 3; the other was the Spanish investigator Santiago Ramón y Cajal (1852–1934). Cajal's early career did not progress altogether smoothly. At one point, he was imprisoned in a solitary cell, limited to one meal a day, and taken out daily for public floggings—at the age of 10—for the crime of not paying attention during his Latin class (Ramón y Cajal, 1937). (And *you* thought *your* teachers were strict!)

Cajal wanted to become an artist, but his father insisted that he study medicine as a safer way to make a living. Cajal managed to combine the two fields, becoming an outstanding anatomical researcher and illustrator. His detailed drawings of the nervous system are still considered definitive today.

Before the late 1800s, microscopy could reveal few details about the nervous system. Then the Italian investigator Camillo Golgi discovered a method of using silver salts to stain nerve cells. For reasons unknown, this method completely stained some cells without affecting others at all. Consequently, it became possible to examine the structure of a single cell. Cajal used Golgi's methods but applied them to infant brains, in which the cells are smaller, more compact, and therefore easier to examine on a single slide. Cajal's research demonstrated the structure of nerve cells and the fact that they remain separate instead of merging into one another.

Philosophically, we can see the appeal of the assumption that neurons merge. We each experience our consciousness as undivided, not as the sum of separate parts, so it seems that all the cells in the brain should be joined together physically as one unit. How the individual cells combine their influences is a complicated and still somewhat mysterious process.

The Structures of an Animal Cell

Figure 2.2 illustrates a neuron from the cerebellum of a mouse (magnified enormously, of course). A neuron has much in common with any other cell in the body, although its shape is certainly distinctive. Let us begin with the properties that all animal cells have in common.

The edge of a cell is a **membrane** (often called a *plasma membrane*), a structure that separates the inside of the cell from the outside environment. It is composed of two layers of fat molecules that are free to flow around one another. (Figure 2.3 shows this arrangement in more detail.) Small uncharged chemicals, such as water, oxygen, and carbon dioxide, move rather freely across the membrane. A few charged ions, such as sodium, potassium, calcium, and chloride, can cross through specialized openings in the membrane called *protein channels.* Most chemicals, however, cannot cross the membrane.

Except for red blood cells, all animal cells have a **nucleus,** the structure that contains the chromosomes. A **mitochondrion** (pl.: mitochondria) is the structure that performs metabolic activities, providing the energy that the cell requires for all its other activities. Mitochondria require fuel and oxygen to function. **Ribosomes** are the sites at which the cell synthesizes

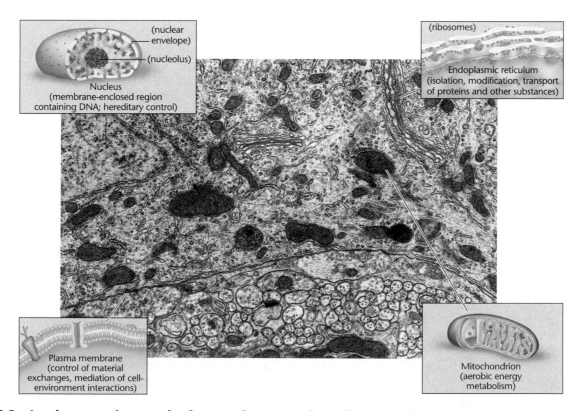

Figure 2.2   An electron micrograph of parts of a neuron from the cerebellum of a mouse, greatly magnified
The nucleus, membrane, and other structures are characteristic of most animal cells. The plasma membrane is the border of the neuron. *Micrograph courtesy of Dennis M. D. Landis*

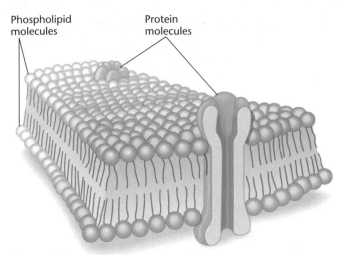

Figure 2.3 The membrane of a neuron
Embedded in the membrane are protein channels that permit certain ions to cross through the membrane at a controlled rate.

new protein molecules. Proteins provide building materials for the cell and facilitate various chemical reactions. Some ribosomes float freely within the cell; others are attached to the endoplasmic reticulum, a network of thin tubes that transport newly synthesized proteins to other locations.

The Structure of a Neuron

A neuron (Figure 2.4) contains a nucleus, a membrane, mitochondria, ribosomes, and the other structures typical of animal cells. The distinctive feature of neurons is their shape.

The larger neurons have these major components: dendrites, a soma (cell body), an axon, and presynaptic

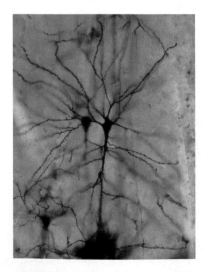

Figure 2.4 Neurons, stained to appear dark
Note the small fuzzy-looking spines on the dendrites.
Source: Photo courtesy of Bob Jacobs, Colorado College

terminals. (The tiniest neurons lack axons and some lack well-defined dendrites.) Contrast the motor neuron in Figure 2.5 and the sensory neuron in Figure 2.6. A **motor neuron** receives excitation from other neurons and conducts impulses from its soma in the spinal cord to muscle or gland cells. Its dendrites enter the soma, and the axon exits from the soma. A **sensory neuron** is specialized at one end to be highly sensitive to a particular type of stimulation, such as touch information from the skin. Different kinds of sensory neurons have different structures; the one shown in Figure 2.6 is a neuron conducting touch information from the skin to the spinal cord. Its dendrites merge directly into the axon, and its soma is located on a little stalk off the main trunk.

The **dendrites** are branching fibers that get narrower near their ends. (The term *dendrite* comes from a Greek root word meaning "tree"; a dendrite is shaped like a tree.) The dendrite's surface is lined with specialized *synaptic receptors,* at which the dendrite receives information from other neurons. (Chapter 3 focuses on the synapses.) The greater the surface area of a dendrite, the more information it can receive. Some dendrites branch widely and therefore have a large surface area. Some also contain dendritic spines, the short outgrowths that increase the surface area available for synapses (Figures 2.4 and 2.7). The shape of dendrites varies enormously from one neuron to another and can even vary from one time to another for a given neuron. The shape of the dendrite has much to do with how the dendrite combines different kinds of input (Häusser, Spruston, & Stuart, 2000).

The **cell body**, or **soma** (Greek for "body"; pl.: somata), contains the nucleus, ribosomes, mitochondria, and other structures found in most cells. Much of the metabolic work of the neuron occurs here. Cell bodies of neurons range in diameter from 0.005 mm to 0.1 mm in mammals and up to a full millimeter in certain invertebrates. Like the dendrites, the cell body is covered with synapses on its surface in many neurons.

The **axon** is a thin fiber of constant diameter, in most cases longer than the dendrites. (The term *axon* is from a Greek word meaning "axis.") The axon is the information-sender of the neuron, conveying an impulse toward either other neurons or a gland or muscle. Many vertebrate axons are covered with an insulating material called a **myelin sheath** with interruptions known as **nodes of Ranvier.** Invertebrate axons do not have myelin sheaths. An axon has many branches, each of which swells at its tip, forming a **presynaptic terminal,** also known as an *end bulb* or *bouton*[1] (French for "button"). This is the point from

---

[1]Unfortunately, many structures in the nervous system have several names. As Candace Pert (1997, p. 64) has put it, "Scientists would rather use each other's toothbrushes than each other's terminology."

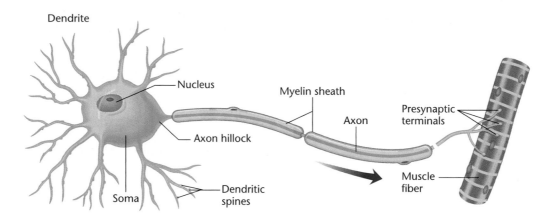

Figure 2.5 The components of a vertebrate motor neuron
The cell body of a motor neuron is in the spinal cord. The various parts are not drawn to scale; in particular, a real axon is much longer in proportion to the size of the soma.

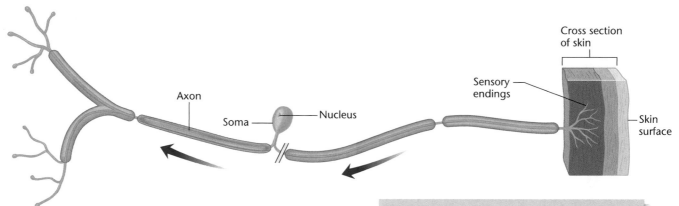

Figure 2.6 A vertebrate sensory neuron
Note that the soma is on a stalk off the main trunk of the axon. (As in Figure 2.5, the various structures are not drawn to scale.)

which the axon releases chemicals that cross through the junction between one neuron and the next.

A neuron can have any number of dendrites but no more than one axon, which may have branches. In most cases, branches depart from the trunk of the axon far from the cell body. Axons vary in length from virtually nonexistent to a meter or more, as in the case of axons from your spinal cord to your feet.

Other terms associated with neurons are *afferent, efferent,* and *intrinsic.* An **afferent axon** brings information into a structure; an **efferent axon** carries information away from a structure. Every sensory neuron is an afferent to the rest of the nervous system; every motor neuron is an efferent from the nervous system. Within the nervous system, a given neuron is an efferent from the standpoint of one structure and an afferent from the standpoint of another. (Remember that *efferent* starts with *e,* as in *exit; afferent* starts with *a,* as in *admission.*) For

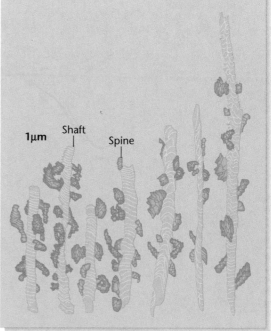

Figure 2.7 Dendritic spines
The dendrites of certain neurons are lined with spines, short outgrowths that receive specialized incoming information. That information apparently plays a key role in long-term changes in the neuron that mediate learning and memory. *Source: K. M. Harris & J. K. Stevens, 1989*

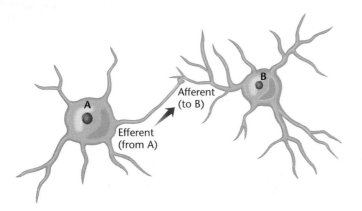

Figure 2.8 Cell structures and axons
It all depends on the point of view. An axon from A to B is an efferent axon from A and an afferent axon to B, just as a train from Washington to New York is exiting Washington and approaching New York.

example, an axon that is efferent from the thalamus may be afferent to the cerebral cortex (Figure 2.8). If a cell's dendrites and axon are entirely within a single

structure, the cell is an **interneuron** or **intrinsic neuron** of that structure. For example, an intrinsic neuron of the thalamus has all its dendrites and axons within the thalamus; it communicates only with other cells of the thalamus.

Variations Among Neurons

Neurons vary enormously in size, shape, and function. The shape of a given neuron determines its connections with other neurons and thereby determines how it contributes to the overall functioning of the nervous system. The wider the branching, the greater the number of connections with other neurons.

The function of a neuron is closely related to its shape (Figure 2.9). For example, the dendrites of the Purkinje cell of the cerebellum (Figure 2.9a) branch extremely widely within a single plane; this cell is capable of integrating an enormous amount of incoming information. The neurons in Figures 2.9c and 2.9e also have widely branching dendrites that receive and integrate information from many sources. By contrast,

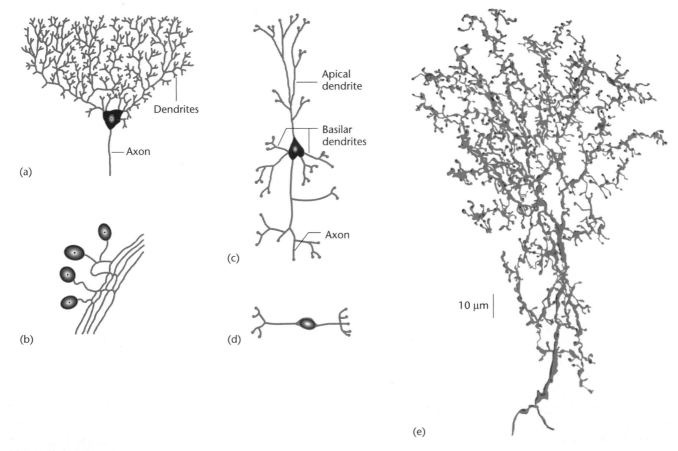

Figure 2.9 The diverse shapes of neurons
(**a**) Purkinje cell, a type found only in the cerebellum; (**b**) sensory neurons from skin to spinal cord; (**c**) pyramidal cell of the motor area of the cerebral cortex; (**d**) bipolar cell of the retina of an eye; (**e**) Kenyon cell, from a honeybee. *Source: Part (e) from R. G. Coss, Brain Research, October 1982. Reprinted by permission of R. G. Coss.*

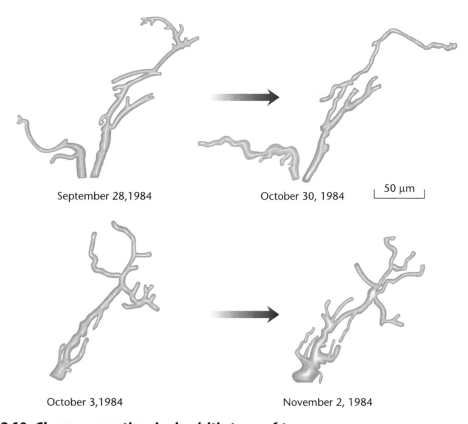

September 28,1984 October 30, 1984 50 μm

October 3,1984 November 2, 1984

Figure 2.10 Changes over time in dendritic trees of two neurons
During one month, some branches elongated and others retracted. The shape of the neuron is in flux even during adulthood. *Source: Reprinted from D. Purves & R. D. Hadley, Nature, 315, pp. 404–406. Copyright ©1985 Macmillan Magazines Ltd. Reprinted by permission.*

certain cells in the retina (Figure 2.9d) have only short branches on their dendrites and therefore pool input from only a few sources.

At one time, researchers believed that neurons never changed their shape. We now know that new experiences continually modify a neuron's shape. Dale Purves and R. D. Hadley (1985) developed a method of injecting a dye that enabled them to examine the structure of a living neuron at different times, days to weeks apart. They demonstrated that some dendritic branches grow and extend, whereas others retract or disappear altogether (Figure 2.10). Evidently, the anatomy of the brain is constantly plastic (i.e., changeable) at the microscopic level.

Glia

Glia (or neuroglia), the other major components of the nervous system, do not transmit information over long distances as neurons do, although they do exchange chemicals with adjacent neurons. The term *glia,* derived from a Greek word meaning "glue," reflects early investigators' idea that glia were like glue that held the neurons together (Somjen, 1988). Although that concept is obsolete, the

term remains. The average glia cell is about one-tenth the size of a neuron. However, because glia are about 10 times more numerous than neurons in the human brain, they occupy about the same total space as the neurons (Figure 2.11).

The functions of glia are numerous (Haydon, 2001). One type of glia, the star-shaped astrocytes, wrap around the presynaptic terminals of several axons, presumably a functionally related group, as shown in Figure 2.12. By taking up chemicals released by those axons and later releasing those chemicals back to the axons, an astrocyte helps synchronize the activity of the axons, enabling them to send messages in waves (Antanitus, 1998). Astrocytes also remove waste material, particularly waste created when neurons die. Microglia, very small cells, also remove waste material as well as viruses, fungi, and other microorganisms. In effect, they function like part of the immune system. Oligodendrocytes (OL-i-go-DEN-druh-sites) in the brain and spinal cord and Schwann cells in the periphery of the body are specialized types of glia that build the myelin sheaths that surround and insulate certain vertebrate axons. Radial glia, a type of astrocyte, guide the migration of neurons and the growth of their axons and dendrites during embryonic development.

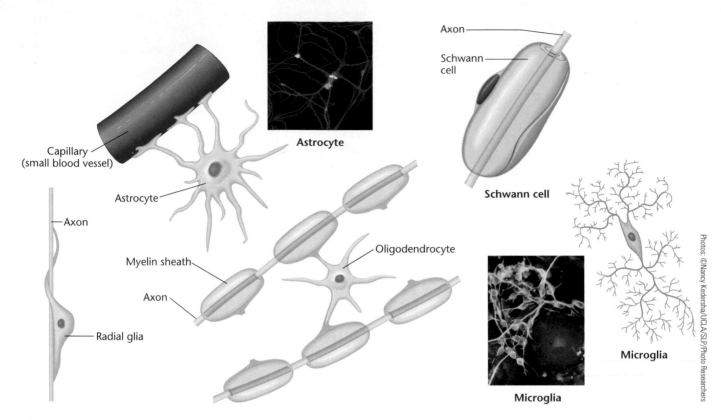

Figure 2.11 Shapes of some glia cells
Oligodendrocytes produce myelin sheaths that insulate certain vertebrate axons in the central nervous system; Schwann cells have a similar function in the periphery. The oligodendrocyte shown here is forming a segment of myelin sheath for two axons; in fact, each oligodendrocyte forms such segments for 30 to 50 axons. Astrocytes pass chemicals back and forth between neurons and blood and among various neurons in an area. Microglia proliferate in areas of brain damage and remove toxic materials. Radial glia guide the migration of neurons during embryonic development. Glia have other functions as well.

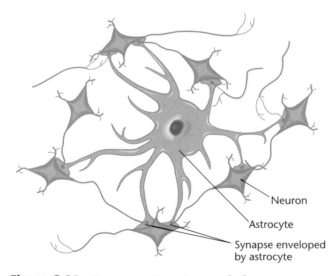

Figure 2.12 How an astrocyte can help synchronize associated axons
Branches of the astrocyte (in the center) surround the presynaptic terminals of several related axons. If a few of them are active at once, they release chemicals, some of which are absorbed by the astrocyte. The astrocyte then temporarily inhibits all the axons to which it is connected. When the inhibition ceases, all the axons are primed to respond again in synchrony. *Source: Based on Antanitus, 1998*

Schwann cells perform a related function after damage to axons in the periphery, guiding a regenerating axon to the appropriate target.

Stop & Check

1. Identify the four major structures that compose a neuron.
2. Which kind of glia cell wraps around the synaptic terminals of axons?

Check your answers on page 38.

THE BLOOD-BRAIN BARRIER

Many drugs that physicians would like to administer cannot enter the brain. For example, certain chemotherapy drugs that fight cancer elsewhere in the body cannot get into the brain to attack brain cancers. Dopamine would be helpful in alleviating Parkinson's disease except that it is also unable to enter the brain. The mechanism that keeps most chemicals out of the vertebrate brain is known as the **blood-brain barrier**. Before we examine how it works, let us consider why we need it.

Why We Need a Blood-Brain Barrier

From time to time, viruses and other harmful substances enter the body. When a virus enters a cell, inner mechanisms extrude a virus particle through the membrane so that various cells of the immune system can find it. When the immune system cells attack the virus, they also kill the cell that contains it. In effect, the cell that exposes the virus through its membrane is committing suicide; it says, "Look, immune system, I'm infected with this virus. Kill me and save the others."

This plan works fine if the virus-infected cell is, say, a skin cell or a blood cell: The body simply makes a replacement. But the mature vertebrate brain does not easily replace damaged neurons. A few parts of the adult brain can make new neurons, but most cannot, and no area can afford to lose many neurons. To minimize the risk, the body literally builds a wall along the sides of the brain's blood vessels. This wall keeps out most viruses, bacteria, and harmful chemicals.

"What happens if a virus does enter the brain?" you might ask. After all, certain viruses do break through the blood-brain barrier. The brain has ways to attack viruses or slow their reproduction (Binder & Griffin, 2001), but not to kill them or the cells they inhabit. Consequently, a virus that enters your nervous system probably remains with you for life. For example, herpes viruses (responsible for chicken pox, shingles, and genital herpes) enter spinal cord cells. No matter how much the immune system attacks the herpes virus outside the nervous system, virus particles remain in the spinal cord and can emerge years later to reinfect you.

How the Blood-Brain Barrier Works

The blood-brain barrier (Figure 2.13) depends on the arrangement of endothelial cells that form the walls of the capillaries (Bundgaard, 1986; Rapoport & Robinson, 1986). In most parts of the body, such cells are separated by gaps large enough to allow the passage of large molecules. In the brain, the endothelial cells are joined so tightly that most molecules cannot pass between them.

Two categories of molecules can cross the blood-brain barrier passively (without the expenditure of energy): *small uncharged molecules,* such as oxygen and carbon dioxide, and *molecules that can dissolve in the fats of the capillary walls.* For example, most psychiatric drugs reach the brain because they dissolve in fats; so do many abused drugs, such as heroin, nicotine,

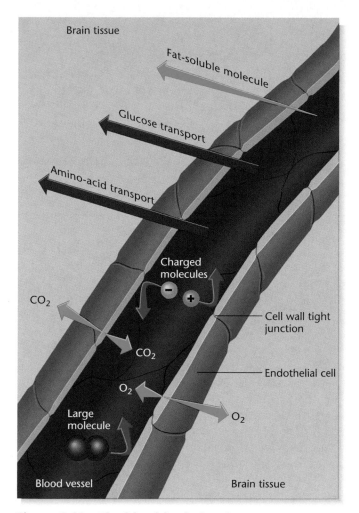

Figure 2.13 The blood-brain barrier
Most large molecules and electrically charged molecules cannot cross from the blood to the brain. A few small uncharged molecules such as O_2 and CO_2 can cross; so can certain fat-soluble molecules. Active transport systems pump glucose and certain amino acids across the membrane.

and cannabinol (the active substance in marijuana). Heroin produces stronger effects on the brain than morphine does because heroin is more fat-soluble.

"If the blood-brain barrier is such a good defense," you might ask, "why don't we have similar walls around our other organs?" The answer is that the barrier that keeps out viruses also keeps out a number of useful chemicals, including most sources of nutrition. To get those chemicals into the brain requires an **active transport**, a protein-mediated process that expends energy to pump chemicals from the blood into the brain. Chemicals known to be actively transported into the brain include glucose (the brain's main fuel), amino acids (the building blocks of proteins), and certain vitamins and hormones (Brightman, 1997). The brain also has an active transport system for moving certain chemicals from the brain to the blood (M. King, Chang, Zuckerman, & Pasternak, 2001).

Stop & Check

3. What is one major advantage of having a blood-brain barrier?

4. What is a disadvantage of the blood-brain barrier?

5. Which chemicals cross the blood-brain barrier on their own?

6. Which chemicals cross the blood-brain barrier by active transport?

Check your answers on this page.

THE NOURISHMENT OF VERTEBRATE NEURONS

Most cells use a wide variety of fuels, but vertebrate neurons depend heavily on glucose, a simple sugar, for their nutrition. (Cancer cells and the testis cells that make sperm also rely overwhelmingly on glucose.) The metabolic pathway that uses glucose requires oxygen; consequently, the neurons consume an enormous amount of oxygen compared with other body organs (Wong-Riley, 1989).

Why do neurons depend so heavily on glucose? Actually, they have the enzymes necessary to metabolize fats and several sugars. However, most other nutrients do not cross the blood-brain barrier in adults, and *ketones,* which do fairly readily cross, are seldom available in large amounts (Duelli & Kuschinsky, 2001). In fact, high ketone levels cause medical complications.

Although neurons require glucose, a glucose shortage is rarely a problem. The liver converts most carbohydrates, proteins, and fats into glucose, so almost any diet provides adequate glucose. If you eat nothing, your body converts your fat stores and even your muscles into glucose. An inability to *use* glucose can be a problem, however. Many chronic alcoholics have a diet deficient in vitamin B$_1$, thiamine, a chemical that is necessary for the use of glucose. Prolonged thiamine deficiency can lead to death of neurons and a condition called *Korsakoff's syndrome,* marked by severe memory impairments (Chapter 13).

MODULE 2.1

In Closing: Neurons

What does the study of individual neurons tell us about behavior? Perhaps the main lesson is that our experience and behavior *do not* follow from the properties of any one neuron. Just as a chemist must know about atoms to make sense of compounds, a biological psychologist must know about cells to understand the nervous system. However, the nervous system is more than the sum of the individual cells, just as water is more than the sum of oxygen and hydrogen. Our behavior emerges from the communication among neurons.

SUMMARY

1. In the late 1800s, Santiago Ramón y Cajal used newly discovered staining techniques to establish that the nervous system is composed of separate cells, now known as neurons. (p. 30)

2. Neurons receive information and convey it to other cells. The nervous system also contains *glia,* cells that serve many functions but do not transmit information over long distances. (pp. 30, 35)

3. Neurons have four major parts: a cell body, dendrites, an axon, and presynaptic terminals. Their shapes vary greatly depending on their functions and their connections with other cells. (p. 32)

4. Glia do not convey information over great distances, but they aid the functioning of neurons in many ways. (p. 35)

5. Because of the blood-brain barrier, many molecules, especially large ones, cannot enter the brain. (p. 36)

6. Adult neurons rely heavily on glucose, the only nutrient that can cross the blood-brain barrier. They need thiamine (vitamin B$_1$) to use glucose. (p. 37)

ANSWERS TO *STOP AND CHECK* QUESTIONS

1. Dendrites, soma (cell body), axon, and presynaptic terminals (p. 36)

2. Astrocytes (p. 36)

3. The blood-brain barrier keeps out most viruses, bacteria, and other harmful substances. (p. 38)

4. The blood-brain barrier also keeps out most nutrients. (p. 38)

5. Small uncharged molecules such as oxygen and molecules that dissolve in fats. (p. 38)

6. Glucose, amino acids, and certain vitamins and hormones. (p. 38)

The Nerve Impulse

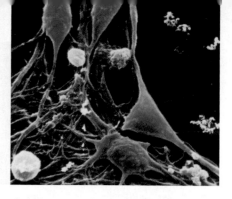

Think about the axons that convey information from your feet's touch receptors toward your spinal cord and brain. If the axons used electrical conduction, they could transfer information at a velocity approaching the speed of light. However, given that your body is made of carbon compounds and not copper wire, the strength of the impulse would decay greatly on the way from your toes to your spinal cord and brain. You would experience a touch on your shoulder much more strongly than a touch on your abdomen, which in turn would feel much stronger than a touch on your toes. Short people would feel their toes better than tall people could.

The way your axons function avoids these problems. Instead of simply conducting an electrical impulse, the axon regenerates an impulse at each point along the way, analogous to the way a burning string conveys a stimulus without loss of strength from its start to its finish. (Unlike a string, of course, an axon can transmit repeated impulses.)

Although the axon's method of transmitting an impulse prevents a touch on your shoulder from feeling stronger than one on your toes, it introduces a different problem: Because the axon transmits information at only a moderate speed (10–100 m/s), a touch on your shoulder will reach your brain *sooner* than will a touch on your toes. Now, if you get a friend to touch you simultaneously on your shoulder and your toe, you probably will not notice that your brain received one stimulus before the other. In fact, if your friend touches you on one hand and then the other, the delay between them has to be longer than 70 ms for you to be more than 80% accurate in recognizing which came first (Yamamoto & Kitazawa, 2001). Your brain is not set up to register small differences in the time of arrival of touch messages. After all, why should it be? You almost never need to know whether a touch on one part of your body occurred slightly before or after a touch somewhere else.

Try It Yourself

With vision, however, your brain *does* need to know whether one stimulus began slightly before or after another one. If two adjacent spots on your retina—let's call them A and B—send impulses at almost the same time, an extremely small difference in timing indicates whether a flash of light moved from A to B or from B to A. To detect movement as accurately as possible, your visual system compensates for the fact that some parts of the retina are slightly closer to your brain than other parts are. Without some sort of compensation, simultaneous flashes arriving at two spots on your retina would reach your brain at different times, and you might perceive a flash of light moving from one spot to the other. What prevents that illusion is the fact that axons from more distant parts of your retina transmit impulses slightly faster than those closer to the brain (L. R. Stanford, 1987)!

In short, the properties of impulse conduction in an axon are well adapted to the exact needs for information transfer in the nervous system. Let us now examine the mechanics of impulse transmission.

THE RESTING POTENTIAL OF THE NEURON

The membrane of a neuron maintains an **electrical gradient,** a difference in electrical charge between the inside and outside of the cell. All parts of a neuron are covered by a membrane about 8 nanometers (nm) thick (just less than 0.00001 mm), composed of two layers (an inner layer and an outer layer) of phospholipid molecules (containing chains of fatty acids and a phosphate group). Embedded among the phospholipids are some cylindrical protein molecules (see Figure 2.3, p. 32). The structure of the membrane provides it with a good combination of flexibility and firmness that retards the flow of chemicals between the inside and outside of the cell.

In the absence of any outside disturbance, the membrane maintains an electrical **polarization,** meaning a difference in electrical charge between two locations. Specifically, the neuron inside the membrane has a slightly negative electrical potential with respect to the outside. This difference in voltage in a resting neuron is called the **resting potential.** The resting potential is mostly the result of negatively charged proteins inside the cell.

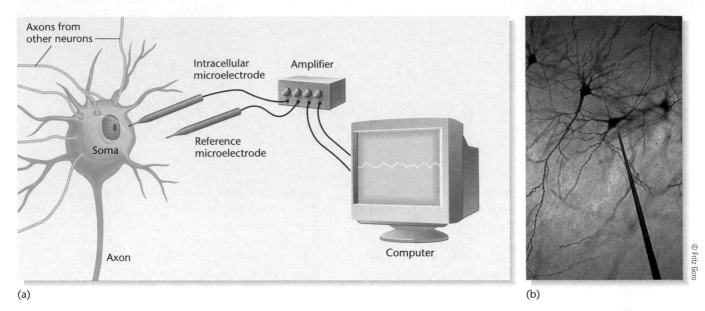

© Fritz Goro

(a)   (b)

Figure 2.14 Methods for recording activity of a neuron
(**a**) Diagram of the apparatus and a sample recording. (**b**) A microelectrode and stained neurons magnified hundreds of times by a light microscope.

Researchers can measure the resting potential by inserting a very thin *microelectrode* into the cell body, as Figure 2.14 shows. The diameter of the electrode must be as small as possible so that it can enter the cell without causing damage. By far the most common electrode is a fine glass tube filled with a concentrated salt solution and tapering to a tip diameter of 0.0005 mm or less. This electrode, inserted into the neuron, is connected to recording equipment. A reference electrode placed somewhere outside the cell completes the circuit. Connecting the electrodes to a voltmeter, we find that the neuron's interior has a negative potential relative to its exterior. The actual potential varies from one neuron to another; a typical level is −70 mV (millivolts), but it can be either higher or lower than that.

Forces Acting on Sodium and Potassium Ions

If charged ions could flow freely across the membrane, the membrane could not maintain its polarization. However, the membrane is selectively permeable—that is, some chemicals can pass through it more freely than others. Most large or electrically charged ions and molecules cannot cross the membrane at all. Oxygen, carbon dioxide, urea, and water cross in both directions through channels that are always open. A few biologically important ions, such as sodium, potassium, calcium, and chloride, cross through membrane channels (or gates) that are sometimes open and sometimes closed. When the membrane is at rest, the sodium channels are closed, preventing almost all sodium flow. These channels are shown in Figure 2.15. As we shall see in Chapter 3, certain kinds of stimulation can open the sodium channels. When the membrane is at rest, potassium channels are nearly but not entirely closed, so potassium flows slowly.

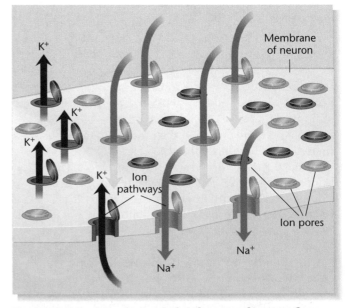

Figure 2.15 Ion channels in the membrane of a neuron
When a channel opens, it permits one kind of ion to cross the membrane. When it closes, it prevents passage of that ion.

Sodium ions are more than 10 times more concentrated outside the membrane than inside because of the **sodium-potassium pump**, a protein complex that repeatedly transports three sodium ions out of the cell while drawing two potassium ions into the cell. The sodium-potassium pump is an active transport requiring energy. Various poisons can stop it and so can an interruption of blood flow.

The sodium-potassium pump is effective only because of the selective permeability of the membrane, which prevents the sodium ions that were pumped out of the neuron from leaking right back in again. As it is, the sodium ions pumped out stay out. However, some of the potassium ions pumped into the neuron do leak out, carrying a positive charge with them. This leakage increases the electrical gradient across the membrane, as shown in Figure 2.16.

When the neuron is at rest, two forces act on sodium, both tending to push it into the cell. First consider the electrical gradient. Sodium is positively charged, and the inside of the cell is negatively charged. Opposite electrical charges attract, so the electrical gradient tends to pull sodium into the cell. Second consider the concentration gradient, the difference in distribution of ions across the membrane. Sodium is more concentrated outside than inside, so by the laws of probability, sodium is more likely to enter the cell than to leave it. (By analogy, imagine two rooms connected by a door. There are 100 cats in room A and only 10 in room B. Are cats more likely to move from A to B or from B to A? The same principle applies to the movement of sodium.) Given that both the electrical gradient and the concentration gradient tend to move sodium ions into the cell, sodium certainly would move rapidly if it had the chance. However, the sodium channels are closed when the membrane is at rest, so almost no sodium flows except for the sodium pushed *out of* the cell by the sodium-potassium pump.

Potassium, however, is subject to competing forces. Potassium is positively charged and the inside of the cell is negatively charged, so the electrical gradient tends to pull potassium in. However, potassium is more concentrated inside the cell than outside, so the concentration gradient tends to drive it out. If the potassium gates were wide open, potassium would flow mostly out of the cell, but not rapidly. That is, for potassium the electrical gradient and concentration gradient are almost in balance. (The sodium-potassium pump keeps pulling potassium in, so the two gradients cannot get completely in balance.)

Why a Resting Potential?

Presumably, evolution could have equipped us with neurons that were electrically neutral at rest. The resting potential must provide enough benefit to justify the energy cost of the sodium-potassium pump. The advantage is that the resting potential prepares the neuron to respond rapidly to a stimulus. As we shall see in the next section, excitation of the neuron opens channels that let sodium enter the cell explosively. Because the membrane did its work in advance by maintaining the concentration gradient for sodium, the cell is prepared to respond strongly and rapidly to a stimulus.

The resting potential of a neuron can be compared to a poised bow and arrow: An archer who pulls the bow in advance and then waits is ready to fire as soon as the appropriate moment comes. Evolution has applied the same strategy to the neuron.

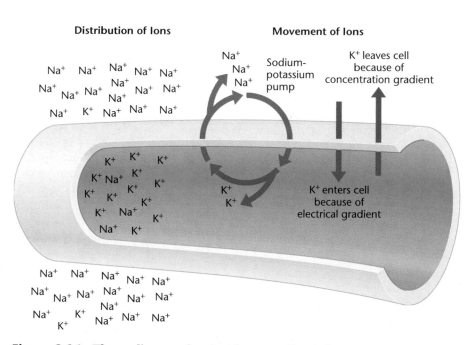

Distribution of Ions

Movement of Ions

Na⁺ Na⁺ Na⁺ Na⁺ Na⁺
Na⁺ Na⁺ Na⁺ Na⁺ Na⁺ Na⁺
Na⁺ Na⁺ Na⁺ Na⁺
Na⁺ K⁺ Na⁺ Na⁺ Na⁺

Na⁺
Na⁺
Na⁺
Na⁺

Sodium-potassium pump

K⁺ leaves cell because of concentration gradient

K⁺ K⁺ K⁺
K⁺ Na⁺ K⁺ K⁺
K⁺ K⁺ K⁺ K⁺
K⁺ K⁺ K⁺
Na⁺ Na⁺ K⁺
Na⁺ K⁺

K⁺
K⁺

K⁺ enters cell because of electrical gradient

Na⁺ Na⁺ Na⁺ Na⁺ Na⁺
Na⁺ Na⁺ Na⁺ Na⁺ Na⁺ Na⁺
Na⁺ Na⁺ Na⁺
Na⁺ K⁺ Na⁺ Na⁺ Na⁺
K⁺

Figure 2.16 The sodium and potassium gradients for a resting membrane
Sodium (Na^+) ions are more concentrated outside the neuron; potassium (K^+) ions are more concentrated inside. Protein and chloride ions (not shown) bear negative charges inside the cell. At rest, very few sodium ions cross the membrane except by means of the sodium-potassium pump. Potassium tends to flow into the cell because of an electrical gradient but to flow out because of the concentration gradient.

THE ACTION POTENTIAL

The resting potential remains stable until the neuron is stimulated. Ordinarily, stimulation of the neuron takes place at synapses, which we consider in Chapter 3. In the laboratory, it is also possible to stimulate a neuron by inserting an electrode into it and applying current.

We can measure a neuron's potential with a microelectrode, as shown in Figure 2.14. When an axon's membrane is at rest, the recordings show a steady negative potential inside the axon. If we now use an additional electrode to apply a negative charge, we can further increase the negative charge inside the neuron. The change is called **hyperpolarization,** which means increased polarization. As soon as the artificial stimulation ceases, the charge returns to its original resting level. The recording looks like this:

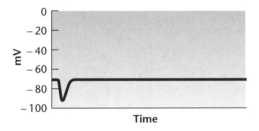

Now, let us apply a current for a slight **depolarization** of the neuron—that is, reduction of its polarization toward zero. If we apply a small depolarizing current, we get a result like this:

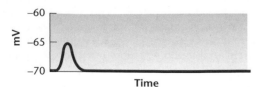

With a slightly stronger depolarizing current, the potential rises slightly higher, but again it returns to the resting level as soon as the stimulation ceases:

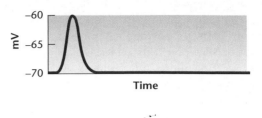

Now, let us see what happens when we apply a still stronger current: Any stimulation beyond a certain level, called the **threshold of excitation,** produces a sudden, massive depolarization of the membrane. When the potential reaches the threshold, the membrane suddenly opens its sodium channels and permits a rapid, massive flow of ions across the membrane. The potential then shoots up far beyond the strength of the stimulus:

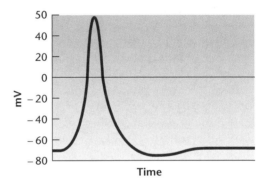

Any *subthreshold* stimulation produces a small response proportional to the amount of current. Any stimulation beyond the threshold, regardless of how far beyond, produces the same response, such as the one just shown. That response, a rapid depolarization and slight reversal of the usual polarization, is referred to as an **action potential.**

The Molecular Basis of the Action Potential

Remember that both the electrical gradient and the concentration gradient tend to drive sodium ions into the neuron. If sodium ions could flow freely across the membrane, they would enter rapidly. Ordinarily, the membrane is almost impermeable to sodium, but during the action potential, its permeability increases sharply.

The membrane proteins that control sodium entry are voltage-activated channels, membrane channels whose permeability depends on the voltage difference across the membrane. At the resting potential, the channels are closed. As the membrane becomes slightly depolarized, the sodium channels begin to open and sodium flows more freely. If the depolarization is less than the threshold, sodium crosses the membrane only slightly more than usual. When the potential across the membrane reaches the threshold, the sodium channels open wide. Sodium ions rush into the neuron explosively until the electrical potential across the membrane passes beyond zero to a reversed polarity, as shown in the following diagram:

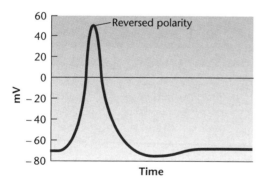

Compared to the total number of sodium ions in and around the axon, only a tiny percentage cross the membrane during an action potential. Even at the peak of the action potential, sodium ions continue to be far more concentrated outside the neuron than inside. An action potential increases the sodium concentration inside a neuron by far less than 1%. Because of the persisting concentration gradient, sodium ions should still tend to diffuse into the cell. However, at the peak of the action potential, the sodium gates snap shut and cannot be opened again, even by a strong stimulation, for at least the next millisecond (ms) or so.

After the peak of the action potential, what brings the membrane back to its original state of polarization? The answer is *not* the sodium-potassium pump, which is too slow for this purpose. After the action potential is well underway, the potassium channels open and potassium ions flow out of the axon, carrying with them a positive charge. Potassium ions leave the axon simply

because they are much more concentrated inside than outside and because they are no longer held inside by a negative charge. Because the potassium channels open wider at this point, enough potassium ions leave to drive the potential a bit beyond the normal resting level to a temporary hyperpolarization. Figure 2.17 summarizes the movements of ions during an action potential.

At the end of this process, the membrane has returned to its resting potential and everything is back to normal, except that the inside of the neuron has slightly more sodium ions and slightly fewer potassium ions than before. Eventually, the sodium-potassium pump restores the original distribution of ions, but this process takes time. In fact, if a series of action potentials occurs at a sufficiently rapid rate, the pump cannot keep up with the action, and sodium may begin to accumulate within the axon. Excessive buildup of sodium can be toxic, even fatal, to a cell. (Excessive stimulation occurs only under

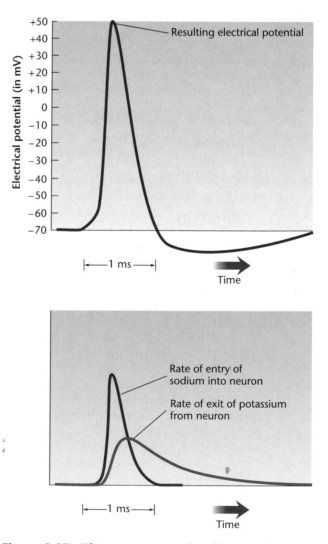

Figure 2.17 The movement of sodium and potassium ions during an action potential
Note that sodium ions cross during the peak of the action potential and that potassium ions cross later in the opposite direction, returning the membrane to its original polarization.

abnormal conditions, however, such as during a stroke or after the use of certain drugs. Don't worry that thinking too hard will start exploding your brain cells.)

For the neuron to function properly, sodium and potassium must flow across the membrane at just the right pace. Scorpion venom attacks the nervous system by keeping sodium channels open and closing potassium channels (Pappone & Cahalan, 1987; Strichartz, Rando, & Wang, 1987). As a result, the membrane goes into a prolonged depolarization that makes it useless for conveying information. **Local anesthetic** drugs, such as Novocain and Xylocaine, attach to the sodium channels of the membrane, preventing sodium ions from entering (Ragsdale, McPhee, Scheuer, & Catterall, 1994). In doing so, such drugs block action potentials in the affected area. If anesthetics are applied to sensory nerves carrying pain messages, they prevent the messages from reaching the brain. **General anesthetics,** such as ether and chloroform, decrease brain activity by opening certain potassium channels wider than usual (Patel et al., 1999). With the potassium channels wide open, as soon as any stimulus starts to excite a neuron by opening sodium channels, potassium ions exit about as fast as the sodium ions enter, preventing most action potentials.

> **5.** During the rise of the action potential, do sodium ions move into the cell or out of it? Why?
>
> **6.** As the membrane reaches the peak of the action potential, what ionic movement brings the potential down to the original resting potential?
>
> *Check your answers on page 48.*

The All-or-None Law

Action potentials occur in axons, and they depend on the fact that axons have voltage-dependent sodium channels. That is, when the voltage reaches a certain level of depolarization (the threshold), these sodium channels open wide to let sodium enter rapidly, and the incoming sodium depolarizes the membrane still further. Dendrites and cell bodies can be depolarized, but they don't have the voltage-dependent sodium channels, so opening the channels a little, letting in a little sodium, doesn't cause them to open even more and let in still more sodium. Thus, dendrites and cell bodies don't produce action potentials.

Within a given axon, all action potentials are approximately equal in amplitude (intensity) and velocity under normal circumstances. This is the **all-or-none law:** The amplitude and velocity of an

action potential are independent of the intensity of the stimulus that initiated it. By analogy, imagine flushing a toilet: You have to make a press of at least a certain strength (the threshold), but pressing even harder does not make the toilet flush any faster or more vigorously.

As a consequence of this law, a neuron's messages are analogous to flicking a light on and off as a signal: The message is conveyed by the time sequence of impulses and pauses. For instance, an axon might signal "weak stimulus" by a low frequency of action potentials per second and "stronger stimulus" by a higher frequency.

The Refractory Period

While the electrical potential across the membrane is returning from its peak toward the resting point, it is still above the threshold. Why does the cell not produce another action potential during this period? Immediately after an action potential, the cell is in a **refractory period during which it resists the production of further action potentials.** In the first part of this period, the **absolute refractory period,** the sodium gates are firmly closed and the membrane cannot produce an action potential, regardless of the stimulation. During the second part, the **relative refractory period,** the sodium gates are reverting to their usual state, but the potassium gates remain open. Because of the free flow of potassium, a stronger than usual stimulus is necessary to initiate an action potential. Most of the axons that have been tested have an absolute refractory period of about 1 ms and a relative refractory period of another 2–4 ms. (To return to the toilet analogy, there is a short time right after you flush a toilet when you cannot make it flush again—an absolute refractory period. Then follows a period when it is possible but difficult to flush it again—a relative refractory period—before it returns to normal.)

> **7.** State the all-or-none law.
>
> **8.** Does the all-or-none law apply to dendrites, somata, axons, or all three?
>
> **9.** Suppose researchers find that axon A can produce up to 1000 action potentials per second (at least briefly, with maximum stimulation), but axon B can never produce more than 200 per second (regardless of the strength of the stimulus). What could we conclude about the refractory periods of the two axons?
>
> *Check your answers on pages 48–49.*

PROPAGATION OF THE ACTION POTENTIAL

Up to this point, we have dealt with the action potential at one location on the axon. Now let us consider how it moves down the axon toward some other cell. Remember that it is important for axons to convey impulses without any loss of strength over distance.

In a motor neuron, an action potential begins on the axon hillock, a swelling where the axon exits the soma (see Figure 2.5, p. 33). Each point along the membrane regenerates the action potential in much the same way that it was generated initially. During the action potential, sodium ions enter a point on the axon. Temporarily, that location is positively charged in comparison with neighboring areas along the axon. The positive ions flow down the axon and across the membrane, as shown in Figure 2.18. Other things being equal, the greater the diameter of the axon, the faster the ions flow (because of decreased resistance). The positive charges now inside the membrane slightly depolarize the adjacent areas of the membrane, causing the next area to reach its threshold and regenerate the action potential. In this manner, the action potential travels like a wave along the axon.

The term **propagation of the action potential** describes the transmission of an action potential down an axon. The propagation of an animal species is the production of babies; in a sense, the action potential gives birth to a new action potential at each point along the axon. In this manner, the action potential can be just as strong at the end of the axon as it was at the beginning. The action potential is much slower than electrical conduction because it requires the diffusion of sodium ions at successive points along the axon. Electrical conduction in a copper wire with free electrons approaches the speed of light, 300 million meters per second (m/s). In an axon, transmission relies on the flow of charged ions through a water medium. In thin axons, action potentials travel at a velocity of less than 1 m/s. Thicker axons and those covered with an insulating shield of myelin conduct with greater velocities.

Let us reexamine Figure 2.18 for a moment. What is to prevent the electrical charge from flowing in the direction opposite that in which the action potential is traveling? Nothing. In fact, the electrical charge does flow in both directions. In that case, what prevents an action potential near the center of an axon from reinvading the areas that it has just passed? The answer is that the areas just passed are still in their refractory period.

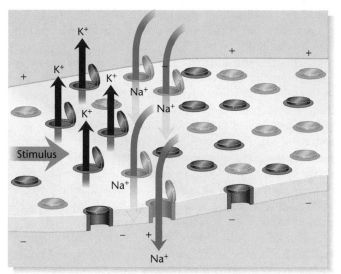

(a)

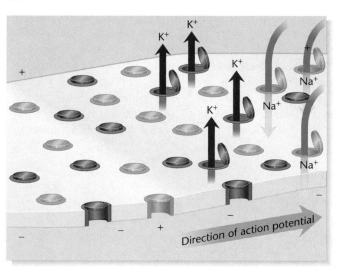

(b)

Figure 2.18
Current that enters an axon at the point of the action potential flows down the axon, thereby depolarizing adjacent areas of the membrane. The current flows more easily through relatively thick axons. Behind the area of sodium entry, potassium ions exit.

THE MYELIN SHEATH AND SALTATORY CONDUCTION

The thinnest axons conduct impulses at less than 1 m/s. Just increasing the diameters increases conduction velocity, but only up to about 10 m/s. At that speed, an impulse from a giraffe's foot takes about 0.5 s to reach its brain. At the slower speeds of thinner unmyelinated axons, a giraffe's brain could be seconds out of date on what was happening to its feet. In some vertebrate axons, sheaths of **myelin**, an insulating material composed of fats and proteins, increase speed to 100 m/s or more.

Consider the following analogy. Suppose it is my job to carry written messages over a distance of 3 kilometers (km) without using any mechanical device. Taking each message and running with it would be reliable but slow, like the propagation of an action potential along an unmyelinated axon. I could try tying each message to a ball and throwing it, but I cannot throw a ball even close to 3 km. The ideal compromise is to station people at moderate distances along the 3 km and throw the message-bearing ball from person to person until it reaches its destination.

The principle behind **myelinated axons**, those covered with a myelin sheath, is the same. Myelinated axons, found only in vertebrates, are covered with a coating composed mostly of fats. The myelin sheath is interrupted at intervals of approximately 1 mm by short unmyelinated sections of axon called **nodes of Ranvier (RAHN-vee-ay)**, as shown in Figure 2.19. Each node is only about 1 micrometer wide.

Suppose that an action potential is initiated at the axon hillock and propagated along the axon until it reaches the first myelin segment. The action

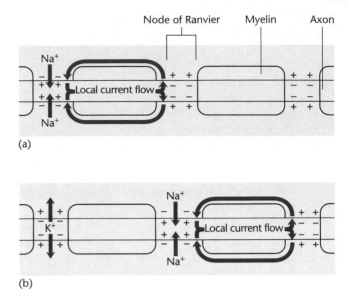

(a)

(b)

Figure 2.20 Saltatory conduction in a myelinated axon
An action potential at the node triggers a flow of current to the next node, where the membrane regenerates the action potential.

potential cannot regenerate along the membrane between nodes because sodium channels are virtually absent in the areas between nodes (Catterall, 1984). After an action potential occurs at a node, sodium ions that enter the axon diffuse in both directions within the axon, repelling positive ions that were already present and thus pushing a chain of positive ions along the axon to the next node, where they regenerate the action potential (Figure 2.20). This flow of ions is considerably faster than the regeneration of an action potential at each point along the axon. The jumping of action potentials from node to node is referred to as **saltatory conduction**, from the Latin word *saltare,* meaning "to jump." (The same root shows up in the word *somersault.*) In addition to providing very rapid conduction of impulses, saltatory conduction has the added benefit of conserving energy: Instead of admitting sodium ions at every point along the axon and then having to pump them out via the sodium-potassium pump, a myelinated axon admits sodium only at its nodes.

Some diseases, including multiple sclerosis, destroy myelin sheaths, thereby slowing down action potentials or stopping them altogether. An axon that has lost its myelin is not the same as one that has never had myelin. A myelinated axon develops sodium channels almost exclusively at its nodes (Waxman & Ritchie, 1985). After the axon loses myelin, it still lacks sodium channels in the areas previously covered with myelin, and many action potentials die out between one node and the next. People with multiple sclerosis suffer a variety of

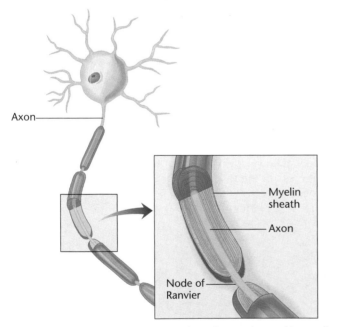

Cutaway view of axon wrapped in myelin

Figure 2.19 An axon surrounded by a myelin sheath and interrupted by nodes of Ranvier
The inset shows a cross section through both the axon and the myelin sheath. Magnification approximately × 30,000. The anatomy is distorted in order to show several nodes; in fact, the distance between nodes is generally about 100 times as large as the nodes themselves.

impairments, including poor muscle coordination.

For an additional review of action potentials, see this Web site:

http://faculty.washington.edu/chudler/ap.html

Stop & Check

---

10. Distinguish between the absolute refractory period and the relative refractory period.

11. In a myelinated axon, how would the action potential be affected if the nodes were much closer together? How might it be affected if the nodes were much farther apart?

Check your answers on page 49.

LOCAL NEURONS

Unlike axons, dendrites and somata do not produce action potentials; they produce small depolarizations and hyperpolarizations, depending on the stimulation affecting them. The action potential, with its all-or-none law, starts at the beginning of the axon. The depolarizations and hyperpolarizations of the dendrites and soma do not follow the all-or-none law but decay as they travel. All these principles apply to relatively large neurons with lengthy axons, but not all neurons fall into that category.

Graded Potentials

Many neurons have only short dendrites and short (if any) axons. They exchange information only with their closest neighbors and are therefore known as **local neurons.** A local neuron does not produce an action potential. It receives information from other neurons in its immediate vicinity and produces **graded potentials,** membrane potentials that vary in magnitude and do not follow the all-or-none law. When a local neuron is stimulated, it depolarizes or hyperpolarizes in proportion to the intensity of the stimulus. The change in membrane potential is conducted to adjacent areas of the cell, in all directions, gradually decaying as it travels. Those various areas of the cell make direct contact onto other neurons, without going through an axon. In Chapter 6, we discuss in some detail a particular local neuron, the *horizontal cell,* which is essential for local interactions within the retina of the eye.

EXTENSIONS AND APPLICATIONS

Small Neurons and Big Misconceptions

Local neurons are somewhat difficult to study; it is almost impossible to insert an electrode into a tiny cell without damaging it. A disproportionate amount of our knowledge therefore has come from large neurons, and that bias in our research methods led to an early, still enduring misconception.

Many years ago, long before neuroscientists could investigate these local neurons, they knew only that they were small. Given that nearly all knowledge about the nervous system was based on the activities of large neurons, the small neurons seemed an anomaly, a mistake. Many scientists assumed that they were "baby" or immature neurons. As one textbook author put it, "Many of these [neurons] are small and apparently undeveloped, as if they constituted a reserve stock not yet utilized in the individual's cerebral activity" (Woodworth, 1934, p. 194). In other words, the small cells would contribute to behavior only if they grew.

Perhaps this misunderstanding was the origin of that widespread, nonsensical belief that "we use only 10% of our brain." It is difficult to imagine any reasonable justification for this belief. Surely, no one maintained that a person could lose 90% of the brain and still behave normally or that only 10% of neurons are active at any given moment. Whatever its source, the belief became popular, presumably because people wanted to believe it. Eventually, they were simply quoting one another long after everyone forgot what evidence they had (or didn't have) for it in the first place.

MODULE 2.2

In Closing: Neural Messages

In this chapter, we have examined what happens within a single neuron, as if each neuron acted independently. It does not, of course; all of its functions depend on communication with other neurons, as we consider in the next chapter. We may as well admit from the start, however, that neural communication is pretty amazing. Unlike human communication, in which a speaker sometimes presents a complicated message to an enormous audience, a neuron delivers only an action potential—a mere on/off message—to only that modest number of other neurons that receive branches of its axon. At various receiving neurons, an "on" message can be converted into either excitation or inhibition (yes or no). From this limited system, all of our behavior and experience emerge.

SUMMARY

1. The inside of a resting neuron has a negative charge with respect to the outside. Sodium ions are actively pumped out of the neuron, and potassium ions are pumped in. Potassium ions are moderately free to flow across the membrane of the neuron, but the flow of sodium ions is greatly restricted. (p. 39)

2. When the charge across the membrane is reduced, sodium ions can flow more freely across the membrane. When the change in membrane potential is sufficient to reach the threshold of the neuron, sodium ions enter explosively, and the charge across the membrane is suddenly reduced and reversed. This event is known as the action potential. (p. 42)

3. The magnitude of the action potential is independent of the size of the stimulus that initiated it; this statement is the all-or-none law. (p. 44)

4. Immediately after an action potential, the membrane enters a refractory period during which it is resistant to starting another action potential. (p. 44)

5. The action potential is regenerated at successive points along the axon by sodium ions flowing through the core of the axon and then across the membrane. The action potential maintains a constant magnitude as it passes along the axon. (p. 45)

6. In axons that are covered with myelin, action potentials form only in the nodes between myelinated segments. Between the nodes, ions flow faster than through axons without myelin. (p. 45)

7. Many small local neurons transmit messages over relatively short distances by graded potentials that decay over time and space instead of by action potentials. (p. 47)

ANSWERS TO *STOP AND CHECK* QUESTIONS

1. Sodium ions are more concentrated outside the cell; potassium is more concentrated inside. (p. 42)

2. When the membrane is at rest, the concentration gradient tends to drive potassium ions out of the cell; the electrical gradient draws them into the cell. The sodium-potassium pump also draws them into the cell. (p. 42)

3. A hyperpolarization is an exaggeration of the usual negative charge within a cell (to a more negative level than usual). A depolarization is a decrease in the amount of negative charge within the cell. (p. 42)

4. A depolarization that passes the threshold produces an action potential. One that falls short of the threshold does not produce an action potential. (p. 42)

5. During the action potential, sodium ions move into the cell. The voltage-dependent sodium gates have opened, so sodium can move freely. Sodium is attracted to the inside of the cell by both an electrical and a concentration gradient. (p. 44)

6. After the peak of the action potential, potassium ions exit the cell, driving the membrane back to the resting potential. (The sodium-potassium pump is not the answer here; it is too slow.) (p. 44)

7. According to the all-or-none law, the size and shape of the action potential are independent of the intensity of the stimulus that initiated it. That is, every depolarization beyond the threshold of excitation produces an action potential of about the same amplitude and velocity for a given axon. (p. 44)

8. The all-or-none law applies only to axons because only axons have action potentials. (p. 44)

9. Axon A must have a shorter absolute refractory period, about 1 ms, whereas B has a longer absolute refractory period, about 5 ms. (p. 44)

10. During the absolute refractory period, the sodium gates are locked and no amount of stimulation can produce another action potential. During the relative refractory period, a stronger than usual amount of stimulation is needed to produce an action potential. (p. 47)

11. If the nodes were closer, the action potential would travel more slowly. If they were much farther apart, the current might not be able to diffuse from one node to the next and still remain above the threshold, so the action potentials might stop. (p. 47)

THOUGHT QUESTIONS

1. Suppose the threshold of a neuron were the same as its resting potential. What would happen? At what frequency would the cell produce action potentials?

2. In the laboratory, researchers can apply an electrical stimulus at any point along the axon, making action potentials travel in both directions from the point of stimulation. An action potential moving in the usual direction, away from the axon hillock, is said to be traveling in the *orthodromic* direction. An action potential traveling toward the axon hillock is traveling in the *antidromic* direction. If we started an orthodromic action potential at the axon hillock and an antidromic action potential at the opposite end of the axon, what would happen when they met at the center? Why? What research might make use of antidromic impulses?

3. If a drug partly blocks a membrane's potassium channels, how does it affect the action potential?

TERMS

absolute refractory period (p. 44)

action potential (p. 42)

active transport (p. 37)

afferent axon (p. 33)

all-or-none law (p. 44)

astrocyte (p. 35)

axon (p. 32)

axon hillock (p. 45)

blood-brain barrier (p. 37)

cell body, or soma (p. 32)

concentration gradient (p. 41)

dendrite (p. 32)

dendritic spine (p. 32)

depolarization (p. 42)

efferent axon (p. 33)

electrical gradient (p. 39)

endoplasmic reticulum (p. 32)

general anesthetic (p. 44)

glia (p. 35)

glucose (p. 38)

graded potential (p. 47)

hyperpolarization (p. 42)

interneuron (p. 34)

intrinsic neuron (p. 34)

local anesthetic (p. 44)

local neuron (p. 47)

membrane (p. 31)

microglia (p. 35)

mitochondrion
    (pl.: mitochondria) (p. 31)

motor neuron (p. 32)

myelin (p. 46)

myelin sheath (p. 32)

myelinated axon (p. 46)

neuron (p. 30)

node of Ranvier (p. 32, 46)

nucleus (p. 31)

oligodendrocyte (p. 35)

polarization (p. 39)

presynaptic terminal (p. 32)

propagation of the action
    potential (p. 45)

radial glia (p. 35)

refractory period (p. 44)

relative refractory period (p. 44)

resting potential (p. 39)

ribosome (p. 31)

saltatory conduction (p. 46)

Schwann cell (p. 35)

selective permeability (p. 40)

sensory neuron (p. 32)

sodium-potassium pump (p. 41)

thiamine (vitamin B1) (p. 38)

threshold of excitation (p. 42)

voltage-activated channel (p. 43)

SUGGESTIONS FOR FURTHER READING

Kimelberg, H. K., & Norenberg, M. D. (1989, April). Astrocytes. *Scientific American, 260*(4), 66–76. An overview of the functions of glia.

Smith, C. U. M. (1996). *Elements of molecular neurobiology* (2nd ed.). New York: Wiley. A detailed treatment of the molecular biology of neurons, including both action potentials and synaptic activity.

WEB SITES TO EXPLORE

You can go to the Biological Psychology Study Center and click this link. While there, you can also check for suggested articles available on InfoTrac College Edition.

- The Biological Psychology Internet address is: **http://psychology.wadsworth.com/ kalatbiopsych8e**

Lights, Camera, Action Potential!
From Eric Chudler's *Neuroscience for Kids.* (But don't assume that it's too childish for adults to appreciate.)
http://faculty.washington.edu/chudler/ap.html

CD-ROM: EXPLORING BIOLOGICAL PSYCHOLOGY

The Parts of a Neuron (animation)

Virtual Reality Neuron (virtual reality)

Neuron Puzzle (drag & drop)

Resting Potential (animation)

Action Potential (AP) (animation)

Action Potential: Na$^+$ Ions (animation)

Critical Thinking (essay questions)

Chapter Quiz (multiple choice questions)

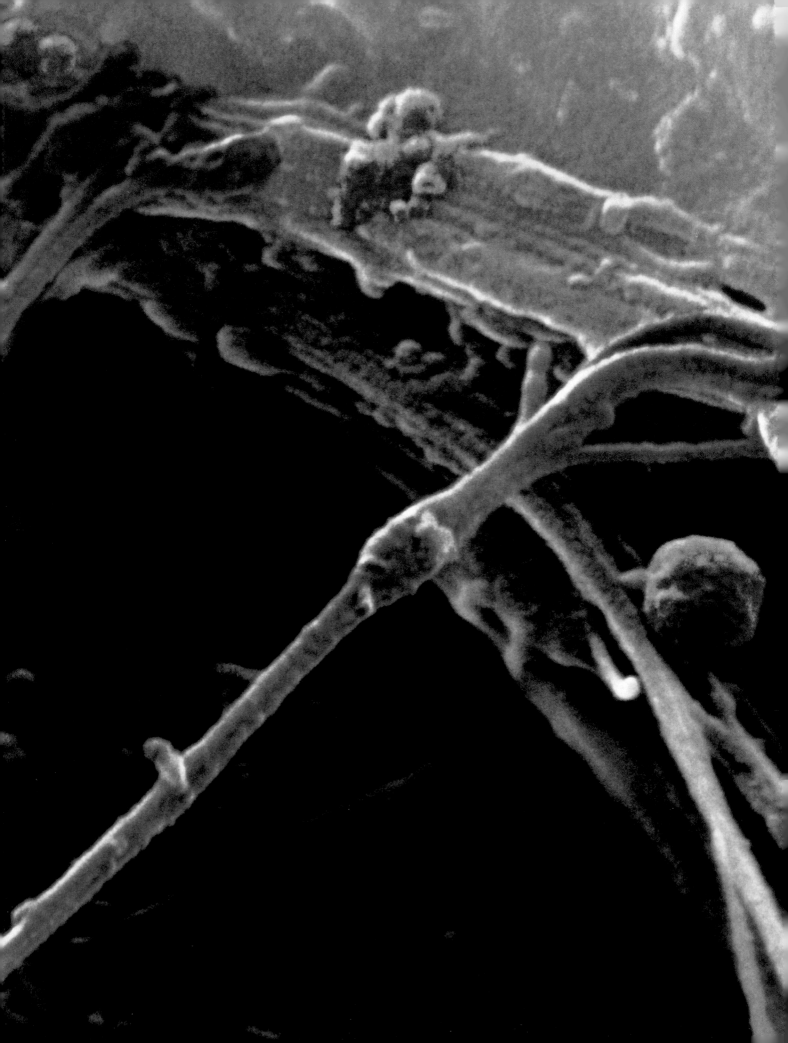

Communication at Synapses

3

Chapter Outline

Main Ideas

1. At a synapse, a neuron releases a chemical known as a neurotransmitter that excites or inhibits another cell.

2. A single release of neurotransmitter produces only a subthreshold response in the receiving cell. This response summates with other subthreshold responses to determine whether or not the cell produces an action potential.

3. Because different neurotransmitters contribute to behavior in different ways, excessive or deficient transmission at a particular type of synapse can lead to abnormal behavior.

If you had to communicate with someone and were not allowed to use speech or any other auditory information, what would you do? Chances are your first choice would be a visual code, such as sign language or written words. If that failed, you might try some sort of touch code or a system of electrical impulses. You might not think of communicating by passing chemicals back and forth. Chemical communication is, however, the primary method of communication for your neurons. Considering how well the human nervous system works, chemical communication is evidently more versatile than we might have guessed. Neurons communicate by transmitting chemicals at specialized junctions called *synapses*. The synapses are central to all comparison and integration of information in the brain.

Opposite:
This electron micrograph, with color added artificially, shows that the surface of a neuron is practically covered with synapses, the connections it receives from other neurons. *Source: ©Eye of Science/Photo Researchers, Inc.*

The Concept of the Synapse

In the late 1800s, Ramón y Cajal demonstrated that neurons do not physically merge into one another and that a narrow gap separates one from the next. As far as anyone knew, information might be transmitted across the gap in the same way it was transmitted along an axon.

Then in 1906, Charles Scott Sherrington inferred that a specialized type of communication occurs at the gap between two neurons, which he labeled the **synapse.** Sherrington also deduced most of the major properties of the synapse. What makes his accomplishment particularly impressive is that he based his conclusions almost entirely on behavioral data. Decades later, when investigators developed techniques for measuring and recording neural processes, nearly all of Sherrington's predictions turned out to be correct.

THE PROPERTIES OF SYNAPSES

Sherrington conducted most of his experiments on **reflexes,** automatic muscular responses to stimuli. In a leg flexion reflex, a sensory neuron excites a second neuron, which in turn excites a motor neuron, which excites a muscle, as Figure 3.1 shows. The circuit from sensory neuron to muscle response is called a **reflex arc.** Because a reflex depends on communication from one neuron to another—not just on the transmission of action potentials along an axon—Sherrington reasoned that the properties of a reflex might reveal some of the special properties of synapses.

In a typical experiment, a dog was strapped into a harness suspended above the ground. Sherrington pinched one of the dog's feet; after a short delay, the dog *flexed* (raised) the pinched leg and *extended* the others. Both the flexion and the extension were reflexive movements—automatic reactions to the stimulus. Furthermore, Sherrington found the same movements after he made a cut that disconnected the spinal cord from the brain; evidently, the flexion and extension were controlled by

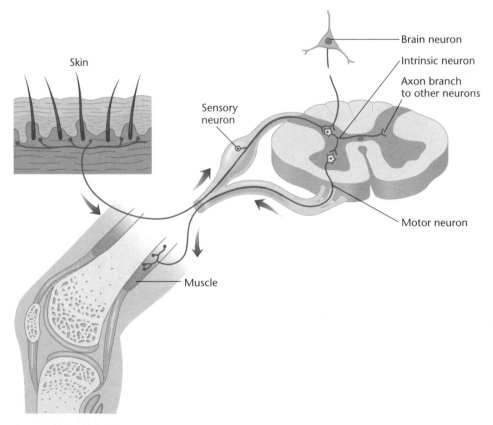

Figure 3.1   A reflex arc for leg flexion
The anatomy has been simplified to show the relationships among sensory, intrinsic, and motor neurons.

the spinal cord itself. In fact, the reflex was more reliable, more consistent in the dog with spinal cord damage. (In an intact animal, messages descending from the brain constantly modify the reflexes. Adult mammals have almost no "pure" reflexes; almost any response can be suppressed, enhanced, or otherwise modified, depending on the situation.)

Sherrington observed several properties of reflexes suggesting that some special process must occur at the junctions between neurons: (a) Reflexes are slower than conduction along an axon; consequently, there must be some delay at the synapses. (b) Several weak stimuli presented at slightly different times or slightly different locations produce a stronger reflex than a single stimulus does. Therefore, the synapse must be able to *summate*, or add together, different stimuli. (c) When one set of muscles becomes excited, a different set becomes relaxed. Apparently, synapses are connected so that the excitation of one leads to a decreased excitation, or even an inhibition, of others. We consider each of these points in some detail.

Speed of a Reflex and Delayed Transmission at the Synapse

When Sherrington pinched a dog's foot, the dog flexed that leg after a short delay. During the delay, an impulse had to travel up an axon from a skin receptor to the spinal cord, and then an impulse had to travel from the spinal cord back down the leg to a muscle. Sherrington measured the total distance that the impulse traveled from skin receptor to spinal cord to muscle and calculated the speed at which the impulse must have traveled to produce a muscle response after the measured delay. He found that the overall speed of conduction through the reflex arc was significantly slower than the known speed of conduction along an axon. Therefore, he deduced, transmission between one neuron and another at the synapse must be slower than transmission along an axon (Figure 3.2).

Temporal Summation

Sherrington's work with reflex arcs suggested that repeated stimuli occurring within a brief time can have a cumulative effect. He referred to this phenomenon as **temporal summation.** When Sherrington pinched a dog's foot very lightly, the leg did not move. However, when he repeated the same light pinch several times in rapid succession, the leg flexed slightly. The more rapid the series of pinches, the greater the response. Sherrington surmised that a single pinch produced a synaptic transmission that

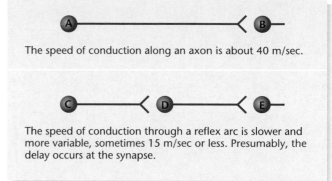

The speed of conduction along an axon is about 40 m/sec.

The speed of conduction through a reflex arc is slower and more variable, sometimes 15 m/sec or less. Presumably, the delay occurs at the synapse.

Figure 3.2 Sherrington's evidence for synaptic delay
An impulse traveling through a synapse in the spinal cord is slower than one traveling a similar distance along an uninterrupted axon.

was too weak to produce an action potential in the next cell. That is, the excitation was less than the threshold of the cell that receives the message, the **postsynaptic neuron.** (The neuron that delivers the synaptic transmission is the **presynaptic neuron.**) Sherrington proposed that this subthreshold excitation begins to decay within a fraction of a second but is capable of combining with a second small excitation that quickly follows it. A rapid succession of pinches produces a series of weak activations at the synapse, each adding its effect to what was left of the previous excitations. If the excitations occur rapidly enough, they combine to exceed the threshold and therefore produce an action potential in the postsynaptic neuron.

Decades after Sherrington conducted his studies, it became possible to measure some of the single-cell properties he had inferred. To record the activity evoked in a neuron by synaptic input, a researcher inserts a microelectrode into the neuron to measure changes in the electrical potential across the membrane. Using this method, John Eccles (1964) demonstrated temporal summation in single cells. He attached stimulating electrodes to some of the axons that formed synapses onto a neuron. He then recorded from the neuron while stimulating one or more approaching axons. For example, after he had briefly stimulated an axon, Eccles recorded a slight depolarization of the membrane of the postsynaptic cell (point 1 in Figure 3.3).

Note that this partial depolarization is a graded potential. Unlike action potentials, which are always depolarizations, graded potentials may be either depolarizations (excitatory) or hyperpolarizations (inhibitory). A graded depolarization is known as an **excitatory postsynaptic potential (EPSP).** Like an action potential, an EPSP results from sodium ions entering the cell (see Chapter 2). The synaptic activation

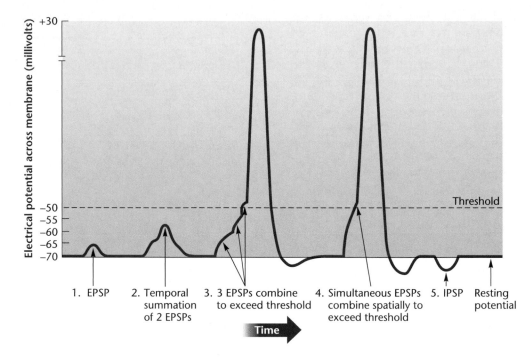

Figure 3.3   Recordings from a postsynaptic neuron during synaptic activation

opens sodium gates and increases the flow of sodium ions across the membrane. However, transmission at a single synapse does not open enough sodium gates to provoke an action potential. Unlike an action potential, an EPSP is a subthreshold event that decays over time and space; that is, its magnitude decreases as it travels along the membrane.

When Eccles stimulated an axon twice in close succession, two consecutive EPSPs were recorded in the postsynaptic cell. If the delay between EPSPs was short enough, temporal summation occurred; that is, the second EPSP added to what was left of the first one (point 2 in Figure 3.3). The summation of two EPSPs might or might not be enough to exceed the threshold of the postsynaptic cell, depending on the size of the EPSPs, the time between them, and the threshold of the postsynaptic cell. In point 3 in Figure 3.3, three consecutive EPSPs combined to exceed the threshold and produce an action potential.

Spatial Summation

Sherrington's work with reflex arcs also suggested that synapses have the property of spatial summation: Several synaptic inputs originating from separate locations can exert a cumulative effect on a neuron. Sherrington again began with a pinch that was too weak to elicit a response. But this time, instead of pinching the dog twice, he gave simultaneous pinches at two points on the foot. Although neither pinch alone elicited a response, the two together did. Sherrington concluded that pinching two points on the foot acti-

vated two sensory neurons, each of which sent an axon to the same target neuron. Excitation from either axon excited a synapse on that neuron, but one excitation was insufficient for an action potential. When both excitations were present at the same time, however, their combined effect exceeded the threshold for producing an action potential (see point 4 in Figure 3.3).

Again Eccles confirmed Sherrington's inference, demonstrating the spatial summation of EPSPs by recording from neurons. Note that temporal and spatial summation produce the same result: Each generates an action potential in the postsynaptic cell (Figure 3.4).

You might guess that the synapses on the cell body or the part of a dendrite closest to the cell body would have a bigger effect—that is, they would add more in spatial summation—than synapses farther away on the dendrites. Certainly, many neuroscientists expected that result. Surprisingly, however, the synapses on remoter parts of the dendrites produce correspondingly larger EPSPs, so their contribution to the cell's response is about the same as that of closer synapses (Magee & Cook, 2000).

Inhibitory Synapses

When Sherrington vigorously pinched a dog's foot, the flexor muscles of that leg contracted and so did the extensor muscles of the other three legs (Figure 3.5). At the same time, the dog relaxed the extensor muscles of the stimulated leg and the flexor muscles of the other legs. Sherrington's explanation for this series of coordinated and adaptive movements depended again on the synapses and in particular on the connections among neurons in the spinal cord: A pinch on the foot sends a message along a sensory neuron to an interneuron (an intermediate neuron) in the spinal cord, which in turn excites the motor neurons connected to the flexor muscles of that leg (Figure 3.6). Sherrington surmised that the interneuron also sends a message that decreases excitation of motor neurons connected to the extensor muscles in the same leg. He did not know whether the interneuron formed an inhibitory synapse onto the motor neuron to the extensor muscles or whether it simply decreased the amount of excitation. In either case, the flexor and extensor muscles of the leg were prevented from contracting at the same time.

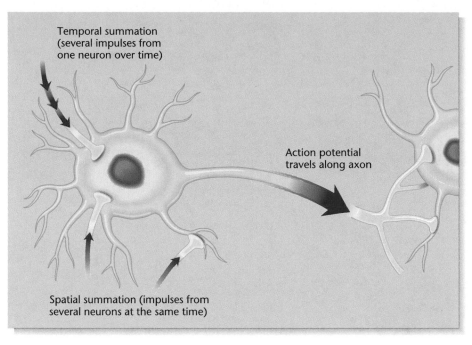

Figure 3.4 **Temporal and spatial summation**

Eccles and later researchers demonstrated that the interneuron actually has inhibitory synapses onto the motor neuron of the extensor muscle. At these synapses, input from the axon hyperpolarizes the postsynaptic cell, increasing the cell's negative charge and decreasing the probability of an action potential by moving the potential further from the threshold (point 5 in Figure 3.3). This temporary hyperpolarization of a membrane—called an **inhibitory postsynaptic potential, or IPSP**—resembles an EPSP in many ways. An IPSP occurs when synaptic input selectively opens the gates for potassium ions to leave the cell (carrying a positive charge with them) or for chloride ions to enter the cell (carrying a negative charge). Inhibition is more than just the absence of excitation; it is an active "brake" that can suppress excitatory responses.

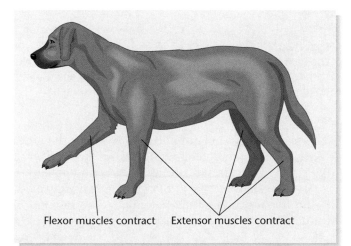

Figure 3.5 **Antagonistic muscles**
Flexor muscles draw an extremity toward the trunk of the body; extensor muscles move an extremity away from the body.

1. What evidence led Sherrington to conclude that transmission at a synapse is different from transmission along an axon?
2. What is the difference between temporal summation and spatial summation?
3. What was Sherrington's evidence for inhibition in the nervous system?
4. What ion gates in the membrane open during an EPSP? What gates open during an IPSP?
Check your answers on page 59.

RELATIONSHIP AMONG EPSP, IPSP, AND ACTION POTENTIAL

A neuron is rarely exposed to a single EPSP or IPSP at a time. A neuron may have thousands of synapses along its surface, some that excite the neuron and others that inhibit it. Any number and combination of synapses may be active at any time, yielding a continuing combination of temporal and spatial summation.

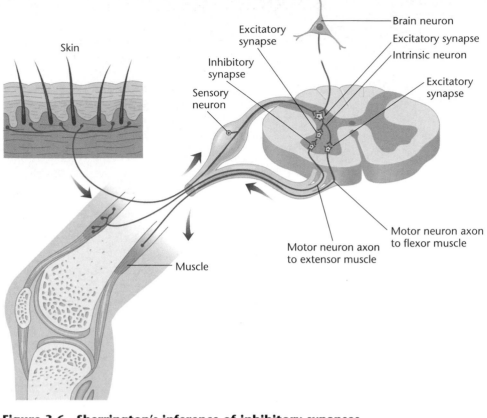

Figure 3.6 Sherrington's inference of inhibitory synapses
When a muscle is excited, the probability of excitation decreases in the paired muscle. Sherrington inferred that the interneuron that excited a motor neuron to one muscle also inhibited a motor neuron connected to the other.

The greater the number of EPSPs, the greater the probability of an action potential; the greater the number of IPSPs, the lower the probability of an action potential.

In many neurons, the EPSPs and IPSPs merely modify the frequency of action potentials that the neuron would fire spontaneously. That is, many neurons have a **spontaneous firing rate,** a periodic production of action potentials even without synaptic input. EPSPs increase the frequency of action potentials in these neurons, whereas IPSPs decrease it. For example, if the neuron's spontaneous firing rate is 10 per second, a steady stream of EPSPs might increase the rate to 15 or 20 or more, whereas a steady stream of IPSPs might decrease the rate to 5 or fewer action potentials per second.

MODULE 3.1

In Closing: The Neuron as Decision Maker

The neuron can be compared to a thermostat, a smoke detector, or any other device that detects something and triggers a response: When input reaches a certain level, the neuron triggers an action potential. That is,

the synapses enable the postsynaptic neuron to integrate information. The EPSPs and IPSPs reaching a neuron at a given moment compete against one another, and the net result is a complicated, not exactly algebraic summation of the two effects. We could regard the summation of EPSPs and IPSPs as a "decision" because it determines whether or not the postsynaptic cell fires an action potential, but we should not imagine that any neuron decides between cereal and pancakes for breakfast. A great many neurons are involved in any behavior, and behavior depends on the whole neural network, not on a single neuron. Moreover, we cannot even assume, for instance, that an inhibitory synapse inhibits bodily activity. Activity at an inhibitory synapse may stop one neuron from inhibiting another neuron and thus yield a net excitation. Such disinhibition (inhibition of inhibition) is commonplace in the nervous system.

SUMMARY

1. The synapse is the point of communication between two neurons. Charles S. Sherrington's observations of reflexes enabled him to infer the properties of synapses. (p. 54)

2. Because transmission through a reflex arc is slower than transmission through an equivalent length of axon, Sherrington concluded that there is a delay of transmission at the synapse. (p. 55)

3. Graded potentials (EPSPs and IPSPs) summate their effects. The summation of graded potentials from stimuli at different times is temporal summation. The summation of graded potentials from different locations is spatial summation. (p. 55)

4. A single stimulation at a synapse produces a brief graded potential in the postsynaptic cell. An excitatory graded potential (depolarizing) is an EPSP. An inhibitory graded potential (hyperpolarizing) is an IPSP. (pp. 55, 57)

5. An EPSP occurs when sodium gates open in the membrane; an IPSP occurs when potassium or chloride gates open. (pp. 56, 57)

6. The EPSPs on a neuron compete with the IPSPs; the balance between the two determines the rate of firing of the neuron. (p. 57)

ANSWERS TO *STOP AND CHECK* QUESTIONS

1. Sherrington found that the velocity of conduction through a reflex arc was significantly slower than the velocity of an action potential along an axon. Therefore, some delay must occur at the junction between one neuron and the next. (p. 57)

2. Temporal summation is the combined effect of quickly repeated stimulation at a single synapse. Spatial summation is the combined effect of several nearly simultaneous stimulations at several synapses onto one neuron. (p. 57)

3. Sherrington found that a reflex that stimulates a flexor muscle sends a simultaneous message that inhibits nerves to the extensor muscles of the same limb. (p. 57)

4. During an EPSP, sodium gates open. During an IPSP, potassium or chloride gates open. (p. 57)

THOUGHT QUESTIONS

1. When Sherrington measured the reaction time of a reflex (i.e., the delay between stimulus and response), he found that the response occurred faster after a strong stimulus than after a weak one. Can you explain this finding? Remember that all action potentials—whether produced by strong or weak stimuli—travel at the same speed along a given axon.

2. A pinch on an animal's right hind foot leads to excitation of an interneuron that excites the motor neurons connected to the flexor muscles of that leg; the interneuron also inhibits the motor neurons connected to the extensor muscles of the leg. In addition, this interneuron sends impulses that reach the motor neuron connected to the extensor muscles of the left hind leg. Would you expect the interneuron to excite or inhibit that motor neuron? (Hint: The connections are adaptive. When an animal lifts one leg, it must put additional weight on the other legs to maintain balance.)

3. Neuron X has a synapse onto neuron Y, and Y has a synapse onto Z. Presume that no other neurons or synapses are present. An experimenter finds that excitation of neuron X causes an action potential in neuron Z after a short delay. However, she determines that the synapse of X onto Y is inhibitory. Explain how the stimulation of X might produce excitation of Z.

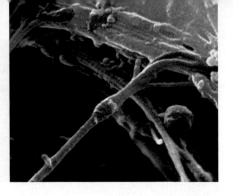

Chemical Events at the Synapse

Although Charles Sherrington accurately inferred many properties of the synapse, he drew one conclusion that was wrong, or at least greatly overstated: Although he knew that synaptic transmission was slower than transmission along an axon, he thought it was still too fast to depend on a chemical process and therefore concluded that it must be electrical. We now know that although some synaptic transmission is indeed electrical (Galarreta & Hestrin, 2001), in most cases it relies on chemical processes that are much faster than Sherrington thought possible and far more versatile than anyone would have guessed.

THE DISCOVERY THAT MOST SYNAPTIC TRANSMISSION IS CHEMICAL

T. R. Elliott, a young British scientist, reported in 1905 that the hormone *adrenaline* closely mimics the effects of the sympathetic nervous system, a set of nerves that control the internal organs (see Chapter 4). For example, stimulation of the sympathetic nerves accelerates the heartbeat, relaxes the stomach muscles, and dilates the pupils of the eyes. Applying adrenaline directly to the surface of the heart, the stomach, and the pupils produces the same effects. Elliott therefore suggested that the sympathetic nerves stimulate muscles by releasing adrenaline or a similar chemical and that synapses in general operate by releasing chemicals. Elliott's evidence was not decisive, however; perhaps adrenaline merely mimicked certain effects that are ordinarily produced by electrical stimulation. At the time, Sherrington's prestige was so great that most scientists ignored Elliott's results and continued to assume that synapses transmitted information by electrical impulses.

Otto Loewi, a German physiologist, was also attracted to the idea that synapses operate by releasing chemicals, but as he did not see how he could test the theory decisively, he set it aside. Then one night in 1920, he was aroused from sleep with a sudden idea. He wrote himself a note and went back to sleep.

Unfortunately, the next morning he could not read his own writing. The following night at 3 A.M., he awoke with the same idea, rushed to the laboratory, and performed the experiment at once.

He repeatedly stimulated the vagus nerve to a frog's heart, causing the heart rate to decrease. He then collected fluid from that heart, transferred it to a second frog's heart, and found that the second heart also decreased its rate of beating. (This experiment is illustrated in Figure 3.7.) In a later experiment, Loewi stimulated the accelerator nerve to the first frog's heart, causing the heart rate to increase. When he collected fluid from that heart and transferred it to the second heart, the heart rate increased. That is, stimulating one nerve released something that inhibited heart rate, and stimulating a different nerve released something else that increased heart rate. Those somethings had to be chemicals, not loose electricity. Therefore, Loewi concluded, nerves send messages by releasing chemicals.

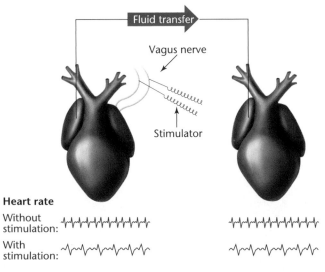

Figure 3.7 Loewi's experiment demonstrating that nerves send messages by releasing chemicals
Loewi stimulated the vagus nerve to one frog's heart, decreasing the heartbeat. Then he transferred fluid from that heart to another frog's heart and observed a decrease in its heartbeat.

Loewi later remarked that if he had thought of this experiment in the light of day, he probably never would have tried it (Loewi, 1960). Even if synapses did release chemicals, his daytime reasoning went, there was little chance that they released enough of the chemicals to make collecting them easy. Fortunately, by the time he realized that the experiment was unlikely to work, he had already completed the research, for which he later won the Nobel Prize.

Despite Loewi's work, researchers believed that chemical transmission occurred only in the peripheral nerves and that the brain and spinal cord operated mostly or entirely by electrical synapses. Finally, in the 1950s, researchers established that chemical transmission is the predominant type of communication in the brain as well. That discovery revolutionized our understanding and made it possible to understand how drugs affect behavior. It also led to research developing new drugs for psychiatric uses (Carlsson, 2001).

THE SEQUENCE OF CHEMICAL EVENTS AT A SYNAPSE

Many medical conditions and drugs affect behavior by altering neurotransmission. Consequently, understanding the chemical events occurring at a synapse is fundamental to much current research in biological psychology. The major events at a synapse are:

1. The neuron synthesizes chemicals that serve as neurotransmitters. It synthesizes the smaller neurotransmitters in the axon terminals and the peptide molecules in the cell body.
2. In the case of peptide neurotransmitters, the neuron transports the chemicals to the axon terminals. Action potentials also travel down the axon.
3. At the presynaptic terminal, an action potential causes calcium to enter the cell, thereby evoking the release of the neurotransmitters from the terminals and into the *synaptic cleft,* the space between the presynaptic and postsynaptic neurons.
4. The released molecules attach to receptors and alter the activity of the postsynaptic neuron.
5. The molecules separate from their receptors and (in some cases) are converted into inactive chemicals.
6. As many of the neurotransmitter molecules as possible are taken back into the presynaptic cell for recycling. In some cells, empty *vesicles* are returned to the cell body.

Figure 3.8 summarizes these steps. We shall discuss each step in more detail. The following Web site offers a brief animation of processes at a synapse, with an advertisement for a more detailed computer program: www.neurosci.tufts.edu/~rhammer/synapse1.html

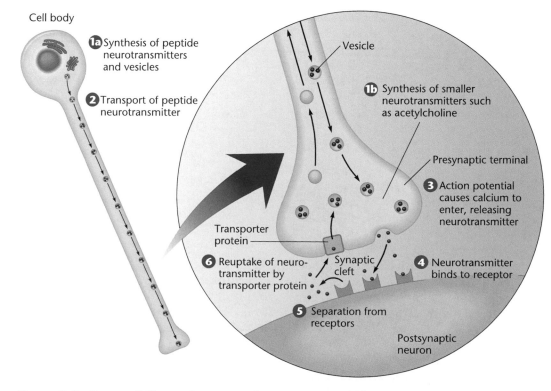

Figure 3.8 Some of the major events in neurotransmission

TABLE 3.1	Neurotransmitters
Amino acids	glutamate, GABA, glycine, aspartate, maybe others
A modified amino acid	acetylcholine
Monoamines (also modified from amino acids)	Indoleamines: serotonin Catecholamines: dopamine, norepinephrine, epinephrine
Peptides (chains of amino acids)	endorphins, substance P, neuropeptide Y, many others
Purines	ATP, adenosine, maybe others
Gases	NO (nitric oxide), maybe others

Types of Neurotransmitters

The chemicals that are released by one neuron at the synapse and that affect another are **neurotransmitters.** Each neuron synthesizes its neurotransmitters from materials in the blood. Neuroscientists believe that dozens of chemicals function as neurotransmitters in the brain, and research has been gradually adding to the list of known or probable neurotransmitters. We shall consider many of these transmitters repeatedly; for now, you should familiarize yourself with some of their names (see Table 3.1). Some major categories are:

amino acids acids containing an amine group (NH_2)

peptides chains of amino acids (A long chain of amino acids is called a *polypeptide;* a still longer chain is a *protein.* The divisions between peptide, polypeptide, and protein are not firm.)

acetylcholine (a one-member "family") a chemical similar to an amino acid, except that the NH_2 group has been replaced by an $N(CH_3)_3$ group

monoamines nonacidic neurotransmitters containing an amine group (NH_2), formed by a metabolic change in certain amino acids

purines a category of chemicals including adenosine and several of its derivatives

gases specifically nitric oxide (NO) and possibly others

The chemicals used as neurotransmitters are a diverse lot. The most surprising is nitric oxide (chemical formula NO), a gas released by many small local neurons. (Do not confuse nitric oxide, NO, with nitrous oxide, N_2O, sometimes known as "laughing gas.") Nitric oxide is poisonous in large quantities and difficult to make by laboratory methods. Yet many neurons contain an enzyme that enables them to make this gas with relatively little energy. Nitric oxide probably serves many functions in the brain. One special function is that the nitric oxide released by active neurons dilates the blood vessels to increase blood flow to the most active areas of the brain (Dawson, Gonzalez-Zulueta, Kusel, & Dawson, 1998). One brain scan technique, known as regional cerebral blood flow, measures relative amounts of blood flow to various brain areas. Nitric oxide is an important part of the explanation for why more blood flows to the active areas.

Synthesis of Transmitters

Every cell in the body uses chemical reactions to build some of the materials it needs, converting substances provided by the diet into other chemicals necessary for normal functioning. The neuron is no exception, synthesizing its neurotransmitters from precursor molecules derived from foods.

Figure 3.9 illustrates the chemical steps in the synthesis of acetylcholine, serotonin, dopamine, epinephrine, and norepinephrine. Note the relationship among epinephrine, norepinephrine, and dopamine—three closely related compounds known as **catecholamines** because they contain a catechol group and an amine group, as shown here:

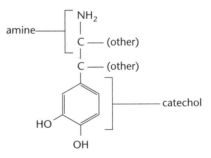

Each pathway in Figure 3.9 begins with substances found in the diet. Acetylcholine, for example, is synthesized from choline, which is abundant in cauliflower and milk. The body can also make choline from lecithin, a component of egg yolks, liver, soybeans, butter, peanuts, and several other foods. The amino acids phenylalanine and tyrosine are precursors of dopamine, norepinephrine, and epinephrine.

The amino acid *tryptophan* is the precursor of serotonin, and a special transport system enables it to cross the blood-brain barrier. The amount of tryptophan in

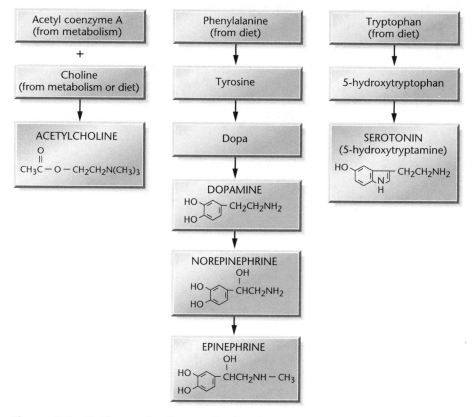

Figure 3.9 Pathways in the synthesis of acetylcholine, dopamine, norepinephrine, epinephrine, and serotonin
Arrows represent chemical reactions.

the diet controls the amount of serotonin in the brain (Fadda, 2000), so serotonin levels are higher after someone eats foods rich in tryptophan, such as soy, than after something low in tryptophan, such as maize (American corn). However, another factor is also at work: Tryptophan shares its transport system with other large amino acids (including phenylalanine) that are abundant in most proteins. One way to increase the amount of tryptophan entering the brain is to eat carbohydrates with the protein. Carbohydrates promote release of the hormone *insulin,* which takes several of the competing amino acids out of the bloodstream and into body cells, thus decreasing the competition against tryptophan for entry into the brain (Wurtman, 1985).

1. What was Loewi's evidence that neurotransmission depends on the release of chemicals?
2. Name the three catecholamine neurotransmitters.

Check your answers on page 69.

Transport of Transmitters

Certain neurotransmitters, such as acetylcholine, are synthesized in the presynaptic terminal, close to where they are released. However, the larger neurotransmitters, including peptides, are synthesized in the cell body and transported from there down the axon to the terminal. The speed of transport varies from only 1 millimeter per day in thin axons to more than 100 mm per day in thicker ones.

Even at the highest speeds, transport from cell body to terminal may take hours or days in the longest axons. Consequently, after releasing peptides, neurons take a long time to replenish their supply. Furthermore, neurons reabsorb and recycle many of the nonpeptide transmitters, but not the peptides. For these reasons, a neuron can exhaust its supply of a peptide relatively quickly in contrast to other transmitters that can be released and re-released.

Release and Diffusion of Transmitters

The presynaptic terminal stores high concentrations of neurotransmitter molecules in vesicles, tiny nearly spherical packets (Figure 3.10). (Nitric oxide, the

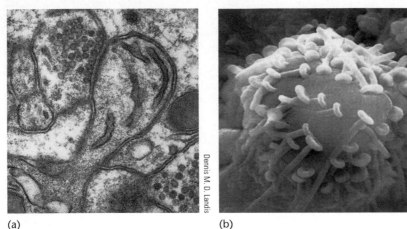

(a)   (b)

Figure 3.10 Anatomy of a synapse
(**a**) An electron micrograph shows a synapse from the cerebellum of a mouse. The small round structures are vesicles. *Source: Landis, 1987*
(**b**) An electron micrograph shows axon terminals onto the soma of a neuron. *Source: E. R. Lewis, Everhart, & Zeevi, 1969*

gaseous neurotransmitter mentioned earlier, is an exception to this rule. Neurons do not store nitric oxide for future use; they release it as soon as they synthesize it.) In addition to the neurotransmitter stored in vesicles, the presynaptic terminal also maintains substantial amounts outside the vesicles.

When an action potential reaches the end of an axon, the depolarization changes the voltage across the membrane and opens voltage-dependent calcium gates in the presynaptic terminal. As calcium flows through specialized channels into the presynaptic terminal, it causes the neuron to excrete neurotransmitter through its membrane and into the synaptic cleft between the presynaptic and postsynaptic neurons—a process called **exocytosis**. Exocytosis is quick, lasting a mere 1 or 2 milliseconds. The result is not the same every time; many action potentials fail to release any transmitter, and even those that succeed do not all release the same amount. The results vary substantially from one synapse to another (A. M. Craig & Boudin, 2001).

After the presynaptic cell releases the neurotransmitter, the chemical diffuses across the synaptic cleft to the postsynaptic membrane, where it attaches to a receptor. The cleft is only 0.02 to 0.05 microns wide, and the neurotransmitter takes no more than 10 microseconds to diffuse across the cleft. The total delay in transmission across the synapse, including the time it takes for the presynaptic cell to release the neurotransmitter, is 2 milliseconds or less (A. R. Martin, 1977; Takeuchi, 1977).

The brain as a whole uses many neurotransmitters—some now estimate close to 100—but no single neuron releases them all. For many years, investigators believed that each neuron released only one neurotransmitter, but now it appears that many, perhaps most, neurons release two, three, or even more transmitters (Hökfelt, Johansson, & Goldstein, 1984). However, each neuron, so far as we know, releases the same combination of transmitters from all branches of its axon. For example, if one branch of the axon releases glutamate and a peptide, then the other branches do also (Eccles, 1986).

Why does a neuron release a combination of transmitters instead of just one? The best guess is that the combination makes the neuron's message more complex. For example, one transmitter might quickly initiate a process and a second transmitter might either prolong it or end it (Jonas, Bischofberger, & Sandkühler, 1998).

Although a neuron releases only a limited number of neurotransmitters, it may receive and respond to many different neurotransmitters at various synapses. For example, it might respond to acetylcholine released at one synapse, serotonin at another synapse, GABA at still another, and so on.

Activation of Receptors of the Postsynaptic Cell

In English, the term *fern* refers to a plant. In German, *fern* means "far away." In French, it means nothing at all. The meaning of any word depends on who hears it or reads it. Similarly, the meaning of a neurotransmitter depends on its receptor. For example, acetylcholine may excite one neuron, inhibit another, and have no effect at all on still another, depending on those neurons' receptors.

Each of the heavily studied neurotransmitters—we can only guess about the others—interacts with several different kinds of receptors. For example, dopamine has at least five types of receptors, and serotonin has more than a dozen. The different receptors have different functions in behavior, and therefore, a drug or a genetic mutation that affects one receptor type may have specific effects on behavior.

A neurotransmitter receptor is a protein embedded in the membrane. When the neurotransmitter attaches to the active site of the receptor, the receptor can directly open a channel—an *ionotropic* effect—or it can exert slower but longer lasting effects—a *metabotropic* effect.

Ionotropic Effects

Some neurotransmitters exert ionotropic effects on the postsynaptic neuron: The neurotransmitter attaches to a receptor on the membrane, almost immediately opening the gates for some type of ion. For example, acetylcholine exerts ionotropic effects at some of its synapses, which are known as *nicotinic* synapses because they also can be stimulated by the drug *nicotine.* When acetylcholine attaches to one of these receptors, as modeled in Figure 3.11, it slightly rotates the walls of the cylindrical channel into a position that lets sodium ions cross through the membrane (Harel et al., 2001). Ionotropic effects are rapid and short-lived, although some are more rapid than others (Scannevin & Huganir, 2000). An example value would be a start of response within 10 ms and a duration of 20 ms (North, 1989; Westbrook & Jahr, 1989). Ionotropic synapses are therefore useful for conveying information about visual and auditory stimulation, muscle movements, and other rapidly changing events. For a very detailed theory about ionotropic mechanisms, see this Web site: www.npaci.edu/features/98/Dec/index.html

The most abundant excitatory transmitter in the vertebrate brain is *glutamate,* which has ionotropic effects at most of its receptors. The most abundant inhibitory transmitter is GABA, which also acts by ionotropic means, except that it opens chloride gates, enabling chloride ions, with their negative charge, to cross the membrane into the cell more rapidly than usual. Glycine is another common inhibitory transmitter (Moss & Smart, 2001).

Metabotropic Effects and Second Messenger Systems

At certain other synapses, neurotransmitters exert **metabotropic effects** by initiating a sequence of metabolic reactions that are slower and longer lasting than ionotropic effects. Metabotropic effects emerge 30 ms or more after the release of the transmitter (North, 1989) and last seconds, minutes, or even hours.

When the neurotransmitter attaches to a metabotropic receptor, it bends the rest of the protein, enabling a portion of the protein inside the neuron to react with other molecules, as shown in Figure 3.12 (Levitzki, 1988; O'Dowd, Lefkowitz, & Caron, 1989). The portion inside the neuron activates a **G-protein,** which is coupled to guanosine triphosphate (GTP), an energy-storing molecule. The activated G-protein in turn increases the concentration of a second messenger, such as cyclic adenosine monophosphate (cyclic AMP), inside the cell. Just as the "first messenger" (the neurotransmitter) carries information to the postsynaptic cell, the **second messenger** communicates to areas within the cell. The effect of the second messenger varies; it may open or close ion channels in the membrane or alter the production of proteins or activate a portion of a chromosome. Note the contrast: An ionotropic synapse has effects localized to one point on the membrane, whereas a metabotropic synapse, by way of its second messenger, influences activity in much or all of the postsynaptic cell.

Researchers sometimes refer to some neurotransmitters, mainly the peptide neurotransmitters, as **neuromodulators,** with the implication that they do not themselves excite or inhibit the postsynaptic cell, but increase or decrease the release of other transmitters or alter the sensitivity of postsynaptic cells. However, neuromodulators act at metabotropic receptors, and in most regards, they resemble other neurotransmitters acting at metabotropic receptors. Peptide transmitters do tend to diffuse widely enough to affect several cells, and their effects are frequently long-lasting, so the term *neuromodulator* is sometimes useful to emphasize these special characteristics.

Hormones

We call a chemical a neurotransmitter or neuromodulator when it is released in small quantities close to its target cells; we call it a hormone when it is released in larger quantities that flow through the blood to targets throughout the body. A neurotransmitter is like a signal on a telephone line: It conveys a message directly and exclusively from the sender to the receiver.

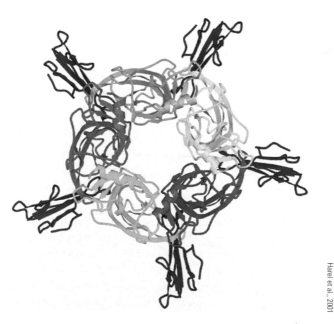

Figure 3.11 Model of the acetylcholine binding protein as seen from above
The protein is composed of five similar but not identical units bound together, surrounding a channel. The receptor molecule, embedded in a neuron's membrane, probably has a similar structure. When the receptor is at rest, the channel is too narrow to let sodium pass through it. When acetylcholine binds to the receptor, it bends the receptor enough to widen the channel and let sodium ions pass. *Source: From M. Harel, R. Kasher, A. Nicolas, J. M. Guss, M. Balass, M. Fredkin, A. B. Smit, K. Brejc, T. K. Sixma, E. Katchalski–Katzir, J. L. Sussman, & S. Fuchs (2001). Neuron, 32, 265–275. Reprinted with permission.*

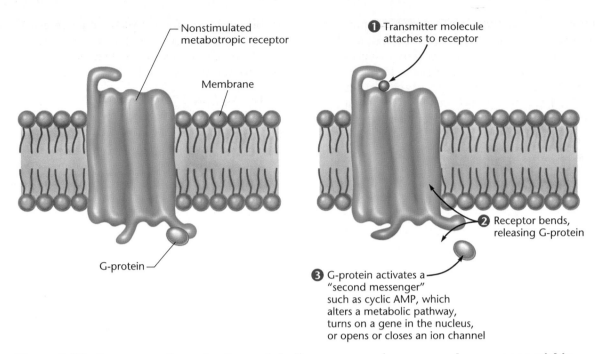

Figure 3.12 Sequence of events at a metabolic synapse, using a second messenger within the postsynaptic neuron

Hormones function more like a radio station: They convey a message to any receiver that happens to be tuned in to their frequency. Many hormones exert effects by the same mechanism as metabotropic neurotransmitters: They attach to receptors on the cell membrane, where they activate an enzyme that produces cyclic AMP or some other second messenger. In fact, many chemicals—including epinephrine, norepinephrine, insulin, and oxytocin—serve as both neurotransmitters and hormones. Chapter 11 discusses hormonal mechanisms in more detail.

Stop & Check

---

3. When the action potential reaches the presynaptic terminal, which ion must enter the presynaptic terminal to evoke release of the neurotransmitter?

4. How do ionotropic and metabotropic synapses differ in speed and duration of effects?

5. Which type of synapse relies on second messengers?

Check your answers on page 69.

Inactivation and Reuptake of Neurotransmitters

A neurotransmitter does not normally linger at the postsynaptic membrane. If it did, it might excite or inhibit the postsynaptic neuron indefinitely. Various neurotransmitters are inactivated in different ways.

After acetylcholine activates a receptor, it is broken down by the enzyme **acetylcholinesterase** (a-SEE-til-ko-lih-NES-teh-raze) into two fragments: acetate and choline. The choline diffuses back to the presynaptic neuron, which takes it up and reconnects it with acetate already in the cell to form acetylcholine again. This recycling process is highly efficient but not perfect and not instantaneous. At any synapse, not just one using acetylcholine, a sufficiently rapid series of action potentials can release the neurotransmitter faster than the presynaptic cell resynthesizes it, thus bringing transmission to a halt (Liu & Tsien, 1995).

If the enzyme acetylcholinesterase is not present in adequate amounts, acetylcholine may remain at the synapse for an abnormally long time and continue to excite it. Drugs that block acetylcholinesterase can be useful for certain purposes. For example, impaired transmission at the acetylcholine synapses of motor neurons onto muscles can lead to myasthenia gravis, a condition characterized by rapid fatigue. One way to alleviate the symptoms is to give drugs that inhibit acetylcholinesterase, thereby prolonging the activity of acetylcholine.

Serotonin and the catecholamines (dopamine, norepinephrine, and epinephrine) are not broken down into inactive fragments at the postsynaptic membrane but simply detach from the receptor. The presynaptic neuron takes up most of these neurotransmitter molecules intact and reuses them. This process, called **reuptake,** occurs through special membrane proteins called **transporters.** Many of the familiar antidepressant drugs, such as fluoxetine (Prozac), act by blocking reuptake and thereby prolonging the effects of the neurotransmitter on its receptor. (We consider antidepressants in more detail in Chapter 15.)

Some of the serotonin and catecholamine molecules, either before or after reuptake, are converted into inactive chemicals that cannot stimulate the receptor. The enzymes that convert catecholamine transmitters into inactive chemicals are **COMT** (catechol-o-methyltransferase) and **MAO** (monoamine oxidase), which affects serotonin as well as catecholamines. We return to MAO in the discussion of antidepressant drugs.

6. What happens to acetylcholine molecules after they stimulate a postsynaptic receptor?

7. What happens to serotonin and catecholamine molecules after they stimulate a postsynaptic receptor?

Check your answers on page 69.

SYNAPSES AND DRUG EFFECTS

What do all these details about synapses have to do with behavior? The rest of this book will provide many examples. Different neurotransmitter receptors mediate different aspects of behavior, so an alteration of function at a particular type of receptor can influence behavior, sometimes in profound ways. In later chapters, we shall consider the evidence linking specific synaptic changes to learning and memory, anxiety, depression, schizophrenia, and so forth.

Furthermore, nearly all drugs with important behavioral effects act on synapses. For example, nicotine, caffeine, opiates, cocaine, and tetrahydrocannabinol all attach to specific brain receptors. When we stop to think about it, that fact should be puzzling: All the chemicals I just mentioned derive from plants (tobacco, coffee beans, poppies, coca, and marijuana). Why are

our brains so sensitive to plant chemicals? The answer is more apparent if we put it the other way: Why do plants produce chemicals that affect our brains?

Part of the answer relates to a surprising fact about animal nervous systems: The chemicals humans use as neurotransmitters are the same as those used by all other animal species (Cravchik & Goldman, 2000). A few exceptions occur to this generalization: Frogs use one or two neurotransmitters that humans don't use, and humans have one or two that insects don't, and so forth. But the exceptions are few. Acetylcholine, serotonin, dopamine, glutamate, and so on—we find them throughout the animal kingdom. So if a plant evolves some chemical to attract wasps to its flowers or to deter caterpillars from eating its leaves, that chemical is likely to affect humans also.

The other part of the answer is that plants themselves use many of the same chemicals that we use as neurotransmitters. Would you have guessed that plants have ionotropic glutamate receptors very similar to our own? They do (Lam et al., 1998). Exactly what these receptors do in plants is uncertain, but presumably, different parts of a plant communicate with one another, even though the plant has no nervous system. Evidently, a small number of chemicals have proved to be so well suited to conveying information that evolution has had no reason to change them.

How Drugs Affect Synapses

As mentioned earlier, nearly all drugs with behavioral effects act at synapses. A drug that blocks the effects of a neurotransmitter is called an **antagonist;** a drug that mimics or increases the effects is called an **agonist.** (The term *agonist* is from a Greek word meaning "contestant." We derive our term *agony* from the same root. An *antagonist* is an "antiagonist," or member of the opposing team.) A drug that is a *mixed agonist-antagonist* is an agonist for some behavioral effects of the neurotransmitter and an antagonist for others or is an agonist at some doses and an antagonist at others.

Drugs influence synaptic activity in many ways. As in Figure 3.13, which illustrates a dopamine synapse, a drug can increase or decrease the synthesis of the neurotransmitter, cause it to leak from its vesicles, increase its release, decrease its reuptake, block its breakdown into inactive chemicals, or directly stimulate or block the postsynaptic receptors.

Investigators say that a drug has an **affinity** for a particular type of receptor if it binds to that receptor, fitting somewhat like a lock and key. Drugs vary in their affinities from strong to weak. The **efficacy** of a drug is its tendency to activate the receptor. So, for example, a drug that binds tightly to a receptor but fails to stimulate it has a high affinity but a low efficacy.

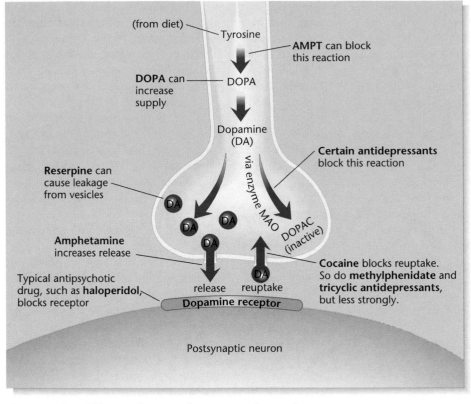

Figure 3.13 Effects of some drugs at a dopamine synapse
Drugs can alter any stage of synaptic processing, from synthesis of the neurotransmitter through release and reuptake.

Such a drug is therefore an antagonist because, by occupying the receptor, it prevents the normal effects of the transmitter.

If you or people you know have ever taken tranquilizers, antidepressants, or other drugs, you may have noticed that the effectiveness and side effects vary from one person to another. Why? One reason is that each drug affects several kinds of synapse. For each neurotransmitter, the brain has several kinds of receptors, each with its own behavioral functions. People vary in their abundance of each kind of receptor. For example, one person might have a relatively large number of dopamine type D_4 receptors and relatively few D_1 or D_2 receptors, whereas someone else has more D_1, fewer D_4, and an average number of D_2 receptors. It is also possible to have a mutant, less sensitive form of a particular receptor. Therefore, a drug with an affinity for some kind of receptor can have noticeably different effects on different people (Cravchik & Goldman, 2000).

Synapses and Personality

People vary in their abundance of various neurotransmitter receptors, and synapses are critical for just about all aspects of behavior. So, could we relate people's personalities to detectable differences in their receptors?

In 1990, researchers studied variations in dopamine receptors and found that people with the less common form of the D_2 receptor (one of five types of dopamine receptors) were more likely than others to develop severe alcoholism. Later research suggested that this gene is not specific to alcoholism but instead increases the probability of a variety of pleasure-seeking behaviors, including alcohol consumption, other recreational drug use, overeating, and habitual gambling (Blum, Cull, Braverman, & Comings, 1996). One hypothesis is that the alternative form of the D_2 receptor is not very sensitive, so everyday experiences are not very reinforcing, and people seek other ways to stimulate their D_2 receptors. However, the link between the alternative D_2 receptor and risky behaviors is statistically weak (Figure 3.14) (Goldman, Urbanek, Guenther, Robin, & Long, 1998; Noble et al., 1998).

Similarly, researchers studying variations in the D_4 receptor found that people with an alternative form of the receptor tend to have a "novelty-seeking" personality as measured by a standardized personality test (Benjamin et al., 1996; Ebstein et al., 1996; Noble et al., 1998). Novelty seeking consists of being impulsive, exploratory, and quick-tempered. Other studies have found that the alternative D_4 receptor is linked to an increased probability of schizophrenia (B. M. Cohen et al., 1999) and delusions (Serretti et al., 1998). However, several other studies have found either no link between D_4 receptor types and personality or only a weak link (Ronai et al., 2001).

How should we interpret these small and inconsistent results? They suggest that variations in a single gene are but one contributor among many to personality. Imagine by analogy 1000 chefs cooking a stew; some use 3 tablespoonfuls of oregano and others use only 1. If they did everything else exactly the same, a gourmet might be able to detect which stews had more oregano and which had less. But if they vary the other ingredients and procedures also, the effect of the oregano may be hard to notice. Something similar may be true for variations in neurotransmitter receptors: Our personal-

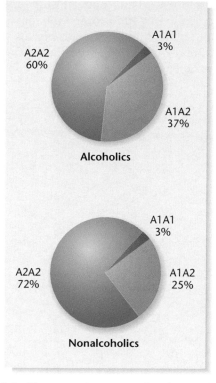

Figure 3.14 These graphs summarize the combined result of 15 studies in which more than 1000 alcoholic and almost as many nonalcoholic adults were tested. A higher percentage of the alcoholics had at least one A1 gene for the D_2 dopamine receptor. The contribution of this gene toward alcoholic predisposition is obviously small.

ities depend on variations in many genes and experiences, as well as health and nutrition. Variations that result from a single gene may be hard to detect.

MODULE 3.2

In Closing: Neurotransmitters and Behavior

The brain uses a great many chemicals as neurotransmitters, and each of the widely investigated neurotransmitters has more than one type of receptor. For example, acetylcholine has at least four types of nicotinic receptors and five types of muscarinic receptors (McCormick, 1989). Dopamine has five types of receptors (Schmauss, 2000), serotonin at least fifteen (Roth, Lopez, & Kroeze, 2000), and glutamate at least sixteen (Westbrook, 1994).

Why are there so many neurotransmitters and so many types of receptors? It is probably for the same reason that our alphabet has more than just three or four letters. The nervous system needs a large number of elements that can be combined in different ways to produce complex behavior. Different transmitters and

different receptors play different roles in brain functioning and behavior. Indeed, one major reason people differ from one another in what we call "personality" may be that their neurotransmitter receptors differ.

SUMMARY

1. Most synapses operate by transmitting a neurotransmitter from the presynaptic cell to the postsynaptic cell. (p. 60)

2. Many chemicals are used as neurotransmitters. As far as we know, each neuron releases the same combination of neurotransmitters from all branches of its axon. (p. 62)

3. At certain synapses, a neurotransmitter exerts its effects by attaching to a receptor that opens the gates to allow a particular ion, such as sodium, to cross the membrane more readily. At other synapses, a neurotransmitter may lead to slower but longer lasting changes inside the postsynaptic cell. (p. 64)

4. After a neurotransmitter has activated its receptor, some of the transmitter molecules reenter the presynaptic cell through transporter molecules in the membrane. This process, known as reuptake, enables the presynaptic cell to recycle its neurotransmitter. (p. 66)

ANSWERS TO STOP AND CHECK QUESTIONS

1. When Loewi stimulated a nerve that increased or decreased a frog's heart rate, he could withdraw some fluid from the area around the heart, transfer it to another frog's heart, and thereby increase or decrease its rate also. (p. 63)

2. Epinephrine, norepinephrine, and dopamine (p. 63)

3. Calcium (p. 66)

4. Ionotropic synapses act more quickly and more briefly. (p. 66)

5. Metabotropic synapses rely on the actions of a second messenger. (p. 66)

6. The enzyme acetylcholinesterase breaks acetylcholine molecules into two smaller molecules, acetate and choline, which are then reabsorbed by the presynaptic terminal. (p. 67)

7. Most serotonin and catecholamine molecules are reabsorbed by the presynaptic terminal. Some of their molecules are broken down into inactive chemicals which then float away in the blood. (p. 67)

THOUGHT QUESTIONS

1. Suppose that axon A enters a ganglion (a cluster of neurons) and axon B leaves on the other side. An experimenter who stimulates A can shortly thereafter record an impulse traveling down B. We want to know whether B is just an extension of axon A or whether A formed an excitatory synapse on some neuron in the ganglion, whose axon is axon B. How could an experimenter determine the answer? You should be able to think of more than one good method. Presume that the anatomy within the ganglion is so complex that you cannot simply trace the course of an axon through it.

2. Transmission of visual and auditory information relies largely on ionotropic synapses. Why is ionotropic better than metabotropic for these purposes? For what purposes might metabotropic synapses be better?

CHAPTER ENDING
Key Terms and Activities

TERMS

acetylcholine (p. 62)

acetylcholinesterase (p. 66)

affinity (p. 67)

agonist (p. 67)

amino acids (p. 62)

antagonist (p. 67)

catecholamine (p. 62)

COMT (p. 67)

efficacy (p. 67)

excitatory postsynaptic potential (EPSP) (p. 55)

exocytosis (p. 64)

G-protein (p. 65)

inhibitory postsynaptic potential (IPSP) (p. 57)

ionotropic effect (p. 64)

MAO (p. 67)

metabotropic effect (p. 65)

monoamines (p. 62)

neuromodulator (p. 65)

neurotransmitter (p. 62)

nitric oxide (p. 62)

peptide (p. 62)

postsynaptic neuron (p. 55)

presynaptic neuron (p. 55)

purines (p. 62)

reflex (p. 54)

reflex arc (p. 54)

reuptake (p. 67)

second messenger (p. 65)

spatial summation (p. 56)

spontaneous firing rate (p. 58)

synapse (p. 54)

temporal summation (p. 55)

transporter (p. 67)

vesicle (p. 63)

SUGGESTION FOR FURTHER READING

Cowan, W. M., Südhof, T. C., & Stevens, C. F. (2001). *Synapses.* Baltimore: Johns Hopkins University Press. I don't recommend that you try to read this one straight through, but if you are curious about some detailed aspect of synapses, this is the best place to look for an answer.

WEB SITES TO EXPLORE

You can go to the Biological Psychology Study Center and click these links. While there, you can also check for suggested articles available on InfoTrac College Edition. The Biological Psychology Internet address is:

**http://psychology.wadsworth.com/
kalatbiopsych8e**

Synapse-The Movie
**http://www.neurosci.tufts.edu/~rhammer/
synapse1.html**

Simulation of Ionic Current Generation
http://www.npaci.edu/features/98/Dec/index.html

CD-ROM: EXPLORING BIOLOGICAL PSYCHOLOGY

Postsynaptic Potentials (animation)

Release of Neurotransmitter (animation)

Cholinergic (animation)

Release of ACh (animation)

AChE Inactivates ACh (animation)

AChE Inhibitors (animation)

Critical Thinking (essay questions)

Chapter Quiz (multiplie choice questions)

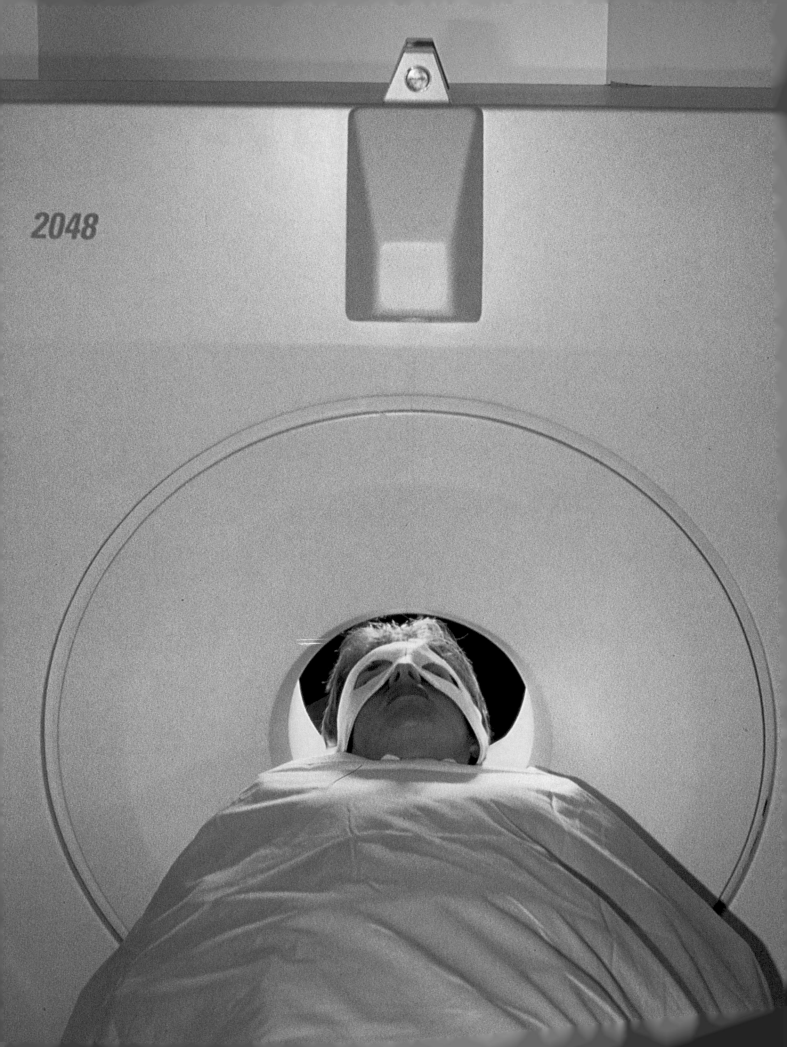

Anatomy of the Nervous System

4

Chapter Outline

Opposite:
This woman is undergoing a PET scan, one of several methods of examining brain structure and activity.
Source: ©Hank Morgan/Rainbow.

Main Ideas

1. It is difficult to conduct research on the functions of the nervous system. Conclusions must come from multiple methods and careful behavioral measurements.

2. Each part of the nervous system has specialized functions, and the parts work together to produce behavior. Damage to different areas results in different types of behavioral deficits.

3. The cerebral cortex, the largest structure in the mammalian brain, elaborately processes sensory information and provides for fine control of movement.

4. As research has identified the different functions of different brain areas, a difficult question has arisen: How do the areas work together to produce unified experience and behavior?

Trying to learn **neuroanatomy** (the anatomy of the nervous system) from a book is like trying to learn geography from a road map. A map can tell you that Mystic, Georgia, is about 40 km north of Enigma, Georgia, and that the two cities are connected by a combination of roads, including U.S. Route 129. Similarly, a book can tell you that the habenula is about 4.6 mm from the interpeduncular nucleus in a rat's brain (slightly farther in a human brain) and that the two structures are connected by a set of axons known as the habenulopeduncular tract (also sometimes known as the fasciculus retroflexus). But these two little gems of information will seem both mysterious and enigmatic unless you are concerned with that part of Georgia or that area of the brain.

This chapter does not provide a detailed road map of the nervous system. It is more like a world globe, describing the large, basic structures (analogous to the continents) and some distinctive features of each.

In the first (very short) module, we examine methods of research. The second introduces key neuroanatomical terms and outlines overall structures of the nervous system. In the third module, we concentrate on the structures and functions of the cerebral cortex, the largest part of the mammalian central nervous system. Be prepared: This chapter, especially the second module, contains a huge number of new terms. You should not expect to memorize all of them at once, and it will pay to review this chapter repeatedly.

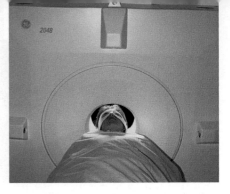

MODULE 4.1

Research Methods

Imagine yourself trying to figure out how some large, complex machine works. You could begin by describing the appearance and location of all the main pieces. That task alone could be quite a chore. However, describing the structure is the easy part compared to what comes next: discovering what each part *does*. If you have never seen a similar machine, your task could be formidable.

Similarly, describing the structure of the brain is a fairly straightforward task in principle, but understanding how it works is quite difficult. Researchers examine the brain's structure with light microscopes and electron microscopes, applying a variety of chemicals that stain or otherwise highlight particular kinds of cells or even parts of cells. Sometimes they pass x-rays through the head to form computerized axial tomography, better known as a CT or CAT scan (Andreasen, 1988). To increase the contrast enough to get a good image, a physician injects a dye into the blood and then places the person's head into a CT scanner like the one shown in Figure 4.1a. X-rays are passed through the head and recorded by detectors on the opposite side. The CT scanner is rotated slowly until a measurement has been taken at each angle of 180°. From the 180 measurements, a computer can reconstruct images of the brain. Figure 4.1b is a CT scan of a normal brain.

How does the amazingly complex brain work? In this module, we consider only the logic of research methods in general. At later points, we examine particular methods in more detail as they become applicable.

The common methods of studying brain function can be grouped into these categories:

1. *Examine the effects of brain damage.* After loss of some brain area, or temporary inactivation, what aspects of behavior are impaired?
2. *Examine the effects of stimulating some part of the brain.* Ideally, a behavior that is impaired by damage to some brain area should be enhanced when the area is stimulated.

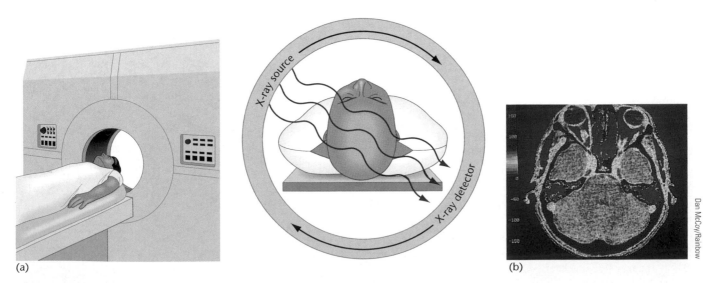

(a) (b)

Figure 4.1 Computerized axial tomography (CT scanning)
(a) A person's head is placed into the device and then a rapidly rotating source sends x-rays through the head while detectors on the opposite side make photographs. A computer then constructs an image of the brain. **(b)** A CT scan of a normal human brain.

3. *During some kind of behavior, record what happens in the brain.* For example, we might record changes in brain activity during fighting, sleeping, finding food, or solving a problem.
4. *Correlate brain anatomy with behavior.* For example, if some people behave differently from others, do their brains differ also? If so, how?

We shall consider the uses and limitations of each of these approaches.

EFFECTS OF BRAIN DAMAGE

In 1861, the French neurologist Paul Broca discovered that when people suddenly lost the ability to speak, usually as a result of a stroke, nearly all of them had damage in part of the frontal part of the left hemisphere of the brain—an area that came to be known as *Broca's area*. This was the first discovery ever about the function of any part of the brain, and with it, Broca pioneered modern neurology. To read biographies of Broca and other pioneering neurologists, check this Web site: www.uic.edu/depts/mcne/founders/

Since then, other researchers have made countless reports of behavioral impairments after brain damage. In humans, the damage can be the result of stroke, disease, genetic impairments, exposure to toxins, nutritional deficiencies, and so forth. The strategy is to describe the behavioral impairment and then examine the brain's anatomy, either under a microscope after the person dies or through brain scan techniques while the person is alive.

From a research standpoint, the lack of control is a problem. If you wanted to study the function of, say, Broca's area, you could find people with damage there, but nearly all would have damage to other areas, too, and probably no two people would have exactly the same damage.

One recently developed method enables researchers to inactivate part of a human brain painlessly, temporarily, and therefore ethically. They apply an intense magnetic field over the scalp, thereby temporarily interrupting activity in the brain area just below it (Walsh & Cowey, 2000). This procedure enables researchers to study a given individual's behavior with the brain area active, then inactive, and then active again.

Research on laboratory animals relies on various kinds of intentional damage, often through an electrode implanted in the head (Methods 5.3, p. 130) or chemicals injected into the brain. Certain chemicals temporarily inactivate one part of the brain or one type of synapse. In the **gene-knockout approach**, researchers use biochemical methods to direct a mutation to a particular gene that is important for certain types of cells, transmitters, or receptors (Joyner & Guillemot, 1994).

With all these approaches, the main problem is to specify exactly how the behavior has changed after the damage. By analogy, suppose you were trying to figure out how a television works, so you cut a wire and discover that the set no longer produces a picture. You would know that this wire was in some way necessary for making a picture, but you could hardly conclude that the wire *makes* the picture. Similarly, if you damage some brain area and find that the animal no longer eats, you cannot conclude that this area produces hunger. All you know so far is that it contributes in some way.

Consider another example. Suppose that after brain damage a rat can no longer learn to go toward a high-frequency sound to get food. Does it have an impairment of hearing, muscle control, hunger, or learning and memory? If the latter, which aspect of learning and memory—storage, consolidation, retrieval, resistance to distraction, or what? Sometimes the effects of damage depend on the exact stimuli used, the frequency of training trials, the time of day of testing, or even how gently the experimenter picks up the rat to carry it to the testing apparatus. Before we can draw any conclusion, we need to test the animal under a wide variety of conditions.

EFFECTS OF BRAIN STIMULATION

If brain damage impairs some behavior, stimulation should increase it. With laboratory animals, researchers can apply brief electrical stimulation to an area. Researchers do not insert electrodes into human brains except during surgery, and even then, it is an unusual procedure. However, it is possible to stimulate an area by applying a magnetic field to the scalp area above it (Fitzgerald, Brown, & Daskalakis, 2002). It was noted earlier that intense magnetic fields applied to the scalp can inactivate the underlying brain area; the difference is that inactivation results from repeated, prolonged, or intense magnetic fields, whereas stimulation results from a briefer, less intense magnetic field. Figure 4.2 shows the apparatus for this procedure.

Another way to stimulate brain activity is to inject a chemical that stimulates a particular kind of receptor. This method, of course, stimulates those receptors wherever they are in the brain, as opposed to electrical or magnetic stimulation, which would activate just one structure.

Stimulating certain areas of the human brain evokes reports of sensations, such as a sound or a flash of light. These reports confirm that a certain area is part of the sensory system. Stimulating other areas can evoke movements. One limitation of any stimulation study is that complex behaviors and experiences depend on the coordinated contributions of many brain areas, not just one, so artificial stimulation produces artificial responses. For example, electrically or magnetically stimulating the primary visual areas of the brain produces reports of sparkling flashing points of light, not the sight of a face or anything else recognizable. Briefly stimulating the motor areas of the brain produces undirected and purposeless movements. In short, it is easier to discover that a brain area is responsible for vision (or movement or whatever) than to discover how it produces a meaningful pattern.

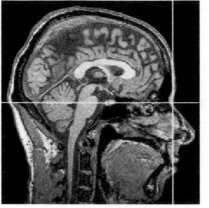
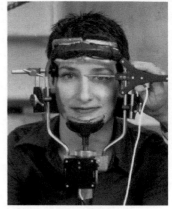

Positioning of the Coil

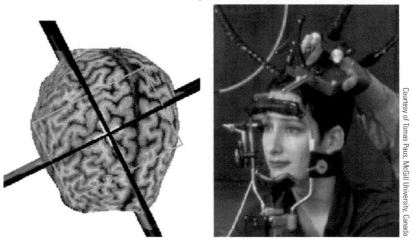

Courtesy of Tomas Paus, McGill University, Canada

Figure 4.2 Apparatus for magnetic stimulation of a human brain.
The procedure is known as transcranial magnetic stimulation, or TMS.

Stop & Check

1. Why does a physician inject someone with a dye before exposing the head to x-rays to make a CT scan?

2. How do the effects of mild, brief magnetic stimulation differ from those of longer, more intense stimulation?

3. Why does electrical or magnetic stimulation of the brain seldom produce complex, meaningful sensations or movements?

Check your answers on page 79.

RECORDING BRAIN ACTIVITY

When you look at a sunset, feel frightened, or solve a mathematical problem, which parts of your brain change their activity and how? With laboratory animals, researchers can record brain activity with electrodes or withdraw chemicals from the brain. Research with humans relies on noninvasive methods—that is, methods that don't require inserting anything into the brain.

One such method is *positron emission tomography,* better known as a *PET scan,* in which the investigator injects a radioactive chemical, such as radioactively labeled glucose, which is absorbed mainly by the brain's

most active cells (Methods 8.1, p. 247). Radioactivity detectors around the head produce a map of which brain areas were the most active. PET scans can also measure the binding of a drug to different brain areas.

In a variant of PET, the **regional cerebral blood flow (rCBF)** method, an investigator injects a chemically inert radioactive chemical that dissolves in the blood and then uses a PET scanner to measure its distribution in the brain. One such substance is the gas xenon (^{133}Xe). After someone inhales xenon, it enters the bloodstream and goes wherever the blood goes. Thus, the radioactivity recorded from a particular part of the brain is proportional to the blood flow in that area, which increases with the brain area's activity.

Unfortunately, PET and rCBF are expensive and require exposing the brain to potentially dangerous radioactivity. Therefore, they are not really noninvasive. For many purposes, they have been replaced by functional magnetic resonance imaging (fMRI), which detects changes in the blood's hemoglobin molecules as they release oxygen, mainly in the brain's most active areas (Methods 6.2, p. 170). An fMRI scan provides fair detail, with spatial resolution of about 1 mm, and it is cheaper and safer than PET. For more information about brain scan techniques and some striking examples of the resulting pictures of the brain, check this Web site: www.musc.edu/psychiatry/fnrd/primer_index.htm

The tricky task in using these methods is to interpret what the images mean. For example, if someone recorded your brain activity while you were reading, a raw measure of brain activity means nothing until we compare it to something else. That is, we want to know which brain areas are *more* active during reading than they would be otherwise. So researchers would record your brain activity at least twice—once while you were reading, and once while you were, well, not reading, but doing what? There is no such thing as doing nothing, at least not for an awake human brain. The choice of comparison task is critical. For example, researchers might compare your activity while reading to the activity while you looked at a page written in some language you do not understand.

After the researchers get the results, they would no doubt find that many areas were more active during reading than during the comparison task. Those areas might have to do with language, memory, visual attention, or something else, so further research would need to identify which areas do what. Furthermore, other brain areas might become *less* active, perhaps because while you are reading you can devote less than usual attention to something else you might have been doing (Gusnard & Raichle, 2001). Interpreting the pattern of increased and decreased activity can be quite a challenge.

One conclusion that sometimes emerges from brain scan studies is that different people can use different brain areas for the same task, depending on their previous experience with it. For example, certain brain areas become highly active when most people do a complex mental calculation or choose the right move in a chess game, but the same areas show little activity in expert calculators or chess players. The experts just look at the question, recognize it, and *remember* the correct answer (Amidzic, Riehle, Fehr, Wienbruch, & Elbert, 2001; Pesenti et al., 2001).

CORRELATING BRAIN ANATOMY WITH BEHAVIOR

Brain anatomy differs from one person to another. The overall shape and organization stay the same, but the size of one structure or another can vary (P.M. Thompson et al., 2001). Do smarter people have bigger brains? Are the motor areas of the brain especially well developed in great athletes? Does any visible brain structure relate to other special talents?

In the 1800s, Franz Joseph Gall observed some people with excellent verbal memories who had protruding eyes. He inferred that verbal memory depended on a part of the brain right behind the eyes that had grown large enough to push the eyes forward. Gall then examined the skulls of people with other talents or personality types, looking for any unusual bulges or depressions. His process of relating skull anatomy to behavioral capacities is known as **phrenology**. Figure 4.3 is a typical phrenological map of the human skull.

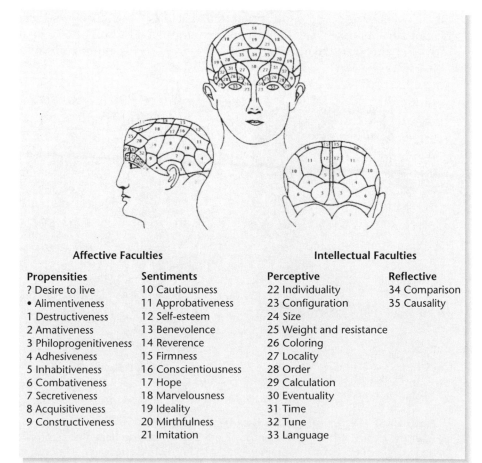

Affective Faculties		Intellectual Faculties	
Propensities	**Sentiments**	**Perceptive**	**Reflective**
? Desire to live	10 Cautiousness	22 Individuality	34 Comparison
• Alimentiveness	11 Approbativeness	23 Configuration	35 Causality
1 Destructiveness	12 Self-esteem	24 Size	
2 Amativeness	13 Benevolence	25 Weight and resistance	
3 Philoprogenitiveness	14 Reverence	26 Coloring	
4 Adhesiveness	15 Firmness	27 Locality	
5 Inhabitiveness	16 Conscientiousness	28 Order	
6 Combativeness	17 Hope	29 Calculation	
7 Secretiveness	18 Marvelousness	30 Eventuality	
8 Acquisitiveness	19 Ideality	31 Time	
9 Constructiveness	20 Mirthfulness	32 Tune	
	21 Imitation	33 Language	

Figure 4.3 A phrenologist's map of the brain
Neuroscientists today also try to localize functions in the brain, but they use more careful methods and they study such functions as vision and hearing, not "secretiveness" and "marvelousness." *Source: Spurzheim, 1908*

The central problem with phrenologists was their uncritical examination of data. Even one person with an unusual personality and a bump on the head was enough to convince them that they had located some function.

Researchers today don't try to relate behavior to the skull. Because of variations in bone thickness, the exterior shape of the skull tells us little about the brain beneath it. Researchers do, however, relate behavior to measurable features of the brain. Here are four examples. The first three will be discussed in more detail in later chapters.

People who have extensively practiced playing stringed instruments have a larger than usual proportion of their brain devoted to sensations from the fingers of the left hand, the one that fingers the strings (Elbert, Pantev, Wienbruch, Rockstroh, & Taub, 1995).

Part of the hippocampus, a brain area important for spatial memories, is larger than normal in highly experienced taxi drivers, who of course rely heavily on their spatial memories (Maguire, Frackowiak, & Frith, 1997).

One part of the hypothalamus, a brain area related to sexual behavior is larger on the average in men than women, and two studies reported that it is larger in heterosexual than homosexual men (Byne et al., 2001; LeVay, 1991).

After the great scientist Albert Einstein died, neuroscientists examined his brain in search of any clues to his genius. They found that one area was larger than normal and had an unusually high ratio of glia to neurons, as shown in Figure 4.4 (M. C. Diamond, Scheibel, Murphy, & Harvey, 1985; Witelson, Kigar, & Harvey, 1999). Of course, we cannot draw conclusions from just one case; a study of this type merely suggests hypotheses for further testing.

One limitation of this approach is something you have probably heard many times in other psychology courses: Correlation does not indicate causation. For example, the finding that homosexual and heterosexual men differ in the structure of one part of the brain could mean that this brain difference led to a difference in behavior, or it could mean that a difference in behavior led to a difference in brain anatomy. We need other kinds of evidence to decide between these possibilities.

Another limitation is that many studies using this approach deal with small samples of people. To a large extent, that limitation is inevitable: If you want to know what kind of brain specialization is associated with extreme levels of genius, well, how many Albert Einsteins are there? Again, the response to this limitation is to compare the conclusions to the results of different kinds of research.

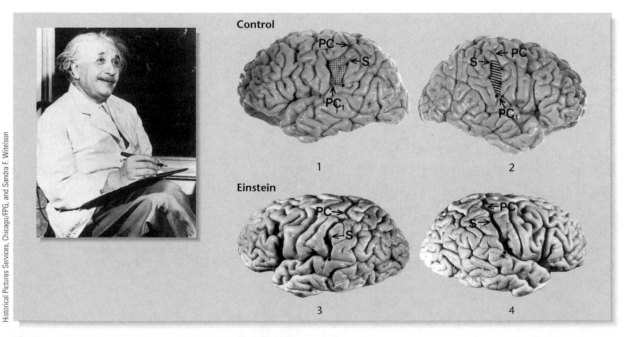

Figure 4.4 What makes a great brain great?
After the death of the great scientist Albert Einstein, researchers dissected his brain in search of clues to his genius. Although Einstein's brain was normal in total size, researchers noted some unusual aspects in its structure. Parts 1 and 2 show the left and right hemispheres of an average brain; the stippled (*left*) and hatched (*right*) sections are an area called the parietal operculum. Parts 3 and 4 show Einstein's brain; the parietal operculum is absent because the inferior parietal lobe has expanded beyond its usual boundaries, occupying the area where one ordinarily finds the parietal operculum.

4. What is meant by "invasive" and "noninvasive" procedures? What is a good example of a non-invasive procedure to study brain functioning?

5. Researchers today sometimes relate differences in people's behavior to differences in their brain anatomy. How does their approach differ from that of the phrenologists?

Check your answers on this page.

MODULE 4.1

In Closing: Methods and Their Limits

Occasionally, one well-designed research study demonstrates clearly that a scientific theory is wrong. Demonstrating that a theory is correct is much more difficult. Indeed, some philosophers of science insist that we can only be sure of which theories are wrong and never be sure of which one is right.

Every research method has some limitation or difficulty of interpretation. At a minimum, every study deals with a limited population of individuals under a certain set of circumstances. If we want to draw widespread conclusions, we need to compare results for different populations under as many circumstances as possible. A conclusion drawn from one study, or even many studies using the same method, is suspect. The more types of evidence point to the same conclusion, the greater our confidence in it.

SUMMARY

1. One way to study brain-behavior relationships is to examine the effects of brain damage. If someone loses a particular ability after brain damage, then the injured area is in some way necessary for the behavior. Of course, we need additional research to discover exactly how it contributes. (p. 75)

2. If stimulation of a brain area increases some behavior, that area presumably contributes to the behavior. Theoretically, we expect that the effects of brain stimulation should be the opposite of those from brain damage. (p. 75)

3. Another method is to record activity in some brain area to see whether it increases, decreases, or remains the same during a given behavior. This method can also compare results for different kinds of people. Noninvasive procedures, such as fMRI, let us study humans without causing any harm. (p. 76)

4. In some cases, it is possible to demonstrate that people who differ with regard to some behavior also differ with regard to their brain anatomy. (p. 77)

5. Each method by itself has limitations, and any conclusion must remain tentative, pending further research using a variety of methods and studying a variety of populations. (p. 79)

ANSWERS TO *STOP AND CHECK* QUESTIONS

1. Without a dye, the various brain areas would show too little contrast for a meaningful picture. (p. 76)

2. Mild, brief magnetic stimulation of the scalp increases activity in the underlying brain areas, whereas longer, more intense stimulation blocks it. (p. 76)

3. Meaningful, complex sensations and movements require a pattern of precisely timed activity in a great many cells, not just a diffuse burst of overall activity in one area. (p. 76)

4. In an invasive procedure, the investigator inserts something, such as an electrode. A noninvasive procedure does nothing that produces any known risk of harm. A good example of a noninvasive procedure is functional magnetic resonance imaging. (p. 79)

5. The phrenologists rashly drew conclusions based on just one or two people with some oddity of skull anatomy or behavior. Researchers today try to compare larger groups, and they examine the anatomy of the brain itself, not the skull above it. (p. 79)

THOUGHT QUESTION

Certain unusual structural aspects were observed in the brain of Albert Einstein. One interpretation is that he was born with neural features that encouraged his scientific and intellectual abilities. What is an alternative interpretation?

Structure of the Vertebrate Nervous System

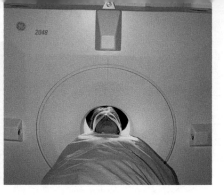

Your nervous system consists of many structures, each with substructures made up of many neurons, each of which receives and makes many synapses. How do all those little parts work together to make one behaving unit, namely, you? Does each neuron have an independent function so that, for example, one cell recognizes your grandmother, another controls your desire for pizzas, and another makes you smile at babies? Or does the brain operate as an undifferentiated whole, with each part doing the same thing as every other part?

The answer is "neither." Individual neurons do have specialized functions, but the activity of a single cell by itself has no more meaning than the letter *h* has out of context. Different brain areas communicate with one another, but they do not funnel all their activity into any central processor or "little person in the head." Meaningful activity emerges from an enormous number of partly independent, partly interdependent processes occurring simultaneously throughout your nervous system.

NERVOUS SYSTEM TERMINOLOGY

Vertebrates have a central nervous system and a peripheral nervous system, which are of course connected (Figure 4.5). The **central nervous system (CNS)** is the brain and the spinal cord, each of which includes a great many substructures. The **peripheral nervous system (PNS)**—the nerves outside the brain and spinal cord—has two divisions: The **somatic nervous system** consists of the nerves that convey messages from the sense organs to the CNS and from the CNS to the muscles and glands. The **autonomic nervous system** controls the heart, the intestines, and other organs.

To follow a road map, you first must understand the terms *north, south, east,* and *west.* Because the nervous system is a complex three-dimensional structure, we need more terms to describe it. As Figure 4.6 and Table 4.1 indicate, **dorsal** means toward the back and **ventral** means toward the stomach. (One way to remember these terms is that a *ventriloquist* is literally a "stomach talker.") In a four-legged animal, the top of the brain (with respect to gravity) is dorsal (on the same side as the animal's back), and the bottom of the brain is ventral (on the stomach side). When humans evolved an upright posture, the

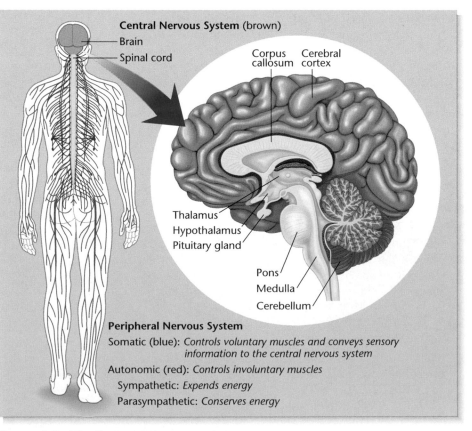

Central Nervous System (brown)
- Brain
- Spinal cord

Corpus callosum · Cerebral cortex

Thalamus
Hypothalamus
Pituitary gland

Pons
Medulla
Cerebellum

Peripheral Nervous System
Somatic (blue): *Controls voluntary muscles and conveys sensory information to the central nervous system*
Autonomic (red): *Controls involuntary muscles*
Sympathetic: *Expends energy*
Parasympathetic: *Conserves energy*

Figure 4.5   The human nervous system
Both the central and the peripheral nervous systems have major subdivisions. The closeup of the brain shows the right hemisphere as seen from the midline.

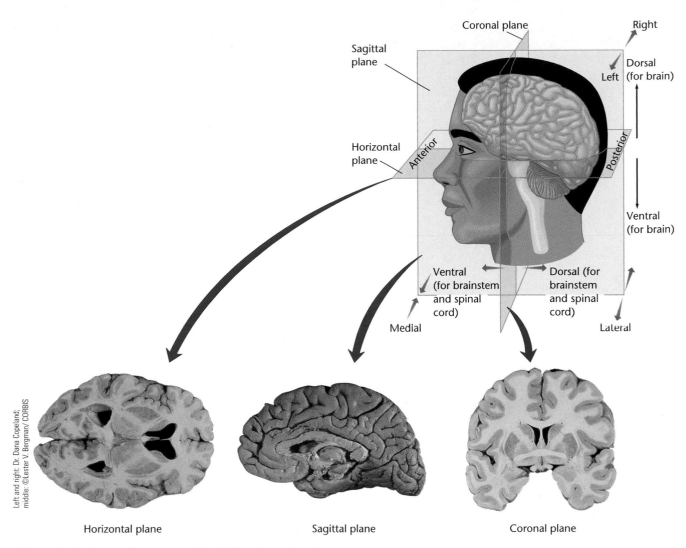

Left and right: Dr. Dana Copeland; middle: ©Lester V. Bergman/ CORBIS

Horizontal plane   Sagittal plane   Coronal plane

Figure 4.6 Terms for anatomical directions in the nervous system
In four-legged animals, dorsal and ventral point in the same direction for the head as they do for the rest of the body. However, humans' upright posture has tilted the head in relation to the spinal cord, so its dorsal and ventral directions are not parallel to the dorsal and ventral directions of the spinal cord.

position of our head changed relative to the spinal cord. For convenience, we still apply the terms *dorsal* and *ventral* to the same parts of the human brain as other vertebrate brains. Consequently, the dorsal–ventral axis of the human brain is at a right angle to the dorsal–ventral axis of the spinal cord. If you picture a person in a crawling position with all four limbs on the ground, but nose pointing forward, the dorsal and ventral positions of the brain will be parallel to those of the spinal cord.

Table 4.2 introduces some additional terminology that relates to clusters of neurons and anatomical structures of the brain. These technical terms may be confusing at first, but they help investigators communicate unambiguously. Tables 4.1 and 4.2 require careful study and review. After you think you have mastered the terms, check yourself with the following.

Stop & Check

1. What does *dorsal* mean, and what term is its opposite?

2. What term means *toward the side, away from the midline,* and what term is its opposite?

3. If two structures are both on the left side of the body, they are _____ to each other. If one is on the left and the other is on the right, they are _____ to each other.

4. The bulges in the cerebral cortex are called _____; the grooves between them are called _____.

Check your answers on page 93.

TABLE 4.1   Anatomical Terms Referring to Directions

Term	Definition
Dorsal	Toward the back, away from the ventral (stomach) side. The top of the brain is considered dorsal because it has that position in four-legged animals.
Ventral	Toward the stomach, away from the dorsal (back) side. (*Venter* is the Latin word for "belly." It also shows up in the word *ventriloquist*, literally meaning "stomach talker.")
Anterior	Toward the front end
Posterior	Toward the rear end
Superior	Above another part
Inferior	Below another part
Lateral	Toward the side, away from the midline
Medial	Toward the midline, away from the side
Proximal	Located close (approximate) to the point of origin or attachment
Distal	Located more distant from the point of origin or attachment
Ipsilateral	On the same side of the body (e.g., two parts on the left or two on the right)
Contralateral	On the opposite side of the body (one on the left and one on the right)
Coronal plane (or frontal plane)	A plane that shows brain structures as seen from the front
Sagittal plane	A plane that shows brain structures as seen from the side
Horizontal plane (or transverse plane)	A plane that shows brain structures as seen from above

THE SPINAL CORD

The **spinal cord** is the part of the CNS found within the spinal column; the spinal cord communicates with the sense organs and muscles below the level of the head. It is a segmented structure, and each segment has on each side both a sensory nerve and a motor nerve, as shown in Figure 4.7. According to the **Bell-Magendie law,** which was one of the first discoveries about the functions of the nervous system, the entering dorsal roots (axon bundles) carry sensory information and the exiting ventral roots carry motor information, to the muscles and glands. The axons to and from the skin and muscles are the peripheral nervous system. The cell bodies of the sensory neurons are located in clusters of neurons outside the spinal cord, called the **dorsal root ganglia.** (*Ganglia* is the plural of *ganglion*, a cluster of neurons.) Cell bodies of the motor neurons are inside the spinal cord.

In the cross section through the spinal cord shown in Figures 4.8 and 4.9, the H-shaped **gray matter** in the center of the cord is densely packed

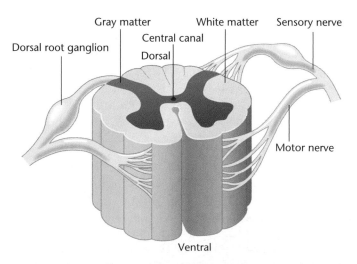

Figure 4.7   Diagram of a cross section through the spinal cord
The dorsal root on each side conveys sensory information to the spinal cord; the ventral root conveys motor commands to the muscles.

TABLE 4.2 Terms Referring to Parts of the Nervous System

Term	Definition
Lamina	A row or layer of cell bodies separated from other cell bodies by a layer of axons and dendrites
Column	A set of cells perpendicular to the surface of the cortex, with similar properties
Tract	A set of axons within the CNS, also known as a *projection*. If axons extend from cell bodies in structure A to synapses onto B, we say that the fibers "project" from A onto B.
Nerve	A set of axons in the periphery, either from the CNS to a muscle or gland or from a sensory organ to the CNS
Nucleus	A cluster of neuron cell bodies within the CNS
Ganglion	A cluster of neuron cell bodies, usually outside the CNS (as in the sympathetic nervous system)
Gyrus (pl.: gyri)	A protuberance on the surface of the brain
Sulcus (pl.: sulci)	A fold or groove that separates one gyrus from another
Fissure	A long, deep sulcus

with cell bodies and dendrites. Many neurons of the spinal cord send axons from the gray matter toward the brain or to other parts of the spinal cord through the **white matter,** which is composed mostly of myelinated axons.

Each segment of the spinal cord sends sensory information to the brain and receives motor commands from the brain. All that information passes through tracts of axons in the spinal cord. If the spinal cord is cut at a given segment, the brain loses sensation from that segment and all segments below it; the brain also loses motor control over all parts of the body served by that segment and the lower ones.

THE AUTONOMIC NERVOUS SYSTEM

The autonomic nervous system is a set of neurons that receives information from and sends commands to the heart, intestines, and other organs. It is comprised of two parts: the sympathetic and parasympathetic

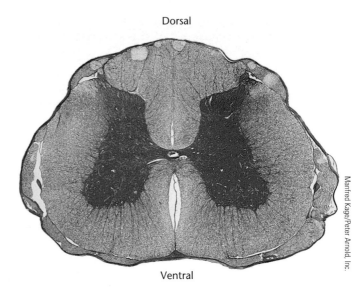

Dorsal

Ventral

Manfred Kage/Peter Arnold, Inc.

Figure 4.8 Photo of a cross section through the spinal cord
The H-shaped structure in the center is gray matter, which is composed largely of cell bodies. The surrounding white matter consists of axons. The axons are organized in tracts; some carry information from the brain and higher levels of the spinal cord downward, while others carry information from lower levels upward.

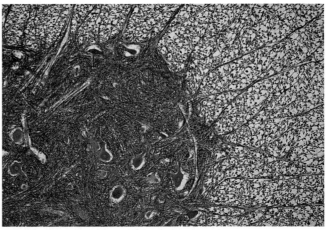

Manfred Kage/Peter Arnold, Inc.

Figure 4.9 A section of gray matter of the spinal cord (lower left) and white matter surrounding it
Cell bodies and dendrites reside entirely in the gray matter. Axons travel from one area of gray matter to another within the white matter.

nervous systems (Figure 4.10). The **sympathetic nervous system,** a network of nerves that prepare the organs for vigorous activity, consists of two paired chains of ganglia lying just to the left and right of the spinal cord in its central regions (the thoracic and lumbar areas) and connected by axons to the spinal cord. Sympathetic axons extend from the ganglia to the organs and activate them for "fight or flight"—increasing breathing and heart rate and decreasing digestive activity. Because all of the sympathetic ganglia are closely linked, they often act as a single system, "in sympathy" with one another, although one part can be more active than the others. The sweat glands, the adrenal glands, the liver, the muscles that constrict blood vessels, and the muscles that erect the hairs of the skin have only sympathetic, not parasympathetic, input.

Erection of the hairs, known as "goose flesh" or "goose bumps," occurs when we are cold. What does this response have to do with the fight-or-flight functions associated with the sympathetic nervous system? Part of the answer is that we also get goose flesh when we are

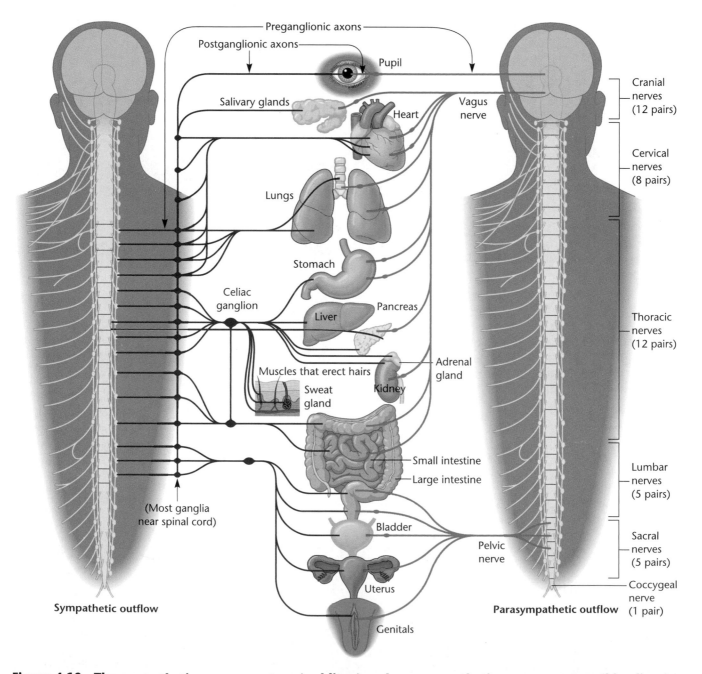

Figure 4.10 The sympathetic nervous system (red lines) and parasympathetic nervous system (blue lines)
Note that the adrenal glands and hair erector muscles receive sympathetic input only. *Source: Adapted from* Biology: The Unity and Diversity of Life, *5ᵗʰ Edition, by C. Starr and R. Taggart, p. 340. Copyright ©1989 Wadsworth.*

frightened. You have heard the expression, "I was so frightened my hairs stood on end." You may also have seen a frightened cat erect its fur. Human body hairs are so short that erecting them accomplishes nothing, but a cat with erect fur looks bigger and potentially frightening. A frightened porcupine erects its quills, which are modified hairs (Richter & Langworthy, 1933). The behavior that makes the quills so useful, their erection in response to fear, evidently evolved before the quills themselves did.

Stop & Check

5. Sensory nerves enter which side of the spinal cord, dorsal or ventral?
6. Which functions are controlled by the sympathetic nervous system? Which are controlled by the parasympathetic nervous system?

Check your answers on page 93.

The **parasympathetic nervous system** facilitates vegetative, nonemergency responses by the organs. The term *para* means "beside" or "related to," and parasympathetic activities are related to, and generally the opposite of, sympathetic activities. For example, the sympathetic nervous system increases heart rate; the parasympathetic nervous system decreases it. The parasympathetic nervous system increases digestive activity; the sympathetic nervous system decreases it. Although the sympathetic and parasympathetic systems act in opposition to one another, they are both constantly active to varying degrees, and many stimuli arouse parts of both systems.

The parasympathetic nervous system is also known as the craniosacral system because it consists of the cranial nerves and nerves from the sacral spinal cord (see Figure 4.10). Unlike the ganglia in the sympathetic system, the parasympathetic ganglia are not arranged in a chain near the spinal cord. Rather, long *preganglionic* axons extend from the spinal cord to parasympathetic ganglia close to each internal organ; shorter *postganglionic* fibers then extend from the parasympathetic ganglia into the organs themselves. Because the parasympathetic ganglia are not linked to one another, they act somewhat more independently than the sympathetic ganglia do.

The parasympathetic nervous system's postganglionic axons release the neurotransmitter acetylcholine. Most of the postganglionic synapses of the sympathetic nervous system use norepinephrine, although a few, including those that control the sweat glands, use acetylcholine. Because the two systems use different transmitters, certain drugs may excite or inhibit one system or the other. For example, over-the-counter cold remedies exert most of their effects either by blocking parasympathetic activity or by increasing sympathetic activity. This action is useful because the flow of sinus fluids is a parasympathetic response; thus, drugs that block the parasympathetic system inhibit sinus flow. The common side effects of cold remedies also stem from their prosympathetic, antiparasympathetic activities: They inhibit salivation and digestion and increase heart rate.

THE HINDBRAIN

The brain itself (as distinct from the spinal cord) consists of three major divisions: the hindbrain, the midbrain, and the forebrain (Figure 4.11 and Table 4.3). Brain investigators unfortunately use a variety of terms synonymously. For example, some people prefer words with Greek roots: rhombencephalon (hindbrain), mesencephalon (midbrain), and prosencephalon (forebrain). You may encounter these terms in other reading.

The **hindbrain**, the posterior part of the brain, consists of the medulla, the pons, and the cerebellum. The medulla and pons, the midbrain, and certain central structures of the forebrain constitute the **brainstem** (Figure 4.12).

The **medulla**, or medulla oblongata, is just above the spinal cord and could be regarded as an enlarged, elaborated extension of the spinal cord, although it is located in the skull. The medulla controls a number of vital reflexes—including breathing, heart rate, vomiting, salivation, coughing,

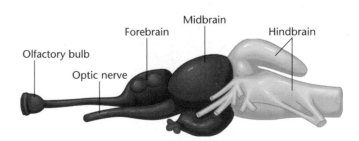

Figure 4.11 Three major divisions of the vertebrate brain
In a fish brain, shown here, the forebrain, midbrain, and hindbrain are clearly visible as separate bulges. In adult mammals, the forebrain grows so large that it surrounds the entire midbrain and part of the hindbrain.

TABLE 4.3   Major Divisions of the Vertebrate Brain

Area	Also Known as	Major Structures
Forebrain	Prosencephalon ("forward-brain")	
	Diencephalon ("between-brain")	Thalamus, hypothalamus
	Telencephalon ("end-brain")	Cerebral cortex, hippocampus, basal ganglia
Midbrain	Mesencephalon ("middle-brain")	Tectum, tegmentum, superior colliculus, inferior colliculus, substantia nigra
Hindbrain	Rhombencephalon (literally, "parallelogram-brain")	Medulla, pons, cerebellum
	Metencephalon ("afterbrain")	Pons, cerebellum
	Myelencephalon ("marrow-brain")	Medulla

and sneezing—through the **cranial nerves,** which control sensations from the head, muscle movements in the head, and much of the parasympathetic output to the organs. Some of the cranial nerves include both sensory and motor components; others have just one or the other. Damage to the medulla is frequently fatal, and large doses of opiates can also be fatal because they suppress activity of the medulla.

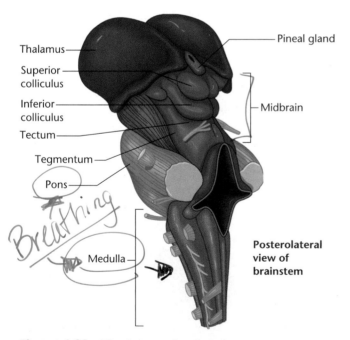

Figure 4.12   **The human brainstem**
This composite structure extends from the top of the spinal cord into the center of the forebrain. The pons, pineal gland, colliculi, and thalamus are ordinarily surrounded by the cerebral cortex.

Just as the lower parts of the body are connected to the spinal cord via sensory and motor nerves, the receptors and muscles of the head and the internal organs are connected to the brain by 12 pairs of cranial nerves (one of each pair on the right of the brain and one on the left), as shown in Table 4.4. Each cranial nerve originates in a *nucleus* (cluster of neurons) that integrates the sensory information, regulates the motor output, or both. The cranial nerve nuclei for nerves V through XII are in the medulla and pons of the hindbrain. Those for cranial nerves I through IV are in the midbrain and forebrain (Figure 4.13).

The **pons** lies anterior and ventral to the medulla; like the medulla, it contains nuclei for several cranial nerves. The term *pons* is Latin for "bridge"; the name reflects the fact that many axons in the pons cross from one side of the brain to the other. This is in fact where axons from each half of the brain cross to the opposite side of the spinal cord, so that the left hemisphere controls the muscles of the right side of the body, and the right hemisphere controls the left side.

The medulla and pons also contain the reticular formation and the raphe system. The **reticular formation** has descending and ascending portions. The descending portion is one of several brain areas that control the motor areas of the spinal cord. The ascending portion sends output to much of the cerebral cortex, selectively increasing arousal and attention in one area or another (Guillery, Feig, & Lozsádi, 1998). The **raphe system** also sends axons to much of the forebrain, increasing or decreasing the brain's readiness to respond to stimuli (Mesulam, 1995).

The **cerebellum** is a large hindbrain structure with a great many deep folds. It has long been known for its contributions to the **control of movement** (see Chapter 8), and many older textbooks describe the cerebellum as important for "balance and coordination." True, people with cerebellar damage are

TABLE 4.4   The Cranial Nerves

Number and Name	Major Functions
I. Olfactory	Smell
II. Optic	Vision
III. Oculomotor	Control of eye movements, pupil constriction
IV. Trochlear	Control of eye movements
V. Trigeminal	Skin sensations from most of the face; control of jaw muscles for chewing and swallowing
VI. Abducens	Control of eye movements
VII. Facial	Taste from the anterior two thirds of the tongue; control of facial expressions, crying, salivation, and dilation of the head's blood vessels
VIII. Statoacoustic	Hearing, equilibrium
IX. Glossopharyngeal	Taste and other sensations from throat and posterior third of the tongue; control of swallowing, salivation, throat movements during speech
X. Vagus	Sensations from neck and thorax; control of throat, esophagus, and larynx; parasympathetic nerves to stomach, intestines, and other organs
XI. Accessory	Control of neck and shoulder movements
XII. Hypoglossal	Control of muscles of the tongue

Cranial nerves III, IV, and VI are coded in red to highlight their similarity: control of eye movements.
Cranial nerves VII, IX, and XII are coded in green to highlight their similarity: taste and control of tongue and throat movements.
Cranial nerve VII has other important functions as well. Nerve X (not highlighed) also contributes to throat movements, although it is primarily known for other functions.

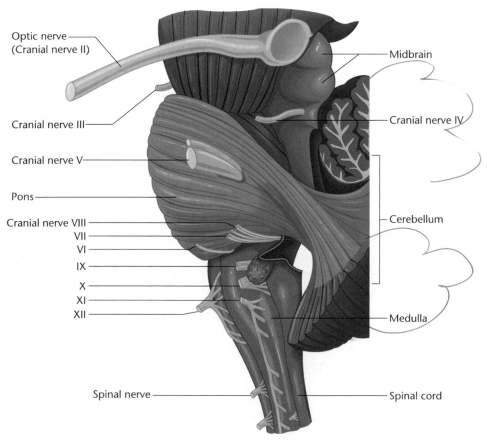

Optic nerve (Cranial nerve II)
Cranial nerve III
Cranial nerve V
Pons
Cranial nerve VIII
VII
VI
IX
X
XI
XII
Spinal nerve

Midbrain
Cranial nerve IV
Cerebellum
Medulla
Spinal cord

clumsy and lose their balance, but the functions of the cerebellum extend far beyond balance and coordination. People with damage to the cerebellum have trouble shifting their attention back and forth between auditory and visual stimuli (Canavan, Sprengelmeyer, Diener, & Hömberg, 1994). They have much difficulty with timing, including sensory timing. For example, they are poor at judging whether one rhythm is faster than another.

Figure 4.13 Cranial nerves II through XII
Cranial nerve I, the olfactory nerve, connects directly to the olfactory bulbs of the forebrain. *Source: Based on Braus, 1960*

THE MIDBRAIN

As the name implies, the **midbrain** is in the middle of the brain, although in adult mammals it is dwarfed and surrounded by the forebrain. In birds, reptiles, amphibians, and fish, the midbrain is a larger, more prominent structure. The roof of the midbrain is called the **tectum**. (*Tectum* is the Latin word for "roof"; the same root shows up in the geological term *plate tectonics*.) The two swellings on each side of the tectum are the **superior colliculus** and the **inferior colliculus** (see Figures 4.12 and 4.16); both are part of important routes for sensory information.

Under the tectum is the **tegmentum**, the intermediate level of the midbrain. (In Latin, *tegmentum* means a "covering," such as a rug on the floor. The tegmentum covers several other midbrain structures, although it is covered by the tectum.) The tegmentum includes the nuclei for the third and fourth cranial nerves, parts of the reticular formation, and extensions of the pathways between the forebrain and the spinal cord or hindbrain. Another midbrain structure is the **substantia nigra,** which gives rise to a dopamine-containing path that deteriorates in Parkinson's disease (see Chapter 8).

THE FOREBRAIN

The **forebrain** is the most anterior and most prominent part of the mammalian brain. The outer portion is the cerebral cortex. (*Cerebrum* is a Latin word meaning "brain"; *cortex* is Latin for "bark" or "covering.") Under the cerebral cortex are other structures, including the thalamus, which is the main source of input to the cerebral cortex. A set of structures known as the basal ganglia plays a major role in certain aspects of movement. A number of other interlinked structures, known as the **limbic system,** form a border (or *limbus*, the Latin word for "border") around the brainstem. These structures are particularly important for motivations and emotions, such as eating, drinking, sexual activity, anxiety, and aggression. The

structures of the limbic system are the olfactory bulb, hypothalamus, hippocampus, amygdala, and cingulate gyrus of the cerebral cortex. Figure 4.14 shows the positions of these structures in three-dimensional perspective. Figures 4.15 and 4.16 show coronal (from the front) and sagittal (from the side) sections through the human brain. Figure 4.15 also includes a view of the ventral surface of the brain.

In describing the forebrain, we begin with the subcortical areas; the next module focuses on the cerebral cortex. In later chapters, we return to each of these areas as they become relevant.

Thalamus

The thalamus and hypothalamus together form the *diencephalon,* a section distinct from the rest of the forebrain, which is known as the *telencephalon.* The **thalamus** is a structure in the center of the forebrain. The term is derived from the Greek word *thalamos,* meaning "anteroom," "inner chamber," or "bridal bed." It resembles two avocados joined side by side, one in the left hemisphere and one in the right. Most sensory information goes first to the thalamus, which then

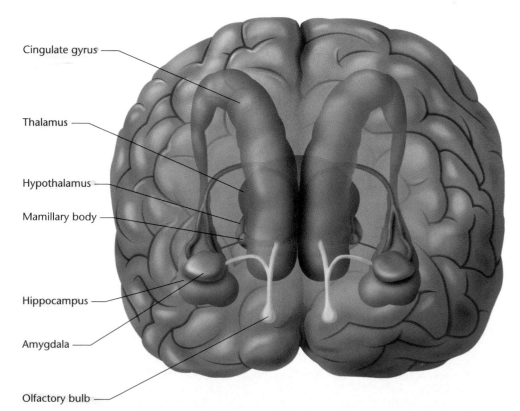

Cingulate gyrus

Thalamus

Hypothalamus

Mamillary body

Hippocampus

Amygdala

Olfactory bulb

Figure 4.14 The limbic system, a set of structures that form a border (or limbus) around the brainstem

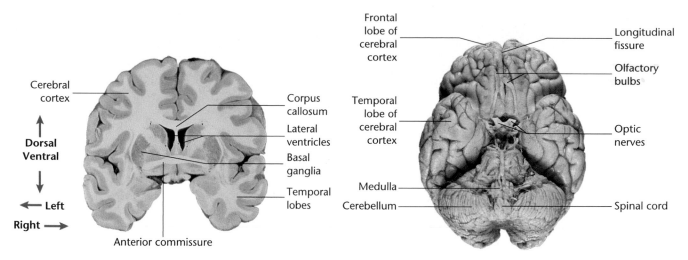

Figure 4.15 Two views of the human brain
Top: A coronal section. Note how the corpus callosum and anterior commissure provide communication between the left and right hemispheres. *Bottom:* The ventral surface. The optic nerves (which are cut here) extend to the eyes. *Source: Photos courtesy of Dr. Dana Copeland*

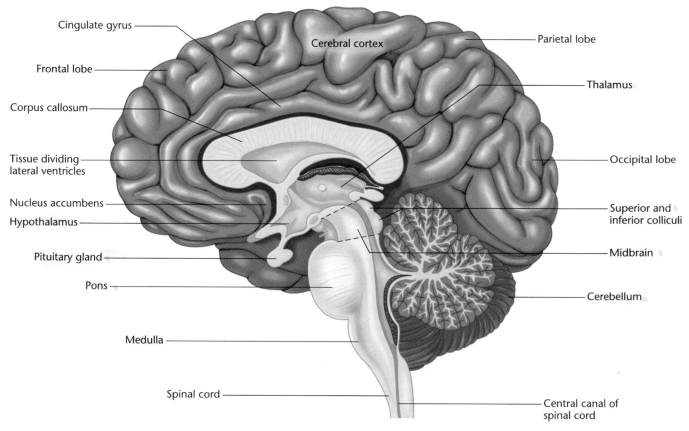

Figure 4.16 A sagittal section through the human brain
Source: After Nieuwenhuys,Voogd, & vanHuijzen 1988

processes it and sends the output to the cerebral cortex. The one clear exception to this rule is olfactory information, which progresses from the olfactory receptors to the olfactory bulbs and from the bulbs directly to the cerebral cortex without passing through the thalamus.

Many nuclei of the thalamus receive their primary input from one of the sensory systems, such as vision, and then transmit the information to a single area of the cerebral cortex, as in Figure 4.17, while receiving feedback from the same area. That feedback modifies

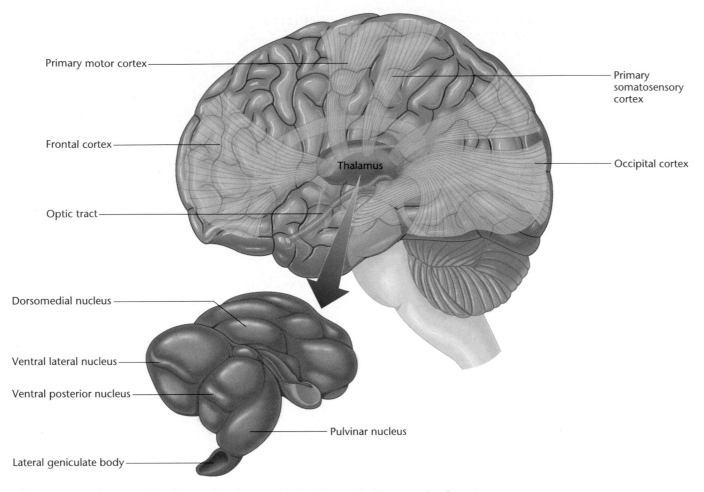

Figure 4.17 Routes of information from the thalamus to the cerebral cortex
Each thalamic nucleus projects its axons to a different location in the cortex. *Source: After Nieuwenhuys, Voogd, & vanHuijzen, 1988*

the continuing input from the thalamus to the cortex and basal ganglia. For example, auditory and visual stimuli excite one nucleus in the posterior thalamus that immediately sends input to the cortex. If those stimuli have previously been associated with reinforcements, the cortex sends messages that prolong further thalamic activity; otherwise, thalamic activity quickly declines (Komura et al., 2001).

Hypothalamus

The **hypothalamus** is a small area near the base of the brain just ventral to the thalamus (see Figures 4.14 and 4.16). It has widespread connections with the rest of the forebrain and the midbrain. The hypothalamus contains a number of distinct nuclei, which we examine in Chapters 10 and 11. Partly through nerves and partly through hypothalamic hormones, the hypothalamus conveys messages to the pituitary gland, altering its release of hormones. Damage to a hypothalamic nucleus leads to abnormalities in one or more motivated behav-

iors, such as feeding, drinking, temperature regulation, sexual behavior, fighting, or activity level. Because of these spectacular effects, the rather small hypothalamus attracts a great deal of research attention.

Pituitary Gland

The **pituitary gland** is an endocrine (hormone-producing) gland attached to the base of the hypothalamus by a stalk that contains neurons, blood vessels, and connective tissue (see Figure 4.16). In response to messages from the hypothalamus, the pituitary synthesizes and releases hormones into the bloodstream, which carries them to other organs.

Basal Ganglia

The **basal ganglia,** a group of subcortical structures lateral to the thalamus, include three major structures: the caudate nucleus, the putamen, and the globus pallidus (Figure 4.18). Some authorities include several other structures. The basal ganglia have been conserved through evolution, and the basic organization is about the same in mammals as in amphibians (Marin, Smeets, & González, 1998).

The basal ganglia have multiple subdivisions, each of which exchanges information with a different part of the cerebral cortex. The connections are most abundant with the frontal areas of the cortex, which are responsible for planning sequences of behavior and for certain aspects of memory and emotional expression (Graybiel, Aosaki, Flaherty, & Kimura, 1994). In conditions such as Parkinson's disease and Huntington's disease, in which the basal ganglia deteriorate, the most prominent symptom is impaired movement, but people also show depression, deficits of memory and reasoning, and attentional disorders.

Basal Forebrain

Several structures lie on the dorsal surface of the forebrain, including the **nucleus basalis,** which receives input from the hypothalamus and basal ganglia, and sends axons that release acetylcholine to widespread areas in the cerebral cortex (Figure 4.19). We might regard the nucleus basalis as an intermediary between the emotional arousal of the hypothalamus and the information processing of the cerebral cortex. The nucleus basalis is a key part of the brain's system for arousal, wakefulness, and attention, as we consider in Chapter 9. Patients with Parkinson's disease and Alzheimer's disease have impairments of attention and intellect because of inactivity or deterioration of their nucleus basalis.

Hippocampus

The **hippocampus** (from a Latin word meaning "sea horse," a shape suggested by the hippocampus) is a large structure between the thalamus and the cerebral cortex, mostly toward the posterior of the forebrain, as shown in Figure 4.14. We consider the hippocampus in more detail in Chapter 13; the gist of that discussion is that the hippocampus is critical for storing certain kinds of memories but not all. A debate continues about how best to describe the class of memories that depend on the hippocampus. People with hippocampal damage have trouble storing new memories, but they do not lose the memories they had before the damage occurred.

7. Of the following, which are in the hindbrain, which in the midbrain, and which in the forebrain: basal ganglia, cerebellum, hippocampus, hypothalamus, medulla, pituitary gland, pons, substantia nigra, superior and inferior colliculi, tectum, tegmentum, thalamus?

8. Which subcortical area is the main source of input to the cerebral cortex?

Check your answers on page 93.

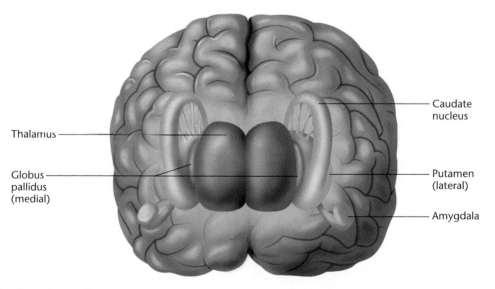

Figure 4.18   The basal ganglia
The thalamus is in the center, the basal ganglia are lateral to it, and the cerebral cortex is on the outside. *Source: After Nieuwenhuys, Voogd, & vanHuijzen, 1988*

THE VENTRICLES

The nervous system begins its development as a tube surrounding a fluid canal. The canal persists into adulthood as the **central canal,** a fluid-filled channel in the center of the spinal cord, and as the **ventricles,** four fluid-filled cavities within the brain. Each hemisphere contains one of the two large lateral ventricles (Figure 4.20). Toward the posterior, they connect to the third ventricle, which connects to the fourth ventricle in the medulla.

The ventricles and the central canal of the spinal cord contain **cerebrospinal fluid (CSF),** a clear fluid similar to blood plasma. CSF is formed by groups of cells, the *choroid plexus,* inside the four ventricles. It flows from the lateral ventricles to the third and fourth ventricles. From the fourth ventricle, some CSF flows into the central canal of the spinal cord, but more goes through an opening into the narrow spaces between the

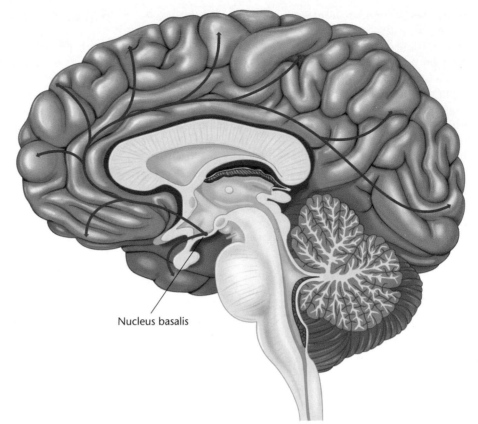

Nucleus basalis

Figure 4.19   The basal forebrain
The nucleus basalis and other structures in this area send axons throughout the cortex, increasing its arousal and wakefulness by releasing of the neurotransmitter acetylcholine. *Source: Adapted from "Cholinergic Systems in Mammalian Brain and Spinal Cord," by N. J. Wolf, Progress in Neurobiology, 37, p. 475–524, 1991. Reprinted by permission of the author.*

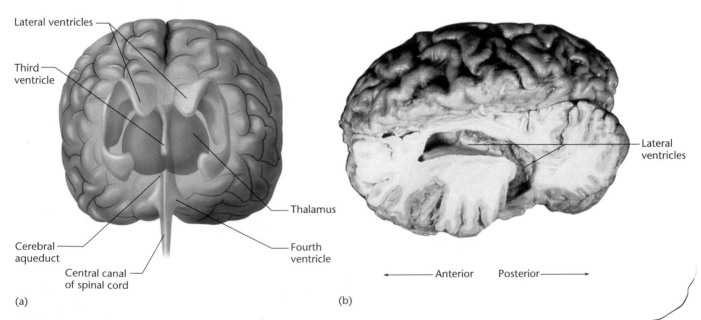

Lateral ventricles

Third ventricle

Cerebral aqueduct

Central canal of spinal cord

(a)

Thalamus

Fourth ventricle

Lateral ventricles

◄——— Anterior   Posterior ———►

(b)

Figure 4.20   The cerebral ventricles
(a) Diagram showing positions of the four ventricles. **(b)** Photo of a human brain, viewed from above, with a horizontal cut through one hemisphere to show the position of the lateral ventricles. Note that the two parts of this figure are seen from different angles. *Source: Photo courtesy of Dr. Dana Copeland*

brain and the thin **meninges,** membranes that surround the brain and spinal cord. (Meningitis is an inflammation of the meninges.) From one of those spaces, the subarachnoid space, CSF is gradually reabsorbed into the blood vessels of the brain.

Cerebrospinal fluid cushions the brain against mechanical shock when the head moves. It also provides buoyancy; just as a person weighs less in water than on land, cerebrospinal fluid helps support the weight of the brain. It also provides a reservoir of hormones and nutrition for the brain and spinal cord.

Sometimes the flow of CSF is obstructed, and it accumulates within the ventricles or in the subarachnoid space, thus increasing the pressure on the brain. When this occurs in infants, the skull bones may spread, causing an overgrown head. This condition, known as *hydrocephalus* (HI-dro-SEFF-ah-luss), is usually associated with mental retardation.

MODULE 4.2

In Closing: Learning Neuroanatomy

The brain is a highly complex structure. This module has introduced a great many terms and facts; do not be discouraged if you have trouble remembering them. You didn't learn world geography all at one time either. It will help to return to this module to review the anatomy of certain structures as you encounter them again in later chapters. Gradually, the material will become more familiar.

It helps to see the brain from different angles and perspectives. Check this fantastic Web site, which includes detailed photos of both normal and abnormal human brains:

www.med.harvard.edu/AANLIB/home.html

You might also appreciate this site, which compares the brains of different species. (Have you ever wondered what a polar bear's brain looks like? Or a dolphin's? Or a weasel's?)

www.brainmuseum.org/Sections/index.html

SUMMARY

1. The main divisions of the vertebrate nervous system are the central nervous system and the peripheral nervous system. The central nervous system consists of the spinal cord, the hindbrain, the midbrain, and the forebrain. (p. 80)

2. Each segment of the spinal cord has a sensory nerve and a motor nerve on each side. Several spinal pathways convey information to the brain. (p. 82)

3. The sympathetic nervous system (one of the two divisions of the autonomic nervous system) activates the body's internal organs for vigorous activities. The parasympathetic system (the other division) promotes digestion and other nonemergency processes. (p. 83)

4. The hindbrain consists of the medulla, pons, and cerebellum. The medulla and pons control breathing, heart rate, and other vital functions through the cranial nerves. The cerebellum contributes to movement. (p. 85)

5. The subcortical areas of the forebrain include the thalamus, hypothalamus, pituitary gland, basal ganglia, and hippocampus. (p. 88)

6. The cerebral cortex receives its sensory information (except for olfaction) from the thalamus. (p. 88)

ANSWERS TO *STOP AND CHECK* QUESTIONS

1. *Dorsal* means toward the back, away from the stomach side. Its opposite is *ventral*. (p. 81)

2. Lateral; medial (p. 81)

3. Ipsilateral; contralateral (p. 81)

4. Gyri; sulci (p. 81)

5. Dorsal (p. 85)

6. The sympathetic nervous system prepares the organs for vigorous fight-or-flight activity. The parasympathetic system increases vegetative responses such as digestion. (p. 85)

7. Hindbrain: cerebellum, medulla, and pons. Midbrain: substantia nigra, superior and inferior colliculi, tectum, and tegmentum. Forebrain: basal ganglia, hippocampus, hypothalamus, pituitary gland, and thalamus. (p. 91)

8. Thalamus (p. 91)

THOUGHT QUESTION

The drug phenylephrine is sometimes prescribed for people suffering from a sudden loss of blood pressure or other medical disorders. It acts by stimulating norepinephrine synapses, including those that constrict blood vessels. One common side effect of this drug is goose bumps. Explain why. What other side effects might be likely?

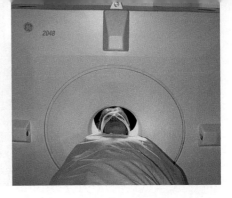

MODULE 4.3

The Cerebral Cortex

The forebrain consists of two cerebral hemispheres, one on the left side and one on the right (Figure 4.21). Each hemisphere is organized to receive sensory information, mostly from the contralateral (opposite) side of the body, and to control muscles, mostly on the contralateral side, through axons to the spinal cord and the cranial nerve nuclei.

The cellular layers on the outer surface of the cerebral hemispheres form gray matter known as the **cerebral cortex** (from the Latin word *cortex*, meaning "bark"). Large numbers of axons extend inward from the cortex, forming the white matter of the cerebral hemispheres (see Figure 4.15). Neurons in each hemisphere communicate with neurons in the corresponding part of the other hemisphere through two bundles of axons, the **corpus callosum** (see Figures 4.15, 4.16, and 4.21) and the smaller **anterior commissure** (see Figure 4.15). Several other commissures (pathways across the midline) link subcortical structures.

ORGANIZATION OF THE CEREBRAL CORTEX

The microscopic structure of the cells of the cerebral cortex varies substantially from one cortical area to another. The differences in appearance relate to differences in function. Much research has been directed toward understanding the relationship between structure and function.

In humans and most other mammals, the cerebral cortex contains up to six distinct **laminae,** layers of cell bodies that are parallel to the surface of the cortex and separated from each other by layers of fibers (Figure 4.22). The laminae vary in thickness and prominence from one part of the cortex to another, and a given lamina may be absent from certain areas. Lamina V, which sends long axons to the spinal cord and other distant areas, is thickest in the motor cortex,

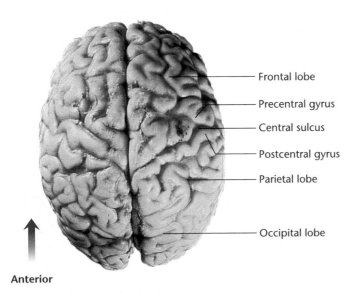

Frontal lobe

Precentral gyrus

Central sulcus

Postcentral gyrus

Parietal lobe

Occipital lobe

Anterior

Posterior

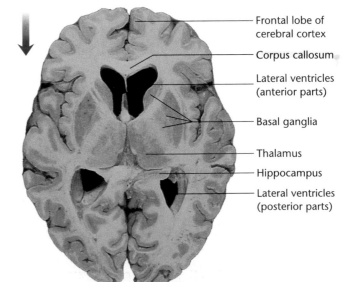

Frontal lobe of cerebral cortex

Corpus callosum

Lateral ventricles (anterior parts)

Basal ganglia

Thalamus

Hippocampus

Lateral ventricles (posterior parts)

Figure 4.21 Dorsal view of the brain surface and a horizontal section through the brain
Source: Photos courtesy of Dr. Dana Copeland

which has the greatest control of the muscles. Lamina IV, which receives axons from the various sensory nuclei of the thalamus, is prominent in all the primary sensory areas (visual, auditory, and somatosensory) but absent from the motor cortex. Anecdotal reports have found lamina IV to be even thicker than normal in the visual cortex of a person with photographic memory and in the auditory cortex of a musician with perfect pitch (Scheibel, 1984).

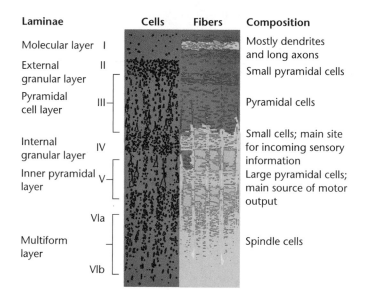

Laminae		Cells	Fibers	Composition
Molecular layer	I			Mostly dendrites and long axons
External granular layer	II			Small pyramidal cells
Pyramidal cell layer	III			Pyramidal cells
Internal granular layer	IV			Small cells; main site for incoming sensory information
Inner pyramidal layer	V			Large pyramidal cells; main source of motor output
Multiform layer	VIa			
	VIb			Spindle cells

Figure 4.22   The six laminae of the human cerebral cortex
Source: From The Anatomy of the Nervous System *by S. W. Ranson and S. L. Clark, 1959. Reprinted by permission of W. B. Saunders Co.*

The cells of the cortex are also organized into **columns** of cells with similar properties, arranged perpendicular to the laminae. Figure 4.23 illustrates the idea of columns, although in fact they do not all have such a straight shape. The cells within a given column have similar or related properties and many connections to one another. For example, if one cell in a given column responds to touch on the palm of the left hand, then the other cells in that column also respond to touch on the palm of the left hand. If one cell responds to a particular pattern of light at a particular location in the retina, then the other cells in the column respond to the same pattern of light in the same location.

We now turn to some of the specific parts of the cortex. Researchers distinguish 50 or more areas of the cerebral cortex based on differences in the thickness of the six laminae and on the appearance of cells and fibers within each lamina. For convenience, we group these areas into four *lobes* named for the skull bones that lie over them: occipital, parietal, temporal, and frontal.

THE OCCIPITAL LOBE

The **occipital lobe,** located at the posterior (caudal) end of the cortex (Figure 4.24), is the main target for axons from the thalamic nuclei that receive visual input. The posterior pole of the occipital lobe is known as the *primary visual cortex,* or *striate cortex,* because of its striped appearance in cross section. Destruction of any part of the striate cortex causes *cortical blindness* in the related part of the visual field. For example, extensive damage to the striate cortex of the right hemisphere causes blindness in the left visual field (the left side of the world from the viewer's perspective). A person with cortical blindness has normal eyes, normal pupillary reflexes, and some eye movements, but no pattern perception and not even visual imagery. People who suffer severe damage to the eyes become blind, but if they have an intact occipital cortex and previous visual experience, they can still imagine visual scenes and have visual dreams (Sabo & Kirtley, 1982).

Surface of cortex

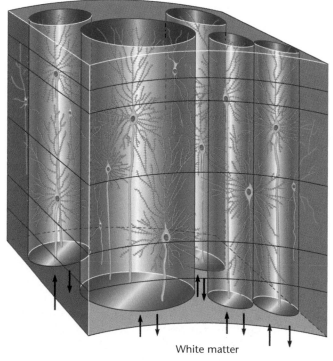

White matter

Figure 4.23   Columns in the cerebral cortex
Each column extends through several laminae. Neurons within a given column have similar properties. For example, in the somatosensory cortex, all the neurons within a given column respond to stimulation of the same area of skin.

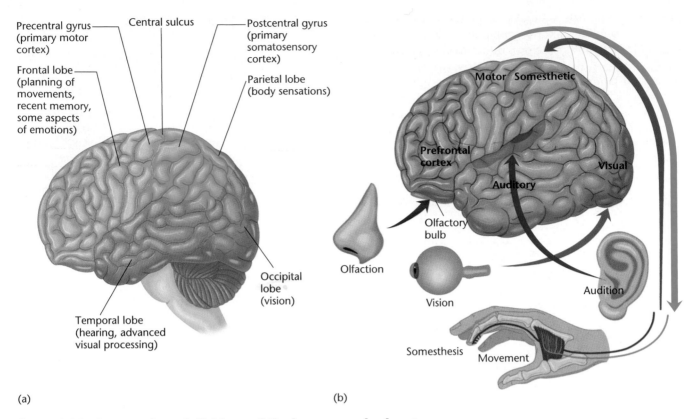

Figure 4.24 Some major subdivisions of the human cerebral cortex
(a) The four lobes: occipital, parietal, temporal, and frontal. **(b)** The primary sensory cortex for vision, hearing, and body sensations; the primary motor cortex; and the olfactory bulb, a noncortical area responsible for the sense of smell.
Source: T.W. Deacon, 1990

THE PARIETAL LOBE

The **parietal lobe** lies between the occipital lobe and the **central sulcus,** which is one of the deepest grooves in the surface of the cortex (see Figure 4.24). The area just posterior to the central sulcus, called the **postcentral gyrus,** or the *primary somatosensory cortex,* is the primary target for touch sensations and information from muscle-stretch receptors and joint receptors. Brain surgeons sometimes use only local anesthesia (anesthetizing the scalp but leaving the brain awake). If during this process they lightly stimulate the postcentral gyrus in one hemisphere, people report "tingling" sensations on the opposite side of the body. The postcentral gyrus includes four bands of cells that run parallel to the central sulcus. Separate areas along each band receive simultaneous information from different parts of the body, as shown in Figure 4.25a (Nicolelis et al., 1998). Two of the bands receive mostly light-touch information, one receives deep-pressure information, and one receives a combination of both (Kaas, Nelson, Sur, Lin, & Merzenich, 1979). In effect, the postcentral gyrus contains four separate representations of the body.

Information about touch and body location is important not only for its own sake but also for interpreting visual and auditory information. For example, if you see something in the upper left portion of the visual field, your brain needs to know which direction your eyes are turned, the position of your head, and the tilt of your body before it can determine the location of the object that you see and therefore the direction you should go if you want to approach or avoid it. The parietal lobe monitors all the information about eye, head, and body positions and passes it to brain areas that control movement (Gross & Graziano, 1995).

THE TEMPORAL LOBE

The **temporal lobe** is the lateral portion of each hemisphere, near the temples (see Figure 4.24). It is the primary cortical target for auditory information. In humans, the temporal lobe—in most cases, the left temporal lobe—is essential for understanding spoken language. The temporal lobe also contributes to some of the more complex aspects of vision, including perception of movement and recognition of faces. A tumor in the temporal lobe may give rise to elaborate auditory or visual hallucinations, whereas a tumor in the occipital lobe ordinarily evokes only simple sensations, such as flashes of light. In fact, when psychiatric patients report hallucinations, brain scans detect extensive activity in the temporal lobes (Dierks et al., 1999).

The temporal lobes also play a part in emotional and motivational behaviors. Temporal lobe damage can lead to a set of behaviors known as the Klüver-Bucy syndrome (named for the investigators who first described it). Previously wild and aggressive monkeys fail to display normal fears and anxieties after temporal lobe damage (Klüver & Bucy, 1939). They put almost anything they find into their mouths and attempt to pick up snakes and lighted matches (which intact monkeys consistently avoid). Interpreting this behavior is difficult. For example, a monkey might handle a snake because it is no longer afraid (an emotional change) or because it no longer recognizes what a snake is (a cognitive change).

THE FRONTAL LOBE

The frontal lobe, which contains the primary motor cortex and the prefrontal cortex, extends from the central sulcus to the anterior limit of the brain (see Figure 4.24).

The posterior portion of the frontal lobe just anterior to the central sulcus, the precentral gyrus, is specialized for the control of fine movements, such as moving one finger at a time. Separate areas are responsible for different parts of the body, mostly on the contralateral (opposite) side but also with slight control of the ipsilateral (same) side. Figure 4.25b shows the traditional map of the precentral gyrus, also known as the *primary motor cortex*. However, the map is only an approximation; for example, what is shown as the arm area does indeed control arm movements, but within that area, there is no one-to-one relationship between brain location and specific muscles of the arm (Graziano, Taylor, & Moore, 2002).

The most anterior portion of the frontal lobe, the prefrontal cortex, forms a large proportion of the brain in species with a large overall brain but only a small portion if the species has a small brain (Figure 4.26). For example, it is large in humans and all the great apes (Semendeferi, Lu, Schenker, & Damasio, 2002). It is not the primary target for any single sensory system, but it receives information from all of them, each projecting to different parts of the prefrontal cortex. Neurons of the prefrontal cortex have large dendrites covered with more dendritic spines (see Figure 2.7) than dendrites in other cortical areas. Prefrontal neurons have up to 16 times as many dendritic spines as neurons in the primary visual cortex in the occipital lobe (Elston, 2000). The result is that the prefrontal cortex can integrate an enormous amount of information.

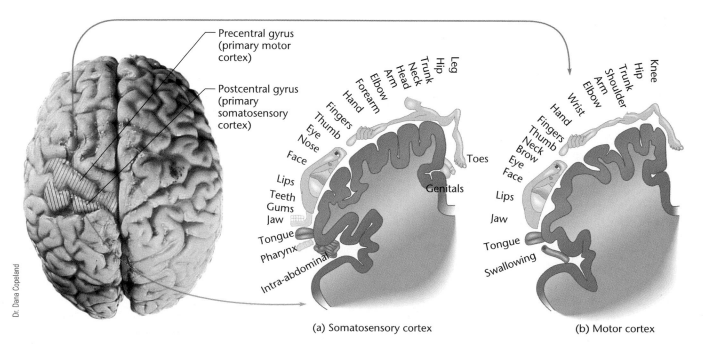

Figure 4.25 Approximate representation of sensory and motor information in the cortex
(a) Each location in the somatosensory cortex represents sensation from a different body part. **(b)** Each location in the motor cortex regulates movement of a different body part. *Source: Adapted from* The Cerebral Cortex of Man *by W. Penfield and T. Rasmussen. Copyright ©1950 Macmillan Publishing Co., Inc. Renewed 1978 by Theodore Rasmussen. Reprinted by permission.*

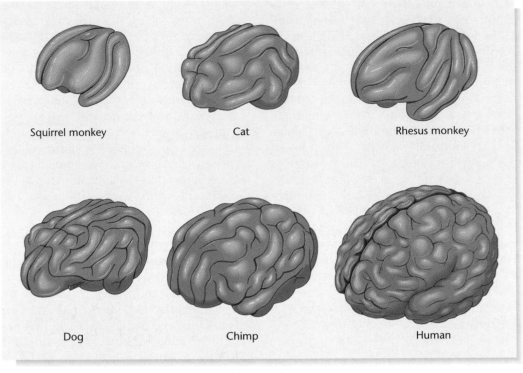

Figure 4.26 Species differences in prefrontal cortex
Note that the prefrontal cortex (blue area) constitutes a larger proportion of the human brain than of these other species. *Source: After* The Prefrontal Cortex *by J. M. Fuster, 1989. Copyright 1989 Ravan Press. Reprinted by permission.*

EXTENSIONS AND APPLICATIONS
The Rise and Fall of Prefrontal Lobotomies

The prefrontal cortex was the target of the infamous **prefrontal lobotomies,** surgical disconnection of the prefrontal cortex from the rest of the brain. The surgery consists of damaging the prefrontal cortex or cutting the connections between it and the rest of the cortex. The lobotomy trend was set in motion by a report that damaging the prefrontal cortex of laboratory primates had made them tamer without impairing their sensory or motor capacities in any striking way. A few physicians reasoned that the same operation might help people who suffered from severe and otherwise untreatable psychiatric disorders.

In the late 1940s and early 1950s, about 40,000 prefrontal lobotomies were performed in the United States (Shutts, 1982), many of them by Walter Freeman, a medical doctor untrained in surgery. His techniques were crude, even by the standards of the time, using such instruments as an electric drill and a metal pick. He performed many operations in his office or in other nonhospital sites. (Freeman carried his equipment in his car, which he called his "lobotomobile.")

Freeman and others became increasingly casual about deciding who should have a lobotomy. At first,

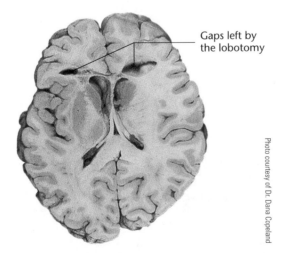

Gaps left by the lobotomy

Photo courtesy of Dr. Dana Copeland

A horizontal section of the brain of a person who had a prefrontal lobotomy many years earlier. The two holes in the frontal cortex are the visible results of the operation.

the technique was used only in cases of severe, untreatable schizophrenia. Lobotomy did calm some schizophrenic people, but the effects were usually disappointing. We now know that the frontal lobes of most schizophrenics are less active than normal; lobotomy was therefore damaging a structure that was already impaired. Later, Freeman lobotomized people with less serious disorders, including some whom we would consider normal by today's standards.

After effective drug therapies became available in the mid-1950s, physicians almost completely abandoned the use of lobotomy, and Freeman faded into the same obscurity as the procedure itself. Few lobotomies were performed after the mid-1950s (Lesse, 1984; Tippin & Henn, 1982).

Among the common consequences of prefrontal lobotomy were apathy, a loss of the ability to plan and take initiative, memory disorders, distractibility, and a loss of emotional expressions (Stuss & Benson, 1984). People with prefrontal damage lose their social inhibitions, ignoring the rules of polite, civilized conduct. They often act impulsively because they fail to calculate adequately the probable outcomes of their behaviors.

Modern View of Functions of the Prefrontal Cortex

Lobotomies added rather little to our understanding of the prefrontal cortex. Later researchers studying brain-damaged people and monkeys found that the prefrontal cortex is important for *working memory,* the ability to remember recent stimuli and events, such as where you parked the car today or what you were talking about before being interrupted (Goldman-Rakic, 1988). The prefrontal cortex is especially important for the **delayed-response task,** in which a stimulus appears briefly, and after some delay, the individual must respond to the remembered stimulus. The prefrontal cortex is much less important for remembering unchanging facts, such as that a green traffic light means "go."

Another description of prefrontal cortex function is that it controls behaviors that depend on the context (E. Miller, 2000). For example, if the phone rang, would you answer it? It depends: If you were at home, you probably would, but if you were at someone else's home, you probably would not. If you saw a good friend from a distance, would you shout out a greeting? Again it depends: At a public park, you probably would, but in a library or during a religious service, you would not. People with prefrontal cortex damage often fail to modify their behavior in relation to the context, so it becomes socially inappropriate or impulsive.

Stop & Check

1. If several neurons of the visual cortex all respond best when the retina is exposed to horizontal lines of light, then those neurons are probably located in the same _____.
2. Which lobe of the cerebral cortex includes the primary auditory cortex? The primary somatosensory cortex? The primary visual cortex? The primary motor cortex?
3. What are the functions of the prefrontal cortex?

Check your answers on page 103.

HOW DO THE PARTS WORK TOGETHER?

We have just considered a list of brain areas, each with its own function. And yet each of us has the sense of being a single person, not just a collection of many parts. The emergence of unified experience from separate parts is a more complicated issue than it might at first seem.

As an example, let's consider the role of the amygdala (see Figure 4.18 on p. 91). Almost any event that arouses fears or anxieties increases activity in the central nucleus of the amygdala, and damage to the central amygdala diminishes fears and anxieties. Rats and mice with this kind of damage walk right up to a cat (Berdoy, Webster, & Macdonald, 2000). People with amygdala damage cannot recognize other people's facial expressions of fear (Adolphs, Tranel, Damasio, & Damasio, 1994). They seem to have forgotten what fear even means. So can we say that activity in the central amygdala *is* fear?

This question is not fully answerable by present methods. If we isolated a group of cells from the central amygdala, kept them alive and healthy in cell culture, and then stimulated them, would they by themselves experience fear? We don't know; cells have no way to tell us! For the amygdala's activity to mean anything, it has to connect to the brain areas responsible for language, muscle actions, and autonomic activities. Ordinarily, it also combines or competes with brain areas that register other kinds of information. (For example, fear intensifies in the presence of pain but diminishes in the presence of a trusted companion.)

The relationship between the whole brain and its various parts is somewhat like that between a sentence and its component words: Each brain area has its own special function, just as each word does. If you damage any part of the brain or delete any word from a sentence, you lose something specific. However, a single brain area can't do much by itself, just as a word has a richer meaning in the context of a sentence than it has by itself.

Given that different brain areas have different functions, how are they put together? In particular, consider the sensory areas of the cerebral cortex. The primary visual area is in the occipital lobe, the primary auditory area is in the temporal lobe, and so forth. How does your brain combine visual, auditory, tactile, and other information into a perception of a unified object?

Consider a few examples of what we need to explain:

- When you hear a ventriloquist's voice while you watch the dummy's mouth move, the dummy appears to be talking. Even infants look at someone whose mouth is moving when they hear speech; somehow they know to attribute sound to moving instead of stationary lips. Somehow we know that sound comes from the object that is moving in synchrony with it.

- If you watch a film in which the picture is slightly out of synchrony with the sound, or a foreign-language film that was badly dubbed, you know that the sound does not match the picture.

- Here is a great demonstration, but you'll need a fake arm (available from almost any magic store). Position someone's arm parallel to a fake arm with a barrier between them so the person sees the fake arm and not the real one. Next, stroke simultaneously a finger of the fake hand and the corresponding finger of the real hand, as in Figure 4.27. Repeat this procedure several times with each finger and other parts of the hand. At each point, the person sees you touching the fake hand while feeling you touch the same part of the real hand. After a minute or two, he or she may say something like, "It feels as if the rubber hand is my own hand" (Botvinick & Cohen, 1998; Pavani, Spence, & Driver, 2000). Finally, vigorously pinch the fake hand and watch the response! This effect doesn't always work. It works best if the person stares at the fake hand and cannot see the real hand at all. But some people are more suggestible than others. When it works, the implication is that the person binds together the touch and visual sensations into a single experience.

The question of how the visual, auditory, and other areas of your brain influence one another to produce a combined perception of a single object is known as the **binding problem** or *large-scale integration* problem (Varela, Lachaux, Rodriguez, & Martinerie, 2001). In an earlier era, researchers thought

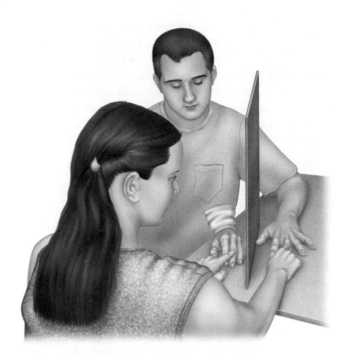

Figure 4.27 Demonstration of touch to "capture" vision
A person looks at a fake arm parallel to his or her actual arm, which is unseen. Someone simultaneously strokes corresponding parts of the fake and real hands. After a minute or two, the person begins to see the fake arm as his or her own. In response to seeing a sudden pinch on the fake arm, the person will startle.

that various kinds of sensory information converged onto what were known as the association areas of the cortex (Figure 4.28). Researchers had identified the primary sensory and motor areas because damage in those areas leads to blindness, hearing impairment, decreased muscle control, and so forth. But what was the function of the remaining areas, where damage caused no obvious loss of sensation or movement? Their guess was that those areas "associate," linking vision with hearing, hearing with touch, or current sensations with memories of previous experiences. This description fit a commonsense view of the mind: First the mind gets sensory information, then it thinks about it, and then it acts.

However, later research found that an "association area" performs advanced processing on a particular sensory system, such as vision or hearing; it does not *combine* vision with hearing. Few cells anywhere in the brain respond to more than one sensory modality. Evidently, the brain has no single site at which all kinds of information funnel to a central integrator—a "little person in the head." Apparently, the only places where all the information comes together are in the cells that prepare and plan for movements (Fuster, Bodner, & Kroger, 2000). The sensory systems that determine what a stimulus *is* attend to only one modality each, such as vision or hearing. The discovery of this fact called attention to the binding problem. Back when researchers believed that all input converged onto some association area, there was no question about how we perceived a connection between what we saw and what we heard. But if the different sensory sytems do not converge on one point, we are left with the problem of how to explain binding.

One hypothesis is that binding of a perception depends on precisely simultaneous activity in various brain areas (Eckhorn et al., 1988; Gray, König, Engel, & Singer, 1989). For example, examine Figure 4.29. These figures are called "Mooney" faces after the investigator who first used them. Most people see a face in parts **b** and **c** but nothing in **a** or **d**. Flip the page upside down and they see faces in **a** and **d** but not in **b** or **c**. Some people fail to see a face at first, even if they view it in the correct position. Researchers found that when people saw a face and *recognized* it as a face, neurons in several areas of their visual cortex produced rapid, synchronized activity known as gamma

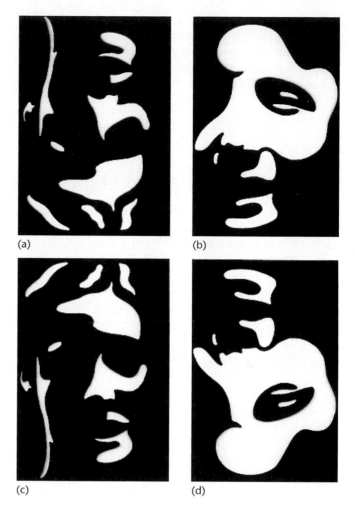

(a) (b)

(c) (d)

Figure 4.29 Four "Mooney" faces
Do you see any faces? Flip the page upside down and try again. Large populations of neurons in the visual cortex produce precisely synchronous activity when we recognize a pattern but not when we look at the same pattern and fail to recognize it.

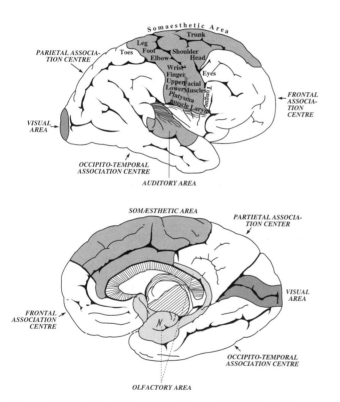

Figure 4.28 An old, somewhat misleading view of the cortex
Note the designation "association centre" in this illustration of the cortex in an old introductory psychology textbook (Hunter, 1923). Researchers today are more likely to regard those areas as "additional sensory areas." They do not associate one kind of sensory information with another.

waves, ranging in frequency at various times from 30 to 80 action potentials per second (Rodriguez et al., 1999). The gamma waves were synchronized to the millisecond in various brain areas. When people failed to recognize a face, the gamma waves did not emerge.

Similarly, when a cat responds to a sudden stimulus, such as a bird that it both sees and hears, it has closely synchronized activity patterns in the occipital, parietal, and frontal areas of its cortex (Roelfsema, Engel, König, & Singer, 1997). At other times, when the cat is not attending to a single object, the activities in various parts of its cortex are unsynchronized and out of phase.

What causes synchrony to develop? The process is hardly well understood, but apparently, synchrony among parts of the cortex distant from one another depends on coordination by the inferior (lower) parietal cortex and the pulvinar nucleus of the basal ganglia. Some people with damage in these areas have trouble binding the different aspects of perception. For example, if they see a display such as

they could report seeing a triangle and a square, one red and one green, but would be almost as likely to call the triangle green as the square (Robertson, Treisman, Friedman-Hill, & Grabowecky, 1997; Ward, Danziger, Owen, & Rafal, 2002). If they see a display such as

they would have trouble stating which circle was moving and which was not (Bernstein & Robertson, 1998). In short, they perceive shape, motion, and color, but they do not bind them into a single perception. Even people with intact brains sometimes make mistakes of this kind if the displays are flashed very briefly, presented in the periphery of vision, or presented while the person is distracted by something else (Holcombe & Cavanagh, 2001; Lehky, 2000). But someone with inferior parietal cortex damage makes such mistakes much more readily.

The results imply that exact synchrony of activity, probably organized by the parietal lobe, is necessary for perceptual binding. Note that the conclusion is *not* that the inferior parietal cortex itself has the sensation of a unified object; rather, it somehow facilitates the ability of the cortex as a whole to maintain synchrony.

However, even if researchers confirm that binding different sensations depends on synchronized neural activity, key questions remain. *Why* does synchrony of various brain areas produce binding? (If a robot has synchronous activity in two circuits, does it interpret the activity in those circuits as representing a single object? Not necessarily.) We still do not understand how a unified experience arises. If we can ever explain this process, we shall have taken a major step toward resolving the mind-brain problem considered in Chapter 1.

Stop & Check

4. What is meant by the "binding problem" and what is one hypothesis to explain it?
   Check your answer on page 103.

MODULE 4.3

In Closing: Functions of the Cerebral Cortex

The human cerebral cortex is so large that we easily slip into thinking of it as "the" brain, with all of the rest of the brain almost trivial. In fact, only mammals have a true cerebral cortex, and many mammals have only a small one. So subcortical areas by themselves can produce very complex behaviors, and a cerebral cortex by itself cannot do anything at all (because it would not be connected to any sense organs or muscles).

What, then, is the function of the cerebral cortex? The primary function seems to be one of elaborating sensory material. Even fish, which have no cerebral cortex, can see and hear and so forth, but they do not recognize and remember all the complex aspects of sensory stimuli that mammals do. In a television advertisement shown frequently in the late 1990s, one company said that it didn't make any products, but it made lots of products better. The same could be said for the cerebral cortex.

SUMMARY

1. The cerebral cortex has six laminae (layers) of neurons. A given lamina may be absent from certain parts of the cortex. The cortex is organized into columns of cells arranged perpendicular to the laminae. (p. 94)

2. Most cortical areas have sensory, associational, and motor functions; the degree of each varies. (p. 94)

3. The occipital lobe of the cortex is primarily responsible for vision. Damage to part of the occipital lobe leads to blindness in part of the visual field. (p. 95)

4. The parietal lobe processes body sensations. The postcentral gyrus contains four separate representations of the body. (p. 96)

5. The temporal lobe contributes to hearing and to complex aspects of vision. (p. 96)

6. The frontal lobe includes the precentral gyrus, which controls fine movements. It also includes the prefrontal cortex, which contributes to memories of current and recent stimuli and planning of movements. (p. 97)

7. Different brain areas have different functions, although no area can do anything by itself. (p. 99)

8. The binding problem is the question of how we connect activities in different brain areas, such as sights and sounds. The various brain areas do not all send their information to a single central processor. (p. 100)

9. One hypothesis to answer the binding problem is that the brain binds activity in different areas when those areas produce precisely synchronous waves of activity. Still, many questions remain. (p. 101)

ANSWERS TO *STOP AND CHECK* QUESTIONS

1. Column (p. 99)

2. Temporal lobe; parietal lobe; occipital lobe; frontal lobe (p. 99)

3. The prefrontal cortex is especially important for working memory (memory for what is currently happening) and for modifying behavior based on the context. (p. 99)

4. The binding problem is the question of how we combine activity in different brain areas to produce unified perception and coordinated behavior. The most prominent hypothesis is that the brain binds activity in different areas when those areas produce precisely synchronized waves of activity. (p. 102)

THOUGHT QUESTION

When monkeys with Klüver-Bucy syndrome pick up lighted matches and snakes, we do not know whether they are displaying an emotional deficit or an inability to identify the object. What kind of research method might help answer this question?

TERMS

anterior (p. 81)

anterior commissure (p. 94)

autonomic nervous system (p. 80)

basal ganglia (p. 90)

Bell-Magendie law (p. 82)

binding problem (p. 100)

brainstem (p. 85)

central canal (p. 92)

central nervous system (CNS) (p. 80)

central sulcus (p. 96)

cerebellum (p. 86)

cerebral cortex (p. 94)

cerebrospinal fluid (CSF) (p. 92)

column (pp. 82, 95)

computerized axial tomography (CT or CAT) (p. 74)

contralateral (p. 82)

coronal plane (p. 82)

corpus callosum (p. 94)

cranial nerve (p. 86)

delayed-response task (p. 99)

distal (p. 82)

dorsal (p. 80)

dorsal root ganglion (p. 82)

fissure (p. 82)

forebrain (p. 88)

frontal lobe (p. 97)

gamma waves (p. 101)

ganglion (pl.: ganglia) (p. 82)

gene-knockout approach (p. 75)

gray matter (p. 82)

gyrus (pl.: gyri) (p. 82)

hindbrain (p. 85)

hippocampus (p. 91)

horizontal plane (p. 82)

hypothalamus (p. 90)

inferior (p. 81)

inferior colliculus (p. 88)

ipsilateral (p. 82)

Klüver-Bucy syndrome (p. 97)

lamina (pl.: laminae) (pp. 82, 94)

lateral (p. 81)

limbic system (p. 88)

medial (p. 82)

medulla (p. 85)

meninges (p. 93)

midbrain (p. 88)

nerve (p. 82)

neuroanatomy (p. 73)

nucleus (p. 82)

nucleus basalis (p. 91)

occipital lobe (p. 95)

parasympathetic nervous system (p. 85)

parietal lobe (p. 96)

peripheral nervous system (PNS) (p. 80)

phrenology (p. 77)

pituitary gland (p. 90)

pons (p. 86)

postcentral gyrus (p. 96)

posterior (p. 81)

precentral gyrus (p. 97)

prefrontal cortex (p. 97)

prefrontal lobotomy (p. 98)

proximal (p. 82)

raphe system (p. 86)

regional cerebral blood flow (rCBF) (p. 76)

reticular formation (p. 86)

sagittal plane (p. 82)

somatic nervous system (p. 80)

spinal cord (p. 82)

substantia nigra (p. 88)

sulcus (pl.: sulci) (p. 82)

superior (p. 81)

superior colliculus (p. 88)

sympathetic nervous system (p. 83)

tectum (p. 88)

tegmentum (p. 88)

temporal lobe (p. 96)

thalamus (p. 88)

tract (p. 82)

ventral (p. 80)

ventricle (p. 92)

white matter (p. 83)

 ## SUGGESTIONS FOR FURTHER READING

Hanaway, J., Woolsey, T. A., Gado, M. H., & Roberts, M. P., Jr. (1998). *The brain atlas.* Bethesda, MD: Fitzgerald Science Press. Outstanding illustrations of all parts of the human brain.

Klawans, H. L. (1988). *Toscanini's fumble and other tales of clinical neurology.* Chicago: Contemporary Books. Fascinating description of human brain damage and other neurological conditions.

WEB SITES TO EXPLORE

You can go to the Biological Psychology Study Center and click these links. While there, you can also check for suggested articles available on InfoTrac College Edition. The Biological Psychology Internet address is:

http://psychology.wadsworth.com/ kalatbiopsych8e

Brain Imaging in Psychiatry
www.musc.edu/psychiatry/fnrd/primer_index.htm

The Whole Brain Atlas (neuroanatomy)
http://www.med.harvard.edu/AANLIB/home.html

Comparative Brain Anatomy
www.brainmuseum.org/sections/index.html

 ## CD-ROM: EXPLORING BIOLOGICAL PSYCHOLOGY

Virtual Reality Head Planes (virtual reality)

Planes Puzzle (drag & drop)

3D Virtual Brain (virtual reality)

Left Hemisphere Function #1 (roll over with text pop-ups)

Cortex Puzzle (drag & drop)

Sagittal Section: Right Hemisphere #1 (roll over with text pop-ups)

Sagittal Section: Right Hemisphere #2 (roll over with text pop-ups)

Sagittal Section: Right Hemisphere #3 (roll over with text pop-ups)

Brain Puzzle (drag & drop)

The Motor Cortex (animation)

The Sensory Cortex (animation)

Neuroimaging (video)

Illustration of Binding (try it yourself)

Critical Thinking (essay questions)

Chapter Quiz (multiple choice questions)

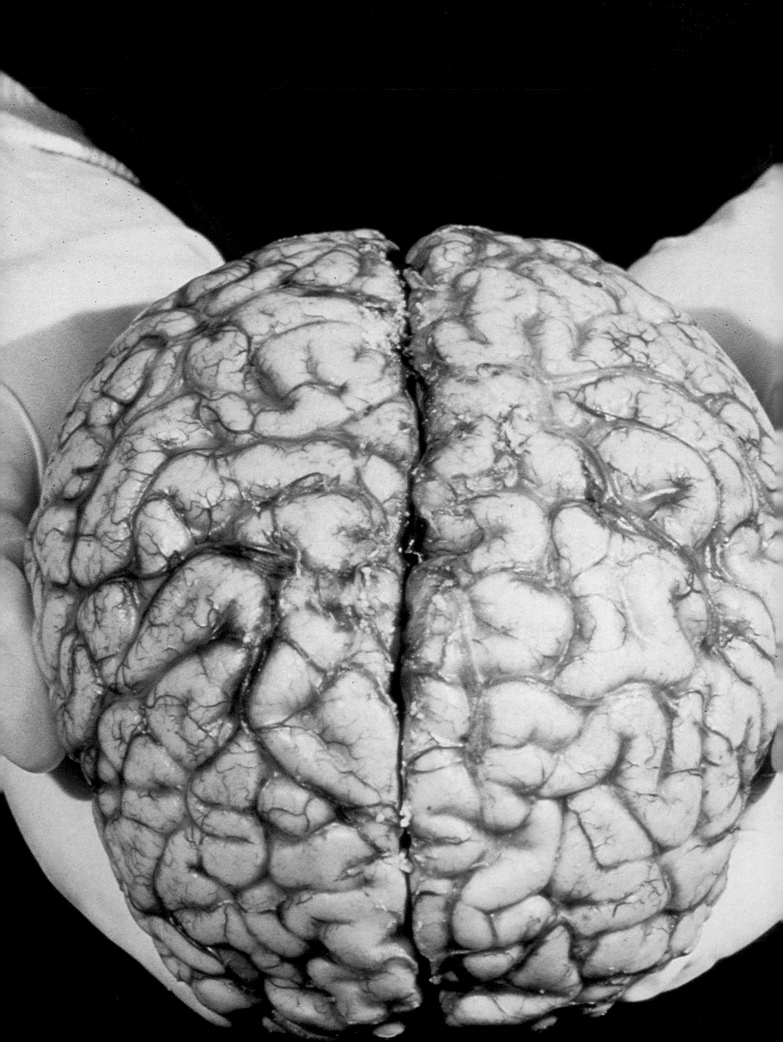

Development and Plasticity of the Brain

Main Ideas

1. The nervous system at first forms far more neurons than it needs and then eliminates those that do not establish suitable connections or receive sufficient input. It also forms more synapses than will survive and discards the less active ones.

2. Axons form connections by a combination of chemical attraction and the effects of experience. Experiences, especially early in life, can alter brain anatomy within limits.

3. The human brain can be damaged by a sharp blow, an interruption of blood flow, and several other types of injury.

4. Many mechanisms contribute to recovery from brain damage, including restoration of undamaged neurons to full activity, regrowth of axons, readjustment of surviving synapses, and behavioral adjustments.

"**S**ome assembly required." Have you ever bought a package with those ominous words? Sometimes all you have to do is attach a few parts. But sometimes you face page after page of incomprehensible instructions. I remember putting together my daughter's bicycle and wondering how something that looked so simple could be so complicated.

The human nervous system requires an enormous amount of assembly, and the instructions are different from those for a bicycle. Instead of, "Put this piece here and that piece there," the instructions are, "Put these axons here and those dendrites there, and then wait to see what happens. Keep the connections that work the best, throw away the others, and then make new ones similar to the ones that you kept. Later, if those connections aren't working well, discard them and try new ones."

Therefore, we say that the brain's anatomy is *plastic;* it is constantly changing, within limits. Major changes in brain anatomy occur during early development and continue as a result of learning and in response to brain damage.

Opposite:
Different parts of the human brain grow and mature at different ages, but all parts continue developing in microscopic ways throughout life. *Source: ©Geoff Tompkinson/SPL/Photo Researchers*

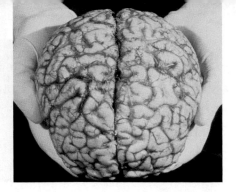

MODULE 5.1

Development of the Brain

As a college student, you can probably perform many feats that you could not have done a few years ago: solve calculus problems, read a foreign language, or convincingly pretend that you understand James Joyce's novels. Have you developed these new skills because your brain has grown? No. Many neurons have changed in microscopic ways, but your brain hasn't actually grown.

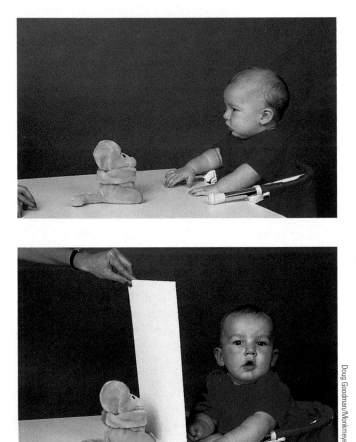

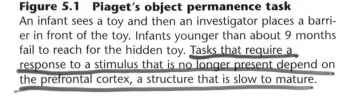

Figure 5.1 Piaget's object permanence task
An infant sees a toy and then an investigator places a barrier in front of the toy. Infants younger than about 9 months fail to reach for the hidden toy. Tasks that require a response to a stimulus that is no longer present depend on the prefrontal cortex, a structure that is slow to mature.

Now think of all the things that 1- or 2-year-old children can do that they could not do at birth. Have *they* developed these new skills because of brain growth? To a large extent, yes. Consider, for example, Jean Piaget's object permanence task, in which an observer shows a toy to an infant and then places it behind a barrier. Generally, a child younger than 9 months does not reach around the barrier to retrieve the toy (Figure 5.1). Why not? The biological explanation is that the prefrontal cortex is necessary for responding to a signal that appears and then disappears, and the synapses of the prefrontal cortex develop massively between the ages of 7 and 12 months (Goldman-Rakic, 1987). The ability to solve the object permanence task requires new neurons and synapses.

Behavioral development does not depend entirely on brain growth, of course; it also requires microscopic readjustments in much the same way as an adult brain does. Furthermore, as we shall see, many processes of brain development depend on experience in complex ways that blur the distinction between learning and maturation. In this module, we consider three major issues: the production of neurons, the growth of axons, and fine-tuning by experience.

GROWTH AND DIFFERENTIATION OF THE VERTEBRATE BRAIN

The human central nervous system begins to form when the embryo is about 2 weeks old. The dorsal surface thickens, and then long thin lips rise, curl, and merge, forming a neural tube surrounding a fluid-filled cavity (Figure 5.2). As the tube sinks under the surface of the skin, the forward end enlarges and differentiates into the hindbrain, midbrain, and forebrain (Figure 5.3); the rest becomes the spinal cord. The fluid-filled cavity within the neural tube becomes the central canal of the spinal cord and the four ventricles of the brain; the fluid is the cerebrospinal fluid (CSF). At birth, the average human brain weighs about 350 grams. At the end of the first year, the brain weighs

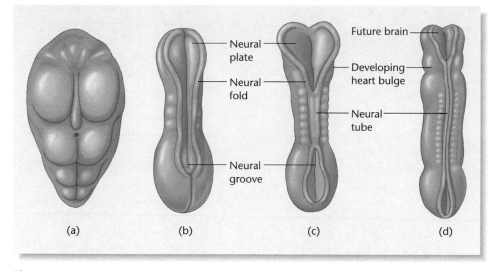

Figure 5.2 Early development of the human central nervous system
The brain and spinal cord begin as folding lips surrounding a fluid-filled canal. The stages shown occur at approximately age 2 to 3 weeks.

1000 g, not much less than the adult weight of 1200 to 1400 g. The developmental process is about the same in all vertebrates, although it varies in speed and duration.

Growth and Development of Neurons

The development of the nervous system naturally includes the production and alteration of neurons. Neuroscientists distinguish these processes in the development of neurons: proliferation, migration, differentiation, myelination, and synaptogenesis.

Proliferation is the production of new cells. Early in development, cells lining the ventricles of the brain divide. Some cells remain where they are (as *stem cells*), continuing to divide and redivide. Others become primitive neurons and glia that migrate (move) toward their eventual destinations in the brain. Different kinds of neurons originate in different locations at different times, and each must migrate substantial distances, following specific chemical paths, to reach its final destination (Marín & Rubenstein, 2001). Some move radially from the inside of the brain to the outside; some move tangentially along the surface of the brain; and some move tangentially and then radially (Nadarajah & Parnavelas, 2002). Any gene or poison that interferes with proliferation or migration can produce mental retardation (Berger-Sweeney & Hohmann, 1997).

At first, a primitive neuron looks like any other cell. Gradually, the neuron differentiates, forming the axon and dendrites that provide its distinctive shape. The axon grows before the dendrites; in fact, it grows while the neuron is migrating. (Some neurons trail an axon growing behind them like a tail.) When the neuron reaches its final location, dendrites begin to form, slowly at first. Most dendritic growth occurs later, when incoming axons are due to arrive.

Neurons in different parts of the brain differ from one another in their shapes and chemical components. When and how does a neuron "decide" which kind of neuron it is going to be? Evidently, it is not a sudden all-or-none decision. In some cases, immature neurons experimentally transplanted from one part of the developing cortex to another develop the properties characteristic of their new location (S. K. McConnell, 1992). However, immature neurons transplanted at a slightly later stage develop some new properties while retaining some old ones (Cohen-Tannoudji, Babinet, & Wassef, 1994). The result resembles the speech of immigrant children: Those who enter a country when very young master the correct pronunciation, whereas slightly older children retain an accent.

After vertebrate axons form, many of them myelinate, as glia cells produce the insulating fatty sheaths that increase transmission speed. In humans, myelin forms first in the spinal cord and then in the hindbrain, midbrain, and forebrain. Unlike the rapid proliferation and migration of neurons, myelination continues gradually for many years, even decades, and perhaps even throughout life (Benes, Turtle, Khan, & Farol, 1994).

The final process, synaptogenesis, or the formation of synapses, continues throughout life. Curiously, cholesterol—a chemical we often think of as something to avoid—is essential for synapse formation (Mauch et al., 2001). As is the case for migration, synaptogenesis fails if the chemical environment is not quite right.

1. What are proliferation and migration of neurons?
2. If an immature neuron is transplanted from one location to another, does it maintain its original properties or adopt those of its new location?

Check your answers on page 124.

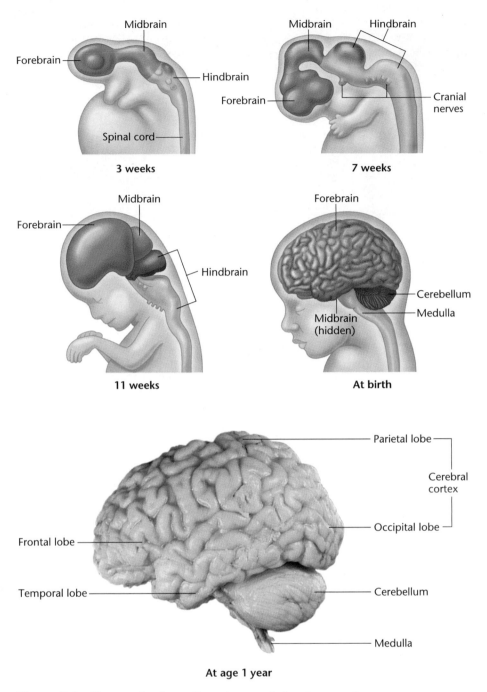

Figure 5.3 Human brain at five stages of development
The brain already shows an adult structure at birth, although it continues to grow during the first year or so. *Source: Dana Copeland*

Determinants of Neuron Survival

Getting just the right number of neurons for each area of the nervous system is more complicated than it might seem. To be of any use, each neuron must receive axons from the right source and send its own axons to a cell in the right area. The various areas do not all develop at the same time, so in many cases, the neurons in an area develop

before any incoming axons have arrived and before any receptive sites are available for its own axons. If we examine a healthy adult nervous system, we find no leftover neurons that failed to make appropriate connections. How does the nervous system get the numbers to come out right?

Consider a specific example. The sympathetic nervous system sends axons to muscles and glands; each ganglion has exactly enough neurons to supply the muscles and glands in its area. Long ago, one explanation was that the muscles sent chemical messages to the sympathetic ganglion to tell it how many neurons to form. Rita Levi-Montalcini was largely responsible for disconfirming this hypothesis. If you were going to plan life circumstances to encourage scientific success, you certainly would not have chosen anything like her early life. She was a young Italian Jewish woman during the Nazi era. World War II was destroying the Italian economy, and almost no one encouraged women to pursue scientific or medical careers. Furthermore, the research projects assigned to her as a young medical student were virtually impossible, as she described in her autobiography (Levi-Montalcini, 1988). Nevertheless, she developed a love for research and eventually discovered that the muscles do not determine how many axons form; they determine how many survive.

When a neuron of the sympathetic nervous system forms a synapse onto an organ muscle, the muscle delivers a protein called nerve growth factor (NGF) that promotes the survival and growth of the axon (Levi-Montalcini, 1987). An axon that does not receive enough NGF degenerates, and its cell body dies. Each neuron starts life with a "suicide program": If its axon does not make contact with an appropriate postsynaptic cell by a certain age, the neuron kills itself through a process called apoptosis, a programmed mechanism of cell death. (Apoptosis is distinct from *necrosis,* which is death caused by an injury or a toxic substance.) NGF cancels the program for apoptosis; it is the postsynaptic cell's way of telling the incoming axon, "I'll be your partner. Don't kill yourself."

Nerve growth factor is a neurotrophin, a chemical that promotes the survival and activity of neurons. (*Trophin* is derived from a Greek word for "nourishment.") In addition to NGF, the nervous system responds to *brain-derived neurotrophic factor* (BDNF) and several other neurotrophins (Airaksinen & Saarma, 2002). The neurotrophins act in several ways. Early in development, axons grow toward a source of neurotrophins, and those that make successful contacts receive enough neurotrophins to survive (K. L. Tucker, Meyer, & Barde, 2001). At later ages, new experiences cause neurons to secrete neurotrophins that increase the branching of incoming axons and thereby facilitate the mechanisms that store memories (Kesslak, So, Choi, Cotman, & Gomez-Pinilla, 1998; Kolb, Gorny, Côté, Ribeiro-da-Silva, & Cuello, 1997). Finally, neurotrophins increase regrowth of axons after brain damage (Ramer, Priestley, & McMahon, 2000).

Not only the sympathetic ganglia but all areas of the developing nervous system initially make far more neurons than will survive into adulthood. Each brain area has a period of massive cell death, becoming littered with dead and dying cells (Figure 5.4). This loss of cells does not indicate that something is wrong; it is a natural part of development (Finlay & Pallas, 1989). In fact, the loss of cells in a particular brain area can indicate that important maturational changes are occurring. For example, parts of the prefrontal cortex mature during the late teens and early 20s for humans. Some aspects of memory dependent on those areas improve at that time (Lewis, 1997), and MRI scans (see Methods 5.1) show increased activity (Sowell, Thompson, Holmes, Jernigan, & Toga, 1999). During the teenage years, the prefrontal cortex and parts of the parietal and temporal cortex show increased growth of white matter (Sowell, Thompson, Tessner, & Toga, 2001) but a *decrease* in the number of neurons (Giedd et al., 1999). Evidently, maturation of appropriate cells and connections is linked to the simultaneous loss of less successful ones.

For a neuron to resist apoptosis and survive, it needs to attach its axon to an appropriate target and receive neurotrophins, and it also needs to receive

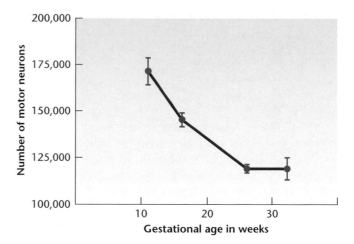

Figure 5.4 Cell loss during development of the nervous system
The graph shows the number of motor neurons in the ventral spinal cord of human fetuses. Note that the number of motor neurons is highest at 11 weeks and drops steadily until about 25 weeks, the age when motor neuron axons make synapses with muscles. Axons that fail to make synapses die. *Source: From "Motoneuronal Death in the Human Fetus," by N. G. Forger and S. M. Breedlove, Journal of Comparative Neurology, 264, p. 118–122. Copyright ©1987 Alan R. Liss, Inc. Reprinted by permission of N. G. Forger.*

adequate incoming stimulation. In one study, researchers examined mice with a genetic defect that prevented all release of neurotransmitters. The brains assembled normal anatomies early in embryological development; however, shortly after that assembly, the neurons started dying in abundance (Verhage et al., 2000). When neurons release neurotransmitters, they simultaneously release neurotrophins, and neurons that fail to release the neurotransmitters withhold the neurotrophins as well (Poo, 2001). In short, survival of a neuron depends on receiving neurotrophins from both incoming axons and the point where its own axon contacts another cell.

Why does the developing CNS produce so many extra neurons? One possibility is that the excess allows for error correction. Even if some axons fail to reach appropriate targets, enough others will. However, researchers find that axon growth is impressively accurate; nearly all axons grow to almost exactly their correct targets (Kozloski, Hamzei-Sichani, & Yuste, 2001). A more likely explanation is that the extra neurons enable the CNS to match the number of incoming axons to the number of receiving cells. For example, when the motor neuron axons begin growing from the spinal cord toward the leg muscles, there is no way to predict exactly how many muscle fibers the leg will have. The spinal cord produces an abundance of neurons at the start and later discards the excess.

[1]Apoptosis is based on the root word *ptosis,* pronounced "TOE-sis," and therefore, some scholars insist that the second *p* in *apoptosis* should be silent. Others argue that *helicopter* is also derived from a root with a silent *p (pteron),* but we pronounce the *p* in *helicopter,* so we should also pronounce the *p* in *apoptosis.* Be prepared to hear and understand either pronunciation.

MRI Scans

One method of examining the anatomy of a living brain is magnetic resonance imaging (MRI), also known as nuclear magnetic resonance (NMR). MRI produces images with a high degree of resolution without exposing the brain to radiation (Warach, 1995). This method is based on the fact that any atom with an odd-numbered atomic weight, such as hydrogen, has an axis of rotation. An MRI device applies a powerful magnetic field (about 25,000 times the magnetic field of the earth), thereby aligning all the axes of rotation, which a brief radio frequency field can then tilt. When the radio frequency field is turned off, the atomic nuclei release electromagnetic energy as they relax and return to their original axis. By measuring that energy, MRI devices form an image of the brain, such as the one in Figure 5.5. Most MRI scans are set to detect the energy released by the hydrogen atoms in water molecules, which are the most abundant molecules in the body. An MRI image can reveal structural defects such as enlargements or shrinkages of various brain areas. One drawback is that the person must lie with the head motionless in a very confining, noisy apparatus. The procedure is not suitable for fidgety people or those who fear enclosed places.

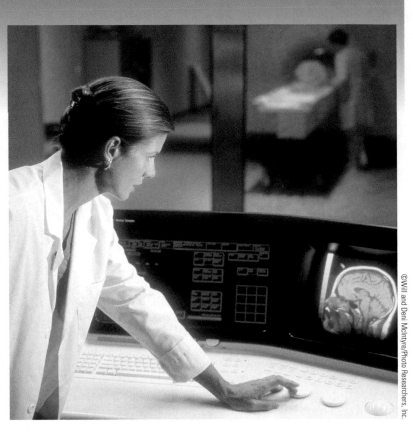

©Will and Deni McIntyre/Photo Researchers, Inc.

Figure 5.5 A view of a living brain generated by magnetic resonance imaging
Any atom with an odd-numbered atomic weight, such as hydrogen, has an inherent rotation. An outside magnetic field can align the axes of rotation. A radio frequency field can then make all these atoms move like tiny gyros. When the radio frequency field is turned off, the atomic nuclei relax, releasing electromagnetic energy. By measuring that energy, we can obtain an image of a structure such as the brain without damaging it.

Stop & Check

3. What process enables the nervous system to have only as many axons as necessary to provide input to the target neurons?

4. What class of chemicals prevents apoptosis?

5. At what age does a person have the greatest number of neurons—as an embryo, newborn, child, adolescent, or adult?

Check your answers on page 124.

PATHFINDING BY AXONS

If you asked someone to run a cable from your desk to another desk in the same room, you wouldn't have to give detailed directions. But imagine asking someone to run a cable from your desk to a friend's thousands of miles away. You would have to give detailed instructions about how to get to the right city, the right building, and eventually the right desk. The developing nervous system faces a similar challenge because it sends some of its axons over enormous distances. How do they find their way?

Chemical Pathfinding by Axons

A famous biologist, Paul Weiss (1924), conducted an experiment in which he grafted an extra leg to a salamander and then waited for axons to grow into it. (Such an experiment could never work with a mammal. Salamanders and other amphibians can regenerate parts of their bodies that mammals cannot. They also generate new axon branches to a grafted-on limb.) After the axons reached the muscles, the extra leg moved in perfect synchrony with the normal leg next to it.

Weiss dismissed as unbelievable the idea that each axon had developed a branch that found its way to exactly the correct muscle in the extra limb. He suggested instead that the nerves attached to muscles at random and then sent a variety of messages, each one tuned to a different muscle. In other words, it did not matter which axon was attached to which muscle. The muscles were like radios, each tuned to a different station: Each muscle received many signals but responded to only one.

Specificity of Axon Connections

Weiss was mistaken. Later evidence supported the interpretation he had rejected: The salamander's extra leg moved in synchrony with its neighbor because each axon had found exactly the correct muscle.

Since the time of Weiss's work, most of the research on axon growth has dealt with how sensory axons find their way to the correct targets in the brain. (The issues are the same as those for axons finding their way to muscles.) In one study, Roger Sperry, a former student of Weiss, cut the optic nerves of some newts. The damaged optic nerve grew back and connected with the *tectum,* which is the main visual area of amphibians, as well as of fish, reptiles, and birds (Figure 5.6). Sperry found that when the new synapses formed, the newt regained normal vision.

Then Sperry (1943) repeated the experiment, but this time, after he cut the optic nerve, he rotated the eye by 180°. When the axons grew back to the tectum, which targets would they contact? Sperry found that the axons from what had originally been the dorsal portion of the retina (which was now ventral) grew back to the area responsible for vision in the dorsal retina. Axons from what had once been the ventral retina (now dorsal) also grew back to their original targets. The newt now saw the world upside down and backward, responding to stimuli in the sky as if they were on the ground and to stimuli on the left as if they were on the right (Figure 5.7). Each axon regenerated to the area of the tectum where it had originally been, presumably by following a chemical trail.

Chemical Gradients

The next question was: How specific a target does an axon have? Must an axon from the retina find the tectal cell with exactly the right chemical marker on its

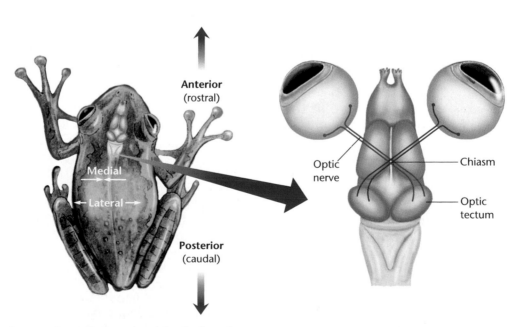

Figure 5.6 Connections from eye to brain in a frog
The optic tectum is a large structure in fish, amphibians, reptiles, and birds. Its location corresponds to the midbrain of mammals, but its function is more elaborate, analogous to what the cerebral cortex does in mammals. *Note:* Connections from eye to brain are different in humans, as described in Chapter 14. *Source: After Romer, 1962*

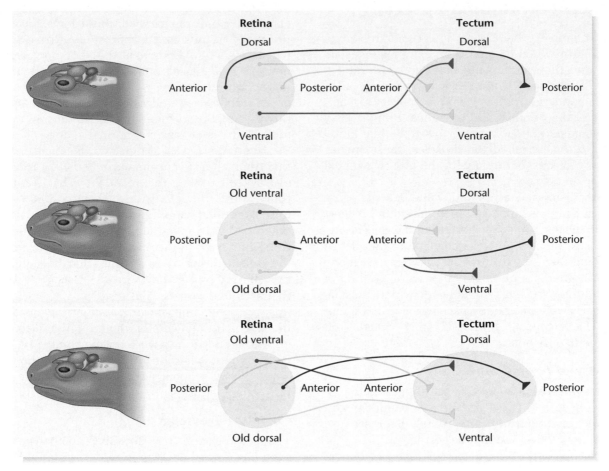

Figure 5.7 Summary of Sperry's experiment on nerve connections in newts
After he cut the optic nerve and inverted the eye, the optic nerve axons grew back to their original targets, not to the targets corresponding to the eye's current position.

surface, like a key finding the right lock? Does the body have to synthesize a separate chemical marker for each of the billions of axons in the nervous system?

No. The current estimate is that humans have only about 30,000 genes total—far too few to mark each neuron individually, even if we did not have to save any genes for any other purpose. A growing axon follows a path of cell-surface molecules, attracted by some chemicals and repelled by others, in a process that steers the axon in the correct direction (Yu & Bargmann, 2001). Some axons follow a trail based on one attractive chemical until they reach an intermediate location, where they become insensitive to that chemical and then follow a different attractant to their final target (Shirasaki, Katsumata, & Murakami, 1998; H. Wang & Tessier-Lavigne, 1999). Then axons sort themselves over the surface of the target area by following a gradient of chemicals. For

example, one chemical in the amphibian tectum is the protein TOP_{DV} (TOP for *top*ography; DV for *d*orso*v*entral). This protein is 30 times more concentrated in the axons of the dorsal retina than of the ventral retina and 10 times more concentrated in the ventral tectum than in the dorsal tectum. As axons from the retina grow toward the tectum, the retinal axons with the greatest concentration of TOP_{DV} connect to the tectal cells with the highest concentration of that chemical; the axons with the lowest concentration connect to the tectal cells with the lowest concentration. A similar gradient of another protein aligns the axons along the anterior–posterior axis (J. R. Sanes, 1993) (Figure 5.8). (By analogy, you could think of men lining up from tallest to shortest, pairing with women who lined up from tallest to shortest, so the tallest man paired with the tallest woman and so forth.)

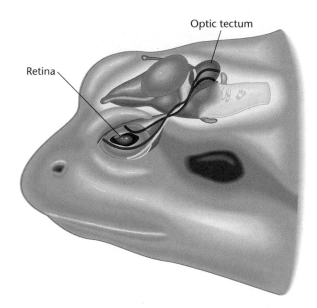

Optic tectum

Retina

Figure 5.8 Retinal axons match up with neurons in the tectum by following two gradients

The protein TOP_{DV} is concentrated mostly in the dorsal retina and the ventral tectum. Axons rich in TOP_{DV} attach to tectal neurons that are also rich in that chemical. Similarly, a second protein directs axons from the posterior retina to the rostral portion of the tectum.

Stop & Check

6. What was Sperry's evidence that axons grow to a specific target presumably by following a chemical gradient instead of attaching at random?

7. If all cells in the tectum of an amphibian produced the same amount of TOP_{DV}, what would be the effect on the attachment of axons?

Check your answers on page 124.

Competition Among Axons as a General Principle

As one might guess from the experiments just described, when axons initially reach their targets, each one forms synapses onto several cells in approximately the correct location, and each target cell receives synapses from a large number of axons. Figure 5.9 summarizes the results: At first, axons make tentative connections with many postsynaptic cells; gradually, the postsynaptic cells strengthen some and reject others.

To some theorists, these results suggest a general principle called **neural Darwinism** (Edelman, 1987). In Darwinian evolution, gene mutations and reassortments produce individuals with variations in their appearance and actions; natural selection favors some variations and weeds out the rest. Similarly, in the development of the nervous system, we start with more neurons and synapses than we keep. Synapses form haphazardly, and then a selection process keeps some and rejects others. In this manner, the most successful axons and combinations survive; the others fail to sustain active synapses.

The principle of competition among axons is an important one, although we should use the analogy with Darwinian evolution cautiously. Mutations in the genes are random events, but neurotrophins steer new axonal branches and synapses in the right direction.

FINE-TUNING BY EXPERIENCE

The genetic instructions for assembling your nervous system are only approximate. Because of the unpredictability of life, our brains have evolved the ability to redesign themselves (within limits) in response to our experience (Shatz, 1992). The plasticity of brain anatomy enables it to custom design an adaptation to our individual activities.

Effects of Experience on Dendritic Branching

Let's start with a simple example. If you live in a complex and challenging environment, you need an elaborate nervous system. Ordinarily, a laboratory rat lives by itself in simple and unchallenging surroundings—a small gray cage. Imagine by contrast 10 or so rats living together in a larger cage with a few little pieces of junk to explore or play with. Researchers sometimes call this an enriched environment, but it is enriched only in contrast to the experience of a typical rat laboratory.

A rat in the more stimulating cage develops a thicker cortex, more dendritic branching, and improved performance on many tests of learning (Greenough, 1975; Rosenzweig & Bennett, 1996). A great deal of this benefit is due to exercise; rats in the group cage move around much more. Simply using a running wheel yields substantial benefits to the rat's brain, even without any other enriched experiences (van Praag, Kempermann, & Gage, 1999). Exercise releases neurotrophins that increase the development of neurons and synapses, and it doesn't even have to be strenuous (Trejo, Carro, & Torres-Alemán, 2001; van Praag, Kempermann, & Gage, 2000). The advice to exercise for your brain's sake is particularly important for older people.

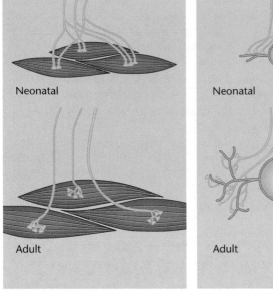

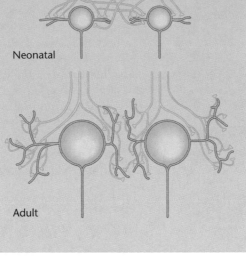

(a) Muscle fibers
(b) Sympathetic ganglion cells

Figure 5.9   Development by elimination of synapses
(**a**) Early in development, each muscle fiber receives synapses from branches of several motor axons. The muscle fiber gradually strengthens its synapse with one axon and rejects the others. (However, an axon can form synapses with many muscle fibers.) (**b**) Early in development, neurons in the ganglia of the sympathetic nervous system receive synapses from many axons. Later, each cell rejects the incoming axons from some neurons and accepts the axons from others. Although the cell as a whole may accept axons from numerous different neurons, each dendrite typically forms lasting synapses with only one axon. That axon may, however, form a great many branches and therefore a great many synapses onto that dendrite. *Source: From "Elimination of Synapses in the Developing Nervous System," by D. Purves and J. W. Lichtman, 1980, Science, 210, p. 153–157. Copyright ©1980 by the AAAs. Reprinted by permission.*

(a)   (b)

Figure 5.10   Effect of a stimulating environment on neuronal branching
(**a**) A jewel fish reared in isolation develops neurons with fewer branches. (**b**) A fish reared with others has more neuronal branches.

An enriched environment enhances sprouting of axons and dendrites in a wide variety of other species (Coss, Brandon, & Globus, 1980) (Figure 5.10). Humans with extensive academic education tend to have longer and more widely branched dendrites than people with less formal education (Jacobs, Schall, & Scheibel, 1993). Two explanations are likely: Learning does increase dendritic branching, but it is also probable that people who already have wider dendrites succeed more in school and therefore stay longer.

Generation of New Neurons

Can the adult vertebrate brain generate any new neurons? The traditional belief, dating back to the work of Cajal in the late 1800s, was that vertebrate brains formed all their neurons during embryological development or during infancy at the latest. Beyond that point, the brain could only lose neurons, never gain. Gradually, researchers found exceptions.

The first was the olfactory receptors which, because they are exposed to the outside world and its toxic chemicals, have a half-life of only 90 days. A population of neurons in the nose remains immature throughout life. Periodically, these neurons divide; one cell remains immature and the other develops to replace a dying olfactory receptor, growing its axon back to the appropriate site in the brain (Gogos, Osborne, Nemes, Mendelsohn, & Axel, 2000; Graziadei & deHan, 1973). Later researchers also found a population of undifferentiated cells, called **stem cells,** in the interior of the brain that sometimes generate "daughter" cells that migrate to the olfactory bulb and transform into glia cells or neurons (Gage, 2000).

Then researchers found evidence of new neuron formation in other brain areas. For example, songbirds have an area in their brain necessary for singing, and in this area, they have a steady replacement of a few kinds of neurons. Old neurons die and new ones take their place (Nottebohm, 2002). The black-capped chickadee, a small nonmigratory North American bird, hides seeds during the late summer and early fall and then finds them during the winter. It grows new neurons in its hippocampus (a brain area important for spatial memory) during the late summer (Smulders,

Shiflett, Sperling, & deVoogd, 2000). Stem cells can also differentiate into new neurons in the adult hippocampus of mammals (Song, Stevens, & Gage, 2002; van Praag et al., 2002).

Development of new neurons in humans and monkeys has been reported but remains controversial (Eriksson et al., 1998; Gould, Reeves, Graziano, & Gross, 1999). It has also been reported that the production of new neurons increases when older cortical cells are dying (Magavi, Leavitt, & Macklis, 2000). However, it is possible that some of what were reported to be new neurons might have been new glia or epithelial cells (Rakic, 2002). In addition, the usual method of demonstrating the presence of new neurons is to inject radioactively labeled chemicals that might get incorporated into the DNA of newly formed cells. Then researchers examine neurons and look for ra-

dioactively labeled DNA. The problem is that this method sometimes confuses new cells with cells undergoing DNA repair (Rakic, 2002). At this point, researchers are not in agreement about the formation of new neurons in adult primates.

Effects of Experience on Human Brain Structures

Cognitive psychologists who have studied experts in various fields have demonstrated that extensively practicing a particular skill, such as playing chess or working crossword puzzles, makes a person ever more adept at that skill, though not necessarily at anything else (Ericsson & Charness, 1994). Presumably, developing expertise at anything changes the brain in ways that im-

---

METHODS 5.2
Magnetoencephalography (MEG)

A **magnetoencephalograph (MEG)** measures the faint magnetic fields generated by brain activity **(Hari, 1994).** Magnetic detectors on the surface of the skull record the net activity over a fairly large area, so an MEG is imprecise in locating activity. However, it has excellent temporal resolution, showing changes from one millisecond to another.

For example, Figure 5.11 shows an MEG record comparing the responses of many brain areas to a brief tone heard in the right ear. The diagram represents a human head as viewed from above, with the nose at the top (Hari, 1994). Using MEG with more complicated tasks, such as naming a picture, researchers can identify the brain location that responds most quickly, the areas that respond slightly later, those that respond still later, and so on. In such a manner, researchers can trace a wave of brain activity from its origin in one area to its processing in another (Salmelin, Hari, Lounasmaa, & Sams, 1994).

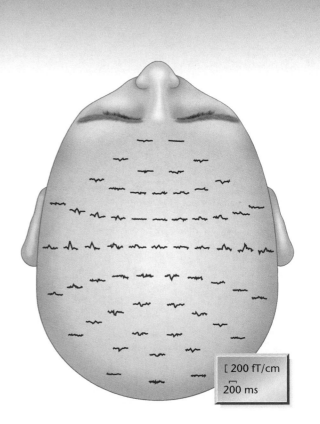

Figure 5.11 A result of magnoencephalography, showing responses to a tone in the right ear
The nose is at the top. For each spot on the diagram, the display shows the changing response over a few hundred ms following the tone. (Note calibration at lower right.) The tone evoked responses in many areas, with the largest responses in the temporal cortex, especially on the left side. *Source: Reprinted from* Neuroscience: From the Molecular to the Cognitive, *by R. Hari, 1994, p. 165, with kind permission from Elsevier Science–NL, Sara Burgerhartstraat 25, 1055 KV Amsterdam, The Netherlands.*

[200 fT/cm

200 ms

prove the required abilities. In a few cases, researchers have identified the brain changes associated with particular kinds of expertise.

One study used magnetoencephalography (MEG; see Methods 5.2) to record responses of the auditory cortex to pure tones. The responses in professional musicians were about twice as large as those for nonmusicians. Then an MRI examination of their brains found that one area of the temporal cortex in the right hemisphere was about 30% larger in the professional musicians (Schneider et al., 2002). Of course, these data do not tell us whether they became professional musicians because they were born with a brain specialization for music or whether extensive early practice encouraged certain brain areas to grow.

A related study used MEG to compare the postcentral gyrus of nonmusicians to people who had extensive experience in playing stringed instruments, in most cases, the violin. As you may recall from Chapter 4, the postcentral gyrus is the primary somatosensory cortex, and each area along the gyrus responds to a particular area of the body. String players use the left hand to finger the strings, and the MEG results showed an expanded representation of the fingers of the left hand in the postcentral gyrus (Elbert, Pantev, Wienbruch, Rockstroh, & Taub, 1995). As shown in Figure 5.12b, the area devoted to the left fingers was larger in those who began learning a stringed instrument early and who had also, of course, practiced for more years at the time of the study.

These results imply that practicing a skill reorganizes the brain, within limits, to maximize performance of that skill. Part of the mechanism of this change is that attention to anything one regards as important releases dopamine, and dopamine acts on cortical areas to expand the representation of stimuli active at the time of the dopamine release (Bao, Chan, & Merzenich, 2001).

Ordinarily, the expanded cortical representation is beneficial in enabling the cortex to pay more attention to a stimulus or process it more extensively. However, in extreme cases, the reorganization creates problems. As mentioned, when people play string instruments many hours a day for years, the representation of the left hand increases in the somatosensory cortex.

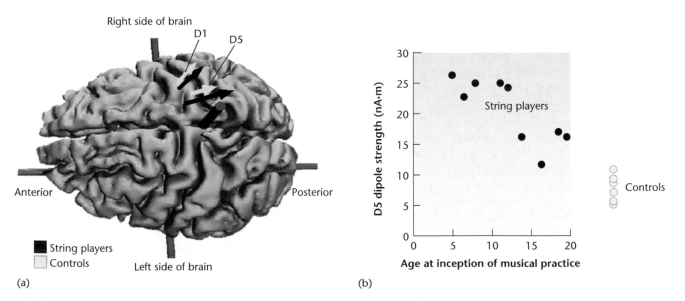

(a)
    (b)

Figure 5.12 Expanded cortical representation of fingers on string players' left hand
(**a**) The yellow and black arrows show the dipole moments (an MEG measure of neuronal activity) in response to stimulation of the thumb (D1) and little finger (D5), superimposed on an MRI brain scan. The red bars show the left–right, dorsoventral, and anterior–posterior axes. Note that the representation of the left thumb is equal for string players and controls, but the representation of the little finger is significantly greater for the string players. Representations of the right hand, not shown in the figure, were equal for musicians and nonmusicians. (**b**) The brain representation of the little finger (D5) was greater in those who had started learning a stringed instrument early than in those who had started late. *Source: reprinted with permission from "Increased Cortical Representation of the Fingers of the Left Hand in Sting Players," by T. Elbert, C. Panter, C. Weinbruch, B. Rockstroh, and E. Taub, Science, 270, p. 305–307. Copyright ©1995 American Association for the Advancement of Science.*

Imagine the normal representation of the fingers in the cortex:

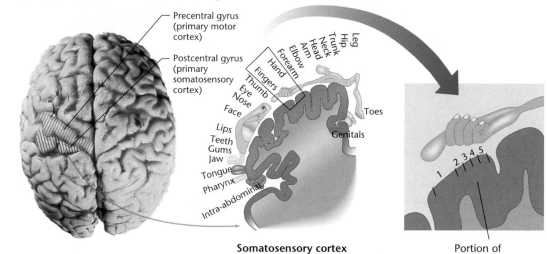

Somatosensory cortex

With extensive musical practice, the representations of the fingers could both grow and spread out like this:

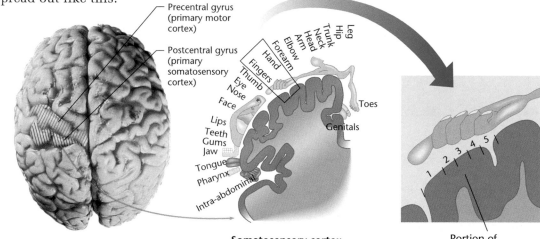

Somatosensory cortex

Or the representations could grow sideways more than they spread out, so the representation of each finger overlaps that of its neighbor:

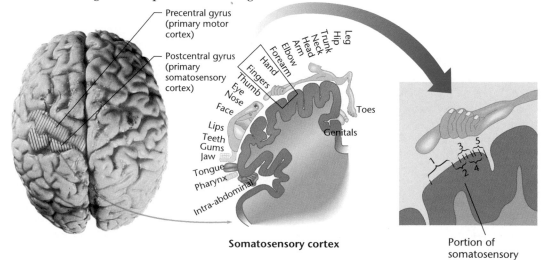

Somatosensory cortex

In some cases, the latter does occur. If the overlap becomes too great, the result is that stimulation on one finger excites the same cortical areas as another finger, and therefore, the person has trouble distinguishing one finger from the other. Someone who can't clearly feel the difference between one finger and another also has trouble controlling them separately. This condition is "musician's cramp"—known more formally as **focal hand dystonia**—in which the fingers become clumsy, fatigue easily, and make involuntary movements that interfere with the task. The condition is long-lasting and, for serious musicians, is a career-ender in most cases. Some people who spend all day handwriting develop the same problem, in which case it is known as "writer's cramp." Traditionally, physicians assumed that the musician's or writer's cramp was an impairment in the hands, but later research indicated that the cause is extensive reorganization of the sensory thalamus and cortex so that touch responses to one finger overlap those of another (Byl, McKenzie, & Nagarajan, 2000; Elbert et al., 1998; Lenz & Byl, 1999; Sanger, Pascual-Leone, Tarsy, & Schlaug, 2001; Sanger, Tarsy, & Pascual-Leone, 2001).

Combinations of Chemical and Experiential Effects

The results discussed so far suggest a two-stage process. First axons find their approximate targets by following a chemical gradient, and then they strengthen some connections and discard others in response to experience. Like most generalizations about the nervous system, this one has exceptions. Even during early prenatal development, when axons are first reaching their destinations, they produce spontaneous action potentials that are necessary for the development of normal connections (Catalano & Shatz, 1998).

What use could action potentials have during prenatal development, when the embryo has only very limited and not very meaningful experience? Consider an example: One part of the thalamus, the *lateral geniculate* (see Figure 4.13, p. 87), receives its input from the retinas of the eyes. During prenatal development, each lateral geniculate cell initially receives input from many retinal axons, which produce spontaneous action potentials. Repeated waves of activity sweep over the retina from one side to the other. Consequently, axons from adjacent areas of the retina are almost simultaneously activated. Each lateral geniculate cell selects a group of axons that are simultaneously active at this time; as a result, it becomes responsive to a group of receptors adjacent to one another on the retina (Meister, Wong, Baylor, & Shatz, 1991).

8. How does the brain of a lifelong string instrument player differ from that of most other people?

9. If axons from the retina were prevented from showing spontaneous activity during early development, what would be the probable effect on development of the lateral geniculate?

Check your answers on page 124.

PROPORTIONAL GROWTH OF BRAIN AREAS

Considering that the human brain enables us to dominate all other species on Earth, it is amazing how similar our brains are to those of other species. Nearly all of our neurotransmitters are found throughout the animal kingdom. The ion channels in our neurons are nearly the same as those of other species, even those of bacteria (Lu, Klem, & Ramu, 2001). The structures of the human brain have nearly the same locations, functions, and detailed anatomies as those of any other mammal, and they have substantial similarities to all vertebrates. Overall brain size is part of the explanation for humans' success, but it cannot be the whole story. The human brain, though larger than that of most mammals (Figure 5.13), is smaller than those of whales, dolphins, and elephants. In Chapter 15, we shall consider the difficult question of how the human brain evolved the capacity for language. Here let us consider how brain anatomy varies among species.

If we compare the brains of different mammals, we find size differences that are far from haphazard. Choose any two major areas of the brain, such as hippocampus and basal ganglia or cerebellum and thalamus. Call one area A and the other B. Now choose any two mammalian species. Even if you know nothing about the two species, you can guess with pretty high confidence that the species with the larger "area A" will also have a larger "area B." This generalization holds remarkably well, unless one of the areas you chose happened to be the olfactory bulb (Finlay & Darlington, 1995). The olfactory bulb is larger in dogs than in humans, for example; its growth is definitely not proportional to that of other brain areas.

You can make even more accurate predictions if you know a rough classification of the species you examined. Figure 5.14 shows the size of the cerebral cortex in comparison to the rest of the brain for insectivores and two suborders of **primates** (monkeys, apes, and

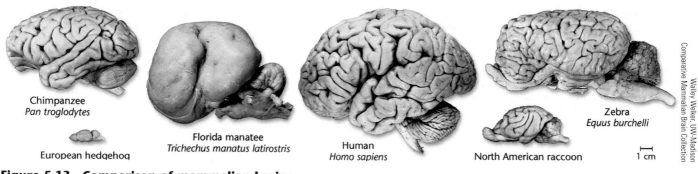

Chimpanzee
Pan troglodytes

Florida manatee
Trichechus manatus latirostris

Human
Homo sapiens

Zebra
Equus burchelli

European hedgehog

North American raccoon

1 cm

Figure 5.13 Comparison of mammalian brains
The human brain is similar in organization to that of all other mammals. The main difference is in overall size.

humans) (Barton & Harvey, 2000). As you can see, the primates have a larger cerebral cortex in proportion to the rest of the brain. Note also that for each group, the size of the cerebral cortex increases in a predictable way as total brain size increases.

Figures 5.15 and 5.16 show the comparisons across species in another way (D. A. Clark, Mitra, & Wang, 2001). For Figure 5.15, the investigators arranged all the insectivores and primates from left to right in terms of what percentage of their brain was devoted to the telencephalon (i.e., the forebrain, which includes the cerebral cortex). They also inserted tree shrews, a species often considered intermediate between insectivores and primates. Note that the forebrain occupies a larger percentage of the brain in *all* primates than it does in *any* of the insectivores. In primates, it increases in percentage mainly at the expense of the midbrain and medulla. The cerebellum

occupies a remarkably constant percentage—approximately 13% of any mammalian brain (Clark, et al., 2001). That is, as the brain gets larger, some areas such as the medulla get larger but less than proportionately to the growth of the whole brain. The cerebral cortex gets more than proportionately larger, and the cerebellum grows almost exactly in proportion to the whole brain. (Why? No one knows.)

In Figure 5.16, the investigators examined the same species but concentrated on only the forebrain. Here they arranged species in terms of progressively increasing percentage of the forebrain devoted to the cerebral cortex. Note that the cerebral cortex forms a substantially larger percentage of the primate than insectivore brains. Note also the near constancy of the basal ganglia and the wide variations in the olfactory bulb.

If we compare one species to another, we also find detailed differences based on way of life. For example, bats that rely heavily on echolocation to catch insects have an unusually large auditory cortex, and monkeys that swing through the trees with their forelimbs have a larger than usual brain representation of the muscles and sense organs of the forelimbs (de Winter & Oxnard, 2001). The brain may not need special genetic mechanisms to tell different areas how to grow. Across species, and even within a species, the size of the adult visual cortex depends on how many visual axons reach it (Stevens, 2001). Similarly, the size of the forelimbs determines the number of incoming sensory axons, and the axons in turn probably determine the amount of brain space to be allotted.

Given that the differences in brain structure across species are almost entirely quantitative, they

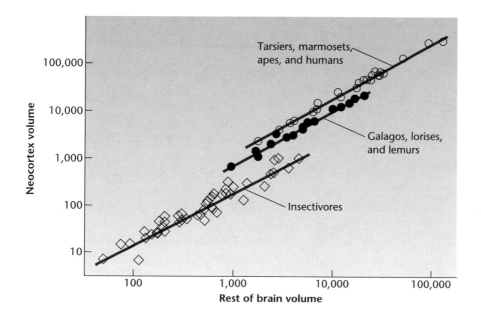

Figure 5.14 Relationship between volume of the cortex and volume of the rest of the brain
For each of the three groups, cortical volume increases quite predictably as a function of the volume of the rest of the brain. However, the lines for the two primate groups are displaced upward. *Source: Barton & Harvey, 2000*

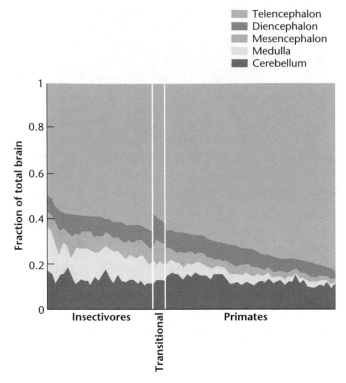

Telencephalon
Diencephalon
Mesencephalon
Medulla
Cerebellum

Neocortex   Piriform cortex
Hippocampus Olfactory bulb
Schizocortex Basal ganglia
Septum

Figure 5.15 Relative sizes of five brain components in insectivores and primates
The forebrain composes a larger percentage of primate than insectivore brains. Note also the near-constant fraction devoted to the cerebellum. *Source: Clark, Mitra, & Wang, 2001*

Figure 5.16 Relative sizes of seven components of the forebrain
The cortex composes a larger percentage of primate brains than those of insectivores. *Neocortex* = cerebral cortex, including white matter and corpus callosum; *schizocortex* = parts of the medial temporal cortex; *septum* = an area ventral to the center of the corpus callosum; *piriform cortex* = olfactory portion of the cortex; *basal ganglia* = caudate nucleus, putamen, and nucleus accumbens. *Source: Clark, Mitra, & Wang, 2001*

probably depend on just a small number of genes. The development of any brain area depends on two factors: how long the embryological development of the brain lasts in days and the number of new neurons produced per day. For example, the main differences between human and chimpanzee brains are due to the fact that neuronal proliferation continues longer in humans (Rakic, 1998; Vrba, 1998). A small amount of genetic change can produce a major difference in outcome.

Stop & Check

10. If you wanted to predict the size of the cerebral cortex in a given species of mammal, what two factors would be most important to know?

11. In mammals with a larger total brain, which brain area occupies a larger percentage of the brain? Which area occupies a nearly constant percentage?

Check your answers on page 124.

THE VULNERABLE DEVELOPING BRAIN

Brain development requires a complicated interplay of precisely timed chemical reactions, and the developing brain is highly vulnerable to malnutrition, toxic chemicals, and infections that would have less serious effects at a later age. For example, impaired thyroid function produces temporary lethargy in adults but permanent mental retardation and slowed body growth in infants. (Thyroid deficiency was common in the past because of iodine deficiencies; it is less common today because table salt is almost always fortified with iodine.) Anesthetic drugs produce only a temporary loss of consciousness in adults; they can kill neurons of infants (Ikonomidou et al., 1999). Diabetes in an adult can produce temporary fluctuations in performance; diabetes that is poorly controlled by a pregnant woman can deprive her fetus of oxygen and glucose during important stages of development and lead

Figure 5.17 Child with fetal alcohol syndrome
Note the facial pattern. Many children exposed to smaller amounts of alcohol before birth have behavioral deficits without facial signs.

to long-term problems in memory and attention (C. A. Nelson et al., 2000).

The infant brain is also highly vulnerable to damage by alcohol. Children of mothers who drink heavily during pregnancy are born with **fetal alcohol syndrome**, a condition marked by decreased alertness, hyperactivity, varying degrees of mental retardation, motor problems, heart defects, and facial abnormalities (Figure 5.17). Dendrites tend to be short with few branches. When children with fetal alcohol syndrome reach adulthood, they have a high risk of alcoholism, drug dependence, depression, and other psychiatric disorders (Famy, Streissguth, & Unis, 1998). Even in children who do not show any facial or other visible abnormalities, the more the mother drank during pregnancy, the more impulsive the child and the worse the school performance (Hunt, Streissguth, Kerr, & Carmichael-Olson, 1995). Researchers now understand the mechanisms of fetal alcohol syndrome: Remember from earlier in this chapter that to prevent apoptosis, a neuron must receive neurotrophins from the incoming axons as well as from its own axon's target cell. Alcohol suppresses the release of glutamate, the brain's main excitatory transmitter, and enhances activity at GABA synapses, the main inhibitory synapses. Consequently, many neurons receive much less total excitation and therefore less neurotrophins, and they undergo apoptosis (Ikonomidou et al., 2000).

Prenatal exposure to other substances can be harmful, too. Children of mothers who use cocaine during pregnancy have a slight decrease in IQ scores compared to normals and a somewhat greater decrease in language skills (Lester, LaGasse, & Seifer, 1998). The effects of cigarette smoking during pregnancy have not been as heavily investigated, but the available results indicate serious harm, possibly greater than that from

cocaine. Children of mothers who smoked during pregnancy are at much increased risk of the following (Brennan, Grekin, & Mednick, 1999; Fergusson, Woodward, & Horwood, 1998; Finette, O'Neill, Vacek, & Albertini, 1998; Milberger, Biederman, Faraone, Chen, & Jones, 1996; Slotkin, 1998):

- Low weight at birth and many illnesses early in life
- Sudden infant death syndrome ("crib death")
- Long-term intellectual deficits
- Attention-deficit hyperactivity disorder (ADHD)
- Impairments of the immune system
- Delinquency and crime later in life (sons especially)

The overall message obviously is that pregnant women should minimize their use of all drugs, even legal ones.

MODULE 5.1

In Closing: Brain Development

Considering the number of ways in which abnormal genes and chemicals can disrupt brain development, let alone the possible varieties of abnormal experience, it is a wonder that any of us develop normally. Evidently, the system has enough margin for error that we can function even if all of our connections do not develop quite perfectly. There are many ways for development to go wrong, but somehow the system usually manages to work.

SUMMARY

1. In vertebrate embryos, the central nervous system begins as a tube surrounding a fluid-filled cavity. Developing neurons proliferate, migrate, differentiate, myelinate, and form synapses. (p. 108)

2. Initially, the nervous system develops far more neurons than will actually survive. As they send out their axons, some make synaptic contacts with cells that release to them nerve growth factor or other neurotrophins. The neurons that receive neurotrophins survive; the others die. (p. 110)

3. Growing axons manage to find their way close to the right locations by following chemicals. (p. 113)

4. Axons attach themselves to a target area by arraying themselves over chemical gradients. (p. 114)

5. Variations in experience can alter overall brain growth and increase or decrease the amount of brain devoted to a particular sensory system. (p. 115)

6. The action potentials of an axon are important in synapse formation even at the earliest stages of development. (p. 120)

7. Among mammals, the size of the brain as a whole correlates positively with the size of its major components. For species with a larger overall brain size, the cerebral cortex comprises a larger percentage of the total, whereas most subcortical areas comprise a smaller percentage, but the cerebellum comprises almost a constant 13%. (p. 120)

8. The cerebral cortex is larger in proportion to the rest of the brain for primates than for other mammals. The relative size of various brain areas depends to some extent on a species' way of life, including the development of its sensory organs. (p. 121)

9. The brain is vulnerable during early development; abnormalities of genes, nutrition, or the chemical environment can produce many behavioral disorders. (p. 122)

ANSWERS TO *STOP AND CHECK* QUESTIONS

1. Proliferation is the formation of new neurons; migration is their movement from the point of origin to their final location. (p. 109)

2. The result depends on the age at transplant. At a very early stage, the neuron will adopt the properties of its new location. At a later stage, it maintains some of the properties of its original location. (p. 109)

3. The nervous system builds far more neurons than it needs and discards through apoptosis those that do not make lasting synapses. (p. 112)

4. Neurotrophins, such as nerve growth factor (p. 112)

5. An embryo has the most neurons. (p. 112)

6. Sperry found that if he cut a newt's eye and inverted it, axons grew back to their original targets, even though they were inappropriate to their new position on the eye. (p. 115)

7. Axons would attach haphazardly instead of arranging themselves according to their dorsoventral position on the retina. (p. 115)

8. In the somatosensory cortex of the right hemisphere, the area devoted to sensation from the fingers of the left hand (which touch the strings) is larger than normal. (p. 120)

9. The axons attach based on a chemical gradient but could not fine-tune the adjustment based on experience. Therefore, the connections would be less precise. (p. 120)

10. The most important fact would be the overall size of the brain. The second fact would be whether the species was a primate. (Primates have a larger cerebral cortex in proportion to the rest of the brain than do other mammalian species.) If you also knew something about the animal's way of life, you could make additional predictions about the size of the auditory cortex and other components of the cortex. (p. 122)

11. The cerebral cortex comprises a larger percentage of larger brains. The cerebellum constitutes almost the same percentage of all mammalian brains. (p. 122)

THOUGHT QUESTIONS

1. Biologists can develop antibodies against nerve growth factor (i.e., molecules that inactivate nerve growth factor). What would happen if someone injected such antibodies into a developing nervous system?

2. Based on material in this chapter, what is one reason a woman should avoid long-lasting anesthesia during delivery of a baby?

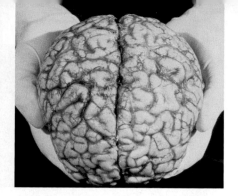

MODULE 5.2

Plasticity After Brain Damage

An American soldier who suffered a wound to the left hemisphere of his brain during the Korean War was at first unable to speak at all. Three months later, he could speak in short fragments. When he was shown the letterhead, "New York University College of Medicine," and was asked to read it, all he could say was, "Doctors—little doctors." Eight years later, when someone asked him again to read the letterhead, he replied, "Is there a catch? It says, 'New York University College of Medicine'" (Eidelberg & Stein, 1974).

Many people show behavioral recovery after brain damage, although it is seldom if ever complete. Given that the mammalian nervous system replaces only a few lost neurons, and only in certain locations, we face the theoretical question of how people recover from brain damage at all. We would like to understand the process so we can facilitate recovery and because studying recovery may yield insights into the functioning of a healthy brain.

CAUSES OF BRAIN DAMAGE

The brain can be damaged in many ways, including tumors, infections, exposure to radiation or toxic substances, and degenerative conditions such as Parkinson's disease and Alzheimer's disease. In young people, the most common cause is **closed head injury,** a sharp blow to the head resulting from a fall, an automobile or motorcycle accident, a sports accident, an assault, or other sudden trauma that does not actually puncture the brain. The damage occurs partly because of rotational forces that drive brain tissue against the inside of the skull. It also results from blood clots that interrupt normal blood flow to the brain (Kirkpatrick, Smielewski, Czosnyka, Menon, & Pickard, 1995). Many people, probably most, have suffered at least one closed head injury. Even a mild injury sometimes (though not often) produces noticeable long-term problems (Satz et al., 1997). Repeated blows to the head, however, such as those suffered by professional boxers, produce serious losses of memory, reasoning, movement control, and emotional balance (Mendez, 1995) (Figure 5.18).

Reducing the Harm From a Stroke

A common cause of brain damage in older people (more rarely in the young) is temporary loss of normal blood flow to a brain area during a **stroke,** also known as a **cerebrovascular accident.** The more common type of stroke is **ischemia,** caused when a blood clot or other obstruction closes an artery; the less common type is **hemorrhage,** caused when an artery ruptures. The two types produce many similar effects. Strokes vary in their severity from barely noticeable to immediately

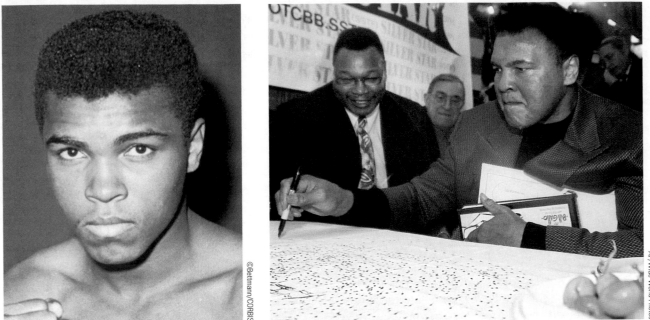

Figure 5.18 Effects of closed head injury
Although a single moderate trauma to the head ordinarily does not produce noticeable problems, repeated blows can cause slowness of speech and movement, as they did for boxer Muhammad Ali.

fatal. Figure 5.19 shows the brains of three people: one who died immediately after a stroke, one who survived long after a stroke, and a bullet wound victim. For a good collection of information about stroke, see this Web site: www.stroke.org/

If one of your relatives had a stroke and you called a hospital, what advice would you probably get? As recently as the 1980s, the staff would have been in no great hurry to see the patient because they

had little to offer anyway. They were likely to recommend keeping the patient warm and providing tranquilizers or similar medications to lower blood pressure. We now know that those procedures probably worsened the condition. Today, it is possible to reduce the effects of a stroke if physicians intervene quickly (Dávalos, Castillo, & Martinez-Vila, 1995).

Cells in the immediate vicinity of the ischemia or hemorrhage die quickly. We have little prospect of

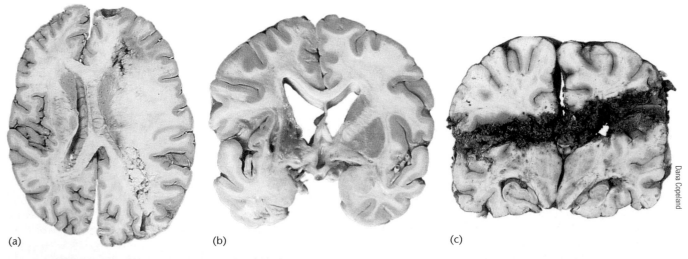

(a) (b) (c)

Figure 5.19 Three damaged human brains
(a) Brain of a person who died immediately after a stroke. Note the swelling on the right side. (b) Brain of a person who survived for a long time after a stroke. Note the cavities on the left side, where many cells were lost. (c) Brain of a person who suffered a gunshot wound and died immediately.

protecting them. However, cells in the penumbra (Latin for "almost shadow"), the region that surrounds the immediate damage, may die over the next few days or weeks but are probably protectable (Ginsberg, 1995a; Hsu, Sik, Gallyas, Horváth, & Buzsáki, 1994; Jonas, 1995).

In ischemia, cells in the penumbra are deprived of blood and therefore lose much of their oxygen and glucose supplies. In hemorrhage, they are flooded with blood and its excess oxygen, calcium, and other products. In either case, they are invaded by waste products from cells that are dead or dying. Potassium ions accumulate outside neurons in the penumbra because the sodium-potassium pump does not have as much energy as usual. Edema (accumulation of fluid) forms because the blood-brain barrier has broken down. The combination of potassium and edema reverses the activity of neurons' glutamate transporters. Instead of facilitating the reuptake of glutamate, the transporter proteins start pumping it out of the cells (Rossi, Oshima, & Attwell, 2000). The excess glutamate (an excitatory transmitter) overstimulates neurons, making it even harder for their sodium-potassium pumps to keep pace. Sodium, calcium, and zinc ions accumulate inside neurons, where they block metabolism in the mitochondria (Stout, Raphael, Kanterewicz, Klann, & Reynolds, 1998). As neurons die, glia cells proliferate, removing waste products and dead neurons. Figure 5.20 summarizes this process. The main point of this figure is that overstimulation kills neurons in both ischemia and hemorrhage.

To the extent that we understand stroke, we may be able to find ways to minimize its damage. One method now in wide use is to administer as quickly as possible a drug called tissue plasminogen activator (tPA), which breaks up blood clots (Barinaga, 1996). This drug is of course recommended for ischemia but not hemorrhage. In addition to dissolving blood clots, tPA has a mixture of helpful and harmful effects on the survival of damaged neurons (Kim, Park, Hong, & Koh, 1999).

Other methods, still in the experimental stage, attempt to prevent overstimulation by blocking glutamate synapses or by preventing calcium and other positive ions from entering neurons. However, most such methods have produced disappointing results (Lee, Zipfel, & Choi, 1999). A somewhat promising new drug opens potassium channels (Gribkoff et al., 2001). As calcium or other positive ions enter a neuron, potassium exits through these open channels, reducing overstimulation.

One possible reason blocking overstimulation has not worked better is that neurons also can die from understimulation (Colbourne, Sutherland, & Auer, 1999; Conti, Raghupathi, Trojanowski, & McIntosh, 1998). An underexcited neuron activates its self-destruct program (apoptosis). In studies of laboratory animals with induced strokes, the drug MK-801, which blocks one type of glutamate receptor (the "NMDA" receptor), improves an animal's recovery if given soon after the stroke but impairs recovery if given later (Barth, Grant, & Schallert, 1990). These results make sense if stroke kills cells initially by overstimulation and later by understimulation.

In search of other solutions, researchers have tried using neurotrophins and other drugs that block apoptosis. Results have been favorable in animal trials using direct injection of the drugs into the brain, but application to humans is doubtful because those drugs do not cross the blood-brain barrier (Barinaga, 1996; Choi-Lundberg et al., 1997; Levivier, Przedborski, Bencsics, & Kang, 1995; Schulz, Weller, & Moskowitz, 1999). Other procedures that have proved helpful in laboratory animal studies include drugs that trap free radicals (Schulz, Matthews, Jenkins, Brar, & Beal, 1995), food restriction (Bruce-Keller, Umberger, McFall, & Mattson, 1999), and cannabinoids—drugs related to marijuana (Nagayama et al., 1999).

The most effective laboratory method so far is to cool the brain. A cooled brain has less activity, lower energy needs, and less risk of overstimulation than does a brain at normal temperature (Barone, Feuerstein, & White, 1997; Colbourne & Corbett, 1995). Humans cannot be cooled safely to the same temperature that rats can, but cooling someone to about 33–36° C (91–97° F) for the first 3 days after a stroke significantly improves survival and long-term behavioral functioning (Steiner, Ringleb, & Hacke, 2001).

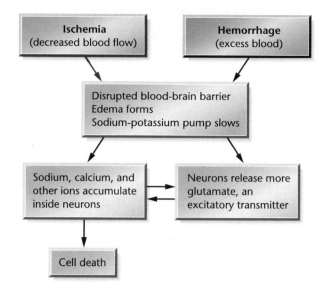

Figure 5.20 Mechanisms of neuron death after stroke
Procedures that can preserve neurons include removing the blood clot, blocking excitatory synapses, stimulating inhibitory synapses, blocking the flow of calcium and zinc, and cooling the brain.

1. In what ways does a stroke overstimulate neurons?

2. Why is tPA not recommended in cases of hemorrhage?

3. If one of your relatives has a stroke and a well-meaning person offers a blanket, what should you say?

Check your answers on page 139.

Effects of Age on Recovery

As you might guess, the elderly do not recover from brain damage as well as younger adults do. People gradually lose neurons throughout life; as they age beyond about 60, many people also begin to have some shrinkage of dendrites in certain brain areas (Jacobs & Scheibel, 1993). The dendrites shrink especially in older people who become senile; they may remain steady or even expand in those who remain alert (Buell & Coleman, 1981). Still, an older person who suffers brain damage is impaired in recovery because other cells are slowly dying off and the remaining cells modify their branching less readily than they used to. As we age, the brain simply becomes less plastic.

If recovery from brain damage is particularly limited in old age, you might expect it to be quite successful in the very young. Sometimes it is. According to the **Kennard principle,** named after Margaret Kennard, who first stated it, recovery is more extensive after youthful brain damage than after similar damage later (Kennard, 1938). For example, rats with amygdala damage at age 10 days recover well; those with similar damage at age 40 days recover less well (Higley, Hermer-Vazquez, Levitsky, & Strupp, 2001). Also, a 2-year-old child who loses the entire left cerebral cortex will probably develop some speech based on altered development of the right cortex, whereas an adult with similar damage would not recover much language.

However, the Kennard principle has many exceptions. Children with left-hemisphere damage vary enormously in how much language they gain, depending on what medical condition caused the injury (Curtiss, de Bode, & Mathern, 2001). Although the young brain is more plastic than the old, it is also more vulnerable to forces that interfere with its development and organization.

For example, after one hemisphere of an infant rat brain is removed, the other hemisphere increases in thickness (Kolb, Sutherland, & Whishaw, 1983).

However, after removal of the anterior portion of the infant cortex, the posterior portion develops less than normally (Kolb & Holmes, 1983). Apparently, the survival of neurons in the posterior cortex requires interaction with neurons in the anterior cortex, so damage to the anterior cortex affects the behavior of infant rats more than it does the behavior of adults.

MECHANISMS OF RECOVERY AFTER BRAIN DAMAGE

People with brain damage generally show some behavioral improvement, especially in the first month after the damage. Even at best, however, the brain is not restored to what it had been. Someone who appears to be functioning normally may have to work harder than usual to achieve the same end and may deteriorate markedly after a couple of beers or a physically tiring effort (Fleet & Heilman, 1986).

As someone is recovering, what is changing in the brain? A simple idea is that another part of the brain takes over the functions of the damaged area, but this assumption is valid only in a limited sense. When a woman who has injured her left leg walks on her right leg and crutches, the arms and right leg are simply performing their own functions in a new way, not really taking over the function of the damaged leg. Similarly, after damage to the motor cortex in one hemisphere, the motor cortex of the remaining hemisphere develops some control of the ipsilateral limb (Chollet & Weiller, 1994). It is not really duplicating the function of the damaged area; it is merely improving the weak ipsilateral pathways that already existed.

Structural changes in the surviving neurons can partially restore lost functions, or the person can learn new ways to solve old problems. Let us consider some of the mechanisms of recovery.

Learned Adjustments in Behavior

Much of the recovery after brain damage is learned; the individual makes better use of unimpaired abilities. For example, someone who has lost vision in all but the center of the visual field may learn to move his or her head back and forth to compensate for the lack of peripheral vision (Marshall, 1985).

A brain-damaged person or animal may also learn to use abilities that at first appeared to be lost but actually were only impaired. For example, in the laboratory, damage to the sensory nerves from a leg eliminates sensation from the affected area (Figure 5.21), but the animal can still control the muscles. The limb

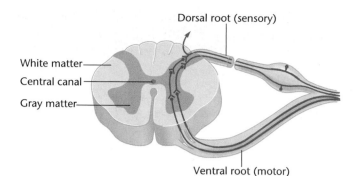

Figure 5.21 Cross section through the spinal cord
A cut through the dorsal root (as shown) deprives the animal of touch sensations from part of the body but leaves the motor nerves intact.

is referred to as **deafferented** because it has lost its afferent (sensory) input. Although the animal can move the muscles, it seldom does. For example, a monkey with a deafferented limb does not spontaneously use it for walking, picking up objects, or any other voluntary behaviors (Taub & Berman, 1968). Investigators initially assumed that the monkey could not use the limb because of the lack of sensory feedback. In a later experiment, however, they cut the afferent nerves of both forelimbs; despite this more extensive damage, the monkey regained use of both deafferented limbs. It could walk moderately fast, climb upward or sideways on the walls of metal cages, and even pick up a raisin between its thumb and forefinger. Apparently, a monkey fails to use one deafferented forelimb only because walking on three limbs is easier than moving the impaired limb. When both limbs are deafferented, the monkey is forced to use both.

Similarly, many people with brain damage find it easier, especially at first, to struggle along without even trying to use an impaired ability. Many are capable of more than they are doing and more than they realize they can do. Therapy for brain-damaged people sometimes focuses on showing them how much they already can do and encouraging them to practice those skills.

Diaschisis

Much research on brain-behavior relationships relies on analyzing the behavior of animals after damage to certain brain areas, as described in Methods 5.3. A behavioral deficit after brain damage reflects more than just the functions of the cells that were destroyed. Ordinarily, activity in any brain area stimulates many other areas. Therefore, damage to one area deprives the other areas of stimulation, perhaps to the point of interfering with their healthy functioning. For example, after damage to part of someone's left frontal cortex (an

area central to language), activity decreases in several distant areas, including the temporal cortex (C. J. Price, Warburton, Moore, Frackowiak, & Friston, 2001). **Diaschisis** (di-AS-ki-sis, from a Greek term meaning "to shock throughout") refers to the decreased activity of surviving neurons after other neurons are damaged. For example, a lesion in the hypothalamus can lead to decreased activity in the cerebral cortex.

If diaschisis is an important contributor to behavioral deficits following brain damage, then stimulant drugs should promote recovery. In a series of experiments, D. M. Feeney and colleagues measured the behavioral effects of cortical damage in rats and cats. Depending on the location of the damage, the animals showed impairments in either coordinated movement or depth perception. Injecting amphetamine (which increases dopamine and norepinephrine activity) significantly enhanced the behaviors, and animals that practiced the behaviors under the influence of amphetamine showed long-lasting benefits. Injecting the drug haloperidol (which blocks most of the same synapses) impaired behavioral recovery (Feeney & Sutton, 1988; Feeney, Sutton, Boyeson, Hovda, & Dail, 1985; Hovda & Feeney, 1989; Sutton, Hovda, & Feeney, 1989).

These results imply that people who have had a stroke should be given stimulant drugs such as amphetamine, not immediately after the stroke, as with clot-busting drugs, but during the following days, when it is important for the person to use as much of the surviving brain as possible. Researchers have found that people's recovery from brain damage is enhanced by amphetamine if it is combined with physical therapy—that is, practice at the impaired skills (Feeney, Weisend, & Kline, 1993; Walker-Batson, Smith, Curtis, Unwin, & Greenlee, 1995). Recovery is impaired by tranquilizers, which among other effects decrease the release of dopamine and norepinephrine (L. B. Goldstein, 1993).

Stop & Check

4. Suppose someone has suffered a spinal cord injury that interrupts all sensation from the left arm. Now he or she uses only the right arm. Of the following, which is the most promising therapy: electrically stimulate the skin of the left arm, tie the right arm behind the person's back, or blindfold the person?

5. Following damage to someone's brain, would it be best (if possible) to direct amphetamine to the cells that were damaged or somewhere else?

Check your answers on page 139.

Lesions

Much of what we know about the human brain comes from studies of people with brain damage. With laboratory animals, researchers sometimes produce damage intentionally, directing it at particular areas. A lesion is damage to a brain area; an ablation is a removal of part of the brain. To damage a structure in the interior of the brain, researchers use a stereotaxic instrument, a device for the precise placement of electrodes in the brain (Figure 5.22). By consulting a stereotaxic atlas (map) of the brain of an animal (e.g., a rat), a researcher can determine the location of a particular area with reference to the position of the ears, landmarks on the animal's skull (Figure 5.23), and so forth. A researcher anesthetizes the animal, drills a small hole in the skull, inserts the electrode, and carefully lowers it to the target area. Later, the researcher passes an electrical current sufficient to damage the cells in that area.

Suppose someone makes a lesion in some brain area, finds that the animal stops eating, and concludes that the area is important for eating. "Wait a minute," you might ask. "How do we know the deficit wasn't caused by anesthetizing the animal, drilling a hole in its skull, and lowering an electrode through part of its brain to reach this target?" To test this possibility, an experimenter produces a sham lesion in a control group, performing all the same procedures but without the electrical current. Any behavioral difference between the lesioned group and the sham-lesioned group must result from the lesion and not from inserting the electrode.

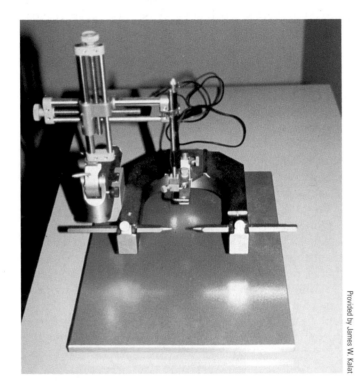

Provided by James W. Kalat

Figure 5.22 A stereotaxic instrument for locating brain areas in small animals
Using this device, researchers can insert an electrode to stimulate, record from, or damage any point in the brain.

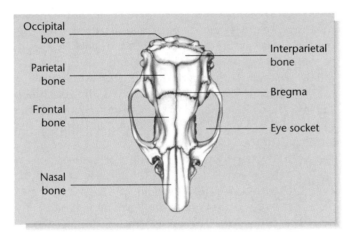

Occipital bone
Parietal bone
Frontal bone
Nasal bone
Interparietal bone
Bregma
Eye socket

Figure 5.23 Skull bones of a rat
Bregma, the point where four bones meet on the top of the skull, is a useful landmark from which to locate areas of the brain.

The Regrowth of Axons

Although a destroyed cell body cannot be replaced, damaged axons do grow back under certain circumstances. A neuron of the peripheral nervous system has its cell body in the spinal cord and an axon that extends into one of the limbs. If the axon is crushed, the degenerated portion grows back toward the periphery at a rate of about 1 mm per day, following the path of the myelin sheath back to its original target. If the axon is cut instead of crushed, the myelin on the two sides of the cut may not line up correctly, and the regenerating axon may not have a sure path to follow. Sometimes a motor nerve attaches to the wrong muscle, as Figure 5.24 illustrates.

Within the mature mammalian brain and spinal cord, damaged axons usually regenerate no more than a millimeter or two (Schwab, 1998). Therefore, paralysis caused by spinal cord injury is permanent. However, in many kinds of fish, axons do regenerate across a cut spinal cord far enough to restore nearly normal functioning (J. J. Bernstein & Gelderd, 1970; Rovainen, 1976; Scherer, 1986; Selzer, 1978). Why do damaged CNS axons regenerate so much better in fish than in mammals? One possibility is that a cut through the adult mammalian spinal cord forms too much scar tissue. The scar tissue not only makes a mechanical barrier to axon growth, but it also synthesizes chemicals called *chondroitin sulphate proteoglycans* that inhibit axon growth. Enzymes that degrade those chemicals can increase the growth of axons in the area around the cut (Bradbury et al., 2002).

Another explanation for the failure of axon growth in mammals and birds is that the myelin in their central nervous systems secretes proteins that inhibit axon growth (Fields, Schwab, & Silver, 1999; McClellan, 1998). Therefore, by the time the CNS is mature, it is full of myelin that prevents additional axons from growing and damaged axons from regenerating. In contrast, the myelin of the peripheral nerves contains chemicals that sustain axon growth, and injecting these chemicals into the CNS helps damaged nerves regrow, at least in mice (Bomze, Bulsara, Iskandar, Caroni, & Skene, 2001).

The hope is that someday such chemicals may help people recover from *hemiplegia,* one-sided paralysis caused by a cut part of the way through the spinal cord.

(When the human spinal cord is cut all the way through, the separated halves pull so far apart that no axon can bridge the gap.) However, here is something to worry about: *Why* do CNS myelin and astrocytes secrete proteins that inhibit axon regrowth? Did we evolve such mechanisms because regrowing axons might connect to the wrong targets and do more harm than good? We have to await more research for the answers.

Sprouting

After damage to a set of axons, the cells that had received input from them react to the loss by secreting neurotrophins that induce nearby uninjured axons to form new branches, or **collateral sprouts,** that attach to the vacant synapses (Ramirez, Finklestein, et al., 1999). Gradually over several months, the sprouts fill in most of the vacated synapses (Figure 5.25). For example, after loss of about half of the cells in a rat's *locus coeruleus* (a hindbrain area), the brain shows an enormous drop in the number of synapses that the locus coeruleus supplies to the forebrain. Over the next 6 months, the surviving axons sprout enough to restore almost completely normal input (Fritschy & Grzanna, 1992).

Sprouting is a normal condition, not one that occurs only after brain damage (Cotman & Nieto-Sampedro, 1982). The brain is continually losing old synapses and sprouting new ones to replace them.

In some cases, when one axon is removed, an unrelated axon sprouts to occupy the vacant synapse. This kind of sprouting is probably useless or harmful because it provides inappropriate information. In other

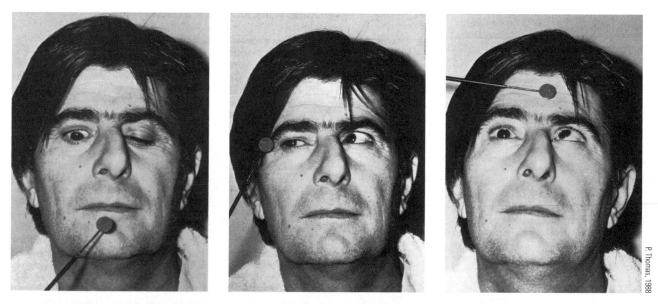

Figure 5.24 What can happen if damaged axons regenerate to incorrect muscles
Damaged axons to the muscles of the patient's right eye regenerated but attached incorrectly. When he looks down, his right eyelid opens wide instead of closing like the other eyelid. His eye movements are frequently misaimed, and he has trouble moving his right eye upward or to the left.

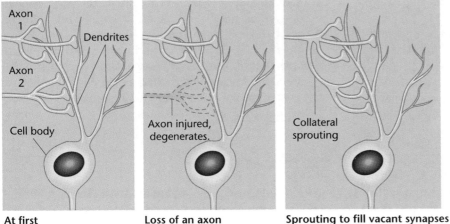

Figure 5.25 Collateral sprouting
A surviving axon grows a new branch to replace the synapses left vacant by a damaged axon.

Labels in figure: Axon 1; Dendrites; Axon 2; Cell body; At first | Axon injured, degenerates. | Loss of an axon | Collateral sprouting | Sprouting to fill vacant synapses

cases, however, the sprouts come from closely related axons. For example, axons from the entorhinal cortex ordinarily terminate in the nearby hippocampus. Damage to part of the left entorhinal cortex stimulates sprouting by axons from the remaining part and from the undamaged right entorhinal cortex. These new branches develop functional synapses within a few days, approximately in the same time it takes for the animal to show behavioral recovery from the damage (Ramirez, Bulsara, Moore, Ruch, & Abrams, 1999). After behavioral recovery, damage to the sprouted path from the right entorhinal cortex greatly impairs the behavior (Ramirez, McQuilkin, Carrigan, MacDonald, & Kelley, 1996). This result is probably the strongest evidence for the beneficial effects of sprouting.

Denervation Supersensitivity

A postsynaptic cell that is deprived of synaptic input for a long time becomes more sensitive to the neurotransmitter. For example, a normal muscle cell responds to the neurotransmitter acetylcholine only at the neuromuscular junction. If the axon is cut, or if it is inactive for days, the muscle cell builds additional receptors, becoming sensitive to acetylcholine over a wider area of its surface (Johns & Thesleff, 1961; Levitt-Gilmour & Salpeter, 1986). The same process occurs in neurons. Heightened sensitivity to a neurotransmitter after the destruction of an incoming axon is known as **denervation supersensitivity** (Glick, 1974). Heightened sensitivity as a result of inactivity by an incoming axon is called **disuse supersensitivity**. The mechanisms of supersensitivity include an increased number of receptors (Kostrzewa, 1995) and increased effectiveness of receptors, perhaps by changes in second-messenger systems.

One way to demonstrate denervation supersensitivity is to use the drug **6-hydroxydopamine (6-OHDA)**, which damages axons that release dopamine. The neurons that release norepinephrine and dopamine recognize 6-OHDA as a related chemical, absorb it, and die after it is oxidized into toxic chemicals. As Figure 5.26 shows, after an injection of 6-OHDA to one side of the brain, postsynaptic cells react by increasing their number of dopamine receptors on that side (LaHoste & Marshall, 1989). Methods 5.4 describes autoradiography, the procedure used in that study.

Denervation supersensitivity contributes to recovery by increasing neurons' responses to the limited amount of dopamine that remains. In one study, experimenters injected 6-OHDA on the left side of rats' brains, damaging dopamine-releasing axons on that side only (Figure 5.27). They waited weeks for postsynaptic neurons to become supersensitive to dopamine. Then they injected the rats with either amphetamine or

METHODS 5.4
Autoradiography

Just as an autograph is a person's signature, an autoradiograph is a chemical's signature. Investigators kill a laboratory animal and slice its brain into thin sections. Then they apply a radioactively labeled chemical to the slices. (For the experiment shown in Figure 5.28, investigators used radioactively labeled spiroperidol, a drug that binds to dopamine type D_2 receptors.) Next they place each section against a piece of x-ray film, which records all the radioactivity that the labeled chemicals emit. From these data, computers create a color display in which red indicates the greatest amount of radioactive binding, followed by yellow, green, and blue. The red and yellow areas are those with the greatest amount of spiroperidol and therefore the greatest density of D_2 receptors.

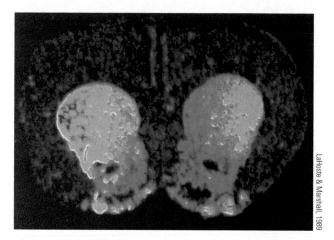

Figure 5.26 Responses of dopamine receptors to decreased input

In this autoradiography procedure, an injection of 6-OHDA destroyed dopamine axons in the hemisphere on the left. The increased amount of red and yellow on the left indicates more binding of the drug to D_2 receptors there. The conclusion is that after loss of dopamine axons, the left hemisphere developed more D_2 receptors.

apomorphine. Amphetamine increases the release of dopamine by surviving axons. Because the left side of the brain was lacking dopamine axons, the amphetamine stimulated only the intact right side of the brain, causing the rats to orient mostly toward stimuli on the left and therefore turn in that direction. Apomorphine is a morphine derivative that directly stimulates dopamine receptors. Because denervation supersensitivity had strengthened receptors on the left side, apomorphine had more effect on that side, so rats were more responsive to stimuli on the right and therefore turned away from the damaged side of the brain (Marshall, Drew, & Neve, 1983). These results (shown in Figure 5.27) indicate that the denervated side of the brain has become supersensitive to dopamine and to drugs that stimulate dopamine receptors.

Denervation supersensitivity helps explain why people can lose most of the axons in some pathways and still maintain nearly normal behavior (Sabel, 1997). The remaining axons increase their release of transmitters, and the receptors on the postsynaptic membrane develop denervation supersensitivity.

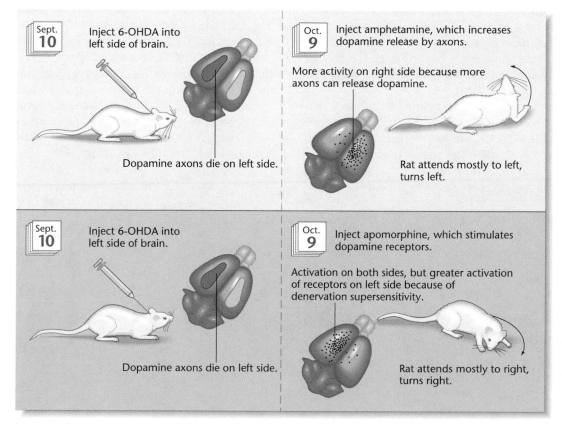

Figure 5.27 Demonstration of denervation supersensitivity

Injecting 6-OHDA destroys axons that release dopamine on one side of the brain. Later, amphetamine stimulates only the intact side of the brain because it cannot cause axons to release dopamine on the damaged side. Apomorphine stimulates the damaged side more strongly because it directly stimulates dopamine receptors, which have become supersensitive on that side.
Source: Based on data from Marshall, Drew, & Neve, 1983

Reorganized Sensory Representations and the Phantom Limb

As we saw earlier in this chapter, experiences can modify the connections within the cerebral cortex. Recall that after someone has played a string instrument for many years, the somatosensory cortex has an enlarged representation of the fingers of the left hand. Similarly, in Braille proofreaders, the brain representation of the index finger is measurably larger at the end of a workday than at the same time on a vacation day (Pascual-Leone, Wasserman, Sadato, & Hallett, 1995). Such changes may represent either collateral sprouting of axons or increased receptor sensitivity by the postsynaptic neurons. A slight reorganization of the cortex gives extra representation to the information that someone uses the most.

A more extensive reorganization of the brain can occur after an amputation. Reexamine Figure 4.25 (p. 97): Along the somatosensory cortex, each section receives input from a different part of the body. Within the part of the cortex marked "fingers" in that figure, a closer examination reveals that each subarea responds more to one finger than to another. Figure 5.28 shows the arrangement for a monkey brain. In one study, experimenters amputated finger 3 in an owl monkey. The cortical cells that previously responded to information from that finger now had no input. As time passed, more and more of them became responsive to finger 2, finger 4, or part of the palm, until eventually the cortex had the pattern of responsiveness we see in Figure 5.28b (Kaas, Merzenich, & Killackey, 1983; Merzenich et al., 1984).

What happens if an entire arm is amputated? For many years, neuroscientists assumed that most of the cortex responsive to that arm became permanently silent because it was too far away from any other axons to evoke sprouting. Then came a surprise. Investigators recorded from the cerebral cortices of monkeys that had had a forelimb deafferented[2] 12 years previously and found that the large stretch of cortex previously responsive to the limb had become responsive to the face (Pons et al., 1991). How did these connections form? The altered responses in the cortex reflected changes that had occurred in several places. After loss of sensory input from the forelimb, the axons representing the forelimb degenerated, leaving vacant synaptic sites at several levels of the CNS. Axons representing the face sprouted into those sites in the spinal cord, brainstem, and thalamus (Florence & Kaas, 1995; E. G. Jones & Pons, 1998). (Or perhaps axons from the face had already innervated those sites but were overwhelmed by the normal input. After removal of the normal input, the weaker synapses became stronger.) Also, lateral connections formed from the face-sensitive cortical areas into the previously hand-sensitive areas of the cortex according to results from *histochemistry* (Florence, Taub, & Kaas, 1998) (see Methods 5.5).

[2]Reminder: To deafferent is to cut the sensory nerves.

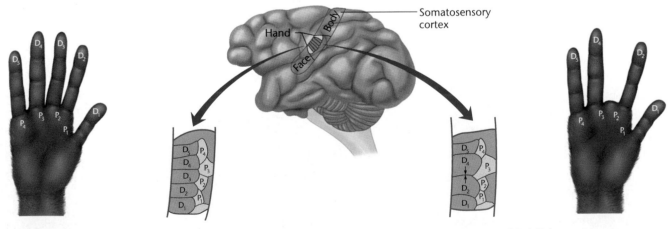

(a) Normal (before amputation)   **(b) After amputation of 3rd digit**

Figure 5.28 Somatosensory cortex of a monkey after a finger amputation
Note that the cortical area previously responsive to the third finger (D₃) becomes responsive to the second and fourth fingers (D₂ and D₄) and part of the palm (P₃). *Source: Redrawn from the Annual Review of Neuroscience, Vol. 6, ©1983 by Annual Reviews Inc.*

Brain scan studies confirm that the same processes occur with humans. Consider what happens when cells in a reorganized cortex become activated. Previously, they responded to an arm, and now they respond to stimulation on the face. But does the response feel like stimulation on the face or on the arm?

The answer: It still feels like the arm (K. D. Davis et al., 1998). Physicians have long noted that many people with amputations experience a **phantom limb,** a continuing sensation of an amputated body part. That experience can range from occasional tingling to intense pain. It is possible to have a phantom hand, intestines, breast, penis, or anything else that has been amputated. Sometimes the phantom sensation fades within days or weeks, but it can last a lifetime (Ramachandran & Hirstein, 1998).

Until the 1990s, no one knew what caused phantom pains, and most believed that the sensations were coming from the stump of the amputated limb. Some physicians even performed additional amputations, removing more and more of the limb in a futile attempt to eliminate the phantom sensations. But modern methods have demonstrated that the greater the reorganization of the somatosensory cortex, the more likely and more intense the phantom sensations (Flor et al., 1995). For example, axons representing the face may come to activate the cortical area previously devoted to an amputated hand. Whenever the face is touched, the person still feels it on the face but also feels a sensation in the phantom hand. It is even possible to map out which part of the face stimulates sensation in which part of the phantom hand (Aglioti, Smania, Atzei, & Berlucchi, 1997) (Figure 5.29). Until a physician or researcher points out the connection, the person ordinarily does not notice that touching the face is what causes the phantom hand sensation.

The connection between phantom sensations and brain reorganization enables us to understand some otherwise puzzling observations. Note in Figure 4.25 (p. 97) that the part of the cortex responsive to the feet is immediately next to the part responsive to the genitals. Two patients, after amputation, felt a phantom

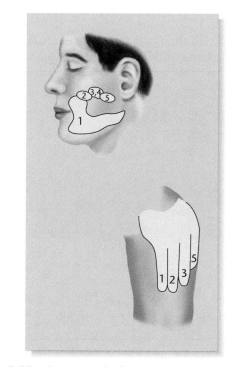

Figure 5.29 Sources of phantom sensation for one person
For this person, stimulation in the areas marked on the cheek produced phantom sensations of digits one (thumb), two, four, and five. Stimulation on the shoulder also evoked phantom sensations of digits one, two, three, and five. *Source: Copyright ©1998 by V. S. Ramachandran, M. D., Ph. D. and Sandra Blakeslee. Used by permission of William Morrow and Company, Inc.*

foot especially during sexual arousal! One in fact reported feeling orgasm not only in the genitals but also in the phantom foot (Ramachandran & Blakeslee, 1998). Evidently, the representation of the genitals had spread into the cortical area responsible for foot sensation. (These particular patients did not complain about their phantom sensations!)

If a phantom sensation is painful, is there any way to relieve it? In some cases, yes. Amputees who learn to use an artificial arm report that their phantom sensations gradually disappear (Lotze et al., 1999). Apparently, they start attributing some sensations to the artificial arm, and in doing so, they displace abnormal connections from the face. Similarly, a study of one man found that after his hands were amputated, the area of his cortex that usually responds to the hands partly shifted to face sensitivity, but after he received hand transplants, his cortex gradually shifted back to hand sensitivity (Giraux, Sirigu, Schneider, & Dubernard, 2001).

In one study, five people with painful phantom limbs who felt "as if fingernails were digging into the skin" sat with a tall mirror perpendicular to the chest, as shown in Figure 5.30, so that they saw a mirror image of their normal arm superimposed on the phantom limb. Four of them found that if they made a fist with the normal hand and looked into the mirror while opening it, they felt the phantom hand

opening also and the pain subsiding (Ramachandran, Rogers-Ramachandran, & Cobb, 1995). Evidently, the combination of visual and tactile experiences had somehow altered the activity in the somatosensory cortex and reduced the phantom pain.

One important message from these studies is that connections in the brain remain plastic throughout life. There are limits on the plasticity, certainly, but they are less strict than researchers once supposed.

8. Is reorganization of the brain helpful or harmful?

Check your answer on page 139.

THERAPIES

After someone suffers brain damage, physicians, physical therapists, and others try to assist recovery. Interventions to promote and guide brain plasticity may well be common in the future; at present, therapy consists mainly of supervised practice of the impaired behaviors.

Behavioral Interventions

You may fail to find your keys either because you accidentally threw them in the trash or because you left them in an odd place. Similarly, brain-damaged people and animals may seem to lack some skill either because it has been destroyed or because they cannot locate it. Therapists help brain-damaged people recover their lost skills or learn to use their remaining abilities more effectively. For example, some people with frontal lobe damage behave in socially inappropriate ways, using obscene language, failing to wash themselves, or making lewd overtures to strangers. Therapists may provide positive reinforcement for polite speech, good grooming, and self-restraint (McGlynn, 1990).

Similarly, a brain-damaged animal that seems to have forgotten a learned skill may still retain it in some hidden manner. After damage to its visual cortex, a rat that previously had learned to approach a white card instead of a black card for food chose randomly between the two cards. Had the rat forgotten the discrimination completely? Evidently not, because it could much more easily relearn to approach the white card than learn to approach the black card (T. E. LeVere & Morlock, 1973). Apparently, some of the original learning survived the brain damage (Figure 5.31). Thomas LeVere (1975) proposed that

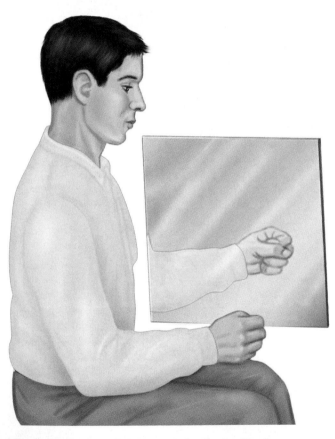

Figure 5.30 A surprising method of relieving phantom pain
People with a phantom limb report sensation in the amputated limb—for example, pain as if fingernails were digging into the skin. By looking in a mirror placed as shown here, such a person can "see" the amputated limb (actually a reflection of the normal limb). If the normal limb moves, the phantom limb now also feels as if it is moving. If the normal fist relaxes, some people with a phantom limb feel their phantom fist relaxing, with consequent reduction of pain.

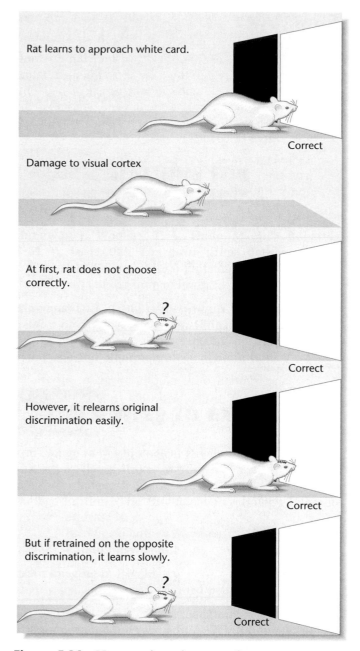

Figure 5.31 Memory impairment after cortical damage
Brain damage impairs retrieval of a memory but does not destroy it completely. *Source: Based on T. E. LeVere & Morlock, 1973*

Rat learns to approach white card.

Correct

Damage to visual cortex

At first, rat does not choose correctly.

?

Correct

However, it relearns original discrimination easily.

Correct

But if retrained on the opposite discrimination, it learns slowly.

?

Correct

such a lesion does not destroy the memory representation but merely impairs the rat's ability to find it.

Humans who have suffered brain damage also may have trouble accessing certain skills and memories. Just as a monkey that has no sensation in one arm may try to get by without using it, a person who has an impaired sensory system may try to do without it (T. E. LeVere, 1980). The task of physical therapists, occupational therapists, and speech therapists is to prod brain-damaged patients into practicing their impaired skills instead of ignoring them.

In an experiment that supports this approach to therapy, N. D. LeVere and T. E. LeVere (1982) trained rats with visual cortex lesions on a discrimination task that included both brightness and tactile cues. For one group of rats, the stimuli were redundant; the rats could solve the problem by responding to either one. This group solved the task rapidly but paid attention only to the tactile stimuli. If they were presented with only brightness stimuli, they responded randomly. For a second group of rats, the tactile stimuli were irrelevant; they could solve the problem only on the basis of brightness. This group took much longer than normal rats to solve the problem because their attention to the tactile stimuli distracted them from the relevant visual cues, but they did eventually solve it. In short, rats with visual cortex lesions can learn about visual stimuli, but they are impaired if other stimuli are available (N. Davis & LeVere, 1982). To help humans with similar brain damage, therapists should either remove the distracting stimuli or teach the individual to concentrate on the relevant stimuli.

Drugs

Several drugs have been shown to aid recovery from brain damage in animals. So far, we do not know their effect on humans.

Nimodipine, a drug that prevents calcium from entering cells, improves memory for visual learning tasks in rats with visual cortex lesions (T. E. LeVere, 1993; T. E. LeVere, Ford, & Sandin, 1992). Calcium blockers administered before brain damage produce modest benefits, presumably by preventing a toxic rush of calcium into neurons, but they produce greater benefits if administered after brain damage, presumably by improving cellular functioning.

Several studies indicate that **gangliosides** (a class of glycolipids—i.e., combined carbohydrate and fat molecules) promote the restoration of damaged brains. The fact that they adhere to neuron membranes suggests that they contribute to the recognition of one neuron by another during development, guiding axons to the correct locations to form synapses. Daily injections of gangliosides aid the recovery of behavior after several kinds of brain damage (Cahn, Borziex, Aldinio, Toffano, & Cahn, 1989; Ramirez, Fass, et al., 1987a, 1987b; Sabel, Slavin, & Stein, 1984). Exactly how they do so is not yet known.

In several studies of laboratory mammals, females have recovered better than males from some aspects of frontal cortex damage, especially if the damage occurred when they had high levels of the hormone *progesterone* (Stein & Fulop, 1998). Progesterone has a variety of effects on the brain, but no one knows which are the relevant ones. Perhaps someday physicians will offer hormonal treatments for brain-damaged patients. It may also be worthwhile to schedule women for certain kinds of brain surgery on days when their progesterone levels are high.

Brain Grafts

One other approach to therapy is the almost Frankensteinian idea of replacing dead brain cells with healthy ones from a donor. We consider this possibility in Chapter 8 in the context of Parkinson's disease, where neural transplants have been tried most frequently. Here let the message be that the method is still in the experimental stage. It is possible to transplant neurons and keep them alive, and the brain has a weak immune system, so tissue rejection is not as serious a problem as it is for other organs. One difficulty is to get suitable donor cells. It is possible to obtain stem cells (which are immature and capable of differentiating into other kinds of cells) from embryos, infants, adults, or recently deceased bodies (Clarke et al., 2000; Horner & Gage, 2000; Palmer et al., 2001). However, each option raises scientific as well as ethical issues, and the long-term potential is still uncertain.

MODULE 5.2

In Closing: Brain Damage and Recovery

In contrast to the multiple ways we have of replacing or temporarily compensating for the loss of blood or skin cells, our mechanisms of recovering from nervous system damage are less numerous and less powerful. Even the responses that do occur, such as collateral sprouting of axons or reorganization of sensory representations, are helpful in some cases and harmful in others. It is tempting to speculate that we did not evolve many mechanisms of recovery from brain damage because, through most of our evolutionary history, a brain-damaged individual was not likely to survive long enough to recover. Modern medicine keeps people with brain and spinal cord damage alive for many years, and we need continuing research on how to improve the recovery mechanisms that evolution has provided.

One measure of how far we have come is that the big question in this field is no longer *whether* we shall someday have good therapies for brain-damaged patients, but *what* those treatments will be. Will the answer be transplanted fetal tissues? Implanted neurotrophins? Drugs with related effects that cross the blood-brain barrier? Or calcium blockers or gangliosides or yet other possibilities? Researchers do not have the answers now, but they have reason to be optimistic.

SUMMARY

1. Brain damage has many causes, including strong or repeated blows to the head. Strokes, a common cause of brain damage in old age, kill neurons largely by overstimulation. Several methods can minimize the damage from stroke if they are applied quickly. (p. 125)

2. Recovery from brain damage may be better or worse in infants than in adults depending on a number of circumstances. (p. 128)

3. Much recovery from brain damage depends on learned changes in behavior that take advantage of the skills that remain. (p. 128)

4. Neurons that are remote from the site of damage may become inactive because they receive less input than usual. Behavioral recovery from brain damage depends partly on increased activity by these remote neurons; stimulant drugs can facilitate activity in surviving cells. (p. 129)

5. A cut axon may regenerate in the peripheral nervous system of a mammal and in either the central or peripheral nervous system of certain fish. Axons usually do not regenerate far in the adult mammalian CNS because of growth-inhibiting chemicals produced by central myelin. (p. 130)

6. When one set of axons dies, neighboring axons may under certain conditions sprout new branches to innervate the vacant synapses. (p. 131)

7. If many of the axons innervating a postsynaptic neuron die or become inactive, the neuron may become responsive to other axons. (p. 132)

8. The cortex and other areas change connections slightly to reflect ongoing experience. They change connections more drastically after an amputation; for example, an area previously responsive to a hand may now respond to stimulation on the face or shoulder. (p. 134)

9. As a result of brain organization, many people with amputations report phantom sensations, such as touch or pain in the amputated limb. These sensations are caused by stimulation in a body area that now connects to the cortex previously sensitive to the limb. (p. 135)

10. Therapy for brain-damaged people consists mostly of helping them practice the abilities that have been impaired but not destroyed. (p. 136)

11. Drugs that enhance memory or guide axonal growth promote recovery after certain kinds of brain damage. (p. 137)

ANSWERS TO *STOP AND CHECK* QUESTIONS

1. In both ischemia and hemorrhage, glia cells dump stored neurotransmitters, including the excitatory transmitter glutamate. Also, the sodium-potassium pump slows, and positive ions accumulate inside the neurons. (p. 128)

2. The drug tPA breaks up blood clots, and the problem in hemorrhage is a ruptured blood vessel, not a blood clot. (p. 128)

3. Refuse the blanket. Recovery will be best if the stroke victim remains cold for the first 3 days. (p. 128)

4. Tie the right arm behind the back to force the person to use the impaired arm instead of only the normal arm. Stimulating the skin of the left arm would accomplish nothing, as the sensory receptors have no input to the CNS. Blindfolding would be either irrelevant or harmful (by decreasing the visual feedback from left-hand movements). (p. 129)

5. It is best to direct the amphetamine to the cells that had been receiving input from the damaged cells. Presumably, the loss of input has produced diaschisis. (p. 129)

6. Axons (p. 134)

7. Dendritic receptors (p. 134)

8. The small-scale reorganization that enables increased representation of a violinist's or Braille reader's fingers is helpful. The larger scale reorganization that occurs after amputation is harmful. (p. 136)

THOUGHT QUESTIONS

1. Ordinarily, patients with advanced Parkinson's disease (who have damage to dopamine-releasing axons) move very slowly if at all. However, during an emergency (e.g., a fire in the building), they may move rapidly and vigorously. Suggest a possible explanation.

2. Drugs that block dopamine synapses tend to impair or slow limb movements. However, after people have taken such drugs for a long time, some experience involuntary twitches or tremors in their muscles. Based on something in this chapter, propose a possible explanation.

Key Terms and Activities

TERMS

ablation (p. 130)

apomorphine (p. 133)

apoptosis (p. 110)

closed head injury (p. 125)

collateral sprout (p. 131)

deafferent (p. 129)

denervation supersensitivity (p. 132)

diaschisis (p. 129)

differentiation (p. 109)

disuse supersensitivity (p. 132)

edema (p. 127)

fetal alcohol syndrome (p. 123)

focal hand dystonia (p. 120)

ganglioside (p. 137)

hemorrhage (p. 125)

ischemia (p. 125)

Kennard principle (p. 128)

lesion (p. 130)

magnetic resonance imaging (MRI) (p. 112)

magnetoencephalograph (MEG) (p. 117)

migration (p. 109)

myelination (p. 109)

nerve growth factor (NGF) (p. 110)

neural Darwinism (p. 115)

neurotrophin (p. 111)

penumbra (p. 127)

phantom limb (p. 135)

primates (p. 120)

proliferation (p. 109)

sham lesion (p. 130)

6-hydroxydopamine (6-OHDA) (p. 132)

stem cells (p. 116)

stereotaxic instrument (p. 130)

stroke (or cerebrovascular accident) (p. 125)

synaptogenesis (p. 109)

tissue plasminogen activator (tPA) (p. 127)

SUGGESTIONS FOR FURTHER READING

Azari, N. P., & Seitz, R. J. (2000). Brain plasticity and recovery from stroke. *American Scientist, 88,* 426–431. Good review of some of the mechanisms of recovery from brain damage.

Levi-Montalcini, R. (1988). *In praise of imperfection.* New York: Basic Books. Autobiography by the discoverer of nerve growth factor.

Ramachandran, V. S., & Blakeslee, S. (1998). *Phantoms in the brain.* New York: Morrow. One of the most interesting and thought-provoking books ever written about human brain damage, including the phantom limb phenomenon.

WEB SITE TO EXPLORE

You can go to the Biological Psychology Study Center and click this link. While there, you can also check for suggested articles available on InfoTrac College Edition.

 • The Biological Psychology Internet address is:
http://psychology.wadsworth.com/ kalatbiopsych8e

National Stroke Association home page
http://www.stroke.org/

CD-ROM: EXPLORING BIOLOGICAL PSYCHOLOGY

Sperry Experiment (animation)

Brains on Ice (video)

Phantom Limb (animation)

Critical Thinking (essay questions)

Chapter Quiz (multiple choice questions)

Vision

6

Chapter Outline

Opposite:
Later in this chapter, you will understand why this prairie falcon has tilted its head. *Source: ©Tom McHugh/Photo Researchers*

Main Ideas

1. Each sensory neuron conveys a particular type of experience; for example, anything that stimulates the optic nerve is perceived as light.

2. Vertebrate vision depends on two kinds of receptors: cones, which contribute to color vision, and rods, which do not.

3. Every cell in the visual system has a receptive field, an area of the visual world that can excite or inhibit it.

4. After visual information reaches the brain, concurrent pathways analyze different aspects, such as shape, color, and movement.

5. Neurons of the visual system establish approximately correct connections and properties through chemical gradients that are present before birth. However, visual experience can fine-tune or alter those properties, especially early in life.

Several decades ago, a graduate student taking his final oral exam for a PhD in psychology was asked, "How far can an ant see?" He suddenly turned pale. He did not know the answer, and evidently, he was supposed to. He mentally reviewed everything he had read about the compound eye of insects. Finally, he gave up and admitted he did not know.

With an impish grin, the professor told him, "Presumably, an ant can see 93 million miles—the distance to the sun." Yes, this was a trick question. However, it illustrates an important point: How far an ant can see, or how far you or I can see, depends on how far the light travels. We see because light strikes our eyes, not because we send out "sight rays." But this principle is far from intuitive. In fact, it was not known until the Arab philosopher Ibn al-Haythem (965–1040) demonstrated that light rays bounce off any object in all directions, but we see only those rays that strike the retina perpendicularly (Gross, 1999). Even today, a distressingly large number of college students believe that energy comes out of their eyes when they see (Winer, Cottrell, Gregg, Fournier, & Bica, 2002). The sensory systems, especially vision, are quite complex and do not match our commonsense notions.

MODULE 6.1

Visual Coding and the Retinal Receptors

Imagine that you are a piece of iron. So there you are, sitting around doing nothing, as usual, when along comes a drop of water. What will be your perception of the water?

You will have the experience of rust. From your point of view, water is above all *rustish*. Now return to your perspective as a human. You know that rustishness is not really a property of water itself but of how it reacts with iron.

The same is true of human perception. In vision, for example, when you look at a tree's leaves, you perceive them as *green*. But green is no more a property of the leaves than rustish is a property of water. Greenness is what happens when the light bouncing off the leaves reacts with the neurons in the back of your eye and eventually with the neurons in your brain. In effect, you color your own world; the greenness is in us—just as the rust is really in the piece of iron.

GENERAL PRINCIPLES OF PERCEPTION

Each receptor is specialized to absorb one kind of energy and transduce it into an electrochemical pattern in the brain. For example, visual receptors can absorb and respond to as little as one photon of light and transduce it into a **receptor potential,** a local depolarization or hyperpolarization of a receptor membrane. The strength of the receptor potential determines the amount of excitation or inhibition the receptor delivers to the next neuron on the way to the brain. After all the information from millions of receptors reaches the brain, how does the brain make sense of it?

From Neuronal Activity to Perception

Let us consider what is *not* an answer. The 17th-century philosopher René Descartes believed that the brain's representation of a physical stimulus had to resemble the stimulus itself. That is, when you look at something, the nerves from the eye would project a picturelike pattern of impulses onto your visual cortex. The problem with this theory is that it assumes a little person in the head who can look at the picture. Even if there were a little person in the head, we would have to explain how he or she perceives the picture. (Maybe there is an even littler person inside that person's head?) Perhaps the early scientists and philosophers would have avoided this error if they had started by studying olfaction instead; we are less tempted to imagine that we create a little flower for a little person in the head to smell.

The main point is that the coding of visual information in your brain *does not duplicate* the shape of the object that you see. For example, when you see a table, the representation of the tabletop does not have to be on the top of your retina or on the top of your head.

Law of Specific Nerve Energies

An important aspect of all sensory coding is *which* neurons are active. A given frequency of impulses may mean one thing when it occurs in one neuron and something different in another. In 1838, Johannes Müller described this basic insight as the **law of specific nerve energies.** Müller held that whatever excited a particular nerve establishes a special kind of energy unique to that nerve. In modern terms, any activity by a particular nerve always conveys the same kind of information to the brain. The brain sees the activity of the optic nerve and hears the activity of the auditory nerve.

We can state the law of specific nerve energies another way: No nerve has the option of sending the message "high C note" at one time, "bright yellow" at another time, and "lemony scent" at yet another. It sends only one kind of message—action potentials. The brain somehow interprets the action potentials from the auditory nerve as sounds, those from the olfactory nerve as odors, and those from the optic nerve as light. (Admittedly, the word "somehow" glosses over a deep mystery.)

If you rub your eyes, you may see spots or flashes of light even if the room is totally dark. The reason is that the mechanical pressure excites receptors in the retina of the eye; anything that excites those receptors is perceived as light. (If you try this experiment, first remove any contact lenses. Then shut your eyes and rub gently.)

If it were possible to cross-transplant the nerves from your eyes and ears so that the visual receptors were connected to the auditory nerve and vice versa, you would literally see sounds and hear lights. That is, of course, a hypothetical experiment. However, researchers discovered that they could perform it on animals with very immature nervous systems. Ferrets, mammals in the weasel family, are born so immature that their optic nerves (from the retina) have not yet reached the thalamus. Researchers rerouted the optic nerve on one side of the brain away from its usual target in the thalamus and into a different thalamic area that usually gets input from the ears. They damaged the axons from the ears to that half of the brain. The result was that the parts of the thalamus and cortex that usually receive input from the ears now received input only from the eyes. Which would you guess happened?

A. The axons from the eyes failed to make functional synapses.
B. What would have been auditory thalamus and cortex reorganized to become visual cortex.
C. The ferrets responded to light stimuli as if they were hearing something.

All right, time for your answer. (Is that your final answer?) The result, surprising to many, was B: What would have been auditory thalamus and cortex reorganized, developing some (but not all) of the characteristic appearance of a visual cortex (Sharma, Angelucci, & Sur, 2000). But how do we know whether the animals treated activity there as visual information? Remember that I said the researchers rerouted information from the optic nerve to the auditory cortex on one side of the brain. They left the other side intact. When the ferrets reached

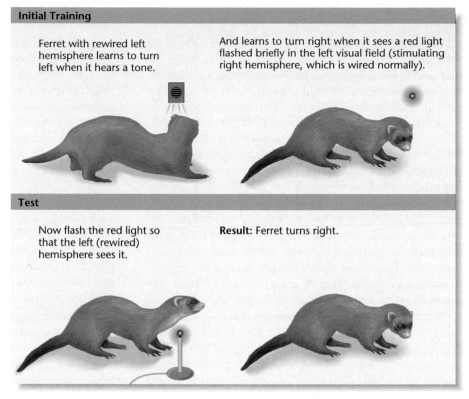

Figure 6.1 Behavior of a ferret with rewired temporal cortex
First the normal (right) hemisphere is trained to respond to a red light by turning to the right. Then the rewired (left) hemisphere is tested with a red light. The fact that the ferret turns to the right indicates that it regards the stimulus as light, not sound.

adulthood, the researchers trained them to turn one direction when they heard something and the other direction when they saw a red light, presenting the visual stimulus so that only the normal side of the brain could see it, as shown in Figure 6.1. After the ferrets learned this task well, the researchers presented a red light that the rewired side could see. The result: The ferrets turned the way they had been taught to turn when they saw something. In short, the rewired temporal cortex, receiving input from the optic nerve, produced visual responses (von Melchner, Pallas, & Sur, 2000).

1. What is the law of specific nerve energies?
2. If the optic nerve is directed into what is ordinarily the auditory portion of the brain, very early in development, what happens?

Check your answers on page 156.

THE EYE AND ITS CONNECTIONS TO THE BRAIN

Light enters the eye through an opening in the center of the iris called the pupil (Figure 6.2). It is focused by the lens (adjustable) and cornea (not adjustable) and projected onto the retina, the rear surface of the eye, which is lined with visual receptors. Light from the left side of the world strikes the right half of the retina, and vice versa. Light from above strikes the bottom half of the retina, and light from below strikes the top half. As in a camera, the image is reversed. However, the inversion of the image poses no problems for the nervous system. Remember, the visual system does not simply duplicate the image. There is no more need to present the image right side up than there is for a computer to use the top of its memory bank to store commands for the top of the screen.

The Route Within the Retina

In a sense, the retina is built inside out. If you or I were designing an eye, we would probably send the receptors' messages directly back to the brain. In the vertebrate retina, however, the receptors, located on the back of the eye, send their messages not toward the brain but to bipolar cells, neurons located closer to the center of the eye. The bipolar cells send their messages to ganglion cells, located still closer to the center of the eye. The ganglion cells' axons join one another, loop around, and travel back to the brain (Figures 6.3 and 6.4). Additional cells called *amacrine cells* get information from bipolar cells and send it to other bipolar cells, other amacrine cells, or ganglion cells. Amacrine cells are numerous and diverse; at least 29 types have been identified so far, providing many options for complex information processing. Figure 6.5 diagrams the various types of cells in the retina (Masland, 2001).

One consequence of this anatomy is that light has to pass through the ganglion cells and bipolar cells before it reaches the receptors. However, because these cells are highly transparent, light passes through them without distortion. A more important consequence of the eye's anatomy is the *blind spot*. The ganglion cell axons band together to form the optic nerve (or optic tract), an axon bundle that exits through the back of the eye. The point at which it leaves (which is also where some major blood vessels leave) is called the blind spot because it has no receptors.

Every person is therefore blind in part of each eye. You can demonstrate your own blind spot using Figure 6.6. Close your left eye and focus your right eye on the o at the top. Then move the page toward you and away, noticing what happens to the x. When the page is about 25 cm (10 inches) away, the x disappears because its image has struck the blind spot of your retina.

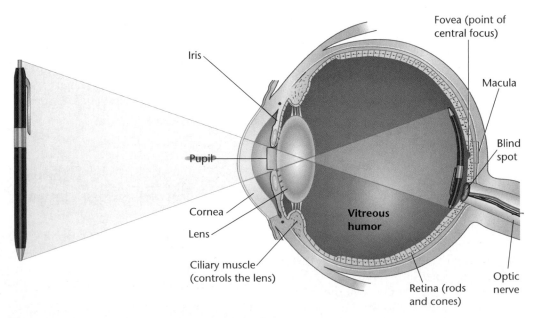

Figure 6.2   Cross section of the vertebrate eye
Note how an object in the visual field produces an inverted image on the retina.

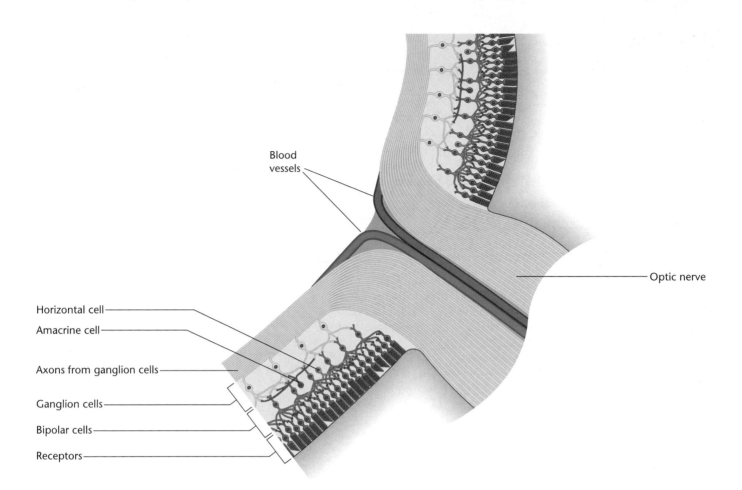

Blood vessels

Optic nerve

Horizontal cell

Amacrine cell

Axons from ganglion cells

Ganglion cells

Bipolar cells

Receptors

Figure 6.3 Visual path within the eyeball
The receptors send their messages to bipolar and horizontal cells, which in turn send messages to the amacrine and ganglion cells. The axons of the ganglion cells loop together to exit the eye at the blind spot. They form the optic nerve, which continues to the brain.

Now repeat the procedure with the lower part of the figure. When the page is again about 25 cm away from your eyes, what do you see? The *gap* disappears!

Some people have a much larger blind spot because glaucoma has destroyed parts of the optic nerve. Generally, they do not notice it any more than you notice your smaller one. Why not? Mainly, what they "see" in their blind areas is not blackness, but simply *nothing*—no sensation at all—the same as you see in your blind spot or out the back of your head.

3. What makes the blind spot of the retina blind?

   Check your answer on page 156.

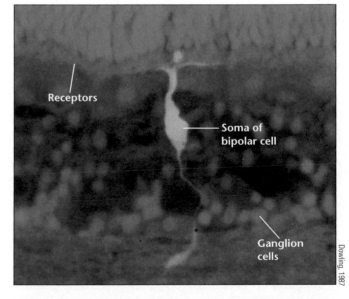

Receptors

Soma of bipolar cell

Ganglion cells

Dowling, 1987

Figure 6.4 A bipolar cell from the retina of a carp, stained with Procion yellow
Bipolar cells get their name from the fact that a fibrous process is attached to each end (or pole) of the neuron.

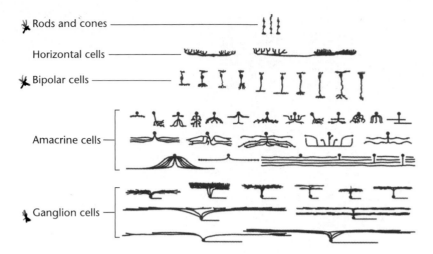

Rods and cones

Horizontal cells

Bipolar cells

Amacrine cells

Ganglion cells

Figure 6.5 Types of cells in the vertebrate retina
Note the huge variation among amacrine cells, which have diverse functions. Note also the variation among ganglion cells. Those in and near the fovea have a narrow span of dendrites and receive input from few receptors. Those in the periphery integrate input from a wide field of receptors. *Source: Reprinted with permission from "The Fundamental Plan of the Retina," by R. H. Masland, Neuroscience, 4, 877-886. Copyright ©2001 Neuroscience.*

Fovea and Periphery of the Retina

When you read or attend to any other detail of vision, you fixate the object on the portion of your retina with the greatest ability to resolve detail. Known as the *macula* (see Figure 6.2), this area measures about 3 mm × 5 mm in the center of the retina. The most precise vision comes from the central portion of the macula, called the **fovea** (meaning "pit"), specialized for acute, detailed vision. Because blood vessels and ganglion cell axons are almost absent near the fovea, it has the least impeded vision available. The tight packing of receptors also aids perception of detail.

Further aiding detailed vision in the human fovea, each receptor connects to a single *bipolar cell,* which in turn connects to a single *ganglion cell,* which then extends its axon to the brain. The ganglion cells in the fovea of humans and other primates are called **midget ganglion cells** because they are small and each receives input from just a single cone. As a result, each cone in the fovea has in effect a direct line to the the brain, which can register the exact location of any point of light in the fovea.

Toward the periphery, more and more receptors converge onto bipolar and ganglion cells. As a result, the brain cannot detect the exact location or shape of a peripheral light source. However, the summation enables perception of very faint lights in the periphery. In short, foveal vision has better *acuity* (sensitivity to detail), and peripheral vision has better sensitivity to dim light.

Peripheral vision can identify a shape much better by itself than if it is surrounded by other objects (Parkes, Lund, Angelucci, Solomon, & Morgan, 2001). For example, fixate your right eye on the x in each of the following displays. With the upper display, you can probably detect the direction of the sloping lines at the right. With the lower display, you probably cannot, at least not clearly. In the lower display, the surrounding elements interfere with detail perception. Note that the interference is great for peripheral vision but not for foveal vision. That is, if you focus on the slanted lines instead of the x, you see them clearly regardless of the surrounding elements.

Try It Yourself

x   ///

```
           #######
x          ##///##
           #######
```

You have heard the expression "eyes like a hawk." In many bird species, the eyes occupy most of the head, compared to only 5% of the head in humans. Furthermore, many bird species have two foveas per eye, one pointing ahead and one pointing to the side

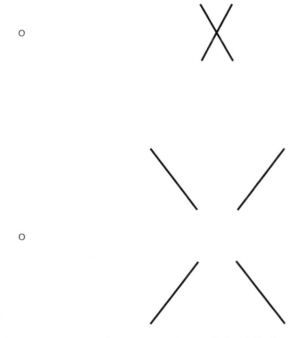

Figure 6.6 Two demonstrations of the blind spot of the retina
Close your left eye and focus your right eye on the o at the top of the figure. Move the page toward you and away, noticing what happens to the x. At a distance of about 25 cm (10 inches), the x disappears. Now repeat this procedure with the bottom of the figure. At that same distance, what do you see?

(Wallman & Pettigrew, 1985). The extra foveas enable perception of detail in the periphery.

Hawks and other predatory birds have a greater density of visual receptors on the top half of their retinas (looking down) than they have on the bottom half (looking up). That arrangement is highly adaptive because predatory birds spend most of their day soaring high in the air looking down. However, when the bird lands and needs to see above it, it must turn its head, as Figure 6.7 shows (Waldvogel, 1990).

Conversely, in many prey species such as rats, the greater density of receptors is on the bottom half of the retina (Lund, Lund, & Wise, 1974). As a result, they can see objects above them better than those below.

VISUAL RECEPTORS: RODS AND CONES

Black

The vertebrate retina contains two types of receptors: rods and cones (Figure 6.8). The **rods**, which are most abundant in the periphery of the human retina, respond to faint light but are bleached by bright light and thus not very useful in bright daylight. **Cones**, which are most abundant in and around the fovea, are less active in dim light, more useful in bright light, and essential for color vision. The differences between foveal and peripheral vision are summarized in Table 6.1. Although rods outnumber cones about 20 to 1 in most mammals, cones have a much more direct route to the brain. Remember the midget ganglion cells: In the fovea (all cones), each receptor has its own line to the brain. In the periphery (mostly rods), each receptor shares a line with tens or hundreds of others. A typical count shows about 10 cone-driven responses in the brain for every rod-driven response (Masland, 2001).

Both rods and cones contain **photopigments**, chemicals that release energy when struck by light. Photopigments consist of 11-*cis*-retinal (a derivative of vitamin A) bound to proteins called *opsins*. The 11-*cis*-retinal is stable in the dark; light energy converts it extremely quickly to another form, all-*trans*-retinal, in the process releasing energy that controls the cell's activities

Colored.

Chase Swift

Figure 6.7 A behavioral consequence of how receptors are arranged on the retina
One owlet has turned its head almost upside down to see above itself. Birds of prey have a great density of receptors on the upper half of the retina, enabling them to see below them in great detail during flight. But they see objects above themselves poorly, unless they turn their heads. Take another look at the prairie falcon at the start of this chapter. It is not a one-eyed bird; it is a bird that has tilted its head. Do you now understand why?

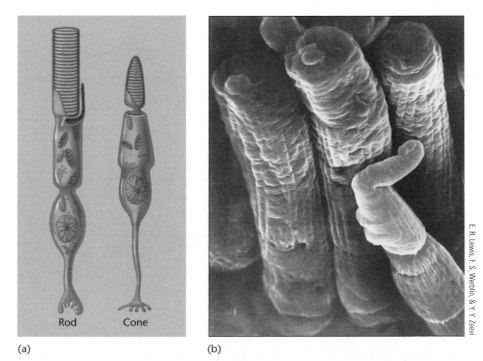

E. R. Lewis, F. S. Werblin, & Y. Y. Zeevi

(a)   (b)

Figure 6.8 Structure of rod and cone
(a) Diagram of a rod and a cone. **(b)** Photo of rods and a cone, produced with a scanning electron microscope. Magnification × 7000.

TABLE 6.1 Human Foveal Vision and Peripheral vision

Characteristic	Foveal Vision	Peripheral Vision
Receptors	Cones in the fovea itself; cones and rods mix in the surrounding area	Proportion of rods increases toward the periphery; the extreme periphery has only rods
Convergence of receptors	One or a few receptors send their input to each postsynaptic cell	Increasing numbers of receptors send input to each postsynaptic cell
Brightness sensitivity	Useful for distinguishing among bright lights; responds poorly to faint lights	Responds well to faint lights; less useful for making distinctions in bright light
Sensitivity to detail	Good detail vision because few receptors funnel their input to a postsynaptic cell	Poor detail vision because so many receptors send their input to the same postsynaptic cell
Color vision	Good (many cones)	Poor (few cones)

(Q. Wang, Schoenlein, Peteanu, Mathies, & Shank, 1994). (The light is absorbed in this process; it does not continue to bounce around in the eye.)

4. You sometimes find that you can see a faint star on a dark night better if you look slightly to the side of the star instead of straight at it. Why?

Check your answer on page 156.

COLOR VISION

Almost all vertebrates have both rods and cones (G. H. Jacobs, 1993). However, color vision requires comparing the responses of different kinds of cones. For example, rats have just one kind of cone (Neitz & Jacobs, 1986) and cannot discriminate one color from another.

In the human visual system, the shortest visible wavelengths, about 350 nm (1 nm = nanometer, or 10^{-9}m), are perceived as violet; progressively longer wavelengths are perceived as blue, green, yellow, orange, and red, near 700 nm (Figure 6.9). Discrimination among colors poses a special coding problem for the nervous system. A cell in the visual system, like any other neuron, can vary only its frequency of action potentials or, in a cell with graded potentials, its membrane polarization. If the cell's response indicates brightness, then it cannot simultaneously signal color. Conversely, if each response indicates a different color, the cell cannot signal brightness. The inevitable conclusion is that no single neuron can simultaneously

indicate brightness and color; our perceptions must depend on patterns of responses by a number of different neurons. Two major interpretations of color vision were described in the 1800s: the trichromatic theory and the opponent-process theory.

The Trichromatic (Young-Helmholtz) Theory

People can distinguish red, green, yellow, blue, orange, pink, purple, greenish-blue, and so forth. Do we have a separate receptor for every distinguishable color? If not, how many different types do we have?

The first person to analyze this question fruitfully was Thomas Young (1773–1829), a British physician and versatile genius. Young was the first to decipher the Rosetta stone, although his version was incomplete. He also founded the modern wave theory of light, defined energy in its modern form, founded the calculation of annuities, introduced the coefficient of elasticity, discovered much about the anatomy of the eye, and made other major contributions to many areas of knowledge (Martindale, 2001). He was among the first to recognize that color required a biological explanation, not a purely physical one. Young proposed that we perceive color by comparing the responses of some small number of receptors, each of which is sensitive to a different part of the range of visible wavelengths.

This theory was later modified by Hermann von Helmholtz and is now known as the trichromatic theory of color vision, or the **Young-Helmholtz theory.** According to this theory, we perceive color through the relative rates of response by three kinds of cones, each kind maximally sensitive to a different set of wavelengths. (*Trichromatic* means "three colors.") How did Helmholtz decide on the number three? He collected **psychophysical observations,** reports by

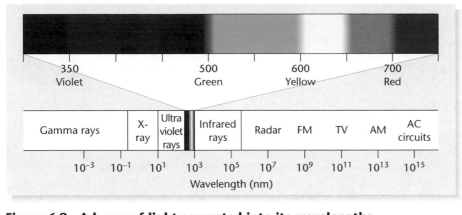

Figure 6.9 A beam of light separated into its wavelengths
Although the wavelengths vary over a continuum, we perceive them as several distinct colors.

observers concerning their perceptions of various stimuli. He found that people could match any color by mixing appropriate amounts of just three wavelengths. Therefore, he concluded that three kinds of receptors—we now call them cones—are sufficient to account for human color vision.

Figure 6.10 shows wavelength-sensitivity functions for the three cone types: *short-wavelength, medium-wavelength,* and *long-wavelength.* Note that each cone responds to a broad band of wavelengths, but to some more than others.

According to the trichromatic theory, we discriminate among wavelengths by the ratio of activity across the three types of cones. For example, light at 500 nm excites the medium-wavelength cone to about 65% of its maximum, the long-wavelength receptor to 40% of its maximum, and the short-wavelength receptor to 10% or 15% of its maximum. This ratio of responses among the three cones determines a perception of blue-green. More intense light increases the activity of all three cones but does not greatly alter the ratio of responses. That is, all receptors respond more strongly, but in the same proportions, so the color appears brighter, but still blue-green. When all three types of cones are equally active, we see white or gray.

Note that any response by one cone is ambiguous. For example, a low response rate by a middle-wavelength cone might indicate low-intensity 540-nm light or brighter 500-nm light or still brighter 460-nm light. A high response rate could indicate

either bright light at 540 nm or bright white light, which includes 540 nm. The nervous system can determine the color and brightness of the light only by comparing the responses of the three types of cones.

Given the desirability of seeing all colors in all locations, we might suppose that the three kinds of cones are equally distributed over the central portion of the retina. In fact, they are not. Long- and medium-wavelength cones are far more abundant than short-wavelength (blue) cones, and consequently, it is easier to see tiny red, yellow, or green dots than blue dots (Roorda & Williams, 1999). Try this: Look at the dots in the following display, first from a close distance and then from greater and greater distances. You probably will notice that the blue dots look blue when close but appear black from a greater distance. The other colors are still visible when the blue is not.

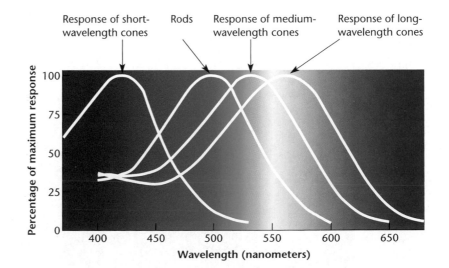

Figure 6.10 Response of rods and three kinds of cones to various wavelengths of light
Note that each kind responds somewhat to a wide range of wavelengths but best to wavelengths in a particular range. *Source: From J. K. Bowmaker and H. J. A. Dartnall, Visual Pigments of Rods and Cones in a Human Retina, Journal of Physiology, 298, 1980, 501–511. Copyright ©1980. Reprinted by permission of the author.*

Furthermore, the three kinds of cones are distributed randomly within the retina (Roorda, Metha, Lennie, & Williams, 2001; Roorda & Williams, 1999). Figure 6.11 shows the distribution of short-, medium-, and long-wavelength cones in two people's retinas, with colors artificially added to distinguish the three cone types. Note how few short-wavelength cones are present. Note also the patches of all medium- or all long-wavelength cones. At a local level, many areas of the retina lack the diversity of receptors needed for full color vision. Near the fovea, that patchy distribution is no problem. However, in the periphery, where cones become scarcer, we have trouble detecting the color of small objects (Martin, Lee, White, Solomon, & Rütiger, 2001). Try this: Get someone to mark a colored dot on the tip of your finger, without telling you what color it is. Slowly move it from behind your head into your field of vision and then gradually toward your fovea. At what point do you see the color? You will see your finger long before you can identify the color. As a rule, the smaller the dot, the farther you will have to move it into your visual field before you can identify the color, especially if it is blue.

The Opponent-Process Theory

The trichromatic theory correctly predicted the discovery of three kinds of cones, but it was originally intended as a theory of all color vision, and for that goal, it is incomplete. For example, try the following demonstration: Stare at the tip of the nose in Figure 6.12 under a bright light, without moving your eyes, for a full minute. (The brighter the light and the longer you stare, the stronger the effect.) Then look at a plain white surface, such as a wall or a blank sheet of paper. Keep your eyes steady. You will now see a **negative color afterimage,** a replacement of the red you had been staring at with green, green with red, yellow and blue with each other, and black and white with each other.

To explain this and related phenomena, Ewald Hering, a 19th-century physiologist, proposed the **opponent-process theory:** We perceive color in terms of paired opposites: red versus green, yellow versus blue, and white versus black (Hurvich & Jameson, 1957). That is, there is no such thing as reddish green, greenish red, or yellowish blue. The brain has some mechanism that perceives color on a continuum from red to green and another from yellow to blue.

Here is one possible mechanism for opponent processes: Consider the bipolar cell diagramed in Figure 6.13. It is excited by short-wavelength (blue) light and inhibited by long-wavelength or medium-wavelength light, but most strongly by a mixture of both, which we see as yellow. An increase in this bipolar cell's activity produces the experience *blue,* and a decrease produces the experience *yellow.* If short-wavelength (blue) light stimulates this cell long enough, the cell becomes fatigued. If we now substitute white light, the cell is more inhibited than excited, responds less than its baseline level, and therefore produces an experience of *yellow.* Many neurons from the bipolar cells through the cerebral cortex are excited by one set of wavelengths and inhibited by another (DeValois & Jacobs, 1968; Engel, 1999).

That explanation of negative color afterimages is appealing because of its simplicity. However, it is probably not the whole story. First, try this: Stare at the x in the following diagram for at least a

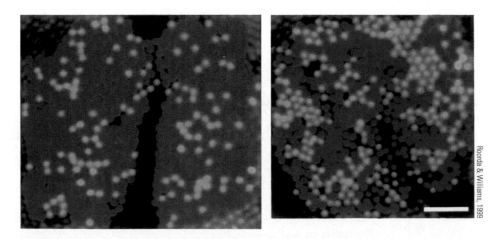

Figure 6.11 Distribution of cones in two human retinas
Investigators artificially colored these images of cones from two people's retinas, indicating the short-wavelength cones with blue, the medium-wavelength with green, and the long-wavelength with red. Note the difference between the two people, the relative rarity of short-wavelength cones, and the patchiness of the distributions.

Figure 6.12 Stimulus for demonstrating negative color afterimages
Stare at any one spot under bright light for about a minute and then look at a white field. You should see a negative afterimage.

minute under the brightest light you can find and then look at a white page. Fixate with your eyes close to the page.

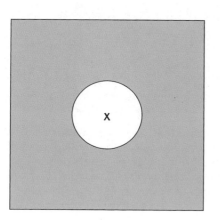

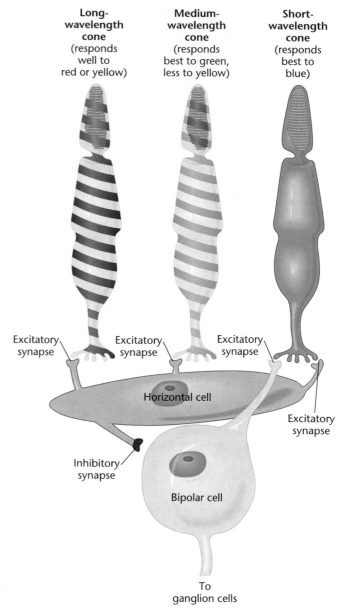

Figure 6.13 Possible wiring for one bipolar cell
Short-wavelength light produces more excitation than inhibition, and the result is seen as blue. Other wavelengths produce mostly inhibition, perceived as yellow. White light produces about equal excitation and inhibition.

For the afterimage of the surrounding box, you saw red, as expected from the theory. But what about the circle inside? Theoretically, you should see a gray or black afterimage (the opposite of white), but in fact, if you used a bright enough light, you saw a green afterimage.

Here is another demonstration: First look at Figure 6.14. Note that although it shows four red quarter circles, you have the illusion of a whole red square. (Look carefully to convince yourself that it is an illusion.) Now stare at the tiny x in Figure 6.14. Again, to get good results, stare for at least a minute under bright lights. Then look at any white surface.

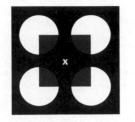

Figure 6.14 An afterimage hard to explain in terms of the retina
Stare at the tiny x under bright light for at least a minute and then look at a white surface. Many people report an alternation between two afterimages, one of them based on the illusion of a red square. *Source: Reprinted with permission from "Afterimage of Perceptually Filled-In Surface," Fig 1A, p. 1678 (left half) by S. Shimojo, Y. Kamitani, and S. Nishida in Science, 293, 1677–1680. Copyright 2001 American Association for the Advancement of Science.*

People usually report that the afterimage fluctuates. Sometimes they see four green quarter circles:

And sometimes they see a whole green square (Shimojo, Kamitani, & Nishida, 2001).

Note that a whole green square is the afterimage of an illusion! The red square you "saw" wasn't really there. This demonstration suggests that afterimages depend at least partly on whatever area of the brain produces the illusion—presumably the cerebral cortex, not the retina itself.

The Retinex Theory

The trichromatic theory and the opponent-process theory are powerful so far as they go, but both are incomplete with regard to some visual phenomena, especially color constancy. **Color constancy** is the ability to recognize the color of an object despite changes in lighting (Kennard, Lawden, Morland, & Ruddock, 1995; Zeki, 1980, 1983). If you put on green-tinted glasses or replace your white light bulb with a green one, you will notice the tint, but you still identify bananas as yellow, paper as white, walls as brown (or whatever), and so forth. You do so by comparing the color of one object with the color of another, in effect subtracting a fixed amount of green from each. Color constancy requires a comparison across all objects in the visual field.

Similarly, our perception of the brightness of an object requires comparing it with other objects. Examine Figure 6.15 (Purves, Shimpi, & Lotto, 1999). You see what appears to be either a divided object or two objects, but in either case, there is a gray top and a white bottom. Now, cover the center (the border between the top and the bottom) with your fingers. You will notice that except around the border, the top of the object has exactly the same brightness as the bottom!

To account for color and brightness constancy, Edwin Land proposed the **retinex theory** (a combination of the words *retin*a and cort*ex*): The cortex compares information from various parts of the retina to determine the brightness and color perception for each area (Land, Hubel, Livingstone, Perry, & Burns, 1983). For example, if the cortex notes a constant amount of green throughout a scene, it subtracts some green from each object to determine its true color.

Figure 6.15 A powerful demonstration of brightness constancy
Do you see a gray object and a white object? With your fingers, cover the border between the two objects and then compare the brightness of the two objects. *Source: From "An Empirical Explanation of Cornsweet Effect," by D. Purves, A. Shimpi, and R. B. Lotto, in Journal of Neuroscience, 19, 8542–8551. Copyright ©1999 by the Society for Neuroscience. Reprinted with permission.*

Dale Purves and colleagues have expressed a similar idea in more general terms: Whenever we see anything, we are making an inference or construction. For example, when you look at the object in Figure 6.15, you ask yourself, "On occasions when I have seen something that looked like this, what did it turn out to be?" The answer, of course, is a gray object and a white object. You go through the same process for perceiving shapes, motion, or anything else: You calculate what objects probably produced the pattern of stimulation you just had (Lotto & Purves, 1999; Purves, Lotto, Williams, Nandy, & Yang, 2001). That is, visual perception requires a kind of reasoning process, not just retinal stimulation.

Stop & Check

5. Suppose a bipolar cell received excitatory input from medium-wavelength cones and inhibitory input from all three kinds of cones. What color of light would most greatly excite the bipolar? What color would most greatly inhibit it?

6. When a television set is off, its screen appears gray. When you watch a program, parts of the screen appear black, even though more light is actually showing on the screen than when the set was off and the screen appeared gray. What accounts for the black perception?

Check your answers on page 156.

Color Vision Deficiency

A colleague once sent a survey to me and many other psychologists asking what discoveries psychologists had made. The encyclopedias are full of examples in astronomy, biology, chemistry, and physics, but what are psychologists' discoveries?

You might give that question some thought. One of my nominations as a major psychological discovery is color blindness, now called **color vision deficiency,** the inability to perceive color differences as most other people do. (Complete color blindness, the inability to perceive anything but shades of black and white, is rare.) Before color vision deficiency was discovered in the 1600s (Fletcher & Voke, 1985), people assumed that vision copies the objects we see. That is, if an object is round, we see the roundness; if it is yellow, we see the yellowness; if it is moving, we see the movement. Investigators *discovered* that it is possible to have otherwise satisfactory vision without seeing color.

We now recognize several types of color vision deficiency. For genetic reasons, some people lack the long-wavelength, medium-wavelength, or short-wavelength cones. Some lack two kinds of cones (Nathans et al., 1989). Other people have all three types of cones but have low numbers or unusual forms of one of them.

In the most common form of color vision deficiency, people have trouble distinguishing red from green because of a gene that causes the long- and medium-wavelength cones to make the same photopigment instead of different ones. The gene causing this deficiency is on the X chromosome. About 8% of men are red-green color blind, compared with less than 1% of women (Bowmaker, 1998). To test yourself for color vision deficiency, and to check for additional information, see this Web site:

http://members.aol.com/protanope/colorblindtest.html

For more information about the retina and vision and vision in general, this site provides an excellent treatment:

webvision.med.utah.edu

MODULE 6.1

In Closing: Visual Receptors

I remember once explaining to my then-teenage son a newly discovered detail about the visual system, only to have him reply, "I didn't realize it would be so complicated. I thought the light strikes your eyes and then you see it." As you should now be starting to realize—and if not, the next module should convince you—vision requires extremely complicated processing. If you tried to build a robot with vision, you would quickly discover that shining light into its eyes accomplishes nothing unless its visual detectors are connected to devices that identify the useful information and use it to select the proper action. We have such devices in our brains, although we are still far from fully understanding them.

SUMMARY

1. Each type of receptor transduces a particular kind of energy into a receptor potential, which is a hyperpolarization or depolarization of its membrane. (p. 144)

2. Sensory information is coded so that the brain can process it. The coded information bears no physical similarity to the stimuli it describes. (p. 144)

3. According to the law of specific nerve energies, the brain interprets any activity of a given sensory neuron as representing the sensory information to which that neuron is tuned. (p. 144)

4. Light passes through the pupil of a vertebrate eye and stimulates the receptors lining the retina at the back of the eye. (p. 146)

5. The axons from the retina loop around to form the optic nerve, which exits from the eye at a point called the blind spot. (p. 146)

6. Visual acuity is greatest in the fovea, the central area of the retina. (p. 148)

7. Because so many receptors in the periphery converge their messages to their bipolar cells, our peripheral vision is highly sensitive to faint light but poorly sensitive to detail. (p. 148)

8. The retina has two kinds of receptors: rods and cones. Rods are more sensitive to faint light; cones are more useful in bright light. Rods are more numerous in the periphery of the eye, cones in the fovea. (p. 149)

9. Light stimulates the receptors by triggering a molecular change in 11-cis-retinal, releasing energy, and thereby activating second messengers within the cell. (p. 149)

10. According to the trichromatic (or Young-Helmholtz) theory of color vision, color perception begins with a given wavelength of light stimulating a distinctive ratio of responses by the three types of cones. (p. 150)

11. According to the opponent-process theory of color vision, visual system neurons beyond the receptors themselves respond with an increase in activity to indicate one color of light and a decrease to indicate the opposite color. The three pairs of opposites are red-green, yellow-blue, and white-black. (p. 152)

12. According to the retinex theory, the cortex compares the responses representing different parts of the retina to determine the brightness and color of each area. (p. 154)

13. For genetic reasons, people with color vision deficiency are unable to distinguish one color from another. Red-green color blindness is the most common type. (p. 155)

ANSWERS TO *STOP AND CHECK* QUESTIONS

1. The law of specific nerve energies is the principle that any impulse in a given nerve sends the same kind of message to the brain. (p. 145)

2. What would have become the auditory cortex instead develops into a visual cortex, and stimulation there produces visual experience. (p. 145)

3. The blind spot has no receptors because it is occupied by exiting axons and blood vessels. (p. 147)

4. If you look slightly to the side, the light falls on an area of the retina that has rods, which are more sensitive to faint light. That portion of the retina also has more convergence of input, which magnifies sensitivity to faint light. (p. 150)

5. It would be most excited by medium-wavelength (green) light. It would be inhibited by either long-wavelength (red) or short-wavelength (blue) light or by a combination of both. However, because the long-wavelength cones are far more abundant than the short-wavelength cones, the cell is mostly excited by green and inhibited by red. (p. 155)

6. The black experience arises by contrast with the other brighter areas. The contrast occurs by comparison within the cerebral cortex, as in the retinex principle of color vision. (p. 155)

THOUGHT QUESTION

How could you test for the presence of color vision in a bee? Examining the retina does not help; invertebrate receptors resemble neither rods nor cones. It is possible to train bees to approach one visual stimulus and not another. The difficulty is that if you trained some bees to approach, say, a yellow card and not a green card, you do not know whether they solved the problem by color or by brightness. Because brightness is different from physical intensity, you cannot assume that two colors that are equally bright to humans are also equally bright to bees. How might you get around the problem of brightness to test color vision in bees?

MODULE 6.2

The Neural Basis of Visual Perception

Long ago, people assumed that anyone who saw an object at all saw everything about it: its shape, its color, its movement. The discovery of colorblindness was a huge surprise in its time, although today you and I take the condition for granted because we have heard about it since early childhood. However, you may be surprised—as were late 20th-century psychologists—by the analogous phenomenon of *motion blindness:* Some people with otherwise satisfactory vision fail to detect that an object is moving, or at least have great trouble determining its direction and speed. "How could anyone not see the movement?" you might ask. Your question is not very different from the question raised in the 1600s: "How could anyone see something without seeing the color?"

The fundamental fact about the visual cortex takes a little getting used to and therefore bears repeating: You have neither a little person in the head nor a central processor that sees every aspect of a visual stimulus at once. Vision is a complex matter; we perceive what an object is, its location, its color, and its movement. Different parts of the cortex process these separate aspects somewhat independently of one another.

AN OVERVIEW OF THE MAMMALIAN VISUAL SYSTEM

Let's begin with a general outline of the anatomy of the mammalian visual system and then examine certain stages in more detail. The rods and cones make synaptic contact with **horizontal cells** and bipolar cells (Figure 6.16). The horizontal cells make inhibitory contact onto bipolar cells, which in turn make synapses onto *amacrine cells* and ganglion cells. All these cells are within the eyeball.

The axons of the ganglion cells form the optic nerve, which leaves the retina and travels along the lower surface of the brain. The optic nerve from the left eye and the optic nerve from the right eye meet at the optic chiasm (Figure 6.17), where, in humans,

half of the axons from each eye cross to the opposite side of the brain. The percentage of crossover varies from one species to another, depending on the location of the eyes. In species with eyes on the sides of the head, such as rabbits and guinea pigs, nearly all the axons cross to the opposite side.

Most of the ganglion cell axons go to the **lateral geniculate nucleus,** a nucleus of the thalamus specialized for visual perception. (The term *geniculate* comes from the Latin root *genu,* meaning "knee." To *genuflect* is to bend the knee. In some species, the lateral geniculate looks a little like a knee if you use some imagination.) Some axons go to the superior colliculus, and even fewer go to several other areas, including a section of the hypothalamus that controls the waking–sleeping schedule (see Chapter 9). At any rate, most of the visual information goes to the lateral geniculate, which in turn sends its axons to other parts of the thalamus and to the visual areas of the cerebral cortex. The cerebral cortex returns many axons to the thalamus, so the input from thalamus to cortex is constantly modified by feedback from previous input to the cortex (Guillery, Feig, & van Lieshout, 2001).

The development of the visual cortex is modified by how many inputs reach it from the thalamus (Sur & Leamey, 2001); the number of incoming axons varies more than we might guess. Some people have two or three times as many axons in their optic nerve as others do and correspondingly more cells in the lateral geniculate and visual cortex (Andrews, Halpern, & Purves, 1997). The variation in number of cells leads to large differences among people in their abilities to detect brief, faint, or rapidly changing visual stimuli (Halpern, Andrews, & Purves, 1999).

The cerebral cortex has many visual areas with distinct functions and ways of analyzing visual information. However, the division of labor begins at the level of the ganglion cells, where several types of cells play different roles in perception. Those cells form different pathways that remain largely separate in the lateral geniculate and in the cerebral cortex. To understand the story of these different pathways, we need to begin with some general principles.

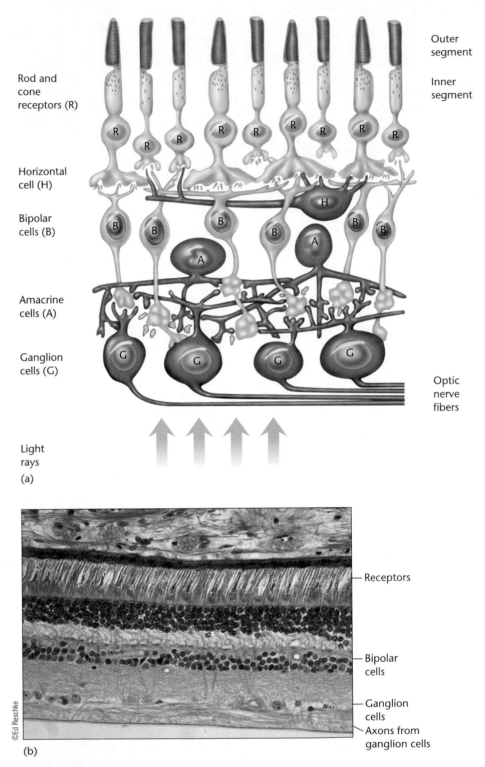

Rod and
cone
receptors (R)

Outer
segment

Inner
segment

Horizontal
cell (H)

Bipolar
cells (B)

Amacrine
cells (A)

Ganglion
cells (G)

Optic
nerve
fibers

Light
rays

(a)

©Ed Reschke

Receptors

Bipolar
cells

Ganglion
cells

Axons from
ganglion cells

(b)

Figure 6.16 The vertebrate retina
(a) Diagram of the neurons of the retina. The top of the figure is the back of the retina. All the optic nerve fibers are grouped together and exit through the back of the
retina, in the "blind spot" of the eye. *Source: Based on "Organization of the Primate
Retina," by J. E. Dowling and B. B. Boycott, Proceedings of the Royal Society of London, B,
1966, 166, p. 80–111. Used by permission of the Royal Society of London and John
Dowling.* **(b)** Photo of a cross section through the periphery of the retina shows relatively few ganglion cells; a slice closer to the fovea would have a greater density.

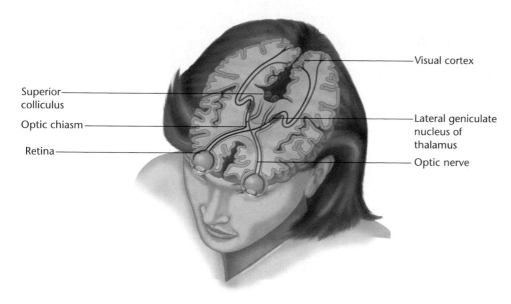

Figure 6.17 Major connections in the visual system of the brain
Part of the visual input goes first to the thalamus and from there to the visual cortex. Another part of the visual input goes to the superior colliculus.

forth, the receptive field of any of these other cells depends on its incoming synapses. For example, if a ganglion cell is connected to a group of receptors, the receptive field of the ganglion cell is the combined receptive fields of those receptors, as shown in Figure 6.18. Then the receptive fields of the ganglion cells converge to form the receptive fields of the next level of cells and so on. The connections from one neuron to another can be either excitatory or inhibitory, so receptive fields can have both excitatory and inhibitory regions.

Stop & Check

1. Where does the optic nerve start and where does it end?

Check your answer on page 176.

MECHANISMS OF PROCESSING IN THE VISUAL SYSTEM

The human retina contains roughly 120 million rods and 6 million cones. We cannot intelligently process 126 million independent messages; we need to extract the meaningful patterns, such as what the objects are, where they are, and whether they are moving.

Receptive Fields

The whole area of the world that you can see at any time is your **visual field.** The part that you see to your left is your left visual field; the part to your right is the right visual field. The part of the visual field to which any one neuron responds is that neuron's **receptive field.** For a receptor, the receptive field is simply the point in space from which light coming into the eye strikes the receptor. Because receptors connect to bipolar cells, which connect to ganglion cells and so

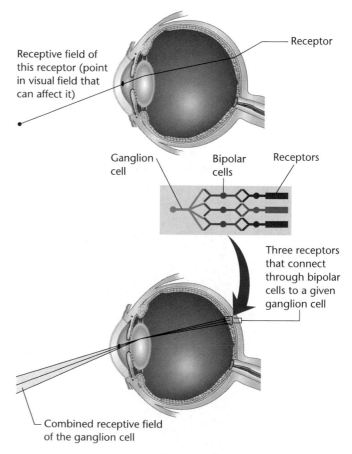

Figure 6.18 Receptive fields
The receptive field of a receptor is simply the area of the visual field from which light strikes that receptor. For any other cell in the visual system, the receptive field is determined by the receptors that connect to the cell in question.

To find a receptive field, an investigator can shine light in various locations while recording from a neuron. If light from a particular spot excites the neuron, then that location is part of the neuron's excitatory receptive field. If it inhibits activity, the location is in the inhibitory receptive field.

Neuroscientists often informally say that a particular neuron in the visual system responds to a particular pattern of light. For example, "This cortical cell responds best to a green horizontal line." The investigator does not mean that light shining on the neuron excites it. Rather the neuron is excited when light shines on its receptive field.

The receptive field of a ganglion cell can be described as a circular center with an antagonistic doughnut-shaped surround. That is, light in the center of the receptive field might be excitatory, with the surround inhibitory, or the opposite.

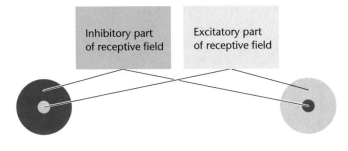

Lateral Inhibition

Neurons in the visual system have complicated receptive fields that we can understand in terms of their synaptic input. One of the most basic examples is lateral inhibition. When you look at any scene, what matters most is borders and edges. Borders identify where one object stops and another starts. Lateral inhibition is the retina's way of sharpening contrasts to make the borders clear.

Let's begin by considering part of the circuitry and then add more. The retina is lined with receptors (rods and cones). They have *inhibitory* synapses onto the bipolar cells and light *decreases* their output, but for simplicity's sake, instead of using double negatives, let's think of their output as excitation of the bipolar cells. Except in the fovea, many receptors connect to each bipolar cell, as shown in Figure 6.3, p. 147; however, for simplicity, let's imagine each receptor connected to just one bipolar. In this diagram, the green arrows represent excitation.

Now let's add the next element, the horizontal cells. Each receptor excites a horizontal cell, which *inhibits* the bipolar cells. Because the horizontal cell spreads widely, excitation of any receptor can inhibit a large group of bipolar cells. However, because

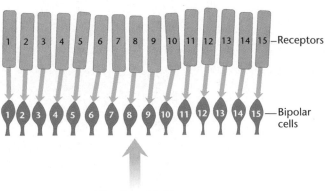

Direction of light

the horizontal cell is a *local cell,* with no axon and no action potentials, its depolarization decays with distance. Mild excitation of, say, receptor 8 excites the bipolar cell to which it connects, bipolar cell 8. Receptor 8 also stimulates the horizontal cell to inhibit bipolars 7 through 9 strongly, bipolars 6 and 10 a bit less, and so on. The result is that bipolar cell 8 shows net excitation; the excitatory synapse here outweighs the effect of the horizontal cell's inhibition. However, the bipolar cells to either side (laterally) get no excitation but some inhibition by the horizontal cell. Bipolars 7 and 9 are strongly inhibited, so their activity falls to well below the spontaneous level. Bipolars 6 and 10 are inhibited somewhat less, so their activity decreases a bit less. In this diagram, green arrows represent excitation from bipolar cells; red arrows represent inhibition from the horizontal cell.

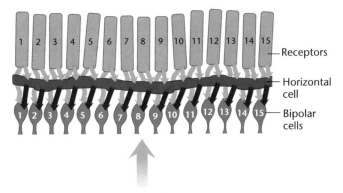

Direction of light

Now imagine what happens if light excites receptors 6–10. These receptors excite bipolar cells 6–10 and the horizontal cell. So bipolar cells 6–10 receive both excitation and inhibition. The excitation from the receptors is stronger than the inhibition from the horizontal cell, so bipolars 6–10 receive net excitation.

However, these bipolar cells do not all receive the same amount of inhibition. Remember, the response of the horizontal cell decays over distance. Bipolar cells 7, 8, and 9 are inhibited by receptors on both sides, but bipolar cells 6 and 10 are each inhibited by receptors on one side and not the other. That is, the bipolar cells on the edge of the excitation are inhibited less than those in the middle. Therefore, the overall result is that bipolar cells 6 and 10 respond *more* than bipolars 7–9.

Now think about bipolar cell 5. What excitation does it receive? None. What inhibition? It is inhibited by the horizontal cell because of the excitation of receptors 6 and 7. Therefore, bipolar 5, receiving inhibition but no excitation, responds even less than bipolars 1–4.

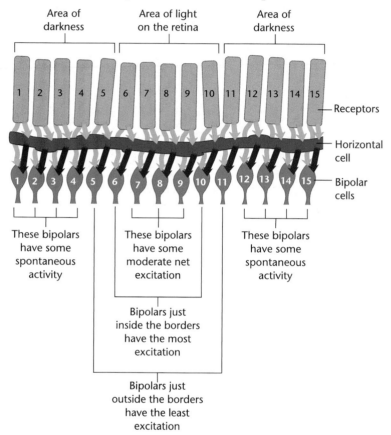

These results illustrate **lateral inhibition,** the reduction of activity in one neuron by activity in neighboring neurons (Hartline, 1949). The main function of lateral inhibition is to heighten the contrasts. When light falls on a surface, as shown here, the bipolars just inside the border are most excited, and those outside the border are the least responsive.

You might (or might not) find this analogy helpful: If I place a wooden block on a surface of gelatin, the block depresses the gelatin beneath it while raising the surrounding surface (Figure 6.19a). The depression is analogous to the excitation of a neuron, and the rise in the surrounding gelatin is analogous to lateral inhibition of surrounding neurons. Then I place a second block next to the first. As the second block sinks into the gelatin, it slightly raises the first (Figure 6.19b). Finally, I try placing a row of blocks on the gelatin. The blocks at the beginning and end of the row sink deeper than the others (Figure 6.19c). Why? Because each block in the

interior of the row is subject to upward pressure from both sides, whereas the blocks at the beginning and end of the row are subject to pressure from one side only.

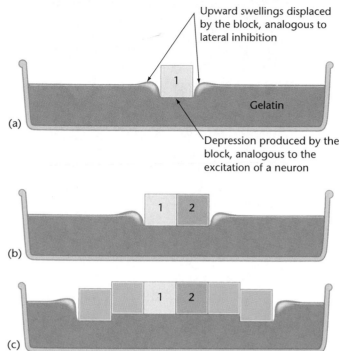

Figure 6.19 Blocks on a surface of gelatin, analogous to lateral inhibition
Each block pushes the gelatin down and the neighboring blocks are therefore pushed up. Blocks at the edge rise up less than those in the center.

2. As we progress from bipolar cells to ganglion cells to later cells in the visual system, are receptive fields ordinarily larger, smaller, or the same size? Why?

3. When light strikes a receptor, what effect does the receptor have on the bipolar cells (excitatory or inhibitory)? What effect does it have on horizontal cells? What effect does the horizontal cell have on bipolar cells?

4. If light strikes only one receptor, what is the net effect (excitatory or inhibitory) on the nearest bipolar cell that is directly connected to that receptor? What is the effect on bipolar cells off to the sides? What causes that effect?

5. Examine Figure 6.20. You should see grayish diamonds at the crossroads among the black squares. Explain why.

Check your answers on page 176.

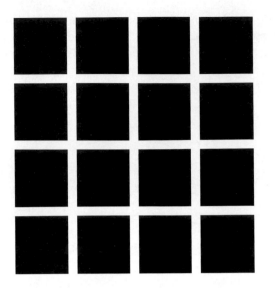

Figure 6.20   An illustration of lateral inhibition
Do you see grayish diamonds at the "crossroads"?

CONCURRENT PATHWAYS IN THE VISUAL SYSTEM

Look out your window. Perhaps you see someone walking by. Although your perception of that person seems to be an integrated whole, different parts of your brain are analyzing different aspects. One set of neurons identifies the person's shape, another set concentrates on the colors, and another sees the speed and direction of movement (Livingstone, 1988; Livingstone & Hubel, 1988; Zeki & Shipp, 1988). Although the various pathways necessarily communicate with one another, they function more independently than we might have imagined.

In the Retina and Lateral Geniculate

Your visual pathway begins its division of labor before it reaches the cerebral cortex. Even at the level of the ganglion cells in the retina, different cells react differently to the same input.

Try this demonstration: Assemble a group of small colored objects, pick one without looking at it, and slowly move it into the extreme periphery of your vision. When you can just barely see it, you cannot detect its shape or color, but if you shake it, you easily notice the movement. Your ability to see movement but not color in part of your retina reflects the presence of one kind of ganglion cell and the absence of another.

Remember that the bipolar cells connect to ganglion cells, whose axons form the optic nerve. Nearly all primate ganglion cells fall into three major categories: parvocellular, magnocellular, and koniocellular (Shapley, 1995). The **parvocellular neurons**, with smaller cell bodies and small receptive fields, are located mostly in or near the fovea. (Parvocellular means "small celled," from the Latin root *parv*, meaning "small.") The **magnocellular neurons**, with larger cell bodies and receptive fields, are distributed fairly evenly throughout the retina. (Magnocellular means "large celled," from the Latin root *magn*, meaning "large." The same root appears in *magnify* and *magnificent*.) The **koniocellular neurons** have small cell bodies, similar to the parvocellular neurons, but they occur throughout the retina instead of being clustered near the fovea. (Koniocellular means "dust celled," from the Greek root meaning dust. They were given this name because of their somewhat granular appearance.)

The parvocellular neurons, with their small receptive fields, are well suited to detect visual details. They are also highly sensitive to color, each excited by some colors and inhibited by others. The high sensitivity to detail and color reflects the fact that parvocellular cells are located mostly in and near the fovea, where we have many cones. Parvocellular neurons connect only to the lateral geniculate nucleus of the thalamus.

The magnocellular neurons, in contrast, have larger receptive fields and are not color sensitive. They respond strongly to moving stimuli and to large overall patterns but not to details. Magnocellular neurons are found throughout the retina, including the periphery, where we are sensitive to movement but not to color or details. Most magnocellular neurons connect to the lateral geniculate nucleus, but a few have connections to other visual areas of the thalamus.

Koniocellular neurons have several kinds of functions, and their axons terminate in several locations (Hendry & Reid, 2000). Various types of koniocellular neurons connect to the lateral geniculate nucleus, other parts of the thalamus, and the superior colliculus. The existence of so many kinds of ganglion cells implies that the visual system analyzes information in several ways from the start. Table 6.2 summarizes the three kinds of primate ganglion cells.

In the Cerebral Cortex

Most visual information from the lateral geniculate area of the thalamus goes first to the **primary visual cortex**, also known as area **V1** or as the *striate cortex* because of its striped appearance. It is the area of the cortex responsible for the first stage of visual processing. It

TABLE 6.2 Three Kinds of Primate Ganglion Cells

	Parvocellular Neurons	Magnocellular Neurons	Koniocellular Neurons
Cell bodies	Smaller	Larger	Small
Receptive fields	Smaller	Larger	Mostly small; variable
Retinal location	In and near fovea	Throughout the retina	Throughout the retina
Color sensitive	Yes	No	Some are
Respond to	Detailed analysis of stationary objects	Movement and broad outlines of shape	Varied and not yet fully described

responds to any kind of visual stimulus and is active even when we close our eyes and imagine visual stimuli (Kosslyn et al., 1999).

The primary visual cortex sends information to the secondary visual cortex (area V2), which processes the information further and transmits it to additional areas, as shown in Figure 6.21. The connections in the visual cortex are reciprocal; for example, V1 sends information to V2 and V2 returns information to V1. Each area also exchanges information with other cortical areas and the thalamus. Neuroscientists have distinguished 30 to 40 visual areas in the brain of a macaque monkey (Van Essen & DeYoe, 1995) and believe that the human brain has even more.

Within the cerebral cortex, the parvocellular and magnocellular pathways split from two pathways into three. A mostly parvocellular pathway continues as a system sensitive to details of shape. A mostly magnocellular pathway has a ventral branch sensitive to movement and a dorsal branch important for integrating vision with action. A mixed parvocellular and magnocellular pathway is sensitive to brightness and color. Many cells in this pathway also show some sensitivity to shape (E. N. Johnson, Hawken, & Shapley, 2001).

Note in Figure 6.21 that although the shape, movement, and color/brightness pathways are separate, they all lead to the temporal cortex. The branch of the mostly magnocellular pathway associated with integrating vision with movement leads to the parietal cortex. Researchers refer collectively to the visual paths in the temporal cortex as the ventral stream, or the "what" pathway, because it is specialized for identify-

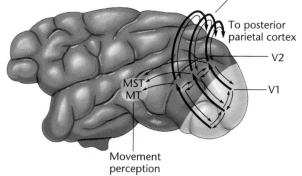

(a) Mostly magnocellular path

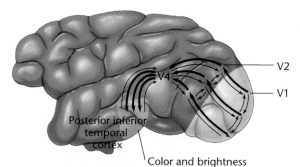

(b) Mixed magnocellular/parvocellular path

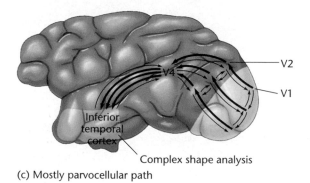

(c) Mostly parvocellular path

Figure 6.21 Three visual pathways in the cerebral cortex
(a) A pathway originating mostly from magnocellular neurons. (b) A mixed magnocellular/parvocellular pathway. (c) A mostly parvocellular pathway. Neurons are only sparsely connected with neurons of other pathways.
Source: Based on DeYoe, Felleman, Van Essen, & McClendon, 1994; Ts'o & Roe, 1995; Van Essen & DeYoe, 1995

ing and recognizing objects. The visual path in the parietal cortex is the **dorsal stream,** or the "where" or "how" pathway, because it helps the motor system find objects and determine how to move toward them, grasp them, and so forth.

People who have damage to the ventral stream (temporal cortex) cannot fully describe the size, shape, or location of the objects they see. However, they can reach for objects, walk toward them, or walk around objects in their way, even though they cannot describe them in words! They are also impaired in their ability to imagine shapes and faces—for example, to recall from memory whether George Washington had a beard (Kosslyn, Ganis, & Thompson, 2001).

In contrast, people who have damage to the dorsal stream (parietal cortex) can accurately describe what they see, but they cannot convert their vision into action. They cannot accurately reach out to grasp an object, even after describing its size, shape, and color (Goodale, 1996; Goodale, Milner, Jakobson, & Carey, 1991). They are also unable to imagine locations or describe them from memory—for example to describe the rooms of a house or the arrangement of furniture in any room (Kosslyn et al., 2001). In short, visually identifying objects is different from perceiving their locations.

Stop & Check

> **6.** What are the differences between the magnocellular and parvocellular systems?
>
> **7.** If you were in a darkened room and researchers wanted to "read your mind" just enough to know whether you were having visual fantasies, what could they do?
>
> *Check your answers on page 176.*

THE CEREBRAL CORTEX: THE SHAPE PATHWAY

In the 1950s, David Hubel and Torsten Wiesel (1959) began a research project in which they shone light patterns on the retina while recording from cells in a cat's or monkey's brain (see Methods 6.1). At first, they presented just dots of light, using a slide projector and a screen, and found little response by cortical cells. The first time they got a big response was when they were moving a slide into place. They quickly realized that the cell was responding to the edge of the slide and had a bar-shaped receptive field (Hubel & Wiesel, 1998). Their research, for which they received a Nobel Prize, has often been called "the research that launched a thousand microelectrodes" because it inspired so much further research. By now, it has probably launched a million microelectrodes.

Hubel and Wiesel's Cell Types in the Primary Visual Cortex

Hubel and Wiesel distinguished several types of cells in the visual cortex. The receptive fields shown in Figure 6.22 are typical of **simple cells,** which are found exclusively in the primary visual cortex. The receptive field of a simple cell has fixed excitatory and inhibitory zones. The more light in the excitatory zone, the more the cell responds. The more light in the inhibitory zone, the less the cell responds. For example, Figure 6.22c shows a vertical receptive field for a simple cell. The cell's response decreases sharply if the bar of light is moved to the left or right or tilted from the vertical because light then strikes the inhibitory regions as well (Figure 6.23). Most simple cells have bar-shaped or edge-shaped receptive fields,

METHODS 6.1
Microelectrode Recordings

David Hubel and Torsten Wiesel pioneered the use of microelectrode recordings to study the properties of individual neurons in the cerebral cortex. In this method, investigators begin by anesthetizing an animal and drilling a small hole in the skull. Then they insert a thin electrode—either a fine metal wire insulated except at the tip or a narrow glass tube containing a salt solution and a metal wire. They direct the electrode either next to or into a single cell and then record its activity while they present various stimuli, such as patterns of light. Researchers use the results to determine what kinds of stimuli do and do not excite the cell.

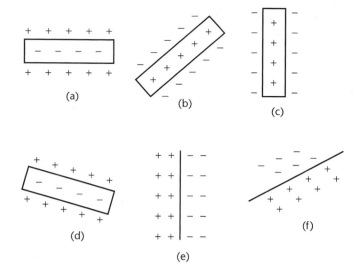

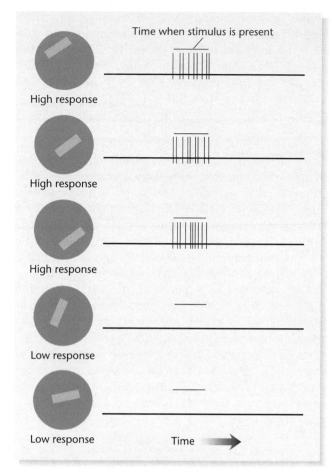

Figure 6.22 Typical receptive fields for simple visual cortex cells of cats and monkeys
Areas marked with a + are the excitatory receptive fields; areas marked with − are the inhibitory receptive fields.
Source: Based on Hubel & Wiesel, 1959

Figure 6.24 The receptive field of a complex cell in the visual cortex
Like a simple cell's, its response depends on the angle of orientation of a bar of light. However, a complex cell responds the same for a bar in any position within the receptive field.

which may be at vertical, horizontal, or intermediate orientations. The vertical and horizontal orientations outnumber the diagonals, and that disparity probably makes sense, considering the importance of horizontal and vertical objects in our world (Coppola, Purves, McCoy, & Purves, 1998).

Unlike simple cells, **complex cells,** located in either area V1 or V2, have receptive fields that cannot be mapped into fixed excitatory and inhibitory zones. A complex cell responds to a pattern of light in a particular orientation (e.g., a vertical bar) anywhere within its large receptive field, regardless of the exact location of the stimulus (Figure 6.24). It responds most

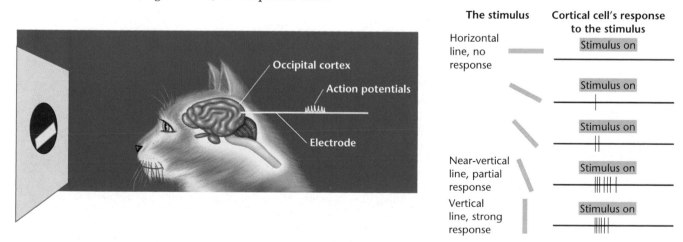

Figure 6.23 Responses of a cat's simple cell to a bar of light presented at varying angles
The rectangles indicate when light is on. *Source: Right, from D. H. Hubel and T. N. Wiesel, "Receptive Fields of Single Neurons in the Cat's Striate Cortex," Journal of Physiology, 148, 1959, 574–591. Copyright ©1959 Cambridge University Press. Reprinted by permission.*

strongly to a stimulus moving perpendicular to its axis—for example, a vertical bar moving horizontally or a horizontal bar moving vertically. If a cell in the visual cortex responds to a bar-shaped pattern of light, the best way to classify the cell is to move the bar slightly in different directions. A cell that responds to the light in only one location is a simple cell; one that responds strongly to the light throughout a large area is a complex cell.

Researchers for decades assumed that complex cells receive input from a combination of simple cells, and eventually, it became possible to demonstrate this point. Researchers used the inhibitory transmitter GABA to block input from the lateral geniculate to the simple cells, and they found that as soon as the simple cells stopped responding, the complex cells stopped, too (Martinez & Alonso, 2001).

End-stopped, or **hypercomplex,** cells resemble complex cells with one additional feature: An end-stopped cell has a strong inhibitory area at one end of its bar-shaped receptive field. The cell responds to a bar-shaped pattern of light anywhere in its broad receptive field provided that the bar does not extend beyond a certain point (Figure 6.25). Table 6.3 summarizes the properties of simple, complex, and end-stopped cells.

The Columnar Organization of the Visual Cortex

Cells having various properties are grouped together in the visual cortex in columns perpendicular to the surface (Hubel & Wiesel, 1977) (see Figure 4.23, p. 95). For example, cells within a given column respond either mostly to the left eye, mostly to the right eye, or to both eyes about equally. In addition, cells within a given column respond best to lines of a single orientation.

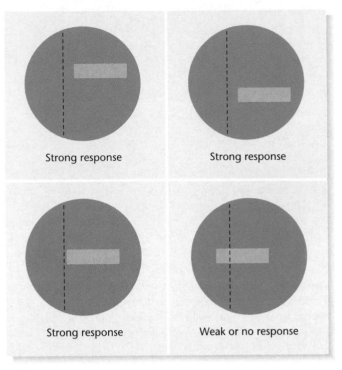

Figure 6.25 The receptive field of an end-stopped cell
The cell responds to a bar in a particular orientation (in this case, horizontal) anywhere in its receptive field, provided that the bar does not extend into a strongly inhibitory area.

Figure 6.26 shows what happens when an investigator lowers an electrode into the visual cortex and records from each cell that it reaches. Each red line represents a neuron and shows the angle of orientation of its receptive field. In electrode path A, the first series of cells are all in one column and show the same orientation preferences. However, after passing through the

TABLE 6.3	Summary of Cells in the Primary Visual Cortex		
Characteristic	Simple Cells	Complex Cells	End-Stopped Cells
Location	V1	V1 and V2	V1 and V2
Binocular input	Yes	Yes	Yes
Size of receptive field	Smallest	Medium	Largest
Receptive field	Bar- or edge-shaped, with fixed excitatory and inhibitory zones	Bar- or edge-shaped, without fixed excitatory or inhibitory zones; responds to stimulus anywhere in receptive field, especially if moving perpendicular to its axis	Same as complex cell, but with strong inhibitory zone at one end

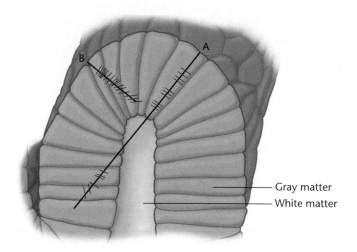

Gray matter
White matter

Figure 6.26 Columns of neurons in the visual cortex
When an electrode passes perpendicular to the surface of the cortex (first part of A), it encounters a sequence of neurons responsive to the same orientation of a stimulus. (The colored lines show the preferred stimulus orientation for each cell.) When an electrode passes across columns (B, or second part of A), it encounters neurons responsive to different orientations. Column borders are shown here to make the point clear; no such borders are visible in the real cortex. *Source: From "The Visual Cortex of the Brain," by David H. Hubel, November 1963, Scientific American, 209, 5, p. 62. Copyright ©Scientific American.*

white matter, the end of path A invades two columns with different preferred orientations. Electrode path B, which is not perpendicular to the surface of the cortex, crosses through three columns and encounters cells with different properties. In short, the cells within a given column process similar information.

Are Visual Cortex Cells Feature Detectors?

Given that neurons in area V1 respond strongly to bar- or edge-shaped patterns, it seems natural to suppose that the activity of such a cell *is* (or at least is necessary for) the perception of a bar, line, or edge. That is, these cells might be feature detectors— neurons whose responses indicate the presence of a particular feature. Cells in later areas of the cortex respond to more complex shapes, and perhaps they are square detectors, circle detectors, and so forth.

Supporting the concept of feature detectors is the fact that prolonged exposure to a given visual feature decreases sensitivity to that feature, as if one has fatigued the relevant detectors. For example, if you stare at a waterfall for a minute or more and then look away, the rocks and trees next to the waterfall appear to be

flowing upward. This effect, the *waterfall illusion,* suggests that you have fatigued the neurons that detect downward motion, leaving unopposed the detectors that detect the opposite motion. You can see the same effect if you watch your computer screen scroll slowly for about a minute and then examine an unmoving display.

However, just as a medium-wavelength cone responds somewhat to the whole range of wavelengths, a cortical cell that responds best to one stimulus also responds to many others. Any object stimulates a large population of cells, and any cell in the visual system responds somewhat to many stimuli (Tsunoda, Yamane, Nishizaki, & Tanifuji, 2001). The response of any cell is ambiguous unless it is compared to the responses of other cells.

Furthermore, Hubel and Wiesel tested only a limited range of stimuli. Later researchers have tried other kinds of stimuli and found that a cortical cell that responds well to a single bar or line

also responds, generally even more strongly, to a sine-wave grating of bars or lines:

Different cortical neurons respond best to gratings of different spatial frequencies (i.e., wide bars or narrow bars), and many are very precisely tuned—that is, they respond strongly to one frequency and hardly at all to a slightly higher or lower frequency (DeValois, Albrecht, & Thorell, 1982). Most visual researchers therefore believe that neurons in area V1 respond to spatial frequencies rather than to bars or edges. How do we translate a series of spatial frequencies into perception? From a mathematical standpoint, sine wave spatial frequencies are easy to work with. In a branch of mathematics called Fourier analysis, it can be demonstrated that a combination of sine waves can produce an unlimited variety of other more complicated patterns. For example, the graph at the top of the following display is the sum of the five sine waves below it:

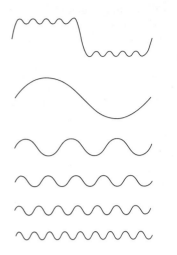

Therefore, a series of spatial frequency detectors, some sensitive to horizontal patterns and others to vertical patterns, could represent anything anyone could see. Still, we obviously do not perceive the world as an assembly of sine waves, and the emergence of object perception remains a puzzle (Hughes, Nozawa, & Kitterle, 1996). Indeed, the activities of areas V1 and V2 are probably preliminary steps that organize visual material and send it to more specialized areas that actually identify objects (Lennie, 1998).

Shape Analysis Beyond Area V1

As visual information goes from the simple cells to the complex cells and then on to later areas of visual processing, the receptive fields become larger and more specialized. For example, in area V2 (next to V1), many cells still respond best to lines, edges, and sine wave gratings, but some cells respond selectively to circles, lines that meet at a right angle, or other complex patterns (Hegdé & Van Essen, 2000). In area V4, many cells respond selectively to a particular slant of a line in three-dimensional space (Hinkle & Connor, 2002).

Response patterns are even more complex in the inferior temporal cortex (see Figure 6.21). Because cells in this area have huge receptive fields, always including the foveal field of vision, their responses provide almost no information about stimulus location. However, many of them respond selectively to complex shapes and are insensitive to many distinctions that are critical for other cells. For example, some cells in the inferior temporal cortex respond about equally to a black square on a white background, a white square on a black background, and a square-shaped pattern of dots moving across a stationary pattern of dots (Sáry, Vogels, & Orban,

1993). On the other hand, a cell that responds about equally to 🔲 and 🔲 may hardly respond at all to 🔲 (Vogels, Biederman, Bar, & Lorincz, 2001). Evidently, cortical neurons can respond specifically to certain details of shape.

Most inferior temporal neurons that respond strongly to a particular shape respond almost equally to its mirror image (Rollenhagen & Olson, 2000). For example, a cell might respond equally to 🦅 and to 🦅. Cells also respond equally after a reversal of contrast, where white becomes black and black becomes white. However, they do not respond the same after a figure-ground reversal. Examine Figure 6.27. Researchers measured responses in monkeys' inferior temporal cortex to a number of stimuli and then to three kinds of transformations. The response of a neuron to each original stimulus correlated highly with its response to the contrast reversal and mirror image but correlated poorly with its response to the figure-ground reversal (Baylis & Driver, 2001). That is, cells in this area detect an object, no matter how it is displayed, and not the amount of light or darkness in any location on the retina.

The ability of inferior temporal neurons to ignore changes in size and direction probably contributes to our capacity for **shape constancy**—the ability to recognize an object's shape even as it changes location or direction. However, although shape constancy

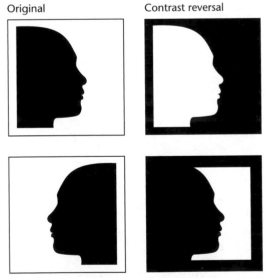

Original   Contrast reversal

Mirror image   Figure-ground reversal

Figure 6.27 Three transformations of an original drawing
In the inferior temporal cortex, cells that respond strongly to the original respond about the same to the contrast reversal and mirror image but not to the figure-ground reversal. Note that the figure-ground reversal resembles the original very strongly in terms of the pattern of light and darkness; however, it is not perceived as the same object.
Source: Based on Baylis & Driver, 2001

helps us recognize an object from different angles, it interferes in reading, where we need to treat mirror image letters as different. (Consider the difficulty some children have in learning the difference between b and d, or p and q.)

Disorders of Object Recognition

Damage to the pattern pathway of the cortex should lead to specialized deficits in the ability to recognize objects. Neurologists have reported such cases for decades, although they frequently met with skepticism. Now that we understand *how* such specialized defects might arise, we find them easier to accept.

An inability to recognize objects despite otherwise satisfactory vision is called **visual agnosia** (meaning "visual lack of knowledge"). A brain-damaged person might be able to point to visual objects and slowly describe them but fail to recognize what they are or mean. For example, when shown a key, one patient said, "I don't know what that is; perhaps a file or a tool of some sort." When shown a stethoscope, he said that it was "a long cord with a round thing at the end." When he could not identify a pipe, the examiner told him what it was. He then replied, "Yes, I can see it now," and pointed out the stem and bowl of the pipe. Then the examiner asked, "Suppose I told you that the last object was not really a pipe?" The patient replied, "I would take your word for it. Perhaps it's not really a pipe" (Rubens & Benson, 1971).

Many other types of agnosia occur. One closed head injury patient could recognize faces of all kinds, including cartoons and face pictures made from objects (Figure 6.28). However, he could not recognize any of the individual objects that composed the face (Moscovitch, Winocur, & Behrmann, 1997).

The opposite disorder—inability to recognize faces—is known as **prosopagnosia** (PROSS-oh-pag-NOH-see-ah). As a rule, people with prosopagnosia can read, and they can recognize familiar people from their voices and sometimes even clothing, so their problem is specific to faces (Farah, Wilson, Drain, & Tanaka, 1998). When they look at a face, they can describe whether the person is old or young, male or female, but they cannot identify the person. One man with prosopagnosia was shown 34 photographs of famous people and was offered a choice of two identifications for each. By chance alone, he should have identified 17 correctly; in fact, he got 18. He remarked that he seldom enjoyed watching movies or television programs because he had trouble keeping track of the characters. Curiously, his favorite movie was *Batman,* in which the main characters wore masks much of the time (Laeng & Caviness, 2001).

Functional MRI scans (as described in Methods 6.2) show that when people with intact brains recognize faces, activity increases in the *fusiform gyrus* of the inferior temporal cortex (Figure 6.30) and in part of the prefrontal cortex (McCarthy, Puce, Gore, & Allison, 1997; Ó Scalaidhe, Wilson, & Goldman-Rakic, 1997). A controversy has developed about how narrowly these areas are specialized for face recognition. Certainly, the fusiform gyrus has cells that respond much more strongly to faces than to any other stimuli, but all of its cells do respond at least somewhat to other stimuli also. Conversely, other visual cortex areas respond

Moscovitch, Winocur & Behrmann, 1997

Figure 6.28 Faces made from other objects
One man, after a closed head injury, could recognize these as faces and could point out the eyes, nose, and so forth, but could not identify any of the component objects. He was not even aware that the faces were composed of objects.

fMRI Scans

Standard MRI scans (discussed in Methods 5.1, p. 112) record the energy released by water molecules after removal of a magnetic field. MRI can resolve details of brain anatomy smaller than a millimeter in diameter. However, MRI doesn't show changes over time because the brain has little net flow of water. A modified version of an MRI that enables researchers to view changes over time is **functional magnetic resonance imaging (fMRI)** (Detre & Floyd, 2001). The fMRI procedure takes advantage of the fact that hemoglobin (the blood protein that binds oxygen) slightly changes its responses to a magnetic field after it releases its oxygen. Because oxygen consumption increases in the brain areas with the greatest activity, researchers can set the fMRI scanner to distinguish between hemoglobin with oxygen and hemoglobin without oxygen and thereby measure the relative activity of various brain areas. An fMRI scan provides reliable information about the amount of stimulation reaching a brain area (Logothetis, Pauls, Augath, Trinath, & Oeltermann, 2001).

An fMRI image has a spatial resolution of 1 or 2 mm (almost as good as standard MRI) and temporal resolution of less than a second (Figure 6.29). Unlike a PET scan, the fMRI procedure does not expose the person to a radiation hazard. It has these drawbacks: First, its large moving magnets are very noisy. Second, the

person has to lie motionless in a device that tightly surrounds most of the body. Very few young children can hold still long enough, and neither can anyone with claustrophobia.

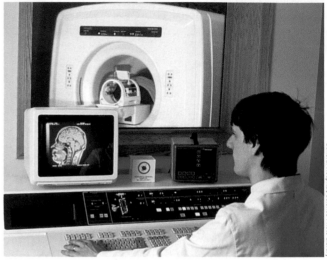

Figure 6.29 An fMRI scan of a human brain
An fMRI produces fairly detailed photos at rates up to about one per second.

somewhat to faces, even though they respond more strongly to some other kind of object. That is, different visual areas have some specialization and some overlap of functions as well (Haxby et al., 2001; Ishai, Ungerleider, Martin, & Haxby, 2000).

Behavioral measures also indicate that the fusiform gyrus is largely but not completely specialized for face recognition. On the one hand, some people develop enough expertise to recognize brands of cars from a distance or to identify hundreds of species of birds, sometimes from just a glance. For those people, looking at a car or a bird activates the fusiform gyrus, and the greater the expertise, the greater the level of activation (Tarr & Gauthier, 2000). People with damage to the fusiform gyrus have trouble recognizing cars, bird species, and so forth (Farah, 1990). Furthermore, when people with intact brains are shown

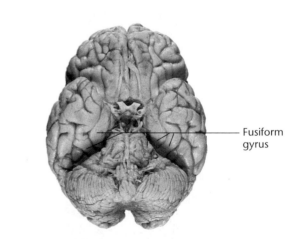

Fusiform gyrus

Figure 6.30 The fusiform gyrus
Many cells here are especially active during recognition of faces. *Source: Courtesy of Dana Copeland*

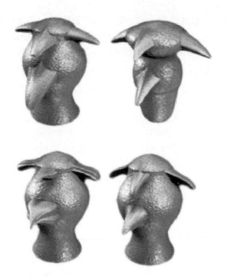

Figure 6.31 Greebles
When people are asked to recognize individual greebles or to sort them into "families" of related individuals, at first they have low accuracy. As they practice and improve, the fusiform gyrus becomes more responsive to greebles.
Source: Gauthier, Tarr, Anderson, Skudlarski, & Gore, 1999

"greebles," the unfamiliar-looking objects shown in Figure 6.31, at first they have trouble recognizing them individually, and the fusiform gyrus responds only weakly. As people gain familiarity and learn to recognize them, the fusiform gyrus becomes more active and reacts to them more like faces (Gauthier, Tarr, Anderson, Skudlarski, & Gore, 1999; Rossion, Gauthier, Goffaux, Tarr, & Crommelinck, 2002). On the other hand, no matter how much expertise people gain with various stimuli, nothing else activates the fusiform gyrus as much as faces (Kanwisher, 2000). So face recognition may indeed be special, not quite like any other kind of expert pattern recognition.

Stop & Check

8. How could a researcher determine whether a given neuron in the visual cortex was simple or complex?

9. What is prosopagnosia and what does its existence tell us about separate shape recognition systems in the visual cortex?

Check your answers on page 176.

THE CEREBRAL CORTEX: THE COLOR PATHWAY

Color perception depends on the parvocellular and koniocellular paths. A path of cells highly sensitive to color emerges in parts of area V1 known as the *blobs*. (These blob-shaped clusters of neurons can be identified by a chemical called cytochrome oxidase that stains them without affecting other cells.) The blobs also have cells of the magnocellular path, which contribute to brightness perception. The cells in the blobs then send their output through particular parts of areas V2, V4, and the posterior inferior temporal cortex, as shown in Figure 6.21b.

Several investigators have found that either area V4 or a nearby area is particularly important for color constancy (Hadjikhani, Liu, Dale, Cavanagh, & Tootell, 1998; Zeki, McKeefry, Bartels, & Frackowiak, 1998). Recall from the discussion of the retinex theory that color constancy is the ability to recognize the color of an object even if the lighting changes. Monkeys with damage to area V4 can learn to pick up a yellow object to get food but cannot find it if the overhead lighting is changed from white to blue (Wild, Butler, Carden, & Kulikowski, 1985). That is, they retain color vision but lose color constancy. In humans also, after damage to an area that straddles the temporal and parietal cortexes, perhaps corresponding to monkey area V4, people recognize and remember colors but lose their color constancy (Rüttiger et al., 1999).

In addition to a role in color vision, area V4 has cells that contribute to visual attention (Leopold & Logothetis, 1996). Animals with damage to V4 have trouble shifting their attention from the larger, brighter stimulus to any less prominent stimulus.

THE CEREBRAL CORTEX: THE MOTION AND DEPTH PATHWAYS

Many of the cells of the magnocellular pathway are specialized for **stereoscopic depth perception,** the ability to detect depth by differences in what the two eyes see. To illustrate, hold a finger in front of your eyes and look at it, first with just the left eye and then just the right eye. Try again, holding your finger at different distances. Note that the two eyes see your finger differently and that the closer your finger is to your face, the greater the difference between the two views.

Certain cells in the magnocellular pathway detect the discrepancy between the two views, presumably mediating stereoscopic depth perception. When you look at something with just one eye, the same cells are almost unresponsive.

Structures Important for Motion Perception

Moving objects grab our attention, and for good reasons. A moving object might be alive. It might be dangerous or it might be useful. In any case, a moving object calls for an immediate decision of whether to chase it, ignore it, or run away from it. Motion detection activates different brain areas from those for shape or color.

Imagine yourself sitting in a small boat on a river. The waves are all flowing one direction, and in the distance, you see rapids. Meanwhile, a duck is swimming slowly against the current, the clouds are moving yet another direction, and your perspective alters every time a wave rocks the boat. In short, you simultaneously see several kinds of motion. Viewing a moving pattern activates many brain areas spread among all four lobes of the cerebral cortex (Sunaert, Van Hecke, Marchal, & Orban, 1999; Vanduffel et al., 2001). Two temporal lobe areas that are consistently and strongly activated by any kind of visual motion are area **MT** (for middle-temporal cortex), also known as area **V5**, and an adjacent region, area **MST** (medial superior temporal cortex) (see Figure 6.21). Areas MT and MST receive their direct input from a branch of the magnocellular path, although they also receive some parvocellular input (Yabuta, Sawatari, & Callaway, 2001). The magnocellular path detects overall patterns, including movement over large areas of the visual field. The parvocellular path includes cells that detect the disparity between the views of the left and right eyes, an important cue to distance (Kasai & Morotomi, 2001).

Most cells in area MT respond selectively to a stimulus moving in a particular direction, almost independently of the size, shape, brightness, or color of the object (Perrone & Thiele, 2001). They also respond somewhat to a still photograph that implies movement, such as a photo of people running or cars

racing (Kourtzi & Kanwisher, 2000). To other kinds of stationary stimuli, they show little response.

Many cells in area MT respond best to moving borders within their receptive fields. Cells in the dorsal part of area **MST** respond best to the expansion, contraction, or rotation of a large visual scene, as illustrated in Figure 6.32. That kind of experience occurs when you move forward or backward or tilt your head. These two kinds of cells—the ones that record movement of single objects and the ones that record movement of the entire background—converge their messages onto neurons in the ventral part of area MST, where cells respond whenever an object moves in a certain direction *relative to its background* (K. Tanaka, Sugita, Moriya, & Saito, 1993) (Figure 6.33).

A cell with such properties is enormously useful in determining the motion of objects. When you move your head or eyes from left to right, all the objects in your visual field move across your retina as if the world itself had moved right to left. (Go ahead and try it.) Yet when you do so, the world looks stationary because the objects are stationary with respect to one another. Many neurons in area MST are silent during eye movements (Thiele, Henning, Kubischik, & Hoffmann, 2002). However, MST neurons respond briskly if an object really is moving during the eye movement—that is, if it is moving relative to the background. In short, MST neurons enable you to distinguish between the result of eye movements and the result of object movements.

Several other brain areas have specialized roles for particular types of motion perception. For example,

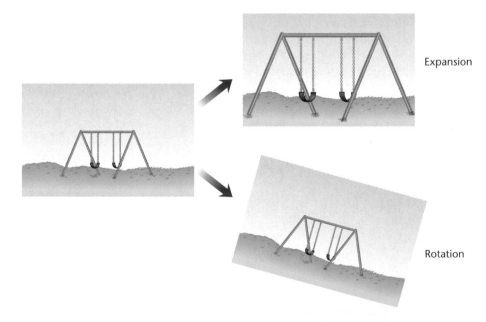

Figure 6.32 Stimuli that excite the dorsal part of area MST
Cells here respond if a whole scene expands, contracts, or rotates. That is, such cells respond if the observer moves forward or backward or tilts his or her head.

Figure 6.33　Stimuli that excite the ventral part of area MST
Cells here respond when an object moves relative to its background. They therefore react either when the object moves or when it is steady and the background moves.

the brain is particularly adept at detecting biological motion—the kinds of motion produced by people and animals. If you attach glow-in-the-dark dots to someone's elbows, knees, hips, shoulders, and a few other points, then when that person moves in an otherwise dark room, you perceive a moving person, even though you are actually seeing only a few spots of light. Perceiving biological motion activates an area near, but not identical with, area MT (Grossman & Blake, 2001; Grossman et al., 2000). Other areas become active when people pay close attention to the speed or direction of movement (Cornette et al., 1998; Sunaert, Van Hecke, Marchal, & Orban, 2000).

Suppressed Vision During Eye Movements

The temporal cortex has cells that distinguish between moving objects and visual changes due to head movements. An additional mechanism prevents confusion or blurring during eye movements. Before the explanation, try this demonstration: Look at yourself in a mirror and focus on your left eye. Then shift your focus to your right eye. *(Please do this now.)* Did you see your eyes move? No, you did not. *(I said to try this. I bet you didn't. None of this is going to make any sense unless you try the demonstration!)*

Why didn't you see your eyes move? Your first impulse is to say that the movement was too small or too fast. Wrong. Try looking at someone else's eyes while he or she focuses first on your left eye and then on your right. You *do* see the other person's eyes move. So an eye movement is neither too small nor too fast for you to see.

One reason you do not see your own eyes move is that your brain decreases activity in the visual cortex during eye movements. In effect, the brain areas that monitor eye movements send the visual cortex the message, "We're about to move the eye muscles, so take a break for the next split second, or you will see nothing but a blur anyway." Consequently, neural activity and blood flow in the visual cortex decrease during eye movements (Burr, Morrone, & Ross, 1994; Paus, Marrett, Worsley, & Evans, 1995). However, neural activity does not cease altogether, and under appropriate conditions, we do detect some visual stimuli during eye movements (García-Pérez & Peli, 2001).

Motion Blindness

Some brain-damaged people become **motion blind,** able to see objects but unable to determine whether they are moving or, if so, in which direction or how fast. Motion-blind people have trouble with the same tasks as monkeys with damage in area MT (Marcar, Zihl, & Cowey, 1997) and probably have damage in that same area (Greenlee, Lang, Mergner, & Seeger, 1995).

One motion-blind patient reported that she felt uncomfortable with people walking around because "people were suddenly here or there but I have not seen them moving." She could not cross a street without help: "When I'm looking at the car first, it seems far away. But then, when I want to cross the road, suddenly the car is very near." Even such a routine task as pouring coffee became difficult; the flowing liquid appeared to be frozen and unmoving, so she did not stop pouring until the cup overfilled (Zihl, von Cramon, & Mai, 1983).

VISUAL ATTENTION

Of all the stimuli striking your retina at any moment, you attend to only a few. A stimulus can grab your attention by its size, brightness, or movement, but you can also voluntarily direct your attention to one stimulus or another in what is called a "top-down" process—that is, one governed by other cortical areas, principally the frontal and parietal cortex. To illustrate, keep your eyes fixated on the central *x* in the following display. Then attend to the *G* at the right, and step by step, shift your attention clockwise around the circle. Notice how you can indeed see different parts of the circle without moving your eyes.

```
          A
     Z         V
   W             R
   B      x      G
   N             K
     F         K
        F  J  P
```

The difference between attended and unattended stimuli is a matter of the amount and duration of activity in a cortical area. For example, suppose you are watching a screen while the letter Q flashes on for a split second. That stimulus automatically produces a brief response in your area V1. If you are attending to something else on the screen, the Q evokes only that brief response and nothing more. However, if you pay attention to the Q (perhaps because someone told you to count the times a letter flashes on the screen), then the brief response in V1 excites V2 and other areas which feed back onto the V1 cells to enhance and prolong their responses (Kanwisher & Wojciulik, 2000; Supér, Spekreijse, & Lamme, 2001). This prolonged or "echoed" response is a clear sign that you have paid attention to the stimulus.

Similarly, if you are told to pay attention to color or motion, activity increases in the areas of your visual cortex responsible for color or motion perception (Chawla, Rees, & Friston, 1999). In fact, activity increases in those areas even before the stimulus (Driver & Frith, 2000). Somehow the instructions prime those areas so that they can magnify their responses to any appropriate stimulus. They in turn feed back to area V1, enhancing that area's response to the stimulus. Again, it appears that the feedback increase in V1 responses is necessary for attention or conscious awareness of a stimulus (Pascual-Leone & Walsh, 2001).

THE BINDING PROBLEM REVISITED: VISUAL CONSCIOUSNESS

In Chapter 4, we encountered the unanswered question of how the brain produces a unified experience, even though different senses activate different brain areas. In this chapter, we have seen that the same problem applies within a single sensory system. The visual cortex has separate paths for shape, color, and motion, with few links among them. So when you see a brown rabbit hopping, how does your visual cortex know that the color, shape, and movement are all part of the same object? And how and where does any of this visual processing become conscious?

Recall the hypothesis that all binding requires precise synchrony of activity in different brain areas. Many researchers follow the same hypothesis for visual binding in particular. In one study, researchers flashed pictures of objects, sometimes on one side or the other and sometimes in the midline, so that each half of the brain saw part of the object. They flashed the pictures for a tenth of a second or less, with interfering patterns before and after, so that the observers could sometimes identify the object and sometimes not. When they did identify an object that they saw in the midline, the visual cortices of the left and right hemispheres produced highly synchronized activity. When they couldn't identify it, the two hemispheres were not synchronized (Mima, Oluwatimilehin, Hiraoka, & Hallett, 2001). That is, we need synchronized activity in the two hemispheres in order to see something that crosses the midline as a single object.

It is possible to have some degree of visual processing without being conscious of it. For example, if you had damage to much of area V1 of your cortex, you would lose experience in much of what had been your visual field. If someone flashed a light in that blind field, you would insist that you saw nothing. However, if someone flashed a light and asked you to point to it or to turn your eyes toward it, you would be surprisingly accurate—surprising even to yourself (Bridgeman & Staggs, 1982; Weiskrantz, Warrington, Sanders, & Marshall, 1974). This ability to localize visual objects within an apparently blind visual field is called **blindsight.**

The explanation for blindsight remains controversial. Even after damage to the lateral geniculate or visual cortex, other branches of the optic nerve deliver some visual information to the superior colliculus (in the midbrain) and several other areas (see Figure 6.17). Perhaps the superior colliculus controls unconscious visually guided movements (Cowey & Stoerig, 1995; Moore, Rodman, Repp, & Gross, 1995). However, if the superior colliculus were capable of doing so, we might expect all people with visual cortex damage to show blindsight. Many do not, and many who do show blindsight have it for only part of their "blind" visual field (Schärli, Harman, & Hogben, 1999; Wessinger, Fendrich, & Gazzaniga, 1997). An alternative explanation is that tiny islands of healthy tissue remain within an otherwise damaged visual cortex, not large enough to provide conscious perception, but nevertheless enough for blindsight (Fendrich, Wessinger, & Gazzaniga, 1992). Some patients experience blindsight after extensive (but not total) damage to the optic nerve, so the "surviving island" theory does appear valid for at least some cases of blindsight (Wüst, Kasten, & Sabel, 2002). In any case, the point is that a brain with no conscious vision can make a few useful responses to visual information.

As you will rightly infer, researchers do not yet understand much about visual consciousness. The dominant hypothesis is that consciousness is distributed over several cortical areas (Zeki, 1998). Perhaps we bind different aspects together because of synchronized simultaneous activity, as discussed in Chapter 4. Still, the fundamental basis of this process remains a challenge to future researchers.

MODULE 6.2

In Closing: Coordinating Separate Visual Pathways

The main points of this module have been as follows:

- Each cell in the visual system has a receptive field, a portion of the visual field to which it responds.
- Each cell in the visual system responds to specific stimulus features in its receptive field, such as shape, color, or movement.
- Separate pathways in the visual system attend to different aspects of the visual system.

- Certain kinds of brain damage can impair specific aspects of visual perception.

Another main point inherent in all of this is that studying the physiology of individual cells in the brain may eventually reveal how we perceive visual scenes. The questions are daunting, but optimism runs high. Questions that were once the realm of philosophical speculation are now subject to scientific investigation.

SUMMARY

1. The optic nerves of the two eyes join at the optic chiasm, where half of the axons from each eye cross to the opposite side of the brain. Most of the axons then travel to the lateral geniculate nucleus of the thalamus, which communicates with the visual cortex. (p. 157)

2. Each neuron in the visual system has a receptive field, an area of the visual field to which it is connected. Light in the receptive field excites or inhibits the neuron depending on the light's location, color, movement, and so forth. (p. 159)

3. Lateral inhibition is a mechanism by which stimulation in any area of the retina suppresses the responses in neighboring areas, thereby enhancing the contrast at light–dark borders. (p. 160)

4. The mammalian vertebrate visual system has a partial division of labor. In general, the parvocellular system is specialized for perception of color and fine details; the magnocellular system is specialized for perception of depth, movement, and overall patterns. (p. 162)

5. One system in the cerebral cortex is responsible for shape perception. Within the primary visual cortex, neuroscientists distinguish simple cells, which have a fixed excitatory and inhibitory field, from complex cells, which respond to a light pattern of a particular shape regardless of its exact location. End-stopped cells are similar to complex cells, except that they have a strong inhibitory field at one end. (p. 164)

6. Within the cortex, cells with similar properties cluster together in columns perpendicular to the surface of the cortex. (p. 166)

7. Neurons sensitive to shapes or other visual aspects may or may not act as feature detectors. In particular, cells of area V1 are highly responsive to spatial frequencies, even though we are not subjectively aware of spatial frequencies in our visual perception. (p. 167)

8. Damage to specific areas beyond the primary visual cortex can impair specific aspects of vision, such as facial recognition, color constancy, and motion perception. (pp. 168–172)

9. An instruction to attend to a particular visual stimulus or a particular aspect of a stimulus magnifies the brain's response to it. (p. 174)

10. Somehow we bind different aspects of visual sensation as a single object, even though shape, color, and motion are processed in different brain areas. Consciousness of some aspects of vision can influence perception of other aspects. Nevertheless, a limited amount of visual perception can occur without conscious awareness. (p. 174)

ANSWERS TO *STOP AND CHECK* QUESTIONS

1. It starts with the ganglion cells in the eye. Most of its axons go to the lateral geniculate nucleus of the thalamus; some go to the hypothalamus, superior colliculus, and elsewhere. (p. 159)

2. They become larger because each cell's receptive field is made by inputs converging at an earlier level. (p. 161)

3. The receptor excites both the bipolar cells and the horizontal cell. The horizontal cell inhibits the same bipolar cell that was excited plus additional bipolar cells in the surround. (p. 161)

4. It produces more excitation than inhibition for the nearest bipolar cells. For surrounding bipolar cells, it produces only inhibition. The reason is that the receptor excites a horizontal cell, which inhibits all bipolar cells in the area. (p. 161)

5. In the parts of your retina that look at the long white arms, each neuron is maximally inhibited by input on two of its sides (either above and below or left and right). In the crossroads, each neuron is maximally inhibited by input on all four sides. Therefore, the response in the crossroads is decreased compared to that in the arms. (p. 161)

6. Neurons of the parvocellular system have small cell bodies with small receptive fields, are located mostly in and near the fovea, and are specialized for detailed and color vision. Neurons of the magnocellular system have large cell bodies with large receptive fields, are located in all parts of the retina, and are specialized for perception of large patterns and movement. (p. 164)

7. Researchers could use fMRI, EEG, or other recording methods to see whether activity was high in your primary visual cortex. (p. 164)

8. First identify a stimulus, such as a horizontal line, that stimulates the cell. Then shine the stimulus at several points in the cell's receptive field. If the cell responds only in one location, it is a simple cell. If it responds in several locations, it is a complex cell. (p. 171)

9. Prosopagnosia is the inability to recognize faces. Its existence implies that the cortical mechanism for identifying faces (and some other complex stimuli) is different from the mechanism for identifying words and many other visual stimuli. (p. 171)

THOUGHT QUESTION

After a receptor cell is stimulated, the bipolar cell receiving input from it shows an immediate strong response. A fraction of a second later, the bipolar's response decreases, even though the stimulation from the receptor cell remains constant. How can you account for that decrease? (Hint: What does the horizontal cell do?)

MODULE 6.3

Development of the Visual System

Suppose that you had lived all your life in the dark. Then today, for the first time, you came out into the light and looked around. Could you make any sense of what you saw?

Unless you were born blind, you did have this experience on the day you were born. At that point, presumably, you could not make much sense of anything you saw. Within months, however, you could recognize faces and crawl toward favorite toys. How did you learn to make sense of what you saw?

INFANT VISION

When cartoonists show us an infant character, they draw the eyes large in proportion to the head. Infant eyes approach full size sooner than the rest of the head does. There is a good reason: The eyes form an enormous number of complex attachments to the brain. If they grew substantially after making those attachments and then sent new axons to the brain, the brain would have to reorganize all those connections to use the additional information.

Human newborns have better developed sensory capacities than psychologists once imagined. Newborns younger than 2 days spend more time looking at faces, circles, or stripes than at patternless displays (Figure 6.34). However, they have trouble shifting their attention. For example, when infants younger than 4 months stare at a highly attractive display, such as twirling dots on a computer screen, they cannot shift their gaze (M. H. Johnson, Posner, & Rothbart, 1991). Occasionally, they stare at something until they start crying in distress! Slightly older infants can look away from an attractive display, but they quickly shift their gaze back to it (Clohessy, Posner, Rothbart, & Veccra, 1991). Not until about age 6 months can an infant shift visual attention from one object to another.

To examine visual development in more detail, investigators turn to studies of animals. The research in this area has greatly expanded our understanding of brain development and has helped alleviate certain human abnormalities.

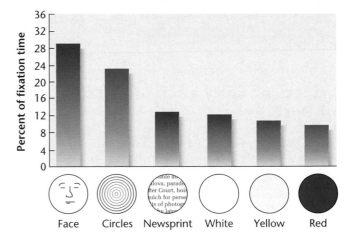

Figure 6.34 Amount of time infants spend looking at various patterns
Even in the first 2 days after birth, infants look more at faces than at most other stimuli. *Source: Based on Fantz, 1963*

EFFECTS OF EXPERIENCE ON VISUAL DEVELOPMENT

Developing axons of the visual system approach their targets by following chemical gradients, as discussed in Chapter 5. In a newborn mammal, the lateral geniculate and visual cortex already resemble an adult's (Gödecke & Bonhoeffer, 1996; Horton & Hocking, 1996), and many of the normal properties will develop even if the eyes are damaged (Rakic & Lidow, 1995; Shatz, 1996) or if the animal is reared in complete darkness (Lein & Shatz, 2001; White, Coppola, & Fitzpatrick, 2001). However, if the darkness continues, those properties diminish. That is, the visual system can mature to a certain point without experience, but it needs visual experience to maintain and fine-tune its connections.

Effects of Early Lack of Stimulation of One Eye

What would happen if a young animal could see with one eye but not the other? For mammals with both eyes pointed in the same direction—cats and primates—

most neurons in the visual cortex receive binocular input (stimulation from both eyes). As soon as a kitten opens its eyes at about age 9 days, each neuron responds to approximately corresponding areas in the two retinas—that is, areas that ordinarily focus on the same point in space (Figure 6.35).

If an experimenter sutures one eyelid shut so that a kitten sees with only the other eye for the first 4 to 6 weeks of life, cells in the visual cortex receive only infrequent random activity from the deprived eye, and their synapses become unresponsive to it (Rittenhouse, Shouval, Paradiso, & Bear, 1999). The kitten becomes almost blind in the deprived eye (Wiesel, 1982; Wiesel & Hubel, 1963).

Effects of Early Lack of Stimulation of Both Eyes

What happens if *both* eyes are kept shut for the first few weeks? We might expect the kitten to become blind in both eyes, but it does not. Evidently, when one eye remains shut during early development, the active synapses from the open eye displace the inactive synapses from the closed eye. If neither eye is active, no axon displaces any other. For at least 3 weeks, the kitten's cortex remains normally responsive to both eyes. If the eyes remain shut still longer, the cortical responses become sluggish and lose their crisp, sharp receptive fields (Crair, Gillespie, & Stryker, 1998). That is, they respond to visual stimuli in many orientations but not very strongly to any of them.

If a person were born blind and got to see later, would the new vision make sense? Sometimes nature does this experiment. Some humans are born blind because of a problem that can be corrected surgically, but they may have no visual experience for years. After the operation, they do respond somewhat to visual stimuli; for example, they can identify the brightness of a light and its approximate location. However, they have trouble learning to identify shapes or objects (Valvo, 1971). Presumably, their cortical cells lack the sharply tuned receptive fields that make such recognition possible. Many people find newly gained vision to be almost useless and prefer to keep their eyes shut much of the time.

Because the effects of abnormal experiences on cortical development depend on age, researchers identify a sensitive period or critical period, when experiences have a particularly strong and long-lasting influence. The length of the sensitive period varies from one species to another and from one part of the cortex to another (Crair & Malenka, 1995); it lasts a bit longer during complete visual deprivation—for example, if a kitten is kept in total darkness—than in the presence of limited experience (Kirkwood, Lee, & Bear, 1995). The onset of the critical period depends on the availability of GABA, the brain's main inhibitory transmitter. GABA becomes abundant in the visual cortex at about the usual time of the sensitive period. If GABA is increased in a mouse's visual cortex shortly after birth, the sensitive period starts sooner than usual. If the cortex is deprived of GABA, the sensitive period does not occur at all, and odd experiences have no effect on the visual cortex (Fagiolini & Hensch, 2000). That is, the changes that occur during the sensitive period require excitation of some synapses coupled with inhibition of others.

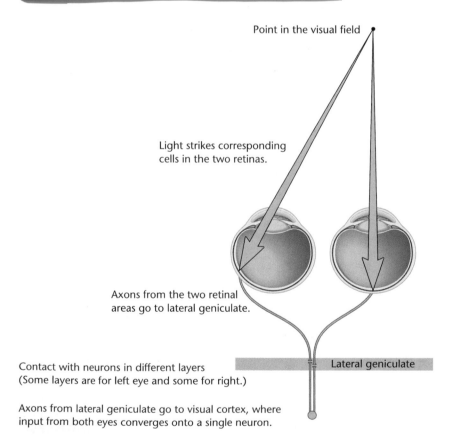

Point in the visual field

Light strikes corresponding cells in the two retinas.

Axons from the two retinal areas go to lateral geniculate.

Lateral geniculate

Contact with neurons in different layers (Some layers are for left eye and some for right.)

Axons from lateral geniculate go to visual cortex, where input from both eyes converges onto a single neuron.

Figure 6.35 The anatomical basis for binocular vision in cats and primates
Light from a point in the visual field strikes points in each retina. Retinal cells send their axons to separate layers of the lateral geniculate, which in turn send axons to a single cell in the visual cortex. That cell is connected (via the lateral geniculate) to corresponding areas of the two retinas.

The duration of the human sensitive period is not known, but abnormal experience during even a brief early period can produce deficits. In one study, investigators examined 14 people who had been born with *cataracts* (cloudy lenses) in both eyes. All of them had their cataracts surgically repaired at ages 2 to 6 months. Although they all eventually developed nearly normal vision, they had lingering problems in subtle regards. For example, for the faces in Figure 6.36, these people had no trouble detecting the difference between the two lower faces, which have different eyes and mouth, but had trouble detecting any difference between the two upper faces, which have the same eyes and mouth moved to slightly different locations (Le Grand, Mondloch, Maurer, & Brent, 2001).

1. What happens to neurons in a kitten's visual cortex if one of its eyes is closed during its early development? What if both eyes are closed?

Check your answers on page 183.

Restoration of Response After Early Deprivation of Vision

After the cortical neurons have become insensitive to the inactive eye, can experience restore their sensitivity? Yes, if the restorative experience comes soon enough. If a kitten is deprived of vision in one eye for a few days during the sensitive period (losing sensitivity to light in that eye) and then receives normal experience with both eyes, it rapidly regains sensitivity to the deprived eye. However, in the long run, it recovers better if it spends a few days with the opposite eye deprived of vision (Mitchell, Gingras, & Kind, 2001). Evidently, the deprived eye can take over more cortical functioning if it doesn't have to overcome a competitor.

This animal research has clear relevance to the human condition called **lazy eye,** also known by the fancier term **amblyopia,** in which a child fails to attend to the vision in one eye, sometimes even letting the eye drift in a different direction from the other one. The animal results imply that the best way to facilitate normal vision in the ignored eye is to prevent the child from using the active eye. A physician puts a patch over the active eye, and the child gradually increases his or her attention to vision in the previously ignored eye. Eventually the child is permitted to use both eyes together. The patch is most effective if it is used early, although no one knows exactly how long the sensitive period lasts in humans.

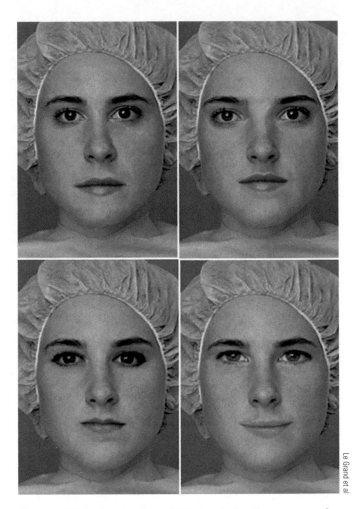

Le Grand et al

Figure 6.36 Faces that differ only in the eyes and mouth
The two upper faces **(a)** have the same eyes and mouth but in slightly different locations. The lower faces **(b)** have different eyes and mouth. People who had cataracts for the first few months of life detect the difference between the faces in **(b)** but have trouble detecting the difference in **(a).** Evidently, the early visual deprivation left deficits that could not be fully remedied by later experience.

Uncorrelated Stimulation in Both Eyes

Almost every neuron in the human visual cortex responds to approximately corresponding areas of both eyes. (Neurons that respond to the extreme left or extreme right of the visual field respond to only one eye.) By comparing the slightly different inputs from the two eyes, you achieve stereoscopic depth perception, a powerful method of perceiving distance.

Stereoscopic depth perception requires the brain to detect **retinal disparity,** the discrepancy between what the left eye sees and what the right eye sees. But how do cortical neurons adjust their connections to detect

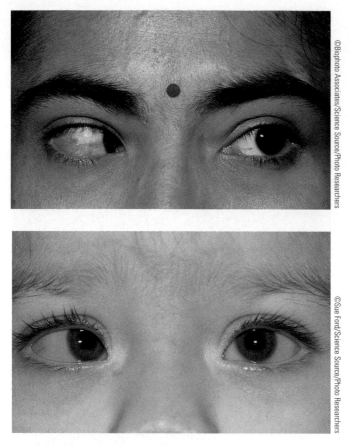

Two examples of "lazy eye."

amblyopia), a condition in which the eyes do not point in the same direction. These children do not develop stereoscopic depth perception; they perceive depth no better with two eyes than with one.

The apparent mechanism is that each cortical cell increases its responsiveness to groups of axons with synchronized activity (Singer, 1986). For example, if a portion of the left retina frequently focuses on the same object as some portion of the right eye, then axons from those two retinal areas frequently carry synchronous messages, and a cortical cell strengthens its synapses with both axons. However, if the eye muscles are damaged, or if one eye at a time is always covered, the cortical cell does not receive simultaneous inputs from the two eyes, and it strengthens its synapses with axons from only one eye (usually the contralateral one).

Recall from Chapter 5 that postsynaptic cells promote the survival of certain axons by delivering nerve growth factor (NGF) or other neurotrophins. The same process apparently occurs in the visual cortex. In one experiment, investigators sealed one eye in several infant ferrets. Ordinarily, this procedure causes cells in the lateral geniculate and visual cortex to become responsive only to the open eye; however, when researchers supplied the brain with extra amounts of the neurotrophin NT-4, all cells remained responsive to both eyes (Riddle, Lo, & Katz, 1995). Apparently, visual experience produces its effects by causing cortical neurons to release neurotrophins to the active axons; if the brain is bathed in extra neurotrophins, all the axons receive them and survive equally.

retinal disparity? Genetic instructions could not by themselves be sufficient; different individuals have slightly different head sizes, and the genes cannot know exactly how far apart the two eyes will be. The fine-tuning of binocular vision must depend on experience.

And indeed it does. Suppose an experimenter sets up a procedure in which a kitten can see with the left eye one day, the right eye the next day, and so forth. The kitten therefore receives the same amount of stimulation in both eyes, but it never sees with both eyes at the same time. After several weeks, almost every neuron in the visual cortex responds to one eye or the other but not to both. The kitten therefore cannot detect retinal disparities and has no stereoscopic depth perception.

Similarly, suppose a kitten has defective or damaged eye muscles so that its two eyes cannot focus in the same direction at the same time. In this case, both eyes are active simultaneously, but no neuron in the visual cortex gets the same message from both eyes at the same time. Again, the result is that each neuron in the visual cortex chooses one eye or the other and becomes fully responsive to it, ignoring the other eye (Blake & Hirsch, 1975; Hubel & Wiesel, 1965).

A similar phenomenon occurs in humans. Certain children are born with **strabismus** (or strabismic

2. What is "lazy eye" and how can it be treated?
3. What early experience is necessary to maintain binocular input to the neurons of the visual cortex?
4. Does an injection of NGF increase or decrease the effects of abnormal visual experience? Why?

Check your answers on page 183.

Early Exposure to a Limited Array of Patterns

If a kitten spends its entire early sensitive period wearing goggles with horizontal lines painted on them (Figure 6.37), nearly all its visual cortex cells become responsive only to horizontal lines (Stryker &

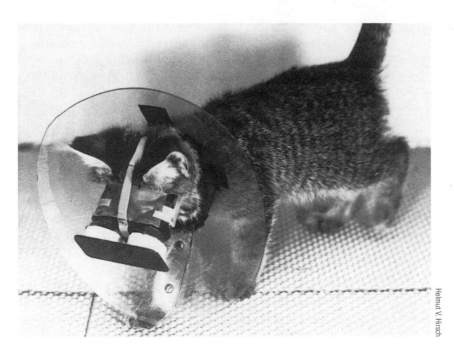

Figure 6.37 Procedure for restricting a kitten's visual experience during early development
For a few hours a day, the kitten wears goggles that show just one stimulus, such as horizontal or diagonal stripes. For the rest of the day, the kitten stays with its mother in a dark room without the mask.

Sherk, 1975; Stryker, Sherk, Leventhal, & Hirsch, 1978). Even after months of later normal experience, the cat does not respond to vertical lines (D. E. Mitchell, 1980).

What happens if human infants are exposed mainly to vertical or horizontal lines instead of both equally? You might wonder how such a bizarre thing could happen. No parents would let an experimenter subject their child to such a procedure, and it never happens accidentally in nature. Right?

Wrong. In fact, it probably happened to you! About 70% of all infants have **astigmatism,** a blurring of vision for lines in one direction (e.g., horizontal, vertical, or one of the diagonals). Astigmatism is caused by an asymmetric curvature of the eyes (Howland & Sayles, 1984). The prevalence of astigmatism declines to about 10% in 4-year-old children as a result of normal growth.

You can informally test yourself for astigmatism with Figure 6.38. Do the lines in some directions look faint or fuzzy? If so, rotate the page. You will notice that the appearance of the lines depends on their position. If you wear corrective lenses, try this demonstration with and without them. If you see a difference in the lines only without your lenses, then the lenses have corrected your astigmatism.

If your eyes had strong astigmatism during the sensitive period for the development of your visual cortex, you saw lines more clearly in one direction than in another direction. If your astigmatism was not corrected early, then the cells of your visual cortex probably became more responsive to the kind of lines you saw more clearly, and you will continue throughout life to see lines in other directions as slightly faint or blurry, even if your eyes are now perfectly spherical (Freedman & Thibos, 1975). However, if you began wearing corrective lenses before age 3 to 4 years, you thereby improved your adult vision (Friedburg & Klöppel, 1996). The moral of the story: Children should be tested for astigmatism early and given corrective lenses as soon as possible.

Adults' cortical neurons can also change in response to altered visual experience, but the effects are smaller. If an adult mammal is trained to respond to a particular stimulus, some of its visual neurons become more responsive to that stimulus and less responsive to other stimuli (Dragoi, Rivadulla, & Sur, 2001; Schoups, Vogels, Qian, & Orban, 2001). If an animal has repeated experiences with a complex stimulus (e.g., as a photograph of an elephant), a cluster of neighboring neurons become highly responsive to that stimulus while other cells that used to respond to it become less responsive (Erickson, Jagadeesh, & Desimone, 2000). In short, the cortex develops specializations for dealing with the patterns it encounters most often. However, these changes are far less drastic than the ones that occur after distorted experiences in infancy.

Figure 6.38 An informal test for astigmatism
Do the lines in one direction look darker or sharper than the other lines? If so, notice what happens when you rotate either the page or your head. The lines really are identical; certain lines appear darker or sharper because of the shape of your eye. If you wear corrective lenses, try this demonstration both with and without them.

Lack of Seeing Objects in Motion

What happens if kittens grow up without seeing anything move? You can imagine the difficulty of arranging such a world; the kitten's head would move, even if nothing else did. Max Cynader and Garry Chernenko (1976) used an ingenious procedure: They raised kittens in an environment illuminated only by a strobe light that flashed eight times a second for 10 microseconds each. In effect, the kittens' visual world was a series of still photographs. After 4 to 6 months in this odd environment, each kitten's visual cortex had neurons that responded normally to shapes but few neurons that responded strongly to moving stimuli. In short, the kittens had become motion blind.

Effects of Blindness on the Cortex

Finally, what happens if someone has no visual stimulation throughout the entire sensitive period? In one experiment, kittens were reared without any visual experience. A section of their parietal lobe that ordinarily responds only to visual stimuli became responsive to auditory or touch stimuli, enabling the kittens to localize sounds with greater accuracy than normal cats do (Rauschecker, 1995).

Similarly, in people who become blind early in life, certain parts of the visual cortex become responsive to auditory and touch stimuli, including Braille symbols. The auditory and touch information invades more of the visual cortex in people who became blind at birth or in infancy than in those who became blind as teenagers or adults (L. G. Cohen et al., 1999). As discussed in Chapter 5, the brain is more plastic when young. Presumably, this observation relates to the fact that people who begin learning Braille as adults do not become as adept as those who start in childhood.

MODULE 6.3

In Closing: The Nature and Nurture of Vision

The nature–nurture issue arises in one disguise or another in almost every area of psychology. In vision, consider what happens when you look out your window. How do you know that what you see are trees, people, and buildings? In fact, how do you know they are objects? How do you know which objects are close and which are distant? Were you born knowing how to interpret what you see or did you have to learn to understand it? The main message of this module is that vision requires a complex mixture of nature and nurture. We are indeed born with a certain amount of understanding, but we need experience to maintain, improve, and refine it. As usual, the influences of heredity and environment are not fully separable.

SUMMARY

1. Humans show some indication of pattern vision even in early infancy. One early deficiency is that they have trouble shifting attention from one object to another. (p. 177)

2. The cells in the visual cortex of infant kittens have nearly normal properties. However, experience is necessary to maintain and fine-tune vision. For example, if a kitten has sight in one eye and not in the other during the early sensitive period, its cortical neurons become responsive only to the open eye. (p. 177)

3. Cortical neurons become unresponsive to axons from the inactive eye mainly because of competition from the active eye. If both eyes are closed, cortical cells remain somewhat responsive to axons from both eyes, although that response becomes sluggish and unselective as the weeks of deprivation continue. (p. 178)

4. Abnormal visual experience has a stronger effect during an early sensitive period than later in life. The sensitive period begins when sufficient GABA levels become available in the visual cortex. (p. 178)

5. If cortical cells have become unresponsive to an eye because it was inactive during the early sensitive period, normal visual experience later does not restore normal responsiveness. However, prolonged closure of the previously active eye can increase the response to the previously inactive eye. (p. 179)

6. Ordinarily, most cortical neurons of cats and primates respond to portions of both retinas. However, if the two eyes are seldom open at the same time during the sensitive period, or if they consistently focus in different directions, then each cortical neuron becomes responsive to the axons from just one eye and not the other. (p. 179)

7. If a kitten sees only horizontal or vertical lines during its sensitive period, most of the neurons in its visual cortex become responsive to such lines only. For the same reason, a young child who has a strong astigmatism may have permanently decreased responsiveness to one kind of line or another. (p. 180)

8. Those who do not see motion early in life lose their ability to see it. (p. 182)

9. In people who are blind throughout early life, parts of the visual cortex become more responsive to auditory and tactile stimulation, enabling greater perception of Braille. (p. 182)

ANSWERS TO *STOP AND CHECK* QUESTIONS

1. If one eye is closed during early development, the cortex becomes unresponsive to it. If both eyes are closed, cortical cells remain somewhat responsive to both eyes for several weeks and then gradually become sluggish and unselective in their responses. (p. 179)

2. "Lazy eye" is inattentiveness to one eye, in most cases an eye that does not move in conjunction with the other eye. It can be treated by closing or patching over the active eye, forcing the child to use the ignored eye. (p. 180)

3. To maintain binocular responsiveness, cortical cells must receive simultaneous activity from both eyes fixating on the same object at the same time. (p. 183)

4. NGF decreases the effects of abnormal experience by facilitating the survival of all axons. (p. 183)

THOUGHT QUESTIONS

1. A rabbit's eyes are on the sides of its head instead of in front. Would you expect rabbits to have many cells with binocular receptive fields—that is, cells that respond to both eyes? Why or why not?

2. Would you expect the cortical cells of a rabbit to be just as sensitive to the effects of experience as are the cells of cats and primates? Why or why not?

Key Terms and Activities

TERMS

astigmatism (p. 181)

binocular input (p. 178)

bipolar cell (p. 146)

blind spot (p. 146)

blindsight (p. 175)

color constancy (p. 154)

color vision deficiency (p. 155)

complex cell (p. 165)

cone (p. 149)

dorsal stream (p. 164)

end-stopped cell (p. 166)

feature detector (p. 167)

fovea (p. 148)

functional magnetic resonance imaging (fMRI) (p. 170)

ganglion cell (p. 146)

horizontal cell (p. 157)

hypercomplex cell (p. 166)

inferior temporal cortex (p. 168)

koniocellular neuron (p. 162)

lateral geniculate nucleus (p. 157)

lateral inhibition (p. 161)

law of specific nerve energies (p. 144)

lazy eye (or amblyopia) (p. 179)

magnocellular neuron (p. 162)

midget ganglion cell (p. 148)

motion blindness (p. 173)

MST (p. 172)

MT (or area V5) (p. 172)

negative color afterimage (p. 152)

opponent-process theory (p. 152)

optic nerve (p. 146)

parvocellular neuron (p. 162)

photopigment (p. 149)

primary visual cortex (or area V1) (p. 162)

prosopagnosia (p. 169)

psychophysical observations (p. 150)

pupil (p. 146)

receptive field (p. 159)

receptor potential (p. 144)

retina (p. 146)

retinal disparity (p. 179)

retinex theory (p. 154)

rod (p. 149)

secondary visual cortex (or area V2) (p. 163)

sensitive period or critical period (p. 178)

shape constancy (p. 168)

simple cell (p. 164)

stereoscopic depth perception (p. 171)

strabismus (or strabismic amblyopia) (p. 180)

trichromatic theory (or Young-Helmholtz theory) (p. 150)

ventral stream (p. 163)

visual agnosia (p. 169)

visual field (p. 159)

SUGGESTIONS FOR FURTHER READING

Hubel, D. H. (1988). *Eye, brain, and vision.* New York: Scientific American Library. Excellent source by cowinner of the Nobel Prize. See especially Chapter 9.

Zeki, S. (1993). *A vision of the brain.* Oxford: Blackwell. Excellent discussion by a leading researcher.

WEB SITES TO EXPLORE

You can go to the Biological Psychology Study Center and click these links. While there, you can also check for suggested articles available on InfoTrac College Edition.

- The Biological Psychology Internet address is:
  **http://psychology.wadsworth.com/
  kalatbiopsych8e**

Color vision testing
**http://members.aol.com/protanope/
colorblindtest.html**

The Primary Visual Cortex, by Matthew Schmolesky
**http://webvision.med.utah.edu/
VisualCortex.html#introduction**

CD-ROM: EXPLORING BIOLOGICAL PSYCHOLOGY

The Retina (animation)

Virtual Reality Eye (virtual reality)

Motion Aftereffect (try it yourself)

Brightness Contrast (try it yourself)

Blind Spot (try it yourself)

Color Blindness in Visual Periphery (try it yourself)

Critical Thinking (essay questions)

Chapter Quiz (multiple choice questions)

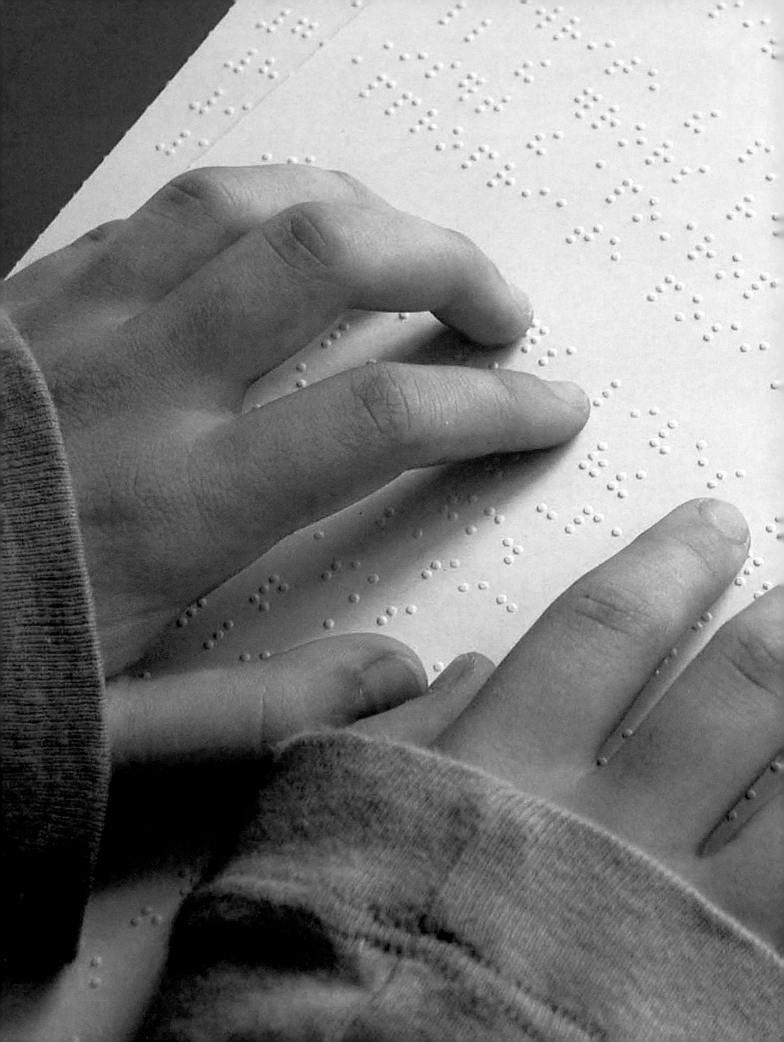

The Other Sensory Systems and Attention

7

Opposite:
Smell, taste, hearing, and other senses receive less research attention than vision, but they are essential to our lives. *Source: ©Susan Van Etten/PhotoEdit*

Main Ideas

1. Our senses have evolved not to give us complete information about all the stimuli in the world but to give us the most useful information.

2. Different sensory systems code information in different ways. As a rule, the activity in a single sensory axon is ambiguous by itself; its meaning depends on its relationship to a pattern across a population of axons.

According to a Native American saying, "A pine needle fell. The eagle saw it. The deer heard it. The bear smelled it" (Herrero, 1985). Different species are sensitive to different kinds of information. Bees and many other insects can see short-wavelength (ultraviolet) light that humans cannot; conversely, humans see long-wavelength (red) light that insects cannot. Bats locate insect prey by echoes from sonar waves that they emit at 20,000 to 100,000 hertz (Hz, cycles per second), well above the range of adult human hearing (Griffin, Webster, & Michael, 1960). Certain cells in a frog's eyes respond selectively to small, dark, moving objects such as insects (Lettvin, Maturana, McCulloch, & Pitts, 1959). The ears of the green tree frog, *Hyla cinerea,* are highly sensitive to sounds at two frequencies—900 and 3000 Hz—prominent in the adult male's mating call (Moss & Simmons, 1986).

Humans' visual and auditory abilities are broader and less specialized than those of frogs, perhaps because a wider range of stimuli is biologically more relevant to us than to them. However, humans also have important sensory specializations. For example, our sense of taste can alert us to the bitterness of certain poisons even at very low concentrations (Richter, 1950; Schiffman & Erickson, 1971), whereas it has virtually no response to substances such as cellulose that are neither helpful nor harmful. Our olfactory systems are unresponsive to gases that it would be useless for us to detect (e.g., nitrogen) and highly responsive to such biologically useful stimuli as the smell of rotting meat. Thus, this chapter concerns not how our sensory systems enable us to perceive reality, but how they process biologically useful information.

MODULE 7.1

Audition

If a tree falls in a forest where no one can hear it, does it make a sound? The answer depends on what we mean by "sound." If we define it simply as a vibration, then of course, a falling tree makes a sound. However, we usually define sound as a psychological phenomenon, a vibration that some organism hears. By the standard definition, a vibration is not a sound unless someone hears it. The human auditory system enables us to hear not only falling trees but also the birds singing in the branches and the wind blowing through the leaves. Some blind people learn to click their heels as they walk and use the echoes to locate obstructions. Our auditory systems are amazingly well adapted for detecting and interpreting useful information.

SOUND AND THE EAR

Sound waves are periodic compressions of air, water, or other media. When a tree falls, both the tree and the ground vibrate, setting up sound waves in the air that strike the ears. If something hit the ground on the moon, where there is no air, people would not hear it—unless, perhaps, they put an ear to the ground.

Physical and Psychological Dimensions of Sound

Sound waves vary in amplitude and frequency. The amplitude of a sound wave is its intensity. A very intense compression of air, such as that produced by a bolt of lightning, produces sound waves of great amplitude, which a listener hears as great loudness. Loudness, the perception of intensity, is not the same as amplitude. If the amplitude of a sound doubles, its loudness increases but it does not double. Many factors influence loudness; for example, a rapidly talking person sounds louder than slow music of the same physical amplitude. So if you complain that television advertisements are louder than the

program, no one should contradict you. Loudness is your perception, and if something sounds louder to you, it is louder.

The frequency of a sound is the number of compressions per second, measured in hertz (Hz, cycles per second). Pitch is a perception closely related to frequency. As a rule, the higher the frequency of a sound, the higher its pitch. Figure 7.1 illustrates the amplitude and frequency of sounds. The height of each wave corresponds to amplitude, and the number of waves per second corresponds to frequency.

Most adult humans can hear air vibrations ranging from about 15 Hz to somewhat less than 20,000 Hz. Children can hear high-frequency sounds much better than adults, whose ability to perceive high frequencies decreases with age and with exposure to loud noises (B. A. Schneider, Trehub, Morrongiello, & Thorpe, 1986). Mice and other small mammals can hear still higher pitches.

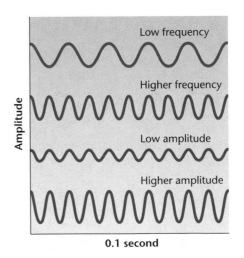

0.1 second

Figure 7.1 Four sound waves
The time between the peaks determines the frequency of the sound, which we experience as pitch. Here, the top line represents five sound waves in 0.1 second, or 50 Hz—a very low-frequency sound that we experience as a very low pitch. The other three lines represent 100 Hz. The vertical extent of each line represents its amplitude or intensity, which we experience as loudness.

Structures of the Ear

Rube Goldberg (1883–1970) drew cartoons about complicated, far-fetched inventions. For example, a person's tread on the front doorstep would pull a string that raised a cat's tail, awakening the cat, which would then chase a bird that had been resting on a balance, which would swing up to strike a doorbell. The functioning of the ear may remind you of a Rube Goldberg device because sound waves are transduced into action potentials through a many-step, roundabout process. Unlike Goldberg's inventions, however, the ear actually works.

Anatomists distinguish among the outer ear, the middle ear, and the inner ear (Figure 7.2). The outer ear includes the *pinna,* the familiar structure of flesh and cartilage attached to each side of the head. By altering the reflections of sound waves, the pinna helps us locate the source of a sound. Rabbits' large movable pinnas enable them to localize sound sources even more precisely.

After sound waves pass through the auditory canal (see Figure 7.2), they strike the **tympanic membrane,** or eardrum, in the middle ear. The tympanic membrane vibrates at the same frequency as the sound waves that strike it. The tympanic membrane is attached to three tiny bones that transmit the vibrations to the **oval window,** a membrane of the inner ear. These bones are sometimes known by their English names (hammer, anvil, and stirrup) and sometimes by their Latin names (malleus, incus, and stapes). The tympanic membrane is about 20 times larger than the footplate of the stirrup, which is connected to the oval window. As in a hydraulic pump, the vibrations of the tympanic membrane are transformed into more forceful vibrations of the smaller stirrup. The net effect of the system is to convert the sound waves into waves of greater pressure on the small oval window. This transformation is important because more force is required to move the viscous fluid behind the oval window than to move the eardrum, which has air on both sides.

In the inner ear is a snail-shaped structure called the **cochlea** (KOCK-lee-uh, Latin for "snail"). A cross section through the cochlea, as in Figure 7.2c, shows three long fluid-filled tunnels: the scala vestibuli, scala

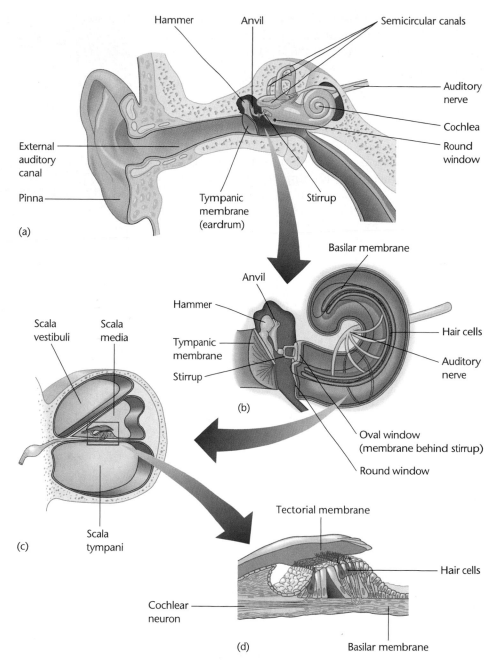

Figure 7.2 **Structures of the ear**
When sound waves strike the tympanic membrane in **(a)**, they cause it to vibrate three tiny bones—the hammer, anvil, and stirrup—that convert the sound waves into stronger vibrations in the fluid-filled cochlea **(b).** Those vibrations displace the hair cells along the basilar membrane in the cochlea. **(c)** A cross section through the cochlea. **(d)** A closeup of the hair cells.

media, and scala tympani. The stirrup makes the oval window vibrate at the entrance to the scala vestibuli, thereby setting in motion all the fluid in the cochlea. The auditory receptors, known as **hair cells,** lie between the basilar membrane of the cochlea on one side and the tectorial membrane on the other (Figure 7.2d). Vibrations in the fluid of the cochlea displace the hair cells. A hair cell responds within microseconds to displacements as small as 10^{-10} meter (0.1 nanometer, about the diameter of one atom), thereby opening ion channels in its membrane (Fettiplace, 1990; Hudspeth, 1985). Figure 7.3 shows electron micrographs of the hair cells of three species. The hair cells have excitatory synapses onto the cells of the auditory nerve, which is part of the eighth cranial nerve.

PITCH PERCEPTION

Our ability to understand speech or enjoy music depends on our ability to differentiate among sounds of different frequencies. How do we do it?

Frequency Theory and Place Theory

According to the early **frequency theory,** the basilar membrane vibrates in synchrony with a sound, causing auditory nerve axons to produce action potentials at the same frequency. For example, a sound at 50 Hz would cause 50 action potentials per second in the auditory nerve. The downfall of this theory in its simplest form is that the refractory period of a neuron is about one thousandth of a second, so a neuron can fire no more than 1000 action potentials per second at most. Nevertheless, we can distinguish tones up to 15,000–20,000 Hz, and many small animals can hear even higher tones.

According to the **place theory,** the basilar membrane resembles the strings of a piano in that each area along the membrane is tuned to a specific frequency and vibrates in its presence. (If you sound one note loud enough with a tuning fork or any musical instrument, you can make the piano string tuned to that note vibrate.) According to this theory, each frequency activates the hair cells at only one place along the basilar membrane, and the nervous system distinguishes among frequencies on the basis of which neurons are activated. The downfall of this theory is that the various parts of the basilar membrane are bound together, and no part can resonate like a piano string.

The current theory combines modified versions of both frequency and place theories. For low-frequency sounds (up to about 100 Hz—more than an octave below middle C in music, which is 264 Hz), the basilar membrane does vibrate in synchrony with the sound waves (in accordance with the frequency theory), and auditory

Figure 7.3 Hair cells from the auditory systems of three species
(a, b) Hair cells from a frog sacculus, an organ that detects ground-borne vibrations. **(c)** Hair cells from the cochlea of a cat. **(d)** Hair cells from the cochlea of a fence lizard. Kc = kinocilium, one of the components of a hair bundle.

nerve axons do generate one action potential per wave. Weak sounds activate few neurons, whereas stronger sounds activate more. Thus, at low frequencies, the frequency of impulses identifies the pitch, and the number of firing cells identifies the loudness.

Because of the refractory period of the axon, as sounds go much above 100 Hz, it is harder and harder for a neuron to continue firing in synchrony with the sound waves. At higher frequencies, it fires on every second, third, fourth, or later wave. Its action potentials are phase-locked to the peaks of the sound waves (i.e., they occur at the same phase in the sound wave), as illustrated here:

Sound wave
(about 1000 Hz)

Action potentials
from one auditory
neuron

Other auditory neurons also produce action potentials that are phase-locked with peaks of the sound wave, but they can be out of phase with one another:

If we consider the auditory nerve as a whole, we find that with a tone of a few hundred Hz, each wave excites at least a few auditory neurons. According to the **volley principle** of pitch discrimination, the auditory nerve as a whole can have volleys of impulses up to about 4000 per second, even though no individual axon can approach that frequency by itself (Rose, Brugge, Anderson, & Hind, 1967). (Beyond about 4000 Hz, even staggered volleys of impulses can't keep pace with the sound waves.) Neuroscientists assume that these volleys contribute to pitch perception, although no one knows quite how the brain uses the information.

Most human hearing takes place below 4000 Hz, the approximate limit of the volley principle. For compari-

son, the highest key on a piano is 4224 Hz. Frequencies much above that level are not important in music or human speech, although rats, mice, bats, and other small animals rely on them heavily. When we hear these very high frequencies, we use a mechanism similar to the place theory. The basilar membrane varies from stiff at its **base,** where the stirrup meets the cochlea, to floppy at the other end of the cochlea, the **apex** (von Békésy, 1956; Yost & Nielsen, 1977) (Figure 7.4). The hair cells along the basilar membrane have different properties based on their location, and they act as tuned resonators that vibrate only for sound waves of a particular frequency. The highest frequency sounds vibrate hair cells near the base, and lower frequency sounds vibrate hair cells farther along the membrane (Warren, 1999).

Stop & Check

1. Through what mechanism do we perceive sounds up to about 100 Hz?
2. How do we perceive sounds from 100 to 4000 Hz?
3. How do we perceive high-frequency sounds (above 4000 Hz)?

Check your answers on page 196.

Pitch Perception in the Cerebral Cortex

Information from the auditory system passes through several subcortical structures, with an important crossover in the midbrain that enables each hemisphere of the forebrain to get its major auditory input from the opposite ear (Glendenning, Baker, Hutson, & Masterton, 1992). The information ultimately reaches the **primary auditory cortex** in the temporal lobes, within part of which cells respond selectively to the location of the sound, as shown in Figure 7.5. In brief, a given cell responds when sounds come from one location and not another (Tian, Reser, Durham, Kustov, & Rauschecker, 2001). In another part of the auditory cortex, cells respond selectively to tones, and the cells that respond best to a given tone cluster together. The auditory cortex provides a kind of map of the sounds—researchers call it a *tonotopic* map— so that the cortical area with the greatest response indicates what frequency is heard, as shown in Figure 7.6. The general principle is the same for all mammals (Scheich & Zuschratter, 1995). The figure is misleading in one regard, however. Although cells in any area respond better to one frequency than to

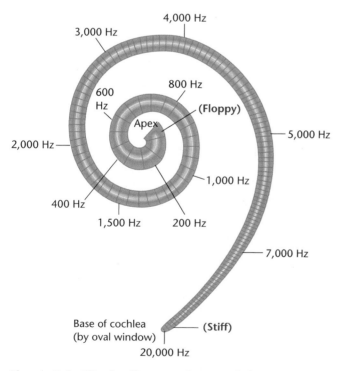

Figure 7.4 The basilar membrane of the human cochlea
High-frequency sounds excite hair cells near the base. Low-frequency sounds excite cells near the apex.

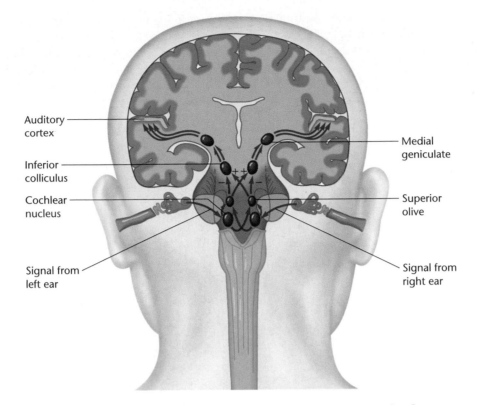

Figure 7.5 Route of auditory impulses from the receptors in the ear to the auditory cortex
The cochlear nucleus receives input from the ipsilateral ear only (the one on the same side of the head). All later stages have input originating from both ears.

any others, most cells do not respond very strongly to any pure tone. Most respond best to combinations or patterns of notes (Griffiths, Uppenkamp, Johnsrude, Josephs, & Patterson, 2001; Wessinger et al., 2001).

Someone who suffers massive damage to the primary visual cortex is blinded. In contrast, people who suffer damage to the primary auditory cortex are not deafened. They can hear and respond to simple sounds reasonably well—such as a beep or buzz—unless the damage extends into subcortical brain areas (Tanaka, Kamo, Yoshida, & Yamadori, 1991). Damage to the primary auditory cortex mainly impairs the ability to recognize combinations or sequences of sounds, like music or speech. Evidently, the cortex is not necessary for all hearing, only for its advanced processing.

HEARING LOSS

Complete deafness is rare. About 99% of hearing-impaired people can hear at least loud noises. We distinguish two categories of hearing impairment: conductive deafness and nerve deafness.

Conductive, or **middle-ear, deafness** occurs if the bones of the middle ear fail to transmit sound waves properly to the cochlea. Such deafness can be caused by diseases, infections, or tumorous bone growth near the middle ear. Conductive deafness is sometimes temporary. If it persists, it can be corrected either by surgery or by hearing aids that amplify the stimulus. Because people with conductive deafness have a normal cochlea and auditory nerve, they hear their own voices, which can be conducted through the bones of the skull directly to the cochlea, bypassing the middle ear. Because they hear only themselves, they may complain that others are talking too softly.

Nerve, or **inner-ear, deafness** results from damage to the cochlea, the hair cells, or the auditory nerve. It can occur in any degree and may be confined to one part of the cochlea, in which case someone cannot hear certain sound frequencies, such as the high frequencies. Hearing aids cannot compensate for extensive nerve damage, but they can help people who have lost receptors in a portion of the cochlea. Nerve deafness can be inherited (A. Wang et al., 1998), or it can develop from a variety of prenatal problems or early childhood disorders (Cremers & van Rijn, 1991; Robillard & Gersdorff, 1986), including:

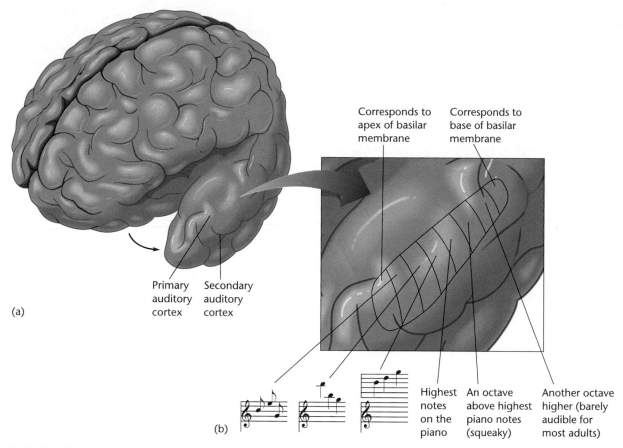

(a)

Corresponds to apex of basilar membrane

Corresponds to base of basilar membrane

Primary auditory cortex

Secondary auditory cortex

(b)

Highest notes on the piano

An octave above highest piano notes (squeaky)

Another octave higher (barely audible for most adults)

Figure 7.6   The human primary auditory cortex
Cells in each area respond mainly to tones of a particular frequency. Note that the neurons are arranged in a gradient, with cells responding to low-frequency tones at one end and cells responding to high-frequency tones at the other end.

- Exposure of the mother to rubella (German measles), syphilis, or other diseases or toxins during pregnancy
- Inadequate oxygen to the brain during birth
- Inadequate activity of the thyroid gland
- Certain diseases, including multiple sclerosis and meningitis
- Childhood reactions to certain drugs, including aspirin
- Repeated exposure to loud noises

Many people with nerve deafness experience **tinnitus** (tin-EYE-tus)—frequent or constant ringing in the ears. Tinnitus is common in old age, probably because so many people lose much of their high-frequency hearing. At least in some cases, tinnitus is due to a phenomenon like phantom limb, discussed in Chapter 5. Recall the example in which someone has an arm amputated, and then the axons reporting facial sensations invade the brain areas previously sensitive to the arm. As a result, stimulation of the face produces a sensation of a phantom arm. Similarly, dam-

age to part of the cochlea is like an amputation: The brain no longer gets its normal input, and axons representing other parts of the body may invade a brain area previously responsive to sounds (usually high-frequency sounds). Several patients have reported ringing in their ears whenever they move their jaws (Lockwood et al., 1998). Presumably, axons representing the lower face invaded their auditory cortex.

For practical information about coping with hearing loss, see this Web site:
www.marky.com/hearing/

4. What are the two major categories of hearing loss? For which type is a hearing aid generally more successful?

Check your answers on page 196.

LOCALIZATION OF SOUNDS

You are walking alone when suddenly you hear a loud noise. You want to know what produced it (friend or foe), but equally, you want to know where it came from (so you can approach or escape). Determining the direction and distance of a sound requires comparing the responses of the two ears—which are in effect just two points in space. And yet this system is accurate enough for you to turn almost immediately toward a sound and for owls in the air to locate mice on the ground in the middle of the night (Konishi, 1995).

One cue for localizing sound is the difference in intensity between the ears. For sounds with a wavelength shorter than the width of the head, the head creates a *sound shadow* (Figure 7.7), making the sound louder for the closer ear. In adult humans, this mechanism produces accurate sound localization for frequencies above 2000 to 3000 Hz. Another method of localization is the difference in *time of arrival* at the two ears. A sound coming from directly in front of a person reaches both ears at the same time. A sound coming directly from the side reaches the closer ear about 600 microseconds (µs) before the other. Sounds coming from intermediate locations reach the two ears at delays between 0 and 600 µs. Time of arrival is most useful for localizing sounds with a sudden onset. Most birds' alarm calls increase gradually in loudness, making them difficult for a predator to localize.

Another cue is the *phase difference* between the ears. Every sound wave has phases with two consecutive peaks 360° apart. Figure 7.8 shows sound waves that are in phase and 45°, 90°, or 180° out of phase. If a sound originates to the side of the head,

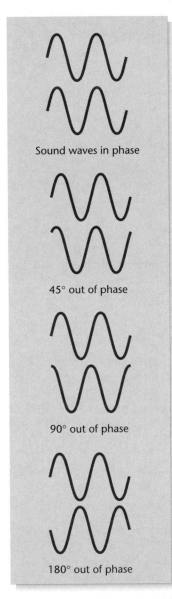

Figure 7.8 Sound waves can be in phase or out of phase
Sound waves that reach the two ears in phase are localized as coming from directly in front of (or behind) the hearer. The more out of phase the waves, the farther the sound source is from the body's midline.

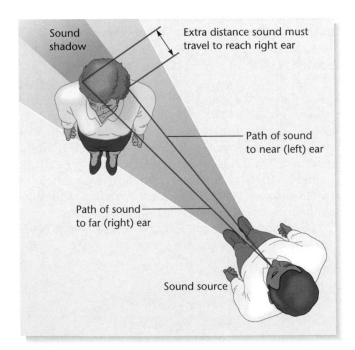

Figure 7.7 Differential loudness and arrival times as cues for sound localization
Sounds reaching the closer ear arrive sooner as well as louder, because the head produces a "sound shadow."
Source: Source: After Lindsay & Norman, 1972

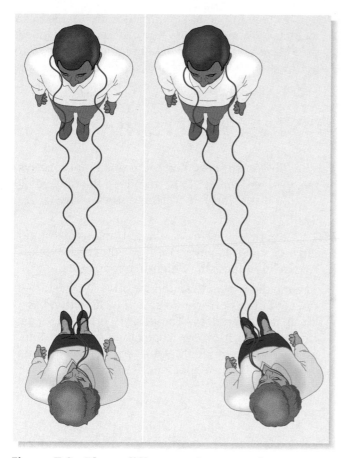

Figure 7.9 Phase differences between the ears as a cue for sound localization
Note that a low-frequency tone from straight ahead **(a)** arrives at the ears slightly in phase. A tone from an angle **(b)** can arrive in different phases at the two ears. With high-frequency sounds, the phases can become ambiguous.

the sound wave strikes the two ears out of phase, as shown in Figure 7.9. How much out of phase depends on the frequency of the sound, the size of the head, and the direction of the sound. Phase differences provide information that is useful for localizing sounds with frequencies up to about 1500 Hz in humans.

In short, humans localize low frequencies by phase differences and high frequencies by loudness differences. We can localize a sound of any frequency by its time of onset if it occurs suddenly enough.

The usefulness of phase and loudness differences depends on the size of the head (Masterton, Heffner, & Ravizza, 1969). Small animals such as mice have their ears close together and can detect neither phase nor loudness differences in low-frequency sounds. A small head casts a good sound shadow, so they are much better at localizing very high-frequency sounds.

Many small rodent species have evolved sensitivity to frequencies of 40,000 Hz or higher. Elephants, which can easily localize low-frequency sounds, have an upper hearing limit of just 10,000 Hz (Heffner & Heffner, 1982). These findings underscore a point made at the beginning of this chapter: Each species is most sensitive to the information that is most useful to it.

5. Which method of sound localization is more effective for an animal with a small head? Which is more effective for an animal with a large head? Why?

Check your answers on page 196.

MODULE 7.1

In Closing: Functions of Hearing

We spend much of our day listening to language, and we sometimes forget that the original, primary function of hearing has to do with simpler but extremely important issues: What do I hear? Where is it? Is it coming closer? Is it a potential mate, a potential enemy, potential food, or something irrelevant? The organization of the auditory system is well suited to resolving these questions.

SUMMARY

1. We detect the pitch of low-frequency sounds by the frequency of action potentials in the auditory system. At intermediate frequencies, we detect volleys of responses across many receptors. We detect the pitch of the highest frequency sounds by the area of greatest response along the basilar membrane. (p. 190)

2. Each cell in the primary auditory cortex responds best to a particular frequency of tones. (p. 191)

3. Deafness may result from damage to the nerve cells or to the bones that conduct sounds to the nerve cells. (p. 192)

4. We localize high-frequency sounds according to differences in loudness between the ears. We localize low-frequency sounds on the basis of differences in phase. (p. 194)

ANSWERS TO *STOP AND CHECK* QUESTIONS

1. At frequencies up to about 100 Hz, the basilar membrane vibrates in synchrony with the sound waves, and each responding axon in the auditory nerve sends one action potential per sound wave. (p. 191)

2. At frequencies from 100 to 4000 Hz, no single axon fires an action potential for each sound wave, but different axons fire for different waves, and so a volley (group) of axons fires for each wave. (p. 191)

3. At high frequencies, the sound causes maximum vibration for the hair cells at one location along the basilar membrane. (p. 191)

4. Conductive deafness (caused by problems with the bones of the middle ear) and nerve deafness (caused by damage to the nerves). Hearing aids are generally successful for conductive deafness; they are not always helpful in cases of nerve deafness. (p. 193)

5. An animal with a small head localizes sounds mainly by differences in loudness because the ears are not far enough apart for differences in onset time to be very large. An animal with a large head localizes sounds mainly by differences in onset time because its ears are far apart and well suited to noting differences in phase or onset time. (p. 195)

THOUGHT QUESTIONS

1. Why do you suppose that the human auditory system evolved sensitivity to sounds in the range of 20 to 20,000 Hz instead of some other range of frequencies?

2. The text explains how we might distinguish loudness for low-frequency sounds. How might we distinguish loudness for a high-frequency tone?

3. The medial part of the superior olive (a structure in the medulla) is critical for sound localization based on phase differences. The lateral part of the superior olive is critical for localization based on loudness. Which part would you expect to be better developed in mice? In elephants?

The Mechanical Senses

The next time you turn on your radio or stereo set, place your hand on its surface. The vibrations you feel in your hand are the same vibrations you hear.

If you practiced enough, could you learn to "hear" the vibrations with your fingers? No, they would remain just vibrations. If an earless species had enough time, might its vibration detectors evolve into sound detectors? Yes! In fact, that is what happened. Primitive animals had touch receptors that ultimately evolved into our organs of hearing. But we also retained receptors that respond to mechanical stimulation.

The *mechanical senses* respond to pressure, bending, or other distortions of a receptor. They include touch, pain, and other body sensations, as well as vestibular sensation, a system that detects the position and movement of the head. Audition is a mechanical sense also because the hair cells are modified touch receptors; we considered it separately because of its complexity and great importance to humans.

VESTIBULAR SENSATION

Try to read this page while you jiggle your head up and down, back and forth. You will find that you can read it fairly easily. Now hold your head steady and jiggle the book up and down, back and forth. Suddenly, you can hardly read it at all. Why?

When you move your head, the vestibular organ adjacent to the cochlea monitors each movement and directs compensatory movements of your eyes. When your head moves left, your eyes move right; when your head moves right, your eyes move left. Effortlessly, you keep your eyes focused on what you want to see (Brandt, 1991). When you move the page, however, the vestibular organ cannot keep your eyes on target. Sensations from the vestibular organ detect the direction of tilt and the amount of acceleration of the head. We are seldom aware of our vestibular sensations except under unusual conditions such as riding a roller coaster; they are nevertheless critical for guiding eye movements and maintaining balance.

The vestibular organ, shown in Figure 7.10, consists of two *otolith organs* (the *saccule* and *utricle*) and three semicircular canals. Like the hearing receptors, the vestibular receptors are modified touch receptors. One otolith organ has a horizontal patch of hairs; the other has a vertical patch. Calcium carbonate particles called *otoliths* lie next to the hair cells. When the head tilts in different directions, the otoliths push against different sets of hair cells and excite them (Hess, 2001).

The three semicircular canals, oriented in three different planes, are filled with a jellylike substance and lined with hair cells. An acceleration of the head at any angle causes the jellylike substance in one of these canals to push against the hair cells. Action potentials initiated by cells of the vestibular system travel through part of the eighth cranial nerve to the brainstem and cerebellum. (The eighth cranial nerve contains both an auditory component and a vestibular component.)

1. Someone with damage to the vestibular system has trouble reading street signs while walking. Why?

Check your answer on page 206.

SOMATOSENSATION

The somatosensory system, the sensation of the body and its movements, is not one sense but many, including discriminative touch (which identifies the shape of an object), deep pressure, cold, warmth, pain, itch, tickle, and the position and movement of joints.

Somatosensory Receptors

The skin is packed with a variety of somatosensory receptors. Some of the major receptor types found in mammalian skin are shown in Figure 7.11. The probable functions of these and other types of somatosensory

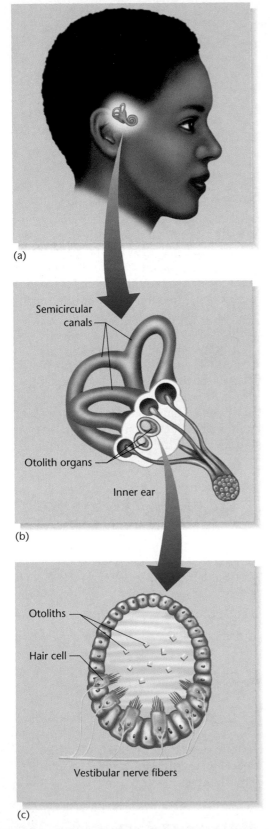

(a)

Semicircular canals

Otolith organs

Inner ear

(b)

Otoliths

Hair cell

Vestibular nerve fibers

(c)

Figure 7.10 Structures for vestibular sensation
(a) Location of the vestibular organs. **(b)** Structures of the vestibular organs. **(c)** Cross section through an otolith organ. Calcium carbonate particles, called otoliths, press against different hair cells, depending on the direction of tilt and rate of acceleration of the head.

receptors are listed in Table 7.1 on page 199 (Iggo & Andres, 1982). However, each receptor probably contributes to several kinds of somatosensory experience. Many respond to more than one kind of stimulus, such as touch and temperature. Others (not on the list) respond to deep stimulation, joint movement, or muscle movement.

A touch receptor may be a simple bare neuron ending (e.g., as many pain receptors), an elaborated neuron ending (Ruffini endings and Meissner's corpuscles), or a bare ending surrounded by nonneural cells that modify its function (Pacinian corpuscles). Stimulation of a touch receptor opens sodium channels in the axon, thereby starting an action potential if the stimulation is strong enough (Price et al., 2000).

One type of receptor, the Pacinian corpuscle, detects sudden displacements or high-frequency vibrations on the skin (Figure 7.12). Inside the onionlike outer structure is a neuron membrane. When mechanical pressure bends the membrane, its resistance to sodium flow decreases, and sodium ions enter, depolarizing the membrane (Loewenstein, 1960). Only a sudden or vibrating stimulus can bend the membrane; the onionlike outer structure provides mechanical support that resists gradual or constant pressure on the skin.

The receptors for heat and cold can be stimulated by certain chemicals as well. The heat receptor responds to capsaicin, the chemical that makes jalapeños and other hot peppers taste hot. We shall return to this point later. The coolness receptor responds to menthol and less strongly to mint (McKemy, Neuhausser, & Julius, 2002). So the next time you see some advertisement saying "with the cool taste of menthol" or mint, you can understand a bit of the reason.

EXTENSIONS AND APPLICATIONS
Tickle

The sensation of tickle is interesting but very poorly understood. Why does it exist at all? Why do you laugh if someone rapidly fingers your armpit, neck, or the soles of your feet? Chimpanzees respond to similar sensations with bursts of panting that resemble laughter. And yet tickling is unlike humor. Most people do not enjoy being tickled for very long—if at all—and certainly not by a stranger. If one joke makes you laugh, you are more likely than usual to laugh at the next joke. But being tickled doesn't change your likelihood of laughing at a joke (C. R. Harris, 1999).

Why can't you tickle yourself? The answer may be similar to why you can't startle yourself. When you touch yourself, your brain compares the resulting stimulation to the "expected" stimulation and generates a relatively small response in the somatosensory cortex

TABLE 7.1 Somatosensory Receptors and Their Possible Functions

Receptor	Location	Responds to
Free nerve ending (unmyelinated or thinly myelinated axons)	Near base of hairs and elsewhere in skin	Pain, warmth, cold
Hair-follicle receptors	Hair-covered skin	Movement of hairs
Meissner's corpuscles	Hairless areas	Sudden displacement of skin; low-frequency vibration (flutter)
Pacinian corpuscles	Both hairy and hairless skin	Sudden displacement of skin; high-frequency vibration
Merkel's disks	Both hairy and hairless skin	Indentation of skin
Ruffini endings	Both hairy and hairless skin	Stretch of skin
Krause end bulbs	Mostly or entirely in hairless areas, perhaps including genitals	Uncertain

and elsewhere. When someone else touches you, the response is much stronger (Blakemore, Wolpert, & Frith, 1998). Evidently, the brain gets messages from motor areas concerning what you are going to do, and these messages subtract from the touch sensations you actually receive. (Some people can tickle themselves—a little—if they tickle the right side of the body with the left hand or the left side with the right hand. Try it.)

Input to the Spinal Cord and the Brain

Information from touch receptors in the head enters the central nervous system (CNS) through the cranial nerves. Information from receptors below the head enters the spinal cord and passes toward the brain through the 31 **spinal nerves** (Figure 7.13), including 8 cervical nerves, 12 thoracic nerves, 5 lumbar nerves, 5 sacral nerves, and 1 coccygeal nerve. Each spinal nerve has a sensory component and a motor component.

Each spinal nerve *innervates,* or connects to, a limited area of the body. The skin area connected to a single sensory spinal nerve is called a **dermatome** (Figure 7.14). For example, the third thoracic nerve (T3) innervates a strip of skin just above the nipples as well as the underarm area. But the borders between dermatomes are not so distinct as Figure 7.14 implies; there is actually an overlap of one third to one half between adjacent pairs.

The sensory information that enters the spinal cord travels in well-defined pathways toward the brain. For example, the touch path-

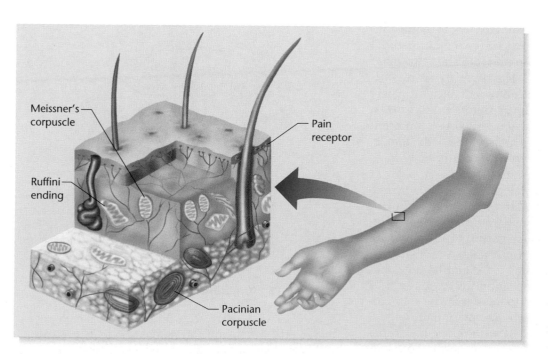

Figure 7.11   Some sensory receptors found in the skin, the human body's largest organ
Different receptor types respond to different stimuli, as described in Table 7.1.

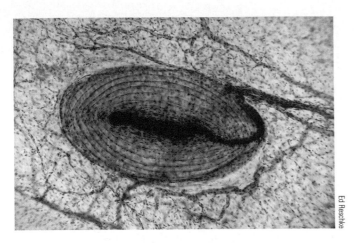

Figure 7.12 A Pacinian corpuscle
Pacinian corpuscles are a type of receptor that responds best to sudden displacement of the skin or to high-frequency vibrations. They respond only briefly to steady pressure on the skin. The onionlike outer structure provides a mechanical support to the neuronal process inside it so that a sudden stimulus can bend it but a sustained stimulus cannot.

in response to such directions as "show me your elbow" or "point to my knee," although she pointed correctly to various nonbody objects in the room. When told to touch her elbow, her most frequent response was to feel her wrist and arm and suggest that the elbow was probably around there, somewhere. She acted as if she had only a blurry map of her own body parts (Sirigu, Grafman, Bressler, & Sunderland, 1991).

way in the spinal cord is separate from the pain pathway, and the pain pathway itself has different populations of axons conveying sharp pain, slow burning pain, and painfully cold sensations (Craig, Krout, & Andrew, 2001). The various areas of the somatosensory thalamus send their impulses to different areas of the somatosensory cortex, located in the parietal lobe. Two parallel strips in the somatosensory cortex respond mostly to touch on the skin; two other parallel strips respond mostly to deep pressure and movement of the joints and muscles (Kaas, 1983). In short, various aspects of somatosensation remain at least partly separate all the way from the receptors to the cortex. Along each strip of somatosensory cortex, different subareas respond to different areas of the body; that is, the somatosensory cortex acts as a map of body location, as shown in Figure 4.25, p. 97.

The somatosensory cortex receives input primarily from the contralateral side of the body, although many cells also receive input across the corpus callosum from the somatosensory cortex of the opposite hemisphere. This crossed input enables somatosensory cortex cells to compare, for example, left-hand sensation and right-hand sensation (Iwamura, Iriki, & Tanaka, 1994). After damage to the somatosensory cortex, people generally experience an impairment of body perceptions. One patient with Alzheimer's disease, who had damage in the somatosensory cortex as well as elsewhere, had much trouble putting her clothes on correctly, and she could not point correctly

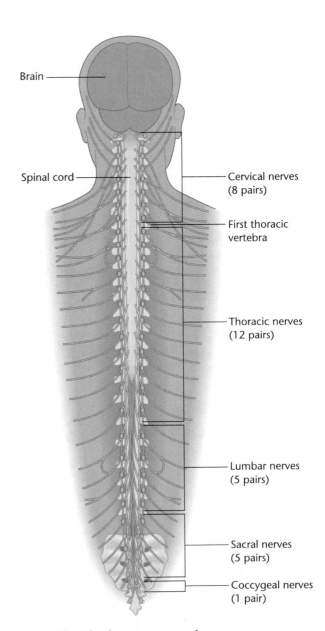

Figure 7.13 The human central nervous system (CNS)
Spinal nerves from each segment of the spinal cord exit through the correspondingly numbered opening between vertebrae. *Source: From Biology: The Unity and Diversity of Life, 5th Edition, by C. Starr and R. Taggart, p. 338. Copyright ©1989 Wadsworth. Reprinted by permission.*

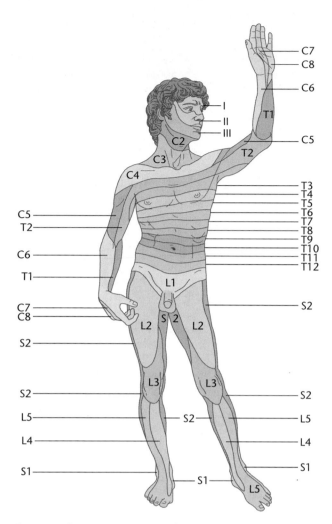

Figure 7.14 Dermatomes innervated by the 31 sensory spinal nerves
Areas I, II, and III of the face are not innervated by the spinal nerves but instead by three branches of the fifth cranial nerve. Although this figure shows distinct borders, the dermatomes actually overlap one another by about one third to one half of their width.

Stop & Check

2. In what way is somatosensation several senses instead of one?

Check your answer on page 206.

PAIN

Pain, the unpleasant emotion and sensation evoked by a harmful stimulus, directs our attention toward a danger. People who are born insensitive to pain incur frequent injuries. Some bite off the tips of their tongues, scorch their mouths with hot drinks, or expose their feet too long to the cold. One woman took a casserole out of the oven with her bare hands. Her husband screamed that she could hurt herself, but she calmly set it on their cardboard table. Not until the table burst into flames did she realize the severity of her mistake (Comings & Amromin, 1974).

Have you ever wondered why morphine decreases pain after surgery but would not during the surgery itself? Or why some people seem to tolerate pain so much better than others? Or why even the slightest touch on sunburn is so painful?

Research on pain partly answers these and other questions. Pain depends on several kinds of axons, several neurotransmitters, and several brain areas, so it is possible to modify different aspects of pain separately.

The Neurotransmitters of Pain

People have long recognized the ability of morphine and other opiates to block pain. To understand how they work, we have to explore the roles of several neurotransmitters. Axons responsible for pain release at least two transmitters. Mild pain releases only glutamate. Stronger pains release both glutamate and **substance P,** a neurotransmitter associated with strong pain (Cao et al., 1998). Mice that lack receptors for substance P react to mild pain the same as other mice, but they react to severe injury the same as to mild injury (DeFelipe et al., 1998). That is, without substance P, they cannot detect the increased intensity.

Pain alerts us to danger, but once we are aware of it, further pain messages accomplish little. Our brains can put the brakes on prolonged pain through **opioid mechanisms**—systems that are responsive to opiate drugs and similar chemicals. Candace Pert and Solomon Snyder (1973) discovered that opiates exert their effects by binding to certain brain receptors. Later researchers found that activating opiate receptors blocks substance P (Figure 7.15). Apparently, opiates produce most of their effects in that way; mice with a genetic defect in their substance P receptors hardly react to opiates at all (Mutra, Sheasby, Hunt, & De Felipe, 2000). The discovery of opiate receptors was exciting because it was the first evidence that opiates exert their main effects in the brain, not the periphery.

The discovery of opiate receptors also implied that the brain must have its own opiatelike chemicals. Two of them are peptide neurotransmitters: *met-enkephalin* and *leu-enkephalin.* The term enkephalin (en-KEFF-ah-lin) reflects the fact that these chemicals were first found in the brain, or encephalon. The two enkephalins are chains of amino acids that are the same except that met-enkephalin ends with the amino acid methionine and

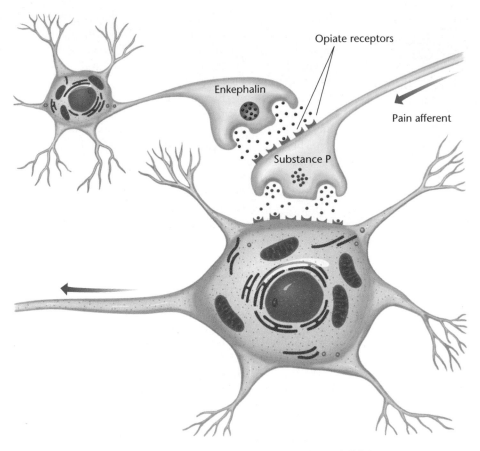

Figure 7.15 Synapses responsible for pain and its inhibition
The pain afferent neuron releases substance P as its neurotransmitter. Another neuron releases enkephalin at presynaptic synapses; the enkephalin inhibits the release of substance P and therefore alleviates pain.

by Ronald Melzack and P. D. Wall (1965). The gate theory was an attempt to explain why one person may scream in agony over pain that someone else takes with no complaint. A little of that discrepancy may relate to genetic differences in neurotransmitter receptors (Wei et al., 2001), but much of it relates to the influence of other stimuli and experiences. According to the **gate theory**, spinal cord areas that receive messages from pain receptors also receive input from other skin receptors and from axons descending from the brain. These other inputs sometimes close the "gates" for the pain messages. Although Melzack and Wall's gate theory included some details that turned out to be wrong, the general principle is valid: Nonpain stimuli can increase or decrease the intensity of pain. You have no doubt noticed this principle yourself. When you have a mild injury, you can decrease the pain by gently rubbing the skin around it. Pain can be reduced in many other ways as well, even by mere distraction.

Stimuli close the pain gates partly by activating neurons that release endorphins in the **periaqueductal gray area** and surrounding areas in the midbrain. Under the influence of the endorphins, the periaqueductal gray area excites cells in the medulla, and then the axons from both the periaqueductal gray area and the medulla send messages to the spinal cord and brainstem, blocking the release of substance P and therefore decreasing pain (Reichling, Kwiat, & Basbaum, 1988). Figure 7.16 summarizes these effects.

Painful Heat

A burn can be intensely painful, but it feels different from the pain of a cut or pinch. The body has special heat receptors, which can also be stimulated by acids. One way to stimulate those heat receptors is to inject **capsaicin,** a chemical found in hot peppers such as jalapeños. Capsaicin directly stimulates pain receptors that ordinarily respond to painful acid or painful heat—above 43°C (110°F). Animals react to capsaicin

leu-enkephalin ends with leucine. Although the enkephalins are chemically unlike morphine, they interact with the same receptors, as do several other brain chemicals, including β-*endorphin.* Collectively, the brain chemicals that attach to the same receptors as morphine are known as **endorphins** (a contraction of *endogenous* morphines) because they are the brain's own morphines.

Both pleasant and unpleasant stimuli can release endorphins and thereby inhibit pain. Inescapable pain is especially potent at stimulating endorphins and inhibiting further pain (Sutton et al., 1997). Presumably, the evolutionary function is that pain alerts an animal to danger, but if the animal can do nothing further about it, there is no advantage to continued panic. Endorphins are released during sex, during the "runner's high" that many long-distance runners report, and when you listen to thrilling music that sends a chill down your spine (A. Goldstein, 1980).

The discovery of endorphins provides physiological details for the gate theory, proposed decades earlier

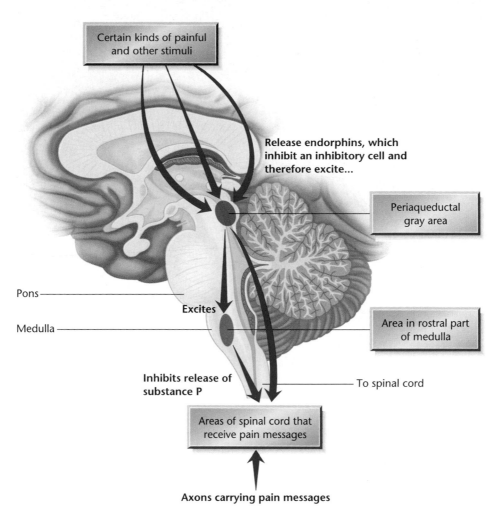

Certain kinds of painful and other stimuli

Release endorphins, which inhibit an inhibitory cell and therefore excite...

Periaqueductal gray area

Pons

Excites

Medulla

Area in rostral part of medulla

Inhibits release of substance P

To spinal cord

Areas of spinal cord that receive pain messages

Axons carrying pain messages

Figure 7.16 The periaqueductal gray area, where electrical stimulation relieves pain
Periaqueductal means "around the aqueduct," a passageway of cerebrospinal fluid between the third and fourth ventricles.

just as they do to heat itself, by sweating or salivating (Caterina et al., 2000). Capsaicin also stimulates neurons to release substance P, thereby producing pain.

When you eat a hot pepper, its capsaicin evokes a sensation of pain and heat. After the sensation abates, you experience relief and decreased sensitivity to further heat and pain on your tongue. The reason is that the capsaicin releases substance P faster than neurons can replace it, so you become temporarily deficient in this pain transmitter. In addition, high doses of capsaicin damage pain receptors.

Similarly, capsaicin rubbed onto a sore shoulder, an arthritic joint, or other painful area produces a temporary burning sensation followed by a longer period of decreased pain. However, do not try eating hot peppers to reduce pain in, say, your legs. Nearly all of the capsaicin you eat passes through the digestive system without entering the blood. Therefore, eating

it will not relieve your pain—unless it is your tongue that hurts (Karrer & Bartoshuk, 1991).

Stop & Check

3. Which neurotransmitters do pain neurons release?

4. What would happen to pain sensation if glutamate receptors were blocked? What happens after substance P receptors are blocked?

5. How do opiates relieve pain?

6. How do jalapeños produce a hot sensation?

Check your answers on page 206–207.

Pain and Emotion

Pain is a sensation, but how much it *hurts* is an emotional reaction, which can differ in intensity from the physical reaction. Some people report much more distress than others do from apparently similar injuries. Athletes and soldiers sometimes ignore serious injuries until the competition or battle is over, although at other times they may react strongly to less severe injuries.

A **placebo** is a drug or other procedure with no pharmacological effects. It is often used as the procedure for a control group in comparison to an experimental group that is given a potentially active therapy. For most medical conditions, placebos have little curative effect, but they do relieve pain, or at least subjective distress (Hróbjartsson & Gøtzsche, 2001). In one study, postsurgical patients were given analgesic (painkilling) drugs. Half received the drugs as injections by a physician; the other half received the same drug at the same times by an infusion machine, so they were not aware of when they were receiving it. The injections by a physician were much more effective at suppressing pain (Amanzio, Pollo, Maggi, & Benedetti, 2001).

One step toward accounting for this variation in effects is to distinguish between the emotional and sensory aspects of pain. The emotional aspect varies more than the sensory aspect. Pain stimulates both a sensory pathway to the somatosensory cortex and a path to the hypothalamus, amygdala, and cingulate cortex—areas known to be important for emotional responses (Hunt & Mantyh, 2001) (Figure 7.17). Surgeons recording activity from the human brain have found that painful stimulation of the skin activates the cingulate cortex, but direct electrical stimulation of the same brain area produces no report of pain (Hutchison, Davis, Lozano, Tasker, & Dostrovsky, 1999). At most, it elicits or deepens a distressed mood. When people are hypnotized and told that a needle prick or similar stimulus "will not hurt," it evokes the usual response in the somatosensory cortex but little response in the cingulate cortex (Rainville, Duncan, Price, Carrier, & Bushnell, 1997).

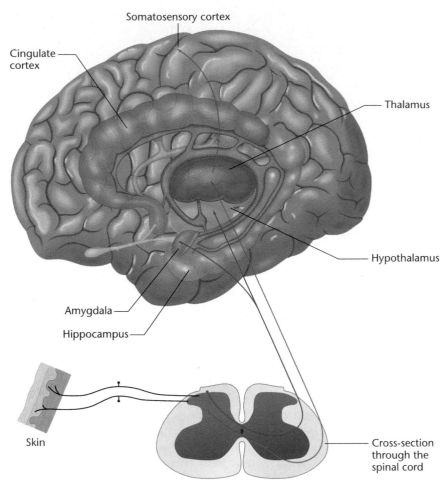

Figure 7.17 Representation of pain in the human brain
One path, to the thalamus and then to the somatosensory cortex, is responsible for the sensory aspects of pain. A separate path to the hypothalamus and amygdala produces the emotional aspects. *Source: Hunt & Mantyh, 2001*

In contrast, if people have been conditioned to expect sharp pain and they receive a moderately warm stimulus instead, their cingulate cortex reacts as if it were painful (Sawamoto et al., 2000). Rats with damage to the cingulate cortex react to pain on their feet by flinching and licking their feet, but they don't learn to avoid the location where they got the pain (Johansen, Fields, & Manning, 2001). In short, the cingulate responds to the emotional aspect of pain, not the sensation.

Sensitization of Pain

In addition to mechanisms for decreasing pain, the body has mechanisms that increase pain. If you have ever been sunburned, you probably remember how badly a light touch could sting. Damaged or inflamed tissue, such as sunburned skin, releases histamine, nerve growth factor, and other chemicals that help repair the damage. However, these chemicals also increase the number of sodium gates in nearby receptors, including pain receptors, and thereby magnify pain responses (Devor, 1996; Tominaga et al., 1998). They also facilitate activity at capsaicin receptors, thus increasing any burning sensations (Chuang et al., 2001).

Nonsteroidal anti-inflammatory drugs, such as ibuprofen, decrease pain by reducing the release of chemicals from damaged tissues (Hunt & Mantyh, 2001). In animal experiments, the neurotrophin GDNF has shown even greater potential to block the heightened pain sensitivity after tissue damage (Boucher et al., 2000).

Pain Control

Morphine and other opiates continue to be the primary drugs for controlling serious pain. They are, of course, potentially addictive, and long-term use can lead to tolerance. Suppose you are about to undergo major surgery. Should you:

A. Start taking morphine before the surgery even starts.
B. Begin morphine soon after awakening from surgery.
C. Postpone the morphine as long as possible and take as little as possible.

Perhaps surprisingly, the research supports answer A: Start taking morphine before the surgery even starts (Keefe & France, 1999). Allowing the brain to be bombarded with pain messages during and after the surgery increases the sensitivity of the pain nerves and their receptors (Malmberg, Chen, Tonagawa, & Basbaum, 1997). People who begin taking morphine before surgery need less than the usual amount afterward. People who take morphine to kill pain while lying in a hospital bed seldom become addicted to it. The experience is not very similar to recreational drug use. (In a hospital, people take only the amount they need in a setting not designed for pleasure.)

Why does morphine block some kinds of pain more than others? Sharp pain, such as feeling a cut, is carried by larger diameter axons, whereas dull pain, such as postsurgical pain, is carried by thinner, slower, unmyelinated axons. Morphine is much more effective at blocking the activity of the thin axons, and therefore, it reduces postsurgical pain but would not by itself provide adequate relief during surgery (Taddese, Nah, & McCleskey, 1995).

For more information about pain, including links to research reports, check either of these Web sites:
www.painnet.com/
www.ampainsoc.org/

ITCH

Have you ever wondered, "What is itch, anyway? Is it a kind of pain? A kind of touch? Or something else altogether?" For many years, no one knew, and we still do not know what kind of receptors are responsible for itch. However, we do know that when your skin rubs against certain plants, when an insect crawls along your skin, or when you have mild tissue damage, your skin releases histamines, and histamines produce an itching sensation.

Researchers have identified a spinal cord pathway of itch sensation (Andrew & Craig, 2001). Histamines in the skin excite axons of this pathway, and other kinds of skin stimuli do not. Even when a stimulus releases histamines, however, this pathway is slow to respond, and when it does respond, the axons transmit impulses at the unusually slow velocity of only about half a meter per second. At that rate, an action potential from your foot needs 3 or 4 seconds to reach your head. For a giraffe or elephant, the delay is even longer. You might try rubbing some rough leaves against your ankle. Note how soon you feel the touch sensation and how much more slowly you notice the itchiness.

Itch is useful because it directs you to scratch the itchy area and presumably remove whatever is irritating your skin. Vigorous scratching produces mild pain, and pain inhibits itch. Opiates, which decrease pain, increase itch (Andrew & Craig, 2001). This inhibitory relationship between pain and itch is the strongest evidence that itch is not just a type of pain.

This research helps explain an experience that you may have had. When a dentist gives you Novocain before drilling a tooth, part of your face becomes numb. An hour or more later, as the Novocain's effects start to wear off, you may feel an intense itchy sensation in the numb portion of your face. But when you try to scratch the itch, you feel nothing because the touch and pain sensations are still numb. (Evidently, the effects of Novocain wear off faster for itch than for touch and pain axons.) The fact that you can feel itch at this time is evidence that it is not just a form of touch or pain. It is interesting that scratching the partly numb skin does not relieve the itch. Evidently, your scratching has to produce some pain to decrease the itch.

7. How do ibuprofen and other nonsteroidal anti-inflammatory drugs decrease pain?

8. Why does morphine relieve dull pain more than sharp pain?

9. Would antihistamine drugs increase or decrease itch sensations? What about opiates?

Check your answers on page 207.

MODULE 7.2

In Closing: Touch, Pain, and Survival

We humans generally pay so much attention to vision and hearing that we take our mechanical senses for granted. However, a mere moment's reflection should reveal how critical they are for survival. At every moment, your vestibular sense tells you whether you are standing or falling; your sense of pain can tell you that you have injured yourself. If you moved to a televisionlike universe with only vision and hearing, you might get by if you had already learned what all the sights and sounds mean. But it is hard to imagine how you could have learned their meaning without much previous experience of touch and pain.

SUMMARY

1. The vestibular system is a sensory system that detects the position and acceleration of the head and adjusts body posture and eye movements accordingly. (p. 197)

2. The somatosensory system depends on a variety of receptors that are sensitive to different kinds of stimulation of the skin and internal tissues. The brain maintains several parallel somatosensory representations of the body. (p. 197)

3. Pain messages are transmitted by axons that release glutamate as their neurotransmitter for moderately painful stimuli and a combination of glutamate and substance P for stronger pains. (p. 201)

4. Opiate drugs attach to the receptors that the brain uses for endorphins, transmitters that decrease pain sensations by blocking the release of substance P. (p. 201)

5. Both pleasant and unpleasant experiences can evoke the release of endorphins and thereby decrease sensitivity to pain. (p. 202)

6. A certain harmful stimulus may give rise to a greater or lesser degree of pain, depending on other current and recent stimuli. According to the gate theory of pain, other stimuli can close certain gates and block the transmission of pain. (p. 202)

7. Capsaicin produces temporary pain by releasing substance P and by stimulating receptors for moderate heat. However, as that pain wears off, the individual becomes less sensitive to pain because the neurons need much time to restore their supply of substance P and because the heat receptors themselves may have been damaged. (p. 202)

8. Pain excites two brain areas, one responsible for the sensory aspect of pain and one for the emotional response to it. (p. 204)

9. Morphine is most effective as a painkiller if it is used promptly. Allowing the nervous system to be bombarded with prolonged pain messages increases the overall sensitivity to pain. Morphine used under medical conditions is seldom addictive. (p. 205)

10. Skin irritation releases histamine, which excites a spinal pathway responsible for itch. The axons of that pathway transmit impulses very slowly. They can be inhibited by pain messages. (p. 205)

ANSWERS TO *STOP AND CHECK* QUESTIONS

1. The vestibular system enables the brain to shift eye movements to compensate for changes in head position. Without feedback about head position, a person would not be able to correct the eye movements and the experience would be like watching a jiggling book page. (p. 197)

2. We have several types of receptors, sensitive to touch, heat, and so forth, and different parts of the somatosensory cortex respond to different kinds of skin stimulation. (p. 201)

3. A mild pain stimulus releases glutamate. A stronger stimulus releases glutamate and substance P. (p. 203)

4. Blocking glutamate receptors would eliminate weak to moderate pain. (However, doing so would not be a good strategy for killing pain. Glutamate is the most abundant transmitter, and blocking it would disrupt practically everything the brain does.) Blocking substance P receptors makes intense pain feel mild. (p. 203)

5. Opiates relieve pain by stimulating the same receptors as endorphins, thereby blocking the release of substance P. (p. 203)

6. Jalapeños and other hot peppers contain capsaicin, which causes pain neurons to release substance P and also directly stimulates receptors that are sensitive to moderate heat. (p. 203)

7. Anti-inflammatory drugs block the release of chemicals from damaged tissues. Damaged tissues would otherwise release chemicals that facilitate capsaicin receptors and increase the number of sodium gates in pain receptors. (p. 206)

8. Morphine and endorphins block activity in thin pain axons, which convey dull pain, but have less effect on thicker pain axons, which convey sharp pain. (p. 206)

9. Antihistamines decrease itch; opiates increase it. (p. 206)

THOUGHT QUESTION

Why is the vestibular sense generally useless under conditions of weightlessness?

MODULE 7.3

The Chemical Senses

Suppose you had the godlike power to create a new species of animal, but you could equip it with only one sensory system. Which sense would you give it?

Your first impulse might be to choose vision or hearing because you know how important they are to humans. But an animal with only one sensory system is not going to be much like humans, is it? To have any chance of survival, it will probably have to be small and slow, maybe even one-celled. What sense will be most useful to such an animal?

Most theorists believe that the first sensory system of the earliest animals was a chemical sensitivity (G. H. Parker, 1922). A chemical sense enables a small animal to cope with the basics of finding food, identifying certain kinds of danger, and even locating mates.

Now imagine that you have to choose one of your senses to lose. Which one will it be? Most of us would not choose to lose vision, hearing, or touch. Losing pain sensitivity can be dangerous. You might choose to sacrifice your smell or taste.

Curious, isn't it? If an animal is going to survive with only one sense, it almost has to be a chemical sense, and yet to humans, who have many other well-developed senses, the chemical senses seem dispensable. Perhaps we underestimate their importance.

GENERAL ISSUES ABOUT CHEMICAL CODING

Suppose you run a bakery and need to send frequent messages to your supplier two blocks away. Suppose further that you can communicate only by ringing three large bells on the roof of your bakery. You would have to work out a code.

One possibility would be to label the three bells: The high-pitched bell means "I need flour." The medium-pitched bell means "I need sugar." And the low-pitched bell means "I need eggs." Then you simply ring the right bell at the right moment. The more you need something, the faster you ring the bell. We shall call this the *labeled-line* code because each bell has a single unchanging label. The problem is that this simple code can signal only flour, sugar, and eggs.

Another possibility would be to set up a code that depends on a relationship among the three bells. Ringing the high and medium bells equally means that you need flour. The medium and low bells together call for sugar; the high and low bells together call for eggs. Ringing all three together means you need vanilla extract. Ringing mostly the high bell while ringing the other two bells slightly means you need hazelnuts. And so forth. We call this the *across-fiber pattern* code because the meaning depends on the pattern across bells. This code is versatile and can be highly useful, unless we make it too complicated.

A sensory system could theoretically use either type of coding. In a system relying on the **labeled-line principle,** each receptor would respond to a limited range of stimuli and send a direct line to the brain. In a system relying on the **across-fiber pattern principle,** each receptor responds to a wider range of stimuli and contributes to the perception of each of them. In other words, a given level of response by a given sensory axon means little unless the brain knows what the other axons are doing at the same time (Erickson, 1982).

Vertebrate sensory systems probably do not have any pure labeled-line codes. The response of any one neuron fluctuates somewhat; the brain gets better information from a combination of responses (Pouget, Dayan, & Zemel, 2000). In color perception, we encountered an example of an across-fiber pattern code: Each color-sensitive cell responds best to certain stimuli, but because it also responds to other stimuli, its message out of context is ambiguous. For example, a medium-wavelength cone might produce the same level of response to a moderately bright green light, a brighter blue light, or a white light. In auditory pitch perception, the responses of the hair cell receptors are narrowly tuned, but even in this case, the meaning of a particular receptor's response depends on the context: A given receptor may respond best to a certain high-frequency tone, but it also responds in phase with a number of low-frequency tones (as do all the other receptors). Each receptor also responds to white noise (static) and to various mixtures of tones. Auditory perception depends on a comparison of responses across all the receptors.

Similarly, each taste and smell stimulus excites several kinds of receptors, and the meaning of a particular response by a particular receptor depends on the context of responses by other receptors. However, our understanding of the chemical senses is limited compared to what we know about the other senses. Even on basic questions of how we code tastes and smells or how many kinds of receptors we have, we cannot draw conclusions with the same confidence as with vision and hearing.

Stop & Check

1. Of the following, which use a labeled-line code and which use an across-fiber pattern code?
   A. A fire alarm
   B. A light switch
   C. The shift key plus another key on a computer or typewriter

Check your answers on page 218.

TASTE

When we talk about the taste of food, we generally mean flavor, which is produced by a combination of taste and smell. Taste refers to the stimulation of the taste buds. Very few people lose their taste buds, and most people who complain of losing their sense of taste actually have an impaired sense of smell. In fact, you don't need very many taste receptors to get a recognizable sensation. Even people who have suffered damage to most of the tongue continue to identify tastes accurately, although they report a loss of intensity (Lehman, Bartoshuk, Catalanotto, Kveton, & Lowlicht, 1995).

Taste Receptors

The receptors for taste are not true neurons but modified skin cells. Like neurons, taste receptors have excitable membranes and release neurotransmitters to excite neighboring neurons, which in turn transmit information to the brain. Like skin cells, however, taste receptors are gradually sloughed off and replaced, each one lasting about 10 to 14 days (Kinnamon, 1987).

Mammalian taste receptors are in taste buds, located in **papillae,** structures on the surface of the tongue (Figure 7.18). A given papilla may contain from zero to ten or more taste buds (Arvidson & Friberg, 1980), and each taste bud contains about 50 receptor cells.

In adult humans, taste buds are located mainly along the outside edge of the tongue, with few or none in the center. You can demonstrate this principle as follows: Soak a small cotton swab in sugar water, salt water, or vinegar. Then touch it lightly on the center of your tongue, not too far toward the back. You will probably experience little taste. Then try it again on the edge of your tongue and notice how much stronger the taste is.

Now change the procedure a bit. Wash your mouth out with water and prepare a cotton swab as before. Touch the soaked portion to one edge of your tongue and then slowly stroke it to the center of your tongue. Now it will seem as if you are moving the taste to the center of your tongue. In fact, you are getting only a touch sensation from the center of your tongue; you attribute the taste you had on the side of your tongue to every other spot you stroke (Bartoshuk, 1991).

How Many Kinds of Taste Receptors?

Traditionally, people in Western society have thought of sweet, sour, salty, and bitter as the "primary" tastes. However, some tastes defy categorization in terms of these four labels (Schiffman & Erickson, 1980; Schiffman, McElroy, & Erickson, 1980). How could we determine how many kinds people have?

EXTENSIONS AND APPLICATIONS
Miracle Berries

One way to answer this question is to find procedures that alter one kind of receptor but not others. For example, chewing a miracle berry (native to West Africa) gives little taste itself but temporarily changes the taste of sour substances. Miracle berries contain a protein, miraculin, that modifies sweet receptors in such a way that they can be stimulated by acids (Bartoshuk, Gentile, Moskowitz, & Meiselman, 1974). If you ever get a chance to chew a miracle berry (and I do recommend it), for about the next half hour all acids will taste sweet in addition to their usual sour taste.

Miraculin was, for a time, commercially available in the United States as a diet aid. The idea was that dieters could coat their tongue with a miraculin pill and then enjoy unsweetened lemonade and so forth, which would taste sweet but provide almost no calories.

A colleague and I once spent an evening experimenting with miracle berries. We drank straight lemon juice, sauerkraut juice, even vinegar. All tasted extremely sweet, but we awoke the next day with mouths full of ulcers.

Other taste-modifying substances include an extract from the plant *Gymnema sylvestre,* which makes people temporarily insensitive to a great variety of sweet tastes (R. A. Frank, Mize, Kennedy, de los Santos, & Green, 1992), and the chemical theophylline, which reduces the bitterness of many substances (Kodama, Fukushima, & Sakata, 1978). After eating artichokes, some people report a sweet taste from water (Bartoshuk, Lee, & Scarpellino, 1972).

Have you ever tasted orange juice just after brushing your teeth? And did you wonder why something that usually tastes so good suddenly tasted so bad? Most toothpastes contain sodium lauryl sulfate, a chemical that intensifies bitter tastes while weakening sweet ones (DeSimone, Heck, & Bartoshuk, 1980; Schiffman, 1983). Evidently, it disrupts the membrane surfaces, preventing molecules from binding to sweetness receptors. Fortunately, the effect wears off in a few minutes.

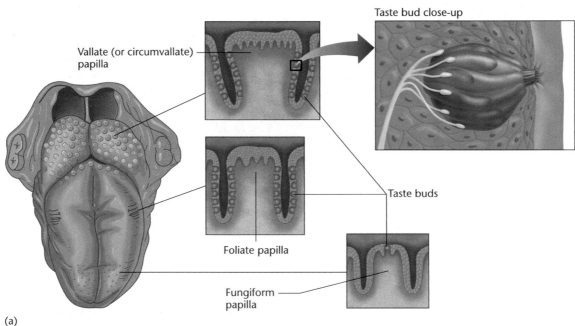

Taste bud close-up

Vallate (or circumvallate) papilla

Taste buds

Foliate papilla

Fungiform papilla

(a)

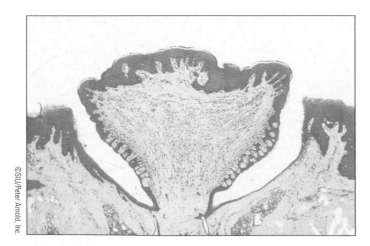

©SIU/Peter Arnold, Inc.

(b)

Figure 7.18 The organs of taste
(a) The tip, back, and sides of the tongue are covered with taste buds. Taste buds are located in papillae. **(b)** Photo showing cross section of a taste bud. Each taste bud contains about 50 receptor cells.

Further behavioral evidence for separate types of taste receptors comes from studies of the following type: Soak your tongue for 15 seconds in a sour solution, such as unsweetened lemon juice. Then try tasting some other sour solution, such as dilute vinegar. You will find that the second solution tastes less sour than usual. Depending on the concentrations of the lemon juice and vinegar, the second solution may not taste sour at all. This phenomenon, called **adaptation**, presumably reflects the fatigue of receptors sensitive to sour tastes. Now try tasting something salty, sweet, or bitter. These substances taste about the same as usual. In short, you experience very little **cross-adaptation**—reduced response to one taste after exposure to another (McBurney & Bartoshuk, 1973).

So we have long known that people have at least four kinds of taste receptors. But several types of evidence suggested a fifth as well, and researchers in fact located a taste receptor for that fifth taste, glutamate, as found in monosodium glutamate (MSG), meats, and broths (Chaudhari, Landin, & Roper, 2000). The taste of glutamate resembles that of unsalted chicken broth. The English language did not have a word for this taste, but Japanese did, so English-speaking researchers have adopted the Japanese word, *umami.*

Mechanisms of Taste Receptors

Neuroscientists have begun to identify and describe the taste receptors (Lindemann, 1996). One is the saltiness detector. Recall that a neuron produces an action potential when sodium ions cross its membrane. A saltiness receptor, which detects the presence of sodium, does not need a specialized membrane site sensitive to sodium. It simply permits sodium ions on the tongue to cross its membrane. The higher the concentration of sodium on the tongue, the greater the receptor's response. Chemicals such as amiloride, which prevents sodium from crossing the membrane, reduce the intensity of salty tastes (DeSimone, et al., 1984; Schiffman, Lockhead, & Maes, 1983).

Sourness receptors operate on a different principle. When an acid binds to the receptor, it closes potassium channels and prevents potassium from leaving the cell. The result is an increased accumulation of positive charges within the neuron and therefore a depolarization of the membrane (Shirley & Persaud, 1990).

Sweetness, bitterness, and umami receptors operate much like a metabotropic synapse (Chapter 3). After a molecule binds to one of these receptors, it activates a G-protein that releases a second messenger within the cell (Lindemann, 1996).

Bitter sensations have long been a puzzle. It is easy to describe the chemicals that produce a sour taste (acids), a salty taste (Na^+ ions), or umami (glutamate). Sweets are more difficult, as they include naturally occurring sugars plus artificial chemicals such as saccharin and aspartame. But bitter substances include a long list of chemicals that apparently have nothing in common with one another, except for the fact that nearly all of them are toxic. What receptor could identify such a large and diverse set of chemicals? The answer is that we have not one bitter receptor but a whole family of them, about 40 to 80 in all (Adler et al., 2000; Matsunami, Montmayeur, & Buck, 2000). Most taste cells sensitive to bitterness contain just a small number of the possible bitter receptors, not all 40 to 80 (Caicedo & Roper, 2001). So it is possible that your brain can distinguish one bitter taste from another, although we have no behavioral evidence that it actually does so.

One consequence of having so many bitter receptors is that we can detect a great variety of dangerous chemicals. The other is that because each type of bitter receptor is present in small numbers, we can't detect very low concentrations of bitter substances, as we can with sour or salty substances, for example.

2. Suppose you find a new, unusual-tasting food. How could you determine whether we have a special receptor for that food or whether we taste it with a combination of the other known taste receptors?

3. If someone injected into your tongue some chemical that blocks the release of second messengers, what would be the effect on your taste experiences?

Check your answers on page 218.

Taste Coding in the Brain

Although you may assume that the five kinds of receptors imply five labeled lines to the brain, research suggests a more complicated system (Hettinger & Frank, 1992). The receptors converge their input onto the next cells in the taste system, each of which responds best to a particular taste, but somewhat to others also. The brain can determine what the tongue is tasting only by comparing the responses of several kinds of taste neurons. In other words, taste depends on a pattern of responses across fibers (R. P. Erickson, DiLorenzo, & Woodbury, 1994).

Information from the receptors in the anterior two thirds of the tongue is carried to the brain along the chorda tympani, a branch of the seventh cranial nerve (the facial nerve). Taste information from the posterior tongue and the throat is carried along branches of the ninth and tenth cranial nerves. What do you suppose would happen if someone anesthetized your chorda tympani? You would no longer taste anything in the anterior part of your tongue, but you probably would not notice because you would still taste with the posterior part. However, the posterior part would become much more sensitive to bitter tastes than before, somewhat more sensitive to most other tastes, and less sensitive to salt. Finally, the probability is about 40% that you would experience taste "phantoms," a little like the phantom limb experience discussed in Chapter 5 (Yanagisawa, Bartoshuk, Catalanotto, Karrer, & Kveton, 1998). That is, you might experience tastes even when nothing was on your tongue. Evidently, the inputs from the anterior and posterior parts of your tongue interact in complex ways. Silencing the anterior part releases the posterior part from inhibition and causes it to report tastes more actively than before.

The taste nerves project to the **nucleus of the tractus solitarius** (NTS), a structure in the medulla (Travers, Pfaffmann, & Norgren, 1986). From the NTS, information branches out, reaching the pons, the lateral hypothalamus, the amygdala, the ventral-posterior thalamus, and two areas of the cerebral cortex (Pritchard, Hamilton, Morse, & Norgren, 1986; Yamamoto, 1984). One of these, the somatosensory cortex, responds to the touch aspects of tongue stimulation. The other area, known as the insula, is the primary taste cortex. Oddly, each hemisphere of the cortex receives input mostly from the ipsilateral side of the tongue (Aglioti, Tassinari, Corballis, & Berlucchi, 2000; Pritchard, Macaluso, & Eslinger, 1999). In contrast, each hemisphere receives mostly contralateral input for vision, hearing, and touch. A few of the major connections are illustrated in Figure 7.19.

Individual Differences in Taste

You may have had a biology instructor who asked you to taste phenythiocarbamide (PTC) and then take samples home for your relatives to try. Some people experience it as bitter, and others hardly taste it at all; the ability to taste it is controlled by a single dominant gene and therefore provides an interesting example for a genetics lab. (Did your instructor happen to mention that PTC is mildly toxic?)

For decades, this difference was widely studied as an interesting, easily measurable difference among

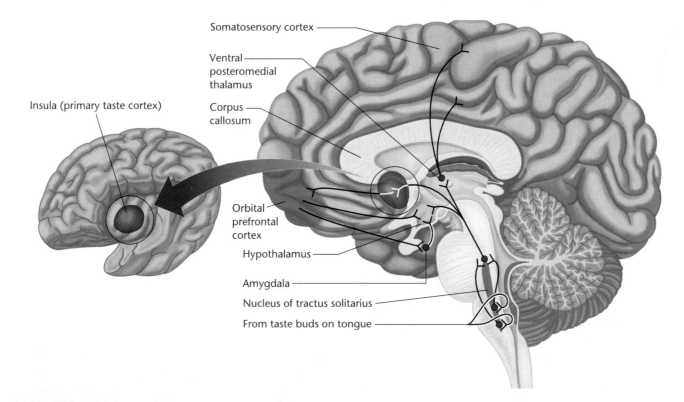

Somatosensory cortex

Ventral posteromedial thalamus

Insula (primary taste cortex)

Corpus callosum

Orbital prefrontal cortex

Hypothalamus

Amygdala

Nucleus of tractus solitarius

From taste buds on tongue

Figure 7.19 Major routes of impulses related to the sense of taste in the human brain
The thalamus and cerebral cortex receive impulses from both the left and the right sides of the tongue.
Source: Based on Rolls, 1995

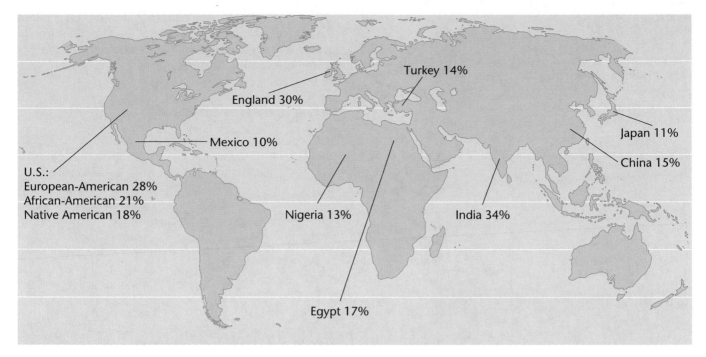

Figure 7.20 Percentage of nontasters in several human populations.
Most of the percentages are based on large samples, including more than 31,000 in Japan and 35,000 in India. *Source: Based on Guo & Reed, 2001*

people that was traceable to genetics, and we have extensive data about the percentage of nontasters in different populations (Guo & Reed, 2001). Figure 7.20 shows some representative results. Although we might expect the prevalence of nontasters to influence cuisine, the figure shows no obvious relationship. For example, nontasters are common in India, but uncommon in Mexico, two countries famous for their spicy food. Nontasters are common in Britain, where the traditional cuisine is bland.

In the 1990s, researchers discovered that people who are insensitive to PTC are also less sensitive than other people to other tastes as well, including other bitter tastes, sours, salts, and so forth. Furthermore, people at the opposite extreme, known as supertasters, have the highest sensitivity to all tastes, as well as to hot peppers, the texture of fats, and apparently mouth sensations in general. Therefore, they are unlikely to enjoy black coffee, strong beer, hot peppers, tart fruits such as lemon and grapefruit, dark bread, and strong-tasting vegetables such as Brussels sprouts, cauliflower, cabbage, and radishes (Drewnowski, Henderson, Shore, & Barratt-Fornell, 1998). However, most food preferences depend on culture and familiarity with various foods. Consequently, even after you think about how much you like or dislike strongly flavored foods, you cannot confidently identify yourself as a supertaster, taster, or nontaster.

The variations in taste sensitivity relate to the number of *fungiform papillae* near the tip of the tongue. Supertasters have the most; nontasters have the fewest. This anatomical difference depends mostly on genetics, although it is also possible to lose taste buds from damage to the tongue. Hormones also modify taste sensitivity. Women's taste sensitivity rises and falls with their monthly hormone cycles and is at maximum during early pregnancy, when estradiol levels are very high (Prutkin et al., 2000). That tendency is probably adaptive: During pregnancy, a woman needs to be more careful than usual to avoid harmful foods.

If you would like to classify yourself as a taster, nontaster, or supertaster, follow these instructions.

Make a quarter-inch hole with a standard hole punch in a piece of wax paper. Dip the cotton swab in blue food coloring. Place the wax paper on the tip of your tongue, just right of the center. Rub the cotton swab over the hole in the wax paper to dye a little part of your tongue. With the flashlight and magnifying glass, count the number of pink, unstained circles in the blue area. They are your fungiform papillae. Compare your results to the following averages.

Supertasters:	25 papillae
Tasters:	17 papillae
Nontasters:	10 papillae

OLFACTION

Olfaction, the sense of smell, is the detection and recognition of chemicals that come in contact with the membranes inside the nose. During an ordinary day, most of us pay little attention to scents, and the deodorant industry is dedicated to removing human body odors from our experience. Nevertheless, we rely on olfaction for discriminating good from bad wine or edible from rotting meat. Natural gas companies add a distinctive odor to their product so that people can smell a leak in the gas line. Odors can call up an array of memories, often nostalgic ones.

Olfactory Receptors

The neurons responsible for smell are the **olfactory cells,** which line the olfactory epithelium in the rear of the nasal air passages (Figure 7.21). In mammals, each olfactory cell has cilia (threadlike dendrites) that extend from the cell body into the mucous surface of the nasal passage. Olfactory receptors are located on the cilia. Each one survives for a little over a month and then is replaced by a new cell that has the same odor sensitivities as the original (Nef, 1998).

Olfaction is subject to rapid adaptation (Kurahashi, Lowe, & Gold, 1994). To demonstrate adaptation, take a bottle of an odorous chemical, such as lemon extract, and determine how far away you can hold the bottle and still smell it. Then hold it up to your nose and inhale deeply and repeatedly for a minute. Now test again: From how far away can you smell it?

When an olfactory receptor is stimulated, its axon carries an impulse to the olfactory bulb (see Figure 4.15, p. 89).

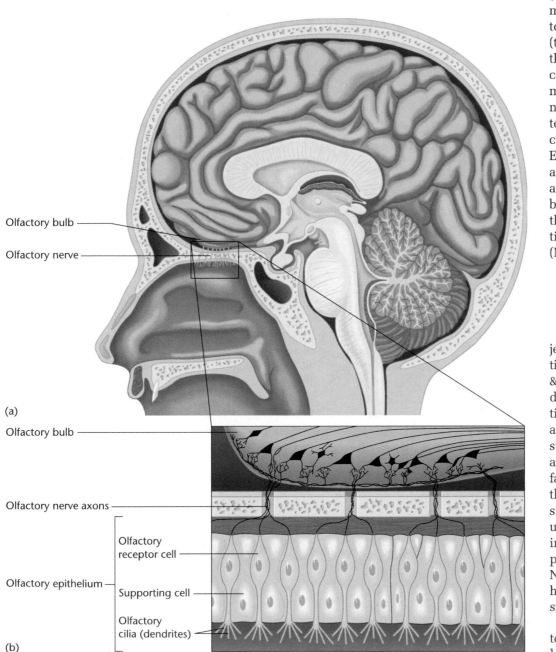

Olfactory bulb
Olfactory nerve

(a)

Olfactory bulb

Olfactory nerve axons

Olfactory epithelium

Olfactory receptor cell

Supporting cell

Olfactory cilia (dendrites)

(b)

Figure 7.21 Olfactory receptors
(a) Location of receptors in nasal cavity. **(b)** Closeup of olfactory cells. Note also the vomeronasal organ, to be discussed later.

Each odorous chemical excites only a limited part of the olfactory bulb. Evidently, olfaction is coded in terms of which area of the olfactory bulb is excited. Chemicals that smell similar to one another excite almost the same areas, whereas chemicals that smell very different excite different areas (Uchida, Takahashi, Tanifuji, & Mori, 2000).

The olfactory bulb sends its axons to several parts of the cortex, and again, the connections are precise. All the receptors sensitive to a given group of chemicals send information to the same small cluster of cells in the cortex, and the organization of the olfactory cortex is almost identical from one individual to another (Zou, Horowitz, Montmayeur, Snapper, & Buck, 2001). From the cortex, information connects to other areas that control feeding and reproduction, two kinds of behavior that are very sensitive to odors.

Stop & Check

> **4.** What is the mean life span of an olfactory receptor?
>
> **5.** If two olfactory receptors are located near each other, in what way are they likely to be similar?
>
> *Check your answers on page 218.*

Behavioral Methods of Identifying Olfactory Receptors

How many kinds of olfactory receptors do we have? Three, seven, twenty, or what? Researchers answered the analogous question for color vision more than a century ago using only behavioral observations. They found that, by mixing various amounts of three colors of light—say, red, green, and blue—they could match any other color that people can see. Researchers therefore concluded that we have three, and probably only three, kinds of color receptors (which we now call cones).

We could imagine doing the same experiment for olfaction. Take a few odors—say, almond, lilac, and skunk spray—and test whether people can mix various proportions of those odors to match all other odors. If three odors are not enough, add more until eventually we can mix them to match every other possible odor. Because we do not know what the "primary odors" are (if indeed there are such odors), we might have to do a great deal of trial-and-error testing to find the best set of odors to use. So far as we know, however, either no one ever tried such an experiment, or everyone who did gave up in discouragement.

A second approach is to study people who have trouble smelling one type of chemical. A general lack of olfaction is known as **anosmia**; the inability to smell a single chemical is a **specific anosmia**. For example, about 2% to 3% of all people are insensitive to the smell of isobutyric acid, the smelly component of sweat (Amoore, 1977). (Few complain about this disability.) Because people can lose the ability to smell just this one chemical, we may assume that there is a receptor specific to isobutyric acid. We might then search for additional specific anosmias on the theory that each specific anosmia represents the loss of a different type of receptor.

One investigator identified at least 5 other specific anosmias—musky, fishy, urinous, spermous, and malty—and less convincing evidence suggested 26 other possible specific anosmias (Amoore, 1977). But the more specific anosmias one finds, the less sure one can be of having found them all.

Biochemical Identification of Receptor Types

Ultimately, the best way to determine the number of olfactory receptor types is to isolate the receptor molecules themselves. Linda Buck and Richard Axel (1991) identified in olfactory receptors a family of proteins, as shown in Figure 7.22. Like many neurotransmitter receptors, each of these proteins traverses the cell membrane seven times and responds to a chemical outside the cell (here an odorant molecule instead of a neurotransmitter) by triggering changes in a G-protein inside the cell; the G-protein then provokes chemical activities that lead to an action potential.

Each olfactory receptor cell expresses only one receptor gene (Serizawa et al., 2000), so it is excited only by a narrow range of chemicals (Araneda, Kini, & Firestein, 2000). The best estimate is that humans have several hundred olfactory receptor proteins, whereas rats and mice have about a thousand types (Zhang & Firestein, 2002). Correspondingly, rats can distinguish among odors that seem the same to humans (Rubin & Kaatz, 2001).

Stop & Check

> **6.** What is a specific anosmia?
>
> **7.** How do olfactory receptors resemble metabotropic neurotransmitter receptors?
>
> *Check your answers on page 218.*

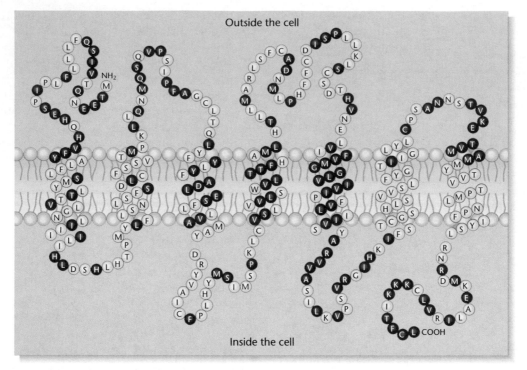

Figure 7.22 One of the olfactory receptor proteins
If you compare this protein with the synaptic receptor protein shown in Figure 3.12 (p. 66), you will notice great similarity. Each protein traverses the membrane seven times; each responds to a chemical outside the cell and triggers activity of a G-protein inside the cell. The protein shown is one of a family; different olfactory receptors contain different proteins, each with a slightly different structure. Each of the little circles in this diagram represents one amino acid of the protein. The white circles represent amino acids that are the same in most of the olfactory receptor proteins; the purple circles represent amino acids that vary from one protein to another. *Source: Based on Buck & Axel, 1991*

Implications for Coding

We have only three kinds of cones and probably five kinds of taste receptors, so it was a surprise to find so many olfactory receptors. Having hundreds makes possible a great specialization of functions. To illustrate, because we have only three kinds of cones with which to see a great variety of colors, each cone must contribute to almost every color perception. In olfaction, we can afford to have receptors that respond to few stimuli. The response of one olfactory receptor might mean, "I smell a fatty acid with a straight chain of about three to five carbon atoms." The response of another receptor might mean, "I smell either a fatty acid or an aldehyde with a straight chain of about four to six carbon atoms." The responses of other cells identify alcohols, alkanes, and so forth (Imamura, Mataga, & Mori, 1992; Mori, Mataga, & Imamura, 1992). In short, the response of one receptor can identify the approximate nature of the molecule, and the response of a larger population of receptors enables more precise recognition.

The question may have occurred to you, "Why did evolution go to the bother of designing so many olfactory receptor types? After all, color vision gets by with just three types of cones." The main reason is that light energy can be arranged along a single di-

mension, wavelength. Olfaction processes an enormous variety of airborne chemicals that are not arranged along any one continuum. To detect them all, we probably need a great variety of receptors. A secondary reason has to do with localization. In olfaction, space is no problem; we arrange our olfactory receptors over the entire surface of the nasal passages. In vision, however, the brain needs to determine precisely where on the retina a stimulus originates. Hundreds of different kinds of wavelength receptors could not be compacted into each spot on the retina.

For more information about olfaction, check these Web sites:
www.senseofsmell.org/home.asp
www.leffingwell.com/olfaction.htm

VOMERONASAL SENSATION AND PHEROMONES

An additional sense is important for most mammals, although less so for humans. The **vomeronasal organ (VNO)** is a set of receptors located near, but separate from, the olfactory receptors. Its receptors cross the cell membrane seven times, just like olfactory receptors. However, the VNO has fewer types of receptors—12 families of them in mice (Rodriguez, Del Punta, Rothman, Ishii, & Mombaerts, 2002)—and they are structurally different from olfactory receptors (Keverne, 1999).

Unlike the olfactory system, which can identify an enormous number of chemicals, the VNO's receptors are specialized to respond only to pheromones, which are chemicals released by an animal that affect the behavior of other members of the same species, especially sexually. For example, if you have ever had a female dog that wasn't neutered, whenever she was in her fertile (estrous) period, even though you kept her indoors, you may have noticed an enormous array of male dogs camped out in your yard. Her pheromones had a far-reaching effect, literally.

Each VNO receptor responds to just one pheromone, such as the smell of a male or a female mouse. It becomes excited by the preferred chemical in concentrations as low as one part in a hundred billion, but it hardly responds at all to other chemicals (Leinders-Zufall et al., 2000). Furthermore, the receptor shows no adaptation to a repeated stimulus. Olfaction, by contrast, shows massive adaptation. Have you ever been in a room that seems smelly at first but not a few minutes later? Your olfactory receptors respond to a new odor but not to a continuing one. The VNO receptors, however, continue responding just as strongly even after prolonged stimulation (Holy, Dulac, & Meister, 2000).

What do you suppose would happen if a male mouse's vomeronasal receptors were inactive because of a genetic abnormality? Results of two studies differed, presumably depending on which vomeronasal receptors were lost. In one study, the males lost practically all sexual behaviors (Del Punta et al., 2002), and in the other, they attempted indiscriminately to mate with both males and females (Stowers, Holy, Meister, Dulac, & Koentges, 2002).

Although the VNO is reasonably prominent in most mammals and easy to find in a human fetus, it is tiny in adult humans (Monti-Bloch, Jennings-White, Dolberg, & Berliner, 1994) (see Figure 7.21). Furthermore, although it is present in adult humans, it apparently has no receptors (Keverne, 1999). It seems to be vestigial—that is, a leftover from our evolutionary past.

Humans nevertheless do respond to pheromones. Researchers have found at least one pheromone receptor in humans. Its structure resembles that of other mammals' pheromone receptors, but for us, it is located in the olfactory mucosa along with normal olfactory receptors, not in the VNO (Rodriguez, Greer, Mok, & Mombaerts, 2000). Other researchers found that when women and men are exposed to each other's skin secretions, the result is increased activity in the hypothalamus, a brain area important for sexual behavior (Savic, Berglund, Gulyas, & Roland, 2001).

The behavioral effects of pheromones apparently occur unconsciously. That is, people respond behaviorally to certain chemicals in human skin that are usually described as "odorless." Exposure to these chemicals alters our skin temperature, sweating, and other autonomic responses (Monti-Bloch, Jennings-White, & Berliner, 1998), even without our awareness.

Several studies indicate a role for pheromones in human sexual behaviors analogous to that in other mammals. The best documented effect relates to the timing of women's menstrual cycles. Women who spend much time together find that their menstrual cycles become more synchronized (McClintock, 1971; Weller, Weller, Koresh-Kamin, & Ben-Shoshan, 1999; Weller, Weller, & Roizman, 1999), unless one of them is taking birth-control pills. To test whether pheromones are responsible for the synchronization, researchers in two studies exposed young volunteer women to the underarm secretions of a donor woman. In both studies, most of the women exposed to the secretions became synchronized to the donor's menstrual cycle (Preti, Cutler, Garcia, Huggins, & Lawley, 1986; Russell, Switz, & Thompson, 1980).

Another study dealt with the phenomenon that a woman who is in an intimate relationship with a man tends to have more regular menstrual periods than other women do. One hypothesis is that the man's pheromones promote this regularity. In the study, young women who were not sexually active were exposed daily to a man's underarm secretions. (Getting volunteers for a study like this isn't easy.) Gradually, over 14 weeks, most of these women's menstrual periods became more regular than before, with a mean of 29 to 30 days each (Cutler et al., 1986). In short, human body secretions apparently do act as pheromones, although the effects are more subtle than in nonhuman mammals, and the mechanism is still uncertain.

MODULE 7.3

In Closing: Different Senses Offer Different Ways of Knowing the World

Ask the average person to describe the current environment, and you will probably get a description of what he or she sees and maybe a description of some sounds. If nonhumans could talk, members of most species would start by describing what they smell. A human, a dog, and a snail may be in the same place, but the environments they perceive are very different.

Humans don't have as many olfactory receptors as mice or dogs, but although we seldom pay much attention to odors, they are nevertheless important for many aspects of our behavior. We don't meet new people by sniffing them, as dogs do, but we care about scents more than we generally realize.

SUMMARY

1. Sensory information can be coded in terms of either a labeled-line system or an across-fiber pattern system. (p. 208)

2. Taste receptors are modified skin cells inside taste buds in papillae on the tongue. (p. 209)

3. According to current evidence, most researchers believe we have five kinds of taste receptors that are sensitive to sweet, sour, salty, bitter, and umami (glutamate) tastes. (p. 211)

4. Salty receptors respond simply to sodium ions crossing the membrane. Sour receptors respond to a stimulus by blocking potassium channels. Sweet, bitter, and umami receptors act by a second messenger within the cell, similar to the way a metabotropic neurotransmitter receptor operates. (p. 211)

5. Mammals have a large number of bitter receptors, enabling them to detect a great variety of harmful substances that are chemically unrelated to one another. However, a consequence of having so many bitter receptors is that we are not highly sensitive to any one bitter chemical at low concentrations. (p. 211)

6. Some people, known as supertasters, have more fungiform papillae than other people do and are more sensitive to a great variety of tastes. They tend to avoid strong-tasting foods. (p. 213)

7. Olfactory receptors are proteins, each of them highly responsive to a few related chemicals and unresponsive to others. Vertebrates have hundreds of olfactory receptors, each contributing to the detection of a few related odors. (p. 215)

8. In most mammals, each vomeronasal organ (VNO) receptor is sensitive to only one chemical, a pheromone. A pheromone is a social signal, usually for mating purposes. Unlike olfactory receptors, VNO receptors show little or no adapation to a prolonged stimulus. Humans also respond somewhat to pheromones, although our receptors are in the olfactory mucosa, not in the VNO. (p. 216)

ANSWERS TO *STOP AND CHECK* QUESTIONS

1. The shift key plus another is an example of an across-fiber pattern code. (The meaning of one key depends on what else is pressed.) A fire alarm and a light switch are labeled lines; they convey only one message. (p. 209)

2. You could test for cross-adaptation. If the new taste cross-adapts with others, then it uses the same receptors. If it does not cross-adapt, it may have a receptor of its own. (p. 211)

3. The chemical would block your experiences of sweet, bitter, and umami but should not prevent you from tasting salty and sour. (p. 211)

4. Most olfactory receptors survive a little more than a month before dying and being replaced. (p. 215)

5. Olfactory receptors located near each other are probably sensitive to structurally similar chemicals. (p. 215)

6. A specific anosmia is a less than normal sensitivity to a particular odorant. (p. 215)

7. Like metabotropic neurotransmitter receptors, an olfactory receptor acts through a G-protein that triggers further events within the cell. (p. 215)

THOUGHT QUESTIONS

1. In the English language, the letter *t* has no meaning out of context; its meaning depends on its relationship to other letters. Indeed, even a word, such as *to,* has little meaning except in its connection to other words. So is language a labeled-line system or an across-fiber pattern system?

2. Suppose a chemist synthesizes a new chemical which turns out to have an odor. Presumably, we do not have a specialized receptor for that chemical. Explain how our receptors detect it.

MODULE 7.4

Attention

Attention is partly an automatic process. For example, if someone in a red sports car zooms by and honks the horn, you will almost certainly notice. Attention can also be deliberate. For example, if three people are talking at once, you can focus on the most interesting or best informed speaker while ignoring the others.

How does your brain control attention? We know far less about it than about the mechanisms of vision, hearing, and the other senses. Attention is, however, a fascinating topic that is central to perception and even to consciousness.

CONSCIOUS AND UNCONSCIOUS, ATTENDED AND UNATTENDED EXPERIENCE

You may have heard that if a message like "Buy Popcorn" is flashed on a movie screen for one frame, people will perceive it subliminally (unconsciously) and feel an irresistible urge to obey. Don't believe it. That claim has been consistently disconfirmed (Bornstein, 1989).

However, a very brief sight or sound that does not register consciously sometimes exerts subtle but demonstrable effects. For example, if you see a face flashed on the screen for less than one thirtieth of a second, followed by an interfering pattern, you will do no better than chance at guessing whether the face was smiling, frowning, or neither. However, your facial muscles will move slightly and briefly in the direction of a smile if you saw a smile and slightly in the direction of a frown if you saw a frown (Dimberg, Thunberg, & Elmehed, 2000). Also, if you see a word (e.g., PENCIL) flashed briefly on a screen, you may not be able to identify it, but you will be quicker than usual to identify the next flashed word if it is closely related (e.g., WRITE) (Dixon, 1981).

So, information can enter your nervous system and slightly influence your behavior even when it doesn't gain your attention. What is the difference between a sensation that becomes conscious and one

that doesn't? In a clever study, researchers flashed a word on a screen for 29 ms. In some cases, it was preceded and followed by a blank screen:

In those cases, people were able to identify the word almost 90% of the time. In other cases, however, the researchers flashed a word for the same 29 ms but preceded and followed it with a masking pattern:

Under these conditions, people could read the word on fewer than 1% of occasions. Although the physical stimulus was the same in both cases—a word flashed for 29 ms—in the first case, it reached consciousness but in the second case, it did not. Using fMRI scans (p. 170), the researchers found that the conscious and unconscious stimuli activated mostly the same areas of the occipital and temporal cortex, but the conscious stimuli activated those areas more strongly. Furthermore, the conscious stimuli activated the prefrontal and parietal cortexes, whereas the unconscious stimuli did not (Dehaene et al., 2001).

These data imply that consciousness of a stimulus depends on how strongly it arouses the brain. Attention to a stimulus can increase by either a "bottom-up" or a "top-down" method, where "bottom" refers to the incoming stimulus and "top" refers to the cerebral cortex. When a stimulus is strong, it increases brain activity (and therefore, attention) in a bottom-up manner. Certain brain areas can also increase the response to a stimulus in a top-down manner (Corbetta & Shulman, 2002). You can easily illustrate the top-down mechanism yourself (Lambie & Marcel, 2002): "Describe the current sensation in your left foot." (Until you read this instruction, you probably didn't have much sensation, certainly not much conscious sensation, in your left foot. Thinking about it increased the representation of that sensation in your brain.)

Studies of people with head injuries further confirm the relationship between consciousness and increased brain activity. One person went into a coma following a suicide attempt. During the period of prolonged unconsciousness, brain metabolism fell to less than two thirds of its normal level. When this person regained consciousness, metabolism and electrical activity recovered, with the parietal cortex showing the biggest increase soon after recovery (Laureys, Lemaire, Maquet, Phillips, & Franck, 1999).

1. In the experiment by Dehaene and colleagues, how were the conscious and unconscious stimuli similar? How were they different?

2. In this experiment, how were the brain's responses different to the conscious and unconscious stimuli?

Check your answers on page 224.

NEGLECT

The opposite of attention is inattention, or neglect. At any moment—now, for example—you are neglecting much of the information that is reaching your senses. For a demonstration, try this: Look straight ahead and describe what you see. You will almost certainly mention what is directly in front of you. Now, without moving your eyes, shift your *attention* up, down, left, and right and describe what you also see in the periphery. (For example, even though you are looking straight ahead, you could shift your attention down and describe the color of your clothing.)

The point of this demonstration is that although we see much in the visual periphery, we seldom pay attention to it. We also ignore many sounds and most touch and smell information. People with certain kinds of brain damage show more widespread neglect. One young man had suffered strokes that destroyed much of his auditory cortex in both hemispheres. Ordinarily, he showed no response to noise. Sudden sounds did not even alter his heart rate or skin conductance. However, if he was given written instructions to pay attention to sounds, he was able to report

when one started or stopped (Engelien et al., 2000). Apparently, the brain has top-down processes (probably originating in the prefrontal cortex) that can increase activity in other brain areas and thereby increase attention to or consciousness of an otherwise ignored stimulus (Sarter, Givens, & Bruno, 2001).

Another kind of brain damage leads to **spatial neglect,** a tendency to ignore the left side of the body and its surroundings, including visual, auditory, and touch stimuli. It occurs after damage in the right hemisphere. (Damage in the left hemisphere does not produce much neglect of the right side.) Researchers formerly believed that neglect stemmed from damage in the parietal and frontal cortex, but many of the patients they studied had widespread damage. A later study found that spatial neglect is most consistently linked with damage to the superior temporal gyrus in the right hemisphere (Karnath, Ferber, & Himmelbach, 2001). The superior temporal gyrus receives auditory input as well as input from both the ventral ("what") and dorsal ("where") visual pathways, so its central role in attention seems reasonable. It also has direct connections to areas of the basal ganglia that are important for attention and movement (Karnath, Himmelbach, & Rorden, 2002).

People with spatial neglect describe only the right side of what they see (Driver & Mattingley, 1998). If they try to describe a familiar scene from memory, they describe only the right side, and when they draw something, they draw only its right side. So the problem is not a sensory impairment; it is impaired attention. They also generally ignore much of what they hear in the left ear and most of what they feel in the left hand, especially if they simultaneously feel something in the right hand. They may put clothes on only the right side of the body.

Various procedures can increase attention to the neglected side. First, simply telling the person to pay attention to the left side helps temporarily. So does having the person look left while at the same time feeling something with the left hand (Vaishnavi, Calhoun, & Chatterjee, 2001) or hearing a sound from the left side of the world (Frassinetti, Pavani, & Làdavas, 2002). Something similar is true for unimpaired people also. Suppose you are staring straight ahead and an experimenter is flashing stimuli very briefly on the left and right sides. Your task is to identify something about the stimulus, such as whether it was on the top or bottom half of the screen. If someone touches you just before a visual stimulus, you will respond slightly faster if the touch was on the same side of the body as the visual stimulus (Kennett, Eimer, Spence, & Driver, 2001). That is, a touch stimulus briefly increases attention to one side of the body or the other.

Some other manipulations also shift the attention of neglect patients to their left side. For example, ordinarily a neglect patient reports feeling nothing with the left hand, especially if the right hand feels something else at the time. However, if you cross one hand over the other as shown in Figure 7.23, the person is more likely to report feeling on the left hand, which is now on the right side of the body (Aglioti, Smania, & Peru, 1999). In addition, the person ordinarily has trouble pointing to anything in the left visual field but has somewhat better success if the hand was so far to the left that he or she would have to move it to the right to point to the object (Mattingley, Husain, Rorden, Kennard, & Driver, 1998). Again, the conclusion is that neglect is not due to a loss of sensation, but a difficulty in directing attention to the left side.

Finally, one study showed that neglect patients have attentional difficulties when two items compete for attention, even if they are in the same spatial location. When the experimenters played a sound directly in front of a patient and asked whether it was a pure tone or a warble, the answer was usually correct. However, if the experimenters played two tones and asked which came first, the high note or the low note, the patient had extreme difficulty, unless the tones were very prolonged (Cusack, Carlyon, & Robertson, 2000). In short, neglect patients have trouble perceiving or attending to two items, either visual or auditory, that are present at approximately the same time.

3. What evidence indicates the possibility of top-down processes to increase attention?

4. What kind of brain damage is most closely linked with spatial neglect?

5. What is the evidence that spatial neglect is a problem in attention, not sensation?

Check your answers on page 224.

ATTENTION-DEFICIT HYPERACTIVITY DISORDER

Attention-deficit hyperactivity disorder (ADHD) is characterized by attention deficits (distractibility), hyperactivity (fidgitiness), impulsivity, mood swings, short temper, high sensitivity to stress, and impaired ability to make and follow plans (Wender, Wolf, & Wasserstein, 2001). These problems affect not only school performance but also social behavior throughout life (DuPaul, McGoey, Eckert, & vanBrakle, 2001; Wender et al., 2001). Some ADHD people have

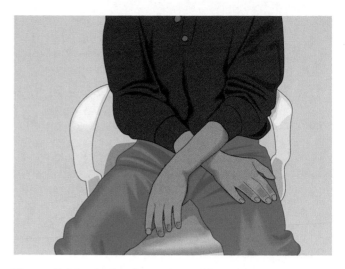

Figure 7.23 A simple way to reduce sensory neglect
Ordinarily, someone with right parietal lobe damage neglects the left arm. However, if the left arm crosses over or under the right, attention to that arm increases.

occupational difficulties or antisocial behaviors in adulthood (Mannuzza, Klein, Bessler, Malloy, & LaPadula, 1998).

In the United States, ADHD has become a very common diagnosis, applied to an estimated 3% to 10% of children and a smaller number of adults. (The diagnosis is far less popular in many European countries.) ADHD is identified about 2 or 3 times as often in males as in females. It is important to study both for the obvious practical reasons and for the theoretical issues of understanding attention.

Research is complicated, however, by the difficulty of making a reliable diagnosis. How distractible is too distractible, how fidgity is too fidgity, and how impulsive is too impulsive? We have no medical test to confirm our opinions. Some teachers and doctors label only the most extreme cases as ADHD, whereas others apply the label to almost any rambunctious child (Panksepp, 1998). Some have given the ADHD label to children as young as 2 years. (How much attention span do they expect from a 2 year old?) Furthermore, therapists need to distinguish ADHD from other disorders that impair attention, such as lead poisoning, fetal alcohol syndrome, epilepsy, allergies to medicines, sleep deprivation, emotional distress, damage to the frontal or parietal cortex, and so forth (Pearl, Weiss, & Stein, 2001).

Measurements of ADHD Behavior

Many people characterize ADHD as a lack of inhibitions, but it is not clear to anyone—frankly, not even to these individuals—exactly what they mean by "lack of inhibitions" (Nigg, 2001). Careful measurements of ADHD people's behavior helps to clarify our descriptions of the condition. Measurements also enable researchers to quantify improvements that might occur after treatment. Here are three examples of tasks on which ADHD people differ, on the average, from other people:

- **The Choice-Delay Task** Which would you prefer, $5 now or $6 tomorrow? Or which would you prefer, a cookie now or a slightly larger cookie 15 minutes from now? The details vary, but the choice is between one reward now and a slightly better reward later. Under a variety of circumstances, ADHD people are more likely than others to choose the smaller but quicker reward (Solanto et al., 2001). This tendency is taken as an indication of impulsivity, or difficulty inhibiting a behavior.
- **The Stop Signal Task** People watch a screen or listen for a sound. When they hear it, they are to press a button as fast as possible. People usually respond in less than a second. However, sometimes another stimulus occurs a split second after the first signal and means "disregard the signal; don't press the button." Obviously, anyone would fail to inhibit the response if it arrived too late, and most people have no trouble inhibiting if the "don't press" signal occurs very quickly. However, with intermediate delays, most ADHD people are more likely than other people to press the button (Rubia, Oosterlaan, Sergeant, Brandeis, & v. Leeuwen, 1998; Solanto et al., 2001). Again, the interpretation is that ADHD people have difficulty inhibiting their behaviors.
- **The Attentional Blink Task** People watch a series of black letters flashed on a screen, a new one every 90 ms. In each set, one of the letters is blue. Another letter, designated as the "probe" letter, might or might not appear after the blue letter. The task is first to name the blue letter and then to say whether or not the probe letter appeared after the blue letter. For example, in the following examples, suppose the probe letter is K:

H U R X G V N K B P   Correct answer: "G, Yes."

D J C W N E M Q Z U   Correct answer: "C, No."

Researchers have found that most people miss the probe letter (that is, they say "no" even though K was present) if it appears about two to seven letters after the blue letter. This tendency is called the *attentional blink;* the idea is that you pay attention to the blue letter for about 200–600 ms after seeing it, so you have trouble paying attention to anything else, as if you had blinked your eyes. The same is even truer for ADHD people; they usually miss the probe letter even if it arrives almost a second after the blue letter (Hollingsworth, McAuliffe, & Knowlton, 2001). The interpretation is that they have trouble controlling their attention; they can't shift it when they need to.

Possible Causes and Brain Differences

ADHD often runs in families, and much evidence suggests fairly high heritability. One form of the dopamine type 4 (D4) receptor gene is more common in ADHD people than other people, but not by much (Faraone, Doyle, Mick, & Biederman, 2001). ADHD probably depends on multiple genes as well as environmental influences (Comings, 2001; Curran et al., 2001).

On the average, people with ADHD have brain volume about 95% of normal, with a smaller than average right prefrontal cortex (Giedd, Blumenthal, Molloy, & Castellanos, 2001; Stefanatos & Wasserstein, 2001). The cerebellum also tends to be a bit smaller than usual, and cerebellar dysfunction is known to be associated with difficulty switching attention (Ravizza & Ivry, 2001). Still, all these differences are small and inconsistent from one person to another. For example, if a doctor is uncertain whether a child has ADHD, a brain scan will not help with the decision.

Treatments

Decades ago, physicians discovered that when they gave amphetamine to epileptic children to calm their seizures—at the time, a fairly common treatment—it sometimes reduced hyperactivity as well. Physicians started using amphetamine to reduce hyperactivity, and today, the most common treatment for ADHD is a stimulant drug such as methylphenidate (Ritalin) or amphetamine (Elia, Ambrosini, & Rapoport, 1999). The drugs increase attentiveness, improve school performance and social relationships, and decrease impulsiveness. They also improve scores on laboratory tests, such as the Stop Signal task (de Wit, Crean, & Richards, 2000). Whether these benefits justify giving drugs to so many children is, of course, a complex issue. One study found that stimulant drugs helped adults with ADHD improve their driving, avoid traffic tickets, keep their attention on the road, and decrease their irritability toward other drivers (Jerome & Segal, 2001).

Amphetamine and methylphenidate increase the availability of dopamine to the postsynaptic receptors. They produce their maximum effects on dopamine about 1 hour after someone takes a pill, and 1 hour is also the time of the maximum behavioral benefit, so researchers are confident that the pills affect behavior through dopamine activity (Volkow et al., 1998). The benefits wear off a few hours later.

Suppose a physician prescribes a stimulant drug, and the child's behavior improves. Does the improvement confirm that the child has ADHD? Many people assume that if the drug helps, the person must have ADHD, but this conclusion does not follow. One study found that stimulant drugs increase the attention span even of normal children (Zahn, Rapoport, & Thompson, 1980).

For more information about methylphenidate (Ritalin), see this Web site:
www.nida.nih.gov/Infofax/ritalin.html

Many behavioral techniques are available as supplements or substitutes for stimulant drugs. Much of the advice is not surprising (Sohlberg & Mateer, 2001):

• Reduce distraction.
• Use lists, calendars, schedules, and so forth to organize your time.
• Practice strategies to pace yourself.
• Learn to relax. Tension and stress can magnify attention deficits.

For links to many kinds of information about ADHD, check this Web site:
www.add-adhd.org/

6. Describe the Choice-Delay and Stop Signal tasks.

7. How does the attentional blink of an ADHD person differ from that of most other people?

8. If a doctor is in doubt about whether a child has ADHD, would a brain scan help? Would trying the effects of stimulant drugs help?

Check your answers on page 224.

MODULE 7.4

In Closing: What Little We Know About Attention

Sometimes it is possible to pay attention to two tasks at once if they are simple or well-practiced, if the stimuli excite different sensory systems, and if the responses don't interfere with each other. For example, you could learn to tap one of three fingers to identify which of three visual patterns you saw, while simultaneously saying "one," "two," or "three" to identify which of three sounds you heard (Schumacher et al., 2001). Usually, however, doing one task or attending to one stimulus interferes with another. Attention is a way of devoting our limited abilities to the most important information and actions.

How attention happens is, obviously, not well understood. As recently as the 1960s, many psychological researchers were not convinced that the concept of attention was useful at all. That is, they believed that all sensory stimuli might influence behavior at all times. We have moved beyond that belief, but as you can tell from this short module, we still have far to go in understanding attention and its brain mechanisms.

SUMMARY

1. A given physical stimulus can be conscious under some circumstances but not others. For example, a brief visual stimulus may be unidentifiable if it is preceded and followed by an interfering pattern. Under conditions when the stimulus becomes conscious, it activates the sensory cortices more strongly than when it is unconscious. Also, when it reaches consciousness, it activates the prefrontal and parietal cortices. (p. 219)

2. Massive damage to the auditory cortex almost eliminates responses to sounds, and damage to the right superior temporal gyrus produces spatial neglect for the left side of the body. Nevertheless, instructions to attend to the neglected information temporarily increase responses to it. (p. 220)

3. Sensory neglect is an attentional phenomenon, not a sensory loss. For example, someone with sensory neglect will describe only the right side of objects even when describing them from memory. (p. 220)

4. People with sensory neglect also have trouble shifting attention from one stimulus to another even when they are in the same place, if they occur at different times. (p. 221)

5. Attention-deficit hyperactivity disorder (ADHD) is a common diagnosis in the United States, but the diagnosis is ambiguous in many cases. The characteristic impulsiveness and impaired attention can be measured by the Choice-Delay task, the Stop Signal task, and the Attentional Blink task. (p. 221)

6. ADHD is probably the result of a number of genes as well as environmental influences. Many ADHD people have mild brain abnormalities, but the pattern is small and inconsistent. (p. 222)

7. Although stimulant drugs improve cognitive performance of ADHD people, they also benefit many normal individuals. Therefore, benefits from the drugs should not be used as evidence that someone has ADHD. (p. 222)

ANSWERS TO *STOP AND CHECK* QUESTIONS

1. The conscious and unconscious stimuli were physically the same (a word flashed on the screen for 29 ms). The difference is that a stimulus did not become conscious if it was preceded and followed by an interfering pattern. (p. 220)

2. If a stimulus became conscious, it activated the same areas of the occipital and temporal cortex as an unconscious stimulus but for a longer period. It also stimulated areas of the parietal and prefrontal cortex that did not respond measurably to the unconscious stimulus. (p. 220)

3. A patient with auditory cortex damage ordinarily does not respond at all to sounds, but can if told to attend to them. Also, we all can increase attention to something we ordinarily ignore—such as the visual periphery—if we are told to do so. (p. 221)

4. Spatial neglect is most closely related to damage to the superior temporal gyrus of the right hemisphere. (p. 221)

5. People with spatial neglect ignore the left side even when they are describing something from memory. They also have trouble shifting attention from one stimulus to another even when they are in the same location, if they occur at slightly different times. (p. 221)

6. In the Choice-Delay task, someone decides between one reward now and a slightly better one later. In the Stop Signal task, someone receives a signal to do something, which is sometimes followed by a second signal to disregard the first one and withhold the response. (p. 223)

7. ADHD people have a longer than normal attentional blink. (p. 223)

8. In both cases, no. Brain scans differ on the average between ADHD people and others, but the differences are too inconsistent to be useful in individual cases. Trying the effects of stimulant drugs would not help because the drugs improve attention even for most children who have no attentional problems. (p. 223)

THOUGHT QUESTION

ADHD is diagnosed far more commonly in the United States today than in the past and far more in the United States than in Europe. What possible explanations can you propose? Are any of them testable?

CHAPTER ENDING
Key Terms and Activities

TERMS

across-fiber pattern principle (p. 208)

adaptation (p. 211)

amplitude (p. 188)

anosmia (p. 215)

apex (p. 191)

attention-deficit hyperactivity disorder (ADHD) (p. 221)

Attentional Blink task (p. 222)

base (p. 191)

capsaicin (p. 202)

Choice-Delay task (p. 222)

cochlea (p. 189)

conductive deafness (middle-ear deafness) (p. 192)

cross-adaptation (p. 211)

dermatome (p. 199)

endorphin (p. 202)

frequency (p. 188)

frequency theory (p. 190)

gate theory (p. 202)

hair cell (p. 190)

labeled-line principle (p. 208)

SUGGESTIONS FOR FURTHER READING

Beauchamp, G. K., & Bartoshuk, L. (1997). *Tasting and smelling.* San Diego, CA: Academic Press. Excellent book covering receptors, psychophysics, and disorders of taste and smell.

Hamill, O. P., & McBride, D. W., Jr. (1995). Mechanoreceptive membrane channels. *American Scientist, 83,* 30–37. Describes the mechanisms of various somatosensory receptors.

Pert, C. B. (1997). *Molecules of emotion.* New York: Simon & Schuster. Autobiographical statement by the woman who, as a graduate student, first demonstrated the opiate receptors.

WEB SITES TO EXPLORE

You can go to the Biological Psychology Study Center and click these links. While there, you can also check for suggested articles available on InfoTrac College Edition. The Biological Psychology Internet address is:

psychology.wadsworth.com/kalatbiopsych8e

Mark Rejhon's Frequently Asked Questions about Hearing Impairment
www.marky.com/hearing/

Pain Net, with many links
www.painnet.com/

American Pain Society
www.ampainsoc.org/

Nontaster, taster, or supertaster?
www.neosoft.com/~bmiller/taste.htm

Sense of Smell Institute
www.senseofsmell.org/home.asp

Olfaction, by John C. Leffingwell
www.leffingwell.com/olfaction.htm

Methylphenidate
www.nida.nih.gov/Infofax/ritalin.html

CD-ROM: EXPLORING BIOLOGICAL PSYCHOLOGY

Hearing Puzzle (puzzle)

Hearing Loss (video)

Somesthetic Experiment (drag & drop)

Attention Deficit Disorder (video)

Critical Thinking (essay questions)

Chapter Quiz (multiple choice questions)

Movement

8

Chapter Outline

Main Ideas

1. Movement depends on overall plans, not just connections between a stimulus and a muscle contraction.

2. Movements vary in sensitivity to feedback, skill, and variability in the face of obstacles.

3. Damage to different brain locations produces different kinds of movement impairment.

4. Brain damage that impairs movement also impairs cognitive processes. That is, control of movement is inseparably linked with cognition.

Before we get started, please try this: Get out a pencil and a sheet of paper and put the pencil in your non-preferred hand. For example, if you are right-handed, put it in your left hand. Now with that hand draw a face in profile—that is, facing one direction or the other but not straight ahead. *Please do this now.*

If you tried the demonstration, you probably notice that your drawing is much more childlike than usual. It is as if some part of your brain stored the way you used to draw as a young child. Now, if you are right-handed and therefore drew the face with your left hand, why did you draw it facing to the right? At least I assume you did, because more than two thirds of right-handers drawing with their left hand draw the profile facing right. Young children, age 5 or so, when drawing with the right hand almost always draw people and animals facing left, but when using the left hand almost always draw them facing right. So, *why* does this occur? The short answer is we don't know. The point is we have much to learn about the control of movement and how it relates to perception, motivation, and other functions.

Opposite:
Ultimately, the goal of all brain activity is to control movement—a far more complex process than it might seem. *Source: ©F. Willingham*

MODULE 8.1

The Control of Movement

Why do we have brains at all? Plants survive just fine without them. So do sponges, which are animals, even if they don't act like it. But plants don't move from place to place, and neither do sponges. A sea squirt swims during its infant stage, and has a brain at that time, but when it transforms into an adult, it attaches to a surface, becomes a stationary filter-feeder, and digests its own brain, as if to say, "Now that I've stopped traveling, I won't need this brain thing anymore."

Brains exist in animals with complex movements. Ultimately, the purpose of a brain is to control behaviors, and all behaviors are movements.

"But wait," you might reply, "we need brains for other things, too, don't we? Like seeing, hearing, finding food, talking, understanding what others say . . ."

Well, what would be the value of seeing and hearing if you couldn't do anything with them? Finding food requires movement, and so does talking. Understanding isn't movement, but again, it doesn't do you much good unless you can do something with it. A great brain without muscles would be like a computer without a monitor, printer, or other peripherals. No matter how powerful the internal processing, it would be useless.

Nevertheless, most psychologists pay little attention to movement. The study of muscle contractions seems somehow less "psychological" than the study of visual perception, learning, social interactions, motivation, or emotion. And yet the rapid movements of a skilled typist, musician, or athlete require very complex brain activities. Understanding movement is a significant challenge for psychologists as well as biologists.

MUSCLES AND THEIR MOVEMENTS

All animal movement depends on the contraction of muscles. Vertebrate muscles fall into three categories (Figure 8.1): **smooth muscles,** which control movements of internal organs; **skeletal,** or **striated, muscles,** which control movements of the body in relation to the environment; and **cardiac muscles** (the heart muscles), which have properties intermediate between those of smooth and skeletal muscles.

Each muscle is composed of many individual fibers, as Figure 8.2 illustrates. A given axon may innervate more than one muscle fiber. For example, the eye muscles have a ratio of about one axon per three muscle fibers, and the biceps muscles of the arm have a ratio of one axon to more than a hundred fibers (Evarts, 1979). This difference allows the eye to move more precisely than the biceps.

A **neuromuscular junction** is a synapse where a motor neuron axon meets a muscle fiber. In skeletal muscles, every axon releases acetylcholine at the neuromuscular junction, and the acetylcholine always excites the muscle to contract. Each muscle can make just one movement—contraction—in just one direction. In the absence of excitation, it relaxes, but it never moves actively in the opposite direction. Moving a leg or arm in two directions requires opposing sets of muscles, called **antagonistic muscles.** An arm, for example, has a **flexor** muscle that flexes or raises it and an **extensor** muscle that extends or straightens it (Figure 8.3). Walking, clapping hands, and other coordinated sequences require a regular alternation between contraction of one set of muscles and contraction of another.

Adult sea squirts attach to a surface, never move again, and digest their own brains.

Gary Bell/Getty Images

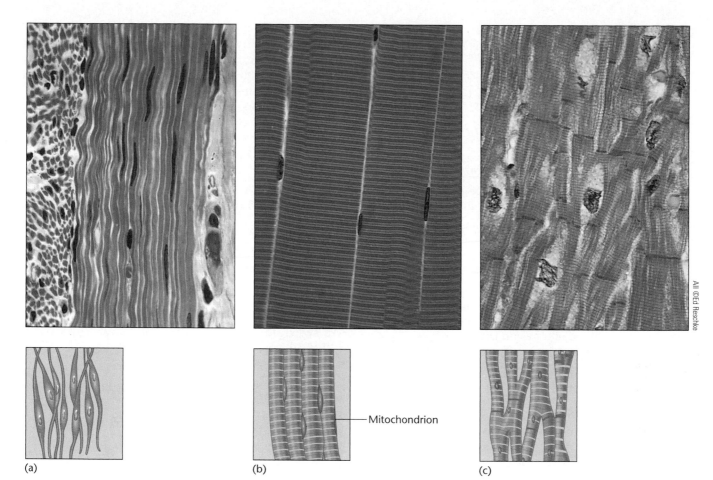

(a)   (b)   —Mitochondrion   (c)

All ©Ed Reschke

Figure 8.1 The three main types of vertebrate muscles
(a) Smooth muscle, found in the intestines and other organs, consists of long, thin cells. **(b)** Skeletal, or striated, muscle consists of long cylindrical fibers with stripes. **(c)** Cardiac muscle, found in the heart, consists of fibers that fuse together at various points. Because of these fusions, cardiac muscles contract together, not independently. *Source: Illustrations after Starr & Taggart, 1989*

Any deficit of acetylcholine or its receptors in the muscles can greatly impair movement. Myasthenia gravis (MY-us-THEE-nee-uh GRAHV-iss) is an *autoimmune disease*, in that the immune system forms antibodies that attack the individual's own body. In myasthenia gravis, the immune system attacks the acetylcholine receptors at neuromuscular junctions (Shah & Lisak, 1993). Myasthenia gravis causes the deaths of 2 or 3 people per 100,000 over the age of 75 each year (Chandra, Bharucha, & Schoenberg, 1984); it also occurs, though rarely, in young people (Evoli et al., 1998).

The symptoms of myasthenia gravis are progressive weakness and rapid fatigue of the skeletal muscles. Here is what happens: Because the muscles have lost many of their acetylcholine receptors, the remaining receptors need the maximum amount of transmitter to move the muscles normally. After any motor neuron fires a few times in quick succession, later action potentials release less acetylcholine. A slight decline is no problem for

healthy people, who have plenty of acetylcholine receptors. In people with myasthenia gravis, transmission at the neuromuscular junction is precarious, and a slight decline in acetylcholine is noticeable (Drachman, 1978).

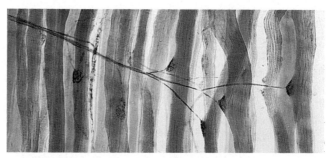

©Ed Reschke

Figure 8.2 An axon branching to innervate separate muscle fibers within a muscle
Movements can be much more precise where each axon innervates only a few fibers, as with eye muscles, than where it innervates many fibers, as with biceps muscles.

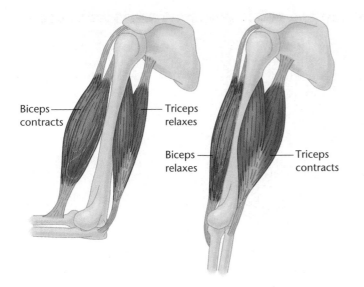

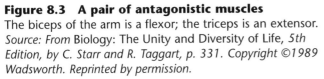

Figure 8.3 A pair of antagonistic muscles
The biceps of the arm is a flexor; the triceps is an extensor.
Source: From Biology: The Unity and Diversity of Life, *5th Edition, by C. Starr and R. Taggart, p. 331. Copyright ©1989 Wadsworth. Reprinted by permission.*

Myasthenia gravis can be treated with drugs that suppress the immune system, thereby decreasing the autoimmune attack on acetylcholine receptors (Shah & Lisak, 1993). However, this approach also weakens the immune system's ability to attack viruses and other intruders. Another approach is to take drugs that inhibit acetylcholinesterase, the enzyme that breaks down acetylcholine, thereby prolonging the acetylcholine's effects at the neuromuscular junction. A physician must monitor the dose carefully, however, as too much acetylcholine is just as troublesome as too little. For more information about myasthenia gravis, see this Web site:

http://pages.prodigy.net/stanley.way/myasthenia/

Fast and Slow Muscles

Imagine that you are a small fish. Your only defense against bigger fish, diving birds, and other predators is your ability to swim away (Figure 8.4). A fish has the same temperature as the water around it, and muscle contractions, being chemical processes, slow down in the cold. So when the water is cold, presumably you will move slowly, right? Strangely, no. You will have to use more muscles than usual, but you will swim just as fast as at higher temperatures (Rome, Loughna, & Goldspink, 1984).

A fish has three kinds of muscles: red, pink, and white. Red muscles produce the slowest movements, but they are not vulnerable to fatigue. White muscles produce the fastest movements, but they fatigue rap-

idly. Pink muscles are intermediate in both speed and susceptibility to fatigue. At high temperatures, a fish relies mostly on its red and pink muscles. At colder temperatures, a fish relies more and more on its white muscles. By recruiting enough white muscles, the fish can swim rapidly even in cold water, although it fatigues much faster.

All right, you can stop imagining that you are a fish. In humans and other mammals, various kinds of muscle fibers are mixed together, not in separate bundles as in fish. Our muscle types range from **fast-twitch fibers** that produce fast contractions but fatigue rapidly to **slow-twitch fibers** that produce less vigorous contractions without fatiguing (Hennig & Lømo, 1985). We rely on our slow-twitch and intermediate fibers for nonstrenuous activities. For example, how long could you talk before your lip muscles fatigued? Practically forever. How long could you walk at a slow comfortable pace? Not forever, but certainly a long time, using slow-twitch fibers. We switch to fast-twitch fibers for running up a steep hill at full speed. (And then we huff and puff.)

Tiu De Roy/Minden Pictures

Figure 8.4 Temperature regulation and movement
Fish are "cold blooded," but many of their predators (such as this pelican) are not. At cold temperatures, a fish must maintain its normal swimming speed, even though every muscle in its body contracts more slowly than usual. To do so, a fish calls upon white muscles that it otherwise uses only for brief bursts of speed.

Slow-twitch fibers do not fatigue because they are **aerobic**—they use air (specifically, oxygen) during their movements. Vigorous use of fast-twitch fibers results in fatigue because the process is **anaerobic**—using reactions that do not require oxygen at the time, although oxygen is eventually necessary for recovery. Anaerobic muscles produce lactate and phosphate, which accumulate to give the experience of muscle fatigue.

One exception to this rule: Goldfish muscles have an enzyme that other animals lack, and as a result, their anaerobic contractions build up ethanol instead of lactate. The ethanol diffuses away and prevents muscle fatigue. This adaptation is one of several reasons goldfish can tolerate periods without oxygen (Nilsson, 2001). Their ability to tolerate low oxygen levels explains why, unlike most other fish, goldfish can survive in a bowl of water without an air pump.

People have varying percentages of fast-twitch and slow-twitch fibers and can increase one type or the other depending on which ones they use. For example, investigators studied one group of male sprinters before and after a 3-month period of intensive training. The athletes increased their number of fast-twitch leg muscle fibers and decreased their slow-twitch fibers (Andersen, Klitgaard, & Saltin, 1994). Conversely, the Swedish ultramarathon runner Bertil Järlaker built up so many slow-twitch fibers in his legs that he once ran 3520 km (2188 mi) in 50 days (an average of 1.7 marathons per day) with only minimal signs of pain or fatigue (Sjöström, Friden, & Ekblom, 1987).

Stop & Check

1. Why can the eye muscles move with greater precision than the biceps muscles?
2. How does an acetylcholinesterase blocker help patients with myasthenia gravis?
3. In what way are fish movements impaired in cold water?
4. Duck breast muscles are red ("dark meat") whereas chicken breast muscles are white. Which species probably can fly longer before fatiguing?
5. Why is an ultramarathoner like Bertil Järlaker probably mediocre or poor at short-distance races?

Check your answers on page 235.

Muscle Control by Proprioceptors

You are walking along on a bumpy road. What happens if the messages from your spinal cord to your leg muscles are not exactly correct? You might set your foot down a little too hard or not quite hard enough. Nevertheless, you adjust your posture almost immediately and maintain your balance without even thinking about it. How do you do that?

A baby is lying on its back. You playfully tug its foot and then let go. At once, the leg bounces back to its original position. How and why?

In both cases, the mechanism is under the control of proprioceptors (Figure 8.5). A **proprioceptor** is a receptor that detects the position or movement of a part of the body—in these cases, a muscle. Muscle proprioceptors detect the stretch and tension of a muscle and send messages that enable the spinal cord to adjust its signals. When a muscle is stretched, the spinal cord sends a reflexive signal to contract it. This **stretch reflex** is *caused* by a stretch; it does not *produce* one.

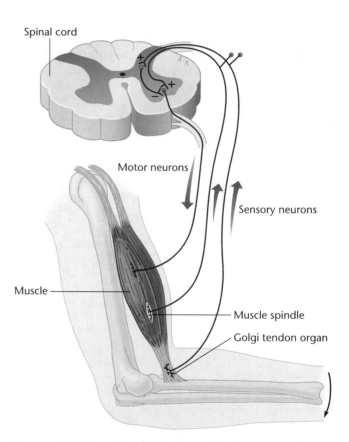

Figure 8.5 Two kinds of proprioceptors regulate the contraction of a muscle
When a muscle is stretched, the nerves from the muscle spindles transmit an increased frequency of impulses, resulting in a contraction of the surrounding muscle. Contraction of the muscle stimulates the Golgi tendon organ, which acts as a brake or shock absorber to prevent a contraction that is too quick or extreme.

One kind of proprioceptor is the **muscle spindle,** a receptor parallel to the muscle that responds to a stretch (Merton, 1972; Miles & Evarts, 1979). Whenever the muscle spindle is stretched, its sensory nerve sends a message to a motor neuron in the spinal cord, which in turn sends a message back to the muscles surrounding the spindle, causing a contraction. Note that this reflex provides for negative feedback: When a muscle and its spindle are stretched, the spindle sends a message that results in a muscle contraction that opposes the stretch.

When you set your foot down on a bump on the road, your knee bends a bit, stretching the extensor muscles of that leg. The sensory nerves of the spindles send action potentials to the motor neuron in the spinal cord, and the motor neuron sends action potentials to the extensor muscle. Contracting the extensor muscle straightens the leg, adjusting for the bump on the road.

A physician who asks you to cross your legs and then taps just below the knee (Figure 8.6) is testing your stretch reflexes. The tap stretches the extensor muscles and their spindles, resulting in a message that jerks the lower leg upward. The same reflex contributes to walking; raising the upper leg reflexively moves the lower leg forward in readiness for the next step. You can find more detail about muscle spindles at this Web site:

www.umds.ac.uk/physiology/mcal/spinmain.html

The **Golgi tendon organ,** another proprioceptor, responds to increases in muscle tension. Located in the tendons at opposite ends of a muscle, it acts as a brake against an excessively vigorous contraction. Some muscles are so strong that they could damage themselves if too many fibers contracted at once. Golgi tendon organs detect the tension that results during a muscle contraction. Their impulses travel to the spinal cord, where they inhibit the motor neurons through messages from interneurons. In short, a vigorous muscle contraction inhibits further contraction by activating the Golgi tendon organs.

The proprioceptors not only control important reflexes but also provide the brain with information. Here is an illusion that you can demonstrate yourself: Find a small, dense object and a larger, less dense object that weighs the same as the small one. Drop one of the objects onto someone's hand while he or she is watching. (The watching is essential.) Then remove it and drop the other object onto the same hand. Most people report that the small one felt heavier. The reason is that with the larger object, people set themselves up with the expectation of a heavier weight. The actual weight displaces their proprioceptors less than expected and therefore yields the perception of a lighter object.

> **6.** If you hold your arm straight out and someone pulls it down slightly, it quickly bounces back. What proprioceptor is responsible?
>
> **7.** What is the function of Golgi tendon organs?
>
> *Check your answers on page 235.*

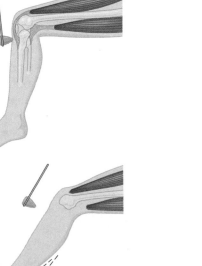

Figure 8.6   The knee-jerk reflex
Here is one example of a stretch reflex.

UNITS OF MOVEMENT

The stretch reflex is a simple example of movement. More complex kinds include speaking, walking, threading a needle, and throwing a basketball through a hoop while off balance and evading two defenders. In many ways, these movements differ from one another and depend on different kinds of control by the nervous system.

Voluntary and Involuntary Movements

Reflexes are consistent automatic responses to stimuli. We generally think of reflexes as *involuntary* because they are insensitive to reinforcements, punishments, and motivations. The stretch reflex is one example; another is the constriction of the pupil in response to bright light.

Infant Reflexes

Actually, humans have rather few reflexes, although infants have several not seen in adults. For example, if you place an object firmly in an infant's hand, the infant will reflexively grasp it tightly (the **grasp reflex**). If you stroke the sole of the foot, the infant will reflexively extend the big toe and fan the others (the **Babinski reflex**). If you touch the cheek of an awake infant, the head will turn toward the stimulated cheek and the infant will begin to suck (the **rooting reflex**). The rooting reflex is not a pure reflex, as its intensity increases when the infant is hungry.

Although such reflexes fade away with time, the connections remain intact, not lost but suppressed by axons from the maturing brain. If the cerebral cortex is damaged, the infant reflexes are released from inhibition. In fact, neurologists and other physicians frequently test adults for infant reflexes. A physician who strokes the sole of your foot during a physical exam is probably looking for evidence of brain damage. This is hardly the most dependable test, but it is among the easiest. If a stroke on the sole of your foot makes you fan your toes like a baby, there may be an impairment of your cerebral cortex.

Infant reflexes sometimes return temporarily if activity in the cerebral cortex is depressed by alcohol, carbon dioxide, or other chemicals. (You might try testing for infant reflexes in a friend who has consumed too much alcohol.)

Infants and children also tend more strongly than adults to have certain allied reflexes. If dust blows in your face, you will reflexively close your eyes and mouth and probably sneeze. These reflexes are allied in the sense that each tends to elicit the others. If you suddenly see a bright light—as when you emerge from a dark theater on a sunny afternoon—you will reflexively close your eyes and you may also close your mouth and perhaps sneeze. Some adults react this way; a higher percentage of young children do (Whitman & Packer, 1993).

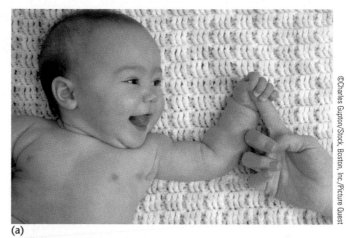

(a)

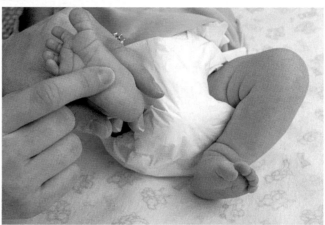

(b)

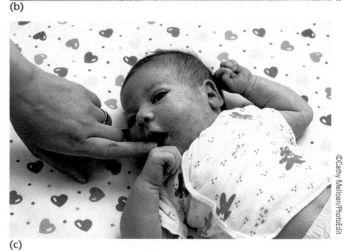

(c)

Three reflexes in infants but ordinarily not in adults:
(a) grasp reflex, **(b)** Babinski reflex, and **(c)** rooting reflex.

Few behaviors can be classified as purely voluntary or involuntary, reflexive or nonreflexive. Take swallowing, for example. You can voluntarily swallow or inhibit swallowing, but only within certain limits. Try to swallow ten times in a row voluntarily (without drinking). The first swallow or two are easy, but soon you will find additional swallows difficult and unpleas- ant. Now try to inhibit swallowing for as long as you can without spitting. Chances are you will not last long.

You might think of a behavior like walking as purely voluntary, but even walking includes involuntary components. When you walk, you automatically compensate for the bumps and irregularities in the road. You probably also swing your arms automatically as an involuntary consequence of walking.

For another example, imagine this task: You are asked to move a computer mouse to draw a straight line on the screen, but you cannot watch your hand or the mouse while you do it. You do, however, watch the screen. Unbeknownst to you, the device is rigged so that actually moving your hand straight will not produce a straight line; you have to curve your hand to the side to make the line straight. Would you notice? Some people do not, even if they have to curve their hand quite far from a straight line (Slachevsky et al., 2001). That is, they make a goal-directed movement with limited awareness of what they are doing. In short, the distinction between voluntary and involuntary is blurry.

Movements With Different Sensitivity to Feedback

The military distinguishes between ballistic missiles and guided missiles. A ballistic missile is simply launched, like a thrown ball, with no way to make a correction if the aim is off. A guided missile, however, detects the target location and adjusts its trajectory one way or the other to correct for error in the original aim.

Similarly, some movements are ballistic and others are corrected by feedback. A **ballistic movement** is executed as a whole: Once initiated, it cannot be altered or corrected. A reflex, such as the stretch reflex or the contraction of the pupils in response to light, is a ballistic movement.

Completely ballistic movements are rare; most behaviors are subject to feedback correction. For example, when you thread a needle, you make a slight movement, check your aim, and then make a readjustment. Similarly, a singer who holds a single note for a prolonged time hears any unintentional wavering of the pitch and corrects it. The importance of the feedback becomes apparent if we distort it. Suppose we equip you with a device that records what you sing and then plays it back over earphones so that you hear what you sang 3 seconds ago. Now when you try to sing one note, you hear the error you made 3 seconds ago and try to correct it. But you will not start to hear your correction for another 3 seconds, and by that time, you have overcorrected. The result is wild swings back and forth.

Sequences of Behaviors

Many of our behaviors consist of rapid sequences, as in speaking, writing, dancing, or playing a musical instrument. In certain cases, we can attribute these sequences to **central pattern generators,** neural mechanisms in the spinal cord or elsewhere that generate rhythmic patterns of motor output. Examples include the spinal cord mechanisms that generate wing flapping in birds, fin movements in fish, and the "wet dog shake." Although a stimulus may activate a central pattern generator, it does not control the frequency of the alternating movements. For example, cats scratch themselves at a rate of three to four strokes per second, and this rhythm is generated by cells in the lumbar segments of the spinal cord (Deliagina, Orlovsky, & Pavlova, 1983). The spinal cord neurons generate this same rhythm even if they are isolated from the brain and even if the muscles are paralyzed.

We refer to a fixed sequence of movements as a **motor program.** A motor program can be either learned or built into the nervous system. For an example of a built-in program, a mouse periodically grooms itself by sitting up, licking its paws, wiping them over its face, closing its eyes as the paws pass over them, licking the paws again, and so forth (Fentress, 1973). Once begun, the sequence is fixed from beginning to end. Many people develop learned but predictable motor sequences. An expert gymnast will produce a familiar pattern of movements as a smooth, coordinated whole; the same can be said for skilled typists, piano players, and so forth. The pattern is automatic in the sense that thinking or talking about it interferes with the action.

By comparing species, we begin to understand how a motor program can be gained or lost through evolution. For example, if you hold a chicken above

Nearly all birds reflexively spread their wings when dropped. However, emus—which lost the ability to fly through evolutionary time—do not spread their wings.

the ground and drop it, its wings will extend and flap. Even chickens with featherless wings make the same movements, though they fail to break their fall (Provine, 1979, 1981). Chickens are, of course, genetically still programmed to fly. On the other hand, penguins, emus, and rheas, which have not used their wings for flight for millions of years, have lost the genes for flight movements and do not extend their wings when they are dropped (Provine, 1984). (You might pause to think about the researcher who found a way to drop an emu to test this hypothesis.)

Do humans have any built-in motor programs? Yawning is one example (Provine, 1986). A yawn consists of a prolonged open-mouth inhalation, often accompanied by stretching, and a shorter exhalation. Yawns are very consistent in duration, with a mean of just under 6 seconds. Certain facial expressions are also programmed, such as smiles, frowns, and the eyebrow-raising greeting.

MODULE 8.1
In Closing: Categories of Movement

Charles Sherrington described a motor neuron in the spinal cord as "the final common path." He meant that regardless of what sensory and motivational processes occupy the brain, the final result was always either a muscle contraction or the delay of a muscle contraction. However, a motor neuron and its associated muscle participate in a great many different kinds of movements, and we need many brain areas to control them.

SUMMARY

1. Vertebrates have skeletal, cardiac, and smooth muscles. (p. 228)

2. Skeletal muscles range from slow muscles that do not fatigue to fast muscles that fatigue quickly. We rely on the slow muscles most of the time, but we recruit the fast muscles for brief periods of strenuous activity. (p. 230)

3. Proprioceptors are receptors sensitive to the position and movement of a part of the body. Two kinds of proprioceptors, muscle spindles and Golgi tendon organs, help regulate muscle movements. (p. 231)

4. Some movements, especially reflexes, proceed as a unit, with little if any guidance from sensory feedback. Other movements, such as threading a needle, are constantly guided and redirected by sensory feedback. (p. 234)

ANSWERS TO *STOP AND CHECK* QUESTIONS

1. Each axon to the biceps muscles innervates about a hundred fibers; therefore, it is not possible to change the movement by just a few fibers more or less. In contrast, an axon to the eye muscles innervates only about three fibers. (p. 231)

2. People with myasthenia gravis have fewer than normal receptors, so they need extra acetylcholine to maintain normal movement. Acetylcholinesterase breaks down acetylcholine after it stimulates a receptor on a muscle. So a drug that blocks acetylcholinesterase increases the amount of acetylcholine. (p. 231)

3. Although a fish can move rapidly in cold water, it fatigues easily. (p. 231)

4. Ducks can fly enormous distances without evident fatigue, as they often do during migration. The white muscle of a chicken breast has the great power that is necessary to get a heavy body off the ground, but it fatigues rapidly. Chickens seldom fly very far at one time. (p. 231)

5. An ultramarathoner builds up large numbers of slow-twitch fibers at the expense of fast-twitch fibers. Therefore, endurance is great but maximum speed is not. (p. 231)

6. The muscle spindle (p. 232)

7. The Golgi tendon organs respond to muscle tension and thereby prevent excessively strong muscle contractions. (p. 232)

THOUGHT QUESTION

Would you expect jaguars, cheetahs, and other great cats to have mostly slow-twitch, nonfatiguing muscles in their legs or mostly fast-twitch, quickly fatiguing muscles? What kinds of animals might have mostly the opposite kind of muscles?

MODULE 8.2

Brain Mechanisms of Movement

What good is it to understand how the brain controls movement? One practical goal is to help people with spinal cord damage or limb amputations. Their brains plan movements, but the messages cannot reach the muscles. Suppose we could listen in on their brain messages and decode what they mean. Then biomedical engineers might route those messages to muscle stimulators or robotic limbs. Researchers have in fact mapped the relationships between rats' brain activity and their movements and then connected wires from the brains to robotic limbs. The rats were able to control the robotic movements with brain activity (Chapin, Moxon, Markowitz, & Nicolelis, 1999). Researchers then did the same for monkeys (Wessberg et al., 2000). In another study, monkeys learned to move a joystick to control a cursor on a computer monitor. Later the joystick was removed, but recordings from the monkey's brain were connected to the screen so that whenever the monkey *thought* about a cursor movement, it happened (Serruya, Hatsopoulos, Paninski, Fellows, & Donoghue, 2002). We can imagine that the monkey was impressed with its apparent psychic powers!

People who suffer severe spinal cord damage continue to produce normal activity in the motor cortex when they want to move (Shoham, Halgren, Maynard, & Normann, 2001), so researchers are encouraged about the possibility of connecting their brains

to robotic limbs as well (Nicolelis, 2001). Understanding the brain mechanisms of movement may improve that technology.

Controlling movement is a more complicated matter than we might have guessed. Figure 8.7 outlines the major motor areas of the mammalian central nervous system. Don't get too bogged down in details at this point; we shall attend to each area in due course.

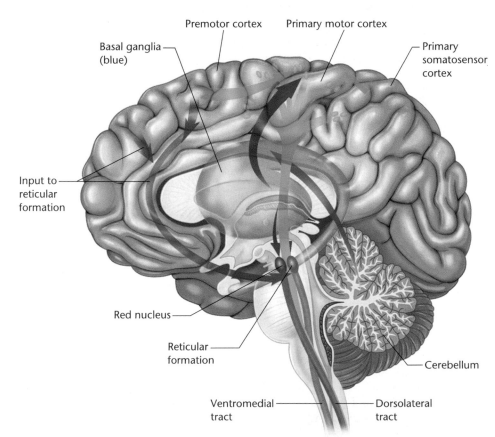

Figure 8.7   The major motor areas of the mammalian central nervous system
The cerebral cortex, especially the primary motor cortex, sends axons directly to the medulla and spinal cord. So do the red nucleus, reticular formation, and other brainstem areas. The medulla and spinal cord control muscle movements. The basal ganglia and cerebellum influence movement indirectly through their communication back and forth with the cerebral cortex and brainstem.

THE ROLE OF THE CEREBRAL CORTEX

Since the pioneering work of Gustav Fritsch and Eduard Hitzig (1870), neuroscientists have known that direct electrical stimulation of the **primary motor cortex,** the precentral gyrus of the frontal cortex, just anterior to the central sulcus (Figure 8.8), elicits movements. However, the motor cortex has no direct connections to the muscles. Some of its axons go to basal ganglia cells, which feed back to control later movements; the other motor cortex axons go to the brainstem and spinal cord (Turner & DeLong, 2000), which have the central pattern generators to control the actual muscle movements (Shik & Orlovsky, 1976). The cerebral cortex is particularly important for complex actions such as writing. It is less important for coughing, sneezing, gagging, laughing, or crying (Rinn, 1984). Granted, your cortex has to process information that tells you when to laugh, cry, and sometimes even when to gag, but the movements themselves are controlled by the medulla and other subcortical areas. (Perhaps this lack of cerebral control explains why it is hard to perform such actions voluntarily. When you do laugh or cough voluntarily, it is not quite the same as when you laugh or cough spontaneously.)

Figure 8.9 (which repeats part of Figure 4.25, p. 97) shows a map of the body along the motor cortex. Stimulating any spot in the motor cortex evokes movements in the body area shown next to it, on the opposite side of the body. For example, the brain area shown next to the hand is active during hand movements. However, don't read this figure as implying that each spot in the motor cortex controls exactly one body area, much less only one muscle. Control is distributed over a population of cells, just as it is for sensation. (Remember the across-fiber pattern principle from Chapter 7.) For example, movement of any one finger or the wrist is associated with activity in a scattered population of cells, and the regions activated by one finger greatly overlap the regions activated by any other finger, as shown in Figure 8.10 (Sanes, Donoghue, Thangaraj, Edelman, & Warach, 1995).

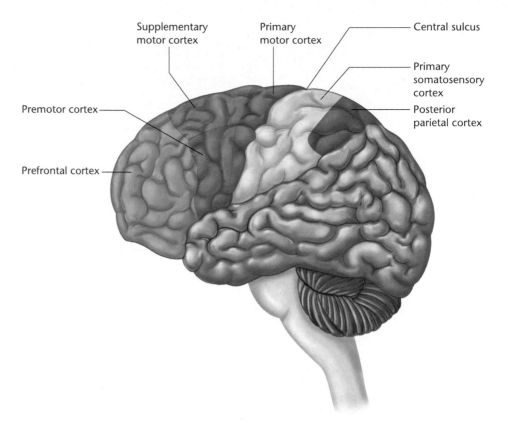

Figure 8.8 Principal areas of the motor cortex in the human brain
Cells in the premotor cortex and supplementary motor cortex are active during the planning of movements, even if the movements are never actually executed.

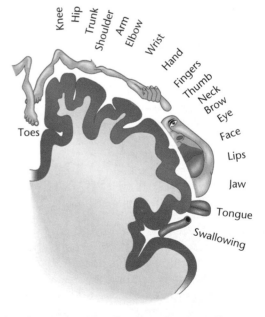

Figure 8.9 Map of body areas in the primary motor cortex
Stimulation at any point in the primary motor cortex is most likely to evoke movements in the body area shown. However, actual results are usually messier than this figure implies: For example, individual cells controlling one finger may be intermingled with cells controlling another finger.
Source: Adapted from Penfield & Rasmussen, 1950

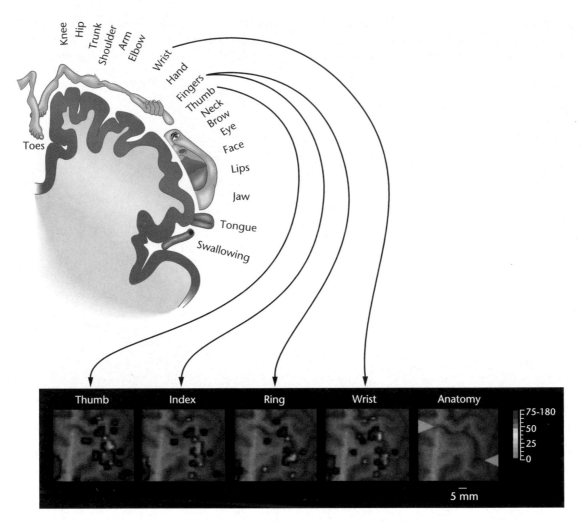

Figure 8.10 Motor cortex during movement of a finger or the wrist
In this functional MRI scan, red indicates the greatest activity, followed in descending order by yellow, green, and blue. Note that each movement activated a scattered population of cells and that the areas activated by any one part of the hand overlapped the areas activated by any other. The scan at the right (anatomy) shows a section of the central sulcus (between the two yellow arrows). The primary motor cortex is just anterior to the central sulcus. *Source: Sanes, Donoghue, Thangaraj, Edelman, & Warach, 1995*

For many years, researchers studied the function of the motor cortex by stimulating various neurons with brief electrical pulses, usually less than 50 ms in duration. The results were brief, isolated muscle twitches. Later researchers found much different results when they changed the procedure. Instead of such brief pulses, they applied electrical stimulation to a monkey's motor cortex for 500 ms (half a second), roughly corresponding to the duration of a normal, integrated movement. Instead of brief twitches, they elicited complex movement patterns. For example, stimulation of one spot in the ventral part of the arm region caused a monkey to make a grasping movement with its hand, move its hand to just in front of the mouth, and open its mouth (Graziano, Taylor, & Moore, 2002). Repeated stimulation of this

same spot elicited the same result every time; the monkey always grasped and moved its hand to its mouth, regardless of what it had been doing at the time and regardless of where or in what position its hand had been. That is, the stimulation produced a certain *outcome*, not a fixed set of muscle movements. Depending on the position of the arm, the stimulation might activate biceps muscles, triceps, or whatever.

Just as the visual cortex becomes active when we imagine seeing something, the motor cortex becomes active when we imagine movements. For example, expert pianists say that when they listen to familiar, well-practiced music, they imagine the finger movements and often start tapping the appropriate fingers as if they were playing the music. Brain recordings have confirmed that the finger area of the motor cortex is active when pianists listen to familiar music, even if they keep their fingers motionless (Haueisen & Knösche, 2001).

Areas Near the Primary Motor Cortex

A number of areas near the primary motor cortex also contribute to movement in diverse ways (see Figure 8.8). In the **posterior parietal cortex,** some neurons respond primarily to visual or somatosensory stimuli, some respond mostly to current or future movements, and some respond to a complicated mixture of the stimulus and the upcoming response (Shadlen & Newsome, 1996). You might think of the posterior parietal cortex as keeping track of the position of the body relative to the world (Snyder, Grieve, Brotchie, & Andersen, 1998). Contrast the effects of posterior parietal damage with those of occipital or temporal damage. People with posterior parietal damage can accurately describe what they see, but they have trouble converting their perception into action. Although they can walk toward something they hear, they cannot walk toward something they see, nor can they reach out to grasp something—even after describing its size, shape, and angle. In contrast, people with damage to certain parts of the occipital cortex cannot describe the size, shape, or location of objects they see, but they can reach out and pick them up, and when walking, they step over or go around objects in their way (Goodale, 1996; Goodale, Milner, Jakobson, & Carey, 1991). In short, the ability to describe what we see is separate from the influence of vision on movement, and we can lose either one without the other.

The primary somatosensory cortex is the main receiving area for touch and other body information, as mentioned in Chapter 7. It sends a substantial number of axons directly to the spinal cord and also provides the primary motor cortex with sensory information. Neurons in this area are especially active when the hand grasps something, responding both to the shape of the object and the type of movement, such as grasping, lifting, or lowering (Gardner, Ro, Debowy, & Ghosh, 1999).

Cells in the prefrontal cortex, premotor cortex, and supplementary motor cortex (see Figure 8.8) actively prepare for a movement, sending messages to the primary motor cortex that actually instigates the movement. These three areas contribute in distinct ways. The **prefrontal cortex** responds to lights, noises, and other sensory signals that lead to a movement. It also calculates probable outcomes of various actions and the values of those outcomes (Tucker, Luu, & Pribram, 1995). Someone with damage in this area has badly planned movements and may shower with clothes on, salt the tea instead of the food, and pour water on the tube of toothpaste instead of the toothbrush (M. F. Schwartz, 1995). Interestingly, this area is inactive during dreams, and the actions we dream about doing are usually haphazard and poorly planned (Braun et al., 1998; Maquet et al., 1996).

The **premotor cortex** is active during preparations for a movement and somewhat active during movement itself. It receives both information about the target in space, to which the body is directing its movement, and information about the current position and posture of the body itself (Hoshi & Tanji, 2000). Both kinds of information are, of course, necessary to move a body part toward some target. The premotor cortex sends output to both the primary motor cortex and the spinal cord, organizing the direction of the movements in space. For example, you would have to use different muscles to move your arm upward depending on whether your hand was palm-up or palm-down at the time, but the same premotor cortex cells would be active in either case (Kakei, Hoffman, & Strick, 2001).

The **supplementary motor cortex** is most active just before a rapid series of movements, such as pushing, pulling, and then turning a stick, in a particular order (Tanji & Shima, 1994). As people practice a rhythm of finger movements, such as you might use when playing a piano, activity increases in the supplementary motor cortex (Ramnani & Passingham, 2001). Damage to the supplementary motor cortex impairs the ability to organize smooth sequences of activities.

Stop & Check

1. How does the posterior parietal cortex contribute to movement? The prefrontal cortex? The premotor cortex? The supplementary motor cortex?

Check your answers on page 248.

Connections From the Brain to the Spinal Cord

All the messages from the brain must eventually reach the medulla and spinal cord, which control the muscles. Diseases of the spinal cord can impair the control of movement in various ways (see Table 8.1). The various outputs from the brain organize into two paths: the dorsolateral tract and the ventromedial tract.

The **dorsolateral tract** of the spinal cord is a set of axons from the primary motor cortex and its surround, and from the **red nucleus,** a midbrain primarily responsible for control of arm muscles (Figure 8.11). The dorsolateral tract axons extend without synaptic interruption to their target neurons in the spinal cord. In bulges of the medulla called *pyramids,* the dorsolateral tract crosses from one side of the brain to the contralateral (opposite) side of the spinal cord. (For this reason, the dorsolateral tract is also called the pyramidal tract.) It controls movements in peripheral areas, such as the hands, fingers, and toes. People with damage to the primary motor cortex or its axons suffer at least a temporary loss of fine movements on the contralateral side.

Why does each hemisphere control the contralateral side instead of its own side? We do not know, but all vertebrates have this pattern. Contralateral control develops gradually. In newborn humans, the immature primary motor cortex has some control over both ipsilateral and contralateral muscles. As the contralateral control improves over the first year and a half of life, it displaces the ipsilateral control, which gradually becomes weaker. In some children with cerebral palsy, the contralateral path fails to mature, and the ipsilateral path remains relatively strong. In fact, sometimes part of the clumsiness of children with cerebral palsy comes from competition between the ipsilateral and contralateral paths (Eyre, Taylor, Villagra, Smith, & Miller, 2001).

In contrast to the dorsolateral tract, the **ventromedial tract** includes axons from the primary motor cortex and supplementary motor cortex and from many other parts of the cortex. It also includes axons that originate from the midbrain tectum, the reticular formation, and the **vestibular nucleus,** the brain area that receives input from the vestibular system (Figure 8.12). Axons of the ventromedial tract go to *both* sides of the spinal cord, not just the contralateral side. The ventromedial tract controls mainly the muscles of the neck, shoulders, and trunk (Kuypers,

TABLE 8.1 Some Disorders of the Spinal Column

Disorder	Description	Cause
Paralysis	Lack of voluntary movement in part of the body.	Damage to spinal cord motor neurons or their axons.
Paraplegia	Loss of sensation and voluntary muscle control in both legs. Reflexes remain. Although no messages pass between the brain and the genitals, the genitals still respond reflexively to touch. Paraplegics have no genital sensations but they can still experience orgasm (Money, 1967).	Cut through the spinal cord above the segments attached to the legs.
Quadriplegia	Loss of sensation and muscle control in all four extremities.	Cut through the spinal cord above the segments controlling the arms.
Hemiplegia	Loss of sensation and muscle control in the arm and leg on one side.	Cut halfway through the spinal cord or (more commonly) damage to one hemisphere of the cerebral cortex.
Tabes dorsalis	Impaired sensation in the legs and pelvic region, impaired leg reflexes and walking, loss of bladder and bowel control.	Late stage of syphilis. Dorsal roots of the spinal cord deteriorate.
Poliomyelitis	Paralysis.	Virus that damages cell bodies of motor neurons
Amyotrophic lateral sclerosis	Gradual weakness and paralysis, starting with the arms and later spreading to the legs. Both motor neurons and axons from the brain to the motor neurons are destroyed.	Unknown.

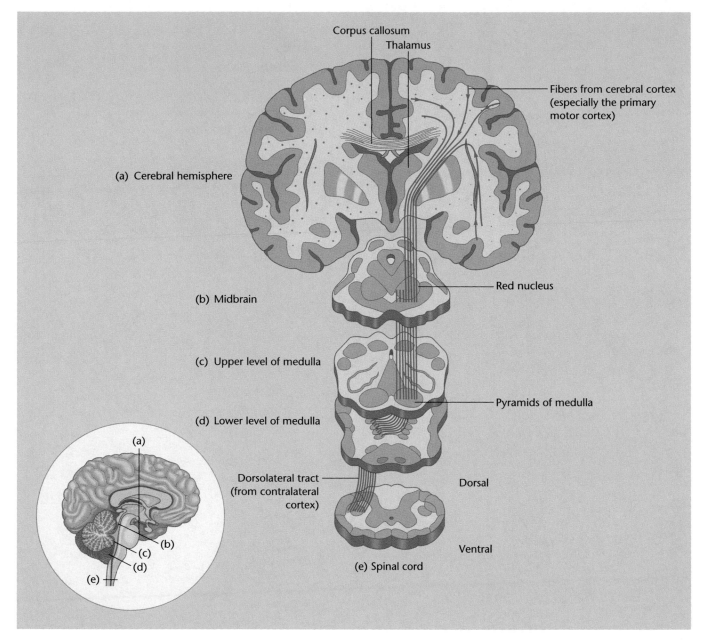

Figure 8.11 **The dorsolateral tract**

This tract originates from the primary motor cortex, neighboring areas, and the red nucleus. It crosses from one side of the brain to the opposite side of the spinal cord, controlling precise and discrete movements of the extremities, such as hands, fingers, and feet.

1989). Note that these movements are necessarily bilateral; you can move your fingers on just one side, but you move your neck on both sides or not at all. Damage to the ventromedial tract impairs bilateral movements such as walking, turning, bending, standing up, and sitting down. Most movements rely on a combination of both the dorsolateral and ventromedial tracts.

2. What kinds of movements are controlled by the dorsolateral tract? By the ventromedial tract?

Check your answers on page 248.

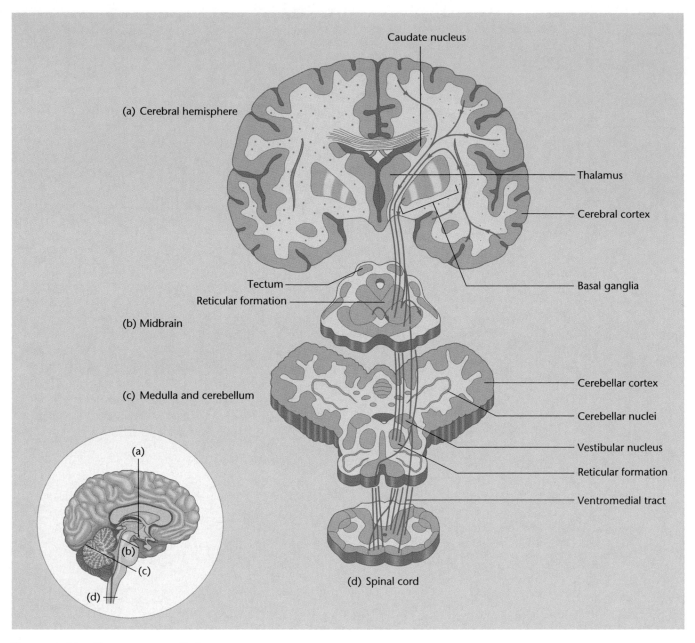

Figure 8.12 The ventromedial tract
This tract originates from many parts of the cerebral cortex and several areas of the midbrain and medulla. It produces bilateral control of trunk muscles for postural adjustments and bilateral movements such as standing, bending, turning, and walking.

THE ROLE OF THE CEREBELLUM

The cerebellum is important for motor control, including learned motor responses. The term *cerebellum* is Latin for "little brain." The cerebellum contains more neurons than the rest of the brain combined (R. W. Williams & Herrup, 1988), and some of those neurons have broad branching with an enormous number of connections. So although the cerebellum is small physically, it is enormous in its potential for processing information.

The most obvious effect of cerebellar damage is trouble with rapid, ballistic movement sequences that require accurate aim and timing. For example, people with cerebellar damage have trouble tapping a rhythm, pointing at a moving object, speaking, writing, typing, playing a musical instrument, most athletic activities, and even hand clapping. However, they have no particular trouble lifting weights because this action does not need precise aim or timing.

The cerebellum is large in most species of birds, which have to time and aim their movements precisely, especially when landing. The sloth, at the other extreme, is a mammal proverbial for its slowness. When M. G. Murphy and J. L. O'Leary (1973) made cerebellar lesions in sloths, they detected no change in the animals' behavior.

Here is one quick way to test how well someone's cerebellum is functioning: Ask the person to focus on one spot and then to move the eyes quickly to another spot. Saccades (sa-KAHDS), ballistic eye movements from one fixation point to another, depend on impulses from the cerebellum and the frontal cortex to the cranial nerves. A normal, healthy person's eyes move from one fixation point to another by a single movement or by one large movement with a small correction at the end. Someone with cerebellar damage, however, has difficulty programming the angle and distance of eye movements (Dichgans, 1984). The eyes make many short movements until, by trial and error, they eventually focus on the intended spot.

Another test of cerebellar damage is the *finger-to-nose test.* The person is instructed to hold one arm straight out and then, at command, to touch his or her nose as quickly as possible. A normal person does so in three steps. First, the finger moves ballistically to a point just in front of the nose. This *move* function depends on the cerebellar cortex (the surface of the cerebellum), which sends messages to the nuclei (clusters of cell bodies in the interior of the cerebellum; Figure 8.13). Second, the finger remains steady at that spot for a fraction of a second. This *hold* function depends on the nuclei alone (Kornhuber, 1974). Finally, the finger moves to the nose by a slower movement that does not depend on the cerebellum.

After damage to the cerebellar cortex, a person has trouble with the initial rapid movement. Either the finger stops too soon or it goes too far, striking the face. If certain cerebellar nuclei have been damaged, the person may have difficulty with the hold segment: The finger reaches a point just in front of the nose and then wavers.

The symptoms of cerebellar damage resemble those of alcohol intoxication: clumsiness, slurred speech, and inaccurate eye movements. A police officer testing someone for drunkenness may use the finger-to-nose test or similar tests because the cerebellum is one of the first brain areas that alcohol affects.

Evidence of a Broad Role

The cerebellum is not only a motor structure. In one study, functional MRI measured cerebellar activity while people performed several tasks with a single set of objects (Gao et al., 1996). When they simply lifted objects, the cerebellum showed little activity. When they felt objects with both hands to decide whether they were the same or different, the cerebellum was much more active. The cerebellum even showed activity when people held their hands steady and the experimenter rubbed an object across them. That is, the cerebellum responded to sensory stimuli that might guide movement, rather than to movement by itself.

What, then, is the role of the cerebellum? Masao Ito (1984) proposed that one key role is to establish new motor programs that enable one to execute a sequence of actions as a whole. Inspired by this idea, many researchers reported evidence that cerebellar damage impairs motor learning. However, such impairment could reflect either slow learning or disrupted movement. In one very clever study, researchers used fMRI to record brain activity while normal, healthy people learned to tap their fingers in a particular way. At first, people were finger tapping while simultaneously performing a difficult distracting task. At that time, their performance did not improve, and the cerebellum showed little increase over its usual level of activity. However, as soon as the distracting task was removed, they *immediately* improved their performance, showing that they had

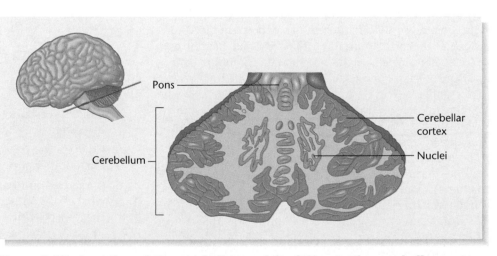

Figure 8.13 Location of the cerebellar nuclei relative to the cerebellar cortex

learned the response during the distraction period. Activity in the cerebellum increased as soon as the performance improved. The conclusion was that increased cerebellar activity was necessary for enhanced performance but not necessarily for motor learning, at least not for all motor learning (Seidler et al., 2002).

Richard Ivry and his colleagues have emphasized the importance of the cerebellum for behaviors that depend on precise timing of fairly short intervals (up to about 1.5 seconds). Any sequence of rapid movements obviously requires timing. Many perceptual and cognitive tasks also require timing—for example, judging which of two visual stimuli is moving faster or listening to two pairs of tones and judging whether the delay was longer between the first or second pair.

People who are accurate at one kind of timed movement, such as tapping a rhythm with a finger, tend to be good at other timed movements, such as tapping a rhythm with a foot, and at judging which visual stimulus moved faster and which intertone delay was longer. People with cerebellar damage are impaired at all of these tasks but unimpaired at controlling the force of a movement or at judging which tone is louder (Ivry & Diener, 1991; Keele & Ivry, 1990). Evidently, the cerebellum is important mainly for tasks requiring timing.

The cerebellum also appears critical for certain aspects of attention. For example, when people are given a signal to shift their attention to a particular visual location, most do so within 100 ms. (They become more accurate at detecting stimuli in that location beginning 100 ms after the signal.) But people with cerebellar damage need a full second to shift their attention (Townsend et al., 1999).

So the cerebellum appears to be linked to habit formation, timing, and certain aspects of attention. Are these really separate functions that just happen to be located in the same place? Or can we somehow reduce them all to a single theme? (For example, maybe shifting attention requires timing or aim. Or maybe shifting attention quickly is a kind of habit.) We don't have an answer now, but note that this unanswered question is really more psychological than neurological.

Cellular Organization

The cerebellum receives input from the spinal cord, from each of the sensory systems by way of the cranial nerve nuclei, and from the cerebral cortex. This information eventually reaches the cerebellar cortex, the surface of the cerebellum (see Figure 8.13).

Figure 8.14 shows the types and arrangements of neurons in the cerebellar cortex. The figure is too complex to understand all at once, but do note these main points:

- The neurons are arranged in a very precise geometrical pattern, with multiple repetitions of the same units.
- The Purkinje cells are flat cells in sequential planes.
- The parallel fibers are axons parallel to one another but perpendicular to the planes of the Purkinje cells.
- Action potentials in varying numbers of parallel fibers excite one Purkinje cell after another. Each Purkinje cell then transmits an inhibitory message to cells in the nuclei of the cerebellum (clusters of cell bodies in the interior of the cerebellum) and the vestibular nuclei in the brainstem, which in turn send information to the midbrain and the thalamus.
- Depending on which and how many parallel fibers are active, they might stimulate only the first few Purkinje cells or a long series of them. Because the parallel fibers' messages reach different Purkinje cells one after another, the greater the number of excited Purkinje cells, the greater their collective *duration* of response. That is, if the parallel fibers stimulate only the first few Purkinje cells, the result is a brief message to the target cells; if they stimulate more Purkinje cells, the message lasts longer. The output of Purkinje cells controls the timing of a movement, including both its onset and offset (Thier, Dicke, Haas, & Barash, 2000).

3. What is a test of cerebellar functioning?
4. Besides control of movement, for what else is the cerebellum important?
5. How are the parallel fibers arranged relative to one another and to the Purkinje cells?
6. If a larger number of parallel fibers are active, what is the effect on the collective output of the Purkinje cells?

Check your answers on page 248.

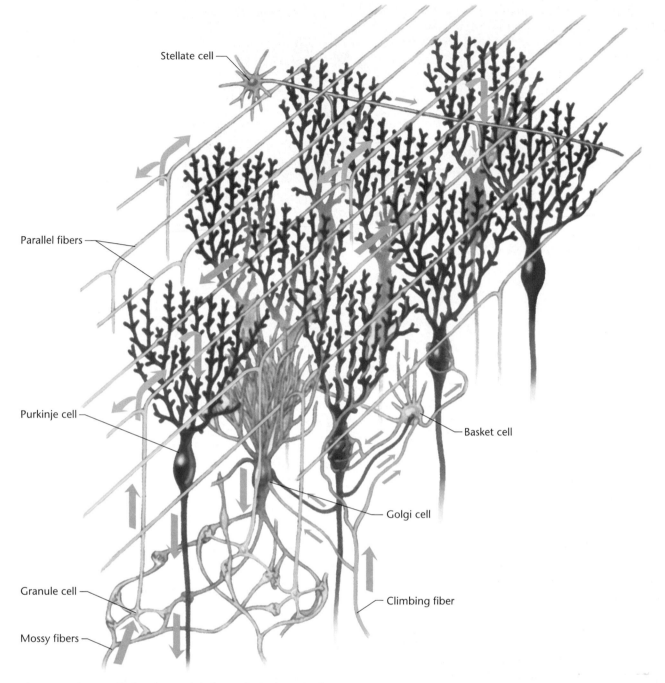

Figure 8.14 Cellular organization of the cerebellum
Parallel fibers (yellow) activate one Purkinje cell after another. Purkinje cells (red) inhibit a target cell in one of the nuclei of the cerebellum (not shown, but toward the bottom of the illustration). The more Purkinje cells that respond, the longer the target cell is inhibited. In this way, the cerebellum controls the duration of a movement.

THE ROLE OF THE BASAL GANGLIA

The term **basal ganglia** applies collectively to a group of large subcortical structures in the forebrain (Figure 8.15).[1] Various authorities differ in which structures they include as part of the basal ganglia, but everyone includes at least the caudate nucleus, the putamen, and the globus pallidus. Each of these areas exchanges information with the others and with the

[1]Ganglia is the plural of ganglion, so the term *basal ganglia* is a plural noun.

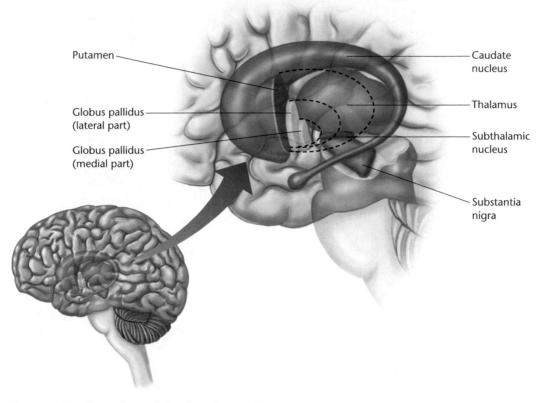

Putamen

Globus pallidus
(lateral part)

Globus pallidus
(medial part)

Caudate
nucleus

Thalamus

Subthalamic
nucleus

Substantia
nigra

Figure 8.15 Location of the basal ganglia
The basal ganglia surround the thalamus and are surrounded by the cerebral cortex.

thalamus and cerebral cortex. The caudate nucleus and the putamen are areas that receive input from sensory areas of the thalamus and the cerebral cortex. The globus pallidus is the output area, sending information to the thalamus, which in turn sends it to the motor cortex and the prefrontal cortex (Hoover & Strick, 1993).

Because information passes back and forth between the basal ganglia and the motor areas of the cortex, the functions of the basal ganglia resemble those of the motor, premotor, and prefrontal cortex: They store sensory information (Vakil, Kahan, Huberman, & Osimani, 2000), use stored information to guide movements (Menon, Anagnoson, Glover, & Pfefferbaum, 2000), learn rules (Filoteo, Maddox, & Davis, 2001), and organize sequences of movements into a smooth, automatic whole (Graybiel, 1998; Koechlin, Corrado, Pietrini, & Grafman, 2000). For example, when you are first learning to drive a car, you have to think about everything you do. After much experience, you can put on your turn signal, turn the wheel, change gears, and change speeds almost effortlessly. The basal ganglia are important for habit learning of this type and so is the cerebral cortex.

The basal ganglia also are active in selecting which response to make or inhibit. In one study, in-

vestigators recorded activity from basal ganglia cells of patients who were undergoing brain surgery, which was performed with only local anesthesia of the scalp. When the patients were given a variety of signals (e.g., to make or inhibit a simple finger response), the caudate nucleus showed much activity after a stimulus that called for an action, but only if it appeared infrequently. The more often the stimulus occurred, the less it excited the caudate nucleus. If it occurred on almost every trial, then the caudate nucleus started becoming active after a stimulus that called for *no* response (Kropotov & Etlinger, 1999).

In another study suggesting the same conclusion, people used a computer mouse to draw lines on a screen while researchers used PET scans to examine brain activity (see Methods 8.1). Drawing a new line activated the basal ganglia and not the cerebellum. However, when people tried to retrace a line as accurately as possible, the cerebellum was much more active than the basal ganglia (Jueptner & Weiller, 1998). Again, the basal ganglia seem critical for the selection of movements; the cerebellum is more important for accurate aim and using feedback to guide further behavior.

One psychiatric condition linked to the basal ganglia is **obsessive-compulsive disorder,** which is

PET Scans

Positron-emission tomography (PET) provides a high-resolution image of activity in a living brain by recording the emission of radioactivity from injected chemicals. First the person receives an injection of glucose or some other chemical with a radioactive label of ^{11}C, ^{18}F, or ^{15}O. These chemicals decay with half-lives of less than 2 hours. Because their half-lives are so short, the investigators must make them in a large device called a cyclotron and then use them almost immediately. Because cyclotrons are large and expensive, PET scans are available only at the largest research hospitals. When a radioactive label decays, it releases a positron that immediately collides with a nearby electron, emitting two gamma rays in exactly opposite directions. The person's head is surrounded by a set of gamma ray detectors (Figure 8.16). When the detectors record two gamma rays at the same time, they identify a spot halfway between the detectors as the point of origin of the gamma rays. A computer uses this information to determine how many gamma rays are coming from each spot in the brain and therefore how much of the radioactive chemical is in each area (Phelps & Mazziotta, 1985).

In a typical experiment, the researchers give the person radioactively labeled glucose, which goes primarily to the most active areas of the brain. Then they present particular kinds of stimuli or ask the person to perform certain tasks and determine which brain areas become the most active.

Figure 8.16   A PET scanner
(No, it's not a state-of-the-art hairdo.) A person engages in a cognitive task while attached to this apparatus that records which areas of the brain become more active and by how much. Red indicates the greatest amount of activity followed in descending order by yellow, green, blue, and purple.

One disadvantage of the PET method is that it requires exposing the brain to a significant amount of radioactivity. No one should undergo repeated PET scans unless necessary for medical diagnosis.

(Burt Glinn/Magnum)

---

marked by repetitive thoughts and actions that the person knows are pointless or nonsensical. The condition is linked with *increased* activity in the caudate nucleus (which is part of the basal ganglia), along with parts of the prefrontal cortex. One hypothesis is that these brain areas are responsible for habit formation, and overactivity in them is linked to excessively strong, even life-dominating habits (Graybiel & Rauch, 2000).

7. How does the function of the basal ganglia differ from that of the cerebellum?

Check your answer on page 248.

MODULE 8.2

In Closing: Movement Control and Cognition

It is tempting to describe behavior in three steps—first we perceive, then we think, and finally we act. As you have seen, the brain does not handle the process in such discrete steps. For example, the posterior parietal cortex monitors the position of the body relative to visual space and therefore helps guide movement. Thus, its functions are sensory, cognitive, and motor. The cerebellum has traditionally been considered a major part of the motor system, but it is now known to be equally important in timing sensory processes. People with basal ganglia damage are slow to start or select a movement; they are also often described as cognitively slow—that is, they hesitate to make any kind of choice. In short, selecting and organizing a movement are not something we tack on at the end of our thinking; they are intimately intertwined with all of our sensory and cognitive processes.

SUMMARY

1. The primary motor cortex is the main source of brain input to the spinal cord. The spinal cord contains central pattern generators that actually control the muscles. (p. 237)

2. Areas near the primary motor cortex—including the prefrontal, premotor, and supplementary motor cortices—are active in detecting stimuli for movement and preparing for a movement. (p. 239)

3. The dorsolateral tract, which controls movements in the periphery of the body, has axons that cross from one side of the brain to the opposite side of the spinal cord. (p. 239)

4. The ventromedial tract controls bilateral movements near the midline of the body. (p. 240)

5. The cerebellum has multiple roles in behavior, including sensory functions related to perception of the timing or rhythm of stimuli. Its role in the control of movement is especially important for timing, aim, and correction of errors. (p. 242)

6. The cells of the cerebellum are arranged in a very regular pattern that enables them to produce outputs of well-controlled duration. (p. 244)

7. The basal ganglia are a group of large subcortical structures that are important for selecting and inhibiting particular movements. (p. 245)

ANSWERS TO *STOP AND CHECK* QUESTIONS

1. The posterior parietal cortex is important for perceiving the location of objects and the position of the body relative to the environment, including those objects. The prefrontal cortex responds to sensory stimuli that call for some movement. The premotor cortex is active in preparing a movement immediately before it occurs. The supplementary motor cortex is especially active in preparing for a rapid sequence of movements. (p. 239)

2. The dorsolateral tract controls detailed movements in the periphery on the contralateral side of the body. (For example, the dorsolateral tract from the left hemisphere controls the right side of the body.) The ventromedial tract controls the trunk muscles bilaterally. (p. 241)

3. Accuracy of saccadic eye movements or finger-to-nose test. (p. 244)

4. Processing sensory stimuli that might guide later movements, any behavior that requires precise timing, habit formation, and certain aspects of attention. (p. 244)

5. The parallel fibers are parallel to one another and perpendicular to the planes of the Purkinje cells. (p. 244)

6. As a larger number of parallel fibers become active, the Purkinje cells increase their duration of response. (p. 244)

7. The cerebellum is important for timing, aim, and correcting errors (using feedback to guide further behavior). The basal ganglia apparently help select the correct movement to make and inhibit inappropriate movements. (p. 247)

THOUGHT QUESTION

Human infants are at first limited to gross movements of the trunk, arms, and legs. The ability to move one finger at a time matures gradually over at least the first year. What hypothesis would you suggest about which brain areas that control movement mature early and which mature later?

Disorders of Movement

Even if your nervous system and muscles are completely healthy, you may sometimes find it difficult to move in the way you like. For example, if you have just finished a bout of unusually strenuous exercise, your muscles may be so fatigued that you can hardly move them voluntarily, even though they keep twitching. Or if your legs "fall asleep" while you are sitting in an awkward position, you may stumble and fall when you try to walk.

Certain neurological disorders produce exaggerated and lasting movement impairments. We consider two examples: Parkinson's disease and Huntington's disease.

PARKINSON'S DISEASE

The symptoms of **Parkinson's disease** (also called *Parkinson disease*) are rigidity, muscle tremors, slow movements, and difficulty initiating physical and mental activity (M. T. V. Johnson et al., 1996; Manfredi, Stocchi, & Vacca, 1995; Pillon et al., 1996). Although the motor problems are the most obvious, the disorder goes beyond movement. Parkinsonian patients are also slow on cognitive tasks, such as imagining movements or mentally counting events, even when they don't have to make any movements (Sawamoto, Honda, Hanakawa, Fukuyama, & Shibasaki, 2002). Most patients become depressed at an early stage, and many show deficits of memory and reasoning. These mental symptoms are probably part of the disease itself, not just a reaction to the muscle failures (Ouchi et al., 1999). Parkinson's disease strikes about 1 person per 100, with onset usually after age 50.

People with Parkinson's disease are not paralyzed or weak; they are impaired at initiating spontaneous movements in the absence of stimuli to guide their actions. Rats with Parkinsonian-type brain damage have few spontaneous movements, but they respond well to strong stimuli (Horvitz & Eyny, 2000). Parkinsonian patients sometimes walk surprisingly well when following a parade, when walking up a flight of stairs, or when walking across lines drawn at one-step intervals (Teitelbaum, Pellis, & Pellis, 1991). In these cases, they have external stimuli to guide their actions.

The immediate cause of Parkinson's disease is the gradual progressive death of neurons, especially in the substantia nigra, which sends dopamine-releasing axons to the caudate nucleus and putamen. People with Parkinson's disease lose these axons and therefore all the effects that their dopamine would have produced. One result is decreased excitation of the cerebral cortex, as shown in Figure 8.17 (Wichmann, Vitek, & DeLong, 1995).

Researchers estimate that the average person over age 45 loses almost 1% of his or her substantia nigra neurons per year. Most of us have enough to spare, but some people either start with fewer or lose them faster. If the number of surviving substantia nigra neurons declines below 20% to 30% of normal, Parkinsonian symptoms begin (Knoll, 1993). The greater the cell loss, the more severe the symptoms.

Possible Causes

About 10 to 20% of Parkinson's patients have a close relative with the same disease. That percentage suggests a possible genetic basis but not a very strong one. In the late 1990s, the news media excitedly reported that researchers had located a gene that causes Parkinson's disease. That report was misleading. Certain families include many members who develop early-onset Parkinson's disease (before age 50), and the affected people have genes leading to the accumulation of a protein called α-synuclein (Shimura et al., 2001). However, this genetic abnormality is not found in people with the more common form of Parkinson's disease that begins later in life.

One study examined Parkinson's patients who had twins. As shown in Figure 8.18, if you have a monozygotic (MZ) twin who develops Parkinson's disease before age 50, you are at great risk, too. However, if your twin develops Parkinson's disease *after* age 50, your risk is increased less, and your risk doesn't depend on whether your twin is monozygotic or dizygotic (Tanner et al., 1999). Equal concordance for dizygotic and monozygotic twins implies low heritability. That is, it implies that the family resemblance depends on shared environment rather than genes. However, this study

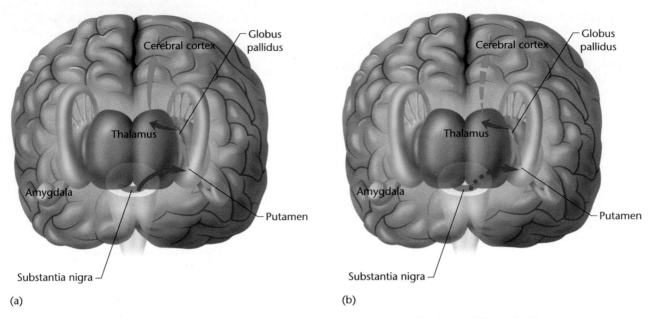

Figure 8.17   Connections from the substantia nigra: (a) normal and (b) in Parkinson's disease
Excitatory paths are shown in green; inhibitory are in red. The substantia nigra's axons inhibit the putamen. Axon loss increases excitatory communication to the globus pallidus. The result is increased inhibition from the globus pallidus to the thalamus and decreased excitation from the thalamus to the cerebral cortex. People with Parkinson's disease show decreased initiation of movement, slow and inaccurate movement, and psychological depression. *Source: Based on Wichmann, Vitek, & DeLong, 1995*

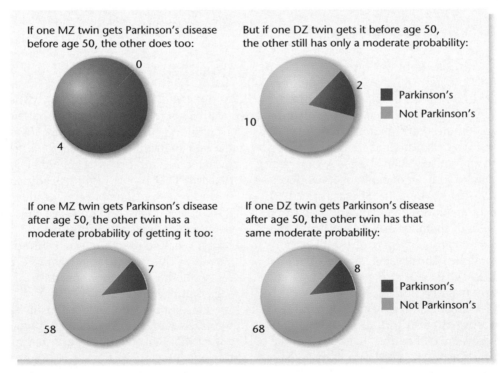

Figure 8.18   Probability of developing Parkinson's disease if you have a twin who developed the disease before or after age 50
Having a monozygotic (MZ) twin develop Parkinson's disease before age 50 means that you are very likely to get it, too. A dizygotic (DZ) twin who gets it before age 50 does not pose the same risk. Therefore, early-onset Parkinson's disease shows a strong genetic component. However, if your twin develops Parkinson's disease later (as is more common), your risk is the same, regardless of whether you are a monozygotic or dizygotic twin. Therefore, late-onset Parkinson's disease has little or no heritability. *Source: Based on data of Tanner et al., 1999*

has two limitations. First, the sample size was small. Second, sometimes one MZ twin develops Parkinson's disease many years before the other twin (Piccini, Burn, Ceravolo, Maraganore, & Brooks, 1999). Therefore, a study with a longer follow-up time might have found different results.

A later study examined the chromosomes of people in 174 families that included more than one person with Parkinson's disease. Researchers looked for genes that were more common in family members who had Parkinson's disease than those who did not. They found no gene that was consistently linked to the disease, but they did find five genes on separate chromosomes that were more common among people with Parkinson's (E. R. Martin et al., 2001; Scott et al., 2001). Presumably, each of these genes increases the risk. However, none is really "a gene for Parkinson's disease." For example, one gene was found in 82% of the people with Parkinson's disease but also in 79% of those without it! Because the study included more than 1000 people, this difference is statistically reliable. However, clearly, the great majority of people with this gene do not get Parkinson's disease. In short, genetics will not take us very far in explaining why some people get the disease and others do not.

What environmental influences might be relevant? Sometimes Parkinson's disease results from exposure to toxins. The first solid evidence was discovered by accident (Ballard, Tetrud, & Langston, 1985). In northern California in 1982, several people aged 22 to 42 developed symptoms of Parkinson's disease after using a drug similar to heroin. At first, physicians resisted diagnosing Parkinson's disease because the patients were so young, but eventually, the diagnosis became clear. Before the investigators could alert the community to the danger of the heroin substitute, many other users had developed symptoms ranging from mild to fatal (Tetrud, Langston, Garbe, & Ruttenber, 1989).

The substance responsible for the symptoms was MPTP, a chemical that the body converts to MPP⁺, which accumulates in, and then destroys, neurons that release dopamine[2] (Nicklas, Saporito, Basma, Geller, & Heikkila, 1992). Postsynaptic neurons compensate for the loss by increasing their number of dopamine receptors (Chiueh, 1988) (Figure 8.19). In many ways, the extra receptors help, but they also produce a jumpy overresponsiveness that creates additional problems (W. C. Miller & DeLong, 1988).

No one supposes that Parkinson's disease is often the result of using illegal drugs. A more likely hypoth-

esis is that people are sometimes exposed to MPTP or similar chemicals in herbicides and pesticides (Figure 8.20), many of which can damage cells of the substantia nigra (Betarbet et al., 2000). However, if exposure to a toxin were the main cause of Parkinson's disease, we should expect to find near epidemics in some geographical regions and almost no cases elsewhere. The patchy distribution of the disease suggests

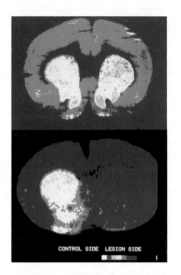

Figure 8.19 Results of injecting MPP⁺ into right hemisphere of the rat brain
The autoradiography above shows D_2 dopamine receptors; the one below shows axon terminals that contain dopamine. Red indicates the highest level of activity, followed in descending order by yellow, green, and blue. Note that the MPP⁺ greatly depleted the number of dopamine axons and that the number of D_2 receptors increased in response to this lack of input. However, the net result is a great decrease in dopamine activity. *Source: From "Dopamine in the Extrapyramidal Motor Function: A Study Based Upon the MPTP-Induced Primate Model of Parkinsonism." by C. C. Chieuh, 1988, Annals of the New York Academy of Sciences, 515, p. 223. Reprinted by permission.*

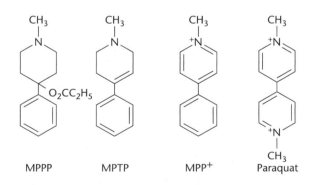

Figure 8.20 The chemical structures of MPPP, MPTP, MPP⁺, and paraquat
Exposure to paraquat and similar herbicides and pesticides may increase the risk of Parkinson's disease.

[2]The full names of these chemicals are 1-methyl-4 phenyl-1,2,3,6-tetrahydropyridine and 1-methyl-4-phenylpyridinium ion. (Let's hear it for abbreviations!)

that toxins are only one cause among several (C. A. D. Smith et al., 1992).

What else might influence the risk of Parkinson's disease? Several studies have compared the lifestyles of people who did and didn't develop the disease. One factor that stands out is cigarette smoking and coffee drinking: People who smoke cigarettes or consume much caffeine have less chance of developing Parkinson's disease (Gorell, Rybicki, Johnson, & Peterson, 1999; Ross et al., 2000; Tanner et al., 2002). (Read that sentence again.) Needless to say, no one should justify smoking for health reasons! Coffee has the benefits without the risks. In either case, the results are theoretically interesting. One hypothesis is that nicotine acts by blocking apoptosis (programmed cell death). Another is that nicotine acts as a "radical scavenger," inactivating the hydoxyl radicals that damage neurons. Unfortunately, the results from mouse studies so far have been inconsistent on whether nicotine decreases the risk of Parkinson's disease (Ferger et al., 1998; Quik & Jeyarasingam, 2000).

In short, Parkinson's disease probably results from a mixture of causes. A gene is responsible for many cases of early-onset Parkinson's disease; exposure to toxins can increase risk; cigarette smoking and caffeine apparently decrease risk. Some researchers believe various diseases and infections, even influenza, sometimes damage substantia nigra cells and predispose to later Parkinson's disease (Calne, 2002). Dopamine-containing neurons are evidently more vulnerable than most other neurons to damage from almost anything that impairs their metabolism (Zeevalk, Manzino, Hoppe, & Sonsalla, 1997), so we may find a variety of causes.

1. Do monozygotic twins resemble each other more than dizygotic twins do for early-onset Parkinson's disease? For late-onset? What conclusion do these results imply?

2. How does MPTP exposure influence the likelihood of Parkinson's disease? What are the effects of cigarette smoking?

Check your answers on page 257.

L-Dopa Treatment

If Parkinson's disease results from a dopamine deficiency, then the goal of therapy should be to restore the missing dopamine. However, a dopamine pill would be ineffective because dopamine does not cross the blood-brain barrier. L-dopa, a precursor to dopamine, does cross the barrier. Taken as a daily pill, L-dopa reaches the brain, where neurons convert it to dopamine. L-dopa is effective for most patients and continues to be the main treatment for Parkinson's disease.

However, L-dopa is disappointing in several ways. First, its effectiveness varies, and for some patients, it provides no relief at all. It is usually effective in the early to intermediate stages of Parkinson's disease but less helpful in the later stages. Second, it does not prevent the continued loss of neurons. In fact, there is some evidence that too much dopamine *kills* dopamine-containing cells (Weingarten & Zhou, 2001). For that reason, L-dopa could do harm as well as good. Third, L-dopa enters not only the brain cells that need extra dopamine but also others, producing harmful side effects that include nausea, restlessness, sleep problems, low blood pressure, repetitive movements, hallucinations, and delusions. Generally, the more severe the patient's symptoms, the more severe the side effects of L-dopa.

Therapies Other Than L-Dopa

Given the limitations of L-dopa, researchers have sought alternatives and supplements. The following possibilities show promise (Dunnett & Björklund, 1999):

- Antioxidant drugs, which may decrease further damage
- Drugs that directly stimulate dopamine receptors
- Drugs that block glutamate (In many cases, dopamine opposes the effects of glutamate; therefore, a deficit of dopamine leads to excess glutamate activity.)
- Neurotrophins to promote survival and growth of the remaining neurons
- Drugs that decrease apoptosis of the remaining neurons
- High-frequency electrical stimulation of the globus pallidus, temporarily inactivating it (This procedure is especially effective for blocking tremor.)
- Surgical damage to the globus pallidus or parts of the thalamus (This procedure produces the same results as electrically inactivating the globus pallidus but is irreversible and therefore riskier.)

Each approach has its limitations. The usual therapy is to combine L-dopa with one or more additional treatments.

A potentially exciting strategy is still in the experimental stage. In a pioneering study, M. J. Perlow and colleagues (1979) injected the chemical 6-OHDA into rats to make lesions in the substantia nigra in one hemisphere, producing Parkinson's-type symptoms in the opposite side of the body. After the movement abnormalities stabilized, the experimenters removed the substantia nigra from rat fetuses and transplanted them into the damaged brains. The grafts survived in 29 of the 30 recipients, making synapses in varying numbers. Four weeks later, most recipients had recovered much of their normal movement. Control animals that suffered the same brain damage without receiving grafts showed little or no behavioral recovery.

If such surgery can work for rats, why not humans? The procedure itself is feasible. Perhaps because the blood-brain barrier protects the brain from foreign substances, the immune system is less active in the brain than elsewhere (Nicholas & Arnason, 1992), and physicians can give drugs to further suppress rejection of the transplanted tissue. However, only brain tissue transplanted from a fetus can make connections, and simply making connections is not enough. The animal still has to relearn the behaviors dependent on those cells (Brasted, Watts, Robbins, & Dunnett, 1999). In effect, the animal has to practice using the transplanted cells.

Ordinarily, scientists test any experimental procedure extensively with laboratory animals before trying it on humans, but with Parkinson's disease, the temptation was too great. People in the late stages have little to lose and are willing to try almost anything. The obvious problem is where to get the donor tissue. Several early studies used tissue from the patient's own adrenal gland. Although that tissue is not composed of neurons, it produces and releases dopamine. Unfortunately, the adrenal gland transplants seldom produced much benefit (Backlund et al., 1985).

Another possibility is to transplant brain tissue from aborted fetuses. Fetal neurons transplanted into the brains of Parkinson's patients sometimes survive for years and do make synapses with the patient's own cells. However, the operation is difficult and expensive, requiring brain tissue from four to eight aborted fetuses. Most patients show only slight benefits within 1 year after surgery (Freed et al., 2001), although some studies show increasing benefits after a longer delay (Isacson, Bjorklund, & Pernaute, 2001). At best, the procedure needs more research.

One problem is that many transplanted cells do not survive or do not form effective synapses, especially in the oldest recipients. As mentioned in Chapter 5, aging brains lose plasticity. They probably produce less neurotrophins than younger brains do. Researchers have found improved success of brain transplants in aging rats if the transplant includes not only fetal neurons but also a source of neurotrophins (Collier, Sortwell, & Daley, 1999).

One way to decrease the need for aborted fetuses is to grow cells in tissue culture, genetically alter them so that they produce large quantities of L-dopa, and then transplant them into the brain (Ljungberg, Stern, &

Wilkin, 1999; Studer, Tabar, & McKay, 1998). This idea is particularly attractive if the cells grown in tissue culture are **stem cells,** immature cells that are capable of differentiating into a wide variety of other cell types depending on where they are in the body. It may be possible to nurture a population of stem cells that are capable of becoming dopamine-releasing neurons and then deposit them into damaged brain areas (Kim et al., 2002).

Yet another possibility is to transplant tissue from fetuses of another species. Although this idea may sound extreme, physicians have indeed transplanted substantia nigra tissue from the brains of pig fetuses into the brains of patients with Parkinson's disease. The investigators did not report the amount of benefit, but a postmortem examination of one patient, who died 7 months after the transplant for unrelated reasons, found that substantial numbers of transplanted pig neurons survived and made synapses with the human neurons (Deacon et al., 1997).

The research on brain transplants has raised yet another possibility for treatment. In several experiments, the transplanted tissue failed to survive, but the recipient showed behavioral recovery anyway. Evidently, the transplanted tissue releases trophic factors that stimulate axon and dendrite growth in the surrounding areas of the recipient's own brain (Bohn, Cupit, Marciano, & Gash, 1987; Dunnett, Ryan, Levin, Reynolds, & Bunch, 1987; Ensor, Morley, Redfern, & Miles, 1993). Further research has demonstrated that brain injections of neurotrophins can significantly benefit brain-damaged rats and monkeys, presumably by enhancing the growth of axons and dendrites (Gash et al., 1996; Kolb, Cote, Ribeiro-da-Silva, & Cuello, 1997). Because neurotrophins do not cross the blood-brain barrier, researchers are developing novel ways to get them into the brain (Kordower et al., 2000).

For the latest information about Parkinson's disease, see the Web site of the World Parkinson Disease Association:

www.wpda.org/

Stop & Check

3. What is the likely explanation for how L-dopa relieves the symptoms of Parkinson's disease?

4. In what ways is L-dopa treatment disappointing?

5. What are some other possible treatments?

Check your answers on page 257.

HUNTINGTON'S DISEASE

Huntington's disease, also known as *Huntington disease* or *Huntington's chorea,* is a severe neurological disorder that strikes about 1 person in 10,000 in the United States (A. B. Young, 1995). Motor symptoms usually begin with arm jerks and then facial twitches; later, tremors spread to other parts of the body and develop into writhing (M. A. Smith, Brandt, & Shadmehr, 2000). (*Chorea* comes from the same root as *choreography;* sometimes the writhings of chorea look a little like dancing.) Gradually, the twitches, tremors, and writhing interfere more and more with the person's walking, speech, and other voluntary movements. The ability to learn and improve new movements is especially limited (Willingham, Koroshetz, & Peterson, 1996). The disorder is associated with gradual, extensive brain damage, especially in the caudate nucleus, putamen, and globus pallidus, but also in the cerebral cortex (Tabrizi et al., 1999) (Figure 8.21).

People with Huntington's disease also suffer psychological disorders, including depression, memory impairment, anxiety, hallucinations and delusions, poor judgment, alcoholism, drug abuse, and sexual disorders ranging from complete unresponsiveness to indiscriminate promiscuity (Shoulson, 1990). In some cases, the psychological disorders develop before the motor disorders, so it is possible for someone in the early stages of Huntington's disease to be misdiagnosed as schizophrenic.

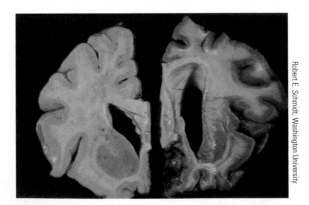

Figure 8.21 Brain of a normal person (left) and a person with Huntington's disease (right)
The angle of cut through the normal brain makes the lateral ventricle look larger in this photo than it actually is. Even so, note how much larger it is in the patient with Huntington's disease. The ventricles expand because of the loss of neurons.

Huntington's disease most often appears between the ages of 30 and 50, although onset can occur at any time from childhood to old age. Once the symptoms emerge, both the psychological and the motor symptoms grow progressively worse and culminate in death. The earlier the onset, the more rapid the deterioration. At this point, no treatment is effective at either controlling the symptoms or slowing the course of the disease. However, mouse research suggests that a stimulating environment can delay the onset of symptoms (van Dellen, Blakemore, Deacon, York, & Hannan, 2000).

Heredity and Presymptomatic Testing

Huntington's disease is controlled by an autosomal dominant gene. As a rule, a mutant gene that causes the loss of a function is recessive. The fact that the Huntington's gene is dominant implies that it produces the gain of some undesirable function.

Imagine that at the age of 20 you learn that your mother or father has Huntington's disease. In addition to your grief about your parent, you know that you have a 50% chance of getting the disease yourself. You worry about it, and your uncertainty about your own health may make it difficult to decide whether to have children and perhaps even what career to choose. Would you want to know in advance whether or not you were going to get the disease?

Investigators worked for many years to discover an accurate presymptomatic test to identify who would or would not develop the disease later. In the 1980s, researchers established that the gene for Huntington's disease is on chromosome number 4, and in 1993, they identified the gene itself (Huntington's Disease Collaborative Research Group, 1993). Now an examination of the chromosomes reveals with almost perfect accuracy who will or will not get Huntington's disease. Not everyone who is at high risk for the disease wants to take the test, but many do.

The critical area of the gene includes a sequence of bases CAG (cytosine, adenine, guanine), repeated 11 to 24 times in most people, sometimes a few more. The result is a string of 11 to 24 glutamines in the resulting protein. People with Huntington's disease have a longer string of CAG sequences. People with 36–38 repeats may or may not get the disease and are likely to be old before they show symptoms. Those with 39–41 repeats are likely to get the disease eventually, but might reach age 75 or older without it. Those with 42 or more repeats are almost certain to get the disease, and the more repetitions they have, the earlier the probable onset, as shown in Figure 8.22 (Brinkman, Mezei, Theilmann, Almqvist, & Hayden, 1997). In

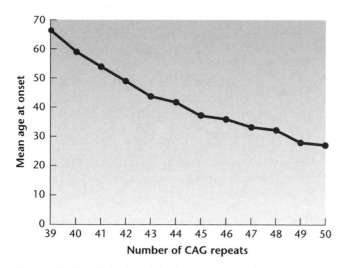

Figure 8.22 Relationship between CAG repeats and age of onset of Huntington's disease
Examining of someone's chromosomes can reveal the number of CAG repeats in the gene for the huntingtin protein. The greater the number of CAG repeats, the earlier the probable onset. People with 36–38 repeats may also get the disease, but they may not get it or may get it only in old age. The ages presented here are, of course, means. For a given individual, a prediction can be made only as an approximation. *Source: Based on data of Brinkmann, Mezei, Theilmann, Almqvist, & Hayden, 1997*

people with more than 50 repeats, the symptoms are likely to begin even younger, although too few such cases have been found to present reliable statistics. In short, a chromosomal examination can predict not only whether a person will get Huntington's disease but also approximately when.

Figure 8.23 shows comparable data for Huntington's disease and seven other neurological disorders. Each is related to an unusually long sequence of CAG repeats in some gene. Note that in each case, the greater the number of CAG repeats, the earlier the probable onset of the disease (Gusella & MacDonald, 2000). Those with a smaller number will be older when they get the disease, and with the right environment (whatever that means), they might not get it at all. You will recall a similar fact about Parkinson's disease: A gene has been identified for early-onset Parkinson's disease, but the late-onset condition is less predictable and appears to depend on environmental factors more than genes. As we shall see in later chapters, genetic factors are clearly important for early-onset Alzheimer's disease, alcoholism, depression, and schizophrenia. For people with later onset, the role of genetics is less certain in each case. In short, the results suggest a consistent pattern: For almost any disorder, the earlier the onset, the greater the probability of a strong genetic influence.

Identification of the gene for Huntington's disease led to the discovery of the protein for which it codes, which has been designated **huntingtin.** Huntingtin occurs throughout the human body, although the mutant form produces no known harm outside the brain. Within the brain, the protein is found inside neurons and not on their membranes. It binds to several other proteins, so an abnormal form of huntingtin interferes with several metabolic pathways (Li, Cheng, Li, & Li, 1999). One of those proteins is necessary for gene expression, so when huntingtin attaches to it, the cell cannot function properly (Nucifora et al., 2001). Even if the cell itself does not die, it fails to release the neurotrophin BDNF, which it ordinarily releases along with its neurotransmitter (Zuccato et al., 2001). Recall from Chapter 5 that neurons undergo apoptosis if they do not receive adequate amounts of neurotrophins from incoming axons. That is, a neuron containing the defective form of huntingtin impairs the survival of other neurons, even if it does not die itself.

Identifying the abnormal huntingtin protein and its cellular functions has enabled investigators to find drugs that reduce the harm, at least in laboratory animals (Steffan et al., 2001). Now for the first time, there is realistic hope of developing drugs that help patients with Huntington's disease.

For the latest information, check the Web site of the Huntington's Disease Society of America: www.hdsa.org

Stop & Check

6. What is a presymptomatic test?
7. What procedure enables physicians to predict who will or will not get Huntington's disease and to estimate the age of onset?

Check your answers on page 257.

Check your answers on page 257.

MODULE 8.3

In Closing: Heredity and Environment in Movement Disorders

Parkinson's disease and Huntington's disease show that genes influence behavior in different ways. Someone who examines the chromosomes can predict almost certainly who will and who will not develop

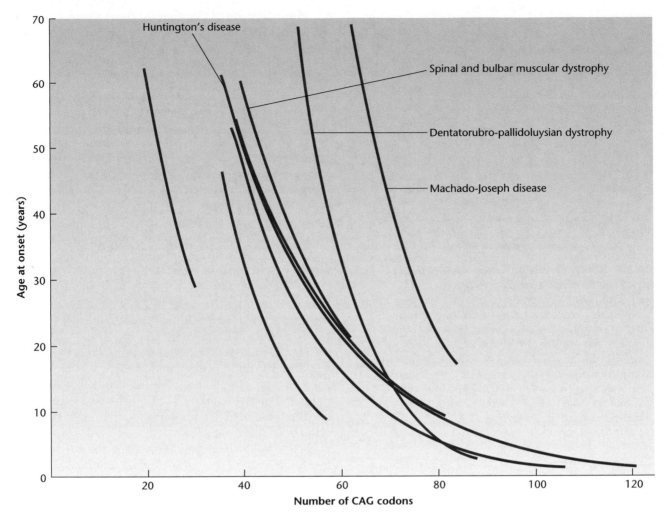

Figure 8.23 Relationship between CAG repeats and age of onset of eight diseases
The x-axis shows the number of CAG repeats; the y-axis shows the mean age at onset of disease. The various lines represent Huntington's disease and seven others. The four unlabeled lines are for four different types of spinocerebellar ataxia. The key point is that for each disease, the greater the number of repeats, the earlier the probable onset of symptoms. *Source: From "Molecular genetics: Unmasking polyglutamine triggers in neurodegenerative disease," by J. F. Gusella and M. E. MacDonald, Fig 1, p. 111 in Neuroscience, 1. 109–115. Reprinted with permission.*

Huntington's disease and with moderate accuracy predict when. A gene has also been identified for early-onset Parkinson's disease, but for the late-onset version, genetic factors play a smaller role, and researchers are looking for environmental influences. In later chapters, especially Chapter 15, we shall discuss other instances in which genes increase the risk of certain disorders, but we will not encounter anything with such a strong heritability as Huntington's disease.

SUMMARY

1. Parkinson's disease is characterized by impaired initiation of activity, slow and inaccurate movements, tremor, rigidity, depression, and cognitive deficits. It is associated with the degeneration of dopamine-containing axons from the substantia nigra to the caudate nucleus and putamen. (p. 249)

2. Early-onset Parkinson's disease has a strong hereditary basis, and the responsible gene has been identified. However, heredity plays only a small role in the ordinary form of Parkinson's disease, with onset after age 50. (p. 249)

3. The chemical MPTP selectively damages neurons in the substantia nigra and leads to the symptoms of Parkinson's disease. Some cases of Parkinson's disease may result in part from exposure to toxins. (p. 251)

4. The most common treatment for Parkinson's disease is L-dopa, which crosses the blood-brain barrier and enters neurons that convert it into

dopamine. However, the effectiveness of L-dopa varies from one patient to another and is sometimes disappointing; it also produces unwelcome side effects. Many other treatments are in use or at least in the experimental stage, including transplant of fetal neurons into the damaged brain. (p. 252)

5. Huntington's disease is a hereditary condition marked by deterioration of motor control as well as depression, memory impairment, and other cognitive disorders. Age of onset is usually between 30 and 50. (p. 254)

6. By examining one gene on chromosome 4, physicians can determine whether someone is likely to develop Huntington's disease later in life. The more CAG repeats in the gene, the earlier the likely onset of symptoms. (p. 254)

7. The gene responsible for Huntington's disease alters the structure of a protein, known as huntingtin, which affects many aspects of neural functioning, although much remains unknown about this protein. (p. 255)

4. L-dopa is ineffective for some people and has only limited benefits for most others. It does not stop the loss of neurons. For people with severe Parkinson's disease, L-dopa produces fewer benefits and more severe side effects. (p. 253)

5. Other possible treatments include antioxidants, drugs that directly stimulate dopamine receptors, drugs that block glutamate, neurotrophins, drugs that decrease apoptosis, high-frequency electrical stimulation of the globus pallidus, and transplants of neurons from a fetus. (p. 253)

6. A presymptomatic test is given to people who do not yet show symptoms of a condition to predict who will eventually develop it. (p. 255)

7. Physicians can examine human chromosome 4. In one identified gene, they can count the number of consecutive repeats of the combination CAG. If the number is fewer than 36, the person will not develop Huntington's disease. If the number is 36 or more, the larger the number, the more certain the person is to develop the disease and the earlier the age of onset. (p. 255)

ANSWERS TO *STOP AND CHECK* QUESTIONS

1. Monozygotic twins resemble each other more than dizygotic twins do for early-onset Parkinson's disease but not for late-onset. The conclusion is that early-onset Parkinson's disease is highly heritable and late-onset is not. (p. 252)

2. Exposure to MPTP can induce symptoms of Parkinson's disease. Cigarette smoking is correlated with decreased prevalence of the disease. (p. 252)

3. L-dopa enters the brain, where neurons convert it to dopamine, thus increasing the supply of a depleted neurotransmitter. (p. 253)

THOUGHT QUESTIONS

1. Haloperidol is a drug that blocks dopamine synapses. What effect would it be likely to have in someone suffering from Parkinson's disease?

2. Neurologists assert that if people lived long enough, sooner or later everyone would develop Parkinson's disease. Why?

Key Terms and Activities

TERMS

aerobic (p. 231)

anaerobic (p. 231)

antagonistic muscles (p. 228)

Babinski reflex (p. 233)

ballistic movement (p. 234)

basal ganglia (caudate nucleus, putamen, globus pallidus) (p. 245)

cardiac muscle (p. 228)

central pattern generator (p. 234)

cerebellar cortex (p. 244)

dorsolateral tract (p. 239)

extensor (p. 228)

fast-twitch fiber (p. 230)

flexor (p. 228)

Golgi tendon organ (p. 232)

grasp reflex (p. 233)

huntingtin (p. 255)

Huntington's disease (p. 254)

L-dopa (p. 252)

motor program (p. 234)

MPTP, MPP$^+$ (p. 251)

muscle spindle (p. 232)

myasthenia gravis (p. 229)

neuromuscular junction (p. 228)

nuclei of the cerebellum (p. 244)

obsessive-compulsive disorder (p. 246)

parallel fibers (p. 244)

Parkinson's disease (p. 249)

positron-emission tomography (PET) (p. 247)

posterior parietal cortex (p. 239)

prefrontal cortex (p. 239)

premotor cortex (p. 239)

presymptomatic test (p. 254)

primary motor cortex (p. 237)

proprioceptor (p. 231)

Purkinje cell (p. 244)

red nucleus (p. 239)

reflex (p. 232)

rooting reflex (p. 233)

skeletal muscle (or striated muscle) (p. 228)

slow-twitch fiber (p. 230)

smooth muscle (p. 228)

stem cell (p. 253)

stretch reflex (p. 231)

supplementary motor cortex (p. 239)

ventromedial tract (p. 240)

vestibular nucleus (p. 240)

SUGGESTIONS FOR FURTHER READING

Cole, J. (1995). *Pride and a daily marathon.* Cambridge, MA: MIT Press. Biography of a man who lost his sense of touch and proprioception from the neck down and eventually learned to control his movements strictly by vision.

Klawans, H. L. (1996). *Why Michael couldn't hit.* New York: Freeman. A collection of fascinating sports examples related to the brain and its disorders.

Lashley, K. S. (1951). The problem of serial order in behavior. In L. A. Jeffress (Ed.), *Cerebral mechanisms in behavior* (pp. 112–136). New York: Wiley. One of the truly classic articles in psychology; thought-provoking appraisal of what a theory of movement should explain.

For more information about Parkinson's disease, contact the American Parkinson Disease Association, 1250 Hylan Blvd., Suite 4B, Staten Island, NY 10305.

For more information about Huntington's disease, contact the Huntington's Disease Society of America, 140 West 22nd St., Sixth Floor, New York, NY 10011–2420.

WEB SITES TO EXPLORE

You can go to the Biological Psychology Study Center and click these links. While there, you can also check for suggested articles available on InfoTrac College Edition.

- The Biological Psychology Internet address is:
http://psychology.wadsworth.com/ kalatbiopsych8e/

Myasthenia gravis links
http://pages.prodigy.net/stanley.way/myasthenia/

Muscle Spindle and Stretch Reflexes, by J. McGarrick
www.umds.ac.uk/physiology/mcal/spinmain.html

World Parkinson Disease Association
www.wpda.org/

Huntington's Disease Society of America
www.hdsa.org

 ## CD-ROM: EXPLORING BIOLOGICAL PSYCHOLOGY

Major Motor Areas (animation)

The Withdrawal Reflex (animation)

The Crossed Extensor Reflex (animation)

The Brain Pacemaker (video)

Critical Thinking (essay questions)

Chapter Quiz (multiple choice questions)

Wakefulness and Sleep

Main Ideas

1. Wakefulness and sleep alternate on a cycle of approximately 24 hours. The brain generates this cycle.
2. Sleep progresses through various stages, which differ in brain activity, heart rate, and other aspects. A special type of sleep, known as paradoxical or REM sleep, is light in some ways and deep in others.
3. Areas in the brainstem and forebrain control arousal and sleep. Localized brain damage can produce prolonged sleep or wakefulness.
4. People have many reasons for failing to sleep well enough to feel rested the following day.
5. Sleep and REM sleep in particular serve important functions, although much about their functions remains uncertain.

Every multicellular animal that we know about has daily rhythms of wakefulness and sleep, and if we are deprived of sleep, we suffer. But if life evolved on another planet with completely different conditions, could animals evolve life without a need for sleep? Imagine a planet that doesn't rotate on its axis. Some animals evolve adaptations to live in the light area, others in the dark area, and still others in the twilight zone separating light from dark. There would be no need for any animal to alternate active periods with inactive periods on any fixed schedule, and perhaps there would be no need at all for prolonged inactive periods. If you were the astronaut who discovered these nonsleeping animals, you might be surprised.

Now imagine the astronauts from the planet where sleep is unknown set out on their first voyage and happen to land on Earth. Imagine *their* surprise to discover animals like ourselves with long inactive periods resembling death. To someone who hadn't seen sleep before, it would seem strange and mysterious indeed. For the purposes of this chapter, let us adopt their perspective and ask why animals as active as we are spend one third of our lives doing so little.

Opposite:
Rock hyraxes at a national park in Kenya.
Source: ©Norbert Wu

MODULE 9.1

Rhythms of Waking and Sleeping

You are, I suspect, not particularly surprised to learn that your body spontaneously generates its own rhythm of wakefulness and sleep. Psychologists of an earlier era, however, considered that idea revolutionary. Many of the behaviorists who dominated experimental psychology from about the 1920s through the 1950s believed that any change in an animal's behavior could be traced to some change in stimulation. For example, alternation between wakefulness and sleep must depend on something in the outside world, such as the cycle of sunrise and sunset or temperature fluctuations. But the research of Curt Richter (1922) and others implied that the body generates its own cycles of activity and inactivity. Gradually, the evidence became stronger that animals generate approximately 24-hour cycles of wakefulness and sleep even in an environment that was as constant as anyone could make it. The idea of self-generated wakefulness and sleep was an important step toward viewing animals as active producers of behaviors.

ENDOGENOUS CYCLES

An animal that produced its behavior entirely in response to current stimuli would be at a serious disadvantage; in many cases, an animal has to prepare for changes in sunlight and temperature before they occur. For example, most migratory birds start on their way toward their winter homes while the weather in their summer homes is still fairly warm. A bird that waited for the first frost would be in serious trouble. Similarly, squirrels begin storing nuts and putting on extra layers of fat in preparation for winter long before food becomes scarce. Animals that mate during only one season of the year change extensively in both their anatomy and their behavior as the reproductive season approaches.

Animals' readiness for a change in seasons comes partly from internal mechanisms. For example, a migratory bird has several cues that tell it when to fly south for the winter, but after it reaches the tropics, it has no external cues to tell it when to fly north in the spring. (In the tropics, the temperature doesn't change much from one time of year to another, and neither does the length

of day or night.) Nevertheless, it flies north at the right time. Even if it is kept in a cage with no cues to the season, it still becomes more active in the spring, and if it is released, it flies north (Gwinner, 1986). Evidently, a mechanism somewhere in the bird's body generates a rhythm, an internal calendar, that prepares the bird for seasonal changes. We refer to that rhythm as an **endogenous circannual rhythm.** (*Endogenous* means "generated from within." *Circannual* comes from the Latin words *circum,* for "about," and *annum,* for "year.")

Similarly, animals ranging from insects to humans produce **endogenous circadian rhythms,** which last about a day. (*Circadian* comes from *circum,* for "about," and *dies,* for "day.") Our most familiar endogenous circadian rhythm controls wakefulness and sleepiness. If you go without sleep all night—as most college students do, sooner or later—you feel sleepier and sleepier as the night goes on, until early morning. But as morning arrives, you actually begin to feel less sleepy. Evidently, your urge to sleep depends largely on the time of day, not just on how recently you have slept.

Figure 9.1 represents the activity of a flying squirrel kept in total darkness for 25 days. Each horizontal line represents one 24-hour day. A thickening in the line represents a period of activity by the animal. Even in this unchanging environment, the animal generates a regular rhythm of activity and sleep. The self-generated cycle may be slightly shorter than 24 hours, as in Figure 9.1, or slightly longer depending on whether the environment is constantly light or constantly dark and on whether the species is normally active in the light or in the dark (Carpenter & Grossberg, 1984). The cycle may also vary from one individual to another, even in the same environment. Nevertheless, the rhythm is highly consistent for a given individual in a given environment, even though the environment provides no clues to time.

Mammals, including humans, have circadian rhythms in their waking and sleeping, frequency of eating and drinking, body temperature, secretion of certain hormones, volume of urination, sensitivity to certain drugs, and many other variables. For example, although we ordinarily think of human body temperature as 37°C, normal temperature fluctuates over the course of a day from a low of about 36.7°C in the mid-

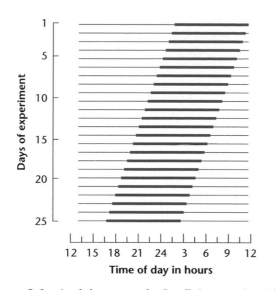

Figure 9.1 Activity record of a flying squirrel kept in constant darkness
The thick segments indicate periods of activity as measured by a running wheel. Note that the free-running activity cycle lasts slightly less than 24 hours. *Source: From "Phase Control of Activity in a Rodent," by P. J. DeCoursey, Cold Spring Harbor Symposia on Quantitive Biology, 1960, 25: 49–55. Reprinted by permission of Cold Spring Harbor Laboratory and P. J. DeCoursey.*

dle of one's sleep to about 37.2°C in late afternoon or early evening (Figure 9.2). Ordinarily, all of these cycles stay in synchrony with one another, suggesting that they depend on a single master clock.

Duration of the Human Circadian Rhythm

It might seem simple to determine the duration of the human circadian rhythm: Put people in an environment with no cues to time and determine what waking–sleeping schedule they follow. But should we make that environment constantly bright, constantly dark, or what? The duration of the rhythm depends on the amount of light (Campbell, 2000). Under constant bright lights, people have trouble sleeping, they complain about the experiment, and their rhythms run faster than 24 hours. In constant darkness, they have trouble waking up, again they complain about the experiment, and their rhythms run slow. In several studies people were allowed to turn on bright lights whenever they chose to be awake and turn them off when they wanted to sleep. Under these conditions, most people followed a cycle closer to 25 than to 24 hours a day. The problem, which experimenters did not realize for years, was that bright light late in the day lengthens the circadian rhythm.

A different way to run the experiment is to provide light and darkness on a cycle that people cannot follow. Researchers had already known that most people can adjust to a 23- or 25-hour day, but not to a 22- or 28-hour day (Folkard, Hume, Minors, Waterhouse, & Watson, 1985; Kleitman, 1963). So later researchers kept 24 healthy adults for a month in rooms with an artificial 28-hour day. None of them could in fact synchronize to that schedule; they all therefore produced their own self-generated rhythms of alertness and body temperature. Those rhythms were all about the same from one person to another, with a mean of 24.2 hours (Czeisler et al., 1999).

MECHANISMS OF THE BIOLOGICAL CLOCK

What kind of biological clock within our body generates our circadian rhythm? Richter (1967) introduced the concept that the brain generates its own rhythms—that is, a biological clock—and he reported that the biological clock is insensitive to most forms of interference. Blind or deaf animals generate nearly normal circadian rhythms, although they slowly drift out of phase with the external world. The circadian rhythm is surprisingly steady despite food or water deprivation, x-rays, tranquilizers, alcohol, anesthesia, lack of oxygen, most kinds of brain damage, or the removal of hormonal organs. Even an hour or so of induced hibernation often fails to reset the biological clock (Gibbs, 1983; Richter, 1975). Evidently, the biological clock is a hardy, robust mechanism.

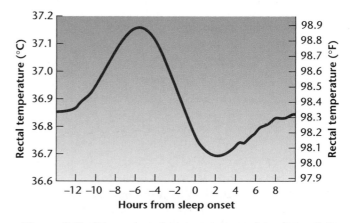

Figure 9.2 Mean rectal temperatures for nine adults
Body temperature reaches its daily low about 2 hours after sleep onset; it reaches its peak about 6 hours before sleep onset. *Source: From: "Sleep-Onset Insomniacs Have Delayed Temperature Rhythms," by M. Morris, L. Lack, and D. Dawson, Sleep, 1990, 13: 1–14. Reprinted by permission.*

The Suprachiasmatic Nucleus (SCN)

The surest way to disrupt the biological clock is to damage an area of the hypothalamus called the **suprachiasmatic** (soo-pruh-kie-as-MAT-ik) **nucleus (SCN).** It gets its name from its location just above the optic chiasm (Figure 9.3). The SCN exerts the main control over the circadian rhythms for sleep and temperature (Refinetti & Menaker, 1992). After damage to the SCN, the body's rhythms are less consistent and no longer synchronized to environmental patterns of light and dark.

The SCN generates circadian rhythms itself in a genetically controlled, unlearned manner. If SCN neurons are disconnected from the rest of the brain or removed from the body and maintained in tissue culture, they continue to produce a circadian rhythm of action potentials (Earnest, Liang, Ratcliff, & Cassone, 1999; Inouye & Kawamura, 1979). Even a single isolated SCN cell can maintain a moderately steady circadian rhythm, although it becomes less steady than a group of cells together (Herzog, Takahashi, & Block, 1998).

One group of experimenters discovered that some hamsters bear a mutant gene that causes them to pro-

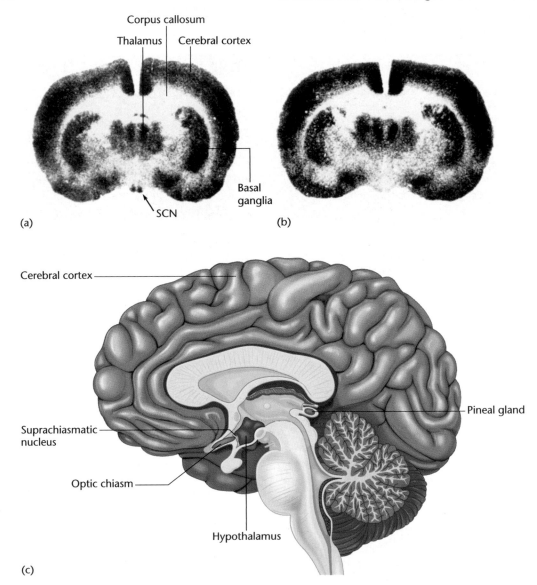

Figure 9.3 The suprachiasmatic nucleus (SCN) of rats and humans
The SCN is located at the base of the brain, just above the optic chiasm. The optic chiasm was torn off when the brain was sliced to make the slides shown in **(a)** and **(b),** which show coronal sections through the plane of the anterior hypothalamus. Each rat was injected with radioactive 2-deoxyglucose, which is absorbed by the most active neurons. A high level of absorption of this chemical produces a dark appearance on the slide. Note that the level of activity in SCN neurons is much higher in section **(a),** in which the rat was injected during the day, than in section **(b),** in which the rat received the injection at night. *Source: W. J. Schwartz & Gainer, 1977* **(c)** A sagittal section through a human brain shows the SCN and the pineal gland.

duce a 20-hour instead of 24-hour rhythm (Ralph & Menaker, 1988). They surgically removed the SCN from adult hamsters and then transplanted SCN tissue from hamster fetuses into the adults. When they transplanted SCN tissue from fetuses with a 20-hour rhythm, the recipients produced a 20-hour rhythm. When they transplanted tissue from fetuses with a 24-hour rhythm, the recipients produced a 24-hour rhythm (Ralph, Foster, Davis, & Menaker, 1990). That is, the rhythm followed the pace of the donors, not the recipients, so again the results show that the rhythms come from the SCN itself.

The Biochemistry of the Circadian Rhythm

What mechanism produces the circadian rhythm? The research began with insects, where the genetic basis was easier to explore because of the faster reproduction. Studies on the fruit fly *Drosophila* discovered genes that interact with the proteins they produce and generate a circadian rhythm (Sehgal, Ousley, Yang, Chen, & Schotland, 1999). Two genes, known as *period* (abbreviated *per*) and *timeless* (*tim*), produce the proteins per and tim that are present in only small amounts early in the morning. They increase throughout the day. By evening, they reach a high level that makes the fly sleepy; that high level also feeds back to the genes to shut them down. During the night, the genes no longer produce these proteins, and their concentration declines until the next morning, when the cycle begins anew. When per and tim levels are high, they interact with a protein called clock to induce sleepiness. When they are low, the result is wakefulness. Furthermore, a pulse of light during the night inactivates the tim protein, so extra light during the evening decreases sleepiness and resets the biological clock. Figure 9.4 summarizes this feedback mechanism.

Why do we care what goes on in flies? The answer is that after researchers knew how the system works in flies, they found that mammals have practically the same genes and proteins, which influence their circadian rhythms (Reick, Garcia, Dudley, & McKnight, 2001; Zheng et al., 1999). The mechanisms are not identical across species, however. For example, light directly alters the tim protein in flies (Shearman et al., 2000), but in mammals, a pulse of light acts by altering input to the SCN, which then alters its release of tim (Crosio, Cermakian, Allis, & Sassone-Corsi, 2000).

Understanding these mechanisms helps make sense of some unusual sleep disorders. Mice with damage to their *clock* gene sleep less than normal (Naylor et al., 2000), and presumably, some cases of decreased sleep in humans might have the same cause. In addition, some people with a mutation in what is apparently their *per* gene have an oddity in their circadian rhythm: They consistently fall asleep and wake up hours ahead of a normal schedule (Toh et al., 2001). Apparently, their altered gene causes their biological clock to run slightly faster than 24 hours, instead of slightly slower as it does in most people (C. R. Jones et al., 1999). Most people find that when they are on vacation with no obligations to meet, they go to bed later than usual and awaken the next morning later than usual. People with the altered *per* gene go to bed even earlier than usual on vacation and awaken even earlier than usual the next morning!

Melatonin

The SCN regulates waking and sleeping by controlling activity levels in other brain areas, including the **pineal gland** (PIN-ee-al, see Figure 9.3), an endocrine gland located just posterior to the thalamus (Aston-Jones, Chen, Zhu, & Oshinsky, 2001; von Gall et al., 2002). The pineal gland releases melatonin, a hormone that increases sleepiness. The human pineal gland secretes melatonin mostly at night, making us sleepy at that time. When people shift to a new time zone and start following a new schedule, they continue to feel sleepy at their old times until the melatonin rhythm shifts (Dijk & Cajochen, 1997). People who have pineal gland tumors or any other impairment of melatonin secretion experience great difficulty falling asleep, sometimes staying awake for days at a time (Haimov & Lavie, 1996).

Melatonin secretion usually starts to increase about 2 or 3 hours before bedtime. Taking a melatonin pill in the evening has little effect on sleepiness because the pineal gland produces melatonin at that time anyway. However, people who take melatonin at other times become sleepy within 2 hours (Haimov & Lavie, 1996). Therefore, some people take melatonin pills when they travel to a new time zone or start a new work schedule and need to sleep at an unaccustomed time.

Melatonin also feeds back to reset the biological clock through its effects on receptors in the SCN (Gillette & McArthur, 1996). A moderate dose of melatonin (0.5 mg) in the afternoon phase-advances the clock; that is, it makes the person get sleepy earlier in the evening and wake up earlier the next morning. A single dose of melatonin in the morning has little effect (Wirz-Justice, Werth, Renz, M üller, & Kräuchi, 2002), although repeated morning doses can phase-delay the clock, causing the person to get sleepy later than usual at night and awaken later the next morning.

Taking melatonin has become something of a fad. Its effect on sleep is well-established, although many

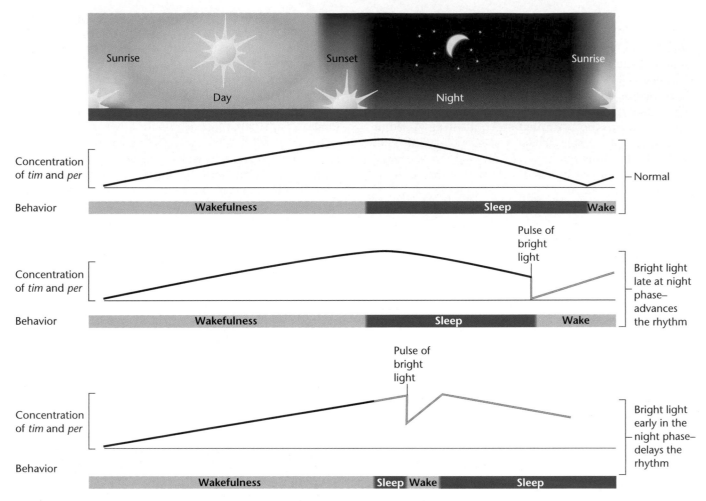

Figure 9.4 Feedback between proteins and genes to control sleepiness
In fruit flies *(Drosophila)*, the tim and per proteins accumulate during the day. When they reach a high level, they induce sleepiness and shut off the genes that produce them. When their levels decline sufficiently, wakefulness returns and so does the gene activity. A pulse of light during the night breaks down the tim protein, thus increasing wakefulness and resetting the circadian rhythm.

people who take melatonin have no sleep problem. Melatonin is an antioxidant, so it has some health benefits (Reiter, 2000). Low pill doses (up to 0.3 mg/day) produce blood levels similar to those that occur naturally and therefore seem unlikely to do any harm. Larger doses seldom produce immediately obvious side effects. However, melatonin increases the movement impairments in rats with symptoms resembling Parkinson's disease (Willis & Armstrong, 1999). Long-term use also impairs animals' reproductive fertility and, if taken during pregnancy, harms the development of the fetus (Arendt, 1997; Weaver, 1997). The long-term effects on humans are not known. Furthermore, no government body regulates the production of melatonin, so the purity varies. Thus the cautious advice therefore is, as with any other medication, don't take it unless you need it.

1. For a migratory bird, what is the advantage of having an endogenous circannual rhythm instead of relying on environmental cues to identify the season?

2. What evidence indicates that humans have an internal biological clock?

3. What evidence indicates that the SCN produces the circadian rhythm itself?

4. How do the proteins tim and per relate to sleepiness in *Drosophila*?

Check your answers on page 269–270.

SETTING AND RESETTING THE BIOLOGICAL CLOCK

Our circadian rhythms have a period close to 24 hours, but they are hardly perfect. We have to readjust our internal workings daily to stay in phase with the outside world. On weekends, when most of us are freer to set our own schedules, we expose ourselves to lights, noises, and activity at night and then awaken late the next morning. By Monday morning, when the electric clock indicates 7 A.M., the biological clock within us says about 5 A.M., and we stagger off to work or school without much pep (Moore-Ede, Czeisler, & Richardson, 1983).

Although circadian rhythms persist in the absence of light, light is critical for periodically resetting them. Consider this analogy: I used to have a windup wristwatch that lost about 2 minutes per day, which would accumulate to an hour per month if I didn't reset it. It had a **free-running rhythm** of 24 hours and 2 minutes—that is, a rhythm that occurs when no stimuli reset or alter it. The circadian rhythm is similar to that wristwatch. The stimulus that resets the circadian rhythm is referred to by the German term **zeitgeber** (TSITE-gay-ber), meaning "time-giver." Light is the dominant zeitgeber for land animals (Rusak & Zucker, 1979). (The tides are important for many marine animals.) But light is not our only zeitgeber; others include exercise (Eastman, Hoese, Youngstedt, & Liu, 1995), noises, meals, and the temperature of the environment (Refinetti, 2000). Even keeping an animal awake for a few hours in the middle of the night by gentle handling can shift the circadian rhythm (Antle & Mistlberger, 2000). Consequently, if you have moved to a new time zone or shifted to a new work schedule and you want to stay awake and alert longer than usual, expose yourself to bright lights, loud noises, and exercise in the evening. But avoid them if you want to get to sleep at your normal time.

What do you suppose would happen if we had no signal to reset our circadian rhythms? Although blind people do not have light to set their rhythms, many can set them by noise, activity, temperature, and so forth. However, many others are not sufficiently sensitive to these secondary zeitgebers. They produce spontaneous circadian rhythms of wakefulness and sleep that run a little longer than 24 hours. When those cycles are in phase with their work schedule, all is well, but when they drift out of phase, the result is insomnia at night and sleepiness during the day (Sack & Lewy, 2001).

One study examined hamsters living under constant light. In some of them, the SCN of the left hemisphere got out of phase with the one in the right hemisphere, and the result was two periods of wakefulness and two periods of sleep every 24 hours (de la Iglesia, Meyer, Carpino, & Schwartz, 2000). (Speculatively, think about all the newborn babies who have short, irregular sleep and wakeful periods throughout the day. Having lived in constant darkness until birth, might they have left and right SCNs out of phase with each other?)

Jet Lag

A disruption of circadian rhythms due to crossing time zones is known as **jet lag.** Travelers complain of sleepiness during the day, sleeplessness at night, depression, and impaired concentration. All these problems stem from the mismatch between internal circadian clock and external time (Haimov & Arendt, 1999). Most of us find it easier to adjust to crossing time zones going west than east. Going west, we expose ourselves to bright lights and activity at night, and then we stay awake late and awaken the next morning already partly adjusted to the new schedule. That is, we *phase-delay* our circadian rhythms. Going east, we have to go to sleep earlier and awaken earlier; we *phase-advance* (Figure 9.5).

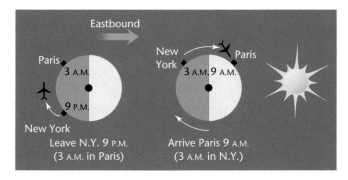

Figure 9.5   Jet lag
Eastern time is later than western time. People who travel six time zones east must wake up when their west-set biological clocks say it is the middle of the night and will try to sleep when their biological clocks indicate late afternoon.

Adjusting to jet lag is stressful, sometimes very stressful. Stress elevates blood levels of the adrenal hormone cortisol, and many studies have shown that prolonged elevations of cortisol can lead to a loss of neurons in the hippocampus, a brain area important for memory. One study examined female flight attendants who had spent the previous 5 years making flights across seven or more time zones, with mostly short breaks (fewer than 6 days) between trips. On the average, they showed smaller than average volumes of the hippocampus and surrounding structures, and they showed some memory impairments (Cho, 2001). These results suggest a danger from repeated adjustments of the circadian rhythm, although the problem here could be air travel itself.

Some people recommend specific diets or vitamin supplements to combat jet lag. These recommendations have not been scientifically tested, however, and their effectiveness is unknown. The best advice is the same as the advice for sleeping anywhere, anytime: Keep the lights bright while you are trying to stay awake and keep the room dark and quiet when you are trying to sleep. If you want to sleep at night, do not nap during the day. If you cannot adjust to the new schedule quickly enough, you might try a melatonin pill for a couple of days 2 or 3 hours before bedtime (Haimov & Arendt, 1999). However, as cautioned before, no one knows about possible long-term effects from frequent use of melatonin.

Shift Work

People who have to sleep irregularly—such as pilots and truck drivers, medical interns, and shift workers in certain factories—find that their duration of sleep depends on what time they go to sleep. When they have to go to sleep in the morning or early afternoon, they sleep only briefly, even though they have been awake for 16 hours or more (Frese & Harwich, 1984; Winfree, 1983).

People who work on a night shift, such as midnight to 8 A.M., sleep during the day. At least, they try to. Even after months or years on such a schedule, many workers adjust incompletely. They continue to feel groggy on the job, they do not sleep soundly during the day, and their body temperature continues to peak when they are trying to sleep during the day instead of while they are working at night. In general, night-shift workers have more accidents than day workers.

Working at night does not reliably shift the circadian rhythm because bright light resets the rhythm more effectively than activity does. Ordinary indoor lighting, around 150–180 lux, as found in most nighttime work settings, is only moderately effective in resetting the rhythm (Boivin, Duffy, Kronauer, & Czeisler, 1996). People adjust best to night work if they sleep in a very dark room during the day and work under very bright lights at night, comparable to the noonday sun (Czeisler et al., 1990).

How Light Resets the SCN

The SCN is located just above the optic chiasm. (Figure 9.3c shows the position in the human brain; the relationship is similar in other mammals.) A small branch

of the optic nerve, known as the *retinohypothalamic path*, extends directly from the retina to the SCN. Axons of that path alter the SCN's settings.

The input to that path, however, does not come from normal retinal receptors. Mice with genetic defects that destroy nearly all their rods and cones nevertheless reset their biological clocks in synchrony with the light (Freedman et al., 1999; Lucas et al., 1999). Or consider blind mole rats (Figure 9.6). Their eyes are covered with folds of skin and fur; they have neither eye muscles nor a lens with which to focus an image. They have fewer than 900 optic nerve axons, as compared with 100,000 in hamsters. Even a bright flash of light evokes no startle response and no measurable change in brain activity. Nevertheless, light resets their circadian rhythms (de Jong, Hendriks, Sanyal, & Nevo, 1990).

The surprising explanation is that the retinohypothalamic path to the SCN comes from a special population of retinal ganglion cells that have their own photopigment, different from the ones found in rods and cones (Hannibal, Hindersson, Knudsen, Georg, & Fahrenkrug, 2001; Lucas, Douglas, & Foster, 2001). These special ganglion cells respond directly to light without any input from rods or cones (Berson, Dunn, & Takao, 2002). The ganglion cells that reset the circadian rhythm are located mainly near the nose, not evenly throughout the retina (Visser, Beersma, & Daan, 1999). They respond to light very slowly and turn off very slowly when the light ceases (Berson et al., 2002). Therefore, they respond to the overall average amount of light, not to instantaneous changes in light. The average intensity over a period of minutes or hours is, of course, exactly the information the SCN needs to gauge the

Figure 9.6 A blind mole rat
Although blind mole rats indeed cannot see, they reset their circadian rhythms in response to light.

time of day. Because the ganglion cells do not contribute to vision, they do not need to respond to momentary changes in light.

5. What stimulus is the most effective zeitgeber for humans?

6. How does light reset the biological clock?

Check your answers on page 270.

MODULE 9.1

In Closing: Sleep-Wake Cycles

Unlike an electrical appliance that stays on until someone turns it off, the brain periodically turns itself on and off. Sleepiness is definitely not a voluntary or optional act. People who try to work when they are sleepy are prone to errors and injuries. Someone who sleeps well may not be altogether healthy or happy, but one who consistently fails to get enough sleep is almost certainly headed for troubles.

SUMMARY

1. Animals, including humans, have internally generated rhythms of activity, lasting about 24 hours. Animals that hibernate or migrate also have internally generated rhythms lasting about a year. (p. 262)

2. The suprachiasmatic nucleus (SCN), a part of the hypothalamus, generates the body's circadian rhythms for sleep and temperature. (p. 264)

3. The genes controlling the circadian rhythm are almost the same in mammals as in insects. Across species, certain proteins increase in abundance during the day and then decrease during the night. (p. 265)

4. The SCN controls the body's rhythm partly by directing the release of melatonin by the pineal gland. The hormone melatonin increases sleepiness; if given at certain times of the day, it can also reset the circadian rhythm. (p. 265)

5. Although the biological clock can continue to operate in constant light or constant darkness, the onset of light resets the clock. The biological clock can reset to match an external rhythm of light and darkness slightly different from 24 hours, but if the discrepancy exceeds about 2 hours, the biological clock generates its own rhythm instead of resetting. (pp. 263, 267)

6. It is easier for people to follow a cycle longer than 24 hours (as when traveling west) than to follow a cycle shorter than 24 hours (as when traveling east). (p. 267)

7. If people wish to work at night and sleep during the day, the best way to shift the circadian rhythm is to have bright lights at night and darkness during the day. (p. 268)

8. Light resets the biological clock partly by a branch of the optic nerve that extends to the SCN. Those axons originate from a special population of ganglion cells that respond directly to light rather than relaying information from rods and cones synapsing onto them. (p. 268)

ANSWERS TO *STOP AND CHECK* QUESTIONS

1. A bird that has migrated to the tropics for the winter will have no cue to identify spring. (The temperature and length of day versus night are invariable through the year.) It therefore needs an endogenous mechanism to identify spring. (p. 266)

2. People who have lived in an environment with a light–dark schedule much different from 24 hours fail to follow that schedule and instead become wakeful and sleepy on about a 24-hour basis. (p. 266)

3. SCN cells produce a circadian rhythm of activity even if they are kept in cell culture isolated from the rest of the body. (p. 266)

4. The proteins tim and per accumulate during the wakeful period. When they reach a high enough level, they trigger sleepiness and turn off the genes that produced them. Therefore, their levels decline until they reach a low enough level for wakefulness to begin anew. (p. 266)

5. Light is the most effective zeitgeber for humans and other land animals. (p. 269)

6. A branch of the optic nerve, the retinohypothalamic path, conveys information about light to the SCN. The axons comprising that path originate from special ganglion cells that respond to light by themselves without needing input from rods or cones. (p. 269)

THOUGHT QUESTIONS

1. Is it possible for the onset of light to reset the circadian rhythms of a blind person? Explain.

2. Why would evolution have enabled blind mole rats to synchronize their SCN activity to light, even though they cannot see well enough to make any use of the light?

3. If you travel across several time zones to the east and want to use melatonin to help reset your circadian rhythm, at what time of day should you take it? What if you travel west?

MODULE 9.2

Stages of Sleep and Brain Mechanisms

Suppose I buy a new radio. After I play it for 4 hours, it suddenly stops. To explain why, I try to discover whether the batteries are dead or whether the radio needs repair. Suppose I later discover that the radio always stops after playing for 4 hours and that it will operate again a few hours later even without repairs or a battery change. I begin to suspect that the manufacturer designed it this way on purpose, perhaps to prevent me from wearing it out too fast or to prevent me from listening to the radio all day. I might then try to find the device that turns it off whenever I play it for 4 hours. Notice that I am now asking a new question. When I thought that the radio stopped because it needed repairs or new batteries, I had not thought to ask which device turned it off. I asked that question only when I thought of stopping the radio as an active process.

Similarly, if we think of sleep as a passive cessation of activity, similar to catching one's breath after running a race, we do not ask which part of the brain is responsible for sleep. But if we think of sleep as a specialized state evolved to serve particular functions, we look for the devices that regulate it.

THE STAGES OF SLEEP

Most advances in scientific research result from improvements in our ability to measure something, and sleep research is no exception. In fact, researchers never even suspected that sleep had separate stages until they accidentally discovered them while measuring brain waves during sleep.

The **electroencephalograph (EEG)**, as described in Methods 9.1, records a gross average of the electrical potentials of the cells and fibers in the brain areas closest to each electrode attached to the scalp (Figures 9.7 and 9.8). That is, if half of the cells in some area increase their electrical potentials while the other half decrease, the EEG recording is flat. The EEG record rises or falls when cells fire in synchrony—doing the same thing at the same time. You might compare it to a record of the noise in a crowded football stadium: It shows only slight fluctuations until some event gets everyone yelling at once. The EEG provides an objective way for brain researchers to determine whether people are awake

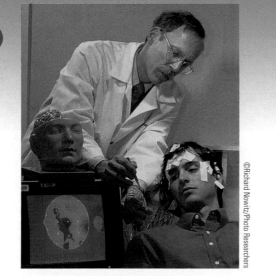

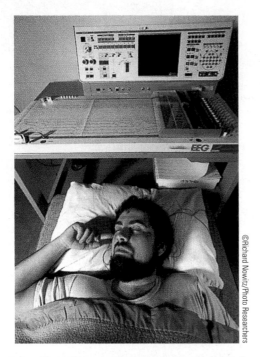

Figure 9.8 Sleeping person with electrodes in place on the scalp for recording brain activity
The printout above his head shows the readings from each electrode.

©Richard Nowitz/Photo Researchers

or asleep and to compare brain activity at different times of night.

Figure 9.9 shows the EEG and eye movements of a male college student during the various stages of sleep. Figure 9.9a begins with a period of relaxed wakefulness for comparison. Note the steady series of **alpha waves** at a frequency of 8 to 12 per second. Alpha waves are characteristic of the relaxed state, not of all wakefulness.

In Figure 9.9b, the young man has just fallen asleep. During this period, called stage 1 sleep, the EEG is dominated by irregular, jagged, low-voltage waves. Overall brain activity is still fairly high, but it is declining. As Figure 9.9c shows, the most prominent characteristics of stage 2 are sleep spindles and K-complexes. A **sleep spindle** consists of 12- to 14-Hz waves during a burst that lasts at least half a second. Sleep spindles result from oscillating interactions between cells in the thalamus and the cortex. A **K-complex** is a sharp high-amplitude negative wave followed by a smaller, slower positive wave. Sudden stimuli can evoke K-complexes during other stages of sleep (Bastien & Campbell, 1992), but they are most common in stage 2.

In each succeeding stage of sleep, heart rate, breathing rate, and brain activity are slower than in the previous stage, and the percentage of slow, large-amplitude waves increases (Figures 9.9d and e). By stage 4, more than half the record includes large waves of at least a half-second duration. Stages 3 and 4 are known together as **slow-wave sleep** (SWS).

Slow waves indicate that neuronal activity is highly synchronized. In stage 1 and wakefulness, the cortex receives almost constant stimuli, which activate different neurons at different times. Thus, the EEG is full of short, rapid, choppy waves. By stage 4, although the sense organs are as responsive as ever, the thalamus stops relaying sensory information to the cortex, unless the stimulation is intense or highly relevant, such as the sound of a baby's cry is to its parents (Coenen, 1995). With sensory input to the cortex mostly silenced, the few remaining inputs synchronize many cells. As an analogy, imagine the stimulation of the waking brain as thousands of rocks dropped

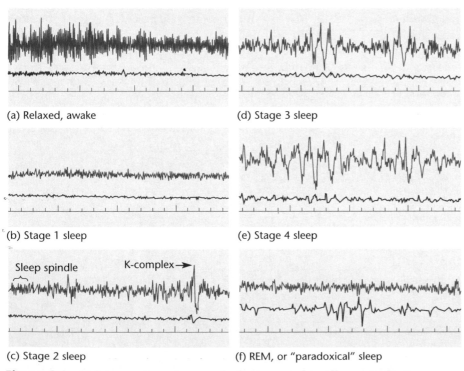

(a) Relaxed, awake

(b) Stage 1 sleep

Sleep spindle   K-complex →

(c) Stage 2 sleep

(d) Stage 3 sleep

(e) Stage 4 sleep

(f) REM, or "paradoxical" sleep

Figure 9.9 Polysomnograph records from a male college student
A polysomnograph includes records of EEG, eye movements, and sometimes other data, such as muscle tension or head movements. For each of these records, the top line is the EEG from one electrode on the scalp; the middle line is a record of eye movements; and the bottom line is a time marker, indicating 1-second units. Note the abundance of slow waves in stages 3 and 4. *Source: Records provided by T. E. LeVere*

into a pond over the course of a minute: The resulting waves are choppy but small because they largely cancel one another out. By contrast, the result of just one rock dropping is fewer but larger waves, such as those in stage 4 sleep.

After stage 4, the person cycles back through stages 3 and 2. But then instead of stage 1, the person enters a new stage, known as *rapid eye movement (REM)* sleep, which has special characteristics.

1. What do long, slow waves on an EEG indicate?

Check your answer on page 283.

PARADOXICAL OR REM SLEEP

A person who has just fallen asleep enters stage 1 sleep. Later in the night people may or may not return to stage 1; usually, they enter a related but very special stage, which two sets of researchers discovered accidentally in the 1950s.

In France, Michel Jouvet was trying to test the learning abilities of cats after complete removal of the cerebral cortex. To cope with the fact that decorticate mammals hardly move at all, Jouvet recorded slight movements of the muscles and EEGs from the hindbrain. During periods of apparent sleep, the cats had high levels of brain activity, but their neck muscles were completely relaxed. Jouvet named this phenomenon **paradoxical sleep** because it is in some ways the deepest sleep and in other ways the lightest. (*Paradoxical* means "apparently self-contradictory.")

Meanwhile, in the United States, Nathaniel Kleitman and Eugene Aserinsky were observing eye movements of sleeping people as a means of measuring depth of sleep, assuming simply that eye movements would decrease during sleep. At first, they recorded only a few minutes of eye movements per hour, partly because the recording paper was expensive and partly because they did not expect to see anything interesting in the middle of the night anyway. When they occasionally found periods of eye movements in people who had been asleep for hours, the investigators assumed that something was wrong with their machines. Only after repeated careful measurements did they conclude that periods of rapid eye movements do exist during sleep (Dement, 1990). They called these periods **rapid eye movement (REM) sleep**

(Aserinsky & Kleitman, 1955; Dement & Kleitman, 1957a) and soon concluded that REM sleep was synonymous with what Jouvet called *paradoxical sleep.* Researchers use the term REM sleep when referring to humans; most prefer the term *paradoxical sleep* for nonhumans because many species lack comparable eye movements.

During paradoxical or REM sleep, the EEG shows irregular, low-voltage fast waves, which suggest a considerable amount of brain activity; in this regard, REM sleep is light. However, during REM sleep, the postural muscles of the body, such as those that support the head, are more relaxed than in any other stage; in this regard, REM sleep is deep. This stage is also associated with erections in males and vaginal moistening in females. Heart rate, blood pressure, and breathing rate are more variable in REM than in stages 2 through 4. In short, REM sleep combines deep sleep, light sleep, and features that are difficult to classify as deep or light. Consequently, it is best to avoid using the terms *deep* and *light* sleep.

In addition to its steady characteristics, REM sleep has certain intermittent characteristics, including facial twitches and the characteristic back-and-forth movements of the eyes. Figure 9.9f provides an example of the **polysomnograph,** a combination of EEG and eye-movement records, for a period of REM sleep. The EEG record is similar to that for stage 1 sleep, but notice how different the eye-movement records are. The stages other than REM are known as **non-REM (NREM) sleep**.

A person who falls asleep enters stage 1 and slowly progresses through stages 2, 3, and 4 in order, although loud noises or other intrusions can cause a reversal of stages or even an awakening. About 60 to 90 minutes after going to sleep, the person gradually begins to cycle back from stage 4 through stages 3 and 2 and then enters a period of REM sleep. The sequence repeats, with each complete cycle lasting about 90 minutes. Early in the night, stages 3 and 4 predominate. Toward morning, the duration of stage 4 grows shorter and the duration of REM sleep grows longer. Figure 9.10 shows typical sequences.

Initially after the discovery of REM, researchers believed it was closely linked with dreaming. William Dement and Nathaniel Kleitman (1957b) awakened adult volunteers during various stages of sleep and found that people awakened during REM sleep reported dreams 80% to 90% of the time. Later researchers, however, found that people awakened during NREM sleep also sometimes reported dreams and usually reported at least some kind of thought process. REM dreams are more likely than NREM dreams to include striking visual imagery and complicated plots, but not always. Some brain-damaged people continue

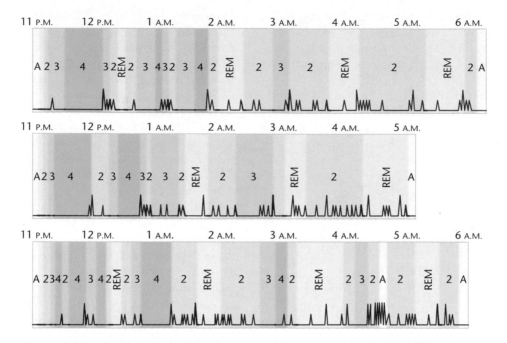

Figure 9.10 Sequence of sleep stages on three representative nights
Columns indicate awake (A) and sleep stages 2, 3, 4, and REM. Deflections in the line at the bottom of each chart indicate shifts in body position. Note that stage 4 sleep occurs mostly in the early part of the night's sleep, whereas REM sleep becomes more prevalent toward the end. *Source: Based on Dement & Kleitman, 1957a*

to have REM sleep but do not report any dreams, and other people continue to report dreams despite no evidence of REM sleep (Solms, 1997). In short, REM tends to intensify dreams, but it is hardly synonymous with dreaming.

Stop & Check

2. How can an investigator determine whether a sleeper is in REM sleep?
3. During which part of a night's sleep is REM most common?

Check your answers on page 283.

BRAIN MECHANISMS OF WAKEFULNESS AND AROUSAL

Recall from Chapter 1 Chalmers's distinction between the "easy" and "hard" problems of consciousness. What he meant by the easy problems were such matters as, "Which brain areas increase overall alertness, and by what kinds of transmitters do they do so?" As you are about to see, that question may be philosophically easy, but it is scientifically complex.

Arousal

After a cut through the midbrain separates the forebrain and part of the midbrain from all the lower structures, an animal enters a prolonged state of sleep, as confirmed by the EEG, for the next week or so, and even after much recovery, the animal shows only brief periods of wakefulness. The explanation might seem simple: The cut isolated the brain from the sensory stimuli that come up from the medulla and spinal cord. However, when a researcher cuts each of the individual tracts that enter the medulla and spinal cord, thus depriving the brain of almost all sensory input, the animal continues to have normal periods of wakefulness and sleep. Evidently, cutting through the midbrain is more disruptive to wakefulness than is cutting all the sensory tracts.

A cut through the midbrain decreases arousal by damaging the reticular formation, a structure that extends from the medulla into the forebrain. The reticular formation contains some neurons with axons ascending into the brain and some with axons descending into the spinal cord. In Chapter 8, we encountered the neurons with descending axons. In 1949, Giuseppe Moruzzi and H. W. Magoun proposed that the reticular formation neurons with ascending axons are well suited to regulate arousal. The term *reticular* (based on the Latin word *rete,* meaning "net") describes the widespread, apparently haphazard connections among neurons in this system, although in fact they are more organized and have more specific functions than researchers once supposed (G. B. Young & Pigott, 1999). One part of the reticular formation that contributes to cortical arousal is the pontomesencephalon (Woolf, 1996). (The term derives from *pons* and *mesencephalon,* or "midbrain.") These neurons receive input from many sensory systems and generate spontaneous activity of their own. They send their axons to the thalamus and basal forebrain, as shown in Figure 9.11, releasing acetylcholine and glutamate and producing excitatory effects at synapses. Those areas of the thalamus and basal forebrain relay arousal to widespread areas of the cortex. In the process, the pontomesencephalon maintains cortical arousal during wakefulness and increases it in response to new or challenging tasks (Kinomura, Larsson, Gulyás, & Roland, 1996). Stimulation of the pontomesencephalon awakens a sleeping individual or increases alertness in someone already awake, shifting the EEG from long, slow waves to short waves at frequencies above 30 Hz (Munk, Roelfsema, König, Engel, & Singer, 1996). However, subsystems within the pontomesencephalon control different sensory modalities, so a stimulus sometimes arouses the visual or auditory areas independently of the others (Guillery, Feig, & Lozsádi, 1998).

However, today neither psychologists nor neuroscientists regard arousal as a single unitary process (Robbins & Everitt, 1995). Waking up, directing attention to a stimulus, storing a memory, and increasing goal-directed effort are different kinds of attention that rely on somewhat distinct brain systems, as shown in Figure 9.11. For instance, the locus coeruleus (LOW-kus ser-ROO-lee-us, literally, "dark blue place"), a small structure in the pons, is inactive at most times, but emits bursts of impulses, releasing norepinephrine, in response to meaningful events. The locus coeruleus is the only major source of norepinephrine axons to the cortex, but its axons spread widely, so this tiny area has a huge influence. Stimulation to the locus coeruleus strengthens the storage of recent memories (Clayton & Williams, 2000).

Many cells in another area, the basal forebrain (the area just anterior and dorsal to the hypothalamus) (Figure 9.12), provide axons to widespread areas of the thalamus and cerebral cortex. Most of these axons release acetylcholine as their transmitter, producing synaptic excitation and behavioral arousal (Mesulam, 1995; Szymusiak, 1995). A smaller population of basal forebrain cells has axons that release GABA, with inhibitory effects on both synapses and behavioral arousal. Damage to the basal forebrain leads to a net decrease in arousal, impaired learning and attention, and increased time spent in non-REM sleep. Because the basal forebrain is heavily damaged in Alzheimer's disease (Chapter 13), these patients have impairments of attention and memory.

The hypothalamus also has separate populations of cells with excitatory and inhibitory effects. In Figure 9.11, note that a couple of paths from the hypothalamus stimulate arousal by releasing histamine as their neurotransmitter (Lin et al., 1996). Antihistamine drugs, often used for allergies, produce drowsiness if they cross the blood-brain barrier.

Getting to Sleep

Sleep requires decreased arousal, and one important step is to decrease the temperature of the brain and the rest of the body's core. (Curiously, a fever also increases sleepiness, but we usually sleep at night when our brains are cooler than during the day.) One of the best predictors of how fast someone will get to sleep is the amount of blood flow to the hands and feet (Kräuchi, Cajochen, Werth, & Wirz-Justice, 1999). People who shift much of their blood flow to the periphery (and therefore *warm* their hands and feet) expose more blood to the environment, which is presumably cooler than the inside of the body, and therefore, they start to *cool* the core of the body. Cooling the body leads to sleep.

A second step is to decrease stimulation (Vellutti, 1997). Obviously, people who want to sleep find a quiet place, close their eyes, and in other ways decrease stimulation, although repetitive vestibular sensation, such as a gentle rocking motion, often helps people (especially babies) get to sleep.

Another important step is to inhibit the arousal systems. One important inhibitor is adenosine (ah-DENN-o-seen). During metabolic activity, adenosine monophosphate (AMP) breaks down into adenosine; thus, when the brain is awake and active, adenosine accumulates. In most of the brain, adenosine has little effect, but the basal forebrain cells responsible for wakeful arousal (see Figure 9.11) have adenosine receptors that inhibit them by releasing a second messenger within the cell. These second messengers increase the activity of certain genes, leading to a long-lasting effect that sustains sleep for hours (Basheer, Rainnie, Porkka-Heiskanen, Ramesh,

& McCarley, 2001). When people go without sleep for a few days, the accumulating adenosine produces sleepiness that may persist for days—a phenomenon known as "sleep debt."

Caffeine, a drug found in coffee, tea, and many soft drinks, increases arousal by blocking adenosine receptors (Rainnie, Grunze, McCarley, & Greene, 1994). It also constricts the blood vessels in the brain, thereby decreasing its blood supply. (Abstention from caffeine after repeated use can increase blood flow to the brain enough to cause a headache.) The message: Just as you might use caffeine to try to

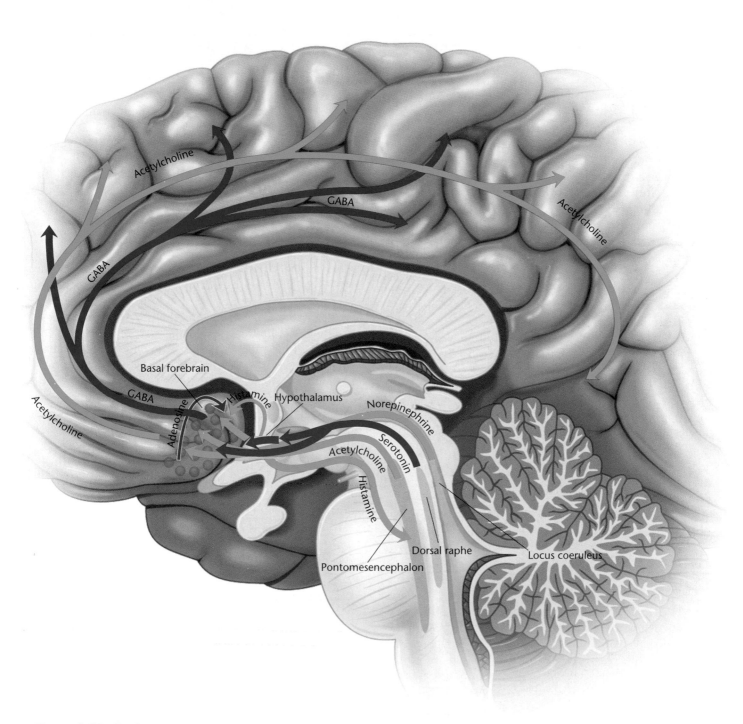

Figure 9.11 Brain mechanisms of sleeping and waking
Green arrows indicate excitatory connections; red arrows indicate inhibitory connections. Neurotransmitters are indicated where they are known. Although adenosine is shown as a small arrow, it is a metabolic product that builds up in the area, not something released by axons. *Source: Based on Lin, Hou, Sakai, & Jouvet, 1996; Robbins & Everitt, 1995; Szymusiak, 1995*

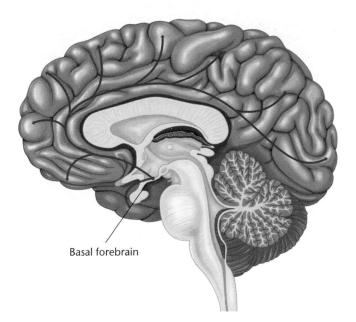

Figure 9.12 Basal forebrain
The basal forebrain is the source of many excitatory axons (releasing acetylcholine) and inhibitory axons (releasing GABA) that regulate arousal of the cerebral cortex.

keep yourself awake, you might try decreasing your caffeine intake if you have trouble sleeping.

Prostaglandins, which also promote sleep, are chemicals present in much of the body; the immune system increases their concentration in response to infection. Like adenosine, prostaglandins build up during the day until they provoke sleep, and they decline during sleep (Ram et al., 1997). They stimulate a cluster of neurons that inhibit the hypothalamic cells that increase arousal (Scamell et al., 1998).

Getting to sleep is partly a matter of decreasing activity in arousal areas but also partly a matter of in-creasing activity in axons that release GABA, an inhibitory transmitter (Gallopin et al., 2000; Szymusiak, 1995) (see Figure 9.11). A lesion to the GABA-releasing cells of the hypothalamus or basal forebrain results in prolonged wakefulness, as do drugs that inhibit GABA. An increase in hypothalamic GABA release produces sleep, and drugs that yield an even greater release produce anesthesia (L. E. Nelson et al., 2002).

These sleep-related cells get much of their input from the anterior and preoptic areas of the hypothalamus (Sherin, Shiromani, McCarley, & Saper, 1996)—areas that are also important for temperature regulation, as we shall see in Chapter 10. One of the effects of fever is sleepiness, and the reason is that during a fever, the preoptic and anterior hypothalamus increase their output to the sleep-related cells.

Table 9.1 summarizes the effects of some key brain areas on arousal and sleep.

Stop & Check

4. Examine Figure 9.11. Would damage to the dorsal raphe system increase or decrease sleep?
5. Why do most antihistamines make people drowsy?
6. How does caffeine increase arousal?
7. Why do people feel sleepy when they get sick? Give two reasons.

Check your answers on page 283.

TABLE 9.1 Brain Structures for Arousal and Sleep

Structure	Neurotransmitter(s) It Releases	Effects on Behavior
Pontomesencephalon	Acetylcholine, glutamate	Increases cortical arousal
Locus coeruleus	Norepinephrine	Increases information storage during wakefulness; suppresses REM sleep
Basal forebrain Most cells	Acetylcholine	Excites thalamus and cortex; increases learning, attention; shifts sleep from NREM to REM
Other cells	GABA	Inhibits thalamus and cortex
Hypothalamus (parts)	Histamine	Increases arousal
Dorsal raphe and pons	Serotonin	Interrupts REM sleep

BRAIN FUNCTION IN REM SLEEP

It might seem simple to use PET scans to determine which human brain areas increase their activity during REM sleep. But PET scans require an injection of a radioactive chemical. How are you going to give sleepers an injection without awakening them? Further, a PET scan yields a clear image only if the head remains motionless during data collection. If the person tosses or turns even slightly, the image is worthless.

To overcome these difficulties, researchers in two studies persuaded some young people to sleep with their heads firmly attached to masks that did not permit any movement. They also inserted a cannula (plastic tube) into each person's left arm so that they could inject radioactive chemicals at various times during the night. So imagine yourself in that setup. You have a cannula in your arm and your head is locked into position. Now try to sleep.

Because the researchers foresaw that it might be difficult to sleep under these conditions (!), they had the men go without sleep the entire night before. Someone who is tired enough can sleep even under trying circumstances. (Maybe.)

Now that you appreciate the heroic nature of the procedures, here are the results. During REM sleep, activity increased in the pons and the limbic system (which is important for emotional responses). Activity decreased in the primary visual cortex, the motor cortex, and the dorsolateral prefrontal cortex but increased in parts of the parietal and temporal cortex (Braun et al., 1998; Maquet et al., 1996). In the next module, we consider what these results imply about dreaming, but for now, note that activity in the pons triggers the onset of REM sleep.

REM sleep is associated with a distinctive pattern of high-amplitude electrical potentials known as **PGO waves,** for pons-geniculate-occipital (Figure 9.13). Waves of neural activity are detected first in the pons, shortly afterward in the lateral geniculate nucleus of the thalamus, and then in the occipital cortex (D. C. Brooks & Bizzi,

1963; Laurent, Cespuglio, & Jouvet, 1974). Each animal maintains a nearly constant amount of PGO waves per day. During a prolonged period of REM deprivation, PGO waves begin to emerge during sleep stages 2 to 4—when they do not normally occur—and even during wakefulness, often in association with strange behaviors, as if the animal were hallucinating. At the end of the deprivation period, when an animal is permitted to sleep without interruption, the REM periods have an unusually high density of PGO waves.

Besides originating the PGO waves, cells in the pons contribute to REM sleep by sending messages to the spinal cord, inhibiting the motor neurons that control the body's large muscles. After damage to the floor of the pons, a cat still has REM sleep periods, but its muscles are not relaxed. During REM, it walks (though awkwardly), behaves as if it were chasing an imagined prey, jumps as if startled, and so forth (Morrison, Sanford, Ball, Mann, & Ross, 1995) (Figure 9.14). Is the cat acting out dreams? We do not know; the cat cannot tell us. Evidently, one function of the messages from the pons to the spinal cord is to prevent action during REM sleep.

REM sleep apparently depends on a relationship between the neurotransmitters serotonin and acetylcholine. Injections of the drug *carbachol,* which stimulates acetylcholine synapses, quickly move a sleeper into REM sleep (Baghdoyan, Spotts, & Snyder, 1993). Note that acetylcholine is important for both wakefulness and REM sleep, two states that activate most of the brain. Serotonin, however, interrupts or shortens

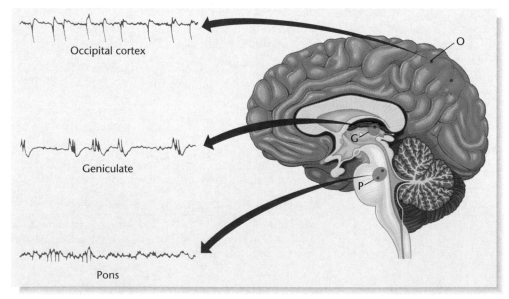

Figure 9.13 PGO waves
PGO waves start in the pons (P) and then show up in the lateral geniculate (G) and the occipital cortex (O). Each PGO wave is synchronized with an eye movement in REM sleep.

Figure 9.14 A cat with a lesion in the pons, wobbling about during REM sleep
Cells of an intact pons send inhibitory messages to the spinal cord neurons that control the large muscles.

Morrison, Sanford, Ball, Mann, & Ross, 1995

REM sleep (Boutrel, Franc, Hen, Hamon, & Adrien, 1999). So does norepinephrine from the locus coeruleus; bursts of activity in the locus coeruleus block REM sleep (Singh & Mallick, 1996).

ABNORMALITIES OF SLEEP

People who work long or irregular hours are especially likely to have sleep problems; so are people with psychiatric problems such as depression, schizophrenia, and substance abuse (Benca, Obermeyer, Thisted, & Gillin, 1992). But a great many otherwise healthy people also have at least occasional sleepless nights. Unsatisfactory sleep is a major cause of accidents on the job, comparable to the effects of drugs and alcohol.

Insomnia

How much sleep is enough? Some people get along fine with 6 hours of sleep per night. For others, 8 hours may not be enough, especially if they awaken repeatedly during the night. The best gauge of insomnia is whether the person feels well rested the following day. Anyone who consistently feels tired during the day is not sleeping enough at night.

Insomnia can have many causes, including excessive noise, worries and stress, drugs and medications, pain, uncomfortable temperatures, sleeping in an unfamiliar place, or trying to fall asleep at the wrong time in one's circadian rhythm. It can also be the result of epilepsy, Parkinson's disease, brain tumors, depression, anxiety, or other neurological or psychiatric conditions. Some children suffer insomnia because they are milk intolerant, and their parents, not realizing the intolerance, give them milk to drink right before bedtime (Horne, 1992). A friend of mine suffered insomnia for months until he realized that he dreaded going to sleep because he hated jogging as soon as he woke up in the morning. He switched his jogging time to late afternoon and no longer had any trouble sleeping. In short, before choosing a method of combating insomnia, try to identify the reasons for your sleep troubles.

It is convenient to distinguish three categories of insomnia: onset insomnia, maintenance insomnia, and termination insomnia. People with **onset insomnia** have trouble falling asleep. Those with **maintenance insomnia** awaken frequently during the night. And those with **termination insomnia** wake up too early and cannot get back to sleep. It is possible to have more than one of the three types.

Certain cases of insomnia are related to abnormalities of biological rhythms (MacFarlane, Cleghorn, & Brown, 1985a, 1985b). Ordinarily, people fall asleep while their temperature is declining and awaken while it is rising, as in Figure 9.15a. Some people's body temperature rhythm is *phase delayed,* as in Figure 9.15b. If they try to fall asleep at the normal time, their body temperature is higher than normal for going to sleep. These people are likely to experience onset insomnia (Morris et al., 1990). Other people's body temperature rhythm is *phase advanced,* as in Figure 9.15c. They are likely to suffer termination insomnia. Irregular fluctuations of circadian rhythms can cause maintenance insomnia.

REM sleep occurs mostly during the rising phase of the temperature cycle. For most people, this is the second half of the night's sleep. For people with termination insomnia or anyone else who falls asleep after the temperature cycle has hit bottom, REM sleep may start soon after sleep begins (Czeisler, Weitzman,

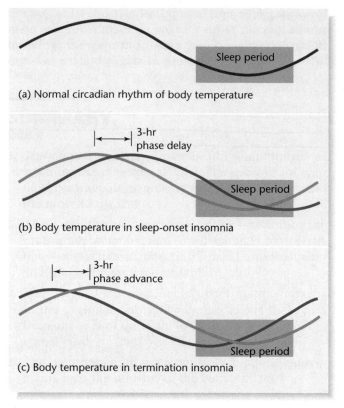

Figure 9.15 Insomnia and circadian rhythms
A delay in the circadian rhythm of body temperature is associated with onset insomnia; an advance is associated with termination insomnia.

(a) Normal circadian rhythm of body temperature

3-hr phase delay

Sleep period

(b) Body temperature in sleep-onset insomnia

3-hr phase advance

Sleep period

(c) Body temperature in termination insomnia

Moore-Ede, Zimmerman, & Knauer, 1980). Because depression is often associated with termination insomnia, most depressed people enter REM sleep earlier in the night than nondepressed people do (see Chapter 15).

Another cause of insomnia is, paradoxically, the use of tranquilizers as sleeping pills. Most sleeping pills operate partly by blocking the activity of norepinephrine, histamine, or other neurotransmitters that increase arousal. Although tranquilizers may help a person fall asleep, taking such drugs a few times may cause dependence on them. Without the pills, the person goes into a withdrawal state that prevents sleep (Kales, Scharf, & Kales, 1978) and may react by taking the sleeping pills again, setting up a cycle from which it is difficult to escape. Much the same problem arises when people use alcohol to try to get to sleep.

Some tranquilizers are long-lasting; others are short-acting. Either kind poses problems. A long-lasting tranquilizer may not wear off by the next morning, leaving the person sleepy during the day. A short-acting tranquilizer may wear off during the night, causing the person to awaken early. In short, frequent use of tranquilizing sleeping pills can relieve one sleep problem while leading to another.

Sleep Apnea

One special cause of insomnia is **sleep apnea,** the inability to breathe while sleeping. Many people breathe irregularly during REM sleep, and most people beyond age 45 have occasional periods of at least 9 seconds without breathing (Culebras, 1996). However, some people go a minute or more without breathing and then awaken, gasping for breath. Some do not remember awakening during the night, although they certainly notice the consequences: sleepiness during the day, impaired attention, depression, and sometimes heart problems. When sleep apnea occurs in infancy, it is one of the possible causes of sudden infant death syndrome, or "crib death." A family that is worried about sleep apnea can use devices that monitor someone's sleep and breathing and alert others when a problem occurs (White, Gibb, Wall, & Westbrook, 1995). Childhood sleep apnea is almost always caused by an obstruction of the breathing passages, which can be widened by removing the tonsils or adenoids.

Obesity is one of several possible causes of sleep apnea. Some obese people, especially men, have narrower than normal airways and have to compensate by breathing more frequently or more vigorously than others do. During sleep, this compensation fails, and the sleep posture narrows the airways even more than usual (Mezzanotte, Tangel, & White, 1992). In other people, especially the elderly, sleep apnea results when brain mechanisms for respiration cease functioning during sleep.

People with sleep apnea are advised to lose weight and avoid alcohol and tranquilizers (which impair the breathing muscles). Medical options include surgery to remove tissue that obstructs the trachea (the breathing passage) or a mask that covers the nose and delivers air under enough pressure to keep the breathing passages open (Figure 9.16).

Narcolepsy

Narcolepsy, a condition characterized by frequent unexpected periods of sleepiness during the day (Aldrich, 1998), strikes about 1 person in 1000. It sometimes runs in families, although no gene for narcolepsy has been identified (Dauvilliers, Neidhart, Lecendreux, Billiard, & Tafti, 2001), and many people with narcolepsy have no close relatives with the disease. Four symptoms are generally associated with narcolepsy, although many patients do not report all four:

1. Gradual or sudden attacks of extreme sleepiness during the day.
2. Occasional **cataplexy**—an attack of muscle weakness while the person remains awake. Cataplexy is often triggered by strong emotions, such as anger or

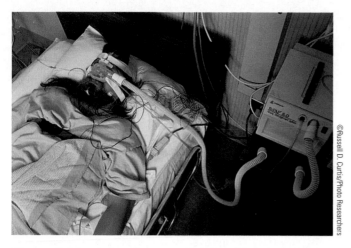

Figure 9.16 A Continuous Positive Airway Pressure (CPAP) mask
The mask fits snugly over the nose and delivers air at a fixed pressure, strong enough to keep the breathing passages open.

great excitement. (One man suddenly collapsed during his own wedding ceremony!)

3. Sleep paralysis—a complete inability to move when falling asleep or waking up. Other people may experience sleep paralysis occasionally, but people with narcolepsy experience it more frequently.

4. *Hypnagogic hallucinations*—dreamlike experiences that the person has trouble distinguishing from reality, often occurring at the onset of sleep.

Each of these symptoms can be interpreted as an intrusion of a REM-like state into wakefulness; REM sleep is associated with muscle weakness (cataplexy), paralysis, and dreams (Mahowald & Schenck, 1992). Some people with narcolepsy have occasional periods of odd behaviors, as if they were acting out a dream—frying their socks, putting business files into the refrigerator, and so forth (Guilleminault, Heinzer, Mignot, & Black, 1998).

One explanation is that narcolepsy results from overactive acetylcholine synapses (Guilleminault et al., 1998). (Recall that acetylcholine is a neurotransmitter necessary for the onset of REM sleep.) Some of those acetylcholine synapses activate the areas of the pons that ordinarily send messages to the spinal cord to suppress muscle activity during REM. Sending these messages during the day produces cataplexy, one of the symptoms of narcolepsy (J. M. Siegel et al., 1991).

Another explanation focuses on a neurotransmitter we have not mentioned until now, known as **orexin** or **hypocretin,** a peptide neurotransmitter released mainly or entirely by neurons with cell bodies in the hypothalamus. Their axons extend widely throughout the forebrain and brainstem, where they stimulate acetylcholine-releasing cells and thereby increase wakefulness and arousal (Kiyashchenko et al., 2002). Certain strains of dogs get narcolepsy, and unlike humans, the dogs' disorder has been traced to a specific gene that controls orexin receptors (Lin et al., 1999). Mice that lack orexin also show symptoms of narcolepsy (Hara, 2001). Humans with narcolepsy lack the hypothalamic cells that produce and release orexin (Thanickal et al., 2000). Why they lack these cells is not known, although one hypothesis is that they have an autoimmune disease that attacks the cells.

Theoretically, we might imagine combating narcolepsy with acetylcholine blockers or drugs that restore orexin. Perhaps someday new drugs of those types will be available. Currently, the most common treatment is stimulant drugs, such as pemoline (Cylert) or methylphenidate (Ritalin), which increase wakefulness.

Periodic Limb Movement Disorder

Another factor occasionally linked to insomnia is **periodic limb movement disorder,** a repeated involuntary movement of the legs and sometimes arms (Edinger et al., 1992). Many people, perhaps most, experience an occasional involuntary kick, especially when starting to fall asleep. Leg movements are not a problem unless they become persistent. In some people, mostly middle-aged and older, the legs kick once every 20 to 30 seconds for a period of minutes or even hours, mostly during NREM sleep. Frequent or especially vigorous leg movements may awaken the person. In some cases, tranquilizers help suppress the movements (Schenck & Mahowald, 1996).

REM Behavior Disorder

For most people, the major postural muscles are relaxed and inactive during REM sleep. However, people with **REM behavior disorder** move around vigorously during their REM periods, apparently acting out their dreams. They frequently dream about defending themselves against attack, and they may punch, kick, and leap about. Most of them injure themselves or other people and damage property (Olson, Boeve, & Silber, 2000). Their behavior is more violent and unrestrained than that of "normal" sleepwalkers.

REM behavior disorder occurs mostly in older people, especially older men with brain diseases such as Parkinson's disease (Olson et al., 2000). Presumably, the damage includes the cells in the pons that send messages to inhibit the spinal neurons that control large muscle movements.

Night Terrors, Sleep Talking, and Sleepwalking

<u>Night terrors</u> are experiences of intense anxiety from which a person awakens screaming in terror. A night terror should be distinguished from a nightmare, which is simply an unpleasant dream. Night terrors occur during NREM sleep and are far more common in children than in adults.

Sleep talking is common and harmless. Many people, probably most, talk in their sleep occasionally. Unless someone hears you talking in your sleep and later tells you about it, you could talk in your sleep for years and never realize it. Sleep talking has about the same chance of occurring during REM sleep as during non-REM sleep (Arkin, Toth, Baker, & Hastey, 1970).

Sleepwalking runs in families, occurs mostly in children, especially ages 2 to 5, and is most common early in the night, during stage 3 or stage 4 sleep. (It does not occur during REM sleep because the large muscles are completely relaxed.) The causes are not known. Sleepwalking is generally harmless both to the sleepwalker and to others. No doubt you have heard people say, "You should never waken someone who is sleepwalking." In fact, it is not harmful or dangerous to awaken a sleepwalker, although the person is likely to feel very confused (Moorcroft, 1993).

In an individual case, it is often difficult to distinguish sleepwalking from REM behavior disorder. One man pleaded "not guilty" to a charge of murder because he had been sleepwalking at the time and did not know what he was doing. The jury agreed with him, partly because he had a family history of sleepwalking. However, especially for a one-time event, it is difficult to know whether he was sleepwalking, subject to REM behavior disorder, or indeed even wide awake at the time (Broughton et al., 1994).

For more information about a variety of sleep disorders, check this Web site:

www.thesleepsite.com/

---

8. Which brain areas are activated by PGO waves?

9. Which neurotransmitter facilitates, and which one inhibits, REM sleep?

10. What is a common cause of sleep apnea in adults?

11. Narcolepsy has been linked to overactive synapses using the neurotrasmitter___ or to a deficit in the neurotransmitter___.

Check your answers on page 283.

In Closing: Stages of Sleep

In many cases, scientific progress depends on drawing useful distinctions. Chemists divide the world into different elements, biologists divide life into different species, and medical doctors distinguish one disease from another. Similarly, psychologists try to recognize the most natural or useful distinctions among types of behavior or experience. The discovery of different stages of sleep was a major landmark in psychology because researchers found a previously unrecognized distinction that is both biologically and psychologically important. It also demonstrated that external measurements—in this case, EEG recordings—can identify internal experiences. We now take it largely for granted that an electrical or magnetic recording from the brain can tell us something about a person's experience, but it is worth pausing to note what a surprising discovery that was in its time.

SUMMARY

1. Over the course of about 90 minutes, a sleeper goes through stages 1, 2, 3, and 4 and then back through stages 3 and 2 to a stage called REM, similar in most ways to stage 1. REM is characterized by rapid eye movements, much brain activity, complete relaxation of the trunk muscles, irregular breathing and heart rate, penile erection or vaginal lubrication, and a high probability of vivid dreams. (p. 271)

2. The brain has multiple systems for arousal. The pontomesencephalon, dorsal raphe, and parts of the hypothalamus control various cell clusters in the basal forebrain that send axons releasing acetylcholine throughout much of the forebrain. (p. 271)

3. The locus coeruleus is active in response to meaningful events. It facilitates attention and new learning; it also blocks the onset of REM sleep. (pp. 275, 279)

4. Sleep is facilitated by decreased core body temperature, decreased stimulation, adenosine and prostaglandins which inhibit the arousal systems of the brain, and increased activity by certain clusters of basal forebrain cells that release GABA throughout much of the forebrain. (p. 275)

5. REM sleep is associated with increased activity in a number of brain areas, including the pons, limbic system, and parts of the parietal and temporal cortex. Activity decreases in the prefrontal cortex, the motor cortex, and the primary visual cortex. (p. 278)

6. REM sleep begins with PGO waves, waves of brain activity transmitted from the pons to the lateral geniculate to the occipital lobe. (p. 278)

7. Insomnia sometimes results from a shift in phase of the circadian rhythm of temperature in relation to the circadian rhythm of sleep and wakefulness. It can also result from difficulty in breathing while asleep, overuse of tranquilizers, and numerous other causes. (p. 279)

8. People with narcolepsy grow very sleepy during the day. Narcolepsy is associated with decreased release of the peptide neurotransmitter orexin (also known as hypocretin). (p. 280)

9. Among other sleep disorders are night terrors, periodic limb movement disorder, sleepwalking, and REM behavior disorder. (p. 281)

ANSWERS TO *STOP AND CHECK* QUESTIONS

1. Long, slow waves indicate a low level of activity, with much synchrony of response among neurons. (p. 273)

2. Examine EEG pattern and eye movements. (p. 274)

3. REM becomes more common toward the end of the night's sleep. (p. 274)

4. Damage to the dorsal raphe decreases arousal and increases sleep. Note that its axons inhibit the basal forebrain cells that send inhibitory messages to the rest of the cortex. Damaging the dorsal raphe decreases that inhibition and therefore leads to greater inhibition of the rest of the cortex. (p. 277)

5. Two paths from the hypothalamus—one to the basal forebrain and one to the pontomesencephalon—use histamine as their neurotransmitter to increase arousal. Antihistamines that cross the blood-brain barrier block those synapses. (p. 277)

6. Caffeine inhibits adenosine, which builds up during wakefulness and inhibits the arousal-inducing cells of the basal forebrain. (p. 277)

7. Illness arouses the immune system, which increases the prostaglandin levels. Prostaglandins stimulate brain areas that inhibit the arousal areas. Also, because of the fever that accompanies illness, the preoptic and anterior hypothalamus increase their stimulation of the basal forebrain cells that inhibit the cortex. (p. 277)

8. The pons, the lateral geniculate nucleus of the thalamus, and the occipital cortex. (p. 282)

9. Acetylcholine facilitates REM sleep, and serotonin inhibits it. (p. 282)

10. Obesity is often associated with adult sleep apnea, especially in men. (p. 282)

11. acetylcholine; orexin (hypocretin) (p. 282)

THOUGHT QUESTION

When cats are deprived of REM sleep and then permitted uninterrupted sleep, the longer the period of deprivation—up to about 25 days—the greater the rebound of REM when they can sleep uninterrupted. However, REM deprivation for more than 25 days produces no additional rebound. Speculate on a possible explanation. (*Hint:* Consider what happens to PGO waves during REM deprivation.)

MODULE 9.3

Why Sleep? Why REM? Why Dreams?

Why do you sleep? "That's easy," you reply. "It's because I get tired." Well, yes, of course, but when you get tired, why can't you just relax and let your body do whatever repairs it has to do right then and there? Why set aside 7 or 8 hours in a row for inactivity? Does your body really need that much time to make repairs? Even on days when you sat around doing almost nothing?

THE FUNCTIONS OF SLEEP

Sleep serves two major functions: to do repairs on the body and to conserve energy during a time of relative inefficiency. The two functions are certainly not in conflict, but some researchers put far more emphasis on one than the other, so we shall consider them as separate theories.

what it Saids what it means

The Repair and Restoration Theory

According to the <u>repair and restoration theory of sleep, the main function of sleep is to enable the body, especially the brain, to repair itself after the exertions of the day.</u> For example, during sleep, the brain rebuilds proteins and replenishes its dwindling reserves of glycogen, an energy store (Kong et al., 2002). One way to examine the restorative functions is to observe the effects of sleep deprivation. People who have gone without sleep for a week or more, either as an experiment or as a publicity stunt, have reported dizziness, impaired concentration, irritability, hand tremors, and hallucinations (Dement, 1972; L. C. Johnson, 1969). A brief period of sleep deprivation enhances certain immune responses (Matsumoto et al., 2001), although longer deprivation impairs the immune system. In short, the body reacts to sleeplessness as it does to illness and stress.

Prolonged sleep deprivation in laboratory animals, mostly rats, has sometimes produced more severe consequences. A major difference is that the animals were forced to stay awake, whereas the human volunteers knew they could quit if necessary. (Stressors take a greater toll when they are unpredictable and uncontrollable.) During a few days of sleep deprivation, rats show increased body temperature, metabolic rate, and appetite, indicating that the body is working harder than usual. With still longer sleep deprivation, the immune system begins to fail, the animal loses its resistance to infection, and brain activity decreases (Everson, 1995; Rechtschaffen & Bergmann, 1995). However, even a 2-week period of sleep deprivation produces no evidence of brain damage (Cirelli, Shaw, Rechtschaffen, & Tononi, 1999).

The restorative functions of sleep are not analogous to catching your breath after running a race. If sleep were restorative in that simple sense, we should expect people to sleep significantly more after a day of great physical or mental exertion than after an uneventful day. But in fact, heavy exertion increases sleep duration only slightly (Horne & Minard, 1985; Shapiro, Bortz, Mitchell, Bartel, & Jooste, 1981). How long we sleep does not depend on our activity level during the day.

Moreover, people vary in their need for sleep. Two men were reported to average only 3 hours of sleep per night and to awaken feeling refreshed (H. S. Jones & Oswald, 1968). A 70-year-old woman was reported to average only 1 hour of sleep per night; many nights she felt no need to sleep at all (Meddis, Pearson, & Langford, 1973).

The Evolutionary Theory

According to an alternative view (Kleitman, 1963; Webb, 1974), the primary or original function of sleep is to conserve energy. In that regard, it would be analogous to hibernation. Hibernation is not a means of "resting up" from the rigors of activity during the warm months; it is merely a way of decreasing energy use during a time when food is scarce. Hibernating animals decrease their body temperature to that of the environment (but they don't let it go low enough for their blood to freeze.) Their heart rate, breathing rate, brain activity, and metabolism decrease to as low as possible, thus saving enough energy to get through the winter.

Hibernation

Here are a few curious facts about hibernation:

1. Hibernation occurs in certain small mammals such as ground squirrels and bats. Whether or not bears hibernate is a matter of definition. Bears sleep most of the winter, but they do not lower their body temperatures as much as small hibernating animals do.

2. Hamsters sometimes hibernate. If you keep your pet hamster in a cold, poorly lit place during the winter and it becomes cold and stops breathing, make sure that it is not hibernating before you bury it!

3. Hibernating animals come out of hibernation briefly every few days, raising their body temperature to about normal. However, they sleep for most of these nonhibernating hours (Barnes, 1996).

4. Hibernation retards the aging process. Hamsters that spend longer times hibernating have proportionately longer life expectancies than other hamsters (Lyman, O'Brien, Greene, & Papafrangos, 1981). Hibernation is also a period of relative invulnerability to infection and other harm. Procedures that would ordinarily damage the brain, such as inserting a needle into it, produce little if any harm during hibernation (Zhou et al., 2001).

Hibernation is a true need; a ground squirrel that is prevented from hibernating can become as disturbed as a person who is prevented from sleeping. However, the function of hibernation is not to recover from a busy summer; it is simply to conserve energy when the environment is hostile.

Similarly, according to the <u>evolutionary theory of sleep,</u> we evolved a need to sleep to force us to conserve energy when we would be relatively inefficient. During sleep, a mammal's body temperature decreases by about 1°C, enough to save a small but noticeable amount of energy. During food shortages, animals either increase their sleep time or decrease their body temperature during sleep (Berger & Phillips, 1995). The evolutionary theory does not deny that we need to sleep; it merely asserts that evolution built that need into us to compel us to conserve energy. It also does not deny that restorative functions occur during sleep, but it emphasizes that even if sleep did not serve restorative functions, we would benefit from it anyway as a means of saving energy.

The evolutionary theory predicts that species should vary in their sleep habits in accordance with how much time each day they must devote to the search for food, how safe they are from predators when they sleep, and other aspects of their way of life. In general, the data support these predictions (Allison & Cicchetti, 1976; Campbell & Tobler, 1984). Cats and bats eat nutrition-rich meals, and while asleep, they face little threat of attack; they sleep many hours per day. Herbivores (plant eaters) need to graze much of the day and need to be alert for predators even while they sleep; their sleep is briefer and easily interrupted (Figure 9.17).

The two views of why we sleep are complementary and compatible. If we need to set aside time for repair and restoration, we may as well do it at times when we are inefficient at doing anything else. And if we are going to decrease body activity to conserve energy, we may as well use that inactive time for some repair and restoration.

Stop & Check

> **1.** Some fish live in caves without light or in the deep ocean, which also has no light. What would the evolutionary theory of sleep predict about the sleep of these fish?
>
> *Check your answer on page 289.*

THE FUNCTIONS OF REM SLEEP

An average person spends about one third of his or her life asleep and about one fifth of sleep in REM, totaling about 600 hours of REM sleep per year. Presumably, REM sleep serves some biological function. But what? To approach this question, we can consider who gets more REM sleep than others and what happens after REM deprivation. Then we consider several hypotheses.

Individual and Species Differences

REM sleep is widespread in mammals and birds, indicating that the capacity for it is part of our ancient evolutionary heritage. Some species, however, have a great deal more than others; as a rule, the species with the most total sleep also have the highest percentage of REM sleep (J. M. Siegel, 1995). Cats spend up to 16 hours a day sleeping, much or most of it in REM sleep. Rabbits, guinea pigs, and sheep sleep much less and spend very little time in REM sleep.

Figure 9.18 illustrates the relationship between age and REM sleep for humans; the trend is the same

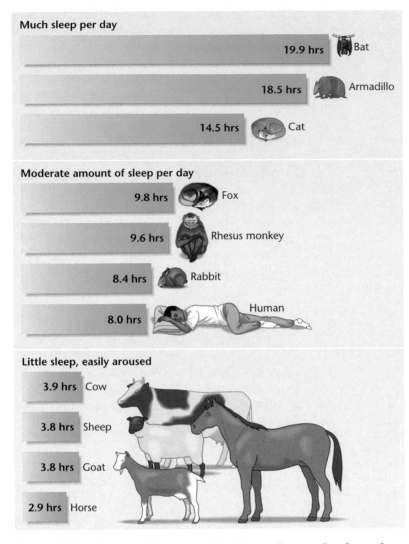

Much sleep per day

19.9 hrs — Bat
18.5 hrs — Armadillo
14.5 hrs — Cat

Moderate amount of sleep per day

9.8 hrs — Fox
9.6 hrs — Rhesus monkey
8.4 hrs — Rabbit
8.0 hrs — Human

Little sleep, easily aroused

3.9 hrs — Cow
3.8 hrs — Sheep
3.8 hrs — Goat
2.9 hrs — Horse

Figure 9.17 Hours of sleep per day for various animal species
Generally, predators and others that are safe when they sleep tend to sleep a great deal; animals in danger of being attacked while they sleep spend less time asleep. (Farm animals are, of course, not in much danger while asleep, but their ancestors were, in recent evolutionary time.)

for other mammalian species. Infants get more REM and more total sleep than adults do, confirming the pattern that more total sleep predicts a higher percentage of REM sleep. Among adult humans, those who get the most sleep per night (9 or more hours) have the highest percentage of REM sleep, and those who get the least sleep (5 or fewer hours) have the lowest percentage of REM.

[handwritten: If we get NO REM we then Fall asleep quicker and we go Right to REM Sleep Sleep]

The Effects of REM Sleep Deprivation

What would happen to someone who had almost no opportunity for REM sleep? William Dement (1960) observed the behavior of eight men who agreed to be

[handwritten: Stages 1 & 2. Go to 3 & 4 & REM]

deprived of REM sleep for 4 to 7 consecutive nights. During that period, they slept only in a laboratory. Whenever the EEG and eye movements indicated that a given subject was entering REM sleep, an experimenter promptly awakened him and kept him awake for several minutes. The subject was then permitted to go back to sleep until he started REM sleep again.

Over the course of the 4 to 7 nights, the experimenters found that they had to awaken the subjects more and more frequently. On the first night, an average subject had to be awakened 12 times. By the final night, this figure had increased to 26 times. That is, the subjects had increased their attempts at REM sleep.

During the deprivation period, most subjects reported mild, temporary personality changes, including irritability, increased anxiety, and impaired concentration. Five of the eight experienced increased appetite and weight gain. Control studies found that a similar number of awakenings not linked to REM sleep did not produce similar effects. The disturbances were therefore due to REM deprivation, not just to the total number of awakenings.

After the deprivation period, seven subjects continued to sleep in the laboratory. During their first uninterrupted night, five of the seven spent more time than usual in REM sleep: 29% of the night, as compared with 19% before the deprivation. One subject showed no REM increase. (The investigators discarded the results from the seventh subject, who came to the laboratory drunk. Alcohol suppresses REM sleep, so results from this subject would be unreliable.)

Similar experiments have been done with laboratory animals, using longer periods of deprivation. Cats have been deprived of paradoxical sleep for up to 70 consecutive days (see Dement, Ferguson, Cohen, & Barchas, 1969). Do not imagine shifts of experimenters monitoring cats 24 hours a day and prodding them whenever they entered paradoxical sleep. Rather they kept each cat on a tiny island surrounded by water. As soon as a cat entered paradoxical sleep, its postural muscles relaxed, it lost its balance, and it fell into the water, awakening immediately. This procedure impaired the cats' behavior and health severely, and note that the cats suffered not only sleep interruptions but also disruption of body temperature from repeated plunges into the water. The results are therefore hard to interpret.

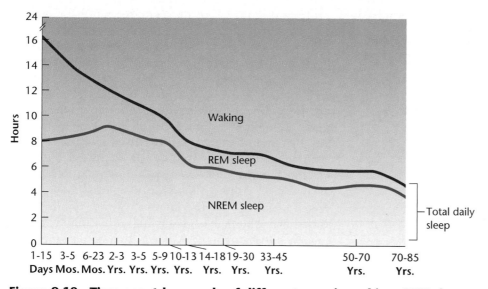

Figure 9.18 Time spent by people of different ages in waking, REM sleep, and NREM sleep
REM sleep occupies about 8 hours a day in newborns but fewer than 2 hours in most adults. The sleep of infants is not quite like that of adults, however, and the criteria for identifying REM sleep are not the same. *Source: From "Ontogenetic Development of Human Sleep-Dream Cycle," by H. P. Roffwarg, J. N. Muzino, and W. C. Dement, Science, 1966, 152: 604–609. Copyright 1966 by the AAAS. Reprinted by permission.*

Hypotheses

The results presented so far suggest that we need some REM sleep, but they do not tell us why. One hypothesis is that REM is important for memory storage or that it helps the brain discard useless connections that formed accidentally during the day (Crick & Mitchison, 1983). Discarding useless connections would help the correct connections stand out by comparison.

The research on this point has yielded mixed and inconclusive results (J. M. Siegel, 2001). For example, some studies have found increased REM sleep following a day with unusual learning experiences, but other studies have not, and many of the learning experiences were stressful (e.g., shock avoidance), so an increase in REM could have explanations other than learning. Some researchers have found that brain areas that were particularly active during the learning become highly active during REM that night (Maquet et al., 2000). However, again, the results of various studies have been inconsistent (J. M. Siegel, 2001). Furthermore, humans awakened during REM sleep seldom report anything similar to what they learned during the previous day, so it is not clear that REM is replaying or reworking the day's learning.

When people learn something and then are tested the next day, their performance is often better the second day than the first, but only if they sleep adequately during the night (Stickgold, James, & Hobson, 2000; Stickgold, Whidbee, Schirmer, Patel, & Hobson,

2000). (The obvious message to students: When you are studying, get enough sleep.) When people practice something repeatedly during one day, sometimes their performance actually deteriorates during the day, but it recovers if they take a short nap (Mednick et al., 2002). Evidently, some aspect of sleep helps to strengthen learning. Still, this evidence merely indicates the importance of sleep for memory, not anything specific about REM sleep.

REM and non-REM sleep may be important for consolidating different types of memories. Depriving people of sleep early in the night (mostly non-REM sleep) impairs verbal learning, such as memorizing a list of words, whereas depriving people of sleep during the second half of the night (more REM) impairs consolidation of learned motor skills (Gais, Plihal, Wagner, & Born, 2000; Plihal & Born, 1997). On the other hand, many people take MAO inhibitors, antidepressant drugs that severely decrease REM sleep. They nevertheless report no memory problems, and research on laboratory animals indicates that the drugs sometimes even enhance memory (Parent, Habib, & Baker, 1999).

A more recent hypothesis sounds oddball just because we have for so long imagined some glamorous role for REM sleep: David Maurice (1998) has proposed that the primary role of REM is to shake the eyeballs back and forth enough to get sufficient oxygen to the corneas of the eyes. The corneas, unlike the rest of the body, ordinarily get much of their oxygen supply directly from the surrounding air, not from the blood. They get some additional oxygen from the fluid behind them (see Figure 6.2, p. 146), but when the eyes are motionless, that fluid can become stagnant. Moving the eyes increases the oxygen supply to the corneas. According to this view, REM is a way of arousing a sleeper just enough to move the eyes back and forth a few times, and all the other manifestations of REM—including dreams—are just by-products. It's an interesting idea, worth further research. However, as mentioned, many people take MAO inhibitors, which greatly restrict REM sleep; they are not known to suffer damage to the cornea. In short, the evidence does not convincingly support any current hypothesis about the function of REM.

2. What kinds of individuals get more REM sleep than others? (Think in terms of age, species, and long vs. short sleepers.)

Check your answer on page 290.

BIOLOGICAL PERSPECTIVES ON DREAMING

What causes dreams? For decades, psychologists were heavily influenced by Sigmund Freud's theory of dreams, which was based on the assumption that they reflect hidden and often unconscious wishes, which were distorted by the brain in an effort to "censor" them. Although it is true that dreams reflect the dreamer's personality and recent experiences, Freud's theory of dreams depended on certain ideas about the nervous system that are now discarded (McCarley & Hobson, 1977). He believed, for example, that brain cells were inactive except when nerves from the periphery brought them energy.

The Activation-Synthesis Hypothesis

Whereas Freud thought the brain actively distorted messages to make a dream, an alternative view holds that a dream represents the brain's effort to make sense of information that is already distorted. According to the **activation-synthesis hypothesis**, dreams begin with periodic bursts of spontaneous activity in the pons—the PGO waves previously described—which partly *activate* many but not all parts of the cortex. The cortex combines this haphazard input with whatever other activity was already occurring, interprets the sum as information, and does its best to *synthesize* a story that makes sense of it all (Hobson & McCarley, 1977; Hobson, Pace-Schott, & Stickgold, 2000; McCarley & Hoffman, 1981). Because activity is suppressed in the primary visual cortex (area V1) and primary somatosensory cortex, normal sensory information cannot compete with the self-generated stimulation, and hallucinations result (Rees, Kreiman, & Koch, 2002). The input from the pons usually activates the amygdala, a portion of the temporal lobe highly important for emotional processing, and therefore, most dreams have strong emotional content. Because much of the

Making Sense of the chaos of our day.

prefrontal cortex is inactive during PGO waves, memory is weak. We not only forget most dreams after we awaken, but we even lose track of what has been happening within a dream, so sudden scene changes are common.

Consider how this theory handles a couple of common dreams. Most people have had occasional dreams of falling or flying. Well, while you are asleep, you lie flat, unlike your posture for the rest of the day. Your brain in its partly aroused condition feels the vestibular sensation of your position and interprets it as flying or falling. Have you ever dreamt that you were trying to move but couldn't? Most people have. An interpretation based on the activation-synthesis theory is that during REM sleep (which accompanies most dreams), your major postural muscles are virtually paralyzed. That is, when you are dreaming, you really *can't* move, you feel your lack of movement, and thus you dream of failing to move.

One controversy about this theory concerns the role of the pons. Patients with damage to the pons continue to report dreams, even though they no longer show the eye movements and other typical features of REM (Solms, 1997). Therefore, some researchers argue that the pons cannot be essential for dreaming. The reply to this criticism is that none of those patients have very extensive damage to the pons. People with extensive damage there are either paralyzed, permanently unconscious, or dead (Hobson et al., 2000). So when people have partial damage to the pons and still have dreams, it is possible that the surviving areas of the pons are essential for the dreams.

Another criticism is that the theory's predictions are vague. If we dream about falling because of the vestibular sensations from lying down, why don't we *always* dream of falling? If we dream we can't move because our muscles are paralyzed during REM sleep, why don't we *always* dream of being paralyzed? This criticism is reasonable, although one could counter that no other theory is any better at predicting anyone's dreams.

Too Random

The Clinico-Anatomical Hypothesis

An alternative view of the biology of dreams has been labeled the **clinico-anatomical hypothesis** because it was derived from clinical studies of dreaming by patients with various kinds of brain damage (Solms, 1997, 2000). In several important regards, this theory resembles the activation-synthesis theory: In both theories, dreams begin with arousing stimuli that are generated within the brain and combined with recent memories and any information the brain is receiving from the senses (which are largely suppressed during sleep). The key difference is that the clinico-anatomical hypothesis puts less emphasis on the pons, PGO waves, or even REM sleep. It regards dreams as just thinking, except that the thinking takes place under unusual conditions.

One of those conditions is that the brain is getting little information from the sense organs, so it is free to generate images without constraints or interference. The primary motor cortex also is suppressed, as are the motor neurons of the spinal cord, so arousal cannot lead to action. Activity is suppressed in the prefrontal cortex, which is important for working memory (memory of very recent events) and for processes loosely described as "use of knowledge." Consequently, the dream is free to wander without the criticisms of "wait a minute; that's not possible!"

Meanwhile, activity is relatively high in the inferior (lower) part of the parietal cortex, an area important for visuospatial perception. Patients with damage here have problems integrating body sensations with vision. They also report no dreams. Fairly high activity is also found in the areas of visual cortex outside V1. These areas are presumably key to the visual imagery that accompanies most dreams. Finally, activity is high in the hypothalamus, amygdala, and other areas important for emotions and motivations. People awakened during dreams usually report some emotion, such as happiness, surprise, anger, or anxiety (Fosse, Stickgold, & Hobson, 2001).

So the idea is that either internal or external stimulation activates parts of the parietal, occipital, and temporal cortex. No sensory input from area V1 overrides the stimulation and no criticism from the prefrontal cortex censors it, so it develops into hallucinatory perceptions. This idea, like the activation-synthesis hypothesis, is hard to test because it does not make specific predictions about who will have what dream and when.

For more information about the content of dreams, see this Web site:

www.dreamresearch.net

3. An adult who sustains extensive damage limited to the primary visual cortex (V1) becomes blind. Would you expect such a person to report visual dreams? Why or why not?

Check your answer on page 290.

In Closing: Our Limited Self-Understanding

I don't want to minimize how much we do understand about sleep, REM, and dreams, but it is noteworthy how many basic questions remain. Our lack of knowledge about activities that occupy so much of our time underscores a point about the biology of behavior: We evolved tendencies to behave in certain ways that lead to survival and reproduction. The behavior can serve its function even when we do not fully understand what that function is.

SUMMARY

1. Sleep probably serves at least two functions: (a) repair and restoration and (b) conservation of energy during a period of relative inefficiency. (p. 284)

2. REM sleep occupies the greatest percentage of sleep in individuals and species that sleep the most total hours. (p. 285)

3. People deprived of REM sleep become irritable and have trouble concentrating. After a period of REM deprivation, people compensate by spending more time than usual in REM sleep. (p. 286)

4. According to the activation-synthesis hypothesis, dreams are the brain's attempts to make sense of the information reaching it, based mostly on haphazard input originating in the pons. (p. 288)

5. According to the clinico-anatomical hypothesis, dreams originate partly with external stimuli but mostly from the brain's own motivations, memories, and arousal. The stimulation often produces peculiar results because it does not have to compete with normal visual input and does not get censored by the prefrontal cortex. (p. 288)

ANSWERS TO *STOP AND CHECK* QUESTIONS

1. The evolutionary theory would predict little if any sleep because these animals are equally efficient at all times of day and have no need to conserve energy at one time more than another. The fish might sleep, however, as a relic left over from ancestors that lived in the light—just as humans

still erect arm hairs in response to cold, a response that was useful for our hairier ancestors but not for us. (p. 285)

2. Much REM sleep is more typical of the young than the old, of those who get much sleep than those who get little, and of species that sleep much of the day and are unlikely to be attacked during their sleep. (p. 288)

3. After adult damage to the primary visual cortex, people become blind but still report visual dreams (Rees et al., 2002). The explanation is that the primary visual cortex is nearly inactive during dreaming anyway, so further suppression is not a problem. However, damage to other parts of the visual cortex, outside V1, do abolish visual imagery in dreams. Also, people who suffered V1 damage in early childhood have no visual imagery in dreams because they never experienced vision to form visual memories. (p. 289)

THOUGHT QUESTION

Why would it be harder to deprive someone of just NREM sleep than just REM sleep?

CHAPTER ENDING
Key Terms and Activities

TERMS

activation-synthesis hypothesis (p. 288)

adenosine (p. 275)

alpha wave (p. 272)

basal forebrain (p. 275)

biological clock (p. 263)

caffeine (p. 276)

cataplexy (p. 280)

clinico-anatomical hypothesis (p. 288)

electroencephalograph (EEG) (p. 271)

endogenous circadian rhythm (p. 262)

endogenous circannual rhythm (p. 262)

evolutionary theory of sleep (p. 285)

free-running rhythm (p. 267)

insomnia (p. 279)

jet lag (p. 267)

K-complex (p. 272)

locus coeruleus (p. 275)

maintenance insomnia (p. 279)

melatonin (p. 265)

narcolepsy (p. 280)

night terror (p. 282)

non-REM (NREM) sleep (p. 273)

onset insomnia (p. 279)

orexin (or hypocretin) (p. 281)

paradoxical sleep (p. 273)

periodic limb movement disorder (p. 281)

PGO wave (p. 278)

pineal gland (p. 265)

polysomnograph (p. 273)

pontomesencephalon (p. 275)

prostaglandin (p. 277)

rapid eye movement (REM) sleep (p. 273)

REM behavior disorder (p. 281)

repair and restoration theory of sleep (p. 284)

reticular formation (p. 274)

sleep apnea (p. 280)

sleep spindle (p. 272)

slow-wave sleep (SWS) (p. 272)

suprachiasmatic nucleus (SCN) (p. 264)

termination insomnia (p. 279)

zeitgeber (p. 267)

SUGGESTIONS FOR FURTHER READING

Culebras, A. (1996). *Clinical handbook of sleep disorders.* Boston: Butterworth-Heinemann. Discusses many kinds of sleep disorders.

Dement, W. C. (1992). *The sleepwatchers.* Stanford, CA: Stanford Alumni Association. Fascinating, entertaining account of sleep research by one of its leading pioneers.

Moorcroft, W. H. (2003). *Understanding sleep and dreaming.* Dordrecht, the Netherlands: Kluwer Academic. Includes discussions of brain mechanisms and sleep disorders.

Refinetti, R. (2000). *Circadian physiology.* Boca Raton, FL: CRC Press. Marvelous summary of research on circadian rhythms and the relevance to human behavior.

Winson, J. (1990, November). The meaning of dreams. *Scientific American, 263*(5), 86–96. Discusses theories of the function of REM sleep and the meaning of dreams.

WEB SITES TO EXPLORE

You can go to the Biological Psychology Study Center and click these links. While there, you can also check for suggested articles available on InfoTrac College Edition. The Biological Psychology Internet address is:

http://psychology.wadsworth.com/ kalatbiopsych8e/

The Sleep Site, specializing in sleep disorders
http://www.thesleepsite.com/

The Quantitative Study of Dreams, by Adam Schneider & G. William Domhoff
http://www.dreamresearch.net

CD-ROM: EXPLORING BIOLOGICAL PSYCHOLOGY

Sleep Cycle (video)

Stages of Sleep on an EEG (static image)

Awake (animation)

Stage 1 (animation)

Stage 2 (animation)

Stage 3 (animation)

Stage 4 (animation)

REM (animation)

Critical Thinking (essay questions)

Chapter Quiz (multiple choice questions)

Internal Regulation

10

Chapter Outline

Main Ideas

1. Many physiological and behavioral processes maintain a near constancy of certain body variables, and they anticipate as well as react to needs.

2. Mammals and birds maintain constant body temperature as a way of staying ready for rapid muscle activity at any temperature of the environment. They use both behavioral and physiological processes to maintain temperature.

3. Thirst mechanisms respond to the osmotic pressure and total volume of the blood.

4. Hunger and satiety are regulated by many factors, including taste, stomach distention, the availability of glucose to the cells, and chemicals released by the fat cells. Many brain peptides help regulate feeding and satiety.

What is life? Life can be defined in different ways, depending on whether our interest is medical, legal, philosophical, or poetic. Biologically, what is necessary for life is *a coordinated set of chemical reactions*. Not all chemical reactions are alive, but without precisely regulated chemical reactions, life as we know it stops.

Every chemical reaction in the body takes place in a water solution at a rate that depends on the identity and concentration of molecules in the water, the temperature of the solution, and the presence of contaminants. Much of our behavior is organized to keep the right chemicals in the right proportions and at the right temperature.

Opposite:
One pelican learned to gulp water from a sprinkler. She brought her babies back to that sprinkler, and they brought the third generation. *Source: Theo Allofs Photography*

MODULE 10.1

Temperature Regulation

Here's an observation that puzzled biologists for years: When a small male garter snake emerges from hibernation in early spring, it emits female pheromones for the first day or two. The pheromones attract larger males, who swarm all over the small male, trying to copulate with it. Presumably, the tendency to release female pheromones must have evolved and must offer the small male some advantage. But what? Biologists speculated about ways in which this pseudomating experience might make the small male better able to attract real females. The truth is simpler: A male that has just emerged from hibernation is cold, usually less than 10°C (50°F). At that temperature, its movements are slow—so slow in fact that it has trouble getting out of its burrow. Most of the larger males emerged from hibernation earlier and had a chance to warm themselves in a sunny place, reaching temperatures above 25°C (77°F). When the larger males swarm all over the smaller male, they warm him and increase his activity level (Shine, Phillips, Waye, LeMaster, & Mason, 2001). The point is that temperature is an important, easily overlooked influence on behavior.

You may not think of temperature regulation as one of your strongest motivations, but it is a very high priority biologically. An average college student expends about 2600 kilocalories (kcal) per day. Where do you suppose all that energy goes? To muscle movements or mental activity, perhaps? No. You use about 1700 kcal (roughly two thirds of the total, and almost the power to light a 100-watt bulb all day) just for basal metabolism, the energy you use to maintain a constant body temperature while at rest (Burton, 1994). Even the most active people spend about half their energy on basal metabolism.

HOMEOSTASIS

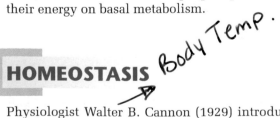

Body Temp.

Physiologist Walter B. Cannon (1929) introduced the term homeostasis (HO-mee-oh-STAY-sis) to refer to temperature regulation and other biological processes that keep certain body variables within a fixed range. To understand how a homeostatic process works, we can use the analogy of a thermostat in a house with both a heating and a cooling system. Someone fixes a set range of temperatures on the thermostat. When the temperature in the house drops below that range, the thermostat triggers the furnace to provide heat until the house temperature returns to the set range. When the temperature rises above the maximum of the range, the thermostat triggers the air conditioner to cool the house.

Similarly, homeostatic processes in animals trigger physiological and behavioral activities that keep certain variables within a set range. In many cases, the range is so narrow that we refer to it as a set point, a single value that the body works to maintain. For example, if calcium is deficient in your diet and its concentration in the blood begins to fall below the set point of 0.16 g/L (grams per liter), storage deposits in your bones release additional calcium into the blood. If the calcium level in the blood rises above 0.16 g/L, part of the excess is stored in the bones and part is excreted. Analogous mechanisms maintain constant blood levels of water, oxygen, glucose, sodium chloride, protein, fat, and acidity (Cannon, 1929). Processes that reduce discrepancies from the set point are known as negative feedback. Most motivated behavior can be described as negative feedback: Something happens to cause a disturbance, and behavior continues in varying ways until it relieves the disturbance.

In the mammalian body, temperature regulation, thirst, and hunger are *nearly* homeostatic processes. They differ from pure or simple homeostasis in several ways:

- They anticipate future needs as well as react to current needs (Appley, 1991). For example, in a frightening situation that might call for vigorous activity, you begin to sweat even before you start to move. (We call it "cold sweat.")
- Set points for body temperature, body fat, and other variables change with time of day, time of year, and other conditions (Mrosovsky, 1990).
- Hunger in particular is governed by some nonhomeostatic influences. For example, people and other animals eat more, and gain weight, when very tasty food is available (de Castro & Plunkett, 2002).

CONTROLLING BODY TEMPERATURE

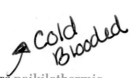
Cold Blooded

Amphibians, reptiles, and most fish are <u>poikilothermic</u> (POY-kih-lo-THER-mik): Their body temperature matches the temperature of their environment. They can control their body temperature by selecting their location, but they lack physiological mechanisms of temperature regulation such as shivering and sweating.

Mammals and birds are <u>homeothermic</u>: They use physiological mechanisms to maintain an almost constant body temperature despite large variations in the environmental temperature. Homeothermy requires effort and therefore fuel. An animal *generates* heat in proportion to its total mass; it *radiates* heat in proportion to its surface area. A small animal, such as a mouse or a hummingbird, has a high surface-to-volume ratio and therefore radiates heat rapidly. Such animals need a great deal of fuel each day to maintain their body temperature. Larger animals are better insulated against heat loss.

Warm Blooded

EXTENSIONS AND APPLICATIONS
Surviving in Extreme Cold

A poikilothermic animal is vulnerable under extreme cold. If the air or water temperature drops below freezing, an animal can burrow into the ground, but with prolonged cold, even the ground freezes. If the animal's blood freezes, ice crystals form, and when water freezes, it expands. The ice crystals therefore tear apart blood vessels and cell membranes, killing the animal.

Amazingly, however, some frogs, fish, and insects survive through northern Canadian winters despite temperatures near −40°C (−40°F). How do they do it? Some insects and fish stock their blood with large

AP/Wide World Photos

Companies will freeze a dead body on the assumption that future technologies can restore the person to life.

amounts of glycerol and other antifreeze chemicals at the start of the winter (Liou, Tocilj, Davies, & Jia, 2000). Wood frogs actually do freeze, but they have several mechanisms to reduce the damage. They start by withdrawing most fluid from their organs and blood vessels and storing it in extracellular spaces. Therefore, ice crystals have plenty of room to expand when they do form, without tearing the blood vessels and cells. They have chemicals that cause ice crystals to form gradually, not in chunks. Finally, they have such enormous blood-clotting capacity that they can quickly repair any blood vessels that do rupture (Storey & Storey, 1999).

As you may have heard, some people have had their bodies frozen immediately after death, with the intention of staying frozen until scientists discover how to cure their disease *and* how to bring a frozen body back to life. What do you think? If you had enough money, would you choose this route to possible life after death?

My advice is don't bother. The wood frogs that survive after freezing begin by dehydrating their organs and blood vessels. Unless a person did this—before dying!—ice crystals are sure to destroy blood vessels and cell membranes throughout the body. It's risky to say something is impossible, but this idea sounds pretty discouraging.

The Advantages of Constant High Body Temperature

Why have we evolved mechanisms to control body temperature? Why is constant body temperature important enough to justify spending so much energy? Primarily, constant body temperature enables an animal to stay active even when the environment turns cold. Recall from Chapter 8 that a fish has trouble maintaining a high activity level at a low temperature. At a high temperature, it can rely on its nonfatiguing slow-twitch muscle fibers; at lower temperatures, it must recruit more and more of its rapidly fatiguing fast-twitch fibers. It can move rapidly in the cold but not for long. Birds and mammals in contrast keep their muscles warm at all times, regardless of air temperature, and therefore keep themselves constantly ready for vigorous activity.

Why did mammals evolve a body temperature of 37°C (98°F) instead of any other possible value? There are two reasons. First, it is easier to keep the body warmer than the environment than to keep it cooler. If the air is cold and you need to heat yourself, you can:

- Find a warmer place. Many small animals burrow underground to keep warm.
- Put on more clothing, if you're a human, thereby increasing your insulation.

- Fluff out your fur, if you're a hairy mammal. (Actually, people also fluff out our "fur" even though our hair is too short to do any good. When we get cold, we get goose bumps by erecting our hairs.)
- Decrease blood flow to the skin, protecting the vital internal organs. You can afford to let your skin get cold, but not your heart or brain.
- Become more active, thereby generating more heat.
- Shiver, thereby generating heat without moving.
- Increase metabolic rate in your brown fat tissue, thereby generating more heat (Lowell & Spiegelman, 2000).
- Huddle or cuddle with others. You might be shy about hugging strangers to keep warm, but many animals are not (Figure 10.1). For example, spectacled eiders (birds in the duck family) spend their winters in the Arctic Ocean, most of which is covered with thick pack ice. With more than 150,000 eiders crowded together, they not only keep one

another warm but also maintain a 20-mile hole in the ice so they can dive for fish all winter long (Weidensaul, 1999).

By contrast, if you need to cool yourself, your options are limited:

- Find a cooler place (Figure 10.2).
- Become less active to avoid overheating.
- Take off clothing or decrease fur thickness.
- Divert more blood to the skin for it to be cooled.
- Sweat. (Or pant if you're a species that doesn't sweat.)

Figure 10.2 One way to cope with the heat
Just like overheated people, overheated animals look for the coolest spot they can find.

If the air is above body temperature, you are reduced to only one mechanism of cooling yourself: evaporation through sweating, panting, or licking yourself. Even evaporation becomes useless if the air is humid as well as hot. Furthermore, if you sweat much, you face the danger of dehydration. On a hot humid day, even healthy young people risk life-threatening heatstroke. In short, it is easier to heat than to cool yourself, and therefore, it is easier to maintain a constant high temperature than a constant low one.

Remember that I said there are two explanations for why human body temperature is around 37°C (98°F). The first is that 37°C is close to the warmest temperatures we frequently face, so we seldom have to cool ourselves below the temperature of the environment. The second, more important reason is that animals gain an advantage by being as warm as they can manage. Other things being equal, a warmer animal has warmer muscles and therefore runs faster and with less fatigue than a cooler animal.

We might have evolved a temperature even higher than 37°C except that proteins begin to break their bonds and lose their useful properties at temperatures above 40° or 41°C (104–106°F). It is possible to evolve proteins that are stable at higher temperatures; indeed, thermophiles survive in water

Figure 10.1 Behavioral regulation of body temperature
A 1-month-old emperor penguin chick is poorly insulated against antarctic temperatures that may drop to –30°C (–22°F) or below. However, many chicks huddled together tightly are like one large well-insulated organism. As those on the outside get cold, they push their way to the inside, and the warm ones on the inside passively drift outward. The process is so effective that a cluster of penguin chicks has to move frequently to prevent melting a hole in the ice!

close to the boiling point (Hoffman, 2001). However, to do so, they need extra bonds to stabilize their proteins. The enzymatic properties of proteins depend on the proteins' flexible structure, so making them rigid enough to withstand high temperatures decreases their versatility and usefulness (Somero, 1996). Birds' body temperatures are about 41°C (105°F), probably about as high as possible for a large animal. Mammals are a little cooler, but not much.

Reproductive cells require a somewhat cooler environment (Rommel, Pabst, & McLellan, 1998). Birds lay eggs and sit on them instead of developing them internally because the birds' internal temperature is too hot for an embryo. Similarly, in most male mammals, the scrotum hangs outside the body because sperm production requires a cooler temperature than the rest of the body. (A man who wears undershorts that are too tight keeps his testes too close to the body, overheats them, and therefore produces fewer healthy sperm cells.) Pregnant women are advised to avoid hot baths and anything else that would overheat a developing fetus.

Stop & Check

1. What is homeostasis?
2. What is the primary advantage of maintaining a constant (high) body temperature?
3. What are two explanations for why we evolved a body temperature of about 37°C (98°F) instead of some other temperature?

Check your answers on page 299.

Physiological Mechanisms

All the physiological changes that defend body temperature—such as shivering, sweating, and changes in blood flow to the skin—depend predominantly on certain areas in and near the hypothalamus, a small structure at the base of the brain (Figure 10.3). The most critical areas for temperature control are the

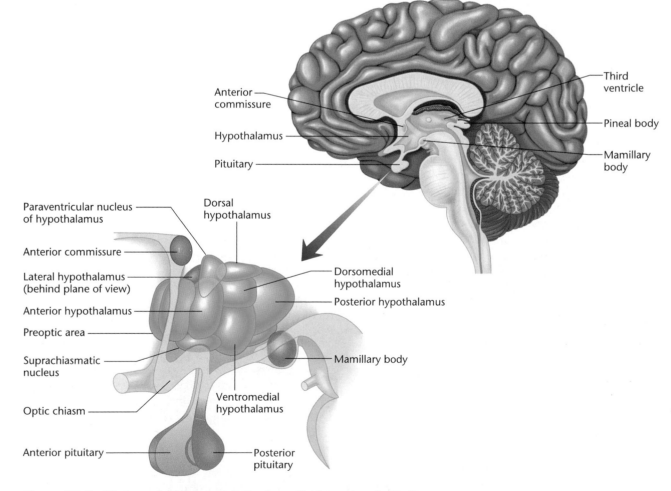

Figure 10.3   Major subdivisions of the hypothalamus and pituitary
Source: After Nieuwenhuys, Voogd, & vanHuijzen, 1988

anterior hypothalamus and the preoptic area, which is just anterior to the anterior hypothalamus. (It is called *preoptic* because it is near the optic chiasm, where the optic nerves cross.) Because of the close relationship between the preoptic area and the anterior hypothalamus, they are often treated as a single area, the **preoptic area/anterior hypothalamus**, or **POA/AH**.

The POA/AH monitors body temperature partly by monitoring its own temperature (Nelson & Prosser, 1981). When an experimenter heats the POA/AH, an animal pants or sweats, even in a cool environment. If the same area is cooled, the animal shivers, even in a warm room. These responses are not simply reflexive. An animal will also react to a heated or cooled POA/AH by pressing a lever or doing other work for cold air or hot air reinforcements (Satinoff, 1964).

Besides monitoring their own temperature, cells of the POA/AH also receive input from temperature-sensitive receptors in the skin and spinal cord. The animal shivers most vigorously when both the POA/AH and the other receptors are cold; it sweats or pants most vigorously when both are hot. Damage to the POA/AH impairs a mammal's ability to regulate temperature, and its body temperature plummets in a cold environment (Satinoff, Valentino, & Teitelbaum, 1976).

Shivering, sweating, and other physiological mechanisms of temperature control develop gradually in newborn mammals, and researchers insufficiently attentive to the problems of temperature regulation have sometimes misinterpreted infant behaviors. For example, psychologists decades ago concluded that infant rats were incapable of odor conditioning and certain controls of eating and drinking. As they studied how these behaviors developed over the first few weeks of life, they eventually discovered that the real problem was temperature control. Researchers generally work at "normal room temperature," about 20–23°C (68–73°F), which is comfortable for adult humans but dangerously cold for an isolated baby rat (Figure 10.4). In a warmer room, even infant rats show abilities that we once assumed required much more brain maturity (Satinoff, 1991).

Behavioral Mechanisms

Although the body temperature of fish, amphibians, and reptiles matches that of their surroundings, it seldom fluctuates wildly because they can choose their location within the environment. A desert lizard burrows into the ground in the middle of the day, when the surface is too hot, and again in the middle of the night, when the surface is too cold. On the surface, it moves from sun to shade as necessary to keep its temperature fairly constant.

Mammals, too, use behavioral means to regulate body temperature. They do not sit on an icy surface shivering when they can build a nest, or sweat and pant in the sun when they can find a shady spot. The more they can regulate their temperature behaviorally, the less they need to rely on physiological efforts (Refinetti & Carlisle, 1986). If the physiological mechanisms fail, as they do after damage to the POA/AH of the hypothalamus, mammals can maintain a fairly constant body temperature by behavioral means alone, such as by seeking a warm or cold place or by pressing a lever to keep a heat lamp on (Satinoff & Rutstein, 1970; Van Zoeren & Stricker, 1977).

Fever

Bacterial and viral infections generally cause fever, an increase in body temperature. As a rule, the fever is not part of the illness; it is part of the body's defense against the illness. When the body is invaded by bacteria, viruses, fungi, or other foreign bodies, it mobilizes, among other things, its *leukocytes* (white blood cells) to attack them. The leukocytes release a protein called *interleukin-1,* which in turn stimulates the production of **prostaglandin E_1** and **prostaglandin E_2,** which cross the blood-brain barrier and stimulate specific receptors in the POA/AH that direct the autonomic nervous system to raise body temperature (Ek et al., 2001). Prostaglandins also increase sleepiness, as we saw in Chapter 9.

Newborn rabbits, whose hypothalamus is immature, do not shiver in response to infections. If given a choice of environments, however, they select an unusually warm spot and thereby raise their body temperature (Satinoff, McEwen, & Williams, 1976). That is, they develop a fever by behavioral rather than physiological means. Fish and reptiles do the same if they can find a warm enough environment (Kluger,

Figure 10.4 The special difficulties of temperature regulation for a newborn rodent
A newborn rat has no hair, thin skin, and little body fat. If it is left exposed in a cool room, its body temperature quickly falls.

1991). Again, the point is that fever is something the animal does to fight an infection.

Does fever do an animal any good? Certain types of bacteria grow less vigorously at high temperatures than at normal mammalian body temperatures. Other things being equal, developing a moderate fever increases an individual's chance of surviving a bacterial infection (Kluger, 1991). However, a fever above about 39°C (103°F) in humans does more harm than good, and a fever of 41–43°C (105–109°F) can be fatal (Rommel, Pabst, McLellan, 1998).

Stop & Check

4. How does the POA/AH monitor body temperature?

5. How can an animal regulate body temperature after damage to the POA/AH?

6. Suppose a drug interferes with the synthesis of prostaglandins. How would it affect fevers?

Check your answers on this page.

MODULE 10.1

In Closing: Temperature and Behavior

It has been said, only partly in jest, that shivering is a sign of stupidity. That is, the physiological mechanisms of temperature regulation (e.g., shivering and sweating) protect us when we have failed to find a place with a comfortable temperature or have worn too much or too little clothing. One of the key themes of this module has been the redundancy of mechanisms—the fact that the body has a variety of ways of accomplishing the same end. We shall see this theme again in the discussions of thirst and hunger.

SUMMARY

1. Homeostasis is a tendency to maintain a body variable near a set point. Temperature, hunger, and thirst are almost homeostatic, but they anticipate future needs as well as react to current needs. (p. 294)

2. A constant body temperature enables a mammal or bird to move rapidly and without fatigue even in a cold environment. (p. 295)

3. A body temperature near 37°C has two advantages: It is usually higher than the air temperature, so we don't have to rely on our inefficient methods of cooling the body. It also keeps the body about as warm as possible, facilitating rapid muscle contractions, without damaging proteins. (p. 295)

4. The preoptic area and anterior hypothalamus (POA/AH) are critical for temperature control. Cells there monitor both their own temperature and that of the skin and spinal cord. (p. 297)

5. Even homeothermic animals rely partly on behavioral mechanisms for temperature regulation, especially in infancy and after damage to the POA/AH. (p. 298)

6. Fever is caused by the release of prostaglandins, which stimulate cells in the POA/AH. A moderate fever helps an animal combat an infection. (p. 298)

ANSWERS TO *STOP AND CHECK* QUESTIONS

1. Homeostasis is a set of processes that keep certain body variables within a fixed range. (p. 297)

2. The primary advantage of a constant (high) body temperature is that it keeps the animal ready for rapid, prolonged muscle activity even if the air is cold. (p. 297)

3. One reason is that we have better mechanisms of heating ourselves than cooling ourselves, so it is best to have a body temperature close to the highest temperatures the environment often reaches. The second reason is that animals gain an advantage in being as warm as possible, and therefore as fast as possible, but proteins lose stability at temperatures much above 37°C (98°F). (p. 297)

4. Cells in the POA/AH monitor their own temperature and that of the skin and spinal cord. (p. 299)

5. It can regulate temperature through behavior, such as by finding a warmer or cooler place. (p. 299)

6. A drug that inhibited prostaglandin formation would lower fevers. Aspirin does in fact lower fever by that route. (p. 299)

THOUGHT QUESTION

Speculate on why birds have higher body temperatures than mammals.

MODULE 10.2

Thirst

Water constitutes about 70% of the mammalian body. Because the concentration of chemicals in water determines the rate of all chemical reactions in the body, the water must be regulated within narrow limits. The body also needs enough fluid in the circulatory system to maintain normal blood pressure. People sometimes survive for weeks without food, but not without water.

MECHANISMS OF WATER REGULATION

Different species have different strategies for maintaining the water they need. Beavers and other species that live in rivers or lakes drink plenty of water, eat moist foods, and excrete copious amounts of dilute urine. In contrast, gerbils and other desert animals may go through their entire lives without drinking. They gain enough water from their food, and they have many adaptations to avoid losing water, including the fact that they excrete very dry feces and very concentrated urine. Unable to sweat, they avoid the heat of the day by burrowing deep under the ground. Their highly convoluted nasal passages minimize water loss when they exhale.

We humans vary our strategy depending on circumstances. If you cannot find enough to drink, or if the water tastes bad, you will conserve water by excreting more concentrated urine, decreasing your sweat, and other autonomic responses. Your posterior pituitary (see Figure 10.3) releases a hormone called **vasopressin**, which raises blood pressure by constricting the blood vessels. (The term *vasopressin* comes from *vascular pressure*.) The increased pressure helps compensate for the decreased volume. Vasopressin is also known as **antidiuretic hormone (ADH)** because it enables the kidneys to reabsorb water and therefore to secrete highly concentrated urine. (*Diuresis* means "urination.") You cannot succeed as well as gerbils, however. Gerbils can drink ocean water, and we certainly cannot.

In most cases, our strategy is closer to that of beavers: We drink more than we need and excrete the excess. (However, if you drink extensively without eating, as many alcoholics do, you may excrete enough body salts to harm yourself.) Most of our drinking is with meals or in social situations, and people in prosperous countries seldom experience intense thirst.

> **1.** If you lacked vasopressin, would you drink like a beaver or like a gerbil? Why?
>
> *Check your answers on page 304.*

OSMOTIC THIRST

Not all thirst is the same. Eating salty foods causes *osmotic* thirst, and losing fluid, such as by bleeding or sweating, induces *hypovolemic* thirst. The two kinds of thirst motivate different kinds of behavior.

The combined concentration of all *solutes* (molecules in solution) in mammalian body fluids remains at a nearly constant level of 0.15 M (molar). (A concentration of 1.0 M has a number of grams of solute equal to the molecular weight of that solute dissolved in 1 liter of solution.) This fixed concentration of solutes can be regarded as a set point, similar to the set point for temperature. Any deviation activates mechanisms that restore the concentration of solutes to the set point.

The solutes inside and outside a cell produce an **osmotic pressure,** the tendency of water to flow across a semipermeable membrane from the area of low solute concentration to the area of higher concentration. A semipermeable membrane is one through which water can pass, but solutes cannot. The membrane surrounding a cell is almost a semipermeable membrane because water flows across it freely and various solutes flow either slowly or not at all between the *intracellular fluid* inside the cell and the *extracellular fluid* outside it. Osmotic pressure occurs when solutes are more concentrated on one side of the membrane than on the other.

If you eat something salty, sodium ions spread through the blood and the extracellular fluid but do not cross the membranes into cells. The result is a higher concentration of solutes outside the cells than inside, and the resulting osmotic pressure draws water from the cells into the extracellular fluid. Certain neurons detect their own loss of water and then trigger osmotic thirst, which helps restore the normal state (Figure 10.5). The kidneys also excrete more concentrated urine to rid the body of excess sodium and maintain as much water as possible.

How does the brain detect osmotic pressure? It gets part of the information from receptors around the third ventricle (Figure 10.6). Of all brain areas, those around the third ventricle have the leakiest blood-brain barrier (Simon, 2000). A weak blood-brain barrier is a disadvantage for most purposes but an advantage for receiving blood chemicals and monitoring their properties, including their overall concentration. The area principally responsible for detecting osmotic pressure is known as the **OVLT** (organum vasculosum laminae terminalis). The brain also gets information from receptors in the periphery, including the stomach, that detect high levels of sodium (Kraly, Kim, Dunham, & Tribuzio, 1995), enabling the brain to anticipate an osmotic need before the rest of the body actually experiences it.

Receptors in the OVLT, the stomach, and elsewhere relay their information to several parts of the hypothalamus, including the **supraoptic nucleus** and the **paraventricular nucleus,** which control the rate at

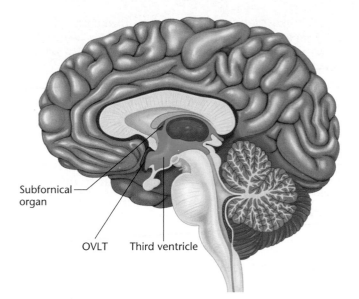

Subfornical organ

OVLT   Third ventricle

Figure 10.6   The brain's receptors for osmotic pressure and blood volume
These neurons are in areas surrounding the third ventricle, where no blood-brain barrier prevents blood-borne chemicals from entering the brain. *Source: Based in part on Weindl, 1973; DeArmond, Fusco, & Dewey, 1974*

which the posterior pituitary releases vasopressin. Receptors also relay information to the **lateral preoptic area** of the hypothalamus, which controls drinking. A lesion in the lateral preoptic area impairs osmotic thirst partly by damage to cell bodies in that area itself and partly by damage to axons passing through or near it (Saad, Luiz, Camargo, Renzi, & Manani, 1996).

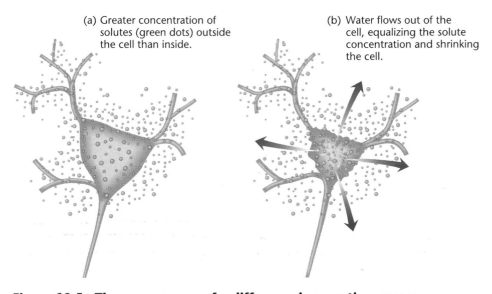

(a) Greater concentration of solutes (green dots) outside the cell than inside.

(b) Water flows out of the cell, equalizing the solute concentration and shrinking the cell.

Figure 10.5   The consequence of a difference in osmotic pressure
(a) A solute such as NaCl is more concentrated outside the cell than inside.
(b) Water flows by osmosis out of the cell until the concentrations are equal. Neurons in certain brain areas detect their own dehydration and trigger thirst.

When osmotic pressure triggers thirst, how do you know when to stop drinking? You do *not* wait until water has restored normal osmotic pressure for the receptors in the brain. The water you drink has to be absorbed through the digestive system and then pumped through the blood to the brain. That process takes 15 minutes or so, and if you continued drinking for all that time, you would consume far too much water. The body monitors swallowing and detects the water contents of the stomach and intestines. These messages can inhibit thirst long enough for water to reach the brain receptors and stop their activation (Huang, Sved, & Stricker, 2000).

HYPOVOLEMIC THIRST

Blood volume may drop sharply after bleeding, diarrhea, or extensive sweating. When blood volume and pressure are low, it is difficult to pump enough blood away from gravity and into the head; it is also difficult to force nutrients out of the blood capillaries and into the cells. The body's response is hypovolemic (HIpo-vo-LEE-mik) thirst, meaning thirst based on low volume. During hypovolemic thirst, the body needs to replenish not only its water but also the lost salts and other solutes.

After a loss of blood volume, an animal will not drink much pure water, which would dilute its body fluids. It drinks slightly salty water in greater amounts (Stricker, 1969). If the animal is offered both pure water and salt, it alternates between the two to yield an appropriate mixture. If sufficient salt is not readily available, it shows a strong craving for salty tastes. That craving develops automatically, as soon as the need exists, even in infant animals (Leshem, 1999; Richter, 1936). In contrast, specific hungers for other vitamins and minerals have to be learned by trial and error (Rozin & Kalat, 1971). People who have lost much salt, such as by extensive sweating or heavy menstrual flow, often crave salty snacks.

Specific sodium hunger depends largely on hormones (Schulkin, 1991). When the body's sodium reserves are low, the adrenal glands produce the hormone aldosterone, which causes the kidneys, salivary glands, and sweat glands to retain salt (Verrey & Beron, 1996). Aldosterone also triggers an increased preference for salty tastes. Angiotensin II increases sodium hunger as well (Sato, Yada, & De Luca, 1996). Aldosterone and angiotensin quickly alter the responses of neurons in the nucleus of the tractus solitarius, part of the taste system (see Figure 7.19). These neurons begin reacting to salt in nearly the same way they would to sugar (McCaughey & Scott, 2000).

Mechanisms

The body has two ways of detecting loss of blood volume (Stricker & Sved, 2000). First, baroreceptors attached to the large veins detect the pressure of blood returning to the heart. They transmit that information to the hypothalamus to increase thirst and secrete vasopressin, the hormone that constricts blood vessels to maintain blood pressure. The second mechanism depends on hormones. When blood volume drops, the kidneys respond by producing the enzyme *renin*. Renin splits a portion off angiotensinogen, a large protein that circulates in the blood, to form angiotensin I, which other enzymes convert to the hormone angiotensin II, which constricts the blood vessels, compensating for the drop in blood pressure (Figure 10.7).

When angiotensin II reaches the brain, it stimulates neurons in areas adjoining the third ventricle. The data are somewhat contradictory about whether angiotensin effects depend more on the OVLT (Fitts, Starbuck, & Ruhf, 2000) or the nearby subfornical organ (SFO), another area adjoining the third ventricle (Mangiapane & Simpson, 1980; Tanaka et al., 2001) (see Figure 10.6). Damage to the subfornical organ impairs drinking in a variety of situations (Starbuck & Fitts, 2001). In any case, angiotensin II receptors relay the information to the hypothalamus, which instigates thirst. Apparently, the axons to the hypothalamus actually use angiotensin II as their neurotransmitter (Tanaka, Hori, & Nomura, 2001).

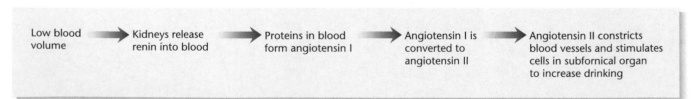

Low blood volume → Kidneys release renin into blood → Proteins in blood form angiotensin I → Angiotensin I is converted to angiotensin II → Angiotensin II constricts blood vessels and stimulates cells in subfornical organ to increase drinking

Figure 10.7 Hormonal response to hypovolemia

That is, angiotensin II is both the stimulus to these axons and their output.

Angiotensin II and baroreceptors have a **synergistic effect** (Epstein, 1983; Rowland, 1980). If two effects are synergistic, their combined effect is more than the sum of the two separate effects. That is, it may take less angiotensin II to stimulate thirst if the baroreceptors also indicate low blood pressure than if they indicate normal blood pressure.

Table 10.1 summarizes the differences between osmotic thirst and hypovolemic thirst.

Stop & Check

2. Would adding salt to the body's extracellular fluids increase or decrease osmotic thirst?

3. Who would drink more pure water—someone with osmotic thirst or someone with hypovolemic thirst?

Check your answers on page 304.

TABLE 10.1 Comparison of Osmotic and Hypovolemic Thirst

Type of Thirst	Stimulus	Best Relieved by Drinking	Receptor Location	Hormone Influences
Osmotic	High solute concentration outside cells causes loss of water from cells	Water	OVLT, a brain area adjoining the third ventricle	Accompanied by vasopressin secretion to conserve water
Hypovolemic	Low blood volume	Water containing solutes	1. Baroreceptors, measuring blood flow returning to the heart 2. Subfornical organ, a brain area adjoining the third ventricle	Increased by angiotensin II

MODULE 10.2

In Closing: The Psychology and Biology of Thirst

You may have thought that temperature regulation happens automatically and that water regulation depends on your behavior. You can see now that the distinction is not entirely correct. You control your body temperature partly by automatic means such as sweating or shivering and also partly by behavioral means such as choosing a warm or a cool place. You control your body water partly by the behavior of drinking and also by hormones that alter kidney activity. If your kidneys cannot regulate your water and sodium adequately, your brain gets signals to change your drinking or sodium intake. In short, keeping your body's chemical reactions going depends on both skeletal and autonomic controls.

SUMMARY

1. Different mammalian species have evolved different ways of maintaining body water, ranging from frequent drinking (beavers) to extreme conservation of fluids (gerbils). Humans alter their strategy depending on the availability of acceptable fluids. (p. 300)

2. An increase in the osmotic pressure of the blood draws water out of cells, causing osmotic thirst. Neurons in the OVLT, an area adjoining the third ventricle, detect changes in osmotic pressure and send information to hypothalamic areas responsible for vasopressin secretion and for drinking. (p. 300)

3. Loss of blood volume causes hypovolemic thirst. Animals with hypovolemic thirst drink more water containing solutes than pure water. (p. 302)

4. Loss of sodium salts from the body triggers sodium-specific cravings. The hormones aldosterone and angiotensin II synergistically stimulate such cravings. (p. 302)

5. Two stimuli have been identified for hypovolemic thirst: signals from the baroreceptors and the hormone angiotensin II, which increases when blood pressure falls. The two stimuli apparently act synergistically. (p. 302)

ANSWERS TO *STOP AND CHECK* QUESTIONS

1. If you lacked vasopressin, you would have to drink more like a beaver. You would not be able to conserve body water, so you would have to drink as much as possible all the time. (p. 300)

2. Adding salt to the extracellular fluids would increase osmotic thirst because it would draw water from the cells into the extracellular spaces. (p. 303)

3. The person with osmotic thirst would have a stronger preference for pure water. The one with hypovolemic thirst would drink more if the solution contained some salts. (p. 303)

THOUGHT QUESTIONS

1. An injection of concentrated sodium chloride triggers osmotic thirst, but an injection of equally concentrated glucose does not. Why not?

2. If all the water you drank leaked out through a tube connected to the stomach, how would your drinking change?

3. Many women crave salt during menstruation or pregnancy. Why?

MODULE 10.3

Hunger

Different species have different strategies for eating. A snake or crocodile might eat a huge meal (Figure 10.8) and then eat nothing more for months. Bears, too, eat as much as they can whenever they can. It is a sensible strategy because bears' main foods—fruits and nuts—are available in large quantities for only short times. Bears' occasional feasts tide them over through times of starvation. You might think of it as survival of the fattest. (Sorry about that one.)

Small birds, at the other extreme, usually eat only what they need at the moment and store almost no fat at all. Such restraint is risky, as a bird can starve quickly if food becomes scarce. The advantage is that a bird that needs to fly away from predators cannot afford to carry any extra weight (Figure 10.9). Even small birds switch strategies, however, and eat larger meals when food is hard to find or if there are no predators around (Gosler, Greenwood, & Perrins, 1995).

Humans eat more than we need at the moment, unlike small birds, but we do not stuff ourselves like bears—not as a rule, anyway. Choosing what to eat

Figure 10.9 A great tit, a small European bird
Ordinarily, when food is abundant, tits eat just what they need each day and maintain very low fat reserves. When food is harder to find, they eat all they can and live off fat reserves between meals. During one era when their predators were scarce, tits started putting on more fat regardless of the food supplies.

and deciding how much to eat are complicated and vitally important. Fortunately, we don't have to make perfect decisions, and we have a wide array of learned and unlearned mechanisms to help in the process.

Figure 10.8 A python swallowing a gazelle
The gazelle weighs about 50% more than the snake. Many reptiles eat huge but infrequent meals, and their total intake over a year is far less than that of a mammal. We mammals need far more fuel because we use so much more energy, mainly for maintaining basal metabolism.

HOW THE DIGESTIVE SYSTEM INFLUENCES FOOD SELECTION

Before discussing hunger, let's quickly examine the digestive system, diagramed in Figure 10.10. Its function is to break food down into smaller molecules that the cells can use. Digestion begins in the mouth, where food mixes with saliva containing enzymes that break down carbohydrates. Swallowed food travels down the esophagus to the stomach, where it mixes with hydrochloric acid and enzymes that digest proteins.

Between the stomach and the intestines is a round sphincter muscle that periodically opens to allow food to enter the intestines. Thus, the stomach stores food as well as digests it.

Food then passes to the small intestine, which contains enzymes that digest proteins, fats, and carbohydrates. It is also the main site for absorbing digested foodstuffs into the bloodstream. Digested materials absorbed through the small intestine are carried by the blood to body cells that use some of the nutrients and store the excess as glycogen, protein, or fat. Later, these reserves are converted into glucose, the body's primary fuel, which is mobilized into the bloodstream. The large intestine absorbs water and minerals and lubricates the remaining materials to pass them as feces.

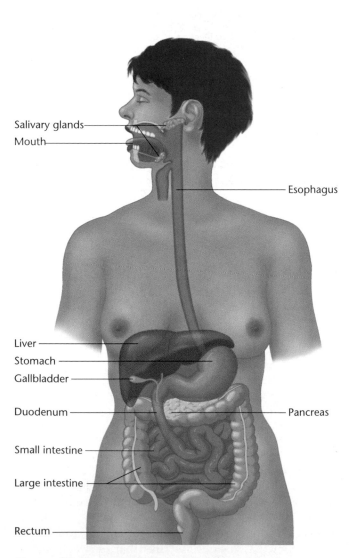

Salivary glands

Mouth

Esophagus

Liver

Stomach

Gallbladder

Duodenum

Pancreas

Small intestine

Large intestine

Rectum

Figure 10.10 The human digestive system

Enzymes and Consumption of Dairy Products

Newborn mammals survive entirely on mother's milk. They stop nursing for several reasons when they grow older: The milk dries up, the mother pushes the infants away, and the infants grow large enough to try other foods. In addition, most mammals beyond the age of weaning lose the intestinal enzyme **lactase**, which is necessary for metabolizing **lactose**, the sugar in milk. From then on, milk consumption can cause stomach cramps and gas (Rozin & Pelchat, 1988). Adult mammals can drink a little milk, as you may have noticed with a pet dog, but generally not much. The declining level of lactase may be an evolved mechanism to encourage weaning at the appropriate time.

Humans are the partial exception to this rule. Many adults have fairly high lactase levels and continue to consume milk and other dairy products throughout life. Worldwide, however, most adults cannot comfortably tolerate large amounts of milk products. About two thirds of all adult humans, including almost all Southeast Asians, have low levels of lactase because of a recessive gene (Flatz, 1987). Most of these people can eat moderate amounts of dairy products (especially cheese and yogurt, which are easier to digest than milk) but develop cramps or gas pains if they consume too much. Figure 10.11 shows the worldwide distribution of lactose tolerance.

Other Influences on Food Selection

For a **carnivore** (meat eater), selecting a satisfactory diet is relatively simple; it eats any animal it can catch. A lion won't become vitamin deficient unless it eats vitamin-deficient zebras. However, **herbivores** (plant eaters) and **omnivores** (those that eat both meat and plants) must distinguish between edible and inedible substances and find a proper balance of vitamins and minerals. One way to do so is to learn from the experiences of others. For example, juvenile rats tend to imitate the food selections of their elders (Galef, 1992). Similarly, children acquire their culture's food preferences, especially the spices, even if they do not like every food their parents enjoy (Rozin, 1990).

But how did their parents learn what to eat? Some individuals at some time must have learned for themselves. If you parachuted onto an uninhabited island covered with unfamiliar plants, you would use many strategies to select edible foods (Rozin & Vollmecke, 1986). First, you would select sweet foods, avoid bitter ones, and use moderation with salty or sour foods. Most sweets are nutritious and nearly all bitter substances are harmful (T. R. Scott & Verhagen, 2000). Second, you would prefer anything that tasted familiar.

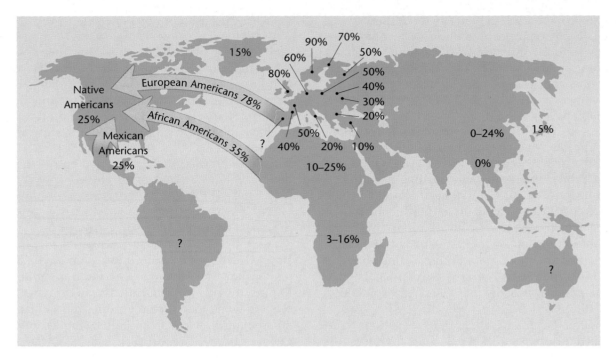

Figure 10.11   Percentage of adults who are lactose tolerant
People in areas with high lactose tolerance (e.g., Scandinavia) are likely to enjoy milk and other dairy products throughout their lives. Adults in areas with low tolerance (including much of Southeast Asia) do not ordinarily drink milk. *Source: Based on Flatz, 1987; Rozin & Pelchat, 1988*

After all, familiar foods are safe, but new foods may not be. What did you think of coffee the first time you tried it? Beer? Hot peppers? Most people like any flavor better after it becomes familiar.

Third, you would learn the consequences of eating each food you try. If you try something, especially something new, and then become ill, even hours later, your brain blames the illness on the food, and it won't taste good the next time you try it (Rozin & Kalat, 1971; Rozin & Zellner, 1985). This phenomenon is known as **conditioned taste aversion.** It is a robust phenomenon that occurs reliably after only a single pairing of food with illness, even if the illness came hours after the food (as it often does). In fact, you will come to dislike a food that is followed by intestinal discomfort even if you know that the nausea came from a thrill ride at the amusement park.

When you eat something
get sick, then you don't
want to eat
that food
any more.

Stop & Check

1. Why do most Southeast Asian cooks not use milk and other dairy products?

Check your answer on page 320.

HOW TASTE AND DIGESTION CONTROL HUNGER AND SATIETY

Eating is far too important to be entrusted to just one mechanism. Your brain gets messages from the mouth, the stomach, the intestines, and elsewhere indicating what to eat, how much, and when.

Oral Factors

You're a busy person, right? If you could get all the nutrition you need by swallowing pills, would you do it? Most of us would not. Never mind how much time we would save; we like to eat. In fact, many people *like* to taste and chew even when they are not hungry. Figure 10.12 shows a piece of 6500-year-old chewing

Battersby, 1997

Figure 10.12   Chewing gum from about 4500 B.C.
This piece of birch-bark tar has small tooth marks, indicating that it was chewed by a child or adolescent.

gum made from birch-bark tar. The tooth marks indicate that it was chewed by a child or teenager. Anthropologists don't know how the ancient people removed the sap to make the gum, and they aren't sure why anyone would chew something that tasted as bad as this gum probably did (Battersby, 1997). Clearly, the urge to chew is strong.

If necessary, could you become satiated without tasting your food? In one experiment, college students consumed lunch 5 days a week by swallowing one end of a rubber tube and then pushing a button to pump a liquid diet into the stomach (Jordan, 1969; Spiegel, 1973). (They were paid for participating.) After a few days of practice, each person established a consistent pattern, pumping in a constant volume of the liquid each day and maintaining a constant body weight. Most found the untasted meals unsatisfying, however, reporting a desire to taste or chew something (Jordan, 1969).

Although taste and other oral sensations contribute to the regulation of eating, they are not sufficient by themselves to end a meal. In **sham-feeding** experiments, everything an animal swallows leaks out of a tube connected to the esophagus or stomach. When sham-feeding, animals eat and swallow far more than normal. They may pause for a while, but then they eat again and again, never becoming satiated (G. P. Smith, 1998). In short, taste and other mouth sensations combine with other cues to produce satiety, but the taste and mouth cues alone are not sufficient.

The Stomach and Intestines

Ordinarily, we end a meal before the food has reached the blood, much less the cells that need fuel. The main signal to end a meal is distention of the stomach. In one experiment, researchers attached an inflatable cuff at the connection between the stomach and the small intestine (Deutsch, Young, & Kalogeris, 1978). When they inflated the cuff, food could not pass from the stomach to the duodenum. They carefully ensured that the cuff was not traumatic to the animal and did not interfere with feeding. The key result was that, with the cuff inflated, an animal ate a normal-size meal and then stopped; that is, it could become satisfied even though the food did not leave the stomach. Evidently, stomach distension is sufficient to produce satiety.

The stomach conveys satiety messages to the brain via the vagus nerve and the splanchnic nerves. The **vagus nerve** (cranial nerve X) conveys information about the stretching of the stomach walls, providing a major basis for satiety. The **splanchnic** (SPLANK-nik) **nerves** convey information about the nutrient contents of the stomach (Deutsch & Ahn, 1986).

Is the stomach the *only* part of the digestive system important for satiety? Later researchers repeated the experiment with the inflatable cuff and replicated the result that a rat ate the same amount regardless of whether the cuff was open or closed, indicating that stomach distension is *sufficient* for satiety. However, when the cuff was open, much food passed to the duodenum before the end of the meal. The **duodenum** (DYOU-oh-DEE-num or dyuh-ODD-ehn-uhm) is the part of the small intestine adjoining the stomach; it is the first digestive site that absorbs a significant amount of nutrients. The rats in this experiment stopped eating when the duodenum was partly distended and the stomach was far from full (Seeley, Kaplan, & Grill, 1995). Evidently, an eater can become satiated when food distends either the stomach or the duodenum. Indeed, people after surgical removal of the stomach still report feeling full, so the stomach cannot be necessary for the sensation.

Food infused directly to the duodenum of human volunteers produces reports of satiety (Lavin et al., 1996), and food infused to the duodenum of rats causes taste neurons in the pons to decrease their responsiveness to sweet tastes (Hajnal, Takenouchi, & Norgren, 1999). Curiously, sugars infused to the duodenum produce satiety much faster than fats do (Horn, Tordoff, & Friedman, 1996). Consequently, it is easy to overeat on a high-fat diet.

Food in the duodenum releases a number of peptides that in various ways decrease meal size (Woods & Seeley, 2000). One of these is the duodenal hormone **cholecystokinin** (ko-leh-SIS-teh-KI-nehn) **(CCK)**, which acts to limit meal size (Gibbs, Young, & Smith, 1973). The main mechanism is that CCK closes the sphincter muscle between the stomach and the duodenum, causing the stomach to hold its contents and fill more quickly than usual (McHugh & Moran, 1985; G. P. Smith & Gibbs, 1998). A shorter version of the CCK molecule also has effects in the brain as a neuromodulator, but the CCK released by the duodenum does not cross the blood-brain barrier. Rather, it stimulates the vagus nerve, causing the vagus to send a message that ultimately stimulates hypothalamic cells to release CCK themselves (G. J. Schwartz, 2000). You might think of this process as gut CCK molecules sending a fax of themselves to the brain. The fact that brain CCK and intestinal CCK have similar behavioral effects suggests that evolution uses the same chemicals in different places for similar purposes.

Glucose, Insulin, and Glucagon

Much of the digested food that enters the bloodstream is in the form of glucose, an important source of energy throughout the body and by far the main fuel of the brain. When the blood's glucose level starts to fall, the liver can convert stored nutrients into glucose. More variable is the amount of glucose available to the cells because that amount depends on two pancreatic hormones: insulin and glucagon. Insulin enables glucose to enter the cells. Most cells use the glucose for current energy needs; fat cells convert it to fat and liver cells convert it to glycogen. Glucagon has the reverse effect, stimulating the liver to convert stored glycogen to glucose, thus raising blood glucose levels. After a meal, insulin levels rise, glucose readily enters the cells, and appetite decreases. Some of the secreted insulin reaches the brain and acts as a satiety hormone, further decreasing hunger (Vanderweele, 1998). As time passes, the blood glucose level falls, receptors detect the drop, and the body instigates actions to increase glucose availability (Pardal & López-Barneo, 2002). One of these mechanisms is that the pancreas releases more glucagon to move glucose into the blood (Figure 10.13). Another mechanism is, of course, increased hunger.

If the insulin level stays high for long, the body continues to move blood glucose into the cells, including the liver cells and fat cells that store it. Consequently, the blood glucose levels drop. For example, in late autumn, migratory and hibernating species have constantly high insulin levels. They rapidly deposit much of each meal as fat and glycogen, grow hungry again, and continue gaining weight in preparation for a period without food (Figure 10.14).

When the insulin level remains constantly low, as in people with diabetes, blood glucose levels may be three or more times the normal level, but little of it enters the cells (Figure 10.15). Diabetic people and animals eat more food than normal because their cells are starving (Lindberg, Coburn, & Stricker, 1984), but they excrete most of their glucose unused, so they lose weight. (Note the paradox that prolonged high or low insulin levels can increase eating, although for different reasons.)

People produce more insulin not only when they eat but also when they are getting ready to eat. Increased insulin before a meal prepares the body to let more glucose enter the cells and to store the excess part of the meal as fats. Obese people produce

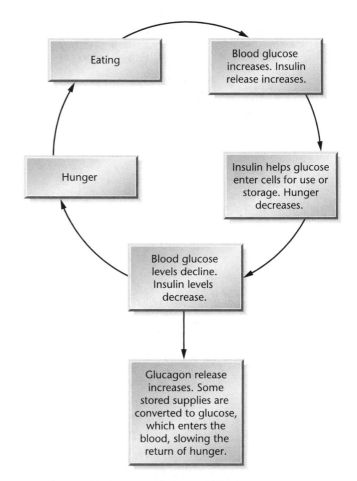

Figure 10.13 Insulin and glucagon feedback system
When glucose levels rise, the pancreas releases the hormone insulin, which causes cells to store the excess glucose as fats and glycogen. The entry of glucose into cells suppresses hunger and decreases eating, thereby lowering the glucose level.

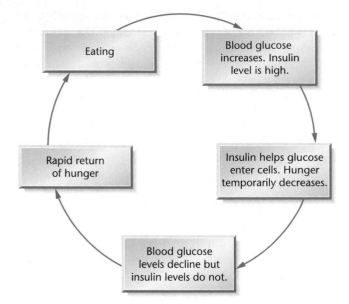

Figure 10.14 Effects of steadily high insulin levels on feeding
Constantly high insulin causes blood glucose to be stored as fats and glycogen. Because it becomes difficult to mobilize the stored nutrients, hunger returns soon after each meal.

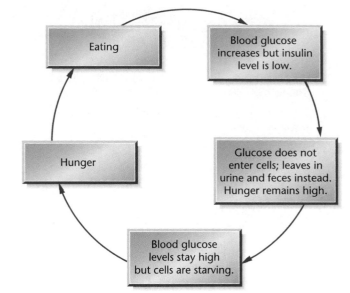

Figure 10.15 Untreated diabetic people eat much but lose weight
Because of their low insulin levels, the glucose in their blood cannot enter the cells either to be stored or used. Consequently, glucose is excreted into the urine, leaving the cells to starve.

more insulin than do people of normal weight (W. G. Johnson & Wildman, 1983). Their high levels of insulin cause more food than normal to be stored as fat, and therefore, their appetite returns soon after a meal (see Figure 10.14).

Stop & Check

6. Why do people with very low insulin levels eat so much? Why do people with constantly high levels eat so much?

7. What would happen to someone's appetite if insulin levels and glucagon levels were both high?

Check your answers on page 320.

THE HYPOTHALAMUS AND FEEDING REGULATION

Damage to small areas of the hypothalamus can produce undereating or overeating. At one time, researchers described the lateral hypothalamus as a feeding center and the ventromedial hypothalamus as a satiety center. We now regard that view as an oversimplification, and we seek a better understanding of how various areas contribute to the control of feeding.

The Lateral Hypothalamus

The **lateral hypothalamus** includes many neuron clusters and passing axons that contribute to feeding in so many and such diverse ways that it has been compared to a city train station (Leibowitz & Hoebel, 1998) (Figure 10.16). It controls insulin secretion, alters taste responsiveness, and influences feeding in other ways. After damage here, an animal refuses food and water, turning its head away as if the food were distasteful. The animal may starve to death unless it is force-fed, but if kept alive, it gradually recovers much of its ability to eat (Figure 10.17). In an intact animal, electrical stimulation of the lateral hypothalamus stimulates eating and food-seeking behaviors. Lateral hypothalamic neurons increase their activity in the presence of tasty food.

Many axons containing dopamine pass through the lateral hypothalamus, so damage to this area interrupts these fibers. To separate the roles of hypothalamic cells from those of passing fibers, investigators developed ways to damage only the axons or only the cells. For example, an injection of 6-hydroxydopamine

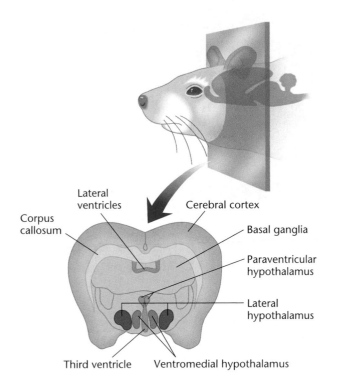

Lateral
ventricles

Cerebral cortex

Corpus
callosum

Basal ganglia

Paraventricular
hypothalamus

Lateral
hypothalamus

Third ventricle   Ventromedial hypothalamus

Figure 10.16 The lateral hypothalamus, ventromedial hypothalamus, and paraventricular hypothalamus
The side view above indicates the plane of the coronal section of the brain below. *Source: After Hart, 1976*

(6-OHDA) damages passing axons containing dopamine. The result is a chronically inactive, unresponsive animal, although it does eat if it has food in its mouth (Berridge, Venier, & Robinson, 1989). There-

fore, the passing axons do not regulate hunger; damage to them stops eating only by blocking all activity.

In other studies, experimenters used chemicals that damage only the cell bodies, or induced lesions in very young rats, before the dopamine axons reached the lateral hypothalamus. The result was a major loss of feeding without loss of arousal and activity (Almli, Fisher, & Hill, 1979; Grossman, Dacey, Halaris, Collier, & Routtenberg, 1978; Stricker, Swerdloff, & Zigmond, 1978).

The question remains: *How* does the lateral hypothalamus contribute to feeding? It contributes in several ways (Leibowitz & Hoebel, 1998) (Figure 10.18):

- Axons from the lateral hypothalamus to the NTS (nucleus of the tractus solitarius), part of the taste pathway (see p. 212), alter the taste sensation and the salivation response to the tastes.
- Some lateral hypothalamic cells increase the pituitary gland's secretion of hormones that increase insulin secretion.
- Axons from the lateral hypothalamus extend into several forebrain structures, facilitating ingestion and swallowing and causing cortical cells to increase their response to the taste, smell, or sight of food (Critchley & Rolls, 1996).
- Dopamine-containing axons that pass through the lateral hypothalamus initiate and reinforce learned behaviors.
- The lateral hypothalamus sends axons to the spinal cord, controlling autonomic responses such as digestive secretions (van den Pol, 1999). After damage to the lateral hypothalamus, the animal has trouble digesting foods.

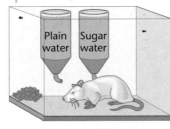 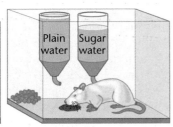 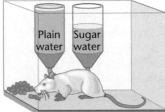 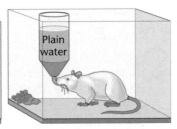

Stage 1. *Aphagia and adipsia.* Rat refuses all food and drink; must be force-fed to keep it alive.

Stage 2. *Anorexia.* Rat eats a small amount of palatable foods and drinks sweetened water. It still does not eat enough to stay alive.

Stage 3. *Adipsia.* The rat eats enough to stay alive, though at a lower-than-normal body weight. It still refuses plain water.

Stage 4. *Near-recovery.* The rat eats enough to stay alive, though at a lower-than-normal body weight. It drinks plain water, but only at mealtimes to wash down its food. Under slightly stressful conditions, such as in a cold room, the rat will return to an earlier stage of refusing food and water.

Figure 10.17 Recovery of feeding after damage to the lateral hypothalamus
At first, the rat refuses all food and drink. If kept alive for several weeks or months by force-feeding, it gradually recovers its ability to eat and drink enough to stay alive. However, even at the final stage of recovery, its behavior is not the same as that of normal rats. *Source: Based on Teitelbaum & Epstein, 1962*

10.3 Hunger   **311**

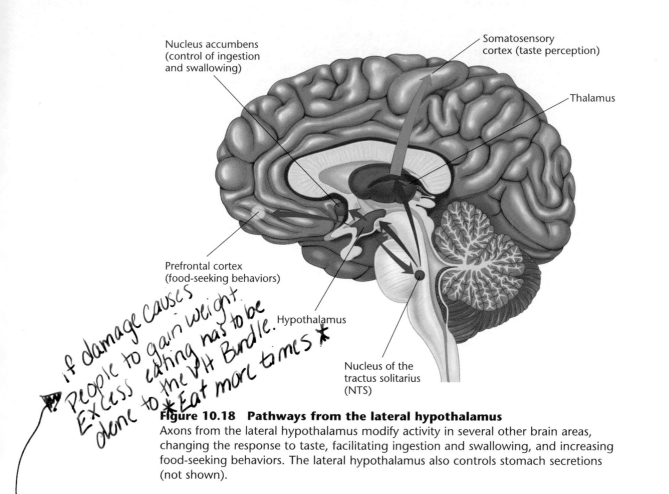

Nucleus accumbens
(control of ingestion
and swallowing)

Somatosensory
cortex (taste perception)

Thalamus

Prefrontal cortex
(food-seeking behaviors)

Hypothalamus

Nucleus of the
tractus solitarius
(NTS)

*[Handwritten note: If damage causes people to gain weight. Excess eating has to be done to the VH Bundle. *Eat more times*]*

Figure 10.18 Pathways from the lateral hypothalamus
Axons from the lateral hypothalamus modify activity in several other brain areas, changing the response to taste, facilitating ingestion and swallowing, and increasing food-seeking behaviors. The lateral hypothalamus also controls stomach secretions (not shown).

Medial Areas of the Hypothalamus

Near the lateral hypothalamus is a set of areas that contribute very differently to feeding. Neuroscientists have known since the 1940s that a large lesion centered on the **ventromedial hypothalamus (VMH)** leads to overeating and weight gain (see Figure 10.16). Some people with a tumor in this area have gained more than 10 kg (22 pounds) per month (Al-Rashid, 1971; Killeffer & Stern, 1970; Reeves & Plum, 1969). Rats with similar damage sometimes double or triple their weight (Figure 10.19). Eventually, body weight levels off at a stable but high set point, and total food intake declines to nearly normal levels.

Although these symptoms have been known as the *ventromedial hypothalamic syndrome,* damage limited to the ventromedial hypothalamic nucleus itself does not consistently increase eating or body weight. To produce a large effect, the lesion must extend outside the ventromedial nucleus to invade nearby medial hypothalamic cells and axons. Excess eating and increased body weight can also result from damage to the ventral noradrenergic bundle (Figure 10.20), an ascending axon pathway through the hypothalamus (Ahlskog & Hoebel, 1973; Ahlskog, Randall, & Hoebel, 1975; Gold, 1973).

Rats with damage in and around the ventromedial hypothalamus show an increased appetite compared to undamaged rats of the same weight (Peters, Sensenig, & Reich, 1973). After they gain much weight, they become finicky eaters. If their diet is bitter or otherwise untasty, they eat less than normal rats do. However, with a normal or sweetened diet, they eat far more than normal (Ferguson & Keesey, 1975; Teitelbaum, 1955). They eat meals of normal size, but they eat more frequently than normal (Hoebel & Hernandez, 1993). One reason is that they have increased stomach motility and secretions, and their stomachs empty faster than normal. The faster the stomach empties, the sooner an animal is ready for its next meal. Another reason for their frequent meals is that the damage increases insulin production (King, Smith, & Frohman, 1984), so a larger than normal percentage of each meal is stored as fat. If animals with this kind of damage are prevented from overeating, they gain weight anyway! Mark Friedman and Edward Stricker (1976) therefore proposed that the animal has to overeat because it stores so much fat that it has little fuel left over for its current needs.

Rats with damage in the nearby **paraventricular nucleus (PVN)** of the hypothalamus also overeat, but for a different reason. Instead of eating more frequent meals, they eat larger meals, as if they were insensitive

[Handwritten note: Causes weight gain but Big Meals.]

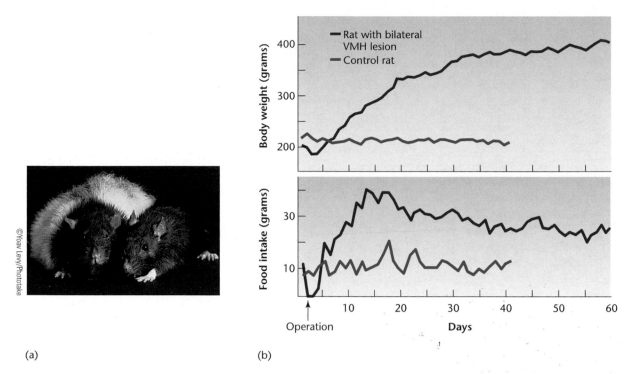

(a)

(b)

Figure 10.19 The effects of damage to the ventromedial hypothalamus
(a) On the right is a normal rat. On the left is a rat after damage to the ventromedial hypothalamus. The brain-damaged rat may weigh up to three times as much as a normal rat. *Source: Yoav Levy/Phototake* **(b)** Changes in weight and eating in a rat after damage to the ventromedial hypothalamus. Within a few days after the operation, the rat begins eating much more than normal. As it gains weight, it eats less, although its intake remains above normal. *Source: Reprinted by permission of the University of Nebraska Press from "Disturbances in Feeding and Drinking Behavior after Hypothalamic Lesions," by P. Teitelbaum, p. 39–69, in M. R. Jones, Ed., 1961, Nebraska Symposium on Motivation. Copyright ©1961 by the University of Nebraska Press. Copyright © renewed 1989 by the University of Nebraska Press.*

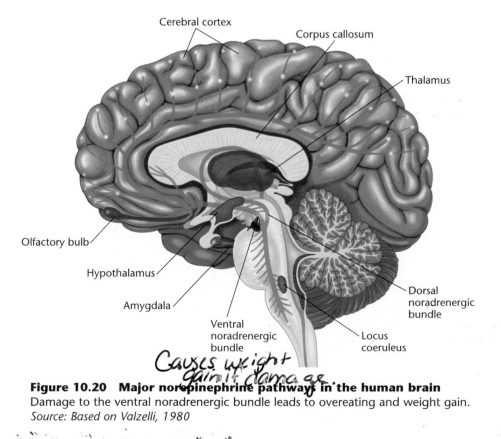

Figure 10.20 Major norepinephrine pathways in the human brain
Damage to the ventral noradrenergic bundle leads to overeating and weight gain.
Source: Based on Valzelli, 1980

to the usual signals for ending a meal (Leibowitz, Hammer, & Chang, 1981). Table 10.2 summarizes the effects of lesions in several areas of the hypothalamus.

TABLE 10.2 Effects of Lesions in Certain Hypothalamic Areas

Hypothalamic Area	Effect of Lesion
Preoptic area	Deficit in physiological mechanisms of temperature regulation
Lateral preoptic area	Deficit in osmotic thirst due partly to damage to cells and partly to interruption of passing axons
Lateral hypothalamus	Undereating, weight loss, low insulin level (because of damage to cell bodies); underarousal, underresponsiveness (because of damage to passing axons)
Ventromedial hypothalamus	Increased meal frequency, weight gain, high insulin level
Paraventricular nucleus	Increased meal size

We eat only partly because of hunger. One researcher asked young adults to keep a 7-day diary of everything they ate and the surrounding circumstances. Meal size showed the following patterns (de Castro, 2000):

- People eat more when they are with other people than when they eat alone, largely because meals last longer in social settings (Figure 10.21).
- The size of a meal depends on time of day, and the difference depends on local customs. In the United States, people eat more in the evening than at noon and feel less satisfied after a small meal late in the day than at noon. In France, people eat more at noon and less at night.
- Americans eat more on weekends, as shown in Figure 10.22. Obviously, this effect is based on cultural customs.
- Americans eat more if they think a food is "low-fat," even if in fact it isn't. If they think a food is high in fat, they decrease their intake during that meal *and* the next.
- People eat more when food tastes good (of course). If they consistently have an abundance of good-tasting food, they eat more than they need and gain weight.
- If people drink an alcoholic beverage with a meal, they eat the same amount as usual but take in more total calories because of the beverage.

Stop & Check

8. What are the effects of damage to the cell bodies in the lateral hypothalamus? Of damage to the axons passing through the lateral hypothalamus?

9. In what way does eating increase after damage in and around the ventromedial hypothalamus? After damage to the paraventricular nucleus?

Check your answers on page 320.

SATIETY CHEMICALS AND EATING DISORDERS

Obesity is considered a medical condition, whereas anorexia and bulimia are considered psychiatric conditions. Nevertheless, any eating disorder includes elements of both biology and psychology.

Obesity = Medical Problem
Anorexia/Bulimia = Psych Problem

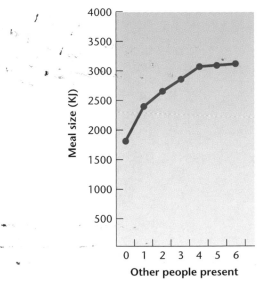

Figure 10.21 Eating in social settings
On the average, the more people present during a meal, the more each person is likely to eat. Meal size is expressed in kilojoules. One kilojoule = approximately 0.25 calorie. *Source: Reprinted from Nutrition, 16, J. M. de Castro, "Eating Behavior: Lessons from the Real World of Humans," p. 800–813, Copyright 2000, with permission from Elsevier Science.*

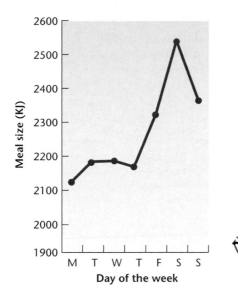

Figure 10.22 Meals throughout the week
On the average, people in the United States eat their biggest meals on weekends, especially Saturdays. *Source: Reprinted from Nutrition, 16, J. M. de Castro, "Eating Behavior: Lessons from the Real World of Humans," p. 800–813, Copyright 2000, with permission from Elsevier Science.*

Physiological studies will not get us far toward understanding these social and cultural influences, but they may help explain why some people eat so much more than others, even when they eat under similar conditions. Research may also help researchers devise new methods to help people control their weight.

Leptin

[handwritten: Peptide — People w/ the obese gene fail to produce leptin]

Figure 10.23 compares two normal mice to a mouse with a gene known as *obese* (Zhang et al., 1994). After researchers located this gene, they identified a previously unknown peptide that the normal gene makes, now known as **leptin** (from the Greek word *leptos,* meaning "slender") (Halaas et al., 1995). In genetically normal mammals (not just mice), fat cells throughout the body produce the peptide leptin: The more fat cells, the more leptin. Leptin circulates through the blood, notifying the rest of the body about the current fat supplies. Mice with the *obese* gene fail to produce leptin.

When leptin levels are high, animals act as if they have plenty of nutrition. They eat less (Campfield, Smith, Guisez, Devos, & Burn, 1995), become more active (Elias, Lee, et al., 1998), and increase the activity of their immune systems (Lord et al., 1998). (If you have enough fat supplies, you can afford to devote energy to your immune system. If you have no fat, you are starving and have to conserve energy wherever you

can.) In adolescence, a certain level of leptin triggers the onset of puberty. (Again, if your fat supply is low, you don't have enough energy to provide for a baby.) On the average, thinner people enter puberty later.

Mice with the obese gene do not make leptin, but they respond to leptin injections by becoming more active and eating less (Pellymounter et al., 1995). As you might imagine, news of this research inspired pharmaceutical companies to hope they could make a fortune by selling leptin. They worried about the potential for abuse: What if thin people (mostly women) trying to get still thinner took leptin and starved themselves to death? But further research found that normal-weight mice did not starve in response to leptin. So leptin looked promising indeed.

[handwritten: overweight people have high levels of leptin — Not]

Unfortunately, almost all overweight people already have high levels of leptin (Considine et al., 1996). (Remember—the more fat, the more leptin.) A very few people have genes that prevent them from producing normal amounts of leptin, and they do become obese (Farooqi et al., 2001). Presumably, leptin would help these people.

If human obesity is seldom due to a lack of leptin, perhaps some people are insensitive to it. A few people have been found with a hereditary defect in the gene controlling the leptin receptor; they become obese, as we would expect (Clément et al., 1998). Could physicians help overweight people lose weight by giving huge doses of leptin to overcome the problem of weak sensitivity to it? Maybe, but caution is necessary. Excess leptin levels increase the risk of diabetes and other medical problems (B. Cohen, Novick, & Rubinstein, 1996; Naggert et al., 1995). The search therefore turns to other chemicals related to satiety.

Figure 10.23 The effects of the obese gene on body weight in mice
A gene that has been located on a mouse chromosome leads to increased eating, decreased metabolic rate, and increased weight gain.

Neuropeptide Y

In a hypothalamic area known as the *arcuate nucleus,* leptin inhibits neurons whose axons release a neuromodulator peptide called **neuropeptide Y (NPY)** (Stephens et al., 1995), one of the most abundant peptides in the brain. Among other effects, NPY powerfully inhibits the paraventricular nucleus (PVN) of the hypothalamus and therefore increases meal size, as tastelessly illustrated in Figure 10.24 (Billington & Levine, 1992; Leibowitz & Alexander, 1991; Morley, Levine, Grace, & Kneip, 1985).

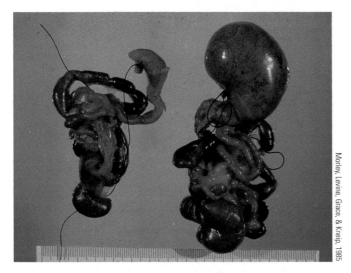

Morley, Levine, Grace, & Kneip, 1985

Figure 10.24 The effects of inhibiting the paraventricular nucleus of the hypothalamus
On the left is the digestive system of a normal rat. On the right is the digestive system of a rat that has had its paraventricular hypothalamus inhibited by injections of peptide YY, a neurotransmitter closely related to neuropeptide Y. The rat continued eating even though its stomach and intestines distended almost to the point of bursting. (All right, I admit this is a little bit disgusting.)

Let's restate for clarity. Activity in the paraventricular nucleus (PVN) limits meal size.

Axons from the arcuate nucleus release NPY to inhibit the PVN and therefore increase meal size.

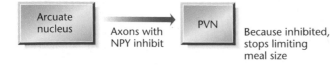

[handwritten note:] Powers the PVN to increase meal size

Leptin inhibits the arcuate nucleus, thereby preventing inhibition of the PVN, with the net result of decreasing eating.

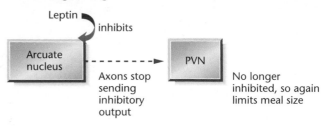

In short, NPY increases meal size and leptin decreases it. Mice without leptin overeat.

Why do many humans overeat? So far as researchers can tell, most obese people produce plenty of leptin and have normal leptin receptors. Possibly, their blood-brain barrier prevents normal amounts of leptin from reaching the brain. Perhaps they have abnormalities of other transmitters in the PVN or elsewhere. And of course, many other explanations are possible.

Other Neuromodulators and Hormones

What other chemicals might influence feeding? Much of the research on these chemicals comes from studies using microdialysis, as described in Methods 10.1. Here is a partial list of neuromodulators and hormones that act on the hypothalamus to influence eating (Di Marzo et al., 2001; Horvath, Diano, Sotonyi, Heiman, & Tschöp, 2001; G. P. Smith, 2000; Wellman, 2000):

Increase Eating	*Decrease Eating*
Neuropeptide Y (NPY)	Leptin
Peptide YY (PYY)	Cholecystokinin (CCK)
Melanocortin (MCH)	Insulin
Orexin A and orexin B	α-Melanocyte-stimulating hormone (α-MSH)
Norepinephrine (at α₂ receptors)	Norepinephrine (at α₁ receptors)
Galanin	Serotonin
Growth-hormone releasing hormone	Glucagon-like peptide-1 (GLP-1)
Agouti-related peptide	Bombesin and related peptides
Ghrelin	Estrogen
Dynorphin and β-endorphin	Corticotropin-releasing hormone
Cannabinoids	Cytokines
	Cocaine- and amphetamine-related transcript

Microdialysis

In microdialysis, an investigator implants into the brain a double fluid-filled tube with a thin membrane tip across which chemicals can diffuse. The experimenter slowly delivers some fluid through one tube, while an equal amount of fluid exits through the other tube and brings with it some of the brain chemicals that have diffused across the membrane. In this manner, researchers discover which neurotransmitters are released during eating and which are released at the point of satiation (e.g., Stanley, Schwartz, Hernandez, Leibowitz, & Hoebel, 1989).

Source: Juan Dominguez, U. Cincinnati College of Medicine

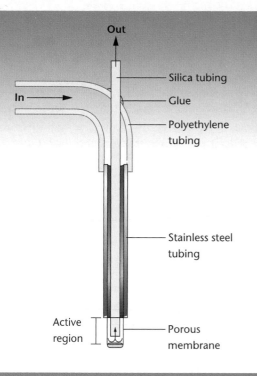

Several general points about these lists are more important than memorizing the names of chemicals. First, we can almost ignore species differences. The structure of insulin and other peptides varies slightly from one species to another, but for the most part, the same chemicals serve the same functions in all animals.

Second, most of these chemicals serve related functions in the periphery and the brain. For example, the peripheral hormone glucagon mobilizes stored food for current use and therefore decreases the need to eat; the very similar peptide GLP-1 acts as a neuromodulator in the brain to decrease eating. CCK from the intestines closes the muscle between the stomach and intestines, thereby increasing stomach distension; CCK in the brain also inhibits feeding. Insulin in the periphery inhibits feeding; so does insulin in the brain (Brüning et al., 2000). The mechanisms are different, but the outcome is the same. Evidently, evolution has been conservative, using the same chemical repeatedly for similar functions (Hoebel, 1988).

Third, most if not all of these chemicals influence other behaviors besides feeding. For example, orexin (or hypocretin), which stimulates feeding, also enhances wakefulness (Willie, Chemelli, Sinton, & Yanagisawa, 2001). As we saw in Chapter 9, narcolepsy is associated with deficient orexin activity.

Fourth, note how many chemicals exert some control over feeding. Obesity in rodents has been related to deficient leptin, deficient CCK (Bi, Ladenheim, Schwartz, & Moran, 2001), deficient melanocortin (Butler et al., 2001), and excessive corticosterones (Masuzaki et al., 2001). Melanocortin is emerging as a key part of the system, influenced by insulin, diet drugs, and many other chemicals known to affect eating (Benoit et al., 2002; Heisler et al., 2002). Undoubtedly, other peptide abnormalities influence feeding as well. Presumably, the complexity of the system reflects the importance of feeding; evolution did not entrust its control to just one or two chemicals. Different chemicals influence feeding in different ways. Several of these chemicals that decrease eating may do so partly by inducing nausea. Some alter metabolism, fat storage, and so forth.

Because of the multiple transmitter contributions, researchers have many options for developing weight-loss drugs, including those influencing the digestive system and others influencing the brain (Halford & Blundell, 2000). For example, one peptide that increases appetite is orexin. A promising drug that blocks orexin receptors decreases meal size in rats (Rodgers et al., 2001). Future research will address its efficacy and safety in humans. Perhaps a combination of drugs that affect several kinds of receptors might be particularly effective.

10. Why are leptin injections probably less helpful for overweight people than for obese mice?

11. What would be the effect on eating from a drug that blocks NPY receptors? One that blocks CCK receptors?

Check your answers on page 320.

Genetics and Human Body Weight

You have probably noticed that most thin parents have thin children and most heavy parents have heavy children. The resemblance no doubt relates in part to the family's food choices, but also to genetics. A Danish study found that the weights of 540 adopted children correlated much more strongly with that of their biological relatives than with that of their adoptive relatives (Stunkard et al., 1986). Overall, researchers estimate that human obesity has a heritability (see p. 11) of about .4 to .7 (Comuzzie & Allison, 1998). For links to useful information about obesity, check this Web site: www.obesity.org/

In some cases, obesity can be traced to the effects of a single gene. The most common of these is a mutation in the gene for the receptor for melanocortin, one of the neuropeptides responsible for hunger. People with a mutation in that gene overeat, become obese in childhood, and maintain the excess weight throughout life (Mergen, Mergen, Ozata, Oner, & Oner, 2001). Researchers have also found evidence for a gene on chromosome 4 that is linked to obesity in women, though not men. Its exact location and nature have not been established (S. Stone et al., 2002).

However, strong single-gene influences on eating are the exception, not the rule. People have genes that influence eating in many ways. For example, comparisons of monozygotic and dizygotic twins indicate that various genes influence how much stomach distension is needed to end a meal, whether we prefer to eat big breakfasts or big dinners, how much we overeat when the food tastes great, and how much we overeat when we are eating in a big friendly group (de Castro, 2002; de Castro & Plunkett, 2002). Researchers have identified several genes that are significantly more common among obese people than others, even though they are not always present in the obese and not always absent in people of normal weight (Feitosa et al., 2002; Hinney et al., 2000).

The actual outcome depends strongly on the environment as well. Far more people are obese today than in previous eras because of changes in diet and lifestyle. (Evolution acts much more slowly.) One hypothesis is that early under- or overfeeding interacts with genes in vulnerable people to modify the brain or digestive organs permanently (Levin, 2000). One illustrative example is diabetes: Overeating can induce diabetes, especially in genetically vulnerable people, and once diabetes begins, it continues even if the person loses weight.

Consider in particular the Native American Pimas of Arizona and Mexico. Most are seriously overweight, apparently because of several genes (Norman et al., 1998), although obesity was not common among them a few decades ago. At that time, they ate a diet of Sonoran Desert plants, which ripen only in brief seasons. The Pimas probably evolved an eating strategy like bears: Eat all you can when food is available because it will have to carry you through a period without food. They also evolved a tendency to be inactive most of the time to conserve energy. Now, with a more typical U.S. diet that is equally available at all times, overeating and inactivity are a maladaptive strategy. In short, their overweight depends on both the genes and the environment; neither one by itself would have this effect.

Weight-Loss Techniques

Losing weight permanently is like quitting smoking, quitting alcohol, or breaking any other strong habit: It is difficult, more people try than succeed, but it can be done.

A survey found that weight-loss specialists agreed on little, except that almost any weight-loss plan should include increased exercise (M. B. Schwartz & Brownell, 1995). Exercise by itself won't trim much weight. For example, walking 4.5 km (a little less than 3 miles) expends about the energy equivalent of a handful of potato chips (Burton, 1994). However, exercise in combination with decreased eating can be effective. Furthermore, exercise lowers blood pressure, lowers cholesterol levels, and improves health, which is the ultimate goal anyway (Campfield, Smith, & Burn, 1998).

Weight loss requires the difficult habit of stopping a meal even when hungry and when the food tastes good. Some people are helped by organized weight-loss programs in which they share encouragement and swap low-calorie recipes with others. Some are also helped by appetite-suppressant drugs. For years, the most effective combination was "fen-phen": *Fenfluramine* increases the release of serotonin and blocks its reuptake. *Phentermine* blocks reuptake of norepinephrine and dopamine. The combination of the two drugs produces brain effects similar to those of a completed meal (Rada & Hoebel, 2000). Unfortunately, fenfluramine often produces medical complications, so it has been withdrawn from use. A replacement drug, *sibutramine* (Meridia), blocks reuptake of both serotonin and norepinephrine. Investigators are also experimenting with drugs that inhibit absorption of dietary fat into the intestines, such as the drug orlistat (Xenical), and drugs that alter nutrient absorption and metabolism (Bray & Tartaglia, 2000).

Anorexia and Bulimia

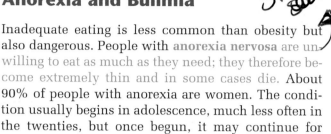

Inadequate eating is less common than obesity but also dangerous. People with **anorexia nervosa** are unwilling to eat as much as they need; they therefore become extremely thin and in some cases die. About 90% of people with anorexia are women. The condition usually begins in adolescence, much less often in the twenties, but once begun, it may continue for years. A genetic predispostion is likely (Grice et al., 2002), although the relationship between the gene and the behavior is not clearly established.

People with anorexia are often interested in food; many enjoy cooking and the taste and smell of food. Their problem is not a lack of appetite but a fear of becoming fat or of losing self-control. Most people with anorexia are hardworking perfectionists who are amazingly active, unlike other people on the verge of starvation. The perfectionism and driven activity resemble obsessive-compulsive behavior, and obsessive-compulsive disorder is common among the relatives of people with anorexia (Lilenfeld et al., 1998). Some people with anorexia also show signs of depression, although few respond well to antidepressant drugs.

For further information about anorexia, see this Web site:

www.mentalhealth.com/dis/p20-et01.html

Bulimia nervosa is a condition in which people (again, mostly women) alternate between extreme dieting and binges of overeating. Some (not all) force themselves to vomit after huge meals. People with bulimia tend to have higher than normal levels of peptide YY (PYY), a neuromodulator with effects similar to NPY (Kaye, Berrettini, Gwirtsman, & George, 1990). They also have lower than normal levels of CCK (Brambilla et al., 1995) and altered serotonin receptors (Kaye et al., 2001). However, we do not know whether these abnormalities are causes or results of bulimia.

One analysis of bulimia compares it to drug addiction (Hoebel, Rada, Mark, & Pothos, 1999). Eating tasty foods activates the same brain areas as addictive drugs. Drug addicts who cannot get drugs sometimes overeat as a substitute, and food-deprived people or animals become more likely than others to use drugs. A cycle of food deprivation followed by overeating strongly stimulates the brain's reinforcement areas in much the same way as drug deprivation followed by more drug use. Researchers examined rats that were food deprived for 12 hours a day, including the first 4 hours of their wakeful period, and then offered a solution of 25% glucose—a

very sweet, syrupy liquid. Over several weeks on this regimen, they drank more and more each day and especially increased how much they drank in the first hour. The eating released dopamine and opiate-like compounds in the brain, similar to the effects of highly addicting drugs (Colantuoni et al., 2001, 2002). If they were then deprived of this liquid, they showed withdrawal symptoms including head shaking and teeth chattering, which could be relieved by an injection of morphine. In other words, they had developed a sugar dependence or addiction. Similarly, it is possible that bulimic cycles of dieting and binge eating may constitute a kind of addiction (Hoebel, et al., 1999). Note the difficulty of quitting this kind of addiction. Someone addicted to heroin or alcohol can try to quit altogether (a difficult task). Someone addicted to bulimia cannot quit eating altogether. The goal is to learn to eat in moderation. Imagine, by analogy, the extreme difficulty for an alcoholic or heroin addict to try to use those substances in moderation.

In Closing: The Multiple Controls of Hunger

Eating is controlled by a number of brain areas, which monitor blood glucose, stomach distention, duodenal contents, body weight, and many other variables. Because the system is so complex, it can produce errors in many ways. However, the complexity of the system also provides a kind of security, a bit like the checks and balances in some governments: If one part of the system makes a mistake, another part can counteract it. We notice people who choose a poor diet or eat the wrong amount. Perhaps we should be even more impressed by how many people eat more or less appropriately. The regulation of eating succeeds not in spite of its complexity but because of it.

SUMMARY

1. The ability to digest a food is one major determinant of preference for that food. For example, people who cannot digest lactose generally do not like to eat dairy products. (p. 306)

2. Other major determinants of food selection include innate preferences for certain tastes, a preference for familiar foods, and the ability to learn about the consequences of foods. (p. 306)

3. People and animals eat partly for the sake of taste. However, a sham-feeding animal, which tastes its foods but does not absorb them, eats far more than normal. (p. 307)

4. Factors controlling hunger include distension of the stomach and intestines, secretion of CCK by the duodenum, and the availability of glucose and other nutrients to the cells. (p. 308)

5. The hormone insulin increases the entry of glucose to the cells, including cells that store nutrients for future use. Glucagon mobilizes stored fuel and converts it to glucose in the blood. Thus, the combined influence of insulin and glucagon determines how much glucose is available at any time. (p. 309)

6. Damage to cells in the lateral hypothalamus leads to decreased eating and loss of weight by affecting taste, salivation, swallowing, food-seeking behaviors, and insulin. (p. 310)

7. Damage to the ventromedial hypothalamus and surrounding areas increases meal frequency; damage to the paraventricular nucleus of the hypothalamus increases meal size. Damage to either of these areas can lead to weight gain. (p. 312)

8. Ordinarily, fat cells produce a protein called leptin, which inhibits hypothalamic secretion of neuropeptide Y (NPY) and thereby limits meal size. If an individual fails to produce leptin or if the leptin fails to inhibit NPY secretion, the result is overeating and obesity. (p. 315)

9. A number of other neurotransmitters also affect eating, and researchers are exploring many possibilities for new appetite-controlling drugs. (p. 316)

10. A few people have single genes that lead almost irresistibly to obesity. Many more people have genes that merely increase the probability of obesity. The actual weight outcome depends on cultural influences, including cuisine and activity patterns. (p. 318)

11. Anorexia nervosa and bulimia nervosa are eating disorders that may be influenced by biological predispositions, although they also certainly depend on cultural pressures. (p. 319)

ANSWERS TO *STOP AND CHECK* QUESTIONS

1. Most Southeast Asian adults lack the digestive enzyme lactase, which is needed to metabolize the sugar in milk. (p. 307)

2. When animals sham-feed (and all the food leaks out of the digestive system), they chew and taste their food but do not become satiated. (p. 309)

3. If a cuff is attached to the junction between the stomach and duodenum so that food cannot leave the stomach, an animal becomes satiated when the stomach is full. (p. 309)

4. If food can leave the stomach, an animal eats the same amount as if it can't leave the stomach. At the time it stops eating, the stomach is less full if food has been free to leave the stomach and enter the duodenum. (p. 309)

5. When the duodenum is distended, it releases CCK, which closes the sphincter muscle between the stomach and duodenum and therefore increases the rate at which the stomach becomes full. Also, neural signals from the intestines cause certain cells in the hypothalamus to release CCK as a neuromodulator, and at its receptors, it triggers decreased feeding. (pp. 309)

6. Those with very low levels, as in diabetes, cannot get glucose to enter their cells, and therefore, they are constantly hungry. They pass much of their nutrition in the urine and feces. Those with constantly high levels deposit much of their glucose into fat and glycogen, so within a short time after a meal, the supply of glucose drops. (p. 310)

7. When glucagon levels rise, stored glycogen is converted to glucose, which enters the blood. If insulin levels are also high, the glucose entering the blood is free to enter all the cells. So the result would be decreased appetite. (p. 310)

8. After damage to cell bodies in the lateral hypothalamus, animals eat less, while remaining active. After damage to the axons passing through the lateral hypothalamus, the animal becomes less aroused and less active. (p. 314)

9. Animals with damage to the ventromedial hypothalamus eat more frequent meals. Animals with damage to the paraventricular nucleus of the hypothalamus eat larger meals. (p. 314)

10. Unlike obese mice, overweight people produce their own leptin in proportion to body fat; however, they may be insensitive to it. Also, very large amounts of leptin can induce diabetes. (p. 318)

11. A drug that blocks NPY receptors would decrease feeding. A drug that blocks CCK receptors would increase feeding. (p. 318)

THOUGHT QUESTION

For most people, insulin levels tend to be higher during the day than at night. Use this fact to explain why people grow hungry a few hours after a daytime meal but not so quickly at night.

Key Terms and Activities

TERMS

aldosterone (p. 302)

angiotensin II (p. 302)

anorexia nervosa (p. 319)

baroreceptor (p. 302)

basal metabolism (p. 294)

bulimia nervosa (p. 319)

carnivore (p. 306)

cholecystokinin (CCK) (p. 308)

conditioned taste aversion (p. 307)

duodenum (p. 308)

glucagon (p. 309)

herbivore (p. 306)

homeostasis (p. 294)

homeothermic (p. 295)

hypovolemic thirst (p. 302)

insulin (p. 309)

lactase (p. 306)

lactose (p. 306)

lateral hypothalamus (p. 310)

lateral preoptic area (p. 301)

leptin (p. 315)

negative feedback (p. 294)

neuropeptide Y (NPY) (p. 316)

omnivore (p. 306)

osmotic pressure (p. 300)

osmotic thirst (p. 301)

OVLT (p. 301)

paraventricular nucleus (PVN) (p. 312)

poikilothermic (p. 295)

preoptic area/anterior hypothalamus (POA/AH) (p. 298)

prostaglandin E_1 and prostaglandin E_2 (p. 298)

set point (p. 294)

sham-feeding (p. 308)

splanchnic nerve (p. 308)

subfornical organ (SFO) (p. 302)

supraoptic nucleus and paraventricular nucleus (p. 301)

synergistic effect (p. 303)

vagus nerve (p. 308)

vasopressin (also known as antidiuretic hormone, ADH) (p. 300)

ventromedial hypothalamus (VMH) (p. 312)

SUGGESTIONS FOR FURTHER READING

Bray, G.A., Bouchard, C., & P. T. James (Eds.). (1998). *Handbook of obesity*. New York: Dekker. Summary of research on causes and treatment of obesity.

Capaldi, E.D. (Ed.). (1996). *Why we eat what we eat*. Washington, DC: American Psychological Association. Discusses the complex motivations that interact in eating and food selection.

Widmaier, E.P. (1998). *Why geese don't get obese (and we do)*. New York: Freeman. Lighthearted and often entertaining discussion of the physiology of eating, thirst, and temperature regulation.

WEB SITES TO EXPLORE

You can go to the Biological Psychology Study Center and click these links. While there, you can also check for suggested articles available on InfoTrac College Edition. The Biological Psychology Internet address is: **http://psychology.wadsworth.com/ kalatbiopsych8e/**

Scientific Obesity-Related Links
http://www.obesity.org/

Internet Mental Health: Anorexia Nervosa
http://www.mentalhealth.com/dis/p20-et01.html

CD-ROM: EXPLORING BIOLOGICAL PSYCHOLOGY

Pathways from the lateral hypothalamus (animation)

Anorexia Patient: Susan (video)

Stress & Fat (video)

Critical Thinking (essay questions)

Chapter Quiz (multiple choice questions)

Reproductive Behaviors

11

Chapter Outline

Main Ideas

1. Sex hormones exert organizing and activating effects. Organizing effects on the genitals and brain occur during a sensitive period of early development and last indefinitely. Activating effects are transient and may occur at any time.

2. In mammals, the presence or absence of testosterone determines whether the genitals and hypothalamus will develop in the male or the female manner, although for certain characteristics testosterone must first be converted to estradiol within the cell.

3. Sex hormones, including testosterone and estradiol, activate specific sexual, parental, and other behaviors.

4. Much about men's and women's sexual behavior, including mate choice, could be the product of evolutionary selection. However, current data do not enable us to determine how much is built-in and how much is determined by our experiences.

5. Certain patterns of genes, hormones, and brain anatomy are related to differences in sexual identity and orientation, but how they interact with experience is not yet clear.

A powerful change comes over people around the time of adolescence. Their bodies change: breast growth and menstruation in females, beard growth and deepening of the voice in males, a growth spurt and onset of pubic hair in both. Their behavior changes, too. Instead of the occasional shy flirtations of preadolescence, people are suddenly preoccupied with sex. Just the sight of a special someone walking by can get the heart thumping.

Those changes are not unique to humans. It is a widespread rule that the time of sexual maturation of the body is also the time of increased interest in sexual behavior. Many questions remain, however. For example, why do some people become sex offenders, and what can we do about it? Why are some people attracted to male partners and others to female partners? What makes people identify themselves as male or female? For questions such as these, hormones are certainly not the whole story. We shall consider the current state of knowledge, but the challenge to future research is to discover how the effects of hormones combine with those of experiences.

Opposite:
Humans may be the only species that plans parenthood, but all species have a strong biological drive that can lead to parenthood. *Source: Art Wolfe*

323

MODULE 11.1

The Effects of Sex Hormones

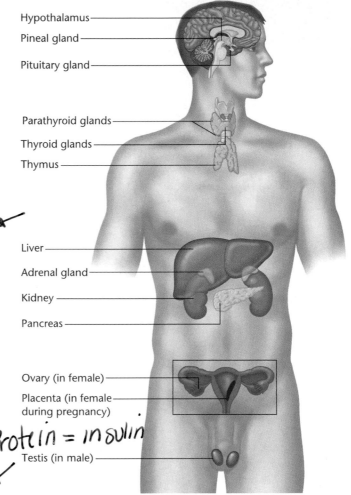

If you want to tell a friend something personal, you say it face to face. If you have a message for everyone—such as the opening of a new store—you place an ad in the newspaper or make an announcement on the radio. The nervous system does its one-to-one communications at synapses. For more widespread messages, it mobilizes hormones.

A **hormone** is a chemical that is secreted by a gland and conveyed by the blood to other organs, whose activity it influences. We already encountered a few examples of hormones in the previous chapter, but now is a good time to discuss hormones in general because of their enormous importance in reproductive behaviors. Figure 11.1 presents the major **endocrine** (hormone-producing) **glands**. Table 11.1 lists some important hormones and their principal effects. (A complete list would be impossible at this time. Many organs release small amounts of many chemicals with unknown functions.)

Hormones are particularly useful for coordinating long-lasting changes in multiple parts of the body. An example from Chapter 10 is leptin, which changes appetite and activity levels. For another example, in early spring, birds that are preparing to migrate secrete hormones that change their eating and digestion to store extra energy for a long journey. The birds also replace their old feathers with brightly colored new ones; they start flying north; they start seeking mates; males start singing; and so forth.

Most hormones fall into a few major classes. One class is composed of protein hormones and peptide hormones, composed of chains of amino acids. (Proteins are longer chains and peptides are shorter.) Insulin, one example of a protein hormone, facilitates the flow of glucose and other nutrients into the cells. Protein and peptide hormones attach to membrane receptors where they activate a second messenger within the cell—exactly the same process as at a metabotropic synapse.

Another major class is the steroid hormones, which contain four carbon rings, as Figure 11.2 shows. Steroids are derived from cholesterol; we are often warned about the risks of excessive cholesterol, but a moderate amount is necessary for generating these important hormones. Steroids exert their effects

Protein = insulin (handwritten)

cholesterol (handwritten)

in two ways. First, they bind to membrane receptors, just as peptide and protein hormones do. Second, they enter cells and attach to receptors in the cytoplasm, which then move to the nucleus of the cell where they determine which genes will be expressed (Figure 11.3). Two important steroids are cortisol, which is predominant in humans, and corticosterone, which is predominant in rodents. Released by the adrenal cortex in response to stressful experiences,

Figure 11.1 Location of some major endocrine glands
Source: Starr & Taggart, 1989

Labels (top to bottom): Hypothalamus, Pineal gland, Pituitary gland, Parathyroid glands, Thyroid glands, Thymus, Liver, Adrenal gland, Kidney, Pancreas, Ovary (in female), Placenta (in female during pregnancy), Testis (in male)

TABLE 11.1 Partial List of Hormone-Releasing Glands

Organ	Hormone	Hormone Functions
Hypothalamus	Various releasing hormones	Promote or inhibit release of various hormones by pituitary
Anterior pituitary	Thyroid-stimulating hormone (TSH)	Stimulates thyroid gland
	Luteinizing hormone (LH)	Increases production of progesterone (female), testosterone (male); stimulates ovulation
	Follicle-stimulating hormone (FSH)	Increases production of estrogen and maturation of ovum (female) and sperm production (male)
	ACTH	Increases secretion of steroid hormones by adrenal gland
	Prolactin	Increases milk production
	Growth hormone (GH), also known as somatotropin	Increases body growth, including the growth spurt during puberty
Posterior pituitary	Oxytocin	Controls uterine contractions, milk release, certain aspects of parental behavior, and sexual pleasure
	Vasopressin, also known as antidiuretic hormone	Constricts blood vessels and raises blood pressure; decreases urine volume
Pineal	Melatonin	Increases sleepiness, influences sleep–wake cycle, also has role in onset of puberty
Thyroid	Thyroxine Triiodothyronine	Increase metabolic rate, growth, and maturation
Parathyroid	Parathyroid hormone	Increases blood calcium and decreases potassium
Adrenal cortex	Aldosterone	Reduces secretion of salts by the kidneys
	Cortisol, corticosterone	Stimulate liver to elevate blood sugar; increase metabolism of proteins and fats
Adrenal medulla	Epinephrine, norepinephrine	Similar to effects of sympathetic nervous system
Pancreas	Insulin	Increases entry of glucose to cells and increases storage as fats
	Glucagon	Increases conversion of stored fats to blood glucose
Ovary	Estrogens	Promote female sexual characteristics
	Progesterone	Maintains pregnancy
Testis	Androgens	Promote sperm production, growth of pubic hair, and male sexual characteristics
Liver	Somatomedins	Stimulate growth
Kidney	Renin	Converts a blood protein into angiotensin, which regulates blood pressure and contributes to hypovolemic thirst
Thymus	Thymosin (and others)	Support immune responses
Fat cells	Leptin	Decreases appetite; increases activity; necessary for onset of puberty

these steroids increase the breakdown of fats and proteins (including muscle proteins) into chemicals the body can use for energy, including glucose. Thus, they increase the body's ability to meet the needs of the immediate situation. For more information about steroid hormones, see this Web site:

www.nida.nih.gov/ResearchReports/Steroids/Anabolic Steroids.html

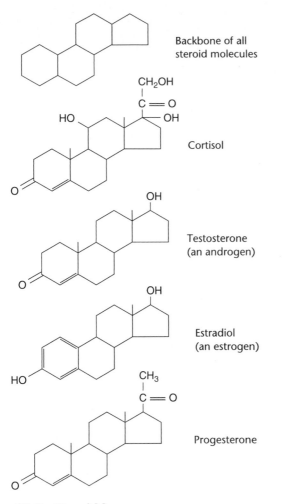

Figure 11.2 Steroid hormones
Note the similarity between the sex hormones testosterone and estradiol.

✻ Steroids

The "sex hormones"—estrogens, progesterone, and the androgens—are a special category of steroids, released mostly by the gonads (testis and ovary), although the adrenal glands also release a small amount. We generally refer to the **androgens,** a group that includes testosterone and several others, as "male hormones" because their level is higher in men. We call the **estrogens,** a group that includes estradiol and others, "female hormones" because their level is higher in women. However, both sexes have both types of hormones. **Progesterone,** another predominantly female hormone, prepares the uterus for the implantation of a fertilized ovum and promotes the maintenance of pregnancy. Sex hormones have effects on the brain, the genitals, and other organs.

Genes that are activated by androgens or estrogens are called **sex-limited genes** because their effects are much stronger in one sex than in the other. For example, estrogen activates the genes responsible for breast

development (much more in women than in men), and androgen activates the genes responsible for the growth of facial hair (much more in men than in women).

Testosterone, other androgens, and synthetic chemicals derived from them are known as **anabolic steroids** because they tend to build up muscles. They increase the synthesis of muscle proteins and enhance the size and strength of muscles, especially in those who exercise (Di Pasquale, 1997). (Cortisol is a *catabolic steroid* because it tends to break down muscles.) Some people, especially male athletes, take anabolic steroids to help develop their muscular strength. One such drug,

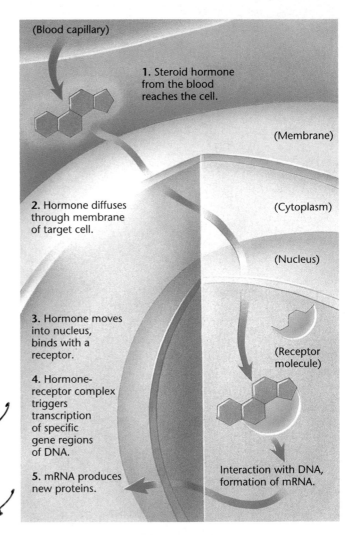

1. Steroid hormone from the blood reaches the cell.

(Blood capillary)

(Membrane)

(Cytoplasm)

2. Hormone diffuses through membrane of target cell.

(Nucleus)

3. Hormone moves into nucleus, binds with a receptor.

4. Hormone-receptor complex triggers transcription of specific gene regions of DNA.

(Receptor molecule)

5. mRNA produces new proteins.

Interaction with DNA, formation of mRNA.

Figure 11.3 One route of action for steroid hormones
The hormone enters a cell, binds with a receptor in the nucleus, and thereby activates particular genes. As a result, the cell increases its production of specific proteins. (Steroid hormones also bind to receptors on the membrane, like peptide hormones.) *Source: Starr & Taggart, 1989*

androstenedione, is often taken as a pill but has doubtful effects, as the digestive system breaks down much or most of it before it has a chance to enter the blood.

You might assume that a drug that increases muscle strength has other masculinizing effects. However, high levels of steroids produce negative feedback on the anterior pituitary, which secretes hormones that control the gonads. The result is breast growth, decreased testis size, increased cholesterol levels, and a high prevalence of depression (Pope & Katz, 1994). The use of anabolic steroids is dangerous and prohibited for those planning to compete in the Olympics and many other organized sports. A high-protein diet can accomplish some of the same goals as the drugs with fewer risks (Di Pasquale, 1997).

In addition to peptide and steroid hormones, other classes are thyroid hormones (released by the thyroid gland, all of them containing iodine) and monoamines (e.g., norepinephrine and dopamine). Several miscellaneous hormones do not fit into any of the described categories.

For more information about hormones in general, try this site:

www.endo-society.org/

CONTROL OF HORMONE RELEASE

Just as circulating hormones modify brain activity, hormones secreted by the brain control the secretion of many other hormones. The **pituitary gland,** attached to the hypothalamus, is sometimes called the "master gland" because its secretions influence so many other glands (Figure 11.4). However, the hypothalamus controls the pituitary, so if any gland is the true master gland, it should be the hypothalamus. The pituitary consists of two distinct glands, the **anterior pituitary** and the **posterior pituitary,** which release different sets of hormones (see Table 11.1, p. 325).

The posterior pituitary, composed of neural tissue, can be considered an extension of the hypothalamus. Neurons in the hypothalamus synthesize the hormones **oxytocin** and **vasopressin** (also known as antidiuretic hormone), plus much smaller amounts of other peptides (J. F. Morris & Pow, 1993). Hypothalamic cells then transport these hormones down their axons to their terminals in the posterior pituitary, as shown in Figure 11.5, which releases the hormones into the blood.

The anterior pituitary, composed of glandular tissue, synthesizes six hormones itself, although the

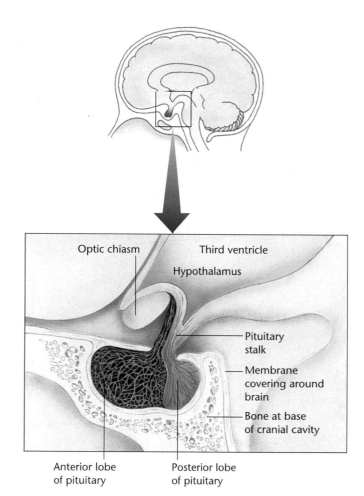

Figure 11.4 Location of the hypothalamus and pituitary gland in the human brain
Source: Starr & Taggart, 1989

hypothalamus controls their release (see Figure 11.5). The hypothalamus secretes **releasing hormones,** which flow through the blood to the anterior pituitary. There they stimulate or inhibit the release of the following hormones:

• Adrenocorticotropic hormone (ACTH)	Controls secretions of the adrenal cortex
• Thyroid-stimulating hormone (TSH)	Controls secretions of the thyroid gland
• Prolactin	Controls secretions of the mammary glands
• Somatotropin, also known as growth hormone (GH)	Promotes growth throughout the body
• Gonadotropins Follicle-stimulating hormone (FSH) Luteinizing hormone (LH)	Control secretions of the gonads

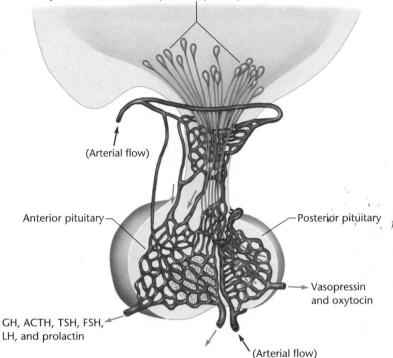

Hypothalamus secretes releasing hormones and inhibiting hormones that control anterior pituitary. Also synthesizes vasopressin and oxytocin, which travel to posterior pituitary.

(Arterial flow)

Anterior pituitary

Posterior pituitary

Vasopressin and oxytocin

GH, ACTH, TSH, FSH, LH, and prolactin

(Arterial flow)

Figure 11.5 Pituitary hormones
The hypothalamus produces vasopressin and oxytocin, which travel to the posterior pituitary (really an extension of the hypothalamus). The posterior pituitary releases these hormones in response to neural signals. The hypothalamus also produces releasing hormones and inhibiting hormones, which travel to the anterior pituitary, where they control the release of six hormones synthesized there.

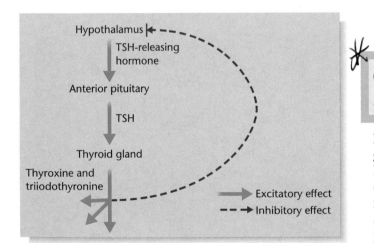

Figure 11.6 Negative feedback in the control of thyroid hormones
The hypothalamus secretes a releasing hormone that stimulates the anterior pituitary to release TSH, which stimulates the thyroid gland to release its hormones. These hormones in turn act on the hypothalamus to decrease its secretion of the releasing hormone.

The hypothalamus maintains fairly constant circulating levels of certain hormones through a negative feedback system. For example, when the level of thyroid hormone is low, the hypothalamus releases *TSH-releasing hormone,* which stimulates the anterior pituitary to release TSH, which in turn causes the thyroid gland to secrete more thyroid hormones. After the level of thyroid hormones has risen, the hypothalamus decreases its release of TSH-releasing hormone (Figure 11.6).

Stop & Check

1. Which has more long-lasting effects, a neurotransmitter or a hormone? Which has effects on more organs?

2. Given the relationship between stress and cortisol and the effects of cortisol and testosterone on muscles, what do you predict would be the effect of stress on testosterone levels?

3. Which part of the pituitary—anterior or posterior—is neural tissue, similar to the hypothalamus? Which part is glandular tissue and produces hormones that control the secretions by other endocrine organs?

Check your answers on page 339.

ORGANIZING EFFECTS OF SEX HORMONES

If we injected estrogens into adult males and androgens into adult females, could we make males act like females and females act like males? Researchers of the 1950s and 1960s, working with a variety of mammals and birds, were surprised to find that the answer was usually *no.* But the same hormones injected early in life have different, more profound effects.

We distinguish between the organizing and activating effects of sex hormones. The **organizing effects** of sex hormones occur mostly at a sensitive stage of development—shortly before and after birth in rats and well before birth in humans—and determine whether the brain and body will develop as a

Happen @ certain development stage

[handwritten: Happens any time]

female or male. **Activating effects** can occur at any time in life, when a hormone temporarily activates a particular response. Activating effects on an organ may last hours, weeks, or even months longer than the hormone remains in an organ, but they do not last indefinitely. The distinction between the two kinds of effects is not absolute; early in life, hormones exert activating effects even while they are organizing body development, and during puberty, hormones can induce long-lasting structural changes as well as activating effects (Arnold & Breedlove, 1985; C. L. Williams, 1986).

Sex Differences in the Gonads and Hypothalamus

[handwritten: Female Gonads. → Ovaries]

Sexual differentiation begins with the chromosomes, although it hardly ends there. A female mammal has an XX chromosome pattern; a male has XY. Most of the effects of the Y gene on brain and behavior depend on testosterone, although a few male–female differences in the brain depend on other genes on the Y chromosome independent of testosterone (Carruth, Reisert, & Arnold, 2002).

During an early stage of prenatal development in mammals, the **gonads** (reproductive organs) of every mammalian fetus are identical, and both male and female have a set of Müllerian ducts and a set of Wolffian ducts. The male's Y chromosome includes the SRY (sex-determining region on the Y chromosome) **gene,** which causes the primitive gonads to develop into masculine structures called **testes,** the

[handwritten: Makes Testes Grow]

sperm-producing organs. (The Y chromosome is small and has few other genes.) The developing testes produce the hormone **testosterone** (an androgen), which increases the growth of the testes, causing them to produce more testosterone and so forth. Testosterone also causes the primitive Wolffian ducts, which are precursors of the male reproductive structures, to develop into *seminal vesicles* (saclike structures that store semen) and the *vas deferens* (a duct from the testis into the penis). A peptide hormone, *Müllerian inhibiting hormone (MIH),* causes degeneration of the **Müllerian ducts,** precursors of the female reproductive structures (oviducts, uterus, and upper vagina) (Graves, 1994). The result of all these testosterone-induced changes is the development of a penis and scrotum. A genetically female fetus (XX) would also develop male structures if she were exposed to large enough amounts of testosterone, but ordinarily she is not. Her gonads develop into **ovaries,** the egg-producing organs. Her Wolffian ducts degenerate, and her primitive Müllerian ducts develop and mature. Figure 11.7 shows the hormone-dependent development of male or female external genitals from the original unisex structures.

[handwritten: Male]

In addition to the obvious differences in the gonads and genitals, the sexes differ in the structure and function of several parts of the nervous system, including parts of the hypothalamus. One area in the anterior hypothalamus, known as the **sexually dimorphic nucleus,** is larger in the male than in the female and contributes to control of sexual behavior in ways not yet well understood. Parts of the female hypothalamus can generate a cyclic pattern of hormone

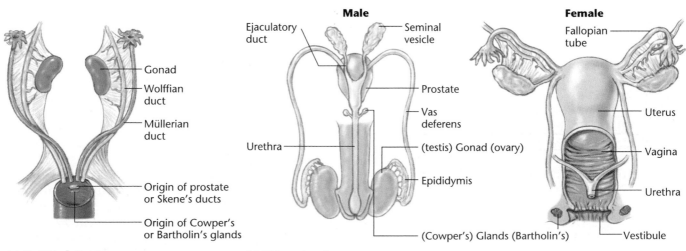

Male
- Ejaculatory duct
- Seminal vesicle
- Prostate
- Vas deferens
- (testis) Gonad (ovary)
- Urethra
- Epididymis
- (Cowper's) Glands (Bartholin's)

Female
- Fallopian tube
- Uterus
- Vagina
- Urethra
- Vestibule

- Gonad
- Wolffian duct
- Müllerian duct
- Origin of prostate or Skene's ducts
- Origin of Cowper's or Bartholin's glands

(a) Undifferentiated

(b) Differentiated

Figure 11.7 Differentiation of human genitals
The male's SRY gene causes the gonad to become a testis, and the testis produces testosterone, which masculinizes development. In the absence of testosterone, development follows the female pattern. *Source: Based on Netter, 1983*

release, as in the human menstrual cycle. The male hypothalamus cannot, and neither can the hypothalamus of a female who was exposed to extra testosterone early in life.

Sexual differentiation depends on the level of testosterone during a **sensitive period**, an early period when a hormone has a long-lasting effect. The human sensitive period for genital formation is about the third and fourth months of pregnancy (Money & Ehrhardt, 1972). In rats, which are less developed than humans at birth, testosterone begins masculinizing the external genitals during the last several days of pregnancy and first few days after birth, but to get the full effect, the testosterone must continue for about a month after birth (Bloch & Mills, 1995; Bloch, Mills, & Gale, 1995; E. C. Davis, Shryne, & Gorski, 1995; Rhees, Shryne, & Gorski, 1990).

A female rat that is injected with testosterone during the last few days before birth or the first few days afterward is partly masculinized, just as if the testosterone had been produced by her own body (Ward & Ward, 1985). Her clitoris grows larger than normal; her other reproductive structures look intermediate between female and male. At maturity, her pituitary and ovaries produce steady levels of hormones instead of the cycles that are characteristic of females. Anatomically, certain parts of her hypothalamus appear more male than female. Her behavior is also masculinized: She mounts other females and makes copulatory thrusting movements rather than arching her back and allowing males to mount her. In short, early testosterone promotes the male pattern and inhibits the female pattern (Gorski, 1985; J. D. Wilson, George, & Griffin, 1981).

Injecting estradiol or other estrogens into a male mammal during the sensitive period does *not* feminize the development of either his external anatomy or behavior. However, he can be feminized or demasculinized in appearance or behavior if he lacks androgen receptors, if he is castrated (deprived of his testes), or if he is exposed to substances that block testosterone effects. The drugs known to have this effect include alcohol, marijuana, haloperidol (an antipsychotic drug), and cocaine (Ahmed, Shryne, Gorski, Branch, & Taylor, 1991; Dalterio & Bartke, 1979; Hull, Nishita, Bitran, & Dalterio, 1984; Raum, McGivern, Peterson, Shryne, & Gorski, 1990).

The overall mechanism of early sexual differentiation has been described by saying that nature's "default setting" is to make every mammal a female. Add early testosterone and the individual becomes a male; without testosterone, it develops as a female, regardless of the amount of estradiol or other estrogens. This generalization, however, is an overstate-

ment. A genetic female that lacks estradiol during the early sensitive period develops approximately normal female external anatomy but does not develop normal sexual behavior. Even if she is given estradiol injections as an adult, she shows little sexual response toward either male or female partners (Bakker, Honda, Harada, & Balthazart, 2002). So estradiol is necessary for normal female development, including brain differentiation.

At least in rodents, testosterone exerts much of its organizing effect on the hypothalamus through a surprising route: After it enters a neuron in early development, it is converted to estradiol! Testosterone and estradiol are chemically very similar, as you can see in Figure 11.2 (p. 326). In organic chemistry, a ring of six carbon atoms containing three double bonds is an *aromatic* compound. An enzyme found in the brain can *aromatize* testosterone into estradiol. Other androgens that cannot be aromatized into estrogens are less effective in masculinizing the hypothalamus. Drugs that prevent testosterone from being aromatized to estradiol block some of the organizing effects of testosterone on sexual development and thereby permanently impair male sexual behavior and fertility (Gerardin & Pereira, 2002; Bochra et al., 2001). Aromatase is particularly abundant in the early sensitive period in brain areas that become larger in males than in females; that is, aromatase occurs in the areas that are to be masculinized (Horvath & Wikler, 1999).

Why, then, is the female not masculinized by her own and her mother's estradiol? During the early sensitive period, immature mammals of many species have in their bloodstream a protein called **alpha-fetoprotein,** which is not present in adults (Gorski, 1980; MacLusky & Naftolin, 1981). Alpha-fetoprotein binds with estrogen and blocks it from leaving the bloodstream and entering the cells that are developing in this early period. Primates have other mechanisms for inactivating estrogen, such as breaking down estrogens into inactive substances. Testosterone is neither bound to alpha-fetoprotein nor metabolized; it is free to enter the cells, where enzymes convert it into estradiol. That is, testosterone is a way of getting estradiol into the cells when estradiol itself cannot leave the blood.

This explanation of testosterone's effects makes sense of an otherwise puzzling fact: Although normal amounts of estradiol have little effect on early development, injecting a larger amount actually masculinizes a female rodent's development. The reason is that normal amounts are bound to alpha-fetoprotein or metabolized, whereas a larger amount exceeds the body's capacity for inactivation; the excess can thus enter the cells and masculinize them.

Sex Differences in Nonreproductive Characteristics

Males and females obviously differ in their reproductive organs and sexual behaviors. But they also differ in many characteristics that are only indirectly related to reproduction, such as size, aggressive behavior, parental behaviors, and life span.

Many of these sex differences depend on the effects of hormones during an early sensitive period before or around the time of birth. For example, female monkeys exposed to testosterone during their sensitive period engage in more rough-and-tumble play than other females, are more aggressive, and make more threatening facial gestures (Quadagno, Briscoe, & Quadagno, 1977; W. C. Young, Goy, & Phoenix, 1964). Human males and females also differ in their patterns of play and aggression, although the role of early hormones is harder to determine. Girls who were exposed to elevated androgen levels during prenatal development (because of a gene that causes excess production of androgens from the adrenal gland) show more interest than their nonandrogenized sisters do in male-typical toys and activities such as football and other sports, electronics, auto mechanics, and hunting. They show little interest in sewing, dolls, fashion, jewelry, or other activities that interested their sisters (Berenbaum, 1999). None of these choices is "wrong"—plenty of women are more interested in sports than in fashion—but the large group difference suggests that the prenatal hormones exert lasting influences on psychological development.

You might wonder whether girls who had a twin brother might be slightly masculinized by androgens that "leak" from the boy fetus to the girl fetus during pregnancy. You could also predict some behavioral masculinization from growing up with a twin brother. However, a comparison of girls who had twin brothers with those who had twin sisters found no differences. On the average, they entered puberty at the same age, developed a similar degree of female-typical interests and attitudes, and had the same probability of bearing children (R. J. Rose et al., 2002).

Males and females differ in several brain areas that have no direct relationship to sexual behavior. For example, women have a greater density of neurons in part of the temporal lobe that is important for language (Witelson, Glezer, & Kigar, 1995). They also tend to have a larger corpus callosum in proportion to total brain size, presumably facilitating greater communication between the hemispheres (S. C. Johnson, Pinkston, Bigler, & Blatter, 1996). The overall size of the cerebral cortex is larger in men than in women but organized somewhat differently, with some areas forming a larger proportion of the total in men, others being proportionately larger in women, and some such as the cerebellum forming an equal proportion for both (Goldstein et al., 2001; Nopoulos, Flaum, O'Leary, & Andreasen, 2000). Actually, males and females start with the same number of neurons, but the period of apoptosis (programmed cell death) continues longer in females, leaving males with more adult cells (Nuñez, Lauschke, & Juraska, 2001). How and why various sex differences develop in the brain are difficult, unresolved questions. Indeed, some of the differences may be by-products of the difference in size between male and female.

ACTIVATING EFFECTS OF SEX HORMONES

At any time in life, not only during an early sensitive period, current levels of testosterone or estradiol exert activating effects, temporarily modifying sexual or other activities. Behaviors can also influence hormonal secretions. For example, when doves court each other, each stage of their behavior initiates hormonal changes that alter the birds' readiness for the next sequence of behaviors, which in turn alters the hormone secretions again (C. Erickson & Lehrman, 1964; Lehrman, 1964; Martinez-Vargas & Erickson, 1973).

In no case do hormones *cause* sexual behavior. They alter the activity in various brain areas to change the way the brain responds to various stimuli. They also change sensitivity in the penis, vagina, and cervix (Etgen, Chu, Fiber, Karkanias, & Morales, 1999).

Research Using Rodents

After removal of the testes from a male rodent or the ovaries from a female, sexual behavior declines as the sex hormone levels in the blood decline. It may not disappear altogether, partly because the adrenal glands also produce steroid hormones. Injections of testosterone into a castrated male restore sexual behavior, as do injections of testosterone's two major metabolites, dihydrotestosterone and estradiol (M. J. Baum & Vreeburg, 1973). A combination of estrogen and progesterone is the most effective combination for females (Matuszewich, Lorrain, & Hull, 2000).

Sex hormones activate sexual behavior partly by enhancing sensations. Estrogens enlarge the area of skin that excites the *pudendal nerve,* which transmits tactile stimulation from the pubic area to the brain (Komisaruk, Adler, & Hutchison, 1972). Sex hormones also facilitate sexual behavior by binding to receptors in the brain and thereby increasing neuronal activity, especially in the hypothalamus.

The ventromedial nucleus and the medial preoptic area (MPOA) and anterior hypothalamus are among the principal areas affected by sex hormones. One anterior hypothalamic area is known as the *sexually dimorphic nucleus (SDN)* because it is distinctly larger in males than in females. The exact importance of the SDN is still unclear. Stimulation of this area increases sex behavior in rats (Bloch, Butler, & Kohlert, 1996), but lesions limited to this area produce only mild deficits in sexual behavior and only in rats with no previous sexual experience (de Jonge et al., 1989). Lesions produce greater deficits if they extend outside the SDN to include more of the medial preoptic area (Yang & Clemens, 2000).

Sex hormones prime the MPOA and several other brain areas to release dopamine. Testosterone primes the release in males; estradiol primes it in females. MPOA neurons release dopamine strongly during sexual activity, and the more dopamine they release, the more likely the male is to copulate (Putnam, Du, Sato, & Hull, 2001). Castrated male rats produce normal amounts of dopamine in the MPOA, but they do not release it in the presence of a receptive female, and they do not attempt to copulate (Hull, Du, Lorrain, & Matuszewich, 1997).

In moderate concentrations, dopamine stimulates mostly type D_1 and D_5 receptors, which facilitate erection of the penis in the male (Hull et al., 1992) and sexually receptive postures in the female (Apostolakis et al., 1996). In higher concentrations, dopamine stimulates type D_2 receptors, which lead to orgasm (Giuliani & Ferrari, 1996; Hull et al., 1992). The effects at D_1 and D_2 receptors tend to inhibit each other. As a result, the early stages of sexual excitement are characterized by arousal but not orgasm; the late stage is marked by orgasm and then a decrease in arousal.

Whereas dopamine stimulates sexual activity, the neurotransmitter serotonin inhibits it, in part by blocking dopamine release (Hull et al., 1999). Many popular antidepressant drugs increase serotonin activity, and one of their side effects is to decrease sexual arousal and impair orgasm.

Sexual Behavior in Humans

Although current hormone levels are less critical for maintaining sexual behavior in humans than in other species, an influence is certainly present. Consequently, it is possible to increase people's sexual arousal through hormones or to decrease it with hormone inhibitors in those with offensive sexual behaviors.

Effects on Men

Among males, sexual excitement is generally highest when testosterone levels are highest, about ages 15 to 25. The hormone oxytocin also may contribute to sexual pleasure. The body releases enormous amounts of oxytocin during orgasm, more than tripling the usual concentration in the blood. Several studies support a relationship between oxytocin and sexual pleasure (M. R. Murphy, Checkley, Seckl, & Lightman, 1990).

Decreases in testosterone levels generally decrease sexual activity. After castration, for example, most men report a decrease in sexual interest and activity (Carter, 1992). However, low testosterone is not the usual basis for impotence, the inability to have an erection. The most common cause is impaired blood circulation, especially in older men. Other common causes include neurological problems, reactions to both legal and illegal drugs, and psychological tension (Andersson, 2001). Part of the basis for an erection is that testosterone increases the release of nitric oxide (NO) in both the hypothalamus and the penis; nitric oxide relaxes the muscles controlling blood flow to the penis, thus producing blood engorgement. One way to help a man get an erection is a drug such as sildenafil (Viagra), which prolongs the effects of nitric oxide (Rowland & Burnett, 2000). In other cases, it is better to deal with overall circulatory problems.

Testosterone reduction has sometimes been tried as a means of controlling sex offenders, including exhibitionists, rapists, child molesters, and committers of incest. Sex offenders are a diverse group. Most have about average testosterone levels (Lang, Flor-Henry, & Frenzel, 1990), and some actually have below average levels, although one study of child molesters found levels above average (Rösler & Witztum, 1998). (The men in that study reported masturbating an average of 32 times per week—that is, about 4 or 5 times a day.) Even for sex offenders who have high testosterone levels, the hormones do not explain their behaviors.

(Many other men with high levels do not engage in offensive behaviors.) Nevertheless, reducing the testosterone levels of sex offenders does reduce their sexual activities, just as it would for any other man.

Some sex offenders have been treated with *cyproterone,* a drug that blocks the binding of testosterone to receptors within cells. Others have been treated with *medroxyprogesterone,* which inhibits gonadotropin, the pituitary hormone that stimulates testosterone production. Within 4 to 8 weeks of treatment with either of these drugs, most sex offenders experience a decrease in sexual fantasies and offensive sexual behaviors. However, these drugs do not completely block testosterone production, and they sometimes fail to reduce the problem behaviors. They also produce unpleasant side effects, including depression, breast growth, weight gain, and blood clots, and their effects wear off quickly if someone stops taking the daily pills.

Thus, researchers have sought a more satisfactory testosterone-blocking procedure. A promising possibility is *triptorelin,* a long-lasting drug that blocks gonadotropin and therefore decreases testosterone production. In one study, monthly injections of triptorelin decreased sex offenders' testosterone levels from 545 ng/dl to a mere 23 ng/dl. The drug also decreased deviant sexual fantasies and abnormal sexual behavior to zero in all participants (Rösler & Witztum, 1998).

Effects on Women

A woman's hypothalamus and pituitary interact with the ovaries to produce the **menstrual cycle,** a periodic variation in hormones and fertility over the course of approximately 1 month (Figure 11.8). After the end of a menstrual period, the anterior pituitary releases **follicle-stimulating hormone (FSH),** which promotes the growth of a follicle in the ovary. The follicle nurtures the *ovum* (egg cell) and produces estrogen. Toward the middle of the menstrual cycle, the follicle builds up more and more receptors to FSH; so even though the actual concentration of FSH in the blood is decreasing, its effects on the follicle increase. As a result, the follicle produces greater amounts of **estradiol,** which is a type of estrogen. (Estrogens and androgens are categories that include several individual hormones. Neither estrogen nor androgen is a specific chemical itself.) The increased release of estradiol causes an increased release of FSH as well as a sudden surge in the release of **luteinizing hormone (LH)** from the anterior pituitary (see the top graph in Figure 11.8). FSH and LH combine to cause the follicle to release an ovum.

The remnant of the follicle (now called the *corpus luteum*) releases the hormone progesterone, which prepares the uterus for the implantation of a fertilized ovum. Progesterone also inhibits the further release of LH. Toward the end of the menstrual cycle, the levels of LH, FSH, estradiol, and progesterone all decline. If the ovum is not fertilized, the lining of the uterus is cast off (menstruation), and the cycle begins again. If the ovum is fertilized, the levels of estradiol and progesterone increase gradually throughout pregnancy. One consequence of high estradiol and progesterone levels is fluctuating activity at the serotonin 3 ($5HT_3$) receptor, responsible for nausea (Rupprecht et al., 2001). For that reason, pregnant women often experience nausea. Figure 11.9 summarizes the interactions between the pituitary and the ovary.

Birth-control pills prevent pregnancy by interfering with the usual feedback cycle between the ovaries and the pituitary. The most widely used birth-control pill, the *combination pill,* containing both estrogen and progesterone, prevents the surge of FSH and LH that would otherwise release an ovum. The estrogen–

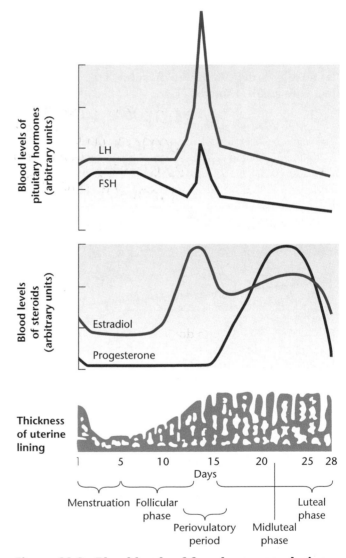

Figure 11.8 Blood levels of four hormones during the human menstrual cycle
Note that estrogen and progesterone are both at high levels during the midluteal phase but drop sharply at menstruation, a short time later.

progesterone combination also thickens the mucus of the cervix, making it harder for a sperm to reach the egg, and prevents an ovum, if released, from implanting in the uterus. Thus, the pill prevents pregnancy in many ways. Note, however, that it does not protect against sexually transmitted diseases such as AIDS or syphilis. "Safe sex" must go beyond the prevention of pregnancy.

Changes in hormones over the menstrual cycle produce small changes in women's sexual interest. The midway point, the periovulatory period, when ovulation occurs, is the time of maximum fertility and generally the highest estrogen levels. According to two studies, women not taking birth-control pills initiate more sexual activity (either with a partner or by masturbation) during the periovulatory period than at other times during the month (Adams, Gold, & Burt, 1978; Udry & Morris, 1968) (Figure 11.10). According to another study, women rate an erotic video as more pleasant and arousing if they watch it during the periovulatory period than if they watch it at other times (Slob, Bax, Hop, Rowland, & van der Werff ten Bosch, 1996). These effects are small, though.

Sex hormones also influence women's preferences for men's faces. Examine the faces in Figure 11.11. For each pair of faces, which do you regard as "more attractive"? Women: For each pair, which would you prefer for a short-term sexual relationship? In one study, women not using oral contraceptives were presented with a computer that enabled them to modify each face to make it look more feminized (the left of each pair) or more masculinized (right). They adjusted the face until it looked most attractive. When they were asked specifically to show the face of the man they would prefer for a "short-term sexual relationship," women who were menstruating or in the luteal phase approaching menstruation usually adjusted the faces to look feminized. Women in the follicular phase (when estrogen and progesterone levels are rising and the probability of becoming pregnant is greatest) preferred a face closer to halfway between feminized and masculinized (Penton-Voak et al., 1999). Women using oral contraceptives, whose hormones are kept more constant throughout the month, did not change their preferences from one time to another. In short, the hormones associated with fertility move women's mate preferences toward more "masculine" looking males.

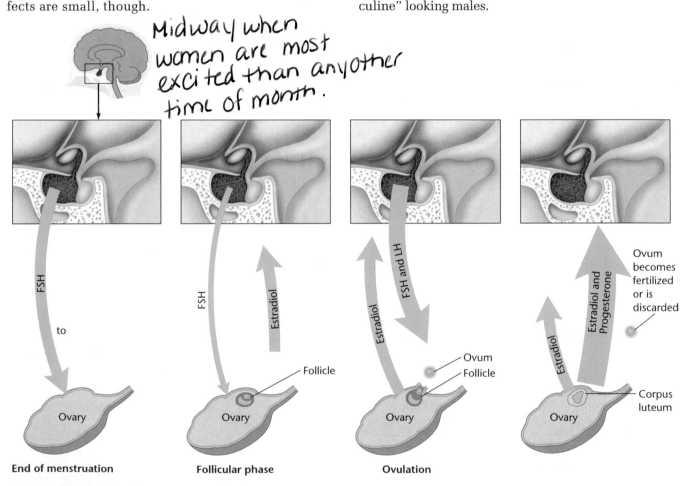

[Handwritten annotation: Midway when women are most excited than anyother time of month.]

Figure 11.9 Interactions between the pituitary and the ovary
FSH from the pituitary stimulates a follicle of the ovary to develop and produce estradiol, triggering a release of a burst of FSH and LH from the pituitary. These hormones cause the follicle to release its ovum and become a corpus luteum. The corpus luteum releases progesterone while the ovary releases estradiol.

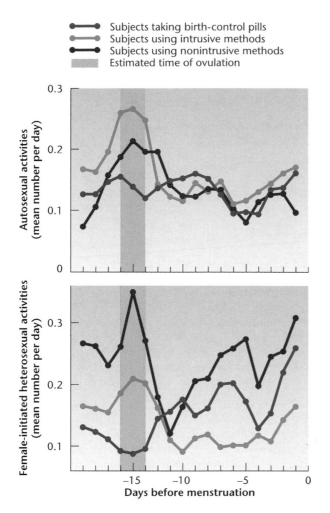

Subjects taking birth-control pills
Subjects using intrusive methods
Subjects using nonintrusive methods
Estimated time of ovulation

Figure 11.10 Female-initiated sexual activities during the monthly cycle

The top graph shows autosexual activities (masturbation and sexual fantasies); the bottom graph shows female-initiated activities with a male partner. "Intrusive" birth-control methods are diaphragm, foam, and condom; "nonintrusive" methods are IUD and vasectomy. Note that women other than pill users increase self-initiated sex activities when their estrogen levels peak. *Source: From "Rise in Female-Initiated Sexual Activity at Ovulation and its Suppression by Oral Contraceptives." by D. B. Adams, A. R. Gold and A. D. Burt, 1978, New England Journal of Medicine, 299. p. 1145–1150. Reprinted by permission from the New England Journal of Medicine.*

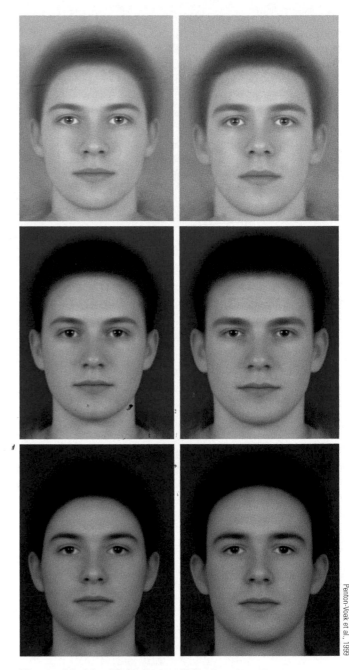

Penton-Voak et al., 1999

Figure 11.11 Male faces differing in apparent femininity or masculinity

Using a computer, women were able to change each face from relatively feminine (left faces) to relatively masculine (right faces). Women at different stages in their menstrual cycle had slightly different preferences. *Source: From Penton-Voak et al., 1999.*

EXTENSIONS AND APPLICATIONS
Premenstrual Syndrome

Some women experience anxiety, irritability, and depression during the days just before menstruation, an experience known as **premenstrual syndrome (PMS)**, or premenstrual dysphoric disorder. The appropriate-

ness of the terms *syndrome* and *disorder* is debatable, as they imply a medical problem requiring medical treatment. Nevertheless, the terms are widely used.

Because PMS occurs at a time of major hormonal changes, it seems likely that those hormones are in some way responsible. Just before menstruation, estradiol and progesterone levels decrease, while levels of cortisol (an adrenal hormone) increase. However, not all women experience PMS, and the swings of estrogen, progesterone, and cortisol are about the same for those with or without PMS (Schmidt, Nieman, Danaceau, Adams, & Rubinow, 1998).

Much research interest now focuses on the metabolism of progesterone. Progesterone is metabolized into several other chemicals, including *allopregnanolone,* which modifies GABA synapses, which control anxiety and stress responses. Several studies have found that women with PMS have normal levels of progesterone but lower than normal levels of allopregnanolone, particularly during the premenstrual period (Follesa et al., 2000; Monteleone et al., 2000; Rapkin et al., 1997).

Nonsexual Behavior

Testosterone increases aggressive behavior in many species of mammals and birds. As a result, males fight mostly during mating season, mainly in competition for mates. We shall consider this relationship further in Chapter 12 when we discuss aggressive behavior in general.

Estrogen and testosterone also produce activating effects on several brain systems with widespread functions. Estrogen stimulates growth of dendritic spines in the hippocampus, blocks apoptosis, and thereby decreases the risk of Alzheimer's disease (Behl, 2002; McEwen, 2001). Increased levels of estrogen also stimulate increased production of dopamine type D_2 receptors and serotonin type $5\text{-}HT_{2A}$ receptors in the nucleus accumbens, the prefrontal cortex, the olfactory cortex, and several other cortical areas (Fink, Sumner, Rosie, Grace, & Quinn, 1996). Those synapses contribute to sexual motivation and reinforcement but also to other types of reinforcement and positive mood. Therefore, increased estrogen would be linked to increased enjoyment of many activities, and decreased estrogen could lead to decreased enjoyment.

Increased estrogen improves female monkeys' learning, memory, and attention (Voytko, 2001). In humans, it improves verbal fluency, verbal memory, attention regulation, and fine motor control. Postmenopausal women taking estrogen replacement perform better on these tasks than women of similar age not taking estrogen (Keenan, Ezzat, Ginsburg, & Moore, 2001; Maki, Zonderman, & Resnick, 2001). Young women perform better on these tasks during the midluteal phase of the menstrual cycle, when estrogen levels are highest. On the other hand, they perform worse at this time, and best when estrogen levels are lower, on certain other kinds of tasks: recognizing an object in a fragmented drawing and visually imagining the rotation of a three-dimensional object (Hausmann,

Slabbekoorn, Van Goozen, Cohen-Kettenis, & Güntürkün, 2000; Kimura & Hampson, 1994; Maki, Rich, & Rosenbaum, 2002). Figure 11.12 shows an example of one such task.

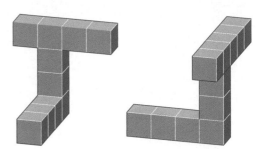

Figure 11.12 A spatial rotation task
People are presented with a series of pairs such as this one and asked whether the first figure could be rotated to match the second. (Here the answer is no.) On the average, men perform better on this task than women, and women perform better while they are menstruating (and their sex hormone levels are low) than at other times. However, women perform verbal fluency and manual dexterity tasks better at other times than they do while menstruating.

Why did we evolve to have a sex hormone influence our intellect? One speculation is that old women are more useful, evolutionarily speaking, than old men because old women are more likely to help with their grandchildren. Therefore, we evolved a hormonal mechanism to help old women stay alive and alert longer (Sapolsky & Finch, 2000). It is an interesting hypothesis, but full of problems. Androgens as wells as estrogens protect intellect in old age (Raber, Bongers, LeFevour, Buttini, & Mucke, 2002), and men's hormones decline less than women's in old age. In fact, Alzheimer's disease is more common in aging women than men, except in those women taking extra hormones as a therapy (Zandi et al., 2002). Furthermore, female rats and voles as well as monkeys perform better on many kinds of memory tasks when their estrogen levels are high but better on spatial tasks when their estrogen is low (Frye, 1995; Galea, Kavaliers, Ossenkopp, & Hampson, 1995; Lacreuse, Verreault, & Herndon, 2001; O'Neal, Means, Poole, & Hamm, 1996; Sandstrom & Williams, 2001). So whatever the explanation for the effect of sex hormones on cognition, it needs to apply across mammalian species.

Unfortunately, estrogen produces harm as well as benefits, especially when given as a supplement to older women. An extensive study of women taking estrogen supplements after menopause found that it increased the risk of heart attack, stroke, and breast cancer, while reducing the risk of hip fractures and colorectal cancer (Writing Group for the Women's Health Initiative Investigators, 2002).

8. How do cyproterone, medroxyprogesterone, and triptorelin decrease male sex drive?

9. At what time in a woman's menstrual cycle are her levels of estrogen and progesterone highest? When are they lowest?

10. What is the relationship between sex hormones and premenstrual syndrome?

Check your answers on page 339.

PARENTAL BEHAVIOR

In most species of mammals and birds, hormonal changes prepare the mother for parental behavior. The mechanisms vary from one species to another. For example, pregnant monkeys become more and more interested in baby monkeys as their pregnancy progresses and their estrogen and progesterone levels increase (Maestripieri & Zehr, 1998). Rats, on the other hand, produce a pattern of hormones late in pregnancy that actually *decreases* their response to infant rats (Mayer & Rosenblatt, 1984). After delivering the babies, mother rats as well as monkeys and all other species become very attentive to their young, largely because of a sudden surge of the hormones prolactin and oxytocin (Pedersen, Caldwell, Walker, Ayers, & Mason, 1994). Hormones act by increasing activity in the medial preoptic area and anterior hypothalamus (Featherstone, Fleming, & Ivy, 2000), and damage to this area eliminates rats' maternal behavior (J. R. Brown, Ye, Bronson, Dikkes, & Greenberg, 1996) (Figure 11.13). (This is the same area that is so impor-

tant for temperature regulation, thirst, and sexual behavior. It's a busy little area.)

Although rat maternal behavior depends on hormones for the first few days, it becomes less dependent at a later stage. If a female that has never been pregnant is left with some 5- to 10-day-old babies, she ignores them at first but gradually becomes more attentive. (Because the babies cannot survive without parental care, the experimenter must periodically replace them with new, healthy babies.) After about 6 days, the adoptive mother builds a nest, assembles the babies in the nest, licks them, and does everything else that a normal mother would, except nurse them. This experience-dependent behavior does not require hormonal changes and occurs even in rats that have had their ovaries removed (Mayer & Rosenblatt, 1979; Rosenblatt, 1967).

An important influence from being with babies is that the mother becomes accustomed to their odors. Infant rats release some chemicals that stimulate the mother's vomeronasal organ, which responds to pheromones (see Chapter 7). We might imagine that evolution would have equipped infants with pheromones that elicit maternal behavior, but actually their pheromones interfere with maternal behavior by stimulating brain areas linked to aggressive behaviors (Sheehan, Cirrito, Numan, & Numan, 2000). For a mother that has just gone through pregnancy, this interference does not matter; her hormones have primed her medial preoptic area so strongly that it overrides objections from elsewhere in the brain. A female without hormonal priming, however, rejects the young unless she has become familiar with their smell (Del Cerro et al., 1995).

Why do mammals need two mechanisms for maternal behavior—one hormone-dependent and one not? In the early phase, hormones compensate for the mother's lack of familiarity with the young. In the later phase, experience maintains the maternal behavior even though the hormones start to decline (Rosenblatt, 1970).

Figure 11.13 Brain development and maternal behavior in mice
The mouse on the left shows normal maternal behavior. The one on the right has a genetic mutation that, among other effects, impairs the development of the preoptic area and anterior hypothalamus.

J. R. Brown, Ye, Bronson, Dikkes, & Greenberg, 1996

What about the father's behavior? For most mammalian species, the answer is simple: The father does not help care for the young. However, in species where the father does contribute, he undergoes hormonal changes similar to those of the mother. For example, in one species of dwarf hamster, males help with the young (unlike most other hamster species). In that species, as the female approaches the end of pregnancy, the male's testosterone level increases, perhaps priming him to defend the nest vigorously. As soon as the mother delivers her babies, however, his testosterone level drops and his prolactin levels increase. The result is nonaggressive parental behavior toward his young (Reburn & Wynne-Edwards, 1999). Prolactin has been found to be critical for fatherly behavior in many species, including fish, amphibians, birds, and those few nonhuman mammals that show paternal care (Schradin & Anzenberger, 1999).

Are hormones important for human parental behavior? Hormonal changes are necessary for a woman to nurse a baby, but otherwise, hormonal changes are not necessary to prepare anyone for infant care. After all, both men and never-pregnant women can adopt children and be excellent parents. It is possible that hormonal changes facilitate or increase some aspects of human parental behavior, but research data are not available on this point.

Stop & Check

11. What factors are responsible for maternal behavior shortly after rats give birth? What factors become more important in later days?

Check your answers on page 339.

MODULE 11.1

In Closing: Sex-Related Behaviors and Motivations

Why do humans and other animals engage in sexual and parental behaviors? You might answer, "to pass on their genes and propagate the species" or "because it feels good." Both answers are correct, and they are linked: Evolution has made reproductive behaviors feel good because the pleasant feeling increases our probability of doing acts that will pass on our genes.

A mother rat licks her babies all over shortly after their birth, providing them with stimulation that is essential for their survival. But the mother presumably does not know the value of the licking for the young; she licks them because she craves the salty taste of the fluid that covers them. She licks them much less if she has access to other salty fluids (Gubernick & Alberts, 1983). In short, animals need not understand the ultimate function of their reproductive behaviors; they have evolved mechanisms that cause them to enjoy and therefore perform the acts.

SUMMARY

1. Among the several types of hormones are peptide hormones and steroid hormones. Peptide hormones attach to membrane receptors and exert effects similar to those of neurotransmitters. Steroid hormones also attach to membrane receptors, and in addition alter the expression of the genes. (p. 324)

2. The hypothalamus controls activity of the pituitary gland through both nerve impulses and releasing hormones. The pituitary in turn secretes hormones that alter the activity of other endocrine glands. (p. 327)

3. The organizing effects of a hormone are exerted during an early sensitive period and bring about relatively permanent alterations in anatomy or in the potential for function. (p. 328)

4. In the absence of sex hormones, an infant mammal develops the female pattern of genitals and hypothalamus. The addition of testosterone shifts development toward the male pattern. Extra estrogen, within normal limits, does not determine whether the individual looks male or female. (p. 329)

5. During early development, testosterone is converted within certain cells to estradiol, which actually masculinizes the development of the brain and external genitals, at least in rodents. Estradiol in the blood does not masculinize development, either because it is bound to proteins in the blood or because it is metabolized. (p. 330)

6. In adulthood, sex hormones can activate sex behaviors, partly by facilitating activity in the medial preoptic area and anterior hypothalamus. Dopamine acts at D_1 receptors to increase sexual arousal and at D_2 receptors to stimulate orgasm. (p. 331)

7. A woman's menstrual cycle depends on a feedback cycle that increases and then decreases the release of several hormones. In many species, females are sexually responsive only when they are fertile. Women can respond sexually at any time in their cycle, although they may have a slight increase in sexual interest around the time of ovulation, when estrogen levels are highest. (p. 333)

8. Hormones released around the time of giving birth facilitate maternal behavior in females of many mammalian species. Nevertheless, mere prolonged exposure to young is also sufficient to induce parental behavior. Hormonal facilitation is not essential to human parental behavior. (p. 337)

ANSWERS TO *STOP AND CHECK* QUESTIONS

1. A hormone has more long-lasting effects. A hormone can affect many parts of the brain as well as other organs; a neurotransmitter affects only the neurons near its point of release. (p. 328)

2. Stress increases the release of cortisol, which breaks down muscles. Testosterone, which builds up muscles, declines during times of stress. (p. 328)

3. The posterior pituitary is neural tissue, like the hypothalamus. The anterior pituitary is glandular tissue and produces hormones that control several other endocrine organs. (p. 328)

4. A mammal exposed to high levels of both male and female hormones will appear male. One exposed to low levels of both will appear female. Genital development depends mostly on the presence or absence of androgens. (p. 331)

5. Pregnant women should avoid alcohol, marijuana, haloperidol, and cocaine because these drugs interfere with masculinization of a genetically male fetus. (p. 331)

6. A female that lacked alpha-fetoprotein would be masculinized by her own estrogens. (p. 331)

7. Unusually high levels of estrogens could exceed the binding capacity of alpha-fetoprotein and therefore enter the cells and masculinize development. (p. 331)

8. Cyproterone prevents testosterone from binding to its receptors. Medroxyprogesterone and triptorelin block gonadotropin, the pituitary hormone that stimulates the testis to produce testosterone. Triptorelin blocks it more effectively and for a longer time. (p. 337)

9. Estrogen and progesterone are highest at the periovulatory phase; they are lowest during and just after menstruation. (p. 337)

10. Premenstrual syndrome is an exaggerated reaction to the normal changes that occur in sex hormones. One hypothesis relates PMS to low levels of one metabolite of progesterone. (p. 337)

11. The early stage of rats' maternal behavior depends on a surge in the release of the hormones prolactin and oxytocin. A few days later, her experience with the young decreases the vomeronasal responses that would tend to make her reject them. Experience with the young maintains maternal behavior after the hormone levels begin to drop. (p. 338)

THOUGHT QUESTIONS

1. The pill RU-486 produces abortions by blocking the effects of progesterone. Explain how this process works.

2. The presence or absence of testosterone determines whether a mammal will differentiate as a male or a female; estrogens have no effect. In birds, the story is the opposite: The presence or absence of estrogen is critical (Adkins & Adler, 1972). What problems would sex determination by estrogen create if that were the mechanism for mammals? Why do those problems not arise in birds? (*Hint:* Think about the difference between live birth and hatching from an egg.)

3. Antipsychotic drugs, such as haloperidol and chlorpromazine, block activity at dopamine synapses. What side effects might they have on sexual behavior?

Variations in Sexual Behavior

People vary considerably in their preferred frequency of sexual activity, preferred types of sexual activity, and sexual orientation. Because sexual activity occurs mostly in private, most of us are not aware of how much diversity exists. In this module, we shall explore some of that diversity, but first we consider a few differences between men and women in general. Several researchers have been trying to go beyond just describing those differences to perhaps explaining them biologically, and the proposed explanations are both fascinating and controversial.

EVOLUTIONARY INTERPRETATIONS OF MATING BEHAVIOR

Let's start with a few common observations: First, men are more likely than women to seek multiple sex partners, especially for short-term encounters. Second, women are more likely than men to be concerned about a potential mate's earning ability, whereas men are more likely to be concerned about a mate's youth. Third, men usually show greater jealousy than women at any indication of sexual infidelity.

Obviously, all of these generalizations vary from person to person. However, the general trends are reasonably consistent across cultures and similar to tendencies seen in many animal species. Granted, a great deal about human mating behavior differs from that of other species, so we should not carelessly generalize from one species to another. Still, several theorists have argued that the different behaviors of men and women reflect the influence of past evolutionary pressures (Buss, 2000). We may or may not accept these arguments, but we should examine them carefully.

Interest in Multiple Mates

First, why are men more likely to be interested in short-term sexual relationships with many partners? Men can adopt either of two mating strategies (Gangestad & Simpson, 2000): Be loyal to one woman and devote your energies to protecting her and her babies or mate with multiple women and hope that some of them can raise your babies without your help. No one needs to be conscious of these strategies, of course. From an evolutionary standpoint, either the one-mate strategy, the multiple-mate strategy, or some compromise can spread the man's genes. Women, however—or so the standard thinking goes—gain nothing by a multiple-mate strategy because a woman can have only a limited number of pregnancies. So evolution may have predisposed men, or at least some men, to be more interested in multiple mates than women would be.

One objection is that a woman does sometimes gain from having multiple sex partners (Hrdy, 2000). If her husband is infertile, mating with another man could be her only way of reproducing. In addition, another man may provide her with valuable gifts and may be kind to her children. (After all, he might be their father!) She also has the possibility of "trading up," abandoning her first mate for a better one. So the prospect of multiple mates may be more appealing to men, but it can have some advantages for women, too.

Another objection is that researchers have no direct evidence that genes influence whether people prefer one mate or many. We shall return to this issue later.

What Men and Women Seek in Their Mates

Men and women both prefer a healthy, intelligent, honest, physically attractive mate. Women have some additional interests that are not prominent for men. For example, women express a much stronger interest than men in finding a mate with an acceptable odor (Herz & Cahill, 1997). (Women probably have more experience with stinky men than men have with stinky women. There are also possible explanations based on a man's odor as a clue to his health and genetic compatibility with the woman.) Also, worldwide, most women prefer mates who are likely to be good providers. As you might guess, this tendency is strongest in societies where women have no jobs or economic power. However, women in all known societies are more interested in men's wealth and success than men care about women's wealth and success (Buss, 2000). According to evolutionary theorists, the reason is clear: While a woman is pregnant or taking care of a small child, she needs help getting food and other requirements. Evolution would have favored any gene that caused women to seek good providers.

Men tend to have a stronger preference for a young partner. An evolutionary explanation is that younger women are much more likely than older women to be fertile, so a man can spread his genes more successfully by mating with a young woman. Men remain fertile into old age, so a woman has less need to insist on youth. A contrary interpretation, of course, is that women prefer young partners, too, when possible, but in many societies, only somewhat older men have enough financial resources to get married.

Differences in Jealousy

Why might men be more jealous about wives' sexual infidelities than women should be about husbands' infidelities? If a man is to pass on his genes—the key point in evolution—he needs to be sure that the children he supports are his own, and an unfaithful wife threatens that certainty. A woman's children are necessarily her own, so she has no similar worry.

One way to test this interpretation is to compare cultures. Attitudes about sexual fidelity differ from one culture to another, ranging from acceptance of extramarital sex to complete prohibition. However, some cultures consider it more acceptable (or less forbidden) for men to have extramarital sex, whereas no known cultures consider it more tolerable for women. Should we be more impressed that jealousy is always at least as strong for men as for women, and usually more, or should we be more impressed that it does vary with culture? Here reasonable people can draw different conclusions.

Which would upset you more: if your partner had a brief sexual affair with someone else, or if he or she became emotionally close to someone else? According to several studies, men say they would be more upset by the sexual infidelity, whereas women would be more upset by the emotional infidelity (Shakelford, Buss, & Bennett, 2002). However, those studies dealt with hypothetical situations. Most men and women who have actually dealt with an unfaithful partner say they were more upset by their partner's becoming emotionally close to someone else than by the sexual affair (C. H. Harris, 2002).

Evolved or Learned?

If a behavior has clear advantages for survival or reproduction and is similar across cultures, can we conclude that it developed by evolution? Not necessarily. Of course the brain has evolved, just like any other organ, and of course our behavioral tendencies are a product of evolution. But the key question is whether evolution has micromanaged our behavior or has set us up so that we can learn appropriately.

Cross-cultural similarity is not strong evidence for any evolved tendency. For example, people throughout the world agree that $2 + 2 = 4$, but we don't assume that they have a gene for that belief. Likewise, it is possible that women throughout the world discover that they gain benefits from marrying a man who can provide well. People of different cultures could show many similar behaviors for reasons unrelated to genetics.

To establish that we evolved a tendency to act in some way, the most decisive evidence would be the demonstration of particular genes with demonstrable effects. For example, if most men have genes influencing them to prefer attractive young women, then presumably, some men would have a mutation in that gene. Perhaps those men would prefer unattractive old women, and so would their sons. Okay, this particular example may not be the best, but the point is this: Unless we find that different genes lead to different behaviors, it is hard to know what any gene produces and hard to separate evolved from learned tendencies.

Conclusions

Discussing these issues is difficult. Ideally, we would like to consider the evidence and logical arguments entirely on their scientific merits. However, when someone describes how evolutionary selection may have led men to be interested in multiple sex partners or to be more jealous than women are, it sometimes sounds like a justification for men to act that way.

The question of right and wrong is different from the science. No gene forces men or women to behave in any particular way. We shall see in Chapter 15 that genes predispose some people to be more likely than others to become alcoholics, but this fact doesn't mean that some people are sure to be alcoholics or other people sure not to be.

Even leaving aside the social implications as far as we can, no firm scientific conclusion emerges. None of the data separate the contributions of genetic predispositions from those of experiences and culture. We need more data, and different kinds of data, before we can draw a conclusion,

1. What evolutionary advantage is suggested for men's tendency to prefer to mate with young women?

2. What is the evolutionary argument for why women are more interested in men's wealth and success than men are interested in the same things about women?

Check your answers on page 351.

DETERMINANTS OF GENDER IDENTITY

The coral goby is a species of fish in which the male and female tend their eggs and young together. If one of them dies, the survivor looks for a new partner. But it does not look far. This is a very stay-at-home kind of fish. If it cannot easily find a partner of the opposite sex, but does find an unmated member of its own sex—oh, well—it simply changes sex and mates with the neighbor. Male-to-female and female-to-male switches are equally common (Nakashima, Kuwamura, & Yogo, 1995).

People cannot switch sexes and remain fertile, but we do have intermediates and variations in sexual development. Sexual development is a very sensitive issue, so let us specify from the start: "Different" does not mean "wrong." People naturally differ in their sexual development just as they do in their height, weight, emotions, and memory.

Gender identity is how we identify sexually and what we call ourselves. The biological differences between males and females are often referred to as *sex differences;* the differences that result from people's thinking about themselves as male or female are *gender differences.* To maintain this useful distinction, we should resist the growing trend to speak of the "gender" of dogs, fruit flies, and so forth. Gender identity is specifically a human characteristic.

Most people accept the gender identity that matches their external appearance, which is ordinarily also the way they were reared. However, some are dissatisfied with their assigned gender, even to such a degree that they insist on a surgical sex change (transsexuals). Might a biological factor, such as prenatal hormones, influence gender identity? Several kinds of human cases shed light on this question, though we have no definitive answers.

Intersexes

Some people are not exactly male or female but something intermediate (Haqq & Donahoe, 1998). For example, some XY males with a mutation in the SRY gene have poorly developed genitals. Some people are born with an XX chromosome pattern but an SRY gene that translocated from the father's Y chromosome onto another chromosome. Despite their XX chromosomes, they have either an ovary and a testis, or two testes, or a mixture of testis and ovary tissue on each side.

Others develop an intermediate appearance because of an atypical hormone pattern. Recall that testosterone masculinizes the development of the genitals and the hypothalamus during early development. If a genetic female is exposed to more testosterone than the average female but less than the average male, her appearance can be partly masculinized. A genetic male who has low levels of testosterone or a mutation of the testosterone receptors may also develop intermediate between male and female or even looking female (Misrahi et al., 1997). Either a male or a female exposed to toxic chemicals, such as the pesticide DDT, can have a loss of sexual behaviors and fertility (Dörner et al., 2001).

A genetically female fetus or (less often) her mother may have an adrenal gland that produces an excess of testosterone and other androgens. Decades ago, some pregnant women took antimiscarriage drugs that mimicked some of the effects of testosterone. (Those drugs are no longer used.) The excess testosterone produces ambiguous external anatomy, as Figure 11.14 illustrates. Note in the figure the structure that appears intermediate between a clitoris and a penis and the swellings that appear intermediate between labia and a scrotum.

Individuals whose genitals do not match the usual development for their genetic sex are referred to as **hermaphrodites** (from Hermes and Aphrodite in Greek mythology). The *true hermaphrodite,* a rarity, has some normal testicular tissue and some normal ovarian tissue—for example, a testis on one side of the body and an ovary on the other. Individuals whose sexual development is intermediate or ambiguous, such as the one in Figure 11.14, are also sometimes called hermaphrodites, but more often called **intersexes** or pseudohermaphrodites. Most dislike the term *pseudohermaphrodite,* which sounds insulting, so we shall use the term *intersex.*

How common are intersexes? According to current estimates, at least 1 child in 100 in the United States is born with some degree of genital ambiguity, and 1 in 2000 has enough ambiguity to make its male or female status uncertain (Blackless et al., 2000). However, the accuracy of these estimates is uncertain, as hospitals and families keep the information private. Maintaining confidentiality is of course important, but an unfortunate

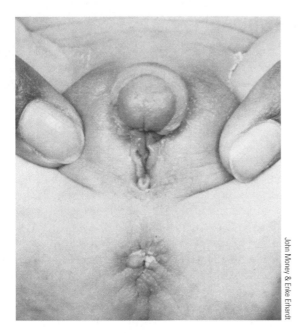

Figure 11.14 External genitals of a genetic female, age 3 months
Masculinized by excess androgens from the adrenal gland before birth, the infant has external anatomy intermediate between male and female.

consequence of secrecy is that intersexed people have trouble finding others who have faced the same problems. For more information, consult the following Web site or contact the following support groups:

www.isna.org/

Ambiguous Genitalia Support Group, P.O. Box 313, Clements, CA 95227

American Educational Gender Information Service, P.O. Box 33724, Decatur, GA 30033–0724

Intersex Society of North America, 4500 9th Ave. NE, Suite 300, Seattle, WA 98105

When a baby is born with an intersex appearance, a decision must be made: Shall we call the child a boy or a girl? Ideally, the label boy or girl should match what the person looks like, acts like, and feels like. Matching the chromosomes is less important because intersexes' chromosomes are a poor predictor of their eventual appearance and behavior.

Beginning in about the 1950s, medical doctors recommended the following: When in doubt, call the child a girl and perform surgery to make her look like a girl (Dreger, 1998). It is difficult surgically to create a satisfactory artificial penis or to enlarge a small one. It is easier to create an artificial vagina or lengthen a short one. After the surgery, the child looks female, or close enough.

And she lives happily ever after, right? Unfortunately, physicians do very few long-term follow-ups on

these people, and the data are sparse (Lerman, McAleer, & Kaplan, 2000). Perhaps some are happy and we never hear from them, but virtually all adult intersexes who have said anything publicly have complained about their treatment. The surgically created or lengthened vagina may be satisfactory to a male partner, but it provides no sensation to the woman and requires almost daily attention to prevent it from scarring over. Many intersexes wish they had their original "abnormal" penis–clitoris instead of the mutilated, insensitive structure left to them by a surgeon. Many develop a male gender identity despite being reared as females. Most of all, intersexes resent the deception. Historian Alice Dreger (1998) describes the case of one intersex:

> As a young person, [she] was told she had "twisted ovaries" that had to be removed; in fact, her testes were removed. At the age of twenty, "alone and scared in the stacks of a [medical] library," she discovered the truth of her condition. Then "the pieces finally fit together. But what fell apart was my relationship with both my family and physicians. It was not learning about chromosome or testes that caused enduring trauma, it was discovering that I had been told lies. I avoided all medical care for the next 18 years. . . . [T]he greatest source of anxiety is not our gonads or karyotype. It is shame and fear resulting from an environment in which our condition is so unacceptable that caretakers lie." (p. 192)

So how *should* such a child be reared? On that question, specialists do not agree. Some continue to insist that any child without a full-size penis should be surgi-

This group of adult intersexed people have gathered to provide mutual support and to protest against the early surgical treatments they received. They requested that their names be used to emphasize their openness about their condition and to emphasize that intersexuality should not be considered shameful. They are from left to right: Martha Coventry, Max Beck, David Vandertie, Kristi Bruce, and Angela Moreno.

cally "corrected" to look like a female and then reared as a girl. A growing number, however, follow these recommendations (Diamond & Sigmundson, 1997):

- Be completely honest with the intersexed person and the family and do nothing without their informed consent. (Some doctors in the past have conducted surgery on infants without even explaining what they were doing or why.)
- Identify the child as male or female based mainly on the predominant external appearance. That is, there should be no bias toward calling every intersex a female.
- Rear the child as consistently as possible, but be prepared that the intersexed person might later be sexually oriented toward males, females, both, or neither.
- Do not perform surgery to reduce the ambiguous penis–clitoris to the size of a normal clitoris. Such surgery impairs the person's erotic sensation and is at best premature, as no one knows how the child's sexual orientation will develop. If the intersexed person makes an informed request for such surgery in adulthood, then it is appropriate, but otherwise it should be avoided.

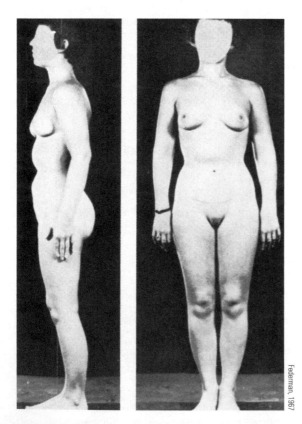

Figure 11.15 A woman with an XY chromosome pattern but insensitivity to androgens
Two undescended testes produce testosterone and other androgens, to which the body is insensitive. The testes and adrenal glands also produce estrogens that are responsible for the pubertal changes.

Testicular Feminization

Certain individuals with the typical male XY chromosome pattern have the genital appearance of a female. This condition is known as **androgen insensitivity,** or **testicular feminization.** Although these individuals produce normal amounts of androgens (e.g., testosterone), they lack the receptor that enables androgens to activate genes in a cell's nucleus. Consequently, the cells are insensitive to androgens, and the external genitals develop almost like those of a normal female. Two abnormalities appear at puberty. First, in spite of breast development and broadening of the hips, menstruation does not begin because the body has two internal testes instead of ovaries and a uterus. (The vagina is short and leads to nothing.) Second, pubic hair does not develop because it depends on androgens in females as well as males (Figure 11.15).

Someone with androgen insensitivity develops a clear female gender identity. Her gender identity should come as no surprise: She looks like a normal female, she has been raised unambiguously as a female, and her cells have been exposed only to estrogens since prenatal development. The only discrepancy is her genetic sex (XY).

Testicular feminization, like any other condition, comes in various degrees. Some look more male than female but with a small penis, lack of body hair, and so forth.

---

3. What would cause a genetic female (XX) to develop an intersex anatomy?
4. What would cause a genetic male (XY) to develop a feminized anatomy?

Check your answers on page 351.

Discrepancies in Sexual Appearance

Most of the evidence from intersexes does not tell us anything indisputable about the roles of rearing and hormones in determining gender identity. From a scientific viewpoint, the most decisive way to settle the issue would be to raise a completely normal male baby as a female or to raise a normal female baby as a male. If the process succeeded in producing an adult who was fully satisfied in the assigned role, we would know that upbringing determines gender identity and that hormones do not. Although no one would perform such an experiment intentionally, it is possible to study accidental events. Here we shall consider examples in which children were apparently exposed to the hormonal pattern of one sex before birth and then reared as the other.

Penis Development Delayed Until Puberty

In one community in the Dominican Republic with apparently much inbreeding, some genetic males have a genetic defect in the enzyme *5α-reductase 2.* This enzyme converts testosterone to *dihydrotestosterone,* an androgen that is more effective than testosterone for masculinizing the genitals. At birth, the penis is so small that it looks like a slightly swollen clitoris, and the child is identified as female and reared as a girl. Nevertheless, the child maintains testosterone levels in the usual male range, and at puberty, the testosterone levels increase enough to cause the penis to grow to about the usual male size.

Women: Imagine that at about age 12 years you had suddenly sprouted a penis and your family wanted to change your name from Juanita to Juan. Would you calmly say, "Yep, okay, I guess I'm a boy now"? Presumably not, but in nearly every case, the girl-turned-boy developed a clear male gender identity and directed his sexual interest toward females (Imperato-McGinley, Guerrero, Gautier, & Peterson, 1974). Remember, these were not "normal" girls; their brains had been exposed to male levels of testosterone (though not dihydrotestosterone) from prenatal life onward. The report of these Dominican Republic families led researchers to look for additional cases, which they found in parts of Brazil and Turkey, again in isolated communities with much inbreeding. In both communities, nearly all the children with 5α-reductase 2 deficiency were originally considered female but switched to male at puberty (Can et al., 1998; Mendonca et al., 1996).

One interpretation of these results is that the prenatal testosterone favored a male gender identity even in children who were reared as females or at least a sufficiently neutral identity that the person could accept either gender more easily than most other people could. Another possibility is that gender identity is established by social influences during adolescence. In either case, the results make it difficult to argue that early rearing experiences determine gender identity.

Stop & Check

---

5. What does the enzyme 5α-reductase 2 do?

Check your answer on page 351.

Accidental Removal of the Penis

Circumcision is the removal of the foreskin of the penis, a common procedure with newborn boys. One physician using an electrical procedure accidentally used too high a current and burned off the entire penis. On the advice of respected and well-meaning authorities, the parents elected to rear the child as a female, with the appropriate corrective surgery. What makes this a particularly interesting case is that the child has a twin brother (whom the parents did not let the physician try to circumcise). If both twins developed satisfactory gender identities, one as a girl and the other as a boy, we would conclude that rearing was decisive in gender identity and that prenatal hormones were not.

Initial reports claimed that the child reared as a girl had a normal female gender identity, though she also had strong tomboyish tendencies (Money & Schwartz, 1978). However, by about age 10, she had figured out that something was wrong and that "she" was really a boy. She had preferred boys' activities and played only with boys' toys. She even tried urinating in a standing position, despite always making a mess. By age 14, she insisted that she wanted to live as a boy. At that time, her (now his) father tearfully explained the earlier events. The child changed names and became known to and accepted by classmates as a boy; at age 25, he married a somewhat older woman and adopted her children. Clearly, the biological predisposition had won out over the family's attempts to rear the child as a girl (Colapinto, 1997; Diamond & Sigmundson, 1997). Could a child who was exposed to the full pattern of male hormones prenatally ever be reared successfully as a female? Well, who knows? There aren't many cases in which it has been tried, and results probably vary (Bradley, Oliver, Chernick, & Zucker, 1998). The point is that no one should feel confident about such a switch, and it was a mistake to impose surgery and hormonal treatments to try to complete the feminization of this child.

POSSIBLE BIOLOGICAL BASES OF SEXUAL ORIENTATION

Why do some people prefer partners of the other sex and some prefer partners of their own sex? This topic is particularly troublesome because of the difficulty of separating scientific issues from social and political disputes. Most of our discussion will focus on male homosexuality, which is more common than female homosexuality and more heavily investigated.

Most people say that their sexual orientation "just happened," generally at an early age, and that they do not know how or why. Sexual orientation, like left- or right-handedness, is not something that people choose or that they can change easily.

Genetics

Homosexual orientation occurs in some animals in captivity, although no one knows how frequently such orientations occur in the wild. Some cases of homosexual orientation in animals can be traced to genetics (Pinckard, Stellflug, Resko, Roselli, & Stormshak, 2000). For example, male *Drosophila* with the *fruitless* gene court only other males.

Several studies of the genetics of human sexual orientation have begun by advertising in gay or lesbian publications for homosexual men or women who have twins. Then they contacted the twins, not telling them how they got their names, and asked them to fill out a questionnaire. The questionnaire included diverse items to conceal the fact that the real interest was sexual orientation. Figure 11.16 shows the results for two such studies. Note that the probability of homosexuality is highest in monozygotic (identical) twins of the originally identified homosexual person, lower in dizygotic twins, and still lower in adopted brothers or sisters (Bailey & Pillard, 1991; Bailey, Pillard, Neale, & Agyei, 1993).

One concern about these studies is that the people who answer ads in gay publications may not be typical of others. To deal with this concern, another study examined the data from 794 pairs of twins who had responded to a national (USA) survey not specifically devoted to sex. Of those 794 pairs, only 43 included at least one homosexual person, so the sample size was relatively small, although it had the advantage of being representative. When one twin (either male or female) had a homosexual orientation, the other did also in 31% of monozygotic pairs and 8% of dizygotic

pairs (Kendler, Thornton, Gilman, & Kessler, 2000). These results support the conclusion of a genetic tendency, although they also confirm that genetic factors are not the only influence. If they were, monozygotic twins would be 100% concordant.

Various studies have not agreed on whether a family with homosexual men is likely also to include homosexual women (Bailey & Bell, 1993; Bailey & Benishay, 1993; Bailey et al., 1999). This inconsistency is disappointing because an answer would tell us whether the factors influencing sexual orientation are the same in men as in women.

One study that examined relatives beyond the immediate family found a higher incidence of homosexuality among the maternal relatives of homosexual men than among the paternal relatives (Hamer, Hu, Magnuson, Hu, & Pattatucci, 1993). These results suggest a relevant gene on the X chromosome, which a man necessarily receives from his mother. However, later studies have not replicated these results (Bailey et al., 1999; Rice, Anderson, Risch, & Ebers, 1999).

If certain genes promote a homosexual orientation, then why has evolution not selected strongly against those genes, which decrease the probability of reproduction? One hypothesis is that homosexual people help their brothers or sisters to rear children and thereby perpetuate genes that the whole family

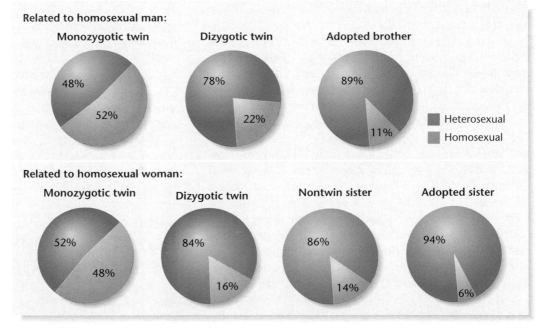

Figure 11.16 Sexual orientations in adult relatives of a homosexual man or woman
Note that the probability of a homosexual orientation is highest among monozygotic twins of a homosexual individual, lower among dizygotic twins, and still lower among adopted brothers or sisters. These data suggest a genetic contribution toward the development of sexual orientation. *Source: Based on the data of Bailey & Pillard, 1991; Bailey, Pillard, Neale, & Agyei, 1993*

shares (LeVay, 1993). However, one survey found that homosexual men were no more likely than heterosexuals to help their brothers, sisters, nephews, or nieces (Bobrow & Bailey, 2001). Indeed, many were quite estranged from their relatives. Of course, we should not generalize too broadly from one study in a single society at a single point in time. A second hypothesis is that certain genes that produce homosexuality in males are disadvantageous to the males but in some way advantageous to their sisters. For example, imagine some gene that makes men interested in sex with other men and also makes their sisters unusually eager to mate with men (or unusually attractive to men). The extra reproduction by the sisters of gay men would maintain the gene at some moderate frequency in the population. The idea is interesting, but as yet researchers have not tested it. A closely related hypothesis is that some gene produces homosexuality in people who are homozygous for that gene but produces some reproductive benefit in people heterozygous for the gene. Still another idea is that male heterosexual development requires an intermediate level of testosterone during prenatal development, and men exposed to either higher or lower testosterone levels might be predisposed to homosexuality (Robinson & Manning, 2000). Obviously, we need more research to decide among these hypotheses, if indeed genes have much to do with sexual orientation.

Hormones

Given the importance of hormones for sexual behavior, it seems natural to look for their possible effects on sexual orientation. We can quickly dismiss the hypothesis that sexual orientation depends on adult hormone levels: Most homosexual men have testosterone and estrogen levels well within the same range as heterosexual men; most lesbian women also have hormone levels well within the typical female range.

A more plausible hypothesis is that sexual orientation depends on testosterone levels during a sensitive period of brain development, which in humans lasts from the early to middle part of pregnancy (Ellis & Ames, 1987). In studies of animals ranging from rats to pigs to zebra finches, males that were exposed to much-decreased levels of testosterone early in life have as adults shown sexual interest in other males (Adkins-Regan, 1988). Females exposed to extra testosterone during that period show an increased probability of attempting to mount sexual partners in the way that males typically do (Figure 11.17). However, in many of these animal studies, the hormonal manipulation also led to physical abnormalities. The animals not only acted (in some ways) like the oppo-

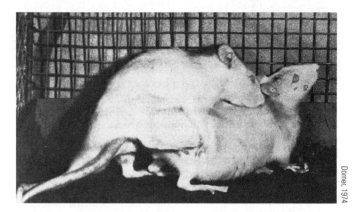

Figure 11.17 A female rat mounting a male
The female was injected with androgens during an early sensitive period; the male was castrated at birth and injected with androgens at adulthood.

site sex but also looked like them. In humans, homosexuality and heterosexuality have no consistent relationship to external anatomy.

Some homosexual men look somewhat feminine, but many others are in fact muscular, athletic, and very masculine-looking. Indeed, some researchers have proposed that male homosexuality might be associated with an excess of testosterone during prenatal development. The evidence here is indirect. First, consider—oddly enough—finger lengths. For most women, the index finger is close to the same length as the ring finger. For most men, the index finger tends to be a bit shorter. Why the sexes differ in finger length is unknown. According to one study, homosexual men have an even smaller ratio of index finger to ring finger length than do other men (Robinson & Manning, 2000). The relative lengths of fingers are nearly constant from the 14th week of prenatal development through adulthood, so finger length is controlled by genes and prenatal hormones, not by anything that happens later. These results suggest that some homosexual men had higher prenatal testosterone levels than the average for other men. (Individual variation is large within all groups. Indeed, some studies show different patterns of results. So you cannot learn a man's sexual orientation by looking at his fingers!)

Similarly, men and women reportedly differ on the average in their patterns of responses in the cochlea when they hear a click. (The differences are complex, depending on the exact number of milliseconds between the click and the measurement.) According to one report, lesbian women have responses similar to those of heterosexual men, and gay men have responses that are an exaggeration of the usual male pattern—even more "male-like" than the average male (McFadden & Champlin, 2000).

Prenatal Stress

One possible source of prenatal hormone changes, other than genetics, is stressful experiences to the mother. Laboratory research has shown that prenatal stress can alter sexual development. In several experiments, rats in the final week of pregnancy had the stressful experience of confinement in tight Plexiglas tubes for more than 2 hours each day under bright lights. In some cases, they were given alcohol as well. These rats' daughters looked and acted approximately normal. The sons, however, had normal male anatomy but, at adulthood, often responded to the presence of another male by arching their backs in the typical rat female posture for sex (I. L. Ward, Ward, Winn, & Bielawski, 1994). Most males who were subjected to either prenatal stress or alcohol developed male sexual behavior in addition to these female sexual behaviors, but those who were subjected to both stress and alcohol showed a decrease of male sexual behaviors (I. L. Ward, Bennett, Ward, Hendricks, & French, 1999).

The effects of prenatal stress varied, depending on social experiences after birth. Prenatally stressed males reared in isolation or with one another developed a sexual responsivity only to males. Those reared with nonstressed males and females became sexually responsive to both males and females (Dunlap, Zadina, & Gougis, 1978; I. L. Ward & Reed, 1985).

Prenatal stress and alcohol may alter brain development through several routes. Stress releases endorphins, some of which cross the placenta and reach the fetus's developing hypothalamus, where they antagonize the effects of testosterone (O. B. Ward, Monaghan, & Ward, 1986). Stress also elevates levels of the adrenal hormones corticosterone and aldosterone (M. T. Williams, Davis, McCrea, Long, & Hennessy, 1999). Corticosterone decreases testosterone release. Alcohol also lowers testosterone release (O. B. Ward, Ward, Denning, French, & Hendricks, 2002). The long-term effects of either prenatal stress or alcohol include several changes in the structure of the nervous system, making the affected males' anatomy closer to that of females (Nosenko & Reznikov, 2001; I. L. Ward, Romeo, Denning, & Ward, 1999).

With regard to human sexual orientation, the rat data are suggestive but have limitations:

- Hormonal influences on sexual behavior vary from one species to another.
- The female sexual behaviors shown by the male rats in these studies (e.g., arching their backs) do not match human behaviors. Homosexual men prefer male partners but do not necessarily prefer female behaviors.
- All these studies demonstrate a role of decreased testosterone on later behavior, whereas the research described in the previous section suggested very

high prenatal testosterone levels for at least some homosexual men.

Nevertheless, the rat studies have prompted investigators to examine possible relationships between prenatal stress and later sexual orientation in humans. One approach is to ask the mothers of homosexual men whether they experienced any unusual stress during pregnancy. Three surveys compared mothers of homosexual sons to mothers of heterosexual sons. In two of the three, the mothers of homosexual sons recalled a greater number of stressful experiences during their pregnancies (Bailey, Willerman, & Parks, 1991; Ellis, Ames, Peckham, & Burke, 1988; Ellis & Cole-Harding, 2001). However, all these studies relied on women's memories of pregnancies more than 20 years earlier. A better but more difficult procedure would be to measure stress during pregnancy and examine the sexual orientation of the sons many years later.

What about the role of hormones in female homosexuality? In the 1950s and early 1960s, certain pregnant women took *diethylstilbestrol (DES)*, a synthetic estrogen, to prevent miscarriage or alleviate other problems. DES can exert masculinizing effects similar to those of testosterone. One study found that of 30 adult women whose mothers had taken DES during pregnancy, 7 reported some degree of homosexual or bisexual responsiveness. By comparison, only 1 of 30 women not prenatally exposed to DES reported any homosexual or bisexual responsiveness (Ehrhardt et al., 1985). These results suggest a role of prenatal hormones, though it could hardly be the sole influence.

Brain Anatomy

On the average, men's brains differ from women's in several ways, including the sizes of several parts of the hypothalamus (Swaab, Chung, Kruijver, Hofman, & Ishunina, 2001). Do the brains of homosexual men differ from those of heterosexual men?

Current evidence shows results that vary from one brain area to another. The anterior commissure (see p. 89) is, on the average, larger in heterosexual women than in heterosexual men; in homosexual men, it is at least as large as it is in women, perhaps even slightly larger (Gorski & Allen, 1992). The implications of this difference are unclear, as the anterior commissure has no known relationship to sexual behavior. The suprachiasmatic nucleus (SCN) is also larger in homosexual men than in heterosexual men (Swaab & Hofman, 1990). Recall from Chapter 9 that the SCN controls circadian rhythms. How might a difference in the SCN relate to sexual orientation? The answer is not clear, but male rats that are deprived of testosterone during early development also show abnormalities in the SCN, and their preference for male or female sexual partners varies with time of day. They make sexual advances toward both male and female partners early in their active period of the day but mostly toward females as the day goes on (Swaab, Slob, Houtsmuller, Brand, & Zhou, 1995). Does human sexual orientation fluctuate depending on time of day? No research has been reported.

The most suggestive studies concern the third interstitial nucleus of the anterior hypothalamus (INAH-3), which is generally more than twice as large in heterosexual men as in women. This area corresponds to part of the sexually dimorphic nucleus, which is larger in male than female rats. Simon LeVay (1991) examined INAH-3 in 41 people who had died between the ages of 26 and 59. Of these, 16 were heterosexual men, 6 were heterosexual women, and 19 were homosexual men. All of the homosexual men, 6 of the 16 heterosexual men, and 1 of the 6 women had died of AIDS. LeVay found that the mean volume of INAH-3 was 0.12 mm^3 in heterosexual men, 0.056 mm^3 in heterosexual women, and 0.051 mm^3 in homosexual men. Figure 11.18 shows typical cross sections for a heterosexual man and a homosexual man. Figure 11.19 shows the distribution of volumes for the three groups. Note that the difference between heterosexual men and the other two groups is fairly large and that the cause of death (AIDS vs. other) has no clear relationship to the results. LeVay (1993) later examined the hypothalamus of a homosexual man who died of lung cancer; he had a small INAH-3, like the homosexual men who died of AIDS.

A later study partly replicated these general trends. Researchers found that the INAH-3 nucleus

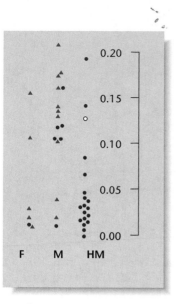

Figure 11.19 Volumes of the interstitial nucleus 3 of the anterior hypothalamus (INAH-3)
Samples are females (F), heterosexual males (M), and homosexual males (HM). Each filled circle represents a person who died of AIDS; each triangle represents a person who died from other causes. The one open circle represents a bisexual man who died of AIDS. *Source: Reprinted with permission from "A Difference in Hypothalamic Structure Between Heterosexual and Homosexual Men," by S. LeVay, Science, 253, p. 1034–1037. Copyright ©1991 American Association for the Advancement of Science.*

was slightly larger in heterosexual than homosexual men, although in this study the homosexual men's INAH-3 nucleus was larger than that of heterosexual women (Byne et al., 2001). Among heterosexual men or women, the INAH-3 nucleus was larger in those who were HIV negative than those who were HIV positive, but even if we look only at HIV positive men, we still find a difference in the hypothalamus between heterosexual and homosexual men. Figure 11.20 displays the means for the five groups. On microscopic examination of the INAH-3, researchers found that heterosexual men had larger neurons than homosexual men but about the same number. (Neither this study nor LeVay's earlier study included homosexual females.)

Interpreting these studies is another matter, however. One possibility is that brain differences predisposed some men to become homosexual and others to become heterosexual. Another possibility is that different kinds of sexual activity produce changes in the size of the adult hypothalamic neurons. Some brain areas do grow or

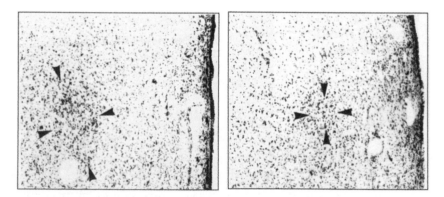

Figure 11.18 Typical sizes of interstitial nucleus 3 of the anterior hypothalamus
On the average, the volume of this structure was more than twice as large in a sample of heterosexual men (left) than in a sample of homosexual men (right), for whom it was about the same size as that in women. Animal studies have implicated this structure as important for male sexual activities. *Source: Reprinted with permission from "A Difference in Hypothalamic Structure Between Heterosexual and Homosexual Men," by S. LeVay, Science, 253, p. 1034–1037. Copyright ©1991 American Association for the Advancement of Science.*

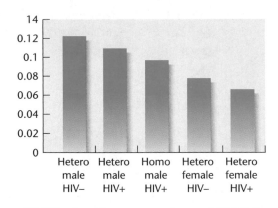

Figure 11.20 Another comparison of INAH-3

Figure 11.20 Another comparison of INAH-3
In this study, the mean volume for homosexual men was larger than that of women but smaller than that of heterosexual men. *Source: Based on data of Byne et al., 2001*

shrink in adults as a result of hormonal or behavioral influences (Cooke, Tabibnia, & Breedlove, 1999).

A further limitation is that we do not know how INAH-3 contributes to sexual behavior. Male rats that have their androgen receptors inactivated throughout the medial preoptic area decrease sexual behaviors but continue to choose female partners (McGinnis, Williams, & Lumia, 1996). Male ferrets with damage to the medial preoptic area, however, do shift to preferring male partners (Baum, Tobet, Cherry, & Paredes, 1996; Kindon, Baum, & Paredes, 1996). The behavioral functions of the medial preoptic area, particularly INAH-3, have not been tested in humans.

Stop & Check

6. What kind of experience in early development can cause a male rat to develop sexual responsiveness to other males and not to females? How does that experience probably produce its effects?

7. What differences have been reported, on the average, between the brains of homosexual and heterosexual men?

Check your answers on page 351.

MODULE 11.2

In Closing: We Are Not All the Same

When Alfred Kinsey conducted the first massive surveys of human sexual behavior, he found that people varied enormously in their frequency of sexual acts, but each person considered his or her own frequency "normal." Many believed that sexual activity much more frequent than their own was excessive, abnormal, and might even lead to insanity (Kinsey, Pomeroy, & Martin, 1948; Kinsey, Pomeroy, Martin, & Gebhard, 1953).

How far have we come since then? People today are more aware of sexual diversity than they were in Kinsey's time and generally more accepting. Still, intolerance remains common. Biological research will not tell us how to treat one another, but it can help us understand how we come to be so different.

SUMMARY

1. Many of the mating habits of people make sense in terms of increasing the probability of passing on our genes. However, we cannot assume a genetic basis, because people may have chosen the behaviors because of their own experiences or cultural influences. (p. 340)

2. People can develop ambiguous genitals or genitals that don't match their chromosomal sex for several reasons. Intersexes are people who experienced a hormonal pattern intermediate between male and female during their prenatal sensitive period for sexual development. (p. 342)

3. Many intersexes do not develop a gender identity that clearly matches their assigned sex. Most resent the surgery that was imposed on them and especially the lack of opportunity to make an informed decision themselves. (p. 343)

4. Testicular feminization is a condition in which someone with XY chromosomes and internal testes lacks the mechanisms that enable testosterone to bind to receptors in the cells. Such people develop with a female appearance and female gender identity. (p. 344)

5. In several parts of the world, some children have a gene that decreases their early production of dihydrotestosterone. Such a child looks female at birth and is considered a girl but develops a penis at adolescence. Most of these people then accept a male gender identity. (p. 345)

6. One genetic male was exposed to normal male hormones until infancy, when his penis was accidentally removed and then his testes intentionally removed. In spite of being reared as a girl, he had typically male interests and eventually insisted on a male gender identity. (p. 345)

7. Plausible biological explanations for homosexual orientation include genetics and prenatal hormones. Hormone levels in adulthood are within the normal range. (p. 345)

8. One part of the hypothalamus is structurally different, on the average, in homosexual men than in heterosexual men. Research does not yet tell us whether the brain difference led to the sexual orientation or whether sexual activities alter brain anatomy. (p. 348)

ANSWERS TO *STOP AND CHECK* QUESTIONS

1. Women are more likely to be fertile while they are young. Age is less critical for fertility in men. (p. 342)

2. During pregnancy and early child care, a female is limited in her ability to get food, and therefore prefers a male partner who can provide for her. A healthy male is not similarly dependent on a female. (p. 342)

3. A genetic female whose adrenal gland produces much more than the usual amount of testosterone will develop an intersex appearance. (p. 344)

4. A genetic male with a gene that prevents testosterone from binding to its receptors will develop a female appearance. (p. 344)

5. The enzyme 5α-reductase 2 catalyzes the conversion of testosterone to dihydrotestosterone, which is more effective in masculinizing the genitals. (p. 345)

6. Stressful experiences given to a rat late in her pregnancy can cause her male offspring to show a later preference for male partners. Evidently, the stress increases the release of endorphins in the hypothalamus, and very high endorphin levels can block the effects of testosterone. (p. 350)

7. Interstitial nucleus 3 of the anterior hypothalamus is larger in the brains of heterosexual than homosexual men. (p. 350)

THOUGHT QUESTIONS

1. In all human cultures, men prefer to mate with attractive young women, and women prefer men who are wealthy and successful (as well as attractive, if possible). It was remarked on page 341 that the similarity across cultures is not sufficient evidence to demonstrate that these preferences depend on genetics. What would be good evidence?

2. On the average, intersexes have IQ scores in the 110 to 125 range, well above the mean for the population (Dalton, 1968; Ehrhardt & Money, 1967; Lewis, Money, & Epstein, 1968). One possible interpretation is that a hormonal pattern intermediate between male and female promotes great intellectual development. Another possibility is that intersexuality may be more common in intelligent families than in less intelligent ones or that the more intelligent families are more likely to bring their intersex children to an investigator's attention. What kind of study would be best for deciding among these hypotheses? (For one answer, see Money & Lewis, 1966.)

3. Recall LeVay's study of brain anatomy in heterosexual and homosexual men (p. 349). Certain critics have suggested that one or more of the men classified as "heterosexual" might actually have been homosexual or bisexual. If so, would that fact strengthen or weaken the overall conclusions?

Key Terms and Activities

TERMS

activating effect (p. 329)

alpha-fetoprotein (p. 330)

anabolic steriods (p. 326)

androgen insensitivity (or testicular feminization) (p. 344)

androgens (p. 326)

anterior pituitary (p. 327)

endocrine glands (p. 324)

estradiol (p. 333)

estrogens (p. 326)

follicle-stimulating hormone (FSH) (p. 333)

gender identity (p. 342)

gonad (p. 329)

hermaphrodite (p. 342)

hormone (p. 324)

impotence (p. 332)

intersex (or pseudohermaphrodite) (p. 342)

luteinizing hormone (LH) (p. 333)

menstrual cycle (p. 333)

Müllerian duct (p. 329)

organizing effect (p. 328)

ovary (p. 329)

oxytocin (p. 327)

peptide hormones (p. 324)

periovulatory period (p. 334)

pituitary gland (p. 327)

posterior pituitary (p. 327)

premenstrual syndrome (PMS) (p. 335)

progesterone (p. 326)

protein hormones (p. 324)

releasing hormones (p. 327)

sensitive period (p. 330)

sex-limited genes (p. 326)

sexually dimorphic nucleus (p. 329)

SRY gene (p. 329)

steroid hormones (p. 324)

testis (p. 329)

testosterone (p. 329)

vasopressin (p. 327)

Wolffian duct (p. 329)

SUGGESTIONS FOR FURTHER READING

Colapinto, J. (2000). *As nature made him: The boy who was raised as a girl.* New York: HarperCollins. Describes the boy whose penis was accidentally removed, as presented on page 345.

Diamond, J. (1997). *Why is sex fun?* New York: Basic Books. Human sexual behavior differs from that of other species in many ways and therefore raises many evolutionary issues, which this book addresses. For example, why do humans have sex at times when the woman cannot become pregnant? Why do women have menopause? Why don't men breast-feed their babies? And what good are men, anyway? If you haven't thought about such questions before, you should read this book.

Dreger, A. D. (1998). *Hermaphrodites and the medical invention of sex.* Cambridge, MA: Harvard University Press. A fascinating history of how the medical profession has treated and mistreated hermaphrodites.

WEB SITES TO EXPLORE

You can go to the Biological Psychology Study Center and click these links. While there, you can also check for suggested articles available on InfoTrac College Edition.

- The Biological Psychology Internet address is:
**http://psychology.wadsworth.com/
kalatbiopsych8e/**

National Institute on Drug Abuse: Anabolic Steroids
**http://www.nida.nih.gov/ResearchReports/Steroids/
AnabolicSteroids.html**

The Endocrine Society
http://www.endo-society.org/

Intersex Society of North America
http://www.isna.org/

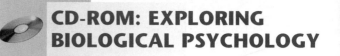

CD-ROM: EXPLORING BIOLOGICAL PSYCHOLOGY

Menstruation Cycle (animation)

Erectile Dysfunction (video)

Sex Dysfunction in Women (video)

Critical Thinking (essay questions)

Chapter Quiz (multiple choice questions)

Emotional Behaviors

12

Chapter Outline

Module 12.1 What Is Emotion?

Emotions and Decision Making
Emotions, Autonomic Arousal, and the
   James-Lange Theory
Brain Areas Associated With Emotion
In Closing: Research on Emotions
Summary
Answers to Stop and Check Questions

Module 12.2 Stress and Health

Stress and the Autonomic Nervous System
Stress and the Hypothalamus-Pituitary-Adrenal
   Cortex Axis
Posttraumatic Stress Disorder
In Closing: Emotions and Body Reactions
Summary
Answers to Stop and Check Questions
Thought Questions

Module 12.3 Attack and Escape Behaviors

Attack Behaviors
Escape, Fear, and Anxiety
In Closing: Doing Something About Emotions
Summary
Answers to Stop and Check Questions
Thought Question

Terms
Suggestions for Further Reading
Web Sites to Explore
CD-ROM: Exploring Biological Psychology

Opposite:
Even a static photo or statue can convey strong emotion, as in this statue, The Angry Boy. With movement we can express even more. *Source: Gunnar Strom*

Main Ideas

1. Emotions are difficult to define or measure.

2. Although panic interferes with good reasoning, moderate emotions are essential to making good decisions.

3. Stress activates the autonomic nervous system and the hypothalamus-pituitary-adrenal cortex axis. Both systems influence health and well-being.

4. Aggressive behavior is associated with decreased serotonin turnover and increased activity in the hypothalamus and amygdala.

5. The amygdala appears to be critical for processing information relevant to emotions.

> [W]e know the meaning [of consciousness] so long as no one asks us to define it.
>
> *William James (1892/1961, p. 19)*

> Unfortunately, one of the most significant things ever said about emotion may be that everyone knows what it is until they are asked to define it.
>
> *Joseph LeDoux (1996, p. 23)*

Consciousness is difficult to define because it is unobservable. I am aware of my own consciousness, but I can only infer anyone else's. Emotions have the same difficulty because our concept of emotion includes a conscious experience. I know how I feel when I am happy, and I infer that you feel the same way when you say you are happy, but I would have a hard time explaining the concept to someone who claimed not to be familiar with the experience.

Because of the difficulty of defining or measuring emotion itself, biological researchers generally focus on emotional behaviors rather than the experience of emotion itself. We can investigate attack and escape behaviors even if we cannot observe anger or fear. However, our understanding of the brain will remain incomplete if we limit ourselves entirely to behavior and never get to the underlying experiences. So to some extent, hesitantly, we also try to investigate the physiology behind emotional experiences, as indicated by people's self-reports. Emotion is a difficult topic for research, but most of us readily agree that it is important and interesting.

What Is Emotion?

Suppose researchers have discovered a new species—let's call it species X—and psychologists begin testing its abilities. They place food behind a green card and nothing behind a red card and find that after a few trials X always goes to the green card. So we conclude that X shows learning, memory, and hunger. Then researchers offer X a green card and a variety of gray cards; X still goes to the green, so it must have color vision and not just brightness discrimination. Next they let X touch a blue triangle which is extremely hot. X makes a loud sound and backs away. Then someone picks up the blue triangle (with padded gloves) and starts moving with it rapidly toward X. As soon as X sees this happening, it makes the same sound, turns, and starts moving rapidly away. Shall we conclude that it feels the emotion of fear?

If you said "yes," now let me add: I said this was a new species, and so it is, but it's a new species of robot, not animal. Do you still think X feels emotions? Most people are willing to talk about artificial learning, memory, intelligence, and maybe even motivation, but not emotions. "The robot was just programmed to make that sound and move away from hot objects," they say. "It doesn't really feel an emotion." (If such behavior isn't adequate evidence for emotion in a robot, is it adequate evidence for an animal?)

One possible approach, advocated by Antonio Damasio (1999), is to identify *emotions* as the observable behaviors (e.g., running away) and to separate them from *feelings* (the private experiences). Scientific study would concentrate on the observable emotions and give them operational definitions. (An *operational definition* specifies the operations one could use to produce something or measure it.) This suggestion has the virtue that it can lead to research progress. However, note that by this definition a robot that runs away from something qualifies as showing an emotion. If we are uncomfortable with that conclusion, we shall need a different definition.

Damasio further argues that it is no coincidence that we infer emotional feelings only when we also infer consciousness. He argues that emotional feelings occur only if consciousness is present. Someone in a coma is not conscious and cannot have feelings. Here is another example: People with an **absence seizure** (a type of epilepsy) have periods of seconds or tens of seconds when they stare blankly without talking or moving. Then they do something without any apparent purpose, such as walking down the hall and sitting in an unfamiliar room. Then, as suddenly as this state began, they suddenly arouse and wonder where they are and what is happening. They have no recollections of the "absent" period, as if they had been unconscious during that time. Furthermore, they show no emotional expressions during the absent period. So apparently, we need a certain level of consciousness and arousal to experience emotions.

1. What do we learn about emotion by studying people with absence seizures?

Check your answer on page 363.

EMOTIONS AND DECISION MAKING

Rightly or wrongly, we base many of our most important decisions partly on emotional considerations—how we think one outcome or another will make us feel. In the words of Antonio Damasio (1999), "Inevitably, emotions are inseparable from the idea of good and evil" (p. 55). Consider the three moral dilemmas illustrated in Figure 12.1.

In each of these dilemmas, you can save five people (and in the lifeboat case, yourself as well) by doing something that kills one person. However, the decisions do not feel the same. Most people say "yes" to pulling the switch in the trolley dilemma, but either say "no" or find it difficult to decide in the footbridge and lifeboat dilemmas. The idea of using your hands to push someone to his death is emotionally upsetting. In fact, brain scans show that contemplating the footbridge or lifeboat dilemma greatly activates brain areas known to

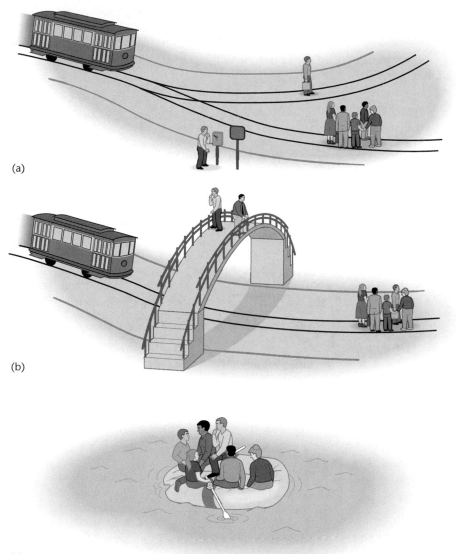

(a)

(b)

(c)

Figure 12.1 Three Moral Dilemmas
(a) *The Trolley Dilemma.* A runaway trolley is headed toward five people on a track. The only way you can prevent their death is to switch the trolley onto another track, where it will kill one person. Would it be right to pull the switch? **(b)** *The Footbridge Dilemma.* You are standing on a footbridge overlooking a trolley track. A runaway trolley is headed toward five people on a track. The only way you can prevent their death is to push a heavy-set stranger off the footbridge and onto the track so that he will block the trolley. Would it be right to push him? **(c)** *The Lifeboat Dilemma.* You and five other people are on a lifeboat in icy waters, but it is overcrowded and starting to sink. If you push one of the people off the boat, the boat will stop sinking and the rest of you will survive. Would it be right to push someone off?

justification afterward (Haidt, 2001).

Are we right to make decisions based on emotions? Often we find it better to calm down, consider the facts, and make a less emotional decision. However, in some cases, your emotional response or "gut feeling" can be a useful guide. In one study, college students viewed a series of slides of snakes and spiders, each presented for just 10 ms, followed by an interfering stimulus. Under these conditions, people cannot identify what they saw, and if they have to guess whether it was a snake or a spider, they guess randomly. For each participant, one kind of stimulus—either the snakes or the spiders—was always followed by a mild shock. Participants were asked to report any perceived changes in their heart rate, which were compared to external measurements of their actual heart rate. Also after each stimulus, they guessed whether a shock was forthcoming. Most people did show stimulus-specific conditioned responses. That is, those shocked after spider pictures showed a bigger heart rate increase after spider pictures, and people shocked after snake pictures showed increased heart rate after snake pictures, even though neither group could consciously identify any of the pictures. Furthermore, those who were most accurate at reporting their heart rate increases were the most accurate at predicting whether they were about to get a shock (Katkin, Wiens, & Öhman, 2001). In short, people who are good at detecting their autonomic responses may have valid "gut feelings" about dangers that they cannot identify consciously.

respond to emotions, including part of the prefrontal cortex, part of the cingulate gyrus, and the angular gyrus—an area of the posterior parietal lobe adjacent to the temporal lobe (Greene, Sommerville, Nystrom, Darley, & Cohen, 2001). When we are making a decision about right and wrong, we seldom work it out rationally. Instead, one decision or the other immediately "feels" right, and we try to think of a logical

People with certain kinds of prefrontal cortex damage have a striking loss of emotions. Although we generally recommend nonemotional decision making, people with a severe loss of emotions make poor decisions. Damasio (1994) examined a man with prefrontal cortex damage who expressed almost no emotions.

Nothing angered him; he was never very sad, even about his own brain damage. Nothing gave him much pleasure, not even music. Far from being purely rational, he frequently made amazingly stupid decisions, losing his job, his marriage, and his savings. When tested in the laboratory, he had no trouble predicting the probable outcomes of various decisions. For example, when asked what would happen if he cashed a check and the bank teller handed him too much money, he knew the probable consequences of either returning it or walking away with it. But he admitted, "And after all this, I still wouldn't know what to do" (Damasio, 1994, p. 49). He could not even imagine feeling good or bad about various outcomes. He knew that one action would win him approval and another would get him in trouble, but it was not obvious to him that he would prefer approval to trouble!

Investigators also studied two young adults who had suffered prefrontal cortex damage in infancy (Anderson, Bechara, Damasio, Tranel, & Damasio, 1999). Not only did they make bad decisions, but apparently, they never learned moral behavior. From childhood onward, they frequently stole, lied, physically and verbally abused others, and failed to show any guilt. Neither had any friends and neither could keep a job.

Here is an experiment to explore further the role of emotions in decision making. People are given a "gambling" task in which they can draw one card at a time from four piles. They always win $100 in play money from decks A and B, $50 from C and D. However, some of the cards also have penalties:

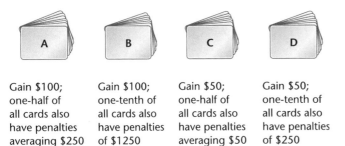

A	B	C	D
Gain $100; one-half of all cards also have penalties averaging $250	Gain $100; one-tenth of all cards also have penalties of $1250	Gain $50; one-half of all cards also have penalties averaging $50	Gain $50; one-tenth of all cards also have penalties of $250

When you see all the payoffs laid out, you can easily calculate the best strategy: Pick cards only from decks C and D. In the experiment, however, people have to discover the payoffs by trial and error. Ordinarily, as people sample from all four decks, they gradually start showing signs of nervous tension whenever they draw a card from A or B, and they start shifting their preference toward C and D. People with damage to either the prefrontal cortex or the amygdala (part of the temporal lobe) show difficulties processing emotional information, and those with prefrontal damage have weak emotional expressions. In this experiment, they do not show any nervous tension associated with

decks A and B, and they continue drawing from those decks (Bechara, Damasio, Damasio, & Lee, 1999). In short, people who can't anticipate the unpleasantness of likely outcomes tend to make bad decisions.

2. Why do people with frontal cortex or amygdala damage make bad decisions?

Check your answer on page 363.

EMOTIONS, AUTONOMIC RESPONSE, AND THE JAMES-LANGE THEORY

When you feel a strong emotion, you are inclined to do something vigorously. If you are afraid, you want to run away; if you are angry, you want to attack. If you are extremely happy, your response is a little less predictable but usually vigorous. The last time your favorite team won a big game, did you jump, scream, and hug nearby people?

Consider for a moment an apparent exception: You're lying in bed when you hear an intruder break into the house. You might lie there frozen with fear, feeling a strong emotion but doing nothing. True, you are not moving, but your heart is racing. You might continue lying there, hoping the intruder will leave without noticing you, but you are ready to run away or attack or do whatever else becomes necessary.

In short, it is hard to imagine an emotion without some readiness for action. The readiness is guided by the two branches of the autonomic nervous system: the sympathetic and the parasympathetic. The sympathetic nervous system prepares the body for brief, intense, vigorous "fight-or-flight" responses. The parasympathetic nervous system increases digestion and other processes that save energy and prepare for later events. (To review the structure of the sympathetic and parasympathetic nervous systems, see Figure 4.10, p. 84.) However, each situation calls for its own special mixture of sympathetic and parasympathetic arousal (Wolf, 1995). For a simple example, running away from danger and swimming away from it require different patterns of blood flow. Nausea includes increased sympathetic stimulation of the stomach (decreasing its contractions and secretions) but also increased salivation and intestinal contractions, which are parasympathetic responses.

Exactly how does the autonomic nervous system relate to emotions? Commonsense holds that first we feel an emotion, which then causes changes in heart rate and so forth. However, according to the **James-Lange theory** (James, 1884), the autonomic arousal and skeletal actions come first; what we experience as an emotion is the label we give to our responses: I am afraid *because* I run away; I am angry *because* I attack.

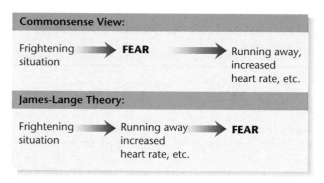

Note that the James-Lange theory assumes that physiological arousal is both necessary and sufficient for emotions. That is, first, the body's response comes before the emotion (which is only a perception of that response anyway); if the body does not respond or the brain does not perceive that response, no emotion results. Second, you discern whether you are angry, frightened, disgusted, happy, sad, or whatever by perceiving your body's actions; anything that causes those actions will be perceived as an emotion. Let's consider the evidence.

Is Physiological Arousal *Necessary* for Emotions?

According to the James-Lange theory, the body's response comes first, followed by our identification of it as an emotion. Whether that is true depends on what we mean by emotion. Today's psychologists distinguish between the cognitive and feeling aspects of an emotion. The cognitive aspect is identifying a situation as one that calls for happiness, one that calls for fear, one that calls for anger, and so forth. The feeling aspect is actually *feeling* the anger.

William James himself did not clearly distinguish between the cognitive and feeling aspects, although certain of his comments suggest that he intended his theory to apply to the feeling aspects. With that interpretation of the James-Lange theory, the data support it.

One's immediate cognitive reaction, such as "this situation calls for happiness," evidently does not require any feedback from the glands or muscles. In one

study, physicians inserted microelectrodes into single cells of the prefrontal cortex in a middle-aged man while he was undergoing brain surgery for severe epilepsy. (Such surgery is sometimes performed with only local anesthesia to the scalp so that the patient remains awake during the procedure. The brain itself has no pain receptors, so the procedure is painless. Sometimes surgeons stimulate a spot in the brain, and the patient says, "Oh, that's the way I feel when I'm about to have one of my seizures." Then the surgeons know they are close to the epileptic focus.) The physicians recorded neuronal responses as they flashed pictures of pleasant or unpleasant scenes and happy or frightened faces. They found that the cells' responses to pleasant scenes or happy faces differed from those to unpleasant scenes or frightened faces, and the differences were detectable as quickly as 120 ms after onset of a picture (Kawasaki et al., 2001). That is, the brain can categorize events as pleasant or unpleasant very quickly, without waiting for feedback from the rest of the body.

With regard to the feeling aspect of emotions, however, feedback from the glands and muscles is important. Consider the case of patients with **pure autonomic failure,** in which output from the autonomic nervous system to the body fails either completely or almost completely. Pure autonomic failure is an uncommon condition, usually beginning in middle-aged adults, with causes unknown. One of its effects occurs when people stand up. When you suddenly stand up, gravity and inertia would pull the blood from your head toward the ground, except that your autonomic nervous system quickly increases your heart rate and constricts the veins in your head. In someone with pure autonomic failure, those reflexes do not occur. To avoid fainting, people have to learn to stand up very slowly. In addition, people with this condition have no changes in heart rate, blood pressure, or sweating during any kind of psychological stress or physical challenge. According to the James-Lange theory, we would expect them to report no emotions. In fact, they report the same emotions as anyone else, but much less intensely (Critchley, Mathias, & Dolan, 2001). Presumably, when they report emotions, they are reporting the cognitive aspect: "Yes, I'm angry; this is a situation that calls for anger." But they do not *feel* much anger.

An even more extreme medical condition is **locked-in syndrome,** in which someone has damage in the ventral part of the brainstem, as shown in Figure 12.2. These people continue to receive sensations (which travel through the dorsal brainstem), but they lose almost all output from the brain to the muscles. The only remaining voluntary movements are a few eye movements, controlled by nerves leaving the brainstem at a level just anterior to the damage. The

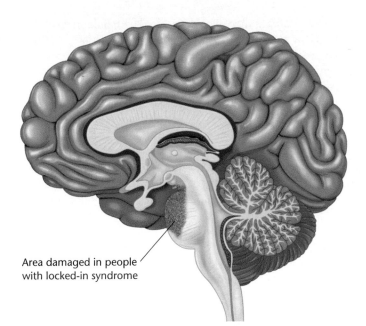

Figure 12.2 Brain damage that causes locked-in syndrome
People with damage in the ventral brainstem receive sensory input but lose almost all voluntary control of their muscles. They can communicate with others only by blinking their eyes.

Area damaged in people with locked-in syndrome

result is mental alertness but total paralysis. It is possible to establish communication with these people. The simplest way is to teach them to blink or move their eyes according to a code to spell out words. How do you think you would feel under those conditions? We might expect that the first message might express terror, depression, or even suicidal wishes. In fact, most of their messages are quite mundane. One woman, just after learning to blink her eyes to spell words, laboriously spelled out "Why do I wear such an ugly shirt?" (Kübler, Kotchoubey, Kaiser, Wolpaw, & Birbaumer, 2001). Most people with locked-in syndrome report feeling tranquil—a bit frustrated and sad, but hardly panicked or depressed. Damasio's (1999) interpretation is that the person cannot send out messages to make the muscles fidget, to cause "butterflies in the stomach," or to produce any other body changes, and therefore, the brain receives messages of tranquillity!

For more information about locked-in syndrome, check these sites:
www.ninds.nih.gov/health_and_medical/disorders/lockedinsyndrome_doc.htm
www.eyegaze.com/doc/csun91.htm

The overall interpretation seems to be that a potentially emotional situation elicits a cognitive component of emotion immediately. That evaluation of the situation

directs the autonomic and skeletal responses, and the perception of those responses produces (as stated by the James-Lange theory) the feeling aspect of emotions.

Situation ⟶ Cognitive appraisal ⟶ Feeling aspect
⟶ Glandular and muscular actions ⟶

Is Physiological Arousal *Sufficient* for Emotions?

The other assumption of the James-Lange theory is that we identify an emotion by its physiological or motor output. Certainly, if you found yourself attacking or running away, you would have no trouble identifying your emotion (presuming that you didn't know already!), but if you were sitting still, could your heart rate, breathing rate, sweating, and so forth tell you whether you were happy, frightened, or angry?

The physiological differences among mild fear, mild anger, or mild happiness are small, and it is uncertain or doubtful that they could identify one emotion from another (Lang, 1994). People's ability to identify emotions from physiological changes is also difficult to test. If an experimenter used drugs or other procedures to raise your heart rate, breathing rate, sweating rate, and so forth to the levels typical of mild anger and you reported no anger, well, maybe anger depends on some other aspect of physiological arousal that the experimenter overlooked.

However, extreme arousal is different. Specifically, some people have occasional periods when their heart rate and breathing rate suddenly increase to enormous levels for no obvious reason, as if they were suffocating (Klein, 1993). Most people quickly identify that experience as extreme fear. If they become afraid of having those attacks, their fear of the fear response becomes part of the problem and triggers even further attacks (Battaglia, Bertella, Ogliari, Bellodi, & Smeraldi, 2001; Gorman et al., 2001). They also learn to associate their attacks with certain locations or situations so that returning to them triggers a new attack as a conditioned response (Bouton, Mineka, & Barlow, 2001). The result is what psychologists call **panic disorder,** a condition marked by episodes of extreme sympathetic nervous system arousal which the person interprets as fear.

What about other emotions? For example, if you find yourself smiling, would you become happier? Again, this is not an easy hypothesis to test. How could we get people to smile without first making them happy? Yes, of course, we could tell them to smile, but if experimenters tell people to smile and then ask whether they are happy, it becomes clear to people what the experiment is about, and the results are unreliable. Some clever researchers did, however, find a way to get people to smile without revealing the purpose of the study, and it is a method you could easily try yourself: Hold a pen in your mouth, either with your teeth or with your lips, as shown in Figure 12.3. Now examine a page of comic strips in your newspaper. Mark each one + for very funny, ✓ for somewhat funny, or − for not funny. Most people rate cartoons funnier when holding a pen with their teeth—which forces a smile—than when holding it with their lips—which prevents a smile (Strack, Martin, & Stepper, 1988). That is, the sensation of smiling increases happiness, at least in this situation and to a small degree. (Telling a depressed person to cheer up and smile does not help.)

One final example: A 16-year-old girl was undergoing brain surgery to remove an epileptic focus. As is often done, the surgeons conducted the surgery with only scalp anesthesia. When they stimulated one particular spot in the frontal cortex (part of the supplementary motor area), she smiled. When they stimulated it again a bit more strongly, she laughed. Whenever they stimulated, she laughed. More to the point, not only did she laugh, but she always found a reason for her laughter such as, "Oh you guys are so funny . . . standing around" (Fried, Wilson, MacDonald, & Behnke, 1998). She interpreted her body's response (laughter) as an emotion (amusement).

The net conclusion: Although it is unlikely that we identify mild emotions from our physiological state, extreme arousal is recognizable as extreme fear or panic. In addition, anything that causes a smile or laughter is regarded as pleasant or amusing. In these

Figure 12.3 Effect of facial expression on emotion
If you hold a pen in your teeth, and are therefore forced to smile, you are more likely to report feelings of amusement or humor than if you hold the pen in your lips, and were therefore prevented from smiling.

regards, the James-Lange theory is largely correct. Our perception of our bodily reactions is a major part of the basis for an emotion.

3. The James-Lange theory assumes that perception of body reactions is necessary for emotion and that it is sufficient to identify an emotion. Although the evidence suggests that this theory is on the right track, what evidence suggests that it cannot be the whole story?

Check your answer on page 363.

BRAIN AREAS ASSOCIATED WITH EMOTION

Do different emotions activate different brain areas, or do they activate the same brain areas in different ways? Moreover, which brain areas react most strongly to emotions?

Traditionally, the **limbic system**—the forebrain areas bordering the brainstem—has been regarded as critical for emotion (Figure 12.4). We shall especially encounter one part of it, the amygdala, later in this chapter. Many other brain areas are important, too. In one study, researchers used PET scans to record brain activity as people recalled in detail their most emotional experiences. High activity levels occurred in the cingulate cortex, the hypothalamus, parts of the somatosensory cortex (see Figure 4.25, p. 97), and the midbrain (A. R. Damasio et al., 2000). People with damage to the cingulate cortex report much reduced levels of tension and anger (R. A. Cohen et al., 2001).

Current researchers are trying to move away from simply identifying the brain areas responsible for emotion in general and instead to distinguish among brain areas responsible for different kinds of emotions (Calder, Lawrence, & Young, 2001). For example, temporary inactivation (by a magnet) of the medial frontal cortex impairs people's ability to identify angry expressions without impairing their identification of happy expressions (Harmer, Thilo, Rothwell, & Goodwin, 2001). Also, the emotional experience we call *disgust* mainly activates the *insular cortex* (or *insula*) (M. L. Phillips et al., 1997). That location is interesting because the insular cortex is the primary taste cortex (see Figure 7.19, p. 212). *Disgust* is literally *dis-gust* or bad-taste. To react with disgust is to react as if something

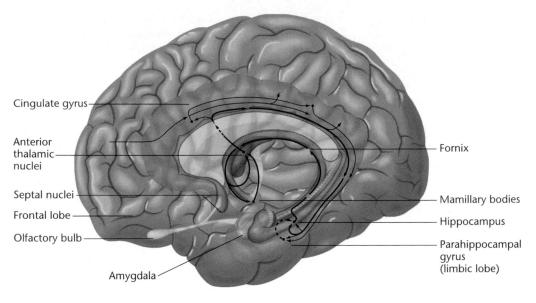

Figure 12.4 The limbic system
The limbic system is a group of structures in the interior of the brain, visible here as if the exterior of the brain were transparent. *Source: Based on MacLean, 1949*

Cingulate gyrus

Anterior thalamic nuclei

Septal nuclei

Frontal lobe

Olfactory bulb

Amygdala

Fornix

Mamillary bodies

Hippocampus

Parahippocampal gyrus (limbic lobe)

tasted bad; we want to spit it out. One man with damage to his insular cortex not only failed to experience disgust but also had trouble recognizing other people's disgust expressions and could not recognize a retching sound as meaning nausea or disgust (Calder, Keane, Manes, Antoun, & Young, 2000).

The right hemisphere appears to be more responsive to emotional stimuli than the left. For example, listening to either laughter or crying activates the right amygdala more than the left (Sander & Scheich, 2001). When people look at faces, drawing their attention to the emotional expression increases the activity in the right temporal cortex (Narumoto, Okada, Sadato, Fukui, & Yonekura, 2001). In one study, experimenters videotaped brain-damaged and non-brain-damaged people while they viewed pleasant and unpleasant slides. Later, other people watched the videotapes and, based on the facial expressions and gestures, tried to guess when people were looking at something pleasant or unpleasant. The raters found it difficult to guess correctly when they watched people with right-hemisphere damage, indicating that those people gave weak emotional expressions. However, when they watched left-hemisphere-damaged patients, their accuracy was slightly *higher* than normal (Buck & Duffy, 1980). Evidently, emotional expressions are strongest if the right hemisphere is active and the left hemisphere inactive.

Another study points to the same conclusion: People watched videotapes of 10 people. All of those 10 described themselves honestly during one speech and completely dishonestly during another. The task of the observers was to guess which of the two interviews was the honest one. The task is more difficult than it might sound; the vast majority of people are no more correct than chance (about 5 of 10). The *only* group tested that performed better than chance was a group of people with left-hemisphere brain damage (Etcoff, Ekman, Magee, & Frank, 2000). They got only 60% correct—not great, but at least they were better than chance. Evidently, the right hemisphere is better not only at expressing emotions but also at detecting other people's emotions, and with the left hemisphere out of the way, the right hemisphere was free to do what it does best.

In yet another study, 11 patients went through a procedure in which one hemisphere at a time was anesthetized by drug injection into one of the carotid arteries, which provide blood to the head. (This procedure, called the Wada procedure, is used before certain kinds of brain surgery, as described in Methods 14.1, p. 424.) All 11 patients had left-hemisphere damage, so they could not be interviewed with the left hemisphere inactivated. When they were tested with the right hemisphere inactivated, something fascinating happened: They could still describe any of the sad, frightening, or irritating events they had experienced in life, but they remembered only the facts, not the emotion. For example, one patient remembered a car wreck, another remembered visiting his mother while she was dying, and another remembered a time his wife threatened to kill him. But they denied they had felt any significant fear, sadness, or anger. When they described the same events with both hemispheres active, they remembered strong emotions indeed. So evidently, when the right hemisphere is inactive, people do not experience strong emotions and cannot even remember feeling them (E. D. Ross, Homan, & Buck, 1994).

The right hemisphere appears to be especially activated by unpleasant emotions (Royet et al., 2000). These patterns in turn relate somewhat to personality: People with greater left-hemisphere activity tend to be more outgoing and fun-loving; people with greater right-hemisphere activity tend to be shy (Schmidt, 1999). We shall return to this point in the Module 15.2.

MODULE 12.1

In Closing: Research on Emotions

If you compare what psychology textbooks today say about memory, perception, child development, and abnormal psychology to what textbooks of 50 years ago said, I think you will be impressed with the progress researchers have made. If you compare textbook treatments of emotion, I am less sure you will be impressed with the progress. Emotions are slippery. They are hard to observe or measure, and progress is difficult.

However, slow progress is not the same as no progress. Some of the recent studies of brain-damaged patients with pure autonomic failure, absence seizures, and locked-in syndrome offer some important insights. The potential from using brain scans has just begun to be realized. The study of emotions is an area to be watched for future progress.

SUMMARY

1. Emotion is difficult to define or measure. We infer it from observable behaviors. (p. 356)

2. When people appear to lack consciousness, as in the case of absence seizures, they also appear to lack emotions. Emotions may be integral to consciousness. (p. 356)

3. Emotions develop quickly, sometimes even when we are not consciously aware of the event that aroused them. Emotions ready us for quick, often vigorous responses which are usually appropriate to the situation. (p. 357)

4. People with severely impaired emotions have trouble imagining which outcome they would prefer because they cannot imagine their emotional responses to those outcomes. Therefore, they make poor decisions. (p. 357)

5. Emotional states activate parts of the autonomic nervous system. The sympathetic nervous system readies the body for vigorous movements, "fight or flight." The parasympathetic nervous system readies the body for energy conservation. (p. 358)

6. According to the James-Lange theory, emotion is one's perception of body changes. That is, the body reacts first, before the experience of emotion, and each emotional state has its own distinctive sensation. (p. 359)

7. One line of support for the James-Lange theory is the observation that people with no autonomic responses (pure autonomic failure) or no muscle movements (locked-in syndrome) have weakened emotions. Also, producing a response, such as a smile, can induce a corresponding emotion. (p. 359)

8. To some extent, different brain areas may be more important for different emotions, although not much research has been done in this area. The right hemisphere is generally more important than the left for responding to and interpreting emotional signals. (p. 361)

ANSWERS TO *STOP AND CHECK* QUESTIONS

1. People with absence seizures have brief periods when they seem to be unconscious. They move around purposelessly and fail to remember the episode later. They also fail to show emotions during these periods, so consciousness may be intimately linked with emotions. (p. 356)

2. People with frontal cortex or amygdala damage have much weakened emotions and cannot imagine how they will feel as a result of various outcomes. Therefore, they do not get nervous when they are about to do something that will probably lead to a bad outcome. (p. 358)

3. First, feedback from the periphery is not necessary for emotion because (a) the brain reacts differently to pleasant and unpleasant stimuli within less than a quarter second, and (b) people who have no autonomic or muscular responses nevertheless report some (weakened) emotions. Second, feedback from the periphery is sufficient to identify amusement or extreme fear, but the physiological differences among emotions are too small to be useful for identifying mild emotions. (p. 361)

MODULE 12.2

Stress and Health

In the early days of scientific medicine, physicians made little allowance for the relation of personality or emotions to health and disease. If someone became ill, the cause had to be structural, like a virus or bacterium. Today, **behavioral medicine** emphasizes the effects on health of diet, smoking, exercise, stressful experiences, and other behaviors. We now accept the idea that emotions and other experiences influence people's illnesses and patterns of recovery. This view does not imply any mystical concept of "mind over matter"; stress and emotions are brain activities, after all.

STRESS AND THE AUTONOMIC NERVOUS SYSTEM

The term *stress,* like the term *emotion,* is difficult to define and quantify. Many people use some variant of Hans Selye's (1979) definition that stress is the nonspecific response of the body to any demand made upon it. Selye included favorable events such as getting married or taking a new job as stressors, and indeed, they can be stressful, but the stressors with the greatest effects on health are the unpleasant ones. Stress activates the autonomic nervous system rapidly and the hypothalamus-pituitary-adrenal cortex axis more slowly; both systems have major effects on health and well-being. We begin with the autonomic system. We have already considered the autonomic nervous system on pages 83–85, which you might want to review. Figure 12.5 provides a reminder of the anatomy.

For access to many Web sites dealing with stress, see this site:

www.stressless.com/AboutSL/StressLinks.cfm

Psychosomatic Illnesses

If the onset of an illness is influenced by someone's personality, emotions, or experiences, we call the illness *psychosomatic.* By that definition, most illnesses are probably psychosomatic—and note that a psychosomatic illness is a real illness, not something imaginary. Many of the clearest examples of psychosomatic influences on illness include some aspect of autonomic nervous system activity.

Ulcers

Beginning in the 1950s, psychologists found evidence that stressful experiences can lead to ulcers. For example, rats were arranged in "yoked" pairs, in which one rat could run in a wheel to avoid shocks, but if it failed to run when it heard the warning signal, both it and its partner received a shock to the tail. The rats without control of the shocks developed more stomach and intestinal ulcerations than the rats with control (Weiss, 1971). (An *ulceration* is a small area of damage.) Note that the ability to control or predict the shocks was critical, as both rats received shocks at the same times and same intensity. Rats with damage to the prefrontal cortex don't show much emotional reactivity to events, as measured by hormone secretions and autonomic responses, and they don't get ulcerations, even when exposed to the situations that cause ulcers in other rats (Sullivan & Gratton, 1999).

In experiments with monkeys, a monkey that could press a lever to avoid shocks ordinarily developed *more* ulcerations than its yoked partner that received shocks at the same times but could not do anything to avoid them (Brady, Porter, Conrad, & Mason, 1958). The key difference from the rat studies was probably the fact that monkeys become extremely good at pressing the lever to avoid shock—so good, in fact, that they almost never get shocks after the first hour of testing. Rats are less efficient at avoiding shock. If a monkey receives uncontrollable shocks, it develops ulcerations just like the rats (Foltz & Millett, 1964).

You might assume the ulcerations develop during the shock-avoidance sessions. In fact, they develop *during the rest periods* between shock sessions (Desiderato, MacKinnon, & Hissom, 1974). During the shock-avoidance sessions, the sympathetic nervous system increases heart rate and decreases stomach secretions and contractions. During the rest period, the parasympathetic nervous system input to the stomach, previously suppressed, undergoes a rebound increase in activation, leading to greater than normal stomach secretions and contractions. If

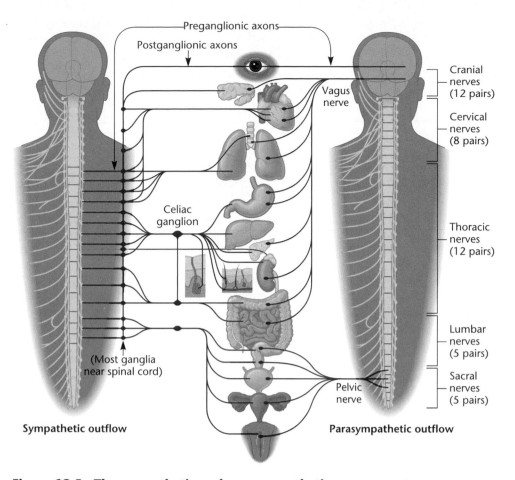

Pregelionic axons
Postgelionic axons

Vagus nerve

Cranial nerves (12 pairs)

Cervical nerves (8 pairs)

Celiac ganglion

Thoracic nerves (12 pairs)

(Most ganglia near spinal cord)

Lumbar nerves (5 pairs)

Sacral nerves (5 pairs)

Pelvic nerve

Sympathetic outflow   **Parasympathetic outflow**

Figure 12.5   The sympathetic and parasympathetic nervous systems
Review pages 83–85 while studying this figure.

there is no food to digest at the moment, what would happen? The stomach secretions attack the lining of the stomach itself.

Until the 1980s, the stress explanation of ulcers seemed pretty well established. True, most animal studies had demonstrated only small ulcerations, not fully developed major ulcers, but most experimenters kept the stress experiences moderate and brief; presumably, more intense stress could produce bigger ulcers. However, the trend shifted in the 1980s with the discovery that as many as 95% of people with ulcers have the bacterium *Helicobacter pylori* in their digestive system and that removing this bacterium cures the ulcers in about 80% of cases. Suddenly, stress seemed irrelevant; the explanation focused on the bacterium.

However, about 70% of people without ulcers also have that bacterium! In fact, of all people with the bacterium, only about 7% develop ulcers (Overmier & Murison, 2000). Granted, eliminating the bacterium usually relieves the ulcers, but the bacterium cannot be the sole cause of ulcers. It may be necessary (or almost necessary), but it is certainly not sufficient. The current thinking is that ulcers arise from the combined

influence of *Helicobacer pylori,* recent stress and past history of stress, and the use of drugs that irritate the digestive system walls, such as ibuprofen (Murison, 2001; Stam, Croiset, Akkermans, & Wiegant, 1999).

Heart Disease

A number of studies have reported that heart disease is more common among people who are frequently hostile than among people who are relaxed and easy-going (Booth-Kewley & Friedman, 1987). In one study, researchers interviewed people, videotaped their facial expressions, and recorded their *transient myocardial ischemias*—brief periods of inadequate blood flow to the muscles of the heart, leading to abnormal heartbeats. Transient myocardial ischemias are usually painless, but they are often precursors to later, more serious heart attacks. The researchers found that people who had a transient myocardial ischemia during the interview produced about twice as many facial expressions of anger as did people without these attacks (Rosenberg et al., 2001). However, all the studies linking heart disease to hostility are correlational, and we cannot draw cause-and-effect conclusions. That is, we do not know whether hostility leads to heart problems, incipient heart problems lead to hostility, or other unidentified factors lead to both.

People who have strong social support—that is, friends and family to help them through trying experiences—tend to keep their heart rate and blood pressure low and therefore maintain better health than people without such support (Uchino, Cacioppo, & Kiecolt-Glaser, 1996). Presumably, the social support acts by moderating influences that would otherwise produce excessive sympathetic nervous system arousal. In particular, people with a successful marriage tend to be healthier than single people or those with troubled marriages. This trend is stronger for men, but it holds for women also (Kiecolt-Glaser & Newton, 2001). The likely reason for the difference is that many women have social support from other friends, whereas many men have fewer close ties.

Voodoo Death and Related Phenomena

Almost everyone knows of someone with a strong will to live who survived well beyond others' expectations and of others who apparently "gave up" and died sooner than expected. An extreme case of the latter is *voodoo death,* in which a healthy person dies apparently just because he or she believes that a curse has destined death.

These phenomena were generally ignored by scientists until Walter Cannon (1942) published a collection of reasonably well-documented reports of voodoo death. In a typical example, a woman who ate a fruit and then learned that it had come from a taboo place died within hours. The common pattern in such cases was that the victims believed that they were sure to die. Friends and relatives, who also believed in the hex, began to treat the victim as a dying person. Overwhelmed with dread and hopelessness, the victim refused food and water and died, usually within 24 to 48 hours. Even in Western societies, people have been known to die of minor injuries because they expected to.

What is the cause of death in such cases? Curt Richter accidentally stumbled on a possible answer while studying the swimming abilities of rats. Why he cared about rat swimming, I don't know, but sometimes researchers experience *serendipity,* the process of stumbling upon something interesting while looking for something less interesting. Ordinarily, rats can swim in turbulent warm water nonstop for 48 hours or more. However, a rat's whiskers are critical to its ability to find its way around, and Richter (1957) found that a rat died quickly if he cut off its whiskers just before placing it into the tank. It swam frantically for a minute or so and then suddenly sank to the bottom, dead. Richter found that under these conditions many, but not all, laboratory rats died quickly. Wild rats, which are more excitable, all died quickly under the same conditions. Autopsies showed that they had not drowned; their hearts had simply stopped beating.

Richter's explanation was that dewhiskering the rat and then suddenly dropping it into water greatly stimulated the rat's sympathetic nervous system and thus its heart rate. After the rat swam frantically for a minute or so and found no escape, its parasympathetic system became highly activated in rebound from the strong sympathetic activation. Massive parasympathetic response may have stopped the rat's heart altogether.

To confirm this explanation, Richter placed a rat in the water several times, rescuing it each time. Then he cut off the rat's whiskers and put it in the water again. The rescues apparently immunized the rat against extreme terror in this situation; it swam successfully for

many hours. Richter's results suggest that certain cases of sudden death in a frightening situation may be due to excessive parasympathetic activity.

However, excessive parasympathetic activity probably accounts for only a small percentage of heart attacks. Most heart attacks begin when excessive sympathetic nervous system activity disrupts the normal rhythmic beating of the heart (Kamarck & Jennings, 1991).

1. Is the immediate cause of ulcer formation more likely to be increased sympathetic or parasympathetic input to the stomach?
2. Did Richter attribute sudden death (voodoo death) to increased sympathetic or parasympathetic input to the heart?

Check your answers on page 371.

STRESS AND THE HYPOTHALAMUS-PITUITARY-ADRENAL CORTEX AXIS

Stress activates two body systems. One is the autonomic nervous system, which reacts quickly. The other is the HPA axis—the hypothalamus, pituitary gland, and adrenal cortex. Activation of the hypothalamus induces the anterior pituitary gland to secrete the hormone adrenocorticotropic hormone (ACTH), which in turn stimulates the human adrenal cortex to secrete cortisol, which elevates blood sugar and enhances metabolism (Figure 12.6). (In rats, it releases corticosterone instead.) Compared to the autonomic nervous system, the HPA axis reacts more slowly, but it becomes increasingly important with prolonged stressors. For example, the government builds a toxic waste dump in your neighborhood; a loved one develops a chronic illness and requires almost constant care; your business is on the verge of failure, and you face a constant worry of paying the bills.

Many researchers refer to cortisol as a "stress hormone" and even use measurements of cortisol level as an indication of someone's recent stress level. Cortisol helps the body mobilize its energies to fight a difficult situation and in the short run is beneficial to health. However, prolonged elevations of cortisol can become harmful. To see why, we start with an overview of the immune system.

[handwritten note: ACTH stimulates the adrenal cortex makes cortisol, elevates blood sugar]

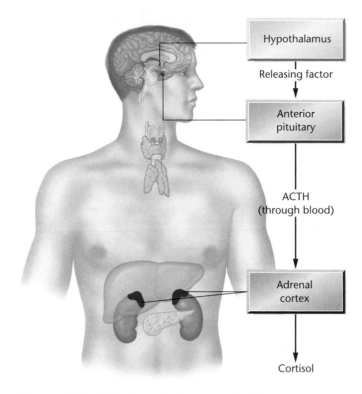

Figure 12.6 The hypothalamus-anterior pituitary-adrenal cortex axis
Prolonged stress leads to the secretion of the adrenal hormone cortisol, which elevates blood sugar and increases metabolism. These changes help the body sustain prolonged activity at the expense of decreased immune system activity.

The Immune System
Protect Body From Viruses & bactria

The **immune system** consists of cells that protect the body against such intruders as viruses and bacteria. The immune system is like a police force: If it is too weak, the "criminals" (viruses and bacteria) run wild and create damage; if it becomes too strong or too unselective, it attacks "law-abiding citizens" (the body's own cells). When the immune system attacks normal cells, we call the result an *autoimmune disease*. Myasthenia gravis, mentioned in Chapter 8, is one example of an autoimmune disease; rheumatoid arthritis is another.

Leukocytes
Cells that protect Body

The most important elements of the immune system are the **leukocytes,** commonly known as white blood cells (Kiecolt-Glaser & Glaser, 1993; O'Leary, 1990). After leukocytes are produced in the bone marrow, they migrate to the thymus gland, the spleen, and the lymph nodes, which store them until needed. The leukocytes patrol the blood and other body fluids, checking each cell. Every body cell has proteins on its surface, and your own body's surface proteins are as unique as your fingerprints. The leukocytes recognize the "self"

proteins and spare those cells. But viruses, bacteria, and organ transplants have different surface proteins, which we call **antigens** (antibody-generator molecules). When a leukocyte finds a cell with antigens, it attacks.

The immune system's specific defense against an intruder begins with two kinds of cells: macrophages and B cells. A **macrophage** surrounds a bacterium or other intruder, exposing its antigens on the macrophage's own surface. A **B cell** (a leukocyte that matures in the bone marrow) also attaches to an intruder and produces specific antibodies to attack the intruder's antigen. **Antibodies** are Y-shaped proteins that circulate in the blood, each kind specifically attaching to one kind of antigen, just as a key fits only one lock. The body develops antibodies against the particular antigens it has encountered. If you ever had measles, for example, your immune system has developed antibodies against the measles virus and protects you against a further outbreak of the same disease. The strategy behind a vaccination is that introducing a weakened form of the virus causes the immune system to develop antibodies against the virus without actually getting the disease. *Two Kinds*

Another kind of leukocytes are T cells (so named because they mature in the thymus), which have two types. The cytotoxic T cells directly attack intruder cells; the helper T cells stimulate other T cells or B cells to multiply more rapidly. Some of the B cells become plasma cells that specialize in producing antibodies against the particular antigen that the original B cell encountered. Others differentiate into *memory cells,* which circulate in search of additional intruders like the first one. Figure 12.7 summarizes this process. *make / attack*

Natural Killer Cells

Blood cells that attach to certain kinds of tumor cells and cells infected with viruses are known as **natural killer cells.** Natural killer cells are relatively nonspecific in their targets. Unlike an antibody or a T cell, each of which attacks only one kind of intruder, a natural killer cell can attack several kinds.

Cytokines
Chemical release to fight diease and Right

When you feel sick, what are your usual symptoms? You will likely think of fever, sleepiness, lack of energy, and lack of appetite. You might not mention decreased sex drive, but that is a common symptom, too. All of these symptoms are brought about by **cytokines** (e.g., interleukin-1, or IL-1), chemicals released by T cells to combat infections and also to communicate with the brain to elicit appropriate behaviors (Maier & Watkins, 1998). In a sense, cytokines are the immune system's way of telling the brain that the body is ill. Ordinarily, only tiny amounts of cytokines cross the blood-brain barrier (although sometimes the blood-brain barrier is

Behavior.

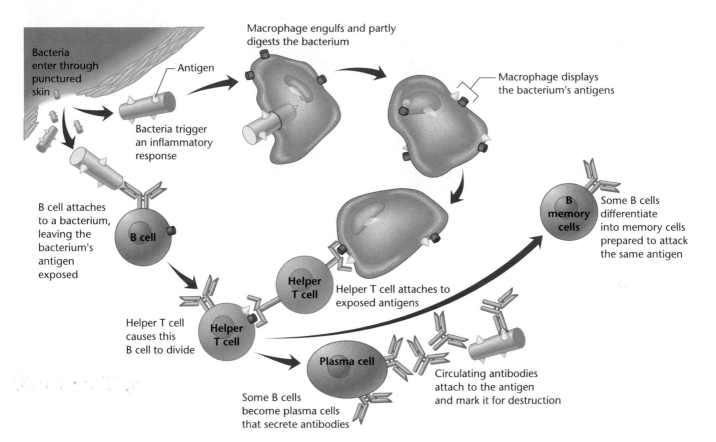

Figure 12.7 Immune system responses to a bacterial infection
A macrophage cell engulfs a bacterial cell and displays one of the bacteria's antigens on its surface. Meanwhile, a B cell also binds to the bacteria and produces antibodies against the bacteria. A helper T cell attaches to both the macrophage and the B cell; it stimulates the B cell to generate copies of itself, called B memory cells, which immunize the body against future invasions by the same kind of bacteria.

weakened during illness). Rather, the cytokines in the periphery stimulate receptors on the vagus nerve (see Figure 4.13, p. 87), which relays a message to cells in the hypothalamus and hippocampus, which then release cytokines themselves. (You might think of it as something like sending a fax, where the original material doesn't travel, but the recipient makes a copy of it.)

The cytokines that are released in the brain instigate a variety of behaviors to attack the infection. Fever, as discussed in Chapter 10, is part of the body's defense against infection because most viruses do not thrive at high temperatures. Sleepiness, decreased muscle activity, and decreased sex drive are useful ways of conserving energy while the body is ill. Cytokines also decrease appetite. The usefulness of decreased appetite is less obvious; we might guess that the body needs extra food when ill. One explanation is that blood iron levels decline during fasting, and many viruses need iron. Another is that finding food is hard work for most animals; it might be better when sick to live off one's stored reserves for a while.

[handwritten] How the immune / central nev system influence each other

Effects of Stress on the Immune System

Contrary to assumptions biologists used to hold, we now know that the nervous system has much control over the immune system. The study of this relationship, called **psychoneuroimmunology,** deals with the ways in which experiences, especially stressful ones, alter the immune system, and how the immune system in turn influences the central nervous system (Ader, 2001).

The body reacts to different stressors in different ways. For example, it treats powerful, inescapable, but temporary stressors like illnesses. Rats subjected to inescapable shocks develop a fever, increase their sleep, and decrease their appetite and sex drive. People under much stress, such as those who are nervous about giving a public speech, show some of the same signs (Maier & Watkins, 1998).

Stress also activates the sympathetic nervous system and HPA axis. Brief activation of either system actually strengthens the immune response and thereby helps to attack viruses and even tumors (Benschop et al., 1995). Even the "negative" emotions of fear and anger boost the activity of the immune system briefly (Mayne, 1999). Brief stress also improves the brain processes believed to underly memory (D. M. Diamond, Bennett, Fleshner, & Rose, 1992).

What is harmful is *long-term* anxiety, anger, or stress. A prolonged increase of cortisol directs energy toward increasing blood sugar and metabolism but therefore away from synthesis of proteins, including the proteins of the immune system. For example, in 1979 at the Three Mile Island nuclear power plant, a major accident was barely contained. The people who continued to live in the vicinity during the next year had lower than normal levels of B cells, T cells, and natural killer cells. They also complained of emotional distress and showed impaired performance on a proofreading task (A. Baum, Gatchel, & Schaeffer, 1983; McKinnon, Weisse, Reynolds, Bowles, & Baum, 1989). A study of research scientists in the antarctic found that a 9-month period of cold, darkness, and social isolation reduced T cell functioning to about half of normal levels (Tingate, Lugg, Muller, Stowe, & Pierson, 1997).

In one study, 276 volunteers filled out an extensive questionnaire about stressful life events before being injected with a moderate dose of common cold virus. (The idea was that those with the strongest immune responses could fight off the cold, but others would succumb.) People who reported stressful experiences lasting less than a month were not significantly more at risk for catching cold than were people who reported no stress. However, for people who reported stress lasting longer than a month, the longer it lasted, the greater the risk of illness (S. Cohen et al., 1998). Other studies have shown that stress is particularly destructive in people who simply resign themselves to it; the immune system is stronger, and therefore health is better, when people attack their problem and gain some sense of control (Olff, 1999).

Prolonged stress can be harmful in another way. High cortisol levels impair memory temporarily (deQuervain, Roozendaal, Nitsch, McGaugh, & Hock, 2000), and prolonged high cortisol levels increase the vulnerability of neurons in the hippocampus so that toxins or overstimulation can kill them (Sapolsky, 1992). High cortisol levels may be responsible for the deterioration of the hippocampus, and therefore the decline of memory, that occurs in many aged people (Cameron & McKay, 1999). Furthermore, hippocampal damage leads to increased cortisol levels, so a vicious cycle can develop:

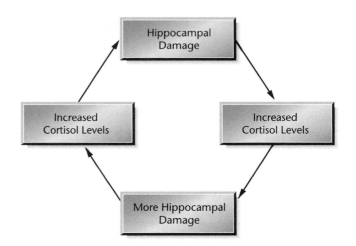

Aged people with the highest cortisol levels tend to be those with the smallest hippocampi and the greatest memory problems (Lupien et al., 1998). Although the data do not tell us whether the problem started with cortisol or with hippocampal damage, the suggestion is that prolonged stress may have led to brain damage.

Stop & Check

> **3.** What is the difference between an antigen and an antibody?
>
> **4.** How do cytokines from the periphery influence brain activity?
>
> **5.** What behavioral changes do cytokines stimulate?
>
> **6.** True or false: Fear and anger are consistently harmful to health.
>
> *Check your answers on page 371.*

POSTTRAUMATIC STRESS DISORDER

People have long recognized that many soldiers returning from battle are prone to continuing anxieties and fears. The condition has been known by such names as *battle fatigue* and *shell shock;* more recently, it has been given the label **posttraumatic stress disorder (PTSD)**, which has become a somewhat common psychiatric diagnosis. PTSD occurs in some people who have been severely injured or threatened or seen other people

Some thing bad happens and nightmares, depressed. etc.

harmed or killed. The symptoms, lasting at least a month after the event, include frequent distressing recollections (flashbacks) and nightmares about the traumatic event, avoidance of reminders of it, and exaggerated arousal in response to noises and other stimuli (Yehuda, 2002). It is common among soldiers, rape victims, kidnap victims, torture victims, survivors of severe automobile accidents, and those who have experienced the sudden death of a loved one.

However, not all people who endure severe traumas develop PTSD. For example, investigators in one study examined 218 people admitted to a hospital emergency ward after severe automobile accidents. All showed about similar stress responses at the time and 1 week later, but the responses declined over time in some and increased in others so that about one sixth of them met the criteria for PTSD 4 months after the accident (Shalev et al., 2000). The ones developing PTSD had not been in consistently worse wrecks than the others; evidently, they were more vulnerable to PTSD.

But why? Studies have found that most PTSD victims have a smaller than average hippocampus (Stein, Hanna, Koverola, Torchia, & McClarty, 1997). This result could represent a biological difference that predisposed these people to PTSD, or it could have developed after PTSD. (The only way to decide would be to test people before and after a severe trauma.) It might seem natural to assume that the relatively small hippocampus in PTSD victims represents damage from prolonged elevations in cortisol secretion. However, PTSD victims show *lower* than normal cortisol levels both immediately after the traumatic event and weeks later (Delahanty, Raimonde, & Spoonster, 2000; Yehuda, 1997). The low levels suggest another hypothesis: Perhaps people with low cortisol levels are ill-equipped to combat stress and therefore more vulnerable to the damaging effects of stress and more prone than other people to PTSD. Certainly, much more research is needed, but the conclusion at present is that PTSD is not just a prolongation of the normal stress response.

7. Name one way in which PTSD differs from a normal stress reaction.

Check your answer on page 371.

MODULE 12.2

In Closing: Emotions and Body Reactions

Research on stress and health is often difficult to interpret. For example, it is sometimes difficult to determine which chemical changes in the brain are symptoms of stress and which are mechanisms of coping with stress (Stanford, 1995). Also, most research on stress and health does not distinguish between direct and indirect effects (S. Cohen & Williamson, 1991). For example, when we find that people with social support recover better from an illness than people without social support, is the difference due to effects of the autonomic and immune systems? Or is it that people with social support are likely to take their prescribed medicines and exercise and eat properly? Determining the relationship between experience and illness is a major long-term research challenge.

SUMMARY

1. Stressful experiences activate the autonomic nervous system, with different responses for different stressors. The results can combine with other influences to affect health. For example, periods of inescapable, unpredictable shocks (rats) or intense work (monkeys) activate the sympathetic nerves that increase heart rate and decrease stomach secretions and contractions. During the rest periods immediately after these sessions, the parasympathetic nerves increase stomach secretions and contractions, increasing the risk of ulcers. (p. 364)

2. Heart disease is more common among people who are frequently hostile and less common in those with much social support. The mechanisms of these effects are not yet established. (p. 365)

3. Rat studies suggest that some cases of voodoo death or other sudden death could be due to strong parasympathetic inhibition of heart rate following a period of intense activation of heart rate by the sympathetic nervous system. (p. 366)

4. The immune system includes several kinds of leukocytes (white blood cells) that attack viruses, bacteria, and other alien cells. (p. 367)

5. In response to infection, the immune system also releases cytokines that stimulate the vagus nerve, which in turn causes cells in the hypothalamus and hippocampus to release their own cytokines. Within the brain, cytokines increase fever and sleepiness and decrease appetite and sex drive. All these responses help fight disease. (p. 367)

6. Stressors activate the HPA axis—hypothalamus, pituitary gland, and adrenal cortex. The adrenal cortex secretes the hormone cortisol, which elevates blood sugar and metabolism. If prolonged, the increased cortisol directs energy away from synthesis of proteins, including those necessary for the immune system. Therefore, prolonged stress increases one's vulnerability to viruses and bacteria. (pp. 366, 368)

7. The high cortisol levels associated with prolonged stress can also damage cells in the hippocampus, thereby impairing memory. (p. 369)

8. Posttraumatic stress disorder (PTSD) shows some special features that differentiate it from other stress. In particular, people with PTSD have, surprisingly, *lower* than normal cortisol levels. (p. 369)

ANSWERS TO *STOP AND CHECK* QUESTIONS

1. Parasympathetic activity contributes to ulcer formation. During a period of high stress, the sympathetic nerves decrease stomach secretions and contractions. Ulcers form during the rest periods, when parasympathetic nerves increase the secretions and contractions. (p. 366)

2. Richter attributed sudden death (similar to voodoo death) to extreme parasympathetic inhibition of heart rate. (p. 366)

3. An antigen is a protein or other large molecule that identifies a cell as being part of the "self" or an "intruder." An antibody is a chemical that the immune system secretes to attack an antigen. (p. 369)

4. Cytokines stimulate receptors on the vagus nerve, which convey a message to cells in the hypothalamus and hippocampus, which then release cytokines themselves. (p. 369)

5. Cytokines influence neurons, especially in the hypothalamus, to increase fever and sleepiness and to decrease appetite and sex drive. (p. 369)

6. False. Fear, anger, or any other stressor impairs health if continued for a long time, but brief experiences arouse the sympathetic nervous system and enhance the activity of the immune system. (p. 369)

7. Ordinarily, stress elevates cortisol levels. People with PTSD have lower than normal cortisol levels. (p. 370)

THOUGHT QUESTIONS

1. If you believe you are at risk for ulcers and you have just had an extremely stressful experience, what might you do to decrease the risk of ulcers?

2. If someone were unable to produce cytokines, what would be the consequences?

Attack and Escape Behaviors

Have you ever watched a cat play with a rat or mouse before killing it? Not all cats do, and some do only occasionally, but when one does, it kicks the rodent, bats it, tosses it in the air, and sometimes picks it up, shakes it, and carries it. Why? Is the cat sadistically tormenting its prey? No. Most of what we call its "play" behaviors are a compromise between attack and escape: When the rodent is facing away, the cat approaches; if the rodent turns around to face the cat, and especially if it bares its teeth, the cat bats it or kicks it defensively (Pellis et al., 1988). A cat usually goes for a quick kill if the rodent is small and inactive or if the cat has been given tranquilizers to lower its anxiety. The same cat withdraws altogether if confronted with a large, menacing rodent. "Play" occurs in intermediate situations (Adamec, Stark-Adamec, & Livingston, 1980; Biben, 1979; Pellis et al., 1988).

Most of the vigorous emotional behaviors we observe in animals fall into the categories of attack and escape, and it is no coincidence that we describe the sympathetic nervous system as the fight-or-flight system. These behaviors and their corresponding emotions—anger and fear—attract much interest from both neuroscience researchers and clinical psychologists.

ATTACK BEHAVIORS

Attack behavior may be wildly passionate or calm and detached. For example, a soldier in battle may feel no anger toward the enemy, and people sometimes make "cold-blooded" attacks for financial gain. We can hardly expect to find a single explanation for all aggressive behaviors.

What actually triggers a vigorous attack is usually some sort of pain or threat, but some individuals attack much more readily than others in response to a given situation, and an individual is more ready to attack at some times than at others. Hamsters provide a clear demonstration. If a hamster intrudes into another hamster's territory, the home hamster sniffs the intruder and eventually attacks, but usually not at once. Suppose the intruder leaves, and a little later, another hamster intrudes. The home hamster attacks faster and

more vigorously than before. The probability of attack remains elevated for 30 minutes or more after the first attack (Potegal, 1994). In other words, shortly after an attack, the hamster is primed for further attacks. You might say it's in a mood for a fight. During that period, activity increases in the corticomedial area of the amygdala, a structure in the temporal lobe (Potegal, Ferris, Hebert, Meyerhoff, & Skaredoff, 1996) (Figure 12.8). In fact, it is possible to bypass the experience and prime an attack by directly stimulating the corticomedial amygdala (Potegal, Hebert, DeCoster, & Meyerhoff, 1996).

We do not have equally good data on the role of the human amygdala in attack priming, but the behaviors are similar: After experiencing an insult or other provocation, people are more aggressive than usual for the next few minutes, and not just against the person who first provoked them (Potegal, 1994). After some stranger has irritated you, you might yell at your roommate. You have probably been told, "If you become angry, count to ten before you act." Counting to a few thousand would work better, but the idea is correct.

Heredity and Environment in Violence

Most people can become violent under some conditions, but some individuals become violent much more easily than others. Research with mice has identified specific genes that may be associated with likelihood of attack (Brodkin, Goforth, Keene, Fossella, & Silver, 2002), but similar research has not yet been done with humans. Studies of human aggressive and criminal behaviors show that monozygotic twins resemble each other more closely than dizygotic twins and that adopted children resemble their biological parents more closely than their adoptive parents (Mason & Frick, 1994). To explore this relationship further, researchers in one study distinguished between juvenile crimes and adult crimes. They found that dizygotic twins resembled each other in juvenile crimes just as much as monozygotic twins did, indicating that juvenile crime had little to do with genetics and presumably much to do with family or neighborhood environment. However, monozygotic twins resembled each other much more

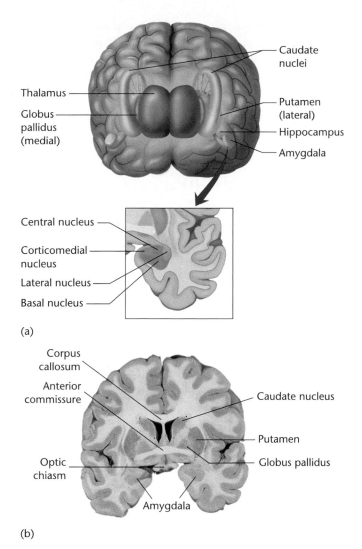

(a)

(b)

Figure 12.8 Location of amygdala in the human brain
The amygdala, located in the interior of the temporal lobe, receives input from many cortical and subcortical areas. Part **(a)** shows a blowup of separate nuclei of the amygdala. *Source: (a) After Nieuwenhuys, Voogd, & vanHuijzen, 1988; Hanaway, Woolsey, Gado, & Roberts, 1998. (b) Photo courtesy of Dana Copeland*

than dizygotic twins did in *adult* crimes, suggesting a probable genetic influence (Lyons et al., 1995). How might a genetic influence become more important in adulthood than in childhood? The researchers suggested that adults have more control over their own environment. Those who are genetically (or otherwise) disposed to criminal behavior choose friends and activities that heighten that tendency and therefore magnify the influence of the genetic predisposition.

Prenatal environment is important also, and as mentioned in Chapter 1, most research studies do not distinguish between the effects of genetics and prenatal environment. One prenatal factor of particular interest is the mother's smoking habits during pregnancy. Two studies found that the more a woman smoked cigarettes during pregnancy, the more likely her son was to be arrested for criminal activities in adolescence and early adulthood (Brennan, Grekin, & Mednick, 1999; Fergusson, Woodward, & Horwood, 1998). The effect was particularly strong if the woman smoked *and* had complications during delivery (Figure 12.9). Of course, these results are correlational, and we do not know whether the women who smoked differed from other women in other ways that might also be important.

In what ways could we imagine genes acting to increase the probability of violent crime? One simple possibility is to influence body size and therefore the probability of winning a fight. One study found that boys taller than usual at age 3 years tended to be relatively fearless and aggressive at that age. They were still relatively aggressive at age 11, even if they were no longer especially tall for their age (Raine, Reynolds, Venables, Mednick, & Farrington, 1998). Perhaps fearlessness and aggressiveness had become habitual.

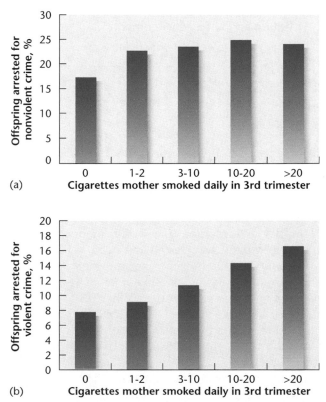

Figure 12.9 Effects of maternal smoking on later criminal behavior by sons
Cigarettes smoked by the mothers during pregnancy correlated with the sons' violent crimes **(b)** much more than the sons' nonviolent crimes **(a)**. *Source: From "Maternal Smoking During Pregnancy and Adult Male Criminal Outcomes," by P. A. Brennan, E. R. Grekin, and S. A. Mednick, Archives of General Psychiatry, 56, p. 215–219. Copyright 1999, American Medical Association. Reprinted by permission.*

Environmental factors combine with genetic factors, of course. One study of adopted children found the highest probability of aggressive behaviors and conduct disorders among those who had biological parents with criminal records *and* adoptive parents with marital discord, depression, substance abuse, or legal problems. A biological predisposition alone or a troubled adoptive family by itself produced only moderate effects (Cadoret, Yates, Troughton, Woodworth, & Stewart, 1995).

1. With regard to criminal behavior, adopted children resemble their biological relatives more closely than their adoptive relatives. One explanation for this observation is a genetic influence. What is the other?

2. What evidence suggests that criminal behavior depends on a combination of biological predisposition and family environment?

Check your answers on page 384.

Hormones

Most fighting throughout the animal kingdom is by males competing for mates or females defending their young. Male aggressive behavior depends heavily on testosterone, which is highest for adult males in the reproductive season.

Similarly, throughout the world, men fight more often than women, get arrested for violent crimes more often, shout insults at each other more often, and so forth. Moreover, the highest incidence of violence, as measured by crime statistics, is in men 15 to 25 years old, who have the highest testosterone levels. The studies that report high rates of violence by women tend to be those that include relatively minor acts (Archer, 2000).

Do the men with the highest testosterone levels also have the highest rates of violent behavior? Yes, although the differences are small (Bernhardt, 1997; Brooks & Reddon, 1996). Figure 12.10 shows the results of one typical study. Note that high testosterone levels were more common among men imprisoned for rape or murder than among those imprisoned for nonviolent crimes. Note also, however, that the differences are not huge. They are also hard to interpret because environmental stressors could affect hormone levels and violent behavior independently.

Testosterone does not compel someone to be violent. Rather, it may alter the way one reacts to various stimuli. In one study, young women who received injections of testosterone showed a greater than usual increase in heart rate when they looked at photographs of angry faces (van Honk et al., 2001). Testosterone may induce people to attend longer and respond more vigorously to situations that include aggression and conflict.

Brain Abnormalities and Violence

Testosterone exerts its effects on aggression by facilitating activity in several brain areas (Delville, Mansour, & Ferris, 1996). Depending on the exact location of the brain activation, an animal might attack another animal or just make a series of undirected growls and facial movements (A. Siegel & Pott, 1988) (Figure 12.11).

Intermittent explosive disorder, a condition marked by occasional outbursts of violent behavior with little or no provocation, is sometimes linked to temporal lobe epilepsy. An epileptic attack occurs when a population of neurons produces a sustained period of synchronous activity. When the epileptic focus is in the temporal lobe, the symptoms include hallucinations, lip smacking or other repetitive acts, and sometimes emotional behaviors (not necessarily angry ones).

Here is a description of one patient with temporal lobe epilepsy and intermittent explosive disorder (Mark & Ervin, 1970):

> Thomas was a 34-year-old engineer, who, at the age of 20, had suffered a ruptured peptic ulcer. The resulting internal bleeding deprived his brain of blood and produced brain damage. Although his intelligence and creativity were unimpaired, there were some serious changes in his behavior, including outbursts of violent rage, sometimes against strangers and sometimes against people he knew. Sometimes his episodes began when he was talking to his wife. He would then interpret something she said as an insult, throw her against the wall and attack her brutally for 5 to 6 minutes. After one of these attacks, he would go to sleep for a half hour and wake up feeling refreshed.
>
> Eventually, he was taken to a hospital, where epileptic activity was found in the temporal lobes of his cerebral cortex. For the next 7 months, he was given a combination of tranquilizers, antiepileptic drugs, and other medications. None of these treatments reduced his violent behavior. He had previously been treated by psychiatrists for 7 years without apparent effect. Eventually, he agreed to a surgical operation to destroy a small part of the amygdala on both sides of the brain. Afterwards, he had no more episodes of rage, although he continued to have periods of confusion and disordered thinking.

Temporal lobe epilepsy is uncommon, but people who have outbursts of unprovoked violence are even

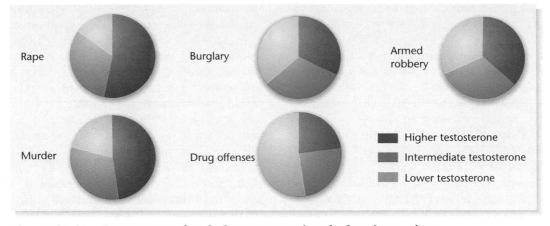

Figure 12.10 Testosterone levels for men convicted of various crimes
Men convicted of rape and murder have higher testosterone levels, on the average, than men convicted of burglary or drug offenses. *Source: Based on Dabbs, Carr, Frady, & Riad, 1995*

rarer. Therefore, although many people with intermittent explosive disorder have temporal lobe epilepsy, most people with temporal lobe epilepsy do not have any violent tendencies. Of those who do, many show abnormalities and loss of cells in the left hemisphere (Tebartz van Elst, Woermann, Lemieux, Thompson, & Trimble, 2000).

Many people with damage in the prefrontal cortex also fight or threaten more frequently than other people or on less provocation (Giancola, 1995). However, people with prefrontal impairments have a

Delgado, 1981

Figure 12.11 Effects of stimulation in the medial hypothalamus
Stimulation of some brain areas can result in a full attack; in this case, the result was undirected growling and facial expressions, a mere fragment of a normal attack.

general loss of inhibitions and a tendency toward many socially inappropriate behaviors, not just violent ones.

Serotonin Synapses and Aggressive Behavior

Several lines of evidence link low serotonin release with increased aggressive behavior.

Nonhuman Animals

Much of the earliest evidence for this conclusion came from studies on mice. Luigi Valzelli (1973) found that 4 weeks of social isolation induced a *decrease in serotonin turnover* in the brains of the male mice. **Turnover is the amount of release and resynthesis of a neurotransmitter by presynaptic neurons.** That is, a brain with low serotonin turnover might have a normal amount of serotonin but releases only relatively small amounts and therefore does not need to resynthesize much of it. Turnover can be inferred from the concentration of **5-hydroxyindoleacetic acid (5-HIAA),** a serotonin metabolite, in the blood, cerebrospinal fluid (CSF), or urine. The greater the amount of serotonin release, the greater the amount of 5-HIAA, and therefore the greater the amount of turnover.

Valzelli further found that when social isolation lowered a male mouse's serotonin turnover, it also induced increased aggressive behavior toward other males. If he placed together two males with low serotonin turnover, they would certainly fight. Comparing different genetic strains of mice, he found that those with the lowest serotonin turnover fought the most (Valzelli & Bernasconi, 1979). Social isolation does not decrease serotonin turnover in female mice in any genetic strain, and it does not make the females aggressive.

Later studies found excessive attack behaviors in mice that are deficient in serotonin receptor type 5-HT$_{1B}$ (Saudou et al., 1994).

In a fascinating natural-environment study, investigators measured 5-HIAA levels in 2-year-old male monkeys and then observed their behavior closely. The monkeys in the lowest quartile for 5-HIAA, and therefore the lowest quartile for serotonin turnover, were the most aggressive, had the greatest probability of attacking larger monkeys, and showed the greatest number of scars and wounds. Most of them died by the age of 6, whereas all monkeys in the highest quartile for serotonin turnover were still alive at 6 (Higley et al., 1996).

If most monkeys with low turnover die young, why hasn't natural selection eliminated the genes for low serotonin turnover? One speculation is that aggressiveness is a high-risk, high-payoff strategy: Sure, if you pick a lot of fights, you'll probably get killed, but if you win enough to survive, you're on your way to being a very dominant male monkey and probably the father of many young.

Another speculation is that the ideal strategy is intermediate aggressiveness. Monkeys with genes for low serotonin turnover fight too much and die young; those with genes at the opposite extreme are too cautious and fearful. Selection favors the heterozygote condition (one gene for high aggression and one for low), and necessarily, some infants will be born with two high-aggression or two low-aggression genes (Trefilov, Berard, Krawczak, & Schmidtke, 2000). More research will be needed to test these hypotheses.

How does low serotonin turnover lead to increased violence? No one knows, but it is not linked specifically to violence. Rather, it is linked to decreased inhibition of impulses (Brunner & Hen, 1997). Mice that lack the 5-HT$_{1B}$ receptor are not only more aggressive than other mice, but they also develop a cocaine addiction faster than normal. In a maze, they move "impulsively" from one arm to another without pausing at the choice points as other mice do. If given a choice between pressing one lever to get a small reward in 4 seconds or a different lever to get a larger reward after 20 seconds, they are more likely than normal mice to choose the quicker but smaller reward. In short, they seem to act without sufficiently pondering the probable outcomes.

Humans

Numerous studies have found low serotonin turnover in people with a history of violent behavior, including people convicted of arson and other violent crimes (Virkkunen, Nuutila, Goodwin, & Linnoila, 1987) and people who commit or attempt suicide by violent means (G. L. Brown et al., 1982; Edman, Åsberg, Levander, & Schalling, 1986; Mann, Arango, & Underwood, 1990; Pandey et al., 1995). Serotonin turnover varies by 5% to 10% from one time of year to another; one study in Belgium found that suicide rates were highest in spring,

when serotonin turnover was lowest, and lowest in fall and winter, when serotonin turnover was highest (Maes et al., 1995).

One study of children and adolescents with a history of aggressive behavior found that those with the lowest serotonin turnover were most likely to get into trouble for additional aggressive behavior during the following 2 years (Kruesi et al., 1992). Follow-up studies on people being released from prison found that those with lower serotonin turnover had a greater probability of further convictions for violent crimes (Virkkunen, DeJong, Bartko, Goodwin, & Linnoila, 1989; Virkkunen, Eggert, Rawlings, & Linnoila, 1996). A follow-up study of people who had survived suicide attempts found that low serotonin turnover levels predicted additional suicide attempts within the next 5 years (Roy, DeJong, & Linnoila, 1989) (Figure 12.12). However, although each of these relationships is statistically reliable, the effects are not strong enough for making decisions about individuals. That is, blood tests would not enable us to pick the potentially dangerous people with enough confidence to do anything about it.

It is possible to alter serotonin synthesis by changes in diet. Neurons synthesize serotonin from tryptophan, an amino acid found in proteins, though seldom in large amounts. Tryptophan crosses the blood-brain barrier by an active transport channel that it shares with phenylalanine and other large amino acids. Thus, a diet high in other amino acids impairs the brain's ability to synthesize serotonin. One study found that many young men on such a diet showed an increase in aggressive behavior a few hours after eating (Moeller et al., 1996). Under the circumstances, it would seem prudent for anyone with aggressive or suicidal tendencies to reduce consumption of aspartame (NutraSweet), which is 50% phenylalanine, and maize (American

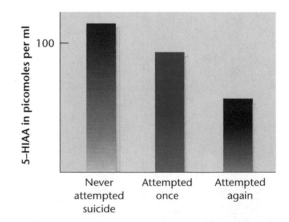

Figure 12.12 Levels of 5-HIAA in the CSF of depressed people
Measurements for the two suicide-attempting groups were taken after the first attempt. Low levels of 5-HIAA indicate low serotonin turnover. *Source: Based on results of Roy, DeJong, & Linnoila, 1989*

corn), which is high in phenylalanine and low in tryptophan (Lytle, Messing, Fisher, & Phebus, 1975).

We shall get to depression in Chapter 15, but if you already know something about depression, you may note a problem: Depression is also linked to low serotonin activity, but most depressed people are not violent. Low serotonin turnover has also been linked to several other psychiatric conditions not related to violence. If some treatment suddenly lowered your serotonin level, would you at once become violent, depressed, or what? When researchers have used drugs or diet to lower serotonin levels suddenly but temporarily, many people with a history of depression became depressed, those with a history of aggressive behavior became aggressive, and those with a history of substance abuse reported a drug craving (Van der Does, 2001). Many normal people became more impulsive (Kaplan, Muldoon, Manuck, & Mann, 1997). Serotonin activity apparently has something to do with suppressing impulses or maintaining a normal mood, but impairing serotonin leads to different problems in different people. Note an interesting psychological implication: People who are frequently violent may not have a much stronger urge to attack than anyone else; they simply have weak mechanisms for inhibiting an impulse to attack (Davidson, Putnam & Larson, 2000).

3. How can one measure the amount of serotonin turnover in the brain?

4. What change in diet can alter the production of serotonin?

Check your answers on page 384.

ESCAPE, FEAR, AND ANXIETY

We distinguish two escape emotions: fear and anxiety. Fear is a temporary experience, like what you feel in a small boat with a storm approaching. If you escape from the danger, the fear is gone. Anxiety is less escapable, such as anxiety about your own mortality.

Fear, Anxiety, and the Amygdala

Do we have any built-in, unlearned fears? Yes, at least one: Even newborns are frightened by loud noises. The response to an unexpected loud noise, known as the **startle reflex,** is extremely fast: Auditory information goes first to the cochlear nucleus in the medulla

and from there directly to an area in the pons that commands the tensing of the muscles, especially the neck muscles. Tensing the neck muscles is important because the neck is so vulnerable to injury. Information reaches the pons within 3 to 8 ms after a loud noise, and the full startle reflex occurs within one fifth of a second (Yeomans & Frankland, 1996).

Although you don't learn your fear of loud noises, your current mood or past experiences can modify your reaction. Your startle reflex is more vigorous if you are already tense. People with posttraumatic stress disorder, who are known for their intense anxiety, show a much stronger than normal startle reflex (Grillon, Morgan, Davis, & Southwick, 1998).

Here's a demonstration you can try on a cooperative roommate or friend. Dim the lights and ask someone to close his or her eyes while you slowly read the following:

Imagine you are walking . . . alone . . . at night . . . through a part of town where you have never been before, and suddenly you realize you have lost your way. You're not sure you want to stop and ask someone for directions, and anyway, you don't see anyone, so you try to find your way by yourself. You walk down a street, hoping to see something familiar, but the street gets darker. Suddenly, the only street light goes out. It's so dark you can hardly see one step in front of yourself. But you can't stay where you are, so you keep walking. Now you hear footsteps. They're growing louder. You realize someone is walking behind you. They're still pretty far away, but the footsteps are growing closer. You decide to step off the sidewalk and hope the other person passes. So you're just standing there. But now you realize you're not alone. Someone else is standing right next to you! . . . [Pause.]

Now slam a shoe or other object onto a table as hard as you can to make a sudden loud noise.

If you build the suspense well, your friend may jump and scream and refuse to participate in any more of your psychology demonstrations. For comparison, make the same loud noise for someone else without reading the story. The point is that a loud noise always produces some startle response, but it produces an even stronger reaction for someone who is tense or frightened.

Studies in Rodents

Psychologists measure the enhancement of a startle reflex as a gauge of fear or anxiety. In research with nonhumans, they typically first measure the normal response to a loud noise. Then they repeatedly pair a stimulus, such as a light, with shock. Finally, they present the light just before the loud noise and determine how much more the animal jumps after the combination of stimuli than after the noise alone. (A control group is tested with a light stimulus that has not been paired with shock.) Results of these studies consis-

We choose our activities partly on the basis of how easily we develop anxiety.

tently show that after animals have learned to associate a stimulus with shock, that stimulus becomes a fear signal; presenting the stimulus just before a loud noise enhances the animal's response to the noise. Conversely, a stimulus previously associated with pleasant stimuli becomes a safety signal that decreases the startle reflex (Schmid, Koch, & Schnitzler, 1995).

By measuring the enhancement of the startle reflex, investigators have determined the role of various brain areas in learned fears. One key area is the amygdala (see Figures 12.8 and 12.13). Many cells in the amygdala, especially in the basolateral and central nuclei, get input from pain fibers as well as vision or hearing, so the circuitry is well suited to establishing conditioned fears (Uwano, Nishijo, Ono, & Tamura, 1995).

Output from the amygdala to the hypothalamus controls autonomic fear responses, such as increased blood pressure. Output from the amygdala to the prefrontal cortex modifies cortical interpretation of potentially frightening stimuli (Garcia, Vouimba, Baudry, & Thompson, 1999). The amygdala also has axons to the *central gray area* in the midbrain, which in turn sends axons to the nucleus in the pons that controls the startle reflex (Fendt, Koch, & Schnitzler, 1996). By this relay, the amygdala can enhance the startle reflex (LeDoux, Iwata, Cicchetti, & Reis, 1988). Figure 12.13 shows the connections.

Although a rat with damage to the amygdala still shows a normal startle reflex, a fear signal before the loud noise does not enhance the reflex. In one typical study, rats were repeatedly exposed to a light followed by shock and then tested for their responses to a loud noise. Intact rats showed a moderate startle reflex to the loud noise and an enhanced response if the light preceded the noise. However, rats with damage at any point along the path from the central amygdala to the hindbrain showed a startle reflex to the loud noise but no enhancement by the light (Hitchcock & Davis, 1991). Other studies have reported similar results (Heldt, Sundin, Willott, & Falls, 2000; Lee, Walker, & Davis, 1996; Phillips & LeDoux, 1992).

Do these results indicate that amygdala damage destroys all fear? Not really; an alternative explanation is that the rats have trouble interpreting or understanding stimuli with emotional consequences. That is, the problem may be that the rats don't know when to be afraid. The same issue arises with humans, as we shall see.

One odd parasite has evolved a way to exploit the consequences of amygdala damage (Berdoy, Webster, & Macdonald, 2000). *Toxoplasma gondii* is a protozoan parasite that affects many mammals but reproduces only in cats. Cats excrete the parasite's eggs in their feces, thereby releasing them into the ground. Rats that burrow in the ground can become infected with the parasite. When the parasite enters a rat, it migrates to the brain where it apparently damages the amygdala. The rat then fearlessly approaches a cat, guaranteeing that the cat will eat the rat and that the parasite will find its way back into a cat!

Studies in Monkeys

The effect of amygdala damage in monkeys was described in classic studies early in the 1900s and known as the *Klüver-Bucy syndrome,* from the names of the primary investigators. Monkeys showing this syndrome are tame and placid. They attempt to pick up lighted matches and other objects that they ordinarily avoid. They display less than the normal fear of snakes or of larger, more dominant monkeys (Kalin, Shelton, Davidson, & Kelley, 2001).

Amygdala damage, with the concomitant decrease of fear, alters monkeys' social behaviors. In one study, male monkeys with amygdala lesions sank to the bottom of the dominance hierarchy because they did not react normally to other monkeys' threat gestures and other social signals (Rosvold, Mirsky, & Pribram, 1954). That is, they approached other monkeys when they should not have.

In another study, monkeys with amygdala lesions became friendlier; that is, they interacted more freely with other monkeys (Emery et al., 2001). (Presumably, in this monkey colony, the other monkeys were less aggressive, so approaches were less risky.) Why might decreased anxiety lead to greater friendliness? Actually, the same has been observed in people who take tranquilizers. We all have a conflict about approaching other people: We desire the interaction but are afraid of rejection. Here the amygdala-damaged monkeys were undeterred by threat expressions because they did not understand them!

Studies in Humans

Several studies have used PET or fMRI scans to measure brain activity while people looked at photos of faces. Photos of people showing emotional expressions evoke much stronger amygdala responses than do neutral faces. If people see the same photo repeatedly, it excites the amygdala strongly the first time but much less on later occasions (Breiter et al., 1996; Büchel et al., 1998). This result corresponds to the experience of a person as a whole: You are likely to react more strongly to an emotional photo the first time you see it than the tenth time. Photos of fearful faces generally evoke more activity than happy faces and in different parts of the amygdala (Hamann, Ely,

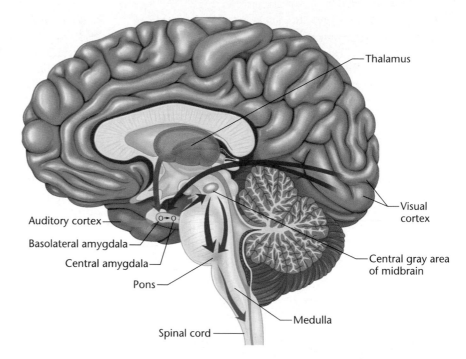

Figure 12.13   Amygdala and connections relevant to learned fears
Cells in the lateral and basolateral parts of the amygdala receive visual and auditory information and then send messages to the central amygdala, which then sends its output to the central gray area of the midbrain, which relays the information to a nucleus in the pons responsible for the startle reflex. Damage at any point along the route from amygdala to pons interferes with learned fears; damage to the pons alone blocks the startle reflex.

Hoffman, & Kilts, 2002; Iidaka et al., 2001; J. S. Morris et al., 1996; Whalen et al., 2001). However, the fact that the amygdala reacts somewhat to happy faces as well indicates that the amygdala is not devoted solely to fear. Furthermore, people with social phobia (a generalized fear of social interactions) show a greater fMRI response to angry and contemptuous faces, but no particularly enhanced response to fearful faces (Stein, Goldin, Sareen, Zorrilla, & Brown, 2002). So, evidently the amygdala responds to strong emotions, regardless of the exact type of emotion.

The amygdala responds to emotional stimuli even if someone cannot identify them consciously. For example, if a face is flashed on a screen very briefly, or if it is flashed in one part of a picture while the person is paying attention to a different part, the person cannot say whether the face was happy or fearful—and perhaps not even whether there was a face. Nevertheless, the amygdala shows its characteristic responses to the emotion and in turn produces changes in sweating and other autonomic responses (Kubota et al., 2000; Vuilleumier, Armony, Driver, & Dolan, 2001). (Recall the earlier discussion about "gut feelings." Sometimes our body reacts emotionally when we do not consciously understand why.)

People with the rare genetic disorder *Urbach-Wiethe disease* suffer skin lesions; many of them also have a gradual atrophy (dying away) of the amygdala as calcium accumulates there. People with this disorder don't show strong dislikes, even in a nonsocial context. If you rated a series of drawings, you probably would rate some as pleasant and others as unpleasant, maybe even ugly. But people with damage to the amygdala rate the drawings as almost equally pleasant (Adolphs & Tranel, 1999). Evidently, they don't interpret new information emotionally in the same way other people do.

Such people also have trouble recognizing other people's facial expressions, especially fear expressions. One woman with this condition had no trouble recognizing familiar faces, but if she looked at photos of people with different emotional expressions, she had much trouble identifying the fearful expressions and a little trouble with the angry and surprised expressions (Adolphs, Tranel, Damasio, & Damasio, 1994). When asked to rate the apparent intensity of the emotional expressions, she rated the intensity in the frightened, angry, or surprised faces much lower than any other observer did. Finally, when she was asked to draw faces showing certain emotions (Figure 12.14), she made good drawings of a happy, sad, surprised, disgusted, and angry face. However, when asked to draw an "afraid" face, she refused at first, saying she did not know what such a face would look like. When the researcher insisted that she try, she drew someone crawling away with hair on end (as cartoonists often indicate fear). Certainly, she seemed much less able to imagine fear than other emotional states (Adolphs, Tranel, Damasio, & Damasio, 1995).

Amygdala damage also interferes with the social judgments that we constantly make about other people. When we look at other people's faces, some of them strike us, rightly or wrongly, as "untrustworthy," and looking at a face we regard as untrustworthy strongly activates the amygdala (Winston, Strange, O'Doherty, & Dolan, 2002). People with damage to the amygdala regard all faces as about equally trustworthy, and they approach people for help indiscriminately, instead of trying to find people who look and act friendly (Adolphs, Tranel, & Damasio, 1998).

People with amygdala damage also fail to shift their attention toward emotional stimuli the way other people do. For example, if a word is briefly flashed on a screen while the viewer's attention is distracted, most people are much more likely to detect an emotionally charged word such as *kill* or *rape* than unemotional words such as *lake* or *pear*. People with amygdala damage are equally unlikely to detect either kind of word (Anderson & Phelps, 2001).

As in the case of rats, it is not clear that amygdala damage has eliminated the capacity to feel fear or any other emotion. In fact, people with amygdala damage report that they continue to feel fear, anger, happiness, and other emotions more or less normally as a result of life events (Anderson & Phelps, 2002). Researchers are now converging to the explanation that amygdala damage impairs people's ability to process information that has emotional meanings (Whalen, 1998). That is, people with amygdala damage don't know when they should become afraid, happy, or whatever, if the signals are subtle or complicated (Baxter & Murray, 2002).

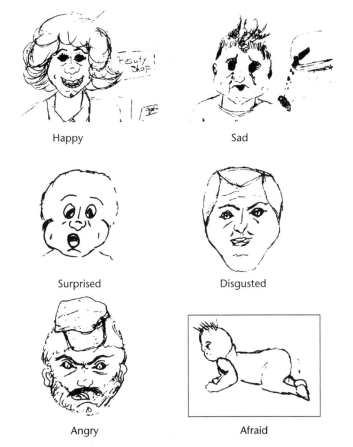

Figure 12.14 Drawings by a woman with a damaged amygdala

Note that the drawings of emotional expressions are fairly realistic and convincing except for the one of fear. The woman at first declined to draw a fearful expression because, she said, she could not imagine it. When urged to try, she remembered that frightened people are often depicted with their hair on end, at least in cartoons.
Source: From "Fear and the Human Amygdala," by R. Adolphs, D. Tranel, H. Damasio, and A. Damasio, Journal of Neuroscience, 15, p. 5879–5891. Copyright ©1995 Oxford University Press. Reprinted by permission.

Stop & Check

5. What brain mechanism enables the startle reflex to be so fast?

6. How could a researcher use the startle reflex to determine whether some stimulus causes a person fear?

7. One hypothesis is that amygdala damage decreases fear. What is another reasonable interpretation of the results?

8. What kind of person has trouble recognizing fear expressions in other people?

Check your answers on page 384.

Genetics of Anxiety Disorders

Many people suffer from excessive anxiety. Individuals with panic disorder and phobia have episodes of extreme fear and sympathetic nervous system arousal. The main difference between the two disorders is that people with phobias are excessively frightened by some object or situation, such as a snake, whereas people with panic disorder have times of excessive fear in unpredictable situations.

Anxiety disorders undoubtedly reflect many determinants, and as with any condition, heredity is one possible cause. Studies of twins and adoptees have pointed to a genetic contribution to excessive fears (Garpenstrand, Annas, Ekblom, Oreland, & Fredrickson, 2001; Gratacòs et al., 2001; Kendler, Myers, Prescott, & Neale, 2001), but many careful studies failed to find any particular gene that was linked to phobia or panic disorder. And then researchers noticed an oddity: Most people with panic disorder and many with other anxiety disorders also have an inherited condition called *joint laxity,* in which the fingers and other joints bend farther and more easily than normal (Martin-Santos et al., 1998). Panic disorder and joint laxity have unrelated symptoms, but apparently, they are controlled by genes on the same part of chromosome 15. Many human genes are repeated; that is, the same genetic segment occurs twice, either on the same or on different chromosomes. For most people, a particular section of chromosome 15 occurs twice, but in people with panic disorder and joint laxity, it occurs three times (Collier, 2002; Gratacòs et al., 2001). Furthermore, this chromosomal segment is apparently unstable: Many people have three copies of it even though their parents didn't, and their children might not, either. So the segment can mutate from two copies to three and possibly mutate back for the next generation. Some people have two copies on some of their chromosomes and three on others in various body parts. Within this chromosomal segment, no one yet knows exactly which gene is related to panic disorder, but the chances are good for researchers to make that determination soon.

We now see why previous researchers failed to find a gene for panic disorder: People with panic disorder do not have any gene that other people lack; they just have more copies of the same gene, and they may not even have those extra copies in every cell. Also, the gene does not always continue from one generation to the next, so studies of twins and adoptees do not indicate high heritability. This episode makes researchers wonder what other conditions might be controlled by similar genetic mechanisms. Perhaps some conditions have greater heritability than current evidence indicates.

Anxiety-Reducing Drugs

A little anxiety can be a useful thing by alerting us to danger. However, some people have exaggerated fears and excessive reactions to frightening events, partly for genetic reasons (Garpenstrand, Annas, Ekblom, Oreland, & Fredrikson, 2001; Gratacòs et al., 2001; Kendler, Myers, Prescott, & Neale, 2001). As you might guess, people with excessive fears have a hyperactive amygdala. One study found that children with panic disorder or generalized anxiety disorder had exaggerated amygdala responses to photos showing fearful faces (K. M. Thomas et al., 2001).

Drugs intended to control anxiety alter activity at amygdala synapses. One of the amygdala's main excitatory neuromodulators is CCK (cholecystokinin), which increases anxiety, and the main inhibitory transmitter is GABA, which inhibits anxiety.

Here is a good experiment showing the role of CCK: Male "intruder" rats were placed in a protected area within a resident male rat's cage, as shown in

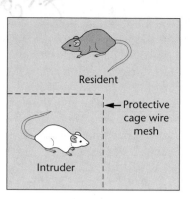

Figure 12.15 Procedure for giving male rats anxiety
New male rats were placed in a cage and kept separate from the resident male by a protective inner cage that was later removed. In some trials, the resident male was removed at the same time, so the intruder was safe. In others, the protection was removed but the resident male was left. The intruders who were attacked (and inevitably defeated) developed great anxiety when replaced in the same location.

Figure 12.15, for 30 minutes at a time, at which point the protective barrier was removed. For some of the intruders, the resident male was removed at the same time as the barrier. For the others, the protection was removed but not the resident. Those intruders were always attacked and defeated. (The "home field advantage" is enormous for rats. A resident male almost always defeats an intruder.) After four repetitions of this experience, the researchers implanted a cannula into the intruder male's brain and used microdialysis (see Methods 10.1, p. 317) to measure brain chemistry. The result was that an intruder male that had been defeated four times by the resident male showed clear signs of anxiety when again placed into that male's cage (motionlessness, defensive postures, and squeals); his prefrontal cortex showed an enormous increase in the release of CCK. However, if he was given a drug that blocked his CCK type B receptors, he showed no anxiety, even when placed in the dangerous cage (Becker et al., 2001). The brain also has CCK type A receptors, less abundant, with different and probably even the opposite effects on behavior (Yamamoto et al., 2000).

Injections of CCK-stimulating drugs into the amygdala enhance the startle reflex (Frankland, Josselyn, Bradwejn, Vaccarino, & Yeomans, 1997), and drugs that block GABA type B receptors can induce an outright panic (Strzelczuk & Romaniuk, 1996). In principle, drugs could reduce anxiety either by blocking CCK or by increasing GABA activity. So far, all marketed tranquilizers (anxiety reducers) have been GABA facilitators, although animal research has shown some potential for CCK blockers (Wiedemann, Jahn, Yassouridis, & Kellner, 2001).

→ Anxiety patient

Benzodiazepines

Decades ago, **barbiturates** were widely used tranquilizers. However, large doses can be fatal, especially if

Slow down
GABA

combined with alcohol. Today, the most commonly used tranquilizers are the **benzodiazepines** (BEN-zo-die-AZ-uh-peens), such as diazepam (trade name Valium), chlordiazepoxide (Librium), and alprazolam (Xanax), all of which can be taken as pills. Like many other drugs, benzodiazepines were found to be effective long before anyone knew how they worked. Then investigators discovered specific benzodiazepine binding sites in the CNS. The receptors are part of the **GABA_A receptor complex**, which includes a site that binds the neurotransmitter GABA as well as sites that bind chemicals that modify the sensitivity of the GABA site (Figure 12.16). (The brain also has other kinds of GABA receptors, such as GABA_B, with different behavioral effects.)

The heart of the GABA_A receptor complex is a chloride channel. When open, it permits chloride ions (Cl^-) to cross the membrane into the neuron, hyperpolarizing the cell. (That is, the synapse is inhibitory.) Surrounding the chloride channel are four units, each containing one or more sites sensitive to GABA. Three of these four units (labeled α in Figure 12.16) also contain a benzodiazepine binding site. When a benzodiazepine molecule attaches, it neither opens nor closes the chloride channel by itself, but it alters the shape of the receptor so that the GABA attaches more easily and binds more tightly (Macdonald, Weddle, & Gross, 1986). Benzodiazepines thus facilitate the effects of GABA. Alcohol also binds to the receptor and facilitates GABA binding.

Benzodiazepines exert their antianxiety effects in the amygdala and the hypothalamus. A minute amount of benzodiazepines injected directly to a rat's amygdala decreases learned shock-avoidance behaviors (Pesold & Treit, 1995), relaxes the muscles, and increases social interactions with unfamiliar partners (Sanders & Shekhar, 1995). However, people don't take benzodiazepines as injections to the amygdala; they take them as pills, so the drug goes to all parts of the brain. When the drug reaches the thalamus and cerebral cortex, it induces sleepiness, blocks epileptic convulsions, and impairs memory (Rudolph et al., 1999). The mixture of effects is a problem. Some people take benzodiazepines to decrease anxiety; others take them as sleeping pills or antiepileptic treatments, but few people need all three effects, and no one wants the memory impairment. Researchers hope to develop drugs that are more specifically targeted to GABA receptors in particular brain

areas, thereby producing more limited behavioral effects (Löw et al., 2000).

Given that benzodiazepines inhibit the amygdala (as well as other areas), might they mimic some of the symptoms related to amygdala damage? Recall that people with amygdala damage have difficulty recognizing facial expressions of fear. People in one study took benzodiazepines or a placebo and then examined photos of facial expressions and rated how much sadness, happiness, anger, disgust, fear, and surprise they showed. Those who had taken the benzodiazepines reported seeing only low levels of fear and anger (Zangara, Blair, & Curran, 2002). That is, people who do not feel much fear or anger—because of either tranquilizers or brain damage—fail to perceive it in others.

Other naturally occurring chemicals bind to the same sites as benzodiazepines. One such chemical is the protein **diazepam-binding inhibitor (DBI),** which blocks the behavioral effects of diazepam and other benzodiazepines (Guidotti et al., 1983). This and several related proteins are also known as **endozepines,** a contraction of "endogenous benzodiazepine," although their effects are actually the opposite of benzodiazepines. So really, an endozepine is an endogenous *anti*benzodiazepine. Keeping a mouse in social isolation elevates the release of endozepines in several brain areas, and presumably, that increase relates to the mouse's fearfulness and aggression when it is again placed with other mice (Dong, Matsumoto, Tohda, Kaneko, & Watanabe, 1999).

Endozepines are still not well understood, but they are an odd kind of neuromodulator. They are released mainly by glia cells, not by neurons (Patte et al., 1999). Why do our brains secrete endozepines and thereby increase our level of fears and anxieties? Presumably, the "right" level of fear varies from time to time, and these chemicals help regulate that level.

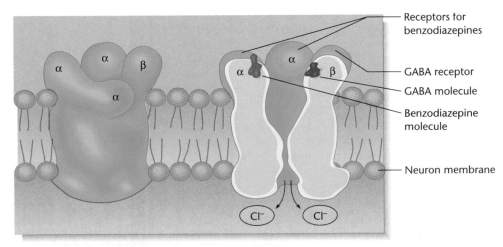

Figure 12.16 The GABA_A receptor complex
Of the four GABA-sensitive receptor sites, the three α sites are also sensitive to benzodiazepines. *Source: Based on Guidotti, Ferrero, Fujimoto, Santi, & Costa, 1986*

EXTENSIONS AND APPLICATIONS

Alcohol as a Tranquilizer

Ethyl alcohol, the beverage alcohol, has behavioral effects similar to those of benzodiazepine tranquilizers. It decreases anxiety and behavioral inhibitions based on the threat of punishment. Moreover, a combination of alcohol and tranquilizers depresses body activities and brain functioning more severely than either drug alone. (A combination of alcohol and tranquilizers can be fatal.) Furthermore, alcohol, benzodiazepines, and barbiturates all exhibit the phenomenon of **cross-tolerance:** An individual who has used one of the drugs enough to develop a tolerance to it will show a partial tolerance to other depressant drugs as well.

Alcohol promotes the flow of chloride ions through the $GABA_A$ receptor complex, just as tranquilizers do (Suzdak et al., 1986), probably by facilitating the binding of GABA to its receptors. Alcohol influences the brain in other ways as well, but the effects on GABA are responsible for alcohol's antianxiety and intoxicating effects. Drugs that block the effects of alcohol on the $GABA_A$ receptor complex also block most of alcohol's behavioral effects. One experimental drug, known as Ro15-4513, is particularly effective in this regard (Suzdak et al., 1986). Besides affecting the $GABA_A$ receptor complex, Ro15-4513 blocks the effects of alcohol on motor coordination, its depressant action on the brain, and its ability to reduce anxiety (Becker, 1988; Hoffman, Tabakoff, Szabo, Suzdak, & Paul, 1987; Ticku & Kulkarni, 1988) (Figure 12.17).

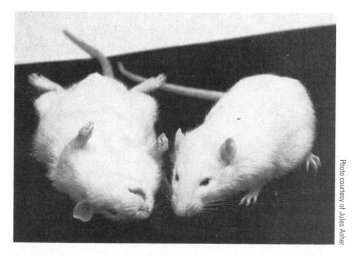

Figure 12.17 Two rats that were given the same amount of alcohol
The rat on the right was later given the experimental drug Ro15-4513. Within 2 minutes, its performance on motor tasks improved significantly.

Photo courtesy of Jules Asher

Could Ro15-4513 be useful as a "sobering-up" pill or as a treatment to help people who want to stop drinking alcohol? Hoffman-LaRoche, the company that discovered it, eventually concluded that the drug would be too risky. People who relied on the pill might think they were sober and try to drive home when they were still somewhat impaired. Furthermore, giving this pill to alcoholics could easily backfire. Alcoholics generally drink to get drunk; a pill that decreased their feeling of intoxication would probably lead them to drink even more. Ro15-4513 reverses the behavioral effects of moderate alcohol doses, but a large dose can still be a health hazard or even fatal (Poling, Schlinger, & Blakely, 1988). For these reasons, Ro15-4513 is used only in experimental laboratories.

Stop & Check

9. Why did researchers for many years fail to find the genetic basis for panic disorder?
10. What would be the effect of benzodiazepines on someone who had no GABA?

Check your answers on page 384.

MODULE 12.3

In Closing: Doing Something About Emotions

Today, we understand the physiology of violence and fearfulness far better than we used to, but clearly, we have a long way to go. If we do make major advances, what then? Imagine we could take a blood sample—measuring 5-HIAA or whatever—plus an fMRI scan and a few other measurements and then with reasonable accuracy predict which people will commit violent crime. Should we use that information to decide who stays in prison and who gets out on parole? Shall we go a step further and use brain tests to prevent crimes before they even occur?

And what about anxiety? Today, we have antianxiety drugs that work moderately well. Suppose research advances to the point that we could modulate people's anxiety precisely without undesirable side effects. Would it be a good idea to use these new methods to assure that everyone had the "right" anxiety level—not too much and not too little? Future research will give us new options and opportunities; deciding what to do with them is another matter.

1. Either a provoking experience, such as fighting, or the direct stimulation of the corticomedial area of the amygdala can produce a temporarily heightened readiness to attack. (p. 372)

2. There is evidence that genetic or prenatal influences can alter the tendency toward violent behavior in conjunction with family environment and other experiences. (p. 372)

3. Testosterone can increase the readiness to attack. (p. 374)

4. A few people with temporal lobe epilepsy have occasional outbursts of unprovoked violence. (p. 374)

5. Low serotonin turnover is associated with an increased likelihood of impulsive behavior, sometimes including violence. (p. 375)

6. Researchers measure enhancement of the startle reflex as an indication of anxiety or learned fears. (p. 377)

7. The startle reflex itself depends on activity in the pons. Enhancement of the startle reflex through learning depends on the amygdala. (p. 378)

8. People and nonhuman animals with damage to the amygdala lose much of their fear or anxiety. People with amygdala damage also have trouble recognizing facial expressions of fear. (p. 378)

9. Most people with panic disorder and many with other anxiety disorders have an extra copy of a particular segment of chromosome 15. That extra copy also produces joint laxity, which depends on a different gene on the same chromosomal segment. (p. 380)

10. Tranquilizers decrease fear by facilitating the binding of the neurotransmitter GABA to the GABA$_A$ receptors, especially in the amygdala. (p. 381)

2. Aggressive behaviors and conduct disorders are most common among those whose biological parents had criminal records and whose adoptive parents had marital discord, depression, substance abuse, or legal problems. (p. 374)

3. One can measure the concentration of 5-HIAA, a serotonin metabolite, in the cerebrospinal fluid or other body fluids. The more 5-HIAA, the more serotonin has been released and presumably resynthesized. (p. 377)

4. To raise production of serotonin, increase consumption of tryptophan or decrease consumption of proteins high in phenylalanine and other large amino acids that compete with tryptophan for entry to the brain. (p. 377)

5. Loud noises activate a path from the cochlea to cells in the pons that directly trigger a tensing of neck muscles. (p. 380)

6. Present the stimulus before giving a loud noise. If the stimulus increases the startle reflex beyond its usual level, then the stimulus produced fear. (p. 380)

7. Perhaps amygdala damage impairs interpretation or understanding of emotional stimuli. That is, the individual is capable of the experience of fear but does not know when to be afraid. (p. 380)

8. People with damage to the amygdala, such as those with Urbach-Wiethe disease, experience little fear themselves and have trouble recognizing the expression in others. (p. 380)

9. Panic disorder is associated with an extra repeat (three copies instead of two) of a particular segment of chromosome 15, and this segment is so unstable that the abnormality does not always continue from one generation to the next or even occur in all cells of the body. (p. 383)

10. Benzodiazepines facilitate the effects of GABA, so a person without GABA would have no response at all to benzodiazepines. (p. 383)

ANSWERS TO *STOP AND CHECK* QUESTIONS

1. The other likely explanation is that families that include members with a criminal record probably do not provide the best prenatal environment; the mothers may smoke or drink during pregnancy or otherwise endanger their fetuses' brain development. (p. 374)

THOUGHT QUESTION

Much of the play behavior of a cat can be analyzed into attack and escape components. Is the same true for children's play?

Key Terms and Activities

TERMS

absence seizure (p. 356)

ACTH (p. 366)

antibody (p. 367)

antigen (p. 367)

B cell (p. 367)

barbiturate (p. 381)

behavioral medicine (p. 364)

benzodiazepine (p. 382)

cortisol (p. 366)

cross-tolerance (p. 383)

cytokines (p. 367)

diazepam-binding inhibitor (DBI) or endozepine (p. 382)

5-hydroxyindoleacetic acid (5-HIAA) (p. 375)

$GABA_A$ receptor complex (p. 382)

HPA axis (p. 366)

immune system (p. 367)

intermittent explosive disorder (p. 374)

James-Lange theory (p. 359)

leukocyte (p. 367)

limbic system (p. 361)

locked-in syndrome (p. 359)

macrophage (p. 367)

natural killer cell (p. 367)

panic disorder (p. 360)

posttraumatic stress disorder (PTSD) (p. 369)

psychoneuroimmunology (p. 368)

pure autonomic failure (p. 359)

startle reflex (p. 377)

stress (p. 364)

T cell (p. 367)

turnover (p. 375)

SUGGESTIONS FOR FURTHER READING

Damasio, A. (1999). *The feeling of what happens.* New York: Harcourt Brace. A neurologist's account of the connection between emotion and consciousness, full of interesting examples.

Niehoff, D. (1999). *The biology of violence.* New York: Free Press. Discusses research on the neural and hormonal mechanisms of aggressive behavior.

Rosen, J. B., & Schulkin, J. (1998). From normal fear to pathological anxiety. *Psychological Review, 105,* 325–350. Reviews brain mechanisms of anxiety, including differences between normal and excessive anxiety.

WEB SITES TO EXPLORE

You can go to the Biological Psychology Study Center and click these links. While there, you can also check for suggested articles available on InfoTrac College Edition.

The Biological Psychology Internet address is:
http://psychology.wadsworth.com/ kalatbiopsych8e/

Stress-related links
http://www.stressless.com/AboutSL/StressLinks.cfm

Locked-in syndrome
http://www.ninds.nih.gov/health_and_medical/ disorders/lockedinsyndrome_doc.htm

Eye-operated communication system in locked-in syndrome
http://www.eyegaze.com/doc/csun91.htm

CD-ROM: EXPLORING BIOLOGICAL PSYCHOLOGY

Amygdala and Fear Conditioning (animation)

Health and Stress (video)

Stress and the Brain (video)

CNS Depressants (animation)

Critical Thinking (essay questions)

Chapter Quiz (multiple choice questions)

The Biology of Learning and Memory

13

Chapter Outline

Opposite:
Learning produces amazingly complex behaviors. Research progress requires distinguishing among various types of learning and memory. *Source: Tim Davis/CORBIS*

Main Ideas

1. To understand the physiology of learning, we must answer two questions: What changes occur in a single cell during learning? How do changed cells work together to produce adaptive behavior?

2. Psychologists distinguish among several types of memory, each of which can be impaired by a different kind of brain damage.

3. During learning, a variety of changes occur that facilitate or decrease the activity at particular synapses. These changes may be the physiological basis of learning and memory.

Suppose you type something on your computer and then store it. A year later you come back, click the correct filename, and retrieve what you wrote. How did the computer remember what to do?

That question is really two questions. One is: How does the computer store a representation of the keys that you typed? To explain how that happened, we need to understand the physics of the silicon chips inside your computer. The second question is: How does the computer convert all those on and off messages on silicon chips into the array on your computer screen? To answer that question, we need to understand the computer's wiring diagram.

Similarly, when we try to explain how you remember some experience, we are really answering two questions. One is: How did a pattern of sensory information create lasting changes in the input–output properties of some of your neurons? That question concerns the biophysics of the neuron. The second question is: After certain neurons change certain properties, how does the nervous system as a whole produce the appropriate behavior? That question concerns the wiring diagram. Learning requires changes in individual cells, but what happens in a single cell may be very different from how the organism learns as a whole.

We begin this chapter by considering how the various areas of the nervous system interact to produce learning and memory. In the second module, we turn to the more detailed physiology of how experience changes the properties of the individual cells and synapses.

MODULE 13.1

Learning, Memory, Amnesia, and Brain Functioning

Suppose you lost the ability to form long-lasting memories. You can remember what you just did and what someone just said to you, but you remember nothing that happened earlier. It's as if you awakened from a long sleep. So you write on a sheet of paper, "Just now, for the first time, I have suddenly become conscious!" A little later, you forget this experience, too. So far as you can tell, you have only now emerged into consciousness after a long sleeplike period. You look at this sheet of paper on which you wrote about becoming conscious, but you don't remember writing it. How odd! You must have written something about being conscious during a time when in fact you were not! Irritated, you cross off that statement and write anew, "*NOW* I am for the first time conscious!" And a minute later, you cross that one off and write it again. And again. Eventually, someone finds this sheet of paper on which you have repeatedly written and crossed out statements about suddenly being conscious for the first time.

Sound far-fetched? It really happened to a patient known as "C" who developed severe memory impairments after encephalitis damaged his temporal cortex (B. A. Wilson, Baddeley, & Kapur, 1995). Life without memory is very unlike life as the rest of us know it.

LOCALIZED REPRESENTATIONS OF MEMORY

What happens in the brain during learning and memory? One early, influential idea was that a connection grew between two brain areas. The Russian physiologist Ivan Pavlov pioneered the investigation of what we now call **classical conditioning** (Figure 13.1a), in which pairing two stimuli changes the response to one of them (Pavlov, 1927). Ordinarily, the experimenter starts by presenting a **conditioned stimulus (CS)**, which initially elicits no response of note, and then presents the **unconditioned stimulus (UCS)**, which automatically elicits the **unconditioned response (UCR)**. After some pairings of the CS and the UCS (perhaps just one or two pairings, perhaps many), the individual begins making a new, learned response to the

CS, called a **conditioned response (CR)**. In his original experiments, Pavlov presented a dog with a sound (CS) followed by meat (UCS), which stimulated the dog to salivate (UCR). After many such pairings, the sound alone (CS) stimulated the dog to salivate (CR). In that case and many others, the CR resembles the UCR, but in some cases, it does not. For example, if a rat experiences a CS paired with shock, the shock elicits screaming and jumping, but the CS elicits a freezing response.

In **operant conditioning**, an individual's response is followed by a reinforcer or punishment (Figure 13.1b). A **reinforcer** is any event that increases the future probability of the response; a **punishment** is an event that suppresses the frequency of the response. For example, when a rat enters one arm of a maze and finds Froot Loops cereal (a potent reinforcer for a rat), the probability of its entering that arm again increases. If it receives a shock instead, the probability decreases. The primary difference between the two kinds of conditioning is that in operant conditioning the individual's response determines the outcome (reinforcer or punishment), whereas in classical conditioning the CS and UCS will be presented at certain times independent of the individual's behavior. (The behavior is useful, however, in anticipating the effects of the UCS.)

Some cases of learning are difficult to label as classical or operant. For example, after a male songbird hears the song of his own species during his first few months, he imitates it the following year. The song that he heard was not paired with any other stimulus, as in classical conditioning. He learned the song without reinforcers or punishments, so we can't call it operant conditioning either. That is, animals have specialized methods of learning other than classical and operant conditioning (Rozin & Kalat, 1971; Rozin & Schull, 1988).

Lashley's Search for the Engram

Pavlov believed that classical conditioning reflected a strengthened connection between a CS center and a UCS center in the brain. That strengthened connection lets any excitation of the CS center flow to the UCS center, evoking the unconditioned response (Figure 13.2).

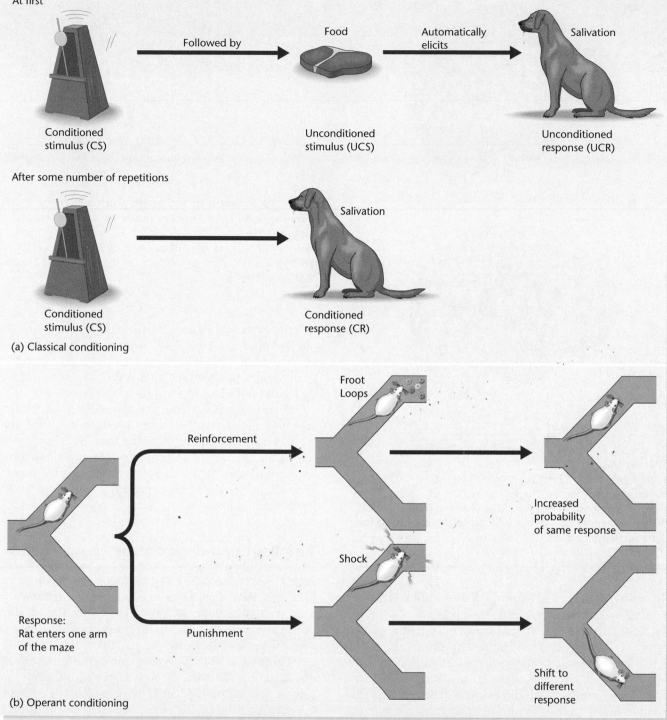

Figure 13.1 Procedures for classical conditioning and operant conditioning
(a) In classical conditioning, two stimuli (CS and UCS) are presented at specific times regardless of what the learner does.
(b) In operant conditioning, the learner's behavior determines the presentation of reinforcer or punishment.

Karl Lashley set out to test this hypothesis. He said that he was searching for the **engram**—the physical representation of what has been learned. (A connection between two brain areas would be one example of an engram but is hardly the only possibility.)

Lashley reasoned that if learning depends on new or strengthened connections between two brain areas,

a knife cut somewhere in the brain should interrupt that connection and abolish the learned response. He trained rats on a variety of mazes and a brightness discrimination task and then made one or more deep cuts in varying locations in their cerebral cortices (Lashley, 1929, 1950) (Figure 13.3). However, no knife cut significantly impaired the rats' performances.

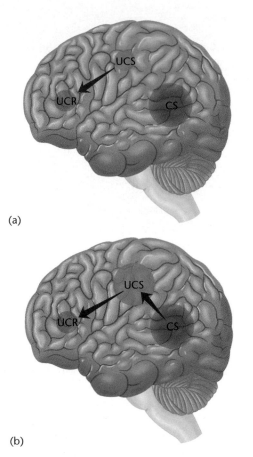

(a)

(b)

Figure 13.2 Pavlov's view of the physiology of learning
Initially **(a),** the UCS excites the UCS center, which then excites the UCR center. The CS excites the CS center, which elicits no response of interest. After training **(b),** excitation in the CS center flows to the UCS center, thus eliciting the same response as the UCS.

Evidently, the types of learning that he studied did not depend on connections across the cortex.

Lashley also tested whether any portion of the cerebral cortex is more important than others for learning. He trained rats on mazes before or after he removed large portions of the cortex. The lesions impaired performance, but the amount of retardation depended more on the amount of brain damage than on its location. Learning and memory apparently did not rely on a single cortical area. Lashley therefore proposed two principles about the nervous system:

- **equipotentiality**—all parts of the cortex contribute equally to complex behaviors such as learning; any part of the cortex can substitute for any other.
- **mass action**—the cortex works as a whole, and the more cortex the better.

Note, however, another interpretation of Lashley's results: Maze learning and visual discrimination learning are more complex tasks than they might appear. A

Figure 13.3 View of rat brain from above, showing cuts that Lashley made in the brains of various rats
He found that no single cut or combination of cuts interfered with a rat's memory of a maze. *Source: Adapted from Lashley, 1950*

rat finding its way to food must attend to visual and tactile stimuli, the location of its body, the position of its head, auditory and olfactory cues if available, and so forth. Learning depends on many cortical areas, but each area could be contributing in a different way.

Eventually, researchers discovered that Lashley's conclusions reflected two unnecessary assumptions: (a) that the cerebral cortex is the best or only place to search for an engram and (b) that all kinds of memory are physiologically the same. As we shall see, investigators who discarded these assumptions came to different conclusions.

The Modern Search for the Engram

Richard F. Thompson and his colleagues used a simpler task than Lashley's and sought the engram of memory not in the cerebral cortex but in the cerebellum, a structure that Masao Ito (1984) had identified as a likely organ of learning.

Thompson and his colleagues studied classical conditioning of eyelid responses in rabbits. They presented first a tone (CS) and then a puff of air (UCS) to the cornea of the rabbit's eye. At first, a rabbit blinked at the air puff but not at the tone; after repeated pairings, classical conditioning occurred and the rabbit blinked at the tone also. Investigators recorded the activity in various brain cells to determine which ones changed their responses during learning.

Thompson and other investigators consistently found changes in cells of one nucleus of the cerebellum, the **lateral interpositus nucleus (LIP)**. At the start of training, these cells showed little response to the tone, but as learning proceeded, their responses increased (Thompson, 1986). The fact that a brain area changed its response does not necessarily mean that the learning took place in that area. Imagine a sequence of brain areas:

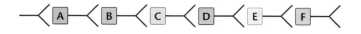

If learning occurs in any one of them (say, area D), we could record changes in D and in every area after it. We could also disrupt the learned response by damaging any of the areas from A through F. (D has to get input from A, B, and C and has to send output to E and F.) How, then, can anyone determine where learning occurs?

Thompson and his colleagues reasoned that if learning occurred in D, then areas E and F need to be active to pass the information along to the muscles, but they wouldn't have to be active while learning itself took place. (Everything up to D would have to be active, of course, to get the information to D.) To investigate the role of the LIP, investigators *temporarily* suppressed activity in that nucleus at the start of training, either by cooling it or by injecting a drug into it. Then they presented the CS and UCS as usual and found no evidence of learning—that is, no responses while the LIP was suppressed. Then they waited for the effects of the cooling or the drugs to wear off and continued training. At that point, the rabbits began to learn, but they learned *at the same speed as animals that had received no previous training.* Evidently, while the LIP was suppressed, the training had no effect.

But did learning actually occur *in* the LIP, or does this area just relay the information to a later area where learning occurs? In the next experiments, investigators suppressed activity in the red nucleus, a midbrain motor area that receives input from the cerebellum: When the red nucleus was suppressed, the rabbits again showed no responses during training. However, as soon as the red nucleus had recovered from the cooling or drugs, the rabbits showed strong learned responses to the tone (R. E. Clark & Lavond, 1993; Krupa, Thompson, & Thompson, 1993). In other words, suppressing the red nucleus temporarily prevented the response but did not prevent learning. The researchers therefore concluded that the learning occurred in the LIP. (The LIP was the last structure in the sequence that had to be awake for learning to occur.) Figure 13.4 summarizes these experiments. Later experiments demonstrated that cooling still other areas failed to impair learning; the key area was always the lateral interpositus nucleus (Bao, Chen, & Thompson, 2000).

The mechanisms for this type of conditioning are probably the same in humans. In one study, PET scans revealed that classical conditioning of the eye blink in young adults produced increased activity in the cerebellum, red nucleus, and several other areas (Logan & Grafton, 1995). People who have damage in the cerebellum are impaired at eye-blink conditioning (Woodruff-Pak, Papka, & Ivry, 1996).

Stop & Check

1. Thompson found a localizable engram, whereas Lashley did not. What key differences in procedures or assumptions were probably responsible for their different results?
2. What evidence indicates that the red nucleus is necessary for performance of a conditioned response but not for learning the response?

Check your answers on page 406.

TYPES OF MEMORY

Although eyelid conditioning and several other kinds of classical conditioning probably depend on the cerebellum, many other kinds of learning and memory do not. You will recall from Chapter 6 that different parts of the brain contribute to different aspects of visual perception. The same principle holds for memory, and much of our progress in understanding the physiology of memory has come from progress in distinguishing among different types of memory.

Short- and Long-Term Memory

Donald Hebb (1949) reasoned that no one mechanism could account for all the phenomena of learning. We can form memories almost instantaneously, and some last a lifetime. Hebb considered it unlikely that any chemical process could occur fast enough to account for immediate memory yet remain stable enough to provide permanent memory. He therefore distinguished between **short-term memory** of events that have just occurred and **long-term memory** of events from previous times. Several types of evidence support this distinction:

↳ longer than 30 sec

• Short-term memory and long-term memory differ in their capacity. As an illustration, read each of these letter sequences and then look away and try to repeat them:

DZLAUV
CYXGMBF
OBGSFKIE
RJNWSCFPT

Most healthy adults can repeat about seven unrelated items in short-term memory—sometimes

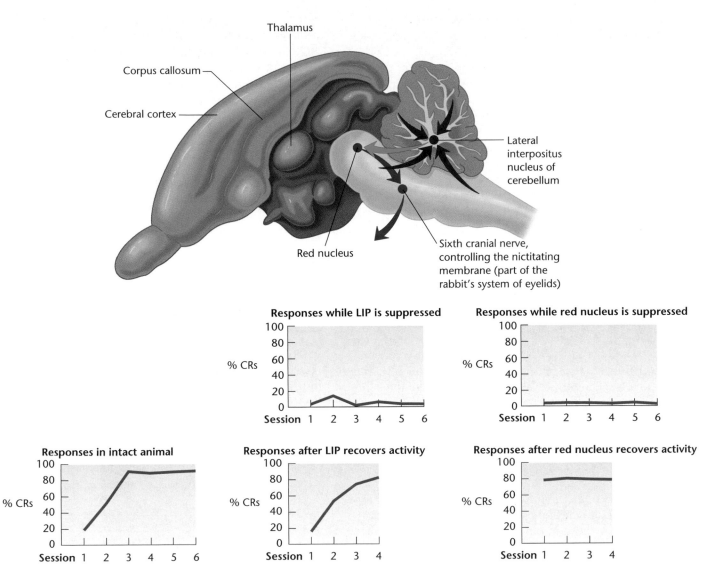

Figure 13.4 Localization of an engram
Rabbits were trained on classical conditioning of an eyelid response. Temporary inactivation of the lateral interpositus nucleus of a rabbit blocked all indications of learning. After the inactivation wore off, the rabbits learned as slowly as rabbits with no previous training. Temporary inactivation of the red nucleus blocked the response during the period of inactivation, but the learned response appeared as soon as the red nucleus recovered. *Source: Based on the experiments of Clark & Lavond, 1993; Krupa, Thompson, & Thompson, 1993*

slightly more or fewer, depending on circumstances. In contrast, long-term memory has a vast, difficult-to-estimate capacity. When you learn something new, you don't have to forget something old to make room for it.

• Short-term memories fade quickly unless you rehearse them. For example, if you read the letter sequence DZLAUV and then something distracts you so that you cannot rehearse those letters, your chance of repeating them correctly is fairly good 5 seconds later, less after 10 seconds, and poor at 20 seconds or beyond (Peterson & Peterson, 1959).

In contrast, you can recall many long-term memories that you haven't thought about in years. Note, however, that the research demonstrating rapid loss of short-term memory has dealt almost entirely with meaningless material. How long would you remember the number sequence 64-57-2-13 without constant rehearsal? Probably not long. How long would you remember "the score is 64 to 57 with 2 minutes and 13 seconds left to play"? Probably longer.

• With short-term memory, once you have forgotten something, it is lost. For example, if you read CYXGMBF and then forget it, you probably won't gain from the hint "starts with CY." With long-term memory, however, you might think you have forgotten something and yet find that some hint helps you reconstruct it. For example, try naming all your high-school teachers. After you have named all you can, you will be able to name still more if someone shows you photos and tells you the teachers' initials.

Consolidation of Long-Term Memories

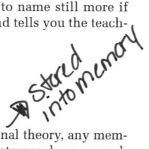
Stored into memory

According to Hebb's (1949) original theory, any memory that stayed in short-term storage long enough would be gradually **consolidated** (strengthened) into a long-term memory. Hebb guessed that a short-term memory might be represented by a *reverberating circuit* of neuronal activity in the brain, with a self-exciting loop of neurons (Figure 13.5). If the reverberating circuit remained active long enough, some permanent chemical or structural change would occur.

Originally, investigators assumed that every memory was either short-term or long-term and that the transition from short-term to long-term took place soon, suddenly, and completely. That is, perhaps an event was stored in short-term memory for, say, 10 seconds, but if it was rehearsed for that long it would then become a long-term memory. To test this idea, researchers gave animals training experiences and then at various delays afterward gave them a powerful shock to the head that should disrupt any reverberating circuit. The idea was to wipe out short-term memories but not long-term memories and therefore tell us how long it took to consolidate a short-term into a long-term memory.

Electroconvulsive shock to the head did indeed impair many memories, but problems arose (Nadel & Land, 2000). In some cases, it wiped out only memories from a

few seconds ago, and in other cases, it wiped out much older memories. Sometimes a memory that appeared to be "wiped out" could be recovered after a reminder.

Later human studies further weakened the idea of a firm distinction between short-term and long-term memory. First, consider your own experience: Right now you probably remember what you ate for dinner last night, who was the last person you talked to, approximately how much money is in your wallet or purse, where you parked your car today, and how well your favorite sports team did in its last game. None of these are classical short-term memories: They happened more than a few seconds ago, and you can recall them without constantly rehearsing them. They are not exactly long-term memories either, as you will forget most of them within hours, days, or weeks.

Researchers have found that the brain produces a chemical that actually interferes with consolidation. When an animal is trained on some simple task, the training activates several genes that promote learning and memory. It also activates a gene that produces *protein phosphatase 1,* a chemical that inactivates the products of the genes promoting learning. The result is forgetting, unless the experience is repeated often enough (Genoux et al., 2002). (Forgetting a single experience is often adaptive. Stated another way, it would not be useful to remember every event you ever experienced.) If the experience is repeated many times within a brief period—a procedure that psychologists call *massed practice*—the protein phosphatase 1 accumulates and interferes with retention. If the same repetitions of the experience are spread out in time—distributed practice—the protein phosphatase 1 declines between one trial and the next, and memory is better. So we now have a physiological explanation for the century-old observation that distributed practice works better than massed practice. In other words, spreading out your study is better than cramming.

Research suggests that even repeated, important items that we would clearly classify as long-term memories go through a gradual consolidation or strengthening process that can continue for a very long time. In one study, eight people aged 60 to 70 years examined photos of people who were famous during one decade of their lives. For example, some were photos of movie actors or actresses who were famous for only a few years. MRI scans found that several areas responded most strongly to faces famous in the 1990s and least to those famous in the 1940s, even though these people recognized the celebrities from the 1940s just as well as those from the 1990s (Haist, Gore, & Mao, 2001). It was as if the brain had to work harder to identify the recent faces, whereas the older faces were stored more firmly. In another study, fMRI scans indicated more temporal lobe activity when people thought about places they had visited within the last

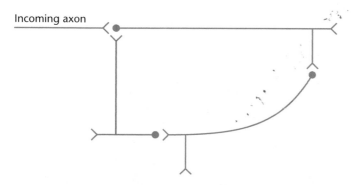
Incoming axon

Figure 13.5 A hypothetical reverberating circuit
According to Hebb, a series of neurons might excite one another approximately as shown, thus maintaining a trace of some stimulation long enough to form a more permanent storage.

2 years than when thinking about places they visited 7 years ago (Niki & Luo, 2002). Again, the implication is that the brain gradually changes how it stores information, with changes occurring over years.

Furthermore, consolidating a long-term memory clearly depends on more than the passage of time. Some long-term memories form rapidly, and others form slowly or not at all, depending mainly on how important or emotionally arousing they seem. Think about your high-school experiences. You probably spent hours trying to memorize names and dates for a history test, and now you can hardly remember them at all. Yet you clearly remember the first time that special person smiled at you, the time you said something foolish in class and people laughed at you, the time you won a major honor, the frightening moment when you heard that a friend was hurt in a car accident. You didn't have to rehearse these events to remember them; you formed strong memories almost at once. Why? Because they were meaningful and emotional.

How does the emotional response enhance consolidation? Remember from Chapter 12 that stressful or emotionally exciting experiences increase the secretion of epinephrine (adrenaline) and cortisol. Epinephrine from the periphery does not cross the blood-brain barrier, but it stimulates receptors on the vagus nerve (cranial nerve X), which sends information that is relayed to the amygdala (C. L. Williams, Men, Clayton, & Gold, 1998). Small to moderate amounts of cortisol also activate the amygdala and hippocampus. Research on humans as well as laboratory animals has demonstrated that direct injections of epinephrine or cortisol enhance the storage and consolidation of recent experiences (Cahill & McGaugh, 1998). The same is true for direct stimulation of the vagus nerve or direct stimulation of the amygdala (Akirav & Richter-Levin, 1999; K. B. Clark, Naritoku, Smith, Browning, & Jensen, 1999). Actually, even rather unexciting kinds of learning activate the amygdala (Fried et al., 2001), but increased excitement activates it more and improves long-term retention. The amygdala in turn stimulates the hippocampus and cerebral cortex, which are both important for memory storage. However, prolonged stress, which releases even more cortisol, impairs memory (deQuervain, Roozendaal, & McGaugh, 1998; Newcomer et al., 1999).

After damage in and around the amygdala, emotional arousal no longer enhances memory storage. For example, imagine yourself memorizing a long list of words. Most are normal everyday words, but a few are emotionally charged "taboo" words such as *penis* or *bitch*. Within the next hour, you will forget many of the words, but you will remember the taboo words. Patients with damage in or near the amygdala are no more likely to remember the taboo words than any others (LaBar & Phelps, 1998).

A Modified Theory: Working Memory

Current researchers no longer regard short-term memory as a temporary holding station on the way to long-term memory. A. D. Baddeley and G. J. Hitch (1994) introduced the term **working memory** to emphasize that temporary storage is not just a station on the way to long-term memory; it is the way we store information while we are working with it or attending to it.

Here is a task you can use to test working memory. Read the following list of words to someone else, or have someone read them to you. After each word, say the *previous word*. That is, when you hear the first word, say nothing. When you hear the second word, say the first word and so forth. Here is the list (you could use any list, of course):

peach, apple, blueberry, melon, orange, mango, raspberry, banana, lemon, papaya, fig, plum, tangerine, grape

Now do it again, but this time say *what was two words back*. That is, say nothing after the first two words; after the third say the first word and so forth. You begin to see that holding material in working memory isn't always easy.

Baddeley and Hitch distinguished three components of working memory:

- a **phonological loop**, which stores auditory information, including words;
- a **visuospatial sketchpad**, which stores visual information; and
- the **central executive**, which directs attention toward one stimulus or another and determines which items will be stored in working memory.

They distinguished the phonological loop from the visuospatial sketchpad because verbal memory seems in many ways independent of visual memory. If you try to memorize a long list of words or a long list of pictures, you will find that one gets confused with another. But if you memorize a mixture of words and pictures, the words and pictures do not interfere with each other (Hale, Myerson, Rhee, Weiss, & Abrams, 1996). Presumably, we also have working memory for touch, smell, and taste, but less is known about these stores.

One common test of working memory is the **delayed response task,** in which one must respond to a stimulus that was heard or seen a short while earlier. For example, a light shines above one of several doors. The light goes off, a delay ensues, and then the individual has to go to the door where it saw the light. The delay can be increased or decreased to test the limits of working memory. Many studies have found that when humans or other mammals perform a delayed response task, cells in the prefrontal cortex, especially the dorso-lateral prefrontal cortex, maintain high activity during the delay, presumably meaning that they are storing the memory (Kikuchi-Yorioka & Sawaguchi, 2000; Leung, Gore, & Goldman-Rakic, 2002). The stronger the activation of this area, the better the individual's performance (Klingberg, Forssberg, & Westerberg, 2002; Sakai, Rowe, & Passingham, 2002). Furthermore, the dorsolateral prefrontal cortex shows similar indications of storing information in experiments where a person or monkey sees a signal and then has to wait until the end of the delay period to get a signal for how it needs to respond to that signal (Constantinidis, Franowicz, & Goldman-Rakic, 2001; Rowe, Toni, Josephs, Frackowiak, & Passingham, 2000). So this area really does store working memories, not only the preparation for a response.

Stop & Check

3. How does epinephrine enhance memory storage? Epinephrine and cortisol enhance emotionally charged memories by activating which brain area?

4. What is the probable brain location and mechanism for working memory?

Check your answers on page 406.

THE HIPPOCAMPUS AND AMNESIA

Amnesia is memory loss. Some people have such serious amnesia that they cannot even remember that they have just finished a meal. One patient ate lunch, about 20 minutes later was offered a second lunch and ate that, too, and then another 20 minutes later started on a third lunch and ate most of it. A few minutes later, he said he would like to "go for a walk and get a good meal" (Rozin, Dow, Moscovitch, & Rajaram, 1998). Many kinds of brain damage can produce amnesia, but one of the most powerful kinds is damage to the hippocampus.

Memory Loss After Hippocampal Damage

In 1953, a man known as H. M. suffered about 10 minor epileptic seizures per day and a major seizure about once a week, despite the use of every antiepileptic drug known at the time. Eventually, he and his neurosurgeon became eager to try almost anything.

Because of evidence suggesting that the hippocampus was sometimes the source of epileptic disorders, the neurosurgeon removed that structure from both hemispheres, as well as several neighboring structures in the temporal cortex. At the time, researchers had done almost no animal studies of the hippocampus, and no one knew what to expect after the surgery. As events turned out, even though the operation reduced H. M.'s epilepsy to no more than two major seizures per year, he almost certainly would have preferred to remain epileptic (Milner, 1959; Penfield & Milner, 1958; Scoville & Milner, 1957). Figure 13.6 shows the normal anatomy of the hippocampus and the damage in H. M. For more about the anatomy of the hippocampus, see this Web site:

rprcsgi.rprc.washington.edu/neuronames/interim/hippocampus.html

After the surgery, H. M.'s intellect and language abilities remained intact; his IQ score even increased slightly, presumably because of the decrease in epileptic interference. His personality remained the same except for what we might call emotional placidity (Eichenbaum, 2002). For example, he rarely complained (even about pain) or requested anything (even food). However, he suffered a massive **anterograde amnesia** (loss of memories for events that happened after brain damage). He could form short-term memories but very few new long-term memories. He also suffered a moderate **retrograde amnesia** (loss of memory for events that occurred shortly before brain damage). That is, he had some trouble recalling events that happened within 1 to 3 years before the operation.

After the operation, he could not learn his way to the hospital bathroom. After reading a story, he could not describe what had happened in it. He could read a magazine repeatedly without losing interest. Sometimes he tells someone about a childhood incident and then minutes later tells the same story again, unaware that he had just finished telling it to the same person (Eichenbaum, 2002).

In one test, Brenda Milner (1959) asked H. M. to remember the number 584. After a 15-minute delay without distractions, he recalled it correctly, explaining, "It's easy. You just remember 8. You see, 5, 8, and 4 add to 17. You remember 8, subtract it from 17, and it leaves 9. Divide 9 in half and you get 5 and 4, and there you are, 584. Easy." A moment later, after his attention had shifted to another subject, he had forgotten both the number and the complicated line of thought he had associated with it.

In 1980, he moved to a nursing home. Four years later, he could not say where he lived or who cared for him. Although he watched the news on television every night, he could recall only a few fragments of events since 1953. For several years after the operation, whenever he was asked his age and the date, he

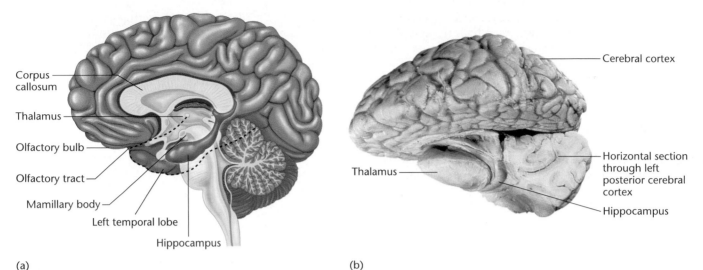

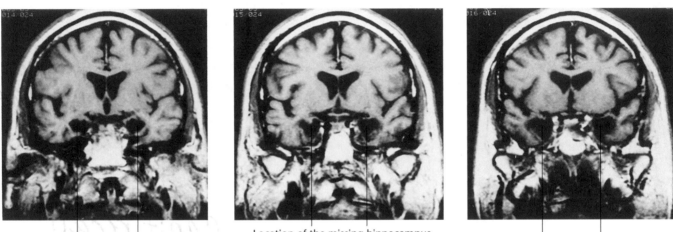

Figure 13.6 The hippocampus
(a) Because the hippocampus is inside the temporal lobe, the left hippocampus is closer to the viewer than the rest of this plane, and the right hippocampus is behind the plane. **(b)** A human brain seen from above. The right hemisphere is intact. The top of the left hemisphere has been cut away to show how the hippocampus loops over (dorsal to) the thalamus, posterior to it, and then below (ventral to) it. *Source: Photo courtesy of Dana Copeland* **(c)** MRI scan of the brain of H. M., showing absence of the hippocampus. Note the large size of this lesion. *Source: Photo courtesy of David Amaral and Suzanne Corkin*

answered "27" and "1953." After a few years he started guessing wildly, generally underestimating his age by 10 years or more and missing the date by as much as 43 years (Corkin, 1984).

Over the years, many new words have entered the English language, such as *Jacuzzi* and *granola*. H. M. cannot define them, and in fact treats them as nonwords (Corkin, 2002). Furthermore, many seldom-used words seem to have dropped out of his vocabulary. When tested beyond age 57, his ability to define common words was about equal to that of other people of the same age and education, but he was impaired at defining infrequently used words, such as *squander* (James & McKay, 2001). A possible explanation is that for any of us, maintaining a weak memory (e.g., the meaning of the word *squander*) requires occasional practice, perhaps even rebuilding of damaged connections in the brain. In someone like H. M., who has such trouble learning, weak memories are vulnerable to damage.

Apparently, however, it is not impossible for him to learn new facts, but he learns them very weakly or slowly (Corkin, 2002). For example, after he moved with his parents to a new house, he did eventually learn the floor plan of the house, although it took many years. When shown photos of people who became famous after his surgery, he could name almost none of them, but he did name some if given both the face and most of the name—for example, Woody A– (Woody Allen), Julie And– (Julie Andrews), Jimmy C– (Jimmy Carter), and Prince Ch– (Prince Charles).

That is, to demonstrate that he forms any new memories, we have to make the task extremely simple, but still it would be wrong to say that he has learned nothing at all.

Many people ask whether he is surprised at his own appearance in a mirror or photo. Yes and no. When asked his age or whether his hair has turned gray, he replies that he does not know. When shown a photo of himself with his mother, he recognizes his mother but not himself. However, when he looks at himself in the mirror, he shows no indication of surprise (Corkin, 2002). He has, of course, seen himself daily in the mirror over all these years. He also has some context of knowing that the person in the mirror must be himself, whereas the person in the photo could be anyone.

Although H. M. has enormous trouble learning new facts and keeping track of current events, he acquires new skills without apparent difficulty. That is, he has impaired **declarative memory**, the ability to state a memory in words, but intact **procedural memory**, the development of motor skills and responses. For example, he has learned to read words written backwards, as they would be seen in a mirror, although he is surprised at this skill because he does not remember having tried it before. Similarly, he has learned to draw something to match what he sees in a mirror (Corkin, 2002). For another example, consider the drawing in Figure 13.7a. Most people are not sure what this represents. If you don't know, check part 13.7b on the next page, then 13.7c on the next page, and so forth. After seeing the complete version, Figure 13.7e, you will "see" the object even in the simplest version, 13.7a, and you will continue to recognize this object even an hour or more later. The Gollins picture test includes a whole series of different objects like this. H. M. does not improve quite as much as normal on this test, but he does improve. That is, after seeing the later versions, he has a better chance of recognizing the simplified originals, even after a delay, and even though he says he does not remember doing this task before (Warrington & Weiskrantz, 1968).

He also shows much more *implicit* than *explicit* memory. **Explicit memory** is deliberate recall of information that one recognizes as a memory. It is tested by such questions as "Who were the main characters in the last novel you read?" **Implicit memory** is the influence of recent experience on behavior, even if one does not realize that one is using memory. For example, you might be talking to someone about sports while other people nearby are carrying on a conversation about the latest movies. You ignore the other conversation, and if asked, you could not say what they were talking about, but suddenly,

Figure 13.7a The Gollins picture test
What is this object? If you are not sure—as most people are not—flip the page to see Figure 13b. If you are still not sure, flip additional pages to see Figure 13c, d, and e. After seeing the complete picture, most people can recognize it in the fragment even an hour or more later. Patient H. M. also improves on this task, even though each time he attempts it he doesn't remember having tried it before.
Source: Gollin, 1960

you comment for no apparent reason, "I wonder what's on at the movies."

Both H. M. and many other amnesic patients show poor explicit memory but nearly normal implicit memory in most but not all situations (Ryan, Althoff, Whitlow, & Cohen, 2000). To explain what is meant by poor explicit and good implicit memory, it is necessary to consider several examples.

First, in one experiment, people viewed a sequence of flashing circles and then were asked whether they guessed that sequence should be called red, yellow, or green. For each sequence, one of those answers was usually considered correct, but not always. After sufficient practice, normal people can describe which sequence is usually associated with which color name. Amnesic patients do not express this explicit memory, but they do guess the correct answer more often than by chance (Ptak, Gutbrod, Perrig, & Schnider, 2001). Their correct answers can be considered a kind of implicit memory.

Here is another example: Have you ever played the video game Tetris? In the game, geometrical forms such as ⬜⬜ and ⬚ fall from the top, and the player must move and rotate them to fill available spaces at the bottom of the screen. Normal people develop a high level of skill within a few hours of playing and can describe the game and its strategy. Amnesic patients after playing the same number of hours cannot describe the game and say they don't remember ever playing it. Nevertheless, they improve—a little—in their performance. Moreover, when they are about to fall asleep, they report seeing images of little piles of blocks falling and rotating (Stickgold, Malia, Maguire, Roddenberry, & O'Connor, 2000). They are puzzled and wondered what these images are all about.

Still another example of implicit memory in an amnesic patient: As an experiment, three hospital workers agreed to act in special ways toward one brain-damaged patient. One was as pleasant as possible at all times; the second was neutral; the third was stern,

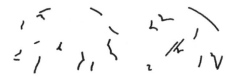

Figure 13.7b   The Gollins picture test
See instruction on page 397.

refused all requests, and made the patient perform boring tasks. After 5 days, the patient was asked to look at photos of the three workers and try to identify them or say anything he knew about them. He said he did not recognize any of them. (He had severe memory problems.) Then he was asked which one he would approach as a possible friend or which one he would ask for help. He was asked this question repeatedly—it was possible to ask repeatedly because he never remembered being asked before—and he usually chose the photo of the "friendly" person and never chose the "unfriendly" person in spite of the fact that the "unfriendly" person was a beautiful woman, smiling in the photograph (Tranel & Damasio, 1993). However, he couldn't say why he preferred one to the other.

In summary, H. M. and similar amnesic patients have:

- Normal short-term or working memory
- Severe anterograde amnesia for declarative memory—that is, difficulty forming new declarative memories
- Moderate retrograde amnesia—loss of some memories from before the brain damage
- Intact procedural memory
- Better implicit than explicit memory

Theories of the Function of the Hippocampus

Exactly how does the hippocampus contribute to memory? H. M. did not lose old memories from before his damage, and neither do other patients with hippocampal damage. Studies on rats and mice confirm that the hippocampus is important for storing long-term memories, but once they are well consolidated, they depend on the cerebral cortex and not the hippocampus (Bontempi, Laurent-Demir, Destrade, & Jaffard, 1999).

Still the hippocampus is more important for storing some kinds of information than others—remember, H. M. could learn new procedures much better than new facts, and his implicit memory is

relatively intact. Researchers have been trying to describe exactly which kinds of memory depend on the hippocampus, and the question has proved to be more difficult than it might appear.

The Hippocampus and Declarative Memory

One hypothesis is that the hippocampus is critical for declarative, explicit memory (Squire, 1992). Certainly, this hypothesis seems to fit the data for H. M. and many other amnesic patients. However, it is difficult to apply this hypothesis to the data for laboratory animals. Nonhuman animals cannot "declare" or explicitly describe any memories.

Can we at least say that hippocampal damage impairs nonhumans on tasks that resemble humans' declarative memories? Consider one example, usually studied in monkeys: In a **delayed matching-to-sample task,** an animal sees an object (the sample) and then, after a delay, gets a choice between two objects, from which it must choose the one that matches the sample. In the **delayed nonmatching-to-sample task,** the procedure is the same except that the animal must choose the object that is different from the sample (Figure 13.8). In both, cases the task is to recognize which stimulus is familiar and which is new.

These tasks, which can be described as declarative memory, are often strongly impaired by hippocampal damage (Zola et al., 2000). The monkey is indicating, "This is like [or unlike] the object I just saw." Unfortunately for theorists, performance varies enormously with what seem like minor changes in procedure. For example, if the delayed matching- or nonmatching-to-sample task uses constantly changing varieties of objects, then hippocampal damage greatly impairs performance. However, if the same two objects are used repeatedly, hippocampal damage has little effect, even though both versions of the task would appear to tap declarative memory (Aggleton, Blindt, & Rawlins, 1989).

In humans, many declarative memories are **episodic memories,** which are memories of single events. Researchers have tried to study whether hippocampally damaged rats are particularly impaired on

Monkey lifts sample object to get food.   Food is under the new object.

Figure 13.8   Procedure for delayed nonmatching-to-sample task

episodic memories. "How could you test that in rats?" you might ask. One attempt is this: The rat digs food out of five piles of sand, each with a different odor. Then it gets a choice between two of the odors and is rewarded if it goes toward the one it smelled first. Intact rats learn to respond correctly, but rats with hippocampal damage do poorly (Fortin, Agster, & Eichenbaum, 2002; Kesner, Gilbert, & Barua, 2002). These results could indicate that hippocampal damage impairs memories for temporal sequences of events or perhaps episodic memories in general. However, another interpretation is simply that hippocampal damage impairs performance on very difficult tasks.

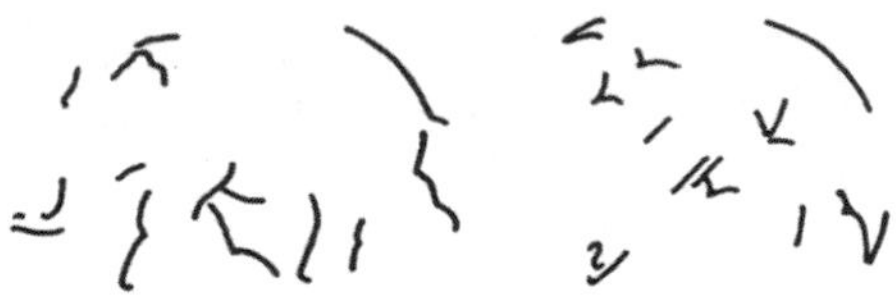

The Hippocampus and Spatial Memory

A second hypothesis is that the hippocampus is especially important for spatial memories. Electrical recordings have indicated that many neurons in a rat's hippocampus are tuned to particular spatial locations, responding best when an animal is in a particular place (O'Keefe & Burgess, 1996) or looking in a particular direction (Dudchenko & Taube, 1997; Rolls, 1996a).

In one study, researchers conducted PET scans on the brains of London taxi drivers as they answered questions such as, "What's the shortest legal route from the Carlton Tower Hotel to the Sherlock Holmes Museum?" (London taxi drivers are well trained and answer with impressive accuracy.) Answering these route questions activated their hippocampus much more than did answering nonspatial questions. MRI scans also revealed that the taxi drivers have a larger than average posterior hippocampus and that, the longer they had been taxi drivers, the larger their posterior hippocampus (Maguire, Frackowiak, & Frith, 2000). This surprising result suggests actual growth of the adult human hippocampus in response to spatial learning experiences.

People with hippocampal damage show impairments on tests of spatial memory. For example, one task is to find your way from one place to another. A second task is to observe objects in a room and then sketch their positions on a map of the room (Bohbot, Allen, & Nadel, 2000).

Consider a couple of nonhuman examples of spatial memory. A radial maze has eight or more arms, some of which have a bit of food or other reinforcer at the end (Figure 13.9). A rat placed in the center can find food by exploring each arm once and only once. In a variation of the task, a rat might have to learn that the arms with a rough floor never have food or that the arms pointing toward the window never have food. So a rat can make a mistake either by entering a never-correct arm or by entering a correct arm twice.

Rats with damage to the hippocampus seldom enter the never-correct arms, but they often enter a correct arm twice. That is, they forget which arms they have already tried (Jarrard, Okaichi, Steward, & Goldschmidt,

Figure 13.7c The Gollins picture test
See instruction on page 397.

1984; Olton & Papas, 1979; Olton, Walker, & Gage, 1978). We might consider this task declarative memory, but note that it also taps spatial memory.

Hippocampal damage impairs performance on another test of spatial memory, the Morris search task, in which a rat must swim through murky water to find a rest platform that is just under the surface (Figure 13.10). (Rats swim as little as they can. Humans are about the only land mammals that swim recreationally.) A rat with hippocampal damage finds the platform. If it always starts from the same place and the rest platform is always in the same place, it gradually learns the route. However, if it has to start from a different location, or if the rest platform occasionally moves from one location to another, the rat has much trouble finding the platform (Eichenbaum, 2000; Liu & Bilkey, 2001). Similarly, if it has to learn on dry land how to get from one place to another, it learns slowly and forgets rapidly compared to rats without hippocampal damage (Ramos, 2001).

Particularly compelling evidence for the role of the hippocampus in spatial memory comes from comparisons of closely related species that differ in their spatial memory. Clark's nutcracker, a member of the jay family, lives year-round at high altitudes in western North America. During the summer and fall, it buries seeds in thousands of locations. Unlike squirrels, which bury nuts but often cannot find them, nut-

Figure 13.9 A radial maze
A rat that reenters one arm before trying other arms has made an error of spatial working memory.

Figure 13.7d The Gollins picture test
See instruction on page 397.

crackers return to their hiding places in the winter and find enough to survive when no other food is available. Pinyon jays, which live at slightly lower elevations, bury less food and depend on it less to survive the winter. Scrub jays and Mexican jays, living at still lower altitudes, depend even less on stored food. Researchers have found that of these four species, the Clark's nutcrackers have the largest hippocampus and perform best on radial mazes and other laboratory tests of spatial memory. Pinyon jays are second best in both respects. On nonspatial tasks, such as color memory, size of the hippocampus does not correlate with success (Basil, Kamil, Balda, & Fite, 1996; Olson, Kamil, Balda, & Nims, 1995) (Figure 13.11). In short, the species comparisons support a link between the hippocampus and spatial memory.

However, even while an animal is performing a single task, some parts of the hippocampus code spatial information, and others code nonspatial aspects of the task (Hampson, Simeral, & Deadwyler, 1999). Thus, the hippocampus is important for spatial tasks, but not exclusively. Hippocampal damage impairs performance on many tasks that have nothing to do with spatial orientation, so the role of the hippocampus cannot be exclusively spatial.

The Hippocampus, Configural Learning, and Binding

The third prominent hypothesis has been modified over the years. An early version of it was that the hippocampus is necessary for **configural learning,** in which the meaning of a stimulus depends on what other stimuli are paired with it. For example, an animal might have to learn that stimulus A signals food, B also signals food, but a combination of both A and B signals no food. Or people might have to learn to choose a square over a triangle, a triangle over a circle, and a circle over a square:

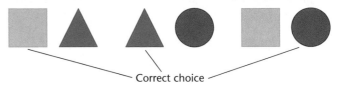

In many cases, hippocampal damage impairs configural learning (Rickard & Grafman, 1998). However, hippocampal damage also impairs memory on nonconfigural tasks when they are sufficiently difficult (Reed & Squire, 1999). In addition, hippocampally damaged animals do eventually (though slowly) learn difficult configural tasks. Consequently, the original idea that the hippocampus is *necessary* for configural learning has been abandoned.

A modified version is that the hippocampus is specialized to quickly record combinations of stimuli that occur together at a single time, whereas the cerebral cortex detects combinations that occur repeatedly (O'Reilly & Rudy, 2001). By this view, the hippocampus is not really necessary for configural learning; the cerebral cortex can handle such learn-

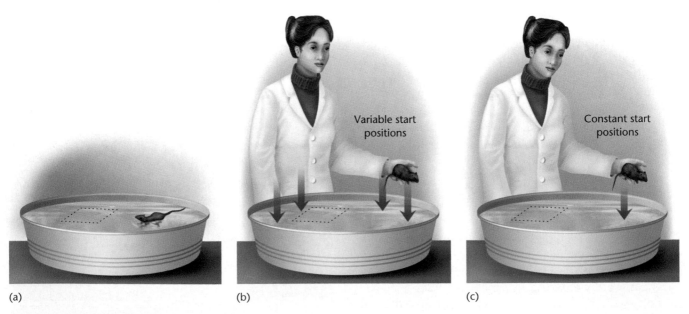

(a) (b) (c)

Figure 13.10 The Morris search task
A rat is placed in murky water. A platform that would provide support is submerged so the rat can feel but not see it. Rats with hippocampal damage have trouble remembering the location of the platform.

ing if given enough opportunity. However, hippocampal damage impairs memory of single events, such as episodic memories.

Here is an elaboration of this theory: At any moment, you experience many sights, sounds, and so forth. Your representation connects them all in some way. Later, you get a reminder, which causes you to reinstate as much of the collection as you can. Memory therefore requires a connection or binding of various pieces of the experience. The role of the hippocampus may be not so much to establish the memory itself, but to bind the pieces together or to lay out a map of where all the separate pieces are stored so that later they can be brought together again. The rich interconnections between the hippocampus and the rest of the forebrain make it well suited to this function (Rolls, 1996b). Obviously, much more research is needed, but this theory has the potential to encompass the importance of the hippocampus in declarative memory and complex spatial memory, as well as single-event configural memory.

The Hippocampus and Adrenal Hormones

According to one final hypothesis, the effect of hippocampal damage on memory is not entirely (maybe not even mainly) due to interruption of its connections with other brain areas but is instead due to the fact that the hippocampus influences the release of hormones from the adrenal gland. After damage to the

Figure 13.7e   The Gollins picture test
See instruction on page 397.

	Habitat	Size of Hippocampus Relative to Rest of Brain	Spatial Memory	Color Memory
Clark's nutcracker 	Lives high in mountains; stores food in summer and relies on finding it to survive the winter.	Largest	Best	Slightly worse
Pinyon jay 	Lives at fairly high altitude; depends on stored food to survive the winter.	Second largest	Second best	Slightly better
Scrub jay 	Stores some food but less dependent on it.	Smaller	Less good	Slightly worse
Mexican jay 	Stores some food but less dependent on it.	Smaller	Less good	Slightly better

Figure 13.11   Hippocampus and spatial memory in jays
Of four species of the jay family, all living in western North America, the species that rely most heavily on stored food to get through the winter have the largest hippocampus and perform best on laboratory tests of spatial memory. They have no consistent advantage on nonspatial memory. *Source: Based on results of Basil, Kamil, Balda, & Fite, 1996; Olson, Kamil, Balda, & Nims, 1995*

hippocampus, adrenal hormone secretion increases. Recall from Chapter 12 that stress releases adrenal hormones, such as cortisol or corticosterone. A small increase in cortisol readies the body for appropriate actions, but prolonged release compromises the brain's activities. Researchers have found that hippocampal damage in rats elevates adrenal hormone release at the same time that it impairs spatial memory. If hippocampally damaged rats receive drugs that block the surge of hormones, then their spatial memory returns to normal (Roozendaal et al., 2001).

This hypothesis does not really compete with the first three. Hippocampal damage still impairs certain kinds of memory more than others. The difference is that we might have to look for a different kind of explanation of why the damage affects memory at all.

---

5. What is the difference between retrograde and anterograde amnesia?

6. Which types of memory are least impaired in H. M.?

7. What are four views of the contribution of the hippocampus to memory formation?

Check your answers on page 406.

OTHER TYPES OF BRAIN DAMAGE AND AMNESIA

Learning and memory depend on many brain areas, and different kinds of brain damage produce different types of amnesia. Here we examine two more disorders: Korsakoff's syndrome and Alzheimer's disease.

Korsakoff's Syndrome and Other Prefrontal Damage

Korsakoff's syndrome, also known as *Wernicke-Korsakoff syndrome,* is brain damage caused by prolonged thiamine deficiency. Severe thiamine deficiency occurs mostly in chronic alcoholics who go for weeks at a time on a diet of nothing but alcoholic beverages, which contain carbohydrates but no vitamins. The brain needs thiamine (vitamin B_1) to metabolize glucose, its primary fuel. Prolonged thiamine deficiency leads to a loss or shrinkage of neurons throughout the brain, especially in the mamillary bodies (part of the hypothalamus) and in the dorsomedial thalamus, a nucleus that sends axons to the prefrontal cortex (Squire, Amaral, & Press, 1990; Victor, Adams, & Collins, 1971). Therefore, the symptoms of Korsakoff's syndrome are similar to those of people with damage to the prefrontal cortex, including apathy, confusion, and both retrograde and anterograde amnesia. Hospitals in large cities report about 1 person with Korsakoff's syndrome per 1000 admissions. Treatment with thiamine sometimes helps, but the longer someone has been thiamine deficient, the poorer the outlook.

To illustrate one aspect of memory in Korsakoff's syndrome, try this demonstration. Here are the first three letters of some words. For each, fill in letters to make any complete word:

met_____ pro_____ con_____
per _____ thi _____ def _____

(Please try the demonstration before reading further.)

Each of these three-letter combinations can start many English words; *pro-, con-,* and *per-* start well over 50 each. Did you happen to fill in any of the following: *metabolize, prolonged, confusion, person, thiamine, deficient?* These six words were in the paragraph just before the demonstration. After you had read the words, you were *primed* to think of them. **Priming,** one type of implicit memory, is the phenomenon that seeing or hearing words temporarily increases one's probability of using them. Patients with Korsakoff's syndrome sometimes read a list of words and then show strong priming effects on a fill-in-the-rest-of-the-word task, even though they don't remember even seeing a list of words, much less remember what the words were (Schacter, 1985). That is, like H. M., people with Korsakoff's syndrome show better implicit than explicit memory.

Korsakoff's patients and other patients with frontal lobe damage have difficulties in reasoning about their memories, such as deciding the order of events (Moscovitch, 1992). Suppose I ask, "Which happened to you most recently—graduation from high school, getting your first driver's license, or reading Chapter 2 of *Biological Psychology?*" You reason it out: "I started driving during my junior year of high school so that came before graduation. *Biological Psychology* is one of my college texts, so I started reading it after high school." A person with frontal lobe damage has trouble with even this simple kind of reasoning.

A distinctive symptom of Korsakoff's syndrome is **confabulation,** in which the patient takes a guess at the answer and then accepts that guess as if it were a memory. For questions about the patient's own life, the guess is almost always an answer that was true in the past but not now, such as, "I went dancing last night." Some patients, though not all, are consistent in their confabulations. For example, when asked how long he had been in the hospital, one patient always responded, "Since yesterday" (Burgess & McNeil, 1999). Much of the problem seems to be that patients have trouble inhibiting an answer they have previously made.

In one study, patients were shown a series of photos and then shown some additional photos and asked which ones matched photos in that series. They did reasonably well up to this point. Then they were shown a second series of photos and again were asked which of several new photos matched the ones in the series they just saw. The patients generally said "yes" to photos that had been on the first list even though they were not on the second (Schnider & Ptak, 1999). They were unable to suppress an answer that was correct previously.

The tendency to confabulate produces a fascinating influence on the strategies for studying. Suppose you had to learn a long list of three-word sentences such as: "Medicine cured hiccups" and "Tourist desired snapshot." Would you simply read the list many times? Or would you alternate between reading the list and testing yourself?

Medicine cured _____.

Tourist desired _____.

Almost everyone learns better the second way. Completing the sentences forces you to be more active and calls your attention to the items you have not yet learned. Korsakoff's patients, however, learn much better the first way, by reading the list over and over. The reason is, when they test themselves, they confabulate. ("Medicine cured headache. Tourist desired passport.") Then they remember their confabulation instead of the correct answer (Hamann & Squire, 1995).

Alzheimer's Disease ✳

Another cause of severe memory loss is **Alzheimer's** (AHLTZ-hime-ers) **disease,** which starts with minor forgetfulness but progresses to serious memory loss, confusion, depression, restlessness, hallucinations, delusions, sleeplessness, and loss of appetite. Most older people experience minor forgetfulness and some decrease in cortical and hippocampal functioning, but Alzheimer's disease is far more severe (Morrison & Hof, 1997). Alzheimer's disease occasionally strikes people younger than age 40 but becomes more common with age, affecting almost 5% of people in the 65–74-year range and almost 50% of people over 85 (D. A. Evans et al., 1989).

The early symptoms of Alzheimer's disease include memory lapses. For example, Daniel Schacter (1983) reported playing golf with an Alzheimer's patient who remembered the rules and jargon of the game correctly but could not remember how many strokes he took on any hole. On five occasions, he teed off, waited for the other player to tee off, and then teed off again, having forgotten his first shot.

As with H. M. and Korsakoff's patients, Alzheimer's patients have better procedural than declarative memory. They learn new hand skills but then are surprised by their good performance on a task they don't remember ever doing before (Gabrieli, Corkin, Mickel, & Growdon, 1993). Alzheimer's patients also show a bigger deficit on explicit than on implicit memory, although they also have moderate impairments on implicit memory as well (Meiran & Jelicic, 1995), probably because of impaired attention (Randolph, Tierney, & Chase, 1995).

The first clue to the genetics of Alzheimer's was the fact that people with *Down syndrome* (a type of mental retardation) almost invariably get Alzheimer's disease if they survive into middle age (Lott, 1982). Down syndrome is caused by having three copies of chromosome 21 rather than the usual two. This fact led investigators to examine chromosome 21, where in fact they did find a gene linked to many cases of early-onset Alzheimer's disease (Goate et al., 1991; Murrell, Farlow, Ghetti, & Benson, 1991). Later researchers found a gene on chromosome 14 that is associated with 70% of early-onset Alzheimer's disease (Schellenberg et al., 1992; Sherrington et al., 1995) and another gene on chromosome 1 that is associated with a few more cases of the early-onset disease (Levy-Lahad et al., 1995).

However, more than 99% of cases have a late onset, after age 60 to 65. Researchers have identified genes on chromosomes 10 and 19 that increase the risk of late-onset Alzheimer's disease (Bertram et al., 2000; Corder et al., 1993; Ertekin-Taner et al., 2000; Myers et al., 2000; Pericak-Vance et al., 1991; Strittmatter & Roses, 1995), but these genes account for only a minority of the cases. In fact, about half of all patients have no known relatives with the disease (St George-Hyslop, 2000).

Further evidence that genes do not hold the whole explanation for late-onset Alzheimer's disease comes from cross-cultural studies. The Yoruba people of Nigeria have a much lower incidence of Alzheimer's than do Americans, including African Americans. Genes that produce a high risk of Alzheimer's disease in the United States occur among the Yoruba but do not elevate their risk. The most likely explanation is that the Yorubas' low-calorie, low-fat, low-sodium diet decreases their vulnerability (Hendrie, 2001).

Although genes do not completely control Alzheimer's disease, understanding their mode of action can shed light on the underlying causes. The emerging pattern is that Alzheimer's disease is caused by brain proteins that fail to fold in the normal way and therefore clump together with one another and interfere with normal neuronal activity. The same general idea holds for Parkinson's disease and several other brain diseases, although each is associated with a different abnormal protein (Taylor, Hardy, & Fischbeck, 2002).

Two kinds of abnormal proteins accumulate in Alzheimer's disease, as shown in Figure 13.12. *Amyloid* produces **plaques,** structures formed from degenerating axons and dendrites. *Tau* produces

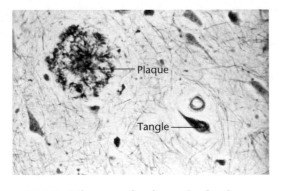

Figure 13.12 Microscopic view of a brain area in an Alzheimer's patient
An amyloid plaque is composed of the protein Aβ₄₂.
A tangle is composed of the protein tau.

tangles, structures formed from degenerating structures within neuronal cell bodies. Tangles form within cells; plaques form in the spaces between neurons.

The genes controlling early-onset Alzheimer's disease lead to the accumulation of amyloid. Brain cells contain a large protein called *amyloid precursor protein,* which is *cleaved* (broken) to form a smaller protein. In most people, it is cleaved mostly into a protein of 40 amino acids, called $A\beta_{40}$, which presumably serves some useful (though currently unknown) function. However, in people with any of the genes for early-onset Alzheimer's disease, amyloid precursor protein is cleaved mostly to a slightly longer protein with 42 amino acids, **amyloid beta protein 42 ($A\beta_{42}$),** which accumulates, clumps with other $A\beta_{42}$ molecules, and damages the membranes of axons and dendrites (Lorenzo et al., 2000). Much evidence favors the importance of $A\beta_{42}$ in the onset of Alzheimer's. Most Alzheimer's patients accumulate amyloid plaques containing $A\beta_{42}$ before the onset of behavioral symptoms (Selkoe, 2000). Amyloid deposits produce widespread atrophy (wasting away) of the cerebral cortex, hippocampus, and other areas, as Figures 13.13 and 13.14 show.

However, the accumulation of $A\beta_{42}$, by itself, impairs certain types of learning and memory (Chen et al., 2000; Walsh et al., 2002) but does not produce the full range of Alzheimer's

symptoms. Along with $A\beta_{42}$, Alzheimer's patients also accumulate an abnormal form of the **tau** protein that is part of the intracellular support structure of neurons; the symptoms of the disease depend on tau as well as $A\beta_{42}$ (Davies, 2000). Tau proteins clump together to form tangles inside neurons, as shown in Figure 13.12.

Analysis of the genes predisposing to late-onset Alzheimer's disease suggests yet another possibility. The late-onset genes alter the receptors for a chemical apolipoprotein E, which is produced mostly by glia although it affects neurons also (Herz & Beffert, 2000). Apolipoprotein E is important for growth of axons and dendrites and perhaps for neuron survival, so an impairment of this protein could lead to cell loss. It is also likely that abnormalities of this protein interfere with the brain's ability to remove $A\beta_{42}$ molecules. (The brain is a complicated organ in which changing any element influences others and then still others.)

Although these biochemical details remain complex and sometimes confusing, the net outcome is clear: The buildup of abnormal chemicals damages many brain areas, prominently including the basal forebrain, whose cells arouse the rest of the cortex (as discussed in Chapter 9). Many of the behavioral problems follow from the impaired arousal and attention.

What can we do to prevent or alleviate Alzheimer's disease? For years, medicine had little to offer. Then researchers found that elevating patients' blood glucose enhanced their memory. This result would seem logical, as the brain depends on glucose for nutrition. However, as you remember from Chapter 10, an increase in blood glucose leads to an increase in insulin secretion, and later researchers have found that insulin enhances memory much more than glucose alone does (Craft et al., 1999). People with Type II (adult-onset) diabetes produce large amounts of insulin but have fewer than

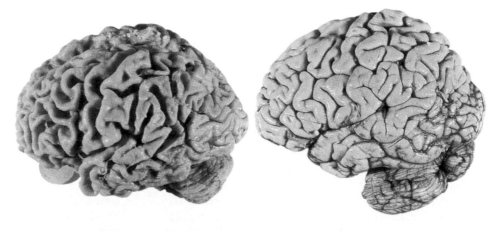

Figure 13.13 Brain atrophy in Alzheimer's disease
In the cerebral cortex of an Alzheimer's patient **(a)**, the gyri are clearly shrunk in comparison with those of a normal person **(b)**. *Source: Photos courtesy of Dr. Robert D. Terry*

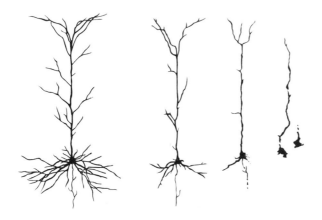

(a)   (b)

Figure 13.14 Neuronal degeneration in Alzheimer's disease
(a) A cell in the prefrontal cortex of a normal human.
(b) Cells from the same area of cortex in Alzheimer's disease patients at various stages of deterioration. Note the shrinkage of the dendritic tree. *Source: After "Dendritic Changes," by A. B. Scheibel, p. 70. In B. Reisberg, Ed.,* Alzheimer's Disease, *1983, Free Press.*

the normal number of insulin receptors. The fact that people with Type II diabetes seldom get Alzheimer's disease further strengthens the suggestion of a relationship between Alzheimer's disease and a deficiency of insulin (Nolan & Wright, 2001).

Another possibility is to give drugs that stimulate acetylcholine receptors or prolong acetylcholine release (McDonald, Willard, Wenk, & Crawley, 1998). One of the main areas damaged is the basal forebrain, which arouses brain activity via axons containing acetylcholine. Enhanced acetylcholine activity increases some aspects of memory even in healthy people (Furey, Pietrini, & Haxby, 2000).

Researchers also are evaluating new ways to block $A\beta_{42}$ production and stimulate surviving cells to become more active (Selkoe, 1999). Even diet shows some prospects. Research with rats indicates that a diet rich in antioxidants guards against a variety of brain degeneration diseases. So eat your spinach and strawberries and take a vitamin E pill (Joseph et al., 1998).

Finally, research with mice suggests this fascinating possibility: One genetic strain of mice, the PDAPP mouse, overproduces $A\beta_{42}$ and develops symptoms resembling human Alzheimer's disease. Researchers have found that if they inject small amounts of $A\beta_{42}$ into a young mouse, the mouse's immune system attacked it and increased its ability to continue attacking it. Later in life, the mouse developed few if any of the learning deficits that usually occur in this strain of mice (Janus et al., 2000; Morgan et al., 2000; Schenk et al., 1999).

For links to more information about Alzheimer's disease, see this Web site:
www.alzforum.org/default.asp

What Amnesic Patients Teach Us

The study of amnesic patients reveals that people do not lose all aspects of memory equally. A patient with great difficulty establishing new memories may be able to remember events from long ago, and someone with greatly impaired factual memory may be able to learn new skills reasonably well. Evidently, people have several somewhat independent kinds of memory that depend on different brain areas.

8. Most people learn a list better if they alternate between studying the list and testing their memory of it. What kind of patient learns best by studying without testing themselves? Why?
9. What is $A\beta_{42}$ and how does it relate to Alzheimer's disease?

Check your answers on page 406.

MODULE 13.1

In Closing: Different Types of Memory

"Overall intelligence," as measured by an IQ test, is a convenient fiction. It is convenient because, under most circumstances, people who are good at one kind of intellectual task are also good at other kinds, so an overall test score makes useful predictions. However, it is a fiction because different kinds of abilities rely on different brain processes, and it is possible to damage one without another. Even memory is composed of separate abilities, and it is possible to lose one type or aspect of memory without impairing others. The study of amnesia shows how the brain operates as a series of partly independent mechanisms serving specific purposes.

SUMMARY

1. Ivan Pavlov suggested that learning depends on the growth of a connection between two brain areas. Karl Lashley showed that learning does *not* depend on new connections across the cerebral cortex. (p. 388)
2. Later researchers have demonstrated that, in certain cases, classical conditioning takes place in small areas within the cerebellum. More complex learning undoubtedly requires more widespread changes. (p. 390)

3. Psychologists distinguish between short-term and long-term memory. Short-term memory holds only a small amount of information and retains it only briefly unless it is constantly rehearsed. Long-term memory retains vast amounts of material indefinitely, but recalling this information sometimes requires great effort. (p. 392)

4. The consolidation of short-term memories into long-term memories depends more on arousal than on the mere passage of time. Arousing events increase the release of epinephrine and cortisol, which directly or indirectly stimulate the amygdala. The amygdala enhances activity in the hippocampus and cerebral cortex. (p. 393)

5. Working memory, a modern alternative to the concept of short-term memory, stores information temporarily while one is using it. The prefrontal cortex and other areas can store working memories through repetitive cellular activity. (p. 394)

6. People with damage to the hippocampus, such as the patient H. M., have great trouble forming new long-term declarative memories, although they can still recall events from before the damage and can still form new procedural memories. (p. 395)

7. The hippocampus is important for some kinds of learning and memory but not all. According to various hypotheses, the hippocampus is critical for declarative memory, spatial memory, or memory of configurations of events that happen together on a single occasion. It appears that much of the impairment caused by hippocampal damage relates to increased release of adrenal stress hormones after the damage. (p. 398)

8. Patients with Korsakoff's syndrome or other types of prefrontal damage have impairments of memory, including difficulty drawing inferences from memories. They often fill in their memory gaps with confabulations, which they then remember as if they were true. (p. 402)

9. Alzheimer's disease is a progressive disease, most common in old age, that is characterized by a severe impairment of memory and attention. It is caused partly by the deposition of amyloid in the brain and partly by an abnormal form of the protein tau. (p. 403)

ANSWERS TO *STOP AND CHECK* QUESTIONS

1. Thompson studied a different, probably simpler type of learning. Also, he looked in the cerebellum instead of the cerebral cortex. (p. 392)

2. If the red nucleus is inactivated during training, the animal makes no conditioned responses during the training, so the red nucleus is necessary for the response. However, as soon as the red nucleus recovers, the animal can show conditioned responses at once, without any further training, so learning occurred while the red nucleus was inactivated. (p. 392)

3. Epinephrine stimulates receptors on the vagus nerve, which excites cells in the brainstem, which in turn activate the amygdala. Epinephrine and cortisol both enhance emotional memories by stimulating the amygdala. (p. 395)

4. The dorsolateral prefrontal cortex maintains activity during the delay, presumably holding a representation of the sensory stimulus. (p. 395)

5. Retrograde amnesia is forgetting events before brain damage; anterograde amnesia is failing to store memories of events after brain damage. (p. 402)

6. H. M. is least impaired on short-term memory, procedural memory, implicit memory, and memory of events that occurred more than 1 to 3 years before his surgery. (p. 402)

7. Various theorists emphasize the importance of the hippocampus for declarative memory, spatial memory, and single-occurrence configural memory. Research also indicates that hippocampal damage impairs brain activity by increasing the release of stress hormones. (p. 402)

8. Patients with Korsakoff's syndrome learn best if they don't test themselves because when they do test themselves they confabulate answers and later remember their confabulations instead of the correct answers. (p. 405)

9. $A\beta_{42}$ is a protein that accumulates in the brains of patients with Alzheimer's disease and causes the growth of plaques. (p. 405)

THOUGHT QUESTIONS

1. Lashley sought to find the engram, the physiological representation of learning. In general terms, how would you recognize an engram if you saw one? That is, what would someone have to demonstrate before you could conclude that a particular change in the nervous system was really an engram?

2. Benzodiazepine tranquilizers impair memory. Use what you have learned in this chapter and the previous one to propose an explanation.

MODULE 13.2

Storing Information in the Nervous System

Anything you see, hear, or do leaves traces in your nervous system. Which of these many traces are important for memory?

If you walk through a field, are the footprints that you leave "memories"? How about the mud that you pick up on your shoes? If the police wanted to know who walked across that field, a forensics expert could check your shoes to answer the question. And yet we would not call these physical traces memories in the usual sense.

Similarly, when a pattern of activity passes through the brain, it leaves a path of physical changes, but not everything that changes is really a memory. The task of finding how the brain stores memories is a little like searching for the proverbial needle in a haystack, and researchers have explored many avenues that seemed promising for a while but now seem fruitless.

EXTENSIONS AND APPLICATIONS
Blind Alleys and Abandoned Mines

Textbooks, this one included, concentrate mostly on successful research that led to our current understanding of a subject. You may get the impression that science progresses smoothly and that each investigator contributes to an ever-accumulating body of knowledge. However, if you look at the old journals or textbooks, you will find discussions of various "promising" or "exciting" findings that we disregard today. Scientific research does not progress straight from ignorance to enlightenment; it explores one direction after another, a little like a rat in a complex maze, abandoning the arms that lead nowhere and pursuing those that lead further.

The problem with the maze analogy is that an investigator seldom runs into a wall that clearly identifies the end of a route. Perhaps a better analogy is a prospector digging in one location after another, never entirely certain whether to abandon an unprofitable spot or to keep digging a little longer. Many once-exciting lines of research in the physiology of learning are now of little more than historical interest. Here are three examples.

1. Wilder Penfield sometimes performed brain surgery for severe epilepsy on conscious patients who had only scalp anesthesia. When he applied a brief, weak electrical stimulus to part of the brain, the patient could describe the experience that the stimulation evoked. Stimulation of the temporal cortex sometimes evoked vivid descriptions such as:

   I feel as though I were in the bathroom at school.

   I see myself at the corner of Jacob and Washington in South Bend, Indiana.

   I remember myself at the railroad station in Vanceburg, Kentucky; it is winter and the wind is blowing outside, and I am waiting for a train.

   Penfield (1955; Penfield & Perot, 1963) suggested that each neuron stores a particular memory, almost like a videotape of one's life. However, brain stimulation very rarely elicited a memory of a specific event, more often evoking vague sights and sounds or repeated experiences such as "seeing a bed" or "hearing a choir sing 'White Christmas.'" Stimulation almost never elicited memories of doing anything—just of seeing and hearing. Also, some patients reported events that they had never actually experienced, such as being chased by a robber or seeing Christ descend from the sky. In short, the stimulation produced something more like a dream than a memory.

2. G. A. Horridge (1962) apparently demonstrated that decapitated cockroaches can learn. First he cut the connections between a cockroach's head and the rest of its body. Then he suspended the cockroach so that its legs dangled just above a surface of water. An electrical circuit was arranged, as Figure 13.15 shows, so that the roach's leg received a shock whenever it touched the water. Each experimental roach was paired with a control roach that got a leg shock whenever the first roach did; only the experimental roach had any control over the shock, however. (This kind of experiment is known as a "yoked-control" design.)

   Over 5 to 10 minutes, roaches in the experimental group "learned" a response of tucking the leg under the body to avoid shocks. Roaches in the control

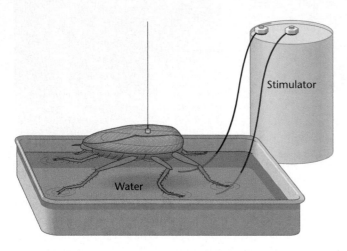

Figure 13.15 Learning in a headless cockroach?
The decapitated cockroach, suspended just above the water, receives a shock whenever its hind leg touches the water. A cockroach in the control group gets a shock whenever the first roach does, regardless of its own behavior. According to some reports, the experimental roach learned to keep its leg out of the water. *Source: From G. A. Horridge, "Learning of Leg Position by the Ventral Nerve Cord in Headless Insects." Proceedings of the Royal Society of London, B, 157, 1962, 33–52. Copyright ©1962 the Royal Society of London. Reprinted by permission of the Royal Society of London and G. A. Horridge.*

group did not, on the average, change their leg position during the training period. Thus, the changed response apparently qualifies as learning and not as some accidental by-product of the shocks.

These experiments initially seemed a promising way to study learning in a very simple nervous system, a single cockroach ganglion (Eisenstein & Cohen, 1965). Unfortunately, decapitated cockroaches learn slowly, and the results vary sharply from one individual to another, limiting the usefulness of the results. After a handful of studies, interest in this line of research faded.

3. In the 1960s and early 1970s, several investigators proposed that each memory is coded as a specific molecule, probably RNA or protein. The boldest test of this hypothesis was an attempt to transfer memories chemically from one individual to another. James McConnell (1962) reported that, when planaria (flatworms) cannibalized other planaria that had been classically conditioned to respond to a light, they apparently "remembered" what the cannibalized planaria had learned. At least they learned the response faster than planaria generally do.

Inspired by that report, other investigators trained rats to approach a clicking sound for food (Babich, Jacobson, Bubash, & Jacobson, 1965). After the rats were well trained, the experimenters ground up their brains, extracted RNA, and injected it into untrained rats. The recipient rats learned to approach the clicking sound faster than rats in the control group did.

That report led to a sudden flurry of experiments on the transfer of training by brain extracts. In *some* of these experiments, rats that received brain extracts from a trained group showed apparent memory of the task, whereas those that received extracts from an untrained group did not (Dyal, 1971; Fjerdingstad, 1973).

The results were inconsistent and unreplicable, however, even within a single laboratory (L. T. Smith, 1975). Many laboratories failed to find any hint of a transfer effect. By the mid-1970s, most biological psychologists saw no point in continuing this research.

LEARNING AND THE HEBBIAN SYNAPSE

The research that seems most promising today began with Ivan Pavlov's concept of classical conditioning. Although, as we have already seen, that theory led Karl Lashley to an unsuccessful search for connections in the cerebral cortex, it also stimulated Donald Hebb to propose a mechanism for change at a synapse.

Hebb suggested that when the axon of neuron A "repeatedly or persistently takes part in firing [cell B], some growth process or metabolic change takes place in one or both cells" that increases the subsequent ability of axon A to excite cell B (Hebb, 1949, p. 62). In other words, an axon that has successfully stimulated cell B in the past becomes even more successful in the future.

Consider how this process relates to classical conditioning. Suppose axon A initially excites cell B slightly, and axon C excites B more strongly. If A and C fire together, their combined effect on B may produce an action potential. You might think of axon A as the CS and axon C as the UCS. Pairing activity in axons A and C causes an increased effect of A on B in the future. Hebb was noncommittal about whether the change occurred in axon A, cell B, or both.

A synapse that increases in effectiveness because of simultaneous activity in the presynaptic and postsynaptic neurons is called a **Hebbian synapse**. In Chapter 5, we encountered many examples of this type of synapse; in the development of the nervous system, postsynaptic neurons increase their responsiveness to combinations of axons that are active at the same time as one another (and therefore at the same time as the postsynaptic neuron). Such synapses may also be critical for many kinds of associative learning. Neuroscientists have discovered much about the mechanisms of Hebbian (or almost Hebbian) synapses.

SINGLE-CELL MECHANISMS OF INVERTEBRATE BEHAVIOR CHANGE

If we are going to look for a needle in a haystack, a good strategy is to look in a small haystack. Therefore, many researchers have turned to studies of invertebrates. Vertebrate and invertebrate nervous systems are organized differently, but the chemistry of the neuron, the principles of the action potential, and even the neurotransmitters are the same. If we identify the physical basis of learning and memory in an invertebrate, we have at least a hypothesis of what *might* work in vertebrates. (Biologists have long used this strategy for studying genetics, embryology, and other biological processes.)

Aplysia as an Experimental Animal

Aplysia, or sea hare, a marine invertebrate related to the common slug, has been a popular animal for studies of the physiology of learning (Figure 13.16). It has fewer neurons than any vertebrate, and many are large and therefore easy to study. Moreover, unlike vertebrates, *Aplysia* neurons are virtually identical from one individual to another so that different investigators can study the properties of the same neuron.

Much of the research on *Aplysia* concerns changes in behavior as a result of experience. Some of these changes may seem simple, and it is a matter of definition whether we call them *learning* or use the broader term *plasticity.* One commonly studied behavior is the withdrawal response: If someone touches the siphon, mantle, or gill of an *Aplysia* (Figure 13.17), the animal vigorously withdraws the irritated structure. Investiga-

Figure 13.16 *Aplysia,* **a marine mollusk**
A full-grown animal is a little larger than the average human hand.

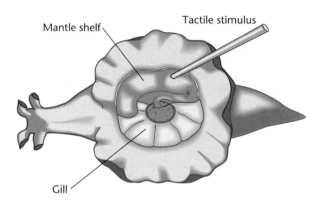

Figure 13.17 Touching an *Aplysia* causes a withdrawal response
The sensory and motor neurons controlling this reaction have been identified and studied.

tors have traced the neural path from the touch receptors through various identifiable interneurons to the motor neurons that direct the withdrawal response. Using this neural pathway, investigators have studied such phenomena as habituation and sensitization.

Habituation in *Aplysia*

Habituation is a decrease in response to a stimulus that is presented repeatedly and accompanied by no change in other stimuli. For example, if your clock chimes each hour, you notice it less after many days. Habituation can be demonstrated in an *Aplysia* by repeatedly stimulating its gills with a brief jet of seawater. At first, it withdraws its gills, but after many repetitions, it stops responding. The decline in response is not due to muscle fatigue because, even after habituation has occurred, direct stimulation of the motor neuron produces a full-sized muscle contraction (Kupfermann, Castellucci, Pinsker, & Kandel, 1970). We can also rule out changes in the sensory neuron. The sensory neuron still gives a full normal response to stimulation; it merely fails to excite the motor neuron as much as before (Kupfermann et al., 1970). We are therefore left with the conclusion that habituation in *Aplysia* depends on a change in the synapse between the sensory neuron and the motor neuron (Figure 13.18).

Sensitization in *Aplysia*

If you experience an unexpected, intense pain, you will probably react more strongly than usual to loud sounds, sharp pinches, and other sudden stimuli in the next few days. This phenomenon is sensitization,

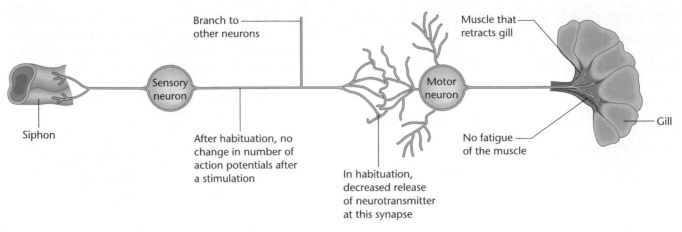

Figure 13.18 Habituation of the gill-withdrawal reflex in *Aplysia*
Touching the siphon causes the gill to withdraw. After many repetitions, the response habituates (declines) because of decreased transmission at the synapse between the sensory neuron and the motor neuron. *Source: Redrawn from "Neuronal Mechanisms of Habituation and Dishabituation of the Gill-Withdrawal Reflex in Aplysia," by V. Castellucci, H. Pinsker, I. Kupfermann, and E. Kandel,* Science, *1970, 167, p. 1745–1748. Copyright ©1970 by the AAAS. Used by permission of AAAS and V. Castellucci.*

an increase in response to mild stimuli as a result of previous exposure to more intense stimuli. Similarly, a strong stimulus almost anywhere on Aplysia's skin can intensify later withdrawal responses to a touch.

Researchers have traced sensitization to changes at identified synapses (Cleary, Hammer, & Byrne, 1989; Dale, Schacher, & Kandel, 1988; Kandel & Schwartz, 1982), as shown in Figure 13.19. Strong stimulation anywhere on the skin excites a particular *facilitating interneuron,* which releases serotonin (5-HT) onto the

presynaptic terminals of many sensory neurons. These are called *presynaptic receptors.* When serotonin attaches to these receptors, it closes potassium channels in the membrane. As you will recall from Chapter 2, potassium flows out of the neuron after the peak of the action potential; the exit of potassium restores the neuron to its usual polarization. When serotonin blocks the potassium channels, the effect is a prolonged action potential in the presynaptic cell and therefore more transmitter release. If the sensitizing stimulus is

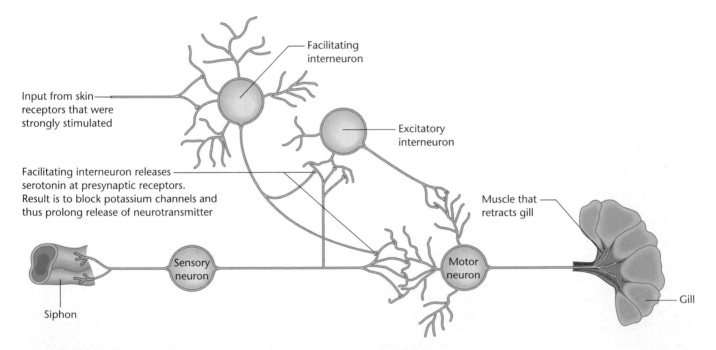

Figure 13.19 Sensitization of the withdrawal response in *Aplysia*
Stimulation of the sensory neuron ordinarily excites the motor neuron, partly by a direct path and partly by stimulation of an excitatory interneuron. Stimulation of a facilitating interneuron releases serotonin to the presynaptic receptors on the sensory neuron, blocking potassium channels and thereby prolonging the release of neurotransmitter. This effect can be long-lasting. *Source: After Kandel & Schwartz, 1982*

repeated, the sensory neuron synthesizes new proteins that produce long-term sensitization (Bailey, Giustetto, Huang, Hawkins, & Kandel, 2000).

The research on *Aplysia* shows us that changes in synaptic activity can produce behavioral plasticity, and in 2000, Eric Kandel won a Nobel Prize for this work. The *Aplysia* research also shows that even sensitization, widely regarded as a fairly simple process, depends on interactions among several neurons and their synapses (Bailey et al., 2000).

Stop & Check

1. How can a Hebbian synapse account for the basic phenomena of classical conditioning?
2. What are the advantages of research on *Aplysia* as compared with vertebrates?
3. When serotonin blocks potassium channels on the presynaptic terminal, what is the effect on transmission?

Check your answers on page 415.

LONG-TERM POTENTIATION IN MAMMALS

Since the work of Sherrington and Cajal, most neuroscientists have assumed that learning depends on some kind of change at the synapses, and the work on *Aplysia* confirms that synaptic changes *can* produce behavioral changes. The first evidence for a similar process among vertebrates came from studies of hippocampal neurons in the 1970s (Bliss & Lømo, 1973). The phenomenon, known as **long-term potentiation (LTP),** is this: One or more axons connected to some dendrite bombard it with a brief but rapid series of stimuli—such as 100 synaptic excitations per second for 1 to 4 seconds. The burst of intense stimulation leaves some of the synapses potentiated (more responsive to new input of the same type) for minutes, days, or weeks.

LTP shows three properties that make it an attractive candidate for a cellular basis of learning and memory:

- **specificity**—If some of the synapses onto a cell have been highly active and others have not, only the active ones become strengthened.
- **cooperativity**—Nearly simultaneous stimulation by two or more axons produces LTP much more

strongly than does repeated stimulation by just one axon. As a result of specificity and cooperativity, if axons A and D are repeatedly active together, while axons B and C are usually inactive, the synapses of A and D become strengthened and those of B and C remain the same or become weaker (Sejnowski, Chattarji, & Stanton, 1990).
- **associativity**—Pairing a weak input with a strong input enhances later response to the weak input. In this regard, the synapses subject to LTP are like Hebbian synapses, except that LTP requires only the depolarization of a dendrite, not necessarily an action potential.

The opposite change, long-term depression, occurs in both the hippocampus (Kerr & Abraham, 1995) and the cerebellum (Ito, 1989, 2002). **Long-term depression (LTD)** is a prolonged decrease in response at a synapse. It occurs when two or more axons have been repeatedly active together but at a low frequency, about one to four times per second.

Biochemical Mechanisms

Determining how LTP or LTD occurs has been a huge research challenge because each neuron receives many incoming synapses—sometimes in the tens of thousands—and each synapse is extremely small. Isolating the chemical changes at any one synapse has taken an enormous amount of careful and creative research, and many of the details are still uncertain. Nevertheless, a consensus has emerged on the basic points (Malenka & Nicoll, 1999). The mechanisms vary among brain areas (Li, Chen, Xing, Wei, & Rogawski, 2001; Mellor & Nicoll, 2001); we shall discuss LTP in the hippocampus, where it is easiest to demonstrate and where its mechanisms have been most extensively studied.

Actions at AMPA and NMDA Synapses
In almost every known case, LTP depends on changes at glutamate synapses. The brain has several types of receptors for glutamate, its most abundant transmitter (Madden, 2002). In previous chapters, you have seen that neuroscientists identify different dopamine receptors by number, such as D_1 and D_2, and different GABA receptors by letter, such as $GABA_A$. For glutamate, they have named the different receptors after drugs that stimulate them. Here we are interested in the AMPA and NMDA type glutamate receptors. The **AMPA** receptor is ordinarily excited only by glutamate, but it can also respond to the drug α-amino-3-hydroxy-5-methyl-4-isoxazolepropionic acid (quite a mouthful). The **NMDA** receptor is also ordinarily excited only by glutamate, but it can respond to the drug N-methyl-D-aspartate.

Both are ionotropic receptors; that is, when they are stimulated, they open a channel to let ions enter the postsynaptic cell. The AMPA receptor opens sodium channels, and it is similar to the other synaptic receptors we have considered. The NMDA receptor, however, is of a type we have not previously discussed: It responds to its transmitter, glutamate, *only when the membrane is already partly depolarized.* Ordinarily, when glutamate attaches to an NMDA receptor, the ion channel is blocked by magnesium ions so that it cannot open. (Magnesium ions, positively charged, are attracted to the negative charge inside the cells but not quite able to fit through the NMDA channel.) Glutamate opens the channel only if the magnesium leaves, and the surest way to detach the magnesium is to depolarize the membrane, decreasing the negative charge that attracts them (Figure 13.20).

Now suppose the axon that releases glutamate is active repeatedly. Better yet, let's activate two axons repeatedly, attached to the same dendrite. So many sodium ions enter through the AMPA channels that the dendrite becomes significantly depolarized, though it does not produce an action potential. (Remember, only axons produce action potentials.) The depolarization of the dendrite displaces the magnesium molecules, enabling glutamate to open the NMDA channel. Both sodium and calcium enter through the NMDA channel (Figure 13.21).

The entry of calcium is the key to the later changes. When calcium enters through the NMDA channel, it activates a protein called CaMKII (α-calcium-calmodulin-dependent proteinkinase II), which is both necessary and sufficient for LTP (Lisman, Schulman, & Cline, 2002). That is, directly increasing CaMKII production increases LTP, and mutations that interfere with CaMKII activation prevent LTP and block consolidation of memories (Frankland, O'Brien, Ohno, Kirkwood, & Silva, 2001). The protein CaMKII sets in motion the following processes:

- AMPA receptors add a phosphate group, becoming more responsive to glutamate.
- The dendrite builds more AMPA receptors or moves old ones into better positions.
- Some "silent" (unresponsive) receptors transform into functional AMPA receptors (Poncer & Malinow, 2001).
- In some cases, the neuron makes more NMDA receptors (Grosshans, Clayton, Coultrap, & Browning, 2002).

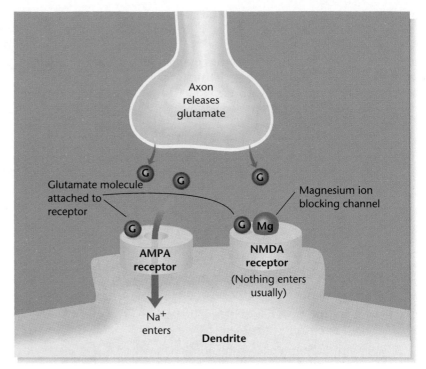

Figure 13.20 The AMPA and NMDA receptors before LTP
Glutamate attaches to both receptors. At the AMPA receptor, it opens a channel to let sodium ions enter. At the NMDA receptor, it binds but usually fails to open the channel, which is blocked by magnesium ions.

- The dendrite may make more branches, thus forming additional synapses with the same axon (Engert & Bonhoeffer, 1999; Toni, Buchs, Nikonenko, Bron, & Muller, 1999) (Figure 13.22). Recall from Chapter 5 that enriched experience also leads to increased dendritic branching.
- Some kinds of learning depend on the release of neurotrophins that promote cellular growth in the hippocampus (Hall, Thomas, & Everitt, 2000), and some depend on the actual formation of new neurons in the hippocampus (Shors et al., 2001). How these processes relate to LTP is not yet known.

Let's summarize: When glutamate massively stimulates AMPA receptors, the resulting depolarization enables glutamate also to stimulate nearby NMDA receptors. Stimulation of the NMDA receptors lets calcium enter the cell, where it sets into motion a series of changes that potentiate the dendrite's future responsiveness to glutamate by increasing either the number of AMPA receptors or their responsiveness. However, the NMDA receptors, which were necessary for the LTP process, do not themselves become potentiated. They act to potentiate the AMPA receptors, but then the NMDA receptors revert to their original condition. The mechanisms of LTP evidently differ from one instance to another.

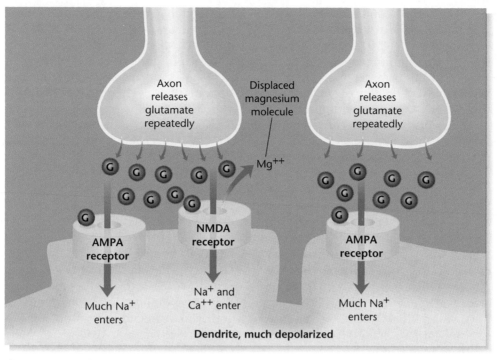

Figure 13.21 The AMPA and NMDA receptors during LTP
If one or (better) more AMPA receptors have been repeatedly stimulated, enough sodium enters to largely depolarize the dendrite's membrane. Doing so displaces the magnesium ions and therefore enables glutamate to stimulate the NMDA receptor. Both sodium and calcium enter through the NMDA receptor's channel.

Once LTP has been established, it no longer depends on NMDA synapses. Drugs that block NMDA synapses prevent the *establishment* of LTP, but they do not interfere with the *maintenance* of LTP that was already established (Gustafsson & Wigström, 1990). In other words, once the NMDA receptors have potentiated the AMPA receptors, the AMPA receptors stay potentiated, regardless of what happens to the NMDAs.

Presynaptic Changes

The changes just described occur in the postsynaptic neuron. For many years, it has been controversial

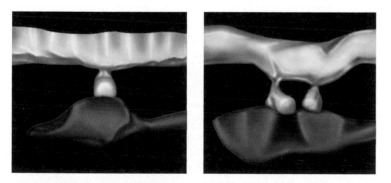

Figure 13.22 One way in which LTP occurs
In some cases, the dendrite makes new branches, which attach to branches of the same axon, thus increasing the overall stimulation.
Source: Based on Toni, Buchs, Nikonenko, Bron, & Muller, 1999

whether LTP depends on postsynaptic changes, presynaptic changes, or both. Evidence has accumulated that the strongest, most enduring forms of LTP require a combination of both presynaptic and postsynaptic changes (Zakharenko, Zablow, & Siegelbaum, 2001). Extensive stimulation of a postsynaptic cell causes it to release a **retrograde transmitter** that travels back to the presynaptic cell to modify it. As a result, a presynaptic neuron decreases its threshold for producing action potentials (Ganguly, Kiss, & Poo, 2000), increases its release of neurotransmitter (Zakharenko et al., 2001), and increases its production of a protein called *GAP-43*, which facilitates the growth and expansion of axons (Routtenberg, Cantallops, Zaffuto, Serrano, & Namgung, 2000). In short, LTP reflects increased activity by the presynaptic neuron as well as increased response to that activity by the postsynaptic neuron.

Consolidation of LTP

Recall the earlier discussion of consolidation of memory: The formation of a reliable long-term memory is a slow, gradual process. The same is true for LTP. After a training experience, one can measure evidence of LTP in the hippocampus quickly. Ordinarily, one can begin to detect changes in the cerebral cortex 90 to 180 minutes later (Izquierdo, 1995). Evidently, the hippocampus stores memories temporarily and then directs information storage in other places (Nagahara, Otto, & Gallagher, 1995). However, if NMDA synapses are blocked, then the consolidation process does not proceed normally. Several studies have reported different results from blocking NMDA synapses. One study found that blocking NMDA synapses within the first week or two after training prevented the consolidation of long-term memories (Shimizu, Tany, Rampon, & Tsien, 2000). In contrast, two other studies found that blocking NMDA synapses for the first week or two after training led to a *prolongation* of LTP and an increase in dendritic branching (Lüthi, Schwyzer, Mateos, Gähwiler, & McKinney, 2001; Villarreal, Do, Haddad, & Derrick, 2002). If so, a possible interpretation is that blocking NMDA synapses prevents later experiences from overriding or competing with the first experience. These effects obviously need to be replicated and investigated further. All we can conclude now is that consolidation is a gradual process over days, weeks, or longer and that NMDA synapses participate in some as yet uncertain way.

Stop & Check

4. Before LTP: In the normal state, what is the effect of glutamate at the AMPA receptors? At the NMDA receptors?

5. During the formation of LTP: When a burst of intense stimulation releases much more glutamate than usual at two or more incoming axons, what is the effect of the glutamate at the AMPA receptors? At the NMDA receptors? Which ions enter at the NMDA receptors?

6. After LTP has formed: After the neuron has gone through LTP, what is the effect of glutamate at the AMPA receptors? At the NMDA receptors?

Check your answers on pages 415–416.

LTP and Behavior

How important is LTP for learning? Is it "the" basis for learning, one of several mechanisms, or just a laboratory curiosity? Laboratory procedures are designed to change synapses in one cell at a time, but the underlying processes should be the same as when a normal experience changes a whole population of neurons. As one set of neurons change, they recruit changes in others. Resesearchers recording from single neurons have found cells that change early in a training period, be-

fore any change is evident in the behavior of the animal as a whole (Repa et al., 2001). We can therefore think of a single-cell change as a part or a preliminary step toward transformation of the animal's behavior.

One key reason for studying LTP is that understanding the biochemistry of learning may enable researchers to understand what could impair or improve memory. Mice with genes that cause abnormalities of the NMDA receptor learn slowly; those with genes causing extra NMDA receptors have better than normal memory (Tang et al., 1999). Mice that lack AMPA receptors also have deficits in both LTP and memory, especially recent memory (Reisel et al., 2002). Drugs that interfere with LTP block learning (Baldwin, Holahan, Sadeghian, & Kelley, 2000), whereas drugs that facilitate LTP enhance learning (Izquierdo & Medina, 1995). One of the mechanisms of LTP is the production of the protein *GAP-43* in the presynaptic neuron, and mice that overproduce this protein show much-enhanced ability to learn and solve problems (Routtenberg et al., 2000). Presumably, drugs that target this protein could have therapeutic value for people with impaired learning.

What about other drugs that might improve memory? The drugs that many people use to improve memory have no apparent connection to LTP, but they may improve learning and memory through other routes. You may have heard claims that memory can be improved by taking the herb *Ginkgo biloba*, or citicoline, phosphatidylcholine, antioxidants, vinpocetine, piracetam, and several other chemicals. Drugs marketed for treating diseases must be approved by the Food and Drug Administration, but naturally occurring supplements face almost no regulation at all. ("Natural" does not mean "safe.") Because supplements are marketed without much research, most scientists have assumed that the claims of their benefits were utterly bogus.

However, careful reviews of the literature have supported neither the extravagant claims of benefits nor complete skepticism. The story appears to be more complicated: Gingko biloba dilates blood vessels and therefore increases blood flow to the brain and may have other effects on the brain. When given to Alzheimer's patients or other people with memory problems, gingko biloba sometimes produces small benefits (Gold, Cahill, & Wenk, 2002). That is, it is neither worthless nor a miracle drug. Similarly, a number of other "memory-boosting" supplements increase blood flow to the brain or increase metabolism. Some studies have shown small memory benefits in laboratory animals or aged people (McDaniel, Maier, & Einstein, 2002). However, apparently no research has examined the effects of taking a combination of "memory chemicals." Results would undoubtedly vary from one population of people to another, from one memory task to another, and from one dose to another. (Doses are often uncertain because the purity of herbal supplements varies from batch to batch.) At this point, it is best to reserve judgment but encourage more research. It is worth noting, however, that the only demonstrated benefits have been for people with circulatory problems and other disorders, not for young people with normal brains. If you want to improve your grades, the best route is to study harder, not to take pills.

MODULE 13.2

In Closing: The Physiology of Memory

In this module, we examined mechanisms such as LTP, which seem remote from the complex behaviors we call learning and memory. And indeed, they are remote; changing one synapse would have little impact by itself. It has to be part of a large interacting network, and researchers are far from understanding how we combine untold numbers of changed synapses to produce complex behaviors.

After we understand the workings of memory more completely, what can we do with the information? Presumably, we will help people overcome or prevent memory deterioration; we can expect much better therapies for Alzheimer's disease and so forth. Should we also look forward to improving memory for normal people? Would you like to have a supermemory?

Maybe, but let's be cautious. Even though I could add memory chips to my computer to store ever-larger quantities of information, I still don't want to keep everything I write or every email message I receive. Similarly, my brain doesn't record a memory of every experience I have, and I'm not sure I would want it to, even if it had unlimited storage capacity. The ideal supermemory would not just record more and more information; it would faithfully record what we need to remember and discard the rest. Indeed, it might not be much different from what you have right now. As the saying goes, "If it ain't broke, don't fix it."

SUMMARY

1. A Hebbian synapse is one that is strengthened if it is active at the same time that the postsynaptic neuron produces an action potential. (p. 408)

2. Habituation of the gill-withdrawal reflex in *Aplysia* depends on a mechanism that decreases the release of transmitter from a particular presynaptic neuron. (p. 409)

3. Sensitization of the gill-withdrawal reflex in *Aplysia* occurs when serotonin blocks potassium channels in a presynaptic neuron and thereby prolongs the release of transmitter from that neuron. (p. 409)

4. Long-term potentiation (LTP) is an enhancement of response at certain synapses because of a brief but intense series of stimuli delivered to a neuron, generally by two or more axons delivering simultaneous inputs. LTP occurs in many brain areas and is particularly prominent in the hippocampus. (p. 411)

5. LTP in hippocampal neurons occurs as follows: Repeated glutamate excitation of AMPA receptors depolarizes the membrane. The depolarization removes magnesium ions that had been blocking NMDA receptors. Glutamate is then able to excite the NMDA receptors, opening a channel for calcium ions to enter the neuron. (p. 411)

6. When calcium enters through the NMDA-controlled channels, it activates a protein that alters the structure of AMPA receptors, converts some NMDA receptors to AMPA receptors, builds more AMPA receptors, and increases the growth of dendritic branches. All these changes increase the later responsiveness of the dendrite to incoming glutamate. (p. 412)

7. Procedures that enhance or impair LTP have similar effects on certain kinds of learning. Research on LTP may lead to drugs that help improve memory. (p. 414)

ANSWERS TO *STOP AND CHECK* QUESTIONS

1. In a Hebbian synapse, pairing the activity of a weaker (CS) axon with a stronger (UCS) axon produces an action potential and in the process strengthens the response of the cell to the CS axon. On later trials, it will produce a bigger depolarization of the postsynaptic cell, which we can regard as a conditioned response. (p. 411)

2. *Aplysia* has fewer cells than vertebrates, and the cells and connections are virtually identical from one individual to another. Therefore, researchers can work out the mechanisms of behavior in great detail. (p. 411)

3. Blocking potassium channels prolongs the action potential and therefore prolongs the release of neurotransmitter, producing an increased response. (p. 411)

4. Before LTP, glutamate stimulates AMPA receptors but usually has little effect at the NMDA receptors because magnesium blocks them. (p. 414)

5. During the formation of LTP, the massive glutamate input strongly stimulates the AMPA receptors, thus depolarizing the dendrite. This depolarization enables glutamate to excite the NMDA receptors also. Both calcium and sodium enter there. (p. 414)

6. After LTP has been established, glutamate stimulates the AMPA receptors more than before. At the NMDA receptors, it is again usually ineffective. (p. 414)

THOUGHT QUESTION

If a synapse has already developed LTP once, should it be easier or more difficult to get it to develop LTP again? Why?

CHAPTER ENDING
Key Terms and Activities

TERMS

Alzheimer's disease (p. 403)

amnesia (p. 395)

AMPA receptor (p. 411)

amyloid beta protein 42 (Aβ$_{42}$) (p. 404)

anterograde amnesia (p. 395)

associativity (p. 411)

central executive (p. 394)

classical conditioning (p. 388)

conditioned response (CR) (p. 388)

conditioned stimulus (CS) (p. 388)

confabulation (p. 402)

configural learning (p. 400)

consolidation (p. 393)

cooperativity (p. 411)

declarative memory (p. 397)

delayed matching-to-sample task (p. 398)

delayed nonmatching-to-sample task (p. 398)

delayed response task (p. 394)

engram (p. 389)

episodic memory (p. 398)

equipotentiality (p. 390)

explicit memory (p. 397)

habituation (p. 409)

Hebbian synapse (p. 408)

implicit memory (p. 397)

Korsakoff's syndrome (p. 402)

lateral interpositus nucleus (LIP) (p. 390)

long-term depression (LTD) (p. 411)

long-term memory (p. 391)

long-term potentiation (LTP) (p. 411)

mass action (p. 390)

Morris search task (p. 399)

NMDA receptor (p. 411)

operant conditioning (p. 388)

phonological loop (p. 394)

plaque (p. 403)

priming (p. 402)

procedural memory (p. 397)

punishment (p. 388)

radial maze (p. 399)

reinforcer (p. 388)

retrograde amnesia (p. 395)

retrograde transmitter (p. 413)

sensitization (p. 409)

short-term memory (p. 391)

specificity (p. 411)

tangle (p. 404)

tau (p. 404)

unconditioned response (UCR) (p. 388)

unconditioned stimulus (UCS) (p. 388)

visuospatial sketchpad (p. 394)

working memory (p. 394)

SUGGESTION FOR FURTHER READING

Eichenbaum, H. (2002). *The cognitive neuroscience of memory.* New York: Oxford University Press. Thoughtful treatment of both the behavioral and physiological aspects of memory.

WEB SITES TO EXPLORE

You can go to the Biological Psychology Study Center and click these links. While there, you can also check for suggested articles available on InfoTrac College Edition.

- The Biological Psychology Internet address is:
  http://psychology.wadsworth.com/ kalatbiopsych8e/

Alzheimer's Research Forum
http://www.alzforum.org/default.asp

Digital anatomist: The hippocampus
http://rprcsgi.rprc.washington.edu/neuronames/ interim/hippocampus.html

CD-ROM: EXPLORING BIOLOGICAL PSYCHOLOGY

Classical Conditioning (video)
Amnestic Patient (video)
Alzheimer's Patient (video)
Implicit Memories (Try it Yourself)
Long-Term Potentiation (Try it Yourself)
Neural Networks and Memory (video)
Critical Thinking (essay questions)
Chapter Quiz (multiple choice questions)

Lateralization and Language

14

Chapter Outline

Main Ideas

1. The left and right hemispheres of the brain communicate primarily through the corpus callosum, although other smaller commissures also exchange some information between the hemispheres. After damage to the corpus callosum, each hemisphere has access to information only from the opposite half of the body and from the opposite visual field.

2. In most people, the left hemisphere is specialized for language and analytical processing. The right hemisphere is specialized for certain complex visuospatial tasks and synthetic processing.

3. The language specializations of the human brain are enormous elaborations of features present in other primates.

4. Abnormalities of the left hemisphere can lead to a great variety of specific language impairments.

Your brain consists of a multitude of neurons, but unlike a society of people who act together at times but still remain independent, the neurons produce a single consciousness. Although your brain parts are many, your experience is one.

What happens if connections among brain areas are broken? After damage to the corpus callosum, which connects the two hemispheres, people act as if they have two fields of awareness—separate "minds," you might say. With damage to certain areas of the left hemisphere, people lose their language abilities, while remaining unimpaired in other ways. Studies of these people offer fascinating clues about how the brain operates and raise equally fascinating unanswered questions.

Opposite:
All species communicate in various ways, but only human language has the flexibility to produce new ways of expressing an endless array of new ideas.
Source: David Young-Wolff/PhotoEdit

419

Lateralization of Function

The left hemisphere of the cerebral cortex is connected to skin receptors and muscles mainly on the right side of the body, except for trunk muscles and facial muscles, which are controlled by both hemispheres. The left hemisphere sees only the right half of the world. The right hemisphere is connected to sensory receptors and muscles mainly on the left half of the body. It sees only the left half of the world. Each hemisphere gets auditory information from both ears but slightly stronger information from the ear on the opposite side. The exceptions to this pattern of crossed input are taste and smell. Each hemisphere gets taste information from its own side of the tongue (Aglioti, Tassinari, Corballis, & Berlucchi, 2000; Pritchard, Macaluso, & Eslinger, 1999) and smell information from the nostril on its own side (Herz, McCall, & Cahill, 1999; Homewood & Stevenson, 2001). No one knows *why* all vertebrates evolved so that each hemisphere controls the contralateral (opposite) side of the body.[1]

At any rate, the left and right hemispheres exchange information through a set of axons called the **corpus callosum** (Figure 14.1; see also Figures 4.15 and 4.16) and through the anterior commissure, the hippocampal commissure, and a couple of other small commissures. Information that initially enters one hemisphere crosses to the opposite hemisphere with only a brief delay.

The two hemispheres are not simply mirror images of each other. In most humans, the left hemisphere is specialized for language; the functions of the right hemisphere are more difficult to summarize, as we shall see later in this chapter. The division of labor between the two hemispheres is known as **lateralization**. If you had no corpus callosum, your left hemisphere could talk only about the information from the right side of your body, and your right hemisphere

could react only to information from the left. Because of the corpus callosum, however, each hemisphere receives information from both sides. Only after damage to the corpus callosum (or to one hemisphere) do we see clear evidence of lateralization.

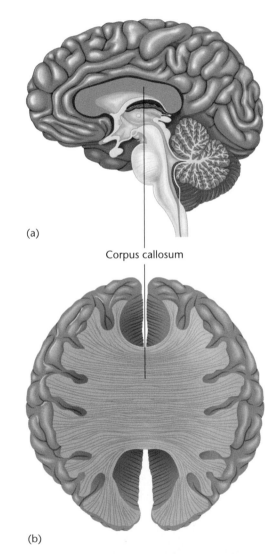

(a)

Corpus callosum

(b)

Figure 14.1 Two views of the corpus callosum
The corpus callosum is a large set of axons that conveys information between the two hemispheres. **(a)** A sagittal section through the human brain. **(b)** A dissection (viewed from above) in which gray matter has been removed to expose the corpus callosum.

---

[1]Here's a wild guess: Maybe each hemisphere had been connected to receptors and muscles on its own side, and then for some reason early in vertebrate evolution, the head flipped upside down so that what used to be the right side of the head was now on the left, but still connected to the right side of the body. As a result, the left hemisphere of the brain would be connected to the muscles and skin on the right side but still connected to taste and smell receptors on the left side (because they are in the head and they flipped sides along with the brain). Why the head might have flipped, I don't know, so admittedly, we would just be exchanging one mystery for another. But it would explain why each hemisphere is connected to smell and touch receptors on its own side of the head.

Before we can discuss lateralization in any detail, we must consider the relation of the eyes to the brain. The connections from the left and right eyes to the left and right hemispheres are more complex than you might expect, and you need to understand them to understand some of the research on split-brain patients.

VISUAL AND AUDITORY CONNECTIONS TO THE HEMISPHERES

The hemispheres are connected to the eyes in such a way that each hemisphere gets input from the opposite half of the visual world; that is, the left hemisphere sees the right side of the world, and the right hemisphere sees the left side. In rabbits and other species that have their eyes far to the side of the head, the connections from eye to brain are easy to describe: The left eye connects to the right hemisphere and the right eye to the left hemisphere. *Your eyes are not connected to the brain in this way.* Both of your eyes face forward. You can see the left side of the world almost as well with your right eye as you can with your left eye.

Figure 14.2 illustrates the connections from the eyes to the brain in humans. Light from the right half of the **visual field**—what is visible at any moment—shines onto the left half of *both* retinas, and light from the left visual field shines onto the right half of both retinas. The left half of *each* retina connects to the left hemisphere, which therefore sees the right visual

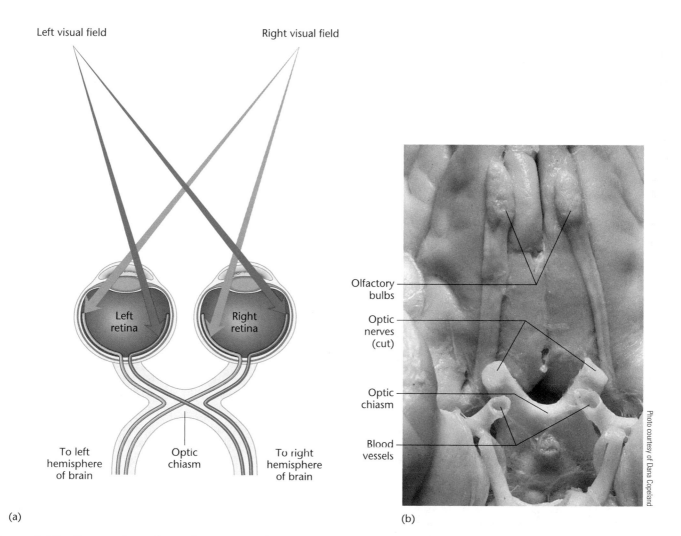

(a)

(b)

Figure 14.2 Connections from the eyes to the human brain
(a) Route of visual input to the two hemispheres of the brain. Note that the left hemisphere is connected to the left half of each retina and thus gets visual input from the right half of the world; the opposite is true of the right hemisphere. **(b)** Closeup of olfactory bulbs and the optic chiasm, where axons from the right half of the left retina cross to the right hemisphere, and axons from the left half of the right retina cross to the left hemisphere.

field. Similarly, the right half of each retina connects to the right hemisphere, which sees the left visual field. A small vertical strip down the center of each retina, covering about 5° of visual arc, connects to both hemispheres (Innocenti, 1980). In Figure 14.2, note how half of the axons from each eye cross to the opposite side of the brain at a place called the **optic chiasm** (literally, the optic "cross").

Right visual field→ left half of each retina→ left hemisphere

Left visual field→ right half of each retina→ right hemisphere

Although touch from each half the body goes to the opposite half of the brain, and vision from half of the visual field goes to the opposite half of the brain, the auditory system is organized differently. Each ear receives sound waves from only one side of the head, but each sends the information to both sides of the brain because any part of the brain that contributes to localizing sounds must receive input from both ears. However, when the two ears receive different information, each hemisphere does pay more attention to the ear on the opposite side (Hugdahl, 1996).

1. The left hemisphere of the brain is connected to the right eye in rabbits. In humans, the left hemisphere is connected to the left half of each retina. Explain the reason for this species difference.

2. In humans, light from the right visual field shines on the _____ half of each retina, which sends its axons to the _____ hemisphere of the brain.

Check your answers on page 432.

CUTTING THE CORPUS CALLOSUM

Damage to the corpus callosum prevents the exchange of information between the two hemispheres. Occasionally, surgeons sever the corpus callosum as a therapy for severe epilepsy. **Epilepsy** is a condition characterized by repeated episodes of excessive synchronized neural activity—that is, many neurons are producing action potentials at the same time—mainly because of decreased release of the inhibitory neurotransmitter GABA (During, Ryder, & Spencer, 1995). It can result from a mutation in a gene controlling the GABA receptor (Baulac et al., 2001). It can also result from trauma or

infection in the brain, brain tumors, or exposure to toxic substance. Often the cause is not known. About 1%–2% of all people have epilepsy. The symptoms vary depending on the location, duration, and frequency of the seizures.

Over the years, medical researchers have developed a large array of antiepileptic drugs, which act mostly by blocking sodium flow across the membrane or by enhancing the effects of GABA. More than 90% of epileptic patients respond well enough to drugs to live a reasonably normal life. Some suffer only the inconvenience of taking a daily pill. A few, however, continue to have frequent seizures despite medication. As a last resort, physicians consider surgically removing the **focus,** or point of origin of the seizure.

However, some people have not one focus but several, so surgical removal is not feasible. Therefore, the idea arose to cut the corpus callosum to prevent epileptic seizures from crossing from one hemisphere to the other. One benefit is that, as predicted, the person's epileptic seizures affect only half the body. (The abnormal activity cannot cross the corpus callosum, so it remains within one hemisphere.) In addition, a surprising bonus is that the seizures become less frequent. Evidently, epileptic activity rebounds back and forth between the hemispheres and prolongs seizures. If it can't bounce back and forth across the corpus callosum, a seizure may not develop at all.

How does severing the corpus callosum affect other aspects of behavior? Following damage to the corpus callosum, laboratory animals show normal sensation, movement, learning and memory, hunger, and thirst. Their responses are abnormal only when sensory stimuli are limited to one side of the body. For example, if they see something in the left visual field, they can reach out to it only with the left forepaw. If they learn to do something with the left forepaw, they then have to learn it again with the right forepaw (Sperry, 1961).

People who have undergone damage to the corpus callosum, referred to as **split-brain people,** show similar tendencies. They maintain their intellect and motivation, and they can still walk without difficulty. They can also use the two hands together on familiar tasks such as tying shoes. Evidently, after many years of tying shoes, the task has become so automatic that it no longer requires much input from the cerebral cortex. Presumably, the basal ganglia or other subcortical areas control the movement. More difficulty arises on unfamiliar tasks. If split-brain patients are asked to pretend they are hitting a golf ball, threading a needle, or attaching a fish hook to a line, they can easily do tasks that were habitual before the surgery, but each patient struggles with whichever tasks are unfamiliar (Franz, Waldie, & Smith, 2000).

Split-brain patients can use their two hands independently in a way that other people cannot. For example, try drawing ∪ with your left hand while simultaneously drawing ⊃ with your right hand. Most people find this task difficult, but split-brain people do it with ease. Or try drawing circles with both hands simultaneously. Most people draw the two circles at the same speed and find it difficult to draw one faster than the other; split-brain people spontaneously draw them at different speeds (Kennerley, Diedrichsen, Hazeltine, Semjen, & Ivry, 2002).

Incidentally, the difficulty of simultaneously moving your left hand one way and your right hand a different way is not a motor limitation but a cognitive one. It is hard to draw a ∪ with one hand and a ⊃ with the other, but if you carefully draw both of them and then try to trace over the ∪ with one hand and a ⊃ with the other, you will find it easier. If you receive a signal such as "SL" meaning "move your left hand a short distance and your right hand a long distance," you will find it hard to do both at once. However, if two targets appear, one just a short distance from your left hand and the other farther from your right hand, you have no trouble reaching out to both at once (Diedrichsen, Hazeltine, Kennerley, & Ivry, 2001). Evidently, it is difficult for you to plan two actions at once unless you have clear targets to direct your movements. Split-brain people have no trouble planning two actions at once.

Research by Roger Sperry and his students (Nebes, 1974) revealed subtle behavioral effects when stimuli were limited to one side of the body. In a typical experiment, a split-brain patient stared straight ahead as words or pictures were flashed on either side of a screen (Figure 14.3). Information that went to one hemisphere could not cross to the other because of the damage to the corpus callosum. The information stayed on the screen long enough to be visible but not long enough for the person to move his or her eyes.

If the experimenter then asked the person to point to the object that had just been shown, the person could point with the left hand only to what the right hemisphere had seen and point with the right hand only to what the left hemisphere had seen. The two halves of the brain had different information, and they could not communicate with each other.

Although both hemispheres can understand speech to some extent (Beeman & Chiarello, 1998), the left hemisphere is dominant for speech comprehension and especially speech production in more than 95% of right-handers and about 80% of left-handers (McKeever, Seitz, Krutsch, & Van Eys, 1995) (see Methods 14.1). The left and right hemispheres respond about equally to nonlanguage sounds, but parts of the left temporal cortex respond selectively to meaningful language (Giraud & Price, 2001). For example, a sentence activates the left hemisphere more than the same words in scrambled order would (Vandenberghe, Nobre, & Price, 2002). An English-speaking person listening to something spoken in Thai or Zulu responds with both hemispheres equally or perhaps even more with the right hemisphere, treating the sounds as if they were music instead of speech (Best & Avery, 1999; Van Lancker & Fromkin, 1973). Also, viewing sign language activates the left hemisphere in deaf people and others who are fluent in sign language, but not in other people (Petitto et al., 2000).

Is there any advantage in having just one hemisphere control speech? Possibly. Many of the people with bilateral control of speech stutter (Fox et al., 2000), although not all people who stutter have bilateral control of speech. It is possible that having two speech centers leads to competing messages to the speech muscles, which need to be tightly coordinated to articulate speech sounds.

Figure 14.3 Effects of damage to the corpus callosum
When the word *hatband* is flashed on a screen, a woman with a split brain can report only what her left hemisphere saw, *band*. However, with her left hand, she can point to a hat, which is what the right hemisphere saw.

Testing Hemispheric Dominance for Speech

Several methods are available to test which hemisphere is dominant for speech in a person with a normal corpus callosum. One is the Wada test, named after its inventor. A physician injects sodium amytal, a barbiturate tranquilizer, into the carotid artery on one side of the head. The drug puts that side of the brain to sleep, enabling researchers to test the capacities of the other hemisphere. For example, a person with left-hemisphere dominance for speech continues speaking after a sodium amytal injection to the right hemisphere but not after an injection to the left hemisphere. The Wada test gives highly accurate information about lateralization, but the procedure is difficult, risky, and sometimes even fatal.

A less accurate, but easier and safer, test is the dichotic listening task, in which a person wears earphones that present different words to the two ears at the same time. The person tries to say either or both words. Ordinarily, someone with left-hemisphere dominance for language identifies mostly the words heard in the right ear; someone with right-hemisphere dominance identifies mostly the words heard in the left ear.

A third method is the Object Naming Latency Task, which measures how fast someone can name an object flashed in the left or right visual field (McKeever et al., 1995). People with left-hemisphere language dominance are faster at naming objects in the right visual field, whereas those with right-hemisphere dominance are faster at naming objects in the left visual field.

A fourth method is to record brain activity while people speak or listen to speech, using PET scans, fMRI scans, or electrical or magnetic evoked responses. This final method is difficult and expensive, but it reveals information that other methods do not. For example, although language activates the left hemisphere more than the right, it does activate the right hemisphere also (Vouloumanos, Kiehl, Werker, & Liddle, 2001).

When a split-brain person views a display briefly in the right visual field, thus seeing it with the left hemisphere, the viewer can name the object easily. But the same person viewing a display in the left visual field (right hemisphere) usually can neither name nor describe it. I say "usually" because a small amount of information travels between the hemispheres through several smaller commissures, as shown in Figure 14.4, and some split-brain patients get enough information to describe some objects at least in part (Berlucchi, Mangun, & Gazzaniga, 1997; Forster & Corballis, 2000). Nevertheless, even a patient who cannot name an object correctly points to it with the left hand. The person sometimes even says, "I don't know," while pointing to the correct choice. (Of course, a split-brain person who watches the left hand point out an object can then name it.)

3. Can a split-brain person name an object after feeling it with the left hand? With the right hand? Explain.

4. After a split-brain person sees something in the left visual field, how can he or she describe or identify the object?

Check your answers on page 432.

Split Hemispheres: Competition and Cooperation

Each hemisphere of a split-brain person can process information and respond independently of the other. For the first weeks after surgery, the hemispheres act like separate people sharing one body. One split-brain person repeatedly took items from the grocery shelf with one hand and returned them with the other (Reuter-Lorenz & Miller, 1998).

Another patient—specifically, his left hemisphere—described his experience as follows (Dimond, 1979, p. 211):

> If I'm reading, I can hold the book in my right hand; it's a lot easier to sit on my left hand, than to hold it with both hands.... You tell your hand—I'm going to turn so many pages in a book—turn three pages—then somehow the left hand will pick up two pages and you're at page 5, or whatever. It's better to let it go, pick it up with the right hand, and then turn to the right page. With your right hand, you correct what the left has done.

Such conflicts are more common soon after surgery than later. The severed halves of the corpus callosum do not grow back together, but the brain learns to use the other smaller connections between the left and right hemispheres (Myers & Sperry, 1985). The left hemisphere somehow suppresses the right hemisphere's interference and simply takes control in some situations. In other situations, the hemispheres learn

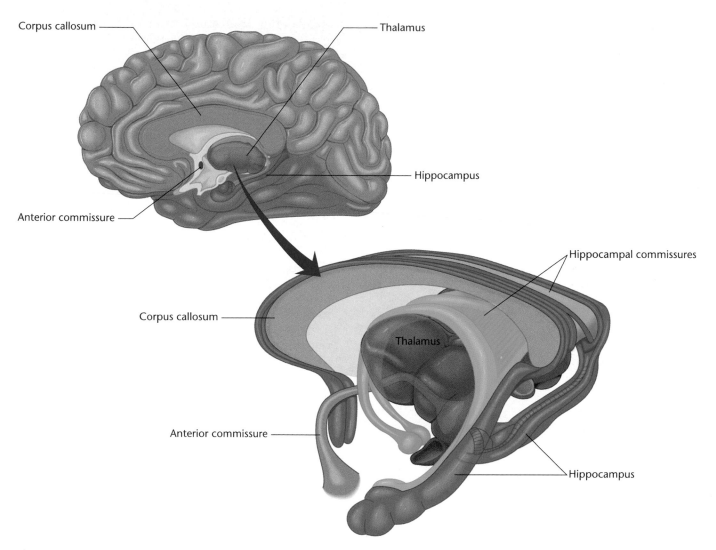

Figure 14.4 The anterior commissure and hippocampal commissures
These commissures allow for the exchange of information between the two hemispheres, as does the larger corpus callosum.
Source: Based on Nieuwenhuys, Voogd, & vanHuijzen, 1988, and others

to cooperate. A split-brain person who was tested with the standard apparatus shown in Figure 14.3 became able to name what he saw in the left visual field, but only when the answers were restricted to two possibilities (e.g., yes–no or true–false) and only when he was allowed to correct himself immediately after making a guess. For example, when something was flashed in the left visual field, the experimenter might ask, "Was it a letter of the alphabet?" The left (speaking) hemisphere would take a guess: "Yes." If that guess was incorrect, the right hemisphere, which knew the correct answer, would then make the face frown. (Both hemispheres can control facial muscles on both sides of the face.) The left hemisphere, feeling the frown, would say, "Oh, I'm sorry. I meant 'no.'"

In another experiment, a split-brain patient saw two words flashed at once, one on each side. He was then asked to draw a picture of what he had read. Each hemisphere saw a full word, but the two words could combine to make a different word. For example,

Left Visual Field *(Right Hemisphere)*	***Right Visual Field*** *(Left Hemisphere)*
hot	dog
honey	moon
sky	scraper
rain	bow

With the right hand, he almost always drew what he had seen in the right visual field (left hemisphere), such as *dog* or *moon.* However, with the left hand, he sometimes drew a literal combination of the two words. For example, after seeing *hot* and *dog,* he drew a dog that was overheated, not a wiener on a bun, and after seeing *sky* and *scraper,* he drew a sky and a scraper (Figure 14.5). The right hemisphere,

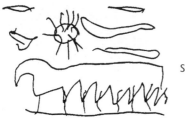

Figure 14.5 Left-hand drawing by a split-brain patient
He saw the word *sky* in the left visual field and *scraper* in the right visual field. His left hemisphere controlled the left hand enough to draw a scraper, and his right hemisphere controlled it enough to draw a sky. Neither hemisphere could combine the two words to make the emergent concept *skyscraper. Source: From "Subcortical Transfer of Higher Order Information: More Illusory than Real?" by A. Kingstone and M. S. Gazzaniga, 1995.* Neuropsychology, 9, *p. 321–328. Copyright ©1995 by the American Psychological Association. Reprinted with permission.*

which predominantly controls the left hand, drew what it saw in the left visual field (*hot* or *sky*). Ordinarily, the left hemisphere doesn't control the left hand, but through the bilateral mechanisms of the ventromedial spinal pathway (described in Chapter 8), it can move the left hand clumsily and, evidently, enough to add what it saw in the right visual field (*dog* or *scraper*). However, neither hemisphere could combine the words into one concept (Kingstone & Gazzaniga, 1995).

The Right Hemisphere

Suppose you watch a series of videotapes of people talking about themselves. Each person speaks twice, once telling the truth and the other time saying nothing but lies. How well do you think you would guess which version was the truth? Most people are very poor at this task. The average score for MIT undergraduates was 47% correct, a bit worse than the 50% expected by random guessing. Most other groups did equally badly, except for one group of people who got 60% correct—still not a great score, but at least better than random guessing (Etcoff, Ekman, Magee, & Frank, 2000). Who do you suppose were these emotional "geniuses" who could detect a liar when they saw one? They were people with left-hemisphere brain damage! They could not understand the words very well, but they were quite adept at reading gestures and facial expressions. As mentioned in Chapter 12, the right hemisphere is better than the left at perceiving the emotions in people's gestures and tone of voice, such as happiness or sadness (Adolphs, Damasio, & Tranel, 2002). If the left hemisphere is damaged

(and therefore prevented from interfering with the right hemisphere), the right-hemisphere is free to make reliable judgments (Buck & Duffy, 1980). In contrast, people with right-hemisphere damage speak in a monotone, do not understand other people's emotional expressions, and usually fail to understand humor and sarcasm (Beeman & Chiarello, 1998).

The hemispheres also contribute differently to emotion in general. Several kinds of studies indicate that happiness and positive interest activate mostly the left hemisphere, whereas fear and anger activate mostly the right (Canli, 1999; Hamann, Ely, Hoffman, & Kilts, 2002; Wiedemann et al., 1999). (You might remember this fact the next time you hear someone talk about "training people to use the right half of the brain.")

However, the right hemisphere is dominant for recognizing emotions in others, including both pleasant and unpleasant emotions (Narumoto, Okada, Sadato, Fukui, & Yonekura, 2001). In a split-brain person, the right hemisphere does better than the left at recognizing whether two photographs show the same or different emotions (Stone, Nisenson, Eliassen, & Gazzaniga, 1996). Moreover, according to Jerre Levy and her colleagues' studies of brain-intact people, when the left and right hemispheres perceive different emotions in someone's face, the response of the right hemisphere dominates. For example, examine the faces in Figure 14.6. Each of these combines half of a smiling face with half of a neutral face. Which looks happier to you: face (a) or face (b)? Most people choose face (a), with the smile on the viewer's left (Heller & Levy, 1981; Hoptman & Levy, 1988). Similarly, a frown on the viewer's left looks sadder than a frown on the viewer's right (Sackeim, Putz, Vingiano, Coleman, & McElhiney, 1988). Remember, what you see in your left visual field directly activates your right hemisphere.

The right hemisphere also appears to be more adept than the left at comprehending spatial relationships. For example, one young woman with damage to her posterior right hemisphere had great trouble finding her way around, even in familiar areas. To reach a destination, she needed directions with specific visual details, such as, "Walk to the corner where you see a building with a statue in front of it. Then turn left and go to the corner that has a flagpole and turn right. . . ." Each of these directions had to include an unmistakable feature; if the instruction was "go to the city government building—that's the one with a tower," she could easily go to a very different building that happened to have a tower (Clarke, Assal, & deTribolet, 1993).

How can we best describe the difference in functions between the hemispheres? According to Robert Ornstein (1997), the left hemisphere focuses more on details and the right hemisphere more on overall patterns. Recall the difference between the parvocellular (detailed shape) and magnocellular (overall patterns and movement) paths of the visual cortex, described in Chapter 6: Much research indicates that the parvocellular path is stronger in the left hemisphere and the magnocellular path is stronger in the right (Roth & Hellige, 1998). One result is that the right hemisphere is better at spatial processing. For example, split-brain patients can arrange puzzle pieces more accurately with the left hand than with the right and can use the left hand better for drawing a box, a bicycle, and similar objects. Also, in one study, brain-intact people examined visual stimuli such as the one in Figure 14.7, in which many repetitions of a small letter compose a different large letter. When they were asked to identify the small letters (in this case, B), activity increased in the left hemisphere, but when asked to identify the large overall letter (H), activity was greater in the right hemisphere (Fink et al., 1996).

Table 14.1 summarizes some key differences between the left and right hemispheres.

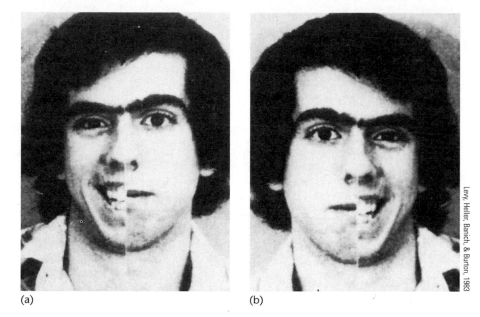
(a)   (b)

Figure 14.6 Half of a smiling face combined with half of a neutral face
Which looks happier to you—**(a)** the one with a smile on your left or **(b)** the one with a smile on your right? Your answer may suggest which hemisphere of your brain is dominant for interpreting emotional expressions.

Levy, Heller, Banich, & Burton, 1983

5. Which hemisphere is dominant for each of the following in most people: speech, expressions of happiness, expressions of anger and fear, emotional inflection of speech, interpreting other people's emotional expressions, spatial relationships, perceiving overall patterns?

Check your answers on page 432.

Hemispheric Specializations in Intact Brains

The differences between the two hemispheres also can be demonstrated in people without brain damage. Most of these differences are, however, small trends.

Here is one demonstration you can try yourself: Tap with a pencil in your right hand on a sheet of paper as many times as you can in 1 minute and then count the tap marks. Rest and repeat with your left hand. Then repeat with both hands while you talk at the same time. Compare results to find out how much faster you tapped when you weren't talking. For most right-handers, talking decreases the tapping rate with the right hand more than with the left hand (Kinsbourne & McMurray, 1975). Evidently, it is more difficult to do two things at once when both activities depend on the same hemisphere.

B   B
B   B
B   B
B   B
B B B B B B B
B   B
B   B
B   B
B   B

Figure 14.7 Stimulus to test analytical and holistic perception
When people were told to name the large composite letter, they had more activity in the right hemisphere. When told to name the small component letters, they had more activity in the left hemisphere. *Source: Based on Fink et al., 1996*

TABLE 14.1 Differences in Function Between the Two Hemispheres

	Contributions of Left Hemisphere	Contributions of Right Hemisphere
Speech	Production and most comprehension	Emotional inflections; understanding humor, sarcasm, other emotional content
Emotions	Expressions of happiness	Expressions of fear, anger, disgust; interpreting others' emotional expressions
Vision	Details; more activity by parvocellular path	Overall pattern; more activity by magnocellular path; spatial processing, such as arranging puzzle pieces or drawing a picture

DEVELOPMENT OF LATERALIZATION AND HANDEDNESS

Because language in most people depends primarily on the left hemisphere, it is natural to ask whether the hemispheres differ anatomically. If so, is the difference present before speech develops or does it develop later? What is the relationship between handedness and hemispheric dominance for speech?

Anatomical Differences Between the Hemispheres

The human brain is specialized to attend to language sounds. If you listen to a repeated syllable ("*pack pack pack pack . . .* ") and then suddenly the vowel sound changes (" *. . . pack pack pack peck . . .* "), the change will catch your attention and will evoke larger electrical responses measured on your scalp. Changing from *pack* to *peck* also increases the evoked response from a baby, even a premature infant born only 30 weeks after conception (Cheour-Luhtanen et al., 1996). Evidently, humans attend to language sounds from the start.

But do the hemispheres differ from the start? Norman Geschwind and Walter Levitsky (1968) found that one section of the temporal cortex, the planum temporale (PLAY-num tem-poh-RAH-lee), is larger in the left hemisphere for 65% of people (Figure 14.8). Smaller but still significant differences are found between left and right hemispheres of chimpanzees and gorillas, so this difference is apparently part of our ancient genetic heritage (Cantalupo & Hopkins, 2001) and presumably prepares us for a left-hemisphere specialization for language.

Sandra Witelson and Wazir Pallie (1973) examined the brains of infants who died before age 3 months and found that the left planum temporale was larger in 12 of 14—on the average, about twice as large. Later studies using MRI scans found that healthy 5- to 12-year-old children with the biggest ratio of left to right planum temporale performed best on language tests, whereas children with nearly equal hemispheres were better on certain nonverbal tasks (Leonard et al., 1996). People who suffer damage to the left hemisphere in infancy eventually develop less language than those with equal damage to the right hemisphere (Stark & McGregor, 1997). In short, the left hemisphere is specialized for language from the start, in most people.

Maturation of the Corpus Callosum

The corpus callosum matures gradually over the first 5 to 10 years of human life (Trevarthen, 1974). The developmental process is not a matter of growing new axons but of selecting certain axons and discarding others. At an early stage, the brain generates far more axons in the corpus callosum than it will have at maturity (Ivy & Killackey, 1981; Killackey & Chalupa, 1986). The reason is that any two neurons connected by the corpus callosum need to have corresponding functions. For example, a neuron in the left hemisphere that responds to light in the very center of the retina should be connected to a right-hemisphere neuron that responds to light in the same location. During early embryonic development, the genes cannot specify exactly where those two neurons will be. Therefore, many connections are made across the corpus callosum, but only the axons that happen to connect very similar cells survive (Innocenti & Caminiti, 1980).

Because the connections take years to develop their mature adult pattern, the behavior of young children in some situations resembles that of split-brain adults. An infant who has one arm restrained will not reach across the midline of the body to pick up a toy on the other side before about age 17 weeks. Evidently, in younger children, each hemisphere has too little access to information from the opposite hemisphere (Provine & Westerman, 1979).

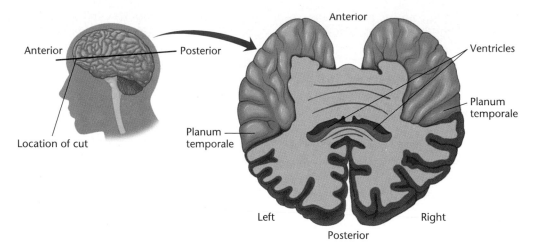

Figure 14.8 Horizontal section through a human brain
This cut, taken just above the surface of the temporal lobe, shows the planum temporale, an area that is critical for speech comprehension. Note that it is substantially larger in the left hemisphere than in the right hemisphere. *Source: From "Human Brain: Left-Right Asymmetries in Temporal Speech Region," by N. Geschwind and W. Levitsky, 1968, Science, 161, p. 186–187. Copyright ©1968 by the AAAS and N. Geschwind.*

In one study, 3- and 5-year-old children were asked to feel two fabrics, either with one hand at two times or with two hands at the same time, and say whether the materials felt the same or different. The 5-year-olds did equally well with one hand or with two. The 3-year-olds made 90% more errors with two hands than with one (Galin, Johnstone, Nakell, & Herron, 1979). The likely interpretation is that the corpus callosum matures sufficiently between ages 3 and 5 to facilitate the comparison of stimuli between the two hands.

Development Without a Corpus Callosum

Rarely, the corpus callosum fails to form or forms incompletely, possibly for genetic reasons, although not necessarily. People born without a corpus callosum are unlike people who have it cut later in life. First, whatever prevented formation of the corpus callosum undoubtedly affects brain development in other ways. Second, the absence or near absence of the corpus callosum induces the remaining brain areas to develop abnormally.

People born without a corpus callosum can perform some tasks that split-brain patients cannot. They can verbally describe what they feel with either hand and what they see in either visual field; they can also feel one object with the left hand and another with the right hand and say whether they are the same or different (Bruyer, Dupuis, Ophoven, Rectem, & Reynaert, 1985; Sanders, 1989). How do they do so? They do not use their right hemisphere for speech (Lassonde, Bryden, & Demers, 1990). Rather each hemisphere develops pathways connect-

ing it to both sides of the body, enabling the left (speaking) hemisphere to feel both the left and right hands. Also, the brain's other commissures become larger than usual. In addition to the corpus callosum, people have the **anterior commissure** (see Figure 4.15, p. 89, and Figure 14.4, p. 425), which connects the anterior parts of the cerebral cortex, the **hippocampal commissure**, which connects the left and right hippocampi (Figure 14.4), and the smaller *posterior commissure* (not shown in Figure 14.4). The extra development of these other commissures partly compensates for the lack of a corpus callosum.

6. A child born without a corpus callosum can name something felt with the left hand, but an adult who suffered damage to the corpus callosum cannot. What are two likely explanations?

Check your answers on page 432.

Handedness and Language Dominance

About 10% of all people are either left-handed or ambidextrous. (Most left-handers are somewhat ambidextrous.) Of all the surviving prehistoric drawings and paintings that show people using tools, more than 90% show the tool in the right hand (Coren & Porac, 1977). Chimpanzees and other primates are also mostly right-handed, although not as strongly as humans (Hopkins, Dahl, & Pilcher, 2001). Thus, right-handedness appears to be part of our ancient heritage, not a recent development.

For more than 95% of right-handed people, the left hemisphere is strongly dominant for speech (McKeever et al., 1995). Left-handers are more variable. Most left-handers have left-hemisphere dominance for speech, just like right-handers, but some have right-hemisphere dominance or a mixture of left and right (Basso & Rusconi, 1998). The same is true for people who were left-handed in early childhood but forced to switch to writing right-handed (Siebner et al., 2002). Many left-handers who have partial right-hemisphere control of speech are also partly reversed for spatial perception, showing more than the usual amount of left-hemisphere contribution. A few left-handers have right-hemisphere dominance for both language and spatial perception (Flöel et al., 2001).

The corpus callosum (especially the anterior corpus callosum) is thicker in left-handers than in right-handers on the average (Moffat, Hampson, & Lee, 1998). Presumably, the larger corpus callosum is needed for communication between the left-hemisphere language areas and the right-hemisphere areas controlling the left hand.

Recovery of Speech After Brain Damage

People usually suffer language impairments after extensive damage to the left hemisphere and sometimes after damage to the right hemisphere. After either kind of damage, some people recover substantially, but others recover only a little. Why the variation? Researchers have long assumed that it depended on how speech was lateralized for a given person. For example, someone with strong left-hemisphere dominance for speech would have a language impairment after left-hemisphere damage and little recovery. Someone with some representation of language in both hemispheres would suffer mild impairment after damage to either hemisphere but would recover relatively well.

New research methods have enabled researchers to test and confirm this hypothesis. First they used fMRI to determine how active each hemisphere became while each participant was talking. Then they applied transcranial magnetic stimulation (see Figure 4.2, p. 76) to temporarily suppress activity in one hemisphere or the other. They found that left-hemisphere inactivation blocked speech in those with strong left-hemisphere dominance, right-hemisphere inactivation blocked it in those with right-hemisphere dominance, and neither kind of inactivation blocked it very strongly in those with bilateral control of speech (Knecht et al., 2002).

When adults with left-hemisphere damage recover speech at all, the recovery requires increased or reorganized activity in the surviving areas of the left hemisphere (Heiss, Kessler, Thiel, Ghaemi, & Karbe, 1999). The basis for recovery is different when young children suffer brain damage. A 2-year-old who loses the entire left hemisphere is speechless at first but gradually develops some language, with the right hemisphere gaining far more language capacity than it could after an adult lesion. The amount of recovery varies greatly from one individual to another.

Researchers have long held that the earlier the damage, the better the language recovery (or development), but the results do not clearly support this view. Children with left-hemisphere damage do generally develop more language than adults with similar damage, but the difference between a 2-year-old child and a 6-year-old child, or perhaps even a 10-year-old child, is less important than what medical problem led to damage of the left hemisphere (Curtiss, de Bode, & Mathern, 2001).

Language recovery is sometimes surprisingly good for children with **Rasmussen's encephalopathy** (en-seff-ah-LOP-ah-thee), a rare condition in which an autoimmune disorder attacks first the glia and then the neurons of one or the other hemisphere of the brain, usually beginning in childhood or adolescence (Whitney & McNamara, 2000). Symptoms include frequent epileptic seizures and a gradual loss of brain tissue on one side. Over time, the seizures become more severe and more frequent, while language deteriorates if the damage is on the left side. Eventually, surgeons remove or disconnect what remains of the damaged hemisphere because it is producing seizures without accomplishing much good. After they do so, language sometimes recovers surprisingly well, though slowly, even in children over 10 years old at the time of surgery (Boatman et al., 1999; Hertz-Pannier et al., 2002). One possible explanation for their relatively good outcomes is that Rasmussen's encephalopathy develops so gradually that while the left hemisphere deteriorates over the years, the right hemisphere may be already starting to reorganize differently in a way that enables it to take over language when needed.

AVOIDING OVERSTATEMENTS

The research on left-brain/right-brain differences sometimes leads to unscientific assertions. Occasionally, you may hear something like, "I don't do well in science because it is a left-brain subject and I am a right-brain person." That kind of statement is based on two reasonable premises and a doubtful one. The scientific ideas are (a) that the hemispheres are specialized for different functions and (b) that certain tasks evoke greater activity in one hemisphere or the other. The doubtful premise is that any individual habitually relies on one hemisphere or the other.

What evidence do you suppose someone has for believing, "I am a right-brain person"? Did he or she undergo an MRI or PET scan to determine which hemisphere was larger or more active? Not likely. Generally, when people say, "I am right-brained," their only evidence is that they perform poorly on logical tasks. Therefore, the statement really means, "I do poorly in science because I do poorly in science." (Of course, saying "I am right-brained" implies that *because* I do poorly on logical tasks, *therefore* I am creative. Unfortunately, illogical is not the same as creative!)

In fact, only the simplest tasks activate just one hemisphere. Here is the evidence, which is a bit complicated: Suppose you are asked to tap one finger as soon as you see a flash of light. You can tap your right finger a few milliseconds faster after you see a flash in the right visual field, and you can tap your left finger a few milliseconds faster if you see a flash in the left visual field. The reason is that you respond faster if the information doesn't have to cross the corpus callosum. Now suppose we do the same kind of experiment but make the task slightly more complicated. Instead of tapping for any light you see, you tap for only certain kinds of light, so you have to process the information in some way before tapping your finger. The result is that you will tap a bit more slowly, and your reaction time won't depend on which finger is tapping or which visual field sees the stimulus (Forster & Corballis, 2000). The reason is that even a slightly difficult task requires you to use both hemispheres anyway, so it doesn't matter where the light started. The same is true in general: Most tasks require cooperation by both hemispheres.

MODULE 14.1

In Closing: One Brain, Two Hemispheres

Imagine that someone asks you a question to which you honestly reply that you do not know, while your left hand points to the correct answer. It must be an unsettling experience. A split-brain person acts at times like two people—two spheres of consciousness.

A brain-intact person acts and feels like a unity. How does a split-brain person feel? We don't know. When we ask, only the left hemisphere can answer, and *it* feels like a unity, but we don't know how the other hemisphere feels. As is so often true when we deal with the mind-brain relationship, many answers are elusive.

SUMMARY

1. The corpus callosum is a set of axons connecting the two hemispheres of the brain. (p. 420)

2. The left hemisphere controls speech in most people, and each hemisphere controls mostly the hand on the opposite side, sees the opposite side of the world, and feels the opposite side of the body. (p. 420)

3. In humans, the left visual field projects onto the right half of each retina, which sends axons to the right hemisphere. The right visual field projects onto the left half of each retina, which sends axons to the left hemisphere. (p. 421)

4. After damage to the corpus callosum, each hemisphere can respond quickly and accurately to questions about the information that reaches it directly and can slowly answer a few questions about information on the other side if it crosses the anterior commissure or one of the other small commissures. (p. 422)

5. Although the two hemispheres of a split-brain person are sometimes in conflict, they find many ways to cooperate and to cue each other. (p. 424)

6. The right hemisphere is dominant for the emotional inflections of speech and for interpreting other people's emotional expressions in either speech or facial expression. The right hemisphere also controls one's own expressions of fear, anger, and disgust. In vision and other modalities, it attends mostly to overall patterns, in contrast to the left hemisphere, which is better for details. (p. 426)

7. The left and right hemispheres differ anatomically even during infancy. Young children have some trouble comparing information from the left and right hands because the corpus callosum is not fully mature. (p. 428)

8. In a child born without a corpus callosum, the rest of the brain develops in unusual ways, and the child does not show the same deficits as an adult who sustains damage to the corpus callosum. (p. 429)

9. The brain of a left-handed person is not simply a mirror image of a right-hander's brain. Most left-handers have left-hemisphere or mixed dominance for speech; few have strong right-hemisphere dominance for speech. (p. 429)

10. Children recover language after left-hemisphere damage better than adults. Even somewhat older children recover well if the left-hemisphere damage developed gradually. (p. 430)

11. Both left and right hemispheres contribute to all but the simplest behaviors. (p. 430)

ANSWERS TO *STOP AND CHECK* QUESTIONS

1. In rabbits, the right eye is far to the side of the head and sees only the right visual field. In humans, the eyes point straight ahead and half of each eye sees the right visual field. (p. 422)

2. Left; left (p. 422)

3. A split-brain person cannot describe something after feeling it with the left hand but can with the right. The right hand sends its information to the left hemisphere, which is dominant for language in most people. The left hand sends its information to the right hemisphere, which cannot speak. (p. 424)

4. After seeing something in the left visual field, a split-brain person could point to the correct answer with the left hand. (p. 424)

5. The left hemisphere is dominant for speech and expressing happiness; the right hemisphere is dominant for all other items listed. (p. 427)

6. In children born without a corpus callosum, the left hemisphere develops more than the usual connections with the left hand, and the anterior commissure and other commissures grow larger than usual. Such growth does not occur after adult brain damage. (p. 429)

THOUGHT QUESTION

When a person born without a corpus callosum moves the fingers of one hand, he or she also is likely to move the fingers of the other hand involuntarily. What possible explanation can you suggest?

MODULE 14.2

Evolution and Physiology of Language

Communication is widespread among animals through visual, auditory, tactile, or chemical (pheromonal) displays. Human language stands out from other forms of communication because of its **productivity,** its ability to produce new signals to represent new ideas. That is, certain monkeys have one call to indicate "eagle or hawk in the air—take cover" and another to indicate "beware—snake on the ground." But they have no way to indicate "snake in the tree above you" or "eagle standing on the ground." Humans can discuss all sorts of new events and invent new expressions when we need them.

Did we evolve this ability out of nothing or from some precursor already present in other species? Why do we have language, whereas other species have at most a rudimentary hint of it? And what brain specializations make language possible? We consider these questions in order.

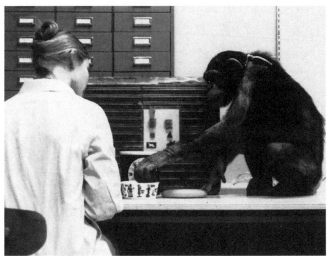

Figure 14.9   One attempt to teach chimpanzees language
One of the Premacks' chimps, Elizabeth, reacts to colored plastic chips that read "Not Elizabeth banana insert—Elizabeth apple wash."

NONHUMAN PRECURSORS OF LANGUAGE

Evolution rarely makes something totally new. Bat wings are modified hands, porcupine quills are modified hairs, and so forth. Nearly all differences among species are modifications of the same structures. So we would expect human language to be a modification of something we can detect in our closest relatives, chimpanzees.

Common Chimpanzees

After many early, unsuccessful attempts to teach chimpanzees to speak, researchers achieved better results by teaching them American Sign Language or other visual systems (B. T. Gardner & Gardner, 1975; Premack & Premack, 1972) (Figure 14.9). In one version, chimps learned to press keys bearing symbols to type messages on a computer (Rumbaugh, 1977), such as "Please machine give apple," "Please machine turn on movie," or (to another chimpanzee), "Please share your chocolate."

Is this use of symbols really language? Not necessarily. For example, when you insert your ATM card into a machine and enter your four-digit PIN, you don't really understand those four digits to mean "Please machine give money." Similarly, when a chimpanzee punches four symbols on a machine, it may not understand them to mean "Please machine give apple." The chimps' use of symbols differed from human language in several regards (Rumbaugh, 1990; Terrace, Petitto, Sanders, & Bever, 1979):

- The chimpanzees seldom used the symbols in new, original combinations, as even very young children do. That is, their use of symbols lacked *productivity*.
- The chimpanzees used their symbols almost always to request, only rarely to describe.
- The chimpanzees produced requests far better than they seemed to understand anyone else's requests. In contrast, young children understand far more than they can say. If you have studied a foreign language, you presumably understand many

sentences that you could not correctly state yourself. However, if you look up how to say something in a foreign-language phrase book, but then can't understand the reply, you don't really understand the language.

Bonobos

Such observations made psychologists skeptical about chimpanzee language. Then some surprising results emerged from studies of a rare endangered species, *Pan paniscus,* known as the bonobo or the pygmy chimpanzee (a misleading name because they are practically the same size as common chimpanzees).

Bonobos' social order resembles humans' in several regards. Males and females form strong, sometimes lasting, personal attachments. They often copulate face-to-face. The female is sexually responsive on almost any day and not just during her fertile period. Unlike most other primates, the males contribute significantly to infant care. Adults often share food with one another. They stand comfortably on their hind legs. In short, they resemble humans more than other primates do.

In the mid-1980s, Sue Savage-Rumbaugh, Duane Rumbaugh, and their associates tried to teach a female bonobo named Matata to press symbols that lit when touched; each symbol represents a word (Figure 14.10). Although Matata made little progress, her infant son Kanzi learned just by watching her. When given a chance to use the symbol board, he quickly excelled without any formal training. Soon researchers noticed that Kanzi understood a fair amount of spoken language. For example, whenever anyone said the word "light," Kanzi would flip the light switch. By age $5\frac{1}{2}$, he understood about 150 English words and could respond to such complex, unfamiliar spoken commands as "Throw your ball in the river" and "Go to the refrigerator and get out a tomato" (Savage-Rumbaugh, 1990; Savage-Rumbaugh, Sevcik, Brakke, & Rumbaugh, 1992). Since then, Kanzi has demonstrated language comprehension comparable to that of a 2- to $2\frac{1}{2}$-year-old child (Savage-Rumbaugh et al., 1993).

Kanzi and his younger sister Mulika use symbols in several ways that resemble humans more than they resemble common chimpanzees (Savage-Rumbaugh, 1991; Savage-Rumbaugh et al., 1993):

- They understand more than they can produce.
- They use symbols to name and describe objects even when they are not requesting them.
- They request items that they do not see, such as "bubbles" (I want to play with the bubble-blower) or "car trailer" (drive me in the car to the trailer).
- They occasionally use the symbols to describe past events. Kanzi once pressed the symbols "Matata bite" to explain the cut that he had received on his hand an hour earlier.
- They frequently make original, creative requests. For example, after Kanzi learned to press symbols to ask someone to play "chase" with him, he asked one person to chase another person while he watched!

Why have Kanzi and Mulika developed such impressive skills where other chimpanzees failed? One likely explanation is a species difference: Perhaps bonobos have more language potential than common chimpanzees. A second explanation is that Kanzi and Mulika began language training when young, unlike the chimpanzees in most other studies. A third reason pertains to the method of training: Perhaps learning by observation and imitation promotes better understanding than the formal

Figure 14.10   Language tests for Kanzi, a bonobo *(Pan paniscus)*
Kanzi listens to questions through the earphones and points to answers on a board. The experimenter with him does not know what the questions are or what answers are expected. *Source: From Georgia State University's Language Research Center, operated with the Yerkes Primate Center of Emory.*

training methods of previous studies (Savage-Rumbaugh et al., 1992).

For more information about bonobos, see this Web site:

www.blockbonobofoundation.org/blinks.htm

Stop & Check

1. In what ways do common chimpanzees' use of symbols differ from language?
2. What are three likely explanations for why bonobos made more language progress than common chimpanzees?

Check your answers on pages 447–448.

Nonprimates

What about nonprimate species? Dolphins have learned to respond to a system of gestures and sounds, each representing one word. For example, after the command "Right hoop left Frisbee fetch," a dolphin takes the Frisbee on the left to the hoop on the right (Herman, Pack, & Morrel-Samuels, 1993). A dolphin responds correctly to new combinations of old words, but only if the result is meaningful. For example, the first time that a dolphin is given the command "Person hoop fetch," it takes the hoop to the person. But when told "Person water fetch," it does nothing (because it has no way to take water to the person). Note that this system offers the dolphins no opportunity to produce language. They cannot tell humans to take the Frisbee to the hoop (Savage-Rumbaugh, 1993).

Spectacular results have been reported for Alex, an African gray parrot (Figure 14.11). Parrots are, of course, famous for imitating human sounds; Irene Pepperberg was the first to argue that parrots can use sounds meaningfully. She kept Alex in a stimulating environment and taught him to say words in conjunction with specific objects. First she and the other trainers would say a word many times and then offer rewards if Alex approximated the same sound. Here is an excerpt from a conversation with Alex early in training (Pepperberg, 1981, p. 142):

Pepperberg: Pasta! *(Takes pasta.)* Pasta! *(Alex stretches from his perch, appears to reach for pasta.)*

Alex: Pa!

Pepperberg: Better . . . what is it?

Alex: Pah-ah.

Pepperberg: Better!

Alex: Pah-ta.

Pepperberg: Okay, here's the pasta. Good try.

Although pasta was used in this example, Pepperberg generally used toys. For example, if Alex said "paper," "wood," or "key," she would give him what he asked for. In no case did she reward him for saying "paper" or "wood" by giving him a piece of food.

Alex gradually learned to give spoken answers to spoken questions. He was shown a tray of 12 small objects and then asked such questions as "What color is the key?" (answer: "green") and "What object is gray?" (answer: "circle"). In one test, he correctly answered 39 of 48 questions. Even many of his incorrect answers were almost correct. In one case, he was asked the color of the block and he responded with the color of the rock (Pepperberg, 1993). He also can answer questions of the form "How many blue key?" in which he has to examine 10 to 14 objects, count the blue keys among objects of two shapes and two colors, and then say the answer, ranging from one to six (Pepperberg, 1994).

Figure 14.11 Language tests for Alex, an African gray parrot
Alex has apparently learned to converse about objects in simple English—for example, giving the correct answer to "What color is the circle?" He receives no food rewards.

Is Alex actually learning language? Pepperberg calls his performance "language-like." She says that she is using the research to study the bird's concept formation, not his language capacities. Still, Alex has made far more progress than most of us would have thought possible.

What do we learn from studies of nonhuman language abilities? At a practical level, we gain insights into how best to teach language to those who do not learn it easily, such as brain-damaged people or autistic children. At a more theoretical level, these studies call attention to the difficulty of defining language: The main reason we have such trouble deciding whether chimpanzees or parrots have language is that we have not specified exactly what language is.

Because bonobos show some potential for language learning, apparently human language evolved from a precursor that was present in the ancient ancestor from which both species derived. But we still don't know what that precursor ability was doing. Do bonobos, and perhaps other primates, have language-type abilities that they use for communication? Perhaps so; the ability for spoken language probably evolved from early communication by gestures (Corballis, 1999). (Gestures are still important for communication; ask someone what a spiral is and then watch their hands move!)

However, the current use of some ability can be very different from the original use. For example, computers were originally invented to make mathematical calculations. Today, most people use them for writing papers, exchanging email, and browsing the Internet. If you looked only at current use, you might not guess the original use. Similarly, it is possible that language evolved from brain circuits devoted to organizing movement or other noncommunicational functions.

HOW DID HUMANS EVOLVE LANGUAGE?

Assuming that humans evolved language from a precursor present in other primates, the question remains: Why did we evolve language? You may think the answer is obvious: "Look at all the ways in which language is useful . . . " True, but if it's so useful, why didn't other animal species evolve at least simple languages? Most theories fall into two main categories: (a) we evolved language as a by-product of overall brain development and (b) we evolved it as an extra part of the brain.

Language as a Product of Overall Intelligence

The simplest view is that humans evolved big brains, and therefore great intelligence, and that language developed as an accidental by-product of increased intelligence. In its simplest form, this hypothesis faces several serious problems.

First Problem: Unclear Relationship Between Brain and Intelligence

If language is a by-product of overall brain development, maybe chimpanzees' brains are not quite big enough for language. If we take this idea seriously, we run into difficulties. Elephants' brains are four times the size of ours, and sperm whales' brains are twice as big as elephants'. But neither has language, at least not as far as we can detect.

An alternative view is that intelligence depends on brain-to-body ratio. Figure 14.12 illustrates the relationship between logarithm of body mass and logarithm of brain mass for various vertebrates (Jerison, 1985). Note that the species we regard as most intelligent—for example, ahem, ourselves—have larger brains in proportion to body size than do the species we consider less impressive, such as frogs. However, as soon as you try to define exactly what you mean by animal intelligence, you will find it a slippery concept (Macphail, 1985). For now, let's not even worry about that one. Humans, it turns out, do *not* have the highest brain-to-body ratio of all species. That honor goes to the squirrel monkey, whose brain constitutes 5% of the monkey's total weight. The human brain weighs only 2% of our total weight. Even the elephant-nose fish, which you might keep in a tropical fish aquarium, beats us in percentage (Figure 14.13). Its brain weighs a mere 0.3 g (as compared to our 1200 to 1400 g), but that's 3% of the total weight of the fish (Nilsson, 1999). So, are squirrel monkeys and elephant-nose fish more intelligent than we are? Consider also the chihuahua problem: Among dogs, chihuahuas have the highest brain-to-body ratio simply because they were selected for small bodies (Deacon, 1997). Are chihuahuas the smartest of dogs? If so, it's going to be news to many people.

What is the relationship between brain size and intelligence among humans? Again, the results are contradictory and confusing. In one study, investigators used MRI scans to estimate brain size in 40 college students and found that the students with the higher IQ scores also had larger brains (Willerman, Schultz, Rutledge, & Bigler, 1991). One study comparing monozygotic to dizygotic twins found

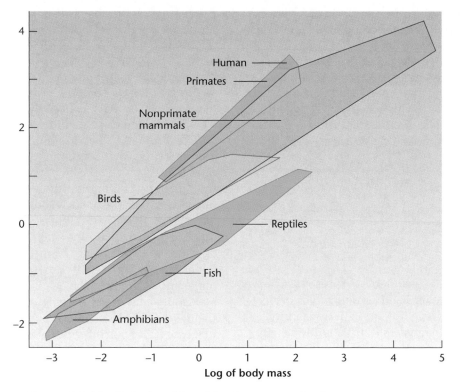

Figure 14.12   Relationship of brain mass to body mass across species
Each species is one point within one of the polygons. In general, log of body mass is a good predictor of log of brain mass. Note that primates in general and humans in particular have a large brain mass in proportion to body mass.
Source: Adapted from Jerison, 1985

evidence for heritability of both brain size and IQ scores, with a strong correlation between the two (Posthuma et al., 2002). However, another study examining pairs of sisters reported very little relationship between which sister had the larger brain and which one had the higher IQ score (Schoenemann, Budinger, Sarich, & Wang, 2000). In short, the relationship between brain size and intelligence is far from clear.

Figure 14.13   An elephant-nose fish
The brain of this odd-looking fish weighs 0.3 g (0.01 ounce), which is 3% of the weight of the whole fish— a vastly higher percentage than most other fish and higher even than humans. What this fish does with so much brain we don't know, but it may relate to the fish's unusual ability to detect electrical fields.

Stop & Check

3. Why are both brain size and brain-to-body ratio unsatisfactory explanations for intelligence?

   Check your answer on page 448.

Second Problem: People With Full-Sized Brains and Impaired Language

If language is a product of overall brain size, then people with full-sized brains and normal overall intelligence should necessarily have normal language. However, not all do. In one family, 16 of 30 people over three generations show severe language deficits despite normal intelligence in other regards. Because of a dominant gene, which has been located and identified, the affected people have serious troubles in pronunciation and virtually all other aspects of language (Fisher, Vargha-Khadem, Watkins, Monaco, & Pembrey, 1998; Gopnik & Crago, 1991; Lai, Fisher, Hurst, Vargha-Khadem, & Monaco, 2001). They fail to master even the simplest grammatical rules, as in the following dialogue about making plurals:

Experimenter	*Respondent*
• This is a wug; these are . . .	• How should I know? *[Later]* These are wug.
• This is a zat; these are . . .	• These are zacko.
• This is a sas; these are . . .	• These are sasss. *[Not sasses]*

In another test, experimenters presented sentences and asked whether each sentence was correct, and if not, how to improve it. People in this family accepted many ungrammatical sentences while labeling many correct sentences as incorrect. (Evidently, they were guessing.) When they tried to correct a sentence, their results were often odd. For example:

Original Item	*Attempted Correction*
• The boy eats three cookie.	• The boys eat four cookie.

In short, a genetic condition that affects brain development can seriously impair language without necessarily impairing other aspects of intelligence. Language requires some sort of specialization of certain parts of the brain, not just a certain quantity of overall brain development.

Third Problem: Williams Syndrome

What about the reverse pattern? Could someone be mentally retarded in most ways and nevertheless have good language? Psychologists long assumed that such a pattern was impossible and that language learning requires good overall intelligence.

Then psychologists discovered a rare condition, affecting about 1 person in 25,000, called **Williams syndrome,** characterized by mental retardation in most regards but (in many cases) skillful use of language. The cause is a deletion of several genes from chromosome 7 (Korenberg et al., 2000), leading to abnormal development of the posterior portions of the cerebral cortex and several subcortical areas (Reiss et al., 2000). Affected people are poor at use of numbers, visuomotor skills (e.g., copying a drawing), and spatial perception (e.g., finding their way home). When asked to estimate the length of a bus, three Williams syndrome people answered "30 inches," "3 inches or 100 inches maybe," and "2 inches, 10 feet" (Bellugi, Lichtenberger, Jones, Lai, & St George, 2000). Throughout life, they require constant supervision and cannot hold even an unskilled job.

Nevertheless, they are close to normal in several other regards. One is their ability to interpret facial expressions, such as relaxed or worried, serious or playful, flirtatious or uninterested (Tager-Flusberg, Boshart, & Baron-Cohen, 1998). Another is social behavior, such as friendliness and openness toward other people. Still another is music, such as the ability to clap a complex rhythm and memorize songs (Levitin & Bellugi, 1998). However, their most spectacular skill is language. Not all people with Williams syndrome have good language abilities (Jarrold, Baddeley, & Hewes, 1998), but some are quite amazing, especially considering their impairments in other regards. For example, if asked to "name as many animals as possible in the next minute," most people list familiar animals such as dog, horse, and squirrel. People with Williams syndrome list odd examples, such as weasel, newt, ibex, unicorn, yak, koala, and triceratops (Bellugi, Wang, & Jernigan, 1994). Figure 14.14 shows the result when a young woman with Williams syndrome and an IQ of 49 was asked to draw an elephant and describe it. Contrast her almost poetic description to the unrecognizable drawing. When shown a picture of a frog in a jar and asked to tell a story about it, one Williams syndrome teenager with an IQ of 50 produced the following:

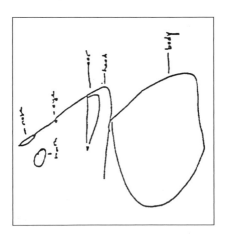

And what an elephant is, it is one of the animals. And what the elephant does, it lives in the jungle. It can also live in the zoo. And what it has, it has long gray ears, fan ears, ears that can blow in the wind. It has a long trunk that can pick up grass, or pick up hay . . . If they're in a bad mood it can be terrible . . . If the elephant gets mad it could stomp; it could charge, like a bull can charge. They have long big tusks. They can damage a car . . . it could be dangerous. When they're in a pinch, when they're in a bad mood it can be terrible. You don't want an elephant as a pet. You want a cat or a dog or a bird . . .

Figure 14.14 A drawing and a description of an elephant by a young woman with Williams syndrome
The labels on the drawing were provided by the investigator, based on what the woman said she was drawing. *Source: From "Williams Syndrome: An unusual Neuropsychological Profile," by U. Bellugi, P. P. Wang, and T. L. Jernigan. In S. H. Broman and J. Grafman, Eds.,* Atypical Cognitive Deficits in Developmental Disorders. *Copyright ©1987 Lawrence Erlbaum. Reprinted by permission.*

Once upon a time when it was dark at night . . . the boy had a frog. The boy was looking at the frog . . . sitting on the chair, on the table, and the dog was looking through . . . looking up to the frog in a jar. That night he slept and slept for a long time, the boy did. But, the frog was not gonna go to sleep. And when the frog went out . . . the boy and the dog were still sleeping. The next morning it was beautiful in the morning. It was bright and the sun was nice and warm. Then suddenly when he opened his eyes . . . he looked at the jar and then suddenly the frog was not there. The jar was empty. There was no frog to found (whispered). (Bellugi, Lichtenberger, Mills, Galaburda, & Korenberg, 1999, p. 199)

Let's not overstate the case. People with Williams syndrome do have some language abnormalities. Their language development is slow in early childhood, and although many of them make spectacular gains later, their grammar continues to be odd (Clahsen & Almazen, 1998; Karmiloff-Smith et al., 1998). If shown a picture of an unfamiliar object and told its name, they are as likely to think the name refers to some part of the object as to the object itself (Stevens & Karmiloff-Smith, 1997). They use fancy words when a common word would work better, such as "I have to evacuate the glass" instead of "empty" or "pour out" the glass (Bellugi et al., 2000). Their language has been compared in some regards to what happens when a normal adult learns a second language (Karmiloff-Smith et al., 1998). In any case, observations of Williams syndrome indicate that language is not simply a by-product of overall intelligence.

Stop & Check

4. Name three arguments against the hypothesis that language evolution depended simply on the overall evolution of brain and intelligence.

5. Describe tasks that people with Williams syndrome do poorly and those that they do well.

Check your answers on page 448.

Language as a Special Module

An alternative view is that language evolved as an extra brain module, a new specialization. This presumed module has been forcefully described by Noam Chomsky (1980) and Steven Pinker (1994) as a **language acquisition device,** a built-in mechanism for acquiring language. The main evidence for this view is the amazing ease with which most children develop language (Trout, 2001). For example, the hearing children of deaf parents gain language almost on schedule despite hearing nothing from their own par-

ents (Lenneberg, 1969). Deaf children quickly learn sign language, and if no one teaches them a sign language, they invent their own and teach it to one another (Goldin-Meadow, McNeill, & Singleton, 1996; Goldin-Meadow & Mylander, 1998).

Advocates of the language acquisition device concept sometimes go beyond saying that children learn language readily, stating instead that people are *born* with language; all they have to do is fill in the words and details. Chomsky defends this idea with the **poverty of the stimulus argument:** Children do not hear many examples of some of the grammatical structures they acquire, and therefore, they could not learn them. For example, even young children will phrase the question

"Is the boy who is unhappy watching Mickey Mouse?"

instead of

"Is the boy who unhappy is watching Mickey Mouse?"

Chomsky and his followers maintain that children have not had enough opportunity to learn that grammatical rule, so they must be born knowing it. Grammars differ among languages, of course, and it is implausible that a child is born knowing all the possible human grammars and then "chooses" the one that fits the language in local use (Nowak, Komarova, & Niyogi, 2002). Adherents of the language acquisition device can counter that they just mean that children are born with an understanding of basic language elements such as subject, verb, and object. However, if that is all they are born with, we are back to puzzling about how children know how to phrase the question about Mickey Mouse.

Most researchers agree that humans have specially evolved *something* that enables them to learn language easily. One part of that something is an identified gene that is necessary for language articulation. Recall earlier (p. 437) the discussion of a family with impairments in both articulation and grammar. The impaired people have a mutation of the gene *FOXP2* on chromosome 7 (Lai et al., 2002). Chimpanzees, gorillas, and other great apes have a corresponding gene that differs from that of humans in just two DNA bases (Enard et al., 2002). Evidently, a very small evolutionary change in one gene, and therefore one protein, made a huge difference in our ability to speak.

One gene change would not be sufficient for language, of course, and language requires more than the ability to articulate sounds. So what else might we have evolved? Many researchers find it implausible that infants would be born literally "knowing" the diverse grammars of thousands of languages (Deacon, 1997; Seidenberg, 1997). Many researchers doubt even that language is a separate, independent "module," like a speech synthesizer attached to an otherwise unchanged computer. Certain brain areas are, to be sure, necessary for language, but language is not the only thing they do. By analogy, you need your elbow to play tennis, but we wouldn't call your elbow "the tennis joint" (Dick et al., 2001). The parts of your brain important for language are also critical for memory (Ullman, 2001), music perception (Maess, Koelsch, Gunter, & Friederici, 2001), and other tasks.

So back to the original question: Why did humans evolve language, whereas no other species did? The honest answer is that we don't know, but language is probably not a by-product of evolving overall intelligence. In fact, the opposite is easier to imagine: Selective pressure for social interactions among people, including those between parents and children, favored the evolution of language, and as language improved, overall intelligence developed as a by-product of language (Deacon, 1992, 1997). Unfortunately, of course, it is difficult to reconstruct early human evolution, especially as it relates to behavior.

Is There a Critical Period for Language Learning?

If humans are specially adapted to learn language, perhaps we are adapted to learn best during a critical period early in life, just as sparrows learn their song best during an early period. One way to test this hypothesis is to see whether people learn a second language better if they start young. The consistent result is that adults are better than children at memorizing the vocabulary of a second language, but children are much more likely to master the pronunciation and the more unfamiliar aspects of the grammar. (For example, the difference between *a* and *the* in English is difficult for adult Chinese speakers, whose native language does not use articles.) A child who overhears a language in the neighborhood, without learning it, has a better chance than other people of mastering the pronunciation if he or she tries to learn the language as an adult (Au, Knightly, Jun, & Oh, 2002).

However, there is no sharp cutoff for learning a second language; starting at age 2 is better than 4, 4 is better than 6, even 13 is better than 16 (Harley & Wang, 1997; Weber-Fox & Neville, 1996). If someone learns a second language well, it activates the same language areas as the first (Paradis, 1998), and the amount of language-area activation depends on the degree of mastery of the second language, *not on the age of starting it* (Perani et al., 1998). Thus, the data on second-language learning are ambiguous with regard to a critical period.

Another way to test the critical-period idea is to study people who were not exposed to language at all during infancy. There are a few cases of children who lived in the wild, raised by wolves or whatever, who were later found and returned to human society. The result is that they were limited in their language learning, but these results are difficult to interpret for many obvious reasons.

Clearer data come from studies of deaf children who at first were not exposed to sign language. If their deafness was profound enough that they could not learn spoken language, they were effectively isolated from all language. Here the result is clear: The earlier a child has a chance to learn sign language, the more skilled he or she will become (Harley & Wang, 1997). A child who learns English early can learn sign language later, and a deaf child who learns sign language early can learn English later (with the obvious exception of pronunciation), but someone who learns no language before starting school will never develop much skill at any language (Mayberry, Lock, & Kazmi, 2002). This observation strongly supports the idea of an early critical period for language learning.

Stop & Check

6. What is the poverty of the stimulus argument?

7. If you learn a second language late in life, does it activate the same brain area as the first language or a different one?

8. What is the strongest evidence in favor of a critical period for language learning?

Check your answers on page 448.

BRAIN DAMAGE AND LANGUAGE

Because almost every healthy child develops language, we infer that the human brain is specialized to make language learning easy. Most of our knowledge about the brain mechanisms of language has come from studies of brain-damaged people.

Broca's Aphasia (Nonfluent Aphasia)

In 1861, a patient who had been mute for 30 years was treated for gangrene by the French surgeon Paul Broca. When the man died 5 days later, Broca did an autopsy and found a lesion in the frontal cortex. In later years, Broca examined the brains of additional patients whose only problem had been aphasia (severe language impairment); in nearly all cases, he found damage that included this same area, a small part of the frontal lobe of the left cerebral cortex near the motor cortex, which is now known as **Broca's area** (Figure 14.15). The usual cause was a stroke (an interruption of blood flow to part of the brain). Broca published his results in 1865, slightly later than papers by other French physicians, Marc and Gustave Dax, who also pointed to the left hemisphere as the seat of language abilities (Finger & Roe, 1996). Broca is given the credit, however, because his description was more detailed and more convincing. This discovery, the first demonstration of a particular function for a particular brain area, paved the way for modern neurology.

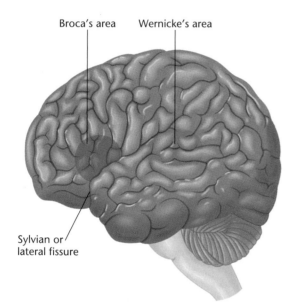

Broca's area   Wernicke's area

Sylvian or / lateral fissure

Figure 14.15 Some major language areas of the cerebral cortex
In most people, only the left hemisphere is specialized for language.

We now know that speaking activates a large area of the brain, mostly in the left hemisphere, and certainly not just Broca's area (Wallesch, Henriksen, Kornhuber, & Paulson, 1985) (Figure 14.16). Damage limited to Broca's area produces only a minor or brief language impairment; serious deficits occur only with extensive damage that extends beyond Broca's area to other cortical and subcortical structures. Also, the symptoms vary and are not completely predictable from the location of the damage (Dick et al., 2001). When brain-damaged people suffer serious impairment of language production, we

call it **Broca's aphasia,** or **nonfluent aphasia,** regardless of the exact location of the damage. People with Broca's aphasia also have comprehension deficits when the meaning of a sentence depends on prepositions, word endings, or unusual word order—in short, when the sentence structure is complicated.

Difficulty in Language Production

People with Broca's aphasia speak slowly and inarticulately, and they have trouble writing and gesturing (Cicone, Wapner, Foldi, Zurif, & Gardner, 1979). The left frontal cortex is just as important for the sign language of the deaf (Neville et al., 1998), and deaf people with Broca's aphasia have trouble producing sign language, although they can use their hands well in other ways (Hickok, Bellugi, & Klima, 1996). So the problem relates to language, not just to the vocal muscles.

When people with Broca's aphasia speak, they omit most pronouns, prepositions, conjunctions, helping verbs, quantifiers, and tense and number endings. At least, they do so in English; when speaking a language such as German or Italian, in which word endings are more important, they use more of the word endings (Blackwell & Bates, 1995). Prepositions, conjunctions, helping verbs, and so forth are known as the *closed class* of grammatical forms because a language rarely adds new prepositions, conjunctions, and the like. In contrast, new nouns and verbs (the *open class*) enter a language frequently. People with Broca's aphasia use nouns and verbs more easily than closed-class words. They find it difficult to repeat a phrase such as "No ifs, ands, or buts," although they can successfully repeat "The general commands the army." Furthermore, patients who cannot read aloud "To be or not to be" can read "Two bee oar knot two bee" (H. Gardner & Zurif, 1975). Clearly, the trouble is with the word meanings, not just pronunciation.

Why do people with Broca's aphasia omit the grammatical words and endings? The simple answer is that they have suffered damage to a "grammar area" in the brain, but there is another possibility: When it is a struggle to speak at all, people leave out the weakest elements. Sometimes people who are in great pain also speak in short, telegraphic expressions like a person with Broca's aphasia (Dick et al., 2001).

Problems in Comprehending Grammatical Words and Devices

People with Broca's aphasia have trouble understanding the same kinds of words that they omit when speaking, such as prepositions and conjunctions. They often misunderstand sentences with complex grammar, such

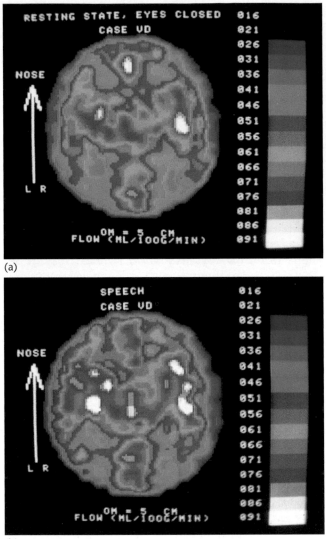

(a)

(b)

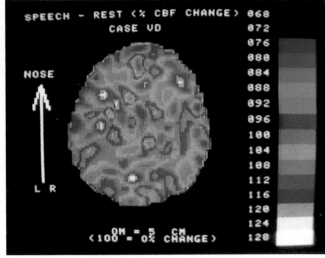

(c)

Figure 14.16 Records showing blood flow for a normal adult
Red indicates the highest level of activity, followed by yellow, green, and blue. **(a)** Blood flow to the brain at rest. **(b)** Blood flow while the subject describes a magazine story. **(c)** Difference between **(b)** and **(a)**. The results in **(c)** indicate which brain areas increased their activity during language production. Note the increased activity in many areas of the brain, especially on the left side. *Source: Wallesch, Henriksen, Kornhuber, & Paulson, 1985*

as "The girl that the boy is chasing is tall" (Zurif, 1980). However, most English sentences follow the subject-verb-object order, and their meaning is clear even without the prepositions and conjunctions. You can demonstrate this for yourself by taking some paragraph and deleting all the prepositions, conjunctions, articles, helping verbs, and word endings to see how it might appear to someone with Broca's aphasia. Here is an example, taken from earlier in this chapter:

Try It Yourself

> What ~~about~~ nonprimate species? Dolphins ~~have~~ learn~~ed~~ ~~to~~ respond ~~to a~~ system ~~of~~ gesture~~s~~ ~~and~~ sounds, ~~each~~ representing one word. ~~For~~ example, ~~after the~~ command "Right hoop left Frisbee fetch," ~~a~~ dolphin take~~s~~ ~~the~~ Frisbee ~~on the~~ left ~~to the~~ hoop ~~on the~~ right. ~~A~~ dolphin responds correct~~ly~~ ~~to~~ new combinations ~~of~~ old words, ~~but~~ only ~~if the~~ result ~~is~~ meaning~~ful~~. ~~For~~ example, ~~the~~ first time ~~that a~~ dolphin ~~is~~ give~~n~~ ~~the~~ command "Person hoop fetch," ~~it~~ takes ~~the~~ hoop ~~to the~~ person. ~~But~~ when told "Person water fetch," ~~it~~ do~~es~~

nothing (~~because it has~~ no way ~~to~~ take water ~~to the~~ person). Note ~~that~~ this system offers ~~the~~ dolphins no opportunity ~~to~~ produce language. ~~They~~ cannot tell humans ~~to~~ take ~~the~~ Frisbee ~~to the~~ hoop.

Still, people with Broca's aphasia have not totally lost their knowledge of grammar. For example, they generally recognize that something is wrong with the sentence "He written has songs," even if they cannot say how to improve it (Wulfeck & Bates, 1991). In many ways, their comprehension resembles that of normal people who are greatly distracted. For example, if you listen to someone speaking rapidly with a heavy accent in a very noisy room, your comprehension will suffer. You will catch bits and pieces of what the speaker says and fill in the rest by inferences. Consequently, you will understand a grammatically simple sentence such as "The boy is chasing a tall girl" but probably not "The girl that the boy is chasing is tall." That is, your understanding and misunderstanding would closely resemble the pattern of Broca's aphasia patients (Blackwell & Bates, 1995; Dick et al., 2001). In fact, even when we hear a sentence clearly, we sometimes ignore the grammar. When people hear "The dog was bitten by the man," many of them assume it was the dog that did the biting (Ferreira, Bailey, & Ferraro, 2002). Broca's aphasia patients just rely on inferences instead of grammar more often than the rest of us.

Wernicke's Aphasia (Fluent Aphasia)

In 1874, Carl Wernicke (usually pronounced WER-nih-kee by English speakers, although the German pronunciation is VER-nih-keh), a 26-year-old junior assistant in a German hospital, discovered that damage in part of the left temporal cortex produced language impairment very different from what Broca had reported. Although patients could speak and write, their language comprehension was poor. Damage in and around Wernicke's area (see Figure 14.15), located near the auditory part of the cerebral cortex, produces Wernicke's aphasia, or fluent aphasia, characterized by impaired ability to remember the names of objects and impaired language comprehension. It is also sometimes known as *fluent aphasia* because the person can still speak smoothly. As with Broca's aphasia, the symptoms vary from person to person even when the actual brain damage appears to be similar. Therefore, we use the term Wernicke's aphasia, or fluent aphasia, to describe a certain pattern of behavior, independent of the exact location of damage. Typical results are as follows:

1. *Articulate speech.* In contrast to Broca's aphasics, Wernicke's aphasics speak clearly, fluently, and rapidly, except for occasional pauses to try to think of the name of something.
2. *Difficulty finding the right word.* People suffering from Wernicke's aphasia have anomia (ay-NOME-ee-uh), difficulty recalling the names of objects. Sometimes they make up names (like "flieber" or "thingamajig") or substitute one name for another, and sometimes they use vague or roundabout expressions such as "the thing that we used to do with the thing that was like the other one." When they do manage to find some of the right words, they arrange them improperly, such as, "The Astros listened to the radio tonight" (instead of "I listened to the Astros on the radio tonight") (R. C. Martin & Blossom-Stach, 1986).
3. *Poor language comprehension.* Wernicke's aphasics have great trouble understanding both spoken and written speech. Although many sentences are clear enough without prepositions, word endings, and grammar (which confuse Broca's aphasics), very

few sentences make sense without nouns and verbs (which trouble Wernicke's patients).

The following conversation is between a woman with Wernicke's aphasia and a speech therapist trying to teach her the names of some objects. (The Duke University Department of Speech Pathology and Audiology provided this dialogue.)

Therapist: *(Holding picture of an apron)* Can you name that one?

Woman: Um . . . you see I can't, I can I can barely do; he would give me sort of umm . . .

T: A clue?

W: That's right . . . just a like, just a . . .

T: You mean, like, "You wear that when you wash dishes or when you cook a meal . . . "?

W: Yeah, something like that.

T: Okay, and what is it? You wear it around your waist, and you cook . . .

W: Cook. Umm, umm, see I can't remember.

T: It's an apron.

W: Apron, apron, that's it, apron.

T: *(Holding another picture)* That you wear when you're getting ready for bed after a shower.

W: Oh, I think that he put under different, something different. We had something, you know, umm, you know.

T: A different way of doing it?

W: No, umm . . . umm . . . *(Pause)*

T: It's actually a bathrobe.

W: Bathrobe. Uh, we didn't call it that, we called it something else.

T: Smoking jacket?

W: No, I think we called it, uh . . .

T: Lounging . . . ?

W: No, no, something, in fact, we called it just . . . *(Pause)*

T: Robe?

W: Robe. Or something like that.

In this conversation, note that the patient still knows the names of objects and recognizes them when she hears them; she just has trouble finding them for herself. In some ways, her speech resembles that of a student called upon to speak in a foreign language class after not studying the vocabulary list very hard.

Why do people with Wernicke's aphasia sometimes use made-up words ("flieber") or roundabout expressions ("the thing that was like the other one")? One hypothesis is that they speak rapidly despite their trouble remembering names of objects. Suppose you take a stack of pictures of unfamiliar objects and activities

TABLE 14.2 Broca's Aphasia and Wernicke's Aphasia

Type	Pronunciation	Content of Speech	Comprehension
Broca's aphasia	Very poor	Mostly nouns and verbs; omits prepositions and other grammatical connectives	Impaired if the meaning depends on complex grammar
Wernicke's aphasia	Unimpaired	Grammatical but often nonsensical; has trouble finding the right word, especially names of objects	Seriously impaired

and force yourself to speak faster than normal and describe each picture in 2 or 3 seconds before going on to the next picture, and then the next, and so forth. You will frequently resort to nonsensical expressions that resemble Wernicke's aphasia (Dick et al., 2001).

Table 14.2 contrasts Broca's aphasia and Wernicke's aphasia. For more information about aphasia and its many forms, see this site:
www.aphasia.org/

Structure and Function: Difficult Inferences

What exactly do Broca's and Wernicke's areas do? If we examine just the language capacities of people with damage in and around these areas, we naturally conclude that they are important for language. But language is not their only, and perhaps not even their primary, function. For example, one proposal links the temporal lobe with declarative memories and the frontal lobe with procedural memories. The names of objects are declarative memories, as are irregular past-tense verbs (e.g., *hit, drove,* and *kept*), and people with Wernicke's aphasia (temporal lobe damage) are impaired in their use of irregular verbs (Tyler et al., 2002; Ullman, 2001). In contrast, we form regular past-tense verbs by using procedural memories (add "–ed"), and the frontal lobe, in and around Broca's area, is apparently critical for regular past tenses (Shapiro, Pascual-Leone, Mottaghy, Gangitano, & Caramazza, 2001; Tyler et al., 2002). In other words, we could explain the language effects of damage to different brain areas without necessarily assuming that those areas are devoted specifically to language.

Inferring structure-function relationships is difficult, partly because a structure can contribute to many abilities and partly because results can be heavily influenced by details of procedure that we might overlook. For example, some results depend on what language someone speaks. Try this: Here is a list

of European birds that are probably unfamiliar to you. Read the list aloud: *capercaillie, gyrfalcon, goshawk, chukar, chough.*

The point is that in English we frequently encounter words we don't know how to pronounce. In particular, how did you pronounce chough? Did you think it would rhyme with *though, through, cough, rough, dough,* or *bough?* You didn't know, and you had to guess—probably incorrectly. (It rhymes with *rough.*) In Italian and other phonetically written languages, the spelling tells you exactly how to say a word, and a correct pronunciation tells you how to spell it. As a result, Italian children learn to read sooner than English-speaking children do, read faster, and seldom get diagnosed as dyslexic. Also—and I'm finally getting to the point—reading aloud activates less of the brain for Italian speakers than it does for English speakers (Paulesu et al., 2000). Reading English requires more work and often requires double-checking ("Did I say that word right?"), a step not necessary in Italian. We need not become discouraged about determining the functions of various brain areas, but we should not draw quick conclusions either.

9. Describe the speech production of people with Broca's aphasia and those with Wernicke's aphasia.

10. Is it reasonable to conclude that Broca's patients have lost their grammar?

11. Describe the speech comprehension of people with Broca's aphasia and those with Wernicke's aphasia.

12. Why does reading aloud require more of the brain in English speakers than Italian speakers?

Check your answers on page 448.

dyslexic adults also made
advanced from a third-gra
level in 4 months (Geiger
first 3 weeks of practice,
special cut-out sheet of pa

One final twist: Of th
went through this proces
would rather return to bei
they could attend to sever
ing to someone, listening
ing a work of art, and so
read one word at a time, tl
perform only one task at a
old way of life. In short,
to their overall attentiona

For more informatic
Web site:
www.bda-dyslexia.org.ul

13. What are four hyp
dyslexia?

Check your answer

MODULE 14.2

In Closing: Lang

Perhaps the best summ
summary of language
guage and reading are
people can become im
reasons. Language is n
all intelligence, but it
intellectual functions e

SUMMARY

1. Chimpanzees can
   gestures or nonvoc
   put does not clos
   Bonobos have ma
   than common chin
   ferences, early onse
   ing methods. (p. 43

2. Even an African g
   language abilities,
   parently not neces

DYSLEXIA

Dyslexia is a specific impairment of reading in a person with adequate vision and adequate skills in other academic areas. It is more common in boys than girls and apparently has a genetic basis, although certainly we cannot attribute all cases to any single gene (Kaplan et al., 2002). Dyslexia is more common among English readers than among readers of, say, Italian, which has purely phonetic spelling. However, even among Italians, some people read better than others, and slow-reading Italians have trouble with the same kinds of language tasks as dyslexic English readers (Paulesu et al., 2001). In other words, a certain number of people in any country have trouble reading, but the problems are more severe in a language with as many odd spellings as English has. (For example, consider the words *phlegm, bivouac, khaki, physique,* and *gnat.*)

Researchers have documented multiple mild abnormalities in the brains of many people with dyslexia, including microscopic details of brain structure (Klingberg et al., 2000). As a rule, a dyslexic person is more likely to have a bilaterally symmetrical cerebral cortex, whereas in other people the planum temporale and certain other areas are larger in the left hemisphere (Galaburda, Sherman, Rosen, Aboitiz, & Geschwind, 1985; Hynd & Semrud-Clikeman, 1989; Jenner, Rosen, & Galaburda, 1999). In some dyslexic people, certain language-related areas are actually larger in the right hemisphere (Duara et al., 1991). Dyslexic people also show signs of weak connections among several brain areas, such that activity in one part of the left cerebral cortex tends to be uncorrelated with activity in other areas of the left cortex, unlike the pattern for normal readers (Horwitz, Rumsey, & Donohue, 1998; Paulesu et al., 1996; Pugh et al., 2000).

Reading is a complicated skill that requires seeing subtle differences as *abode* versus *adobe,* hearing subtle differences as *symphony* versus *sympathy,* and connecting the sound patterns to the visual symbols. In the often confusing literature about dyslexia, the one point that stands out clearly is that different people have different kinds of reading problems, and no one explanation works for all. Some researchers distinguish between *dysphonetic dyslexics* and *dyseidetic dyslexics* (Flynn & Boder, 1991). Dysphonetic dyslexics have trouble sounding out words, so they try to memorize words as wholes, and when they don't recognize a word, they guess based on context. For example, they might read the word *laugh* as "funny." Dyseidetic readers sound out words well enough, but they fail to recognize a word as a whole. They read slowly and have particular trouble with irregularly spelled words. This distinction is sometimes useful, and different types of dyslexia probably have different genetic bases (Fisher & DeFries, 2002). However, many

researchers doubt that dyslexic people fall into two neat categories (Farmer & Klein, 1995).

Various researchers have emphasized different hypotheses to explain dyslexia. One hypothesis has been that dyslexic people have an unresponsive magnocellular path in the visual system (Livingstone, Rosen, Drislane, & Galaburda, 1991). Recall from Chapter 6 that the magnocellular path deals with overall patterns and moving objects. Someone who cannot see words normally would certainly have trouble reading them. However, most studies have found only mild and inconsistent evidence for visual deficits (Cornelissen, Richardson, Mason, Fowler, & Stein, 1995; Skottun, 2000). It is still possible that dyslexic people do not attend to the right visual cues, but most of them apparently see the cues well enough.

According to another hypothesis, dyslexia reflects a subtle hearing impairment. Brain scans have shown that dyslexics' brains show less than normal responses to speech sounds, especially consonants (Helenius, Salmelin, Richardson, Leinonen, & Lyytinen, 2002; McCrory, Frith, Brunswick, & Price, 2000). Many dyslexic people tend to have particular trouble detecting the temporal order of sounds, such as noticing the difference between beep-click-buzz and beep-buzz-click (Farmer & Klein, 1995; Kujala et al., 2000; Nagarajan et al., 1999). They also have much difficulty making Spoonerisms—that is, trading the first consonants of two words, such as listening to "dear old queen" and saying "queer old dean" or listening to "way of life" and saying "lay of wife" (Paulesu et al., 1996). Doing so, of course, requires close attention to sounds and their order. Many dyslexic people have trouble with nonauditory temporal order tasks as well, such as tapping a regular rhythm with the fingers (Wolff, 1993). In fact, even slow-reading college students, not diagnosed as dyslexic, also have trouble tapping rapid finger rhythms (Carello, LeVasseur, & Schmidt, 2002).

However, granting these temporal order problems, the question remains, how might impaired perception of temporal order lead to dyslexia? One proposal is that people with dyslexia have trouble hearing the difference between similar words and therefore confuse them when they try to read them (Carello et al., 2002). However, presumably, someone who cannot hear the differences among various words would not be able to pronounce them correctly, whereas dyslexic people as a rule speak clearly. Therefore, the relation between dyslexia and impaired temporal order processing remains unclear.

Another hypothesis is that the problem in dyslexia is not simply vision or sound but converting one to the other, as if one part of the brain were poorly connected to another. In one study, dyslexics performed about the same as normals at watching nonsense words flashed on the screen and saying whether they were the same or

different. (For example, bra
and *sond-snod* would be
equal to normals at listenir
and saying whether they we
paired only when they had
on the screen and then say v
nonsense word they heard (

A final hypothesis rela
in attention. Here is a demo
on the central dot in each
moving your eyes back an
dle letter of each three-lett

NOE

WSH

CTN

HCW

IEY

HNO

Figure 14.17 Identif
Normal readers identify
letters become more rei
of the fixation point, ye
of fixation. *Source: Repri*
1992, Cognitive Brain R
KV Amsterdam, The Netl

---

2. Bonobos may be more predisposed to language than common chimpanzees. The bonobos started training at an earlier age. They learned by imitation instead of formal training techniques. (p. 435)

3. If we define intelligence in terms of human-type intelligence, including language, there are species with larger overall brain volume or with a larger brain-to-body ratio that lack language. (p. 437)

4. First, overall intelligence, as defined by humans, has no simple relationship to brain size. Second, some people have normal brain size but very poor language. Third, some people are mentally retarded but nevertheless develop nearly normal language. (p. 439)

5. Poor: self-care skills, numbers, visuomotor skills, and spatial perception. Relatively good: language, interpretation of facial expressions, social behaviors, some aspects of music. (p. 439)

6. The poverty of the stimulus argument is the claim that children say complex sentences without adequate opportunity to learn them, so they must be born with an innate grammar. (p. 440)

7. If you learn a second language well, it activates the same brain areas as your first language regardless of the age at which you learned it. (p. 440)

8. Deaf children who are not exposed to sign language until later in life (and who did not learn spoken language while they were young) never become as proficient at it as those who started younger. (p. 440)

9. People with Broca's aphasia speak slowly and with poor pronunciation, but their speech includes nouns and verbs and is usually meaningful. They omit prepositions, conjunctions, and other grammatical words that have no meaning out of context. People with Wernicke's aphasia

speak fluently and grammatically but omit most nouns and verbs and therefore make little sense. (p. 444)

10. No. They can usually recognize incorrect grammar, even if they cannot state how to correct it. Their speech is like that of someone who finds it painful to speak (leaving out the words with the least meaning), and their comprehension is like that of someone listening to inarticulate speech in a noisy room. (p. 444)

11. People with Broca's aphasia understand most speech unless the meaning depends on grammatical devices or complex sentence construction. People with Wernicke's aphasia understand little speech. (p. 444)

12. Reading English requires more of the brain because it is more difficult. Italian is spelled phonetically and English is not. (p. 444)

13. Four hypotheses are that dyslexia relates to visual problems, hearing problems (especially processing temporal order), connecting vision to hearing, and attention to the proper area of the visual field. (p. 447)

THOUGHT QUESTIONS

1. Most people with Broca's aphasia suffer from partial paralysis on the right side of the body. Most people with Wernicke's aphasia do not. Why?

2. In a syndrome called *word blindness,* a person loses the ability to read (even single letters), although the person can still see and speak. What is a possible neurological explanation? That is, can you imagine a pattern of brain damage that might produce this result?

CHAPTER ENDING
Key Terms and Activities

TERMS

anomia (p. 443)
anterior commissure (p. 429)
aphasia (p. 441)
Broca's aphasia (p. 441)

Broca's area (p. 441)
chihuahua problem (p. 436)
corpus callosum (p. 420)
dichotic listening task (p. 424)
dyslexia (p. 445)
epilepsy (p. 422)

SUGGESTIONS FOR FURTHER READING

Deacon, T. (1997). *The symbolic species.* New York: Norton. Deep analysis of the evolution of language and intelligence.

McManus, C. (2002). *Right hand left hand.* Cambridge, MA: Harvard University Press. Review of almost everything about left-handedness and right-handedness.

Pinker, S. (1994). *The language instinct.* New York: Morrow. Discussion of both behavioral and biological aspects of language.

WEB SITES TO EXPLORE

You can go to the Biological Psychology Study Center and click these links. While there, you can also check for suggested articles available on InfoTrac College Edition.

The Biological Psychology Internet address is:
http://psychology.wadsworth.com/kalatbiopsych8e/

National Aphasia Association
http://www.aphasia.org/

The Bonobo Foundation
http://www.blockbonobofoundation.org/blinks.htm

The British Dyslexia Association
http://www.bda-dyslexia.org.uk

CD-ROM: EXPLORING BIOLOGICAL PSYCHOLOGY

Hemisphere Control (Try it Yourself)

Hemispheric Specialization (Try it Yourself)

Lateralization and Language (animation)

Critical Thinking (essay questions)

Chapter Quiz (multiple choice questions)

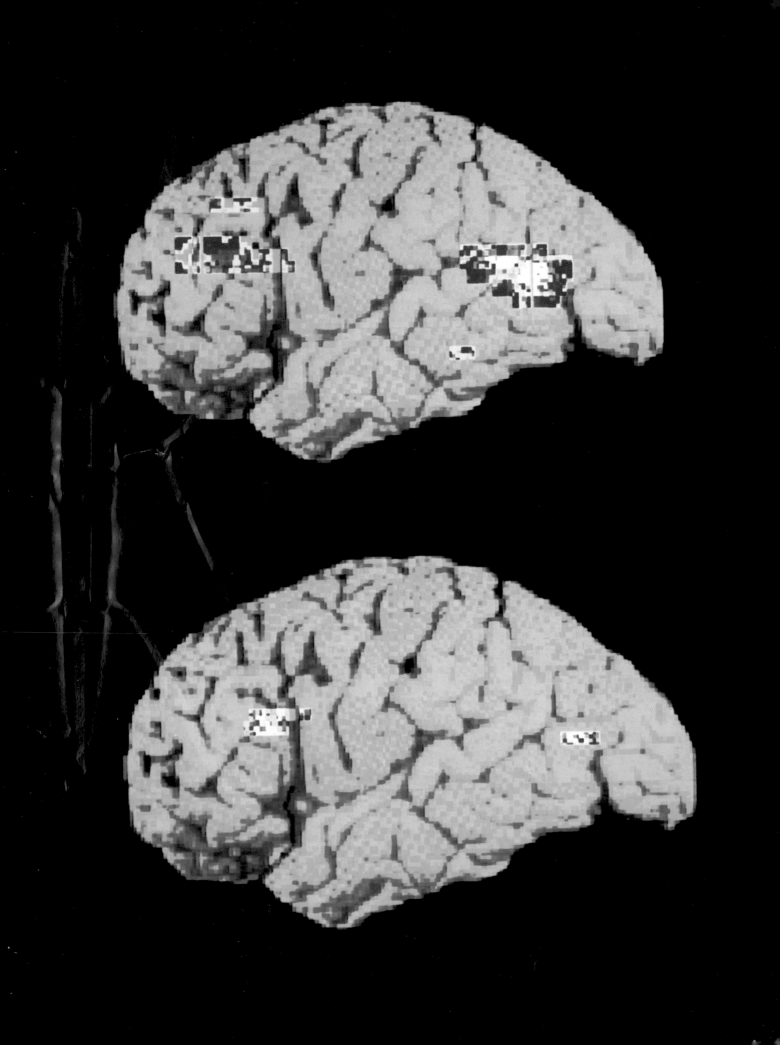

Psychological Disorders

15

Chapter Outline

Main Ideas

1. Psychological disorders result from a combination of biological and environmental influences.

2. Some people have genetic predispositions that increase their risk of psychological disorders. Researchers continue to investigate how these genes act and how they interact with experience.

3. Nearly all abused drugs increase the release of dopamine in the nucleus accumbens.

4. Various drugs for treating depression and schizophrenia alter transmission at various synapses. The drugs' effectiveness suggests that the disorders may be caused in part by problems affecting particular neurotransmitters.

5. A number of nonpharmaceutical biological treatments are also effective against certain kinds of mood disorder, including electroconvulsive shock, changes in sleep patterns, exposure to bright light, and lithium salts.

6. Schizophrenia may be the result of genetic or other problems that impair early development of the brain.

Are mental illnesses really *illnesses,* analogous to tuberculosis or influenza? Or are they normal reactions to abnormal experiences? In general, neither of these characterizations is accurate. Psychological disorders are complex outcomes of biological predispositions and experiential influences, and to control them we need a good understanding of both aspects.

In this chapter, the emphasis is strongly on the biological components of mental illnesses; *Biological Psychology* is, after all, the title of the book. But this emphasis does not imply that other aspects are unimportant.

Opposite:
PET scans of the left hemisphere of a depressed person (top) and a person who has recovered from depression (bottom). Areas coded in red or yellow show less than normal levels of neural activity. *Source: Wellcome Dept. of Cognitive Neurology/Science Photo Library*

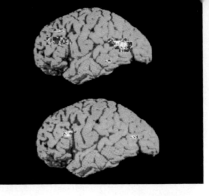

MODULE 15.1

Substance Abuse

The American Psychiatric Association (1994), in its *Diagnostic and Statistical Manual* (4th ed.), defines **substance abuse** as a maladaptive pattern of substance use leading to clinically significant impairment or distress (p. 182). Almost any substance can be abused, although some are certainly abused more often than others.

What is the difference between good drugs and bad ones? None, really. Many drugs that we regard as dangerous—including cocaine, morphine, and amphetamine—have medical uses as well. The difference is between the good and bad use of drugs, which depends on the amount taken and the motivation for taking it. We would like to understand the effects of various drugs and why some people use drugs to the point of endangering their health, well-being, careers, and even lives. We begin with some general issues and later turn to specific drugs.

SYNAPSES, REINFORCEMENT, AND DRUG USE

Why are many drugs habit-forming or addictive? We could ask the same question about gambling, video games, and other powerful habits that do not involve drugs. The answers are incomplete, but the gist is that habit-forming or addictive behaviors have something to do with dopamine synapses. The story begins with an accidental discovery by researchers who were trying to answer a much different question.

Electrical Self-Stimulation of the Brain

Decades ago, two young scientists, James Olds and Peter Milner (1954), put rats in a situation in which they had to choose between turning left and turning right. Olds and Milner wanted to test whether stimulation of a particular brain area influences the direction in which the rat turns. However, they accidentally implanted the electrode in an unintended area of the brain, the septum. To their surprise, when the rat re-

ceived the brain stimulation, it sometimes sat up, looked around, and sniffed, as if reacting to a favorable stimulus. Olds and Milner later placed rats in Skinner boxes, where the rats could produce **self-stimulation of the brain** by pressing a lever for electrical brain stimulation as a reinforcer (Figure 15.1). Rats worked extremely vigorously to stimulate certain brain areas, in some cases pressing a lever 2000 times per hour until they collapsed from exhaustion (Olds, 1958).

The results of later experiments have indicated that, with few exceptions, brain stimulation is reinforcing only if it stimulates axons that release dopamine (Wise, 1996). Many other kinds of reinforcing experiences, ranging from sexual activity to video games, also stimulate the release of dopamine, especially in the **nucleus accumbens,** a small subcortical area rich in dopamine receptors (Figure 15.2).

Many people have therefore regarded the nucleus accumbens as a pleasure area and dopamine as a pleasure chemical. However, a reinforcer is merely whatever causes an individual to repeat an act, not necessarily something enjoyable. You might work very hard to prepare for a test, even without expecting your grade to make you very happy. Drug addicts will work hard to get a drug even after they have developed so much tolerance that the "high" is minimal. Furthermore, a presumably pleasant event such as food increases dopamine release only when the event is surprising (unpredicted). If a stimulus fully

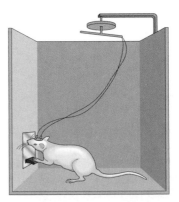

Figure 15.1 A rat pressing a lever for self-stimulation of its brain

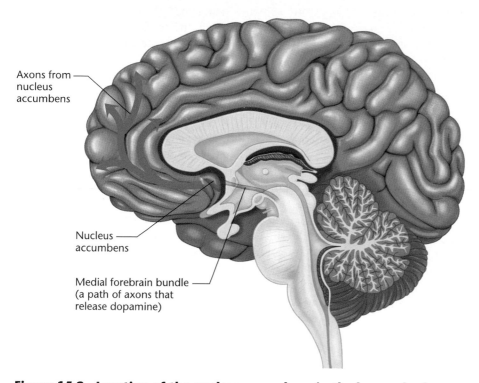

Axons from
nucleus
accumbens

Nucleus
accumbens

Medial forebrain bundle
(a path of axons that
release dopamine)

Figure 15.2 Location of the nucleus accumbens in the human brain
A wide variety of procedures that yield reinforcement inhibit the activity of the nucleus accumbens. Therefore, this area is considered essential for reinforcement or reward.

predicts the food, then the food releases no dopamine (Waelti, Dickinson, & Schultz, 2001). Of course, to some extent, the same is true of pleasure; we enjoy almost any pleasant event more when it is a surprise (Melters & McGraw, 2001).

Drugs and Reinforcement

What, then, is the role of the dopamine synapses and the nucleus accumbens? One hypothesis is that they relate to the arousal or attention-getting potential of an event (Berridge & Robinson, 1998). Addictive drugs have a tremendous ability to dominate the user's attention and cravings, even if the drug experience is not dependably pleasant (Berridge & Robinson, 1995). Informative events, including both food and shock, are also attention-getting, whereas a fully expected event draws rather little attention (Schultz, 2000). On the other hand, dopamine is also released in many situations such as classical conditioning that do not require attention in the usual sense.

Nearly all addicting drugs increase dopamine release in the nucleus accumbens. However, those same dopamine synapses also respond to other strong habits, even if they do not involve drug use. For example, sexual excitement releases dopamine (Damsma, Pfaus, Wenkstern, Philips, & Fibiger, 1992;

Lorrain, Riolo, Matuszewich, & Hull, 1999), as does video game playing, at least in habitual players (Koepp et al., 1998). No doubt dopamine release could also be demonstrated in compulsive gamblers, sports fans, and so forth. In one fascinating study, young heterosexual men viewed photos of faces and rated each of them for attractiveness. They could also press a key to view a face longer. They pressed the key only to sustain the attractive female faces, and only those attractive female faces activated the men's nucleus accumbens, as indicated by fMRI scans (Aharon et al., 2001). Although they reported that certain men's faces were "attractive," viewing those faces actually *decreased* stimulation of their nucleus accumbens, as if viewing these attractive men's faces was threatening or unpleasant.

An understanding of the reinforcement properties of drugs may someday lead to treatments for drug addiction. One drug, ibogaine, is already known to decrease the reinforcement value of drugs in the nucleus accumbens and therefore to weaken cravings and addictions. However, it not only weakens the reinforcing properties of drugs but the reinforcing values of everything else as well, so although some drug user may stop taking drugs, he or she does not do anything else instead. Researchers are experimenting with new drugs that appear to weaken drug reinforcement without harming other motivations (Glick & Maisonneuve, 2000).

We hope that such endeavors will succeed, but addiction is probably not that simple. We know a good deal about the short-term effects of drugs on synapses, but addiction is a long term process, and we know much less about what happens long term (Hyman & Malenka, 2001). At one time, psychologists believed that addiction was based largely on attempts to escape from the withdrawal effects people suffer when they quit a drug. However, people who quit cocaine suffer relatively mild withdrawal effects for only hours or days but feel cravings long afterward. People who suddenly quit taking nasal decongestant drugs get withdrawal effects, but they do not develop an addiction to nasal decongestants. People who quit cigarettes can experience powerful cravings months or even years later, long after the end of the withdrawal symptoms. These cravings are poorly understood, but they will have to be controlled if we are to deal with addictions. Part of the problem is that any stimulus that reminds someone of past drug experiences can trigger a craving; even rats that are given a stimulus previously paired with cocaine show increased efforts to get cocaine (Kruzich, Congleton, & See, 2001).

COMMON DRUGS AND THEIR SYNAPTIC EFFECTS

We categorize drugs based on their predominant action. For example, amphetamine and cocaine are stimulants; opiates are narcotics; LSD and phencyclidine are hallucinogens. Marijuana does not fit into any simple classification. Despite their differences, however, nearly all of these drugs increase activity at dopamine synapses, either by increasing the release of dopamine or by decreasing its reuptake by the presynaptic cell. We shall survey each of these drugs, leaving alcohol for a separate discussion of greater length. You could check the following Web site for a complete text on drugs and behavior online:
www.rci.rutgers.edu/~lwh/drugs/

Stimulant Drugs

Many highly addictive drugs are **stimulant drugs,** producing excitement, alertness, elevated mood, decreased fatigue, and sometimes increased motor activity. Each of these drugs directly increases activity at dopamine receptors, especially at dopamine receptor types D_2, D_3, and D_4 (R. A. Harris, Brodie, & Dunwiddie, 1992; Wise & Bozarth, 1987).

Amphetamine stimulates dopamine synapses by increasing the release of dopamine from the presynaptic terminal. The presynaptic terminal ordinarily reabsorbs released dopamine through a protein called the *dopamine transporter.* Amphetamine reverses the transporter, causing the cell to excrete dopamine instead of reabsorb it (Giros, Jaber, Jones, Wightman, & Caron, 1996). Amphetamine also blocks certain synapses that inhibit dopamine release, so it enhances dopamine release in at least two ways (Paladini, Fiorillo, Morikawa, & Williams, 2001). **Cocaine** blocks the reuptake of dopamine, norepinephrine, and serotonin, thus prolonging their effects. Several kinds of evidence indicate that the behavioral effects of cocaine depend mainly on increasing dopamine effects and secondarily on serotonin effects (Rocha et al., 1998; Volkow, Wang, Fischman, et al., 1997). Because both amphetamine and cocaine increase dopamine activity, their behavioral effects are similar.

The effects of cocaine and amphetamine on dopamine synapses are intense but short-lived. By increasing the release of dopamine or decreasing its reuptake, the drugs increase the accumulation of dopamine in the synaptic cleft. However, the excess dopamine washes away from the synapse faster than the presynaptic cell can synthesize more dopamine. Furthermore, the excess dopamine in the synaptic cleft activates autoreceptors on the presynaptic terminal, exerting a negative feedback effect that reduces further release of dopamine (North, 1992). The net result is that, within hours after taking amphetamine or cocaine, a user "crashes" into a depressed state.

The effects of stimulant drugs are also limited by the tolerance that a user develops. After someone has used cocaine repeatedly, the drug releases less dopamine and more of a transmitter called *dynorphin,* which counteracts the reinforcing properties of cocaine (Carlezon et al., 1998; Volkow, Wang, Fowler, et al., 1997). Similarly, after a rat has learned to press a lever to self-stimulate dopamine-releasing axons, further stimulation releases less and less dopamine (Garris et al., 1999). Repeated and predictable reinforcers become less effective in changing behavior. Note the implication: Once a strong habit is formed, it can continue even with weak or erratic reinforcement.

Methylphenidate (Ritalin), another stimulant drug, is often prescribed for people with attention-deficit disorder (ADD), a condition marked by impulsiveness and poor control of attention, as described in Chapter 7. Methylphenidate and cocaine block the reuptake of dopamine in the same way at the same brain receptors. The differences are due to dose and time course. Drug abusers, of course, use large doses of cocaine, whereas anyone following a physician's directions uses only small amounts of methylphenidate. Furthermore, when people take methylphenidate in pill form (as directed), its concentration in the brain increases gradually over an hour and then declines with a half-life of more than an hour and a half. In contrast, sniffed or injected cocaine produces a four to five times faster rise and fall of effects (Volkow, Wang, & Fowler, 1997; Volkow, Wang, Fowler, et al., 1998). Therefore, methylphenidate does not produce the sudden rush of excitement, the strong withdrawal effects, the cravings, or the addiction that are common with cocaine. If people injected large amounts of methylphenidate, its effects would resemble cocaine's. Methylphenidate also increases serotonin release, which may have some calming effects on hyperactive people (Gainetdinov et al., 1999).

Many people wonder whether prolonged use of methylphenidate in childhood makes people more likely to abuse drugs later. This question is difficult to answer because it is hard to get a suitable control group of children with the same ADD problems but no use of methylphenidate. However, experimenters tried giving methylphenidate to juvenile rats at low to moderate doses. Later, when the rats reached adulthood, the experimenters let the rats learn one response to get cocaine and another response to avoid it. Unlike most rats, which learn to get the cocaine, the rats exposed to methylphenidate in their earlier life actually avoided cocaine (Andersén, Arvanitogiannis, Pliakas, LeBlanc, & Cárlezon, 2002). The results suggest that although methylphenidate may produce other problems, it does not appear to increase the risk of cocaine abuse later. If anything, it may decrease the risk.

Because dopamine is mostly an inhibitory transmitter, drugs that increase activity at dopamine synapses decrease the activity in much of the brain. Figure 15.3 shows the results of a PET scan, which measures relative amounts of activity in various brain areas (London et al., 1990) (see Methods 8.1). How, you might wonder, could drugs that decrease brain activity lead to behavioral arousal? One hypothesis is that high dopamine activity mostly decreases "background noise" in the brain and therefore increases the signal-to-noise ratio (Mattay et al., 1996).

Stimulant drugs are known primarily for their short-term effects, but repeated use of high doses can produce long-term problems. Cocaine users suffer

lasting changes in brain metabolism and blood flow, thereby increasing their risk of stroke, epilepsy, and memory impairments (Strickland, Miller, Kowell, & Stein, 1998). The drug methylenedioxymethamphetamine (MDMA, or "ecstasy") stimulates the release of dopamine at low doses. At higher doses (comparable to the doses people use recreationally), it also stimulates serotonin synapses, producing hallucinogenic effects similar to those of LSD. In monkey studies, MDMA not only stimulates axons that release dopamine and serotonin but also destroys them (McCann, Lowe, & Ricaurte, 1997), as shown in Figure 15.4. Damage to a moderate number of dopamine and serotonin neurons could increase the later risk of depression or Parkinson's disease (Ricaurte, Yuan, Hatzidimitriou, Cord, & McCann, 2002).

In humans, it is difficult to get equally detailed data for obvious reasons. One study using PET scans reported a decrease in serotonin synapses by current MDMA users but nearly normal levels in those who had quit for more than a year. However, even those who had quit showed below-average performance on memory tests (Reneman et al., 2001). These results are difficult to interpret, as most of those who quit MDMA switched to marijuana. Furthermore, we don't know whether the former MDMA users may have had memory problems from the start. That is, maybe people with poorer cognitive skills are more likely than others to become MDMA users. Still, the risk of long-term damage should be a concern to anyone considering the use of MDMA.

Stop & Check

1. How does amphetamine influence dopamine synapses?
2. How does cocaine influence dopamine synapses?
3. Why is methylphenidate generally less disruptive to behavior than cocaine is despite the drugs' similar mechanisms?
4. Does cocaine increase or decrease overall brain activity?

Check your answers on page 463.

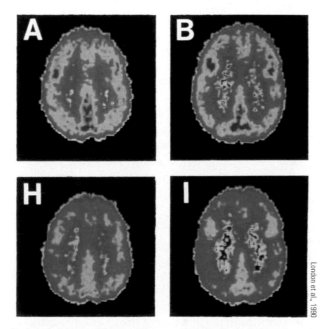

London et al., 1990

Figure 15.3 Effects of cocaine on the brain
Sometimes "your brain on drugs" is not like something in a frying pan, a popular analogy; it is more like something in the refrigerator. As these positron emission tomography (PET) scans show, the brain has lower metabolism and lower overall activity under the influence of cocaine than it has ordinarily. Red indicates highest activity, followed by yellow, green, and blue. A and B represent brain activity under normal conditions; H and I show activity after a cocaine injection.

Nicotine

Nicotine, a compound present in tobacco, has long been known to stimulate one type of acetylcholine receptor, conveniently known as the *nicotinic receptor*, which is found both in the central nervous system and at the

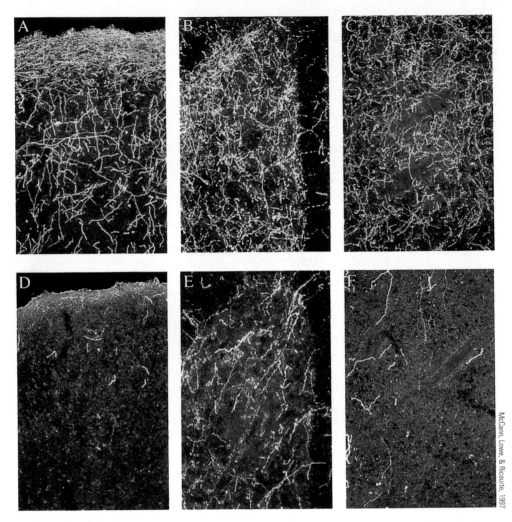

Figure 15.4 Brain damage produced by MDMA
These slices through monkey brains have been stained with a chemical that makes axons containing serotonin glow white. Photos in the top row are from a normal monkey; those below are from a monkey that was exposed to MDMA ("ecstasy") a year and a half earlier. Notice the decreased density of serotonin axons in the photos below.

McCann, Lowe, & Ricaurte, 1997

Opiates

Opiate drugs are derived from (or similar to those derived from) the opium poppy. Familiar opiates include morphine, heroin, and methadone. Opiates relax people, decrease their attention to real-world problems, and decrease their sensitivity to pain. Although opiates are known as highly addictive, people who take them as pain-killers under medical supervision almost never abuse them. Addiction is not simply a product of the drug; it depends on the person, the reasons for taking the drug, the dose, and even the social setting.

People smoked or injected morphine and other opiates for centuries before anyone knew how they affected the brain. Then Candace Pert and Solomon Snyder found that opiates attach to specific receptors in the brain (Pert & Snyder, 1973). It was a safe guess that vertebrates had not evolved such receptors just to enable us to become drug addicts; the brain must produce its own chemical that attaches to these receptors. Indeed, investigators soon found that the brain produces peptides now known as the *endorphins*—a contraction of *endo*-genous *morphines*. One reason this discovery was exciting was that it indicated opiates relieve pain by acting on receptors in the brain, not just out in the skin or organs where people felt the pain. This discovery also implied that the brain may have other peptides that regulate emotions and motivations. Much research has confirmed this hypothesis, and much remains to be learned about the brain's peptides.

Endorphin synapses may contribute directly to certain kinds of reinforcement (Nader, Bechara, Roberts, & van der Kooy, 1994), but they also act indirectly by way of dopamine. Endorphin synapses inhibit ventral tegmental neurons (in the midbrain) that release GABA, a transmitter that inhibits the firing of dopamine neurons (North, 1992). Thus, through

nerve-muscle junction of skeletal muscles. Acetylcholine stimulation at other kinds of receptors is not reinforcing, but nicotinic receptors are abundant on dopamine-releasing axon terminals in the nucleus accumbens, so nicotine increases dopamine release there (Levin & Rose, 1995; Pontieri, Tanda, Orzi, & DiChiara, 1996). In fact, nicotine increases dopamine release in mostly the same cells in the nucleus accumbens as cocaine does (Pich et al., 1997). One consequence of repeated exposure to nicotine, as demonstrated in rat studies, is that after the end of nicotine use, the nucleus accumbens cells responsible for reinforcement become less responsive than usual (Epping-Jordan, Watkins, Koob, & Markou, 1998). That is, many events, not just nicotine itself, become less reinforcing than they used to be. Some people who are trying to quit smoking find it helpful to take antidepressant drugs (Hall et al., 1998).

inhibition of an inhibitor, the net effect is to increase dopamine release. Endorphins also block the locus coeruleus, an area that we considered in Chapter 9. The locus coeruleus responds to arousing or stressful stimuli by releasing norepinephrine, which facilitates memory storage. When endorphins or opiate drugs block this area, the result is decreased response to stress and decreased memory storage—two effects common among opiate users (Curtis, Bello, & Valentine, 2001).

For extensive information specifically about heroin use, see this Web site:

www.uphs.upenn.edu/recovery/pros/opioids.html

5. How does nicotine influence dopamine synapses?

6. How do opiates influence dopamine synapses?

Check your answers on page 463.

Marijuana

The leaves of the marijuana plant contain the chemical Δ^9-tetrahydrocannabinol (Δ^9-THC) and other **cannabinoids** (chemicals related to Δ^9-THC), which people absorb when they smoke or eat the leaves. Marijuana has been used medically to relieve pain or nausea and to combat glaucoma (an eye disorder), although laws in the United States greatly restrict its medical use. Common psychological effects of marijuana include an intensification of sensory experience and an illusion that time is passing very slowly.

Many users also experience cognitive impairments. Many studies have reported significant memory impairments in heavy users of marijuana. This observation by itself could mean either that marijuana impairs memory or that people with memory impairments are more likely to use marijuana. However, it has also been found that former users recover normal memory after 4 weeks of abstention from the drug (Pope, Gruber, Hudson, Huestis, & Yurgelun-Todd, 2001). The recovery supports the interpretation that marijuana impairs memory.

Cannabinoids dissolve in the body's fats and leave the body slowly. One consequence is that someone who quits marijuana can test positive for cannabinoids in the urine days or weeks later. Another consequence is that quitting marijuana does not produce intense withdrawal symptoms like those of opiates. Heavy marijuana smokers who abstain do report a moderate amount of irritability, restlessness, anxiety, depression, stomach pain, sleep difficulties, craving for marijuana, and loss of appetite (Budney, Hughes, Moore, & Novy, 2001).

Investigators could not explain the effects of marijuana on the brain until 1988, when researchers finally identified cannabinoids receptors (Devane, Dysarz, Johnson, Melvin, & Howlett, 1988). Most of the psychological and behavioral effects of marijuana depend on these receptors (Huestis et al., 2001). The receptors are now known to be widespread in the animal kingdom, having been reported in mammals, birds, amphibians, fish, sea urchins, leeches, mussels, and even hydra. Curiously, they are not found in insects, although insects otherwise use virtually the same neurotransmitters as vertebrates (McPartland, DiMarzo, de Petrocellis, Mercer, & Glass, 2001). Cannabinoid receptors are abundant in the human brain, including the hippocampus, the basal ganglia, and the cerebellum (Herkenham, 1992; Herkenham, Lynn, de Costa, & Richfield, 1991). However, they are sparse in the medulla and the rest of the brainstem. That near absence is significant because the medulla includes the neuron clusters that control breathing and heartbeat. You have no doubt heard of people being rushed to the hospital after overdosing on opiates or cocaine, but how often have you heard of anyone fatally overdosing on marijuana? Marijuana has little effect on heartbeat or breathing.

Just as the discovery of opiate receptors in the brain led to a successful search for the brain's endogenous opiates, the discovery of cannabinoid receptors prompted investigators to search for a brain chemical that binds to cannabinoid receptors. Researchers first identified **anandamide** (from the Sanskrit word *ananda,* meaning "bliss") (Calignano, LaRana, Giuffrida, & Piomelli, 1998; DiMarzo et al., 1995) and later the more abundant cannabinoid *sn*-2 arachidonylglycerol, abbreviated **2-AG** (Stella, Schweitzer, & Piomelli, 1997). The cannabinoid receptors are peculiar in being located on the *pre*synaptic neuron, not the postsynaptic one. When one of the familiar transmitters such as glutamate or GABA stimulates the postsynaptic neuron, the postsynaptic neuron releases a cannabinoid chemical (anandamide or 2-AG), which travels back to the presynaptic neuron and temporarily decreases further release (Kreitzer & Regehr, 2001; Wilson & Nicoll, 2002). That is, it provides negative feedback, putting the brakes on transmitter release. In some cases, the inhibited neuron has a wide expanse, so inhibiting it decreases release of transmitter to neighboring neurons also (Kreitzer, Carter, & Regehr, 2002). Because cannabinoids limit the release of both glutamate (excitatory) and GABA (inhibitory), we cannot classify cannabinoids as either stimulants or depressants (Kreitzer & Regehr, 2001; Ohno-Shosaku,

Maejima, & Kano, 2001; Wilson & Nicoll, 2001). Maybe we should call them "leveler-outers"?

The cellular mechanism of cannabinoids suggests an explanation for an otherwise puzzling finding: At least in animal studies, cannabinoids decrease the brain damage caused by a stroke (Glass, 2001; Panikashvili et al., 2001). Recall from Chapter 6 that strokes kill neurons in two ways—first by overstimulating with excess glutamate and later by prolonged lack of stimulation. Presumably, cannabinoids decrease both risks by limiting either excessive stimulation or excessive inhibition. However, although marijuana may be useful shortly after a stroke, habitual use poses multiple problems. Besides the memory problems mentioned earlier and probable increase in lung cancer risk, marijuana also increases the risk of Parkinson's disease (Glass, 2001).

Researchers have started to explain some of marijuana's other effects as well. Cannabinoids relieve nausea by inhibiting serotonin type 3 synapses (5-HT_3), which are known to be important for nausea (Fan, 1995). Mice that lack cannabinoid receptors learn normally in a classical-conditioning situation, but they fail to extinguish when the conditioned stimulus no longer predicts the unconditioned stimulus (Marsicano et al., 2002). Presumably, extra cannabinoids (e.g., from smoking marijuana) would lead to more rapid extinction and therefore losses of learned behaviors. Cannabinoid receptors are abundant in areas of the hypothalamus that influence feeding, and mice lacking these receptors fail to increase their appetite appropriately after a period of food deprivation (DiMarzo et al., 2001). Thus, we begin to understand why marijuana users often report increased appetite.

The report that "time passes more slowly" under marijuana's influences is harder to explain, but whatever the cause, we can demonstrate it in rats as well: Consider a rat that has learned to press a lever for food on a fixed-interval schedule such that only the first press during any 30-second period produces food. With practice, each rat learns to wait a certain period of time after each press before it starts pressing again. Under the influence of marijuana, rats press sooner after each reinforcer. That is, instead of waiting 20 seconds, a rat might wait only 10 or 15. Evidently, the 10 or 15 seconds *felt like* 20 seconds; time was passing more slowly (Han & Robinson, 2001).

Finally, let us return to the observation that marijuana sometimes impairs memory. Recall from Chapter 13 that during long-term potentiation (LTP), the postsynaptic neuron releases a "retrograde" transmitter that signals the presynaptic neuron to make changes. The same is true during long-term depression (LTD), and in that case, the retrograde transmitters are known to be cannabinoids (Gerdeman, Ronesi, & Lovinger, 2002). LTD, when it occurs naturally, is a helpful process of weakening connections that should be weakened. However, marijuana has the potential to produce LTD inappropriately and therefore to weaken connections that should be maintained.

7. What are the effects of cannabinoids on neurons?

Check your answer on page 463.

Hallucinogenic Drugs

Drugs that distort perception are called **hallucinogenic drugs.** Many hallucinogenic drugs, such as lysergic acid diethylamide (LSD), chemically resemble serotonin (Figure 15.5) and stimulate serotonin type 2A (5-HT_{2A}) receptors at inappropriate times or for longer than usual durations. Contrast this mode of action to that of amphetamine, which acts by releasing norepinephrine and dopamine from the presynaptic neurons. If the neurons have a low supply of these neurotransmitters, amphetamine is ineffective. In contrast, even after chemical damage to a rat's serotonin-releasing neurons, LSD still exerts its full effect. It may even produce a greater than normal effect: After the loss of the incoming serotonin, the postsynaptic neuron compensates by developing an increased number of serotonin receptors, making LSD more effective (B. L. Jacobs, 1987). Note that we understand the chemistry better than the psychology. LSD exerts its effects at 5-HT_{2A} receptors, but *why* do effects at those receptors produce hallucinations?

Table 15.1 summarizes the effects of some commonly abused drugs.

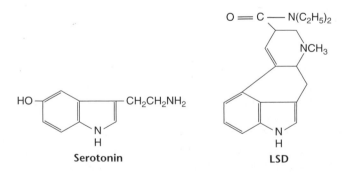

Figure 15.5 Resemblance of the neurotransmitter serotonin to LSD, a hallucinogenic drug

TABLE 15.1 Summary of Some Drugs and Their Effects

Drugs	Main Effects on Behavior	Main Effects on Synapses
Amphetamine	Excitement, alertness, elevated mood, decreased fatigue	Increases release of dopamine and several other neurotransmitters
Cocaine	Excitement, alertness, elevated mood, decreased fatigue	Blocks reuptake of dopamine and several other neurotransmitters
Methylphenidate	Increased concentration	Blocks reuptake of dopamine and others, but more gradually than cocaine does
Nicotine	Mostly stimulant effects	Stimulates nicotinic-type acetylcholine receptor, which (among other effects) increases dopamine release in nucleus accumbens
Opiates	Relaxation, withdrawal, decreased pain	Stimulates endorphin receptors
Cannabinoids (marijuana)	Intensified sensory experiences, distorted sense of time, decreased pain and nausea	Excites negative-feedback receptors on presynaptic cells; thereby puts the brakes on release of either glutamate or GABA
LSD	Distorted sensations	Stimulates serotonin type 2 receptors (5-HT$_2$)
Alcohol	Relaxation, decreased attention	Facilitates GABA$_A$ receptor

ALCOHOL AND ALCOHOLISM

Alcohol is the most widely used recreational drug in most of the world. In moderate amounts, it helps people relax and may even help prevent heart attacks (although the evidence on this point is suggestive and not conclusive). In greater amounts, it damages the liver and other organs, impairs judgment, and ruins lives. Even after people recognize that alcohol is harming their lives, quitting is difficult. Alcoholism or alcohol dependence is the continued use of alcohol despite medical or social harm, even after people have decided to quit or decrease their drinking. Many people insist "I am not an alcoholic" because they don't drink every day, sometimes drink without getting drunk, and manage to hold a successful job in spite of their drinking. However, being an alcoholic does not require severe deterioration; many people have drinking problems only on weekends or during some weeks and not others. The deciding factor is whether the alcohol is interfering with the person's life.

Alcohol inhibits the flow of sodium across the membrane, expands the surface of membranes, decreases serotonin activity (Fils-Aime et al., 1996), facilitates response by the GABA$_A$ receptor (Mihic et al., 1997), blocks glutamate receptors (Tsai et al., 1998), and increases dopamine activity (Phillips et al., 1998). With such diverse effects on the nervous system, no wonder it has so many effects on behavior.

Genetics

Recall that early-onset Parkinson's disease has a clear genetic basis; late-onset Parkinson's disease does not. The same is true for Alzheimer's disease. With Huntington's disease, people with many C-A-G repeats on the *huntingtin* gene develop the disease early in life, whereas those with fewer repeats get it later or not at all. Similarly, early-onset alcoholism has a stronger genetic basis than late-onset alcoholism.

Researchers distinguish two major types of alcoholism (Brown, Babor, Litt, & Kranzler, 1994; Devor, Abell, Hoffman, Tabakoff, & Cloninger, 1994):

Type I (or Type A) alcoholism	Type II (or Type B) alcoholism
• Later onset (usually after 25)	• Earlier onset (usually before 25)
• Gradual onset	• More rapid onset
• Fewer genetic relatives with alcoholism	• More genetic relatives with alcoholism
• Men and women about equally	• Men far more than women
• Generally less severe	• Often severe, often associated with criminality

Recall from Chapter 12 that low serotonin turnover is associated with impulsive behavior, which can include violence. Low serotonin turnover is highly characteristic of Type II alcoholics (Fils-Aime et al., 1996), as is a history of impulsive and violent behaviors (Virkkunen et al., 1994). Not only does impulsiveness predispose someone to overindulge in alcohol, but research on rats demonstrates that alcohol increases impulsive behavior, such as choosing a small immediate reward instead of a larger delayed reward (Poulos, Parker, & Lê, 1998). In short, Type II alcoholism, impulsiveness, and low serotonin turnover are all interrelated.

Evidence for a genetic basis of Type II alcoholism includes the finding that monozygotic twins have greater concordance for alcohol abuse than do dizygotic twins. One study estimated a .55 heritability for alcoholism (True et al., 1999). Additional evidence is that biological children of alcoholics have an increased risk of alcoholism themselves, even if they are adopted by nonalcoholics (Cloninger, Bohman, & Sigvardsson, 1981; Vaillant & Milofsky, 1982). However, this evidence is subject to the criticism that many of the mothers were drinking during pregnancy, and thus, what appears to be a genetic effect could be due to prenatal environment. Overall, most researchers believe genetics contributes to alcoholism, although they disagree about how much (Cadoret, Troughton, & Woodworth, 1994). Several genes have been found to occur more frequently in alcoholics than in other people, but so far, each of these genes appears to be, by itself, a minor contributor. For example, one gene was found to occur in about 5% of alcoholics and 2% of other people—a statistically significant but not terribly impressive result (Lappalainen et al., 2002).

Stop & Check

8. Which type of alcoholism has a stronger genetic basis? Which type has earlier onset?

Check your answer on page 463.

Alcohol Metabolism and Antabuse

Part of the genetic influence on alcoholism probably relates to a tendency toward impulsiveness. Another genetic effect relates to the way the body metabolizes alcohol. After someone drinks ethyl alcohol (as opposed to methyl alcohol or isopropyl alcohol, which are poisonous if drunk), enzymes in the liver metabolize it to acetaldehyde, a poisonous substance. An enzyme, acetaldehyde dehydrogenase, then converts acetaldehyde to acetic acid, a chemical that the body can use as a source of energy.

Ethyl alcohol $\longrightarrow$ Acetaldehyde $\xrightarrow{\text{Acetaldehyde dehydrogenase}}$ Acetic acid

People with an abnormal gene for acetaldehyde dehydrogenase metabolize acetaldehyde more slowly. If they drink much alcohol, they accumulate acetaldehyde, which can produce flushing of the face, increased heart rate, nausea, headache, abdominal pain, difficult breathing, and potential damage to internal organs. As you can imagine, people who can't metabolize acetaldehyde are unlikely to drink much alcohol. About half of the people in China and Japan have the gene that slows acetaldehyde metabolism; probably for that reason, alcohol abuse has historically been uncommon in those countries (Tu & Israel, 1995) (Figure 15.6). In other words, one gene affects alcohol abuse through effects in the liver, not the brain.

James W. Kalat

Figure 15.6 Robin Kalat (the author's daughter) finds an alcohol vending machine in Tokyo
The Japanese have traditionally been casual about preventing people from buying alcohol, presumably because severe alcoholism has been uncommon. One reason is that many Japanese people cannot quickly metabolize acetaldehyde to acetic acid. However, in 2000, increasing alcohol abuse prompted the banning of public alcohol vending machines.

The drug *disulfiram*, which goes by the trade name Antabuse, antagonizes the effects of acetaldehyde dehydrogenase by binding to its copper ion. People who take Antabuse cannot drink alcohol without getting sick. The strategy is to prescribe Antabuse, hoping that alcoholics will associate alcohol with illness and stop drinking.

Most studies find that Antabuse is only moderately effective (Hughes & Cook, 1997). When it works at all, it supplements the alcoholic's own commitment to stop drinking. By taking a daily pill and thinking about the illness that could follow a drink of alcohol, the person reaffirms a decision to abstain. In that case, of course, it doesn't matter whether the pill really contains Antabuse or not; someone who never drinks will never experience the threatened illness (Fuller & Roth, 1979). Those who drink in spite of taking the pill become ill, but unfortunately, they are as likely to quit taking the pill as to quit drinking alcohol. Antabuse treatment is more effective if steps are taken to urge continued use of the drug, such as by having friends or relatives make sure the person takes the pill daily (Azrin, Sisson, Meyers, & Godley, 1982).

Stop & Check

9. Who would be likely to drink more alcohol—someone who metabolizes acetaldehyde to acetic acid rapidly or one who metabolizes it slowly?

10. How does Antabuse work?

Check your answers on page 463.

Risk Factors for Alcohol Abuse

Once someone has developed a severe alcohol problem, the prospects for recovery are not encouraging. Many researchers have tried to identify alcoholism as early as possible in hopes of intervening more successfully.

Most of the research follows this design: First identify a group of sons of alcoholic fathers. Generally, researchers study sons who are in their late teens or early twenties, who have not yet become problem drinkers. Because of the strong familial tendency of alcoholism, they expect that many of these young men are future alcoholics. (Researchers have focused on men instead of women because almost all Type II alcoholics are men. They study sons of alcoholic fathers instead of mothers to increase the chance that they will see genetic instead of prenatal influences.) The researchers compare them to other young men of the same age with similar drinking habits but no alcoholic relatives. The idea is that any behavior more common in the sons of alcoholics is probably a predictor of future alcoholism (Figure 15.7).

This method has led to these findings:

- Sons of alcoholics show *less* than average intoxication after drinking a moderate amount of alcohol. They report feeling less drunk, show less body sway, and register less change on an EEG (Schuckit & Smith, 1996; Volavka et al., 1996). Presumably, someone who begins to feel tipsy after a drink or two stops at that point; one who "holds his liquor well" continues drinking, perhaps enough to impair his judgment.

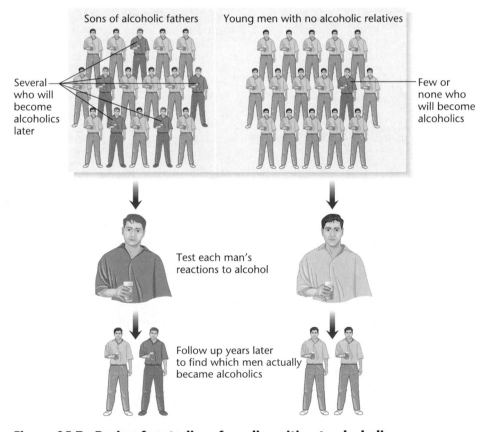

Figure 15.7   Design for studies of predisposition to alcoholism
Sons of alcoholic fathers are compared to other young men of the same age and same current drinking habits. Any behavior that is more common in the first group is presumably a predictor of later alcoholism.

A follow-up study found that men who report low intoxication after moderate drinking are much more likely than others to become alcohol abusers within the next 8 years (Schuckit & Smith, 1996).

- Sons of alcoholics also experience more than average relief from tension after drinking alcohol (Levenson, Oyama, & Meek, 1987). That is, in a difficult situation, alcohol decreases stress for most people, but it decreases it even more for sons of alcoholics.
- Sons of alcoholics have some brain peculiarities, including a smaller than normal amygdala in the right hemisphere (S. Hill et al., 2001). The amygdala is important for emotions, although how the emotional deficit relates to alcoholism is not yet clear. Note that these young men were not yet alcohol abusers themselves, so the brain abnormality is a potential predisposition to alcoholism, not a result of it.

Here is another clever study to determine what predisposes people to alcoholism: The issue is whether a sensation-seeking personality predisposes to alcoholism. In the overall population, sensation-seeking correlates positively with alcoholism, but the correlation could mean that sensation-seeking happens to be common in the same ethnic groups or social classes that have much alcoholism. To separate these factors, the researchers identified families in which one brother or sister scored high in sensation-seeking and another scored low. They found that the person higher in sensation-seeking was consistently more likely to be a heavy alcohol drinker (Dick, Johnson, Viken, & Rose, 2000). Note that the clever design of this study means that the differences could be due to personality differences but could not be due to ethnicity or social class.

In short, the combination that puts someone at greatest risk for alcoholism is to feel much relief from stress but not much intoxication after drinking a moderate amount of alcohol and to have a sensation-seeking personality. Such people can be identified. Now the question is whether it is possible to steer them toward moderate drinking or abstention by intervening soon enough.

11. What are two ways in which sons of alcoholics differ, on average, from sons of nonalcoholics?

Check your answer on page 463.

In Closing: Drugs and Behavior

Basic research on the nervous system helps us understand and treat psychological disorders, such as substance abuse. The reverse is true also: Research on substance abuse and other disorders leads to new understanding about the nervous system in general. We have learned, for example, that abused drugs have much in common with other reinforcing events, in that nearly all of them increase dopamine activity in the nucleus accumbens.

The fact that all kinds of addictions have so much in common is important to remember. Gambling, video game playing, and Internet use can become addictive and consuming of time and energy, much like drug addictions, and they probably affect the nucleus accumbens in similar ways. So we should beware of attributing the addictive properties of alcohol or anything else to the pharmacological properties of the substance itself. The addiction isn't in the drug; it's in the user.

SUMMARY

1. Reinforcing brain stimulation, reinforcing experiences, and most self-administered drugs act largely by increasing the activity of axons that release dopamine (a predominantly inhibitory transmitter) in the nucleus accumbens. Dopamine is probably better described as mediating attention rather than reward or pleasure. (p. 452)

2. Amphetamine acts mostly by increasing the release of dopamine. Cocaine and methylphenidate act by decreasing the reuptake of dopamine after its release. (p. 454)

3. Nicotine excites acetylcholine receptors on axon terminals that release dopamine in the nucleus accumbens. (p. 455)

4. Opiate drugs stimulate endorphin receptors, which inhibit the release of GABA, which would otherwise inhibit the release of dopamine. Thus, the net effect of opiates is increased dopamine release. (p. 456)

5. Marijuana activates receptors on the presynaptic cell, mimicking an endogenous chemical with a negative feedback effect. That is, when a presynaptic terminal releases either an excitatory or inhibitory transmitter, the postsynaptic cell releases a marijuanalike chemical that puts the brakes on further release. (p. 457)

6. Hallucinogens act by stimulating certain kinds of serotonin receptors. (p. 458)

7. Type I alcoholism has a slower onset, is usually less severe, and affects men and women about equally. Type II alcoholism starts faster and sooner, is more severe, affects mostly men, and is sometimes associated with criminality and impulsiveness. (p. 459)

8. Ethyl alcohol is metabolized to acetaldehyde, which is then metabolized to acetic acid. People who, for genetic reasons, are deficient in that second reaction tend to become ill after drinking and therefore are unlikely to drink heavily. (p. 460)

9. Antabuse, a drug sometimes used as a supplemental treatment for alcoholics, blocks the conversion of acetaldehyde to acetic acid. (p. 460)

10. Sons of alcoholics are less likely than other young men of the same age to show signs of intoxication after moderate drinking and are more likely to report significant relief from stress after drinking. (p. 461)

ANSWERS TO *STOP AND CHECK* QUESTIONS

1. Amphetamine causes the dopamine transporter to release dopamine instead of reabsorb it. (p. 455)

2. Cocaine interferes with the reuptake of released dopamine. (p. 455)

3. The effects of a methylphenidate pill develop and decline in the brain much more slowly than do those of cocaine. (p. 455)

4. Cocaine decreases total activity in the brain because it stimulates activity of dopamine, which is an inhibitory transmitter in most cases. (p. 455)

5. Nicotine excites acetylcholine receptors on neurons that release dopamine and thereby increases dopamine release. (p. 457)

6. Opiates stimulate endorphin synapses, which inhibit GABA synapses on certain cells that release dopamine. By inhibiting an inhibitor, opiates increase the release of dopamine. (p. 457)

7. Cannabinoids released by the postsynaptic neuron attach to receptors on the presynaptic neuron, where they inhibit further release of either excitatory (glutamate) or inhibitory (GABA) transmitters. That is, they provide negative feedback. (p. 458)

8. For both parts of the question, Type II. (p. 460)

9. People who metabolize it rapidly would be more likely to drink alcohol because they suffer fewer unpleasant effects. (p. 461)

10. Antabuse blocks the enzyme that converts acetaldehyde to acetic acid and, therefore, Antabuse makes people sick if they drink alcohol. Potentially, it could teach people an aversion to alcohol, but more often it works as a way for the person to make a daily recommitment to abstain from drinking. (p. 461)

11. Sons of alcoholics show less intoxication, including less body sway, after drinking a moderate amount of alcohol. They also show greater relief from stress after drinking alcohol. (p. 462)

THOUGHT QUESTIONS

1. People who take methylphenidate (Ritalin) for control of attention-deficit disorder often report that, although the drug increases their arousal for a while, they feel a decrease in alertness and arousal a few hours later. Explain.

2. Some people who use MDMA ("ecstasy") report that after repeated use it becomes less effective. Offer an explanation other than the usual mechanisms of tolerance that apply to other drugs.

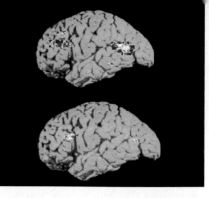

MODULE 15.2

Mood Disorders

Depression can be easy to diagnose in many cases. Depressed people act depressed; they look depressed (Figure 15.8); they tell you they are depressed. The problem is that many people who seem depressed may have other problems that lead to the depression, such as hormonal problems, head injuries (Holsinger et al., 2002), brain tumors, or other illnesses. Many people have depression comorbid with (i.e., combined with) substance abuse, anxiety, schizophrenia, or Parkinson's disease. The consequence for research is inconsistent results because of differences from one patient sample to another. The consequence for an individual patient is the possibility of being treated for one disorder while another one is overlooked.

MAJOR DEPRESSIVE DISORDER

At times, almost everyone feels sad, discouraged, lacking in energy. The difference between ordinary sadness and major depression depends on intensity and duration. According to *DSM–IV* (American Psychiatric As-

Figure 15.8 The face of depression
Depressed people show their condition in their face, their walk, their voice, their whole appearance.

sociation, 1994), people with a **major depression** feel sad and helpless every day for weeks at a time. They have little energy, feel worthless, contemplate suicide, have trouble sleeping, cannot concentrate, get little pleasure from sex or food, and in many cases can hardly even imagine being happy again. Major depression is diagnosed about twice as often in women as in men. It can occur at any time from adolescence to old age (rarely in children). Estimates vary concerning the prevalence of depression, and most of the variation results from whether one includes only severe cases or also somewhat milder cases. One survey reported that within any given year about 5% of adults in the United States have "clinically significant" (i.e., fairly severe) depression (Narrow, Rae, Robins, & Regier, 2002).

Genetics

Depression tends to run in families (Erlenmeyer-Kimling et al., 1997), and adopted children resemble their biological parents more than their adoptive parents with regard to depression (Wender et al., 1986). However, the impact of genes varies among different types of depression. You are at seriously increased risk of depression if you have close relatives who had severe early-onset depression (i.e., beginning before age 30), especially if those relatives were female (Bierut et al., 1999; Kendler, Gardner, & Prescott, 1999; Lyons et al., 1998). Compare this pattern to alcoholism: You are at increased risk of alcoholism if you had male relatives with early-onset alcoholism.

So far, efforts to find a single gene linked to depression have failed to identify any one gene with a strong link (Wong & Licinio, 2001). Evidently, depression depends on many genes that increase the risk, combined with a variety of environmental factors.

Life Events

Depression offers a classic example of the interaction between heredity and environment. Most depressed people can point to a life event that seemed to precipitate or aggravate their depression. Most also have evidence of genetic or other biological predispositions to depression. The most severe episodes occur when someone who has always been a little depressed, perhaps because of a biological predisposition, then has a traumatic experience. For example, after the California earthquake of 1989, almost everyone in the area became temporarily depressed, but those who had already been somewhat depressed before the earthquake became more severely depressed and remained depressed longer than the others (Nolen-Hoeksema & Morrow, 1991).

Hormones

Depression occurs in episodes rather than constantly. Someone may feel normal for weeks, months, or years, and then something triggers a new episode of depression. One likely trigger is stress, which releases cortisol, as described in Chapter 12. Cortisol readies the body for action and is helpful in the short term, but if prolonged, it can exhaust the body's energies, impair sleep, impair the immune system, and in short, set the stage for an episode of depression.

The role of sex hormones is less certain. Most women feel some emotional distress for a day or two after giving birth, and about 20% experience a moderately serious postpartum depression—that is, a depression after giving birth. About 1 woman in 1000 enters a more serious, long-lasting depression (Hopkins, Marcus, & Campbell, 1984). Most of these women had already suffered several previous episodes of depression; the postpartum events aggravated, but didn't really cause, depression (Schöpf, Bryois, Jonquière, & Le, 1984). One study found that after a drug-induced drop in estradiol and progesterone levels, women with a history of postpartum depression suddenly show new symptoms of depression, whereas other women do not (Bloch et al., 2000). That is, some women are more vulnerable to depression than others, and hormonal changes can trigger an episode of depression for the vulnerable women. Another study found that estradiol supplements relieved depression in many middle-aged women going through menopause (Soares, Almeida, Joffe, & Cohen, 2001).

Depression is more common among women than men for unknown reasons. Childhood depression is about equally common (actually, equally uncommon) in boys and girls. Beginning at puberty, depression is more common in females than males in all cultures for which we have data (Cyranowski, Frank, Young, & Shear, 2000; Silberg et al., 1999). The extra vulnerability of women is found even when researchers survey a town for undiagnosed cases, so it is not just a result of women seeking treatment more often than men. However, the probability of depression does not correlate strongly with hormone levels (Roca, Schmidt, & Rubinow, 1999). (Neither does PMS, as you may recall from Chapter 11.)

Abnormalities of Hemispheric Dominance

Studies of normal people have found a fairly strong relationship between happy mood and increased activity in the left prefrontal cortex (G. D. Jacobs & Snyder, 1996). Most depressed people have decreased activity in the left and increased activity in the right prefrontal cortex (Davidson, 1984; Starkstein & Robinson, 1986). Here's something you can try: Ask someone to solve a cognitive problem, such as "See how many words you can think of that start with hu-" or "Try to remember all the ingredients you've ever seen on a pizza." Then unobtrusively watch the person's eye movements to see whether they gaze right or left. Most people gaze to the right during verbal tasks, but most depressed people gaze to the left (Lenhart & Katkin, 1986).

Many people become seriously depressed after left-hemisphere damage; fewer do after right-hemisphere damage (Vataja et al., 2001). Occasionally, people with right-hemisphere damage become manic, the opposite of depressed (Robinson, Boston, Starkstein, & Price, 1988). We shall return to this point when we discuss the effects of electroconvulsive shock to the left or right hemisphere.

1. Some people offer to train you to use the right hemisphere of your brain more strongly, allegedly to increase creativity. If they were successful, can you see any disadvantage?

Check your answer on page 475.

Viruses

A few cases of depression may be linked to a viral infection. As recently as the 1980s, Borna disease was known only as an infection of European farm animals. Gradually, investigators discovered that a much greater variety of species are vulnerable, over a much wider geographical range. In severe cases, the virus is fatal; in milder cases, Borna disease is noted mostly by its behavioral effects, such as periods of frantic activity alternating with periods of inactivity (Figure 15.9).

Many viruses are passed between humans and other species, although the effects on humans may be quite different or even undetectable. In 1985, investigators reported the results of a blood test given to 370 people (Amsterdam et al., 1985). Only 12 people tested positive for Borna disease virus, but *all 12 were*

(a)

(b)

Bode & Ludwig, 1997

Figure 15.9 Symptoms of Borna disease
Farm animals infected with Borna disease have periods of
frantic activity alternating with inactivity, much like a person
with bipolar disorder. **(a)** Horse with Borna disease.
(b) Same horse after recovery.

suffering from major depression or bipolar disorder.
These 12 were a small percentage of the 265 depressed
people tested; still, none of the 105 undepressed people had the virus.

During the 1990s, thousands of people were tested
in Europe, Asia, and North America. The Borna virus
was found in about 2% of normal people, 30% of severely depressed patients, and 13% to 14% of people
with chronic brain diseases (Bode, Ferszt, & Czech,
1993; Bode, Riegel, Lange, & Ludwig, 1992). However,
later studies found the Borna virus in people with
other psychiatric diseases as well as depression
(Herzog et al., 1997). Evidently, the Borna virus predisposes people to psychiatric difficulties in general,
but not specifically depression.

Antidepressant Drugs

It is logical to assume that investigators would first figure out the causes of a psychological disorder and
then develop a treatment to address it. But the

opposite sequence has been more common: First investigators find a drug or other treatment that seems
helpful, and then they try to figure out how it works.
Like many other psychiatric drugs, the early antidepressants were discovered by accident.

> ### EXTENSIONS AND APPLICATIONS
> ### Accidental Discoveries of Psychiatric Drugs
>
> Nearly all of the earliest psychiatric drugs were dis-
> covered by accident. Disulfiram, for example, was
> originally used in the manufacture of rubber. Someone
> noticed that workers in a certain rubber factory devel-
> oped a distaste for alcohol and traced the cause to
> disulfiram, which had altered the workers' metabo-
> lism so they became ill after drinking any alcohol
> (Schwartz & Tulipan, 1933). Disulfiram became the
> drug Antabuse, often prescribed for people who are
> trying to avoid alcohol.
>
> The use of bromides to control epilepsy was origi-
> nally based on a theory, but the theory was all wrong
> (Friedlander, 1986; Levitt, 1975). People in the 1800s
> who believed that masturbation caused epilepsy
> thought that bromides reduced sexual drive. There-
> fore, the reasoning went, bromides should reduce
> epilepsy. It turns out that bromides do relieve
> epilepsy, but for altogether different reasons.
>
> The earliest antidepressants and antipsychotics
> were also stumbled upon haphazardly, and at first, no
> one had any idea how they worked. Each drug had
> multiple effects on the body, any one of which might
> be relevant. Only after researchers had identified a few
> of them could they try to figure out what those drugs
> had in common with one another.
>
> For decades, researchers sought new drugs en-
> tirely by trial and error. Today, because we largely un-
> derstand how drugs affect synapses, researchers can
> evaluate new chemicals in test tubes or tissue samples
> until they find one with a potential for stronger or
> more specific effects on neurotransmission. The result
> is the use of fewer laboratory animals as well as fewer
> human research participants.

Types of Antidepressants

Antidepressant drugs fall into four major categories:
tricyclics, MAOIs, selective serotonin reuptake inhibitors, and atypical antidepressants (Figure 15.10).
The **tricyclics** (e.g., imipramine, trade name Tofranil)
operate by preventing the presynaptic neuron from
reabsorbing serotonin or catecholamines after releasing them; thus, the neurotransmitters remain longer
in the synaptic cleft and continue stimulating the

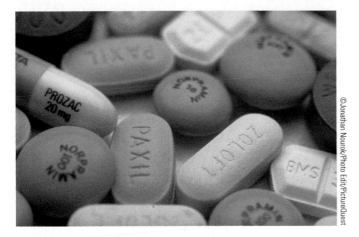

Figure 15.10 Antidepressant pills
Tricyclic drugs block the reuptake of catecholamines and serotonin by presynaptic terminals. Monoamine oxidase inhibitors block the breakdown of catecholamines and serotonin after their release into the synaptic cleft. Selective serotonin reuptake inhibitors, such as Prozac, have effects that are more limited to the neurotransmitter serotonin.

postsynaptic cell. However, the tricyclics also block histamine receptors, acetylcholine receptors, and certain sodium channels (Horst & Preskorn, 1998). As mentioned in Chapter 9, blocking histamine produces drowsiness. Blocking acetylcholine leads to dry mouth and difficulty urinating. Blocking sodium channels causes heart irregularities, among other problems. Many people have to limit their use of tricyclics because of the side effects.

The **monoamine oxidase inhibitors (MAOIs)** (e.g., as phenelzine, trade name Nardil) block the enzyme monoamine oxidase (MAO), a presynaptic terminal enzyme that metabolizes catecholamines and serotonin into inactive forms. When MAOIs block this enzyme, the presynaptic terminal has more of its transmitter available for release. The tricyclics are usually more effective, but MAOIs help many patients who do not respond to tricyclics (Thase, Trivedi, & Rush, 1995). People taking MAOIs must avoid foods containing tyramine, including cheese, raisins, liver, pickles, licorice, and a long list of others. Tyramine combines effects with MAOIs to increase blood pressure, sometimes fatally.

The **selective serotonin reuptake inhibitors (SSRIs)** are similar to tricyclics but specific to the neurotransmitter serotonin. For example, fluoxetine (trade name Prozac) blocks the reuptake of serotonin by the presynaptic terminal. SSRIs produce only mild side effects, mainly mild nausea or headache (Feighner et al., 1991). However, they sometimes produce nervousness and are not recommended for patients with both depression and anxiety. Other common SSRIs include sertraline (Zoloft), fluvoxamine (Luvox), citalopram (Celexa), and paroxetine (Paxil or Seroxat).

The **atypical antidepressants** are a miscellaneous group of drugs with antidepressant effects but only mild side effects (Horst & Preskorn, 1998). They are often effective for patients who failed to respond to the other drugs. One atypical antidepressant is bupropion (Wellbutrin), which inhibits reuptake of dopamine and to some extent norepinephrine but not serotonin. Another is venlafaxin, which mostly inhibits the reuptake of serotonin but also somewhat that of norepinephrine and slightly that of dopamine. A third is nefazodone, which specifically blocks serotonin type 2A receptors and also weakly blocks reuptake of serotonin and norepinephrine. Figure 15.11 summarizes the mechanisms of tricyclics, MAOIs, and SSRIs.

In addition, many people use St. John's wort, an herb. Because it is marketed as a nutritional supplement instead of a drug, it is not regulated by the Food and Drug Administration in the United States, and the purity varies from one batch to another. It has the advantage of being less expensive than other antidepressant drugs. An advantage or disadvantage, depending on

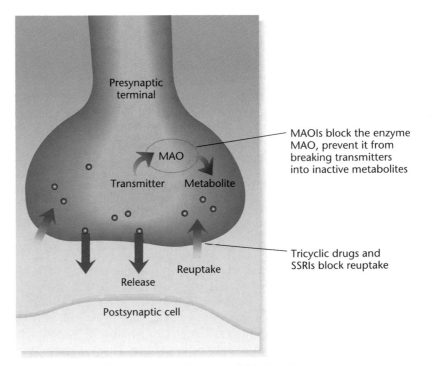

Figure 15.11 Routes of action of antidepressants
Tricyclics block the reuptake of dopamine, norepinephrine, or serotonin. SSRIs specifically block the reuptake of serotonin. MAOIs block the enzyme MAO, which converts dopamine, norepinephrine, and serotonin into inactive chemicals. Atypical antidepressants have varying effects.

your point of view, is that it is available without prescription, and therefore, people can get it easily but may take inappropriate amounts or combine it inappropriately with other drugs. Apparently, it works the same way as the SSRIs. Depending on which study you believe, it is either a little more effective than standard SSRIs, about equal to them, or totally ineffective (Barnes, Anderson, & Phillipson, 2001; Hypericum Depression Trial Study Group, 2002). However, it has one little-known and potentially dangerous side effect: All mammals have a liver enzyme that breaks down a wide variety of plant toxins. St. John's wort increases the effectiveness of that enzyme. Increasing the action of an enzyme that breaks down toxins sounds like a good thing, and sometimes it is (Kliewer & Willson, 2002). However, the enzyme also breaks down many medicines. Therefore, taking St. John's wort decreases the effectiveness of many other drugs you might be taking—including other antidepressant drugs, cancer drugs, AIDS drugs, even birth-control pills (Moore et al., 2000).

Antidepressant drugs have delayed effects that limit the excitation of the postsynaptic cell. One such effect is to decrease the sensitivity of the postsynaptic receptors. Recall from Chapter 5 the concept of disuse supersensitivity: A receptor that receives little input becomes more sensitive to future input. The opposite is also true: A receptor that receives excess input decreases its sensitivity. A second effect depends on a special kind of receptor that we have not encountered earlier in this text, called an *autoreceptor*. An **autoreceptor** is a negative feedback receptor on the presynaptic terminal. After an axon releases much of its neurotransmitter, some of the molecules come back to stimulate the autoreceptors, which then decrease further release of the neurotransmitter. In other words, any increase in transmitter release is followed by a decrease. In effect, the autoreceptors put on the brakes (Figure 15.12). When antidepressant drugs prolong the presence of serotonin or other transmitters in the synapse, the extra molecules stimulate the autoreceptors and thereby decrease further release.

Exactly How Do Antidepressants Work?

We know the effects of antidepressant drugs up to a certain point; for example, tricyclics and SSRIs block reuptake of certain transmitters, and MAOIs block the breakdown of certain transmitters. However, these known effects may not be the main basis for the antidepressant effects. The main problem is that the time course of known synaptic effects does not match the time course of the behavioral effects. Antidepressant drugs produce their effects on catecholamine and serotonin synapses within hours, varying from one drug to another. However, no one experiences antidepressant benefits within

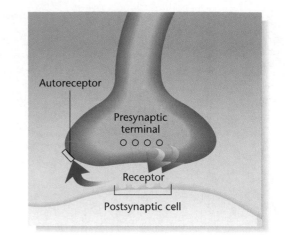

Figure 15.12   An autoreceptor
After an axon releases a neurotransmitter, some of the molecules attach to autoreceptors on the presynaptic terminal itself, feeding back to limit further release of the transmitter.

hours. Typically, the benefits begin after 2 or 3 weeks. One study found that most benefits occurring in less than 2 weeks are placebo effects; the patients continue reporting the benefits even if the physician substitutes an inactive pill (Stewart et al., 1998). In contrast, methylphenidate (Ritalin) has benefits for attention-deficit disorder in which the time courses do match: The drug produces its peak effect on the synapses in 60 minutes and its peak effect on behavior also in 60 minutes (Volkow et al., 1998). So the effect of methylphenidate on attention-deficit disorder probably does depend on those synaptic effects, but the benefits of antidepressant drugs require further investigation.

One likely explanation for antidepressant drugs pertains to the fact that neurons in certain parts of the hippocampus and cerebral cortex shrink when people become depressed (Cotter, Mackay, Landau, Kerwin, & Everall, 2001). When drugs (or anything else) increase dopamine release, the axons releasing dopamine also release a neurotrophin called *brain-derived neurotrophic factor* (Guillin et al., 2001). Recall from Chapter 5 that neurotrophins aid in survival, growth, and connections of neurons. As antidepressant drugs increase dopamine release, they also increase the neurotrophin release and thereby increase cell size in the brain areas that had shown decreases (Duman, Heninger, & Nestler, 1997). The growth is gradual, and studies on mice suggest that the neurotrophins' effects are necessary for the behavioral effects of antidepressant drugs (Saarelainen et. al., 2003).

2. What are the effects of tricyclic drugs?

3. What are the effects of MAOIs?

4. What are the effects of SSRIs?

5. What are the atypical antidepressants?

6. Why are the immediate effects of antidepressants at synapses probably not the explanation for their effects on behavior?

Check your answers on page 475.

Other Therapies

An alternative to antidepressant drugs is cognitive therapy or other forms of psychotherapy. Drug therapies and psychotherapy produce remarkably similar effects. Brain scans show that antidepressant drugs increase metabolism in certain brain areas, and successful psychotherapy produces almost the same changes (Brody et al., 2001; S. D. Martin et al., 2001). This similarity should not be terribly surprising to one who accepts the mind-body identity position. If mental activity really is the same thing as brain activity, then changing someone's thoughts should indeed change brain chemistry.

In comparison to drug therapy, psychotherapy has one important advantage: Someone who recovers by means of psychotherapy is less likely to relapse into a renewed episode of depression (M. D. Evans et al., 1992). In other words, its benefits are more likely to be long-lasting. Drugs, however, have their own advantages. They are cheaper than psychotherapy and more convenient. (Being a busy person, which would you rather do today—take a pill or spend an hour talking to a therapist?) Finally, someone taking drugs can expect benefits in 2 or 3 weeks, whereas the benefits of psychotherapy generally develop gradually over 2 months or more.

When depressed patients get no treatment at all, about one third to one half improve over time anyway. If given antidepressant drugs, about two thirds improve. If given cognitive therapy, again about two thirds improve. If given antidepressant drugs and cognitive therapy—guess what—still two thirds improve (Thase et al., 1997). Evidently, those likely to improve on the drugs are the same people likely to improve with cognitive therapy. We are left with one third of patients who do not respond well to either

drugs or cognitive therapy. What can anyone offer them? Let us consider two possibilities: electroconvulsive therapy and sleep alterations.

Electroconvulsive Therapy (ECT)

Treatment through an electrically induced seizure, known as **electroconvulsive therapy (ECT),** has had a stormy history (Fink, 1985). It originated with the observation that people with both epilepsy and schizophrenia sometimes have a decrease in the symptoms of one when they have an increase in the symptoms of the other (Trimble & Thompson, 1986). In the 1930s, a Hungarian physician, Ladislas Meduna, tried to relieve schizophrenia by inducing convulsive seizures. Soon other physicians were doing the same, inducing seizures with a large dose of insulin. Insulin shock is a dreadful experience, however, and difficult to control. An Italian physician, Ugo Cerletti, after years of experimentation with animals, developed a method of inducing seizures with an electric shock through the head (Cerletti & Bini, 1938). Electroconvulsive therapy is quick, and most patients awaken calmly without remembering it.

When ECT proved to be not very effective with schizophrenia, you might guess that psychiatrists would abandon it. Instead, they tried it for other mental hospital patients, despite having no theoretical reason to expect success. ECT did indeed seem helpful for many depressed patients and soon became a common treatment. Its misuse, especially during the 1950s, earned it a bad reputation, as some patients were given ECT hundreds of times without their consent.

When antidepressant drugs became available in the late 1950s, the use of ECT declined abruptly. However, it made a partial comeback in the 1970s when it became clear that many depressed patients do not respond well to drug treatments. ECT is used only with informed consent, usually for patients who have not responded to antidepressant drugs (Scovern & Kilmann, 1980; Weiner, 1979). It is also sometimes recommended for patients with strong suicidal tendencies because it works faster than antidepressant drugs: Feeling better in 1 week instead of 2 may be the difference between life and death.

ECT is usually applied every other day for about 2 weeks, sometimes longer. Patients are given muscle relaxants or anesthetics to minimize discomfort and the possibility of injury (Figure 15.13). Because the shock is less intense than in earlier years, the risk of provoking a heart attack is low except in elderly patients.

The most common side effect of ECT is memory loss, but if physicians limit the shock to the right hemisphere, the antidepressant effects occur without memory impairment (McElhiney et al., 1995). (Recall that

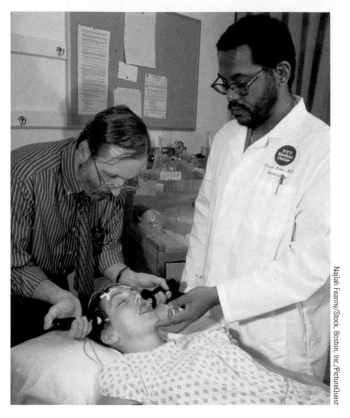

Figure 15.13 Electroconvulsive therapy (ECT)
In contrast to the practices of an earlier era, ECT today is administered with muscle relaxants or anesthetics to minimize discomfort. It can be used only if the patient gives informed consent.

right-hemisphere activity is more associated with unpleasant mood.) Because depression is associated with decreased activity of the left hemisphere, right-hemisphere ECT may either promote a better balance of activity between the two hemispheres or somehow enhance activity in the left hemisphere.

Besides the threat of memory loss, the other serious drawback to ECT is that about half of the people who respond well to it relapse into another episode of depression within 6 months (Riddle & Scott, 1995). After ECT has relieved someone's depression, the usual strategy is to try to prevent a relapse by means of either drugs, psychotherapy, or additional ECT treatments every few weeks (Swoboda, Conca, König, Waanders, & Hansen, 2001.

More than half a century after the introduction of ECT, no one is yet sure how it relieves depression. It stimulates the production of additional dopamine type D_1 and D_2 receptors in the nucleus accumbens (S. Smith, Lindefors, Hurd, & Sharp, 1995), decreases the number of norepinephrine receptors at postsynaptic cells (Kellar & Stockmeier, 1986; Lerer & Shapira, 1986), and exerts a wide variety of other effects. We do not know, however, which effect is critical.

A more recent, similar treatment is repetitive transcranial magnetic stimulation. An intense magnetic field is applied to the scalp, temporarily disabling all the neurons just below the magnet. This procedure resembles ECT both in its level of effectiveness and in the fact that no one knows why it is effective (George et al., 1997).

Altered Sleep Patterns

Most depressed people report sleep problems, and people with sleep problems are much more likely than others to become depressed (Ford & Cooper-Patrick, 2001). The usual sleep disturbance in depression suggests a disorder of biological rhythms. Recall from Chapter 9 that most people who go to bed at the normal time first enter REM sleep about 80 minutes after falling asleep; the amount of REM sleep remains low for the first half of the night and increases in the second half. That trend is controlled by the time of day, not by how long the person has been asleep. Someone who goes to sleep later than usual on a given night is likely to enter REM sleep relatively soon (Figure 15.14).

Most depressed people enter REM sleep within 45 minutes after going to bed, as Figure 15.14 illustrates. They also have trouble staying asleep and awaken early. During the day, they feel drowsy. As they recover from depression, their sleep improves (Dew et al., 1996).

Surprisingly, although we might guess that keeping a depressed person awake all night would make the depression worse, it actually relieves the depression in most cases (Ringel & Szuba, 2001). In fact, one night of total sleep deprivation is the quickest known method of relieving depression.

Sleep deprivation is particularly helpful to patients with low levels of dopamine turnover, mild thyroid abnormalities, or elevated metabolism in the prefrontal cortex (Gillin, Buchsbaum, Wu, Clark, & Bunney, 2001; Orth et al., 2001; Ringel & Szuba, 2001). That is, careful screening can identify which patients are the best prospects for trying this procedure.

Unfortunately, the antidepressant effects from sleep deprivation are short-lived. Most patients become depressed again after the next night's sleep and sometimes even after a brief nap. It is possible to extend the benefits by altering the sleep schedule on later days. For example, go without sleep altogether for one day and then start a schedule of sleeping from 5 P.M. until midnight instead of the usual later time. This schedule relieves depression for at least a week in most patients, and it is possible to permit the patient to readjust the sleep schedule gradually back toward the usual time (Riemann et al., 1999).

Researchers cannot yet explain how sleep deprivation or rescheduling produces mood benefits. Both total deprivation and shifting sleep to an earlier time yield a decrease in REM sleep, and most antidepressant drugs also reduce REM (Winokur et al., 2001). Thus, it is possible that reducing REM has antidepressant effects. However, far more research will be needed to clarify what is happening during sleep deprivation. A better understanding might lead to other still better treatments for depression.

Stop & Check

7. For what kinds of patients is ECT recommended?

8. What change in sleep habits sometimes relieves depression?

Check your answers on page 475.

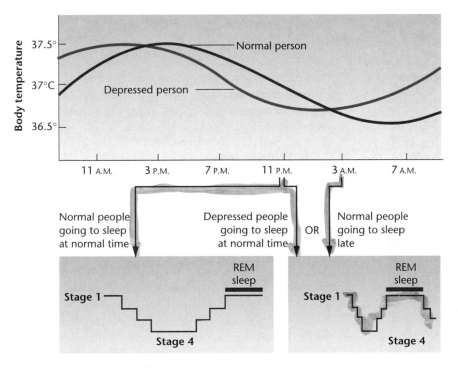

Figure 15.14   Sleep, REM, and the circadian rhythm of body temperature

Nondepressed people going to bed at their normal time get much stage 4 sleep for the first few hours and increasing amounts of REM sleep later during the night. Most depressed people have their circadian rhythms advanced by several hours; when they go to sleep at 11 P.M., they sleep as a normal person does at about 3 A.M. *Source: Adapted from* Sleep *by J. Allan Hobson. Scientific American Library, 1989. Reprinted by permission of W. H. Freeman and Company.*

BIPOLAR DISORDER

Depression is either a unipolar or a bipolar disorder. People with **unipolar disorder** experience only one pole, or extreme; they vary between feeling normal and feeling depressed. People with **bipolar disorder**—formerly known as **manic-depressive disorder**—alternate between two poles: depression and its opposite, mania. **Mania** is characterized by restless activity, excitement, laughter, self-confidence, rambling speech, and loss of inhibitions. In extreme cases, manic people are dangerous to themselves and others. People who have full-blown episodes of mania are said to have **bipolar I disorder**. People with **bipolar II disorder** have much milder manic phases, called hypomania, which are characterized mostly by agitation or anxiety. About 1% of people have at least a mild case of bipolar disorder at some time in life, with an average age of onset in the early twenties (Craddock & Jones, 1999).

A cycle from depression to mania and back to depression again may last as little as a couple of days or as much as a couple of years (Bunney, Murphy, Goodwin, & Borge, 1972). Figure 15.15 represents the rise and fall of a manic episode in one hospitalized patient.

The rate of glucose metabolism is a good indicator of overall brain activity. As Figure 15.16 shows, glucose use is higher than normal during mania and lower than normal during depression (Baxter et al., 1985). Bipolar patients have some brain abnormalities, including a larger than normal amygdala (Strakowski et al., 1999). As mentioned in Chapter 12, the amygdala is an important area for emotions.

Genetics

Several lines of evidence suggest a hereditary basis for bipolar disorder (Craddock & Jones, 1999). If one monozygotic twin has bipolar disorder, the other has at least a 50% chance of getting it also, whereas the dizygotic twins, brothers, sisters, or children of a bipolar patient have about a 5% to 10% probability. Adopted children who develop bipolar disorder are likely to have biological relatives with mood disorders.

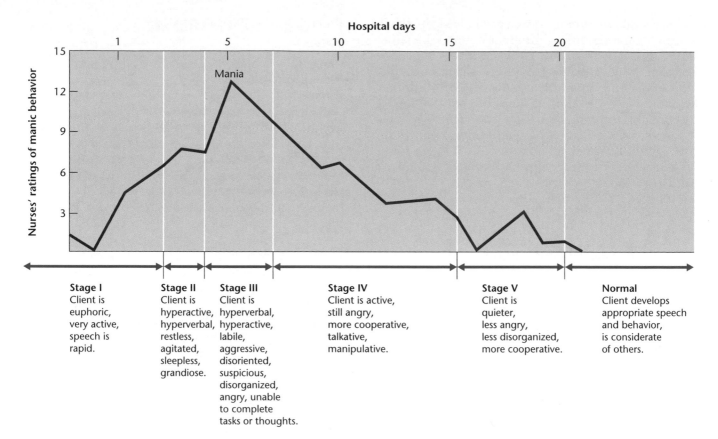

Hospital days

Figure 15.15 **Observations of a 3-week manic episode** *Source: From* Psychiatric Mental Health Nursing *by E. Janosik and J. Davies, p. 173. Copyright ©1986 Jones and Bartlet Publishers. Reprinted with permission.*

Stage I
Client is euphoric, very active, speech is rapid.

Stage II
Client is hyperactive, hyperverbal, restless, agitated, sleepless, grandiose.

Stage III
Client is hyperverbal, hyperactive, labile, aggressive, disoriented, suspicious, disorganized, angry, unable to complete tasks or thoughts.

Stage IV
Client is active, still angry, more cooperative, talkative, manipulative.

Stage V
Client is quieter, less angry, less disorganized, more cooperative.

Normal
Client develops appropriate speech and behavior, is considerate of others.

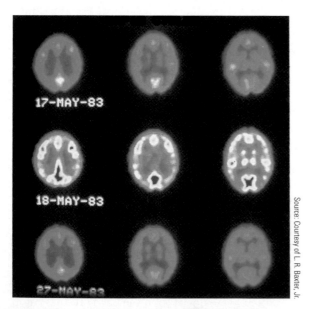

Source: Courtesy of L. R. Baxter, Jr.

Figure 15.16 **PET scans of a bipolar patient**
Horizontal planes through three levels of the brain are shown for each day. On May 17 and May 27, when the patient was depressed, brain metabolic rates were low. On May 18, when the patient was in a cheerful, hypomanic mood, the brain metabolic rate was high. Red indicates the highest metabolic rate, followed by yellow, green, and blue.

Comparisons of chromosomes in several populations have identified several genes that are somewhat more common than average among people with bipolar disorder (Badenhop et al., 2001; Blackwood et al., 1996; Degn et al., 2001; Egeland et al., 1987; Freimer et al., 1996; Ginns et al., 1996; McMahon et al., 2001). However, no specific gene is so strongly linked that it appears to be a major cause.

Treatments

The first successful treatment for bipolar disorder was lithium salts, which continue to be used today. The effectiveness of lithium was discovered accidentally by an Australian investigator, J. F. Cade, who believed that uric acid might relieve mania and depression. Cade mixed uric acid with a lithium salt to help it dissolve and then gave the solution to patients. It was indeed helpful, although investigators eventually realized that lithium was the effective agent, not uric acid.

Lithium stabilizes the mood of a bipolar patient, preventing a relapse into either mania or depression. The use of lithium must be regulated carefully, as a low dose is ineffective and a high dose is toxic

(Schou, 1997). Two other effective drugs are valproic acid (trade names Depakene, Depakote, and others) and carbamazepine. Valproic acid and carbamazepine are often recommended for patients with bipolar II disorder, characterized by depression and only mild manic phases. Lithium appears to be more effective for people with bipolar I disorder, with depression and stronger manic phases (Kleindienst & Greil, 2000).

Lithium, valproic acid, and carbamazepine each have a variety of effects on the brain. A good research strategy is to assume that the way they relieve bipolar disorder depends on some effect they have in common. For example, valproic acid and carbamazepine increase activity at GABA synapses but lithium does not, so that effect is presumably not central to relieving bipolar disorder. One finding is that all three drugs block the synthesis of a brain chemical called *inositol,* and giving extra inositol abolishes the benefits of lithium, valproic acid, or carbamazepine (R. S. B. Williams, Cheng, Mudge, & Harwood, 2002). Inositol is a chemical with many known useful effects. It contributes to membrane formation, helps transport and break down fats, and is a precursor to a second messenger in neurons. In fact, it is often sold as a dietary supplement to increase sleep, combat anxiety, and relieve depression. Nevertheless, it is possible that excessive inositol causes problems for some people. However, researchers so far have found no abnormality of inositol synthesis in bipolar patients (Atack, 1996).

Another finding is that lithium and valproic acid block the synthesis of a brain chemical called *arachidonic acid,* which is generally produced during brain inflammation (Rapoport & Bosetti, 2002). Arachidonic acid attaches to phospholipids, which are part of a neuronal membrane. The effects of arachidonic acid are counteracted by polyunsaturated fatty acids, such as are found abundantly in most seafood, and epidemiological studies suggest that people who eat much seafood may have a decresed risk of bipolar disorder (Noaghiul, Hibbeln, & Weissman, in press). At this point, researchers are not sure how lithium and other drugs alleviate bipolar disorder; more research is needed on both the inositol and arachidonic acid hypotheses.

One further possible treatment deserves more attention: Bipolar patients during the depressed phase tend to go to bed late and stay in bed for many hours. During the manic phase, they go to bed early but awaken quickly, sleeping perhaps only 3 or 4 hours. Researchers talked one bipolar patient into keeping a consistent schedule of staying in bed (in a dark, quiet room) for at least 10 hours per night. This procedure greatly reduced the intensity of his mood swings (Wehr et al., 1998). The researchers speculate that the artificial lights, television, and other technology of our society tempts us into staying up late at night and may in the process increase the prevalence of bipolar disorder.

9. What are two common treatments for bipolar disorder?

10. What dietary supplement should bipolar patients probably avoid, and why?

Check your answers on page 475.

SEASONAL AFFECTIVE DISORDER (SAD)

Another form of depression is seasonal affective disorder, conveniently abbreviated SAD, which is depression that regularly recurs during a particular season, such as winter. SAD is most prevalent near the poles, where the winter nights are very long (Haggarty et al., 2002), less common in moderate climates, and unheard-of in the tropics. Most people feel happier and more active in the summer, when there are many hours of sunlight, than in winter (Madden, Heath, Rosenthal, & Martin, 1996). SAD appears to be an exaggeration of this common tendency.

In many ways, SAD differs from other types of depression; for example, SAD patients have phase-delayed sleep and temperature rhythms, unlike most other depressed patients, whose rhythms are phase-advanced (Teicher et al., 1997) (Figure 15.17). Also, SAD is seldom severe, contrary to major depression in general.

It is possible to treat SAD with very bright lights (e.g., 2500 lux) for an hour or more each day. The bright light treatment is effective in morning, afternoon, or evening, but most research indicates that it has its strongest effect if presented in the morning (Eastman, Young, Fogg, Liu, & Meaden, 1998; Lewy et al., 1998; Terman, Terman, & Ross, 1998).

Researchers do not yet know what causes seasonal affective disorder or why bright light alleviates it. The most likely hypotheses are that bright light affects serotonin synapses and alters circadian rhythms. Regardless of how it works, it produces bigger, more reliable benefits than either antidepressant drugs or psychotherapy does for other types of depression. Consequently, some therapists have begun recommending

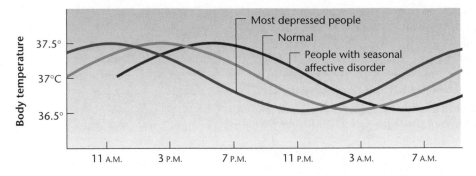

Figure 15.17 Circadian rhythms for normal, depressed, and SAD people
Note that SAD patients are phase-delayed while most other depressed patients are phase-advanced.

bright light therapy for nonseasonal depression, even though no research has yet been done for that application (Wirz-Justice, 1998).

The following Web site provides much information about light therapy and biological rhythms:
www.sltbr.org/

11. In what parts of the world are people most likely to experience seasonal affective disorder?

Check your answer on page 475.

Check your answer on page 475.

MODULE 15.2

In Closing: The Biology of Mood Swings

Do you feel sad because of events that have happened to you or because of your brain chemistry? According to biological psychologists, that is a meaningless question. Your experiences are changes in your brain state; you cannot have one without the other. The better question is: Are some people more likely than others to become depressed because of a preexisting condition in their brain chemistry? The answer to that one is "probably." It is difficult to get from "probably" to "definitely" because it is difficult to do research on human moods. At each stage in life, brain structure and chemistry alter one's reactions to events, and experience in turn alters the brain, affecting the reaction to the next event. Studying an adult brain has the same challenge as watching only a few minutes in the middle of a complex movie and trying to guess how events led up to that point.

SUMMARY

1. People with major depression feel sad, helpless, and lacking in energy for weeks at a time. For most, depression occurs as a series of episodes, each triggered by life events or biological changes. (p. 464)

2. Depression shows a strong family tendency, especially for women, implying a genetic contribution. However, no individual genes have yet been located. (p. 464)

3. Most severe cases of depression are an interaction between a biological predisposition and life events that trigger an episode. (p. 464)

4. Depression is associated with decreased activity in the left hemisphere of the cortex. (p. 465)

5. Four kinds of antidepressant drugs are in wide use. Tricyclics block reuptake of serotonin and catecholamines but produce strong side effects. MAOIs block an enzyme that breaks down catecholamines and serotonin. SSRIs block reuptake of serotonin. Atypical antidepressants are a miscellaneous group with diverse effects. (p. 466)

6. The antidepressants alter synaptic activity quickly, but their effects on behavior build up over weeks. The benefits apparently depend on gradual effects of neurotrophins released with the neurotransmitters. (p. 468)

7. Other therapies for depression include cognitive psychotherapy, electroconvulsive therapy, and altered sleep patterns. Each has its own pattern of benefits. (p. 469)

8. People with bipolar disorder alternate between two extremes: depression and mania. Bipolar disorder has a probable genetic basis. Effective therapies include lithium salts and certain drugs. How these drugs benefit people with bipolar disorder is uncertain, but current work focuses on the fact that both lithium and the drugs decrease the synthesis of inositol and arachidonic acid. (p. 471)

9. Seasonal affective disorder is marked by recurrent depression during one season of the year. Exposure to bright lights is usually effective in treating it. (p. 473)

ANSWERS TO *STOP AND CHECK* QUESTIONS

1. People with predominant right-hemisphere activity and decreased left activity tend to become depressed. (p. 465)

2. Tricyclic drugs block reuptake of serotonin and catecholamines. They also block histamine receptors, acetylcholine receptors, and certain sodium channels, thereby producing unpleasant side effects. (p. 469)

3. MAOIs block the enzyme MAO, which breaks down catecholamines and serotonin. The result is increased availability of these transmitters. (p. 469)

4. SSRIs selectively inhibit the reuptake of serotonin. (p. 469)

5. Atypical antidepressants are a miscellaneous group that does not fall into any of the other groups. They have diverse effects on serotonin and other synapses. (p. 469)

6. The antidepressants produce their known effects on the synapses quickly, but their behavioral benefits develop gradually over 2 to 3 weeks. (p. 469)

7. ECT is recommended for depressed people who did not respond to other therapies and for those who are an immediate suicide risk (because ECT acts faster than other therapies). (p. 471)

8. Getting depressed people to go to bed earlier sometimes relieves depression. (p. 471)

9. The common treatments for bipolar disorder are lithium salts and the drugs valproat and carbamazepine.(p. 473)

10. Bipolar patients probably should avoid the nutritional supplement inositol because of evidence that it blocks the effectiveness of lithium and other drugs generally prescribed for bipolar patients. (p. 473)

11. Seasonal affective disorder is more common toward the poles, where the difference between summer and winter is greatest. (p. 474)

THOUGHT QUESTION

Some people have suggested that ECT relieves depression by causing people to forget the events that caused it. What evidence opposes this hypothesis?

Schizophrenia

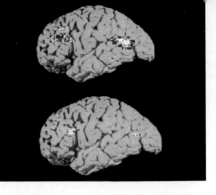

Here is a conversation between two people diagnosed with schizophrenia (Haley, 1959, p. 321):

A: Do you work at the air base?

B: You know what I think of work. I'm 33 in June, do you mind?

A: June?

B: 33 years old in June. This stuff goes out the window after I live this, uh—leave this hospital. So I can't get my vocal cords back. So I lay off cigarettes. I'm in a spatial condition, from outer space myself . . . .

A: I'm a real spaceship from across.

B: A lot of people talk that way, like crazy, but "Believe It or Not," by Ripley, take it or leave it—alone—it's in the *Examiner,* it's in the comic section, "Believe It or Not," by Ripley, Robert E. Ripley, Believe it or not, but we don't have to believe anything, unless I feel like it. Every little rosette—too much alone.

A: Yeah, it could be possible.

B: I'm a civilian seaman.

A: Could be possible. I take my bath in the ocean.

B: Bathing stinks. You know why? 'Cause you can't quit when you feel like it. You're in the service.

People with schizophrenia say and do things that other people (including other people with schizophrenia) find difficult to understand. The causes of the disorder are still not well understood, but they apparently include a large biological component.

CHARACTERISTICS

According to *DSM–IV*, schizophrenia is a disorder characterized by deteriorating ability to function in everyday life and by some combination of hallucinations, delusions, thought disorder, movement disorder, and inappropriate emotional expressions (American Psychiatric Association, 1994). The symptoms vary greatly. Hallucinations and delusions are prominent for some; thought disorders are dominant for others; some have clear signs of brain damage, but others do not. In short, you could easily find several people who have all been diagnosed with schizophrenia who nevertheless have almost nothing in common (Andreasen, 1999). What we call schizophrenia may turn out to be more than one disorder.

Schizophrenia was originally called *dementia praecox,* which is Latin for "premature deterioration of the mind." In 1911, Eugen Bleuler introduced the term *schizophrenia,* which has become the established term even though it confuses many people. Although schizophrenia is Greek for "split mind," it is *not* the same as *dissociative identity disorder* (previously known as *multiple personality*), a condition in which someone alternates among different personalities and identities. A person with schizophrenia has only one personality. What Bleuler meant by *schizophrenia* was a split between the emotional and intellectual aspects of the person: The person's emotional expression or lack of it seems unconnected with current experiences. For example, the person might giggle or cry for no apparent reason or listen to bad news and show no response. Not all patients show this detachment of emotion from intellect, but the term lives on.

This Web site provides a good source of information on many aspects of schizophrenia: www.schizophrenia.com/

Behavioral Symptoms

Schizophrenia is characterized by **positive symptoms** (behaviors that are present that should be absent) and **negative symptoms** (behaviors that are absent that should be present). The typical negative symptoms are weak social interactions, emotional expression, speech, and working memory. Negative symptoms tend to be stable over time and difficult to treat. Positive symptoms, which are more sporadic, fall into two clusters that do not correlate strongly with each other (Andreasen, Arndt, Alliger, Miller, & Flaum, 1995). The *psychotic* cluster consists of **delusions** (unfounded beliefs, such as the conviction that one is being persecuted or that outer space aliens are trying to control one's behavior) and **hallucinations** (abnormal sensory experiences, such as hearing voices when no one else is speaking). PET scans have determined that hallucinations occur during periods of increased activity in the thalamus, hippocampus, and parts of the cortex—including many of the areas activated by actual hearing (Shergill, Brammer, Williams, Murray, & McGuire, 2000; Silbersweig et al., 1995) (Figure 15.18).

The *disorganized* cluster of positive symptoms consists of inappropriate emotions (expressing great happiness or sadness for no apparent reason), bizarre behaviors, and thought disorder. The most typical thought disorder of schizophrenia is a difficulty understanding and using abstract concepts. For example, a schizophrenic person would take literally a proverb such as, "When the cat's away, the mice will play." Schizophrenic people also organize their thoughts loosely, as in a dream.

Of all these symptoms, which if any is the primary or central problem? According to Nancy Andreasen (1999), one of the leading investigators of schizophrenia, the main problem is disordered thoughts, which result from abnormal interactions between the cortex and the thalamus and cerebellum. The disordered thinking may result in hallucinations and delusions, but those are not the fundamental problem.

Schizophrenia can be either acute or chronic. An acute condition has a sudden onset and good prospects for recovery. A chronic condition has a gradual onset and a long-term course. In other words, some people have permanent schizophrenia, whereas others have one or two episodes followed by a return to normality with no need for further treatment (Wiersma, Nienhuis, Slooff, & Giel, 1998).

Before antischizophrenic drugs became available in the mid-1950s, most schizophrenic people were confined to mental hospitals, where they generally deteriorated for the rest of their lives. Today, many people with schizophrenia manage to live normally with the aid of drugs and outpatient treatment, and many others live normal lives most of the time, with an occasional need for hospitalization.

EXTENSIONS AND APPLICATIONS
Differential Diagnosis of Schizophrenia

Schizophrenia is difficult to diagnose. Suppose you're a psychiatrist and you meet a patient who has recently deteriorated in everyday functioning and has hallucinations, delusions, thought disorder, and disorganized speech. You are ready to enter a diagnosis of schizophrenia and begin treatment, right?

Not so fast. According to *DSM–IV* (American Psychiatric Association, 1994), before making a diagnosis of schizophrenia, one must first rule out other conditions that might produce similar symptoms. A **differential diagnosis** is one that identifies one condition as distinct from all other conditions with similar symptoms. Here are a few conditions that sometimes resemble schizophrenia:

- *Mood disorder with psychotic features:* Depressed people frequently have delusions, especially delusions of guilt or failure. Some report hallucinations also.

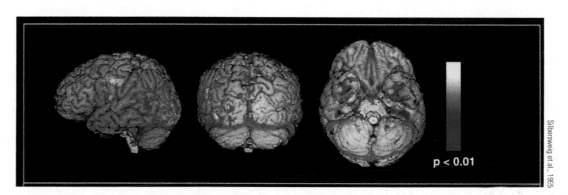

Figure 15.18 Brain areas activated during hallucinations
Researchers made PET scans of the brain of a schizophrenic patient during both auditory and visual hallucinations and compared activity to his resting state. Yellow indicates areas of greatest activation, and red is next greatest. Note the widespread areas of activation; note also the lack of activation in Broca's area, where we might have expected activity if the hallucinations were due to inner speech. *Source: Silbersweig et al., 1995.*

- *Substance abuse:* Many of the symptoms, especially the positive symptoms, of schizophrenia can develop from prolonged use of amphetamine, methamphetamine, cocaine, LSD, or phencyclidine ("angel dust"). Someone who stops taking the drugs is likely, though not certain, to recover from these symptoms. Substance abuse often produces visual hallucinations, which are less common in schizophrenia, so if you encounter someone with visual hallucinations, check on the possibility of drug abuse.
- *Brain damage:* Lesions to the temporal or prefrontal cortex can produce symptoms resembling schizophrenia. Presumably, no competent therapist would confuse schizophrenia with the effects of a stroke, but one might easily overlook the possibility of a brain tumor.
- *Undetected hearing deficits:* On occasion, someone who is starting to have trouble hearing thinks that everyone else is whispering and therefore starts to worry, "They're whispering about me!" If someone's main problem is delusions of persecution, it is wise to do a hearing test.
- *Huntington's disease:* The symptoms of Huntington's disease include hallucinations, delusions, and disordered thinking. Ordinarily, the motor symptoms come first, and the psychotic thinking develops later, but not always. And after all, one rare type of schizophrenia, called *catatonic schizophrenia,* includes motor abnormalities, so a mixture of psychological and motor symptoms could represent either schizophrenia or Huntington's disease. A family medical history usually calls attention to the possibility of Huntington's disease, but some people do not know their family's medical history.
- *Nutritional abnormalities:* Niacin deficiency can produce hallucinations and delusions (Hoffer, 1973); so can prolonged deficiency of vitamin C or an allergy to milk proteins (not the same as lactose intolerance). Some people cannot tolerate wheat gluten or other proteins and react with hallucinations and delusions (Reichelt, Seim, & Reichelt, 1996). Most psychiatrists consider dietary deficiencies or allergies to be a rare cause of schizophrenic reactions, but if we almost never test for the possibility, how do we know?

Demographic Data

[handwritten: All Groups Get this! earlier in men]

The possibility of confusing schizophrenia with other disorders makes any statistic on its prevalence suspect. Nevertheless, one survey of U.S. adults reported that about 1% of all people suffer from schizophrenia at any given time (Narrow, et al., 2002). That estimate could rise or fall depending on whether we include mild cases or only severe cases.

Since the mid-1900s, the reported prevalence of schizophrenia has been declining in many countries (Suvisaari, Haukka, Tanskanen, & Lönnqvist, 1999). Has schizophrenia actually become less common, or are psychiatrists diagnosing it differently? No one knows, and this is not an easy question to answer. However, even when it is diagnosed today, it appears to be less severe than it often used to be. Perhaps our society is doing something that helps to prevent schizophrenia even though we don't know what it is!

Schizophrenia occurs in all ethnic groups and all parts of the world, although it is 10 to 100 times more common in the United States and Europe than in most Third World countries (Torrey, 1986). Part of this discrepancy could be due to differences in diagnostic standards and recordkeeping, but there are other possibilities. Schizophrenia is more common for those born in crowded cities than for those born in small towns or on farms, and the longer people have lived in a large city, the greater the risk of schizophrenia (Pedersen & Mortensen, 2001; Torrey, Bowler, & Clark, 1997). Large cities are, of course, more common in the United States and Europe than in most Third World countries. (Why living in a big city increases the risk of schizophrenia is not known.) Also, in the United States or Europe, someone with schizophrenia is likely to live with parents or other immediate family members. Sooner or later, almost anyone with full-time responsibility for a schizophrenic relative loses patience, and the resultant hostile expressions, known to psychiatrists as **expressed emotion,** seriously aggravate the condition (Butzlaff & Hooley, 1998). In more traditional cultures, notably India and the Arab countries, a large extended family takes care of any schizophrenic relative. Caregivers seldom lose their patience, and when schizophrenia does occur, it is generally not severe (El-Islam, 1982; Leff et al., 1987).

Lifetime prevalence of schizophrenia is about equal for men and women, but the usual age of onset is early twenties for men and late twenties for women. Some women have their first onset around the age of menopause, age 45–50. The reasons for this difference are unknown; one hypothesis is that estrogen has some protective effect against schizophrenia (Häfner et al., 1998).

Childhood-onset schizophrenia is much less common and may have different causes. Unlike the adult-onset version, childhood schizophrenia is associated with identifiable genetic abnormalities

(Burgess et al., 1998) and gradually increasing brain damage (Rapoport et al., 1999; P. M. Thompson et al., 2001b). The brain abnormalities are also more severe, as a rule (Nopoulos, Giedd, Andreasen, & Rapoport, 1998).

One more little unexplained oddity: The older a father is at the time of a baby's birth, the greater the risk of schizophrenia in that baby (Malaspina et al., 2001). The age of the mother is apparently unimportant. One hypothesis is that older fathers have more mutations in their genes, but the evidence for this explanation is not strong.

Stop & Check

1. Why are hallucinations considered a "positive symptom"?
2. Has schizophrenia been increasing, decreasing, or staying the same in prevalence?

Check your answers on pages 489–490.

GENETICS

Huntington's disease (Chapter 8) can be called a genetic disease: Almost everyone with Huntington's disease has an abnormality in the same gene, and anyone with that abnormal gene will get Huntington's disease. At one time, many researchers believed that schizophrenia might be a genetic disease in the same sense, and they considered it appropriate to seek "the" gene for schizophrenia.

As evidence has accumulated since the 1980s, it has become clear that many genes influence schizophrenia, but schizophrenia is not a one-gene disorder. Let's consider the evidence for a genetic contribution and the limitations of the evidence.

Twin Studies

The more closely you are biologically related to someone with schizophrenia, the greater your own probability of schizophrenia, as shown in Figure 15.19 (Gottesman, 1991). One of the most important points in Figure 15.19, confirmed by other studies since then (Cardno et al., 1999), is that having a monozygotic twin with schizophrenia increases the risk far

more than does a dizygotic twin with schizophrenia. For monozygotic twins, there is about a 50% concordance (agreement) for schizophrenia (varying from one study to another), as compared to a 15% to 20% concordance for dizygotic twins. Furthermore, twin pairs who are really monozygotic, but thought they weren't, are more concordant for schizophrenia than twin pairs who thought they were, but really aren't (Kendler, 1983). That is, *being* monozygotic is more critical than *being treated as* monozygotic.

The high concordance for monozygotic twins has long been taken as strong evidence for a genetic influence. However, note three problems:

- Monozygotic twins have only about 50% concordance, not 100%. Clearly, heredity can't be the only factor. Monozygotic twins could sometimes differ because a gene is activated in one individual and suppressed in another (Tsujita et al., 1998), or they could differ because of some environmental influence.

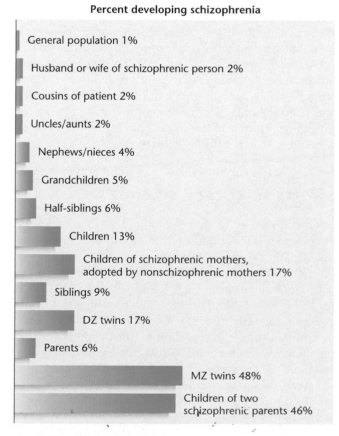

Figure 15.19 Probabilities of developing schizophrenia
The closer the genetic relationship to someone with schizophrenia, the higher the probability of developing it oneself.
Source: Based on data from I. I. Gottesman, 1991

- In Figure 15.19, note the greater similarity between dizygotic twins than between siblings. Dizygotic twins have the same genetic resemblance as siblings but greater environmental similarity, including that of prenatal and early postnatal life.

- As mentioned in Chapter 1, most monozygotic twins develop in a single chorion, whereas dizygotic twins always develop in separate chorions. It is therefore possible that part of what we have been attributing to genetics might instead be due to similarity of prenatal environment.

Adopted Children Who Develop Schizophrenia

When an adopted child develops schizophrenia, it is more common among his or her biological relatives than adopting relatives. One Danish study found schizophrenia in 12.5% of the immediate biological relatives and none of the adopting relatives (Kety et al., 1994). Note in Figure 15.19 that children of a schizophrenic mother have a 17% chance of schizophrenia, even if adopted by nonschizophrenic parents.

These results suggest a genetic basis, but they are also consistent with a prenatal influence. Consider a pregnant woman with schizophrenia. True, she passes her genes to her child, but she also provides the prenatal environment, which may be less than healthy. Many women with schizophrenia have poor nutrition, smoke and drink heavily, and fail to get medical care during pregnancy. If their children develop schizophrenia, we cannot be sure that the influence is genetic.

Efforts to Locate a Gene

There are reasons to question a strong role of genetics. One is the fact mentioned earlier that schizophrenia has declined in prevalence in many countries since about the mid-1900s. If it were based solely on genetics, we could not have seen such a rapid decline. Another problem is that people with schizophrenia tend to die younger than other people and tend to have fewer children than average. If it is under strong genetic control, presumably natural selection would have reduced the frequency of the responsible gene to nearly zero.

The strongest evidence for a genetic influence would be to locate a gene that is consistently linked with schizophrenia. Recall from earlier chapters that researchers have located a gene that is strongly linked with Huntington's disease and genes linked with the early-onset forms of Parkinson's and Alzheimer's diseases. Many researchers have sought to locate a similar gene for schizophrenia. Two

studies examined all the chromosomes, looking for any genetic marker that was more common in schizophrenic people than in others. One study found several genes with a mild link to schizophrenia (Blouin et al., 1998); the other found nothing especially promising (Levinson et al., 1998). Other studies have looked at specific chromosomal areas suspected of a link to schizophrenia. Several studies have found apparent links, but the results have been hard to replicate in other populations (Egan et al., 2001; Levinson et al., 2002; Maziade et al., 2001; McGinnis et al., 2001; Sklar et al., 2001; Vaswani & Kapur, 2001). Even when apparent linkages do emerge, they are generally small effects. For example, one study found a gene that was present in 70% of schizophrenic patients and 60% of other people (Saleem et al., 2001). If we assume that 1% of the population has schizophrenia, the math works out that someone without this gene has about a 0.7% risk of schizophrenia and someone with the gene has a 1.2% risk.

What shall we conclude? One possibility is that our diagnoses of schizophrenia are just too sloppy for genetic purposes; clinicians are diagnosing schizophrenia in people who don't have it and failing to diagnose it in many who do, so it is hard to find any gene linked to the real condition. Another possibility is that schizophrenia depends on a combination of genes. Perhaps there are many genes, any one of which by itself adds only slightly to the risk of schizophrenia, but the more of those genes one has, the greater the risk.

And of course, the other possibility is that some people develop schizophrenia because of genetics, others because of prenatal or early postnatal environment, and still others because of a combination of genetic and environmental factors. If so, it might be difficult to locate the relevant genes because they would not be linked to schizophrenia consistently enough. About the only point we can conclude with confidence is that schizophrenia is not a single-gene disorder.

Stop & Check

3. The higher concordance between monozygotic than dizygotic twins implies a probable genetic basis for schizophrenia. What other interpretation is possible?

4. The fact that adopted children who develop schizophrenia usually have biological relatives with schizophrenia implies a probable genetic basis. What other interpretation is possible?

Check your answers on page 490.

THE NEURODEVELOPMENTAL HYPOTHESIS

According to the neurodevelopmental hypothesis now popular among biomedical researchers, schizophrenia is based on abnormalities in the prenatal (before birth) or neonatal (newborn) development of the nervous system, which lead to subtle but important abnormalities of brain anatomy and major abnormalities in behavior (Weinberger, 1996). The hypothesis holds that stressful experiences can aggravate the symptoms and that supportive relatives and friends can decrease them, but environmental factors by themselves do not cause schizophrenia.

The argument for the neurodevelopmental hypothesis is that (a) in addition to genetics, several kinds of prenatal or neonatal abnormalities that impair brain development are linked to later schizophrenia; (b) people with schizophrenia have a number of minor brain abnormalities that apparently originate early in life; and (c) it is plausible that certain abnormalities of early brain development could produce behavioral abnormalities in adulthood.

Prenatal and Neonatal Environment

Many people with schizophrenia had problems before or shortly after birth that could have affected their brain development, including poor nutrition during pregnancy (Dalman, Allebeck, Cullberg, Grunewald, & Köstler, 1999), premature birth or low birth weight (P. B. Jones, Rantakallio, Hartikainen, Isohanni, & Sipila, 1998), and complications during delivery, such as excessive bleeding or prolonged labor (Hultman, Öhman, Cnattingius, Wieselgren, & Lindström, 1997; Verdoux et al., 1997).

Schizophrenia also has been linked to problems in early or middle pregnancy. During the winter of 1944–1945, near the end of World War II, Germany blockaded the Netherlands, which depended heavily on imported food. The Dutch people endured a near-starvation diet until the Allies liberated them in May. Women who were in the earliest stage of pregnancy during the starvation period gave birth to a high percentage of babies who later developed schizophrenia (Susser et al., 1996).

If a mother is Rh-negative and her baby is Rh-positive, a small amount of the baby's Rh-positive blood factor may leak into the mother's blood supply, triggering an immunological rejection response. The response is weak with the woman's first Rh-positive baby but stronger during later pregnancies, and it is more intense with boy than girl babies. Second- and later-born boy babies with Rh incompatibility have an increased risk of hearing deficits, mental retardation, and several other problems, and about twice the usual probability of schizophrenia (Hollister, Laing, & Mednick, 1996).

A further implication of prenatal difficulties stems from the season-of-birth effect: the tendency for people born in winter to have a slightly (5% to 8%) greater probability of developing schizophrenia than people born at other times of the year. This tendency occurs only in nontropical climates (where the weather changes by season) and is particularly pronounced for schizophrenic people who have no schizophrenic relatives and those born in large cities (Torrey, Miller, Rawlings, & Yolken, 1997).

What might account for the season-of-birth effect? One possibility is complications of delivery or early nutrition. Another is viral infection. Influenza and other viral epidemics are most common in the fall. Therefore, the reasoning goes, many pregnant women become infected in the fall with a virus that impairs a crucial stage of brain development in a baby who will be born in the winter. A virus that affects the mother does not cross the placenta into the fetus's brain, but it does give the mother a fever, and heat can damage the fetal brain. A fever of just 38.5°C (101°F) slows the division of fetal neurons, and a fever of 40°C (104°F) kills them (Laburn, 1996). (Exercise during pregnancy does *not* overheat the abdomen and is not dangerous to the fetus. Hot baths and saunas are risky, however.)

To test the role of prenatal infection, it would be best to examine which mothers had infections and at which stage of pregnancy and then relate these data to the eventual psychiatric outcome of their children. No one keeps good records of influenza or most other infections, but one study examined mothers who had rubella ("German measles") during pregnancy and found that 11 of 53 of their children developed schizophrenia or closely related disorders (A. S. Brown et al., 2001). Another study retrieved blood samples that a hospital had taken from pregnant women and stored for decades. The researchers found that the mothers whose children eventually became schizophrenic had elevated levels of several immune system proteins, indicating that they were fighting off various infections (Buka et al., 2001). In short, maternal infection during pregnancy is one route to schizophrenia and is an alternative or supplement to genetics and other influences.

Mild Brain Abnormalities

In accord with the neurodevelopmental hypothesis, some (though not all) people with schizophrenia show mild abnormalities of brain anatomy. MRI scans indicate that people with schizophrenia have slightly less

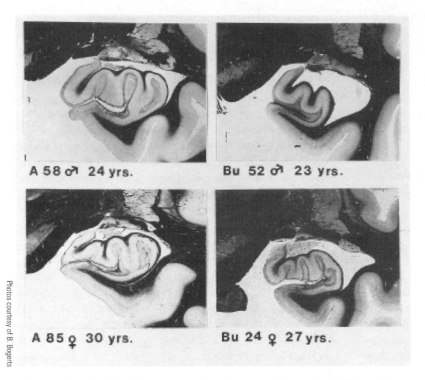

A 58 ♂ 24 yrs.　Bu 52 ♂ 23 yrs.

A 85 ♀ 30 yrs.　Bu 24 ♀ 27 yrs.

Figure 15.20　The hippocampus of normal people (left) and people with schizophrenia (right)
Notice the atrophy of the brains on the right. *Source: Bogerts, Meertz, & Schönfeldt-Bausch, 1985*

gray matter than normal in the prefrontal cortex, temporal cortex, and hippocampus, especially in the left hemisphere (Barch et al., 2001; Gur, Cowell, et al., 2000; Gur, Turetsky, et al., 2000; Velakoulis et al., 1999; Wright et al., 2000) (Figure 15.20). The ventricles (fluid-filled spaces within the brain) are larger than normal (Wolkin et al., 1998; Wright et al., 2000) (Figure 15.21). Signs of brain damage are especially common in schizophrenic people who had a history of complications during pregnancy or at birth (Stefanis et al., 1999).

The areas with the most consistent signs of abnormality are those that mature most slowly, especially the dorsolateral prefrontal cortex (Berman, Torrey, Daniel, & Weinberger, 1992; Fletcher et al., 1998; Gur, Cowell, et al., 2000). People with schizophrenia also have fewer than the normal number of synapses in the prefrontal cortex (Glantz & Lewis, 1997, 2000). As you might predict, people with schizophrenia

perform poorly at working memory tasks, which depend on the prefrontal cortex (Goldberg, Weinberger, Berman, Pliskin, & Podd, 1987; Spindler, Sullivan, Menon, Lim, & Pfefferbaum, 1997). On a variety of neuropsychological tests, schizophrenic patients tend to show deficits of memory and attention similar to those of people with damage to the temporal or prefrontal cortex (Park, Holzman, & Goldman-Rakic, 1995) (see Methods 15.1).

At a microscopic level, the most reliable finding is that cell bodies are smaller than normal, especially in the hippocampus and prefrontal cortex (Pierri, Volk, Auh, Sampson, & Lewis, 2001; Rajkowska, Selemon, & Goldman-Rakic, 1998; Selemon, Rajkowska, & Goldman-Rakic, 1995; Weinberger, 1999). In addition, some neurons fail to arrange themselves in the neat, orderly manner typical of normal brains (Benes & Bird, 1987) (Figure 15.22).

Lateralization is also different from the normal pattern. In most people, the left hemisphere is slightly larger than the right, especially in the planum temporale of the temporal lobe, but in schizophrenic people, the right hemisphere is slightly larger (Kwon et al., 1999). Schizophrenic people have lower than normal overall activity in the left hemisphere (Gur & Chin, 1999) and are more likely than other people to be left-handed (Satz & Green, 1999). All these results suggest a subtle change in early brain development.

The reasons behind the brain abnormalities are not certain. Most researchers have been careful to limit their studies to patients who have never taken,

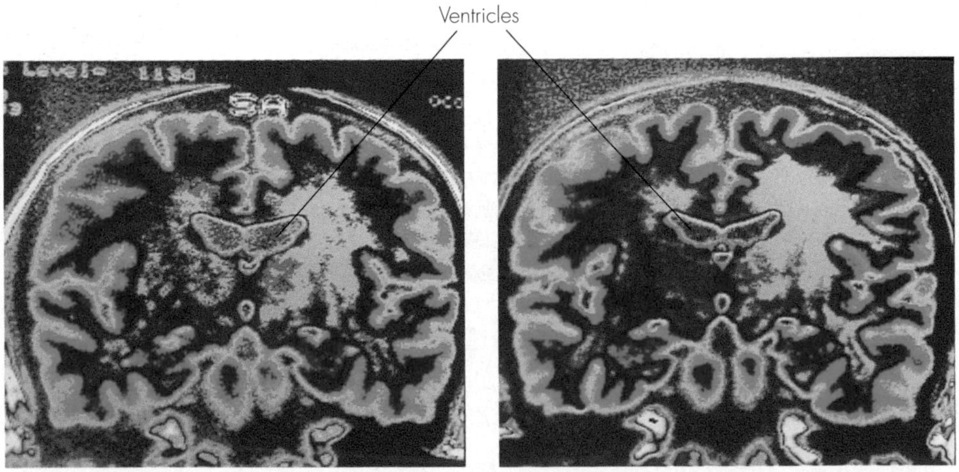

Ventricles

Figure 15.21　Coronal sections for identical twins
The twin on the left has schizophrenia; the twin on the right does not. Note that the ventricles (near the center of each brain) are larger in the twin with schizophrenia.

or who have not recently taken, antipsychotic drugs, so the deficits are probably not a by-product of treatments for schizophrenia. However, one study found damage to the cerebellum only in schizophrenic patients who were also alcohol abusers (Sullivan et al., 2000). Most studies have not examined the possible role of alcohol and other drugs, and it is possible that some of the brain damage we associate with schizophrenia may really be the result of years of abusing alcohol or other drugs.

The results are inconclusive as to whether the brain damage associated with schizophrenia is *progressive*—that is, whether it increases over time. The brain damage associated with Parkinson's disease, Huntington's disease, and Alzheimer's disease gets worse and worse as the person ages. Brain abnormalities are found in young schizophrenic patients shortly after diagnosis

(Lieberman et al., 2001), and most studies find that the brain abnormalities are no greater in older schizophrenic patients (Andreasen, Swayze, et al., 1990; Censits, Ragland, Gur, & Gur, 1997; Russell, Munro, Jones, Hemsley, & Murray, 1997; Selemon et al., 1995). One study reported some shrinkage of the cerebral cortex and expansion of the ventricles during the first year after patients were diagnosed as schizophrenic (Cahn et al., 2002), and a few studies have reported slightly increased damage as patients age (Hulshoff et al., 2001; Mathalon, Sullivan, Lim, & Pfefferbaum, 2001). Nevertheless, other researchers doubt these results (Weinberger & McClure, 2002) because brains of schizophrenic people do not show the two typical signs that accompany neuron death—proliferation of glia cells and activation of the genes responsible for repair after injury (Arnold, 2000; Benes, 1995; Lim et

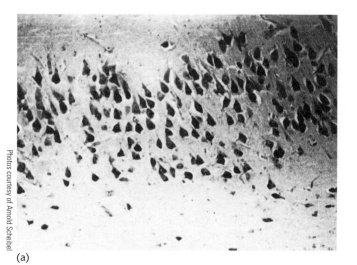

(a)

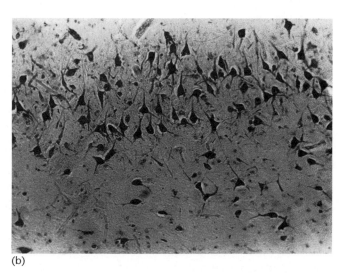

(b)

Photos courtesy of Arnold Scheibel

Figure 15.22 Hippocampal disorganization in schizophrenia
Neurons of a normal person **(a)** show an orderly arrangement; those of someone with schizophrenia **(b)** appear more haphazard and disorganized.

al., 1998). One possible reconciliation of these results is that neurons of schizophrenic people may be shrinking without actually dying. We shall need more research.

Early Development and Later Psychopathology

One question may have struck you by now. How can we reconcile the evidence for abnormalities of early brain development with the fact that the disorder is usually diagnosed after age 20? The time course may not be so puzzling as it seems at first (Weinberger, 1996). The prefrontal cortex, the area that shows the most consistent signs of damage in schizophrenia, matures very slowly, not reaching full competence until the late teens (Lewis, 1997; Sowell, Thompson, Holmes, Jernigan, & Toga, 1999). In one study, researchers damaged this area in infant monkeys and tested the monkeys later. At age 1 year, the monkeys' behavior was nearly normal, but by age 2 years, it had deteriorated markedly (P. S. Goldman, 1971, 1976). That is, the effects of the brain damage actually grew worse over time. Presumably, the effects of brain damage were minimal at age 1 year because the dorsolateral prefrontal cortex doesn't do much at that age anyway. Later, when it should begin assuming important functions, the damage begins to make a difference (Figure 15.23).

The current status of the neurodevelopmental hypothesis is best described as plausible but not firmly established. Many studies link schizophrenia to probable prenatal damage and mild brain abnormalities, but the effects are small, vary from one sample of patients to another, and are often subject to alternative interpretations (Weinberger, 1996). Additional research will be necessary to test the hypothesis more thoroughly.

5. What is the season-of-birth effect?

6. If schizophrenia is due to abnormal brain development, why do behavioral symptoms not become apparent until later in life?

Check your answers on page 490.

NEUROTRANSMITTERS AND DRUGS

As presented earlier in this module, researchers once stated confidently that schizophrenia was a genetic disorder, but the evidence hasn't solidified that position as neatly as expected. Something similar has happened regarding neurotransmitters. Researchers were once convinced—and many still are—that schizophrenia is due to excess activity at dopamine synapses. But again, this view faces problems that haven't gone away. We consider the evidence for the dopamine hypothesis, the problems with that hypothesis, and then an alternative.

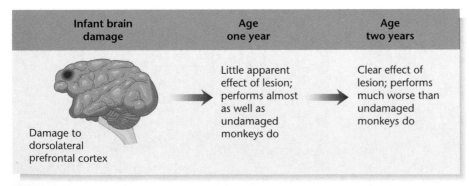

Figure 15.23 Delayed effects of brain damage in infant monkeys
After damage to the dorsolateral prefrontal cortex, monkeys seem relatively unimpaired at age 1 year but are more severely impaired later, when this area ordinarily matures. Researchers speculate that similar damage in humans might produce behavioral deficits not apparent until adulthood; thus, an abnormality of early brain development might produce schizophrenia in adults. *Source: Based on P. S. Goldman, 1976*

The Dopamine Hypothesis

According to the dopamine hypothesis of schizophrenia, schizophrenia results from excess activity at certain dopamine synapses. The main evidence for this hypothesis comes from studies of drugs that relieve or aggravate the symptoms of schizophrenia.

Antipsychotic Drugs

The most persuasive evidence for the dopamine hypothesis comes from studies of drugs that relieve schizophrenia. In the 1950s, psychiatrists were surprised to discover that one tranquilizer, chlorpromazine (trade name Thorazine), frequently relieves the positive symptoms of schizophrenia. Previously, most schizophrenic patients who entered a mental hospital never left. Chlorpromazine and related drugs halt the progression of the disease in many cases if treatment begins early. Often a patient must continue taking the drug indefinitely, although some patients recover and can stop taking it. About one fourth of schizophrenic patients do not benefit from the drugs.

Researchers later discovered that most other antipsychotic or neuroleptic drugs (drugs that tend to relieve schizophrenia and similar conditions) belong to two chemical families: the phenothiazines (FEE-no-THI-uh-zeens), which include chlorpromazine, and the butyrophenones (BYOO-tir-oh-FEE-noans), which include haloperidol (trade name Haldol). Figure 15.24 illustrates the correlation between the therapeutic effects of various drugs and their ability to block postsynaptic dopamine receptors. For each drug, researchers determined the mean dose prescribed for schizophrenic patients (displayed along the horizontal axis) and the amount needed to block dopamine receptors (displayed along the vertical axis). As the figure shows, the drugs that are most effective against schizophrenia (and therefore used in the smallest doses) are the most effective at blocking dopamine receptors (Seeman, Lee, Chau-Wong, & Wong, 1976).

Drugs That Can Provoke Schizophrenic Symptoms

Large, repeated doses of certain drugs can provoke substance-induced psychotic disorder, characterized by hallucinations and delusions (positive symptoms of schizophrenia). Among the drugs that commonly produce these symptoms are amphetamine, methamphetamine, and cocaine,

all of which increase the activity at dopamine synapses, as noted in Module 15.1. LSD also produces psychotic symptoms; LSD is best known for its effects on serotonin synapses, but it also increases activity at dopamine synapses.

Problems With the Dopamine Hypothesis

Recall from Module 15.2 that antidepressant drugs alter the activity at dopamine and serotonin synapses quickly but improve mood only after 2 or 3 weeks of treatment. The same issue arises for schizophrenia: Antipsychotic drugs block dopamine synapses within minutes, but their effects on behavior build up gradually over 2 or 3 weeks. So blocking dopamine synapses may be an important first step for an antipsychotic drug, but clearly, something else must develop later.

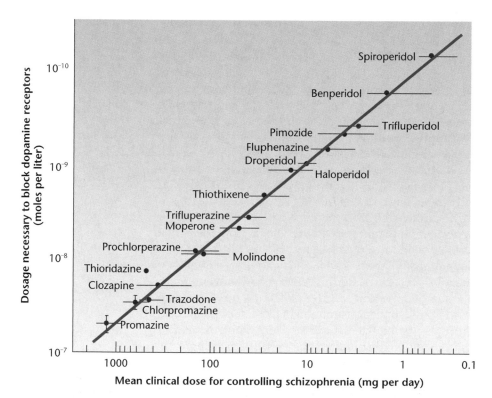

Figure 15.24 Dopamine-blocking effects of antipsychotic drugs
Drugs are arranged along the horizontal axis in terms of the average daily dose prescribed for schizophrenic patients. (Horizontal lines indicate common ranges of dosage.) Note that *larger* doses are to the left and *smaller* doses are to the right so that *more effective* drugs are to the right. (Less is needed of a more effective drug to achieve the same effect.) The vertical axis shows the amount of each drug required to achieve a certain degree of blockage of postsynaptic dopamine receptors. Again, *larger* doses are toward the bottom and *smaller* doses are toward the top so that the drugs on top are *more effective* in blocking dopamine synapses. A drug's effectiveness in blocking dopamine synapses is almost perfectly correlated with its ability to control schizophrenia. *Source: From "Antipsychotic Drug Doses and Neuroleptic/Dopamine Receptors." by P. Seeman, T. Lee, M. Chan-Wong, and K. Wong, 1976,* Nature, *261, pp. 717–719. Copyright ©1976 Macmillan Magazines Ltd. Reprinted by permission of* Nature *and Phillip Seeman.*

Furthermore, direct measurements of dopamine and its metabolites generally find approximately normal levels in people with schizophrenia (Jaskiw & Weinberger, 1992). Studies of dopamine receptors have yielded complicated results. According to most studies, the density of type D_1 and D_2 receptors is below normal, and the levels of D_3 and D_4 are above normal (Gurevich et al., 1997; Murray et al., 1995; Okubo et al., 1997; Suhara et al., 2002). However, some studies have failed to replicate this pattern (Karlsson, Farde, Halldin, & Sedvall, 2002). Presumably, one reason is that no two people with schizophrenia are quite the same, and any result varies from one sample to another.

Additional Support for the Dopamine Hypothesis

Synaptic activity is a complex process, and activity at dopamine synapses could be modified by the amount of dopamine released, the number of receptors, the amount of reuptake by the presynaptic neuron, and so forth. Rather than try to measure each step separately, one group of researchers set out to measure the number of dopamine receptors occupied at a given moment—probably as good an indication as any of how much dopamine stimulation occurs. Their procedure was first to use a radioactively labeled drug, IBZM, that binds to dopamine type D_2 receptors, measuring the number of receptors bound by the drug. Because IBZM can bind only to dopamine receptors that were not already bound to dopamine, this procedure in effect counts the number of vacant dopamine receptors. Then the researchers used a second drug, AMPT, that blocks all synthesis of dopamine and again used IBZM to count the number of vacant D_2 receptors. Because AMPT had prevented production of dopamine, *all* D_2 receptors should be vacant at this time, so the researchers got a count of all of them. Then they subtracted the first count from the second count, yielding the number of D_2 receptors occupied by dopamine at the first count:

- First count: IBZM binds to all D_2 receptors not already attached to dopamine.
- Second count: IBZM binds to all D_2 receptors (because AMPT prevented production of dopamine, and no dopamine is bound to D_2 receptors).
- Second count minus first count = number of D_2 receptors bound to dopamine at the first count.

Comparing results from schizophrenic and normal people, the researchers found that schizophrenic people had about twice as many D_2 receptors occupied as normal (Abi-Dargham et al., 2000). This study provides good evidence of excessive dopamine release (or binding) in schizophrenic people. Another study found that among schizophrenic patients, the greater the amount of D_2 receptor activation in the prefrontal cortex, the greater the cognitive impairment (Meyer-Lindenberg et al., 2002).

The Glutamate Hypothesis

According to an alternative possibility, the glutamate hypothesis of schizophrenia, the underlying problem is (at least in part) a deficient activity at glutamate synapses, especially in the prefrontal cortex. In many brain areas, dopamine inhibits glutamate release, or glutamate stimulates neurons that inhibit dopamine release, or glutamate excites neurons that dopamine inhibits. Therefore, increased dopamine would produce about the same effects as decreased glutamate, and drugs that block dopamine increase glutamate effects. So the antipsychotic effects of drugs like chlorpromazine and haloperidol are equally compatible with the dopamine hypothesis (too much dopamine, which needs to be blocked) or the glutamate hypothesis (too little glutamate, which needs to be enhanced). In fact, one experiment examined mice that had a severe deficit of NMDA-type glutamate receptors but normal amounts of dopamine. Dopamine-blocking drugs such as haloperidol decreased the behavioral abnormalities of these mice (Mohn, Gainetdinov, Caron, & Koller, 1999).

The glutamate hypothesis is supported by data from measurements of glutamate activity in the brain, the effects of the drug phencyclidine, and the possible effectiveness of certain glutamate-enhancing drugs as antipsychotic drugs.

Measurements of Glutamate

Researchers have found that the brains of schizophrenic people release lower than normal amounts of glutamate in the prefrontal cortex and hippocampus (Akbarian et al., 1995; Tsai et al., 1995). Schizophrenic people also have lower than normal levels of glutamate receptors (Ibrahim et al., 2000). These findings are consistent with the glutamate hypothesis, although much more research is needed.

The Effects of Phencyclidine

Recall that dopamine-stimulating drugs such as amphetamine and cocaine can induce positive symptoms of schizophrenia. **Phencyclidine (PCP)** ("angel dust"), a drug that inhibits glutamate type NMDA receptors, at low doses produces intoxication and slurred speech, somewhat like the effects of alcohol. At larger doses, it produces both positive and negative symptoms of schizophrenia, including hallucinations, thought disorder, loss of emotions, and memory loss. Studies on monkeys show that it impairs the functioning of the prefrontal cortex, including the activity at dopamine synapses (Jentsch et al., 1997). PCP is an interesting model for schizophrenia in other regards (Farber, Newcomer, & Olney, 1999; Olney & Farber, 1995):

- PCP and the related drug *ketamine* produce little if any psychotic response in preadolescents. Just as the symptoms of schizophrenia usually begin to emerge well after puberty, so do the psychotic effects of PCP and ketamine.
- LSD, amphetamine, and cocaine produce temporary schizophrenic symptoms in almost anyone that are not much worse in people with a history of schizophrenia than in anyone else. However, for someone who has recovered from schizophrenia, PCP induces a long-lasting relapse.

Drugs That Enhance Glutamate Activity

It might seem that the best test of the glutamate hypothesis would be to administer glutamate itself. However, recall from Chapter 5 that strokes kill neurons by overstimulating glutamate synapses. Significantly increasing overall brain glutamate would be too risky.

However, glutamate affects several types of receptors, and it may be possible to find drugs that act just at the appropriate synapses in the prefrontal cortex. One drug, with the not-very-catchy name *LY 354740,* which selectively stimulates one type of metabotropic glutamate receptor, blocks the behavioral effects of PCP on rats and prevents its disruption of activity in the prefrontal cortex (Moghaddam & Adams, 1998). This drug has not yet been tried with humans. Another possibility is the amino acid glycine. The type-NMDA glutamate receptor has a primary site that is activated by glutamate but also a secondary cotransmitter site that is activated by glycine (Figure 15.25). Glycine by itself does not activate the receptor, but it increases the effectiveness of glutamate. Thus, an increase in glycine can gently increase the activity at NMDA synapses without the risk of overstimulating glutamate throughout the brain. Researchers have found that although glycine is not an effective antipsychotic drug by itself, it increases the effects of other antipsychotic drugs, especially with regard to negative symptoms (Heresco-Levy et al., 1999). Cycloserine, a drug that attaches less strongly to the glycine site but

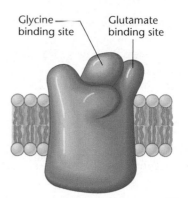

Figure 15.25   An NMDA glutamate receptor
NMDA glutamate receptors have a primary binding site for glutamate and a secondary binding site for glycine. Glycine by itself does not activate the receptor, but it increases the effect of glutamate. Cycloserine also attaches to the glycine site, about half as effectively as glycine.

crosses the blood-brain barrier more easily, also improves the effectiveness of antipsychotic drugs, especially for negative symptoms (Goff et al., 1999).

The dopamine hypothesis of schizophrenia is much more heavily investigated and more widely accepted than the glutamate hypothesis. Nevertheless, enough evidence suggests an important role for glutamate to encourage additional research. Furthermore, schizophrenia is a sufficiently complex disorder that both dopamine and glutamate may play important roles, perhaps to different degrees in different individuals.

7. How fast do antipsychotic drugs affect dopamine synapses? How fast do they alter behavior?

8. What drugs induce mainly the positive symptoms of schizophrenia? What drug can induce both positive and negative symptoms?

9. Why are so many drug results equally compatible with the dopamine hypothesis and the glutamate hypothesis?

Check your answers on page 490.

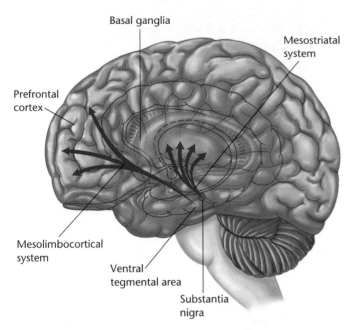

Basal ganglia

Mesostriatal system

Prefrontal cortex

Mesolimbocortical system

Ventral tegmental area

Substantia nigra

Figure 15.26 Two major dopamine pathways
The mesolimbocortical system is apparently responsible for the symptoms of schizophrenia; the path to the basal ganglia is probably responsible for tardive dyskinesia, a movement disorder. *Source: Adapted from Valzelli, 1980*

Once tardive dyskinesia emerges, it can last for years, even if the person quits the drug (Kiriakakis et al., 1998). Consequently, the best strategy is to prevent it from starting. Certain new drugs called atypical antipsychotics, such as clozapine, alleviate schizophrenia but seldom if ever produce movement problems (Figure 15.27). The atypical antipsychotics have briefer or less intense effects on dopamine type D_2 receptors but stronger effects on type D_4 receptors and serotonin type 5-HT_2 receptors (Kapur et al., 2000; Meltzer, Matsubara, & Lee, 1989; Mrzljak et al., 1996; Roth, Willins, Kristiansen, & Kroeze, 1999). They also increase the release of glutamate (Melone et al., 2001). Behaviorally, whereas most antipsychotic drugs reduce hallucinations and delusions but seldom help with the negative symptoms, atypical antipsychotics decrease both positive and negative symptoms, including depression and the risk of suicide (Meltzer, 2001; Stip, 2000). Unfortunately, atypical antipsychotics produce their own side effects, including increased risk of diabetes (Newcomer et al., 2002) and an impairment of the immune system. People taking atypical antipsychotics therefore need frequent, expensive blood tests. More research is needed to find the best drug treatments for schizophrenia.

The Search for Improved Drugs

The commonly used antipsychotic drugs block dopamine receptors throughout the brain. Presumably, the benefits result from effects on the dopamine neurons in the mesolimbocortical system, a set of neurons that project from the midbrain tegmentum to the limbic system. However, the drugs also block dopamine neurons in other locations, including those in the basal ganglia (Figure 15.26). The result is tardive dyskinesia (TARD-eev dis-kih-NEE-zhee-uh), characterized by tremors and other involuntary movements that develop gradually over periods ranging from a few days of medication to more than 20 years (Kiriakakis, Bhatia, Quinn, & Marsden, 1998). Tardive dyskinesia may result from denervation supersensitivity (Chapter 5): Prolonged blockage of dopamine transmission causes the postsynaptic neurons to increase in sensitivity and respond vigorously to even small amounts of dopamine. After receptors in the basal ganglia become supersensitive, even slight stimulation causes bursts of involuntary movements.

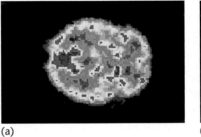

(a)   (b)

©Hank Morgan/Science Source/Photo Researchers

Figure 15.27 PET scans of a patient with schizophrenia
These PET scans of a patient with schizophrenia **(a)** taking clozapine and **(b)** during a period off the drug demonstrate that clozapine increases brain activity in many brain areas. (Red indicates the highest activity, followed by yellow, green, and blue.) Clozapine helps relieve both positive and negative symptoms of schizophrenia.

MODULE 15.3

In Closing: The Fascination of Schizophrenia

A good mystery novel presents an array of clues, mixing important clues with irrelevant information, and the reader's challenge is to figure out who committed the crime. Schizophrenia research is similar, except that we want to know *what* is to blame, not *who*. As with a mystery novel, we have to sort through an enormous number of clues and false leads, looking for a pattern. One difference is that, unlike the reader of a mystery novel, we have the option of collecting new evidence of our own.

I trust it is clear to you that researchers have not yet solved the mystery of schizophrenia. But it should also be clear that they have made progress. The hypotheses they are considering today are almost certainly not completely correct, but they have much more evidence behind them than the hypotheses of decades past. The future looks exciting for this area of research.

SUMMARY

1. Positive symptoms of schizophrenia (characteristics not present in most other people) include hallucinations, delusions, inappropriate emotions, bizarre behaviors, and thought disorder. (p. 476)

2. Negative symptoms (normal characteristics absent in people with schizophrenia) include deficits of social interaction, emotional expression, and speech. (p. 476)

3. Studies of twins and adopted children imply a genetic predisposition to schizophrenia. However, concordance between monozygotic twins is only about 50%, not 100%, and prevalence of the disorder has declined since the mid-1900s, so schizophrenia cannot be purely a genetic disorder. (p. 479)

4. The evidence does not tell us how much of the predisposition is due to genetics and how much is due to prenatal environment. So far, researchers have not located any gene that is strongly linked with schizophrenia. (p. 480)

5. According to the neurodevelopmental hypothesis, either genes or difficulties early in life impair brain development in ways that lead to behavioral abnormalities beginning in early adulthood. (p. 481)

6. The probability of schizophrenia is higher than average for those who were subjected to prenatal malnutrition, Rh incompatibility, or maternal fever. (p. 481)

7. Some people with schizophrenia show mild abnormalities of early brain development. Most (but not all) studies conclude that the brain damage is nonprogressive; that is, it does not increase over time, as brain damage does with Alzheimer's disease or Huntington's disease. (p. 481)

8. Parts of the prefrontal cortex are very slow to mature. It is plausible that early disruption of these areas might produce behavioral symptoms that become manifest as schizophrenia in young adults. (p. 484)

9. According to the dopamine hypothesis, schizophrenia is due to excess dopamine activity. The main support for this hypothesis is that drugs that block dopamine synapses reduce the positive symptoms of schizophrenia, and drugs that increase dopamine activity can induce the positive symptoms. However, direct measurements of dopamine and its receptors have not strongly supported this theory. (p. 484)

10. According to the glutamate hypothesis, the problem is deficient glutamate activity. Evidence supporting this view is that phencyclidine, which blocks NMDA glutamate synapses, produces both positive and negative symptoms of schizophrenia, especially in people predisposed to schizophrenia. (p. 486)

11. Prolonged use of antipsychotic drugs may produce tardive dyskinesia, a movement disorder. The atypical antipsychotic drug clozapine relieves both positive and negative symptoms without producing tardive dyskinesia, but it produces other dangerous side effects of its own. (p. 488)

ANSWERS TO *STOP AND CHECK* QUESTIONS

1. Hallucinations are considered a positive symptom because they are present when they should be absent. A "positive" symptom is not a "good" symptom. (p. 479)

2. Schizophrenia has been decreasing in prevalence. (p. 479)

3. Monozygotic twins could resemble each other partly because they shared more of their prenatal environment than did dizygotic twins. (p. 480)

4. A biological mother can influence her child's development through prenatal environment as well as genetics, even if the child is adopted early. (p. 480)

5. The season-of-birth effect is the observation that schizophrenia is slightly more common among people born in the winter. (p. 484)

6. Parts of the prefrontal cortex are very slow to reach maturity; therefore, early disruption of this area's development might not produce any symptoms early in life, when the prefrontal cortex is contributing little anyway. (p. 484)

7. They alter dopamine synaptic activity within minutes. They take 2 to 3 weeks to alter behavior. (p. 487)

8. Amphetamine, cocaine, and LSD in large doses induce positive symptoms, such as hallucinations and delusions. Phencyclidine induces both positive and negative symptoms. (p. 487)

9. Dopamine inhibits glutamate cells in many areas, and glutamate stimulates neurons that inhibit dopamine. Therefore, the effects of increasing dopamine are similar to those of decreasing glutamate. (p. 487)

THOUGHT QUESTIONS

1. With some illnesses, a patient who at first fails to respond is offered higher and higher doses of medication. However, if a schizophrenic patient does not respond to antipsychotic drugs, it is generally not a good idea to increase the dosages. Why not?

2. Long-term use of antipsychotic drugs can induce tardive dyskinesia. However, if a person with tardive dyskinesia stops taking the drugs, the symptoms actually grow worse, at least temporarily. Why?

3. Why might it sometimes be difficult to find effective drugs for someone who suffers from both depression and schizophrenia?

Key Terms and Activities

TERMS

acetaldehyde (p. 460)

acetic acid (p. 460)

acute (p. 477)

2-AG (p. 457)

alcoholism (or alcohol dependence) (p. 459)

amphetamine (p. 454)

anandamide (p. 457)

Antabuse (p. 460)

antipsychotic (or neuroleptic) drug (p. 485)

atypical antidepressants (p. 467)

atypical antipsychotics (p. 488)

autoreceptor (p. 468)

bipolar disorder (or manic-depressive disorder) (p. 471)

bipolar I disorder (p. 471)

bipolar II disorder (p. 471)

Borna disease (p. 465)

butyrophenone (p. 485)

cannabinoids (p. 457)

chlorpromazine (p. 485)

chronic (p. 477)

cocaine (p. 454)

concordance (p. 479)

Δ^9-*tetrahydrocannabinol (Δ^9-THC)* (p. 457)

delusion (p. 476)

differential diagnosis (p. 477)

dopamine hypothesis of schizophrenia (p. 484)

electroconvulsive therapy (ECT) (p. 469)

expressed emotion (p. 478)

glutamate hypothesis of schizophrenia (p. 486)

hallucination (p. 477)

hallucinogenic drugs (p. 458)

lithium (p. 472)

major depression (p. 464)

mania (p. 471)

mesolimbocortical system (p. 488)

methylphenidate (p. 454)

monoamine oxidase inhibitors (MAOIs) (p. 467)

negative symptom (p. 476)

neurodevelopmental hypothesis (p. 481)

nicotine (p. 455)

nucleus accumbens (p. 452)

opiate drugs (p. 456)

phencyclidine (PCP) (p. 486)

phenothiazine (p. 485)

positive symptom (p. 476)

postpartum depression (p. 465)

schizophrenia (p. 476)

seasonal affective disorder (SAD) (p. 473)

season-of-birth effect (p. 481)

selective serotonin reuptake inhibitors (SSRIs) (p. 467)

self-stimulation of the brain (p. 452)

stimulant drugs (p. 454)

substance abuse (p. 452)

substance-induced psychotic disorder (p. 485)

tardive dyskinesia (p. 488)

thought disorder (p. 477)

tricyclic (p. 466)

Type I alcoholism (p. 459)

Type II alcoholism (p. 459)

unipolar disorder (p. 471)

SUGGESTIONS FOR FURTHER READING

Andreasen, N. C. (1994). *Schizophrenia: From mind to molecule.* Washington, DC: American Psychiatric Press. Discusses the behavior, biology, and treatment of schizophrenia.

McKim, W. A. (2003). *Drugs and behavior* (5th ed.). Upper Saddle River, NJ: Prentice-Hall. Concise, highly informative text on drugs and drug abuse.

Waddington, J. L., & Buckley, P. F. (1996). *The neurodevelopmental basis of schizophrenia.* Austin, TX: Landes Co. Discusses season-of-birth effect and possible roles of viruses, obstetric complications, and other early influences on the later development of schizophrenia.

WEB SITES TO EXPLORE

You can go to the Biological Psychology Study Center and click these links. While there, you can also check for suggested articles available on InfoTrac College Edition. The Biological Psychology Internet address is:

**http://psychology.wadsworth.com/
kalatbiopsych8e/**

Drugs, Brains, and Behavior by C. Robin Timmons and Leonard W. Hamilton
http://www.rci.rutgers.edu/~lwh/drugs/

Heroin Use, Addiction and Treatment by Charles P. O'Brien
http://www.uphs.upenn.edu/recovery/pros/opioids.html

Society for Light Treatment and Biological Rhythms
http://www.sltbr.org/

Schizophrenia information and support
http://www.schizophrenia.com/

CD-ROM: EXPLORING BIOLOGICAL PSYCHOLOGY

Understanding Addiction (video)

CNS Stimulants (animation)

Opiate Narcotics (animation)

Barbara 1 (video)

Barbara 2 (video)

Mary 1 (video)

Mary 2 (video)

Mary 3 (video)

Frontal Neglect and the Wisconsin Card Sorting Task (video)

Schizophrenia (video)

Etta 1 (video)

Etta 2 (video)

Critical Thinking (essay questions)

Chapter Quiz (multiple choice questions)

Brief, Basic Chemistry

MAIN IDEAS

1. All matter is composed of a limited number of elements that combine in endless ways.

2. Atoms, the component parts of an element, consist of protons, neutrons, and electrons. Most atoms can gain or lose electrons, or share them with other atoms.

3. The chemistry of life is predominantly the chemistry of carbon compounds.

INTRODUCTION

To understand certain aspects of biological psychology, particularly the action potential and the molecular mechanisms of synaptic transmission, you need to know a little about chemistry. If you have taken a high school or college course and remember the material reasonably well, you should have no trouble with the chemistry in this text. If your knowledge of chemistry is pretty hazy, this appendix will help. (If you plan to take other courses in biological psychology, you should study as much biology and chemistry as possible.)

ELEMENTS AND COMPOUNDS

If you look around, you will see an enormous variety of materials—dirt, water, wood, plastic, metal, cloth, glass, your own body. Every object is composed of a small number of basic building blocks. If a piece of wood catches fire, it breaks down into ashes, gases, and water vapor. The same is true of your body. An investigator could take those ashes, gases, and water and break them down by chemical and electrical means into carbon, oxygen, hydrogen, nitrogen, and a few other materials. Eventually, however, the investigator arrives at a set of materials that cannot be broken down further: Pure carbon or pure oxygen, for example, cannot be converted into anything simpler, at least not by ordinary chemical means. (High-power bombardment with subatomic particles is another story.) The matter we see is composed of elements (materials that cannot be broken down into other materials) and compounds (materials made up by combining elements).

Chemists have found 92 elements in nature, and they have constructed more in the laboratory. (Actually, one of the 92—technetium—is so rare as to be virtually unknown in nature.) Figure A.1, the periodic table, lists each of these elements. Of these, only a few are important for life on Earth. Table A.1 shows the elements commonly found in the human body.

Note that each element has a one- or two-letter abbreviation, such as O for oxygen, H for hydrogen, and Ca for calcium. These are internationally accepted symbols that facilitate communication among chemists who speak different languages. For example, element number 19 is called potassium in English, potassio in Italian, kālijs in Latvian, and draslík in Czech. But chemists in all countries use the symbol K (from *kalium,* the Latin word for "potassium"). Similarly, the symbol for sodium is Na (from *natrium,* the Latin word for "sodium"), and the symbol for iron is Fe (from the Latin word *ferrum*).

A compound is represented by the symbols for the elements that compose it. For example, NaCl stands for sodium chloride (common table salt). H_2O, the symbol for water, indicates that water consists of two parts of hydrogen and one part of oxygen.

Atoms and Molecules

A block of iron can be chopped finer and finer until it is divided into tiny pieces that cannot be broken down any further. These pieces are called atoms. Every element is composed of atoms. A compound, such as water, can also be divided into tinier and tinier pieces. The smallest possible piece of a compound is called a molecule. A molecule of water can be further decomposed into two atoms of hydrogen and one atom of oxygen, but when that happens the compound is broken and is no longer water. A molecule is the smallest piece of a compound that retains the properties of the compound.

An atom is composed of subatomic particles, including protons, neutrons, and electrons. A proton has a positive electrical charge, a neutron has a neutral charge, and an electron has a negative charge. The nucleus of an atom—its center—contains one or more protons plus a number of neutrons. Electrons are found in the space around the nucleus. Because an atom has the same number of protons as electrons, the electrical charges balance out. (Ions, which we shall consider in a moment, have an imbalance of positive and negative charges.)

The difference between one element and another is in the number of protons in the nucleus of the atom. Hydrogen has just one proton, for example, and oxygen has eight. The number of protons is the atomic number of the element; in the periodic table it is recorded at the top of the square for each element. The

TABLE A.1 The Elements That Compose Almost All of the Human Body

Element	Symbol	Percentage by Weight in Human Body
Oxygen	O	65
Carbon	C	18
Hydrogen	H	10
Nitrogen	N	3
Calcium	Ca	2
Phosphorus	P	1.1
Potassium	K	0.35
Sulfur	S	0.25
Sodium	Na	0.15
Chlorine	Cl	0.15
Magnesium	Mg	0.05
Iron	Fe	Trace
Copper	Cu	Trace
Iodine	I	Trace
Fluorine	F	Trace
Manganese	Mn	Trace
Zinc	Zn	Trace
Selenium	Se	Trace
Molybdenum	Mo	Trace

Periodic Table of the Elements

Period	1 IA (Alkali Metals)	2 IIA (Alkaline Earth Metals)	3 IIIB	4 IVB	5 VB	6 VIB	7 VIIB	8 VIIIB	9 VIIIB	10 VIIIB	11 IB	12 IIB	13 IIIA	14 IVA	15 VA	16 VIA	17 VIIA (Halogens)	18 VIIA (Noble Gases)
			Transition Elements															
1	1 **H** hydrogen 1.008																	2 **He** helium 4.003
2	3 **Li** lithium 6.941	4 **Be** beryllium 9.012											5 **B** boron 10.81	6 **C** carbon 12.011	7 **N** nitrogen 14.007	8 **O** oxygen 16.0	9 **F** fluorine 18.999	10 **Ne** neon 20.179
3	11 **Na** sodium 22.99	12 **Mg** magnesium 24.305											13 **Al** aluminum 26.982	14 **Si** silicon 28.085	15 **P** phosphorous 30.974	16 **S** sulfur 32.060	17 **Cl** chlorine 35.453	18 **Ar** argon 39.948
4	19 **K** potassium 39.098	20 **Ca** calcium 40.08	21 **Sc** scandium 44.955	22 **Ti** titanium 47.90	23 **V** vanadium 50.941	24 **Cr** chromium 51.996	25 **Mn** manganese 54.938	26 **Fe** iron 55.847	27 **Co** cobalt 58.933	28 **Ni** nickel 58.70	29 **Cu** copper 63.546	30 **Zn** zinc 65.38	31 **Ga** gallium 69.72	32 **Ge** germanium 72.59	33 **As** arsenic 74.922	34 **Se** selenium 78.96	35 **Br** bromine 79.904	36 **Kr** krypton 83.80
5	37 **Rb** rubidium 85.468	38 **Sr** strontium 87.62	39 **Y** yttrium 88.906	40 **Zr** zirconium 91.22	41 **Nb** niobium 92.906	42 **Mo** molybdenum 95.940	43 **Tc** technetium (97)	44 **Ru** ruthenium 101.07	45 **Rh** rhodium 102.905	46 **Pd** palladium 106.40	47 **Ag** silver 107.868	48 **Cd** cadmium 112.41	49 **In** indium 114.82	50 **Sn** tin 118.69	51 **Sb** antimony 121.75	52 **Te** tellurium 127.60	53 **I** iodine 126.904	54 **Xe** xenon 131.30
6	55 **Cs** cesium 132.905	56 **Ba** barium 137.33	57 **La** lanthanum 138.906 †	72 **Hf** hafnium 178.49	73 **Ta** tantalum 180.948	74 **W** tungsten 183.85	75 **Re** rhenium 186.207	76 **Os** osmium 190.20	77 **Ir** iridum 192.22	78 **Pt** platinum 195.09	79 **Au** gold 196.967	80 **Hg** mercury 200.59	81 **Tl** thallium 204.37	82 **Pb** lead 207.20	83 **Bi** bismuth 208.980	84 **Po** polonium (209)	85 **At** astatine (210)	86 **Rn** radon (222)
7	87 **Fr** francium (223)	88 **Ra** radium 226.025	89 **Ac** actinium (227) ‡	104 **Rf** rutherfordium (261)	105 **Db** dubnium (262)	106 **Sg** seaborgium (263)	107 **Bh** bohrium (262)	108 **Hs** hassium (265)	109 **Mt** meitnerium (266)	110 **Uun** ununnilium (269)	111 **Uuu** unununium (272)	112 **Uub** ununbium (277)	113	114 **Uuq** ununquadium (289)	115	116 **Uuh** ununhexium (289)	117	118 **Uuo** ununoctium (293)

Inner Transition Elements

† Lanthanides 6	58 **Ce** cerium 140.12	59 **Pr** praseodymium 140.908	60 **Nd** neodymium 144.24	61 **Pm** prometheum (145)	62 **Sm** samarium 150.40	63 **Eu** europium 151.96	64 **Gd** gadolinium 157.25	65 **Tb** terbium 158.925	66 **Dy** dysprosium 162.50	67 **Ho** holmium 164.93	68 **Er** erbium 167.26	69 **Tm** thulium 168.934	70 **Yb** ytterbium 173.04	71 **Lu** lutetium 174.97
‡ Actinides 7	90 **Th** thorium 232.038	91 **Pa** protactinium 231.036	92 **U** uranium 238.029	93 **Np** neptunium (237)	94 **Pu** plutonium (244)	95 **Am** americium (243)	96 **Cm** curium (247)	97 **Bk** berkelium (247)	98 **Cf** californium (251)	99 **Es** einsteinium (254)	100 **Fm** fermium (257)	101 **Md** mendelevium (258)	102 **No** nobelium (255)	103 **Lr** lawrencium (260)

Key

atomic number — 1
symbol of element — **H**
element name — hydrogen
atomic weight — 1.008

Figure A.1 The periodic table of chemistry
It is called "periodic" because certain properties show up at periodic intervals. For example, the column from lithium down consists of metals that readily form salts. The column at the far right consists of gases that do not readily form compounds. Elements 110–118 have only tentative names and symbols.

number at the bottom is the element's **atomic weight,** which indicates the weight of an atom relative to the weight of one proton. A proton has a weight of one unit, a neutron has a weight just trivially greater than one, and an electron has a weight just trivially greater than zero. The atomic weight of the element is the number of protons in the atom plus the average number of neutrons. For example, most hydrogen atoms have one proton and no neutrons; a few atoms per thousand have one or two neutrons, giving an average atomic weight of 1.008. Sodium ions have 11 protons; most also have 12 neutrons, and the atomic weight is slightly less than 23. (Can you figure out the number of neutrons in the average potassium atom? Refer to Figure A.1.)

Ions and Chemical Bonds

An atom that has gained or lost one or more electrons is called an **ion.** For example, if sodium and chloride come together, the sodium atoms readily lose one electron each and the chloride atoms gain one each. The result is a set of positively charged sodium ions (indicated Na^+) and negatively charged chloride ions (Cl^-). Potassium atoms, like sodium atoms, tend to lose an electron and to become positively charged ions (K^+); calcium ions tend to lose two electrons and gain a double positive charge (Ca^{++}).

Because positive charges attract negative charges, sodium ions attract chloride ions. When dry, sodium and chloride form a crystal structure, as Figure A.2 shows. (In water solution, the two kinds of ions move about haphazardly, occasionally attracting one another

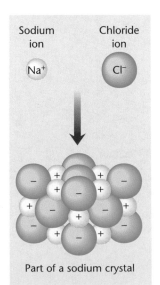

Figure A.2   The crystal structure of sodium chloride
Each sodium ion is surrounded by chloride ions, and each chloride ion is surrounded by sodium ions; no ion is bound to any other single ion in particular.

Figure A.3   Structure of a hydrogen molecule
A hydrogen atom has one electron; in the compound the two atoms share the two electrons equally.

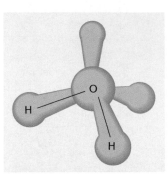

Figure A.4   Structure of a water molecule
The oxygen atom shares a pair of electrons with each hydrogen atom. Oxygen holds the electrons more tightly, making the oxygen part of the molecule more negatively charged than the hydrogen part of the molecule.

but then pulling apart.) The attraction of positive ions for negative ions forms an **ionic bond.** In other cases, instead of transferring an electron from one atom to another, some pairs of atoms share electrons with each other, forming a **covalent bond.** For example, two hydrogen atoms bind, as shown in Figure A.3, and two hydrogen atoms bind with an oxygen atom, as shown in Figure A.4. Atoms that are attached by a covalent bond cannot move independently of one another.

REACTIONS OF CARBON ATOMS

Living organisms depend on the enormously versatile compounds of carbon. Because of the importance of these compounds for life, the chemistry of carbon is known as organic chemistry.

Carbon atoms form covalent bonds with hydrogen, oxygen, and a number of other elements. They also form covalent bonds with other carbon atoms. Two carbon atoms may share from one to three pairs of electrons. Such bonds can be indicated as follows:

C–C   Two atoms share one pair of electrons.

C=C   Two atoms share two pairs of electrons.

C≡C   Two atoms share three pairs of electrons.

Each carbon atom ordinarily forms four covalent bonds, either with other carbon atoms, with hydrogen atoms, or with other atoms. Many biologically important compounds include long chains of carbon compounds linked to one another, such as:

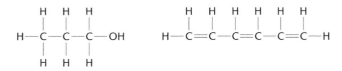

Note that each carbon atom has a total of four bonds, counting each double bond as two. In some molecules, the carbon chain loops around to form a ring:

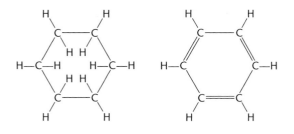

Ringed structures are common in organic chemistry. To simplify the diagrams chemists often omit the hydrogen atoms. You can simply assume that each carbon atom in the diagram has four covalent bonds and that all the bonds not shown are with hydrogen atoms. To further simplify the diagrams, chemists often omit the carbon atoms themselves, showing only the carbon-to-carbon bonds. For example, the two molecules shown in the previous diagram might be rendered as follows:

If a particular carbon atom has a bond with some atom other than hydrogen, the diagram shows the exception. For example, in each of the two molecules diagrammed below, one carbon has a bond with an oxygen atom, which in turn has a bond with a hydrogen atom. All the bonds that are not shown are carbon–hydrogen bonds.

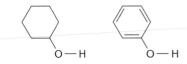

Figure A.5 illustrates some carbon compounds that are critical for animal life. Purines and pyrimidines form the central structure of DNA and RNA, the chemicals responsible for heredity. Proteins, fats, and carbohydrates are the primary types of fuel that the body uses. Figure A.6 displays the chemical structures of seven neurotransmitters that are extensively discussed in this text.

Chemical Reactions in the Body

A living organism is an immensely complicated, coordinated set of chemical reactions. Life requires that the rate of each reaction be carefully regulated. In many cases one reaction produces a chemical that enters into another reaction, which produces another chemical that enters into another reaction, and so forth. If any one of those reactions is too rapid compared to the others, the chemical it produces will accumulate to possibly harmful levels. If a reaction is too slow, it will not produce enough product and the next reaction will be stalled.

Figure A.5 Structures of some important biological molecules
The R in the protein represents a point of attachment for various chains that differ from one amino acid to another. Actual proteins are much longer than the chemical shown here.

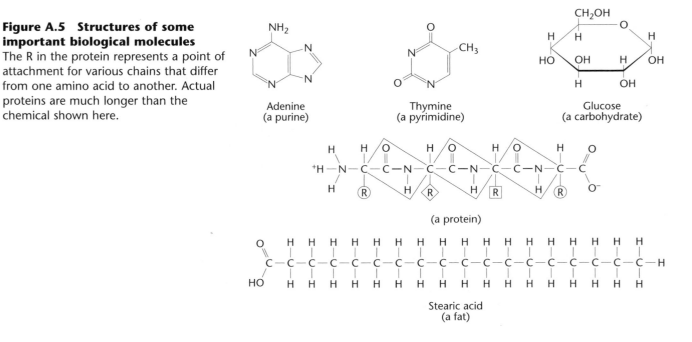

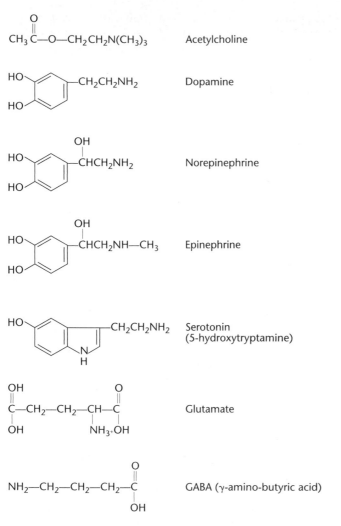

Figure A.6 Chemical structures of seven abundant neurotransmitters

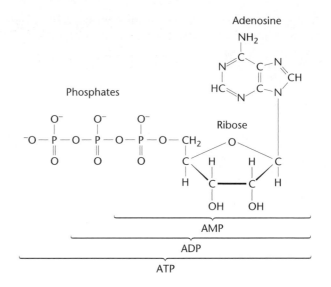

Figure A.7 ATP, composed of adenosine, ribose, and three phosphates
ATP can lose one phosphate group to form ADP (adenosine diphosphate) and then lose another one to form AMP (adenosine monophosphate). Each time it breaks off a phosphate group, it releases energy.

Enzymes are proteins that control the rate of chemical reactions. Each reaction is controlled by a particular enzyme. Enzymes are a type of catalyst. A catalyst is any chemical that facilitates a reaction among other chemicals, without being altered itself in the process.

The Role of ATP

The body relies on ATP (adenosine triphosphate) as its main way of sending energy where it is needed (Figure A.7). Much of the energy derived from food goes into forming ATP molecules that eventually provide energy for the muscles and other body parts.

ATP consists of adenosine bound to ribose and three phosphate groups (PO_3). Phosphates form high-energy covalent bonds. That is, a large amount of energy is required to form the bonds and a large amount of energy is released when they break. ATP can break off one or two of its three phosphates to provide energy.

SUMMARY

1. Matter is composed of 92 elements that combine to form an endless variety of compounds. (p. 494)

2. An atom is the smallest piece of an element. A molecule is the smallest piece of a compound that maintains the properties of the compound. (p. 494)

3. The atoms of some elements can gain or lose an electron, thus becoming ions. Positively charged ions attract negatively charged ions, forming an ionic bond. In some cases two or more atoms may share electrons, thus forming a covalent bond. (p. 496)

4. The principal carrier of energy in the body is a chemical called ATP. (p. 498)

TERMS

atom (p. 494)

atomic number (p. 494)

atomic weight (p. 496)

ATP (adenosine triphosphate) (p. 498)

compound (p. 494)

covalent bond (p. 496)

element (p. 494)

enzyme (p. 498)

ion (p. 496)

ionic bond (p. 496)

molecule (p. 494)

Society for Neuroscience Policies on the Use of Animals and Human Subjects in Neuroscience Research

POLICY ON THE USE OF ANIMALS IN NEUROSCIENCE RESEARCH

The Policy on the Use of Animals in Neuroscience Research affects a number of the Society's functions that involve making decisions about animal research conducted by individual members. These include the scheduling of scientific presentations at the Annual Meeting, the review and publication of original research papers in *The Journal of Neuroscience,* and the defense of members whose ethical use of animals in research is questioned by antivivisectionists. The responsibility for implementing the policy in each of these areas will rest with the relevant administrative body (Program Committee, Publications Committee, Editorial Board, and Committee on Animals in Research, respectively), in consultation with Council.

Introduction

The Society for Neuroscience, as a professional society for basic and clinical researchers in neuroscience, endorses and supports the appropriate and responsible use of animals as experimental subjects. Knowledge generated by neuroscience research on animals has led to important advances in the understanding of diseases and disorders that affect the nervous system and in the development of better treatments that reduce suffering in humans and animals. This knowledge also makes a critical contribution to our understanding of ourselves, the complexities of our brains, and what makes us human. Continued progress in understanding how the brain works and further advances in treating and curing disorders of the nervous system require investigation of complex functions at all levels in the living nervous system. Because no adequate alternatives exist, much of this research must be done on animal subjects. The Society takes the position that neuroscientists have an obligation to contribute to this progress through responsible and humane research on animals.

Several functions of the Society are related to the use of animals in research. A number of these involve decisions about research conducted by individual members of the Society, including the scheduling of scientific presentations at the Annual Meeting, the review and publication of original research papers in *The Journal of Neuroscience,* and the defense of members whose ethical use of animals in research is questioned by antivivisectionists. Each of these functions, by establishing explicit support of the Society for the research of individual members, defines a relationship between the Society and its members. The purpose of this document is to outline the policy that guides that relationship. Compliance with the following policy will be an important factor in determining the suitability of research for presentation at the Annual Meeting or for publication in *The Journal of Neuroscience,* and in situations where the Society is asked to provide public and active support for a member whose use of animals in research has been questioned.

General Policy

Neuroscience research uses complicated, often invasive methods, each of which is associated with different problems, risks, and specific technical considerations. An experimental method that would be deemed inappropriate for one kind of research may be the method of choice for another kind of research. It is therefore impossible for the Society to define specific policies and procedures for the care and use of all research animals and for the design and conduct of every neuroscience experiment.

The U.S. *Public Health Service Policy on Humane Care and Use of Laboratory Animals* (PHS Policy) and the *Guide for the Care and Use of Laboratory Animals* (the Guide) describe a set of general policies and procedures designed to ensure the humane and appropriate use of live vertebrate animals in all forms of biomedical research. The Society finds the policies and procedures set forth in the PHS Policy and the Guide to be both necessary and sufficient to ensure a high standard of animal care and use and adopts them as its official "Policy on the Use of Animals in Neuroscience Research" (Society Policy). All Society members are expected to conduct their animal research in compliance with the Society Policy and are required to verify that they have done so when submitting abstracts for presentation at the Annual Meeting or manuscripts for publication in *The Journal of Neuroscience.* Adherence to the Society Policy is also an important step toward receiving help from the Society in responding to questions about a member's use of animals in research. A complete description of the Society's policy and procedures for defending members whose research comes under attack is given in the Society's *Handbook for the Use of Animals in Neuroscience Research.*

Local Committee Review

An important element of the Society Policy is the establishment of a local committee that is charged with reviewing and approving all proposed animal care and use procedures. In addition to scientists experienced in research involving animals and a veterinarian, the membership of this local committee should include an individual who is not affiliated with the member's institution in any other way. In reviewing a proposed use of animals, the committee should evaluate the adequacy of institutional policies, animal husbandry, veterinary care, and the physical plant. Specific attention should be paid to proposed procedures for animal procurement, quarantine and stabilization, separation by species, disease diagnosis and treatment, anesthesia and analgesia, surgery and postsurgical care, and euthanasia. The review committee also should ensure that procedures involving live vertebrate animals are designed and performed with due consideration of their relevance to human or animal health, the advancement of knowledge, or the good of society. This review and approval of a member's use of live vertebrate animals in research by a local committee is an essential component of the Society Policy. Assistance in developing appropriate animal care and use procedures and establishing a local review committee can be obtained from the documents listed here and from the Society.

Other Laws, Regulations, and Policies

In addition to complying with the policy described above, Regular Members (i.e., North American residents) of the Society must also adhere to all relevant national, state, or local laws and/or regulations that govern their use of animals in neuroscience research. Thus, U.S. members must observe the U.S. Animal

Welfare Act (as amended in 1985) and its implementing regulations from the U.S. Department of Agriculture. Canadian members must abide by the *Guide to the Care and Use of Experimental Animals,* and members in Mexico must comply with the *Reglamento de la Ley General de Salud en Materia de Investigacion para la Salud* of the Secretaria de Salud (published on Jan. 6, 1987). Similarly, in addition to complying with the laws and regulations of their home countries, Foreign Members of the Society should adhere to the official Society Policy outlined here.

Recommended References

"Anesthesia and paralysis in experimental animals." *Visual Neuroscience,* 1:421–426. 1984.

The Biomedical Investigator's Handbook for Researchers Using Animal Models. 1987. Foundation for Biomedical Research, 818 Connecticut Ave., N.W., Suite 303, Washington, D.C. 20006.

Guide for the Care and Use of Laboratory Animals, 7th edition. 1996. NRC (National Research Council), Institute of Laboratory Animal Resources, National Academy of Sciences, 2101 Constitution Ave., N.W., Washington, D.C. 20418.

Guide to the Care and Use of Experimental Animals, 2nd edition, vol. 1. 1993. Canadian Council on Animal Care, 350 Albert St., Suite 315, Ottawa, Ontario, Canada K1R 1B1.

Handbook for the Use of Animals in Neuroscience Research. 1991. Society for Neuroscience, 11 Dupont Circle, N.W., Suite 500, Washington, D.C. 20036.

OPRR Public Health Service Policy on Humane Care and Use of Laboratory Animals (revised Sept. 1986). Office for Protection from Research Risks, NIH, 6100 Executive Blvd., Suite 3B01-MSC 7507, Rockville, MD 20892-7507.

Preparation and Maintenance of Higher Mammals During Neuroscience Experiments. Report of a National Institutes of Health Workshop. NIH Publication No. 91-3207, March 1991. National Eye Institute, Bldg. 31, Rm. 6A47, Bethesda, MD 20892.

Seventh Title of the Regulations of the General Law of Health, Regarding Health Research. In: *Laws and Codes of Mexico.* Published in the Porrua Collection, 12th updated edition, pp. 430–431. Porrua Publishers, Mexico, 1995.

The following principles, based largely on the PHS *Policy on Humane Care and Use of Laboratory*

Animals, can be a useful guide in the design and implementation of experimental procedures involving laboratory animals.

Animals selected for a procedure should be of an appropriate species and quality and the minimum number required to obtain valid results.

Proper use of animals, including the avoidance or minimization of discomfort, distress, and pain, when consistent with sound scientific practices, is imperative.

Procedures with animals that may cause more than momentary or slight pain or distress should be performed with appropriate sedation, analgesia, or anesthesia. Surgical or other painful procedures should not be performed on unanesthetized animals paralyzed by chemical agents.

Postoperative care of animals shall be such as to minimize discomfort and pain and, in any case, shall be equivalent to accepted practices in schools of veterinary medicine.

Animals that would otherwise suffer severe or chronic pain or distress that cannot be relieved should be painlessly killed at the end of the procedure or, if appropriate, during the procedure. If the study requires the death of the animal, the animal must be killed in a humane manner.

Living conditions should be appropriate for the species and contribute to the animals' health and comfort. Normally, the housing, feeding, and care of all animals used for biomedical purposes must be directed by a veterinarian or other scientist trained and experienced in the proper care, handling, and use of the species being maintained or studied. In any case, appropriate veterinary care shall be provided.

Exceptions to these principles require careful consideration and should only be made by an appropriate review group such as an institutional animal care and use committee.

POLICY ON THE USE OF HUMAN SUBJECTS IN NEUROSCIENCE RESEARCH

Experimental procedures involving human subjects must have been conducted in conformance with the policies and principles contained in the Federal Policy for the Protection of Human Subjects (United States Office of Science and Technology Policy) and in the Declaration of Helsinki. When publishing a paper in *The Journal of Neuroscience* or submitting an abstract for presentation at the Annual Meeting, authors must sign a statement of compliance with this policy.

Recommended References

Declaration of Helsinki. (Adopted in 1964 by the 18th World Medical Assembly in Helsinki, Finland, and revised by the 29th World Medical Assembly in Tokyo in 1975.) In: *The Main Issue in Bioethics Revised Edition.* Andrew C. Varga, Ed. New York: Paulist Press, 1984.

Federal Policy for the Protection of Human Subjects; Notices and Rules. *Federal Register.* Vol. 56, No. 117 (June 18, 1991), pp. 28002–28007.

http://www.apa.org/science/anguide.html
This Web site presents the ethical guidelines adopted by the American Psychological Association. They are largely similar to those of the Neuroscience Society.

References

Numbers in parentheses following citations indicate the chapter in which a reference is cited.

Abi-Dargham, A., Rodenhiser, J., Printz, D., Zea-Ponce, Y., Gil, R., Kegeles, L. S., Weiss, R., Cooper, T. B., Mann, J. J., Van Heertum, R. L., Gorman, J. M. & Laruelle, M. (2000). Increased baseline occupancy of D_2 receptors by dopamine in schizophrenia. *Proceedings of the National Academy of Sciences, USA, 97,* 8104-8109. (15)

Adamec, R. E., Stark-Adamec, C., & Livingston, K. E. (1980). The development of predatory aggression and defense in the domestic cat (*Felis catus*): 3. Effects on development of hunger between 180 and 365 days of age. *Behavioral and Neural Biology, 30,* 435–447. (12)

Adams, D. B., Gold, A. R., & Burt, A. D. (1978). Rise in female-initiated sexual activity at ovulation and its suppression by oral contraceptives. *New England Journal of Medicine, 299,* 1145–1150. (11)

Ader, R. (2001). Psychoneuroimmunology. *Current Directions in Psychological Science, 10,* 94–98. (12)

Adkins, E. K., & Adler, N. T. (1972). Hormonal control of behavior in the Japanese quail. *Journal of Comparative and Physiological Psychology, 81,* 27–36. (11)

Adkins-Regan, E. (1988). Sex hormones and sexual orientation in animals. *Psychobiology, 16,* 335–347. (11)

Adler, E., Hoon, M. A., Mueller, K. L., Chandrashekar, J., Ryba, N. J. P., & Zuker, C. S. (2000). A novel family of mammalian taste receptors. *Cell, 100,* 693–702. (7)

Adolphs, R., Damasio, H., & Tranel, D. (2002). Neural systems for recognition of emotional prosody: A 3-D lesion study. *Emotion, 2,* 23–51. (14)

Adolphs, R., & Tranel, D. (1999). Preferences for visual stimuli following amygdala damage. *Journal of Cognitive Neuroscience, 11,* 610–616. (12)

Adolphs, R., Tranel, D., & Damasio, A. R. (1998). The human amygdala in social judgment. *Nature, 393,* 470–474. (4, 12)

Adolphs, R., Tranel, D., Damasio, H., & Damasio, A. (1994). Impaired recognition of emotion in facial expressions following bilateral damage to the human amygdala. *Nature, 372,* 669–672. (12)

Adolphs, R., Tranel, D., Damasio, H., & Damasio, A. (1995). Fear and the human amygdala. *Journal of Neuroscience, 15,* 5879–5891. (12)

Aggleton, J. P., Blindt, H. S., & Rawlins, J. N. P. (1989). Effects of amygdaloid and amygdaloid-hippocampal lesions on object recognition and spatial working memory in rats. *Behavioral Neuroscience, 103,* 962–974. (13)

Aglioti, S., Smania, N., Atzei, A., & Berlucchi, G. (1997). Spatio-temporal properties of the pattern of evoked phantom sensations in a left index amputee patient. *Behavioral Neuroscience, 111,* 867–872. (5)

Aglioti, S., Smania, N., & Peru, A. (1999). Frames of reference for mapping tactile stimuli in brain-damaged patients. *Journal of Cognitive Neuroscience, 11,* 67–79. (7)

Aglioti, S., Tassinari, G., Corballis, M. C., & Berlucchi, G. (2000). Incomplete gustatory localization as shown by analysis of taste discrimination after callosotomy. *Journal of Cognitive Neuroscience, 12,* 238–245. (7, 14)

Aharon, I., Etcoff, N., Ariely, D., Chabris, C. F., O'Connor, E., & Breiter, H. C. (2001). Beautiful faces have variable reward value: fMRI and behavioral evidence. *Neuron, 32,* 537–551. (15)

Ahlskog, J. E., & Hoebel, B. G. (1973). Overeating and obesity from damage to a noradrenergic system in the brain. *Science, 182,* 166–169. (10)

Ahlskog, J. E., Randall, P. K., & Hoebel, B. G. (1975). Hypothalamic hyperphagia: Dissociation form hyperphagia following destruction of noradrenergic neurons. *Science, 190,* 399–401. (10)

Ahmed, I. I., Shryne, J. E., Gorski, R. A., Branch, B. J., & Taylor, A. N. (1991). Prenatal ethanol and the prepubertal sexually dimorphic nucleus of the preoptic area. *Physiology & Behavior, 49,* 427–432. (11)

Airaksinen, M. S., & Saarma, M. (2002). The GDNF family: Signalling, biological functions and therapeutic value. *Nature Reviews Neuroscience, 3,* 383–394. (5)

Akbarian, S., Kim, J. J., Potkin, S. G., Hagman, J. O., Tafazzoli, A., Bunney, W. E., Jr., & Jones, E. G. (1995). Gene expression for glutamic acid decarboxylase is reduced without loss of neurons in prefrontal cortex of schizophrenics. *Archives of General Psychiatry, 52,* 258–266 (15)

Akirav, I., & Richter-Levin, G. (1999). Biphasic modulation of hippocampal plasticity by behavioral stress and basolateral amygdala stimulation in the rat. *Journal of Neuroscience, 19,* 10530–10535. (13)

Albright, T. D., Jessell, T. M., Kandel, E. R., & Posner, M. I. (2001). Progress in the neural sciences in the century after Cajal (and the mysteries that remain).

Annals of the New York Academy of Sciences, 929, 11–40. (2)

Aldrich, M. S. (1998). Diagnostic aspects of narcolepsy. *Neurology, 50* (Suppl. 1), S2-S7. (9)

Allison, T., & Cicchetti, D. V. (1976). Sleep in mammals: Ecological and constitutional correlates. *Science, 194*, 732–734. (9)

Almli, C. R., Fisher, R. S., & Hill, D. L. (1979). Lateral hypothalamus destruction in infant rats produces consummatory deficits without sensory neglect or attenuated arousal. *Experimental Neurology, 66*, 146–157. (10)

Al-Rashid, R. A. (1971). Hypothalamic syndrome in acute childhood leukemia. *Clinical Pediatrics, 10*, 53–54. (10)

Amanzio, M., Pollo, A., Maggi, G., & Benedetti, F. (2001). Response variability to analgesics: A role for non-specific activation of endogenous opioids. *Pain, 90*, 205–215. (7)

American Psychiatric Association. (1994). *Diagnostic and statistical manual of mental disorders* (4th ed.). Washington, DC: Author. (12, 15)

Amidzic, O., Riehle, H. J., Fehr, T., Wienbruch, C., & Elbert, T. (2001). Pattern of focal γ-bursts in chess players. *Nature, 412*, 603. (4)

Amoore, J. E. (1977). Specific anosmia and the concept of primary odors. *Chemical Senses and Flavor, 2*, 267–281. (7)

Amsterdam, J. D., Winokur, A., Dyson, W., Herzog, S., Gonzalez, F., Rott, R., & Koprowski, H. (1985). Borna disease virus. *Archives of General Psychiatry, 42*, 1093–1096. (15)

Andersen, J. L., Klitgaard, H., & Saltin, B. (1994). Myosin heavy chain isoforms in single fibres from m. vastus lateralis of sprinters: Influence of training. *Acta Physiologica Scandinavica, 151*, 135–142. (8)

Andersen, S. L., Arvanitogiannis, A., Pliakas, A. M., LeBlanc, C., & Carlezon, W. A., Jr. (2002). Altered responsiveness to cocaine in rats exposed to methylphenidate during development. *Nature Neuroscience, 5*, 13–14. (15)

Anderson, A. K., & Phelps, E. A. (2001). Lesions of the human amygdala impair enhanced perception of emotionally salient events. *Nature, 411*, 305-309. (12)

Anderson, A. K., & Phelps, E. A. (2002). Is the human amygdala critical for the subjective experience of emotion? Evidence of intact dispositional affect in patients with amygdala lesions. *Journal of Cognitive Neuroscience, 14*, 709–720. (12)

Anderson, S. W., Bechara, A., Damasio, H., Tranel, D., & Damasio, A. R. (1999). Impairment of social and moral behavior related to early damage in human prefrontal cortex. *Nature Neuroscience, 2*, 1032–1037. (12)

Andersson, K.-E. (2001). Pharmacology of penile erection. *Pharmacological Reviews, 53*, 417–450. (11)

Andreasen, N. C. (1988). Brain imaging: Applications in psychiatry. *Science, 239*, 1381–1388. (4)

Andreasen, N. C. (1999). A unitary model of schizophrenia. *Archives of General Psychiatry, 56*, 781–787. (15)

Andreasen, N. C., Arndt, S., Alliger, R., Miller, D., & Flaum, M. (1995). Symptoms of schizophrenia: Methods, meanings, and mechanisms. *Archives of General Psychiatry, 52*, 341–351. (15)

Andreasen, N. C., Swayze, V. W., II, Flaum, M., Yates, W. R., Arndt, S., & McChesney, C. (1990). Ventricular enlargement in schizophrenia evaluated with computed tomographic scanning. *Archives of General Psychiatry, 47*, 1008–1015. (15)

Andrew, D., & Craig, A. D. (2001). Spinothalamic lamina I neurons selectively sensitive to histamine: A central neural pathway for itch. *Nature Neuroscience, 4*, 72–77. (7)

Andrews, T. J., Halpern, S. D., & Purves, D. (1997). Correlated size variations in human visual cortex, lateral geniculate nucleus, and optic tract. *Journal of Neuroscience, 17*, 2859–2868. (6)

Antanitus, D. S. (1998). A theory of cortical neuron-astrocyte interaction. *Neuroscientist, 4*, 154–159. (2)

Antle, M. C., & Mistlberger, R. E. (2000). Circadian clock resetting by sleep deprivation without exercise in the Syrian hamster. *Journal of Neuroscience, 20*, 9326–9332. (9)

Apostolakis, E. M., Garai, J., Fox, C., Smith, C. L., Watson, S. J., Clark, J. H., & O'Malley, B. W. (1996). Dopaminergic regulation of progesterone receptors: Brain D5 dopamine receptors mediate induction of lordosis by D1-like agonists in rats. *Journal of Neuroscience, 16*, 4823–4834. (11)

Appley, M. H. (1991). Motivation, equilibrium, and stress. In R. Dienstbier (Ed.), Nebraska *Symposium on Motivation 1990* (pp. 1–67). Lincoln: University of Nebraska Press. (10)

Araneda, R. C., Kini, A. D., & Firestein, S. (2000). The molecular receptive range of an odorant receptor. *Nature Neuroscience, 3*, 1248–1255. (7)

Archer, J. (2000). Sex differences in aggression between heterosexual partners: A meta-analytic review. *Psychological Bulletin, 126*, 651–680. (12)

Arendt, J. (1997). Safety of melatonin in long-term use(?). *Journal of Biological Rhythms, 12*, 673–681. (9)

Arkin, A. M., Toth, M. F., Baker, J., & Hastey, J. M. (1970). The frequency of sleep talking in the laboratory among chronic sleep talkers and good dream recallers. *Journal of Nervous and Mental Disease, 151*, 369–374. (9)

Arnold, A. P., & Breedlove, S. M. (1985). Organizational and activational effects of sex steroids on brain and behavior: A reanalysis. *Hormones and Behavior, 19*, 469–498. (11)

Arnold, S. E. (2000). Cellular and molecular neuropathology of the parahippocampal region in schizophrenics. *Annals of the New York Academy of Sciences, 911*, 275–292. (15)

Arvidson, K., & Friberg, U. (1980). Human taste: Response and taste bud number in fungiform papillae. *Science, 209*, 807–808. (7)

Aserinsky, E., & Kleitman, N. (1955). Two types of ocular motility occurring in sleep. *Journal of Applied Physiology, 8*, 1–10. (9)

Asston-Jones, G., Chen, S., Zhu, Y., & Oshinsky, M. L. (2001). A neural circuit for circadian regulation of arousal. *Nature Neuroscience, 4*, 732–738. (9)

Atack, J. R. (1996). Inositol monophosphatase, the putative therapeutic target for lithium. *Brain Research Reviews, 22*, 183–190. (15)

Au, T. K., Knightly, L. M., Jun, S.-A., & Oh, J. S. (2002). Overhearing a language during childhood. *Psychological Science, 13*, 238–243. (14)

Azrin, N. H., Sisson, R. W., Meyers, R., & Godley, M. (1982). Alcoholism treatment by disulfiram and community reinforcement therapy. Journal of Behavior *Therapy and Experimental Psychiatry, 13*, 105–112. (15)

Babich, F. R., Jacobson, A. L., Bubash, S., & Jacobson, A. (1965). Transfer of a response to naive rats by injection of ribonucleic acid extracted from trained rats. *Science, 149*, 656–657. (13)

Backlund, E.-O., Granberg, P.-O., Hamberger, B., Sedvall, G., Seiger, A., & Olson, L. (1985). Transplantation of adrenal medullary tissue to striatum in Parkinsonism. In A. Björklund & U. Stenevi (Eds.), *Neural grafting in the mammalian CNS* (pp. 551–556). Amsterdam: Elsevier. (8)

Baddeley, A. D., & Hitch, G. J. (1994). Developments in the concept of working memory. *Neuropsychology, 8*, 485–493. (13)

Badenhop, R. F., Moses, M. J., Scimone, A., Mitchell, P. B., Ewen, K. R., Rosso, A., Donald, J. A., Adams, L. J., & Schofield, P. R. (2001). A genome screen of a large bipolar affective disorder pedigree supports evidence for a susceptibility locus on chromosome 13q. *Molecular Psychiatry, 6*, 396–403. (15)

Baghdoyan, H. A., Spotts, J. L., & Snyder, S. G. (1993). Simultaneous pontine and basal forebrain microinjections of carbachol suppress REM sleep. *Journal of Neuroscience, 13*, 229–242. (9)

Bailey, C. H., Giustetto, M., Huang, Y.-Y., Hawkins, R. D., & Kandel, E. R. (2000). Is heterosynaptic modulation essential for stabilizing Hebbian plasticity and memory?

Nature Reviews Neuroscience, 1, 11–20. (13)

Bailey, J. M., & Bell, A. P. (1993). Familiality of female and male homosexuality. *Behavior Genetics, 23*, 313–322. (11)

Bailey, J. M., & Benishay, D. S. (1993). Familial aggregation of female sexual orientation. *American Journal of Psychiatry, 150*, 272–277. (11)

Bailey, J. M., & Pillard, R. C. (1991). A genetic study of male sexual orientation. *Archives of General Psychiatry, 48*, 1089–1096. (11)

Bailey, J. M., Pillard, R. C., Dawood, K., Miller, M. B., Farrer, L. A., Trivedi, S., & Murphy, R. L. (1999). A family history study of male sexual orientation using three independent samples. *Behavior Genetics, 29*, 79–86. (11)

Bailey, J. M., Pillard, R. C., Neale, M. C., & Agyei, Y. (1993). Heritable factors influence sexual orientation in women. *Archives of General Psychiatry, 50*, 217–223. (11)

Bailey, J. M., Willerman, L., & Parks, C. (1991). A test of the maternal stress theory of human male homosexuality. *Archives of Sexual Behavior, 20*, 277–293. (11)

Bakker, J., Honda, S.-I., Harada, N., & Balthazart, J. (2002). The aromatase knock-out mouse provides new evidence that estradiol is required during development in the female for the expression of sociosexual behaviors in adulthood. *Journal of Neuroscience, 22*, 9104–9112. (11)

Baldwin, A. E., Holahan, M. R., Sadeghian, K., & Kelley, A. E. (2000). *N*-methyl-D-aspartate receptor-dependent plasticity within a distributed corticostriatal network mediates appetitive instrumental learning. *Behavioral Neuroscience, 114*, 84–98. (13)

Ballard, P. A., Tetrud, J. W., & Langston, J. W. (1985). Permanent human parkinsonism due to 1-methyl-4-phenyl-1,2,3,6-tetrahydropyridine (MPTP). *Neurology, 35*, 949–956. (8)

Bao, S., Chan, V. T., & Merzenich, M. M. (2001). Cortical remodeling induced by activity of ventral tegmental dopamine neurons. *Nature, 412*, 79–83. (5)

Bao, S., Chen, L., & Thompson, R. F. (2000). Learning- and cerebellum-dependent neuronal activity in the lateral pontine nucleus. *Behavioral Neuroscience, 114*, 254–261. (13)

Barch, D. M., Carter, C. S., Braver, T. S., Sabb, F. W., MacDonald, A. III, Noll, D. C., & Cohen, J. D. (2001). Selective deficits in prefrontal cortex function in medication-naive patients with schizophrenia. *Archives of General Psychiatry, 58*, 280–288. (15)

Barinaga, M. (1996). Finding new drugs to treat stroke. *Science, 272*, 664–666. (5)

Barnes, B. M. (1996, September/October). Sang froid. *The Sciences, 36*(5), 13–14. (9)

Barnes, J., Anderson, L. A., & Phillipson, J. D. (2001). St John's wort (*Hypericum perforatum L.*): A review of its chemistry, pharmacology and clinical properties. *Journal of Pharmacy and Pharmacology, 53*, 583–600. (15)

Barone, F. C., Feuerstein, G. Z., & White, R. F. (1997). Brain cooling during transient focal ischemia provides complete neuroprotection. *Neuroscience and Biobehavioral Reviews, 21*, 31–44. (5)

Barth, T. M., Grant, M. L., & Schallert, T. (1990). Effects of MK-801 on recovery from sensorimotor cortex lesions. *Stroke, 21*(Suppl. III), III-153-III-157. (5)

Barton, R. A., & Harvey, P. H. (2000). Mosaic evolution of brain structure in mammals. *Nature, 405*, 1055–1058. (5)

Bartoshuk, L. M. (1991). Taste, smell, and pleasure. In R. C. Bolles (Ed.), *The hedonics of taste* (pp. 15–28). Hillsdale, NJ: Erlbaum. (7)

Bartoshuk, L. M. (2000). Comparing sensory experiences across individuals: Recent psychophysical advances illuminate genetic variation in taste perception. *Chemical Senses, 25*, 447–460. (7)

Bartoshuk, L. M., Gentile, R. L., Moskowitz, H. R., & Meiselman, H. L. (1974). Sweet taste induced by miracle fruit (*Synsephalum dulcificum*). *Physiology & Behavior, 12*, 449–456. (7)

Bartoshuk, L. M., Lee, C.-H., & Scarpellino, R. (1972). Sweet taste of water induced by artichoke (*Cynara scolymus*). *Science, 178*, 988–990. (7)

Basheer, R., Rainnie, D. G., Porkka-Heiskanen, T., Ramesh, V., & McCarley, R. W. (2001). Adenosine, prolonged wakefulness, and A1-activated NF-kB DNA binding in the basal forebrain of the rat. *Neuroscience, 104*, 731–739. (9)

Basil, J. A., Kamil, A. C., Balda, R. P., & Fite, K. V. (1996). Differences in hippocampal volume among food storing corvids. *Brain, Behavior and Evolution, 47*, 156–164. (13)

Basso, A., & Rusconi, M. L. (1998). Aphasia in left-handers. In P. Coppens, Y. Lebrun, & A. Basso (Eds.), *Aphasia in atypical populations* (pp. 1–34). Mahwah, NJ: Erlbaum. (14)

Bastien, C., & Campbell, K. (1992). The evoked K-complex: All-or-none phenomenon? *Sleep, 15*, 236–245. (9)

Battaglia, M., Bertella, S., Ogliari, A., Bellodi, L., & Smeraldi, E. (2001). Modulation by muscarinic antagonists of the response to carbon dioxide challenge in panic disorder. *Archives of General Psychiatry, 58*, 114–119. (12)

Battersby, S. (1997). Plus c'est le même chews. *Nature, 385*, 679. (10)

Baulac, S., Huberfeld, G., Gourfinkel-An, I., Mitropoulou, G., Beranger, A., Prud'homme, J.-F., Baulac, M., Brice, A., Bruzzone, R., & LeGuern, E. (2001). First genetic evidence of GABAA receptor dysfunction in epilepsy: A mutation in the γ2-subunit gene. *Nature Genetics, 28*, 46–48. (14)

Baum, A., Gatchel, R. J., & Schaeffer, M. A. (1983). Emotional, behavioral, and physiological effects of chronic stresss at Three Mile Island. *Journal of Consulting and Clinical Psychology, 51*, 565–582. (12)

Baum, M. J., Tobet, S. A., Cherry, J. A., & Paredes, R. G. (1996). Estrogenic control of preoptic area development in a carnivore, the ferret. *Cellular and Molecular Neurobiology, 16*, 117–128. (11)

Baum, M. J., & Vreeburg, J. T. M. (1973). Copulation in castrated male rats following combined treatment with estradiol and dihydrotestosterone. Science, 182, 283–285. (11)

Baxter, L. R., Phelps, M. E., Mazziotta, J. C., Schwartz, J. M., Gerner, R. H., Selin, C. E., & Sumida, R. M. (1985). Cerebral metabolic rates for glucose in mood disorders. *Archives of Gener-al Psychiatry, 42*, 441–447. (15)

Baxter, M. G., & Murray, E. A. (2002). The amygdala and reward. *Nature Reviews Neuroscience, 3*, 563–573. (12)

Baylis, G. C., & Driver, J. (2001). Shape-coding in IT cells generalizes over contrast and mirror reversal but not figure-ground reversal. *Nature Neuroscience, 4*, 937–942. (6)

Bechara, A., Damasio, H., Damasio, A. R., & Lee, G. P. (1999). Different contributions of the human amygdala and ventromedial prefrontal cortex to decision-making. *Journal of Neuroscience, 19*, 5473–5481. (12)

Becker, C., Thiébot, M.-H., Touitou, Y., Hamon, M., Cesselin, F., & Benoliel, J.-J. (2001). Enhanced cortical extracellular levels of cholecystokinin-like material in a model of anticipation of social defeat in the rat. *Journal of Neuroscience, 21*, 262–269. (12)

Becker, H. C. (1988). Effects of the imidazobenzodiazepine Ro15-4513 on the stimulant and depressant actions of ethanol on spontaneous locomotor activity. *Life Sciences, 43*, 643–650. (12)

Beeman, M. J., & Chiarello, C. (1998). Complementary right- and left-hemisphere language comprehension. *Current Directions in Psychological Science, 7*, 2–8. (14)

Behl, C. (2002). Oestrogen as a neuroprotective hormone. *Nature Reviews Neuroscience, 3*, 433–442. (11)

Békésy, G.—See von Békésy, G.

Bellugi, U., Lichtenberger, L., Jones, W., Lai, Z., & St George, M. (2000). I. The neurocognitive profile of Williams syndrome: A complex pattern of strengths and weaknesses. *Journal of Cognitive Neuroscience, 12*(Suppl.), 7–29. (14)

Bellugi, U., Lichtenberger, L., Mills, D., Galaburda, A., & Korenberg, J. R. (1999). Bridging cognition, the brain and molecular genetics: Evidence from Williams syndrome. *Trends in Neurosciences, 22*, 197–207. (14)

Bellugi, U., Wang, P. P., & Jernigan, T. L. (1994). Williams syndrome: An unusual neuropsychological profile. In S. H. Broman & J. Grafman (Eds.), *Atypical cognitive deficits in developmental disorders* (pp. 23–56). Hillsdale, NJ: Erlbaum. (14)

Benca, R. M., Obermeyer, W. H., Thisted, R. A., & Gillin, J. C. (1992). Sleep and psychiatric disorders. *Archives of General Psychiatry, 49*, 651–668. (9)

Benes, F. M. (1995). Is there a neuroanatomic basis for schizophrenia? An old question revisited. *The Neuroscientist, 1*, 104–115. (15)

Benes, F. M., & Bird, E. D. (1987). An analysis of the arrangement of neurons in the cingulate cortex of schizophrenic patients. *Archives of General Psychiatry, 44*, 608–616. (15)

Benes, F. M., Turtle, M., Khan, Y., & Farol, P. (1994). Myelination of a key relay zone in the hippocampal formation occurs in the human brain during childhood, adolescence, and adulthood. *Archives of General Psychiatry, 51*, 477–484. (5)

Benjamin, J., Li, L., Patterson, C., Greenberg, B. D., Murphy, D. L., & Hamer, D. H. (1996). Population and familial association between the D4 dopamine receptor gene and measures of novelty seeking. *Nature Genetics, 12*, 81–84. (3)

Benoit, S. C., Air, E. L., Coolen, L. M., Strauss, R., Jackman, A., Clegg, D. J., Seeley, R. J., & Woods, S. C. (2002). The catabolic action of insulin in the brain is mediated by melanocortins. *Journal of Neuroscience, 22*, 9048–9052. (10)

Benschop, R. J., Godaert, G. L. R., Geenen, R., Brosschot, J. F., DeSmet, M. B. M., Olff, M., Heijnen, C. J., & Beilleux, R. E. (1995). Relationships between cardiovascular and immunologic changes in an experimental stress model. *Psychological Medicine, 25,* 323–327. (12)

Berdoy, M., Webster, J. P., & Macdonald, D. W. (2000). Fatal attraction in rats infected with *Toxoplasma gondii. Proceedings of the Royal Society of London, B, 267,* 1591–1594. (12)

Berenbaum, S. A. (1999). Effects of early androgens on sex-typed activities and interests in adolescents with congenital adrenal hyperplasia. *Hormones and Behavior, 35,* 102–110. (11)

Berger, R. J., & Phillips, N. H. (1995). Energy conservation and sleep. *Behavioural Brain Research, 69,* 65–73. (9)

Berger-Sweeney, J., & Hohmann, C. F. (1997). Behavioral consequences of abnormal cortical development: Insights into developmental disabilities. *Behavioural Brain Research, 86,* 121–142. (5)

Berlucchi, G., Mangun, G. R., & Gazzaniga, M. S. (1997). Visuospatial attention and the split brain. *News in Physiological Sciences, 12,* 226–231. (14)

Berman, K. F., Torrey, E. F., Daniel, D. G., & Weinberger, D. R. (1992). Regional cerebral blood flow in monozygotic twins discordant and concordant for schizophrenia. *Archives of General Psychiatry, 49,* 927–934. (15)

Bernhardt, P. C. (1997). Influences of serotonin and testosterone in aggression and dominance: Convergence with social psychology. *Current Directions in Psychological Science, 6,* 44–48. (12)

Bernstein, J. J., & Gelderd, J. B. (1970). Regeneration of the long spinal tracts in the goldfish. *Brain Research, 20,* 33–38. (5)

Bernstein, L. J., & Robertson, L. C. (1998). Illusory conjunctions of color and motion with shape following bilateral parietal lesions. *Psychological Science, 9,* 167–175. (4)

Berridge, K. C., & Robinson, T. E. (1995). The mind of an addicted brain: Neural sensitization of wanting versus liking. *Current Directions in Psychological Science, 4,* 71–76. (15)

Berridge, K. C., & Robinson, T. E. (1998). What is the role of dopamine in reward: Hedonic impact, reward learning, or incentive salience? *Brain Research Reviews, 28,* 309–369. (15)

Berridge, K. C., Venier, I. L., & Robinson, T. E. (1989). Taste reactivity analysis of 6-hydroxydopamine-induced aphagia: Implications for arousal and anhedonia hypotheses of dopamine function. *Behavioral Neuroscience, 103,* 36–45. (10)

Berson, D. M., Dunn, F. A., & Takao, M. (2002). Phototransduction by retinal ganglion cells that set the circadian clock. *Science, 295,* 1070–1073. (9)

Bertram, L., Blacker, D., Mullin, K., Keeney, D., Jones, J., Basu, S., Yhu, S., McInnis, M. G., Go, R. C. P., Vekrellis, K., Selkow, D. J., Saunders, A. J., & Tanzi, R. E. (2000). Evidence for genetic linkage of Alzheimer's disease to chromosome 10q. *Science, 290,* 2302–2303. (13)

Best, C. T., & Avery, R. A. (1999). Left-hemisphere advantage for click consonants is determined by linguistic significance and experience. *Psychological Science, 10,* 65–70. (14)

Betarbet, R., Sherer, T. B., MacKenzie, G., Garcia-Osuna, M., Panov, A. V., & Greenamyre, J. T. (2000). Chronic systemic pesticide exposure reproduces features of Parkinson's disease. *Nature Neuroscience, 3,* 1301–1306. (8)

Bi, S., Ladenheim, E. E., Schwartz, G. J., & Moran, T. H. (2001). A role for NPY overexpression in the dorsomedial hypothalamus in hypoerphagia and obesity of OLETF rats. *American Journal of Physiology, 281,* R254–R260. (10)

Biben, M. (1979). Predation and predatory play behaviour of domestic cats. *Animal Behaviour, 27,* 81–94. (12)

Bierut, L. J., Heath, A. C., Bucholz, K. K., Dinwiddie, S. H., Madden, P. A. F., Statham, D. J., Dunne, M. P., & Martin, N. G. (1999). Major depressive disorder in a community-based twin sample. *Archives of General Psychiatry, 56,* 557–563. (15)

Billington, C. J., & Levine, A. S. (1992). Hypothalamic neuropeptide Y regulation of feeding and energy metabolism. *Current Opinion in Neurobiology, 2,* 847–851. (10)

Binder, G. K., & Griffin, D. E. (2001). Interferon-g-mediated site-specific clearance of alphavirus from CNS neurons. *Science, 293,* 303–306. (2)

Blackless, M., Charuvastra, A., Derryck, A., Fausto-Sterling, A., Lauzanne, K., & Lee, E. (2000). How sexually dimorphic are we? Review and synthesis. *American Journal of Human Biology, 12,* 151–166. (11)

Blackwell, A., & Bates, E. (1995). Inducing agrammatic profiles in normals: Evidence for the selective vulnerability of morphology under cognitive resource limitation. *Journal of Cognitive Neuroscience, 7,* 228–257. (14)

Blackwood, D. H. R., He, L., Morris, S. W., McLean, A., Whitton, C., Thomson, M., Walker, M. T., Woodburn, K., Sharp, C. M., Wright, A. F., Shibasaki, Y., St. Clair, D. M., Porteous, D. J., & Muir, W. J. (1996). A locus for bipolar affective disorder on chromosome 4p. *Nature Genetics, 12,* 427–430. (15)

Blake, R., & Hirsch, H. V. B. (1975). Deficits in binocular depth perception in cats after alternating monocular deprivation. *Science, 190,* 1114–1116. (6)

Blakemore, S.-J., Wolpert, D. M., & Frith, C. D. (1998). Central cancellation of self-produced tickle sensation. *Nature Neuroscience, 1,* 635–640. (7)

Bliss, T. V. P., & Lømo, T. (1973). Long-lasting potentiation of synaptic transmission in the dentate area of the anaesthetized rabbit following stimulation of the perforant path. *Journal of Physiology* (London), *232,* 331–356. (13)

Bloch, G. J., Butler, P. C., & Kohlert, J. G. (1996). Galanin microinjected into the medial preoptic nucleus facilitates female- and male-typical sexual behaviors in the female rat. *Physiology & Behavior, 59,* 1147–1154. (11)

Bloch, G. J., & Mills, R. (1995). Prepubertal testosterone treatment of neonatally gonadectomized male rats: Defeminization and masculinization of behavioral and endocrine function in adulthood. *Neuroscience and Biobehavioral Reviews, 19,* 187–200. (11)

Bloch, G. J., Mills, R., & Gale, S. (1995). Prepubertal testosterone treatment of female rats: Defeminization of behavioral and endocrine function in adulthood. *Neuroscience and Biobehavioral Reviews, 19,* 177–186. (11)

Bloch, M., Schmidt, P. J., Danaceau, M., Murphy, J., Nieman, L., & Rubinow, D. R. (2000). Effects of gonadal steroids in women with a history of postpartum depression. *American Journal of Psychiatry, 157,* 924–930. (15)

Blouin, J.-L., Dombroski, B. A., Nath, S. K., Lasseter, V. K., Wolyniec, P. S., Nestadt, G., Thornquist, M., Ullrich, G., McGrath, J., Kasch, L., Lamacz, M., Thomas, M. G., Gehrig, C., Radhakrishna, U., Snyder, S. E., Balk, S. E., Neufeld, K., Swartz, K. L., DeMarchi, N., Papadimitriou, G. N., Dikeos, D. G., Stefanis, C. N., Chakravarti, A., Childs, B., Housman, D. E., Kazazian, H. H., Antonarakis, S. E., & Pulver, A. E. (1998). Schizophrenia susceptibility loci on chromosomes 13q32 and 8p21. *Nature Genetics, 20,* 70–73. (15)

Blum, D. (1994). *The monkey wars.* New York: Oxford University Press. (1)

Blum, K., Cull, J. G., Braverman, E. R., & Comings, D. E. (1996). Reward deficiency syndrome. *American Scientist, 84,* 132–145. (3)

Boatman, D., Freeman, J., Vining, E., Pulsifer, M., Miglioretti, D., Minahan, R., Carson, B., Brandt, J., & McKhann, G. (1999). Language recovery after left hemispherectomy in children with late-onset seizures. *Annals of Neurology, 46,* 579–586. (14)

Bobrow, D., & Bailey, J. M. (2000). Is male homosexuality maintained via kin selection? *Evolution and Human Behavior, 22,* 361–368. (11)

Bode, L., Ferszt, R., & Czech, G. (1993). Borna disease virus infection and affective disorders in man. *Archives of Virology* (Suppl. 7), 159–167. (15)

Bode, L., & Ludwig, H. (1997). Clinical similarities and close genetic relationship of human and animal Borna disease virus. *Archives of Virology* (Suppl. 13), 167–182. (15)

Bode, L., Riegel, S., Lange, W., & Ludwig, H. (1992). Human infections with Borna disease virus: Seroprevalence in patients with chronic diseases and healthy individuals. *Journal of Medical Virology, 36,* 309–315. (15)

Bogerts, B., Meertz, E., & Schönfeldt-Bausch, R. (1985). Basal ganglia and limbic system pathology in schizophrenia. *Archives of General Psychiatry, 42,* 784–791. (15)

Bohbot, V. D., Allen, J. J. B., & Nadel, L. (2000). Memory deficits characterized by patterns of lesions to the hippocampus and parahippocampal cortex. *Annals of the New York Academy of Sciences, 911,* 355–368. (13)

Bohn, M. C., Cupit, L., Marciano, F., & Gash, D. M. (1987). Adrenal medulla grafts enhance recovery of striatal dopaminergic fibers. *Science, 237,* 913–916. (8)

Boivin, D. B., Duffy, J. F., Kronauer, R. E., & Czeisler, C. A. (1996). Dose-response relationships for resetting of human circadian clock by light. *Nature, 379,* 540–542. (9)

Bomze, H. M., Bulsara, K. R., Iskandar, B. J., Caroni, P., & Skene, J. H. P. (2001). Spinal axon regeneration evoked by replacing two growth cone proteins in adult neurons. *Nature Neuroscience, 4,* 38–43. (5)

Bontempi, B., Laurent-Demir, C., Destrade, C., & Jaffard, R. (1999). Time-dependent reorganization of brain circuitry underlying long-term memory storage. *Nature, 400,* 671–675. (13)

Booth-Kewley, S., & Friedman, H. S. (1987). Psychological predictors of heart disease: A quantitative review. *Psychological Bulletin, 101,* 343–362. (12)

Bornstein, R. F. (1989). Subliminal techniques as propaganda tools: Review and critique. *Journal of Mind and Behavior, 10,* 231–262. (7)

Botvinick, M., & Cohen, J. (1998). Rubber hands "feel" touch that eyes see. *Nature, 391,* 756. (4)

Boucher, T. J., Okuse, K., Bennett, D. L. H., Munson, J. B., Wood, J. N., & McMahon, S. B. (2000). Potent analgesic effects of GDNF in neuropathic pain states. *Science, 290,* 124–127. (7)

Bouton, M. E., Mineka, S., & Barlow, D. H. (2001). A modern learning theory perspective on the etiology of panic disorder. *Psychological Review, 108,* 4–32. (12)

Boutrel, B., Franc, B., Hen, R., Hamon, M., & Adrien, J. (1999). Key role of 5-HT1B receptors in the regulation of paradoxical sleep as evidenced in 5-HT1B knock-out mice. *Journal of Neuroscience, 19,* 3204–3212. (9)

Bowmaker, J. K. (1998). Visual pigments and molecular genetics of color blindness. *News in Physiological Sciences, 13,* 63–69. (6)

Bowmaker, J. K., & Dartnall, H. J. A. (1980). Visual pigments of rods and cones in a human retina. *Journal of Physiology* (London), *298,* 501–511. (6)

Bradbury, E. J., Moon, L. D. F., Popat, R. J., King, V. R., Benett, G. S., Patel, P. N., Fawcett, J. W., & McMahon, S. B. (2002). Chondroitinase ABC promotes functional recovery after spinal cord injury. *Nature, 416,* 636–640. (5)

Bradley, S. J., Oliver, G. D., Chernick, A. B., & Zucker, K. J. (1998). Experiment of nature: Ablatio penis at 2 months, sex reassignment at 7 months, and a psychosexual follow-up in young adulthood. *Pediatrics, 102,* p. e9. (11) Retrieved from http://www.pediatrics.org/cgi/content/full/102/1/e9

Brady, J. V., Porter, R. W., Conrad, D. G., & Mason, J. W. (1958). Avoidance behavior and the development of gastroduodenal ulcers. *Journal of the Experimental Analysis of Behavior, 1,* 69–72. (12)

Brambilla, F., Brunetta, M., Draisci, A., Peirone, A., Perna, G., Sacerdote, P., Manfredi, B., & Panerai, A. E. (1995). T-lymphocyte concentrations of cholecystokinin-8 and beta-endorphin in eating disorders: II. Bulimia nervosa. *Psychiatry Research, 59,* 51–56. (10)

Brandt, T. (1991). Man in motion: Historical and clinical aspects of vestibular function. *Brain, 114*, 2159–2174. (7)

Brasted, P. J., Watts, C., Robbins, T. W., & Dunnett, S. B. (1999). Associative plasticity in striatal transplants. *Proceedings of the National Academy of Sciences, USA, 96*, 10524–10529. (8)

Braun, A. R., Balkin, T. J., Wesensten, N. J., Guadry, F., Carson, R. E., Varga, M., Baldwin, P., Belenky, G., & Herscovitch, P. (1998). Dissociated pattern of activity in visual cortices and their projections during human rapid eye movement sleep. *Science, 279*, 91–95. (8, 9)

Braus, H. (1960). *Anatomie des Menschen, 3. Band: Periphere Leistungsbahnen II. Centrales Nervensystem, Sinnesorgane. 2. Auflage* [Human anatomy: Vol. 3. Peripheral pathways II. Central nervous system, sensory organs (2nd ed.)]. Berlin: Springer-Verlag. (4)

Bray, G. A., & Tartaglia, L. A. (2000). Medicinal strategies in the treatment of obesity. *Nature, 404*, 672–677. (10)

Breiter, H. C., Etcoff, N. L., Whalen, P. J., Kennedy, W. A., Rauch, S. L., Buckner, R. L., Strauss, M. M., Hyman, S. E., & Rosen, B. R. (1996). Response and habituation of the human amygdala during visual processing of facial expression. *Neuron, 17*, 875–887. (12)

Brennan, P. A., Grekin, E. R., & Mednick, S. A. (1999). Maternal smoking during pregnancy and adult male criminal outcomes. *Archives of General Psychiatry, 56*, 215–219. (5, 12)

Bridgeman, B., & Staggs, D. (1982). Plasticity in human blindsight. *Vision Research, 22*, 1199–1203. (6)

Brightman, M. W. (1997). Blood-brain barrier: Penetration by solutes and cells. In G. Adelman & B. H. Smith (Eds.), *Elsevier encyclopedia of neuroscience.* New York: Elsevier. (2)

Brinkmann, R. R., Mezei, M. M., Theilmann, J., Almqvist, E., & Hayden, M. R. (1997). The likelihood of being affected with Huntington disease by a particular age, for a specific CAG size.

American Journal of Human Genetics, 60, 1202–1210. (8)

Brodkin, E. S., Goforth, S. A., Keene, A. H., Fossella, J. A., & Silver, L. M. (2002). Identification of quantitative trait loci that affect aggressive behavior in mice. *Journal of Neuroscience, 22*, 1165–1170. (12)

Brody, A. L., Saxena, S., Stoesssel, P., Gillies, L. A., Fairbanks, L. A., Alborzian, S., Phelps, M. E., Huang, S.-C., Wu, H.-M., Ho, M. L., Ho, M. K., Au, S. C., Maidment, K., & Baxter, L. R., Jr. (2001). Regional brain metabolic changes in patients with major depression treated with either paroxetine or interpersonal therapy. *Archives of General Psychiatry, 58*, 631–640. (15)

Brooks, D. C., & Bizzi, E. (1963). Brain stem electrical activity during deep sleep. *Archives Italiennes de Biologie, 101*, 648–665. (9)

Brooks, J. H., & Reddon, J. R. (1996). Serum testosterone in violent and nonviolent young offenders. *Journal of Clinical Psychology, 52*, 475–483. (12)

Broughton, R., Billlings, R., Cartwright, R., Doucette, D., Edmeads, J., Edwardh, M., Ervin, F., Orchard, B., Hill, R., & Turrell, G. (1994). Homicidal somnambulism: A case report. *Sleep, 17*, 253–264. (9)

Brown, A. S., Cohen, P., Harkavy-Friedman, J., Babulas, V., Malaspina, D., Gorman, J. M., & Susser, E. S. (2001). Prenatal rubella, premorbid abnormalities, and adult schizophrenia. *Biological Psychiatry, 49*, 473–486. (15)

Brown, G. L., Ebert, M. H., Goyer, P. F., Jimerson, D. C., Klein, W. J., Bunney, W. E., & Goodwin, F. K. (1982). Aggression, suicide, and serotonin: Relationships of CSF amine metabolites. *American Journal of Psychiatry, 139*, 741–746. (12)

Brown, J., Babor, T. F., Litt, M. D., & Kranzler, H. R. (1994). The type A/type B distinction. *Annals of the New York Academy of Sciences, 708*, 23–33. (15)

Brown, J. R., Ye, H., Bronson, R. T., Dikkes, P., & Greenberg, M. E. (1996). A defect in nurturing in

mice lacking the immediate early gene *fos B. Cell, 86*, 297–309. (11)

Bruce-Keller, A. J., Umberger, G., McFall, R., & Mattson, M. P. (1999). Food restriction reduces brain damage and improves behavioral outcome following excitotoxic and metabolic insults. *Annals of Neurology, 45*, 8–15. (5)

Brüning, J. C., Gautham, D., Burks, D. J., Gillette, J., Schubert, M., Orban, P. C., Klein, R., Krone, W., Müller-Wieland, D., & Kahn, C. R. (2000). Role of brain insulin receptor in control of body weight and reproduction. *Science, 289*, 2122–2125. (10)

Brunner, D., & Hen, R. (1997). Insights into the neurobiology of impulsive behavior from serotonin receptor knockout mice. *Annals of the New York Academy of Sciences, 836*, 81–105. (12)

Bruyer, R., Dupuis, M., Ophoven, E., Rectem, D., & Reynaert, C. (1985). Anatomical and behavioral study of a case of asymptomatic callosal agenesis. *Cortex, 21*, 417–430. (14)

Brysbaert, M., Vitu, F., & Schroyens, W. (1996). The right visual field advantage and the optimal viewing position effect: On the relation between foveal and parafoveal word recognition. *Neuropsychology, 10*, 385–395. (14)

Büchel, C., Morris, J., Dolan, R. J., & Friston, K. J. (1998). Brain systems mediating aversive conditioning: An event-related fMRI study. *Neuron, 20*, 947–957. (12)

Buck, L., & Axel, R. (1991). A novel multigene family may encode odorant receptors: A molecular basis for odor recognition. *Cell, 65*, 175–187. (7)

Buck, R., & Duffy, R. J. (1980). Nonverbal communication of affect in brain-damaged patients. *Cortex, 16*, 351–362. (12, 14)

Budney, A. J., Hughes, J. R., Moore, B. A., & Novy, P. L. (2001). Marijuana abstinence effects in marijuana smokers maintained in their home environment. *Archives of General Psychiatry, 58*, 917–924. (15)

Buell, S. J., & Coleman, P. D. (1981). Quantitative evidence for selective dendritic growth in normal human aging but not in senile dementia. *Brain Research, 214*, 23–41. (5)

Buka, S. L., Tsuang, M. T., Torrey, E. F., Klebanoff, M. A., Bernstein, D., & Yolken, R. H. (2001). Maternal infections and subsequent psychosis among offspring. *Archives of General Psychiatry, 58,* 1032–1037. (15)

Bundgaard, M. (1986). Pathways across the vertebrate blood-brain barrier: Morphological viewpoints. *Annals of the New York Academy of Sciences, 481,* 7–19. (2)

Bunney, W. E., Jr., Murphy, D. L., Goodwin, F. K., & Borge, G. F. (1972). The "switch process" in manic-depressive illness. *Archives of General Psychiatry, 27,* 295–302. (15)

Burgess, C. E., Lindblad, K., Sigransky, E., Yuan, Q.-P., Long, R. T., Breschel, T., Ross, C. A., McInnis, M., Lee, P., Ginns, E., Lenane, M., Kumra, S., Jacobsen, L., Rapoport, J., & Schalling, M. (1998). Large CAG/CTG repeats are associated with childhood-onset schizophrenia. *Molecular Psychiatry, 3,* 321–327. (15)

Burgess, P. W., & McNeil, J. E. (1999). Content-specific confabulation. *Cortex, 35,* 163–182. (13)

Burr, D. C., Morrone, M. C., & Ross, J. (1994). Selective suppression of the magnocellular visual pathway during saccadic eye movements. *Nature, 371,* 511–513. (6)

Burton, R. F. (1994). *Physiology by numbers.* Cambridge, England: Cambridge University Press. (10)

Buss, D. M. (1994). The strategies of human mating. *American Scientist, 82,* 238–249. (11)

Buss, D. M. (2000). Desires in human mating. *Annals of the New York Academy of Sciences, 907,* 39–49. (11)

Butler, A. A., Marks, D. L., Fan, W., Kuhn, C. M., Bartholome, M., & Cone, R. D. (2001). Melanocortin-4 receptor is required for acute homeostatic responses to increased dietary fat. *Nature Neuroscience, 4,* 605–611. (10)

Butzlaff, R. L., & Hooley, J. M. (1998). Expressed emotion and psychiatric relapse. *Archives of General Psychiatry, 55,* 547–552. (15)

Byl, N. N., McKenzie, A., & Nagarajan, S. S. (2000). Differences in somatosensory hand organization in a healthy flutist and a flutist with focal hand dystonia: A case report. *Journal of Hand Therapy, 13,* 302–309. (5)

Byne, W., Tobet, S., Mattiace, L. A., Lasco, M. S., Kemether, E., Edgar, M. A., Morgello, S., Buchsbaum, M. S., & Jones, L. B. (2001). The interstitial nuclei of the human anterior hypothalamus: An investigation of variation with sex, sexual orientation, and HIV status. *Hormones and Behavior, 40,* 86–92. (11)

Cadoret, R., Troughton, E., & Woodworth, G. (1994). Evidence of heterogeneity of genetic effect in Iowa adoption studies. *Annals of the New York Academy of Sciences, 708,* 59–71. (15)

Cadoret, R. J., Yates, W. R., Troughton, E., Woodworth, G., & Stewart, M. A. (1995). Genetic-environmental interaction in the genesis of aggressivity and conduct disorders. *Archives of General Psychiatry, 52,* 916–924. (12)

Cahill, L., & McGaugh, J. L. (1998). Mechanisms of emotional arousal and lasting declarative memory. *Trends in Neurosciences, 21,* 294–299. (13)

Cahn, R., Borziex, M.-G., Aldinio, C., Toffano, G., & Cahn, J. (1989). Influence of monosialoganglioside inner ester on neurologic recovery after global cerebral ischemia in monkeys. *Stroke, 20,* 652–656. (5)

Cahn, W., Hulshoff, H. E., Lems, E. B. T. E., van Haren, N. E. M., Schnack, H. G., van der Linden, J. A., Schothorst, P. F., van Engeland, H., & Kahn, R. S. (2002). Brain volume changes in first-episode schizophrenia. *Archives of General Psychiatry, 59,* 1002–1010. (15)

Caicedo, A., & Roper, S. D. (2001). Taste receptor cells that discriminate between bitter stimuli. *Science, 291,* 1557–1560. (7)

Cajal, S. R. (1937). Recollections of my life. *Memoirs of the American Philosophical Society, 8.* (Original work published 1901–1917) (2)

Calder, A. J., Keane, J., Manes, F., Antoun, N., & Young, A. W. (2000). Impaired recognition and experience of disgust following brain injury. *Nature Neuroscience, 3,* 1077–1078. (12)

Calder, A. J., Lawrence, A. D., & Young, A. W. (2001). Neuropsychology of fear and loathing. *Nature Reviews Neuroscience, 2,* 352–363. (12)

Calignano, A., LaRana, G., Giuffrida, A., & Piomelli, D. (1998). Control of pain initiation by endogenous cannabinoids. *Nature, 394,* 277–281. (15)

Calne, D. B. (2002, Spring). What triggers the "shaking palsy"? *Cerebrum, 4*(2), 58–70. (8)

Cameron, H. A., & McKay, R. D. G. (1999). Restoring production of hippocampal neurons in old age. *Nature Neuroscience, 2,* 894–897. (12)

Campbell, S. (2000). Is there an intrinsic period of the circadian clock? *Science, 288,* 1174. (9)

Campbell, S. S., & Tobler, I. (1984). Animal sleep: A review of sleep duration across phylogeny. *Neuroscience and Biobehavioral Reviews, 8,* 269–300. (9)

Campfield, L. A., Smith, F. J., & Burn, P. (1998). Strategies and potential molecular targets for obesity treatment. *Science, 280,* 1383–1387. (10)

Campfield, L. A., Smith, F. J., Guisez, Y., Devos, R., & Burn, P. (1995). Recombinant mouse OB protein: Evidence for a peripheral signal linking adiposity and central neural networks. *Science, 269,* 546–552. (10)

Can, S., Zhu, Y.-S., Cai, L.-Q., Ling, Q., Katz, M. D., Akgun, S., Shackleton, C. H. L., & Imperato-McGinley, J. (1998). The identification of 5α-reductase 2 and 17β-hydrosteroid dehydrogenase-3 gene defects in male pseudohermaphrodites from a Turkish kindred. *Journal of Clinical Endocrinology & Metabolism, 83,* 560–569. (11)

Canavan, A. G. M., Sprengelmeyer, R., Diener, H.-C., & Hömberg, V. (1994). Conditional associative learning is impaired in cerebellar disease in humans. *Behavioral Neuroscience, 108,* 475–485. (4)

Canli, T. (1999). Hemispheric asymmetry in the experience of emotion: A perspective from functional imaging. *Neuroscientist, 5,* 201–207. (14)

Cannon, W. B. (1929). Organization for physiological homeostasis. *Physiological Reviews, 9,* 399–431. (10)

Cannon, W. B. (1942). "Voodoo" death. *American Anthropologist, 44,* 169–181. (12)

Cannon, W. B. (1945). *The way of an investigator.* New York: Norton. (inside cover)

Cantalupo, C., & Hopkins, W. D. (2001). Asymmetric Broca's area in great apes. *Nature, 414,* 505. (14)

Cao, Y. Q., Mantyh, P. W., Carlson, E. J., Gillespie, A.-M., Epstein, C. J., & Basbaum, A. I. (1998). Primary afferent tachykinins are required to experience moderate to intense pain. *Nature, 392,* 390–394. (7)

Cardno, A. G., Marshall, E. J., Coid, B., Macdonald, A. M., Ribchester, T. R., Davies, N. J., Venturi, P., Jones, L. A., Lewis, S. W., Sham, P. C., Gottesman, I. I., Farmer, A. E., McGuffin, P., Reveley, A. M., & Murray, R. M. (1999). Heritability estimates for psychotic disorders. *Archives of General Psychiatry, 56,* 162–168. (15)

Carello, C., LeVasseur, V. M., & Schmidt, R. C. (2002). Movement sequencing and phonological fluency in (putatively) nonimpaired readers. *Psychological Science, 13,* 375–379. (14)

Carlezon, W. A., Jr., Thome, J., Olson, V. G., Lane-Ladd, S. B., Brodkin, E. S., Hiroi, N., Duman, R. S., Neve, R. L., & Nestler, E. J. (1998). Regulation of cocaine reward by CREB. *Science, 282,* 2272–2275. (15)

Carlsson, A. (2001). A paradigm shift in brain research. *Science, 294,* 1021–1024. (3)

Carpenter, G. A., & Grossberg, S. (1984). A neural theory of circadian rhythms: Aschoff's rule in diurnal and nocturnal mammals. *American Journal of Physiology, 247,* R1067–R1082. (9)

Carruth, L. L., Reisert, I., & Arnold, A. P. (2002). Sex chromosome genes directly affect brain sexual differentiation. *Nature Neuroscience, 5,* 933–934. (11)

Carter, C. S. (1992). Hormonal influences on human sexual behavior. In J. B. Becker, S. M. Breedlove, &

D. Crews (Eds.), *Behavioral endocrinology* (pp. 131–142). Cambridge, MA: MIT Press. (11)

Castellucci, V. F., Pinsker, H., Kupfermann, I., & Kandel, E. (1970). Neuronal mechanisms of habituation and dishabituation of the gill-withdrawal reflex in *Aplysia. Science, 167,* 1745–1748. (13)

Catalano, S. M., & Shatz, C. J. (1998). Activity-dependent cortical target selection by thalamic axons. *Science, 281,* 559–562. (5)

Catchpole, C. K., & Slater, P. J. B. (1995). *Bird song: Biological themes and variations.* Cambridge, England: Cambridge University Press. (1)

Caterina, M. J., Leffler, A., Malmberg, A. B., Martin, W. J., Trafton, J., Petersen-Zeitz, K. R., Koltenburg, M., Basbaum, A. I., & Julius, D. (2000). Impaired nociception and pain sensation in mice lacking the capsaicin receptor. *Science, 288,* 306–313. (7)

Catterall, W. A. (1984). The molecular basis of neuronal excitability. *Science, 223,* 653–661. (2)

Censits, D. M., Ragland, J. D., Gur, R. C., & Gur, R. E. (1997). Neuropsychological evidence supporting a neurodevelopmental model of schizophrenia: A longitudinal study. *Schizophrenia Research, 24,* 289–298. (15)

Cerletti, U., & Bini, L. (1938). L'Elettro-shock [Electroshock]. *Archivio Generale di Neurologia e Psichiatria e Psicoanalisi, 19,* 266–268. (15)

Chalmers, D. J. (1995). Facing up to the problem of consciousness. *Journal of Consciousness Studies, 2,* 200–219. (1)

Chandra, V., Bharucha, N. E., & Schoenberg, B. S. (1984). Mortality data for the U.S. for deaths due to and related to twenty neurologic diseases. *Neuroepidemiology, 3,* 149–168. (8)

Chapin, J. K., Moxon, K. A., Markowitz, R. S., & Nicolelis, M. A. L. (1999). Real-time control of a robot arm using simultaneously recorded neurons in the motor cortex. *Nature Neuroscience, 2,* 664–670. (8)

Chase, T. N., Wexler, N. S., & Barbeau, A. (1979). *Advances in*

neurology: Vol. 23. Huntington's disease. New York: Raven Press. (8)

Chaudhari, N., Landin, A. M., & Roper, S. D. (2000). A metabotropic glutamate receptor variant functions as a taste receptor. *Nature Neuroscience, 3,* 113–119. (7)

Chawla, D., Rees, G., & Friston, K. J. (1999). The physiological basis of attentional modulation in extrastriate visual areas. *Nature Neuroscience, 2,* 671–676. (6)

Chen, G., Chen, K. S., Knox, J., Inglis, J., Bernard, A., Martin, S. J., Justice, A., McConlogue, L., Games, D., Freedman, S. B., & Morris, R. G. M. (2000). A learning deficit related to age and β–amyloid plaques in a mouse model of Alzheimer's disease. *Nature, 408,* 975–979. (13)

Cheour-Luhtanen, M., Alho, K., Sainio, K., Rinne, T., Reinikainen, K., Pohjavuoir, M., Renlund, M., Aaltonen, O., Eerola, O., & Näätänen, R. (1996). The ontogenetically earliest discriminative response of the human brain. *Psychophysiology, 33,* 478–481. (14)

Chiueh, C. C. (1988). Dopamine in the extrapyramidal motor function: A study based upon the MPTP-induced primate model of Parkinsonism. *Annals of the New York Academy of Sciences, 515,* 226–248. (8)

Cho, K. (2001). Chronic "jet lag" produces temporal lobe atrophy and spatial cognitive deficits. *Nature Neuroscience, 4,* 567–568. (9)

Choi-Lundberg, D. L., Lin, Q., Chang, Y.-N., Chiang, Y. L., Hay, C. M., Mohajeri, H., Davidson, B. L., & Bohn, M. C. (1997). Dopaminergic neurons protected from degeneration by GDNF gene therapy. *Science, 275,* 838–841. (5)

Chollet, F., & Weiller, C. (1994). Imaging recovery of function following brain injury. *Current Opinion in Neurobiology, 4,* 226–230. (5)

Chomsky, N. (1980). *Rules and representations.* New York: Columbia University Press. (14)

Chuang, H., Prescott, E. D., Kong, H., Shields, S., Jordt, S.-E., Basbaum,

A. I., Chao, M. V., & Julius, D. (2001). Bradykinin and nerve growth factor release the capsaicin receptor from PtdIns(4,5)P2-mediated inhibition. *Nature, 411,* 957–962. (7)

Churchland, P. S. (1996). The hornswoggle problem. *Journal of Consciousness, 3,* 402–408. (1)

Cicone, N., Wapner, W., Foldi, N. S., Zurif, E., & Gardner, H. (1979). The relation between gesture and language in aphasic communication. *Brain and Language, 8,* 324–349. (14)

Cirelli, C., Shaw, P. J., Rechtschaffen, A., & Tononi, G. (1999). No evidence of brain cell degeneration after long-term sleep deprivation in rats. *Brain Research, 840,* 184–193. (9)

Clahsen, H., & Almazen, M. (1998). Syntax and morphology in Williams syndrome. *Cognition, 68,* 167–198. (14)

Clark, D. A., Mitra, P. P., & Wang, S. S.-H. (2001). Scalable architecture in mammalian brains. *Nature, 411,* 189–193. (5)

Clark, K. B., Naritoku, D. K., Smith, D. C., Browning, R. A., & Jensen, R. A. (1999). Enhanced recognition memory following vagus nerve stimulation in human subjects. *Nature Neuroscience, 2,* 94–98. (13)

Clark, R. E., & Lavond, D. G. (1993). Reversible lesions of the red nucleus during acquisition and retention of a classically conditioned behavior in rabbits. *Behavioral Neuroscience, 107,* 264–270. (13)

Clarke, D. L., Johansson, C. B., Wilbertz, J., Veress, B., Nilsson, E., Karlström, H., Lendahl, U., & Frisén, J. (2000). Generalized potential of adult neural stem cells. *Science, 288,* 1660–1663. (5)

Clarke, S., Assal, G., & deTribolet, N. (1993). Left hemisphere strategies in visual recognition, topographical orientation and time planning. *Neuropsychologia, 31,* 99–113. (14)

Clayton, E. C., & Williams, C. L. (2000). Glutamatergic influences on the nucleus paragigantocellularis: Contribution to performance in avoidance and spatial memory tasks. *Behavioral Neuroscience, 114,* 707–712. (9)

Cleary, L. J., Hammer, M., & Byrne, J. H. (1989). Insights into the cellular mechanisms of short-term sensitization in *Aplysia*. In T. J. Carew & D. B. Kelley (Eds.), *Perspectives in neural systems and behavior* (pp. 105–119). New York: Liss. (13)

Clément, K., Vaisse, C., Lahlou, N., Cabrol, S., Pelloux, V., Cassuto, D., Gourmelen, M., Dina, C., Chambaz, J., Lacorte, J.-M., Basdevant, A., Bougnères, P., Lebouc, Y., Froguel, P., & Guy-Grand, B. (1998). A mutation in the human leptin receptor gene causes obesity and pituitary dysfunction. *Nature, 392,* 398–401. (10)

Clohessy, A. B., Posner, M. I., Rothbart, M. K., & Veccra, S. P. (1991). The development of inhibition of return in early infancy. *Journal of Cognitive Neuroscience, 3,* 345–350. (6)

Cloninger, C. R., Bohman, M., & Sigvardsson, S. (1981). Inheritance of alcohol abuse: Cross-fostering of adopted men. *Archives of General Psychiatry, 38,* 861–868. (15)

Clutton-Brock, T. H., O'Riain, M. J., Brotherton, P. N. M., Gaynor, D., Kansky, R., Griffin, A. S., & Manser, M. (1999). Selfish sentinels in cooperative mammals. *Science, 284,* 1640–1644. (1)

Coenen, A. M. L. (1995). Neuronal activities underlying the electroencephalogram of sleeping and waking: Implications for information processing. *Neuroscience and Biobehavioral Reviews, 19,* 447–463. (9)

Cohen, B., Novick, D., & Rubinstein, M. (1996). Modulation of insulin activities by leptin. *Science, 274,* 1185–1188. (10)

Cohen, B. M., Ennulat, D. J., Centorrino, F., Matthysse, S., Konieczna, H., Chu, H.-M., & Cherkerzian, S. (1999). Polymorphisms of the dopamine D$_4$ receptor and response to antipsychotic drugs. *Psychopharmacology, 141,* 6–10. (3)

Cohen, L. G., Weeks, R. A., Sadato, N., Celnik, P., Ishii, K., & Hallett, M. (1999). Period of susceptibility for cross-modal plasticity in the blind. *Annals of Neurology, 45,* 451–460. (6)

Cohen, R. A., Paul, R., Zawacki, T. M., Moser, D. J., Sweet, L., & Wilkinson, H. (2001). Emotional and personality changes following cingulotomy. *Emotion, 1,* 38–50. (12)

Cohen, S., Frank, E., Doyle, W. J., Skoner, D. P., Rabin, B. S., & Swaltney, J. M., Jr. (1998). Types of stressors that increase susceptibility to the common cold in healthy adults. *Health Psychology, 17,* 214–223. (12)

Cohen, S., & Williamson, G. M. (1991). Stress and infectious disease in humans. *Psychological Bulletin, 109,* 5–24. (12)

Cohen-Tannoudji, M., Babinet, C., & Wassef, M. (1994). Early determination of a mouse somatosensory cortex marker. *Nature, 368,* 460–463. (5)

Colantuoni, C., Rada, P., McCarthy, J., Patten, C., Avena, N. M., Chadeayne, A., & Hoebel, B. G. (2002). Evidence that intermittent, excessive sugar intake causes endogenous opioid dependence. *Obesity Research, 10,* 478–488. (10)

Colantuoni, C., Schwenker, J., McCarthy, J., Rada, P., Ladenheim, B., Cadet, J.-L., Schwartz, G. J., Moran, T. H., & Hoebel, B. G. (2001). Excessive sugar intake alters binding to dopamine and mu-opioid receptors in the brain. *NeuroReport, 12,* 3549–3552. (10)

Colapinto, J. (1997, December 11). The true story of John/Joan. *Rolling Stone,* pp. 54–97. (11)

Colbourne, F., & Corbett, D. (1995). Delayed postischemic hypothermia: A six-month survival study using behavioral and histological assessments of neuroprotection. *Journal of Neuroscience, 15,* 7250–7260. (5)

Colbourne, F., Sutherland, G. R., & Auer, R. N. (1999). Electron microscopic evidence against apoptosis as the mechanism of neuronal death in global ischemia. *Journal of Neuroscience, 19,* 4200–4210. (5)

Collier, D. A. (2002). FISH, flexible joints and panic: Are anxiety disorders really expressions of instability in the human genome? *British Journal of Psychiatry, 181,* 457–459. (12)

Collier, T. J., Sortwell, C. E., & Daley, B. F. (1999). Diminished viability, growth, and behavioral efficacy of fetal dopamine neuron grafts in aging rats with long-term dopamine depletion: An argument for neurotrophic supplementation. *Journal of Neuroscience, 19,* 5563–5573. (8)

Comings, D. E. (2001). Clinical and molecular genetics of ADHD and Tourette syndrome. *Annals of the New York Academy of Sciences, 931,* 50–83. (7)

Comings, D. E., & Amromin, G. D. (1974). Autosomal dominant insensitivity to pain with hyperplastic myelinopathy and autosomal dominant indifference to pain. *Neurology, 24,* 838–848. (7)

Comuzzie, A. G., & Allison, D. B. (1998). The search for human obesity genes. *Science, 280,* 1374–1377. (10)

Considine, R. V., Sinha, M. K., Heiman, M. L., Kriauciunas, A., Stephens, T. W., Nyce, M. R., Ohannesian, J. P., Maarco, C. C., McKee, L. J., Bauer, T. L., & Caro, J. F. (1996). Serum immunoreactive-leptin concentrations in normal-weight and obese humans. *New England Journal of Medicine, 334,* 292–295. (10)

Constantinidis, C., Franowicz, W. N., & Goldman-Rakic, P. S. (2001). The sensory nature of mnemonic representation in the primate prefrontal cortex. *Nature Neuroscience, 4,* 311–316. (13)

Conti, A. C., Raghupathi, R., Trojanowski, J. Q., & McIntosh, T. K. (1998). Experimental brain injury induces regionally distinct apoptosis during the acute and delayed post-traumatic period. *Journal of Neuroscience, 18,* 5663–5672. (5)

Cooke, B. M., Tabibnia, G., & Breedlove, S. M. (1999). A brain sexual dimorphism controlled by adult circulating androgens. *Proceedings of the National Academy of Sciences, USA, 96,* 7538–7540. (11)

Coppola, D. M., Purves, H. R., McCoy, A. N., & Purves, D. (1998). The distribution of oriented contours in the real world. *Proceedings of the National Academy of Sciences, USA, 95,* 4002–4006. (6)

Corballis, M. C. (1999). The gestural origins of language. *American Scientist, 87,* 138–145. (14)

Corbetta, M., & Shulman, G. L. (2002). Control of goal-directed and stimulus-driven attention in the brain. *Nature Reviews Neuroscience, 3,* 201–215. (7)

Corder, E. H., Saunders, A. M., Strittmatter, W. J., Schmechel, D. E., Gaskell, P. C., Small, G. W., Roses, A. D., Haines, J. L., & Pericak-Vance, M. A. (1993). Gene dose of apolipoprotein E type 4 allele and the risk of Alzheimer's disease in late onset families. *Science, 261,* 921–923. (13)

Coren, S., & Porac, C. (1977). Fifty centuries of right-handedness: The historical record. *Science, 198,* 631–632. (14)

Corkin, S. (1984). Lasting consequences of bilateral medial temporal lobectomy: Clinical course and experimental findings in H. M. *Seminars in Neurology, 4,* 249–259. (13)

Corkin, S. (2002). What's new with the amnesic patient H. M.? *Nature Reviews Neuroscience, 3,* 153–159. (13)

Cornelissen, P., Richardson, A., Mason, A., Fowler, S., & Stein, J. (1995). Contrast sensitivity and coherent motion detection measured at photopic luminance levels in dyslexics and controls. *Vision Research, 35,* 1483–1494. (14)

Cornette, L., Dupont, P., Rosier, A., Sunaert, S., Van Hecke, P., Michiels, J., Mortelmans, L., & Orban, G. A. (1998). Human brain regions involved in direction discrimination. *Journal of Neurophysiology, 79,* 2749–2765. (6)

Coss, R. G., Brandon, J. G., & Globus, A. (1980). Changes in morphology of dendritic spines on honeybee calycal interneurons associated with cumulative nursing and foraging experiences. *Brain Research, 192,* 49–59. (5)

Cotman, C. W., & Nieto-Sampedro, M. (1982). Brain function, synapse renewal, and plasticity. *Annual Review of Psychology, 33,* 371–401. (5)

Cotter, D., Mackay, D., Landau, S., Kerwin, R., & Everall, I. (2001). Reduced glial cell density and neuronal size in the anterior cingulate cortex in major depressive disorder. *Archives of General Psychiatry, 58,* 545–553. (15)

Cowey, A., & Stoerig, P. (1995). Blindsight in monkeys. *Nature, 373,* 247–249. (6)

Crabbe, J. C., Wahlsten, D., & Dudek, B. C. (1999). Genetics of mouse behavior: Interactions with laboratory environment. *Science, 284,* 1670–1672. (1)

Craddock, N., & Jones, I. (1999). Genetics of bipolar disorder. *Journal of Medical Genetics, 36,* 585–594. (15)

Craft, S., Asthana, S., Newcomer, J. W., Wilkinson, C. W., Matos, I. T., Baker, L. D., Cherrier, M., Lofgreen, C., Latandresse, S., Petrova, A., Plymate, S., Raskind, M., Grimwood, K., & Veith, R. C. (1999). Enhancement of memory in Alzheimer's disease with insulin and somatostatin, but not glucose. *Archives of General Psychiatry, 56,* 1135–1140. (13)

Craig, A. D., Krout, K., & Andrew, D. (2001). Quantitative response characteristics of thermoreceptive and nociceptive lamina I spinothalamic neurons in the cat. *Journal of Neurophysiology, 86,* 1459–1480. (7)

Craig, A. M., & Boudin, H. (2001). Molecular heterogeneity of central synapses: Afferent and target regulation. *Nature Neuroscience, 4,* 569–578. (3)

Crair, M. C., Gillespie, D. C., & Stryker, M. P. (1998). The role of visual experience in the development of columns in cat visual cortex. *Science, 279,* 566–570. (6)

Crair, M. C., & Malenka, R. C. (1995). A critical period for long-term potentiation at thalamocortical synapses. *Nature, 375,* 325–328. (6)

Cravchik, A., & Goldman, D. (2000). Neurochemical individuality. *Archives of General Psychiatry, 57,* 1105–1114. (3)

Cremers, C. W. R. J., & van Rijn, P. M. (1991). Acquired causes of deafness in childhood. *Annals of* the *New York Academy of Sciences, 630*, 197–202. (7)

Crick, F., & Mitchison, G. (1983). The function of dream sleep. *Nature, 304*, 111–114. (9)

Critchley, H. D., Mathias, C. J., & Dolan, R. J. (2001). Neuroanatomical basis for first- and second-order representations of bodily states. *Nature Neuroscience, 4*, 207–212. (12)

Critchley, H. D., & Rolls, E. T. (1996). Hunger and satiety modify the responses of olfactory and visual neurons in the primate orbito-frontal cortex. *Journal of Neuro-physiology, 75*, 1673–1686. (10)

Crosio, C., Cermakian, N., Allis, C. D., & Sassone-Corsi, P. (2000). Light induces chromatin modification in cells of the mammalian circadian clock. *Nature Neuroscience, 3*, 1241–1247. (9)

Culebras, A. (1996). *Clinical handbook of sleep disorders.* Boston: Butterworth-Heinemann. (9)

Curran, S., Mill, J., Tahir, E., Kent, L., Richards, S., Gould, A., Huckett, L., Sharp, J. Batten, C., Fernando, S., Ozbay, F., Yazgan, Y., Simonoff, E., Thompson, M., Taylor, E., & Asherson, P. (2001). Association study of a dopamine transporter polymorphism and attention deficit hyperactivity disorder in UK and Turkish samples. *Molecular Psychiatry, 6*, 425–428. (7)

Curtis, A. L., Bello, N. T., & Valentine, R. J. (2001). Evidence for functional release of endogenous opioids in the locus ceruleus during stress termination. *Journal of Neuroscience, 21*, RC 152: 1–5. (15)

Curtiss, S., de Bode, S., & Mathern, G. W. (2001). Spoken language outcomes after hemispherectomy: Factoring in etiology. *Brain and Language, 79*, 379–396. (5, 14)

Cusack, R., Carlyon, R. P., & Robertson, I. H. (2000). Neglect between but not within auditory objects. *Journal of Cognitive Neuroscience, 12*, 1056–1065. (7)

Cutler, W. B., Preti, G., Krieger, A., Huggins, G. R., Garcia, C. R., & Lawley, H. J. (1986). Human axillary secretions influence women's menstrual cycles: The role of

donor extract from men. *Hormones and Behavior, 20*, 463–473. (7)

Cynader, M., & Chernenko, G. (1976). Abolition of direction selectivity in the visual cortex of the cat. *Science, 193*, 504–505. (6)

Cyranowski, J. M., Frank, E., Young, E., & Shear, K. (2000). Adolescent onset of the gender difference in lifetime rates of major depression. *Archives of General Psychiatry, 57*, 21–27. (15)

Czeisler, C. A., Duffy, J. F., Shanahan, T. L., Brown, E. N., Mitchell, J. F., Rimmer, D. W., Ronda, J. M., Silva, E. J., Allan, J. S., Emens, J. S., Dijk, D.-J., & Kronauer, R. E. (1999). Stability, precision, and near-24-hour period of the human circadian pacemaker. *Science, 284*, 2177–2181. (9)

Czeisler, C. A., Johnson, M. P., Duffy, J. F., Brown, E. N., Ronda, J. M., & Kronauer, R. E. (1990). Exposure to bright light and darkness to treat physiologic maladaptation to night work. *New England Journal of Medicine, 322*, 1253–1259. (9)

Czeisler, C. A., Weitzman, E. D., Moore-Ede, M. C., Zimmerman, J. C., & Knauer, R. S. (1980). Human sleep: Its duration and organization depend on its circadian phase. *Science, 210*, 1264–1267. (9)

Dabbs, J. M., Jr., Carr, T. S., Frady, R. L., & Riad, J. K. (1995). Testosterone, crime, and misbehavior among 692 male prison inmates. *Personality and Individual Differences, 18*, 627–633. (12)

Dale, N., Schacher, S., & Kandel, E. R. (1988). Long-term facilitation in Aplysia involves increase in transmitter release. *Science, 239*, 282–285. (13)

Dalman, C., Allebeck, P., Cullberg, J., Grunewald, C., & Köstler, M. (1999). Obstetric complications and the risk of schizophrenia. *Archives of General Psychiatry, 56*, 234–240. (15)

Dalterio, S., & Bartke, A. (1979). Perinatal exposure to cannabinoids alters male reproductive function in mice. *Science, 205*, 1420–1422. (11)

Dalton, K. (1968). Ante-natal progesterone and intelligence. *British*

Journal of Psychiatry, 114, 1377–1382. (11)

Damasio, A. (1999). *The feeling of what happens.* New York: Harcourt Brace. (12)

Damasio, A. R. (1994). *Descartes' error.* New York: Putnam's Sons. (12)

Damasio, A. R., Grabowski, T. J., Bechara, A., Damasio, H., Ponto, L. L. B., Parvizi, J., & Hichwa, R. D. (2000). Subcortical and cortical brain activity during the feeling of self-generated emotions. *Nature Neuroscience, 3*, 1049–1056. (12)

Damsma, G., Pfaus, J. G., Wenkstern, D., Phillips, A. G., & Fibiger, H. C. (1992). Sexual behavior increases dopamine transmission in the nucleus accumbens and striatum of male rats: A comparison with novelty and locomotion. *Behavioral Neuroscience, 106*, 181–191. (15)

Darwin, C. (1859). *The origin of species.* New York: D. Appleton. (1)

Dauvilliers, Y., Neidhart, E., Lecendreux, M., Billiard, M., & Tafti, M. (2001). MAO-A and COMT polymorphisms and gene effects in narcolepsy. *Molecular Psychiatry, 6*, 367–372. (9)

Dávalos, A., Castillo, J., & Martinez-Vila, E. (1995). Delay in neurological attention and stroke outcome. *Stroke, 26*, 2233–2237. (5)

Davidson, R. J. (1984). Affect, cognition, and hemispheric specialization. In C. E. Izard, J. Kagan, & R. B. Zajonc (Eds.), *Emotions, cognition, & behavior* (pp. 320–365). Cambridge, England: Cambridge University Press. (15)

Davidson, R. J., Putnam, K. M., & Larson, C. L. (2000). Dysfunction in the neural circuitry of emotion regulation: A possible prelude to violence. *Science, 289*, 591–594. (12)

Davies, P. (2000). A very incomplete comprehensive theory of Alzheimer's disease. *Annals of the New York Academy of Sciences, 924*, 8–16. (13)

Davis, E. C., Shryne, J. E., & Gorski, R. A. (1995). A revised critical period for the sexual differentiation of the sexually dimorphic nucleus of the preoptic area in the rat. *Neuroendocrinology, 62,* 579–585. (11)

Davis, K. D., Kiss, Z. H. T., Luo, L., Tasker, R. R., Lozano, A. M., & Dostrovsky, J. O. (1998). Phantom sensations generated by thalamic microstimulation. *Nature, 391,* 385–387. (5)

Davis, N., & LeVere, T. E. (1982). Recovery of function after brain damage: The question of individual behaviors or functionality. *Experimental Neurology, 75,* 68–78. (5)

Dawkins, R. (1989). *The selfish gene* (new ed.). Oxford, England: Oxford University Press. (1)

Dawson, T. M., Gonzalez-Zulueta, M., Kusel, J., & Dawson, V. L. (1998). Nitric oxide: Diverse actions in the central and peripheral nervous system. *Neuroscientist, 4,* 96–112. (3)

de Castro, J. M. (2000). Eating behavior: Lessons from the real world of humans. *Nutrition, 16,* 800–813. (10)

de Castro, J. M. (2002). Independence of heritable influences on the food intake of free-living humans. *Nutrition, 18,* 11–16. (10)

de Castro, J. M., & Plunkett, S. (2002). A general model of intake regulation. *Neuroscience and Biobehavioral Reviews, 26,* 581–595. (10)

de Jong, W. W., Hendriks, W., Sanyal, S., & Nevo, E. (1990). The eye of the blind mole rat (Spalax ehrenbergi): Regressive evolution at the molecular level. In E. Nevo & O. A. Reig (Eds.), *Evolution of subterranean mammals at the organismal and molecular levels* (pp. 383–395). New York: Liss (9)

de Jonge, F. H., Louwerse, A. L., Ooms, M. P., Evers, P., Endert, E., & Van De Poll, N. E. (1989). Lesions of the SDN-POA inhibit sexual behavior of male Wistar rats. *Brain Research Bulletin, 23,* 483–492. (11)

de la Iglesia, H. O., Meyer, J., Carpino, A., Jr., & Schwartz, W. J. (2000). Antiphase oscillation of the left and right suprachiasmatic nuclei. *Science, 290,* 799–801. (9)

De Luca, M., Di Page, E., Judica, A., Spinelli, D., & Zoccolotti, P. (1999). Eye movement patterns in linguistic and non-linguistic tasks in developmental surface dyslexia. *Neuropsychologia, 37,* 1407–1420. (14)

de Winter, W., & Oxnard, C. E. (2001). Evolutionary radiations and convergences in the structural organization of mammalian brains. *Nature, 409,* 710–714. (5)

de Wit, H., Crean, J., & Richards, J. B. (2000). Effects of d-amphetamine and ethanol on a measure of behavioral inhibition in humans. *Behavioral Neuroscience, 114,* 830–837. (7)

Deacon, T., Schumacher, J., Dinsmore, J., Thomas, C., Palmer, P., Kott, S., Edge, A., Penney, D., Kassissieh, S., Dempsey, P., & Isacson, O. (1997). Histological evidence of fetal pig neural cell survival after transplantation into a patient with Parkinson's disease. *Nature Medicine, 3,* 350–353. (8)

Deacon, T. W. (1990). Problems of ontogeny and phylogeny in brain-size evolution. *International Journal of Primatology, 11,* 237–282. (4)

Deacon, T. W. (1992). Brain-language coevolution. In J. A. Hawkins & M. Gell-Mann (Eds.), *The evolution of human languages* (pp. 49–83). Reading, MA: Addison-Wesley. (14)

Deacon, T. W. (1997). *The symbolic species.* New York: Norton (14)

DeArmond, S. J., Fusco, M. M., & Dewey, M. M. (1974). *Structure of the human brain.* New York: Oxford University Press. (10)

DeCoursey, P. (1960). Phase control of activity in a rodent. *Cold Spring Harbor symposia on quantitative biology, 25,* 49–55. (9)

DeFelipe, C., Herrero, J. F., O'Brien, J. A., Palmer, J. A., Doyle, C. A., Smith, A. J. H., Laird, J. M. A., Belmonte, C., Cervero, F., & Hunt, S. P. (1998). Altered nociception, analgesia and aggression in mice lacking the receptor for substance P. *Nature, 392,* 394–397. (7)

Degn, B., Lundorf, M. D., Wang, A., Vang, M., Ors, O., Kruse, T. A., & Ewald, H. (2001). Further evidence for a bipolar risk gene on chromosome 12q24 suggested by investigation of haplotype sharing and allelic association in patients from the Faroe Islands. *Molecular Psychiatry, 6,* 450–455. (15)

Dehaene, S., Naccache, L., Cohen, L., LeBihan, D., Mangin, J.-F., Poline, J.-B., & Rivière, D. (2001). Cerebral mechanisms of word masking and unconscious repetition priming. *Nature Neuroscience, 4,* 752–758. (7)

Del Cerro, M. C. R., Perez Izquierdo, M. A., Rosenblatt, J. S., Johnson, B. M., Pacheco, P., & Komisaruk, B. R. (1995). Brain 2-deoxyglucose levels related to maternal behavior-inducing stimuli in the rat. *Brain Research, 696,* 213–220. (11)

Del Punta, K., Leinders-Zufall, T., Rodriguez, I., Jukam, D., Wysocki, C. J., Ogawa, S., Zufall, F., & Mombaerts, P. (2002). Deficient pheromone responses in mice lacking a cluster of vomeronasal receptor genes. *Nature, 419,* 70–74. (7)

Delahanty, D. L., Raimonde, A. J., & Spoonster, E. (2000). Initial post-traumatic urinary cortisol levels predict subsequent PTSD symptoms in motor vehicle accident victims. *Biological Psychiatry, 48,* 940–947. (12)

Delgado, J. M. R. (1981). Neuronal constellations in aggressive behavior. In L. Valzelli & L. Morgese (Eds.), *Aggression and violence: A psycho/biological and clinical approach* (pp. 82–98). Milan, Italy: Edizioni Saint Vincent. (12)

Deliagina, T. G., Orlovsky, G. N., & Pavlova, G. A. (1983). The capacity for generation of rhythmic oscillations is distributed in the lumbosacral spinal cord of the cat. *Experimental Brain Research, 53,* 81–90. (8)

Delville, Y., Mansour, K. M., & Ferris, C. F. (1996). Testosterone facilitates aggression by modulating vasopressin receptors in the hypothalamus. *Physiology & Behavior, 60,* 25–29. (12)

Dement, W. (1960). The effect of dream deprivation. *Science, 131,* 1705–1707. (9)

Dement, W. (1972). *Some must watch while some must sleep.* San Francisco: Freeman. (9, inside cover)

Dement, W. C. (1990). A personal history of sleep disorders medicine. *Journal of Clinical Neurophysiology, 7,* 17–47. (9)

Dement, W., Ferguson, J., Cohen, H., & Barchas, J. (1969). Non-chemical methods and data using a biochemical model: The REM quanta. In A. J. Mandell & M. P. Mandell (Eds.), *Psychochemical research in man* (pp. 275–325). New York: Academic Press. (9)

Dement, W., & Kleitman, N. (1957a). Cyclic variations in EEG during sleep and their relation to eye movements, body motility, and dreaming. *Electroencephalography and Clinical Neurophysiology, 9,* 673–690. (9)

Dement, W., & Kleitman, N. (1957b). The relation of eye movements during sleep to dream activity: An objective method for the study of dreaming. *Journal of Experimental Psychology, 53,* 339–346. (9)

Dennett, D. C. (1991). *Consciousness explained.* Boston, MA: Little, Brown. (1, 6)

Dennett, D. C. (1996). Facing backwards on the problem of consciousness. *Journal of Consciousness, 3,* 4–6. (1)

deQuervain, D. J.-F., Roozendaal, B., & McGaugh, J. L. (1998). Stress and glucocorticoids impair retrieval of long-term spatial memory. *Nature, 394,* 787–790. (13)

deQuervain, D. J.-F., Roozendaal, B., Nitsch, R. M., McGaugh, J. L., & Hock, C. (2000). Acute cortisone administration impairs retrieval of long-term declarative memory in humans. *Nature Neuroscience, 3,* 313–314. (12)

Desiderato, O., MacKinnon, J. R., & Hissom, H. (1974). Development of gastric ulcers in rats following stress termination. *Journal of Comparative and Physioloigcal Psychology, 87,* 208–214. (12)

DeSimone, J. A., Heck, G. L., & Bartoshuk, L. M. (1980). Surface active taste modifiers: A comparison of the physical and psychophysical properties of gymnemic acid and sodium lauryl sulfate. *Chemical Senses, 5,* 317–330. (7)

DeSimone, J. A., Heck, G. L., Mierson, S., & DeSimone, S. K. (1984). The active ion transport properties of canine lingual epithelia in vitro. *Journal of General Physiology, 83,* 633–656. (7)

Detre, J. A., & Floyd, T. F. (2001). Functional MRI and its applica-tions to the clinical neurosciences. *Neuroscientist, 7,* 64–79. (6)

Deutsch, J. A., & Ahn, S. J. (1986). The splanchnic nerve and food intake regulation. *Behavioral and Neural Biology, 45,* 43–47. (10)

Deutsch, J. A., Young, W. G., & Kalogeris, T. J. (1978). The stomach signals satiety. *Science, 201,* 165–167. (10)

DeValois, R. L., Albrecht, D. G., & Thorell, L. G. (1982). Spatial frequency selectivity of cells in macaque visual cortex. *Vision Research, 22,* 545–559. (6)

DeValois, R. L., & Jacobs, G. H. (1968). Primate color vision. *Science, 162,* 533–540. (6)

Devane, W. A., Dysarz, F. A. III, Johnson, M. R., Melvin, L. S., & Howlett, A. C. (1988). Determination and characterization of a cannabinoid receptor in rat brain. *Molecular Pharmacology, 34,* 605–613. (15)

Devor, E. J., Abell, C. W., Hoffman, P. L., Tabakoff, B., & Cloninger, C. R. (1994). Platelet MAO activity in Type I and Type II alcoholism. *Annals of the New York Academy of Sciences, 708,* 119–128. (15)

Devor, M. (1996). Pain mechanisms. *The Neuroscientist, 2,* 233–244. (7)

Dew, M. A., Reynolds, C. F., III, Buysse, D. J., Houck, P. R., Hoch, C. C., Monk, T. H., & Kupfer, D. J. (1996). Electroencephalographic sleep profiles during depression. *Archives of General Psychiatry, 53,* 148–156. (15)

DeYoe, E. A., Felleman, D. J., Van Essen, D. C., & McClendon, E. (1994). Multiple processing streams in occipitotemporal visual cortex. *Nature, 371,* 151–154. (6)

Di Pasquale, M. (1997). *Amino acids and proteins for the athlete: The anabolic edge.* Boca Raton, FL: CRC Press. (11)

Diamond, D. M., Bennett, M. C., Fleshner, M., & Rose, G. M. (1992). Inverted-U relationship between the level of peripheral corticosterone and the magnitude of hippocampal primed burst potentiation. *Hippocampus, 2,* 421–430. (12)

Diamond, M., & Sigmundson, H. K. (1997). Management of intersexuality: Guidelines for dealing with persons with ambiguous genitalia. *Archives of Pediatrics and Adolescent Medicine, 151,* 1046–1050. (11)

Diamond, M. C., Scheibel, A. B., Murphy, G. M., & Harvey, T. (1985). On the brain of a scientist: Albert Einstein. *Experimental Neurology, 88,* 198–204. (4)

Dichgans, J. (1984). Clinical symptoms of cerebellar dysfunction and their topodiagnostic significance. *Human Neurobiology, 2,* 269–279. (8)

Dick, D. M., Johnson, J. K., Viken, R. J., & Rose, R. J. (2000). Testing between-family associations in within-family comparisons. *Psychological Science, 11,* 409–413. (15)

Dick, F., Bates, E., Wulfeck, B., Utman, J. A., Dronkers, N., & Gernsbacher, M. A. (2001). Language deficits, localization, and grammar: Evidence for a distributive model of language breakdown in aphasic patients and neurologically intact individuals. *Psychological Review, 108,* 759–788. (14)

Dickens, W. T., & Flynn, J. R. (2001). Heritability estimates versus large environmental effects: The IQ paradox resolved. *Psychological Review, 108,* 346–369. (1)

Diedrichsen, J., Hazeltine, E., Kennerley, S., & Ivry, R. B. (2001). Moving to directly cued locations abolishes spatial interference during bimanual actions. *Psychological Science, 12,* 493–498. (14)

Dierks, T., Linden, D. E. J., Jandl, M., Formisano, E., Goebel, R., Lanfermann, H., & Singer, W. (1999). Activation of Heschl's gyrus during auditory hallucinations. *Neuron, 22,* 615–621. (4)

Dijk, D.-J., & Cajochen, C. (1997). Melatonin and the circadian regulation of sleep initiation, consolidation, structure, and the sleep EEG. *Journal of Biological Rhythms, 12,* 627–635. (9)

DiMarzo, V., Fontana, A., Cadas, H., Schinelli, S., Cimino, G., Schwartz, J.-C., & Piomelli, D. (1994). Formation and inactivation of endogenous cannabinoid anandamide in central neurons. *Nature, 372,* 686–691. (15)

DiMarzo, V., Goparaju, S. K., Wang, L., Liu, J., Bátkai, S., Járai, Z.,

Fessa, F., Miura, G. I., Palmiter, R. D., Sugiura, T., & Kunos, G. (2001). Leptin-regulated endocannabinoids are involved in maintaining food intake. *Nature, 410,* 822–825. (10, 15)

Dimberg, U., Thunberg, M., & Elmehed, K. (2000). Unconscious facial reactions to emotional facial expressions. *Psychological Science, 11,* 86–89. (7)

Dimond, S. J. (1979). Symmetry and asymmetry in the vertebrate brain. In D. A. Oakley & H. C. Plotkin (Eds.), *Brain, behaviour, and evolution* (pp. 189–218). London: Methuen. (14)

Dixon, N. F. (1981). *Preconscious processing.* New York: Wiley. (7)

Dong, E., Maatsumoto, K., Tohda, M., Kaneko, Y., & Watanabe, H. (1999). Diazepam binding inhibitor (DBI) gene expression in the brains of socially isolated and group-housed mice. *Neuroscience Research, 33,* 171–177. (12)

Dörner, G. (1974). Sex-hormone-dependent brain differentiation and sexual functions. In G. Dörner (Ed.), *Endocrinology of sex* (pp. 30–37). Leipzig: Barth. (11)

Dörner, G., Götz, F., Rohde, W., Plagemann, A., Lindner, R., Peters, H., & Ghanaati, Z. (2001). Genetic and epigenetic effects on sexual brain organization mediated by sex hormones. *Neuroendocrinology Letters, 22,* 403–409. (11)

Dowling, J. E. (1987). *The retina.* Cambridge, MA: Harvard University Press. (6)

Dowling, J. E., & Boycott, B. B. (1966). Organization of the primate retina. *Proceedings of the Royal Society of London, B, 166,* 80–111. (6)

Drachman, D. B. (1978). Myasthenia gravis. *New England Journal of Medicine, 298,* 136–142, 186–193. (8)

Dragoi, V., Rivadulla, C., & Sur, M. (2001). Foci of orientation plasticity in visual cortex. *Nature, 411,* 80–86. (6)

Dreger, A. D. (1998). *Hermaphrodites and the medical invention of sex.* Cambridge, MA: Harvard University Press. (11)

Drewnowski, A., Henderson, S. A., Shore, A. B., & Barratt-Fornell, A. (1998). Sensory responses to 6-*n*-propylthiouracil (PROP) or sucrose solutions and food preferences in young women. *Annals of the New York Academy of Sciences, 855,* 797–801. (7)

Driver, J., & Frith, C. (2000). Shifting baselines in attention research. *Nature Reviews Neuroscience, 1,* 147–148. (6)

Driver, J., & Mattingley, J. B. (1998). Parietal neglect and visual awareness. *Nature Neuroscience, 1,* 17–22. (7)

Duara, R., Kushch, A., Gross-Glenn, K., Barker, W. W., Jallad, B., Pascal, S., Loewenstein, D. A., Sheldon, J., Rabin, M., Levin, B., & Lubs, H. (1991). Neuroanatomic differences between dyslexic and normal readers on magnetic resonance imaging scans. *Archives of Neurology, 48,* 410–416. (14)

Dudchenko, P. A., & Taube, J. S. (1997). Correlation between head direction cell activity and spatial behavior on a radial arm maze. *Behavioral Neuroscience, 111,* 3–19. (13)

Duelli, R., & Kuschinsky, W. (2001). Brain glucose transporters: Relationship to local energy demand. *News in Physiological Sciences, 16,* 71–76. (2)

Duman, R. S., Heninger, G. R., & Nestler, E. J. (1997). A molecular and cellular theory of depression. *Archives of General Psychiatry, 54,* 597–606. (15)

Dunlap, J. L., Zadina, J. E., & Gougis, G. (1978). Prenatal stress interacts with prepubertal social isolation to reduce male copulatory behavior. *Physiology & Behavior, 21,* 873–875. (11)

Dunnett, S. B., & Björklund, A. (1999). Prospects for new restorative and neuroprotective treatments in Parkinson's disease. *Nature, 399*(Suppl.), A32–A39. (8)

Dunnett, S. B., Ryan, C. N., Levin, P. D., Reynolds, M., & Bunch, S. T. (1987). Functional consequences of embryonic neocortex transplanted to rats with prefrontal cortex lesions. *Behavioral Neuroscience, 101,* 489–503. (8)

DuPaul, G. J., McGoey, K. E., Eckert, T. L., & vanBrakle, J. (2001). Preschool children with attention-deficit/hyperactivity disorder: Impairments in behavioral, social, and school functioning. *Journal of the American Academy of Child & Adolescent Psychiatry, 40,* 508–515. (7)

During, M. J., Ryder, K. M., & Spencer, D. D. (1995). Hippocampal GABA transporter function in temporal-lobe epilepsy. *Nature, 376,* 174–177. (14)

Dyal, J. A. (1971). Transfer of behavioral bias: Reality and specificity. In E. J. Fjerdingstad (Ed.), *Chemical transfer of learned information* (pp. 219–263). New York: American Elsevier. (13)

Earnest, D. J., Liang, F.-Q., Ratcliff, M., & Cassone, V. M. (1999). Immortal time: Circadian clock properties of rat suprachiasmatic cell lines. *Science, 283,* 693–695. (9)

Eastman, C. I., Hoese, E. K., Youngstedt, S. D., & Liu, L. (1995). Phase-shifting human circadian rhythms with exercise during the night shift. *Physiology & Behavior, 58,* 1287–1291. (9)

Eastman, C. I., Young, M. A., Fogg, L. F., Liu, L., & Meaden, P. M. (1998). Bright light treatment of winter depression. *Archives of General Psychiatry, 55,* 883–889. (15)

Ebstein, R. P., Novick, O., Umansky, R., Priel, B., Osher, Y., Blaine, D., Bennett, E. R., Nemanov, L., Katz, M., & Belmaker, R. H. (1996). Dopamine D4 receptor (D4DR) exon III polymorphism associated with the personality trait of Novelty Seeking. *Nature Genetics, 12,* 78–80. (3)

Eccles, J. C. (1964). *The physiology of synapses.* Berlin: Springer-Verlag. (3)

Eccles, J. C. (1986). Chemical transmission and Dale's principle. In T. Hökfelt, K. Fuxe, & B. Pernow (Eds.), *Progress in brain research* (Vol. 68, pp. 3–13). Amsterdam: Elsevier. (3)

Eckhorn, R., Bauer, R., Jordan, W., Brosch, M., Kruse, W., Munk, M., & Reitboeck, H. J. (1988). Coherent oscillations: A mechanism of feature linking in the visual cortex? *Biological Cybernetics, 60,* 121–130. (4)

Edelman, G. M. (1987). *Neural Darwinism.* New York: Basic Books. (5)

Edelman, G. (2001). Consciousness: The remembered present. *Annals of the New York Academy of Sciences, 929*, 111–122. (1)

Edinger, J. D., McCall, W. V., Marsh, G. R., Radtke, R. A., Erwin, C. W., & Lininger, A. (1992). Periodic limb movement variability in older DIMS patients across consecutive nights of home monitoring. *Sleep, 15*, 156–161. (9)

Edman, G., Åsberg, M., Levander, S., & Schalling, D. (1986). Skin conductance habituation and cerebrospinal fluid 5-hydroxyindoleacetic acid in suicidal patients. *Archives of General Psychiatry, 43*, 586–592. (12)

Egan, M. F., Goldberg, T. E., Kolachana, B. S., Callicott, J. H., Mazzanti, C. M., Straub, R. E., Goldman, D., & Weinberger, D. R. (2001). Effect of COMT Val$^{108/158}$ Met genotype on frontal lobe function and risk for schizophrenia. *Proceedings of the National Academy of Sciences, USA, 98*, 6917–6922. (15)

Egeland, J. A., Gerhard, D. S., Pauls, D. L., Sussex, J. N., Kidd, K. K., Allen, C. R., Hostetter, A. M., & Housman, D. E. (1987). Bipolar affective disorders linked to DNA markers on chromosome 11. *Nature, 325*, 783–787. (15)

Ehrhardt, A. A., Meyer-Bahlburg, H. F. L., Rosen, L. R., Feldman, J. F., Veridiano, N. P., Zimmerman, I., & McEwen, B. S. (1985). Sexual orientation after prenatal exposure to exogenous estrogen. *Archives of Sexual Behavior, 14*, 57–77. (11)

Ehrhardt, A. A., & Money, J. (1967). Progestin-induced hermaphroditism: IQ and psychosexual identity in a study of ten girls. *Journal of Sex Research, 3*, 83–100. (11)

Eichenbaum, H. (2000). A cortical-hippocampal system for declarative memory. *Nature Reviews Neuroscience, 1*, 41–50.(13)

Eichenbaum, H. (2002). *The cognitive neuroscience of memory.* New York: Oxford University Press. (13)

Eidelberg, E., & Stein, D. G. (1974). Functional recovery after lesions of the nervous system. *Neurosciences Research Program Bulletin, 12*, 191–303. (5)

Eisenstein, E. M., & Cohen, M. J. (1965). Learning in an isolated prothoracic insect ganglion. *Animal Behaviour, 13*, 104–108. (13)

Ek, M., Engblom, D., Saha, S., Blomqvist, A., Jakobsson, P.-J., & Ericsson-Dahlstrand, A. (2001). Pathway across the blood-brain barrier. *Nature, 410*, 430–431. (10)

Elbert, T., Candia, V., Altenmüller, E., Rau, H., Sterr, A., Rockstroh, B., Pantev, C., & Taub, E. (1998). Alteration of digital representations in somatosensory cortex in focal hand dystonia. *Neuroreport, 9*, 3571–3575. (5)

Elbert, T., Pantev, C., Wienbruch, C., Rockstroh, B., & Taub, E. (1995). Increased cortical representation of the fingers of the left hand in string players. *Science, 270*, 305–307. (4, 5)

Elia, J., Ambrosini, P. J., & Rapoport, J. L. (1999). Treatment of attention-deficit hyperactivity disorder. *New England Journal of Medicine, 340*, 780–788. (7)

Elias, C. F., Lee, C., Kelly, J., Aschkenazi, C., Ahima, R. S., Couceyro, P. R., Kuhar, M. J., Saper, C. B., & Elmquist, J. K. (1998). Leptin activates hypothalamic CART neurons projecting to the spinal cord. *Neuron, 21*, 1375–1385. (10)

El-Islam, M. F. (1982). Rehabilitation of schizophrenics by the extended family. *Acta Psychiatrica Scandinavica, 65*, 112–119. (15)

Elliott, T. R. (1905). The action of adrenalin. *Journal of Physiology* (London), *32*, 401–467. (3)

Ellis, L., & Ames, M. A. (1987). Neurohormonal functioning and sexual orientation: A theory of homosexuality-heterosexuality. *Psychological Bulletin, 101*, 233–258. (11)

Ellis, L., Ames, M. A., Peckham, W., & Burke, D. (1988). Sexual orientation of human offspring may be altered by severe maternal stress during pregnancy. *Journal of Sex Research, 25*, 152–157. (11)

Ellis, L., & Cole-Harding, S. (2001). The effects of prenatal stress, and of prenatal alcohol and nicotine exposure, on human sexual orientation. *Physiology & Behavior, 74*, 213–226. (11)

Elston, G. N. (2000). Pyramidal cells of the frontal lobe: All the more spinous to think with. *Journal of Neuroscience, 20*, RC95: 1–4. (4)

Emery, N. J., Capitanio, J. P., Mason, W. A., Machado, C. J., Mendoza, S. P., & Amaral, D. G. (2001). The effects of bilateral lesions of the amygdala on dyadic social interactions in rhesus monkeys (*Macaca mulatta*). *Behavioral Neuroscience, 115*, 515–544. (12)

Enard, W., Przeworski, M., Fisher, S. E., Lai, C. S. L., Wiebe, V., Kitano, T., Monaco, A. P., & Pääbo, S. (2002). Molecular evolution of *FOXP2*, a gene involved in speech and language. *Nature, 418*, 869–872. (14)

Engel, S. A. (1999). Using neuroimaging to measure mental representations: Finding color-opponent neurons in visual cortex. *Current Directions in Psychological Science, 8*, 23–27. (6)

Engelien, A., Huber, W., Silbersweig, D., Stern, E., Frith, C. D., Döring, W., Thron, A., & Frackowiak, R. S. J. (2000). The neural correlates of "deaf hearing" in man: Conscious sensory awareness enabled by attentional modulation. *Brain, 123*, 532–545. (7)

Engert, F., & Bonhoeffer, T. (1999). Dendritic spine changes associated with hippocampal long-term synaptic plasticity. *Nature, 399*, 66–70. (13)

Ensor, D. M., Morley, J. S., Redfern, R. M., & Miles, J. B. (1993). The activity of an analogue of MPF (b-endorphin 28-31) in a rat model of Parkinson's disease. *Brain Research, 610*, 166–168. (8)

Epping-Jordan, M. P., Watkins, S. S., Koob, G. F., & Markou, A. (1998). Dramatic decreases in brain reward function during nicotine withdrawal. *Nature, 393*, 76–79. (15)

Epstein, A. N. (1983). The neuropsychology of drinking behavior. In E. Satinoff & P. Teitelbaum (Eds.), *Handbook of behavioral neurobiology: Vol. 6. Motivation* (pp. 367–423). New York: Plenum Press. (10)

Erickson, C. A., Jagadeesh, B., & Desimone, R. (2000). Clustering of perirhinal neurons with similar properties following visual experience in adult monkeys. *Nature Neuroscience, 3*, 1143–1148. (6)

Erickson, C., & Lehrman, D. (1964). Effect of castration of male ring doves upon ovarian activity of females. *Journal of Comparative and Physiological Psychology, 58*, 164–166. (11)

Erickson, R. P. (1982). The across-fiber pattern theory: An organizing principle for molar neural function. *Contributions to Sensory Physiology, 6*, 79–110. (7)

Erickson, R. P., DiLorenzo, P. M., & Woodbury, M. A. (1994). Classification of taste responses in brain stem: Membership in fuzzy sets. *Journal of Neurophysiology, 71*, 2139–2150. (7)

Ericsson, K. A., & Charness, N. (1994). Expert performance: Its structure and acquisition. *American Psychologist, 49*, 725–747. (5)

Eriksson, P. S., Perfilieva, E., Björk-Eriksson, T., Alborn, A.-M., Nordborg, C., Peterson, D. A., & Gage, F. H. (1998). Neurogenesis in the adult human hippocampus. *Nature Medicine, 4*, 1313–1317. (5)

Erlenmeyer-Kimling, L., Adamo, U. H., Rock, D., Roberts, S. A., Bassett, A. S., Squires-Wheeler, E., Cornblatt, B. A., Endicott, J., Pape, S., & Gottesman, I. I. (1997). The New York high-risk project. *Archives of General Psychiatry, 54*, 1096–1102. (15)

Ertekin-Taner, N., Graff-Radford, N., Younkin, L. H., Eckman, C., Baker, M., Adamson, J., Ronald, J., Blangero, J., Hutton, M., & Younkin, S. G. (2000). Linkage of plasma Aβ42 to a quantitative locus on chromosome 10 in late-onset Alzheimer's disease pedigrees. *Science, 290*, 2303–2304. (13)

Etcoff, N. L., Ekman, P., Magee, J. J., & Frank, M. G. (2000). Lie detection and language comprehension. *Nature, 405*, 139. (12, 14)

Etgen, A. M., Chu, H.-P., Fiber, J. M., Karkanias, G. B., & Morales, J. M. (1999). Hormonal integration of neurochemical and sensory signals governing female reproductive behavior. *Behavioural Brain Research, 105*, 93–103. (11)

Evans, D. A., Funkenstein, H. H., Albert, M. S., Scherr, P. A., Cook, N. R., Chown, M. J., Hebert, L. E., Hennekens, C. H., & Taylor, J. O. (1989). Prevalence of Alzheimer's disease in a community population of older persons. *Journal of the American Medical Association, 262*, 2551–2556. (13)

Evans, M. D., Hollon, S. D., DeRubeis, R. J., Piasecki, J. M., Grove, W. M., Garvey, M. J., & Tuason, V. B. (1992). Differential relapse following cognitive therapy and pharmacotherapy for depression. *Archives of General Psychiatry, 49*, 802–808. (15)

Evarts, E. V. (1979). Brain mechanisms of movement. *Scientific American, 241*(3), 164–179. (8)

Everson, C. A. (1995). Functional consequences of sustained sleep deprivation in the rat. *Behavioural Brain Research, 69*, 43–54. (9)

Evoli, A., Batocchi, A. P., Bartoccioni, E., Lino, M. M., Minisci, C., & Tonali, P. (1998). Juvenile myasthenia gravis with prepubertal onset. *Neuromuscular Disorders, 8*, 561–567. (8)

Eyre, J. A., Taylor, J. P., Villagra, F., Smith, M., & Miller, S. (2001). Evidence of activity-dependent withdrawal of corticospinal projections during human development. *Neurology, 57*, 1543–1554. (8)

Fadda, F. (2000). Tryptophan-free diets: A physiological tool to study brain serotonin function. *News in Physiological Sciences, 15*, 260–264. (3)

Fagiolini, M., & Hensch, T. K. (2000). Inhibitory threshold for critical-period activation in primary visual cortex. *Nature, 404*, 183–186. (6)

Famy, C., Streissguth, A. P., & Unis, A. S. (1998). Mental illness in adults with fetal alcohol syndrome or fetal alcohol effects. *American Journal of Psychiatry, 155*, 552–554. (5)

Fan, P. (1995). Cannabinoid agonists inhibit the activation of 5-HT3 receptors in rat nodose ganglion neurons. *Journal of Neurophysiology, 73*, 907–910. (15)

Fantz, R. L. (1963). Pattern vision in newborn infants. *Science, 140*, 296–297. (6)

Farah, M. J. (1990). *Visual agnosia.* Cambridge, MA: MIT Press. (6)

Farah, M. J., Wilson, K. D., Drain, M., & Tanaka, J. N. (1998). What is "special" about face perception? *Psychological Review, 105*, 482–498. (6)

Faraone, S. V., Doyle, A. E., Mick, E., & Biederman, J. (2001). Meta-analysis of the association between the 7-repeat allele of the dopamine D4 receptor gene and attention deficit hyperactivity disorder. *American Journal of Psychiatry, 158*, 1052–1057. (7)

Farber, N. B., Newcomer, J. W., & Olney, J. W. (1999). Glycine agonists: What can they teach us about schizophrenia? *Archives of General Psychiatry, 56*, 13–17. (15)

Farmer, M. E., & Klein, R. M. (1995). The evidence for a temporal processing deficit linked to dyslexia: A review. *Psychonomic Bulletin & Review, 2*, 460–493. (14)

Farooqi, I. S., Keogh, J. M., Kamath, S., Jones, S., Gibson, W. T., Trussell, R., Jebb, S. A., Lip, G. Y. H., & O'Rahilly, S. (2001). Partial leptin deficiency and human adiposity. *Nature, 414*, 34–35. (10)

Faust, M., Kravetz, S., & Babkoff, H. (1993). Hemispheric specialization or reading habits: Evidence from lexical decision research with Hebrew words and sentences. *Brain and Language, 44*, 254–263. (14)

Featherstone, R. E., Fleming, A. S., & Ivy, G. O. (2000). Plasticity in the maternal circuit: Effects of experience and partum condition on brain astrocyte number in female rats. *Behavioral Neuroscience, 114*, 158–172. (11)

Federman, D. D. (1967). *Abnormal sexual development.* Philadelphia: Saunders. (11)

Feeney, D. M. (1987). Human rights and animal welfare. *American Psychologist, 42*, 593–599. (1)

Feeney, D. M., & Sutton, R. L. (1988). Catecholamines and recovery of function after brain damage. In D. G. Stein & B. A. Sabel (Eds.), *Pharmacological approaches to the treatment of brain and spinal cord injury* (pp. 121–142). New York: Plenum Press. (5)

Feeney, D. M., Sutton, R. L., Boyeson, M. G., Hovda, D. A., & Dail, W. G. (1985). The locus coeruleus and cerebral metabolism: Recovery of function after cerebral injury. *Physiological Psychology, 13,* 197–203. (5)

Feeney, D. M., Weisend, M. P., & Kline, A. E. (1993). Noradrenergic pharmacotherapy, intracerebral infusion and adrenal transplantation promote functional recovery after cortical damage. *Journal of Neural Transplantation & Plasticity, 4,* 199–213. (5)

Feighner, J. P., Gardner, E. A., Johnston, J. A., Batey, S. R., Khayrallah, M. A., Ascher, J. A., & Lineberry, C. G. (1991). Double-blind comparison of bupropion and fluoxetine in depressed outpatients. *Journal of Clinical Psychiatry, 52,* 329–335. (15)

Feitosa, M. F., Borecki, I. B., Rich, S. S., Arnett, D. K., Sholinsky, P., Myers, R. H., Leppert, M., & Province, M. A. (2002). Quantitative-trait loci influencing body-mass index reside on chromosomes 7 and 13: The National Heart, Lung, and Blood Institute family heart study. *American Journal of Human Genetics, 70,* 72–82. (10)

Fendrich, R., Wessinger, C. M., & Gazzaniga, M. S. (1992). Residual vision in a scotoma: Implications for blindsight. *Science, 258,* 1489–1491. (6)

Fendt, M., Koch, M., & Schnitzler, H.-U. (1996). Lesions of the central gray block conditioned fear as measured with the potentiated startle paradigm. *Behavioural Brain Research, 74,* 127–134. (12)

Fentress, J. C. (1973). Development of grooming in mice with amputated forelimbs. *Science, 179,* 704–705. (8)

Ferger, B., Spratt, C., Earl, C. D., Teisman, P., Oertel, W. H., & Kuschinsky, K. (1998). Effects of nicotine on hydroxyl free radical formation in vitro and on MPTP-induced neurotoxicity in vivo. *Naunyn-Schmiedeberg's Archives of Pharmacology, 358,* 351–359. (8)

Ferguson, N. B. L., & Keesey, R. E. (1975). Effect of a quinine-adulterated diet upon body weight maintenance in male rats with ventromedial hypothalamic lesions. *Journal of Comparative and Physiological Psychology, 89,* 478–488. (10)

Fergusson, D. M., Woodward, L. J., & Horwood, J. (1998). Maternal smoking during pregnancy and psychiatric adjustment in late adolescence. *Archives of General Psychiatry, 55,* 721–727. (5, 12)

Ferreira, F., Bailey, K. G. D., & Ferraro, V. (2002). Good-enough representations in language comprehension. *Current Directions in Psychological Science, 11,* 11–15. (14)

Fettiplace, R. (1990). Transduction and tuning in auditory hair cells. *Seminars in the Neurosciences, 2,* 33–40. (7)

Fields, R. D., Schwab, M. E., & Silver, J. (1999). Does CNS myelin inhibit axon regeneration? *Neuroscientist, 5,* 12–18. (5)

Filoteo, J. V., Maddox, W. T., & Davis, J. D. (2001). A possible role of the striatum in linear and non-linear category learning: Evidence from patients with Huntington's disease. *Behavioral Neuroscience, 115,* 786–798. (8)

Fils-Aime, M.-L., Eckardt, M. J., George, D. T., Brown, G. L., Mefford, I., & Linnoila, M. (1996). Early-onset alcoholics have lower cerebrospinal fluid 5-hydroxyindoleacetic acid levels than late-onset alcoholics. *Archives of General Psychiatry, 53,* 211–216. (15)

Finette, B. A., O'Neill, J. P., Vacek, P. M., & Albertini, R. J. (1998). Gene mutations with characteristic deletions in cord blood T lymphocytes associated with passive maternal exposure to tobacco smoke. *Nature Medicine, 4,* 1144–1151. (5)

Finger, S., & Roe, D. (1996). Gustave Dax and the early history of cerebral dominance. *Archives of Neurology, 53,* 806–813. (14)

Fink, G., Sumner, B. E. H., Rosie, R., Grace, O., & Quinn, J. P. (1996). Estrogen control of central neurotransmission: Effect on mood, mental state, and memory. *Cellular and Molecular Neurobiology, 16,* 325–344. (11)

Fink, G. R., Halligan, P. W., Marshall, J. C., Frith, C. D., Frackowiak, R. S. J., & Dolan, R. J. (1996). Where in the brain does visual attention select the forest and the trees? *Nature, 382,* 626–628. (14)

Fink, M. (1985). Convulsive therapy: Fifty years of progress. *Convulsive Therapy, 1,* 204–216. (15)

Finlay, B. L., & Darlington, R. B. (1995). Linked regularities in the development and evolution of mammalian brains. *Science, 268,* 1578–1584. (5)

Finlay, B. L., & Pallas, S. L. (1989). Control of cell number in the developing mammalian visual system. *Progress in Neurobiology, 32,* 207–234. (5)

Fisher, S. E., & DeFries, J. C. (2002). Developmental dyslexia: Genetic dissection of a complex cognitive trait. *Nature Reviews Neuroscience, 3,* 767–780. (14)

Fisher, S. E., Vargha-Khadem, F., Watkins, K. E., Monaco, A. P., & Pembrey, M. E. (1998). Localisation of a gene implicated in a severe speech and language disorder. *Nature Genetics, 18,* 168–170. (14)

Fitts, D. A., Starbuck, E. M., & Ruhf, A. (2000). Circumventricular organs and ANGII-induced salt appetite: Blood pressure and connectivity. *American Journal of Physiology, 279,* R2277–R2286. (10)

Fitzgerald, P. B., Brown, T. L., & Daskalakis, Z. J. (2002). The application of transcranial magnetic stimulation in psychiatry and neurosciences research. *Acta Psychiatrica Scandinavica, 105,* 324–340. (4)

Fjerdingstad, E. J. (1973). Transfer of learning in rodents and fish. In W. B. Essman & S. Nakajima (Eds.), *Current biochemical approaches to learning and memory* (pp. 73–98). Flushing, NY: Spectrum. (13)

Flatz, G. (1987). Genetics of lactose digestion in humans. *Advances in Human Genetics, 16,* 1–77. (10)

Fleet, W. S., & Heilman, K. M. (1986). The fatigue effect in hemispatial neglect. *Neurology, 36*(Suppl. 1), 258. (5)

Fletcher, P. C., McKenna, P. J., Frith, C. D., Grasby, P. M., Friston, K. J., & Dolan, R. J. (1998). Brain activations in schizophrenia during a graded memory task studied with functional neuroimaging. *Archives of General Psychiatry, 55,* 1001–1008. (15)

Fletcher, R., & Voke, J. (1985). *Defective colour vision.* Bristol, England: Hilger. (6)

Flöel, A., Knecht, S., Lohmann, H., Deppe, M., Sommer, J., Dräger, B., Ringelstein, E.-B., & Henningsen, H. (2001). Language and spatial attention can lateralize to the same hemisphere in healthy humans. *Neurology, 57,* 1018–1024. (14)

Flor, H., Elbert, T., Knecht, S., Wienbruch, C., Pantev, C., Birbaumer, N., Larbig, W., & Taub, E. (1995). Phantom-limb pain as a perceptual correlate of cortical reorganization following arm amputation. *Nature, 375,* 482–484. (5)

Florence, S. L., & Kaas, J. H. (1995). Large-scale reorganization at multiple levels of the somatosensory pathway follows therapeutic amputation of the hand in monkeys. *Journal of Neuroscience, 15,* 8083–8095. (5)

Florence, S. L., Taub, H. B., & Kaas, J. H. (1998). Large-scale sprouting of cortical connections after peripheral injury in adult macaque monkeys. *Science, 282,* 1117–1121. (5)

Flynn, J. M., & Boder, E. (1991). Clinical and electrophysiological correlates of dysphonetic and dyseidetic dyslexia. In J. F. Stein (Ed.), *Vision and visual dyslexia* (pp. 121–131). Vol. 13 of J. R. Cronly-Dillon (Ed.), *Vision and visual dysfunction.* Boca Raton, FL: CRC Press. (14)

Folkard, S., Hume, K. I., Minors, D. S., Waterhouse, J. M., & Watson, F. L. (1985). Independence of the circadian rhythm in alertness from the sleep/wake cycle. *Nature, 313,* 678–679. (9)

Follesa, P., Serra, M., Cagetti, E., Pisu, M. G., Porta, S., Floris, S., Massa, F., Sanna, E., & Biggio, G. (2000). Allopregnanolone synthesis in cerebellar granule cells: Roles in regulation of GABAA receptor expression and function during progesterone treatment and withdrawal. *Molecular Pharmacology, 57,* 1262–1270. (11)

Foltz, E. L., & Millett, F. E. (1964). Experimental psychosomatic disease states in monkeys: I. Peptic ulcer—"executive monkeys." *Journal of Surgical Research, 4,* 445–453. (12)

Ford, D. E., & Cooper-Patrick, L. (2001). Sleep disturbances and mood disorders: An epidemiological perspective. *Depression and Anxiety, 14,* 3–6. (15)

Forger, N. G., & Breedlove, S. M. (1987). Motoneuronal death during human fetal development. *Journal of Comparative Neurology, 264,* 118–122. (5)

Forster, B., & Corballis, M. C. (2000). Interhemispheric transfer of colour and shape information in the presence and absence of the corpus callosum. *Neuropsychologia, 38,* 32–45. (14)

Fortin, N. J., Agster, K. L., & Eichenbaum, H. B. (2002). Critical role of the hippocampus in memory for sequences of events. *Nature Neuroscience, 5,* 458–462. (13)

Fox, P. T., Ingham, R. J., Ingham, J. C., Zamarripa, F., Xiong, J.-H., & Lancaster, J. L. (2000). Brain correlates of stuttering and syllable production: A PET performance-correlation analysis. *Brain, 123,* 1985–2004. (14)

Frank, R. A., Mize, S. J. S., Kennedy, L. M., de los Santos, H. C., & Green, S. J. (1992). The effect of Gymnema sylvestre extracts on the sweetness of eight sweeteners. *Chemical Senses, 17,* 461–479. (7)

Frankland, P. W., Josselyn, S. A., Bradwejn, J., Vaccarino, F. J., & Yeomans, J. S. (1997). Activation of amygdala cholecystokinin B receptors potentiates the acoustic startle response in the rat. *Journal of Neuroscience, 17,* 1838–1847. (12)

Frankland, P. W., O'Brien, C., Ohno, M., Kirkwood, A., & Silva, A. J. (2000). α-CaMKII-dependent plasticity in the cortex is required for permanent memory. *Nature, 411,* 309–313. (13)

Franz, E. A., Waldie, K. E., & Smith, M. J. (2000). The effect of callosotomy on novel versus familiar bimanual actions: A neural dissociation between controlled and automatic processes? *Psychological Science, 11,* 82–85. (14)

Frassinetti, F., Pavani, F., & Làdavas, E. (2002). Acoustical vision of neglected stimuli: Interaction among spatially converging audiovisual inputs in neglect patients. *Journal of Cognitive Neuroscience, 14,* 62–69. (7)

Freed, C. R., Greene, P. E., Breeze, R. E., Tsai, W.-Y., DuMouchel, W., Kao, R., Dillon, S., Winfield, H., Culver, S., Trojanowski, J. Q., Eidelberg, D., & Fahn, S. (2001). Transplantation of embryonic dopamine neurons for severe Parkinson's disease. *New England Journal of Medicine, 344,* 710–719. (8)

Freedman, M. S., Lucas, R. J., Soni, B., von Schantz, M., Muñoz, M., David-Gray, Z., & Foster, R. (1999). Regulation of mammalian circadian behavior by non-rod, non-cone, ocular photoreceptors. *Science, 284,* 502–504. (9)

Freedman, R. D., & Thibos, L. N. (1975). Contrast sensitivity in humans with abnormal visual experience. *Journal of Physiology, 247,* 687–710. (6)

Freimer, N. B., Reus, V. I., Escamilla, M. A., McInnes, L. A., Spesny, M., Leon, P., Service, S. K., Smith, L. B., Silva, S., Rojas, E., Gallegos, A., Meza, L., Fournier, E., Baharloo, S., Blankenship, K., Tyler, D. J., Batki, S., Vinogradov, S., Weissenbach, J., Barondes, S. H., & Sandkuijl, L. A. (1996). Genetic mapping using haplotype, association and linkage methods suggests a locus for severe bipolar disorder (BP1) at 18q22-q23. *Nature Genetics, 12,* 436–441. (15)

Frese, M., & Harwich, C. (1984). Shiftwork and the length and quality of sleep. *Journal of Occupational Medicine, 26,* 561–566. (9)

Fried, I., Wilson, C. L., MacDonald, K. A., & Behnke, E. J. (1998). Electric current stimulates laughter. *Nature, 391,* 650. (12)

Fried, I., Wilson, C. L., Morrow, J. W., Cameron, K. A., Behnke, E. D., Ackerson, L. C., & Maidment, N. T. (2001). Increased dopamine release in the human amygdala during performance of cognitive tasks. *Nature Neuroscience, 4,* 201–206. (13)

Friedburg, D., & Klöppel, K. P. (1996). Frühzeitige Korrektion von Hyperopie und Astigmatismus bie Kindern führt zu besserer Entwicklung des Sehschärfe. *Klinische Monatsblatt der*

Augenheilkunde, 209, 21–24. (6)

Friedlander, W. J. (1986). Who was "the father of bromide treatment of epilepsy"? *Archives of Neurology, 43*, 505–507. (15)

Friedman, M. I., & Stricker, E. M. (1976). The physiological psychology of hunger: A physiological perspective. *Psychological Review, 83*, 409–431. (10)

Fritsch, G., & Hitzig, E. (1870). Über die elektrische Erregbarkeit des Grosshirns [Concerning the electrical stimulability of the cerebrum]. *Archiv für Anatomie Physiologie und Wissenschaftliche Medicin, 300*–332. (8)

Fritschy, J.-M., & Grzanna, R. (1992). Degeneration of rat locus coeruleus neurons is not accompanied by an irreversible loss of ascending projections. *Annals of the New York Academy of Sciences, 648*, 275–278. (5)

Frye, C. A. (1995). Estrus-associated decrements in a water maze task are limited to acquisition. *Physiology & Behavior, 57*, 5–14. (11)

Fuller, R. K., & Roth, H. P. (1979). Disulfiram for the treatment of alcoholism: An evaluation in 128 men. *Annals of Internal Medicine, 90*, 901–904. (15)

Furey, M. L., Pietrini, P., & Haxby, J. V., (2000). Cholinergic enhancement and increased selectivity of perceptual processing during working memory. *Science, 290*, 2315–2319. (13)

Fuster, J. M. (1989). *The prefrontal cortex* (2nd ed.). New York: Raven Press. (4)

Fuster, J. M., Bodner, M., & Kroger, J. K. (2000). Cross-modal and cross-temporal associations in neurons of frontal cortex. *Nature, 405*, 347–351. (4)

Gabrieli, J. D. E., Corkin, S., Mickel, S. F., & Growdon, J. H. (1993). Intact acquisition of mirror-tracing skill in Alzheimer's disease and in global amnesia. *Behavioral Neuroscience, 107*, 899–910. (13)

Gage, F. H. (2000). Mammalian neural stem cells. *Science, 287*, 1433–1438. (5)

Gainetdinov, R. R., Wetsel, W. C., Jones, S. R., Levin, E. D., Jaber, M., & Caron, M. G. (1999). Role of serotonin in the paradoxical calming effect of psychostimulants on hyperactivity. *Science, 283*, 397–401. (15)

Gais, S., Plihal, W., Wagner, U., & Born, J. (2000). Early sleep triggers memory for early visual discrimination skills. *Nature Neuroscience, 3*, 1335–1339. (9)

Galaburda, A. M., Sherman, G. F., Rosen, G. D., Aboitiz, F., & Geschwind, N. (1985). Developmental dyslexia: Four consecutive patients with cortical anomalies. *Annals of Neurology, 18*, 222–233. (14)

Galarreta, M., & Hestrin, S. (2001). Electrical synapses between GABA releasing interneurons. *Nature Reviews Neuroscience, 2*, 425–433. (3)

Galea, L. A. M., Kavaliers, M., Ossenkopp, K.-P., & Hampson, E. (1995). Gonadal hormone levels and spatial learning performance in the Morris water maze in male and female meadow voles, *Microtus pennsylvanicus. Hormones and Behavior, 29*, 106–125. (11)

Galef, B. G., Jr. (1992). Weaning from mother's milk to solid foods: The developmental psychobiology of self-selection of foods by rats. *Annals of the New York Academy of Sciences, 662*, 37–52. (10)

Galin, D., Johnstone, J., Nakell, L., & Herron, J. (1979). Development of the capacity for tactile information transfer between hemispheres in normal children. *Science, 204*, 1330–1332. (14)

Gallopin, T., Fort, P., Eggermann, E., Cauli, B., Luppi, P.-H., Rossier, J., Audinat, E., Mühlethaler, M., & Serafin, M. (2000). Identification of sleep-promoting neurons *in vitro. Nature, 404*, 992–995. (9)

Gangestad, S. W., & Simpson, J. A. (2000). The evolution of human mating: Trade-offs and strategic pluralism. *Behavioral and Brain Sciences, 23*, 573–644. (11)

Ganguly, K., Kiss, L., & Poo, M. (2000). Enhancement of presynaptic neuronal excitability by correlated presynaptic and postsynaptic spiking. *Nature Neuroscience, 3*, 1018–1026. (13)

Gao, J.-H., Parsons, L. M., Bower, J. M., Xiong, J., Li, J., & Fox, P. T. (1996). Cerebellum implicated in sensory acquisition and discrimination rather than motor control. *Science, 272*, 545–547. (8)

Garcia, R., Vouimba, R.-M., Baudry, M., & Thompson, R. F. (1999). The amygdala modulates prefrontal cortex activity relative to conditioned fear. *Nature, 402*, 294–296. (12)

García-Pérez, M. A., & Peli, E. (2001). Intrasaccadic perception. *Journal of Neuroscience, 21*, 7313–7322. (6)

Gardner, E. P., Ro, J. Y., Debowy, D., & Ghosh, S. (1999). Facilitation of neuronal activity in somatosensory and posterior parietal cortex during prehension. *Experimental Brain Research, 127*, 329–354. (8)

Gardner, B. T., & Gardner, R. A. (1975). Evidence for sentence constituents in the early utterances of child and chimpanzee. *Journal of Experimental Psychology: General, 104*, 244–267. (14)

Gardner, H., & Zurif, E. B. (1975). Bee but not be: Oral reading of single words in aphasia and alexia. *Neuropsychologia, 13*, 181–190. (14)

Garpenstrand, H., Annas, P., Ekblom, J., Oreland, L., & Fredrikson, M. (2001). Human fear conditioning is related to dopaminergic and serotonergic biological markers. *Behavioral Neuroscience, 115*, 358–364. (12)

Garris, P. A., Kilpatrick, M., Bunin, M. A., Michael, D., Walker, Q. D., & Wightman, R. M. (1999). Dissociation of dopamine release in the nucleus accumbens from intracranial self-stimulation. *Nature, 398*, 67–69. (15)

Gash, D. M., Zhang, Z., Ovadia, A., Cass, W. A., Yi, A., Simmerman, L., Russell, D., Martin, D., Lapchak, P. A., Collins, F., Hoffer, B. J., & Gerhardt, G. A. (1996). Functional recovery in parkinsonian monkeys treated with GDNF. *Nature, 380*, 252–255. (8)

Gauthier, I., Tarr, M. J., Anderson, A. W., Skudlarski, P., & Gore, J. C. (1999). Activation of the middle fusiform "face area" increases with experience in recognizing novel objects. *Nature Neuroscience, 2*, 568–573. (6)

Geiger, G., Lettvin, J. Y., & Fahle, M. (1994). Dyslexic children learn a new visual strategy for reading: A controlled experiment. *Vision Research, 34*, 1223–1233. (14)

Geiger, G., Lettvin, J. Y., & Zegarra-Moran, O. (1992). Task-determined strategies of visual process. *Cognitive Brain Research, 1*, 39–52. (14)

Gell-Mann, M. (2001). Consciousness, reduction, and emergence. *Annals of the New York Academy of Sciences, 929*, 41–49. (1)

Genoux, D., Haditsch, U., Knobloch, M., Michalon, A., Storm, D., & Mansuy, I. M. (2002). Protein phosphatase 1 is a molecular constraint on learning and memory. *Nature, 418*, 970–975. (13)

George, D. T., Nutt, D. J., Walker, W. V., Porges, S. W., Adinoff, B., & Linnoila, M. (1989). Lactate and hyperventilation substantially attenuate vagal tone in normal volunteers. *Archives of General Psychiatry, 46*, 153–156. (12)

George, M. S., Wasserman, E. M., Kimbrell, T. A., Little, J. T., Williams, W. E., Danielson, A. L., Greenberg, B. D., Hallett, M., & Post, R. M. (1997). Mood improvement following daily left prefrontal repetitive transcranial magnetic stimulation in patients with depression: A placebo-controlled crossover trial. *American Journal of Psychiatry, 154*, 1752–1756. (15)

Gerardin, D. C. C., & Pereira, O. C. M. (2002). Reproductive changes in male rats treated perinatally with an aromatase inhibitor. *Pharmacology Biochemistry and Behavior, 71*, 309–313. (11)

Gerdeman, G. L., Ronesi, J., & Lovinger, D. M. (2002). Post-synaptic endocannabinoid release is critical to long-term depression in the striatum. *Nature Neuroscience, 5*, 446–451. (15)

Geschwind, N. (1965). Disconnexion syndromes in animals and man. *Brain, 88*, 237–294, 585–644. (inside cover)

Geschwind, N., & Levitsky, W. (1968). Human brain: Left-right asymmetries in temporal speech region. *Science, 161*, 186–187. (14)

Ghosh, E. P., Ro, J. Y., Debowy, D., & Ghosh, S. (1999). Facilitation of neuronal activity in somatosensory and posterior parietal cortex dur-ing prehension. *Experimental Brain Research, 127*, 329–354. (8)

Giancola, P. R. (1995). Evidence for dorsolateral and orbital prefrontal cortical involvement in the expression of aggressive behavior. *Aggressive Behavior, 21*, 431–450. (12)

Gibbs, F. P. (1983). Temperature dependence of the hamster circadian pacemaker. *American Journal of Physiology, 244*, R607–R610. (9)

Gibbs, J., Young, R. C., & Smith, G. P. (1973). Cholecystokinin decreases food intake in rats. *Journal of Comparative and Physiological Psychology, 84*, 488–495. (10)

Giedd, J. N., Blumenthal, J., Jeffries, N. O., Castellanos, F. X., Liu, H., Zijdenbos, A., Paus, T., Evans, A. C., & Rapoport, J. L. (1999). Brain development during childhood and adolescence: A longitudinal MRI study. *Nature Neuroscience, 2*, 861–863. (5)

Giedd, J. N., Blumenthal, J., Molloy, E., & Castellanos, F. X. (2001). Brain imaging of attention deficit/hyperactivity disorder. *Annals of the New York Academy of Sciences, 931*, 33–49. (7)

Gillette, M. U., & McArthur, A. J. (1996). Circadian actions of melatonin at the suprachiasmatic nucleus. *Behavioural Brain Research, 73*, 135–139. (9)

Gillin, J. C., Buchsbaum, M., Wu, J., Clark, C., & Bunney, W., Jr. (2001). Sleep deprivation as a model experimental antidepressant treatment: Findings from functional brain imaging. *Depression and Anxiety, 14*, 37–49. (15)

Ginns, E. I., Ott, J., Egeland, J. A., Allen, C. R., Fann, C. S. J., Pauls, D. L., Weissenbach, J., Carulli, J. P., Falls, K. M., Keith, T. P., & Paul, S. M. (1996). A genome-wide search for chromosomal loci linked to bipolar affective disorder in the Old Order Amish. *Nature Genetics, 12*, 431–435. (15)

Ginsberg, M. D. (1995). Neuroprotection in brain ischemia: An update (Part I). The *Neuroscientist, 1*, 95–103. (5)

Giraud, A. L., & Price, C. J. (2001). The constraints functional neuroimaging places on classical models of auditory word processing.

Journal of Cognitive Neuroscience, 13, 754–765. (14)

Giraux, P., Sirigu, A., Schneider, F., & Dubernard, J.-M. (2001). Cortical reorganization in motor cocrtex after graft of both hands. *Nature Neuroscience, 4*, 691–692. (5)

Giros, B., Jaber, M., Jones, S. R., Wightman, R. M., & Caron, M. G. (1996). Hyperlocomotion and indifference to cocaine and amphetamine in mice lacking the dopamine transporter. *Nature, 379*, 606–612. (15)

Giuliani, D., & Ferrari, F. (1996). Differential behavioral response to dopamine D2 agonists by sexually naive, sexually active, and sexually inactive male rats. *Behavioral Neuroscience, 110*, 802–808. (3, 11)

Glantz, L. A., & Lewis, D. A. (1997). Reduction of synaptophysin immunoreactivity in the prefrontal cortex of subjects with schizophrenia. *Archives of General Psychiatry, 54*, 660–669. (15)

Glantz, L. A., & Lewis, D. A. (2000). Decreased dendritic spine density on prefrontal cortical pyramidal neurons in schizophrenia. *Archives of General Psychiatry, 57*, 65–73. (15)

Glass, M. (2001). The role of cannabinoids in neurodegenerative diseases. *Progress in Neuro-Psychopharmacology & Biological Psychiatry, 25*, 743–765. (15)

Glendenning, K. K., Baker, B. N., Hutson, K. A., & Masterton, R. B. (1992). Acoustic chiasm V: Inhibition and excitation in the ipsilateral and contralateral projections of LSO. *Journal of Comparative Neurology, 319*, 100–122. (7)

Glick, S. D. (1974). Changes in drug sensitivity and mechanisms of functional recovery following brain damage. In D. G. Stein, J. J. Rosen, & N. Butters (Eds.), *Plasticity and recovery of function in the central nervous system* (pp. 339–372). New York: Academic Press. (5)

Glick, S. D., & Maisonneuve, I. M. (2000). Development of novel medications for drug addiction: The legacy of an African shrub. *Annals of the New York Academy of Sciences, 909*, 88–103. (15)

Goate, A., Chartier-Harlin, M. C., Mullan, M., Brown, J., Crawford, F., Fidani, L., Giuffra, L., Haynes, A., Irving, N., James, L., Mant, R., Newton, P., Rooke, K., Roques, P., Talbot, C., Pericak-Vance, M., Roses, A., Williamson, R., Rossor, M., Owen, M., & Hardy, J. (1991). Segregation of a missense mutation in the amyloid precursor protein gene with familial Alzheimer's disease. *Nature, 349*, 704–706. (13)

Gödecke, I., & Bonhoeffer, T. (1996). Development of identical orientation maps for two eyes without common visual experience. *Nature, 379*, 251–254. (6)

Goff, D. C., Tsai, G., Levitt, J., Amico, E., Manoach, D., Schoenfeld, D. A., Hayden, D. L., McCarley, R., & Coyle, J. T. (1999). A placebo-controlled trial of D-cycloserine added to conventional neuroleptics in patients with schizophrenia. *Archives of General Psychiatry, 56*, 21–27. (15)

Gogos, J. A., Osborne, J., Nemes, A., Mendelsohn, M., & Axel, R. (2000). Genetic ablation and restoration of the olfactory topographic map. *Cell, 103*, 609–620. (5)

Gold, P. E., Cahill, L., & Wenk, G. L. (2002). Gingko biloba: A cognitive enhancer? *Psychological Science in the Public Interest, 3*, 2–11. (13)

Gold, R. M. (1973). Hypothalamic obesity: The myth of the ventromedial hypothalamus. *Science, 182*, 488–490. (10)

Goldberg, T. E., Weinberger, D. R., Berman, K. F., Pliskin, N. H., & Podd, M. H. (1987). Further evidence for dementia of the prefrontal type in schizophrenia? *Archives of General Psychiatry, 44*, 1008–1014. (15)

Goldin-Meadow, S., McNeill, D., & Singleton, J. (1996). Silence is liberating: Removing the handcuffs on grammatical expression in the manual modality. *Psychological Review, 103*, 34–55. (14)

Goldin-Meadow, S., & Mylander, C. (1998). Spontaneous sign systems created by deaf children in two cultures. *Nature, 391*, 279–281. (14)

Goldman, D., Urbanek, M., Guenther, D., Robin, R., & Long, J. C. (1998). A functionally deficient DRD2 variant [Ser311Cys] is not linked to alcoholism and substance abuse. *Alcohol, 16*, 47–52. (3)

Goldman, P. S. (1971). Functional development of the prefrontal cortex in early life and the problem of neuronal plasticity. *Experimental Neurology, 32*, 366–387. (15)

Goldman, P. S. (1976). The role of experience in recovery of function following orbital prefrontal lesions in infant monkeys. *Neuropsychologia, 14*, 401–412. (15)

Goldman-Rakic, P. S. (1987). Development of cortical circuitry and cognitive function. *Child Development, 58*, 601–622. (5)

Goldman-Rakic, P. S. (1988). Topography of cognition: Parallel distributed networks in primate association cortex. *Annual Review of Neuroscience, 11*, 137–156. (inside cover, 4)

Goldstein, A. (1980). Thrills in response to music and other stimuli. *Physiological Psychology, 8*, 126–129. (7)

Goldstein, J. M., Seidman, L. J., Horton, N. J., Makris, N., Kennedy, D. N., Caviness, V. S., Jr., Faraone, S. V., & Tsuang, M. T. (2001). Normal sexual dimorphism of the adult human brain assessed by in vivo magnetic resonance imaging. *Cerebral Cortex, 11*, 490–497. (11)

Goldstein, L. B. (1993). Basic and clinical studies of pharmacologic effects on recovery from brain injury. *Journal of Neural Transplantation & Plasticity, 4*, 175–192. (5)

Gollin, E. S. (1960). Developmental studies of visual recognition of incomplete objects. *Perceptual and Motor Skills, 11*, 289–298. (13)

Goodale, M. A. (1996). Visuomotor modules in the vertebrate brain. *Canadian Journal of Physiology and Pharmacology, 74*, 390–400. (6, 8)

Goodale, M. A., Milner, A. D., Jakobson, L. S., & Carey, D. P. (1991). A neurological dissociation between perceiving objects and grasping them. *Nature, 349*, 154–156. (6, 8)

Gopnik, M., & Crago, M. B. (1991). Familial aggregation of a developmental language disorder. *Cognition, 39*, 1–50. (14)

Gorell, J. M., Rybicki, B. A., Johnson, C. C., & Peterson, E. L. (1999). Smoking and Parkinson's disease: A dose-response relationship. *Neurology, 52*, 115–119. (8)

Gorman, J. M., Kent, J., Martinez, J., Browne, S., Coplan, J., & Papp, L. A. (2001). Physiological changes during carbon dioxide inhalation in patients with panic disorder, major depression, and premenstrual dysphoric disorder. *Archives of General Psychiatry, 58*, 125–131. (12)

Gorski, R. A. (1980). Sexual differentiation of the brain. In D. T. Krieger & J. C. Hughes (Eds.), *Neuroendocrinology* (pp. 215–222). Sunderland, MA: Sinauer. (11)

Gorski, R. A. (1985). The 13th J. A. F. Stevenson memorial lecture. Sexual differentiation of the brain: Possible mechanisms and implications. *Canadian Journal of Physiology and Pharmacology, 63*, 577–594. (11)

Gorski, R. A., & Allen, L. S. (1992). Sexual orientation and the size of the anterior commissure in the human brain. *Proceedings of the National Academy of Sciences, USA, 89*, 7199–7202. (11)

Gosler, A. G., Greenwood, J. J. D., & Perrins, C. (1995). Predation risk and the cost of being fat. *Nature, 377*, 621–623. (10)

Gottesman, I. I. (1991). *Schizophrenia genesis*. New York: Freeman. (15)

Gould, E., Reeves, A. J., Graziano, M. S. A., & Gross, C. G. (1999). Neurogenesis in the neocortex of adult primates. *Science, 286*, 548–552. (5)

Gratacòs, M., Nadal, M., Martín-Santos, R., Pujana, M. A., Gago, J., Peral, B., Armengol, L., Ponsa, I., Miró, R., Bulbena, A., & Estivill, X. (2001). A polymorphic genomic duplication on human chromosome 15 is a susceptibility factor for panic and phobic disorders. *Cell, 106*, 367–379. (12)

Graves, J. A. M. (1994). Mammalian sex-determining genes. In R. V. Short & E. Balaban (Eds.), *The differences between the sexes* (pp. 397–418). Cambridge, England: Cambridge University Press. (11)

Gray, C. M., König, P., Engel, A. K., & Singer, W. (1989). Oscillatory responses in cat visual cortex exhibit inter-columnar synchronization which reflects global stimulus properties. *Nature, 338*, 334–337. (4)

Graybiel, A. M. (1998). The basal ganglia and chunking of action repertoires. *Neurobiology of Learning and Memory, 70*, 119–136. (8)

Graybiel, A. M., Aosaki, T., Flaherty, A. W., & Kimura, M. (1994). The basal ganglia and adaptive motor control. *Science, 265*, 1826–1831. (4)

Graybiel, A. M., & Rauch, S. L. (2000). Toward a neurobiology of obsessive-compulsive disorder. *Neuron, 28*, 343–347. (8)

Graziadei, P. P. C., & deHan, R. S. (1973). Neuronal regeneration in frog olfactory system. *Journal of Cell Biology, 59*, 525–530. (5)

Graziano, M. S. A., Taylor, C. S. R., & Moore, T. (2002). Complex movements evoked by microstimulation of precentral cortex. *Neuron, 34*, 841–851. (4, 8)

Greene, J. D., Sommerville, R. B., Nystrom, L. E., Darley, J. M., & Cohen, J. D. (2001). An fMRI investigation of emotional engagement in moral judgment. *Science, 293*, 2105–2108. (12)

Greenlee, M. W., Lang, H.-J., Mergner, T., & Seeger, W. (1995). Visual short-term memory of stimulus velocity in patients with unilateral posterior brain damage. *Journal of Neuroscience, 15*, 2287–2300. (6)

Greenough, W. T. (1975). Experiential modification of the developing brain. *American Scientist, 63*, 37–46. (5)

Gribkoff, V. K., Starrett, J. E., Jr., Dworetzky, S. I., Hewawasam, P., Boissard, C. G., Cook, D. A., Frantz, S. W., Heman, K., Hibbard, J. R., Huston, K., Johnson, G., Krishnan, B. S., Kinney, G. G., Lombardo, L. A., Meanwell, N. A., Molinoff, P. B., Myers, R. A., Moon, S. L., Ortiz, A., Pajor, L., Pieschl, R. L., Post-Munson, D. J., Signor, L. J., Srinivas, N., Taber, M. T., Thalody, G., Trojnacki, J. T., Wiener, H., Yeleswaram, K., & Yeola, S. W. (2001). Targeting acute ischemic stroke with a calcium-sensitive opener of maxi-K potassium channels. *Nature Medicine, 7*, 471–477. (5)

Grice, D. E., Halmi, K. A., Fichter, M. M., Strober, M., Woodside, D. B., Treasure, J. T., Kaplan, A. S., Magistretti, P. J., Goldman, D., Bulik, C. M., Kaye, W. H., & Berrettini, W. H. (2002). Evidence for a susceptibility gene for anorexia nervosa on chromosome 1. *American Journal of Human Genetics, 70*, 787–792. (10)

Griffin, D. R., Webster, F. A., & Michael, C. R. (1960). The echolocation of flying insects by bats. *Animal Behaviour, 8*, 141–154. (7)

Griffiths, T. D., Uppenkamp, S., Johnsrude, I., Josephs, O., & Patterson, R. D. (2001). Encoding of the temporal regularity of sound in the human brainstem. *Nature Neuroscience, 4*, 633–637. (7)

Grillon, C., Morgan, C. A., III, Davis, M., & Southwick, S. M. (1998). Effect of darkness on acoustic startle in Vietnam veterans with PTSD. *American Journal of Psychiatry, 155*, 812–817. (12)

Gross, C. G. (1999). The fire that comes from the eye. *The Neuroscientist, 5*, 58–64. (6)

Gross, C. G., & Graziano, M. S. A. (1995). Multiple representations of space in the brain. *The Neuroscientist, 1*, 43–50. (4)

Grosshans, D. R., Clayton, D. A., Coultrap, S. J., & Browning, M. D. (2002). LTP leads to rapid surface expression of NMDA but not AMPA receptors in adult rat CA1. *Nature Neuroscience, 5*, 27–33. (13)

Grossman, E. D., & Blake, R. (2001). Brain activity evoked by inverted and imagined biological motion. *Vision Research, 41*, 1475–1482. (6)

Grossman, E., Donnelly, M., Price, R., Pickens, D., Morgan, V., Neighbor, G., & Blake, R. (2000). Brain areas involved in perception of biological motion. *Journal of Cognitive Neuroscience, 12*, 711–720. (6)

Grossman, S. P., Dacey, D., Halaris, A. E., Collier, T., & Routtenberg, A. (1978). Aphagia and adipsia after preferential destruction of nerve cell bodies in hypothalamus. *Science, 202*, 537–539. (10)

Gubernick, D. J., & Alberts, J. R. (1983). Maternal licking of young: Resource exchange and proximate controls. *Physiology & Behavior, 31*, 593–601. (11)

Guidotti, A., Ferrero, P., Fujimoto, M., Santi, R. M., & Costa, E. (1986). Studies on endogenous ligands (endocoids) for the benzodiazepine/beta carboline binding sites. *Advances in Biochemical Pharmacology, 41*, 137–148. (12)

Guidotti, A., Forchetti, C. M., Corda, M. G., Konkel, D., Bennett, C. D., & Costa, E. (1983). Isolation, characterization, and purification to homogeneity of an endogenous polypeptide with agonistic action on benzodiazepine receptors. *Proceedings of the National Academy of Sciences, USA, 80*, 3531–3535. (12)

Guilleminault, C., Heinzer, R., Mignot, E., & Black, J. (1998). Investigations into the neurologic basis of narcolepsy. *Neurology, 50*(Suppl. 1), S8–S15. (9)

Guillery, R. W., Feig, S. L., & Lozsádi, D. A. (1998). Paying attention to the thalamic reticular nucleus. *Trends in Neurosciences, 21*, 28–32. (4, 9)

Guillery, R. W., Feig, S. L., & van Lieshout, D. P. (2001). Connections of higher order visual relays in the thalamus: A study of corticothalamic pathways in cats. *Journal of Comparative Neurology, 438*, 66–85. (6)

Guillin, O., Diaz, J., Carroll, P., Griffon, N., Schwartz, J-C., & Sokoloff P. (2001). BDNF controls dopamine D₃ receptor expression and triggers behavioural sensitization. *Nature, 412*, 86–89. (15)

Guo, S.-W., & Reed, D. R. (2001). The genetics of phenylthiocarbamide perception. *Annals of Human Biology, 28*, 111–142. (7)

Gur, R. E., & Chin, S. (1999). Laterality in functional brain imaging studies of schizophrenia. *Schizophrenia Bulletin, 25*, 141–156. (15)

Gur, R. E., Cowell, P. E., Latshaw, A., Turetsky, B. I., Grossman, R. I., Arnold, S. E., Bilker, W. B., & Gur, R. C. (2000). Reduced dorsal and orbital prefrontal gray matter volumes in schizophrenia. *Archives of General Psychiatry, 57,* 761–768. (15)

Gur, R. E., Turetsky, B. I., Cowell, P. E., Finkelman, C., Maany, V., Grossman, R. I., Arnold, S. E., Bilker, W. B., & Gur, R. C. (2000). Temporolimbic volume reductions in schizophrenia. *Archives of General Psychiatry, 57,* 769–775. (15)

Gurevich, E. V., Bordelon, Y., Shapiro, R. M., Arnold, S. E., Gur, R. E., & Joyce, J. N. (1997). Mesolimbic dopamine D$_3$ receptors and use of antipsychotics in patients with schizophrenia. *Archives of General Psychiatry, 54,* 225–232. (15)

Gusella, J. F., & MacDonald, M. E. (2000). Molecular genetics: Unmasking polyglutamine triggers in neurodegenerative disease. *Nature Reviews Neuroscience, 1,* 109–115. (8)

Gusnard, D. A., & Raichle, M. E. (2001). Searching for a baseline: Functional imaging and the resting human brain. *Nature Reviews Neuroscience, 2,* 685–694. (4)

Gustafsson, B., & Wigström, H. (1990). Basic features of long-term potentiation in the hippocampus. *Seminars in the Neurosciences, 2,* 321–333. (13)

Gwinner, E. (1986). Circannual rhythms in the control of avian rhythms. *Advances in the Study of Behavior, 16,* 191–228. (9)

Hadjikhani, N., Liu, A. K., Dale, A. M., Cavanagh, P., & Tootell, R. B. H. (1998). Retinotopy and color sensitivity in human visual cortical area V8. *Nature Neuroscience, 1,* 235–241. (6)

Häfner, H., an der Heiden, W., Behrens, S., Gattaz, W. F., Hambrecht, M., Löffler, W., Maurer, K., Munk-Jørgensen, P., Nowotny, B., Riecher-Rössler, A., & Stein, A. (1998). Causes and consequences of the gender difference in age of onset of schizophrenia. *Schizophrenia Bulletin, 24,* 99–113. (15)

Haggarty, J. M., Cernovsky, Z., Husni, M., Minor, K., Kermean, P., & Merskey, H. (2002). Seasonal affective disorder in an arctic community. *Acta Psychiatrica Scandinavica, 105,* 378–384. (15)

Haidt, J. (2001). The emotional dog and its rational tail: A social intuitionist approach to moral judgment. *Psychological Review, 108,* 814–834. (12)

Haimov, I., & Arendt, J. (1999). The prevention and treatment of jet lag. *Sleep Medicine Reviews, 3,* 229–240. (9)

Haimov, I., & Lavie, P. (1996). Melatonin—A soporific hormone. *Current Directions in Psychological Science, 5,* 106–111. (9)

Haist, F., Gore, J. B., & Mao, H. (2001). Consolidation of human memory over decades revealed by functional magnetic resonance imaging. *Nature Neuroscience, 4,* 1139–1145. (13)

Hajnal, A., Takenouchi, K., & Norgren, R. (1999). Effect of intraduodenal lipid on parabrachial gustatory coding in awake rats. *Journal of Neuroscience, 19,* 7182–7190. (10)

Halaas, J. L, Gajiwala, K. S., Maffei, M., Cohen, S. L., Chait, B. T., Rabinowitz, D., Lallone, R. L., Burley, S. K., & Friedman, J. M. (1995). Weight-reducing effects of the plasma protein encoded by the *obese* gene. *Science, 269,* 543–546. (10)

Hale, S., Myerson, J., Rhee, S. H., Weiss, C. S., & Abrams, R. A. (1996). Selective interference with the maintenance of location information in working memory. *Neuropsychology, 10,* 228–240. (13)

Haley, J. (1959). An interactional description of schizophrenia. *Psychiatry, 22,* 321–332. (15)

Halford, J. C. G., & Blundell, J. E. (2000). Pharmacology of appetite suppression. *Progress in Drug Research, 54,* 25–58. (10)

Hall, J., Thomas, K. L., & Everitt, B. J. (2000). Rapid and selective induction of BDNF expression in the hippocampus during contextual learning. *Nature Neuroscience, 3,* 533–535. (13)

Hall, S. M., Reus, V. I., Muñoz, R. F., Sees, K. L., Humfleet, G., Hartz, D. T., Frederick, S., & Triffleman, E. (1998). Nortriptyline and cognitive-behavioral therapy in the treatment of cigarette smoking. *Archives of General Psychiatry, 55,* 683–690. (15)

Halpern, S. D., Andrews, T. J., & Purves, D. (1999). Interindividual variation in human visual performance. *Journal of Cognitive Neuroscience, 11,* 521–534. (6)

Hamann, S. B., Ely, T. D., Hoffman, J. M., & Kilts, C. D. (2002). Ecstasy and agony: Activation of the human amygdala in positive and negative emotion. *Psychological Science, 13,* 135–141. (12, 14)

Hamann, S. B., & Squire, L. R. (1995). On the acquisition of new declarative knowledge in amnesia. *Behavioral Neuroscience, 109,* 1027–1044. (13)

Hamer, D. H., Hu, S., Magnuson, V. L., Hu, N., & Pattatucci, A. M. L. (1993). A linkage between DNA markers on the X chromosome and male sexual orientation. *Science, 261,* 321–327. (11)

Hameroff, S. (2001). Consciousness, the brain, and spacetime geometry. *Annals of the New York Academy of Sciences, 929,* 74–104. (1)

Hamilton, W. D. (1964). The genetical evolution of social behavior (I and II). *Journal of Theoretical Biology, 7,* 1–16; 17–52. (1)

Hampson, R. E., Simeral, J. D., & Deadwyler, S. A. (1999). Distribution of spatial and nonspatial information in dorsal hippocampus. *Nature, 402,* 610–614. (13)

Han, C. J., & Robinson, J. K. (2001). Cannabinoid modulation of time estimation in the rat. *Behavioral Neuroscience, 115,* 243–246. (15)

Hanaway, J., Woolsey, T. A., Gado, M. H., & Roberts, M. P., Jr. (1998). *The brain atlas.* Bethesda, MD: Fitzgerald Science Press. (12)

Hannibal, J., Hindersson, P., Knudsen, S. M., Georg, B., & Fahrenkrug, J. (2001). The photopigment melanopsin is exclusively present in pituitary adenylate cyclase-activating polypeptide-containing retinal ganglion cells of the retinohypothalamic tract. *Journal of Neuroscience, 21,* RC191: 1–7. (9)

Haqq, C. M., & Donahoe, P. K. (1998). Regulation of sexual dimorphism in mammals. *Physiological Reviews, 78,* 1–33. (11)

Hara, J., Beuckmann, C. T., Nambu, T., Willie, J. T., Chemelli, R. M., Sinton, C. M., Sugiyama, F., Yagami, K.-i., Goto, K., Yanagisawa, M., & Sakurai, T. (2001). Genetic ablation of orexin neurons in mice results in narcolepsy, hypophagia, and obesity. *Neuron, 30*, 345–354. (9)

Harel, M., Kasher, R., Nicolas, A., Guss, J. M., Balass, M., Fridkin, M., Smith, A. B., Brejc, K., Sixma, T. K., Katchalski-Katzir, E., Sussman, J. L., & Fuchs, S. (2001). The binding site of acetylcholine receptor as visualized in the x-ray structure of a complex between a-bungarotoxin and a mimotope peptide. *Neuron, 32*, 265–275. (3)

Hari, R. (1994). Human cortical functions revealed by magnetoencephalography. *Progress in Brain Research, 100*, 163–168. (5)

Harley, B., & Wang, W. (1997). The critical period hypothesis: Where are we now? In A. M. B. deGroot & J. F. Knoll (Eds.), *Tutorials in bilingualism* (pp. 19–51). Mahwah, NJ: Erlbaum. (14)

Harmer, C. J., Thilo, K. V., Rothwell, J. C., & Goodwin, G. M. (2001). Transcranial magnetic stimulation of medial-frontal cortex impairs the processing of angry facial expressions. *Nature Neuroscience, 4*, 17–18. (12)

Harris, C. H. (2002). Sexual and romantic jealousy in heterosexual and homosexual adults. *Psychological Science, 13*, 7–12. (11)

Harris, C. R. (1999, July/August). The mystery of ticklish laughter. *American Scientist, 87*(4), 344–351. (7)

Harris, K. M., & Stevens, J. K. (1989). Dendritic spines of CA1 pyramidal cells in the rat hippocampus: Serial electron microscopy with reference to their biophysical characteristics. *Journal of Neuroscience, 9*, 2982–2997. (2)

Harris, R. A., Brodie, M. S., & Dunwiddie, T. V. (1992). Possible substrates of ethanol reinforcement: GABA and dopamine. *Annals of the New York Academy of Sciences, 654*, 61–69. (15)

Hart, B. L. (Ed.). (1976). *Experimental psychobiology.* San Francisco: Freeman. (10)

Hartline, H. K. (1949). Inhibition of activity of visual receptors by illuminating nearby retinal areas in the limulus eye. *Federation Proceedings, 8*, 69. (6)

Haueisen, J., & Knösche, T. R. (2001). Involuntary motor activity in pianists evoked by music perception. *Journal of Cognitive Neuroscience, 13*, 786–792. (8)

Hausmann, M., Slabbekoorn, D., Van Goozen, S. H. M., Cohen-Kettenis, P. T., & Güntürkün, O. (2000). Sex hormones affect spatial abilities during the menstrual cycle. *Behavioral Neuroscience, 114*, 1245–1250. (11)

Häusser, M., Spruston, N., & Stuart, G. J. (2000). Diversity and dynamics of dendritic signaling. *Science, 290*, 739–744. (2)

Haxby, J. V., Gobbini, M. I., Furey, M. L., Ishai, A., Schouten, J. L., & Pietrini, P. (2001). Distributed and overlapping representations of faces and objects in ventral temporal cortex. *Science, 293*, 2425–2430. (6)

Haydon, P. G. (2001). Glia: Listening and talking to the synapse. *Nature Reviews Neuroscience, 2*, 185–193. (2)

Hebb, D. O. (1949). *Organization of behavior.* New York: Wiley. (inside cover, 13)

Heffner, R. S., & Heffner, H. E. (1982). Hearing in the elephant (*Elephas maximus*): Absolute sensitivity, frequency discrimination, and sound localization. *Journal of Comparative and Physiological Psychology, 96*, 926–944. (7)

Hegdé, J., & Van Essen, D. C. (2000). Selectivity for complex shapes in primate visual area V2. *Journal of Neuroscience, 20*, RC61:1–6. (6)

Heisler, L. K., Cowley, M. A., Tecott, L. H., Fan, W., Low, M. J., Smart, J. L., Rubinstein, M., Tatro, J. B., Marcus, J. N., Holstege, H., Lee, C. E., Cone, R. D., & Elmquist, J. K. (2002). Activation of central melanocortin pathways by fenfluramine. *Science, 297*, 609–611. (10)

Heiss, W.-D., Kessler, J., Thiel, A., Ghaemi, M., & Karbe, H. (1999). Differential capacity of left and right hemispheric areas for compensation of poststroke aphasia.

Annals of Neurology, 45, 430–438. (14)

Heldt, S., Sundin, V., Willott, J. F., & Falls, W. A. (2000). Posttraining lesions of the amygdala interfere with fear-potentiated startle to both visual and auditory conditioned stimuli in C56BL/6J mice. *Behavioral Neuroscience, 114*, 749–759. (12)

Helenius, P., Salmelin, R., Richardson, U., Leinonen, S., & Lyytinen, H. (2002). Abnormal auditory cortical activation in dyslexia 100 msec after speech onset. *Journal of Cognitive Neuroscience, 14*, 603–617. (14)

Heller, W., & Levy, J. (1981). Perception and expression of emotion in right-handers and left-handers. *Neuropsychologia, 19*, 263–272. (14)

Hendrie, H. C. (2001). Exploration of environmental and genetic risk factors for Alzheimer's disease: The value of cross-cultural studies. *Current Directions in Psychological Science, 10*, 98–101. (13)

Hendry, S. H. C., & Reid, R. C. (2000). The koniocellular pathway in primate vision. *Annual Review of Neuroscience, 23*, 127–153. (6)

Hennig, R., & Lømo, T. (1985). Firing patterns of motor units in normal rats. *Nature, 314*, 164–166. (8)

Heresco-Levy, U., Javitt, D. C., Ermilov, M., Mordel, C., Silipo, G., & Lichtenstein, M. (1999). Efficacy of high-dose glycine in the treatment of enduring negative symptoms of schizophrenia. *Archives of General Psychiatry, 56*, 29–36. (15)

Herkenham, M. (1992). Cannabinoid receptor localization in brain: Relationship to motor and reward systems. *Annals of the New York Academy of Sciences, 654*, 19–32. (15)

Herkenham, M., Lynn, A. B., de Costa, B. R., & Richfield, E. K. (1991). Neuronal localization of cannabinoid receptors in the basal ganglia of the rat. *Brain Research, 547*, 267–274. (15)

Herman, L. M., Pack, A. A., & Morrel-Samuels, P. (1993). Representational and conceptual skills of dolphins. In H. L. Roitblat, L. M. Herman, & P. E. Nachtigall

(Eds.), *Language and communication: Comparative perspectives* (pp. 403–442). Hillsdale, NJ: Erlbaum. (14)

Herrero, S. (1985). *Bear attacks: Their causes and avoidance.* Piscataway, NJ: Winchester. (7)

Hertz-Pannier, L., Chiron, C., Jampaqué, I., Renaux-Kieffer, V., Van de Moortele, P.-F., Delalande, O., Fohlen, M., Brunelle, F., & Le Bihan, D. (2002). Late plasticity for language in a child's non-dominant hemisphere. A pre- and post-surgery fMRI study. *Brain, 125,* 361–372. (14)

Herz, J., & Beffert, U. (2000). Apoliprotein E receptors: Linking brain development and Alzheimer's disease. *Nature Reviews Neuroscience, 1,* 51–58. (13)

Herz, R. S., & Cahill, E. D. (1997). Differential use of sensory information in sexual behavior as a function of gender. *Human Nature, 8,* 275–286. (11)

Herz, R. S., McCall, C., & Cahill, L. (1999). Hemispheric lateralization in the processing of odor pleasantness versus odor names. *Chemical Senses, 24,* 691–695. (14)

Herzog, E. D., Takahashi, J. S., & Block, G. D. (1998). Clock controls circadian period in isolated suprachiasmatic nucleus neurons. *Nature Neuroscience, 1,* 708–713. (9)

Herzog, S., Pfeuffer, I., Haberzettl, K., Feldmann, H., Frese, K., Bechter, K., & Richt, J. A. (1997). Molecular characterization of Borna disease virus from naturally infected animals and possible links to human disorders. *Archives of Virology* (Suppl. 13), 183–190. (15)

Hess, B. J. M. (2001). Vestibular signals in self-orientation and eye movement control. *News in Physiological Sciences, 16,* 234–238. (7)

Hettinger, T. P., & Frank, M. E. (1992). Information processing in mammalian gustatory systems. *Current Opinion in Neurobiology, 2,* 469–478. (7)

Hickok, G., Bellugi, U., & Klima, E. S. (1996). The neurobiology of sign language and its implications for the neural basis of language. *Nature, 381,* 699–702. (14)

Higley, J. D., Mehlman, P. T., Higley, S. B., Fernald, B., Vickers, J., Lindell, S. G., Taub, D. M., Suomi, S. J., & Linnoila, M. (1996). Excessive mortality in young free-ranging male nonhuman primates with low cerebrospinal fluid 5-hydroxyindoleacetic acid concentrations. *Archives of General Psychiatry, 53,* 537–543. (12)

Higley, M. J., Hermer-Vazquez, L., Levitsky, D. A., & Strupp, B. J. (2001). Recovery of associative function following early amygdala lesions in rats. *Behavioral Neuroscience, 115,* 154–164. (5)

Hill, S. Y., De Bellis, M. D., Keshavan, M. S., Lowers, L., Shen, S., Hall, J., & Pitts, T. (2001). Right amygdala volume in adolescents and young adult offspring from families at high risk for developing alcoholism. *Biological Psychiatry, 49,* 894–905. (15)

Hinkle, D. A., & Connor, C. E. (2002). Three-dimensional orientation tuning in macaque area V4. *Nature Neuroscience, 5,* 665–670. (6)

Hinney, A., Ziegler, A., Oeffner, F., Wedewardt, C., Vogel, M., Wulftange, H., Geller, F., Stübing, K., Siegfried, W., Goldschmidt, H.-P., Remschmidt, H., & Hebebrand, J. (2000). Independent confirmation of a major locus for obesity on chromosome 10. *Journal of Clinical Endocrinology & Metabolism, 85,* 2962–2965. (10)

Hitchcock, J. M., & Davis, M. (1991). Efferent pathway of the amygdala involved in conditioned fear as measured with the fear-potentiated startle paradigm. *Behavioral Neuroscience, 105,* 826–842. (12)

Hobson, J. A. (1989). *Sleep.* New York: Scientific American Library. (15)

Hobson, J. A., & McCarley, R. W. (1977). The brain as a dream state generator: An activation-synthesis hypothesis of the dream process. *American Journal of Psychiatry, 134,* 1335–1348. (9)

Hobson, J. A., Pace-Schott, E. F., & Stickgold, R. (2000). Dreaming and the brain: Toward a cognitive neuroscience of conscious states. *Behavioral and Brain Sciences, 23,* 793–1121. (9)

Hoebel, B. G. (1988). Neuroscience and motivation: Pathways and peptides that define motivational systems. In R. C. Atkinson, R. J. Herrnstein, G. Lindzey, & R. D. Luce (Eds.), *Stevens' handbook of experimental psychology* (2nd ed.) (pp. 547–625). New York: Wiley. (10)

Hoebel, B. G., & Hernandez, L. (1993). Basic neural mechanisms of feeding and weight regulation. In A. J. Stunkard & T. A. Wadden (Eds.), *Obesity: Theory and therapy* (2nd ed.) (pp. 43–62). New York: Raven Press. (10)

Hoebel, B. G., Rada, P. V., Mark, G. P., & Pothos, E. (1999). Neural systems for reinforcement and inhibition of behavior: Relevance to eating, addiction, and depression. In D. Kahneman, E. Diener, & N. Schwartz (Eds.), *Well-being: Foundations of hedonic psychology* (pp. 560–574). New York: Russell Sage Foundation. (10)

Hoffer, A. (1973). Mechanism of action of nicotinic acid and nicotinamide in the treatment of schizophrenia. In D. Hawkins & L. Pauling (Eds.), *Orthomolecular psychiatry* (pp. 202–262). San Francisco: Freeman. (15)

Hoffman, P. L., Tabakoff, B., Szabó, G., Suzdak, P. D., & Paul, S. M. (1987). Effect of an imidazobenzodiazepine, Ro15-4513, on the incoordination and hypothermia produced by ethanol and pentobarbital. *Life Sciences, 41,* 611–619. (12)

Hoffman, R. (2001). Thermophiles in Kamchatka. *American Scientist, 89,* 20–23. (10)

Hökfelt, T., Johansson, O., & Goldstein, M. (1984). Chemical anatomy of the brain. *Science, 225,* 1326–1334. (3)

Holcombe, A. O., & Cavanagh, P. (2001). Early binding of feature pairs for visual perception. *Nature Neuroscience, 4,* 127–128. (4)

Hollingsworth, D. E., McAuliffe, S. P., & Knowlton, B. J. (2001). Temporal allocation of visual attention in adult attention deficit hyperactivity disorder. *Journal of Cognitive Neuroscience, 13,* 298–305. (7)

Hollister, J. M., Laing, P., & Mednick, S. A. (1996). Rhesus incompatibility as a risk factor for schizophrenia in male adults. *Archives of General Psychiatry, 53,* 19–24. (15)

Holsinger, T., Steffens, D. C., Phillips, C., Helms, M. J., Havlik, R. J., Breitner, J. C. S., Guralnik, J. M., & Plassman, B. L. (2002). Head injury in early adulthood and the lifetime risk of depression. *Archives of General Psychiatry, 59,* 17–22. (15)

Holy, T. E., Dulac, C., & Meister, M. (2000). Responses of vomeronasal neurons to natural stimuli. *Science, 289,* 1569–1572. (7)

Homewood, J., & Stevenson, R. J. (2001). Differences in naming accuracy of odors presented to the left and right nostrils. *Biological Psychology, 58,* 65–73. (14)

Hoover, J. E., & Strick, P. L. (1993). Multiple output channels in the basal ganglia. *Science, 259,* 819–821. (8)

Hopkins, J., Marcus, M., & Campbell, S. B. (1984). Postpartum depression: A critical review. *Psychological Bulletin, 95,* 498–515. (15)

Hopkins, W. D., Dahl, J. F., & Pilcher, D. (2001). Genetic influence on the expression of hand preferences in chimpanzees (Pan troglodytes): Evidence in support of the right-shift theory and developmental instability. *Psychological Science, 12,* 299–303. (14)

Hoptman, M. J., & Levy, J. (1988). Perceptual asymmetries in left- and right-handers for cartoon and real faces. *Brain and Cognition, 8,* 178–188. (14)

Horn, C. C., Tordoff, M. G., & Friedman, M. I. (1996). Does ingested fat produce satiety? *American Journal of Physiology, 270,* R761–R765. (10)

Horne, J. A. (1992). Sleep and its disorders in children. *Journal of Child Psychology & Psychiatry & Allied Disorders, 33,* 473–487. (9)

Horne, J. A., & Minard, A. (1985). Sleep and sleepiness following a behaviourally "active" day. *Ergonomics, 28,* 567–575. (9)

Horner, P. J., & Gage, F. H. (2000). Regenerating the damaged central nervous system. *Nature, 407,* 963–970. (5)

Horridge, G. A. (1962). Learning of leg position by the ventral nerve cord in headless insects. *Proceedings of the Royal Society of London, B, 157,* 33–52. (13)

Horst, W. D., & Preskorn, S. H. (1998). Mechanisms of action and clinical characteristics of three atypical antidepressants: Venlafaxine, nefazodone, bupropion. *Journal of Affective Disorders, 51,* 237–254. (15)

Horton, J. C., & Hocking, D. R. (1996). An adult-like pattern of ocular dominance columns in striate cortex of newborn monkeys prior to visual experience. *Journal of Neuroscience, 16,* 1791–1807. (6)

Horvath, T. L., Diano, S., Sotonyi, P., Heiman, M., & Tschöp, M. (2001). Minireview: Ghrelin and the regulation of energy balance—A hypothalamic perspective. *Endocrinology, 142,* 4163–4169. (10)

Horvath, T. L., & Wikler, K. C. (1999). Aromatase in developing sensory systems of the rat brain. *Journal of Neuroendocrinology, 11,* 77–84. (11)

Horvitz, J. C., & Eyny, Y. S. (2000). Dopamine D2 receptor blockade reduces response likelihood but does not affect latency to emit a learned sensory-motor response: Implications for Parkinson's disease. *Behavioral Neuroscience, 114,* 934–939. (8)

Horwitz, B., Rumsey, J. M., & Donohue, B. C. (1998). Functional connectivity of the angular gyrus in normal reading and dyslexia. *Proceedings of the National Academy of Sciences, USA, 95,* 8939–8944. (14)

Hoshi, E., & Tanji, J. (2000). Integration of target and body-part information in the premotor cortex when planning action. *Nature, 408,* 466–470. (8)

Hovda, D. A., & Feeney, D. M. (1989). Amphetamine-induced recovery of visual cliff performance after bilateral visual cortex ablation in cats: Measurements of depth perception thresholds. *Behavioral Neuroscience, 103,* 574–584. (5)

Howland, H. C., & Sayles, N. (1984). Photorefractive measurements of astigmatism in infants and young children. *Investigative Ophthalmology and Visual Science, 25,* 93–102. (6)

Hrdy, S. B. (2000). The optimal number of fathers. *Annals of the New York Academy of Sciences, 907,* 75–96. (11)

Hróbjartsson, A., & Gøtzsche, P. C. (2001). Is the placebo powerless? *New England Journal of Medicine, 344,* 1594–1602. (7)

Hsu, M., Sik, A., Gallyas, F., Horváth, Z., & Buzsáki, G. (1994). Short-term and long-term changes in the postischemic hippocampus. *Annals of the New York Academy of Sciences, 743,* 121–140. (5)

Huang, W., Sved, A. F., & Stricker, E. M. (2000). Water ingestion provides an early signal inhibiting osmotically stimulated vasopressin secretion in rats. *American Journal of Physiology, 279,* R756–R760. (10)

Hubel, D. H. (1963, November). The visual cortex of the brain. *Scientific American, 209*(5), 54–62. (6)

Hubel, D. H., & Wiesel, T. N. (1959). Receptive fields of single neurons in the cat's striate cortex. *Journal of Physiology, 148,* 574–591. (6)

Hubel, D. H., & Wiesel, T. N. (1965). Binocular interaction in striate cortex of kittens reared with artificial squint. *Journal of Neurophysiology, 28,* 1041–1059. (6)

Hubel, D. H., & Wiesel, T. N. (1977). Functional architecture of macaque monkey visual cortex. *Proceedings of the Royal Society of London, B, 198,* 1–59. (6)

Hubel, D. H., & Wiesel, T. N. (1998). Early exploration of the visual cortex. *Neuron, 20,* 401–412. (6)

Hudspeth, A. J. (1985). The cellular basis of hearing: The biophysics of hair cells. *Science, 230,* 745–752. (7)

Huestis, M. A., Gorelick, D. A., Heishman, S. J., Preston, K. L., Nelson, R. A., Moolchan, E. T., & Frank, R. A. (2001). Blockade of effect of smoked marijuana by the CB1-selective cannabinoid receptor antagonist SR141716. *Archives of General Psychiatry, 58,* 322–328. (15)

Hugdahl, K. (1996). Brain laterality—beyond the basics. *European Psychologist, 1,* 206–220. (14)

Hughes, II. C., Nozawa, G., & Kitterle, F. (1996). Global precedence, spatial frequency channels, and the statistics of natural images. *Journal of Cognitive Neuroscience, 8*, 197–230. (6)

Hughes, J. C., & Cook, C. C. H. (1997). The efficacy of disulfiram: A review of outcome studies. *Addiction, 92*, 381–395. (15)

Hull, E. M., Du, J., Lorrain, D. S., & Matuszewich, L. (1997). Testosterone, preoptic dopamine, and copulation in male rats. *Brain Research Bulletin, 44*, 327–333. (11)

Hull, E. M., Eaton, R. C., Markowski, V. P., Moses, J., Lumley, L. A., & Loucks, J. A. (1992). Opposite influence of medial preoptic D_1 and D_2 receptors on genital reflexes: Implications for copulation. *Life Sciences, 51*, 1705–1713. (11)

Hull, E. M., Lorrain, D. S., Du, J., Matuszewich, L., Lumley, L. A., Putnam, S. K., & Moses, J. (1999). Hormone-neurotransmitter interactions in the control of sexual behavior. *Behavioural Brain Research, 105*, 105–116. (11)

Hull, E. M., Nishita, J. K., Bitran, D., & Dalterio, S. (1984). Perinatal dopamine-related drugs demasculinize rats. *Science, 224*, 1011–1013. (11)

Hulshoff, H. E., Schnack, H. G., Mandl, R. C. W., van Haren, N. E. M., Koning, H., Collins, L., Evans, A. C., & Kahn, R. S. (2001). Focal gray matter density changes in schizophrenia. *Archives of General Psychiatry, 58*, 1118–1125. (15)

Hultman, C. M., Öhman, A., Cnattingius, S., Wieselgren, I.-M., & Lindström, L. H. (1997). Prenatal and neonatal risk factors for schizophrenia. *British Journal of Psychiatry, 170*, 128–133. (15)

Hunt, E., Streissguth, A. P., Kerr, B., & Carmichael-Olson, H. (1995). Mothers' alcohol consumption during pregnancy: Effects on spatial-visual reasoning in 14-year-old children. *Psychological Science, 6*, 339–342. (5)

Hunt, S. P., & Mantyh, P. W. (2001). The molecular dynamics of pain control. *Nature Reviews Neuroscience, 2*, 83–91. (7)

Hunter, W. S. (1923). *General psychology* (Rev. ed.). Chicago: University of Chicago Press. (4)

Huntington's Disease Collaborative Research Group. (1993). A novel gene containing a trinucleotide repeat that is expanded and unstable on Huntington's disease chromosomes. *Cell, 72*, 971–983. (8)

Hurvich, L. M., & Jameson, D. (1957). An opponent-process theory of color vision. *Psychological Review, 64*, 384–404. (6)

Hutchison, W. D., Davis, K. D., Lozano, A. M., Tasker, R. R., & Dostrovsky, J. O. (1999). Pain-related neurons in the human cingulate cortex. *Nature Neuroscience, 2*, 403–405. (7)

Hyman, S. E., & Malenka, R. C. (2001). Addiction and the brain: The neurobiology of compulsion and its persistence. *Nature Reviews Neuroscience, 2*, 695–703. (15)

Hynd, G. W., & Semrud-Clikeman, M. (1989). Dyslexia and brain morphology. *Psychological Bulletin, 106*, 447–482. (14)

Hypericum Depression Trial Study Group. (2002). Effect of Hypericum perforatum (St John's wort) in major depressive disorder. *Journal of the American Medical Association, 287*, 1807–1814. (15)

Ibrahim, H. M., Hogg, A. J., Jr., Healy, D. J., Haroutunian, V., Davis, K. L., & Meador-Woodruff, J. H. (2000). Ionotropic glutamate receptor binding and subunit mRNA expression in thalamic nuclei in schizophrenia. *American Journal of Psychiatry, 157*, 1811–1823. (15)

Iggo, A., & Andres, K. H. (1982). Morphology of cutaneous receptors. *Annual Review of Neuroscience, 5*, 1–31. (7)

Iidaka, T., Omori, M., Murata, T., Kosaka, H., Yonekura, Y., Okada, T., & Sadato, N. (2001). Neural interaction of the amygdala with the prefrontal and temporal cortices in the processing of facial expressions as revealed by fMRI. *Journal of Cognitive Neuroscience, 13*, 1035–1047. (12)

Ikonomidou, C., Bittigau, P. Ishimaru, M. J., Wozniak, D. F., Koch, C., Genz, K., Price, M. T., Stefovska, V., Hörster, F., Tenkova, T., Dikranian, K., & Olney, J. W. (2000). Ethanol-induced apoptotic neurodegeneration and fetal alcohol syndrome. *Science, 287*, 1056–1060. (5)

Ikonomidou, C., Bosch, F., Miksa, M., Bittigau, P., Vöckler, J., Dikranian, K., Tenkova, T. I., Stefovska, V., Turski, L., & Olney, J. W. (1999). Blockade of NMDA receptors and apoptotic neurodegeneration in the developing brain. *Science, 283*, 70–74. (5)

Imamura, K., Mataga, N., & Mori, K. (1992). Coding of odor molecules by mitral/tufted cells in rabbit olfactory bulb: I. Aliphatic compounds. *Journal of Neurophysiology, 68*, 1986–2002. (7)

Imperato-McGinley, J., Guerrero, L., Gautier, T., & Peterson, R. E. (1974). Steroid 5 alpha-reductase deficiency in man: An inherited form of male pseudohermaphroditism. *Science, 186*, 1213–1215. (11)

Innocenti, G. M. (1980). The primary visual pathway through the corpus callosum: Morphological and functional aspects in the cat. *Archives Italiennes de Biologie, 118*, 124–188. (14)

Innocenti, G. M., & Caminiti, R. (1980). Postnatal shaping of callosal connections from sensory areas. *Experimental Brain Research, 38*, 381–394. (14)

Inouye, S. T., & Kawamura, H. (1979). Persistence of circadian rhythmicity in a mammalian hypothalamic "island" containing the suprachiasmatic nucleus. *Proceedings of the National Academy of Sciences, USA, 76*, 5962–5966. (9)

Isacson, O., Bjorklund, L., & Pernaute, R. S. (2001). Parkinson's disease: Interpretations of transplantation study are erroneous. *Nature Neuroscience, 4*, 553. (8)

Ishai, A., Ungerleider, L. G., Martin, A., & Haxby, J. V. (2000). The representation of objects in the human occipital and temporal cortex. *Journal of Cognitive Neuroscience, 12*(Suppl. 2), 35–51. (6)

Ito, M. (1984). *The cerebellum and neural control.* New York: Raven Press. (8, 13)

Ito, M. (1989). Long-term depression. *Annual Review of Neuroscience, 12*, 85–102. (13)

Ito, M. (2002). The molecular organization of cerebellar long-term depression. *Nature Reviews Neuroscience, 3*, 896–902. (13)

Ivry, R. B., & Diener, H. C. (1991). Impaired velocity perception in patients with lesions of the cerebellum. *Journal of Cognitive Neuroscience, 3*, 355–366. (8)

Ivy, G. O., & Killackey, H. P. (1981). The ontogeny of the distribution of callosal projection neurons in the rat parietal cortex. *Journal of Comparative Neurology, 195*, 367–389. (14)

Iwamura, Y., Iriki, A., & Tanaka, M. (1994). Bilateral hand representation in the postcentral somatosensory cortex. *Nature, 369*, 554–556. (7)

Izquierdo, I. (1995). Role of the hippocampus, amygdala, and entorhinal cortex in memory storage and expression. In J. L. McGaugh, F. Bermúdez-Rattoni, & R. A. Prado-Alcalá (Eds.), *Plasticity in the central nervous system* (pp. 41–56). Mahwah, NJ: Erlbaum. (13)

Izquierdo, I., & Medina, J. H. (1995). Correlation between the pharmacology of long-term potentiation and the pharmacology of memory. *Neurobiology of Learning and Memory, 63*, 19–32. (13)

Jacobs, B., Schall, M., & Scheibel, A. B. (1993). A quantitative dendritic analysis of Wernicke's area in humans: II. Gender, hemispheric, and environmental factors. *Journal of Comparataive Neurology, 327*, 97–111. (5)

Jacobs, B., & Scheibel, A. B. (1993). A quantitative dendritic analysis of Wernicke's area in humans: I. Lifespan changes. *Journal of Comparative Neurology, 327*, 83–96. (5)

Jacobs, B. L. (1987). How hallucinogenic drugs work. *American Scientist, 75*, 386–392. (15)

Jacobs, G. D., & Snyder, D. (1996). Frontal brain asymmetry predicts affective style in men. *Behavioral Neuroscience, 110*, 3–6. (15)

Jacobs, G. H. (1993). The distribution and nature of colour vision among the mammals. *Biological Reviews, 68*, 413–471. (6)

James, L. E., & MacKay, D. G. (2001). H. M., word knowledge, and aging: Support for a new theory of long-term retrograde amnesia. *Psychological Science, 12*, 485–492. (13)

James, W. (1884). What is an emotion? *Mind, 9*, 188–205. (12)

James, W. (1961). *Psychology: The briefer course.* New York: Harper. (Original work published 1892). (12)

Janosik, E. H., & Davies, J. L. (1986). *Psychiatric mental health nursing.* Boston: Jones & Bartlett. (15)

Janus, C., Pearson, J., McLaurin, J., Mathews, P. M., Jiang, Y., Schmidt, S. D., Chishti, M. A., Horne, P., Heslin, D., French, J., Mount, H. T. J., Nixon, R. A., Mercken, M., Bergeron, C., Fraser, P. E., St George-Hyslop, P., & Westaway, D. (2000). Aβ peptide immunization reduces behavioural impairment and plaques in a model of Alzheimer's disease. *Nature, 408*, 979–982. (13)

Jarrard, L. E., Okaichi, H., Steward, O., & Goldschmidt, R. B. (1984). On the role of hippocampal connections in the performance of place and cue tasks: Comparisons with damage to hippocampus. *Behavioral Neuroscience, 98*, 946–954. (13)

Jarrold, C., Baddeley, A. D., & Hewes, A. K. (1998). Verbal and nonverbal abilities in the Williams syndrome phenotype: Evidence for diverging developmental trajectories. *Journal of Child Psychology and Psychiatry and Allied Disciplies, 39*, 511–523. (14)

Jaskiw, G. E., & Weinberger, D. R. (1992). Dopamine and schizophrenia—a cortically corrective perspective. *Seminars in the Neurosciences, 4*, 179–188. (15)

Jenner, A. R., Rosen, G. D., & Galaburda, A. M. (1999). Neuronal asymmetries in primary visual cortex of dyslexic and nondyslexic brains. *Annals of Neurology, 46*, 189–196. (14)

Jentsch, J. D., Redmond, D. E., Jr., Elsworth, J. D., Taylor, J. R., Youngren, K. D., & Roth, R. H. (1997). Enduring cognitive deficits and cortical dopamine dysfunction in monkeys after long-term administration of phencyclidine. *Science, 277*, 953–955. (15)

Jerison, H. J. (1985). Animal intelligence as encephalization. *Philosophical Transactions of the Royal Society of London, B, 308*, 21–35. (14)

Jerome, L., & Segal, A. (2001). Benefit of long-term stimulants on driving in adults with ADHD. *Journal of Nervous and Mental Disease, 189*, 63–64. (7)

Johansen, J. P., Fields, H. L., & Manning, B. H. (2001). The affective component of pain in rodents: Direct evidence for a contribution of the anterior cingulate cortex. *Proceedings of the National Academy of Sciences, USA, 98*, 8077–8082. (7)

Johns, T. R., & Thesleff, S. (1961). Effects of motor inactivation on the chemical sensitivity of skeletal muscle. *Acta Physiologica Scandinavica, 51*, 136–141. (5)

Johnson, E. N., Hawken, M. J., & Shapley, R. (2001). The spatial transformation of color in the primary visual cortex of the macaque monkey. *Nature Neuroscience, 4*, 409–416. (6)

Johnson, L. C. (1969). Physiological and psychological changes following total sleep deprivation. In A. Kales (Ed.), *Sleep: Physiology & pathology* (pp. 206–220). Philadelphia: Lippincott. (9)

Johnson, M. H., Posner, M. I., & Rothbart, M. K. (1991). Components of visual orienting in early infancy: Contingency learning, anticipatory looking, and disengaging. *Journal of Cognitive Neuroscience, 3*, 335–344. (6)

Johnson, M. T. V., Kipnis, A. N., Coltz, J. D., Gupta, A., Silverstein, P., Zwiebel, F., & Ebner, T. J. (1996). Effects of levodopa and viscosity on the velocity and accuracy of visually guided tracking in Parkinson's disease. *Brain, 119*, 801–813. (8)

Johnson, S. C., Pinkston, J. B., Bigler, E. D., & Blatter, D. D. (1996). Corpus callosum morphology in normal controls and traumatic brain injury: Sex differences, mechanisms of injury, and neuropsychological correlates.

Neuropsychology, 10, 408–415. (11)

Johnson, W. G., & Wildman, H. E. (1983). Influence of external and covert food stimuli on insulin secretion in obese and normal subjects. *Behavioral Neuroscience, 97*, 1025–1028. (10)

Jonas, P., Bischofberger, J., & Sandkühler, J. (1998). Corelease of two fast neurotransmitters at a central synapse. *Science, 281*, 419–424. (3)

Jonas, S. (1995). Prophylactic pharmacologic neuroprotection against focal cerebral ischemia. *Annals of the New York Academy of Sciences, 765*, 21–25. (5)

Jones, C. R., Campbell, S. S., Zone, S. E., Cooper, F., DeSano, A., Murphy, P. J., Jones, B., Czajkowski, L., & Ptáçek, L. J. (1999). Familial advanced sleep-phase syndrome: A short-period circadian rhythm variant in humans. *Nature Medicine, 5*, 1062–1065. (9)

Jones, E. G., & Pons, T. P. (1998). Thalamic and brainstem contributions to large-scale plasticity of primate somatosensory cortex. *Science, 282*, 1121–1125. (5)

Jones, H. S., & Oswald, I. (1968). Two cases of healthy insomnia. *Electroencephalography and Clinical Neurophysiology, 24*, 378–380. (9)

Jones, P. B., Rantakallio, P., Hartikainen, A.-L., Isohanni, M., & Sipila, P. (1998). Schizophrenia as a long-term outcome of pregnancy, delivery, and perinatal complications: A 28-year follow-up of the 1966 North Finland general population birth cohort. *American Journal of Psychiatry, 155*, 355–364. (15)

Jordan, H. A. (1969). Voluntary intragastric feeding. *Journal of Comparative and Physiological Psychology, 68*, 498–506. (10)

Joseph, J. A., Shukitt-Hale, B., Denisova, N. A., Prior, R. L., Cao, G., Martin, A., Taglialatela, G., & Bickford, P. C. (1998). Long-term dietary strawberry, spinach, or vitamin E supplementation retards the onset of age-related neuronal signal-transduction and cognitive behavioral deficits. *Journal of Neuroscience, 18*, 8047–8055. (13)

Joyner, A. L., & Guillemot, F. (1994). Gene targeting and development of the nervous system. *Current Opinion in Neurobiology, 4*, 37–42. (4)

Jueptner, M., & Weiller, C. (1998). A review of differences between basal ganglia and cerebellar control of movements as revealed by functional imaging studies. *Brain, 121*, 1437–1449. (8)

Kaas, J. H. (1983). What, if anything, is SI? Organization of first somatosensory area of cortex. *Physiological Reviews, 63*, 206–231. (7)

Kaas, J. H., Merzenich, M. M., & Killackey, H. P. (1983). The reorganization of somatosensory cortex following peripheral nerve damage in adult and developing mammals. *Annual Review of Neuroscience, 6*, 325–356. (5)

Kaas, J. H., Nelson, R. J., Sur, M., Lin, C.-S., & Merzenich, M. M. (1979). Multiple representations of the body within the primary somatosensory cortex of primates. *Science, 204*, 521–523. (4)

Kakei, S., Hoffman, D. S., & Strick, P. L. (2001). Direction of action is represented in the ventral premotor cortex. *Nature Neuroscience, 4*, 1020–1025. (8)

Kales, A., Scharf, M. B., & Kales, J. D. (1978). Rebound insomnia: A new clinical syndrome. *Science, 201*, 1039–1041. (9)

Kalin, N.H., Shelton, S. E., Davidson, R. J., & Kelley, A. E. (2001). The primate amygdala mediates acute fear but not the behavioral and physiological components of anxious temperament. *Journal of Neuroscience, 21*, 2067–2074. (12)

Kamarck, T., & Jennings, J. R. (1991). Biobehavioral factors in sudden cardiac death. *Psychological Bulletin, 109*, 42–75. (12)

Kandel, E. R., & Schwartz, J. H. (1982). Molecular biology of learning: Modulation of transmitter release. *Science, 218*, 433–443. (13)

Kanwisher, N. (2000). Domain specificity in face perception. *Nature Neuroscience, 3*, 759–763. (6)

Kanwisher, N., & Wojciulik, E. (2000). Visual attention: Insights from brain imaging. *Nature Reviews Neuroscience, 1*, 91–100. (6)

Kaplan, D. E., Gayán, J., Ahn, J., Won, T.-W., Pauls, D., Olson, R. K., DeFries, J. C., Wood, F., Pennington, B. F., Page, G. P., Smith, S. D., & Gruen, J. R. (2002). Evidence for linkage and association with reading disability, on 6p21.3-22. *American Journal of Human Genetics, 70*, 1287–1298. (14)

Kaplan, J. R., Muldoon, M. F., Manuck, S. B., & Mann, J. J. (1997). Assessing the observed relationship between low cholesterol and violence-related mortality. *Annals of the New York Academy of Sciences, 836*, 57–80. (12)

Kapur, S., Zipusky, R., Jones, C., Shammi, C. S., Remington, G., & Seeman, P. (2000). A positron emission tomography study of quetiapine in schizophrenia. *Archives of General Psychiatry, 57*, 553–559. (15)

Karlsson, P., Farde, L., Halldin, C., & Sedvall, G. (2002). PET study of D1 dopamine receptor binding in neuroleptic-naive patients with schizophrenia. *American Journal of Psychiatry, 159*, 761–767. (15)

Karmiloff-Smith, A., Tyler, L. K., Voice, K., Sims, K., Udwin, O., Howlin, P., & Davies, M. (1998). Linguistic dissociations in Williams syndrome: Evaluating receptive syntax in on-line and off-line tasks. *Neuropsychologia, 36*, 343–351. (14)

Karnath, H.-O., Ferber, S., & Himmelbach, M. (2001). Spatial awareness is a function of the temporal not the posterior parietal lobe. *Nature, 411*, 950–953. (7)

Karnath, H.-O., Himmelbach, M., & Rordan, C. (2002). The subcortical anatomy of human spatial neglect: Putamen, caudate nucleus and pulvinar. *Brain, 125*, 350–360. (7)

Karrer, T., & Bartoshuk, L. (1991). Capsaicin desensitization and recovery on the human tongue. *Physiology & Behavior, 49*, 757–764. (7)

Kasai, T., & Morotomi, T. (2001). Event-related brain potentials during selective attention to depth and form in global stereopsis.

Vision Research, 41, 1379–1388. (6)

Katkin, E. S., Wiens, S., & Öhman, A. (2001). Nonconscious fear conditioning, visceral perception, and the development of gut feelings. *Psychological Science, 12,* 366–370. (12)

Kawasaki, H., Adolphs, R., Kaufman, O., Damasio, H., Damasio, A. R., Granner, M., Bakken, H., Hori, T., & Howard, M. A., III. (2001). Single-neuron responses to emotional visual stimuli recorded in human ventral prefrontal cortex. *Nature Neuroscience, 4,* 15–16. (12)

Kaye, W. H., Berrettini, W., Gwirtsman, H., & George, D. T. (1990). Altered cerebrospinal fluid neuropeptide Y and peptide YY immunoreactivity in anorexia and bulimia nervosa. *Archives of General Psychiatry, 47,* 548–556. (10)

Kaye, W. H., Frank, G. K., Meltzer, C. C., Price, J. C., McConaha, C. W., Crossan, P. J., Klump, K. L., & Rhodes, L. (2001). Altered serotonin 2A receptor activity in women who have recovered from bulimia nervosa. *American Journal of Physiology, 158,* 1152–1155. (10)

Keefe, F. J., & France, C. R. (1999). Pain: Biopsychosocial mechanisms and management. *Current Directions in Psychological Science, 8,* 137–141. (7)

Keele, S. W., & Ivry, R. (1990). Does the cerebellum provide a common computation for diverse tasks? *Annals of the New York Academy of Sciences, 608,* 179–207. (8)

Keenan, P. A., Ezzat, W. H., Ginsburg, K., & Moore, G. J. (2001). Prefrontal cortex as the site of estrogen's effect on cognition. *Psychoneuroendocrinology, 26,* 577–590. (11)

Kellar, K. J., & Stockmeier, C. A. (1986). Effects of electroconvulsive shock and serotonin axon lesions on beta-adrenergic and serotonin-2 receptors in rat brain. *Annals of the New York Academy of Sciences, 462,* 76–90. (15)

Kendler, K. S. (1983). Overview: A current perspective on twin studies of schizophrenia. *American Journal of Psychiatry, 140,* 1413–1425. (15)

Kendler, K. S. (2001). Twin studies of psychiatric illness. *Archives of General Psychiatry, 58,* 1005–1014. (1)

Kendler, K. S., Gardner, C. O., & Prescott, C. A. (1999). Clinical characteristics of major depression that predict risk of depression in relatives. *Archives of General Psychiatry, 56,* 322–327. (15)

Kendler, K. S., Myers, J., Prescott, C. A., & Neale, M. C. (2001). The genetic epidemiology of irrational fears and phobias in men. *Archives of General Psychiatry, 58,* 257–265. (12)

Kendler, K. S., Thornton, L. M., Gilman, S. E., & Kessler, R. C. (2000). Sexual orientation in a U.S. national sample of twin and nontwin sibling pairs. *American Journal of Psychiatry, 157,* 1843–1846. (11)

Kennard, C., Lawden, M., Morland, A. B., & Ruddock, K. H. (1995). Colour identification and colour constancy are impaired in a patient with incomplete achromatopsia associated with prestriate cortical lesions. *Proceedings of the Royal Society of London, B, 260,* 169–175. (6)

Kennard, M. A. (1938). Reorganization of motor function in the cerebral cortex of monkeys deprived of motor and premotor areas in infancy. *Journal of Neurophysiology, 1,* 477–496. (5)

Kennerley, S. W., Diedrichsen, J., Hazeltine, E., Semjen, A., & Ivry, R. B. (2002). Callosotomy patients exhibit temporal uncoupling during continuous bimanual movements. *Nature Neuroscience, 5,* 376–381. (14)

Kennett, S., Eimer, M., Spence, C., & Driver, J. (2001). Tactile-visual links in exogenous spatial attention under different postures: Convergent evidence from psychophysics and ERPs. *Journal of Cognitive Neuroscience, 13,* 462–478. (7)

Kenrick, D. T. (2001). Evolutionary psychology, cognitive science, and dynamical systems: Building an integrative paradigm. *Current Directions in Psychological Science, 10,* 13–17. (11)

Kerr, D. S., & Abraham, W. C. (1995). Cooperative interactions among afferents govern the induction of homosynaptic long-term depression in the hippocampus. *Proceedings of the National Academy of Sciences, USA, 92,* 11637–11641. (13)

Kesner, R. P., Gilbert, P. E., & Barua, L. A. (2002). The role of the hippocampus in meaning for the temporal order of a sequence of odors. *Behavioral Neuroscience, 116,* 286–290. (13)

Kesslak, J. P., So, V., Choi, J., Cotman, C. W., & Gomez-Pinilla, F. (1998). Learning upregulates brain-derived neurotrophic factor messenger ribonucleic acid: A mechanism to facilitate encoding and circuit maintenance? *Behavioral Neuroscience, 112,* 1012–1019. (5)

Kety, S. S., Wender, P. H., Jacobson, B., Ingraham, L. J., Jansson, L., Faber, B., & Kinney, D. K. (1994). Mental illness in the biological and adoptive relatives of schizophrenic adoptees. *Archives of General Psychiatry, 51,* 442–455. (15)

Keverne, E. B. (1999). The vomeronasal organ. *Science, 286,* 716–720. (7)

Kiecolt-Glaser, J. K., & Glaser, R. (1993). Mind and immunity. In D. Goleman & J. Gurin (Eds.), *Mind/body medicine* (pp. 39–61). Yonkers, NY: Consumer Reports Books. (12)

Kiecolt-Glaser, J. K., & Newton, T. L. (2001). Marriage and health: His and hers. *Psychological Bulletin, 127,* 472–503. (12)

Kikuchi-Yorioka, Y., & Sawaguchi, T. (2000). Parallel visuospatial and audiospatial working memory processes in the monkey dorsolateral prefrontal cortex. *Nature Neuroscience, 3,* 1075–1076. (13)

Killackey, H. P., & Chalupa, L. M. (1986). Ontogenetic change in the distribution of callosal projection neurons in the postcentral gyrus of the fetal rhesus monkey. *Journal of Comparative Neurology, 244,* 331–348. (14)

Killeffer, F. A., & Stern, W. E. (1970). Chronic effects of hypothalamic injury. *Archives of Neurology, 22,* 419–429. (10)

Kim, J.-H., Auerbach, J. M., Rodriguez-Gómez, J. A., Velasco, I.,

Gavin, D., Lumelsky, N., Lee, S. H., Nguyen, J., Sánchez-Pernaute, R., Bankiewicz, K, & McKay, R. (2002). Dopamine neurons derived from embryonic stem cells function in an animal model of Parkinson's disease. *Nature, 418*, 50–56. (8)

Kim, Y.-H., Park, J.-H., Hong, S. H., & Koh, J.-Y. (1999). Nonproteolytic neuroprotection by human recombinant tissue plasminogen activator. *Science, 284*, 647–650. (5)

Kimura, D., & Hampson, E. (1994). Cognitive pattern in men and women is influenced by fluctuations in sex hormones. *Current Directions in Psychological Science, 3*, 57–61. (11)

Kindon, H. A., Baum, M. J., & Paredes, R. J. (1996). Medial preoptic/anterior hypothalamic lesions induce a female-typical profile of sexual partner preference in male ferrets. *Hormones and Behavior, 30*, 514–527. (11)

King, B. M., Smith, R. L., & Frohman, L. A. (1984). Hyperinsulinemia in rats with ventromedial hypothalamic lesions: Role of hyperphagia. *Behavioral Neuroscience, 98*, 152–155. (10)

King, M., Su, W., Chang, A., Zuckerman, A., & Pasternak, G. W. (2001). Transport of opioids from the brain to the periphery by P-glycoprotein: Peripheral actions of central drugs. *Nature Neuroscience, 4*, 268–274. (2)

Kingstone, A., & Gazzaniga, M. S. (1995). Subcortical transfer of higher order information: More illusory than real? *Neuropsychology, 9*, 321–328. (14)

Kinnamon, J. C. (1987). Organization and innervation of taste buds. In T. E. Finger & W. L. Silver (Eds.), *Neurobiology of taste and smell* (pp. 277–297). New York: Wiley. (7)

Kinomura, S., Larsson, J., Gulyás, B., & Roland, P. E. (1996). Activation by attention of the human reticular formation and thalamic intralaminar nuclei. *Science, 271*, 512–515. (9)

Kinsbourne, M., & McMurray, J. (1975). The effect of cerebral dominance on time sharing between speaking and tapping by preschool children. *Child Development, 46*, 240–242. (14)

Kinsey, A. C., Pomeroy, W. B., & Martin, C. E. (1948). *Sexual behavior in the human male.* Philadelphia: Saunders. (11)

Kinsey, A. C., Pomeroy, W. B., Martin, C. E., & Gebhard, P. H. (1953). *Sexual behavior in the human female.* Philadelphia: Saunders. (11)

Kiriakakis, V., Bhatia, K. P., Quinn, N. P., & Marsden, C. D. (1998). The natural history of tardive dyskinesia: A long-term follow-up study of 107 cases. *Brain, 121*, 2053–2066. (15)

Kirkpatrick, P. J., Smielewski, P., Czosnyka, M., Menon, D. K., & Pickard, J. D. (1995). Near-infrared spectroscopy in patients with head injury. *Journal of Neurosurgery, 83*, 963–970. (5)

Kirkwood, A., Lee, H.-K., & Bear, M. F. (1995). Co-regulation of long-term potentiation and experience-dependent synaptic plasticity in visual cortex by age and experience. *Nature, 375*, 328–331. (6)

Kiyashchenko, L. I., Mileykovskiy, B. Y., Maidment, N., Lam, H. A., Wu, M.-F., John, J., Peever, J., & Siegel, J. M. (2002). Release of hypocretin (orexin) during waking and sleeping states. *Journal of Neuroscience, 22*, 5282–5286. (9)

Klein, D. F. (1993). False suffocation alarms, spontaneous panics, and related conditions. *Archives of General Psychiatry, 50*, 306–317. (12)

Kleindienst, N., & Greil, W. (2000). Differential efficacy of lithium and carbamazepine in the prophylaxis of bipolar disorder: Results of the MAP study. *Neuropsychobiology, 42*(Suppl. 1), 2–10. (15)

Kleitman, N. (1963). *Sleep and wakefulness* (Rev. ed.). Chicago: University of Chicago Press. (9)

Kliewer, S. A., & Willson, T. M. (2002). Regulation of xenobiotic and bile acid metabolism by the nuclear pregnane X receptor. *Journal of Lipid Research, 43*, 359–364. (15)

Klingberg, T., Forssberg, H., & Westerberg, H. (2002). Increased brain activity in frontal and parietal cortex underlies the development of visuospatial working memory capacity during childhood. *Journal of Cognitive Neuroscience, 14*, 1–10. (13)

Klingberg, T., Hedehus, M., Temple, E., Salz, T., Gabrieli, J. D. E., Moseley, M. E., & Poldrack, R. A. (2000). Microstructure of temporoparietal white matter as a basis for reading ability: Evidence from diffusion tensor magnetic resonance imaging. *Neuron, 25*, 493–500. (14)

Kluger, M. J. (1991). Fever: Role of pyrogens and cryogens. *Physiological Reviews, 71*, 93–127. (10)

Klüver, H., & Bucy, P. C. (1939). Preliminary analysis of functions of the temporal lobes in monkeys. *Archives of Neurology and Psychiatry, 42*, 979–1000. (4)

Knecht, S., Flöel, A., Dräger, B., Breitenstein, C., Sommer, J., Henningsen, H., Ringelstein, E. B., & Pascual-Leone, A. (2002). Degree of language lateralization determines susceptibility to unilateral brain lesions. *Nature Neuroscience, 5*, 695–699. (14)

Knoll, J. (1993). The pharmacological basis of the beneficial effects of (2) deprenyl (selegiline) in Parkinson's and Alzheimer's diseases. *Journal of Neural Transmission*, (Suppl. 40), 69–91. (8)

Koch, C., & Crick, F. (2001). The zombie within. *Nature, 411*, 893. (1)

Kodama, J., Fukushima, M., & Sakata, T. (1978). Impaired taste discrimination against quinine following chronic administration of theophylline in rats. *Physiology & Behavior, 20*, 151–155. (7)

Koechlin, E., Corrado, G., Pietrini, P., & Grafman, J. (2000). Dissociating the role of the medial and lateral anterior prefrontal cortex in human planning. *Proceedings of the National Academy of Sciences, USA, 97*, 7651–7656. (8)

Koepp, M. J., Gunn, R. N., Lawrence, A. D., Cunningham, V. J., Dagher, A., Jones, T., Brooks, D. J., Bench, C. J., & Grasby, P. M. (1998). Evidence for striatal dopamine release during a video game. *Nature, 393*, 266–268. (15)

Kolb, B., Côté, S., Ribeiro-da-Silva, A., & Cuello, A. C. (1997). Nerve growth factor treatment prevents dendritic atrophy and promotes recovery of function after cortical injury. *Neuroscience, 76,* 1139–1151. (5, 8)

Kolb, B., Gorny, G., Côté, S., Ribeiro-da-Silva, A., & Cuello, A. C. (1997). Nerve growth factor stimulates growth of cortical pyramidal neurons in young adult rats. *Brain Research, 751,* 289–294. (5)

Kolb, B., & Holmes, C. (1983). Neonatal motor cortex lesions in the rat: Absence of sparing of motor behaviors and impaired spatial learning concurrent with abnormal cerebral morphogenesis. *Behavioral Neuroscience, 97,* 697–709. (5)

Kolb, B., Sutherland, R. J., & Whishaw, I. Q. (1983). Abnormalities in cortical and subcortical morphology after neonatal neocortical lesions in rats. *Experimental Neurology, 79,* 223–244. (5)

Komisaruk, B. R., Adler, N. T., & Hutchison, J. (1972). Genital sensory field: Enlargement by estrogen treatment in female rats. *Science, 178,* 1295–1298. (11)

Komura, Y., Tamura, R., Uwano, T., Nishijo, H., Kaga, K., & Ono, T. (2001). Retrospective and prospective coding for predicted reward in the sensory thalamus. *Nature, 412,* 546–549. (4)

Kong, J., Shepel, P. N., Holden, C. P., Mackiewicz, M., Pack, A. I., & Geiger, J. D. (2002). Brain glycogen decreases with increased periods of wakefulness: Implications for homeostatic drive to sleep. *Journal of Neuroscience, 22,* 5581–5587. (9)

Konishi, M. (1995). Neural mechanisms of auditory image formation. In M. S. Gazzaniga (Ed.), *The cognitive neurosciences* (pp. 269–277). Cambridge, MA: MIT Press. (7)

Konishi, S., Nakajima, K., Uchida, I., Kameyama, M., Nakahara, K., Sekihara, K., & Miyashita, Y. (1998). Transient activation of inferior prefrontal cortex during cognitive set shifting. *Nature Neuroscience, 1,* 80–84. (15)

Korchmaros, J. D., & Kenny, D. A. (2001). Emotional closeness as a mediator of the effect of genetic relatedness on altruism. *Psychological Science, 12,* 262–265. (1)

Kordower, J. H., Emborg, M. E., Bloch, J., Ma, S.Y., Chu, Y., Leventhal, L., McBride, J., Chen, E.-Y., Palfi, S., Roitberg, B. Z., Brown, W. D., Holden, J. E., Pyzalski, R., Taylor, M. D., Carvey, P., Ling, Z. D., Trono, D., Hantraye, P., Déglon, N., & Aebischer, P., (2000). Neurodegeneration prevented by lentiviral vector delivery of GDNF in primate models of Parkinson's disease. *Science, 290,* 767–773. (8)

Korenberg, J. R., Chen, X.-N., Hirota, H., Lai, Z., Bellugi, U., Burian, D., Roe, B., & Matsuoka, R. (2000). VI. Genome structure and cognitive map of Williams syndrome. *Journal of Cognitive Neuroscience, 12*(Suppl.), 89–107. (14)

Kornhuber, H. H. (1974). Cerebral cortex, cerebellum, and basal ganglia: An introduction to their motor functions. In F. O. Schmitt & F. G. Worden (Eds.), *The neurosciences: Third study program* (pp. 267–280). Cambridge, MA: MIT Press. (8)

Kosslyn, S. M., Ganis, G., & Thompson, W. L. (2001). Neural foundations of imagery. *Nature Reviews Neuroscience, 2,* 635–642. (6)

Kosslyn, S. M., Pascual-Leone, A., Felician, O., Camposano, S., Kennan, J. P., Thompson, W. L., Ganis, G., Sukel, K. E., & Alpert, N. M. (1999). The role of area 17 in visual imagery: Convergent evidence from PET and rTMS. *Science, 284,* 167–170. (6)

Kostrzewa, R. M. (1995). Dopamine receptor supersensitivity. *Neuroscience and Biobehavioral Reviews, 19,* 1–17. (5)

Kourtzi, Z., & Kanwisher, N. (2000). Activation in human MT/MST by static images with implied motion. *Journal of Cognitive Neuroscience, 12,* 48–55. (6)

Kozloski, J., Hamzei-Sichani, F., & Yuste, R. (2001). Stereotyped position of local synaptic targets in neocortex. *Science, 293,* 868–872. (5)

Kraly, F. S., Kim, Y.-M., Dunham, L. M., & Tribuzio, R. A. (1995). Drinking after intragastric NaCl without increase in systemic plasma osmolality in rats. *American Journal of Physiology, 269,* R1085–R1092. (10)

Kräuchi, K., Cajochen, C., Werth, E., & Wirz-Justice, A. (1999). Warm feet promote the rapid onset of sleep. *Nature, 401,* 36–37. (9)

Kreitzer, A. C., Carter, A. G., & Regehr, W. G. (2002). Inhibition of interneuron firing extends the spread of endocannabinoid signaling in the cerebellum. *Neuron, 34,* 787–796. (15)

Kreitzer, A. C., & Regehr, W. G. (2001). Retrograde inhibition of presynaptic calcium influx by endogenous cannabinoids at excitatory synapses onto Purkinje cells. *Neuron, 29,* 717–727. (15)

Kropotov, J. D., & Etlinger, S. C. (1999). Selection of actions in the basal ganglia-thalamocortical circuits: Review and model. *International Journal of Psychophysiology, 31,* 197–217. (8)

Kruesi, M. J. P., Hibbs, E. D., Zahn, T. P., Keysor, C. S., Hamburger, S. D., Bartko, J. J., & Rapoport, J. L. (1992). A 2-year prospective follow-up of children and adolescents with disruptive behavior disorders. *Archives of General Psychiatry, 49,* 429–435. (12)

Krupa, D. J., Thompson, J. K., & Thompson, R. F. (1993). Localization of a memory trace in the mammalian brain. *Science, 260,* 989–991. (13)

Kruzich, P. J., Congleton, K. M., & See, R. E. (2001). Conditioned reinstatement of drug-seeking behavior with a discrete compound stimulus classically conditioned with intravenous cocaine. *Behavioral Neuroscience, 115,* 1086–1092. (15)

Kübler, A., Kotchoubey, B., Kaiser, J., Wolpaw, J. R., & Birbaumer, N. (2001). Brain-computer communication: Unlocking the locked-in. *Psychological Bulletin, 127,* 358–375. (12)

Kubota, Y., Sato, W., Murai, T., Toichi, M., Ikeda, A., & Sengoku, A. (2000). Emotional cognition without awareness after unilateral temporal lobectomy in humans. *Journal of Neuroscience, 20,* RC97, 1–5. (12)

Kujala, T., Myllyviita, K., Tervaniemi, M., Alho, K., Kallio, J., & Näätänen, R. (2000). Basic auditory dysfunction in dyslexia as demonstrated by brain activity measurements. *Psychophysiology, 37*, 262–266. (14)

Kupfermann, I., Castellucci, V., Pinsker, H., & Kandel, E. (1970). Neuronal correlates of habituation and dishabituation of the gill withdrawal reflex in *Aplysia*. *Science, 167*, 1743–1745. (13)

Kurahashi, T., Lowe, G., & Gold, G. H. (1994). Suppression of odorant responses by odorants in olfactory receptor cells. *Science, 265*, 118–120. (7)

Kuypers, H. G. J. M. (1989). Motor system organization. In G. Adelman (Ed.), *Neuroscience year* (pp. 107–110). Boston: Birkhäuser. (8)

Kwon, J. S., McCarley, R. W., Hirayasu, Y., Anderson, J. E., Fischer, I. A., Kikinis, R., Jolesz, F. A., & Shenton, M. E. (1999). Left planum temporale volume reduction in schizophrenia. *Archives of General Psychiatry, 56*, 142–148. (15)

LaBar, K. S., & Phelps, E. A. (1998). Arousal-mediated memory consolidation: Role of the medial temporal lobe in humans. *Psychological Science, 9*, 490–493. (13)

Laburn, H. P. (1996). How does the fetus cope with thermal challenges? *News in Physiological Sciences, 11*, 96–100. (15)

Lacreuse, A., Verreault, M., & Herndon, J. G. (2001). Fluctuations in spatial recognition memory across the menstrual cycle in female rhesus monkeys. *Psychoneuroendocrinology, 26*, 623–639. (11)

Laeng, B., & Caviness, V. S. (2001). Prosopagnosia as a deficit in encoding curved surfaces. *Journal of Cognitive Neuroscience, 13*, 556–576. (6)

LaHoste, G. J., & Marshall, J. F. (1989). Non-additivity of D_2 receptor proliferation induced by dopamine denervation and chronic selective antagonist administration: Evidence from quantitative autoradiography indicates a single mechanism of action. *Brain Research, 502*, 223–232. (5)

Lai, C. S. L., Fisher, S. E., Hurst, J. A., Vargha-Khadem, F., & Monaco, A. P. (2001). A forkhead-domain gene is mutated in a severe speech and language disorder. *Nature, 413*, 519–523. (14)

Lake, R. I. E., Eaves, L. J., Maes, H. H. M., Heath, A. C., & Martin, N. G. (2000). Further evidence against the environmental transmission of individual differences in neuroticism from a collaborative study of 45,850 twins and relatives on two continents. *Behavior Genetics, 30*, 223–233. (1)

Lam, H.-M., Chiu, J., Hsieh, M.-H., Meisel, L., Oliveira, I. C., Shin, M., & Coruzzi, G. (1998). Glutamate-receptor genes in plants. *Nature, 396*, 125–126. (3)

Lambie, J. A., & Marcel, A. J. (2002). Consciousness and the varieties of emotion experience: A theoretical framework. *Psychological Review, 109*, 219–259. (7)

Land, E. H., Hubel, D. H., Livingstone, M. S., Perry, S. H., & Burns, M. M. (1983). Colour-generating interactions across the corpus callosum. *Nature, 303*, 616–618. (6)

Landis, D. M. D. (1987). Initial junctions between developing parallel fibers and Purkinje cells are different from mature synaptic junctions. *Journal of Comparative Neurology, 260*, 513–525. (3)

Lang, P. J. (1994). The varieties of emotional experience: A meditation on James-Lange theory. *Psychological Review, 101*, 211–221. (12)

Lang, R. A., Flor-Henry, P., & Frenzel, R. R. (1990). Sex hormone profiles in pedophilic and incestuous men. *Annals of Sex Research, 3*, 59–74. (11)

Lappalainen, J., Kranzler, H. R., Malison, R., Price, L. H., Van Dyck, C., Rosenheck, R. A., Cramer, J., Southwick, S., Charney, D., Krystal, J., & Gelernter, J. (2002). A functional neuropeptide Y Leu 7 Pro polymorphism associated with alcohol dependence in a large population sample from the United States. *Archives of General Psychiatry, 59*, 825–831. (15)

Lashley, K. S. (1929). *Brain mechanisms and intelligence*. Chicago: University of Chicago Press. (13)

Lashley, K. S. (1930). Basic neural mechanisms in behavior. *Psychological Review, 37*, 1–24. (inside cover)

Lashley, K. S. (1950). In search of the engram. *Symposia of the Society for Experimental Biology, 4*, 454–482. (13)

Lassonde, M., Bryden, M. P., & Demers, P. (1990). The corpus callosum and cerebral speech lateralization. *Brain and Language, 38*, 195–206. (14)

Laurent, J.-P., Cespuglio, R., & Jouvet, M. (1974). Dèlimitation des voies ascendantes de l'activité ponto-géniculo-occipitale chez le chat [Demarcation of the ascending paths of ponto-geniculo-occipital activity in the cat]. *Brain Research, 65*, 29–52. (9)

Laureys, S., Lemaire, C., Maquet, P., Phillips, C., & Franck, G. (1999). Cerebral metabolism during vegetative state and after recovery to consciousness. *Journal of Neurology Neurosurgery & Psychiatry, 67*, 121. (7)

Lavin, J. H., Wittert, G., Sun, W.-M., Horowitz, M., Morley, J. E., & Read, N. W. (1996). Appetite regulation by carbohydrate: Role of blood glucose and gastrointestinal hormones. *American Journal of Physiology, 271*, E209–E214. (10)

Le Grand, R., Mondloch, C. J., Maurer, D., & Brent, H. P. (2001). Early visual experience and face processing. *Nature, 410*, 890. (6)

LeDoux, J. (1996). *The emotional brain*. New York: Simon & Schuster. (12)

LeDoux, J. E., Iwata, J., Cicchetti, P., & Reis, D. J. (1988). Different projections of the central amygdaloid nucleus mediate autonomic and behavioral correlates of conditioned fear. *Journal of Neuroscience, 8*, 2517–2529. (12)

Lee, J.-M., Zipfel, G. J., & Choi, D. W. (1999). The changing landscape of ischaemic brain injury mechanisms. *Nature, 399*(Suppl.), A7–A14. (5)

Lee, Y., Walker, D., & Davis, M. (1996). Lack of a temporal gradient of retrograde amnesia following NMDA-induced lesions of the basolateral amygdala assessed with the fear-potentiated startle paradigm. *Behavioral Neuroscience, 110,* 836–839. (12)

Leff, J., Wig, N. N., Chosh, A., Bedi, H., Menon, D. K., Kuipers, L., Korten, A., Ernberg, G., Day, R., Sartorius, N., & Jablensky, A. (1987). Expressed emotion and schizophrenia in North India: III. Influence of relatives' expressed emotion on the course of schizophrenia in Changigarh. *British Journal of Psychiatry, 151,* 166–173. (15)

Lehky, S. R. (2000). Deficits in visual feature binding under isoluminant conditions. *Journal of Cognitive Neuroscience, 12,* 383–392. (4)

Lehman, C. D., Bartoshuk, L. M., Catalanotto, F. C., Kveton, J. F., & Lowlicht, R. A. (1995). Effect of anesthesia of the chorda tympani nerve on taste perception in humans. *Physiology & Behavior, 57,* 943–951. (7)

Lehrman, D. S. (1964). The reproductive behavior of ring doves. *Scientific American, 211*(5), 48–54. (11)

Leibowitz, S. F., & Alexander, J. T. (1991). Analysis of neuropeptide Y-induced feeding: Dissociation of Y_1 and Y_2 receptor effects on natural meal patterns. *Peptides, 12,* 1251–1260. (10)

Leibowitz, S. F., Hammer, N. J., & Chang, K. (1981). Hypothalamic paraventricular nucleus lesions produce overeating and obesity in the rat. *Physiology & Behavior, 27,* 1031–1040. (10)

Leibowitz, S. F., & Hoebel, B. G. (1998). Behavioral neuroscience of obesity. In G. A. Bray, C. Bouchard, & P. T. James (Eds.), *Handbook of obesity* (pp. 313–358). New York: Dekker. (10)

Lein, E. S., & Shatz, C. J. (2001). Neurotrophins and refinement of visual circuitry. In W. M. Cowan, T. C. Südhof, & C. F. Stevens (Eds.), *Synapses* (pp. 613–649). Baltimore: Johns Hopkins University Press. (6)

Leinders-Zufall, T., Lane, A. P., Puche, A. C., Ma, W., Novotny, M. V., Shipley, M. T., & Zufall, F. (2000). Ultrasensitive pheromone detection by mammalian vomeronasal neurons. *Nature, 405,* 792–796. (7)

Lenhart, R. E., & Katkin, E. S. (1986). Psychophysiological evidence for cerebral laterality effects in a high-risk sample of students with sub-syndromal bipolar depressive disorder. *American Journal of Psychiatry, 143,* 602–607. (15)

Lenneberg, E. H. (1969). On explaining language. *Science, 164,* 635–643. (14)

Lennie, P. (1998). Single units and visual cortical organization. *Perception, 27,* 889–935. (6)

Lenz, F. A., & Byl, N. N. (1999). Reorganization in the cutaneous core of the human thalamic principal somatic sensory nucleus (ventral caudal) in patients with dystonia. *Journal of Neurophysiology, 82,* 3204–3212. (5)

Leonard, C. M., Lombardino, L. J., Mercado, L. R., Browd, S. R., Breier, J. I., & Agee, O. F. (1996). Cerebral asymmetry and cognitive development in children: A magnetic resonance imaging study. *Psychological Science, 7,* 89–95. (14)

Leopold, D. A., & Logothetis, N. K. (1996). Activity changes in early visual cortex reflect monkeys' percepts during binocular rivalry. *Nature, 379,* 549–553. (6)

Lerer, B., & Shapira, B. (1986). Neurochemical mechanisms of mood stabilization. *Annals of the New York Academy of Sciences, 462,* 367–375. (15)

Lerman, S. E., McAleer, I. M., & Kaplan, G. W. (2000). Sex assignment in cases of ambiguous genitalia and its outcome. *Urology, 55,* 8–12. (11)

Leshem, M. (1999). The ontogeny of salt hunger in the rat. *Neuroscience and Biobehaioral Reviews, 23,* 649–659. (10)

Lesse, S. (1984). Psychosurgery. *American Journal of Psychotherapy, 38,* 224–228. (4)

Lester, B. M., LaGasse, L. L., & Seifer, R. (1998). Cocaine exposure and children: The meaning of subtle effects. *Science, 282,* 633–634. (5)

Lettvin, J. Y., Maturana, H. R., McCulloch, W. S., & Pitts, W. H. (1959). What the frog's eye tells the frog's brain. *Proceedings of the Institute of Radio Engineers, 47,* 1940–1951. (7)

Leung, H.-C., Gore, J. C., & Goldman-Rakic, P. S. (2002). Sustained mnemonic response in the human middle frontal gyrus during on-line storage of spatial memoranda. *Journal of Cognitive Neuroscience, 14,* 659–671. (13)

LeVay, S. (1991). A difference in hypothalamic structure between heterosexual and homosexual men. *Science, 253,* 1034–1037. (4, 11)

LeVay, S. (1993). *The sexual brain.* Cambridge, MA: MIT Press. (11)

Levenson, R. W., Oyama, O. N., & Meek, P. S. (1987). Greater reinforcement from alcohol for those at risk: Parental risk, personality risk, and sex. *Journal of Abnormal Psychology, 96,* 242–253. (15)

LeVere, N. D., & LeVere, T. E. (1982). Recovery of function after brain damage: Support for the compensation theory of the behavioral deficit. *Physiological Psychology, 10,* 165–174. (5)

LeVere, T. E. (1975). Neural stability, sparing and behavioral recovery following brain damage. *Psychological Review, 82,* 344–358. (5)

LeVere, T. E. (1980). Recovery of function after brain damage: A theory of the behavioral deficit. *Physiological Psychology, 8,* 297–308. (5)

LeVere, T. E. (1993). Recovery of function after brain damage: The effects of nimodipine on the chronic behavioral deficit. *Psychobiology, 21,* 125–129. (5)

LeVere, T. E., Ford, K., & Sandin, M. (1992). Recovery of function after brain damage: The benefits of diets supplemented with the calcium channel blocker nimodipine. *Psychobiology, 20,* 219–222. (5)

LeVere, T. E., & Morlock, G. W. (1973). Nature of visual recovery following posterior neodecortication in the hooded rat. *Journal of Comparative and Physiological Psychology, 83,* 62–67. (5)

Levi-Montalcini, R. (1987). The nerve growth factor 35 years later. *Science, 237,* 1154–1162. (5)

Levi-Montalcini, R. (1988). *In praise of imperfection.* New York: Basic Books. (5, inside cover)

Levin, B. E. (2000). Metabolic imprinting on genetically predisposed neural circuits perpetuates obesity. *Nutrition, 16*, 909–915. (10)

Levin, E. D., & Rose, J. E. (1995). Acute and chronic nicotine interactions with dopamine systems and working memory performance. *Annals of the New York Academy of Sciences, 757*, 245–252. (15)

Levinson, D. F., Holmans, P. A., Leurent, C., Riley, B., Pulver, A. E., Gejman, P. V., Schwab, S. G., Williams, N. M., Owen, M. J., Wildenauer, D. B., Sanders, A. R., Nestadt, G., Mowry, B. J., Wormley, B., Bauché, S., Soubigou, S., Ribble, R., Nertney, D. A., Liang, K. Y., Martinolich, L., Maier, W., Norton, N., Williams, H., Albus, M., Carpenter, E. B., deMarchi, N., Ewen-White, K. R., Walsh, D., Jay, M., Deleuze, J.-F., O'Neill, F. A., Papadimitrou, G., Weilbaecher, A., Lerer, B., O'Donovan, M. C., Dikeos, D., Silverman, J. M., Kendler, K. S., Mallet, J., Crowe, R. R., & Walters, M. (2002). No major schizophrenia locus detected on chromosome 1q in a large multicenter sample. *Science, 296*, 739–741. (15)

Levinson, D. F., Mahtani, M. M., Nancarrow, D. J., Brown, D. M., Kruglyak, L., Kirby, A., Hayward, N. K., Crowe, R. R., Andreasen, N. C., Black, D. W., Silverman, J. M., Endicott, J., Sharpe, L., Mohs, R. C., Siever, L. J., Walters, M. K., Lennon, D. P., Jones, H. L., Nertney, D. A., Daly, M. J., Gladis, M., & Mowry, B. J. (1998). Genome scan of schizophrenia. *American Journal of Psychiatry, 155*, 741–750. (15)

Levitin, D. J., & Bellugi, U. (1998). Musical abilities in individuals with Williams syndrome. *Music Perception, 15*, 357–389. (14)

Levitt, R. A. (1975). *Psychopharmacology*. Washington, DC: Hemisphere. (15)

Levitt-Gilmour, T. A., & Salpeter, M. M. (1986). Gradient of extrajunctional acetylcholine receptors early after denervation of mammalian muscle. *Journal of Neuroscience, 6*, 1606–1612. (5)

Levitzki, A. (1988). From epinephrine to cyclic AMP. *Science, 241*, 800–806. (3)

Levivier, M., Przedborski, S., Bencsics, C., & Kang, U. J. (1995). Intrastriatal implantation of fibroblasts genetically engineered to produce brain-derived neurotrophic factor prevents degeneration of dopaminergic neurons in a rat model of Parkinson's disease. *Journal of Neuroscience, 15*, 7810–7820. (5)

Levy, J., Heller, W., Banich, M. T., & Burton, L. A. (1983). Asymmetry of perception in free viewing of chimeric faces. *Brain and Cognition, 2*, 404–419. (14)

Lewis, D. A. (1997). Development of the prefrontal cortex during adolescence: Insights into vulnerable neural circuits in schizophrenia. *Neuropsychopharmacology, 16*, 385–398. (5, 15)

Lewis, E. R., Everhart, T. E., & Zeevi, Y. Y. (1969). Studying neural organization in Aplysia with the scanning electron microscope. *Science, 165*, 1140–1143. (3)

Lewis, V. G., Money, J., & Epstein, R. (1968). Concordance of verbal and nonverbal ability in the adrenogenital syndrome. *Johns Hopkins Medical Journal, 122*, 192–195. (11)

Lewy, A. J., Bauer, V. K., Cutler, N. L., Sack, R. L., Ahmed, S., Thomas, K. H., Blood, M. L., & Jackson, J. M. L. (1998). Morning vs. evening light treatment of patients with winter depression. *Archives of General Psychiatry, 55*, 890–896. (15)

Li, H., Chen, A., Xing, G., Wei, M.-L., & Rogawski, M. A. (2001). Kainate receptor-mediated heterosynaptic facilitation in the amygdala. *Nature Neuroscience, 4*, 612–620. (13)

Li, S.-H., Cheng, A. L., Li, H., & Li, X.-J. (1999). Cellular defects and altered gene expression in PC12 cells stably expressing mutant huntingtin. *Journal of Neuroscience, 19*, 5159–5172. (8)

Lieberman, J., Chakos, M., Wu, H., Alvir, J., Hoffman, E., Robinson, D., & Bilder, R. (2001). Longitudinal study of brain morphology in first episode schizophrenia. *Biological Psychiatry, 49*, 487–499. (15)

Lilenfeld, L. R., Kaye, W. H., Greeno, C. G., Merikangas, K. R., Plotnicov, K., Pollice, C., Rao, R., Strober, M., Bulik, C. M., & Nagy, L. (1998). A controlled family study of anorexia nervosa and bulimia nervosa. *Archives of General Psychiatry, 55*, 603–610. (10)

Lim, K. O., Adalsteinsson, E., Spielman, D., Sullivan, E. V., Rosenbloom, M. J., & Pfefferbaum, A. (1998). Proton magnetic resonance spectroscopic imaging of cortical gray and white matter in schizophrenia. *Archives of General Psychiatry, 55*, 346–352. (15)

Lin, J.-S., Hou, Y., Sakai, K., & Jouvet, M. (1996). Histaminergic descending inputs to the mesopontine tegmentum and their role in the control of cortical activation and wakefulness in the cat. *Journal of Neuroscience, 16*, 1523–1537. (9)

Lin, L., Faraco, J., Li, R., Kadotani, H., Rogers, W., Lin, X., Qiu, X., de Jong, P. J., Nishino, S., & Nignot, E. (1999). The sleep disorder canine narcolepsy is caused by a mutation in the hypocretin (orexin) receptor 2 gene. *Cell, 98*, 365–376. (9)

Lindberg, N. O., Coburn, C., & Stricker, E. M. (1984). Increased feeding by rats after subdiabetogenic streptozotocin treatment: A role for insulin in satiety. *Behavioral Neuroscience, 98*, 138–145. (10)

Lindemann, B. (1996). Taste reception. *Physiological Reviews, 76*, 719–766. (7)

Lindsay, P. H., & Norman, D. A. (1972). *Human information processing*. New York: Academic Press. (7)

Liou, Y.-C., Tocilj, A., Davies, P. L., & Jia, Z. (2000). Mimicry of ice structure by surface hydroxyls and water of a b-helix antifreeze protein. *Nature, 406*, 322–324. (10)

Lisman, J., Schulman, H., & Cline, H. (2002). The molecular basis of CaMKII function in synaptic and behavioural memory. *Nature Reviews Neuroscience, 3*, 175–190. (13)

Liu, G., & Tsien, R. W. (1995). Properties of synaptic transmission at single hippocampal synaptic boutons. *Nature, 375*, 404–408. (3)

Liu, P., & Bilkey, D. K. (2001). The effect of excitotoxic lesions centered on the hippocampus or perirhinal cortex in object recognition and spatial memory tasks.

Behavioral Neuroscience, 115, 94–111. (13)

Livingstone, M. S. (1988, January). Art, illusion and the visual system. *Scientific American, 258*(1), 78–85. (6)

Livingstone, M. S., & Hubel, D. (1988). Segregation of form, color, movement, and depth: Anatomy, physiology, and perception. *Science, 240,* 740–749. (6)

Livingstone, M. S., Rosen, G. D., Drislane, F. W., & Galaburda, A. M. (1991). Physiological and anatomical evidence for a magnocellular defect in developmental dyslexia. *Proceedings of the National Academy of Sciences, USA, 88,* 7943–7947. (14)

Ljungberg, M. C., Stern, G., & Wilkin, G. P. (1999). Survival of genetically engineered, adult-derived rat astrocytes grafted into the 6-hydroxydopamine lesioned adult rat striatum. *Brain Research, 816,* 29–37. (8)

Lockwood, A. H., Salvi, R. J., Coad, M. L., Towsley, M. L., Wack, D. S., & Murphy, B. W. (1998). The functional neuroanatomy of tinnitus: Evidence for limbic system links and neural plasticity. *Neurology, 50,* 114–120. (7)

Loewenstein, W. R. (1960, August). Biological transducers. *Scientific American, 203*(2), 98–108. (7)

Loewi, O. (1960). An autobiographic sketch. *Perspectives in Biology, 4,* 3–25. (3)

Logan, C. G., & Grafton, S. T. (1995). Functional anatomy of human eyeblink conditioning determined with regional cerebral glucose metabolism and positron-emission tomography. *Proceedings of the National Academy of Sciences, USA, 92,* 7500–7504. (13)

Logothetis, N. K., Pauls, J., Augath, M., Trinath, T., & Oeltermann, A. (2001). Neurophysiological investigtion of the basis of the fMRI signal. *Nature, 412,* 150–157. (6)

London, E. D., Cascella, N. G., Wong, D. F., Phillips, R. L., Dannals, R. F., Links, J. M., Herning, R., Grayson, R., Jaffe, J. H., & Wagner, H. N. (1990). Cocaine-induced reduction of glucose utilization in human brain. *Archives of General Psychiatry, 47,* 567–574. (15)

Lord, G. M., Matarese, G., Howard, J. K., Baker, R. J., Bloom, S. R., & Lechler, R. I. (1998). Leptin modulates the T-cell immune response and reverses starvation-induced immunosuppression. *Nature, 394,* 897–901. (10)

Lorenzo, A., Yuan, M., Zhang, Z., Paganetti, P. A., Sturchler-Pierrat, C., Stauferbiel, M., Mautino, J., Sol Vigo, F., Sommer, B., & Yankner, B. A. (2000). Amyloid β interacts with the amyloid precursor protein: A potential toxic mechanism in Alxheimer's disease. *Nature Neuroscience, 3,* 460–464. (13)

Lorrain, D. S., Riolo, J. V., Matuszewich, L., & Hull, E. M. (1999). Lateral hypothalamic serotonin inhibits nucleus accumbens dopamine: Implications for sexual refractoriness. *Journal of Neuroscience, 19,* 7648–7652. (15)

Lott, I. T. (1982). Down's syndrome, aging, and Alzheimer's disease: A clinical review. *Annals of the New York Academy of Sciences, 396,* 15–27. (13)

Lotto, R. B., & Purves, D. (1999). The effects of color on brightness. *Nature Neuroscience, 2,* 1010–1014. (6)

Lotze, M., Grodd, W., Birbaumer, N., Erb, M., Huse, E., & Flor, H. (1999). Does use of a myoelectric prosthesis prevent cortical reorganization and phantom limb pain? *Nature Neuroscience, 2,* 501–502. (5)

Löw, K., Crestani, F., Keist, R., Benke, D., Brünig, I., Benson, J. A. Fritschy, J.-M., Rülicke, T., Bluethmann, H., Möhler, H., & Rudolph, U. (2000). Molecular and neuronal substrate for the selective attenuation of anxiety. *Science, 290,* 131–134. (12)

Lowell, B. B., & Spiegelman, B. M. (2000). Towards a molecular understanding of adaptive thermogenesis. *Nature, 404,* 652–660. (10)

Lu, Z., Klem, A. M., & Ramu, Y. (2001). Ion conduction pore is conserved among potassium channels. *Nature, 413,* 809–813. (5)

Lucas, R. J., Douglas, R. H., & Foster, R. G. (2001). Characterization of an ocular photopigment capable of driving pupillary constriction in mice. *Nature Neuroscience, 4,* 621–626. (9)

Lucas, R. J., Freedman, M. S., Muñoz, M., Garcia-Fernández, J.-M., & Foster, R. G. (1999). Regulation of the mammalian pineal by non-rod, non-cone ocular photoreceptors. *Science, 284,* 505–507. (9)

Lund, R. D., Lund, J. S., & Wise, R. P. (1974). The organization of the retinal projection to the dorsal lateral geniculate nucleus in pigmented and albino rats. *Journal of Comparative Neurology, 158,* 383–404. (6)

Lupien, S. J., de Leon, M., de Santi, S., Convit, A., Tarshish, C., Nair, N. P. V., Thakur, M., McEwen, B. S., Hauger, R. L., & Meaney, M. J. (1998). Cortisol levels during human aging predict hippocampal atrophy and memory deficits. *Nature Neuroscience, 1,* 69–73. (12)

Lüthi, A., Schwyzer, L., Mateos, J. M., Gähwiler, B. H., & McKinney, R. A. (2001). NMDA receptor activation limits the number of synaptic connections during hippocampal development. *Nature Neuroscience, 4,* 1102–1107. (13)

Lyman, C. P., O'Brien, R. C., Greene, G. C., & Papafrangos, E. D. (1981). Hibernation and longevity in the Turkish hamster *Mesocricetus brandti. Science, 212,* 668–670. (9)

Lyons, M. J., Eisen, S. A., Goldberg, J., True, W., Lin, N., Meyer, J. M., Toomey, R., Faraone, S. V., Merla-Ramos, M., & Tsuang, M. T. (1998). A registry-based twin study of depression in men. *Archives of General Psychiatry, 55,* 468–472. (15)

Lyons, M. J., True, W. R., Eisen, S. A., Goldberg, J., Meyer, J. M., Faraone, S. V., Eaves, L. J., & Tsuang, M. T. (1995). Differential heritability of adult and juvenile antisocial traits. *Archives of General Psychiatry, 52,* 906–915. (12)

Lytle, L. D., Messing, R. B., Fisher, L., & Phebus, L. (1975). Effects of long-term corn consumption on brain serotonin and the response to electric shock. *Science, 190,* 692–694. (12)

Macdonald, R. L., Weddle, M. G., & Gross, R. A. (1986). Benzodiazepine, β-carboline, and barbiturate actions on GABA responses. *Advances in Biochemical Psychopharmacology*, *41*, 67–78. (12)

MacFarlane, J. G., Cleghorn, J. M., & Brown, G. M. (1985a). Melatonin and core temperature rhythms in chronic insomnia. In G. M. Brown & S. D. Wainwright (Eds.), *The pineal gland: Endocrine aspects* (pp. 301–306). New York: Pergamon Press. (9)

MacFarlane, J. G., Cleghorn, J. M., & Brown, G. M. (1985b, September). *Circadian rhythms in chronic insomnia.* Paper presented at the 4th World Congress of Biological Psychiatry, Philadelphia. (9)

MacLean, P. D. (1949). Psychosomatic disease and the "visceral brain": Recent developments bearing on the Papez theory of emotion. *Psychosomatic Medicine*, *11*, 338–353. (12)

MacLusky, N. J., & Naftolin, F. (1981). Sexual differentiation of the central nervous system. *Science*, *211*, 1294–1303. (11)

Macphail, E. M. (1985). Vertebrate intelligence: The null hypothesis. *Philosophical Transactions of the Royal Society of London*, B, *308*, 37–51. (14)

Madden, D. R. (2002). The structure and function of glutamate receptor ion channels. *Nature Reviews Neuroscience*, *3*, 91–101. (13)

Madden, P. A. F., Heath, A. C., Rosenthal, N. E., & Martin, N. G. (1996). Seasonal changes in mood and behavior. *Archives of General Psychiatry*, *53*, 47–55. (15)

Maes, M., Scharpé, S., Verkerk, R., D'Hondt, P., Peeters, D., Cosyns, P., Thompson, P., De Meyer, F., Wauters, A., & Neels, H. (1995). Seasonal availability in plasma L-tryptophan availability in healthy volunteers. *Archives of General Psychiatry*, *52*, 937–946. (12)

Maess, B., Koelsch, S., Gunter, T. C., & Friederici, A. D. (2001). Musical syntax is processed in Broca's area: An MEG study. *Nature Neuroscience*, *4*, 540–545. (14)

Maestripieri, D., & Zehr, J. L. (1998). Maternal responsiveness increases during pregnancy and after estrogen treatment in macaques. *Hormones and Behavior*, *34*, 223–230. (11)

Magavi, S. S., Leavitt, B. R., & Macklis, J. D. (2000). Induction of neurogenesis in the neocortex of adult mice. *Nature*, *405*, 951–955. (5)

Magee, J. C., & Cook, E. P. (2000). Somatic EPSP amplitude is independent of synapse location in hippocampal pyramidal neurons. *Nature Neuroscience*, *3*, 895–903. (3)

Maguire, E. A., Frackowiak, R. S. J., & Frith, C. D. (1997). Recalling routes around London: Activation of the right hippocampus in taxi drivers. *Journal of Neuroscience*, *17*, 7103–7110. (4, 13)

Maguire, E. A., Gadian, D. G., Johnsrude, I. S., Good, C. D., Ashburner, J., Frackowiak, R. S. J., & Frith, C. D. (2000). Navigation-related structural change in the hippocampi of taxi drivers. *Proceedings of the National Academy of Sciences, USA*, *97*, 4398–4403. (13)

Mahowald, M. W., & Schenck, C. H. (1992). Dissociated states of wakefulness and sleep. *Neurology*, *42*(Suppl. 6), 44–52. (9)

Maier, S. F., & Watkins, L. R. (1998). Cytokines for psychologists: Implications of bidirectional immune-to-brain communication for understanding behavior, mood, and cognition. *Psychological Review*, *105*, 83–107. (12)

Maki, P. M., Rich, J. B., & Rosenbaum, R. S. (2002). Implicit memory varies across the menstrual cycle: Estrogen effects in young women. *Neuropsychologia*, *40*, 518–529. (11)

Maki, P. M., Zonderman, A. B., & Resnick, S. M. (2001). Enhanced verbal memory in nondemented elderly women receiving hormone-replacement therapy. *American Journal of Psychiatry*, *158*, 227–233. (11)

Malamed, F., & Zaidel, E. (1993). Language and task effects on lateralized word recognition. *Brain and Language*, *45*, 70–85. (14)

Malaspina, D., Harlap, S., Fennig, S., Heiman, D., Nahon, D., Feldman, D., & Susser, E. S. (2001). Advancing paternal age and the risk of schizophrenia. *Archives of General Psychiatry*, *58*, 361–367. (15)

Malenka, R. C., & Nicoll, R. A. (1999). Long-term potentiation—A decade of progress? *Science*, *285*, 1870–1874. (13)

Malmberg, A. B., Chen, C., Tonegawa, S., & Basbaum, A. I. (1997). Preserved acute pain and reduced neuropathic pain in mice lacking PKCγ. *Science*, *278*, 179–283. (7)

Manfredi, M., Stocchi, F., & Vacca, L. (1995). Differential diagnosis of parkinsonism. *Journal of Neural Transmission* (Suppl. 45), 1–9. (8)

Mangiapane, M. L., & Simpson, J. B. (1980). Subfornical organ: Forebrain site of pressor and dipsogenic action of angiotensin II. *American Journal of Physiology*, *239*, R382–R389. (10)

Mann, J. J., Arango, V., & Underwood, M. D. (1990). Serotonin and suicidal behavior. *Annals of the New York Academy of Sciences*, *600*, 476–485. (12)

Mannuzza, S., Klein, R. G., Bessler, A., Malloy, P., & LaPadula, M. (1998). Adult psychiatric status of hyperactive boys grown up. *American Journal of Psychiatry*, *155*, 493–498. (5)

Maquet, P., Laureys, S., Peigneux, P., Fuchs, S., Petiau, C., Phillips, C., Aerts, J., DelFiore, G., Degueldre, C., Meulemans, T., Luxen, A., Frank, G., Van Der Linden, M., Smith, C., & Cleeremans, A. (2000). Experience-dependent changes in cerebral activation during human REM sleep. *Nature Neuroscience*, *3*, 831–836. (9)

Maquet, P., Peters, J.-M., Aerts, J., Delfiore, G., Degueldre, C., Luxen, A., & Franck, G. (1996). Functional neuroanatomy of human rapid-eye-movement sleep and dreaming. *Nature*, *383*, 163–166. (8, 9)

Marcar, V. L., Zihl, J., & Cowey, A. (1997). Comparing the visual deficits of a motion blind patient with the visual deficits of monkeys with area MT removed. *Neuropsychologia*, *35*, 1459–1465. (6)

Marín, O., & Rubenstein, J. L. R. (2001). A long, remarkable journey: Tangential migration in the telencephalon. *Nature Reviews Neuroscience*, *2*, 780–790. (5)

Marin, O., Smeets, W. J. A. J., & González, A. (1998). Evolution of the basal ganglia in tetrapods: A new perspective based on recent studies in amphibians. *Trends in Neurosciences, 21,* 487–494. (4)

Mark, V. H., & Ervin, F. R. (1970). *Violence and the brain.* New York: Harper & Row. (12)

Marshall, J. F. (1985). Neural plasticity and recovery of function after brain injury. *International Review of Neurobiology, 26,* 201–247. (5)

Marshall, J. F., Drew, M. C., & Neve, K. A. (1983). Recovery of function after mesotelencephalic dopaminergic injury in senescence. *Brain Research, 259,* 249–260. (5)

Marsicano, G., Wotjak, C. T., Azad, S. C., Bisogno, T., Rammes, G., Cascio, M. G., Hermann, H., Tang, J., Hofmann, C., Zieglgänsberger, W., Di Marzo, V., & Lutz, B. (2002). The endogenous cannabinoid system controls extinction of aversive memories. *Nature, 418,* 530–534. (15)

Martin, A. R. (1977). Junctional transmission: II. Presynaptic mechanisms. In E. R. Kandel (Ed.), *Handbook of physiology* (Sect. 1, Vol. 1, Pt. 1, pp. 329–355). Bethesda, MD: American Physiological Society. (3)

Martin, E. R., Scott, W. K., Nance, M. A., Watts, R. L., Hubble, J. P., Koller, W. C., Lyons, K., Pahwa, R., Stern, M. B., Colcher, A., Hiner, B. C., Hankovic, J., Ondo, W. G., Allen, F. H., Jr., Goetz, C. G., Small, G. W., Masterman, D., Mastaglia, F., Laing, N. G., Stajich, J. M., Ribble, R. C., Booze, M. W., Rogala, A., Hauser, M. A., Zhang, F., Gibson, R. A., Middleton, L. T., Roses, A. D., Haines, J. L., Scott, B. L., Pericak-Vance, M. A., & Vance, J. M. (2001). Association of single-nucleotide polymorphisms of the tau gene with late-onset Parkinson disease. *Journal of the Americal Medical Association, 286,* 2245–2250. (8)

Martin, P. R., Lee, B. B., White, A. J. R., Solomon, S. G., & Rütiger, L. (2001). Chromatic sensitivity of ganglion cells in the peripheral primate retina. *Nature, 410,* 933–936. (6)

Martin, R. C., & Blossom-Stach, C. (1986). Evidence of syntactic deficits in a fluent aphasic. *Brain and Language, 28,* 196–234. (14)

Martin, S. D., Martin, E., Rai, S. S., Richardson, M. A., Royall, R., & Eng, C. (2001). Brain blood flow changes in depressed patients treated with interpersonal psychotherapy or venlafaxine hydrochloride. *Archives of General Psychiatry, 58,* 641–648. (15)

Martin-Santos, R., Bulbena, A., Porta, M., Gago, J., Molina, L., & Duró, J. C. (1998). Association between joint hypermobility syndrome and panic disorder. *American Journal of Psychiatry, 155,* 1578–1583. (12)

Martindale, C. (2001). Oscillations and analogies: Thomas Young, MD, FRS, genius. *American Psychologist, 56,* 342–345. (6)

Martinez, L. M., & Alonso, J.-M. (2001). Construction of complex receptive fields in cat primary visual cortex. *Neuron, 32,* 515–525. (6)

Martinez-Vargas, M. C., & Erickson, C. J. (1973). Some social and hormonal determinants of nest-building behaviour in the ring dove (*Streptopelia risoria*). *Behaviour, 45,* 12–37. (11)

Masland, R. H. (2001). The fundamental plan of the retina. *Nature Neuroscience, 4,* 877–886. (6)

Mason, D. A., & Frick, P. J. (1994). The heritability of antisocial behavior: A meta-analysis of twin and adoption studies. *Journal of Psychopathology and Behavioral Assessment, 16,* 301–323. (12)

Masterton, B., Heffner, H., & Ravizza, R. (1969). The evolution of human hearing. *Journal of the Acoustical Society of America, 45,* 966–985. (7)

Masuzaki, H., Paterson, J., Shinyama, H., Morton, N. M., Mullins, J. J., Seckl, J. R., & Flier, J. S. (2001). A transgenic model of visceral obesity and the metabolic syndrome. *Science, 294,* 2166–2170. (10)

Mathalon, D. H., Sullivan, E. V., Lim, K. O., & Pfefferbaum, A. (2001). Progressive brain volume changes and the clinical course of schizophrenia in men. *Archives of General Psychiatry, 58,* 148–157. (15)

Matsumoto, Y., Mishima, K., Satoh, K., Tozawa, T., Mishima, Y.,

Shimizu, T., & Hishikawa, Y. (2001). Total sleep deprivation induces an acute and transient increase in NK cell activity in healthy young volunteers. *Sleep, 24,* 804–809. (9)

Matsunami, H., Montmayeur, J.-P., & Buck, L. B. (2000). A family of candidate taste receptors in human and mouse. *Nature, 404,* 601–604. (7)

Mattay, V. S., Berman, K. F., Ostrem, J. L., Esposito, G., Van Horn, J. D., Bigelow, L. B., & Weinberger, D. R. (1996). Dextroamphetamine enhances "neural network-specific" physiological signals: A positron-emission tomography rCBF study. *Journal of Neuroscience, 15,* 4816–4822. (15)

Mattingley, J. B., Husain, M., Rorden, C., Kennard, C., & Driver, J. (1998). Motor role of human inferior parietal lobe revealed in unilateral neglect patients. *Nature, 392,* 179–182. (7)

Matuszewich, L., Lorrain, D. S., & Hull, E. M. (2000). Dopamine release in the medial preoptic area of female rats in response to hormonal manipulation and sexual activity. *Behavioral Neuroscience, 114,* 772–782. (11)

Mauch, D. H., Nägler, K., Schumacher, S., Göritz, C., Müller, E.-C., Otto, A., & Pfrieger, F. W. (2001). CNS synaptogenesis promoted by glia-derived cholesterol. *Science, 294,* 1354–1357. (5)

Maurice, D. M. (1998). The Von Sallmann lecture of 1996: An ophthalmological explanation of REM sleep. *Experimental Eye Research, 66,* 139–145. (9)

May, P. R. A., Fuster, J. M., Haber, J., & Hirschman, A. (1979). Woodpecker drilling behavior: An endorsement of the rotational theory of impact brain injury. *Archives of Neurology, 36,* 370–373. (5)

Mayberry, R. I., Lock, E., & Kazmi, H. (2002). Linguistic ability and early language exposure. *Nature, 417,* 38. (14)

Mayer, A. D., & Rosenblatt, J. S. (1979). Hormonal influences during the ontogeny of maternal behavior in female rats. *Journal of Comparative and Physiological Psychology, 93,* 879–898. (11)

Mayer, A. D., & Rosenblatt, J. S. (1984). Postpartum changes in maternal responsiveness and nest defense in Rattus norvegicus. *Journal of Comparative Psychology, 98,* 177–188. (11)

Mayne, T. J. (1999). Negative affect and health: The importance of being earnest. *Cognition and Emotion, 13,* 601–635. (12)

Maziade, M., Roy, M.-A., Rouillard, É., Bissonnette, L., Fournier, J.-P., Roy, A., Garneau, Y., Montgrain, N., Potvin, A., Cliché, D., Dion, D., Wallot, H., Fournier, A., Nicole, L., Lavallée, J.-C., & Mérette, C. (2001). A search for specific and common susceptibility loci for schizophrenia and bipolar disorder: A linkage study in 13 target chromosomes. *Molecular Psychiatry, 6,* 684–693. (15)

McBurney, D. H., & Bartoshuk, L. M. (1973). Interactions between stimuli with different taste qualities. *Physiology & Behavior, 10,* 1101–1106. (7)

McCann, U. D., Lowe, K. A., & Ricaurte, G. A. (1997). Long-lasting effects of recreational drugs of abuse on the central nervous system. *The Neuroscientist, 3,* 399–411. (15)

McCarley, R. W., & Hobson, J. A. (1977). The neurobiological origins of psychoanalytic dream theory. *American Journal of Psychiatry, 134,* 1211–1221. (9)

McCarley, R. W., & Hoffman, E. (1981). REM sleep, dreams, and the activation-synthesis hypothesis. *American Journal of Psychiatry, 138,* 904–912. (9)

McCarthy, G., Puce, A., Gore, J. C., & Allison, T. (1997). Face-specific processing in the human fusiform gyrus. *Journal of Cognitive Neuroscience, 9,* 605–610. (6)

McCaughey, S. A., & Scott, T. R. (2000). Rapid induction of sodium appetite modifies taste-evoked activity in the rat nucleus of the solitary tract. *American Journal of Physiology, 279,* R1121–1131. (10)

McClellan, A. D. (1998). Spinal cord injury: Lessons from locomotor recovery and axonal regeneration in lower vertebrates. *The Neuroscientist, 4,* 250–263. (5)

McClintock, M. K. (1971). Menstrual synchrony and suppression. *Nature, 229,* 244–245. (7)

McConnell, J. V. (1962). Memory transfer through cannibalism in planarians. *Journal of Neuropsychiatry, 3*(Suppl. 1), 42–48. (13)

McConnell, S. K. (1992). The genesis of neuronal diversity during development of cerebral cortex. *Seminars in the Neurosciences, 4,* 347–356. (5)

McCormick, D. A. (1989). Acetylcholine: Distribution, receptors, and actions. *Seminars in the Neurosciences, 1,* 91–101. (3)

McCrory, E., Frith, U., Brunswick, N., & Price, C. (2000). Abnormal functional activation during a simple word repetition task: A PET study of adult dyslexics. *Journal of Cognitive Neuroscience, 12,* 753–762. (14)

McDaniel, M. A., Maier, S. F., & Einstein, G. O. (2002). "Brain-specific" nutrients: A memory cure? *Psychological Science in the Public Interest, 3,* 12–38. (13)

McDonald, M. P., Willard, L. B., Wenk, G. L., & Crawley, J. N. (1998). Coadministration of galanin antagonist M40 with a muscarinic M$_1$ agonist improves delayed nonmatching to position choice accuracy in rats with cholinergic lesions. *Journal of Neuroscience, 18,* 5078–5085. (13)

McElhiney, M. C., Moody, B. J., Steif, B. L., Prudic, J., Devanand, D. P., Nobler, M. S., & Sackeim, H. A. (1995). Autobiographical memory and mood: Effects of electroconvulsive therapy. *Neuropsychology, 9,* 501–517. (15)

McEwen, B. S. (2001). Invited review: Estrogen effects on the brain: Multiple sites and molecular mechanisms. *Journal of Applied Physiology, 91,* 2785–2801. (11)

McFadden, D., & Champlin, C. A. (2000). Comparison of auditory evoked potentials in heterosexual, homosexual, and bisexual males and females. *Journal of the Association for Research in Otolaryngology, 01,* 89–99. (11)

McGinnis, M. Y., Williams, G. W., & Lumia, A. R. (1996). Inhibition of male sex behavior by androgen receptor blockade in preoptic area or hypothalamus, but not amygdala or septum. *Physiology & Behavior, 60,* 783–789. (11)

McGinnis, R. E., Fox, H., Yates, P., Cameron, L.-A., Barnes, M. R., Gray, I. C., Spurr, N. K., Hurko, O., & St Clair, D. (2001). Failure to confirm *NOTCH4* association with schizophrenia in a large population-based sample from Scotland. *Nature Genetics, 28,* 128–129. (15)

McGlynn, S. M. (1990). Behavioral approaches to neuropsychological rehabilitation. *Psychological Bulletin, 108,* 420–441. (5)

McGuire, S., & Clifford, J. (2000). Genetic and environmental contributions to loneliness in children. *Psychological Science, 11,* 487–491. (1)

McHugh, P. R., & Moran, T. H. (1985). The stomach: A conception of its dynamic role in satiety. *Progress in Psychobiology and Physiological Psychology, 11,* 197–232. (10)

McKeever, W. F., Seitz, K. S., Krutsch, A. J., & Van Eys, P. L. (1995). On language laterality in normal dextrals and sinistrals: Results from the bilateral object naming latency task. *Neuropsychologia, 33,* 1627–1635. (14)

McKemy, D. D., Neuhausser, W. M., & Julius, D. (2002). Identification of a cold receptor reveals a general role for TRP channels in thermosensation. *Nature, 416,* 52–58. (7)

McKinnon, W., Weisse, C. S., Reynolds, C. P., Bowles, C. A., & Baum, A. (1989). Chronic stress, leukocyte-subpopulations, and humoral response to latent viruses. *Health Psychology, 8,* 389–402. (12)

McMahon, F. J., Simpson, S. G., McInnis, M. G., Badner, J. A., MacKinnon, D. F., & DePaulo, R. (2001). Linkage of bipolar disorder to chromosome 18q and the validity of bipolar II disorder. *Archives of General Psychiatry, 58,* 1025–1031. (15)

McPartland, J., DiMarzo, V., de Petrocellis, L., Mercer, A., & Glass, M. (2001). Cannabinoid receptors are absent in insects. *Journal of Comparative Neurology, 436,* 423–429. (15)

Meddis, R., Pearson, A. J. D., & Langford, G. (1973). An extreme case of healthy insomnia. *EEG and Clinical Neurophysiology, 35*, 213–214. (9)

Mednick, S. C., Nakayama, K., Cantero, J. L., Atienza, M., Levin, A. A., Pathak, N., & Stickgold, R. (2002). The restorative effect of naps on perceptual deterioration. *Nature Neuroscience, 5*, 677–681. (9)

Meiran, N., & Jelicic, M. (1995). Implicit memory in Alzheimer's disease: A meta-analysis. *Neuropsychology, 9*, 291–303. (13)

Meister, M., Wong, R. O. L., Baylor, D. A., & Shatz, C. J. (1991). Synchronous bursts of action potentials in ganglion cells of the developing mammalian retina. *Science, 252*, 939–943. (5)

Mellor, J., & Nicoll, R. A. (2001). Hippocampal mossy fiber LTP is independent of postsynaptic calcium. *Nature Neuroscience, 4*, 125–126. (13)

Melone, M., Vitellaro-Zuccarello, L., Vallejo-Illarramendi, A., Pérez-Samartin, A., Matute, C., Cozzi, A., Pellegrini-Giampietro, D. E., Rothstein, J. D., & Conti, F. (2001). The expression of glutamate transporter GLT-1 in the rat cerebral cortex is down-regulated by the antipsychotic drug clozapine. *Molecular Psychiatry, 6*, 380–386. (15)

Melters, B. A., & McGraw, A. P. (2001). Anticipated emotions as guides to choice. Current *Directions in Psychological Science, 10*, 210–214. (15)

Meltzer, H. Y. (2001). Treatment of suicidality in schizophrenia. *Annals of the New York Academy of Sciences, 932*, 44–58. (15)

Meltzer, H. Y., Matsubara, S., & Lee, J.-C. (1989). Classification of typical and atypical antipsychotic drugs on the basis of dopamine D-1, D-2 and serotonin$_2$ pKi values. *Journal of Pharmacology and Experimental Therapeutics, 251*, 238–246. (15)

Melzack, R., & Wall, P. D. (1965). Pain mechanisms: A new theory. *Science, 150*, 971–979. (7)

Mendez, M. F. (1995). The neuropsychiatric aspects of boxing.

International Journal of Psychiatry in Medicine, 25, 249–262. (5)

Mendonca, B. B., Inacio, M., Costa, E. M. F., Arnhold, I. J. P., Silva, F. A. Q., Nicolau, W., Bloise, W., Russell, D. W., & Wilson, J. D. (1996). Male pseudohermaphroditism due to steroid 5α-reductase 2 deficiency. *Medicine, 75*, 64–76. (11)

Menon, V., Anagnoson, R. T., Glover, G. H., & Pfefferbaum, A. (2000). Basal ganglia involvement in memory-guided movement sequencing. *NeuroReport, 11*, 3641–3645. (8)

Mergen, M., Mergen, H., Ozata, M., Oner, R., & Oner, C. (2001). A novel melanocortin 4 receptor (MC4R) gene mutation associated with morbid obesity. *Journal of Clinical Endocrinology & Metabolism, 86*, 3448–3451. (10)

Merton, P. A. (1972). How we control the contraction of our muscles. *Scientific American, 226*(5), 30–37. (8)

Merzenich, M. M., Nelson, R. J., Stryker, M. P., Cynader, M. S., Schoppman, A., & Zook, J. M. (1984). Somatosensory cortical map changes following digit amputation in adult monkeys. *Journal of Comparative Neurology, 224*, 591–605. (5)

Mesulam, M.-M. (1995). Cholinergic pathways and the ascending reticular activating system of the human brain. *Annals of the New York Academy of Sciences, 757*, 169–179. (4, 9)

Meyer-Lindenberg, A., Miletich, R. S., Kohn, P. D., Esposito, G., Carson, R. E., Quarantelli, M., Weinberger, D. R., & Berman, K. F. (2002). Reduced prefrontal activity predicts exaggerated striatal dopaminergic function in schizophrenia. *Nature Neuroscience, 5*, 267–271. (15)

Mezzanotte, W. S., Tangel, D. J., & White, D. P. (1992). Waking genioglossal electromyogram in sleep apnea patients versus normal controls (a neuromuscular compensatory mechanism). *Journal of Clinical Investigation, 89*, 1571–1579. (9)

Mihic, S. J., Ye, Q., Wick, M. J., Koltchine, V. V., Krasowski, M. D., Finn, S. E., Mascia, M. P., Valenzuela, C. F., Hanson, K. K.,

Greenblatt, E. P., Harris, R. A., & Harrison, N. L. (1997). Sites of alcohol and volatile anaesthetic action on GABA$_A$ and glycine receptors. *Nature, 389*, 385–389. (15)

Milberger, S., Biederman, J., Faraone, S. V., Chen, L., & Jones, J. (1996). Is maternal smoking during pregnancy a risk factor for attention deficit hyperactivity disorder in children? *American Journal of Psychiatry, 153*, 1138–1142. (5)

Miles, F. A., & Evarts, E. V. (1979). Concepts of motor organization. *Annual Review of Psychology, 30*, 327–362. (8)

Miles, L. E. M., Raynal, D. M., & Wilson, M. A. (1977). Blind man living in normal society has circadian rhythms of 24.9 hours. *Science, 198*, 421–423. (9)

Miller, E. (2000). The prefrontal cortex and cognitive control. *Nature Reviews Neuroscience, 1*, 59–65. (4)

Miller, W. C., & DeLong, M. R. (1988). Parkinsonian symptomatology: An anatomical and physiological analysis. *Annals of the New York Academy of Sciences, 515*, 287–302. (8)

Milner, B. (1959). The memory defect in bilateral hippocampal lesions. *Psychiatric Research Reports, 11*, 43–58. (13)

Mima, T., Oluwatimilehin, T., Hiraoka, T., & Hallett, M. (2001). Transient interhemispheric neuronal synchrony correlates with object recognition. *Journal of Neuroscience, 21*, 3942–3948. (6)

Misrahi, M., Meduri, G., Pissard, S., Bouvattier, C., Beau, I., Loosfelt, H., Jolivet, A., Rappaport, R., Milgrom, E., & Bougneres, P. (1997). Comparison of immunocytochemical and molecular features with the phenotype in a case of incomplete male pseudohermaphroditism associated with a mutation of the luteinizing hormone receptor. *Journal of Clinical Endocrinology & Metabolism, 82*, 2159–2165. (11)

Mitchell, D. E. (1980). The influence of early visual experience on visual perception. In C. S. Harris (Ed.), *Visual coding and adaptability* (pp. 1–50). Hillsdale, NJ: Erlbaum. (6)

Mitchell, D. E., Gingras, G., & Kind, P. C. (2001). Initial recovery of vision after early monocular deprivation in kittens is faster when both eyes are open. *Proceedings of the National Academy of Sciences, 98*, 11662–11667. (6)

Moeller, F. G., Dougherty, D. M., Swann, A. C., Collins, D., Davis, C. M., & Cherek, D. R. (1996). Tryptophan depletion and aggressive responding in healthy males. *Psychopharmacology, 126*, 97–103. (12)

Moffat, S. D., Hampson, E., & Lee, D. H. (1998). Morphology of the planum temporale and corpus callosum in left-handers with evidence of left and right hemisphere speech representation. *Brain, 121*, 2369–2379. (14)

Moghaddam, B., & Adams, B. W. (1998). Reversal of phencyclidine effects by a group II metabotropic glutamate receptor agonist in rats. *Science, 281*, 1349–1352. (15)

Mohn, A., Gainetdinov, R. R., Caron, M. G., & Koller, B. H. (1999). Mice with reduced NMDA receptor expression display behaviors related to schizophrenia. *Cell, 98*, 427–436. (15)

Money, J. (1967). Sexual problems of the chronically ill. In C. W. Wahl (Ed.), *Sexual problems: Diagnosis and treatment in medical practice* (pp. 266–287). New York: Free Press. (8)

Money, J., & Ehrhardt, A. A. (1972). *Man & woman, boy & girl.* Baltimore, MD: Johns Hopkins University Press. (11)

Money, J., & Lewis, V. (1966). IQ, genetics and accelerated growth: Adrenogenital syndrome. *Bulletin of the Johns Hopkins Hospital, 118*, 365–373. (11)

Money, J., & Schwartz, M. (1978). Biosocial determinants of gender identity differentiation and development. In J. B. Hutchison (Ed.), *Biological determinants of sexual behaviour* (pp. 765–784). Chichester, England: Wiley. (11)

Monteleone, P., Luisi, S., Tonetti, A., Bernardi, F., Genazzani, A. D., Luisi, M., Petraglia, F., & Genazzani, A. R. (2000). Allopregnanolone concentrations and premenstrual syndrome. *European Journal of Endocrinology, 142*, 269–273. (11)

Monti-Bloch, L., Jennings-White, C., & Berliner, D. L. (1998). The human vomeronasal system: A review. *Annals of the New York Academy of Sciences, 855*, 373–389. (7)

Monti-Bloch, L., Jennings-White, C., Dolberg, D. S., & Berliner, D. L. (1994). The human vomeronasal system. *Psychoneuroendocrinology, 19*, 673–686. (7)

Moorcroft, W. H. (1993). *Sleep, dreaming, & sleep disorders* (2nd ed.). Lanham, MD: University Press of America. (9)

Moore, L. B., Goodwin, B., Jones, S. A., Wisely, G. B., Serabjit-Singh, C. J., Willson, T. M., Collins, J. L., & Kliewer, S. A. (2000). St. John's wort induces hepatic drug metabolism through activation of the pregnane X receptor. *Proceedings of the National Academy of Sciences, USA, 97*, 7500–7502. (15)

Moore, T., Rodman, H. R., Repp, A. B., & Gross, C. G. (1995). Localization of visual stimuli after striate cortex damage in monkeys: Parallels with human blindsight. *Proceedings of the National Academy of Sciences, USA, 92*, 8215–8218. (6)

Moore-Ede, M. C., Czeisler, C. A., & Richardson, G. S. (1983). Circadian timekeeping in health and disease. *New England Journal of Medicine, 309*, 469–476. (9)

Morgan, D., Diamond, D. M., Gottschall, P. E., Ugen, K. E., Dickey, C., Hardy, J., Duff, K., Jantzen, P., DiCarlo, G., Wilcock, D., Connor, K., Hatcher, J., Hope, C., Gordon, M., & Arendash, G. W. (2000). Aβ peptide vaccination prevents memory loss in an animal model of Alzheimer's disease. *Nature, 408*, 982–985. (13)

Mori, K., Mataga, N., & Imamura, K. (1992). Differential specificities of single mitral cells in rabbit olfactory bulb for a homologous series of fatty acid odor molecules. *Journal of Neurophysiology, 67*, 786–789. (7)

Morley, J. E., Levine, A. S., Grace, M., & Kneip, J. (1985). Peptide YY (PYY), a potent orexigenic agent. *Brain Research, 341*, 200–203. (10)

Morris, J. F., & Pow, D. V. (1993). New anatomical insights into the inputs and outputs from hypothalamic magnocellular neurons. *Annals of the New York Academy of Sciences, 689*, 16–33. (11)

Morris, J. S., Frith, C. D., Perrett, D. I., Rowland, D., Young, A. W., Calder, A. J., & Dolan, R. J. (1996). A differential neural response in the human amygdala to fearful and happy expressions. *Nature, 383*, 812–815. (12)

Morris, M., Lack, L., & Dawson, D. (1990). Sleep-onset insomniacs have delayed temperature rhythms. *Sleep, 13*, 1–14. (9)

Morrison, A. R., Sanford, L. D., Ball, W. A., Mann, G. L., & Ross, R. J. (1995). Stimulus-elicited behavior in rapid eye movement sleep without atonia. *Behavioral Neuroscience, 109*, 972–979. (9)

Morrison, J. H., & Hof, P. R. (1997). Life and death of neurons in the aging brain. *Science, 278*, 412–419. (13)

Moruzzi, G., & Magoun, H. W. (1949). Brain stem reticular formation and activation of the EEG. *Electroencephalography and Clinical Neurophysiology, 1*, 455–473. (9)

Moscovitch, M. (1992). Memory and working-with-memory: A component process model based on modules and central systems. *Journal of Cognitive Neuroscience, 4*, 257–267. (13)

Moscovitch, M., Winocur, G., & Behrmann, M. (1997). What is special about face recognition? Nineteen experiments on a person with visual object agnosia and dyslexia but normal face recognition. *Journal of Cognitive Neuroscience, 9*, 555–604. (6)

Moss, C. F., & Simmons, A. M. (1986). Frequency selectivity of hearing in the green treefrog, Hyla cinerea. *Journal of Comparative Physiology, A, 159*, 257–266. (7)

Moss, S. J., & Smart, T. G. (2001). Constructing inhibitory synapses. *Nature Reviews Neuroscience, 2*, 240–250. (3)

Mrosovsky, N. (1990). *Rheostasis: The physiology of change.* New York: Oxford University Press. (10)

Mrzljak, L., Bergson, C., Pappy, M., Huff, R., Levenson, R., & Goldman-

Rakic, P. S. (1996). Localization of dopamine D4 receptors in GABAergic neurons of the primate brain. *Nature, 381,* 245–248. (15)

Munk, M. H. J., Roelfsema, P. R., König, P., Engel, A. K., & Singer, W. (1996). Role of reticular activation in the modulation of intracortical synchronization. *Science, 272,* 271–274. (9)

Murison, R. (2001). Is there a role for psychology in ulcer disease? *Integrative Physiological and Behavioral Science, 36,* 75–83. (12)

Murphy, M. G., & O'Leary, J. L. (1973). Hanging and climbing functions in raccoon and sloth after total cerebellectomy. *Archives of Neurology, 28,* 111–117. (8)

Murphy, M. R., Checkley, S. A., Seckl, J. R., & Lightman, S. L. (1990). Naloxone inhibits oxytocin release at orgasm in man. *Journal of Clinical Endocrinology & Metabolism, 71,* 1056–1058. (11)

Murray, A. M., Hyde, T. M., Knable, M. B., Herman, M. M., Bigelow, L. B., Carter, J. M., Weinberger, D. R., & Kleinman, J. E. (1995). Distribution of putative D4 dopamine receptors in postmortem striatum from patients with schizophrenia. *Journal of Neuroscience, 15,* 2186–2191. (15)

Murrell, J., Farlow, M., Ghetti, B., & Benson, M. D. (1991). A mutation in the amyloid precursor protein associated with hereditary Alzheimer's disease. *Science, 254,* 97–99. (13)

Mutra, P., Sheasby, A. M., Hunt, S. P., & De Felipe, C. (2000). Rewarding effects of opiates are absent in mice lacking the receptor for substance P. *Nature, 405,* 180–183. (7)

Myers, A., Holmans, P., Marshall, H., Kwon, J., Meyer, D., Ramic, D., Shears, S., Booth, J., DeVrieze, F. W., Crook, R., Hamshere, M., Abraham, R., Tunstall, N., Rice, F., Carty, S., Lillystone, S., Kehoe, P., Rudrasingham, V., Jones, L., Lovestone, S., Perez-Tur, J., Williams, J., Owen, M. J., Hardy, J., & Goate, A. M. (2000). Susceptibility locus for Alzheimer's disease on chromosome 10. *Science, 290,* 2304–2305. (13)

Myers, J. J., & Sperry, R. W. (1985). Interhemispheric communication after section of the forebrain commissures. *Cortex, 21,* 249–260. (14)

Nadarajah, B., & Parnavelas, J. G. (2002). Modes of neuronal migration in the developing cerebral cortex. *Nature Reviews Neuroscience, 3,* 423–432. (5)

Nadel, L., & Land, C. (2000). Memory traces revisited. *Nature Reviews Neuroscience, 1,* 209–212. (13)

Nader, K., Bechara, A., Roberts, D. C. S., & van der Kooy, D. (1994). Neuroleptics block high- but not low-dose heroin place preferences: Further evidence for a two-system model of motivation. *Behavioral Neuroscience, 108,* 1128–1138. (15)

Nagahara, A. H., Otto, T., & Gallagher, M. (1995). Entorhinal-perirhinal lesions impair performance of rats on two versions of place learning in the Morris water maze. *Behavioral Neuroscience, 109,* 3–9. (13)

Nagarajan, S., Mahncke, H., Salz, T., Tallal, P., Roberts, T., & Merzenich, M. M. (1999). Cortical auditory signal processing in poor readers. *Proceedings of the National Academy of Sciences, 96,* 6483–6488. (14)

Nagayama, T., Sinor, A. D., Simon, R. P., Chen, J., Graham, S. H., Jin, K., & Greenberg, D. A. (1999). Cannabinoids and neuroprotection in global and focal cerebral ischemia and in neuronal cultures. *Journal of Neuroscience, 19,* 2987–2995. (5)

Naggert, J. K., Fricker, L. D., Varlamov, O., Nishina, P. M., Rouille, Y., Steiner, D. F., Carroll, R. J., Paigen, B. J., & Leiter, E. H. (1995). Hyperproinsulinaemia in obese fat/fat mice associated with a carboxypeptidase E mutation which reduces enzyme activity. *Nature Genetics, 10,* 135–142. (10)

Nakashima, Y., Kuwamura, T., & Yogo, Y. (1995). Why be a both-ways sex changer? *Ethology, 101,* 301–307. (11)

Narrow, W. E., Rae, D. S., Robins, L. N., & Regier, D. A. (2002). Revised prevalence estimates of mental disorders in the United States.

Archives of General Psychiatry, 59, 115–123. (15)

Narumoto, J., Okada, T., Sadato, N., Fukui, K., & Yonekura, Y. (2001). Attention to emotion modulates fMRI activity in human right superior temporal sulcus. *Cognitive Brain Research, 12,* 225–231. (12, 14)

Nathans, J., Davenport, C. M., Maumenee, I. H., Lewis, R. A., Hejtmancik, J. F., Litt, M., Lovrien, E., Weleber, R., Bachynski, B., Zwas, F., Klingaman, R., & Fishman, G. (1989). Molecular genetics of human blue cone monochromacy. *Science, 245,* 831–838. (6)

Naylor, E., Bergmann, B. M., Krauski, K., Zee, P. C., Takahashi, J. S., Vitaterna, M. H., & Turek, F. W. (2000). The circadian clock mutation alters sleep homeostasis in the mouse. *Journal of Neuroscience, 20,* 8138–8143. (9)

Nebes, R. D. (1974). Hemispheric specialization in commissurotomized man. *Psychological Bulletin, 81,* 1–14. (14)

Nef, P. (1998). How we smell: The molecular and cellular bases of olfaction. *News in Physiological Sciences, 13,* 1–5. (7)

Neitz, J., & Jacobs, G. H. (1986). Reexamination of spectral mechanisms in the rat (*Rattus norvegicus*). *Journal of Comparative Psychology, 100,* 21–29. (6)

Nelson, C. A., Wewerka, S., Thomas, K. M., Tribby-Walbridge, S., deRegnier, R., & Georgieff, M. (2000). Neurocognitive sequelae of infants of diabetic mothers. *Behavioral Neuroscience, 114,* 950–956. (5)

Nelson, D. O., & Prosser, C. L. (1981). Intracellular recordings from thermosensitive preoptic neurons. *Science, 213,* 787–789. (10)

Nelson, L. E., Guo, T. Z., Lu, J., Saper, C. B., Franks, N. P., & Maze, M. (2002). The sedative component of anesthesia is mediated by $GABA_A$ receptors in an endogenous sleep pathway. *Nature Neuroscience, 5,* 979–984. (9)

Netter, F. H. (1983). *CIBA collection of medical illustrations: Vol. 1.*

Nervous system. New York: CIBA.
(11)

Neville, H. J., Bavelier, D., Corina,
D., Rauschecker, J., Karni, A.,
Lalwani, A., Braun, A., Clark, V.,
Jezzard, P., & Turner, R. (1998).
Cerebral organization for language
in deaf and hearing subjects:
Biological constraints and effects
of experience. *Proceedings of the
National Academy of Sciences,
USA, 95,* 922–929. (14)

Newcomer, J. W., Haupt, D. W.,
Fucetola, R., Melson, A. K.,
Schweiger, J. A., Cooper, B. P., &
Selke, G. (2002). Abnormalities in
glucose regulation during antipsy-
chotic treatment of schizophrenia.
Archives of General Psychiatry, 59,
337–345. (15)

Newcomer, J. W., Selke, G., Melson,
A. K., Hershey, T., Craft, S.,
Richards, K., & Alderson, A. L.
(1999). Decreased memory performance in healthy humans induced by stress-level cortisol treatment. *Archives of General
Psychiatry, 56,* 527–533. (13)

Nicholas, M. K., & Arnason, B. G. W.
(1992). Immunologic responses in
central nervous system transplantation. *Seminars in the
Neurosciences, 4,* 273–283. (8)

Nicklas, W. J., Saporito, M., Basma,
A., Geller, H. M., & Heikkila, R. E.
(1992). Mitochondrial mechanisms
of neurotoxicity. *Annals of the
New York Academy of Sciences,
648,* 28–36. (8)

Nicolelis, M. A. L. (2001). Actions
from thoughts. *Nature, 409,*
403–407. (8)

Nicolelis, M. A. L., Ghazanfar, A. A.,
Stambaugh, C. R., Oliveira, L. M.
O., Laubach, M., Chapin, J. K.,
Nelson, R. J., & Kaas, J. H. (1998).
Simultaneous encoding of tactile
information by three primate corti-
cal areas. *Nature Neuroscience, 1,*
621–630. (4)

Nieuwenhuys, R., Voogd, J., &
vanHuijzen, C. (1988). *The human
central nervous system* (3rd Rev.
ed.). Berlin: Springer-Verlag. (4, 10,
12, 14)

Nigg, J. T. (2001). Is ADHD a disin-
hibitory disorder? *Psychological
Bulletin, 127,* 571–598. (7)

Niki, K., & Luo, J. (2002). An fMRI
study on the time-limited role of
the medial temporal lobe in long-
term topographical autobiographic
memory. *Journal of Cognitive
Neuroscience, 14,* 500–507. (13)

Nilsson, G. E. (1999, December). The
cost of a brain. *Natural History,
108,* 66–73. (14)

Nilsson, G. E. (2001). Surviving
anoxia with the brain turned on.
*News in Physiological Sciences,
16,* 217–221. (8)

Noaghiul, S., Hibbeln, J. R., &
Weissman, M. M. (in press). Cross-
national comparisons of seafood
consumption and rates of bipolar
disorder. *American Journal of
Psychiatry.* (15)

Noble, E. P., Ozkaragoz, T. Z.,
Ritchie, T. L., Zhang, X., Belin, T.
R., & Sparkes, R. S. (1998). D_2 and
D_4 dopamine receptor polymorphisms and personality. *American
Journal of Medical Genetics, 81,*
257–267. (3)

Nolan, J. H., & Wright, C. E. (2001).
Evidence of impaired glucose tolerance and insulin resistance in
patients with Alzheimer's disease.
*Current Directions in
Psychological Science, 10,*
102–105. (13)

Nolen-Hoeksema, S., & Morrow, J.
(1991). A prospective study of
depression and posttraumatic
stress symptoms after a natural
disaster: The Loma Prieta earthquake. *Journal of Personality and
Social Psychology, 61,* 115–121.
(15)

Nopoulos, P., Flaum, M., O'Leary,
D., & Andreasen, N. C. (2000).
Sexual dimorphism in the human
brain: Evaluation of tissue volume,
tissue composition and surface
anatomy using magnetic resonance
imaging. *Psychiatry Research:
Neuroimaging Section, 98,* 1–13.
(11)

Nopoulos, P. C., Giedd, J. N.,
Andreasen, N. C., & Rapoport, J. L.
(1998). Frequency and severity of
enlarged cavum septi pellucidi in
childhood-onset schizophrenia.
*American Journal of Psychiatry,
155,* 1074–1079. (15)

Norman, R. A., Tatarranni, P. A.,
Pratley, R., Thompson, D. B.,
Hanson, R. L., Prochazka, M.,
Baier, L., Ehm, M. G., Sakul, H.,
Foroud, T., Garvey, W. T., Burns,
D., Knowler, W. C., Bennett, P. H.,
Bogardus, C., & Ravussin, E.
(1998). Autosomal genomic scan
for loci linked to obesity and en-
ergy metabolism in Pima Indians.
*American Journal of Human
Genetics, 62,* 659–668. (10)

North, R. A. (1989).
Neurotransmitters and their receptors: From the clone to the clinic.
Seminars in the Neurosciences, 1,
81–90. (3)

North, R. A. (1992). Cellular actions
of opiates and cocaine. *Annals of
the New York Academy of
Sciences, 654,* 1–6. (15)

Nosenko, N. D., & Reznikov, A. G.
(2001). Prenatal stress and sexual
differentiation of monoaminergic
brain systems. *Neurophysiology,
33,* 197–206. (11)

Nottebohm, F. (2002). Why are some
neurons replaced in adult brain?
Journal of Neuroscience, 22,
624–628. (5)

Nowak, M. A., Komarova, N. L., &
Niyogi, P. (2002). Computational
and evolutionary aspects of language. *Nature, 417,* 611–617. (14)

Nucifora, F. C., Jr., Sasaki, M.,
Peters, M. F., Huang, H., Cooper, J.
K., Yamada, M., Takahashi, H.,
Tsuji, S., Tronscoso, J., Dawson, V.
L., Dawson, T. M., & Ross, C. A.
(2001). Interference by huntingtin
and atrophin-1 with CBP-mediated
transcription leading to cellular
toxicity. *Science, 291,* 2423–2428.
(8)

Nuñez, J. L., Lauschke, D. M., &
Juraska, J. M. (2001). Cell death in
the development of the posterior
cortex in male and female rats.
*Journal of Comparative Neurology,
436,* 32–41. (11)

Ó Scalaidhe, S. P., Wilson, F. A. W.,
& Goldman-Rakic, P. S. (1997).
Areal segregation of face-process-
ing neurons in prefrontal cortex.
Science, 278, 1135–1138. (6)

O'Dowd, B. F., Lefkowitz, R. J., &
Caron, M. G. (1989). Structure of
the adrenergic and related receptors. *Annual Review of
Neuroscience, 12,* 67–83. (3)

Ohno-Shosaku, T., Maejima, T., &
Kano, M. (2001). Endogenous
cannabinoids mediate retrograde
signals from depolarized postsynaptic neurons to presynaptic
terminals. *Neuron, 29,* 729–738.
(15)

O'Keefe, J., & Burgess, N. (1996). Geometric determinants of the place fields of hippocampal neurons. *Nature, 381*, 425–434. (13)

Okubo, Y., Suhara, T., Suzuki, K., Kobayashi, K., Inoue, O., Terasaki, O., Someya, Y., Sassa, T., Sudo, Y., Matsushima, E., Iyo, M., Tateno, Y., & Toru, M. (1997). Decreased prefrontal dopamine D1 receptors in schizophrenia revealed by PET. *Nature, 385*, 634–636. (15)

Olds, J. (1958). Satiation effects in self-stimulation of the brain. *Journal of Comparative and Physiological Psychology, 51*, 675–678. (15)

Olds, J., & Milner, P. (1954). Positive reinforcement produced by electrical stimulation of the septal area and other regions of the rat brain. *Journal of Comparative and Physiological Psychology, 47*, 419–428. (15)

O'Leary, A. (1990). Stress, emotion, and human immune function. *Psychological Bulletin, 108*, 363–382. (12)

Olff, M. (1999). Stress, depression and immunity: The role of defense and coping styles. *Psychiatry Research, 85*, 7–15. (12)

Olney, J. W., & Farber, N. B. (1995). Glutamate receptor dysfunction and schizophrenia. *Archives of General Psychiatry, 52*, 998–1007. (15)

Olson, D. J., Kamil, A. C., Balda, R. P., & Nims, P. J. (1995). Performance of four seed-caching corvid species in operant tests of nonspatial and spatial memory. *Journal of Comparative Psychology, 109*, 173–181. (13)

Olson, E. J., Boeve, B. F., & Silber, M. H. (2000). Rapid eye movement sleep behaviour disorder: Demographic, clinical and laboratory findings in 93 cases. *Brain, 123*, 331–339. (9)

Olton, D. S., & Papas, B. C. (1979). Spatial memory and hippocampal function. *Neuropsychologia, 17*, 669–682. (13)

Olton, D. S., Walker, J. A., & Gage, F. H. (1978). Hippocampal connections and spatial discrimination. *Brain Research, 139*, 295–308. (13)

O'Neal, M. F., Means, L. W., Poole, M. C., & Hamm, R. J. (1996). Estrogen affects performance of ovariectomized rats in a two-choice water-escape working memory task. *Psychoneuroendocrinology, 21*, 51–65. (11)

O'Reilly, R. C., & Rudy, J. W. (2001). Conjunctive representations in learning and memory: Principles of cortical and hippocampal function. *Psychological Review, 108*, 311–345. (13)

Ornstein, R. (1997). *The right mind.* New York: Harcourt Brace. (14)

Orth, D. N., Shelton, R. C., Nicholson, W. E., Beck-Peccoz, P., Tomarken, A. J., Persani, L., & Loosen, P. T. (2001). Serum thyrotropin concentrations and bioactivity during sleep deprivation in depression. *Archives of General Psychiatry, 58*, 77–83. (15)

Ouchi, Y., Yoshikawa, E., Okada, H., Futatsubashi, M., Sekine, Y., Iyo, M., & Sakamoto, M. (1999). Alterations in binding site density of dopamine transporter in the striatum, orbitofrontal cortex, and amygdala in early Parkinson's disease: Compartment analysis for β-CFT binding with positron emission tomography. *Annals of Neurology, 45*, 601–610. (8)

Overmier, J. B., & Murison, R. (2000). Anxiety and helplessness in the face of stress predisposes, precipitates, and sustains gastric ulceration. *Behavioural Brain Research, 110*, 161–174. (12)

Paladini, C. A., Fiorillo, C. D., Morikawa, H., & Williams, J. T. (2001). Amphetamine selectively blocks inhibitory glutamate transmission in dopamine neurons. *Nature Neuroscience, 4*, 275–281. (15)

Palmer, T. D., Schwartz, P. H., Taupin, P., Kaspar, B., Stein, S. A., & Gage, F. H. (2001). Progenitor cells from human brain after death. *Nature, 411*, 42–43. (5)

Pandey, G. N., Pandey, S. C., Dwivedi, Y., Sharma, R. P., Janicak, P. G., & Davis, J. M. (1995). Platelet serotonin-2A receptors: A potential biological marker for suicidal behavior. *American Journal of Psychiatry, 152*, 850–855. (12)

Panikashvili, D., Simeonidou, C., Ben-Shabat, S., Hanus, L., Breuer, A., Mechoulam, R., & Shohami, E. (2001). An endogenous cannabinoid (2-AG) is neuroprotective after brain injury. *Nature, 413*, 527–531. (15)

Panksepp, J. (1998). Attention deficit hyperactivity disorders, psychostimulants, and intolerance of childhood playfulness: A tragedy in the making? *Current Directions in Psychological Science, 7*, 91–98. (7)

Pappone, P. A., & Cahalan, M. D. (1987). Pandinus imperator scorpion venom blocks voltage-gated potassium channels in nerve fibers. *Journal of Neuroscience, 7*, 3300–3305. (2)

Paradis, M. (1998). Aphasia in bilinguals: How atypical is it? In P. Coppens, Y. Lebrun, & A. Basso (Eds.), *Aphasia in atypical populations* (pp. 35–66). Mahwah, NJ: Erlbaum. (14)

Pardal, R., & López-Barneo, J. (2002). Low glucose-sensing cells in the carotid body. *Nature Neuroscience, 5*, 197–198. (10)

Parent, M. B., Habib, M. K., & Baker, G. B. (1999). Task-dependent effects of the antidepressant/antipanic drug phenelzine on memory. *Psychopharmacology, 142*, 280–288. (9)

Park, S., Holzman, P. S., & Goldman-Rakic, P. S. (1995). Spatial working memory deficits in the relatives of schizophrenic patients. *Archives of General Psychiatry, 52*, 821–828. (15)

Parker, G. H. (1922). *Smell, taste, and allied senses in the vertebrates.* Philadelphia: Lippincott. (7)

Parkes, L., Lund, J., Angelucci, A., Solomon, J. A., & Morgan, M. (2001). Compulsory averaging of crowded orientation signals in human vision. *Nature Neuroscience, 4*, 739–744. (6)

Pascual-Leone, A., & Walsh, V. (2001). Fast backprojections from the motion to the primary visual area necessary for visual awareness. *Science, 292*, 510–512. (6)

Pascual-Leone, A., Wasserman, E. M., Sadato, N., & Hallett, M. (1995). The role of reading activity on the modulation of motor cortical outputs to the reading hand in Braille readers. *Annals of Neurology, 38*, 910–915. (5)

Patel, A. J., Honoré, E., Lesage, F., Fink, M., Romey, G., & Lazdunski, M. (1999). Inhalation anesthetics activate two-pore-domain background K⁺ channels. *Nature Neuroscience, 2*, 422–426. (2)

Patte, C., Gandolfo, P., Leprince, J., Thoumas, J. L., Fontaine, M., Vaudry, H., & Tonon, M. C. (1999). GABA inhibits endozepine release from cultured rat astrocytes. *Glia, 25*, 404–411. (12)

Paulesu, E., Démonet, J.-F., Fazio, F., McCrory, E., Chanoine, V., Brunswick, N., Cappa, S. F., Cossu, G., Habib, M., Frith, C. D., & Frith, U. (2001). Dyslexia: Cultural diversity and biological unity. *Science, 291*, 2165–2167. (14)

Paulesu, E., Frith, U., Snowling, M., Gallagher, A., Morton, J., Frackowiak, R. S. J., & Frith, C. D. (1996). Is developmental dyslexia a disconnection syndrome? *Brain, 119*, 143–157. (14)

Paulesu, E., McCrory, E., Fazio, F., Mononcello, L., Brunswick, N., Cappa, S.F., Cotelli, M., Cossu, G., Corte, F., Lorusso, M., Pesenti, S., Gallagher, A., Perani, D., Price, C., Frith, C. D., & Frith, U. (2000). A cultural effect on brain function. *Nature Neuroscience, 3*, 91–96. (14)

Paus, T., Marrett, S., Worsley, K. J., & Evans, A. C. (1995). Extraretinal modulation of cerebral blood flow in the human visual cortex: Implications for saccadic suppression. *Journal of Neurophysiology, 74*, 2179–2183. (6)

Pavani, F., Spence, C., & Driver, J. (2000). Visual capture of touch: Out-of-the-body experiences with rubber gloves. *Psychological Science, 11*, 353–359. (4)

Pavlov, I. P. (1927). *Conditioned reflexes*. Oxford, England: Oxford University Press. (13)

Pearl, P. L., Weiss, R. E., & Stein, M. A. (2001). Medical mimics. *Annals of the New York Academy of Sciences, 931*, 97–112. (7)

Pedersen,, C. A., Caldwell, J. D., Walker, C., Ayers, G., & Mason, G. A. (1994). Oxytocin activates the postpartum onset of rat maternal behavior in the ventral tegmentum and medial preoptic areas. *Behavioral Neuroscience, 108*, 1163–1171. (11)

Pedersen, C. B., & Mortensen, P. B. (2001). Evidence of a dose-response relationship between urbanicity during upbringing and schizophrenia risk. *Archives of General Psychiatry, 58*, 1039–1046. (15)

Pellis, S. M., O'Brien, D. P., Pellis, V. C., Teitelbaum, P., Wolgin, D. L., & Kennedy, S. (1988). Escalation of feline predation along a gradient from avoidance through "play" to killing. *Behavioral Neuroscience, 102*, 760–777. (12)

Pellymounter, M. A., Cullen, M. J., Baker, M. B., Hecht, R., Winters, D., Boone, T., & Collins, F. (1995). Effects of the obese gene product on body weight regulation in *ob/ob* mice. *Science, 269*, 540–543. (10)

Penfield, W. (1955). The permanent record of the stream of consciousness. *Acta Psychologica, 11*, 47–69. (13)

Penfield, W., & Milner, B. (1958). Memory deficit produced by bilateral lesions in the hippocampal zone. *Archives of Neurology and Psychiatry, 79*, 475–497. (13)

Penfield, W., & Perot, P. (1963). The brain's record of auditory and visual experience. *Brain, 86*, 595–696. (13)

Penfield, W., & Rasmussen, T. (1950). *The cerebral cortex of man*. New York: Macmillan. (4, 8)

Penton-Voak, I. S., Perrett, D. I., Castles, D. L., Kobayashi, T., Burt, D. M., Murray, L. K., & Minamisawa, R. (1999). Menstrual cycle alters face preference. *Nature, 399*, 741–742. (11)

Pepperberg, I. M. (1981). Functional vocalizations by an African grey parrot. *Zeitschrift für Tierpsychologie, 55*, 139–160. (14)

Pepperberg, I. M. (1993). Cognition and communication in an African Grey parrot (*Psittacus erithacus*): Studies on a nonhuman, nonprimate, nonmammalian subject. In H. L. Roitblat, L. M. Herman, & P. E. Nachtigall (Eds.), *Language and communication: Comparative perspectives* (pp. 221–248). Hillsdale, NJ: Erlbaum. (14)

Pepperberg, I. M. (1994). Numerical competence in an African gray parrot (*Psittacus erithacus*). *Journal of Comparative Psychology, 108*, 36–44. (14)

Perani, D., Paulesu, E., Galles, N. S., Dupoux, E., Dehaene, S., Bettinardi, V., Cappa, S. F., Fazio, F., & Mehler, J. (1998). The bilingual brain: Proficiency and age of acquisition of the second language. *Brain, 121*, 1841–1852. (14)

Pericak-Vance, M. A., Bebout, J. L., Gaskell, P. C., Jr., Yamaoka, L. H., Hung, W.-Y., Alberts, M. J., Walker, A. P., Bartlett, R. J., Haynes, C. A., Welsh, K. A., Earl, N. L., Heyman, A., Clark, C. M., & Roses, A. D. (1991). Linkage studies in familial Alzheimer disease: Evidence for chromosome 19 linkage. *American Journal of Human Genetics, 48*, 1034–1050. (13)

Perlow, M. J., Freed, W. J., Hoffer, B. J., Seiger, A., Olson, L., & Wyatt, R. J. (1979). Brain grafts reduce motor abnormalities produced by destruction of nigrostriatal dopamine system. *Science, 204*, 643–647. (8)

Perrone, J. A., & Thiele, A. (2001). Speed skills: Measuring the visual speed analyzing properties of primate MT neurons. *Nature Neuroscience, 4*, 526–532. (6)

Pert, C. B. (1997). *Molecules of emotion*. New York: Touchstone. (2)

Pert, C. B., & Snyder, S. H. (1973). The opiate receptor: Demonstration in nervous tissue. *Science, 179*, 1011–1014. (7, 15)

Pesenti, M., Zago, L., Crivello, F., Mellet, E., Samson, D., Duroux, B., Seron, X., Mazoyer, B., & Tzourio-Mazoyer, N. (2001). Mental calculation in a prodigy is sustained by right prefrontal and medial temporal areas. *Nature Neuroscience, 4*, 103–107. (4)

Pesold, C., & Treit, D. (1995). The central and basolateral amygdala differentially mediate the anxiolytic effect of benzodiazepines. *Brain Research, 671*, 213–221. (12)

Peters, R. H., Sensenig, L. D., & Reich, M. J. (1973). Fixed-ratio performance following ventromedial hypothalamic lesions in rats. *Physiological Psychology, 1*, 136–138. (10)

Peterson, L. R., & Peterson, M. J. (1959). Short-term retention of individual verbal items. *Journal of Experimental Psychology, 58*, 193–198. (13)

Petitto, L. A., Zatorre, R. J., Gauna, K., Nikelski, E. J., Dostie, D., &

Evans, A. C. (2000). Speech-like cerebral activity in profoundly deaf people processing signed languages: Implications for the neural basis of human language. *Proceedings of the National Academy of Sciences, USA, 97,* 13961–13966. (14)

Phelps, M. E., & Mazziotta, J. C. (1985). Positron emission tomography: Human brain function and biochemistry. *Science, 228,* 799–809. (8)

Phillips, M. L., Young, A. W., Senior, C., Brammer, M., Andrew, C., Calder, A. J., Bullmore, E. T., Perrett, D. I., Rowland, D., Williams, S. C. R., Gray, J. A., & David, A. S. (1997). A specific neural substrate for perceiving facial expressions of disgust. *Nature, 389,* 495–498. (12)

Phillips, R. G., & LeDoux, J. E. (1992). Differential contribution of amygdala and hippocampus to cued and contextual fear conditioning. *Behavioral Neuroscience, 106,* 274–285. (12)

Phillips, T. J., Brown, K. J., Burkhart-Kasch, S., Wenger, C. D., Kelly, M. A., Rubinstein, M., Grandy, D. K., & Low, M. J. (1998). Alcohol preference and sensitivity are markedly reduced in mice lacking dopamine D_2 receptors. *Nature Neuroscience, 1,* 610–615. (15)

Piccini, P., Burn, D. J., Ceravolo, R., Maraganore, D., & Brooks, D. J. (1999). The role of inheritance in sporadic Parkinson's disease: Evidence from a longitudinal study of dopaminergic function in twins. *Annals of Neurology, 45,* 577–582. (8)

Pich, E. M., Pagliusi, S. R., Tessari, M., Talabot-Ayer, D., van Huijsduijnen, R. H., & Chiamulera, C. (1997). Common neural substrates for the addictive properties of nicotine and cocaine. *Science, 275,* 83–86. (15)

Pierri, J. N., Volk, C. L. E., Auh, S., Sampson, A., & Lewis, D. A. (2001). Decreased somal size of deep layer 3 pyramidal neurons in the prefrontal cortex of subjects with schizophrenia. *Archives of General Psychiatry, 58,* 466–473. (15)

Pillon, B., Ertle, S., Deweer, B., Sarazin, M., Agid, Y., & Dubois, B. (1996). Memory for spatial location is affected in Parkinson's disease. *Neuropsychologia, 34,* 77–85. (8)

Pinckard, K. L., Stellflug, J., Resko, J. A., Roselli, C. E., & Stormshak, F. (2000). Review: Brain aromatization and other factors affecting male reproductive behavior with emphasis on the sexual orientation of rams. *Domestic Animal Endocrinology, 18,* 83–96. (11)

Pinker, S. (1994). *The language instinct.* New York: HarperCollins. (14)

Plihal, W., & Born, J. (1997). Effects of early and late nocturnal sleep on declarative and procedural memory. *Journal of Cognitive Neuroscience, 9,* 534–547. (9)

Plomin, R., Corley, R., DeFries, J. C., & Fulker, D. (1990). Individual differences in television viewing in early childhood: Nature as well as nurture. *Psychological Science, 1,* 371–377. (1)

Poling, A., Schlinger, H., & Blakely, E. (1988). Failure of the partial inverse benzodiazepine agonist Ro15-4513 to block the lethal effects of ethanol in rats. *Pharmacology, 31,* 945–947. (12)

Pollatsek, A., Bolozky, S., Well, A. D., & Rayner, K. (1981). Asymmetries in the perceptual span for Israeli readers. *Brain and Language, 14,* 174–180. (14)

Poncer, J. C., & Malinow, R. (2001). Postsynaptic conversion of silent synapses during LTP affects synaptic gain and transmission dynamics. *Nature Neuroscience, 4,* 989–996. (13)

Pons, T. P., Garraghty, P. E., Ommaya, A. K., Kaas, J. H., Taub, E., & Mishkin, M. (1991). Massive cortical reorganization after sensory deafferentation in adult macaques. *Science, 252,* 1857–1860. (5)

Pontieri, F. E., Tanda, G., Orzi, F., & DiChiara, G. (1996). Effects of nicotine on the nucleus accumbens and similarity to those of addictive drugs. *Nature, 382,* 255–257. (15)

Poo, M.-m. (2001). Neurotrophins as synaptic modulators. *Nature Reviews Neuroscience, 2,* 24–32. (5)

Pope, H. G., Jr., Gruber, A. J., Hudson, J. I., Huestis, M. A., & Yurgelun-Todd, D. (2001). Neuropsychological performance in long-term cannabis users. *Archives of General Psychiatry, 58,* 909–915. (15)

Pope, H. G., & Katz, D. L. (1994). Psychiatric and medical effects of anabolic-androgenic steroid use. *Archives of General Psychiatry, 51,* 375–382. (11)

Posner, S. F., Baker, L., Heath, A., & Martin, N. G. (1996). Social contact, social attitudes, and twin similarity. *Behavior Genetics, 26,* 123–133. (1)

Posthuma, D., De Geus, E. J. C., Baaré, W. F. C., Pol, H. E. H., Kahn, R. S., & Boomsma, D. I. (2002). The association between brain volume and intelligence is of genetic origin. *Nature Neuroscience, 5,* 83–84. (14)

Potegal, M. (1994). Aggressive arousal: The amygdala connection. In M. Potegal & J. F. Knutson (Eds.), *The dynamics of aggression* (pp. 73–111). Hillsdale, NJ: Erlbaum. (12)

Potegal, M., Ferris, C., Hebert, M., Meyerhoff, J. M., & Skaredoff, L. (1996). Attack priming in female Syrian golden hamsters is associated with a *c-fos* coupled process within the corticomedial amygdala. *Neuroscience, 75,* 869–880. (12)

Potegal, M., Hebert, M., DeCoster, M., & Meyerhoff, J. L. (1996). Brief, high-frequency stimulation of the corticomedial amygdala induces a delayed and prolonged increase of aggressiveness in male Syrian golden hamsters. *Behavioral Neuroscience, 110,* 401–412. (12)

Pouget, A., Dayan, P., & Zemel, R. (2000). Information processing with population codes. *Nature Reviews Neuroscience, 1,* 125–132. (7)

Poulos, C. X., Parker, J. L., & Lê, D. A. (1998). Increased impulsivity after injected alcohol predicts later alcohol consumption in rats: Evidence for "loss-of-control drinking" and marked individual differences. *Behavioral Neuroscience, 112,* 1247–1257. (15)

Premack, A. J., & Premack, D. (1972). Teaching language to an ape. *Scientific American, 227*(4), 92–99. (14)

Preti, G., Cutler, W. B., Garcia, C. R., Huggins, G. R., & Lawley, H. J. (1986). Human axillary secretions influence women's menstrual cycles: The role of donor extract of females. *Hormones and Behavior, 20*, 474–482. (7)

Price, C. J., Warburton, E. A., Moore, C. J., Frackowiak, R. S. J., & Friston, K. J. (2001). Dynamic diaschisis: Anatomically remote and context-sensitive human brain lesions. *Journal of Cognitive Neuroscience, 13*, 419–429. (5)

Price, M. P., Lewin, G. R., McIlwrath, S. L., Cheng, C., Xie, J., Heppenstall, P. A., Stucky, C. L., Mannsfeldt, A. G., Brennan, T. J., Drummond, H. A., Qiao, J., Benson, C. J., Tarr, D. E., Hrstka, R. F., Yang, B., Williamson, R. A., & Welsh, M. J. (2000). The mammalian sodium channel BNC1 is required for normal touch sensation. *Nature, 407*, 1007–1011. (7)

Pritchard, T. C., Hamilton, R. B., Morse, J. R., & Norgren, R. (1986). Projections of thalamic gustatory and lingual areas in the monkey, Macaca fascicularis. *Journal of Comparative Neurology, 244*, 213–228. (7)

Pritchard, T. C., Macaluso, D. A., & Eslinger, P. J. (1999). Taste perception in patients with insular cortex lesions. *Behavioral Neuroscience, 113*, 663–671. (7, 14)

Provine, R. R. (1979). "Wing-flapping" develops in wingless chicks. *Behavioral and Neural Biology, 27*, 233–237. (8)

Provine, R. R. (1981). Wing-flapping develops in chickens made flightless by feather mutations. *Developmental Psychobiology, 14*, 48 B 1–486. (8)

Provine, R. R. (1984). Wing-flapping during development and evolution. *American Scientist, 72*, 448–455. (8)

Provine, R. R. (1986). Yawning as a stereotyped action pattern and releasing stimulus. *Ethology, 72*, 109–122. (8)

Provine, R. R., & Westerman, J. A. (1979). Crossing the midline: Limits of early eye-hand behavior. *Child Development, 50*, 437–441. (14)

Prutkin, J., Duffy, V. B., Etter, L., Fast, K., Gardner, E., Lucchina, L. A., Snyder, D. J., Tie, K., Weiffenbach, J., & Bartoshuk, L. M. (2000). Genetic variation and inferences about perceived taste intensity in mice and men. *Physiology & Behavior, 69*, 161–173. (7)

Ptak, R., Gutbrod, K., Perrig, W., & Schnider, A. (2001). Probabilistic contingency learning with limbic or prefrontal damage. *Behavioral Neuroscience, 115*, 993–1001. (13)

Puca, A. A., Daly, M. J., Brewster, S. J., Matise, T. C., Barrett, J., Shea-Drinkwater, M., Kang, S., Joyce, E., Nicoli, J., Benson, E., Kunkel, L. M., & Perls, T. (2001). A genome-wide scan for linkage to human exceptional longevity identifies a locus on chromosome 4. *Proceedings of the National Academy of Sciences, USA, 98*, 10505–10508. (1)

Pugh, K. R., Mencl, W. E., Shaywitz, B. A., Shaywitz, S. E., Fulbright, R. K., Constable, R. T., Skudlarski, P., Marchione, K. E., Jenner, A. R., Fletcher, J. M., Liberman, A. M., Shankweiler, D. P., Katz, L., Lacadie, C., & Gore, J. C. (2000). The angular gyrus in developmental dyslexia: Task-specific differences in functional connectivity within parietal cortex. *Psychological Science, 11*, 51–56. (14)

Purves, D., & Hadley, R. D. (1985). Changes in the dendritic branching of adult mammalian neurones revealed by repeated imaging *in situ. Nature, 315*, 404–406. (2)

Purves, D., & Lichtman, J. W. (1980). Elimination of synapses in the developing nervous system. *Science, 210*, 153–157. (5)

Purves, D., Lotto, R. B., Williams, S. M., Nandy, S., & Yang, Z. (2001). Why we see things the way we do: Evidence for a wholly empirical strategy of vision. *Philosophical Transactions of the Royal Society of London, 356*, 285–297. (6)

Purves, D., Shimpi, A., & Lotto, R. B. (1999). An empirical explanation of the Cornsweet effect. *Journal of Neuroscience, 19*, 8542–8551. (6)

Putnam, S. K., Du, J., Sato, S., & Hull, E. M. (2001). Testosterone restoration of copulatory behavior correlates with medial preoptic dopamine release in castrated male rats. *Hormones and Behavior, 39*, 216–224. (11)

Quadagno, D. M., Briscoe, R., & Quadagno, J. S. (1977). Effect of perinatal gonadal hormones on selected nonsexual behavior patterns: A critical assessment of the non-human and human literature. *Psychological Bulletin, 84*, 62–80. (11)

Quik, M., & Jeyarasingam, G. (2000). Nicotinic receptors and Parkinson's disease. *European Journal of Pharmacology, 393*, 223–230. (8)

Raber, J., Bongers, G., LeFevour, A., Buttini, M., & Mucke, L. (2002). Androgens protect against apolipoprotein E4-induced cognitive deficits. *Journal of Neuroscience, 22*, 5204–5209. (11)

Rada, P. V., & Hoebel, B. G. (2000). Supraadditive effect of δ-fenfluramine plus phentermine on extracellular acetylcholine in the nucleus accumbens: Possible mechanism for inhibition of excessive feeding and drug abuse. *Pharmacology Biochemistry and Behavior, 65*, 369–373. (10)

Ragsdale, D. S., McPhee, J. C., Scheuer, T., & Catterall, W. A. (1994). Molecular determinants of state-dependent block of Na$^+$ channels by local anesthetics. *Science, 265*, 1724–1728. (2)

Raine, A., Reynolds, C., Venables, P. H., Mednick, S. A., & Farrington, D. P. (1998). Fearlessness, stimulation-seeking, and large body size at age 3 as early predispositions to childhood aggression at age 11 years. *Archives of General Psychiatry, 55*, 745–751. (12)

Rainnie, D. G., Grunze, H. C. R., McCarley, R. W., & Greene, R. W. (1994). Adenosine inhibition of mesopontine cholinergic neurons: Implications for EEG arousal. *Science, 263*, 689–692. (9)

Rainville, P., Duncan, G. H., Price, D. D., Carrier, B., & Bushnell, M. C. (1997). Pain affect encoded in human anterior cingulate but not somatosensory cortex. *Science, 277*, 968–971. (7)

Rajkowska, G., Selemon, L. D., & Goldman-Rakic, P. S. (1998). Neuronal and glial somal size in the prefrontal cortex. *Archives of General Psychiatry, 55*, 215–224. (15)

Rakic, P. (1998). Cortical development and evolution. In M. S. Gazzaniga & J. S. Altman (Eds.), *Brain and mind: Evolutionary perspectives* (pp. 34–40). Strasbourg, France: Human Frontier Science Program. (5)

Rakic, P. (2002). Neurogenesis in adult primate neocortex: An evaluation of the evidence. *Nature Reviews Neuroscience, 3*, 65–71. (5)

Rakic, P., & Lidow, M. S. (1995). Distribution and density of monoamine receptors in the primate visual cortex devoid of retinal input from early embryonic stages. *Journal of Neuroscience, 15*, 2561–2574. (6)

Ralph, M. R., Foster, R. G., Davis, F. C., & Menaker, M. (1990). Transplanted suprachiasmatic nucleus determines circadian period. *Science, 247*, 975–978. (9)

Ralph, M. R., & Menaker, M. (1988). A mutation of the circadian system in golden hamsters. *Science, 241*, 1225–1227. (9)

Ram, A., Pandey, H. P., Matsumura, H., Kasahara-Orita, K., Nakajima, T., Takahata, R., Satoh, S., Terao, A., & Hayaishi, O. (1997). CSF levels of prostaglandins, especially the level of prostaglandin D_2, are correlated with increasing propensity towards sleep in rats. *Brain Research, 751*, 81–89. (9)

Ramachandran, V. S., & Blakeslee, S. (1998). *Phantoms in the brain.* New York: Morrow. (5)

Ramachandran, V. S., & Hirstein, W. (1998). The perception of phantom limbs: The D. O. Hebb lecture. *Brain, 121*, 1603–1630. (5)

Ramachandran, V. S., Rogers-Ramachandran, D., & Cobb, S. (1995). Touching the phantom limb. *Nature, 377*, 489–490. (5)

Ramer, M. S., Priestley, J. V., & McMahon, S. B. (2000). Functional regeneration of sensory axons into the adult spinal cord. *Nature, 403*, 312–316. (5)

Ramirez, J. J., Bulsara, K. R., Moore, S. C., Ruch, K., & Abrams, W. (1999). Progressive unilateral damage of the entorhinal cortex enhances synaptic efficacy of the crossed entorhinal afferent to dentate granule cells. *Journal of Neuroscience, 19*:RC42, 1–6. (5)

Ramirez, J. J., Fass, B., Karpiak, S. E., & Steward, O. (1987a). Ganglioside treatments reduce locomotor hyperactivity after bilateral lesions of the entorhinal cortex. *Neuroscience Letters, 75*, 283–287. (5)

Ramirez, J. J., Fass, B., Kilfoil, T., Henschel, B., Grones, W., & Karpiak, S. E. (1987b). Ganglioside-induced enhancement of behavioral recovery after bilateral lesions of the entorhinal cortex. *Brain Research, 414*, 85–90. (5)

Ramirez, J. J., Finklestein, S. P., Keller, J., Abrams, W., George, M. N., & Parakh, T. (1999). Basic fibroblast growth factor enhances axonal sprouting after cortical injury in rats. *NeuroReport, 10*, 1201–1204. (5)

Ramirez, J. J., McQuilkin, M., Carrigan, T., MacDonald, K., & Kelley, M. S. (1996). Progressive entorhinal cortex lesions accelerate hippocampal sprouting and spare spatial memory in rats. *Proceedings of the National Academy of Sciences, USA, 93*, 15512–15517. (5)

Ramnani, N., & Passingham, R. E. (2001). Changes in the human brain during rhythm learning. *Journal of Cognitive Neuroscience, 13*, 952–966. (8)

Ramón y Cajal, S. (1937). Recollections of my life. *Memoirs of the American Philosophical Society, 8*, parts 1 and 2. (inside cover)

Ramos, J. M. J. (2001). Rats with hippocampal lesions can learn a place response, but how long can they retain it? *Behavioral Neuroscience, 115*, 1048–1058. (13)

Randolph, C., Tierney, M. C., & Chase, T. N. (1995). Implicit memory in Alzheimer's disease. *Journal of Clinical and Experimental Neuropsychology, 17*, 343–351. (13)

Ranson, S. W., & Clark, S. L. (1959). *The anatomy of the nervous system: Its development and function* (10th ed.). Philadelphia: Saunders. (4)

Rapkin, A. J., Morgan, M., Goldman, L., Brann, D. W., Simone, D., & Mahesh, V. B. (1997). Progesterone metabolite allopregnanolone in women with premenstrual syndrome. *Obstetrics & Gynecology, 90*, 709–714. (11)

Rapoport, J. L., Giedd, J. N., Blumenthal, J., Hamburger, S., Jeffries, N., Fernandez, T., Nicolson, R., Bedwell, J., Lenane, M., Zijdenbos, A., Paus, T., & Evans, A. (1999). Progressive cortical change during adolescence in childhood-onset schizophrenia. *Archives of General Psychiatry, 56*, 649–654. (15)

Rapoport, S. I., & Bosetti, F. (2002). Do lithium and anticonvulsants target the brain arachidonic acid cascade in bipolar patients? *Archives of General Psychiatry, 59*, 592–596. (15)

Rapoport, S. I., & Robinson, P. J. (1986). Tight-junctional modification as the basis of osmotic opening of the blood-brain barrier. *Annals of the New York Academy of Sciences, 481*, 250–267. (2)

Raum, W. J., McGivern, R. F., Peterson, M. A., Shryne, J. H., & Gorski, R. A. (1990). Prenatal inhibition of hypothalamic sex steroid uptake by cocaine: Effects on neurobehavioral sexual differentiation in male rats. *Developmental Brain Research, 53*, 230–236. (11)

Rauschecker, J. P. (1995). Developmental plasticity and memory. *Behavioural Brain Research, 66*, 7–12. (6)

Ravizza, S. M., & Ivry, R. B. (2001). Comparison of the basal ganglia and cerebellum in shifting attention. *Journal of Cognitive Neuroscience, 13*, 285–297. (7)

Reburn, C. J., & Wynne-Edwards, K. E. (1999). Hormonal changes in males of a naturally biparental and a uniparental mammal. *Hormones and Behavior, 35*, 163–176. (11)

Rechtschaffen, A., & Bergmann, B. M. (1995). Sleep deprivation in the rat by the disk-over-water method. *Behavioural Brain Research, 69*, 55–63. (9)

Reed, J. M., & Squire, L. R. (1999). Impaired transverse patterning in human amnesia is a special case of impaired memory for two-choice discrimination tasks. *Behavioral Neuroscience, 113*, 3–9. (13)

Rees, G., Kreiman, G., & Koch, C. (2002). Neural correlates of consciousness in humans. *Nature Reviews Neuroscience, 3*, 261–270. (9)

Reeves, A. G., & Plum, F. (1969). Hyperphagia, rage, and dementia accompanying a ventromedial hypothalamic neoplasm. *Archives of Neurology, 20*, 616–624. (10)

Refinetti, R. (2000). *Circadian physiology*. Boca Raton, FL: CRC Press. (9)

Refinetti, R., & Carlisle, H. J. (1986). Complementary nature of heat production and heat intake during behavioral thermoregulation in the rat. *Behavioral and Neural Biology, 46*, 64–70. (10)

Refinetti, R., & Menaker, M. (1992). The circadian rhythm of body temperature. *Physiology & Behavior, 51*, 613–637. (9)

Regan, T. (1986). The rights of humans and other animals. *Acta Physiologica Scandinavica, 128*(Suppl. 554), 33–40. (1)

Reichelt, K. L., Seim, A. R., & Reichelt, W. H. (1996). Could schizophrenia be reasonably explained by Dohan's hypothesis on genetic interaction with a dietary peptide overload? *Progress in Neuro-Psychopharmacology & Biological Psychiatry, 20*, 1083–1114. (15)

Reichling, D. B., Kwiat, G. C., & Basbaum, A. I. (1988). Anatomy, physiology, and pharmacology of the periaqueductal gray contribution to antinociceptive controls. In H. L. Fields & J.-M. Besson (Eds.), *Progress in brain research* (Vol. 77, pp. 31–46). Amsterdam: Elsevier. (7)

Reick, M., Garcia, J. A., Dudley, C., & McKnight, S. L. (2001). NPAS2: An analog of clock operative in the mammalian forebrain. *Science, 293*, 506–509. (9)

Reisel, D., Bannerman, D. M., Schmitt, W. B., Deacon, R. M. J., Flint, J., Borchardt, T., Seeburg, P. H., & Rawlins, J. N. P. (2002). Spatial memory dissociations in mice lacking GluR1. *Nature Neuroscience, 5*, 868–873. (13)

Reiss, A. L., Eliez, S., Schmitt, J. E., Straus, E., Lai, Z., Jones, W., & Bellugi, U. (2000). IV. Neuroanatomy of Williams syndrome: A high-resolution MRI study. *Journal of Cognitive Neuroscience, 12*(Suppl.), 65–73. (14)

Reiter, R. J. (2000). Melatonin: Lowering the high price of free radicals. *News in Physiological Sciences, 15*, 246–250. (9)

Reneman, L., Lavalaye, J., Schmand, B., de Wolff, F. A., van den Brink, W., den Heeten, G. J., & Booij, J. (2001). Cortical serotonin transporter density and verbal memory in individuals who stopped using 3,4-methylenedioxymethamphetamine (MDMA or "ecstasy"). *Archives of General Psychiatry, 58*, 901–906. (15)

Repa, J. C., Muller, J., Apergis, J., Dessrochers, T. M., Zhou, Y., & LeDoux, J. E. (2001). Two different lateral amygdala cell populations contribute to the initiation and storage of memory. *Nature Neuroscience, 4*, 724–731. (13)

Reuter-Lorenz, P. A., & Miller, A. C. (1998). The cognitive neuroscience of human laterality: Lessons from the bisected brain. *Current Directions in Psychological Science, 7*, 15–20. (14)

Rhees, R. W., Shryne, J. E., & Gorski, R. A. (1990). Onset of the hormone-sensitive perinatal period for sexual differentiation of the sexually dimorphic nucleus of the preoptic area in female rats. *Journal of Neurobiology, 21*, 781–786. (11)

Ricaurte, G. A., Yuan, J., Hatzidimitriou, G., Cord, B. J., & McCann, U. D. (2002). Severe dopaminergic neurotoxicity in primates after a common recreational dose regimen of MDMA ("ecstasy"). *Science, 297*, 2260–2263. (15)

Rice, G., Anderson, C., Risch, N., & Ebers, G. (1999). Male homosexuality: Absence of linkage to microsatellite markers at Xq28. *Science, 284*, 665–667. (11)

Richter, C. P. (1922). A behavioristic study of the activity of the rat. *Comparative Psychology Monographs, 1*, 1–55. (9)

Richter, C. P. (1936). Increased salt appetite in adrenalectomized rats. *American Journal of Physiology, 115*, 155–161. (10)

Richter, C. P. (1950). Taste and solubility of toxic compounds in poisoning of rats and humans. *Journal of Comparative and Physiological Psychology, 43*, 358–374. (7)

Richter, C. P. (1957). On the phenomenon of sudden death in animals and man. *Psychosomatic Medicine, 19*, 191–198. (12)

Richter, C. P. (1967). Psychopathology of periodic behavior in animals and man. In J. Zubin & H. F. Hunt (Eds.), *Comparative psychopathology* (pp. 205–227). New York: Grune & Stratton. (9)

Richter, C. P. (1975). Deep hypothermia and its effect on the 24-hour clock of rats and hamsters. *Johns Hopkins Medical Journal, 136*, 1–10. (9)

Richter, C. P., & Langworthy, O. R. (1933). The quill mechanism of the porcupine. *Journal für Psychologie und Neurologie, 45*, 143–153. (4)

Rickard, T. C., & Grafman, J. (1998). Losing their configural mind: Amnesic patients fail on transverse patterning. *Journal of Cognitive Neuroscience, 10*, 509–524. (13)

Riddle, D. R., Lo, D. C., & Katz, L. C. (1995). NT-4-mediated rescue of lateral geniculate neurons from effects of monocular deprivation. *Nature, 378*, 189–191. (6)

Riddle, W. J. R., & Scott, A. I. F. (1995). Relapse after successful electroconvulsive therapy: The use and impact of continuation antidepressant drug treatment. *Human Psychopharmacology, 10*, 201–205. (15)

Riemann, D., König, A., Hohagen, F., Kiemen, A., Voderholzer, U., Backhaus, J., Bunz, J., Wesiack, B., Hermle, L., & Berger, M. (1999). How to preserve the antidepressive effect of sleep deprivation: A comparison of sleep phase advance and sleep phase delay. *European Archives of Psychiatry and Clinical Neuroscience, 249*, 231–237. (15)

Ringel, B. L., & Szuba, M. P. (2001). Potential mechanisms of the sleep therapies for depression. *Depression and Anxiety, 14*, 29–36. (15)

Rinn, W. E. (1984). The neuropsychology of facial expression: A review of the neurological and psychological mechanisms for producing facial expressions. *Psychological Bulletin, 95*, 52–77. (8)

Rittenhouse, C. D., Shouval, H. Z., Paradiso, M. A., & Bear, M. F. (1999). Monocular deprivation induces homosynaptic long-term depression in visual cortex. *Nature, 397,* 347–350. (6)

Robbins, T. W., & Everitt, B. J. (1995). Arousal systems and attention. In M. S. Gazzaniga (Ed.), *The cognitive neurosciences* (pp. 703–720). Cambridge, MA: MIT Press. (9)

Robertson, L., Treisman, A., Friedman-Hill, S., & Grabowecky, M. (1997). The interaction of spatial and object pathways: Evidence from Balint's syndrome. *Journal of Cognitive Neuropsychology, 9,* 295–317. (4)

Robillard, T. A. J., & Gersdorff, M. C. H. (1986). Prevention of pre- and perinatal acquired hearing defects: Part I. Study of causes. *Journal of Auditory Research, 26,* 207–237. (7)

Robinson, R. G., Boston, J. D., Starkstein, S. E., & Price, T. R. (1988). Comparison of mania and depression after brain injury: Causal factors. *American Journal of Psychiatry, 145,* 172–178. (15)

Robinson, S. J., & Manning, J. T. (2000). The ratio of 2nd to 4th digit length and male homosexuality. *Evolution and Human Behavior, 21,* 333–345. (11)

Roca, C. A., Schmidt, P. J., & Rubinow, D. R. (1999). Gonadal steroids and affective illness. *Neuroscientist, 5,* 227–237. (15)

Rocha, B. A., Fumagalli, F., Gainetdinov, R. R., Jones, S. R., Ator, R., Giros, B., Miller, G. W., & Caron, M. G. (1998). Cocaine self-administration in dopamine-transporter knockout mice. *Nature Neuroscience, 1,* 132–137. (15)

Rochira, V., Balestrieri, A., Madeo, B., Baraldi, E., Faustini-Fustini, M., Granata, A. R. M., & Carani, C. (2001). Congenital estrogen deficiency: In search of the estrogen role in human male reproduction. *Molecular and Cellular Endocrinology, 178,* 107–115. (11)

Rodgers, R. J., Halford, J. C. G., Nunes de Souza, R. L., Canto de Souza, A. L., Piper, D. C., Arch, J. R. S., Upton, N., Porter, R. A., Johns, A., & Blundell, J. E. (2001). SB-334867, a selective orexin-1 receptor antagonist, enhances behavioural satiety and blocks the hyperphagic effect of orexin-A in rats. *European Journal of Neuroscience, 13,* 1444–1452. (10)

Rodriguez, E., George, N., Lachaux, J.-P., Martinerie, J., Renault, B., & Varela, F. J. (1999). Perception's shadow: Long-distance synchronization of human brain activity. *Nature, 397,* 430–433. (4)

Rodriguez, I., Del Punta, K., Rothman, A., Ishii, T., & Mombaerts, P. (2002). Multiple new and isolated families within the mouse superfamily of Vlr vomeronasal receptors. *Nature Neuroscience, 5,* 134–140. (7)

Rodriguez, I., Greer, C. A., Mok, M. Y., & Mombaerts, P. A. (2000). A putative pheromone receptor gene expressed in human olfactory mucosa. *Nature Genetics, 26,* 18–19. (7)

Roelfsema, P. R., Engel, A. K., König, P., & Singer, W. (1997). Visuomotor integration is associated with zero time-lag synchronization among cortical areas. *Nature, 385,* 157–161. (4)

Roffwarg, H. P., Muzio, J. N., & Dement, W. C. (1966). Ontogenetic development of human sleep-dream cycle. *Science, 152,* 604–609. (9)

Rollenhagen, J. E., & Olson, C. R. (2000). Mirror-image confusion in single neurons of the macaque inferotemporal cortex. *Science, 287,* 1506–1508. (6)

Rolls, E. T. (1995). Central taste anatomy and neurophysiology. In R. L. Doty (Ed.), *Handbook of olfaction and gustation* (pp. 549–573). New York: Dekker. (7)

Rolls, E. T. (1996a) The representation of space in the primate hippocampus, and its relation to memory. In K. Ishikawa, J. L. McGaugh, and H. Sakata (Eds.), *Brain processes and memory* (pp. 203–227). Amsterdam: Elsevier. (13)

Rolls, E. T. (1996b). A theory of hippocampal function in memory. *Hippocampus, 6,* 601–620. (13)

Rome, L. C., Loughna, P. T., & Goldspink, G. (1984). Muscle fiber activity in carp as a function of swimming speed and muscle temperature. *American Journal of Psychiatry, 247,* R272–R279. (8)

Romer, A. S. (1962). *The vertebrate body.* Philadelphia: Saunders. (5)

Rommel, S. A., Pabst, D. A., & McLellan, W. A. (1998). Reproductive thermoregulation in marine mammals. *American Scientist, 86,* 440–448. (10)

Ronai, Z., Szekely, A., Nemoda, Z., Lakatos, K., Gervai, J., Staub, M., & Sasvari-Szekely, M. (2001). Association between novelty seeking and the −521 C/T polymorphism in the promoter region of the DRD4 gene. *Molecular Psychiatry, 6,* 35–38. (15)

Roorda, A., Metha, A. B., Lennie, P., & Williams, D. R. (2001). Packing arrangement of the three cone classes in primate retina. *Vision Research, 41,* 1291–1306. (6)

Roorda, A., & Williams, D. R. (1999). The arrangement of the three cone classes in the living human eye. *Nature, 397,* 520–522. (6)

Roozendaal, B., Phillips, R. G., Power, A. E., Brooke, S. M., Sapolsky, R. M., & McGaugh, J. L. (2001). Memory retrieval impairment induced by hippocampal CA3 lesions is blocked by adrenocortical suppression. *Nature Neuroscience, 4,* 1169–1171. (13)

Rose, J. E., Brugge, J. F., Anderson, D. J., & Hind, J. E. (1967). Phase-locked response to low-frequency tones in single auditory nerve fibers of the squirrel monkey. *Journal of Neurophysiology, 30,* 769–793. (7)

Rose, R. J., Kaprio, J., Winter, T., Dick, D. M., Viken, R. J., Pulkkinen, L., & Koskenvuo, M. (2002). Femininity and fertility in sisters with twin brothers: Prenatal androgenization? Cross-sex socialization? *Psychological Science, 13,* 263–267. (11)

Rosenberg, E. L., Ekman, P., Jiang, W., Babyak, M., Coleman, R. E., Hanson, M., O'Connor, C., Waugh, R., & Blumenthal, J. A. (2001). Linkages between facial expressions of anger and transient myocardial ischemia in men with coronary artery disease. *Emotion, 1,* 107–115. (12)

Rosenblatt, J. S. (1967). Nonhormonal basis of maternal behavior in the rat. *Science, 156,* 1512–1514. (11)

Rosenblatt, J. S. (1970). Views on the onset and maintenance of maternal behavior in the rat. In L. R. Aronson, E. Tobach, D. S. Lehrman, & J. S. Rosenblatt (Eds.), *Development and evolution of behavior* (pp. 489–515). San Francisco: Freeman. (11)

Rosenzweig, M. R., & Bennett, E. L. (1996). Psychobiology of plasticity: Effects of training and experience on brain and behavior. *Behavioural Brain Research, 78*, 57–65. (5)

Rösler, A., & Witztum, E. (1998). Treatment of men with paraphilia with a long-acting analogue of gonadotropin-releasing hormone. *New England Journal of Medicine, 338*, 416–422. (11)

Ross, E. D., Homan, R. W., & Buck, R. (1994). Differential hemispheric lateralization of primary and social emotions. *Neuropsychiatry, Neuropsychology, and Behavioral Neurology, 7*, 1–19. (12)

Ross, G. W., Abbott, R. D., Petrovitch, H., Morens, D. M., Grandinetti, A., Tung, K.-H., Tanner, C. M., Masaki, K. H., Blanchette, P. L., Burb, J. D., Popper, J. S., & White, L. R. (2000). Association of coffee and caffeine intake with the risk of Parkinson's disease. *Journal of the American Medical Association, 283*, 2674–2679. (8)

Rossi, D. J., Oshima, T., & Attwell, D. (2000). Glutamate release in severe brain ischaemia is mainly by reversed uptake. *Nature, 403*, 316–321. (5)

Rossion, B., Gauthier, I., Goffaux, V., Tarr, M. J., & Crommelinck, M. (2002). Expertise training with novel objects leads to left-lateralized facelike electrophysiological responses. *Psychological Science, 13*, 250–257. (6)

Rosvold, H. E., Mirsky, A. F., & Pribram, K. H. (1954). Influence of amygdalectomy on social behavior in monkeys. *Journal of Comparative and Physiological Psychology, 47*, 173–178. (12)

Roth, B. L., Lopez, E., & Kroeze, W. K. (2000). The multiplicity of serotonin receptors: Uselessly diverse molecules or an embarrassment of riches? *Neuroscientist, 6*, 252–262. (3)

Roth, B. L., Willins, D. L., Kristiansen, K., & Kroeze, W. K. (1999). Activation is hallucinogenic and antagonism is therapeutic: Role of 5-HT$_{2A}$ receptors in atypical antipsychotic drug actions. *Neuroscientist, 5*, 254–262. (15)

Roth, E. C., & Hellige, J. B. (1998). Spatial processing and hemispheric asymmetry: Contributions of the transient/magnocellular visual system. *Journal of Cognitive Neuroscience, 10*, 472–484. (14)

Routtenberg, A., Cantallops, I., Zaffuto, S., Serrano, P., & Namgung, U. (2000). Enhanced learning after genetic overexpression of a brain growth protein. *Proceedings of the National Academy of Sciences, USA, 97*, 7657–7662. (13)

Rovainen, C. M. (1976). Regeneration of Müller and Mauthner axons after spinal transection in larval lampreys. *Journal of Comparative Neurology, 168*, 545–554. (5)

Rowe, J. B., Toni, I., Josephs, O., Frackowiak, R. S. J., & Passingham, R. E. (2000). The prefrontal cortex: Response selection or maintenance within working memory? *Science, 288*, 1656–1660. (13)

Rowland, D. L., & Burnett, A. L. (2000). Pharmacotherapy in the treatment of male sexual dysfunction. *Journal of Sex Research, 37*, 226–243. (11)

Rowland, N. (1980). Drinking behavior: Physiological, neurological, and environmental factors. In T. M. Toates & T. R. Halliday (Eds.), *Analysis of motivational processes* (pp. 39–59). London: Academic Press. (10)

Roy, A., DeJong, J., & Linnoila, M. (1989). Cerebrospinal fluid monoamine metabolites and suicidal behavior in depressed patients. *Archives of General Psychiatry, 46*, 609–612. (12)

Royet, J.-P., Zald, D., Versace, R., Costes, N., Lavenne, F., Koenig, O., & Gervais, R. (2000). Emotional responses to pleasant and unpleasant olfactory, visual, and auditory stimuli: A positron emission tomography study. *Journal of Neuroscience, 20*, 7752–7759. (12)

Rozin, P. (1990). Getting to like the burn of chili pepper. In B. G. Green, J. R. Mason, & M. R. Kare (Eds.), *Chemical senses* (Vol. 2, pp. 231–269). New York: Dekker. (10)

Rozin, P., Dow, S., Moscovitch, M., & Rajaram, S. (1998). What causes humans to begin and end a meal? A role for memory for what has been eaten, as evidenced by a study of multiple meal eating in amnesic patients. *Psychological Science, 9*, 392–396. (13)

Rozin, P., & Kalat, J. W. (1971). Specific hungers and poison avoidance as adaptive specializations of learning. *Psychological Review, 78*, 459–486. (10, 13)

Rozin, P., & Pelchat, M. L. (1988). Memories of mammaries: Adaptations to weaning from milk. *Progress in Psychobiology and Physiological Psychology, 13*, 1–29. (10)

Rozin, P., & Schull, J. (1988). The adaptive-evolutionary point of view in experimental psychology. In R. C. Atkinson, R. J. Herrnstein, G. Lindzey, & R. D. Luce (Eds.), *Stevens' handbook of experimental psychology* (2nd ed.): Vol. 1. *Perception and motivation* (pp. 503–546). New York: Wiley (13)

Rozin, P., & Vollmecke, T. A. (1986). Food likes and dislikes. *Annual Review of Nutrition, 6*, 433–456. (10)

Rozin, P., & Zellner, D. (1985). The role of Pavlovian conditioning in the acquisition of food likes and dislikes. *Annals of the New York Academy of Sciences, 443*, 189–202. (10)

Rubens, A. B., & Benson, D. F. (1971). Associative visual agnosia. *Archives of Neurology, 24*, 305–316. (6)

Rubia, K., Oosterlaan, J., Sergeant, J. A., Brandeis, D., & v. Leeuwen, T. (1998). Inhibitory dysfunction in hyperactive boys. *Behavoural Brain Research, 94*, 25–32. (7)

Rubin, B. D., & Katz, L. C. (2001). Spatial coding of enantiomers in the rat olfactory bulb. *Nature Neuroscience, 4*, 355–356. (7)

Rudolph, U., Crestani, F., Benke, D., Brünig, I., Benson, J. A., Fritschy, J.-M., Martin, J. R., Bluethmann, H., & Möhler, H. (1999). Benzodiazepine actions mediated by specific g-aminobutyric acidA receptor subtypes. *Nature, 401,* 796–800. (12)

Rumbaugh, D. M. (Ed.). (1977). *Language learning by a chimpanzee: The Lana Project.* New York: Academic Press. (14)

Rumbaugh, D. M. (1990). Comparative psychology and the great apes: Their competency in learning, language, and numbers. *Psychological Record, 40,* 15–39. (14)

Rupprecht, R., di Michele, F., Hermann, B., Ströhle, A., Lancel, M., Romeo, E., & Holsboer, F. (2001). Neuroactive steroids: Molecular mechanisms of action and implications for neuropsychopharmacology. *Brain Research Reviews, 37,* 59–67. (11)

Rusak, B., & Zucker, I. (1979). Neural regulation of circadian rhythms. *Physiological Reviews, 59,* 449–526. (9)

Russell, A. J., Munro, J. C., Jones, P. B., Hemsley, D. R., & Murray, R. M. (1997). Schizophrenia and the myth of intellectual decline. *American Journal of Psychiatry, 154,* 635–639. (15)

Russell, M. J., Switz, G. M., & Thompson, K. (1980). Olfactory influences on the human menstrual cycle. *Pharmacology, Biochemistry, and Behavior, 13,* 737–738. (7)

Rutter, M., Pickles, A., Murray, R., & Eaves, L. (2001). Testing hypotheses on specific environmental causal effects on behavior. *Psychological Bulletin, 127,* 291–324. (1)

Rüttiger, L., Braun, D. I., Gegenfurtner, K. R., Petersen, D., Schönle, P., & Sharpe, L. T. (1999). Selective color constancy deficits after circumscribed unilateral brain lesions. *Journal of Neuroscience, 19,* 3094–3106. (6)

Ryan, J. D., Althoff, R. R., Whitlow, S., & Cohen, N. J. (2000). Amnesia is a deficit in relational memory. *Psychological Science, 11,* 454–461. (13)

Saad, W. A., Luiz, A. C., Camargo, L. A. A., Renzi, A., & Manani, J. V. (1996). The lateral preoptic area plays a dual role in the regulation of thirst in the rat. *Brain Research Bulletin, 39,* 171–176. (10)

Saarelainen, T., Hendolin, P., Lucas, G., Koponen, E., Sairanen, M., MacDonald, E., Agerman, K., Haapasalo, A., Nawa, H., Aloyz, R., Ernfors, P., & Castrén, E. (2003). Activation of the TrkB neurotrophin receptor is induced by antidepressant drugs and is required for antidepressant-induced behavioral effects. *Journal of Neuroscience, 23,* 349-357. (15)

Sabel, B. A. (1997). Unrecognized potential of surviving neurons: Within-systems plasticity, recovery of function, and the hypothesis of minimal residual structure. *The Neuroscientist, 3,* 366–370. (5)

Sabel, B. A., Slavin, M. D., & Stein, D. G. (1984). GM₁ ganglioside treatment facilitates behavioral recovery from bilateral brain damage. *Science, 225,* 340–342. (5)

Sabo, K. T., & Kirtley, D. D. (1982). Objects and activities in the dreams of the blind. *International Journal of Rehabilitation Research, 5,* 241–242. (4)

Sack, R. L., & Lewy, A. J. (2001). Circadian rhythm sleep disorders: Lessons from the blind. *Sleep Medicine Reviews, 5,* 189–206. (9)

Sackeim, H. A., Putz, E., Vingiano, W., Coleman, E., & McElhiney, M. (1988). Lateralization in the processing of emotionally laden information: I. Normal functioning. *Neuropsychiatry, Neuropsychology, and Behavioral Neurology, 1,* 97–110. (14)

Sakai, K., Rowe, J. B., & Passingham, R. E. (2002). Active maintenance in prefrontal area 46 creates distractor-resistant memory. *Nature Neuroscience, 5,* 479–484. (13)

Saleem, Q., Dash, D., Gandhi, C., Kishore, A., Benegal, V., Sherrin, T., Mukherjee, O., Jain, S., & Brahmachari, S. K. (2001). Association of CAG repeat loci on chromosome 22 with schizophrenia and bipolar disorder. *Molecular Psychiatry, 6,* 694–700. (15)

Salmelin, R., Hari, R., Lounasmaa, O. V., & Sams, M. (1994). Dynamics of brain activation during picture naming. *Nature, 368,* 463–465. (5)

Sander, K., & Scheich, H. (2001). Auditory perception of laughing and crying activates human amygdala regardless of attentional state. *Cognitive Brain Research, 12,* 181–198. (12)

Sanders, R. J. (1989). Sentence comprehension following agenesis of the corpus callosum. *Brain and Language, 37,* 59–72. (14)

Sanders, S. K., & Shekhar, A. (1995). Anxiolytic effects of chlordiazepoxide blocked by injection of GABA_A and benzodiazepine receptor antagonists in the region of the anterior basolateral amygdala of rats. *Biological Psychiatry, 37,* 473–476. (12)

Sandstrom, N. J., & Williams, C. L. (2001). Memory retention is modulated by acute estradiol and progesterone replacement. *Behavioral Neuroscience, 115,* 384–393. (11)

Sanes, J. N., Donoghue, J. P., Thangaraj, V., Edelman, R. R., & Warach, S. (1995). Shared neural substrates controlling hand movements in human motor cortex. *Science, 268,* 1775–1777. (8)

Sanes, J. R. (1993). Topographic maps and molecular gradients. *Current Opinion in Neurobiology, 3,* 67–74. (5)

Sanger, T. D., Pascual-Leone, A., Tarsy, D., & Schlaug, G. (2001). Nonlinear sensory cortex response to simultaneous tactile stimuli in writer's cramp. *Movement Disorders, 17,* 105–111. (5)

Sanger, T. D., Tarsy, D., & Pascual-Leone, A. (2001). Abnormalities of spatial and temporal sensory discrimination in writer's cramp. *Movement Disorders, 16,* 94–99. (5)

Sapolsky, R. M. (1992). *Stress, the aging brain, and the mechanisms of neuron death.* Cambridge, MA: MIT Press. (12)

Sapolsky, R. M., & Finch, C. E. (2000). Alzheimer's disease and some speculations about the evolution of its modifiers. *Annals of the New York Academy of Sciences, 924,* 99–103. (11)

Sarter, M., Givens, B., & Bruno, J. P. (2001). The cognitive neuroscience of sustained attention: Where top-down meets bottom-up. *Brain Research Reviews, 35,* 146–160. (7)

Sáry, G., Vogels, R., & Orban, G. A. (1993). Cue-invariant shape selectivity of macaque inferior temporal neurons. *Science, 260,* 995–997. (6)

Satinoff, E. (1964). Behavioral thermoregulation in response to local cooling of the rat brain. *American Journal of Physiology, 206,* 1389–1394. (10)

Satinoff, E. (1991). Developmental aspects of behavioral and reflexive thermoregulation. In H. N. Shanir, G. A. Barr, & M. A. Hofer (Eds.), *Developmental psychobiology: New methods and changing concepts* (pp. 169–188). New York: Oxford University Press. (10)

Satinoff, E., McEwen, G. N., Jr., & Williams, B. A. (1976). Behavioral fever in newborn rabbits. *Science, 193,* 1139–1140. (10)

Satinoff, E., & Rutstein, J. (1970). Behavioral thermoregulation in rats with anterior hypothalamic lesions. *Journal of Comparative and Physiological Psychology, 71,* 77–82. (10)

Satinoff, E., Valentino, D., & Teitelbaum, P. (1976). Thermoregulatory cold-defense deficits in rats with preoptic/anterior hypothalamic lesions. *Brain Research Bulletin, 1,* 553–565. (10)

Sato, M. A., Yada, M. M., & De Luca, L. A., Jr. (1996). Antagonism of the renin-angiotensin system and water deprivation-induced NaCl intake in rats. *Physiology & Behavior, 60,* 1099–1104. (10)

Satz, P., & Green, M. F. (1999). Atypical handedness in schizophrenia: Some methodological and theoretical issues. *Schizophrenia Bulletin, 25,* 63–78. (15)

Satz, P., Zaucha, K., McCleary, C., Light, R., Asarnow, R., & Becker, D. (1997). Mild head injury in children and adolescents: A review of studies (1970–1995). *Psychological Bulletin, 122,* 107–131. (5)

Saudou, F., Amara, D. A., Dierich, A., LeMeur, M., Ramboz, S., Segu, L., Buhot, M.-C., & Hen, R. (1994). Enhanced aggressive behavior in mice lacking 5-HT$_{1B}$ receptor. *Science, 265,* 1875–1878. (12)

Savage-Rumbaugh, E. S. (1990). Language acquisition in a nonhuman species: Implications for the innateness debate. *Developmental Psychobiology, 23,* 599–620. (14)

Savage-Rumbaugh, E. S. (1991). Language learning in the bonobo: How and why they learn. In N. A. Kresnegor, D. M. Rumbaugh, R. L. Schiefelbusch, & M. Studdert-Kennedy (Eds.), *Biological and behavioral determinants of language development* (pp. 209–233). Hillsdale, NJ: Erlbaum. (14)

Savage-Rumbaugh, E. S. (1993). Language learnability in man, ape, and dolphin. In H. L. Roitblat, L. M. Herman, & P. E. Nachtigall (Eds.), *Language and communication: Comparative perspectives* (pp. 457–473). Hillsdale, NJ: Erlbaum. (14)

Savage-Rumbaugh, E. S., Murphy, J., Sevcik, R. A., Brakke, K. E., Williams, S. L., & Rumbaugh, D. M. (1993). Language comprehension in ape and child. *Monographs of the Society for Research in Child Development, 58*(Serial no. 233). (14)

Savage-Rumbaugh, E. S., Sevcik, R. A., Brakke, K. E., & Rumbaugh, D. M. (1992). Symbols: Their communicative use, communication, and combination by bonobos (*Pan paniscus*). In L. P. Lipsitt & C. Rovee-Collier (Eds.), *Advances in infancy research* (Vol. 7, pp. 221–278). Norwood, NJ: Ablex. (14)

Savic, I., Berglund, H., Gulyas, B., & Roland, P. (2001). Smelling of odorous sex hormone-like compounds causes sex-differentiated hypothalamic activations in humans. *Neuron, 31,* 661–668. (7)

Sawamoto, N., Honda, M., Okada, T., Hanakawa, T., Kanda, M., Fukuyama, H., Konishi, J., & Shibasaki, H. (2000). Expectation of pain enhances responses to nonpainful somatosensory stimulation in the anterior cingulate cortex and parietal operculum/posterior insula: An event-related functional magnetic resonance imaging study. *Journal of Neuroscience, 20,* 7438–7445. (7)

Sawamoto, N., Honda, M., Hanakawa, T., Fukuyama, H., & Shibasaki, H. (2002). Cognitive slowing in Parkinson's disease: A behavioral evaluation independent of motor slowing. *Journal of Neuroscience, 22,* 5198–5203. (8)

Scamell, T., Gerashchenko, D., Urade, Y., Onoe, H., Saper, C., & Hayaishi, O. (1998). Activation of ventrolateral preoptic neurons by the somnogen prostaglandin D$_2$. *Proceedings of the National Academy of Sciences, USA, 95,* 7754–7759. (9)

Scannevin, R. H., & Huganir, R. L. (2000). Postsynaptic organization and regulation of excitatory synapses. *Nature Reviews Neuroscience, 1,* 133–141. (3)

Schacter, D. L. (1983). Amnesia observed: Remembering and forgetting in a natural environment. *Journal of Abnormal Psychology, 92,* 236–242. (13)

Schacter, D. L. (1985). Priming of old and new knowledge in amnesic patients and normal subjects. *Annals of the New York Academy of Sciences, 444,* 41–53. (13)

Schärli, H., Harman, A. M., & Hogben, J. H. (1999). Blindsight in subjects with homonymous visual field defects. *Journal of Cognitive Neuroscience, 11,* 52–66. (6)

Scheibel, A. B. (1983). Dendritic changes. In B. Reisberg (Ed.), *Alzheimer's disease* (pp. 69–73). New York: Free Press. (13)

Scheibel, A. B. (1984). A dendritic correlate of human speech. In N. Geschwind & A. M. Galaburda (Eds.), *Cerebral dominance* (pp. 43–52). Cambridge, MA: Harvard University Press. (4)

Scheich, H., & Zuschratter, W. (1995). Mapping of stimulus features and meaning in gerbil auditory cortex with 2-deoxyglucose and c-fos antibodies. *Behavioural Brain Research, 66,* 195–205. (7)

Schellenberg, G. D., Bird, T. D., Wijsman, E. M., Orr, H. T., Anderson, L., Nemens, E., White, J. A., Bonnycastle, L., Weber, J. L., Alonso, M. E., Potter, H., Heston, L. L., & Martin, G. M. (1992). Genetic linkage evidence for a familial Alzheimer's disease locus on chromosome 14. *Science, 258,* 668–671. (13)

Schenck, C. H., & Mahowald, M. W. (1996). Long-term, nightly benzodiazepine treatment of injurious parasomnias and other disorders of disrupted nocturnal sleep in 170 adults. *American Journal of Medicine, 100,* 333–337. (9)

Schenk, D., Barbour, R., Dunn, W., Gordon, G., Grajeda, H., Guido, T., Hu, K., Huang, J., Johnson-Wood, K., Khan, K., Kholodenko, D., Lee, M., Liao, Z., Lieberburg, I., Motter, R., Mutter, L., Soriano, F., Shopp, G., Vasquez, N., Vandevert, C., Walker, S., Wogulis, M., Yednock, T., Games, D., & Seubert, P. (1999). Immunization with amyloid-β attenuates Alzheimer-disease-like pathology in the PDAPP mouse. *Nature, 400,* 173–177. (13)

Scherer, S. S. (1986). Reinnervation of the extraocular muscles in goldfish is nonselective. *Journal of Neuroscience, 6,* 764–773. (5)

Schiermeier, Q. (1998). Animal rights activists turn the screw. *Nature, 396,* 505. (1)

Schiffman, S. S. (1983). Taste and smell in disease. *New England Journal of Medicine, 308,* 1275–1279, 1337–1343. (7)

Schiffman, S. S., & Erickson, R. P. (1971). A psychophysical model for gustatory quality. *Physiology & Behavior, 7,* 617–633. (7)

Schiffman, S. S., & Erickson, R. P. (1980). The issue of primary tastes versus a taste continuum. *Neuroscience and Biobehavioral Reviews, 4,* 109–117. (7)

Schiffman, S. S., Lockhead, E., & Maes, F. W. (1983). Amiloride reduces the taste intensity of Na$^+$ and Li$^+$ salts and sweeteners. *Proceedings of the National Academy of Sciences, USA, 80,* 6136–6140. (7)

Schiffman, S. S., McElroy, A. E., & Erickson, R. P. (1980). The range of taste quality of sodium salts. *Physiology & Behavior, 24,* 217–224. (7)

Schmauss, C. (2000). Dopamine receptors: Novel insights from biochemical and genetic studies. *Neuroscientist, 6,* 127–138. (3)

Schmid, A., Koch, M., & Schnitzler, H.-U. (1995). Conditioned pleasure attenuates the startle response in rats. *Neurobiology of Learning and Memory, 64,* 1–3. (12)

Schmidt, L. A.(1999). Frontal brain electrical activity in shyness and sociability. *Psychological Science, 10,* 316–320. (12)

Schmidt, P. J., Nieman, L. K., Danaceau, M. A., Adams, L. F., & Rubinow, D. R. (1998). Differential behavioral effects of gonadal steroids in women with and in those without premenstrual syndrome. *New England Journal of Medicine, 338,* 209–216. (11)

Schneider, B. A., Trehub, S. E., Morrongiello, B. A., & Thorpe, L. A. (1986). Auditory sensitivity in preschool children. *Journal of the Acoustical Society of America, 79,* 447–452. (7)

Schneider, P., Scherg, M., Dosch, G., Specht, H. J., Gutschalk, A., & Rupp, A. (2002). Morphology of Heschl's gyrus reflects enhanced activation in the auditory cortex of musicians. *Nature Neuroscience, 5,* 688–694. (5)

Schnider, A., & Ptak, R. (1999). Spontaneous confabulators fail to suppress currently irrelevant memory traces. *Nature Neuroscience, 2,* 677–681. (13)

Schoenemann, P. T., Budinger, T. F., Sarich, V. M., & Wang, W. S.-Y. (2000). Brain size does not predict general cognitive ability within families. *Proceedings of the National Academy of Sciences, USA, 97,* 4932–4937. (14)

Schöpf, J., Bryois, C., Jonquière, M., & Le, P. K. (1984). On the nosology of severe psychiatric post-partum disorders. *European Archives of Psychiatry and Neurological Sciences, 234,* 54–63. (15)

Schou, M. (1997). Forty years of lithium treatment. *Archives of General Psychiatry, 54,* 9–13. (15)

Schoups, A., Vogels, R., Qian, N., & Orban, G. (2001). Practising orientation identification improves orientation coding in V1 neurons. *Nature, 412,* 549–553. (6)

Schradin, C., & Anzenberger, G. (1999). Prolactin, the hormone of paternity. *News in Physiological Sciences, 14,* 223–231. (11)

Schuckit, M. A., & Smith, T. L. (1996). An 8-year follow-up of 450 sons of alcoholic and control subjects. *Archives of General Psychiatry, 53,* 202–210. (15)

Schulkin, J. (1991). *Sodium hunger: The search for a salty taste.* Cambridge, England: Cambridge University Press. (10)

Schultz, W. (2000). Multiple reward signals in the brain. *Nature Reviews Neuroscience, 1,* 199–207. (15)

Schulz, J. B., Matthews, R. T., Jenkins, B. G., Brar, P., & Beal, M. F. (1995). Improved therapeutic window for treatment of histotoxic hypoxia with a free radical spin trap. *Journal of Cerebral Blood Flow and Metabolism, 15,* 948–952. (5)

Schulz, J. B., Weller, M., & Moskowitz, M. A. (1999). Caspases as treatment targets in stroke and neurodegenerative diseases. *Annals of Neurology, 45,* 421–429. (5)

Schumacher, E. H., Seymour, T. L., Glass, J. M., Fencsik, D. E., Lauber, E. J., Kieras, D. E., & Meyer, D. E. (2001). Virtually perfect time sharing in dual-task performance: Uncorking the central cognitive bottleneck. *Psychological Science, 12,* 101–108. (7)

Schwab, M. E. (1998). Regenerative nerve fiber growth in the adult central nervous system. *News in Physiological Sciences, 13,* 294–298. (5)

Schwartz, G. J. (2000). The role of gastrointestinal vagal afferents in the control of food intake: Current prospects. *Nutrition, 16,* 866–873. (10)

Schwartz, L., & Tulipan, L. (1933). An outbreak of dermatitis among workers in a rubber manufacturing plant. *Public Health Reports, 48,* 809–814. (15)

Schwartz, M. B., & Brownell, K. D. (1995). Matching individuals to weight loss treatments: A survey of obesity experts. *Journal of Consulting and Clinical Psychology, 63,* 149–153. (10)

Schwartz, M. F. (1995). Re-examining the role of executive functions in routine action production. *Annals of the New York Academy of Sciences, 769,* 321–335. (8)

Schwartz, W. J., & Gainer, H. (1977). Suprachiasmatic nucleus: Use of 14C-labeled deoxyglucose uptake as a functional marker. *Science, 197,* 1089–1091. (9)

Scott, T. R., & Verhagen, J. V. (2000). Taste as a factor in the management of nutrition. *Nutrition, 16,* 874–885. (10)

Scott, W. K., Nance, M. A., Watts, R. L., Hubble, J. P., Koller, W. C., Lyons, K., Pahwa, R., Stern, M. B., Colcher, A., Hiner, B. C., Jankovic,

J., Ondo, W. G., Allen, F. H., Jr., Goetz, C. G., Small, G. W., Masterman, D., Mastaglia, F., Laing, N. G., Stajich, J. M., Slotterbeck, B., Booze, M. W., Ribble, R. C., Rampersaud, E., West, S. G., Gibson, R. A., Middleton, L. T., Roses, A. D., Haines, J. L., Scott, B. L., Vance, J. M., & Pericak-Vance, M. A. (2001). Complete genomic screen in Parkinson disease. *Journal of the American Medical Association, 286,* 2239–2244. (8)

Scovern, A. W., & Kilmann, P. R. (1980). Status of electroconvulsive therapy: Review of the outcome literature. *Psychological Bulletin, 87,* 260–303. (15)

Scoville, W. B., & Milner, B. (1957). Loss of recent memory after bilateral hippocampal lesions. *Journal of Neurology, Neurosurgery, and Psychiatry, 20,* 11–21. (13)

Searle, J. R. (1992). *The rediscovery of the mind.* Cambridge, MA: MIT Press. (1)

Seeley, R. J., Kaplan, J. M., & Grill, H. J. (1995). Effect of occluding the pylorus on intraoral intake: A test of the gastric hypothesis of meal termination. *Physiology & Behavior, 58,* 245–249. (10)

Seeman, P., Lee, T., Chau-Wong, M., & Wong, K. (1976). Antipsychotic drug doses and neuroleptic/dopamine receptors. *Nature, 261,* 717–719. (15)

Sehgal, A., Ousley, A., Yang, Z., Chen, Y., & Schotland, P. (1999). What makes the circadian clock tick: Genes that keep time? *Recent Progress in Hormone Research, 54,* 61–85. (9)

Seidenberg, M. S. (1997). Language acquisition and use: Learning and applying probabilistic constraints. *Science, 275,* 1599–1603. (14)

Seidler, R. D., Purushotham, A., Kim, S.-G., Uğurbil, K., Willingham, D., & Ashe, J. (2002). Cerebellum activation associated with performance change but not motor learning. *Science, 296,* 2043–2046. (8)

Sejnowski, T. J., Chattarji, S., & Stanton, P. K. (1990). Homosynaptic long-term depression in hippocampus and neocortex. *Seminars in the Neurosciences, 2,* 355–363. (13)

Selemon, L. D., Rajkowska, G., & Goldman-Rakic, P. S. (1995). Abnormally high neuronal density in the schizophrenic cortex. *Archives of General Psychiatry, 52,* 805–818. (15)

Selkoe, D. J. (1999). Translating cell biology into therapeutic advances in Alzheimer's disease. *Nature, 399*(Suppl.), A23–A31. (13)

Selkoe, D. J. (2000). Toward a comprehensive theory for Alzheimer's disease. *Annals of the New York Academy of Sciences, 924,* 17–25. (13)

Selye, H. (1979). Stress, cancer, and the mind. In J. Taché, H. Selye, & S. B. Day (Eds.), *Cancer, stress, and death* (pp. 11–27). New York: Plenum Press. (12)

Selzer, M. E. (1978). Mechanisms of functional recovery and regeneration after spinal cord transection in larval sea lamprey. *Journal of Physiology, 277,* 395–408. (5)

Semendeferi, K., Lu, A., Schenker, N., & Damasio, H. (2002). Humans and great apes share a large frontal cortex. *Nature Neuroscience, 5,* 272–276. (4)

Serizawa, S., Ishii, T., Nakatani, H., Tsuboi, A., Nagawa, F., Asano, M., Sudo, K., Sakagami, J., Sakano, H., Ijiri, T., Matsuda, Y., Suzuki, M., Yamamori, T., Iwakura, Y., & Sakano, H. (2000). Mutually exclusive expression of odorant receptor transgenes. *Nature Neuroscience, 3,* 687–693. (7)

Serretti, A., Macciardi, F., Cusin, C., Lattuada, E., Lilli, R., & Smeraldi, E. (1998). Dopamine receptor D_4 gene is associated with delusional symptomatology in mood disorders. *Psychiatry Research, 80,* 129–136. (3)

Serruya, M. D., Hatsopoulos, N. G., Paninski, L., Fellows, M. R., & Donoghue, J. P. (2002). Instant neural control of a movement signal. *Nature, 416,* 141–142. (8)

Shadlen, M. N., & Newsome, W. T. (1996). Motion perception: Seeing and deciding. *Proceedings of the National Academy of Sciences, USA, 93,* 628–633. (8)

Shah, A., & Lisak, R. P. (1993). Immunopharmacologic therapy in myasthenia gravis. *Clinical Neuropharmacology, 16,* 97–103. (8)

Shakelford, T. K., Buss, D. M., & Bennett, K. (2002). Forgiveness or breakup: Sex differences in responses to a partner's infidelity. *Cognition and Emotion, 16,* 299–307. (11)

Shalev, A. Y., Peri, T., Brandes, D., Freedman, S., Orr, S. P., & Pitman, R. K. (2000). Auditory startle response in trauma survivors with posttraumatic stress disorder: A prospective study. *American Journal of Psychiatry, 157,* 255–261. (12)

Shapiro, C. M., Bortz, R., Mitchell, D., Bartel, P., & Jooste, P. (1981). Slow-wave sleep: A recovery period after exercise. *Science, 214,* 1253–1254. (9)

Shapiro, K. A., Pascual-Leone, A., Mottaghy, F. M., Gangitano, M., & Caramazza, A. (2001). Grammatical distinctions in the left frontal cortex. *Journal of Cognitive Neuroscience, 13,* 713–720. (14)

Shapley, R. (1995). Parallel neural pathways and visual function. In M. S. Gazzaniga (Ed.), *The cognitive neurosciences* (pp. 315–324). Cambridge, MA: MIT Press. (6)

Sharma, J., Angelucci, A., & Sur, M. (2000). Induction of visual orientation modules in auditory cortex. *Nature, 404,* 841–847. (6)

Shatz, C. J. (1992, September). The developing brain. *Scientific American, 267*(9), 60–67. (5)

Shatz, C. J. (1996). Emergence of order in visual-system development. *Proceedings of the National Academy of Sciences, USA, 93,* 602–608. (6)

Shearman, L. P., Sriram, S., Weaver, D. R., Maywood, E. S., Chaves, I., Zheng, B., Kume, K., Lee, C. C., van der Horst, G. T. J., Hastings, M. H., & Reppert, S. M. (2000). Interacting molecular loops in the mammalian circadian clock. *Science, 288,* 1013–1019. (9)

Sheehan, T. P., Cirrito, J., Numan, M. J., & Numan, M. (2000). Using c-Fos immunocytochemistry to identify forebrain regions that may inhibit maternal behavior in rats. *Behavioral Neuroscience, 114,* 337–352. (11)

Shergill, S. S., Brammer, M. J., Williams, S. C. R., Murray, R. M., & McGuire, P. K. (2000). Mapping auditory hallucinations in schizophrenia using functional magnetic resonance imaging. *Archives of General Psychiatry, 57*, 1033–1038. (15)

Sherin, J. E., Shiromani, P. J., McCarley, R. W., & Saper, C. B. (1996). Activation of ventrolateral preoptic neurons during sleep. *Science, 271*, 216–219. (9)

Sherrington, C. S. (1906). *The integrative action of the nervous system.* New York: Scribner's. (2nd ed.). New Haven, CT: Yale University Press, 1947. (3)

Sherrington, C. S. (1941). *Man on hs nature.* New York: Macmillan. (inside cover)

Sherrington, R., Rogaev, E. I., Liang, Y., Rogaeva, E. A., Levesque, G., Ikeda, M., Chi, H., Lin, C., Li, G., Holman, K., Tsuda, T., Mar, L., Foncin, J.-F., Bruni, A. C., Montesi, M. P., Sorbi, S., Rainero, I., Pinessi, L., Nee, L., Chumakov, I., Pollen, D., Brookes, A., Sanseau, P., Polinsky, R. J., Wasco, W., DaSilva, H. A. R., Haines, J. L., Pericak-Vance, M. A., Tanzi, R. E., Roses, A. D., Fraser, P. E., Rommens, J. M., & St George-Hyslop, P. H. (1995). Cloning of a gene bearing missense mutations in early-onset familial Alzheimer's disease. *Nature, 375*, 754–760. (13)

Shik, M. L., & Orlovsky, G. N. (1976). Neurophysiology of locomotor automatism. *Physiological Reviews, 56*, 465–501. (8)

Shimizu, E., Tang, Y.-P., Rampon, C., & Tsien, J. Z. (2000). NMDA receptor-dependent synaptic reinforcement as a crucial process for memory consolidation. *Science, 290*, 1170–1174. (13)

Shimojo, S., Kamitani, Y., & Nishida, S. (2001). Afterimage of perceptually filled-in surface. *Science, 293*, 1677–1680. (6)

Shimura, H., Schlossmacher, M. G., Hattori, N., Frosch, M. P., Trockenbacher, A., Schneider, R., Mizuno, Y., Kosik, K. S., & Selkoe, D. J. (2001). Ubiquitination of a new form of a-synuclein by parkin from human brain: Implications for Parkinson's disease. *Science, 293*, 263–269. (8)

Shine, R., Phillips, B., Waye, H., LeMaster, M., & Mason, R. T. (2001). Benefits of female mimicry in snakes. *Nature, 414*, 267. (10)

Shirasaki, R., Katsumata, R., & Murakami, F. (1998). Change in chemoattractant responsiveness of developing axons at an intermediate target. *Science, 279*, 105–107. (5)

Shirley, S. G., & Persaud, K. C. (1990). The biochemistry of vertebrate olfaction and taste. *Seminars in the Neurosciences, 2*, 59–68. (7)

Shoham, S., Halgren, E., Maynard, E. M., & Normann, R. A. (2001). Motor-cortical activity in tetraplegics. *Nature, 413*, 793. (8)

Shors, T. J., Miesegaes, G., Beylin, A., Zhao, M., Rydel, T., & Gould, E. (2001). Neurogenesis in the adult is involved in the formation of trace memories. *Nature, 410*, 372–376. (13)

Shoulson, I. (1990). Huntington's disease: Cognitive and psychiatric features. *Neuropsychiatry, Neuropsychology, and Behavioral Neurology, 3*, 15–22. (8)

Shutts, D. (1982). *Lobotomy: Resort to the knife.* New York: Van Nostrand Reinhold. (4)

Siebner, H. R., Limmer, C., Peinemann, A., Drzezga, A., Bloom, B. R., Schwaiger, M., & Conrad, B. (2002). Long-term consequences of switching handedness: A positron emission tomography study on handwriting in "converted" left-handers. *Journal of Neuroscience, 22*, 2816–2825. (14)

Siegel, A., & Pott, C. B. (1988). Neural substrates of aggression and flight in the cat. *Progress in Neurobiology, 31*, 261–283. (12)

Siegel, J. M. (1995). Phylogeny and the function of REM sleep. *Behavioural Brain Research, 69*, 29–34. (9)

Siegel, J. M. (2001). The REM sleep-memory consolidation hypothesis. *Science, 294*, 1058–1063. (9)

Siegel, J. M., Nienhuis, R., Fahringer, H. M., Paul, R., Shiromani, P., Dement, W. C., Mignot, E., & Chiu, C. (1991). Neuronal activity in narcolepsy: Identification of cataplexy-related cells in the medial medulla. *Science, 252*, 1315–1318. (9)

Silberg, J., Pickles, A., Rutter, M., Hewitt, J., Simonoff, E., Maes, H., Carbonneau, R., Murrelle, L., Foley, D., & Eaves, L. (1999). The influence of genetic factors and life stress on depression among adolescent girls. *Archives of General Psychiatry, 56*, 225–232. (15)

Silbersweig, D. A., Stern, E., Frith, C., Cahill, C., Holmes, A., Grootoonk, S., Seaward, J., McKenna, P., Chua, S. E. Schnorr, L., Jones, T., & Frackowiak, R. S. J. (1995). A functional neuroanatomy of hallucinations in schizophrenia. *Nature, 378*, 176–179. (15)

Simon, E. (2000). Interface properties of circumventricular organs in salt and fluid balance. *News in Physiological Sciences, 15*, 61–67. (10)

Singer, W. (1986). Neuronal activity as a shaping factor in postnatal development of visual cortex. In W. T. Greenough & J. M. Jusaska (Eds.), *Developmental neuropsychobiology* (pp. 271–293). Orlando, FL: Academic Press. (6)

Singh, S., & Mallic, B. N. (1996). Mild electrical stimulation of pontine tegmentum around locus coeruleus reduces rapid eye movement sleep in rats. *Neuroscience Research, 24*, 227–235. (9)

Sirigu, A., Grafman, J., Bressler, K., & Sunderland, T. (1991). Multiple representations contribute to body knowledge processing. Evidence from a case of autopagnosia. *Brain, 114*, 629–642. (7)

Sjöström, M., Friden, J., & Ekblom, B. (1987). Endurance, what is it? Muscle morphology after an extremely long distance run. *Acta Physiologica Scandinavica, 130*, 513–520. (8)

Sklar, P., Schwab, S. G., Williams, N. M., Daly, M., Schaffner, S., Maier, W., Albus, M., Trixler, M., Eichhammer, P., Lerer, B., Hallmayer, J., Norton, N., Williams, H., Zammit, S., Cardno, A. G., Jones, S., McCarthy, G., Milanova, V., Kirov, G., O'Donovan, M. C., Lander, E. S., Owen, M. J., & Wildenauer, D. B. (2001). Association analysis of *NOTCH4* loci in schizophrenia using family and population-based controls. *Nature Genetics, 28*, 126–128. (15)

Skottun, B. C. (2000). The magnocellular deficit theory of dyslexia: The evidence from contrast sensitivity. *Vision Research, 40*, 111–127. (14)

Slachevsky, A., Pillon, B., Fourneret, P., Pradat-Diehl, P., Jeannerod, M., & Dubois, B. (2001). Preserved adjustment but impaired awareness in a sensory-motor conflict following prefrontal lesions. *Journal of Cognitive Neuroscience, 13*, 332–340. (8)

Slob, A. K., Bax, C. M., Hop, W. C. J., Rowland, D. L., & van der Werff ten Bosch, J. J. (1996). Sexual arousability and the menstrual cycle. *Psychoneuroendocrinology, 21*, 545–558. (11)

Slotkin, T. A. (1998). Fetal nicotine or cocaine exposure: Which is worse? *Journal of Pharmacology and Experimental Therapeutics, 285*, 931–945. (5)

Smith, C. A. D., Gough, A. C., Leigh, P. N., Summers, B. A., Harding, A. E., Maranganore, D. M., Sturman, S. G., Schapira, A. H. V., Williams, A. C., Spurr, N. K., & Wolf, C. R. (1992). Debrisoquine hydroxylase gene polymorphism and susceptibility to Parkinson's disease. *Lancet, 339*, 1375–1377. (8)

Smith, G. P. (1998). Pregastric and gastric satiety. In G. P. Smith (Ed.), *Satiation: From gut to brain* (pp. 10–39). New York: Oxford University Press. (10)

Smith, G. P. (2000). The controls of eating: A shift from nutritional homeostasis to behavioral neuroscience. *Nutrition, 16*, 814–820. (10)

Smith, G. P., & Gibbs, J. (1998). The satiating effects of cholecystokinin and bombesin-like peptides. In G. P. Smith (Ed.), *Satiation: From gut to brain* (pp. 97–125). New York: Oxford University Press. (10)

Smith, L. T. (1975). The interanimal transfer phenomenon: A review. *Psychological Bulletin, 81*, 1078–1095. (13)

Smith, M. A., Brandt, J., & Shadmehr, R. (2000). Motor disorder in Huntington's disease begins as a dysfunction in error feedback control. *Nature, 403*, 544–549. (8)

Smith, S., Lindefors, N., Hurd, Y., & Sharp, T. (1995). Electroconvulsive shock increases dopamine D1 and D2 receptor mRNA in the nucleus accumbens of the rat. *Psychopharmacology, 120*, 333–340. (15)

Smulders, T. V., Shiflett, M. W., Sperling, A. J., & DeVoogd, T. J. (2000). Seasonal changes in neuron numbers in the hippocampal formation of a food-hoarding bird: The black-capped chickadee. *Journal of Neurobiology, 44*, 414–422. (5)

Snowling, M. J. (1980). The development of grapheme-phoneme correspondence in normal and dyslexic readers. *Journal of Experimental Child Psychology, 29*, 294–305. (14)

Snyder, L. H., Grieve, K. L., Brotchie, P., & Andersen, R. A. (1998). Separate body- and world-referenced representations of visual space in parietal cortex. *Nature, 394*, 887–891. (8)

Soares, C. deN., Almeida, O. P., Joffe, H., & Cohen, L. S. (2001). Efficacy of estradiol for the treatment of depressive disorders in perimenopausal women. *Archives of General Psychiatry, 58*, 529–534. (15)

Sohlberg, M. M., & Mateer, C. A. (2001). Improving attention and managing attentional problems. *Annals of the New York Academy of Sciences, 931*, 359–375. (7)

Solanto, M. V., Abikoff, H., Sonuga-Barke, E., Schachar, R., Logan, G. D., Wigal, T., Hechtman, L., Hinshaw, S., & Turkel, E. (2001). The ecological validity of delay aversion and response inhibition as measures of impulsivity in AD/HD: A supplement to the NIMH multimodal treatment study of AD/HD. *Journal of Abnormal Child Psychology, 29*, 215–228. (7)

Solms, M. (1997). *The neuropsychology of dreams.* Mahwah, NJ: Erlbaum. (9)

Solms, M. (2000). Dreaming and REM sleep are controlled by different brain mechanisms. *Behavioral and Brain Sciences, 23*, 843–850. (9)

Somero, G. N. (1996). Temperature and proteins: Little things can mean a lot. *News in Physiological Sciences, 11*, 72–77. (10)

Somjen, G. G. (1988). Nervenkitt: Notes on the history of the concept of neuroglia. *Glia, 1*, 2–9. (2)

Song, H., Stevens, C. F., & Gage, F. H. (2002). Neural stem cells from adult hippocampus develop essential properties of functional CNS neurons. *Nature Neuroscience, 5*, 438–445. (5)

Sowell, E. R., Thompson, P. M., Holmes, C. J., Jernigan, T. L., & Toga, A. W. (1999). In vivo evidence for post-adolescent brain maturation in frontal and striatal regions. *Nature Neuroscience, 2*, 859–861. (5, 15)

Sowell, E. R., Thompson, P. M., Tessner, K. D., & Toga, A. W. (2001). Mapping continued brain growth and gray matter density reduction in dorsal frontal cortex: Inverse relationships during postadolescent brain maturation. *Journal of Neuroscience, 21*, 8819–8829. (5)

Sperry, R. W. (1943). Visuomotor coordination in the newt (Triturus viridescens) after regeneration of the optic nerve. *Journal of Comparative Neurology, 79*, 33–55. (5)

Sperry, R. W. (1961). Cerebral organization and behavior. *Science, 133*, 1749–1757. (14)

Sperry, R. W. (1975). In search of psyche. In F. G. Worden, J. P. Swazey, & G. Adelman (Eds.), *The neurosciences: Paths of discovery* (pp. 425-434). Cambridge, MA: MIT Press. (inside cover)

Spiegel, T. A. (1973). Caloric regulation of food intake in man. *Journal of Comparative and Physiological Psychology, 84*, 24–37. (10)

Spindler, K. A., Sullivan, E. V., Menon, V., Lim, K. O., & Pfefferbaum, A. (1997). Deficits in multiple systems of working memory in schizophrenia. *Schizophrenia Research, 27*, 1–10. (15)

Spurzheim, J. G. (1908). *Phrenology* (Rev. ed.) Philadelphia: Lippincott. (4)

Squire, L. R. (1992). Memory and the hippocampus: A synthesis from findings with rats, monkeys, and humans. *Psychological Review, 99*, 195–231. (13)

Squire, L. R., Amaral, D. G., & Press, G. A. (1990). Magnetic resonance imaging of the hippocampal formation and mammillary nuclei distinguish medial temporal lobe and diencephalic amnesia. *Journal of Neuroscience, 10*, 3106–3117. (13)

St George-Hyslop, P. H. (2000). Genetic factors in the genesis of

Alzheimer's disease. *Annals of the New York Academy of Sciences, 924,* 1–7. (13)

Stam, R., Croiset, G., Akkermans, L. M. A., & Wiegant, V. M. (1999). Psychoneurogastroenterology: Interrelations in stress-induced colonic motility and behavior. *Physiology & Behavior, 65,* 679–684. (12)

Stanford, L. R. (1987). Conduction velocity variations minimize conduction time differences among retinal ganglion cell axons. *Science, 238,* 358–360. (2)

Stanford, S. C. (1995). Central noradrenergic neurones and stress. *Pharmacology & Therapeutics, 68,* 297–342. (12)

Stanley, B. G., Schwartz, D. H., Hernandez, L., Leibowitz, S. F., & Hoebel, B. G. (1989). Patterns of extracellular 5-hydroxyindoleacetic acid (5-HIAA) in the paraventricular hypothalamus (PVN): Relation to circadian rhythm and deprivation-induced eating behavior. *Pharmacology, Biochemistry, & Behavior, 33,* 257–260. (10)

Starbuck, E. M., & Fitts, D. A. (2001). Influence of the subfornical organ on meal-associated drinking in rats. *American Journal of Physiology, 280,* R669–R677. (10)

Stark, R. E., & McGregor, K. K. (1997). Follow-up study of a right- and a left-hemispherectomized child: Implications for localization and impairment of language in children. *Brain and Language, 60,* 222–242. (14)

Starkstein, S. E., & Robinson, R. G. (1986). Cerebral lateralization in depression. *American Journal of Psychiatry, 143,* 1631. (15)

Starr, C., & Taggart, R. (1989). *Biology: The unity and diversity of life.* Pacific Grove, CA: Brooks/Cole. (4, 7, 8, 11)

Stefanatos, G. A., & Wasserstein, J. (2001). Attention deficit/hyperactivity disorder as a right hemisphere syndrome. *Annals of the New York Academy of Sciences, 931,* 172–195. (7)

Stefanis, N., Frangou, S., Yakeley, J., Sharma, T., O'Connell, P., Morgan, K., Sigmudsson, T., Taylor, M., & Murray, R. (1999). Hippocampal volume reduction in schizophrenia: Effects of genetic risk and pregnancy and birth complications. *Biological Psychiatry, 46,* 689–696. (15)

Steffan, J. S., Bodai, L., Pallos, J., Poelman, M., McCampbell, A., Apostol, B. L., Kazantsev, A., Schmidt, E., Zhu, Y.-Z., Greenwald, M., Kurokawa, R., Housman, D. E., Jackson, G. R., Marsh, J. L., & Thompson, L. M. (2001). Histone deacetylase inhibitors arrest polyglutamine-dependent neurodegeneration in *Drosophila. Nature, 413,* 739–743. (8)

Stein, D. G., & Fulop, Z. L. (1998). Progesterone and recovery after traumatic brain injury: An overview. *Neuroscientist, 4,* 435–442. (5)

Stein, M. B., Goldin, P. R., Sareen, J., Zorrilla, L. T. E., & Brown, G. G. (2002). Increased amygdala activation to angry and contemptuous faces in generalized social phobia. *Archives of General Psychiatry, 59,* 1027–1034. (12)

Stein, M. B., Hanna, C., Koverola, C., Torchia, M., & McClarty, B. (1997). Structural brain changes in PTSD. *Annals of the New York Academy of Sciences, 821,* 76–82. (12)

Steiner, T., Ringleb, P., & Hacke, W. (2001). Treatment options for large hemispheric stroke. *Neurology, 57*(Suppl 2), S61–S68. (5)

Stella, N., Schweitzer, P., & Piomelli, D. (1997). A second endogenous cannabinoid that modulates long-term potentiation. *Nature, 382,* 677–678. (15)

Stephens, T. W., Basinski, M., Bristow, P. K., Bue-Valleskey, J. M., Burgett, S. G., Craft, L., Hale, J., Hoffman, J., Hsiung, H. M., Kriauciunas, A., MacKellar, W., Rosteck, P. R., Jr., Schoner, B., Smith, D., Tinsley, F. C., Zhang, W.-Y., & Heiman, M. (1995). The role of neuropeptide Y in the antiobesity action of the *obese* gene product. *Nature, 377,* 530–532. (10)

Stevens, C. F. (2001). An evolutionary scaling law for the primate visual system and its basis in cortical function. *Nature, 411,* 193–195. (5)

Stevens, T., & Karmiloff-Smith, A. (1997). Word learning in a special population: Do individuals with Williams syndrome obey lexical constraints? *Journal of Child Language, 24,* 737–765. (14)

Stewart, J. W., Quitkin, F. M., McGrath, P. J., Amsterdam, J., Fava, M., Fawcett, J., Reimherr, F., Rosenbaum, J., Beasley, C., & Roback, P. (1998). Use of pattern analysis to predict differential relapse of remitted patients with major depression during 1 year of treatment with fluoxetine or placebo. *Archives of General Psychiatry, 55,* 334–343. (15)

Stickgold, R., James, L., & Hobson, J. A. (2000). Visual discrimination learning requires sleep after training. *Nature Neuroscience, 3,* 1237–1238. (9)

Stickgold, R., Malia, A., Maguire, D., Roddenberry, D., & O'Connor, M. (2000). Replaying the game: Hypnagogic images in normals and amnesics. *Science, 290,* 350–353. (13)

Stickgold, R., Whidbee, D., Schirmer, B., Patel, V., & Hobson, J. (2000). Visual discrimination task improvement: A multi-step process occurring during sleep. *Journal of Cognitive Neuroscience, 12,* 246–254. (9)

Stip, E. (2000). Novel antipsychotics: Issues and controversies. Typicality of atypical antipsychotics. *Journal of Psychiatry & Neuroscience, 25,* 137–153. (15)

Stone, S., Abkevich, V., Hunt, S. C., Gutin, A., Russell, D. L., Neff, C. D., Riley, R., Frech, G. C., Hensel, C. H., Jammulapati, S., Potter, J., Sexton, D., Tran, T., Gibbs, D., Iliev, D., Gress, R., Bloomquist, B., Amatruda, J., Rae, P. M. M., Adams, T. D., Skolnick, M. H., & Shattuck, D. (2002). A major predisposition locus for severe obesity, at 4p15-p14. *American Journal of Human Genetics, 70,* 1459–1468. (10)

Stone, V. E., Nisenson, L., Eliassen, J. C., & Gazzaniga, M. S. (1996). Left hemisphere representations of emotional facial expressions. *Neuropsychologia, 34,* 23–29. (14)

Stoolmiller, M. (1999). Implications of the restricted range of family environments for estimates of heritability and non-shared environment in behavior-genetic adoption studies. *Psychological Bulletin, 125*, 392–409. (1)

Storey, K. B., & Storey, J. M. (1999, May/June). Lifestyles of the cold and frozen. *The Sciences, 39*(3), 33–37. (10)

Stout, A. K., Raphael, H. M., Kanterewicz, B. I., Klann, E., & Reynolds, I. J. (1998). Glutamate-induced neuron death requires mitochondrial calcium uptake. *Nature Neuroscience, 1*, 366–373. (5)

Stowers, L., Holy, T. E., Meister, M., Dulac, C., & Koentges, G. (2002). Loss of sex discrimination and male-male aggression in mice deficient for TRP2. *Science, 295*, 1493–1500. (7)

Strack, F., Martin, L. L., & Stepper, S. (1988). Inhibiting and facilitating conditions of the human smile: A nonobtrusive test of the facial feedback hypothesis. *Journal of Personality and Social Psychology, 54*, 768–777. (12)

Strakowski, S. M., Del Bello, M. P., Sax, K. W., Zimmerman, M. E., Shear, P. K., Hawkins, J. M., & Larson, E. R. (1999). Brain magnetic resonance imaging of structural abnormalities in bipolar disorder. *Archives of General Psychiatry, 56*, 254–260. (15)

Strichartz, G., Rando, T., & Wang, G. K. (1987). An integrated view of the molecular toxinology of sodium channel gating in excitable cells. *Annual Review of Neuroscience, 10*, 237–267. (2)

Stricker, E. M. (1969). Osmoregulation and volume regulation in rats: Inhibition of hypovolemic thirst by water. *American Journal of Physiology, 217*, 98–105. (10)

Stricker, E. M., & Sved, A. F. (2000). Thirst. *Nutrition, 16*, 821–826. (10)

Stricker, E. M., Swerdloff, A. F., & Zigmond, M. J. (1978). Intrahypothalamic injections of kainic acid produce feeding and drinking deficits in rats. *Brain Research, 158*, 470–473. (10)

Strickland, T. L., Miller, B. L., Kowell, A., & Stein, R. (1998). Neurobiology of cocaine-induced organic brain impairment: Contributions from functional neuroimaging. *Neuropsychology Review, 8*, 1–9. (15)

Strittmatter, W. J., & Roses, A. D. (1995). Apolipoprotein E: Emerging story in the pathogenesis of Alzheimer's disease. *The Neuroscientist, 1*, 298–306. (13)

Stryker, M. P., & Sherk, H. (1975). Modification of cortical orientation selectivity in the cat by restricted visual experience: A reexamination. *Science, 190*, 904–906. (6)

Stryker, M. P., Sherk, H., Leventhal, A. G., & Hirsch, H. V. B. (1978). Physiological consequences for the cat's visual cortex of effectively restricting early visual experience with oriented contours. *Journal of Neurophysiology, 41*, 896–909. (6)

Strzelczuk, M., & Romaniuk, A. (1996). Fear induced by the blockade of GABA$_A$-ergic transmission in the hypothalamus of the cat: Behavioral and neurochemical study. *Behavioural Brain Research, 72*, 63–71. (12)

Studer, L., Tabar, V., & McKay, R. D. G. (1998). Transplantation of expanded mesencephalic precursors leads to recovery in parkinsonian rats. *Nature Neuroscience, 1*, 290–295. (8)

Stunkard, A. J., Sorensen, T. I. A., Hanis, C., Teasdale, T. W., Chakraborty, R., Schull, W. J., & Schulsinger, F. (1986). An adoption study of human obesity. *New England Journal of Medicine, 314*, 193–198. (10)

Stuss, D. T., & Benson, D. F. (1984). Neuropsychological studies of the frontal lobes. *Psychological Bulletin, 95*, 3–28. (4)

Suhara, T., Okubo, Y., Yasuno, F., Sudo, Y., Inoue, M., Ichimiya, T., Nakashima, Y., Nakayama, K., Tanada, S., Suzuki, K., Halldin, C., & Farde, L. (2002). Decreased dopamine D$_2$ receptor binding in the anterior cingulate cortex in schizophrenia. *Archives of General Psychiatry, 59*, 25–30. (15)

Sullivan, E. V., Deshmukh, A., Desmond, J. E., Mathalon, D. H., Rosenbloom, M. J., Lim, K. O., & Pfefferbaum, A. (2000). Contribution of alcohol abuse to cerebellar volume deficits in men with schizophrenia. *Archives of General Psychiatry, 57*, 894–902. (15)

Sullivan, R. M., & Gratton, A. (1999). Lateralized effects of medial pre-

frontal cortex lesions on neuroendocrine and autonomic stress responses in rats. *Journal of Neuroscience, 19*, 2834–2840. (12)

Sunaert, S., Van Hecke, P., Marchal, G., & Orban, G. A. (1999). Motion-responsive regions of the human brain. *Experimental Brain Research, 127*, 355–370. (6)

Sunaert, S., Van Hecke, P., Marchal, G., & Orban, G. A. (2000). Attention to speed of motion, speed discrimination, and task difficulty: An fMRI study. *NeuroImage, 11*, 612–623. (6)

Supér, H., Spekreijse, H., & Lamme, V. A. F. (2001). Two distinct modes of sensory processing observed in monkey primary visual cortex (V1). *Nature Neuroscience, 4*, 304–310. (6)

Sur, M., & Leamey, C. A. (2001). Development and plasticity of cortical areas and networks. *Nature Reviews Neuroscience, 2*, 251–262. (6)

Susser, E., Neugebauer, R., Hoek, H. W., Brown, A. S., Lin, S., Labovitz, D., & Gorman, J. M. (1996). Schizophrenia after prenatal famine. *Archives of General Psychiatry, 53*, 25–31. (15)

Sutton, L. C., Lea, E., Will, M. J., Schwartz, B. A., Hartley, C. E., Poole, J. C., Watkins, L. R., & Maier, S. F. (1997). Inescapable shock-induced potentiation of morphine analgesia. *Behavioral Neuroscience, 111*, 1105–1113. (7)

Sutton, R. L., Hovda, D. A., & Feeney, D. M. (1989). Amphetamine accelerates recovery of locomotor function following bilateral frontal cortex ablation in rats. *Behavioral Neuroscience, 103*, 837–841. (5)

Suvisaari, J. M., Haukka, J. K., Tanskanen, A. J., & Lönnqvist, J. K. (1999). Decline in the incidence of schizophrenia in Finnish cohorts born from 1954 to 1965. *Archives of General Psychiatry, 56*, 733–740. (15)

Suzdak, P. D., Glowa, J. R., Crawley, J. N., Schwartz, R. D., Skolnick, P., & Paul, S. M. (1986). A selective imidazobenzodiazepine antagonist of ethanol in the rat. *Science, 234*, 1243–1247. (12)

Swaab, D. F., Chung, W. C. J., Kruijver, F. P. M., Hofman, M. A., &

Ishunina, T. A. (2001). Structural and functional sex differences in the human hypothalamus. *Hormones and Behavior, 40,* 93–98. (11)

Swaab, D. F., & Hofman, M. A. (1990). An enlarged suprachiasmatic nucleus in homosexual men. *Brain Research, 537,* 141–148. (11)

Swaab, D. F., Slob, A. K., Houtsmuller, E. J., Brand, T., & Zhou, J. N. (1995). Increased number of vasopressin neurons in the suprachiasmatic nucleus (SCN) of "bisexual" adult male rats following perinatal treatment with the aromatase blocker ATD. *Developmental Brain Research, 85,* 273–279. (11)

Swoboda, E., Conca, A., König, P., Waanders, R., & Hansen, M. (2001). Maintenance electroconvulsive therapy in affective and schizoaffective disorders. *Neuropsychobiology, 43,* 23–28. (15)

Szymusiak, R. (1995). Magnocellular nuclei of the basal forebrain: Substrates of sleep and arousal regulation. *Sleep, 18,* 478–500. (9)

Tabrizi, S. J., Cleeter, M. W. J., Xuereb, J., Taanman, J.-W., Cooper, J. M., & Schapira, A. H. V. (1999). Biochemical abnormalities and excitotoxicity in Huntington's disease brain. *Annals of Neurology, 45,* 25–32. (8)

Taddese, A., Nah, S. Y., & McCleskey, E. W. (1995). Selective opioid inhibition of small nociceptive neurons. *Science, 270,* 1366–1369. (7)

Tager-Flusberg, H., Boshart, J., & Baron-Cohen, S. (1998). Reading the windows to the soul: Evidence of domain-specific sparing in Williams syndrome. *Journal of Cognitive Neuroscience, 10,* 631–639. (14)

Takeuchi, A. (1977). Junctional transmission: I. Postsynaptic mechanisms. In E. R. Kandel (Ed.), *Handbook of physiology Section 1: Neurophysiology, Vol. 1. Cellular biology of neurons* (Pt. 1, pp. 295–327). Bethesda, MD: American Physiological Society. (3)

Tanaka, J., Hayashi, Y., Nomura, S., Miyakubo, H., Okumura, T., &

Sakamaki, K. (2001). Angiotensinergic and noradrenergic mechanisms in the hypothalamic paraventricular nucleus participate in the drinking response induced by activation of the subfornical organ in rats. *Behavioural Brain Research, 118,* 117–122. (10)

Tanaka, J., Hori, K., & Nomura, M. (2001). Dipsogenic response induced by angiotensinergic pathways from the lateral hypothalamic area to the subfornical organ in rats. *Behavioural Brain Research, 118,* 111–116. (10)

Tanaka, K., Sugita, Y., Moriya, M., & Saito, H.-A. (1993). Analysis of object motion in the ventral part of the medial superior temporal area of the macaque visual cortex. *Journal of Neurophysiology, 69,* 128–142. (6)

Tanaka, Y., Kamo, T., Yoshida, M., & Yamadori, A. (1991). "So-called" cortical deafness. *Brain, 114,* 2385–2401. (7)

Tang, Y.-P., Shimizu, E., Dube, G. R., Rampon, C., Kerchner, G. A., Zhuo, M., Liu, G., & Tsien, J. Z. (1999). Genetic enhancement of learning and memory in mice. *Nature, 401,* 63–69. (13)

Tanji, J., & Shima, K. (1994). Role for supplementary motor area cells in planning several movements ahead. *Nature, 371,* 413–416. (8)

Tanner, C. M., Goldman, S. M., Aston, D. A., Ottman, R., Ellenberg, J., Mayeux, R., & Langston, J. W. (2002). Smoking and Parkinson's disease in twins. *Neurology, 58,* 581–588. (8)

Tanner, C. M., Ottman, R., Goldman, S. M., Ellenberg, J., Chan, P., Mayeux, R., & Langston, J. W. (1999). Parkinson disease in twins: An etiologic study. *Journal of the American Medical Association, 281,* 341–346. (8)

Tarr, M. J., & Gauthier, I. (2000). FFA: A flexible fusiform area for subordinate-level visual processing automatized by experience. *Nature Neuroscience, 3,* 764–769. (6)

Taub, E., & Berman, A. J. (1968). Movement and learning in the absence of sensory feedback. In S. J. Freedman (Ed.), *The neuropsychology of spatially oriented behavior* (pp. 173–192). Homewood, IL: Dorsey. (5)

Taylor, J. P., Hardy, J., & Fischbeck, K H. (2002). Toxic proteins in neurodegenerative disease. *Science, 296,* 1991–1995. (13)

Tebartz van Elst, L. T., Woermann, F. G., Lemieux, L., Thompson, P. J., & Trimble, M. R. (2000). Affective aggression in patients with temporal lobe epilepsy. *Brain, 123,* 234–243. (12)

Teicher, M. H., Glod, C. A., Magnus, E., Harper, D., Benson, G., Krueger, K., & McGreenery, C. E. (1997). Circadian rest-activity disturbances in seasonal affective disorder. *Archives of General Psychiatry, 54,* 124–130. (15)

Teitelbaum, P. (1955). Sensory control of hypothalamic hyperphagia. *Journal of Comparative and Physiological Psychology, 48,* 156–163. (10)

Teitelbaum, P. (1961). Disturbances in feeding and drinking behavior after hypothalamic lesions. In M. R. Jones (Ed.), *Nebraska Symposia on Motivation 1961* (pp. 39–69). Lincoln: University of Nebraska Press. (10)

Teitelbaum, P., & Epstein, A. N. (1962). The lateral hypothalamic syndrome. *Psychological Review, 69,* 74–90. (10)

Teitelbaum, P., Pellis, V. C., & Pellis, S. M. (1991). Can allied reflexes promote the integration of a robot's behavior? In J. A. Meyer & S. W. Wilson (Eds.), *From animals to animats: Simulation of animal behavior* (pp. 97–104). Cambridge, MA: MIT Press/Bradford Books. (8)

Terman, M., Terman, J. S., & Ross, D. C. (1998). A controlled trial of timed bright light and negative air ionization for treatment of winter depression. *Archives of General Psychiatry, 55,* 875–882. (15)

Terrace, H. S., Petitto, L. A., Sanders, R. J., & Bever, T. G. (1979). Can an ape create a sentence? *Science, 206,* 891–902. (14)

Tetrud, J. W., Langston, J. W., Garbe, P. L., & Ruttenber, A. J. (1989). Mild parkinsonism in persons exposed to 1-methyl-4-phenyl-1,2,3,6-tetrahydropyridine (MPTP). *Neurology, 39,* 1483–1487. (8)

Thanickal, T. C., Moore, R. Y., Nienhuis, R., Ramanathan, L., Gulyani, S., Aldrich, M., Cornford, M., & Siegel, J. M. (2000). Reduced number of hypocretin neurons in human narcolepsy. *Neuron, 27,* 469–474. (9)

Thase, M. E., Greenhouse, J. B., Frank, E., Reynolds, C. F., III, Pilkonis, P. A., Hurley, K., Grochocinski, V., & Kupfer, D. J. (1997). Treatment of major depression with psychotherapy or psychotherapy-psychopharmacology combinations. *Archives of General Psychiatry, 54,* 1009–1015. (15)

Thase, M. E., Trivedi, M. H., & Rush, A. J. (1995). MAOIs in the contemporary treatment of depression. *Neuropsychopharmacology, 12,* 185–219. (15)

Thiele, A., Henning, P., Kubischik, K.-P., & Hoffman, K.-P. (2002). Neural mechanisms of saccadic suppression. *Science, 295,* 2460–2462. (6)

Thier, P., Dicke, P. W., Haas, R., & Barash, S. (2000). Encoding of movement time by populations of cerebellar Purkinje cells. *Nature, 405,* 72–76. (8)

Thomas, K. M., Drevets, W. C., Dahl, R. E., Ryan, N. D., Birmaher, B., Eccard, C. H., Axelson, D., Whalen, P. J., & Casey, B. J. (2001). Amygdala response to fearful faces in anxious and depressed children. *Archives of General Psychiatry, 58,* 1057–1063. (12)

Thomas, P. K. (1988). Clinical aspects of PNS regeneration. In S. G. Waxman (Ed.), *Advances in neurology* (Vol. 47, pp. 9–29). New York: Raven Press. (5)

Thompson, P. M., Cannon, T. D., Narr, K. L., van Erp, T., Poutanen, V.-P., Huttunen, M., Lönnqvist, J., Standertskjöld-Nordenstam, C.-G., Kaprio, J., Khaledy, M., Dail, R., Zoumalan, C. I., & Toga, A. W. (2001a). Genetic influences on brain structure. *Nature Neuroscience, 4,* 1253–1258. (1, 4)

Thompson, P. M., Vidal, C., Giedd, J. N., Gochman, P., Blumenthal, J., Nicolson, R., Toga, A. W., & Rapoport, J. L. (2001b). Mapping adolescent brain change reveals dynamic wave of accelerated gray matter loss in very early-onset schizophrenia. *Proceedings of the National Academy of Sciences, USA, 98,* 11650–11655. (15)

Thompson, R. F. (1986). The neurobiology of learning and memory. *Science, 233,* 941–947. (13)

Tian, B., Reser, D., Durham, A., Kustov, A., & Rauschecker, J. P. (2001). Functional specialization in rhesus monkey auditory cortex. *Science, 292,* 290–293. (7)

Ticku, M. K., & Kulkarni, S. K. (1988). Molecular interactions of ethanol with GABAergic system and potential of Ro15-4513 as an ethanol antagonist. *Pharmacology Biochemistry and Behavior, 30,* 501–510. (12)

Tinbergen, N. (1951). *The study of instinct.* Oxford, England: Oxford University Press. (1)

Tinbergen, N. (1973). The search for animal roots of human behavior. In N. Tinbergen (Ed.), *The animal in its world* (Vol. 2, pp. 161–174). Cambridge, MA: Harvard University Press. (1)

Tingate, T. R., Lugg, D. J., Muller, H. K., Stowe, R. P., & Pierson, D. L. (1997). Antarctic isolation: Immune and viral studies. *Immunology and Cell Biology, 75,* 275–283. (12)

Tippin, J., & Henn, F. A. (1982). Modified leukotomy in the treatment of intractable obsessional neurosis. *American Journal of Psychiatry, 139,* 1601–1603. (4)

Toh, K. L., Jones, C. R., He, Y., Eide, E. J., Hinz, W. A., Virshup, D. M., Ptáček, L. J., & Fu, Y.-H. (2001). An h*Per₂* phosphorylation site mutation in familial advanced sleep phase syndrome. *Science, 291,* 1040–1043. (9)

Tominaga, M., Caterina, M. J., Malmberg, A. B., Rosen, T. A., Gilbert, H., Skinner, K., Raumann, B. E., Basbaum, A. I., & Julius, D. (1998). The cloned capsaicin receptor integrates multiple pain-producing stimuli. *Neuron, 21,* 531–543. (7)

Toni, N., Buchs, P.-A., Nikonenko, I., Bron, C. R., & Muller, D. (1999). LTP promotes formation of multiple spine synapses between a single axon terminal and a dendrite. *Nature, 402,* 421–425. (13)

Torrey, E. F. (1986). Geographic variations in schizophrenia. In C. Shagass, R. C. Josiassen, W. H. Bridger, K. J. Weiss, D. Stoff, & G. M. Simpson (Eds.), *Biological*

psychiatry 1985 (pp. 1080–1082). New York: Elsevier. (15)

Torrey, E. F., Bowler, A. E., & Clark, K. (1997). Urban birth and residence as risk factors for psychoses: An analysis of 1880 data. *Schizophrenia Research, 25,* 169–176. (15)

Torrey, E. F., Miller, J., Rawlings, R., & Yolken, R. H. (1997). Seasonality of births in schizophrenia and bipolar disorder: A review of the literature. *Schizophrenia Research, 28,* 1–38. (15)

Townsend, J., Courchesne, E., Covington, J., Westerfield, M., Harris, N. S., Lyden, P., Lowry, T. P., & Press, G. A. (1999). Spatial attention deficits in patients with acquired or developmental cerebellar abnormality. *Journal of Neuroscience, 19,* 5632–5643. (8)

Tranel, D., & Damasio, A. (1993). The covert learning of affective valence does not require structures in hippocampal system or amygdala. *Journal of Cognitive Neuroscience, 5,* 79–88. (13)

Travers, S. P., Pfaffmann, C., & Norgren, R. (1986). Convergence of lingual and palatal gustatory neural activity in the nucleus of the solitary tract. *Brain Research, 365,* 305–320. (7)

Trefilov, A., Berard, J., Krawczak, M., & Schmidtke, J. (2000). Natal dispersal in rhesus macaques is related to serotonin transporter gene promoter variation. *Behavior Genetics, 30,* 295–301. (12)

Trejo, J. L., Carro, E., & Torres-Alemán, I. (2001). Circulating insulin-like growth factor I mediates exercise-induced increases in the number of new neurons in the adult hippocampus. *Journal of Neuroscience, 21,* 1628–1634. (5)

Trevarthen, C. (1974). Cerebral embryology and the split brain. In M. Kinsbourne & W. L. Smith (Eds.), *Hemispheric disconnection and cerebral function* (pp. 208–236). Springfield, IL: Thomas. (14)

Trimble, M. R., & Thompson, P. J. (1986). Neuropsychological and behavioral sequelae of spontaneous seizures. *Annals of the New York Academy of Sciences, 462,* 284–292. (15)

Trivers, R. L. (1985). *Social evolution*. Menlo Park: Benjamin/Cummings. (1)

Trout, J. D. (2001). The biological basis of speech: What to infer from talking to the animals. *Psychological Review, 108*, 523–549. (14)

True, W. R., Xian, H., Scherer, J. F., Madden, P. A. F., Bucholz, K. K., Heath, A. C., Eisen, S. A., Lyons, M. J., Goldberg, J., & Tsuang, M. (1999). Common genetic vulnerability for nicotine and alcohol dependence in men. *Archives of General Psychiatry, 56*, 655–661. (15)

Tsai, G., Passani, L. A., Slusher, B. S., Carter, R., Baer, L., Kleinman, J. E., & Coyle, J. T. (1995). Abnormal excitatory neurotransmitter metabolism in schizophrenic brains. *Archives of General Psychiatry, 52*, 829–836. (15)

Tsai, G. E., Ragan, P., Chang, R., Chen, S., Linnoila, M. I., & Coyle, J. T. (1998). Increased glutamatergic neurotransmission and oxidative stress after alcohol withdrawal. *American Journal of Psychiatry, 155*, 726–732. (15)

Ts'o, D. Y., & Roe, A. W. (1995). Functional compartments in visual cortex: Segregation and interaction. In M. S. Gazzaniga (Ed.), *The cognitive neurosciences* (pp. 325–337). Cambridge, MA: MIT Press. (6)

Tsujita, T., Niikawa, N., Yamashita, H., Imamura, A., Hamada, A., Nakane, Y., & Okazaki, Y. (1998). Genomic discordance between monozygotic twins discordant for schizophrenia. *American Journal of Psychiatry, 155*, 422–424. (15)

Tsunoda, K., Yamane, Y., Nishizaki, M., & Tanifuji, M. (2001). Complex objects are represented in macaque inferotemporal cortex by the combination of feature columns. *Nature Neuroscience, 4*, 832–838. (6)

Tu, G. C., & Israel, Y. (1995). Alcohol consumption by Orientals in North America is predicted largely by a single gene. *Behavior Genetics, 25*, 59–65. (15)

Tucker, D. M., Luu, P., & Pribram, K. H. (1995). Social and emotional self-regulation. *Annals of the New York Academy of Sciences, 769*, 213–239. (8)

Tucker, K. L., Meyer, M., & Barde, Y.-A. (2001). Neurotrophins are required for nerve growth during development. *Nature Neuroscience, 4*, 29–37. (5)

Turner, R. S., & DeLong, M. R. (2000). Corticostriatal activity in primary motor cortex of the macaque. *Journal of Neuroscience, 20*, 7096–7108. (8)

Tyler, L. K., deMornay-Davies, P., Anokhina, R., Longworth, C., Randall, B., & Marslen-Wilson, W. D. (2002). Dissociations in processing past tense morphology: Neuropathology and behavioral studies. *Journal of Cognitive Neuroscience, 14*, 79–94. (14)

Uchida, N., Takahashi, Y. K., Tanifuji, M., & Mori, K., (2000). Odor maps in the mammalian olfactory bulb: Domain organization and odorant structural features. *Nature Neuroscience, 3*, 1035–1043. (7)

Uchino, B. N., Cacioppo, J. T., & Kiecolt-Glaser, J. K. (1996). The relationship between social support and physiological processes: A review with emphasis on underlying mechanisms and implications for health. *Psychological Bulletin, 119*, 488–531. (12)

Udry, J. R., & Morris, N. M. (1968). Distribution of coitus in the menstrual cycle. *Nature, 220*, 593–596. (11)

Ullman, M. T. (2001). A neurocognitive perspective on language: The declarative/procedural model. *Nature Reviews Neuroscience, 2*, 717–726. (14)

Uwano, T., Nishijo, H., Ono, T., & Tamura, R. (1995). Neuronal responsiveness to various sensory stimuli, and associative learning in the rat amygdala. *Neuroscience, 68*, 339–361. (12)

Vaillant, G. E., & Milofsky, E. S. (1982). The etiology of alcoholism: A prospective viewpoint. *American Psychologist, 37*, 494–503. (15)

Vaishnavi, S., Calhoun, J., & Chatterjee, A. (2001). Binding personal and peripersonal space: Evidence from tactile extinction. *Journal of Cognitive Neuroscience, 13*, 181–189. (7)

Vakil, E., Kahan, S., Huberman, M., & Osimani, A. (2000). Motor and non-motor sequence learning in patients with basal ganglia lesions: The case of serial reaction time (SRT). *Neuropsychologia, 38*, 1–10. (8)

Valvo, A. (1971). *Sight restoration after long-term blindness*. New York: American Foundation for the Blind. (6)

Valzelli, L. (1973). The "isolation syndrome" in mice. *Psychopharmacologia, 31*, 305–320. (12)

Valzelli, L. (1980). *An approach to neuroanatomical and neurochemical psychophysiology*. Torino, Italy: C. G. Edizioni Medico Scientifiche. (10, 15)

Valzelli, L., & Bernasconi, S. (1979). Aggressiveness by isolation and brain serotonin turnover changes in different strains of mice. *Neuropsychobiology, 5*, 129–135. (12)

van den Pol, A. N. (1999). Hypothalamic hypocretin (orexin): Robust innervation of the spinal cord. *Journal of Neuroscience, 19*, 3171–3182. (10)

Van der Does, A. J. W. (2001). The effects of tryptophan depletion on mood and psychiatric symptoms. *Journal of Affective Disorders, 64*, 107–119. (12)

van Dellen, A., Blakemore, C., Deacon, R., York, D., & Hannan, A. J. (2000). Delaying the onset of Huntington's in mice. *Nature, 404*, 721–722. (8)

Van Essen, D. C., & DeYoe, E. A. (1995). Concurrent processing in the primate visual cortex. In M. S. Gazzaniga (Ed.), *The cognitive neurosciences* (pp. 383–400). Cambridge, MA: MIT Press. (6)

van Honk, J., Tuiten, A., Hermans, E., Putman, P., Koppenschaar, H., Thijssen, J., Verbaten, R., & van Doornen, L. (2001). A single administration of testosterone induces cardiac accelerative responses to angry faces in healthy young women. *Behavioral Neuroscience, 115*, 238–242. (12)

Van Lancker, D., & Fromkin, V. A. (1973). Hemispheric specialization for pitch and "tone": Evidence from Thai. *Journal of Phonetics, 1*, 101–109. (14)

van Praag, H., Kempermann, G., & Gage, F. H. (1999). Running increases cell proliferation and neurogenesis in the adult mouse dentate gyrus. *Nature Neuroscience, 2*, 266–270. (5)

van Praag, H., Kempermann, G., & Gage, F. H. (2000). Neural consequences of environmental enrichment. *Nature Reviews Neuroscience, 1*, 191–198. (5)

van Praag, H., Schinder, A. F., Christie, B. R., Toni, N., Palmer, T. D., & Gage, F. H. (2002). Functional neurogenesis in the adult hippocampus. *Nature, 415*, 1030–1034. (5)

Van Zoeren, J. G., & Stricker, E. M. (1977). Effects of preoptic, lateral hypothalamic, or dopamine-depleting lesions on behavioral thermoregulation in rats exposed to the cold. *Journal of Comparative and Physiological Psychology, 91*, 989–999. (10)

van Zutphen, B. (2001). European researchers encourage improvement in lab animal welfare. *Nature, 409*, 452. (1)

Vandenberghe, R., Nobre, A. C., & Price, C. J. (2002). The response of left temporal cortex to sentences. *Journal of Cognitive Neuroscience, 14*, 550–560. (14)

Vanderweele, D. A. (1998). Insulin as a satiating signal. In G. P. Smith (Ed.), *Satiation: From gut to brain* (pp. 198–216). New York: Oxford University Press. (10)

Vanduffel, W., Fize, D., Mandeville, J. B., Nelissen, K., Van Hecke, P., Rosen, B. R., Tottell, R. B. H., & Orban, G. A. (2001). Visual motion processing investigated using contrast agent-enhanced fMRI in awake behaving monkeys. *Neuron, 32*, 565–577. (6)

Varela, F., Lachaux, J.-P., Rodriguez, E., & Martinerie, J. (2001). The brainweb: Phase synchronization and large-scale integration. *Nature Reviews Neuroscience, 2*, 229–239. (4)

Vaswani, M., & Kapur, S. (2001). Genetic basis of schizophrenia: Trinucleotide repeats an update. *Progress in Neuro-Psychopharmacology & Biological Psychiatry, 25*, 1187–1201. (15)

Vataja, R., Pohjasvaara, T., Leppävuori, A., Mäantylä, R., Aronen, H. J., Salonen, O., Kastre, M., & Erkinjuntti, T. (2001). Magnetic resonance imaging correlates of depression after ischemic stroke. *Archives of General Psychiatry, 58*, 925–931. (15)

Velakoulis, D., Pantelis, C., McGorry, P. D., Dudgeon, P., Brewer, W., Cook, M., Desmond, P., Bridle, N., Tierney, P., Murrie, V., Singh, B., & Copolov, D. (1999). Hippocampal volume in first-episode psychoses and chronic schizophrenia. *Archives of General Psychiatry, 56*, 133–140. (15)

Vellutti, R. A. (1997). Interactions between sleep and sensory physiology. *Journal of Sleep Research, 6*, 61–77. (9)

Verdoux, H., Geddes, J. R., Takei, N., Lawrie, S. M., Bovet, P., Eagles, J. M., Heun, R., McCreadie, R. G., McNeil, T. F., O'Callaghan, E., Stöber, G., Williger, U., Wright, P., & Murray, R. M. (1997). Obstetric complications and age at onset in schizophrenia: An international collaborative meta-analysis of individual patient data. *American Journal of Psychiatry, 154*, 1220–1227. (15)

Verhage, M., Maia, A. S., Plomp, J. J., Brussard, A. B., Heeroma, J. H., Vermeer, H., Toonen, R. F., Hammer, R. E., van den Berg, T. K., Missler, M., Geuze, H. J., & Südhof, T. C. (2000). Synaptic assembly of the brain in the absence of neurotransmitter secretion. *Science, 287*, 864–869. (5)

Verrey, F., & Beron, J. (1996). Activation and supply of channels and pumps by aldosterone. *News in Physiological Sciences, 11*, 126–133. (10)

Victor, M., Adams, R. D., & Collins, G. H. (1971). *The Wernicke-Korsakoff syndrome*. Philadelphia: Davis. (13)

Villarreal, D. M., Do, V., Haddad, E., & Derrick, B. E. (2002). NMDA receptor antagonists sustain LTP and spatial memory: Active processes mediate LTP decay. *Nature Neuroscience, 5*, 48–52. (13)

Virkkunen, M., DeJong, J., Bartko, J., Goodwin, F. K., & Linnoila, M. (1989). Relationship of psychobiological variables to recidivism in violent offenders and impulsive fire setters. *Archives of General Psychiatry, 46*, 600–603. (12)

Virkkunen, M., Eggert, M., Rawlings, R., & Linnoila, M. (1996). A prospective follow-up study of alcoholic violent offenders and fire setters. *Archives of General Psychiatry, 53*, 523–529. (12)

Virkkunen, M., Nuutila, A., Goodwin, F. K., & Linnoila, M. (1987). Cerebrospinal fluid monoamine metabolite levels in male arsonists. *Archives of General Psychiatry, 44*, 241–247. (12)

Virkkunen, M., Rawlings, R., Tokola, R., Poland, R. E., Guidotti, A., Nemeroff, C., Bissette, G., Kalogeras, K., Karonen, S.-L., & Linnoila, M. (1994). CSF biochemistries, glucose metabolism, and diurnal activity rhythms in alcoholic, violent offenders, fire setters, and healthy volunteers. *Archives of General Psychiatry, 51*, 20–27. (15)

Visser, E. K., Beersma, G. M., & Daan, S. (1999). Melatonin suppression by light in humans is maximal when the nasal part of the retina is illuminated. *Journal of Biological Rhythms, 14*, 116–121. (9)

Vogels, R., Biederman, I., Bar, M., & Lorincz, A. (2001). Inferior temporal neurons show greater sensitivity to nonaccidental than to metric shape differences. *Journal of Cognitive Neuroscience, 13*, 444–453. (6)

Volavka, J., Czobor, P., Goodwin, D. W., Gabrielli, W. F., Penick, E. C., Mednick, S. A., Jensen, P., Knop, J., & Schulsinger, F. (1996). The electroencephalogram after alcohol administration in high-risk men and the development of alcohol use disorders 10 years later. *Archives of General Psychiatry, 53*, 258–263. (15)

Volkow, N. D., Wang, G.-J., Fischman, M. W., Foltin, R. W., Fowler, J. S., Abumrad, N. N., Vitkum, S., Logan, J., Gatley, S. J., Pappas, N., Hitzemann, R., & Shea, C. E. (1997). Relationship between subjective effects of cocaine and dopamine transporter occupancy. *Nature, 386*, 827–830. (15)

Volkow, N. D., Wang, G.-J., & Fowler, J. S. (1997). Imaging studies of cocaine in the human brain and studies of the cocaine addict. *Annals of the New York Academy of Sciences, 820*, 41–55. (15)

Volkow, N. D., Wang, G.-J., Fowler, J. S., Gatley, S. J., Logan, J., Ding, Y.-S., Hitzemann, R., & Pappas, N. (1998). Dopamine transporter occupancies in the human brain induced by therapeutic doses of oral methylphenidate. *American Journal of Psychiatry, 155*, 1325–1331. (7, 15)

Volkow, N. D., Wang, G.-J., Fowler, J. S., Logan, J., Gatley, S. J., Hitzemann, R., Chen, A. D., Dewey, S. L., & Pappas, N. (1997). Decreased striatal dopaminergic responsiveness in detoxified cocaine-dependent subjects. *Nature, 386*, 830–833. (15)

von Békésy, G. (1956). Current status of theories of hearing. *Science, 123*, 779–783. (7)

von Gall, C., Garabette, M. L., Kell, C. A., Frenzel, S., Dehghani, F., Schumm-Draeger, P. M., Weaver, D. R., Korf, H.-W., Hastings, M. H., & Stehle, J. H., (2002). Rhythmic gene expression in pituitary depends on heterologous sensitization by the neurohormone melatonin. *Nature Neuroscience, 5*, 234–238. (9)

von Melchner, L., Pallas, S. L., & Sur, M. (2000). Visual behaviour mediated by retinal projections directed to the visual pathway. *Nature, 404*, 871–876. (6)

Vouloumanos, A., Kiehl, K. A., Werker, J. F., & Liddle, P. F. (2001). Detection of sounds in the auditory stream: Event-related fMRI evidence for differential activation to speech and nonspeech. *Journal of Cognitive Neuroscience, 13*, 994–1005. (14)

Voytko, M. L. (2002). Estrogen and the cholinergic system modulate visuospatial attention in monkeys (*Macaca fascicularis*). *Behavioral Neuroscience, 116*, 187–197. (11)

Vrba, E. S. (1998). Multiphasic growth models and the evolution of prolonged growth exemplified by human brain evolution. *Journal of Theoretical Biology, 190*, 227–239. (5)

Vuilleumier, P., Armony, J. L., Driver, J., & Dolan, R. J. (2001). Effects of attention and emotion on face processing in the human brain: An event-related fMRI study. *Neuron, 30*, 829–841. (12)

Waelti, P., Dickinson, A., & Schultz, W. (2001). Dopamine responses comply with basic assumptions of formal learning theory. *Nature, 412*, 43–48. (15)

Wagner, A. D., Schacter, D. L., Rotte, M., Koutstaal, W., Maril, A., Dale, A. M., Rosen, B. R., & Buckner, R. L. (1998). Building memories: Remembering and forgetting of verbal experiences as predicted by brain activity. *Science, 281*, 1188–1191. (6)

Waisbren, S. R., Brown, M. J., de Sonneville, L. M. J., & Levy, H. L. (1994). Review of neuropsychological functioning in treated phenylketonuria: An information-processing approach. *Acta Paediatrica, 83*(Suppl. 407), 98–103. (1)

Waldvogel, J. A. (1990). The bird's eye view. *American Scientist, 78*, 342–353. (6)

Walker-Batson, D., Smith, P., Curtis, S., Unwin, H., & Greenlee, R. (1995). Amphetamine paired with physical therapy accelerates motor recovery after stroke: Further evidence. *Stroke, 26*, 2254–2259. (5)

Wallesch, C.-W., Henriksen, L., Kornhuber, H.-H., & Paulson, O. B. (1985). Observations on regional cerebral blood flow in cortical and subcortical structures during language production in normal man. *Brain and Language, 25*, 224–233. (14)

Wallman, J., & Pettigrew, J. D. (1985). Conjugate and disjunctive saccades in two avian species with contrasting oculomotor strategies. *Journal of Neuroscience, 5*, 1418–1428. (6)

Walsh, D. M., Klyubin, I., Fadeeva, J. V., Cullen, W. K., Anwyl, R., Wolfe, M. S., Rowan, M. J., & Selkoe, D. J. (2002). Naturally secreted oligomers of amyloid β protein potently inhibit hippocampal long-term potentiation *in vivo*. *Nature, 416*, 535–539. (13)

Walsh, V., & Cowey, A. (2000). Transcranial magnetic stimulation and cognitive neuroscience. *Nature Reviews Neuroscience, 1*, 73–79. (4)

Wang, A., Liang, Y., Fridell, R. A., Probst, F. J., Wilcox, E. R., Touchman, J. W., Morton, C. C., Morell, R. J., Noben-Trauth, K., Camper, S. A., & Friedman, T. B. (1998). Associations of unconventional myosin *MYO15* mutations with human nonsyndromic deafness *DFNB3*. *Science, 280*, 1447–1451. (7)

Wang, H., & Tessier-Lavigne, M. (1999). *En passant* neurotrophic action of an intermediate axonal target in the developing mammalian CNS. *Nature, 401*, 765–769. (5)

Wang, Q., Schoenlein, R. W., Peteanu, L. A., Mathies, R. A., & Shank, C. V. (1994). Vibrationally coherent photochemistry in the femtosecond primary event of vision. *Science, 266*, 422–424. (6)

Wang, T., Okano, Y., Eisensmith, R., Huang, S. Z., Zeng, Y. T., Wilson, H. Y. L., & Woo, S. L. (1989). Molecular genetics of phenylketonuria in Orientals: Linkage disequilibrium between a termination mutation and haplotype 4 of the phenylalanine hydroxylase gene. *American Journal of Human Genetics, 45*, 675–680. (1)

Warach, S. (1995). Mapping brain pathophysiology and higher cortical function with magnetic resonance imaging. *The Neuroscientist, 1*, 221–235. (5)

Ward, I. L., Bennett, A. L., Ward, O. B., Hendricks, S. E., & French, J. A. (1999). Androgen threshold to activate copulation differs in male rats prenatally exposed to alcohol, stress, or both factors. *Hormones and Behavior, 36*, 129–140. (11)

Ward, I. L., & Reed, J. (1985). Prenatal stress and prepubertal social rearing conditions interact to determine sexual behavior in male rats. *Behavioral Neuroscience, 99*, 301–309. (11)

Ward, I. L., Romeo, R. D., Denning, J. H., & Ward, O. B. (1999). Fetal alcohol exposure blocks full masculinization of the dorsolateral nucleus in rat spinal cord. *Physiology & Behavior, 66*, 571–575. (11)

Ward, I. L., Ward, B., Winn, R. J., & Bielawski, D. (1994). Male and female sexual behavior potential of male rats prenatally exposed to the influence of alcohol, stress, or both factors. *Behavioral Neuroscience, 108,* 1188–1195. (11)

Ward, I. L., & Ward, O. B. (1985). Sexual behavior differentiation: Effects of prenatal manipulations in rats. In N. Adler, D. Pfaff, & R. W. Goy (Eds.), *Handbook of behavioral neurobiology,* Vol. 7 (pp. 77–98). New York: Plenum Press. (11)

Ward, O. B., Monaghan, E. P., & Ward, I. L. (1986). Naltrexone blocks the effects of prenatal stress on sexual behavior differentiation in male rats. *Pharmacology Biochemistry and Behavior, 25,* 573–576. (11)

Ward, O. B., Ward, I. L., Denning, J. H., French, J. A., & Hendricks, S. E. (2002). Postparturitional testosterone surge in male offspring of rats stressed and/or fed ethanol during late pregnancy. *Hormones and Behavior, 41,* 229–235. (11)

Ward, R., Danziger, S., Owen, V., & Rafal, R. (2002). Deficits in spatial coding and feature binding following damage to spatiotopic maps in the human pulvinar. *Nature Neuroscience, 5,* 99–100. (4)

Warren, R. M. (1999). *Auditory perception.* Cambridge, England: Cambridge University Press. (7)

Warrington, E. K., & Weiskrantz, L. (1968). New method for testing long-term retention with special reference to amnesic patients. *Nature, 217,* 972–974. (13)

Waxman, S. G., & Ritchie, J. M. (1985). Organization of ion channels in the myelinated nerve fiber. *Science, 228,* 1502–1507. (2)

Weaver, D. R. (1997). Reproductive safety of melatonin: A "wonder drug" to wonder about. *Journal of Biological Rhythms, 12,* 682–689. (9)

Webb, W. B. (1974). Sleep as an adaptive response. *Perceptual and Motor Skills, 38,* 1023–1027. (9)

Weber-Fox, C. M., & Neville, H. J. (1996). Maturational constraints on functional specializations for language processing: ERP and behavioral evidence in bilingual speakers. *Journal of Cognitive Neuroscience, 8,* 231–256. (14)

Wehr, T. A., Turner, E. H., Shimada, J. M., Lowe, C. H., Barker, C., &

Leinbenluft, E. (1998). Treatment of a rapidly cycling bipolar patient by using extended bed rest and darkness to stabilize the timing and duration of sleep. *Biological Psychiatry, 43,* 822–828. (15)

Wei, F., Wang, G.-D., Kerchner, G. A., Kim, S. J., Xu, H.-M., Chen, Z.-F., & Zhuo, M. (2001). Genetic enhancement of inflammatory pain by forebrain NR2B overexpression. *Nature Neuroscience, 4,* 164–169. (7)

Weidensaul, S. (1999). *Living on the wind.* New York: North Point Press. (10)

Weinberger, D. R. (1996). On the plausibility of "the neurodevelopmental hypothesis" of schizophrenia. *Neuropsychopharmacology, 14,* 1S–11S. (15)

Weinberger, D. R. (1999). Cell biology of the hippocampal formation in schizophrenia. *Biological Psychiatry, 45,* 395–402. (15)

Weinberger, D. R., & McClure, R. K. (2002). Neurotoxicity, neuroplasticity, and magnetic resonance imaging morphometry: What is happening in the schizophrenic brain? *Archives of General Psychiatry, 59,* 553–558. (15)

Weindl, A. (1973). Neuroendocrine aspects of circumventricular organs. In W. F. Ganong & L. Martini (Eds.), *Frontiers in neuroendocrinology 1973* (pp. 3–32). New York: Oxford University Press. (10)

Weiner, R. D. (1979). The psychiatric use of electrically induced seizures. *American Journal of Psychiatry, 136,* 1507–1517. (15)

Weingarten, P., & Zhou, Q.-Y. (2001). Protection of intracellular dopamine cytotoxicity by dopamine disposition and metabolism factors. *Journal of Neurochemistry, 77,* 776–785. (8)

Weiskrantz, L., Warrington, E. K., Sanders, M. D., & Marshall, J. (1974). Visual capacity in the hemianopic field following a restricted occipital ablation. *Brain, 97,* 709–728. (6)

Weiss, J. M. (1971). Effects of coping behavior in different warning signal conditions on stress pathology in rats. *Journal of Comparative and Physiological Psychology, 77,* 1–13. (12)

Weiss, P. (1924). Die funktion transplantierter amphibienextremitäten. Aufstellung einer resonanztheorie der motorischen nerventätigkeit auf grund abstimmter endorgane [The function of transplanted amphibian limbs. Presentation of a resonance theory of motor nerve action upon tuned end organs]. *Archiv für Mikroskopische Anatomie und Entwicklungsmechanik, 102,* 635–672. (5)

Weller, L., Weller, A., Koresh-Kamin, H., & Ben-Shoshan, R. (1999). Menstrual synchrony in a sample of working women. *Psychoneuroendocrinology, 24,* 449–459. (7)

Weller, L., Weller, A., & Roizman, S. (1999). Human menstrual synchrony in families and among close friends: Examining the importance of mutual exposure. *Journal of Comparative Psychology, 113,* 261–268. (7)

Wellman, P. J. (2000). Norepinephrine and the control of food intake. *Nutrition, 16,* 837–842. (10)

Wender, P. H., Kety, S. S., Rosenthal, D., Schulsinger, F., Ortmann, J., & Lunde, I. (1986). Psychiatric disorders in the biological and adoptive families of adopted individuals with affective disorders. *Archives of General Psychiatry, 43,* 923–929. (15)

Wender, P. H., Wolf, L. E., & Wasserstein, J. (2001). Adults with ADHD. *Annals of the New York Academy of Sciences, 931,* 1–16. (7)

Wessberg, J., Stambaugh, C. R., Kralik, J. D., Beck, P. D., Laubach, M., Chapin, J. K., Kim, J., Biggs, S. J., Srinivasan, M. A., & Nicolelis, M. A. L. (2000). Real-time prediction of hand trajectory by ensembles of cortical neurons in primates. *Nature, 408,* 361–365. (8)

Wessinger, C. M., Fendrich, R., & Gazzaniga, M. S. (1997). Islands of residual vision in hemianopic patients. *Journal of Cognitive Neuropsychology, 9,* 203–221. (6)

Wessinger, C. M., VanMeter, J., Tian, B., Van Lare, J., Pekar, J., & Rauschecker, J. P. (2001). Hierarchical organization of the human auditory cortex revealed by functional magnetic resonance imaging. *Journal of Cognitive Neuroscience, 13*, 1–7. (7)

Westbrook, G. L. (1994). Glutamate receptor update. *Current Opinion in Neurobiology, 4*, 337–346. (3)

Westbrook, G. L., & Jahr, C. E. (1989). Glutamate receptors in excitatory neurotransmission. *Seminars in the Neurosciences, 1*, 103–114. (3)

Whalen, P. J. (1998). Fear, vigilance, and ambiguity: Initial neuroimaging studies of the human amygdala. *Current Directions in Psychological Science, 7*, 177–188. (12)

Whalen, P. J., Shin, L. M., McInerney, S. C., Fischer, H., Wright, C. I., & Rauch, S. L. (2001). A functional MRI study of human amygdala responses to facial expressions of fear versus anger. *Emotion, 1*, 70–83. (12)

White, D. P., Gibb, T. J., Wall, J. M., & Westbrook, P. R. (1995). Assessment of accuracy and analysis time of a novel device to monitor sleep and breathing in the home. *Sleep, 18*, 115–126. (9)

White, L. E., Coppola, D. M., & Fitzpatrick, D. (2001). The contribution of sensory experience to the maturation of orientation selectivity in ferret visual cortex. *Nature, 411*, 1049–1052. (6)

Whitman, B. W., & Packer, R. J. (1993). The photic sneeze reflex: Literature review and discussion. *Neurology, 43*, 868–871. (8)

Whitney, K. D., & McNamara, J. O. (2000). GluR3 autoantibodies destroy neural cells in a complement-dependent manner modulated by complement regulatory proteins. *Journal of Neuroscience, 20*, 7307–7316. (14)

Wichmann, T., Vitek, J. L., & DeLong, M. R. (1995). Parkinson's disease and the basal ganglia: Lessons from the laboratory and from neurosurgery. *The Neuroscientist, 1*, 236–244. (8)

Wiedemann, G., Pauli, P., Dengler, W., Lutzenberger, W., Birbaumer, N., & Buchkremer, G. (1999). Frontal brain asymmmetry as a biological substrate of emotions in patients with panic disorders. *Archives of General Psychiatry, 56*, 78–84. (14)

Wiedemann, K., Jahn, H., Yassouridis, A., & Kellner, M. (2001). Anxiolyticlike effects of atrial natriuretic peptide on cholecystokinin tetrapeptide-induced panic attacks. *Archives of General Psychiatry, 58*, 371–377. (12)

Wiersma, D., Nienhuis, F. J., Slooff, C. J., & Giel, R. (1998). Natural course of schizophrenic disorders: A 15-year follow-up of a Dutch incidence cohort. *Schizophrenia Bulletin, 24*, 75–85. (15)

Wiesel, T. N. (1982). Postnatal development of the visual cortex and the influence of environment. *Nature, 299*, 583–591. (6, inside cover)

Wiesel, T. N., & Hubel, D. H. (1963). Single-cell responses in striate cortex of kittens deprived of vision in one eye. *Journal of Neurophysiology, 26*, 1003–1017. (6)

Wild, H. M., Butler, S. R., Carden, D., & Kulikowski, J. J. (1985). Primate cortical area V4 important for colour constancy but not wavelength discrimination. *Nature, 313*, 133–135. (6)

Willerman, L., Schultz, R., Rutledge, J. N., & Bigler, E. D. (1991). In vivo brain size and intelligence. *Intelligence, 15*, 223–228. (5)

Williams, C. L. (1986). A reevaluation of the concept of separable periods of organizational and activational actions of estrogens in development of brain and behavior. *Annals of the New York Academy of Sciences, 474*, 282–292. (11)

Williams, C. L., Men, D., Clayton, E. C., & Gold, P. E. (1998). Norepinephrine release in the amygdala after systemic injection of epinephrine or escapable footshock: Contribution of the nucleus of the solitary tract. *Behavioral Neuroscience, 112*, 1414–1422. (13)

Williams, M. T., Davis, H. N., McCrea, A. E., Long, S. J., & Hennessy, M. B. (1999). Changes in the hormonal concentrations of pregnant rats and their fetuses following multiple exposures to a stressor during the third trimester. *Neurotoxicology and Teratology, 21*, 403–414. (11)

Williams, R. S. B., Cheng, L., Mudge, A. W., & Harwood, A. J. (2002). A common mechanism of action for three mood-stabilizing drugs. *Nature, 417*, 292–295. (15)

Williams, R. W., & Herrup, K. (1988). The control of neuron number. *Annual Review of Neuroscience, 11*, 423–453. (2, 8)

Williams, T. (1999, May–June). Management by majority. *Audubon, 101*(3), 40–49. (1)

Willie, J. T., Chemelli, R. M., Sinton, C. M., & Yanagisawa, M. (2001). To eat or to sleep? Orexin in the regulation of feeding and wakefulness. *Annual Review of Neuroscience, 24*, 429–458. (10)

Willingham, D. B., Koroshetz, W. J., & Peterson, E. W. (1996). Motor skills have diverse neural bases: Spared and impaired skill acquisition in Huntington's disease. *Neuropsychology, 10*, 315–321. (8)

Willis, G. L., & Armstrong, S. M. (1999). A therapeutic role for melatonin antagonism in experimental models of Parkinson's disease. *Physiology & Behavior, 66*, 785–795. (9)

Wilson, B. A., Baddeley, A. D., & Kapur, N. (1995). Dense amnesia in a professional musician following herpes simplex virus encephalitis. *Journal of Clinical and Experimental Neuropsychology, 17*, 668–681. (13)

Wilson, D. S., & Sober, E. (1994). Reintroducing group selection to the human behavioral sciences. *Behavioral and Brain Sciences, 17*, 585–654. (1)

Wilson, J. D., George, F. W., & Griffin, J. E. (1981). The hormonal control of sexual development. *Science, 211*, 1278–1284. (11)

Wilson, R. I., & Nicoll, R. A. (2001). Endogenous cannabinoids mediate retrograde signalling at hippocampal synapses. *Nature, 410*, 588–592. (15)

Wilson, R. I., & Nicoll, R. A. (2002). Endocannabinoid signaling in the brain. *Science, 296*, 678–682. (15)

Winer, G. A., Cottrell, J. F., Gregg, V., Fournier, J. S., & Bica. L. A. (2002). Fundamentally misunderstanding visual perception: Adults' belief in visual emissions. *American Psychologist, 57*, 417–424. (6)

Winfree, A. T. (1983). Impact of a circadian clock on the timing of human sleep. *American Journal of Physiology, 245,* R497–R504. (9)

Winokur, A., Gary, K. A., Rodner, S., Rae-Red, C., Fernando, A. T., & Szuba, M. P. (2001). Depression, sleep physiology, and antidepressant drugs. *Depression and Anxiety, 14,* 19–28. (15)

Winston, J. S., Strange, B. A., O'Doherty, J., & Dolan, R. J. (2002). Automatic and intentional brain responses during evaluation of trustworthiness of faces. *Nature Neuroscience, 5,* 277–283. (12)

Wirz-Justice, A. (1998). Beginning to see the light. *Archives of General Psychiatry, 55,* 861–862. (15)

Wirz-Justice, A., Werth, E., Renz, C., Müller, S., & Kräuchi, K. (2002). No evidence for a phase delay in human circadian rhythms after a single morning melatonin administration. *Journal of Pineal Research, 32,* 1–5. (9)

Wise, R. A. (1996). Addictive drugs and brain stimulation reward. *Annual Review of Neuroscience, 19,* 319–340. (15)

Wise, R. A., & Bozarth, M. A. (1987). A psychomotor stimulant theory of addiction. *Psychological Review, 94,* 469–492. (15)

Witelson, S. F., Glezer, I. I., & Kigar, D. L. (1995). Women have greater density of neurons in posterior temporal cortex. *Journal of Neuroscience, 15,* 3418–3428. (11)

Witelson, S. F., Kigar, D. L., & Harvey, T. (1999). The exceptional brain of Albert Einstein. *Lancet, 353,* 2149–2153. (4)

Witelson, S. F., & Pallie, W. (1973). Left hemisphere specialization for language in the newborn: Neuroanatomical evidence of asymmetry. *Brain, 96,* 641–646. (14)

Wolf, S. (1995). Dogmas that have hindered understanding. *Integrative Physiological and Behavioral Science, 30,* 3–4. (12)

Wolff, P. H. (1993). Impaired temporal resolution in developmental dyslexia. *Annals of the New York Academy of Sciences, 682,* 87–103. (14)

Wolkin, A., Rusinek, H., Vaid, G., Arena, L., Lafargue, T., Sanfilipo, M., Loneragan, C., Lautin, A., &

Rotrosen, J. (1998). Structural magnetic resonance image averaging in schizophrenia. *American Journal of Psychiatry, 155,* 1064–1073. (15)

Wong, M.-L., & Licinio, J. (2001). Research and treatment approaches to depression. *Nature Reviews Neuroscience, 2,* 343–351. (15)

Wong-Riley, M. T. T. (1989). Cytochrome oxidase: An endogenous metabolic marker for neuronal activity. *Trends in Neurosciences, 12,* 94–101. (2)

Woodruff-Pak, D. S., Papka, M., & Ivry, R. B. (1996). Cerebellar involvement in eyeblink classical conditioning in humans. *Neuropsychology, 10,* 443–458. (13)

Woods, S. C., & Seeley, R. J. (2000). Adiposity signals and the control of energy homeostasis. *Nutrition, 16,* 894–902. (10)

Woodworth, R. S. (1934). *Psychology* (3rd ed.). New York: Holt. (2)

Woolf, N. J. (1991). Cholinergic systems in mammalian brain and spinal cord. *Progress in Neurobiology, 37,* 475–524. (4)

Woolf, N. J. (1996). Global and serial neurons form a hierarchically arranged interface proposed to underlie memory and cognition. *Neuroscience, 74,* 625–651. (9)

Wright, I. C., Rabe-Hesketh, S., Woodruff, P. W. R., David, A. S., Murray, R. M., & Bullmore, E. T. (2000). Meta-analysis of regional brain volumes in schizophrenia. *American Journal of Psychiatry, 157,* 16–25. (15)

Writing Group for the Women's Health Initiative Investigators. (2002). Risks and benefits of estrogen plus progestin in healthy postmenopausal women. *Journal of the American Medical Association, 288,* 321–333. (11)

Wulfeck, B., & Bates, E. (1991). Differential sensitivity to errors of agreement and word order in Broca's aphasia. *Journal of Cognitive Neuroscience, 3,* 258–272. (14)

Wurtman, J. J. (1985). Neurotransmitter control of carbohydrate consumption. *Annals of the New York Academy of Sciences, 443,* 145–151. (3)

Wüst, S., Kasten, E., & Sabel, B. A. (2002). Blindsight after optic nerve injury indicates functionality of spared fibers. *Journal of Cognitive Neuroscience, 14,* 243–253. (6)

Yabuta, N. H., Sawatari, A., & Callaway, E. M. (2001). Two functional channels from primary visual cortex to dorsal visual cortical areas. *Science, 292,* 297–300. (6)

Yamamoto, S., & Kitazawa, S. (2001). Reversal of subjective temporal order due to arm crossing. *Nature Neuroscience, 4,* 759–765. (2)

Yamamoto, T. (1984). Taste responses of cortical neurons. *Progress in Neurobiology, 23,* 273–315. (7)

Yamamoto, Y., Akiyoshi, J., Kiyota, A., Katsuragi, S., Tsutsumi, T., Isogawa, K., & Nagayama, H. (2000). Increased anxiety behavior in OLETF rats without cholecystokinin-A receptor. *Brain Research Bulletin, 53,* 789–792. (12)

Yanagisawa, K., Bartoshuk, L. M., Catalanotto, F. A., Karrer, T. A., & Kveton, J. F. (1998). Anesthesia of the chorda tympani nerve and taste phantoms. *Physiology & Behavior, 63,* 329–335. (7)

Yang, L.-Y., & Clemens, L. G. (2000). MPOA lesions affect female pacing of copulation in rats. *Behavioral Neuroscience, 114,* 1191–1202. (11)

Yehuda, R. (1997). Sensitization of the hypothalamic-pituitary-adrenal axis in posttraumatic stress disorder. *Annals of the New York Academy of Sciences, 821,* 57–75. (12)

Yehuda, R. (2002). Post-traumatic stress disorder. *New England Journal of Medicine, 346,* 108–114. (12)

Yeomans, J. S., & Frankland, P. W. (1996). The acoustic startle reflex: Neurons and connections. *Brain Research Reviews, 21,* 301–314. (12)

Yost, W. A., & Nielsen, D. W. (1977). *Fundamentals of hearing.* New York: Holt, Rinehart & Winston. (7)

Young, A. B. (1995). Huntington's disease: Lessons from and for molecular neuroscience. *The Neuroscientist, 1,* 51–58. (8)

Young, G. B., & Pigott, S. E. (1999). Neurobiological basis of consciousness. *Archives of Neurology, 56,* 153–157. (9)

Young, W. C., Goy, R. W., & Phoenix, C. H. (1964). Hormones and sexual behavior. *Science, 143,* 212–218. (11)

Yu, T. W., & Bargmann, C. I. (2001). Dynamic regulation of axon guidance. *Nature Neuroscience Supplement, 4,* 1169–1176. (5)

Zaccato, C., Ciammola, A., Rigamonti, D., Leavitt, B. R., Goffredo, D., Conti, L., MacDonald, M. E., Friedlander, R. M., Silani, V., Hayden, M. R., Timmusk, T., Sipione, S., & Cattaneo, E. (2001). Loss of huntingtin-mediated BDNF gene transcription in Huntington's disease. *Science, 293,* 493–498. (8)

Zahn, T. P., Rapoport, J. L., & Thompson, C. L. (1980). Autonomic and behavioral effects of dextroamphetamine and placebo in normal and hyperactive prepubertal boys. *Journal of Abnormal Child Psychology, 8,* 145–160. (7)

Zakharenko, S. S., Zablow, L., & Siegelbaum, S. A. (2001). Visualization of changes in presynaptic function during long-term synaptic plasticity. *Nature Neuroscience, 4,* 711–717.(13)

Zandi, P. P., Carlson, M. C., Plassman, B. L., Welsh-Bohmer, K. A., Mayer, L. S., Steffens, D. C., & Breitner, J. C. S. (2002). Hormone replacement therapy and incidence of Alzheimer disease in older women. *Journal of the American Medical Association, 288,* 2123–2129. (11)

Zangara, A., Blair, R. J. R., & Curran, H. V. (2002). A comparison of the effects of a b-adrenergic blocker and a benzodiazepine upon the recognition of human facial expressions. *Psychopharmacology, 163,* 36–41. (12)

Zeevalk, G. D., Manzino, L., Hoppe, J., & Sonsalla, P. (1997). In vivo vulnerability of dopamine neurons to inhibition of energy metabolism. *European Journal of Pharmacology, 320,* 111–119. (8)

Zeki, S. (1980). The representation of colours in the cerebral cortex. *Nature, 284,* 412–418. (6)

Zeki, S. (1983). Colour coding in the cerebral cortex: The responses of wavelength-selective and colour-coded cells in monkey visual cortex to changes in wavelength composition. *Neuroscience, 9,* 767–781. (6)

Zeki, S. (1998). Parallel processing, asynchronous perception, and a distributed system of consciousness in vision. *Neuroscientist, 4,* 365–372. (6)

Zeki, S., McKeefry, D. J., Bartels, A., & Frackowiak, R. S. J. (1998). Has a new color area been discovered? *Nature Neuroscience, 1,* 335. (6)

Zeki, S., & Shipp, S. (1988). The functional logic of cortical connections. *Nature, 335,* 311–317. (6)

Zeman, A. (2001). Consciousness. *Brain, 124,* 1263–1289. (1)

Zhang, X., & Firestein, S. (2002). The olfactory receptor gene superfamily of the mouse. *Nature Neuroscience, 5,* 124–133. (7)

Zhang, Y., Proenca, R., Maffei, M., Barone, M., Leopold, L., & Friedman, J. M. (1994). Positional cloning of the mouse *obese* gene and its human homologue. *Nature, 372,* 425–432. (10)

Zheng, B., Larkin, D. W., Albrecht, U., Sun, Z. S., Sage, M., Eichele, G., Lee, C. C., & Bradley, A. (1999). The *mPer2* gene encodes a functional component of the mammalian circadian clock. *Nature, 400,* 169–173. (9)

Zhou, F., Zhu, X., Castellani, R. J., Stimmelmayr, R., Perry, G., Smith, M. A., & Drew, K. L. (2001). Hibernation, a model of neuroprotection. *American Journal of Pathology, 158,* 2145–2151. (9)

Zihl, J., von Cramon, D., & Mai, N. (1983). Selective disturbance of movement vision after bilateral brain damage. *Brain, 106,* 313–340. (6)

Zola, S. M., Squire, L. R., Teng, E., Stefanacci, L., Buffalo, E. A., & Clark, R. E. (2000). Impaired recognition memory in monkeys after damage limited to the hippocampal region. *Journal of Neuroscience, 20,* 451–463. (13)

Zou, Z., Horowitz, L. F., Montmayeur, J.-P., Snapper, S., & Buck, L. B. (2001). Genetic tracing reveals a stereotyped sensory map in the olfactory cortex. *Nature, 414,* 173–179. (7)

Zurif, E. B. (1980). Language mechanisms: A neuropsychological perspective. *American Scientist, 68,* 305–311. (14)

Credits

Chapter 1

James Balog/Getty Images **2:** Courtesy of Dr. Dana Copeland **3:** top left, © Dan McCoy/Rainbow **3:** © Dorr/Premium Stock/PictureQuest **3:** bottom right, © Steve Maslowski/Photo Researchers **4:** Gary Bell/Seapics.com **4:** left, © Frank Siteman/Stock Boston **5:** From Descartes', Treaties on Man. **13:** Courtesy of Professor Bruce Dudek **16:** bottom left, © Alain Le Garsmeur/CORBIS **16:** top right, © F. J. Hierschel/Okapia/Photo Researchers **18:** © Nigel J. Dennis; Gallo Images/CORBIS **22:** bottom left, Barbara Aulicino/American Scientist **22:** center left, © David M. Barron/Animals Animals **22:** top left, © Gonfier/Photo Researchers **22:** center right, © Frans Lanting/Photo Researchers **23:** Courtesy of the Foundation for Biomedical Research

Chapter 2

28: © CNRI/Photo Researchers **31:** Micrograph courtesy of Dennis M. D. Landis **32:** Photo courtesy of Bob Jacobs, Colorado College **33:** From K. M. Harris and J. K. Stevens, Society for Neuroscience, Dendritic Spines of CA1 Pyramidal Cells in the Rat Hippocampus: Serial Electron Microscopy with Reference to their Biophysical Characteristics, Journal of Neuroscience, 9, 1989, 2982–2997. Copyright © 1989 Society for Neuroscience. Reprinted by permission. **34:** Part e, from R. G. Coss, Brain Research, October 1982. Reprinted by permission of R. G. Coss. **35:** Reprinted from "Changes in Dendritic Branching of Adult Mammalian Neurons Revealed by Repeated Imaging in Situ," by D. Purves and R. D. Hadley, Nature, 315, pp. 404–406. Copyright © 1985 Macmillan Magazines, Ltd. Reprinted by permission of D. Purves and Macmillan Magazines, Ltd. **36:** top, © Nancy Kedersha/UCLA/SLP/Photo Researchers **36:** right, © Nancy Kedersha/UCLA/SLP/Photo Researchers **40:** © Fritz Goro

Chapter 3

52: © Eye of Science/Photo Researchers **64:** Dennis M. D. Landis **64:** top right, From, "Studying neural organization and aplysia with the scanning electron micrograph" by E. R. Lewis, et al., Science, 1969, 165:1142. Copyright 1969 by the AAAS. Reprinted with permission of AAS and E.R. Lewis **65:** From M. Harel, R. Kasher, A. Nicolas, J. M. Guss, M. Balass, M. Fredkin, A. B. Smit, K. Brejc, T. K. Sixma, E. Katzir, J. L. Sussman, & S. Fuchs (2001). Neuron, 32, 265–275. Reprinted with permission. **65:** From M. Kasher, A. Nicolas, J. M. Guss, M. Balass, M. Fredkin, A. B. Smit, K. Brejc, T. K. Sixma, E. Katachalski-Katzir, J. L. Sussman, & S. Fuchs (2001). Neuron, 32, 265–275. Reprinted with permission.

Chapter 4

72: © Hank Morgan/Rainbow **74:** Dan McCoy/Rainbow **76:** Courtesy Tomas Paus, McGill University. From Paus, T. Combination of Transcranial Magnetic Stimulation with Brain Imaging. In: J. Mazziotta, A. Toga (Eds.). Brain Mapping: The Methods. Second Edition Academic Press, pp. 691–705, 2002. Figure 1. **78:** Historical Pictures Services, Chicago/Getty Images and Sandra F. Witelson **78:** left, © Stock Montage; right (all) Figure 2, p. 2151, From Witelson, S. F., Kigar, D. L. & Harvey T. (1999). The exceptional brain of Albert Einstein, Lancet, 353, 2149–2153. **81:** Left and right: Dr. Dana Copeland; middle: © Lester V. Bergman/CORBIS **83:** top, Manfred Kage/Peter Arnold, Inc. **83:** bottom, Manfred Kage/Peter Arnold, Inc. **84:** Adapted from Biology: The Unity and Diversity of Life, 5th Edition, by C. Starr and R. Taggart, p. 340. Copyright © 1989 Wadsworth. **89:** Photos courtesy of Dr. Dana Copeland **92:** Adapted from "Cholinergic Systems in Mammalian Brain and Spinal Cord," by N. J. Woolf, Progress in Neurobiology, 37, pp. 475–524, 1991. Reprinted by permission of the author. **92:** Photos courtesy of Dr. Dana Copeland **94:** Photos courtesy of Dr. Dana Copeland **95:** From S. W. Ranson and S. L. Clark, The Anatomy of the Nervous System, 1959, Copyright © 1959 W. B. Saunders Co.. Reprinted by permission. **96:** T. W. Deacon, 1990. **97:** Adapted from The Cerebral Cortex of Man by W. Penfield and T. Rasmussen, Macmillan Library Reference. Reprinted by permission of The Gale Group. **98:** After The Prefrontal Cortex by J. M. Fuster, 1989, Raven Press. Reprinted by permission. **101:** Figure 2.2, page 391, of commentary by W. Singer referring to article: E. Rodriguez et al. (1999). Perception's shadow: long-distance synchronization of human brain activity. Nature, 397, 430–433. Used with permission of the author.

Chapter 5

106: © Geoff Tompkinson/SPL/Photo Researchers **108:** Both; Doug Goodman/Photo Researchers **110:** Dana Copeland **111:** From N. G. Forger and S. M. Breedlove, Motoneuronal Death in the Human Fetus, Journal of Comparative Neurology, 264, 1987, 118–122. Copyright © 1987 Alan R. Liss, Inc.. Reprinted by permission of N. G. Forger. **112:** © Will and Demi McIntyre/Photo Researchers **116:** From D. Purves and J. W. Lichtman, Elimination of Synapses in the Developing Nervous System, Science, 210, 1980, 153–157. Copyright © 1980 American Association for the Advancement of Science. Reprinted by permission. **116:** top right, Richard Coss **117:** Reprinted from Neuroscience: From the Molecular to the Cognitive, by R. Hari, 1994, p. 165, with kind permission from Elsevier Science-NL, Sara Burgerhartstraat 25, 1055 KV Amsterdam, The Netherlands. **118:** Reprinted with permission from "Increased Cortical Representation of the Fingers of the Left Hand in String Players," by T. Elbert, C. Panter, C. Weinbruch, B. Rockstrah, and E. Taub, Science 2, 270, pp. 305–307. Copyright © 1995 American Association for the Advancement of Science. **118:** Reprinted with permission from "Increased Cortical Representation of the Finges of the Left Hand in String Players," by T. Elbert, C. Panter, C. Weinbruch, and E. Taub, Science, 270, pp. 305–307. Copyright © 1995 AAAS. **121:** Fig 1, p. 1055 in R. A. Barton & R. H. Harvey, "Mosaic evolution of brain structure in mammals." Nature, 405, pp. 1055–1058.

P. Teitelbaum, pp. 39–69, in M. R. Jones, Ed., 1961, Nebraska Symposium on Motivation. Copyright © 1961 by the University of Nebraska Press. Copyright © renewed 1989 by the University of Nebraska Press. **313:** Yoav Levy/Phototake **314:** Reprinted from Nutrition, 16, J. M. de Castro, "Eating Behavior: Lessons from the Real World of Humans," pp. 800–813, copyright 2000, with permission from Elsevier Science. **315:** Reprinted from Nutrition, 16, J. M. de Castro, "Eating Behavior: Lessons from the Real World of Humans," pp. 800–813, copyright 2000, with permission from Elsevier Science. **315:** Zhang et al., 1994. Photo courtesy John Sholtis/The Rockefeller University **316:** From "Peptide YY (PYY), a potent orexigenic agent," by J. E. Morley, A. S. Levine, M. Grace, and J. Kneip, Brain Research, 1985, 341, 200–203. **317:** Reprinted with permission from Dr. Juan Dominguez.

Chapter 11
322: Art Wolfe **335:** From "Rise in Female-Initiated Sexual Activity at Ovulation and Its Suppression by Oral Contraceptives," by D. B. Adams, A. R. Gold, and A. D. Burt, 1978, New England Journal of Medicine, 299, pp. 1145–1150. Reprinted by permission of The New England Journal of Medicine. **337:** From " A defect in nurturing in mice lacking the immediate early gene fosB," by Brown, J. R., Ye H. Bronson, R. T., Dikkes, P., and Greenberg, M. E., Cell, 86, 297–309. **343:** bottom right, Courtesy of Intersex Society of North America **343:** top, "Man-Woman/Boy-Girl," 1972/John Money & Enke Erhardt, Baltimore/John Hopkins University Press **344:** From Abnormal Sexual Development by D. D. Federman, 1967, Used by permission of W. B. Saunders Company. **347:** From "Sex-hormone-dependent brain differntiation and sexual functions" by G. Dorner, in G. Dorner (ed), Endocrinology of sex. Copyright 1975 by permission of Johann Ambrosius Barth **349:** left, Both, reprinted with permission from "A Difference in Hypothalamic Structure Between Heterosexual and Homosexual Men," by S. LeVay, Science, 253, pp. 1034–1037. Copyright © 1991 American Association for the Advancement of Science. **349:** Reprinted with permission from "A Difference in Hypothalamic Structure Between Heterosexual and Homosexual Men," by S. LeVay, Science, 253, pp. 1034–1037. Copyright © 1991 American Association for the Advancement of Science. **349:** Reprinted with permission from "A Difference in Hypothalamic Structure Between Heterosexual and Homosexual Men," by S. LeVay, Science, 253, pp. 1034–1037. Copyright © 1991 American Association for the Advancement of Science.

Chapter 12
354: Gunnar Strom **361:** © Kathleen Olson **373:** From "Maternal Smoking During Pregnancy and Adult Male Criminal Outcomes," by P. A. Brennan, E. R. Grekin, and S. A. Mednick, Archives of General Psychiatry, 56, p. 219. Copyright © 1999 American Medical Association. Reprinted by permission. **373:** Photo courtesy of Dana Copeland **375:** From "Neuronal constellations in aggressive behavior" by Jose Delgado, in L. Valzellis and L. Morgese (eds) Aggression and violence: A psycho/biological and clinical approach, Edizioni Saint Vincent, 1981. **378:** © Joe McBride/Getty Images **380:** From "Fear and the Human Amygdala," by R. Adolphs, D. Tranel, H. Damasio, and A. Damasio, Journal of Neuroscience, 15, pp. 5879–5891. Copyright © 1995 Oxford University Press. Reprinted by permission. **383:** Courtesy of Jules Asher. From "New Drug Counters Alcohol Intoxication" by G. Kolata, 1986, Science, 234: 1199. Copyright 1986 by the AAAS. Used by permission of AAAS.

Chapter 13
386: Tim Davis/CORBIS **396:** top right, courtesy Dr. Dana Copeland; bottom, (all) courtesy David Amaral and Suzanne Corkin **397:** Reproduced with permission of author and publisher from Gollins, E. S. Developmental studies of visual recognition of incomplete objects. Perceptual and Motor Skills, 1960, 11, 289–298. © Southern Universities Press 1960. **398:** Reproduced with permission of author and publisher from Gollins, E. S. Developmental studies of visual recognition of incomplete objects. Perceptual and Motor Skills, 1960, 11, 289–298. © Southern Universities Press 1960. **399:** Reproduced with permission of author and publisher from Gollins, E. S. Developmental studies of visual recognition of incomplete objects. Perceptual and Motor Skills, 1960, 11, 289–298. © Southern Universities Press 1960. **399:** © Robert Folz/Visuals Unlimited, Inc. **400:** Reproduced with permission of author and publisher from Gollins, E. S. Developmental studies of visual recognition of incomplete objects. Perceptual and Motor Skills, 1960, 11, 289–298. © Southern Universities Press 1960. **400:** Reproduced with permission of author and publisher from Gollins, E. S. Developmental studies of visual recognition of incomplete objects. Perceptual and Motor Skills, 1960, 11, 289–298. © Southern Universities Press 1960. **401:** all, © Tom Vezo/The Wildlife Collection **404:** top, Dr. M. Goedert/Science Photo Library/Photo Researchers **404:** both, courtesy of Dr. Robert D. Terry, Department of Neurosciences, School of Medicine, University of California at San Diego **405:** After "Dendritic changes," by A. B. Scheibel, p. 70. In B. Reisberg, Ed.,

Alzheimer's Disease, 1983. Free Press. **408:** From G. A. Horridge, "Learning of Leg Position by the Ventral Nerve Cord in Headless Insects." Proceedings of the Royal Society of London, B, 157, 1962, 33–52. Copyright © 1962 The Royal Society of London. Reprinted by permission of the Royal Society of London and G. A. Horridge. **409:** © H. Chaumeton/Nature **410:** Redrawn from "Neuronal Mechanisms of Habituation and Dishabituation of the Gill-Withdrawal Reflex in Aplysia," by V. Castellucci, H. Pinsker, I. Kupfermann, and E. Kandel, Science, 1970, 167, pp. 1745–1748. Copyright © 1970 by AAAS. Used by permission of AAAS and V. Castellucci.

Chapter 14
418: © David Young-Wolff/PhotoEdit **421:** Photo Courtesy of Dana Copeland **426:** From "Subcortical Transfer of Higher Order Information: More Illusory than Real?," by A. Kingstone and M. S. Gazzaniga, 1995. Neuropsychology, 9, pp. 321–328. Copyright © 1995 American Psychological Association. Reprinted with permission. **427:** From "Asymmetry of perception in free viewing of chimeric faces" by J. Levy, W. Heller, M. T. Banich and L. A. Burton, Brain and Cognition, 1983, 2:404–419. Used by permission of Academic Press. **429:** From "Human Brain: Left-Right Asymmetries in Temporal Speech Region," by N. Geschwind and W. Levitsky, 1968, Science, 161, pp. 186–187. Copyright © 1968 by AAAS and N. Geschwind. Reprinted with permission. **433:** Photo courtesy of Ann Premack **434:** From Georgia State University's Language Research Center, operated with Yerkes Primate Center of Emory. Photo courtesy of Duane Rumbaugh **435:** David Carter **437:** © Michael Dick/Animals Animals **438:** From "Williams Syndrome: An Unusual Neuropsychological Profile," by U. Bellugi, P. O. Way, and T. L. Jernigan, S. H. Broman and J. Grafman, Eds., Atypical Cognitive Deficits in Developmental Disorders. Copyright © 1987 Lawrence Erlbaum. Reprinted by permission. **442:** Wallesch, Henriksen, Kornhuber, & Paulson, 1985 **446:** Reprinted from "Task-Determined Strategies of Visual Process," by G. Geiger, J. Y. Lettvin, & U. Zagarra-Moran, 1992, Cognitive Brain Research, 1, pp. 39–52, 1992, with kind permission of Elsevier Science-NL, Sara Burgerhartstraat 25, 1055 KV Amsterdam, The Netherlands.

Chapter 15
427: From Psychiatric Mental Health Nursing by E. Janosik and J. Davies, p. 173. Copyright © 1986 Jones and Bartlett Publishers. Reprinted with permission. **450:** Wellcome Dept. of Cognitive Neurology/Science Photo

Name Index

Subject Glossary/Index

Note: Italicized page numbers refer to figures, illustrations, and tables.

Aβ_{42}. *See* Amyloid beta protein
Abducens nerve, *87*
Ablation the removal of a structure, 130
Absence seizure a type of epilepsy in which people have brief periods, less than a minute, when they stare blankly without talking or moving; then they do something without any apparent purpose, 356
Absolute refractory period the time immediately after an action potential, when the sodium gates close and the membrane cannot produce an action potential in response to stimulation of any intensity, 44
Accessory nerve, *87*
Acetaldehyde a toxic substance produced by the metabolism of alcohol, 460
Acetic acid a chemical that the body uses as a source of energy, 460
Acetylcholine a chemical similar to an amino acid, except that the NH_2 group has been replaced by an $N(CH_3)_3$ group; a neurotransmitter:
 and Alzheimer's disease, 405
 and arousal, 275
 inactivation and reuptake of, 66
 and muscles, 229–230
 and parasympathetic nervous system, 85
 receptors for, 65, *65*
 and sleep, 278, 281
 synthesis of, 62, 63, *63*
Acetylcholinesterase an enzyme that breaks acetylcholine into acetate and choline, 66
Across-fiber pattern principle the notion that each receptor responds to a wide range of stimuli and contributes to the perception of every

stimulus in its system, 208, 212, 237
ACTH (adrenocorticotropic hormone) a hormone that stimulates the human adrenal cortex to release cortisol and the rat adrenal gland to release corticosterone, *325*, 327, 366
Action potential rapid depolarization and slight reversal of the usual polarization caused by stimulation beyond the threshold, 42–47, *42, 43*
 and audition, 190–191
 and brain development, 120
 and color vision, 150
 and muscles, 229, 232
 and myelin sheaths, 45–47, *46*
 propagation of, 45, *45*
 and vestibular sensation, 197
Activating effect temporary effect of a hormone on behavior or anatomy, occurring only while the hormone is present, 329, 331–337
Activation-synthesis hypothesis the view that during dreams, various parts of the cortex are activated by the input arising from the pons plus whatever stimuli are present in the room, and the cortex synthesizes a story to make sense of all the activity, 288
Active transport protein-mediated process that expends energy to pump chemicals from the blood into the brain, 37
Acute conditions conditions having a sudden onset and a strong possibility of ending quickly, 477
Adaptation decreased response to a stimulus as a result of recent exposure to it, 211
Addictive behavior. *See* Substance abuse
Adenosine breakdown product of AMP that forms during metabolic activity; a neuromodulator

that inhibits the basal forebrain cells that promote arousal and wakefulness, 62, 275–276
Adenosine triphosphate (ATP) a compound that stores energy; also used as a neuromodulator, 498, *498*
ADH. *See* Antidiuretic hormone
ADHD. *See* Attention-deficit/hyperactivity disorder
Adoption studies, 11, 12. *See also* specific research subjects
Adrenal cortex, *325*, 366, *367*
Adrenal hormones, 324, *325*, 326, 366, 369, 394, 401–402
Adrenaline, 60
Adrenal medulla, *325*
Adrenocorticotrophic hormone. *See* ACTH
Aerobic fibers muscle fibers that use air during their movements, 231
Afferent axon neuron that brings information into a structure, 33–34, *34*
Affinity tendency of a drug to bind to a particular type of receptor, 67–68
African gray parrot, 435–436, *435*
2-AG (sn-2 arachidonylglycerol) a chemical that is produced in large quantities by the brain and that attaches to cannabinoid receptors, 457
Age:
 and brain damage recovery, 128
 and mate selection, 341
 and sleep, 285–286, *287*
Aggressive behavior. *See* Attack behaviors
Agonist drug that mimics or increases the effects of a neurotransmitter, 67
Alcohol, 459–462
 and anxiety, 382, 383
 and cerebellum, 243
 dependence on, 68, *69*, 402, 459–462, *461*
 fetal exposure to, 123, *123*, 348
 and infant reflexes, 233
 and sleep, 280

Alcoholism (alcohol dependence) the inability to quit drinking or to limit intake of alcohol in spite of strong intentions to do so, ~~68, 69, 402, 459–462, 461~~
Aldosterone adrenal hormone that causes the kidneys to conserve sodium when excreting urine, 302, *325*
Allied reflexes, 233
Allopregnanolone, 335
All-or-none law principle stating that the size, amplitude, and velocity of the action potential are independent of the intensity of the stimulus that initiated it, 44
Alpha-fetoprotein protein that binds with estrogen in the bloodstream of many immature mammals, 330
Alpha wave rhythm of 8 to 12 brain waves per second, generally associated with relaxation, 272
Alprazolam (Xanax), 382
Altruistic behavior behavior that benefits someone other than the individual engaging in the behavior, 17–18
Alzheimer's disease condition characterized by memory loss, confusion, depression, restlessness, hallucinations, delusions, sleeplessness, and loss of appetite, 403–405, *404, 405*
 and basal forebrain, 275, 404, 405
 and nucleus basalis, 91
 and sex hormones, 335, 336
 and somatosensory cortex, 200
Amacrine cells, 146, *148*, 157
Amblyopia (lazy eye) reduced vision resulting from disuse of one eye, usually associated with failure of the two eyes to point in the same direction, 179, *180*
American Scientist, 25
Amino acids acids containing an amine group, 37, 62

Amnesia memory loss, 402–405
    and Alzheimer's disease, 403–405, *404, 405*
    and hippocampus, 395–398, *396, 397, 398*
    and Korsakoff's syndrome, 38, 402–403
AMPA receptor glutamate receptor that also responds to the drug a-amino-3-hydroxy-5-methyl-4-isoxazolepropionic acid, 411–413, *412, 413*
Amphetamine stimulant drug that increases the release of dopamine, 454
    and ADHD, 222
    and brain damage recovery, 129, 133
    and schizophrenia, 478, 485, 487
Amplitude intensity of a sound or other stimulus, 188
AMPT, 486
Amputated limbs, 134–136, *134, 135, 136*
Amygdala, 88
    and alcoholism, 462
    and attack behaviors, 372, *373*
    and bipolar disorder, 471
    and dreams, 288, 289
    and emotions, 361
    and escape behaviors, 377–380, *379, 380, 381, 382*
    and memory, 394
    and pain, 204
Amyloid beta protein 42 (Aβ₄₂) protein with 42 amino acids, which accumulates in the brain and impairs the functions of neurons and glia cells, leading to Alzheimer's disease, 404
Amyloid precursor protein, 404
Amyloid proteins, 403–404, *404*
Amyotrophic lateral sclerosis, 240
Anabolic steroid a steroid chemical, especially a derivative-3 of testosterone, that tends to build up muscles, 326–327
Anaerobic process a process that does not require oxygen at the time, 231
Anandamide naturally occurring brain chemical that binds to the same receptors as cannabinoids, 457
Anatomical terminology, 2, 80–82, *81, 82*
Androgen class of steroid hormones that are more abundant in males than in females for most

species, *325,* 326, 331. *See also* Sex hormones
Androgen insensitivity condition in which a person lacks the mechanism that enables androgens to bind to genes in a cell's nucleus, 344, *344*
Androstenedione, 327
Angel dust. *See* Phencyclidine
Angiotensin II hormone that constricts the blood vessels, contributing to hypovolemic thirst, 302–303
Animal research, 20–24, *21, 22,* 499–501
Anomia difficulty recalling the names of objects, 443
Anorexia nervosa condition characterized by unwillingness to eat, severe weight loss, and sometimes death, 319
Anosmia general lack of olfaction, 215
Antabuse (disulfiram) a drug that helps people break an alcohol habit by impairing their ability to convert acetaldehyde to acetic acid, 460–461, 466
Antagonist drug that blocks the effects of a neurotransmitter, 67–68
Antagonistic muscles pairs of muscles that move a limb in opposite directions (for example, extensor and flexor), 56–57, *57, 228, 230*
Anterior toward the front end, *82*
Anterior commissure set of axons connecting the two cerebral hemispheres; smaller than the corpus callosum, 94, *425,* 429
Anterior pituitary portion of the pituitary gland, *325,* 327, 366, *367*
Anterograde amnesia loss of memory for events that happened after brain damage, 395
Antibody Y-shaped protein that fits onto an antigen and weakens it or marks it for destruction, 367
Antidepressant drugs, 67, 466–469, *467, 468*
Antidiuretic hormone (ADH) (vasopressin) pituitary hormone that raises blood pressure and enables the kidneys to reabsorb water and therefore to secrete highly concentrated urine, 300, 302, *325,* 327
Antigen protein on the surface of a microorganism in response to which the immune system generates antibodies, 367

Antihistamine drugs, 275
Antioxidants, 405
Antipsychotic drug that relieves schizophrenia, 484–485, *485,* 488–489, *488*
Anxiety, 377–383, *381*
    and amygdala, 377–380, *379, 380,* 381, 382
    drugs for, 381–383, *382, 383*
    See also Fear
Anxiety disorders, 380–381
Apex one end of the cochlea, farthest from the point where the stirrup meets the cochlea, 191
Aphasia severe impairment of language, 440–444, *444*
Aplysia, 409–411, *409,* 410
Apolipoprotein E, 404
Apomorphine morphine derivative that stimulates dopamine receptors, 133
Apoptosis developmental program by which a neuron kills itself at a certain age unless inhibited from doing so, 110–111, 123, 127, 252, 331, 335
Appetite-supressant drugs, 318–319
Arachidonic acid, 473
Arcuate nucleus, 316
Aromatase, 330
Aromatization, 330
Arousal, 274–277, *276, 277,* 358–361, 404, 453
Artificial selection change in the frequencies of various genes in a population because of a breeder's selection of desired individuals for mating purposes, 14
Associativity tendency for pairing a weak input with a stronger input to enhance the later effectiveness of the weaker input, 411
Astigmatism blurring of vision for lines in one direction because of the nonspherical shape of the eye, 181
Astrocyte (astroglia) relatively large star-shaped glia cell, 35, *36*
Atomic number the number of protons in the nucleus of an atom, 494
Atomic weight number indicating the weight of an atom relative to a weight of one for a proton, 496
Atom piece of an element that cannot be divided any further, 494, 496
ATP. *See* Adenosine triphosphate
Attack behaviors, 372–377

    and brain, 374–377, *375, 376*
    and genetics, 372–374, *373*
    and testosterone, 335
Attention, 219–224
    and dyslexia, 446–447
    and substance abuse, 453
    visual, 174
Attention-deficit/hyperactivity disorder (ADHD) condition marked by excesses of impulsiveness, activity, and shifts of attention, 221–223, 454
Attraction. *See* Sexual behavior
Atypical antidepressants miscellaneous group of drugs with antidepressant effects but only mild side effects, 467
Atypical antipsychotics drugs that block dopamine activity in the pathways to the prefrontal cortex, especially at dopamine type D₄ receptors, but have little effect on the D₂ receptors, and also block serotonin type 5–HT2 receptors, 488, *488*
Audition, 188–196
    and dyslexia, 445
    and ear structure, 188–190, *189, 190, 191*
    hearing loss, 192–193
    and lateralization, 422
    pitch perception, 190–192, *191, 192, 193*
    sound localization, 194–195, *194, 195*
Autoimmune diseases, 229–230, 367
Autonomic nervous system set of neurons that regulates functioning of the internal organs, 80, 83–85, *84*
    and emotions, 358–361, *359, 360, 361*
    and stress, 364–366, *365*
Autoradiography, 132
Autoreceptor presynaptic receptor that is stimulated by the neurotransmitter released by the presynaptic cell itself, feeding back to decrease further release of the transmitter, 468, *469*
Autosomal gene a gene on any of the chromosomes other than the sex chromosomes (X and Y), 10
Axon hillock swelling of the soma, the point where the axon begins, 45
Axons single thin fibers of constant diameter that extend from a neuron, 32, 33

and astrocytes, 35, *36*
collateral sprouting of, 131–132, *133*
development of, 109
impulse transmission in, 39
and muscles, 228, *229*
myelinated, 46–47, *46*, 83, 109
pathfinding, 112–115, *113, 114, 115*
regrowth of, 130–131, *131*
See also Action potential

Babinski reflex the reflexive flexion of the big toe when the sole of the foot is stimulated, 233, *233*

Ballistic movement motion that proceeds as a single organized unit that cannot be redirected once it begins, 234

Barbiturates class of drugs sometimes used as tranquilizers, 381–382

Baroreceptor a receptor that detects the blood pressure in the largest blood veins, 302, 303

Basal forebrain the forebrain area anterior and dorsal to the hypothalamus; includes cell clusters that promote wakefulness and other cell clusters that promote sleep, 91, *92*, 275, *277*
and Alzheimer's disease, 275, 404, 405

Basal ganglia set of subcortical forebrain structures lateral to the hypothalamus including the caudate nucleus, putamen, and globus pallidus, 88, 90–91, *91*, 237, 245–247, *246*, 488

Basal metabolism rate of energy use while the body is at rest, used largely for maintaining a constant body temperature, 294

Base the part of the tympanic membrane closest to the stirrup, 191

Basilar membrane the floor of the scala media, within the cochlea, 190, 191

Battle fatigue. *See* Posttraumatic stress disorder

B cell type of leukocyte that matures in the bone marrow; attaches to an intruder and produces specific antibodies to attack the intruder's antigen, 367

Behavior:
altruistic, 17–18

attack behaviors, 335, 372–377, *373, 375, 376*
biological explanations of, 3–4
and body temperature, 296, *296*, 298
and brain anatomy, 77–78, *78*
and brain damage recovery, 128–129
and emotions, 356
and genetics, 13–14, 18
and homeostasis, 294
and long-term potentiation, 414–415
motor sequences of, 234–235
parental, 337–338, *337*
schizophrenic, 476–477
See also Escape behaviors; Sexual behavior

Behavioral interventions, 136–137

Behavioral medicine field that includes the influence of eating and drinking habits, smoking, stress, exercise, and other behavioral variables on health, 364

Behavioral neuroscientists, 25

Bell-Magendie law observation that the dorsal roots of the spinal cord carry sensory information and that the ventral roots carry motor information toward the muscles and glands, 82

Benzodiazepines a class of widely used antianxiety drugs, 381–382, *382*

Binding problem question of how the visual, auditory, and other areas of the brain influence one another to produce a combined perception of a single object, 99–102, *100, 101*, 174–175

Binocular vision based on the simultaneous stimulation of two eyes, 178, *178*

Biological clock internal mechanism for controlling rhythmic variations in a behavior, 263–266, *264, 266*
resetting, 267–269, *268*

Biological psychology study of the physiological, evolutionary, and developmental mechanisms of behavior and experience:
careers in, 25
importance of, 2

Bipolar cells type of neuron in the retina that receives input directly from the receptors, *34*, 146, *147*, 157
and color vision, 152, *153*

and foveal vs. peripheral vision, 148
and lateral inhibition, 160–161, *160, 161, 162*

Bipolar disorder condition in which a person alternates between the two poles of mania and depression, 471–473, *472*

Birdsong, 4

Birth-control pills, 333–334

Blindness, 95, 182. *See also* Vision

Blindsight ability to localize objects within an apparently blind visual field, 175

Blind spot point in the retina that lacks receptors because the optic nerve exits at this point, 146–147, *148*

Blobs, 171

Blood-brain barrier the mechanism that keeps many chemicals out of the brain, 36–38, *37*
and edema, 127
and immune system, 367–368
and neurotransmitter synthesis, 62
and Parkinson's disease, 252, 253
and thirst, 301

Blood volume, 302

Body temperature, 294–299
and circadian rhythms, 262–263, *263*, 279–280
homeostasis, 294
and movement, 230, *230*
and sleep, 275, 279

Body weight:
and hypothalamus, 312, *313*
weight-loss techniques, 317, 318–319
See also Obesity

Bonobos, 434–435, *434*

Borna disease viral infection that affects the nervous system, producing results that range from exaggerated activity fluctuations to death, 465–466, *466*

Bouton (presynaptic terminal), 32–33

Brain, 85–93, *86, 89, 94*
and Alzheimer's disease, 403–404, *404*
and amputated limbs, 134–136
animal vs. human, 20, *21*
and arousal, 274–275, *277*
and attack behaviors, 374–377, *375, 376*
binding problem, 99–102
and biopolar disorder, 471, *472, 473*
and body temperature, 297–298, *297*
brainstem, 85, *86*

and consciousness, 5–7
cranial nerves, 86, *87*
and eating regulation, 308, 310–314, *311, 312, 313*
electrical self-stimulation experiments, 452–453, *452*
and emotions, 357–358, 361–363, *362*
eye connections with, 146–149, *147, 148*
forebrain, 88–91, 311
hindbrain, 85–87
and immune system, 367–368
and learning, 388–392, *390*, 393, 411–415, *412, 413*
major divisions of, 85, *86*
midbrain, 88
and nitric oxide, 62
and pain, 201–202, *202, 203*
recording activity in, 76–77
sagittal section, *90*
and schizophrenia, 477, *477*
and sex hormones, 332, 335
and sexual differentiation, 329–330
and sexual orientation, 348–350, *349, 350*
size of, 77–78, *78*
and sleep, 273, 275–279, *276, 277, 278*
somatosensory input to, 199–200
stimulation of, 75–76
and taste, 211–212, *212*
terminology, 2, 80–82, *81, 82*
and thirst, 301, *301*
tissue transplants, 253
ventricles, 90, 92–93, 482, *482*
See also Blood-brain barrier; Brain and movement; Brain damage; Cerebral cortex; Lateralization; Nervous system; Neurotransmitters

Brain and movement, 236–247, *236*
basal ganglia, 245–247, *246*
cerebellum, 242–244, *243, 245*
cerebral cortex, 237–241, *237, 238, 241, 242*
primary motor cortex, 237–239, *237, 238*
spinal cord connections, 239–241, *241, 242*

Brain damage, 125–139
and age, 128
and axon regrowth, 130–131, *131*
and behavioral adjustments, 128–129
and cannabinoids, 458
causes of, 125–127, *126, 127*

and collateral sprouting, 131–132, *133*

and denervation super-sensitivity, 132–134, *133*

and diaschisis, 129

and emotions, 359–360, *360*

Korsakoff's syndrome, 38, 402–403

and language, 440–444, *441, 442, 444*

and lateralization, 422–426, *423*, 430

and locked-in syndrome, 359–360, *360*

and prefrontal lobotomies, 99

and REM behavior disorder, 281

and research, 75

and schizophrenia, 478, 481–484, *482, 483, 484*

and stress, 369, *369*

therapies for, 136–138, *137*

and vision, 169–171, 173–174

See also Alzheimer's disease

Brain-derived neurotrophic factor (BDNF), 111, 468

Brain development, 107–124, *110*

abnormalities in, 122–123, *123*

adult neuron generation, 116–117

axon pathfinding, 112–115, *113, 114, 115*

collateral sprouting, 131–132, *133*

and experience, 115–120, *116, 118, 119*

and language, 436–440, *437, 438*

and lateralization, 428–429

neuron development, 109

neuron survival, 110–112, *111*, 180

proportional growth, 120–122, *121, 122*

and schizophrenia, 481–484, *482, 483, 484*

Brain grafts, 138

Brain size:

comparison among animals, 120–121, *121, 122*

and intelligence, 436–437, *437*

Brainstem hindbrain, midbrain, and posterior central structures of the forebrain, 86, *86*

Brain-to-body ratio, 436, *437*

Brightness constancy, 154

Broca's aphasia (nonfluent aphasia) condition marked by loss of fluent speech and impaired use and understanding of prepositions, word endings, and other grammatical devices, 440–442, *444*

Broca's area portion of the human left frontal lobe associated with certain aspects of language, especially language production, 441, *441*

Bromides, 466

Bulimia nervosa condition characterized by alternation between dieting and overeating, 319

Bupropion (Wellbutrin), 467

Butyrophenones class of antipsychotic drugs that includes haloperidol, 485

Caffeine drug present in coffee and other drinks that constricts blood vessels to the brain and prevents adenosine from inhibiting the release of dopamine and acetylcholine, 252, 276–277

Calcium blockers, 137

CaMKII, 412

Cannabinoids chemicals related to Δ^9–THC, the component of marijuana that alters experience, 457–458

Capsaicin chemical that causes neurons containing substance P to release it suddenly and also directly stimulates pain receptors sensitive to moderate heat, 202–203

Carbachol, 278

Carbamazepine, 473

Carbon atoms, 496–498, *497, 498*

Cardiac muscles the muscles of the heart, 228, *229*

Careers in biological psychology, 25

Carnivores animals that eat meat, 306

Catabolic steroids, 326

Cataplexy attack of muscle weakness while a person remains awake, 280–281

Cataracts, 179

Catatonic schizophrenia, 478

Catecholamines compounds such as dopamine, norepinephrine, and epinephrine that contain both catechol and an amine (NH_2), 62, 67

Catechol-o-methyltransferase. *See* COMT

Caudate nucleus large subcortical structure, one part of the basal ganglia, 90, 245, 246

CCK. *See* Cholecystokinin

Celexa (citalopram), 467

Cell body (soma) the structure of a cell that contains the nucleus, 32, 482

Cell structure, 31–34

Central canal fluid-filled channel in the center of the spinal cord, 92

Central executive mechanism that directs attention toward one stimulus or another and determines which items will be stored in working memory, 394

Central gray area, 378

Central nervous system (CNS) the brain and spinal cord, 80, *200*

prenatal development, 108–109, *109*

and somatosensory system, 199–200, *199, 200, 201*

See also Brain; Spinal cord

Central pattern generator neural mechanism in the spinal cord or elsewhere that generates rhythmic patterns of motor output, 234

Central sulcus large groove in the surface of the primate cerebral cortex, separating frontal from parietal cortex, 96

Cerebellar cortex the outer covering of the cerebellum, 243, 244, *245*

Cerebellum the large, highly convoluted structure in the hindbrain, 86–87

and memory, 390–391

and movement, 242–244, *243, 245*

Cerebral cortex the layer of cells on the outer surface of the cerebral hemispheres of the forebrain, 88, 89, 94–99, *97*, 102

and Alzheimer's disease, 404, *404*

and arousal, 275

and audition, 191–192, *192*

and binding problem, 100–102, *101*

and depression, 468

development of, 120–121, *121*

frontal lobe, 97–99, *98*

and infant reflexes, 233

and language, 441, *441*, 445

and learning, 390

and movement, 237–241, *237, 238, 241, 242*

occipital lobe, 95

organization of, 94–95, *95*

parietal lobe, 96

and Parkinson's disease, 249, *250*

and schizophrenia, 483

sex differences in, 331

subdivision illustration, *96*

and thalamus, 89–90, *90*

and vision, 157, 162–163, *163*

See also Corpus callosum

Cerebral palsy, 240

Cerebral ventricles, 90, 92, *92*

Cerebrospinal fluid (CSF) liquid similar to blood serum, found in the ventricles of the brain and in the central canal of the spinal cord, 92–93, 108

Cerebrovascular accident. *See* Stroke

Cerebrum, 25

Chemical senses, 208–218

and chemical coding, 208–209

olfaction, 89, 214–216, *214, 216,* 337

vomeronasal sensation, 216–217, 337

See also Taste

Chemistry, 493–498

carbon, 496–498, *497, 498*

elements and compounds, 494, *494, 495, 496, 496*

Chihuahua problem observation that chihuahuas have an unusually high brain-to-body ratio because they were selected for small bodies, not for large brains, 436

Chimpanzees, 433–434, *433*

Chlordiazepoxide (Librium), 382

Chloride channels, 382, 383

Chlorpromazine (Thorazine) the first drug found to relieve the positive symptoms of schizophrenia, 485

Cholecystokinin (CCK) hormone released by the duodenum in response to food distention, 308, 317, 319, 381

Cholesterol, 324

Chondroitin sulphate proteoglycans, 131

Chorda tympani, 212

Choroid plexus, 92

Chromosome strand of DNA bearing the genes, 9–11

Chronic conditions conditions having a gradual onset and long duration, 477

Cigarette smoking, 455–456

and Parkinson's disease, 252

prenatal effects of, 123, 373, *373*

Cingulate cortex, 88, 204

Circadian rhythms, 261–270

biological clock mechanisms, 263–266, *264, 266*

and biopolar disorder, 473

and body temperature, 262–263, *263,* 279–280

definitions, 262–263

and depression, 470–471, *471*

and insomnia, 479–480

and jet lag, 267, *268*

resetting, 267–269, *268*

and seasonal affective disorder, 473, *474*

Circannual rhythms, 262

Citalopram (Celexa), 467

Classical conditioning a type of conditioning produced by the pairing of two stimuli, one of which evokes an automatic response, 388–392, *389, 390, 392,* 408, 458

Clinico-anatomical hypothesis the view that regards dreams as just thinking that takes place under unusual conditions, 288–289

Closed head injury sharp blow to the head resulting from a fall, an automobile or motorcycle accident, an assault, or other sudden trauma that does not actually puncture the brain, 125, *126*

Clozapine, 488, *488*

CNS. *See* Central nervous system

Cocaine stimulant drug that increases the stimulation of dopamine synapses by blocking the reuptake of dopamine by the presynaptic neuron, 123, 454, *455,* 478, 485, 487

Cochlea structure in the inner ear containing auditory receptors, 189–190, *191*

Cognition:

and movement, 247–248

and sex hormones, 335–336, *336*

See also Learning; Memory

Cold receptors, 198

Collateral sprout newly formed branch from an uninjured axon that attaches to a synapse vacated when another axon was destroyed, 131–132, *133*

Color blindness, 10–11, 155

Color constancy ability to recognize the color of an object despite changes in lighting, 154, 171

Color vision, 149, 150–155, *151, 152, 153, 154,* 171

Color vision deficiency inability to perceive color differences as most other people do, 10–11, 155

Column collection of cells having similar properties, arranged perpendicular to the laminae, *83, 95, 95,* 166–167, *167*

Commissures of the brain, 94, *425,* 429

Comparative psychologists, 25

Complex cell a cell type of the visual cortex that responds best to a light stimulus of a particular shape anywhere in its receptive field; its receptive field cannot be mapped into fixed excitatory and inhibitory zones, 165–166, *165*

Compound material made by combining elements, 494

Computerized axial tomography (CT scan, CAT scan) method of visualizing a living brain by injecting a dye into the blood and then passing x-rays through the head and recording them by detectors on the other side, 74, *74*

COMT (catechol-o-methyl-transferase) an enzyme that converts catecholamines into synaptically inactive forms, 67

Concordance agreement (pair of twins is concordant for a trait if both of them have it or if neither has it), 479

Conditioned response (CR) a response evoked by a conditioned stimulus after it has been paired with an unconditioned stimulus, 388

Conditioned stimulus (CS) a stimulus that evokes a particular response only after it has been paired with an unconditioned stimulus, 388

Conditioned taste aversions learned avoidance of a food whose consumption is followed by illness, 307

Conductive (middle-ear) deafness hearing loss that occurs if the bones of the middle ear fail to transmit sound waves properly to the cochlea, 192

Cone a type of retinal receptor that contribute to color perception, 149–150, *149,* 150, 151, 152, *152,* 155

Confabulation making up an answer to a question and then accepting the invented information as if it were a memory, 402–403

Configural learning performance of a task in which the meaning of a stimulus depends on what other stimuli are paired with it, 400–401

Consciousness:

and attention, 219–220

and mind-body problem, 6–7

visual, 174–175

Consolidation conversion of short-term memories into long-term memories and strengthening of those memories, 393

Continuous Positive Airway Pressure (CPAP) mask, 280, *281*

Contraception, 333–334

Contralateral on the opposite side of the body (left or right), *82,* 240

Cooperativity tendency for nearly simultaneous stimulation by two or more axons to produce LTP much more effectively than stimulation by just one, 411

Cornea, 146

Coronal plane the plane that shows brain structures as they would be seen from the front, *81, 82*

Corpus callosum the large set of axons that connects the two hemispheres of the cerebral cortex, 94

damage to, 422–426, *423*

development of, 428–429

and handedness, 430

and lateralization, 420, *420*

sex differences, 331

Corpus luteum, 333

Cortical blindness, 95

Corticosterone, 324, *325,* 402

Cortisol hormone released by the adrenal cortex that elevates blood sugar and enhances metabolism, 324, *325,* 326, 366, 369, 394, 402

Covalent bond chemical bond between two atoms that share electrons, 496–497, *496*

CPAP (Continuous Positive Airway Pressure) mask, 280, *281*

Cranial nerves part of a set of nerves controlling sensory and motor information of the head, connecting to nuclei in the medulla, pons, midbrain, or forebrain, 86, *87*

Craniosacral system. *See* Parasympathetic nervous system

Criminal behavior. *See* Attack behaviors

Critical (sensitive) period stage of development when experiences have a particularly strong and long-lasting influence, 178, 330, 440

Cross-adaptation reduced response to one stimulus because of recent exposure to some other stimulus, 211

Crossing over exchange of parts between two chromosomes during replication, 10

Cross-tolerance tolerance of a drug because of exposure to a different drug, 383

CR. *See* Conditioned response

CS. *See* Conditioned stimulus

CSF. *See* Cerebrospinal fluid

CT/CAT scan. *See* Computerized axial tomography

Cycloserine, 487

Cyproterone, 333

Cytokines chemicals released by the immune system that attack infections and communicate with the brain to elicit anti-illness behaviors, 367–368

Δ^9–tetrahydrocannabinol (Δ^9–THC) chemical found in the leaves of marijuana plants, 457

DBI. *See* Diazepam-binding inhibitor

Deafferent to remove the sensory nerves from a body part, 129

Deafness, 192–193, 440. *See also* Audition

Decision making, 356–358, *357, 358*

Declarative memory a memory that a person can state in words, 397, 398–399

Delayed matching-to-sample task a task in which an animal sees a sample object and then after a delay must choose an object that matches the sample, 398

Delayed nonmatching-to-sample task a task in which an animal sees an object and then after a delay must choose an object that does not match the sample, 398, *398*

Delayed-response task an assignment in which an animal must respond on the basis of a signal that it remembers but that is no longer present, 99, 394–395

Delusions beliefs that other people regard as unfounded, such as the belief that one is being severely persecuted, 476–477

Dementia praecox. *See* Schizophrenia

Dendrite branching fiber that emanates from a neuron,

growing narrower as it extends from the cell body toward the periphery, 32, 109

Dendritic branching, 34–35, *35*, 115–116, *116*, 412, 414

Dendritic spine short outgrowth along the dendrites, 32, *33*, 335

Denervation supersensitivity increased sensitivity by a postsynaptic cell after removal of an axon that formerly innervated it, 132–134, *133*, 488

Deoxyribonucleic acid (DNA) double-stranded chemical that composes the chromosomes; it serves as a template for the synthesis of RNA, 9, *9*

Depolarization reduction in the level of polarization across a membrane, 42, 44, 55–56

Depression, 464–471, *464*
and antidepressant drugs, 67, 466–469, *467, 468*
and bipolar disorder, 471–473, *472*
and electroconvulsive therapy, 469–470, *470*
seasonal affective disorder, 473–474, *474*
and serotonin, 376–377, *376*, 467
and sleep, 280, 470–471, *471*
and viral infections, 465–466, *466*

Depth perception, 171–172, 179–180

Dermatome area of skin connected to a particular spinal nerve, 199

Diabetes, 122–123, 309, *310*, 318, 404–405

Diaschisis decreased activity of surviving neurons after other neurons are damaged, 129

Diazepam (Valium), 382

Diazepam-binding inhibitor (DBI) brain protein that blocks the behavioral effects of diazepam and other benzodiazepines, 382

Dichotic listening task procedure in which a person wears earphones that present different words to the two ears at the same time; the person tries to say either or both words, 424

Diencephalon, 88

Diet, 63, 405, 478. *See also* Eating regulation

Diethylstilbestrol (DES), 348

Differential diagnosis identification of a condition as distinct from all similar conditions, 477–478

Differentiation formation of the axon and dendrites that gives a neuron its distinctive shape, 109

Digestive system, 305–307, *306*. *See also* Eating regulation

Directions, anatomical, 80–82, *81, 82*

Disgust, 361–362

Distal located more distant from the point of origin or attachment, *82*

Disulfiram (Antabuse) a drug that helps people break an alcohol habit by impairing their ability to convert acetaldehyde to acetic acid, 460–461, 466

Disuse supersensitivity increased sensitivity by a postsynaptic cell because of decreased input by incoming axons, 132

Dizygotic twins fraternal (non-identical) twins, 11, 12, *12*. *See also specific research subjects*

DNA. *See* Deoxyribonucleic acid

Dolphins, 435

Dominant gene gene that shows a strong effect in either the homozygous or heterozygous condition, 10

Dopamine a neurotransmitter:
and ADHD, 222
and alcohol, 68, *69*, 459
and brain damage recovery, 133
and brain development, 118
and depression, 467, 468, 470
drug effects on, *68*
and eating regulation, 310–311
and Parkinson's disease, 249, 251, 252
and personality, 68
reuptake of, 67
and schizophrenia, 484–486, *485*, 488
and sex hormones, 332, 335
and substance abuse, 68, *69*, 452–454, *452, 453*, 455, 456
synthesis of, 62, *63*

Dopamine hypothesis of schizophrenia proposal that schizophrenia is due to excess activity at certain dopamine synapses, 484–486, *485*

Dopamine transporter, 454

Dorsal toward the back, away from the ventral (stomach) side, 2, *2*, 80, 81, *82*

Dorsal root ganglia set of sensory neuron somas on the dorsal side of the spinal cord, 82

Dorsal stream visual path in the parietal cortex, some-

times known as the "where" or "how" pathway, 164

Dorsolateral prefrontal cortex area of the prefrontal cortex, 395

Dorsolateral tract path of axons in the spinal cord from the contralateral hemisphere of the brain, controlling movements of peripheral muscles, 239–240, *241*

Dorsomedial thalamus, 402

Down syndrome, 403

Dreams, 273–274, 288–289

Drugs:
for ADHD, 222–223, 454–455
for alcoholism, 460–461
for Alzheimer's disease, 405
amphetamine, 129, 133, 222, 454, 478, 485, 487
anabolic steroids, 326–327
anesthetic, 44
antidepressant, 67, 466–469, *467, 468*
antihistamine, 275
antipsychotic, 484–485, *485*, 488–489, *488*
anxiety-reducing, 381–383, *382, 383*
appetite-suppressant, 318–319
for bipolar disorder, 472–473
and blood-brain barrier, 37
for brain damage recovery, 127, 129, 137–138
for epilepsy, 422
hallucinogenic, 458, *458*
marijuana, 457–458
and memory, 414
morphine, 205
nicotine, 455–456
opiates, 201, 205, 456–457
for pain, 201, 205
and parasympathetic nervous system, 85
and Parkinson's disease, 251
phencyclidine, 478, 486–487
prenatal effects of, 122, 123
for schizophrenia, 484–485, *485*, 488–489, *488*
and synaptic activity, 67–68, *68*
testosterone-reducing, 332–333
tranquilizers, 129, 280
See also Stimulant drugs; Substance abuse

Dualism belief that mind and body are different kinds of substance, existing independently, that somehow interact, 5

Duodenum part of the small intestine adjoining the stomach; the first part of the digestive system that absorbs food, 308

Dynorphin, 454

Dyslexia specific reading difficulty in a person with adequate vision and at least average skills in other academic areas, 445–447, *446*

DZ twins. *See* **Dizygotic twins**

Ears, 188–190, *189, 190, 191*. *See also* Audition

Easy problems questions pertaining to certain concepts that are termed *consciousness*, such as the difference between wakefulness and sleep, and the mechanisms that enable us to focus our attention, 5

Eating disorders, 319

Eating regulation, 305–320
chemical influences, 315–318, *315, 316*
digestive system, 305–307, *306*
eating disorders, 319
and hypothalamus, 310–314, *311, 312, 313, 314*
and immune system, 368
satiety, 307–310
social influences, 314–315, *314, 315*

Ecstasy (MDMA), 455, *456*

ECT. *See* Electroconvulsive therapy

Edema accumulation of fluid, 127

EEG. *See* Electroencephalograph

Efferent axon neuron that carries information away from a structure, 33–34, *34*

Efficacy tendency of a drug to activate a particular kind of receptor, 67–68

Electrical gradient difference in positive and negative charges across a membrane, 39

Electroconvulsive therapy (ECT) electrically inducing a convulsion in an attempt to relieve depression or other disorder, 393, 469–470, *470*

Electroencephalograph (EEG) device that measures the brain's electrical activity through electrodes on the scalp, 271–272

Electrons, 494

Elements materials that cannot be broken down into other materials, 494–495, *494, 495*

Elevated plus maze, 13, *14*

Emotions, 355–385

attack behaviors, 335, 372–377, *373, 375, 376*
and autonomic nervous system, 358–361, *359, 360, 361*
and brain areas, 357–358, 361–363, *362*
and cataplexy, 280–281
and decision making, 356–358, 357, *358*
definitions of, 356
and dreams, 288, 289
escape behaviors, 377–383, *379, 380*
and lateralization, 362, 426, *427*
and memory, 394
and pain, 204
See also Stress
End bulb (presynaptic terminal), 32–33
Endocrine gland organ that produces and releases hormones, 324, *324, 325*
Endogenous circadian rhythm self-generated rhythm that lasts about a day, 262
Endogenous circannual rhythm self-generated rhythm that lasts about a year, 262
Endogenous cycles, 262–263, *263*
Endoplasmic reticulum network of thin tubes within a cell that transports newly synthesized proteins to other locations, 32
Endorphins category of chemicals the body produces that stimulate the same receptors as do opiates, 202, 456–457
Endothelial cells, 37
Endozepines brain protein that blocks the behavioral effects of diazepam and other benzodiazepines, 382
End-stopped (hypercomplex) cell a cell of the visual cortex that responds best to stimuli of a precisely limited type, anywhere in a large receptive field, with a strong inhibitory field at one end of its field, 166, *166*
Engram the physical representation of what has been learned, 388–392, *392*
Enkephalins, 201–202
Environmental factors, 12, 13
and brain development, 115–116, *116*
and Parkinson's disease, 251–252
Enzymes any proteins that catalyze biological reactions, 9, 306, 498

Epilepsy condition characterized by repeated episodes of excessive, synchronized neural activity, mainly because of decreased release of the inhibitory transmitter GABA, 356, 374–375, 422, 466
Epinephrine also known as adrenaline; a hormone; also used as a neurotransmitter, 62, *63*, 67, *325*, 394
Episodic memories memories of single events, 398–399, 401
EPSP. *See* Excitatory postsynaptic potential
Equipotentiality concept that all parts of the cortex contribute equally to complex behaviors such as learning; that any part of the cortex can substitute for any other, 390
Escape behaviors, 377–383
and amygdala, 377–380, *379, 380,* 381, 382
Estradiol one type of estrogen, 330, 333, 465
Estrogen class of steroid hormones that are more abundant in females than in males for most species, *325,* 326, 333, 335–336, 478. *See also* Sex hormones
Ethical issues, 20–21, 23–24, 499–501
Evolution change in the frequencies of various genes in a population over generations, 14–18, *15*
and animal research, 20
and brain development, 115
and genetics, 11
misunderstandings about, 14–16
and sociobiology, 16–18
See also Evolutionary explanations
Evolutionary explanations understanding in terms of the evolutionary history of a species, 3–4, 284–285, 336
attack behaviors, 376
language, 436–440, *437*
sexual behavior, 340–342
sexual orientation, 346–347
sleep, 284–285
Evolutionary psychology. *See* Sociobiology
Evolutionary theory of sleep concept that the function of sleep is to conserve energy at times of relative inefficiency, 284–285
Evolutionary trees, 14, *15*
Excitatory neurotransmitters, 65

Excitatory postsynaptic potential (EPSP) the graded depolarization of a neuron, 55–56, *56, 57*–58
Exercise, 115, 318
Exocytosis excretion of neurotransmitter through the membrane of a presynaptic terminal and into the synaptic cleft between the presynaptic and postsynaptic neurons, 64
Experience:
and brain development, 115–120, *116*
and visual development, 177–182, *177, 181*
See also Environmental factors
Explicit memory the deliberate recall of information that one recognizes as a memory, detectable by direct testing such as asking a person to describe a past event, 397, 403
Expressed emotion hostility expressed toward a patient by frustrated family members, 478
Extensor muscle that extends a limb, 228, *230*
Eyes, 146–150, *146, 147, 148, 149. See also* Vision

Face recognition, 169–171
Facial nerve, *87*
Facilitating interneurons, 410
Fast-twitch fibers muscle fibers that produce fast contractions but fatigue rapidly, 230–231
Fat cells, 315, *325*
Fear, 377–380. *See also* Anxiety
Feature detector neuron whose responses indicate the presence of a particular feature, 167–168, *167, 168*
Feeding process. *See* Eating regulation
Feelings, 356. *See also* Emotions
Fenfluramine, 318
Fen-phen, 318
Fetal alcohol syndrome condition resulting from prenatal exposure to alcohol and marked by decreased alertness, hyperactivity, varying degrees of mental retardation, motor problems, heart defects, and facial abnormalities, 123, *123*
Fetal development. *See* Prenatal development
Fever, 277, 298–299, 368
Finger-to-nose test, 243
Fissure a long, deep sulcus, *83*
Fitness number of copies of one's genes that endure in later generations, 16

Flexor muscle that flexes a limb, 228, *230*
Fluent aphasia (Wernicke's aphasia) a condition marked by poor language comprehension and great difficulty remembering the names of objects, 443–444, *444*
Fluoxetine (Prozac), 67, 467, *467*
Fluvoxamine (Luvox), 467
FMRI. *See* Functional magnetic resonance imaging
Focal hand dystonia "musician's cramp," a condition in which the touch responses to one finger overlap those of another, leading to clumsiness, fatigue, and involuntary movements, 120
Follicle-stimulating hormone (FSH) anterior pituitary hormone that promotes the growth of follicles in the ovary, *79, 325,* 327, 333
Food selection, 306–307. *See also* Diet; Eating regulation
Forebrain most anterior part of the brain, including the cerebral cortex and other structures, 88–91, 311. *See also* Cerebral cortex; Hypothalamus
Fourier analysis, 167–168
Fovea area in the center of the human retina specialized for acute, detailed vision, 148, 149
Foveal vision, 149, *150*
Fraternal twins. *See* Dizygotic twins
Free-running rhythm circadian or circannual rhythm that is not being periodically reset by light or other cues, 267
Frequency number of sound waves per second, 188
Frequency theory concept that pitch perception depends on differences in frequency of action potentials by auditory neurons, 190
Frontal lobe section of cerebral cortex extending from the central sulcus to the anterior limit of the brain, containing the primary motor cortex and the prefrontal cortex, 97–99
FSH. *See* Follicle-stimulating hormone
Functional explanations understanding why a structure or behavior evolved as it did, 4, 16–17
Functional magnetic resonance imaging (fMRI) a modified version of MRI

that measures energies released by hemoglobin molecules in an MRI scan, and then determines the brain areas receiving the greatest supply of blood and oxygen, 76–77, 170

Fungiform papillae, 213

Fusiform gyrus, 169–171, *170*

GABA (gamma amino butyric acid) the most abundant inhibitory neurotransmitter:
and alcohol, 123, 459
and anxiety, 381, *382, 382, 383*
and arousal, 275, 277
and biopolar disorder, 473
and epilepsy, 422
and ionotropic effects, 65
and premenstrual syndrome, 335
and sensitive period, 178
and substance abuse, 456

GABA_A receptor complex structure that includes a site that binds GABA, as well as sites that bind other chemicals that modify the sensitivity of the GABA site, 382

Gamma amino butyric acid. *See* GABA

Gamma waves repetitive activity in neurons at a rhythm of 30 to 80 action potentials per second, 101

Ganglion cluster of neuron cell bodies, usually outside the CNS, *83*

Ganglion cell type of neuron in the retina that receives input from the bipolar cells, 146, 148, *148,* 157, 162, *163*

Ganglioside molecule composed of carbohydrates and fats, 137

GAP-43, 413, 414

Gases, 62

Gate theory assumption that stimulation of certain nonpain axons in the skin or in the brain can inhibit transmission of pain messages in the spinal cord, 202

Gender identity the sex with which a person identifies, 342–345, *343, 344*

Gene unit of heredity that maintains its structural identity from one generation to another, 9–11. *See also* Genetics

Gene-knockout approach use of biochemical methods to direct a mutation to a particular gene that is important for certain types of cells, transmitters, or receptors, 75

General anesthetics drugs that decrease brain activity by opening potassium channels wider than usual, 44

Genetic drift, 4

Genetics, 9–14
and alcoholism, 459–460
and Alzheimer's disease, 403
and anxiety, 380–381
and attack behaviors, 372–374, *373*
and behavior, 13–14, 18
and bipolar disorder, 471–472
and body weight, 315, 318
and circadian rhythms, 265, *266*
and color vision deficiency, 155
and depression, 464
and heritability, 11–13
and Huntington's disease, 254–255
and language, 439
Mendelian, 9–11, *10*
and schizophrenia, 479–480, *479*
and sex hormones, 326
and sexual orientation, 346–347, *346*
See also Heritability

Genitals, 329–330, *329*

Gingko biloba, 414

Glia type of cell in the nervous system that, in contrast to neurons, does not conduct impulses to other cells, 30, 35–36, *36,* 382

Globus pallidus large subcortical structure, one part of the basal ganglia, 90, 245, 246

Glossopharyngeal nerve, *87*

Glucagon-like peptide-1 (GLP-1), 317

Glucagon pancreatic hormone that stimulates the liver to convert stored glycogen to glucose, 309, *309, 310,* 317, *325*

Glucose a simple sugar, the main fuel of vertebrate neurons:
and active transport, 37
and Alzheimer's disease, 404–405
and bipolar disorder, 471, *472*
and insulin, 309, *309,* 310
and neuron nourishment, 38

Glutamate the most abundant excitatory neurotransmitter, 65
and alcohol, 123, 459
and arousal, 275
and long-term potentiation, 411–413, *412, 413*
and schizophrenia, 486–487, *487,* 488

and strokes, 127

Glutamate hypothesis of schizophrenia proposal that schizophrenia is due to deficient activity at certain glutamate synapses, 486–487, *487*

Glycine, 487

Glycogen, 284

Golgi tendon organ receptor that responds to the contraction of a muscle, 232

Gollins picture test, 397, *397, 398, 399, 400, 401*

Gonadotropins, 327

Gonad reproductive organ, 329. *See also* Ovaries; Testes

Goose bumps, 3–4, 84–85

G-protein protein coupled to GTP (guanosine triphosphate, an energy-storing molecule), 65

Graded potential membrane potential that varies in magnitude and does not follow the all-or-none law, 47, 55–56
and color vision, 150

Grasp reflex reflexive grasp of an object placed firmly in the hand, 233, *233*

Gray matter areas of the nervous system with a high density of cell bodies and dendrites, with few myelinated axons, 83, *83*

Group selection, 17

Growth hormone (GH) (somatotropin), *325,* 327

GTP (guanosine triphosphate), 65

Guanosine triphosphate (GTP), 65

Gyrus (pl: gyri) a protuberance or elevation of the brain, separated from another gyrus by a sulcus, *83, 404*

Habituation decrease in response to a stimulus that is presented repeatedly and that is accompanied by no change in other stimuli, 409, *410*

Hair cell type of sensory receptor shaped like a hair; auditory receptors are hair cells, 190, *190,* 191, 197

Hair erection, 4, 84–85

Haldol (haloperidol), 129, 485, 486

Hallucination sensory experience that does not correspond to reality, 477, *477,* 478

Hallucinogenic drugs drugs that grossly distort perception, such as LSD, 458, *458*

Haloperidol (Haldol), 129, 485, 486

Handedness, 429–430

Hard problem philosophical question of why and how any kind of brain activity is associated with consciousness, 6

Head injuries, 125, *126*

Hearing. *See* Audition

Hearing loss, 192–193, 478

Heart disease, 365

Heat:
and pain, 202–203
receptors for, 198

Hebbian synapse a synapse that increases in effectiveness because of simultaneous activity in the presynaptic axon and the postsynaptic neuron, 408

Helicobacter pylori, 365

Hemiplegia, 131, *240*

Hemispheres of the brain. *See* Lateralization

Hemorrhage the rupture of an artery, 125, 127

Herbivores animals that eat plants, 306

Heritability estimate, ranging from 0 to 1.0, indicating the degree to which variance in a characteristic depends on variations in heredity for a given population, 11–13
of bipolar disorder, 471–472
of Huntington's disease, 254–256, *255*
of obesity, 318
of Parkinson's disease, 249, *250,* 251, 255–256
of schizophrenia, 479–480, *479*
See also Genetics

Hermaphrodite individual whose genitals do not match the usual development for his or her genetic sex, 342. *See also* Intersex

Hertz (Hz), 188

Heterozygous having two unlike genes for a given trait, 10

5-HIAA. *See* 5-Hydroxyindoleacetic acid

Hibernation, 284–285

Hindbrain most posterior part of the brain, including the medulla, pons, and cerebellum, 85–87

Hippocampal commissure set of axons that connects the left and right hippocampi, *425,* 429

Hippocampus large forebrain structure between the thalamus and cortex, 88
and Alzheimer's disease, 404
and amnesia, 395–398, *396, 397, 398*
and depression, 468

and immune system, 368
long-term potentiation in, 411–415
memory functions of, 91, 398–402, *401,* 413–414
and schizophrenia, 482, *482, 483,* 486
and sex hormones, 335
and stress, 369, *369*
Histamines, 205, 275, 280
Histochemistry, 134, 135
Homeostasis tendency to maintain a variable, such as temperature, within a fixed range, 294
Homeothermic maintaining nearly constant body temperature over a wide range of environmental temperatures, 295
Homosexuality. *See* Sexual orientation
Homozygous having two identical genes for a given characteristic, 10
Horizontal cell type of cell that receives input from receptors and delivers inhibitory input to bipolar cells, 47, 157, 160
Horizontal plane the plane that shows brain structures as they would be seen from above, *81, 82*
Hormones chemicals secreted by glands and conveyed by the blood to other organs, which are influenced by their activity, 65–66, 324–328, *326*
and active transport, 37
adrenal, 324, *325,* 326, 366, 369, 394, 401–402
and attack behaviors, 374, *375*
and brain damage recovery, 137–138
and depression, 465
and eating regulation, 316–317
and hypothalamus, 90, *325,* 327–328, *327*
partial list of, *325*
release control, 327–328, *327, 328*
and sexual orientation, 347
and taste, 213
and thirst, 302, *302*
See also Sex hormones
HPA axis the hypothalamus, pituitary gland, and adrenal cortex, 366, *367,* 368–369
Hunger, 294. *See also* Eating regulation
Huntingtin protein produced by the gene whose mutation leads to Huntington's disease, 255
Huntington's disease an inherited disorder characterized initially by

jerky arm movements and facial twitches, later by tremors, writhing movements, and psychological symptoms, including depression, memory impairment, hallucinations, and delusions, 91, 254–255, *254, 255,* 478
Hydrocephalus, 93
6-Hydroxydopamine (6-OHDA) a chemical that is absorbed by neurons that release dopamine or norepinephrine; it then oxidized into toxic chemicals that kill those neurons, 132, 252–253, 310–311
5-Hydroxyindoleacetic acid (5-HIAA) a serotonin metabolite, 375, 376
Hypercomplex (end-stopped) cell a cell of the visual cortex that responds best to stimuli of a precisely limited type, anywhere in a large receptive field, with a strong inhibitory field at one end of its field, 166, *166*
Hyperpolarization increased polarization across a membrane, 42
Hypnagogic hallucinations, 281
Hypocretin (orexin) neurotransmitter that stimulates acetylcholine-releasing cells and thereby increases wakefulness and arousal, 281, 317
Hypoglossal nerve, *87*
Hypomania, 471
Hypothalamus forebrain structure near the base of the brain just ventral to the thalamus, 88, 90
and anxiety, 382
and arousal, 275, 277
and body temperature, 297–298, *297*
and dreams, 289
and eating regulation, 310–314, *311, 312, 313, 314*
and hormones, 90, *325,* 327–328, *327*
and immune system, 368
and memory, 402
and menstrual cycle, 333
and pain, 204
and parental behavior, 337
and sexual differentiation, 329–330
and sexual orientation, 349–350, *349, 350*
and stress, 366, *367*
and thirst, 301, 302
and vision, 157
Hypovolemic thirst thirst provoked by low blood

volume, 302–303, *302, 303*
IBZM, 486
Identical twins. *See* Monozygotic twins
Identity position view that mental processes are the same as certain kinds of brain processes, but described in different terms, 5–6
Immune system set of structures that protects the body against viruses and bacteria, 367–369, *368, 369*
Implicit memory influence of recent experience on memory, even if one does not recognize that influence or realize that one is using memory at all, 397–398, 402, 403
Impotence inability to have an erection, 332
INAH-3 (third interstitial nucleus of the anterior hypothalamus), 349, *349, 350*
Infants, 177, 233, *233*
Inferior below another part, *82*
Inferior colliculus swelling on each side of the tectum in the midbrain, 88
Inferior parietal cortex, 102
Inferior temporal cortex portion of the cortex where neurons are highly sensitive to complex aspects of the shape of visual stimuli within very large receptive fields, 168–169
Inhibitory neurotransmitters, 65
Inhibitory postsynaptic potential (IPSP) temporary hyperpolarization of a membrane, 57–58
Inhibitory synapses, 56–57, *58*
Inner-ear (nerve) deafness hearing loss that results from damage to the cochlea, the hair cells, or the auditory nerve, 192
Inositol, 473
Insomnia lack of sleep, leaving the person feeling poorly rested the following day, 279–280
Insular cortex (insula), 212, 361–362
Insulin pancreatic hormone that facilitates the entry of glucose into the cells, 63, 309–310, *309, 310, 325,* 404
Intelligence, 436–439, *437, 438. See also* Cognition
Interleukin-1, 298
Intermittent explosive disorder a condition marked by occasional

outbursts of violent behavior with little or no provocation, sometimes linked to temporal lobe epilepsy, 374–375
Internal regulation. *See* Body temperature; Eating regulation; Hunger; Thirst
Interneurons, 34, 57
Intersex an individual whose sexual development is intermediate or ambiguous, 342–344, *343*
Intestines, 306
Intrinsic neuron a neuron whose axons and dendrites are all confined within a given structure, 34
Involuntary movements, 232. *See also* Reflex
Ion an atom that has gained or lost one or more electrons, 496, *496*
Ion channels, 40, *40,* 43
Ionic bond chemical attraction between two ions of opposite charge, 496, *496*
Ionotropic effect synaptic effect that depends on the rapid opening of some kind of gate in the membrane, 64–65, *65*
Ipsilateral on the same side of the body (left or right), *82*
IPSP. *See* Inhibitory postsynaptic potential
Ischemia local insufficiency of blood because a blood clot or other obstruction has closed an artery, 125, 127
Itching, 205

James-Lange theory the proposal that an event first provokes autonomic and skeletal responses and that emotion is the perception of those responses, 359–361, *359, 361*
Jealousy, 341
Jet lag the disruption of biological rhythms caused by travel across time zones, 267, *268*
Joint laxity, 381

K-complex sharp, high-amplitude, negative wave followed by a smaller, slower, positive wave, 272
Kennard principle generalization (not always correct) that it is easier to recover from brain damage early in life than later, 128
Kenyon cell, *34*
Ketamine, 487
Ketones, 38

Kidneys, 302, *325*

Kin selection the selection for a gene because it benefits the individual's relatives, 18

Klüver-Bucy syndrome the condition in which monkeys with damaged temporal lobes fail to display normal fears and anxieties, 97, 103, 378

Koniocellular neurons ganglion cells located throughout the retina, 162, *163*

Korsakoff's syndrome a type of brain damage caused by thiamine deficiency, characterized by apathy, confusion, and memory impairment, 38, 402–403

Labeled-line principle concept that each receptor responds to a limited range of stimuli and has a direct line to the brain, 208

Lactase enzyme necessary for lactose metabolism, 306

Lactose the sugar in milk, 306, *307*

Lamarckian evolution a discredited theory that evolution proceeds through the inheritance of acquired characteristics, 14–15

Lamina (plural: laminae) layer of cell bodies parallel to the surface of the cortex and separated from other laminae by layers of fibers, *83*, 94–95, *95*

Language, 433–447
   and brain damage, 440–444, *441, 442, 444*
   and brain development, 436–440, *437, 438*
   dyslexia, 445–447, *446*
   evolutionary explanations, 436–440, *437*
   and lateralization, 424, 428, 430
   nonhuman precursors, 433–436, *433, 434, 435*

Language acquisition device built-in mechanism for acquiring language, 439

Large-scale integration problem. *See* Binding problem

Lateral toward the side, away from the midline, *82*

Lateral geniculate nucleus thalamic nucleus that receives incoming visual information, 157

Lateral hypothalamus area of the hypothalamus that is important for the control of eating and drinking, 310–312, *311, 312*

Lateral inhibition restraint of activity in one neuron by activity in a neighboring neuron, 160–161, *160, 161, 162*

Lateral interpositus nucleus (LIP) a nucleus of the cerebellum that is critical for classical conditioning of the eye-blink response, 390–392

Lateralization the division of labor between the two hemispheres of the brain, 419–432
   and anatomical differences, 428, *429*
   and brain development, 428–429
   and corpus callosum damage, 422–426, *423*
   and depression, 465
   and emotions, 362, 426, *427*
   and handedness, 429–430
   and hemisphere functions, 426–427, *427*
   misconceptions, 430–431
   and schizophrenia, 482
   and sensory systems, 420, 421–422, 425–426, *426*

Lateral preoptic area portion of the hypothalamus that includes some cells that facilitate drinking and some that inhibit it, as well as passing axons that are important for osmotic thirst, 301

Law of specific nerve energies the statement that each nerve always conveys the same kind of information to the brain, 144–145

Lazy eye (amblyopia) reduced vision resulting from disuse of one eye, usually associated with failure of the two eyes to point in the same direction, 179, *180*

L-dopa chemical precursor of dopamine and other catecholamines, 252

Learning, 408–415
   classical conditioning, 388–392, *389, 390, 392*, 408, 458
   and Hebbian synapses, 408
   invertebrate studies, 409–411, *409, 410*
   and long-term potentiation, 411–415, *412, 413*
   past research, 407–408, *408*
   and sleep, 287
   See also Memory

Lens (eye), 146

Leptin peptide released by fat cells; tends to decrease eating, partly by inhibiting release of neuropeptide Y in the hypothalamus, 315, *325*

Lesion damage to a structure, 130

Leu-enkephalin chain of five amino acids believed to function as a neurotransmitter that inhibits pain, 201–202

Leukocyte white blood cell, a component of the immune system, 298, 367

LH. *See* Luteinizing hormone

Librium (Chlordiazepoxide), 382

Light:
   and seasonal affective disorder, 473
   and suprachiasmatic nucleus, 268–269
   wavelengths, 151, *151, 152*

Limbic system set of forebrain areas traditionally regarded as critical for emotion, which form a border around the brainstem, including the olfactory bulb, hypothalamus, hippocampus, amygdala, cingulate gyrus of the cerebral cortex, and several other smaller structures, 88, 88, 278, 361, *362*

LIP. *See* Lateral interpositus nucleus

Lithium element whose salts are often used as a therapy for bipolar disorder, 472–473

Liver, *325*

Lobotomies, prefrontal, 98–99, *98*

Local anesthetic drug that attaches to the sodium channels of the membrane, preventing sodium ions from entering and thereby blocking action potentials, 44

Localization of sounds, 194–195, *194, 195*

Local neuron small neuron with no axon or a very short one, 47

Locked-in syndrome a condition caused by damage to the ventral brainstem, in which the person almost completely loses brain control of the muscles, 359–360, *360*

Locus coeruleus small hindbrain structure whose widespread axons send bursts of norepinephrine in response to meaningful stimuli, 275, 279, 457

Long-term depression (LTD) prolonged decrease in response to an axonal input that has been repeatedly paired with some other input, generally at a low frequency, 411, 458

Long-term memory the memory of an event that is not currently held in attention, 391, 393–394

Long-term potentiation (LTP) phenomenon that after one or more axons bombard a dendrite with a rapid series of stimuli, the synapses between those axons and the dendrite become more sensitive for minutes, days, or weeks, 411–415, *412, 413*, 458

Loudness perception of the intensity of a sound, 188

LSD (lysergic acid diethylamide), 458, 478, 485, 487

LTD. *See* Long-term depression

LTP. *See* Long-term potentiation

Luteinizing hormone (LH) anterior pituitary hormone that stimulates the release of an ovum, *325*, 327, 333

Luvox (fluvoxamine), 467

LY 354740, 487

Machine consciousness, 7, 8

Macrophage immune system cell that surrounds a bacterium or other intruder, digests it, and exposes its antigens on the macrophage's own surface, 367

Macula, 148

Magnetic resonance imaging (MRI) method of imaging a living brain by using a magnetic field and a radio frequency field to make atoms with odd atomic weights all rotate in the same direction and then removing those fields and measuring the energy that the atoms release, 76–77, 112, 170

Magnetoencephalograph (MEG) a device that measures the faint magnetic fields generated by the brain's activity, 117–118

Magnocellular neuron large-celled neuron of the visual system that is sensitive to changing or moving stimuli in a relatively large visual field, 162, *163*, 171, 172, 445

Maintenance insomnia frequent awakening during the night, 279

Major depression state of feeling sad, helpless, and lacking in energy and pleasure for weeks at a time, 464–471, *464, 466, 467, 468, 470*

Mamillary bodies, 402

Mania condition of restless activity, excitement, laughter, self-confidence, and few inhibitions, 471

Manic-depressive disorder. *See* Bipolar disorder

MAO (monoamine oxidase) enzyme that converts catecholamines and serotonin into synaptically inactive forms, 67

MAOI. *See* Monoamine oxidase inhibitor

Marijuana, 457–458

Mass action theory that the cortex works as a whole, and the more cortex the better, 390

Massed practice, 393

Materialism view that everything that exists is material, or physical, 5

Maternal behavior. *See* Parental behavior

Mating behavior. *See* Sexual behavior

Matter, 6

MDMA (ecstasy), 455, *456*

Mechanical senses, 197–207
  itch, 205
  pain, 135–136, 201–205, *202, 203, 204*
  somatosensation, 197–201, *199, 200, 201*
  vestibular sensation, 197, *198*

Medial toward the midline, away from the side, *82*

Medial frontal cortex, 361

Medial preoptic area (MPOA), 332, 337

Medications. *See* Drugs

Medroxyprogesterone, 333

Medulla hindbrain structure located just above the spinal cord; the medulla could be regarded as an enlarged, elaborated extension of the spinal cord, 85–86, 212, 457

MEG. *See* Magnetoencephalograph

Melanocortin, 317, 318

Melatonin hormone that among other effects induces sleepiness, 265–266, *325*

Membrane structure that separates the inside of a cell from the outside, 31, *32*, 39

Memory, 387–408
  and Alzheimer's disease, 403–405, *404, 405*
  brain localization of, 388–392, *389, 390, 392*
  and dreams, 288, 289
  and electroconvulsive therapy, 469–470

and hippocampus, 91, 395–402, *396, 397, 398, 401,* 413–414
  and Korsakoff's syndrome, 38, 402–403
  and prefrontal cortex, 99, 395, 402
  and REM sleep, 287
  and schizophrenia, 482
  and stress, 369, *369,* 402
  and substance abuse, 455, 457
  types of, 391–395
  See also Learning

Memory cells, 367

Mendelian genetics, 9–11, *10*

Meninges membranes surrounding the brain and spinal cord, 93

Meningitis, 93

Menstrual cycle in women, periodic variation in hormones and fertility over the course of approximately 1 month, 333–334, *333, 334,* 335

Mentalism view that only the mind really exists, 5

Meridia (sibutramine), 318–319

Mesencephalon. *See* Midbrain

Mesolimbocortical system set of neurons that project from the midbrain tegmentum to the limbic system, 488

Metabolic rate, 471, *472*

Metabotropic effect the effect at a synapse that produces a relatively slow but long-lasting effect through metabolic reactions, 65, *66*

Met-enkephalin chain of five amino acids believed to function as a neurotransmitter that inhibits pain, 201–202

Methamphetamine, 478, 485

Methylphenidate (Ritalin) stimulant drug that increases the stimulation of dopamine synapses by blocking the reuptake of dopamine by the presynaptic neuron, 222, 454–455, 468

Microdialysis, 317

Microelectrodes, 40, *41,* 42, 164

Microglia very small cells, 35, *36*

Midbrain middle part of the brain, including superior colliculus, inferior colliculus, tectum, and tegmentum, 88

Middle-ear (conductive) deafness hearing loss that occurs if the bones of the middle ear fail to transmit sound waves properly to the cochlea, 192

Midget ganglion cells ganglion cells in the fovea of

humans and other primates, 148, 149

Migration the movement of neurons toward their eventual destinations in the brain, 109

MIH (Müllerian inhibiting hormone), 329

Mind. *See* Brain; Consciousness; Mind-body problem

Mind-body problem or **mind-brain problem** the question of how the mind is related to the brain, 5–7

Miraculin, 209–210

Mitochondrion (plural: mitochondria) the structure where the cell performs the metabolic activities that provide energy, 31

MK-801, 127

Molecule the smallest possible piece of a compound that retains the properties of the compound, 494

Monism the theory that only one kind of substance exists in the universe (not separate physical and mental substances), 5–6

Monoamine nonacidic neurotransmitter containing an amine group (NH_2), formed by a metabolic change of certain amino acids, 62

Monoamine oxidase. *See* MAO

Monoamine oxidase inhibitor (MAOI) drug that blocks the enzyme monoamine oxidase (MAO), a presynaptic terminal enzyme that metabolizes catecholamines and serotonin into inactive forms, 287, 467

Monozygotic twins identical twins, 11, 12, *12. See also specific research subjects*

Mood disorders, 464–475
  bipolar disorder, 471–473, *472*
  major depression, 464–471, *464, 466, 467, 468, 470*
  and schizophrenia, 477
  seasonal affective disorder, 473–474, *474*

"Mooney" faces, 101, *101*

Morphine, 205

Morris search task procedure in which a subject must find his or her way to a slightly submerged platform that is not visible in murky water or other opaque substance, *399, 400*

Motion blindness impaired ability to perceive the direction or speed of

movement, despite otherwise satisfactory vision, 157, 173–174

Motion perception, 172–174, *172, 173,* 182

Motor cortex, *97,* 237–238, *237, 238*

Motor neuron a neuron that receives excitation from other neurons and conducts impulses from its soma in the spinal cord to muscle or gland cells, 32, *33,* 82

Motor program a fixed sequence of movements that occur as a single unit, 234–235

Movement, 227–259
  and body temperature, 230, *230*
  and cognition, 247–248
  and muscles, 228–232
  units of, 232–235, *233*
  See also Brain and movement; Movement disorders

Movement disorders, 249–257, *256*
  Huntington's disease, 89, 254–255, *254, 255,* 478
  Parkinson's disease, 88, 89, 90, 138, 249–253, *250, 251,* 281

MPTP, MPP+ chemicals known to be toxic to the dopamine-containing cells in the substantia nigra, capable of producing the symptoms of Parkinson's disease, 251

MRI. *See* Magnetic resonance imaging

MST medial superior temporal cortex, an area in which neurons are sensitive to expansion, contraction, or rotation of the visual field or to the movement of an object relative to its background, 172

MT (area V5) a portion of the middle temporal cortex, where neurons are highly sensitive to the speed and direction of movement of visual stimuli, 172

Müllerian ducts early precursors to female reproductive structures (the oviducts, uterus, and upper vagina), 329

Müllerian inhibiting hormone (MIH), 329

Multiple sclerosis, 46–47

Multiplier effect a tendency for small genetic or prenatal influences to change the environment in a way that magnifies the change, 12

Muscles, 228–232, *229, 231, 232,* 326–327
  antagonistic, 56–57, *57,* 228, *230*
Muscle spindle receptor parallel to the muscle that responds to the stretch of a muscle, 232
Mutation the change in a gene during reproduction, 11, 14
Myasthenia gravis a disease in which the immune system attacks the acetylcholine receptors at the nerve-muscle junctions, 66, 229–230
Myelinated axon an axon covered with a myelin sheath, 46–47, *46,* 83, 109
Myelination development of a myelin sheath that insulates an axon, 109
Myelin sheath insulating material that covers many vertebrate axons, 32, 46–47, *46,* 131
MZ twins. *See* **Monozygotic twins**

Narcolepsy a condition characterized by unexpected periods of sleepiness during the day, 280–281
Natural killer cell a type of leukocyte that destroys certain kinds of tumor cells and cells infected with viruses, 367
Necrosis, 111
Nefazodone, 467
Negative color afterimage the result of prolonged staring at a colored display and then looking at a white surface, in which one sees green where the display had been red, red where it had been green, yellow where it had been blue, blue where it had been yellow, black where it had been white, and white where it had been black, 152–154
Negative feedback in homeostasis, processes that reduce discrepancies from the set point, 294
Negative symptom the absence of a behavior ordinarily seen in normal people, for example, lack of emotional expression, 476
Neglect the tendency to ignore the contralateral side of the body and the world after damage to the parietal lobe in one hemisphere (usually the right), 220–221, *221*
Nerve (inner-ear) deafness hearing loss that results

from damage to the cochlea, the hair cells, or the auditory nerve, 192
Nerve growth factor (NGF) protein that promotes the survival and growth of axons in the sympathetic nervous system and certain axons in the brain, 110–111, 180
Nerves sets of axons in the periphery, either from the CNS to a muscle or gland or from a sensory organ to the CNS, *83*
Nervous system, 29–48, *80*
  autonomic, 80, 84–85, *84*
  blood-brain barrier, 36–38, *37*
  cell structure, 31–36
  forebrain, 88–90
  hindbrain, 85–88, *86*
  local neurons, 47
  midbrain, 88
  neuron nourishment, 38
  resting potential, 39–42, *41, 42*
  terminology, 2, 80–82, *81, 82*
  See also Action potential; Brain; Research methods; Spinal cord; Synapses
Neural Darwinism the principle that, in the development of the nervous system, synapses form haphazardly at first, and then a selection process keeps some and rejects others, 115
Neuroanatomy the anatomy of the nervous system, 73
Neurochemists, 25
Neurodevelopmental hypothesis the proposal that schizophrenia is based on abnormalities in the prenatal or neonatal development of the nervous system, which lead to subtle but important abnormalities of brain anatomy and major abnormalities in behavior, 481–484, *482, 483, 484*
Neuroglia. *See* **Glia**
Neuroleptic drug that relieves schizophrenia, 485
Neurologists, 25
Neuromodulator chemical that has properties intermediate between those of a neurotransmitter and those of a hormone, 65, 316–317
Neuromuscular junction the synapse where a motor neuron's axon meets a muscle fiber, 228
Neuronal branching. *See* Dendritic branching
Neurons cells that receive information and transmit

it to other cells by conducting electrochemical impulses, 2, *3,* 30, *31, 32*
  adult generation of, 116–117
  cerebellar cortex, 244, *245*
  development of, 109
  importance of, 47–48
  local, 47
  and neurotransmitters, 64
  nourishment of, 38
  number of, *30*
  resting potential, 39–42, *41, 42*
  structure of, 32–34
  survival determinants, 110–112, *111,* 180
  variations among, 34–35, *34*
  See also Action potential; Synapses
Neuropeptide Y (NPY) a peptide found in the brain, especially the hypothalamus; it inhibits activity of the paraventricular nucleus and thereby increases meal size, 316, *316*
Neuropsychologists, 25
Neuroscientists, 25
Neurosurgeons, 25
Neurotransmitters chemicals released by neurons that affect other neurons, 62–67
  chemical structures of, *498*
  and drugs, 67–68, *68*
  inactivation/reuptake of, 66–67
  and pain, 201–202, *202*
  and personality, 68–69, *69*
  and receptor effects, 64–66
  and schizophrenia, 484–487, *485, 487*
  synthesis of, 62–63, *62, 63*
  types of, 62, *62*
Neurotrophin a chemical that promotes the survival and activity of neurons, 111, 115, 127, 253, 412
Neutrons, 494
NGF. *See* Nerve growth factor
Niacin deficiency, 478
Nicotine a drug found in tobacco that, among other effects, stimulates certain acetylcholine receptors, 455–456. *See also* Cigarette smoking
Nicotinic receptor, 455–456
Nicotinic synapses, 65
Night terror the experience of intense anxiety during sleep from which a person awakens screaming in terror, 282
Nimodipine, 137
Nitric oxide gas released by many small neurons and

used as a neuromodulator, 62, 63–64, 332
NMDA receptor glutamate receptor that also responds to the drug *N*-methyl-D-aspartate, 411–413, *412, 413,* 486, 487, *487*
NMR (nuclear magnetic resonance). *See* Magnetic resonance imaging
Node of Ranvier short unmyelinated section of axon between segments of myelin, 32, 46, *46*
Nonfluent aphasia (Broca's aphasia) condition marked by loss of fluent speech and impaired use and understanding of prepositions, word endings, and other grammatical devices, 440–442, *444*
Non-REM (NREM) sleep the sleep stages other than REM sleep, 273
Norepinephrine a neurotransmitter:
  and depression, 467
  and eating regulation, *313,* 319
  reuptake of, 67
  and sleep, 279, 280
  source of, *325*
  and substance abuse, 457
  and sympathetic nervous system, 85
  synthesis of, 62, *63*
NREM sleep. *See* Non-REM (NREM) sleep
NTS. *See* Nucleus of the tractus solitarius
Nuclear magnetic resonance (NMR). *See* Magnetic resonance imaging
Nuclei of the cerebellum clusters of neurons in the interior of the cerebellum that send axons to motor-controlling areas outside the cerebellum, 244
Nucleus accumbens small subcortical brain area that is rich in dopamine receptors and evidently a major part of the brain's reinforcement system, 452, 453, *453,* 456, 470
Nucleus basalis the area on the dorsal surface of the forebrain; a major source of axons that release acetylcholine to widespread areas in the cerebral cortex, 91
Nucleus of the tractus solitarius (NTS) the area in the medulla that receives input from taste receptors, 212, 311
Nucleus a structure within a cell that contains the chromosomes (b) cluster of neuron cell bodies within the CNS, 31, *83,* 86

Obesity:
and genetics, 315, 318
and insulin production,
309–310
and sleep apnea, 280
See also Body weight
Object Naming Latency Task
procedure that measures
how fast a person can
name an object flashed
in the left or right visual
field, 424
Object permanence task, 108,
108
Object recognition disorders,
169–170, *169*
**Obsessive-compulsive disor-
der (OCD)** a disorder
linked to the basal gan-
glia, marked by repeti-
tive thoughts and actions
that the person knows
are pointless and non-
sensical, 246–247
Occipital lobe the posterior
(caudal) section of the
cerebral cortex, 95
OCD. *See* Obsessive-compulsive disorder
Oculomotor nerve, *87*
6-OHDA. *See* 6-
Hydroxydopamine
Olfaction the sense of smell,
89, 214–216, *214, 216,*
337
Olfactory bulb, 88, 89,
214–215
Olfactory cells the neurons
responsible for the sense
of smell, located on the
olfactory epithelium in
the rear of the nasal air
passages, 214
Olfactory nerve, *87*
Olfactory receptors, 89, 116,
214–215, *214, 216*
Oligodendrocytes glia cells
that surround and insu-
late certain axons in the
vertebrate brain and
spinal cord, 35, *36*
Omnivores animals that eat
both meat and plants, 306
Onset insomnia difficulty
falling asleep, 279
Ontogenetic explanations
understanding in terms
of how a structure or a
behavior develops, 3, 4
Operant conditioning a type
of conditioning in which
reinforcement or punish-
ment changes the future
probabilities of a given
behavior, 388, *389*
Opiates class of drugs derived
from, or similar to those
derived from, opium
poppies, 201, 205,
456–457
Opioid mechanisms systems
responsive to opiate
drugs and similar chemi-
cals, 201
Opponent-process theory the
theory that we perceive

color in terms of paired
opposites: white versus
black, red versus green,
and blue versus yellow,
152–154
Opsins, 149
Optic chiasm the point at
which parts of the optic
nerves cross from one
side of the brain to the
other, 422
Optic nerve (or optic tract)
the bundle of axons that
travel from the ganglion
cells of the retina to the
brain, *87,* 146, 147, 157
Orexin (hypocretin) neurotransmitter that stimu-
lates acetylcholine-
releasing cells and
thereby increases wake-
fulness and arousal, 281,
317
Organizing effect long-lasting
effect of a hormone that
is present during a sensitive period early in
development, 328–330
Organum vasculosum lami-
nae terminalis. *See*
OVLT
Orlistat (Xenical), 319
Osmotic pressure the tendency of water to flow
across a semipermeable
membrane from the area
of low solute concentra-
tion to the area of high
solute concentration,
300–302, *301*
Osmotic thirst the thirst that
results from an increase
in the concentration of
solutes in the body,
300–302, *301, 303*
Otolith organs, 197
Oval window a membrane of
the inner ear, adjacent to
the stirrup, 189
Ovaries the female gonads
that produce eggs, *325,*
329, 333, *334*
**OVLT (organum vasculosum
laminae terminalis)** a
brain structure on the
border of the third ven-
tricle, highly sensitive to
the osmotic pressure of
the blood, 301, 302
Oxygen, 38, 231
Oxytocin a hormone released
by the posterior pitu-
itary; also a neurotrans-
mitter; important for
sexual and parental
behaviors, *325,* 327

Pacinian corpuscle a receptor
that responds to a sud-
den displacement of the
skin or high-frequency
vibration on the skin,
198, *200*
Pain, 201–205, *202, 203, 204*
and phantom limbs,
135–136

Pancreas, 309, *325*
Panic disorder a condition
characterized by occa-
sional attacks of extreme
fear, breathlessness,
heart palpitations, fa-
tigue, and dizziness, 360,
381
Papilla (plural: papillae)
structure on the surface
of the tongue containing
taste buds, 209
Paradoxical sleep. *See* REM
(rapid eye movement)
sleep
Parallel fibers axons that run
parallel to one another
but perpendicular to the
planes of the Purkinje
cells in the cerebellum,
244, *245*
Paralysis, *240*
Paraplegia, *240*
**Parasympathetic nervous
system (PNS)** the system
of nerves that facilitate
vegetative, nonemer-
gency responses by the
body's organs, *84, 85,*
358
and stress, 364–365, *365,*
366
Parathyroid gland, *325*
Parathyroid hormone, *325*
**Paraventricular nucleus
(PVN)** the area of the
hypothalamus in which
activity tends to limit
meal size and damage
leads to excessively large
meals, 301, *311,* 312,
314, 316
Parental behavior, 337–338,
337
Parietal lobe the section of
the cerebral cortex be-
tween the occipital lobe
and the central sulcus,
96, 289
Parkinson's disease malady
caused by damage to a
dopamine pathway,
resulting in slow move-
ments, difficulty initiating movements, rigidity
of the muscles, and
tremors:
and brain structure, 88,
89, 90, 249–253,
250, 251
and REM behavior disor-
der, 281
therapies for, 138,
252–253
Paroxetine (Paxil or Seroxat),
467
Parrots, 435–436, *435*
Parvocellular neuron small-
celled neuron of the
visual system that is
sensitive to color differences and visual details
in its small visual field,
162, *163,* 172
Paxil (paroxetine), 467
PCP. *See* Phencyclidine

Penumbra area of endangered
cells surrounding an area
of primary damage, 127
Peptide a chain of amino
acids, 62, 63, 456
Peptide hormone a hormone
composed of a short
chain of amino acids,
324
Perception:
binding of, 99–102, *100,*
101
principles of, 144–145,
145
See also Sensory systems
Periaqueductal gray area the
area of the brainstem
that is rich in enkephalin
synapses, 202, *203*
**Periodic limb movement
disorder** repeated involuntary movement of the
legs and sometimes arms
during sleep, 281
Periodic table of elements,
495
Periovulatory period the time
just before and after the
release of the ovum,
when fertility is highest,
334
**Peripheral nervous system
(PNS)** the nerves outside
the brain and spinal
cord, 80
Peripheral vision, 148, 149,
150, 220
Personality, 68–69, *69*
PET. *See* Positron emission
tomography
PGO wave a pattern of high-
amplitude electrical
potentials that occurs
first in the pons, then in
the lateral geniculate,
and finally in the occipital cortex, 278, *278,* 288
Phantom limb the continuing
sensation of an ampu-
tated body part,
134–136, *134, 135, 136,*
193
Phase differences, 194–195,
195
Phencyclidine (PCP) a drug
that inhibits type NMDA
glutamate receptors; at
low doses produces
intoxication and slurred
speech, and at higher
doses produces both
positive and negative
symptoms of schizophre-
nia, 478, 486–487
Phenothiazines the class of
antipsychotic drugs that
includes
chlorpromazine, 485
Phentermine, 318
Phenylalanine, 376–377
Phenylephrine, 93
Phenylketonuria (PKU) the
inherited inability to
metabolize phenylala-
nine, leading to mental
retardation unless the

afflicted person stays on a strict low-phenylalanine diet throughout childhood, 13

Phenythiocarbamide (PTC), 10, 212–213

Pheromone a chemical released by one animal that affects the behavior of other members of the same species, 217, 337

Phonological loop the aspect of working memory that stores auditory information, including words, 394

Phospholipids, 473

Photopigment a chemical that releases energy when struck by light, 149–150

Phrenology the pseudoscience that claimed a relationship between skull anatomy and behavioral capacities, 77–78, 77

Physiological explanations understanding in terms of the activity of the brain and other organs, 3, 4

Pineal gland a small unpaired gland in the brain, just posterior to the thalamus, that releases the hormone melatonin, 5, 265, 325

Pinna the outer-ear structure of flesh and cartilage that sticks out from each side of the head, 189

Pitch the experience that corresponds to the frequency of a sound, 188, 190–192, 192, 193

Pituitary gland endocrine gland attached to the base of the hypothalamus, 90, 311, 327–328, 327, 328
and menstrual cycle, 333, 334

Pituitary gland endocrine gland attached to the base of the hypothalamus and stress, 366, 367

PKU. See Phenylketonuria

Placebo a drug or other procedure with no pharmacological effects, 204, 468

Placebo effect deriving benefit due to the expectation of improvement or to the mere passage of time, 204

Place theory the concept that pitch perception depends on which part of the inner ear has cells with the greatest activity level, 190

Planum temporale the area of the temporal cortex that for most people is larger in the left hemisphere than in the right hemisphere, 428, 429

Plaque the structure formed from degenerating axons and dendrites in the brains of people with Alzheimer's disease, 403–404

Plasma membrane, 31

Plasticity, 136, 409, 411

PMS. See Premenstrual syndrome

PNS. See Parasympathetic nervous system; Peripheral nervous system

POA/AH. See Preoptic area/anterior hypothalamus

Poikilothermic maintaining the body at the same temperature as the environment, 295

Polarization the electrical gradient across a membrane, 39

Poliomyelitis, 240

Polypeptides, 62

Polysomnograph the combination of EEG and eye-movement records, and sometimes other data, for a sleeping person, 273

Pons hindbrain structure, anterior and ventral to the medulla, 86, 278, 288, 377

Pontomesencephalon part of the reticular formation that contributes to cortical arousal by axons that release acetylcholine and glutamate in the basal forebrain and thalamus, 275

Positive symptom the presence of a behavior not seen in normal people, 476

Positron emission tomography (PET) a method of mapping activity in a living brain by recording the emission of radioactivity from injected chemicals, 76, 247, 278

Postcentral gyrus a gyrus of the cerebral cortex just posterior to the central gyrus; a primary projection site for touch and other body sensations, 96, 118, 239

Posterior commissure, 429

Posterior parietal cortex an area with a mixture of visual, somatosensory, and movement functions, particularly in monitoring the position of the body relative to objects in the world, 239

Posterior pituitary a portion of the pituitary gland, 300, 325, 327

Posterior toward the rear end, 82

Postganglionic fibers, 85

Postpartum depression depression after giving birth, 465

Postsynaptic neuron a neuron on the receiving end of a synapse, 55, 56, 110–111, 180, 408, 411–413, 468

Posttraumatic stress disorder (PTSD) a condition resulting from a severe traumatic experience, leading to a long-lasting state of frequent distressing recollections (flashbacks) and nightmares about the traumatic event, avoidance of reminders of it, and exaggerated arousal in response to noises and other stimuli, 369–370, 377

Potassium ions, 40, 43, 44, 127, 410

Poverty of the stimulus argument the claim that children do not hear many examples of some of the grammatical structures they acquire and therefore that they could not learn them, 439

Precentral gyrus the gyrus of the cerebral cortex just anterior to the central sulcus, site of the primary motor cortex, 97

Prefrontal cortex the anterior portion of the frontal lobe of the cortex, which responds mostly to the sensory stimuli that signal the need for a movement, 97–99, 98
and attack behaviors, 375
and depression, 465
development of, 111
and emotions, 357–358
and memory, 99, 395, 402
and movement, 239
prefrontal lobotomies, 98–99, 98
and schizophrenia, 482, 483, 484, 484, 486, 487

Prefrontal lobotomy the surgical disconnection of the prefrontal cortex from the rest of the brain, 98–99, 98

Preganglionic axons, 85

Pregnancy. See Prenatal development

Premenstrual syndrome (PMS) a condition of anxiety, irritability, and depression during the days just before menstruation, 335

Premotor cortex the area of the frontal cortex, just anterior to the primary motor cortex, active

during the planning of a movement, 239

Prenatal development:
and alcohol exposure, 123, 123, 348
and attack behaviors, 373, 373
and body temperature, 297
and schizophrenia, 481
sexual differentiation, 329–330
and sexual orientation, 347, 348
twins, 12, 12
See also Brain development

Preoptic area/anterior hypothalamus (POA/AH) brain area important for temperature control, 297, 298

Presymptomic test an exam to predict the onset of a disease, conducted before any symptoms appear, 254

Presynaptic neuron a neuron on the releasing end of a synapse, 55, 413, 466

Presynaptic receptor the receptor located on the terminal at the tip of an axon, 410–411

Presynaptic terminal the tip of an axon, the point from which the axon releases chemicals, 32–33

Primary auditory cortex area in the temporal lobes in which cells respond best to tones of a particular frequency, 191–192, 192, 193

Primary motor cortex area of the frontal cortex just anterior to the central sulcus; a primary point of origin for axons conveying messages to the spinal cord, 97, 237–239, 237, 238

Primary somatosensory cortex. See Postcentral gyrus

Primary visual cortex (V1) the area of the cortex responsible for the first stage of visual processing, 95, 162–163
cell types in, 164–166, 165, 166
columnar organization of, 166–167, 167
feature detectors in, 167–168, 167, 168

Primates monkeys, apes, and humans, 120–121

Priming the phenomenon that seeing or hearing a word or words temporarily increases one's probability of using them, 402

Problem of other minds difficulty of knowing

whether other people (or animals) have conscious experiences, 7, 20

Procedural memory the memory of motor skills, 397

Productivity the ability of language to produce new signals to represent new ideas, 433

Progesterone a steroid hormone which, among other functions, prepares the uterus for the implantation of a fertilized ovum and promotes the maintenance of pregnancy, 137–138, *325, 326, 333, 335*

Prolactin, *325, 327*

Proliferation the production of new cells, 109

Propagation of the action potential the transmission of an action potential down an axon, 45, *45, 46*

Proprioceptor a receptor that is sensitive to the position and movement of a part of the body, 231–232, *231, 232*

Prosencephalon. *See* Forebrain

Prosopagnosia an impaired ability to recognize or identify faces, 169

Prostaglandin E_1 and E_2 chemicals produced during an infection, which stimulate increased body temperature (fever) and increased sleep, 298

Prostaglandins body chemicals that promote sleep, 277

Protein channels, 31

Protein hormone a hormone composed of a long chain of amino acids, 324

Protein phosphatase 1, 393

Proteins, 9, 32, 62, 255, 296–297, 403–404

Protons, 494

Proximal located close (approximate) to the point of origin or attachment, *82*

Prozac (Fluoxetine), 67, 467, *467*

Pseudohermaphrodite. *See* Intersex

Psychiatric drugs. *See* Drugs

Psychiatrists, 25

Psychological disorders. *See* Mood disorders; Schizophrenia; Substance abuse

Psychoneuroimmunology the study of the ways in which experiences, especially stressful ones, alter the immune system and how the immune

system in turn influences the central nervous system, 368–369

Psychophysical observations reports by observers concerning their perceptions of various stimuli, 150–151

Psychophysiologists, 25

Psychosomatic illnesses, 364–365

Psychotherapy, 469

Psychotic symptoms, 476–477

PTSD. *See* Posttraumatic stress disorder

Pudendal nerve, 332

Pulvinar nucleus, 102

Punishment an event that suppresses the frequency of the preceding response, 388

Pupil the opening in the center of the iris through which light enters, 146

Pure autonomic failure a condition in which output from the autonomic nervous system to the body fails, 359

Purines the category of chemicals including adenosine, 62

Purkinje cell a neuron type in the cerebellum; a very flat cell in a plane perpendicular to that of other Purkinje cells, *34, 244, 245*

Putamen a large subcortical structure, one part of the basal ganglia, 90, 245, 246

PVN. *See* Paraventricular nucleus

Pyramids, 240

Quadriplegia, *240*

Radial glia type of glia cells that guides the migration of neurons and the growth of their axons and dendrites during embryological development, 35

Radial maze an apparatus with many arms radiating from a central point; reinforcement is put at the ends of some or all of the arms, 399, *399*

Raphe system a group of neurons in the pons and medulla whose axons extend throughout much of the forebrain, 86

Rapid eye movement sleep. *See* REM (rapid eye movement) sleep

Rasmussen's encephalopathy a rare condition in which an autoimmune disorder attacks first the glia and then the neurons of one or the other

hemisphere of the brain, 430

RCBF. *See* Regional cerebral blood flow

Reading ability: and brain damage, 441–443
dyslexia, 445–447, *446*
See also Language

Receptive field the part of the visual field to which any one neuron responds, 159, *159, 160*

Receptor potential the local depolarization or hyperpolarization of a receptor membrane, 144

Recessive gene gene that shows its effects only in the homozygous condition, 10, 11

Reciprocal altruism helping individuals who may later be helpful in return, 18

Recombination the reassortment of genes during reproduction, leading to a characteristic that is not apparent in either parent, 11, 14

Red nucleus a nucleus midbrain structure whose axons join the dorsolateral tract of the spinal cord, controlling distal muscles of the body such as those in the hands and feet, 239–240

Reflex a consistent, automatic response to a stimulus, 54–55, *54,* 232
as ballistic movement, 234
infant, 233, *233*
and medulla, 85–86
stretch, 231, 232, *232*

Reflex arc circuit of neurons from the sensory neurons to muscle responses that produces a reflex, 54, *54,* 56

Refractory period the brief period following an action potential, when the cell resists the production of further action potentials, 44

Regional cerebral blood flow (rCBF) method of estimating activity of different areas of the brain by dissolving a radioactive chemical such as xenon in the blood and measuring radioactivity from different brain areas, 76

Reinforcement an event that increases the future probability of the preceding response, 453–454

Reinforcer an event that increases the future probability of the preceding response, 388

Relative refractory period the time after the absolute refractory period, when potassium gates remain open wider than usual, requiring a stronger than usual stimulus to initiate an action potential, 44

Releasing hormone a hormone released by the hypothalamus that flows through the blood to the anterior pituitary, 327

REM behavior disorder a condition in which people move around vigorously during REM sleep, 281

REM (rapid eye movement) sleep the sleep stage with rapid eye movements, high brain activity, and relaxation of the large muscles, 273–274, 278–280, *278, 279*
functions of, 285–288, *286, 287*
and narcolepsy, 281

Renin, 302, *325*

Repair and restoration theory of sleep the concept that the function of sleep is to enable the body to repair itself after the exertions of the day, 284

Reproductive behaviors. *See* Sex hormones; Sexual behavior

Research: on animals, 20–24, *21, 22,* 499–501
blind alleys in, 407–408
on human subjects, 501
See also Research methods

Research methods, 74–79
autoradiography, 132
electroencephalograph, 271
histochemistry, 135
and lateralization, 424
lesions, 130
magnetic resonance imaging, 76–77, 112, 170
microdialysis, 317
microelectrodes, 40, *41, 42,* 164
positron emission tomography, 76, 247, 278
Wisconsin Card Sorting Task, 483

Resting potential the electrical potential across a membrane when a neuron is not being stimulated, 39–42, *41, 42*

Reticular formation a network of neurons in the medulla and other parts of the brainstem; the descending portion controls motor areas of the spinal cord; the ascending portion selectively increases arousal and attention in various forebrain areas, 86, 274–275

Retina the rear surface of the eye, lined with visual receptors, 146–149, *147, 148, 158*
  and color vision, *152*
  lateral inhibition in, 160–161, *160, 161, 162*
  neural pathways in, 162, *163*
  visual receptors in, 149–150, *149*

Retinal disparity discrepancy between what the left eye sees and what the right eye sees, 179–180

Retinex theory the concept that when information from various parts of the retina reaches the cortex, the cortex compares each of the inputs to determine the color perception in each area, 154–155

Retinohypothalamic path, 268

Retrograde amnesia the loss of memory for events that occurred before brain damage, 395

Retrograde transmitter a transmitter, released by a postsynaptic cell under extensive stimulation, that travels back to the presynaptic cell to modify it, 413, 458

Reuptake the reabsorption of a neurotransmitter by the presynaptic terminal, 67

Reverberating circuit, 393, *393*

Rh incompatibility, 481

Rhombencephalon. *See* Hindbrain

Ribonucleic acid (RNA) a single strand chemical; one type of an RNA molecule serves as a template for the synthesis of protein molecules, 9, *9*

Ribosome the site at which the cell synthesizes new protein molecules, 31–32

Ritalin (methylphenidate) stimulant drug that increases the stimulation of dopamine synapses by blocking the reuptake of dopamine by the presynaptic neuron, 222, 454–455, 468

RNA. *See* Ribonucleic acid

Ro15-4513 experimental drug, 383

Robots, 7, 8

Rod a type of retinal receptor that does not contribute to color perception, 149–150, *149*

Rooting reflex the reflexive head turning and sucking after a touch on the cheek, 233, *233*

Saccade ballistic movement of the eyes from one fixation point to another, 243

SAD. *See* Seasonal affective disorder

Sagittal plane the plane that shows brain structures as they would be seen from the side, *81, 82*

Saliva, 305

Saltatory conduction the jumping of action potentials from one node to another by the flow of positive ions, 45–47, *46*

Satiety, 307–310. *See also* Eating regulation

Schizophrenia a disorder characterized both by a deteriorating ability to function in everyday life and by some combination of hallucinations, delusions, thought disorder, movement disorder, and inappropriate emotional expressions, 476–489
  characteristics of, 476–479, *477*
  drugs for, 484–485, *485,* 488–489, *488*
  and electroconvulsive therapy, 469
  and genetics, 479–480, *479*
  neurodevelopmental hypothesis, 481–484, *482, 483, 484*
  neurotransmitter hypotheses, 484–487, *485, 487*

Schwann cell a glia cell that surrounds and insulates certain axons in the periphery of the vertebrate body, 35, 36, *36*

Scientific American, 25

SCN. *See* Suprachiasmatic nucleus

SDN. *See* Sexually dimorphic nucleus

Seasonal affective disorder (SAD) a period of depression that recurs seasonally, such as in winter, 473–474, *474*

Season-of-birth effect the tendency for people born in winter to have a greater probability of developing schizophrenia than people born in other seasons, 481

Secondary visual cortex (V2) the area of the visual cortex responsible for the second stage of visual processing, 163

Second messenger the chemical within a neuron that, when activated by a neurotransmitter, initiates processes that carry messages to several areas within the neuron, 65, 275

Selective permeability the ability of certain chemicals to pass more freely than others through a membrane, 40

Selective serotonin reuptake inhibitor (SSRI) a drug that blocks the reuptake of serotonin into the presynaptic terminal, 467, *467*

Self-stimulation of the brain behavior that is reinforced by direct electrical stimulation of a brain area, 452–453, *452*

Semicircular canal a canal lined with hair cells and oriented in three planes, sensitive to the direction of tilt of the head, 197

Seminal vesicles, 329

Sensitive (critical) period the time early in development during which some event (such as an experience or the presence of a hormone) has a strong and long-lasting effect, 178, 330, 440

Sensitization an increase in the response to mild stimuli as a result of previous exposure to more intense stimuli, 409–410, *410*

Sensory neuron a neuron specialized to be highly sensitive to a specific type of stimulation, 32, *33, 34*

Sensory systems, 187
  and binding problem, 100–101, *101*
  and brain structure, 88–90, 96, *97,* 102
  and lateralization, 420, 421–422, 425–426, *426*
  See also Audition; Chemical senses; Mechanical senses; Vision

Serendipity, 366

Serotonin a neurotransmitter:
  and alcoholism, 459–460
  and attack behaviors, 375–377, *376*
  and cannabinoids, 458
  and depression, 376–377, *376,* 467
  and hallucinogenic drugs, 458
  reuptake of, 67
  and sensitization, 410–411
  and sexual behavior, 332
  and sleep, 278–279

and stimulant drugs, 454
  synthesis of, 62–63, *63*
  and weight loss, 319

Seroxat (paroxetine), 467

Sertraline (Zoloft), 467

Set point the level at which homeostatic processes maintain a variable, 294

Sex differences, 331, 465, 478. *See also* Gender identity

Sex hormones, 328–339
  and cognition, 335–336, *336*
  and depression, 465
  and endocrine glands, 324, *324, 325*
  and intersexes, 342
  and menstrual cycle, 333–334, *333, 334,* 335
  organizing effects of, 328–331, *329*
  and parental behavior, 337–338, *337*
  and sexual behavior, 331, 332–333, 334, *335, 336*

Sex-limited gene a gene that exerts its effects primarily in one sex because of activation by androgens or estrogens, although members of both sexes may have the gene, 11, 326

Sex-linked gene a gene on either the X or the Y chromosome, 10–11

Sex offenders, 332–333

Sexual behavior, 323
  evolutionary explanations, 340–342
  and hormones, 331, 332–333, 334
  and pheromones, 217
  and sex hormones, 331, 332–333, 334, *335, 336*
  See also Sexual orientation

Sexually dimorphic nucleus (SDN) a part of the medial preoptic nucleus of the hypothalamus, larger in males than in females and linked to male sexual behavior, 329–330, 332

Sexual orientation, 345–351
  and brain anatomy, 348–350, *349, 350*
  and genetics, 346–347, *346*
  and hormones, 347
  and prenatal development, 347, 348

SFO. *See* Subfornical organ

Sham-feeding a procedure in which everything that an animal swallows leaks out a tube connected to the esophagus or stomach, 308

Sham lesion a control procedure for an experiment,

in which an investigator inserts an electrode into a brain but does not pass a current, 130

Shape constancy the ability to perceive the shape of an object despite the movement or rotation of the object, 168–169

Shape perception, 164–171
  and columnar organization, 166–167, *167*
  disorders of, 169–170, *169*
  feature detectors, 167–168, *167, 168*
  and fusiform gyrus, 169–171, *170, 171*
  and inferior temporal cortex, 168–169
  primary visual cortex cell types, 164–166, *165, 166*

Shell shock. *See* Posttraumatic stress disorder

Shift work, 268

Shivering, 298

Short-term memory the memory of an event that just happened, 391–393

Sibutramine (Meridia), 318–319

SIDS (sudden infant death syndrome), 280

Sight. *See* Vision

Sildenafil (Viagra), 332

Simple cell a type of visual cortex cell that has fixed excitatory and inhibitory zones in its receptive field, 164–165, *165*

Skeletal (striated) muscles muscles that control the movement of the body in relation to the environment (such as arm and leg muscles), 228, *229*

Skin, *199*

Sleep:
  abnormalities of, 279–282, *280*
  and arousal, 275–277, *276, 277*
  and depression, 280, 470–471, *471*
  and dreams, 273–274, 288–289
  evolutionary explanations, 284–285
  functions of, 284–287, *286, 287*
  and melatonin, 265–266
  stages of, 271–273, *272, 274*
  See also Circadian rhythms; REM (rapid eye movement) sleep

Sleep apnea the inability to breathe while sleeping, 280, *281*

Sleep deprivation, 276, 284, 286, 470–471

Sleep paralysis, 281

Sleep spindle 12- to 14-Hz brain waves in bursts that last at least half a second, 272

Sleep talking, 282

Sleepwalking, 282

Slow-twitch fibers muscle fibers that produce less vigorous contractions without fatiguing, 230–231

Slow-wave sleep (SWS) stages 3 and 4 of sleep, which are occupied largely by slow, large-amplitude brain waves, 272–273

Smell. *See* Olfaction

Smoking. *See* Cigarette smoking

Smooth muscles muscles that control the movements of internal organs, 228, *229*

Society for Neuroscience, 499–501

Sociobiology the field concerned with how and why various social behaviors evolved, 16–18, 25

Sodium ions, 41, 43–44, 56, 211, 301, 459

Sodium-potassium pump the mechanism that actively transports three sodium ions out of the cell while simultaneously drawing in two potassium ions, 41, *41*

Sodium-specific cravings, 302

Solipsism the philosophical position that I alone exist or I alone am conscious, 6

Solutes, 300–301

Soma (cell body) the structure of a cell that contains the nucleus, 32, 482

Somatic nervous system nerves that convey messages from the sense organs to the CNS and from the CNS to muscles and glands, 80

Somatomedins, *325*

Somatosensory cortex, 134–136, *134*, 200, 212

Somatosensory receptors, 197–198, *199*

Somatosensory system the sensory network that monitors the surface of the body and its movements, 197–201, *199, 200, 201*, 212
  and amputated limbs, 134–136, *134, 135, 136*

Somatotropin (growth hormone), *325*, 327

Sound localization, 194–195, *194, 195*

Sound shadow, 194

Sound waves, 188, *188, 194*

Spatial memory, 399–400, *401, 402*

Spatial neglect a tendency to ignore the left side of the body and its surroundings, 220–221, *221*

Spatial summation combination of effects of activity from two or more synapses onto a single neuron, 56, *57*

Specific anosmia inability to smell one type of chemical, 215

Specificity the property (found in long-term potentiation) that highly active synapses become strengthened but less active synapses do not, 411

Speech, 424, 430. *See also* Language

Spinal cord the part of the CNS found within the spinal column; it communicates with the sense organs and muscles below the level of the head, 82–83, *82, 83, 129*
  brain connections to, 239–241, *241, 242*
  disorders of, *240*
  and somatosensory system, 199–200, *200*

Spinal nerves nerves that convey information between the spinal cord and either sensory receptors or muscles in the periphery, 199, *200, 201*

Splanchnic nerves nerves carrying impulses from the thoracic and lumbar parts of the spinal cord to the digestive organs and from the digestive organs to the spinal cord; they convey information about the nutrient content of food in the digestive system, 308

Split-brain people those who have undergone damage to the corpus callosum, 422–426, *423, 426*

Spontaneous firing rate the periodic production of action potentials by a neuron in the absence of synaptic input, 58

SRY gene sex-region Y gene, which causes the primitive gonads to develop into testes, 329

SSRI. *See* Selective serotonin reuptake inhibitor

Startle reflex the response that one makes after a sudden, unexpected loud noise or similar sudden stimulus, 377–378

Statoacoustic nerve, *87*

Stem cells undifferentiated cells that can divide and produce daughter cells that develop more specialized properties, 109, 116, 138, 253

Stereoscopic depth perception the sensation of depth by comparing the slightly different inputs from the two eyes, 171–172, 179–180

Stereotaxic instrument a device for the precise placement of electrodes in the head, 130

Steroid hormone a hormone that contains four carbon rings, 324–325, 326–327, *326*

Stimulant drugs drugs that tend to produce excitement, alertness, elevated mood, decreased fatigue, and sometimes increased motor activity:
  and ADHD, 222–223, 454
  and brain damage recovery, 129
  and narcolepsy, 281
  and prenatal development, 123
  and schizophrenia, 478, 485, 487
  and substance abuse, 454–455, *455*

St. John's wort, 467–468

Stomach, 305–306, 308

Strabismus a condition in which the two eyes point in different directions, 180

Stress the nonspecific response of the body to any demand made upon it, 364–371
  and autonomic nervous system, 364–366, *365*
  and HPA axis, 366, *367*, 368–369
  and immune system, 367–369, *368, 369*
  and memory, 369, *369*, 402
  posttraumatic stress disorder, 369–370, *377*

Stretch reflex the reflexive contraction of a muscle in response to a stretch of that muscle, 231, 232, *232*

Striate cortex. *See* Primary visual cortex

Striated (skeletal) muscles muscles that controls the movement of the body in relation to the environment (such as arm and leg muscles), 228, *229*

Stroke (cerebrovascular accident) the temporary loss of normal blood flow to a brain area, 125–127, *126, 127*, 458

Subarachnoid space, 93

with a strong genetic basis and rapid onset early in life; much more common in men, 459–460

UCR. *See* Unconditioned response
UCS. *See* Unconditioned stimulus
Ulcers, 364–365
Unconditioned response (UCR) a response automatically evoked by an unconditioned stimulus, 388
Unconditioned stimulus (UCS) a stimulus that automatically evokes an unconditioned response, 388
Unipolar disorder a mood disorder with only one extreme (or pole), generally depression, 471
Urbach-Wiethe disease, 379

Vagus nerve the tenth cranial nerve, which has branches to and from the stomach and several other organs; it conveys information about the stretching of the stomach walls, *87*, 308, 394
Valium (Diazepam), 382
Valproic acid, 473
Vas deferens, 329
Vasopressin (antidiuretic hormone) pituitary hormone that raises blood pressure and enables the kidneys to reabsorb water and therefore to secrete highly concentrated urine, 300, 302, *325*, 327
Venlaxafine, 467
Ventral toward the stomach, away from the dorsal (back) side, 2, *2*, 80, 81, *81*
Ventral stream visual paths in the temporal cortex, sometimes known as the "what" pathway, 163–164
Ventral tegmental neurons, 456
Ventricles any of the four fluid-filled cavities in the brain, 92–93, *92*, 482, *482*
Ventromedial hypothalamus (VMH) the region of the hypothalamus, in which

damage leads to faster stomach emptying and increased secretion of insulin, *311*, 312, *313*, 332
Ventromedial tract the path of axons in the spinal cord providing bilateral control of the trunk muscles, 240–241, *242*, 426
Vesicles the tiny, nearly spherical packets near the axon terminals filled with the neurotransmitter, 61, 63, *64*
Vestibular nucleus the cluster of neurons in the brainstem, primarily responsible for motor responses to vestibular sensation, 240
Vestibular organ the component in the inner ear that detects tilt of the head, 197, *198*
Vestibular sensation, 197, *198*
Viagra (sildenafil), 332
Violent behavior. *See* Attack behaviors
Viruses:
    and blood-brain barrier, 37
    and mood disorders, 465–466, *466*
    and schizophrenia, 481
Vision, 143–183
    and binding problem, 174–175
    color, 149, 150–155, *151, 152, 153, 154*, 171
    depth perception, 171–172, 179–180
    development of, 177–182, *177, 181*
    and dyslexia, 445
    eye-brain connections, 146–149, *147, 148*
    and lateralization, 421–422, 425–426, *426*
    motion perception, 157, 172–174, *172, 173, 182*
    and neural pathways, 162–164, *163*
    and principles of perception, 144–145, *145*
    processing mechanics, 159–161, *159, 160, 161*
    shape perception, 164–171, *165, 166, 167, 168, 169, 170, 171*
    system overview, 157–159, *159*

visual attention, 174
visual receptors, 146, 149–150, *149*
Visual agnosia the impaired ability to identify visual objects despite otherwise satisfactory vision, 169
Visual attention, 174
Visual cortex, 163, 167–168, *167, 168*, 289
Visual field the area of the world that an individual can see at any time, 159, 421, 425–426
Visual receptors, 146, 149–150, *149*
Visuospatial sketchpad an aspect of working memory that stores visual information, 394
VMH. *See* Ventromedial hypothalamus
VNO. *See* Vomeronasal organ
Volley principle the tenet that a sound wave of a moderately high pitch may produce a volley of impulses by various fibers even if no individual fiber can produce impulses in synchrony with the sound waves, 191
Voltage-activated channel a membrane channel whose permeability to sodium (or some other ion) depends on the voltage difference across the membrane, 43
Vomeronasal organ (VNO) the set of receptors located near, but separate from, the olfactory receptors, 216–217, 337
Voodoo death, 366

Wada test a procedure in which a physician injects sodium amytal, a barbiturate tranquilizer, into the carotid artery on one side of the head; the drug puts that side of the brain to sleep, enabling researchers to test the capacities of the other hemisphere, 362, 424
Wakefulness, 274–275
Wakefulness/sleep cycles. *See* Circadian rhythms; Sleep
Water regulation, 300–303
Weight regulation. *See* Body weight; Obesity
Wellbutrin (bupropion), 467

Wernicke-Korsakoff syndrome, 38, 402–403
Wernicke's aphasia (fluent aphasia) a condition marked by poor language comprehension and great difficulty remembering the names of objects, 443–444, *444*
Wernicke's area the portion of the human left temporal lobe associated with language comprehension, *441*, 443
White matter area of the nervous system consisting mostly of myelinated axons, 83, *83*
Williams syndrome a type of mental retardation in which the person has good language skills in spite of extremely limited abilities in other regards, 438–439, *438*
Wisconsin Card Sorting Task, 483
Wolffian ducts early precursors to male reproductive structures, 329
Woodpeckers, 125
Working memory the temporary storage of memories while we are working with them or attending to them, 99, 289, 394–395, 482

Xanax (Alprazolam), 382
X chromosome the chromosome of which female mammals have two and males have one, 10–11
Xenical (orlistat), 319

Yawning, *3*, 235
Y chromosome the chromosome of which female mammals have none and males one, 10–11
Young-Helmholtz (trichomatic) theory the theory that we perceive color through the relative rates of response by three kinds of cones, with each kind maximally sensitive to a different set of wavelengths, 150–152

Zeitgeber a stimulus that resets a biological clock, 267
Zoloft (sertraline), 467

COMMENTS FROM SOME NOTED BIOLOGICAL PSYCHOLOGISTS

Nancy C. Andreasen

Being a scientist and a clinician is a double privilege. We actually get paid to spend our time asking both scientific and clinical questions that everyone would like to ask and have answered, and people grant us the trust of sharing their most intimate thoughts and experiences with us.

William C. Dement

The average person would not, at first blush, pick watching people sleep as the most apparent theme for a spine-tingling scientific adventure thriller. However, there is a subtle sense of awe and mystery surrounding the "short death" we call sleep.

Masao Ito

Brains seem to be built on several principles such that numerous neurons interact with each other through excitation and inhibition, that synaptic plasticity provides memory elements, that multi-layered neuronal networks bear a high computational power, and that combination of neuronal networks, sensors and effectors constitutes a neural system representing a brain function. Thus, Hebbian tradition has provided a very successful paradigm in modern neuroscience, but we may have to go beyond it in order to understand the entire functions of brains.

Roger W. Sperry (1913–1994)

When subjective values have objective consequences . . . they become part of the content of science. . . . Science would become the final determinant of what is right and true, the best source and authority available to the human brain for finding ultimate axioms and guideline beliefs to live by, and for reaching an intimate understanding and rapport with the forces that control the universe and created man.

David Hubel

Brain science is difficult and tricky, for some reason; consequently one should not believe a result (one's own or anyone else's) until it is proven backwards and forwards or fits into a framework so highly evolved and systematic that it couldn't be wrong.

Patricia S. Goldman-Rakic

The question of how the brain organizes its subsystems to produce integrated behavior is perhaps the most challenging that can be posed.

Charles Scott Sherrington (1857–1952)

A rainbow every morning who would pause to look at? The wonderful which comes often or is plentifully about us is soon taken for granted. That is practical enough. It allows us to get on with life. But it may stultify if it cannot on occasion be thrown off. To recapture now and then childhood's wonder, is to secure a driving force for occasional grown-up thoughts.

Eric R. Kandel

The questions posed by higher cognitive processes such as learning and memory are formidable, and we have only begun to explore them. Although elementary aspects of simple forms of learning have been accessible to molecular analysis in invertebrates, we are only now beginning to know a bit about the genes and proteins involved in more complex, hippocampus based, learning processes of mammals.

Carla J. Shatz

The functioning of the brain depends upon the precision and patterns of its neural circuits. How is this amazing computational machine assembled and wired during development? The biological answer is so much more wonderful than anticipated! The adult precision is sculpted from an early imprecise pattern by a process in which connections are verified by the functioning of the neurons themselves. Thus, the developing brain is not simply a miniature version of the adult. Moreover, the brain works to wire itself, rather than assembling itself first and then flipping a switch, as might happen in the assembly of a computer. This kind of surprise in scientific discovery opens up new vistas of understanding and possibility and makes the process of doing science infinitely exciting and fascinating.

Frank A. Beach (1911–1988)

Grant money comes from taxes; taxes come from a lot of folks who don't have much money. Spend that money wisely. To what degree should my choice of research work be governed by human needs, by social imperatives, and how am I going to justify spending all of my energies on any research that does not bear directly on pressing human problems? . . . The solution, or rationalization, that I have finally come up with is that it is a perfectly worthwhile way of spending one's life to do your level best to increase human knowledge, and it is not necessary nor is it always even desirable to be constrained by possible applicability of what you find to immediate problems. This may sound very peculiar to some young people, but it is a value judgement which I myself have made and which I can live with.

Duane Rumbaugh and Sue Savage-Rumbaugh with chimpanzee Austin

Chimpanzees and bonobos are outstanding teachers of psychology. They never presume that we, as their students, know a damn thing about who they are. And, they certainly aren't impressed with our degrees. Consequently, they are able to teach all manner of important things about what it means to be human and to be ape—that is, if we as students are quiet, listen carefully, and let them tell us as only they can.

James L. McGaugh

Memory is perhaps the most critical capacity that we have as humans. Memory is not simply a record of experiences; it is the basis of our knowledge of the world, our skills, our hopes and dreams and our ability to interact with others and thus influence our destinies. Investigation of how the brain enables us to bridge our present existence with our past and future is thus essential for understanding human nature. Clearly, the most exciting challenge of science is to determine how brain cells and systems create our memories.

Donald O. Hebb (1904–1985)

Modern psychology takes completely for granted that behavior and neural function are perfectly correlated. . . . There is no separate soul or life force to stick a finger into the brain now and then and make neural cells do what they would not otherwise. . . . It is quite conceivable that some day the assumption will have to be rejected. But it is important also to see that we have not reached that day yet. . . . One cannot logically be a determinist in physics and chemistry and biology, and a mystic in psychology.

Jerre Levy

Despite the quite amazing progress of the last half century in neuroscientific understanding, we are still, in my view, as distant now as ever in knowing what questions to ask about how and why brains make minds. It is simply evading the issue to say, as some philosophers do, that our mental experiences are just the inside view of the stuff we measure on the outside. Why is the inside view so utterly different from our external measurements? Even if we specified all the critical spatiotemporal neural dynamics that were necessary and sufficient for a given mental experience, this would not tell us why those dynamics give rise to any experience at all. . . . Nature will answer if we ask the right questions.

Walter B. Cannon (1871–1945)

As a matter of routine I have long trusted unconscious processes to serve me. . . . [One] example I may cite was the interpretation of the significance of bodily changes which occur in great emotional excitement, such as fear and rage. These changes— the more rapid pulse, the deeper breathing, the increase of sugar in the blood, the secretion from the adrenal glands—were very diverse and seemed unrelated. Then, one wakeful night, after a considerable collection of these changes had been disclosed, the idea flashed through my mind that they could be nicely integrated if conceived as bodily preparations for supreme effort in flight or in fighting.

Curt P. Richter (1894–1988)

I enjoy research more than eating.

Larry R. Squire

Memory is personal and evocative, intertwined with emotion, and it provides us with a sense of who we are. During the past two decades there has been a revolution in our understanding of what memory is and what happens in the brain when we learn and remember. At the beginning of the 21st century, one has the sense that memory may be the first mental faculty that will be understandable in terms of molecules, cells, brain systems, and behavior. Yet, even with all the progress, there can be no doubt that the study of the brain is still a young science, rich with opportunity for the student and beginning scientist. This is a good time to hear about the promise and excitement of neuroscience. The best is yet to come.